South-East Asia
on a shoestring

Chris Taylor
Peter Turner
Joe Cummings
Brendan Delahunty
Paul Greenway
James Lyon
Jens Peters
Robert Storey
David Willett
Tony Wheeler

South-East Asia

9th edition

Published by
Lonely Planet Publications
Head Office: PO Box 617, Hawthorn, Vic 3122, Australia
Branches: 155 Filbert St, Suite 251, Oakland, CA 94607, USA
10 Barley Mow Passage, Chiswick, London W4 4PH, UK
71 bis rue du Cardinal Lemoine, 75005 Paris, France

Printed by
SNP Printing Pte Ltd, Singapore

Photographs by

Glenn Beanland (GB)	Joe Cummings (JC)	Hugh Finlay (HF)	Richard I'Anson (RI)
Peter Morris (PM)	Bernard Napthine (BN)	Richard Nebesky (RN)	Joanna O'Brien (JO)
Jens Peters (JP)	Chris Taylor (CT)	Tony Wheeler (TW)	

Front cover: Umbrella at Nusa Dua in Bali, Indonesia. Larry Dale Gordon (The Image Bank)

First Published
1975

This Edition
April 1997

National Library of Australia Cataloguing in Publication Data

South-East Asia.

9th ed.
Includes index.
ISBN 0 86442 412 4.

1. Asia, Southeastern – Guidebooks. I. Turner, Peter.
(Series: Lonely Planet on a shoestring).

915.90453

text & maps © Lonely Planet 1997
photos © photographers as indicated 1997

Chris Taylor

Chris grew up in England and Australia and has spent much of his adult life based variously in Melbourne, Tokyo and Taipei. He joined Lonely Planet to work on the phrasebook series, later departing to contribute to *Japan, China, Tibet, Cambodia* and *Malaysia, Singapore & Brunei*, as well as other Lonely Planet guidebooks. He is based in Taiwan, where he works as a freelance writer.

Peter Turner

Peter was born in Melbourne and studied Asian studies, politics and English before setting off on the Asian trail. His long-held interest in South-East Asia has seen him make numerous trips to the region. He has worked on Lonely Planet's *Singapore city guide*, *Jakarta city guide*, *Java, Indonesia, New Zealand* and *Malaysia, Singapore & Brunei*.

Joe Cummings

Joe has travelled extensively in South-East Asia. Before travel writing became a full-time job, he was a Peace Corps volunteer in Thailand, a graduate student of Thai language and Asian art history at the University of California at Berkeley, an East-West Center Scholar in Hawaii, a university lecturer in Malaysia and a bilingual studies consultant in the USA and Taiwan. Joe is also the author of Lonely Planet's *Thailand, Bangkok, Laos* and *Myanmar* guidebooks and the *Thai* and *Lao* phrasebooks.

Brendan Delahunty

After years in journalism, peppered with varied stints as an editor, outreach educator, farmer and teacher of Indonesian to pre-school toddlers, the prospect of unemployment brought Brendan into the Lonely Planet fold in 1994. With LP's support, he established an alliance between far-sighted HIV/AIDS educators in Ujung Pandang and Australia, and goes 'home' to Sulawesi as often as possible. Brendan is now working as a legal researcher in Sydney.

Paul Greenway

During his research for the Indonesia chapter, Paul managed to avoid serious rioting in Jayapura and Timika by a few days, but was not so lucky during an earthquake in Biak. Paul also caught a bad fever in Nabire, was violently ill during a 40 hour boat trip to the Sula Islands and, worst of all, missed all of the World Cup cricket competition on TV. He is now based in his mother's spare bedroom in Adelaide, South Australia. Paul updated the latest edition of *Mongolia* and co-wrote *Indian Himalaya*.

James Lyon

James is a sceptic by nature and a social scientist by training. He worked for five years as an editor at Lonely Planet's Melbourne office, then 'jumped the fence' to become a researcher and writer. He has travelled in Bali both by himself and with his wife, Pauline, and their two young children. A keen gardener, he finds the flowers and landscapes of Bali a special delight, and he's a recent convert to the underwater world and the beauty of coral gardens.

Jens Peters

Born in Germany, Jens studied advertising, communications and arts education in Berlin. Since 1970 he has travelled for several months each year in countries outside Europe. So far he has visited the Philippines more than 50 times and spent over eight years there. He has worked as a freelance journalist for various travel magazines and published several guidebooks about tropical countries.

Robert Storey

Experienced budget traveller and renowned cheapskate, Robert has spent much of his time trekking around the world on a shoestring. During his travels, he survived a number of near-death experiences, including marriage and riding the subway in New York City. Robert now lives in Taiwan, where he has devoted himself to safe and serious pursuits such as writing books, studying Chinese, computer hacking and motorcycle stunt-driving.

David Willett

David is a freelance journalist based near Bellingen on the north coast of New South Wales, Australia. He grew up in Hampshire, England, and wound up in Australia after stints on newspapers in Iran (1975-8) and Bahrain. He spent two years as a subeditor on the Melbourne *Sun* newspaper before trading a steady job for a warmer climate. He has previously worked on LP's *Greece*, *North Africa*, *Indonesia* and *Australia* guidebooks.

Tony Wheeler

Tony was born in England but spent most of his youth overseas. He returned to England to do a university degree in engineering, worked as an automotive design engineer, returned to university to complete an MBA and then dropped out on the Asian overland trail with his wife, Maureen. They've been travelling, writing and publishing guidebooks ever since, having set up Lonely Planet Publications in the mid-70s. Travel for the Wheelers is now considerably enlivened by their daughter, Tashi, and their son, Kieran.

This Book

The comprehensive update of this book, the 9th edition of *South-East Asia on a shoestring*, required lots of people and lots of days on the road. Chris Taylor was the coordinating author for northern South-East Asia and also updated the chapters on Cambodia, Brunei, Malaysia (Sabah, Sarawak and the east coast of the peninsula) and Indonesia (Kalimantan), as well as the introductory chapters.

Peter Turner covered Singapore, the west coast of Peninsular Malaysia, and Java and Nusa Tenggara in Indonesia and coordinated southern South-East Asia. Indonesia, by virtue of its size, required a considerable effort to update. Brendan Delahunty returned to Sulawesi, Paul Greenway went to Irian Jaya and Maluku, David Willett researched Sumatra and James Lyon updated the Bali and Lombok sections.

Joe Cummings updated the Thailand, Laos and Myanmar chapters, and Jens Peters travelled throughout the Philippines to update that chapter. Robert Storey prepared the chapters on Hong Kong, Macau and Vietnam.

From the Publisher

This book was produced in LP's Melbourne office. Linda Suttie and Greg Alford coordinated the editing, Sally Gerdan oversaw the mapping, with assistance from Adam McCrow, and Adam designed and laid out the book. Editing was done by David Andrew, Miriam Cannell, Anne Mulvaney and Kristin Odijk and Linda proofread the book. Indexing was done by Sharon Wertheim and Anne. The cover was designed by Simon Bracken and Adam. And thanks to computer guru Dan Levin for helping out with the Lao fonts.

Warning & Request

Things change – prices go up, schedules change, good places go bad and bad places go bankrupt – nothing stays the same. So, if you find things better or worse, recently opened or long since closed, please tell us and help make the next edition even more accurate and useful.

We value all of the feedback we receive from travellers. Julie Young coordinates a small team who read and acknowledge every letter, postcard and email, and ensure that every morsel of information finds its way to the appropriate authors, editors and publishers.

Everyone who writes to us will find their name in the next edition of the appropriate guide and will also receive a free subscription to our quarterly newsletter, *Planet Talk*. The very best contributions will be rewarded with a free Lonely Planet guide.

Excerpts from your correspondence may appear in updates (which we add to the end pages of reprints); new editions of this guide; in our newsletter, *Planet Talk*; or in the Postcards section of our Web site – so please let us know if you don't want your letter published or your name acknowledged.

Thanks

Thanks to all the travellers who wrote in to share their experiences of life on the road in South-East Asia. We apologise if we've omitted or misspelt your name.

Ken & Ina, R & D Abbotts, Lisa Abram, Garry Adams, Zimran Ahmed, Grell Albrecht, Alison Allgaier, Einar Andersen, S Andersen, Aaron Anderson, Mike Ashby, Ivar Austin, Paul Authur, Ingvill Baeko, Al & Joan Bailey, Anna Baker, Nicole Bakker, Maya Bar, Lyndsay Barnes, David Barnhill, John Barraco, D Bates, Amanda Bauhofer, Janet Beale, Geoff Beattie, Glenn Behrman, Cheralyn Bell, Didier Bellet, Miguel Benito, S Bennet, Jurgen Berger, T Berndt, Liz Berry, Steve Beutler, Lisa Blanch, Holger Blanck, Laurie Bloomgarten, Susan Bohdan, F Bolle, Jean-Marie Boone, Denis Borle, Keith Bortock, Antoinette Bouwens, David Boyall, JD Boyes, Bradley Brainard, J Bramson, Coen Bravenboer, Robert Brookfield, Richard Brooks, Karen Brooks, Danny Brown, Family Brown, Sean Bruce-Cullen, Justin Brumelle, Angela Buckingham, Geoff Budge, Mat Burbery, Simone Burgon, P Butler, Thomas Sean Butler, Lisa & Paul Byrne

Heather Cameron, Colin Campbell, Ruth Campbell, Natalie Capelett, Debbie Carr, Mathew & Alena Casey, W Casker, Federico Cesati, Haywood Chapman, Jacques & Liliaue Chapon, Sophia Chiang, Al Chin, Scott Chosed, Lee Sek Chu, Chris Clark, Jackie Clement, Carl & Diana Clifford, Donn Colby, M Cook, Neil Cooper, Gerald Coulter, Jerry Creedon, Patricia Creighton, David Cross

Pat Dagger, Annet Damen, Pat Daniel & the

Medpower Team, Will David, Michael Davidson, Lucinda Davies, Adrian Davis, Scott Davis, Maurice de Rooij, Sophie de Lara, Alberto Deacon-Morey, Bennett Dean, S Deane, Shane Delphine, Annemarie den Broeder, Kari Diggins, Doni & Tim Dilworth, Bjorn Donnis, Mark Donovan, Julia Dotson, P Doucette, Catherine Douxchamps, J Downham, K Downham, Annick Duflos, Jason Dumphry, Ian & Sonia Duncan, Trang Duong, BPF Du Sautoy, Hans Durrer, Jayne Dyer, T Dykstra, Thomas Dyvik, Suzanne Ecklund, RB Edminson, RP Edwards, Sandy Edwards, Bert Eijnthoven, Andy & Pravina Ellis, Cathy Ellis, Usha Engel, H Jonas Eriksson, EV Estey, Sue Evans, J Evans, Sara Evans, Andrew Ewart

Teresa Farnes, James Farrell, Evan Fearn, Andrew Fearnside, Lyndsay & Jamie Finn, Syd Fisher, Matthew Flattery, Peter Flegg, Sarah Ford, Jane & Alan Fowler, R Steve Fox, J Fram, Robert Francis, Bruce & Margaret Fraser, Michael Fris-Madsen, Monique Gallway, Sean Garrity, William Gaultier, Richard Gee, J Gibbons, Roger Gilbert, Jane Gindin, Margarita Ginty, Katherine Glover, Erica Goedegebuure, J E Goldsworthy, Arvid Goletz, Daren Gooddy, Mark Gooding, Tim Gourlay, Antonia Gowan, NS Gower, JA Graham, Martin Gray, Clare Green, Michelle Green, Peter & Sanne Griffin, Kathryn Guest, Cathy Gulkin

Art Hacker, Bill Haigh, Peter Hajssmann, Debbie Hall, Glen Hall, John Hall, U Hanke, Peter Hardie, Jean Harrison, Julie Harrison, Daniel Hart, Claire Hawkins, Lucinda Hayward, C Malcolm Heath, Paul Heester, John Heinzel, Jenifer Henderson, Mark Henley & Co, Katri Hentula, Jonathon Hill, Dave Hirst, Graham Hodge, Marie Hodgeman, Jonathon Hoey, Joanne Holmes, Andy Hopewell, Nick Horesh, Leow Chun Hui, Rodney Jackson, Tim Jacobi, Ali James, Saffron James, Helmut Jansch, Tim Jeffreys, Helen Jeffs, Adrian Johnson, Samuel Johnson, Chris Jones, Nicolas Jones, N Jones, Richard Juterbock, Jan Willem Kaal, L Kahansky, Pertti Kantanen, David Kàrlsson, Mel Kay, Joseph Kellegher, Charlotte Kelly, Tony Kenyon, Neil Kerfoot, Christopher Kickham, Julia Kimber, Heather Knox, Julien Kozak, Tim Kretser, L Kahansky, Wai Shing Kwan

Michael Laird, Yin Lan Lo, D Langley, Eleanor & George Lawson, Alex Layarfd, Darren Le Poidevin, Tim Leffel, Chris Leslie, Wim Leuppens, Matt & Gail Lewis, Sheila Lewis, Cas Liber, Steve Lidgey, Inge Light, Alison Linsday, Richard Londesborough, Paul Lovichi, Lorraine Luciano, Sally Luke, Ben Lupton, John MacGregor, Sophia Wai Chee Mah, J Marges, Will Markle, Trevor Marshall, Ricky Martin, Ian & Tina Mathiason, Steinunn Matthiasovir, Roland Mayer, Annette McAllister, Lesley McCann, Francis McEntee, TJ McIntyre, J McLoughlin, I Mende, Marilyn Meyers, Annette Miller, Greg Mitchell, John Mitchell, Vit Mlcoch, Alistair Moes, Sheila Montague, N Moore, Christopher Morden, Michael Mortensen, Kristian Muller, Diana Mundi

Kerryn Newton, Kevin Nicholls, Ian Nicholson, A Nidecker, Jos Nieuwenhuis, David Nightingale, Kala Nobbs, V Noonan, Adrian Nordenborg, Ray Norton, Claire Notman, Johan Nygren, Gail O'Connell, Wendy Okafuji, Karen Okun, Claes Olesen, Diane Oliver, Enrico & Alma Orbitani, Tina Ottman, Kathy Palmer, Paul & Sherrie Panther, Arnaud Parienty, Nick Park, Ros Passmore, Emma Patricio, Lynn Patterson, Jonathan Paul, Andrea Payne, Scott Pegg, Diana Peh, Rena Penna, Oliver Perceval, Mattijs Perdeck, Matthew Peregrine-Jones, Stuart Perkins, Ann Perrelli, Raymond Peter, Christian Pfeiffer, Jochen Pfeuffer, Hoa Pham, Dale & Nigel Philips, John Piekarski, Jonathon Platt, Sally Platt, Bine Pohner, Julie Polk, M Porup, Alex Potocki

Al & Robyn Raam, Clem Read, J Redfern, Malin Regebro, David Reid, Lynette & Anthea Reid, Katrin Reiter, Renee Renjel, N Rickaby, Bert Rietmeijer, Jennifer & Alan Robins, Ashley Rogers, Nick Rogl, Steve Rogowski, Isabel Romero, Joost Rompa, Ron Rook, Johan Ros, Russell Rose, Daphne Rose-Jevremor, Nina Rosenbladt, Yancey Rousek, Peter Rowan, EJ Rowley, Jay Ruchamkin, Minco Ruiter, Greg Runyon, Denise Rushton, Petra Russi

A Saez, Jeff Sagalewicz, Sean Salloux, Arla Sase, RW Saunders, Kathy Sawdon, Alain Schellinckx, Jesper Schmidt, Jetta Schmidt-Pedersen, Marianne Schodt, Ralph Schwer, Alison Scott, Steve Scott, Frank Sear, Mijk Searchfield, Clive Searle, Paul Seddon, Anton Segal, Jack Sellner, Phil & Louise Shambrook, Jenny Shaw, Louise Sheaman, M Shepherd, Ann Siebert, Ge Sijm, Matthew Simmonds, Carl Simpson, Ricki Singer, Ron Singer, Robert Skuy, Joseph Smallwood, Carole Smith, Heather Smith, Michael Smith, Patrick & Mary Smith, CJ Smith, Janine Smith, Anna Soliguo, Lorrain Solomon, John Spheeris, Amy Spilane, Martin Sprinzl & Co, DJ Staveley, Craig Steed, Tatjana Steinecke, S Stolk, Bill Stoughton, Robert Strang, John Straube, Patrick Sullivan, Wanda & Barry Syner, AA Tan-Keultjes, Marie Tatham, Jurgen Ten-Brummeler, Alison Thackray, Howard Thain, Bob Thomas, G Thompson, Les Thompson, Bill Thomson, David Thorne, Andy Tindle, Lisa Ting, KE Titchener, Jacques Trouman, Hamish Trumbull

Derek Uhlemann, AW van der Ban, Mark van der Berg, Cathy van der Zee, Ray van Seeters, Jan Maarten van Sonsbeek, Herbert Vollmer, Luc & Jose de Vries, Chris Wagstaff, Janet Walker, David Wall, Arthur Walton, Jacob Weismann, Peter Weisshaar, Don Welch, Peter Wellens, Carina Westling, Francis Wetzel, L Wharam, Debbie Whitehead, Charlie Wicke, Chrissie Williams, Laura Williams, Louise Williams, NG Williams, Henry Wilson, Stefan Winkler, Mike Witcombe, J Withers, Monica & Christina Wojtaszewski, Ronald Wolff, Rohan Wood, Andy Woodhouse, Jackie Wright, Ricky Yu, YB Yuen, Justin Zaman, RA Zambardino, Yoav Zand

Contents

LAOS 395

Map Legend

BOUNDARIES

— International Boundary
— Regional Boundary

ROUTES

Freeway
Highway
Major Road
Unsealed Road or Track
City Road
City Street
Railway
Underground Railway
Tram
Walking Track
Walking Tour
Ferry Route
Cable Car or Chairlift

AREA FEATURES

Parks
Built-Up Area
Pedestrian Mall
Market
Cemetery
Reef
Beach or Desert
Rocks

HYDROGRAPHIC FEATURES

Coastline
River, Creek
Intermittent River or Creek
Rapids, Waterfalls
Lake, Intermittent Lake
Canal
Swamp

SYMBOLS

✪ CAPITAL .... National Capital
◉ Capital .... Regional Capital
⬤ CITY .... Major City
● City .... City
● Town .... Town
● Village .... Village

■ ▼ .... Place to Stay, Place to Eat
☕ 🍴 .... Cafe, Pub or Bar
✉ ☎ .... Post Office, Telephone
ℹ $ .... Tourist Information, Bank
◉ P .... Transport, Parking
🏛 ⬆ .... Museum, Youth Hostel
⚏ ▲ .... Caravan Park, Camping Ground
✝ ➡ .... Church, Cathedral
☾ ✡ .... Mosque, Synagogue
卍 卐 .... Buddhist Temple, Hindu Temple
△ ☬ .... Stupa, Sikh Temple

◎ ⛽ .... Embassy, Petrol Station
✈ ✚ .... Airport, Airfield
🏊 ✿ .... Swimming Pool, Gardens
❖ 🐘 .... Shopping Centre, Zoo
✚ ★ .... Hospital, Police Station
← A25 .... One-Way Street, Route Number
🏛 ▲ .... Stately Home, Monument
⛳ ▣ .... Golf Course, Tomb
⌓ ⌂ .... Cave, Hut or Chalet
▲ ☀ .... Mountain or Hill, Lookout
🗼 ☒ .... Lighthouse, Shipwreck
)(◎ .... Pass, Spring
🏖 .... Beach, Surf Beach
∴ .... Archaeological Site or Ruins
.... Ancient or City Wall
⟹ ⟸ .... Cliff or Escarpment, Tunnel
⊢⊣ .... Railway Station

Note: not all symbols displayed above appear in this book

Introduction

South-East Asia has so many highlights it is difficult to know where to begin. Soaring mountains, deep jungles, ancient temples, hustle-bustle cities, palm-fringed beaches and spellbinding ritual – South-East Asia has it all. Indeed there is nowhere in the world where trains, buses and boats (the occasional flight is required, unfortunately) can whisk the traveller through such a diversity of cultures and geography.

Most travellers arrive at one of the sprawling Asian gateways. Don't be put off by first impressions. True, most Asian capitals are polluted snarls of honking traffic and hastily thrown together shopping malls – at least that's probably the view you'll have coming in on the bus from the airport. But probe beneath the surface and you'll find fascinating markets, back-street temples, raucous street vendors and, at times, an almost overwhelming air of go-get-it vibrancy. Hong Kong is a bustling economic powerhouse; Jakarta is the melting pot of Indonesia; push-and-shove Bangkok is in your face – at turns shocking, at turns seductive – but provides an earthy contrast to sanitised Singapore, where 'shocking Asia' morphs into 'shopping Asia'.

Mind you, the occasional quiet backwater capital lingers on (though probably not for much longer). Vientiane is lazily stirring itself from a long nap. Yangon (Rangoon), the capital of Myanmar (Burma), is a decrepit (some say 'charming') lesson in how not to run your country. Hanoi has unhurried French charm and wide, clean socialist boulevards. Even Phnom Penh, overlooked by many travellers, is a city rich in colonial history.

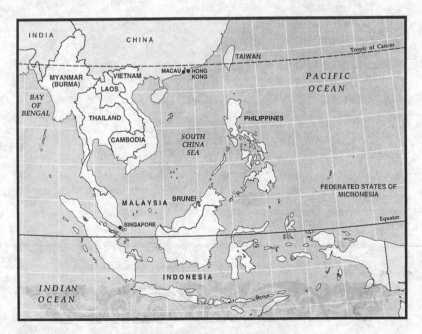

15

But for most visitors Asia's real sights are in the countryside: in the Philippines, Mayon, the 'most perfect' volcano; in Java, the moonscapes of Gunung Bromo; in Malaysian Borneo, Mt Kinabalu; in Sumatra, the unforgettable panorama presented by Lake Toba; and in Flores, the bizarre three-coloured lakes of Keli.

Trying to choose the best beaches is a good way to start an argument. Thailand probably takes the prize with Phuket and the islands of Ko Samui, Ko Pha-Ngan, Ko Tao, Ko Phi Phi, Ko Chang...the list keeps growing. The east coast of Peninsular Malaysia has a few contenders, notably Tioman and the Perhentian islands. The Philippines is no slouch in the sea and sand department – Boracay is the most famed, but there's also Puerto Galera, Malapascua and dozens of other resorts. Indonesia also has its fair share scattered around the archipelago, from Nias Island to Bali's Kuta Beach and the Gili Islands off Lombok. Vietnam is the new kid on the block, but beaches like Nha Trang are already well on the way to big resort status. If you want to find that deserted paradise, Indonesia and the Philippines have hundreds of islands to choose from.

And of course there's the history too. Ancient temple complexes, such as Cambodia's Angkor, Myanmar's Bagan and Indonesia's Borobudur are awe-inspiring sights that are simply not to be missed. Other temples around the region jostle for your attention, but – without a doubt – the most fabulous is the Shwedagon Pagoda: a gilded, jewel-encrusted treasure that dominates the city of Yangon.

More? Well there's great food, jungle trekking, giant lizards, superb coral reefs...in South-East Asia deciding what *not* to do is the problem.

A	B	C
D	E	F
G	H	I

A: Songkhla, Thailand (RN)
B: Bangkok, Thailand (JO)
C: Sanur, Bali, Indonesia (PM)
D: Chinatown, Singapore (RN)
E: Angkor, Cambodia (CT)
F: Hat Yai, Thailand (JC)
G: Halong Bay, Vietnam (RI)
H: Vientiane, Laos (RI)
I: Shwesandaw Paya, Bagan, Myanmar (BN)

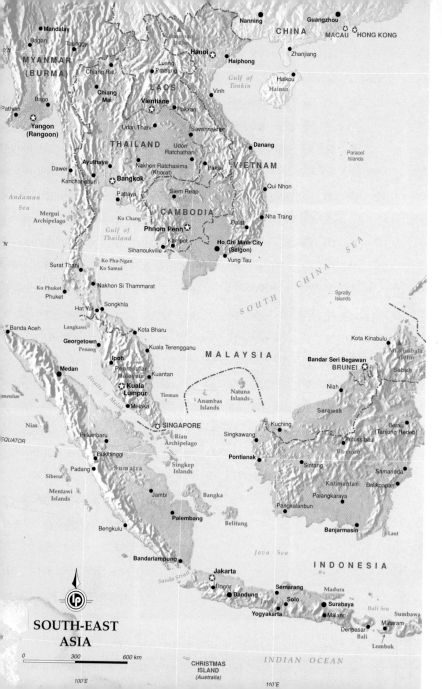

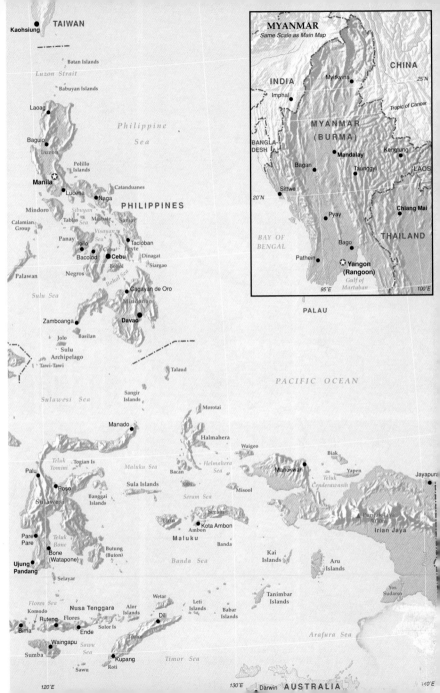

A	B	C
D	E	F
G	H	I

A: Mandalay, Myanmar (JC)
B: Banaue, Luzon, Philippines (JP)
C: Wat Si Saket, Vientiane, Laos (JC)
D: Nha Trang, Vietnam (GB)
E: Borobudur, Java, Indonesia (PM)

F: Kampung Ayer, Brunei (HF)
G: Ratchaburi, Thailand (RN)
H: Lantau Island, Hong Kong (TW)
I: Panay, Philippines (JP)

Regional Facts for the Visitor

PLANNING

When to Go

Any time for any amount of time might be the answer to this one.

Although there are wet and dry seasons, monsoonal activity is rarely an impediment to travel in South-East Asia. Throughout the region, the rainy season is usually marked by sudden downpours of torrential rain followed just as suddenly by sunshine – bring an umbrella and you'll be fine.

As a rule of thumb, from Singapore north (including the Philippines), rainfall peaks between the months of May and September; south and east of Singapore (Indonesia) rainfall is at its heaviest between December and March. Check the climate charts at the back of this book for more details.

Maps

There's very little in the way of decent maps that cover the whole of South-East Asia. Bartholomew's *Asia, South-East World Travel Map* is a fold-out affair with a scale of 1:5,800,000. Very similar is International Travel Maps' *South-East Asia*, at a scale of 1:6,000,000. Nelles Verlag publishes the *South-East Asia Map*, and Ravenstein has the *South & East Asia Road Map* at a scale of 1:9,000,000. Periplus, a Singaporean publisher, is producing a range of South-East Asian regional maps, but as yet there is no map of the entire region. Look out too for Lonely Planet's travel atlases for *Thailand*, *Vietnam* and *Laos*.

What to Bring

As little as possible is the best policy – but not so little that you have to scrounge off other travellers, as some of the 'super lightweight' travellers do. It's very easy to find almost anything you need along the way – it's better to start with too little than too much.

Clothes Clothing is generally cheaper in South-East Asia than in the west, so it makes sense to bring as little as possible and shop for what you need as you travel. Many travellers flying into Bangkok or Bali seem to stock up on a whole wardrobe within days of arriving.

For those who like to be prepared, a checklist of clothing to bring might include:

- underwear & swimming gear
- a pair of jeans & a pair of shorts
- a few T-shirts & shirts
- a sweater for cold nights
- a pair of runners or shoes
- sandals or thongs
- a lightweight jacket or raincoat
- a dress-up set of clothes (an optional possibility that most budget travellers dispense with)

Bear in mind that modesty is rated highly in Asian countries, especially for women. Wearing shorts (or skimpier apparel) away from the beach is generally perceived as undignified.

Other Needs There is a host of travel accessories you might bring besides a basic wardrobe. A medical kit is well worth considering (see the Health section in the appendix). A good pair of sunglasses with UV protection is essential in the tropical sun, as is high-factor sunscreen, and you might also bring:

- washing gear
- sewing kit
- padlock
- Swiss army knife
- umbrella
- money belt
- extra camera batteries
- water bottle
- torch (flashlight)
- compass

A padlock is useful to lock your bag to a train or bus luggage rack, or to fortify your hotel room – which often locks with a latch. A folding umbrella will almost certainly come in handy – these are readily available throughout the region. Soap, toothpaste and so on are always easy to get, but toilet paper and tampons can be difficult to find in remote areas.

Sleeping Bag Should you, shouldn't you? The fact is, in South-East Asia you will get very few opportunities to use a sleeping bag. If you are planning to hike up mountains or do some serious trekking in areas that see few foreigners (there are not many places like this left), it may be worth bringing one; otherwise, you are probably better off saving the space in your pack for something else. Many travellers find that a locally bought sarong serves perfectly as a sheet, as well as functioning as a towel, a beach wrap or a dressing gown.

How to Carry It A backpack is still the best way to carry gear because it's commodious and perfect for walking. On the debit side, a backpack is awkward to load on and off buses and trains; it doesn't offer too much protection for your valuables; the straps tend to get caught on things; and some airlines may refuse to take responsibility if it's damaged or broken into. Fortunately, backpacks no longer have the 'pack equals hippy' and 'hippy equals bad' connotation they once had.

Travelpacks – a combination of backpack and shoulder bag – are also popular. The backpack straps zip away inside the pack when not needed so you almost have the best of both worlds. Although not really suitable for long hiking trips, they're much easier to carry than a bag. Access to your gear is also easier – the top zips open so you don't have to take out everything to find something at the bottom – and they are easier to lock than a backpack. Another alternative is a large, soft zip bag with a wide shoulder strap so it can be carried with relative ease. Backpacks and travelpacks can be made reasonably thief-proof with small padlocks. Forget suitcases.

The secret of successful packing is plastic bags, also called 'stuff bags' – they not only separate the items in your pack, they keep them clean and dry.

Airlines do lose bags from time to time, but you've got a much better chance of it not being yours if you tag it with your name and address *inside* the bag, as well as outside. Outside tags can fall off or be removed.

SUGGESTED ITINERARIES

This section could easily get out of hand – there are just too many possibilities! Travellers can create their own itineraries based on the information in the following Highlights section. Also see the Getting Around chapter.

Unless you have unlimited funds, and years to spend, you can rule out going everywhere. You could spend two months each in the Philippines and Indonesia and only see a tiny fraction of what these two vast archipelagos have to offer. And assuming you are on a six-month trip, this only leaves two months for Singapore, Malaysia, Thailand, Myanmar, Vietnam, Laos, Cambodia and Hong Kong. Most people end up deciding on a route through the region that takes in some of the highlights, perhaps indulges some special interests and includes some R&R on a beach retreat.

There are two basic itineraries on the South-East Asian trail: north or south, up or down. A flight to Bali or to Timor, for example, allows you to travel through Java, Sumatra, Peninsular Malaysia (and Singapore), Thailand and Laos without once taking a flight. From Bangkok you might fly to Myanmar, Vietnam or Cambodia; there are also cheap flights from Vientiane in Laos to Vietnam and Cambodia. From Hanoi in Vietnam you even have the option nowadays of travelling overland to China and from there to Hong Kong, though the China leg of this trip is not covered by this book – look out for Lonely Planet's *China – travel survival kit* if you are planning this trip.

The north-south trail is, however, just part of the story. Assuming you fly into Bangkok (the most popular entry point), there are any number of possible itineraries you might follow. Bangkok allows easy access to the rest of Thailand, to Myanmar, to Indochina or even to Hong Kong. From southern Thailand, overland travel to Peninsular Malaysia,

Singapore and Indonesia has long been a standard South-East Asian route.

The wild cards on the South-East Asian trail are the Philippines, Malaysian and Indonesian Borneo, and outlying islands of Indonesia, such as Sulawesi, Maluku and Irian Jaya. These are all very much detours from the main circuit and thus see much lower volumes of tourist traffic – if you want to get away from banana pancakes and Bob Marley tapes, these places give you the opportunity to do so.

HIGHLIGHTS

South-East Asia is packed with highlights. Listed here are some of the more interesting/fun highlights of a trip through the region.

Beaches

There are excellent beaches in the Philippines, Indonesia and Malaysia; there are even some OK beaches in Vietnam and Cambodia. But it's Thailand that pulls in the crowds.

Most of Thailand's best beaches are on islands in the south. Phuket (largely upmarket these days) and Ko Samui were two of the earliest islands to be developed, and consequently they now offer a wide range of accommodation, dining and entertainment options. Ko Pha-Ngan, not far from Ko Samui, is no longer the quiet retreat from Samui it once was – it has achieved fame as the venue for massive full-moon parties. Ko Tao is a small, remote island, accessible from Ko Pha-Ngan, and is the place to get away from it all. Ko Phi Phi, on the western side of the isthmus, is arguably overdeveloped but still a popular beach retreat. Other popular islands are Ko Samet (with easy access from Bangkok) and Ko Chang, which is close to the Cambodian border.

The Philippines' most celebrated beaches are on Boracay, a small island just off the northern tip of Panay. On the east coast of Peninsular Malaysia there's a string of resorts and budget beach havens. The most popular places are Tioman Island, Cherating and the stunning but alcohol-free and

slightly boring Perhentian Islands – Malaysian beaches are generally more straightlaced than those elsewhere in the region.

Bali's famous beaches, such as Kuta, are a favourite of package tours these days, but Indonesia's most stunning beaches are further afield. Pulau Bunaken in Sulawesi, Nias off the Sumatran coast, or the islands of Maluku have some great beaches.

Historical Sights

South-East Asia has two historical sights that vie with each other for top billing: Bagan (Pagan) in Myanmar and Angkor in Cambodia. At Bagan there are more than 5000 temples to explore. Angkor doesn't quite rival Bagan in numbers, but there are few sights in the world that measure up to the grandeur of Angkor Wat.

Indonesia's prime historical attractions are in Java. The most famous is Borobudur, which predates the temples of Bagan and all but the very earliest Angkorian structures (there are probably historical connections between the makers of Borobudur and the early temples of Angkor). Less well known, but also impressive, is the temple complex at Prambanan.

Thailand is brimming with wats but it has no world-famous historical attractions. The best places to get a glimpse of Thailand's past are Ayuthaya, the capital until 1767, and Lopburi, its 10th century capital. Chiang Mai is something of a noisy tourist trap these days, but it also has some good historical sights.

Colonial Legacy

There's still a great deal of colonial architecture lingering in the region. The British left their mark in Singapore, parts of Malaysia (mainly on the west coast of the peninsula), Myanmar and Hong Kong; the French in Indochina; the Dutch in Indonesia; and the Spanish in the Philippines.

If it's derelict colonial architecture you're interested in, you'll have to head to Myanmar or Indochina. Much of Yangon in Myanmar, however, remains in a photogenic state of disrepair. The most charming of the

Indochinese cities is Hanoi, with its leafy boulevards and French villas; Phnom Penh, too, is not without its charm.

Most travellers tend to forget the Philippines when it comes to colonial architecture, but there are some fine sights here too. In northern Luzon, Vigan is probably the best preserved Spanish town in the whole archipelago – a stay here is a wonderful trip back in time. Nearby Laoag has some wonderful Spanish churches.

Finally, amid all the new, Singapore, Malaysia and Hong Kong have some worthwhile colonial architecture. Singapore's Colonial District is an interesting area to explore on foot and contains famous landmarks like the Raffles Hotel – renovated but still evocative of the past. In Malaysia, Kuala Lumpur and Melaka have some good historical buildings. Jakarta has some of the oldest colonial architecture in the east.

Places to Hang Out

For many travellers, South-East Asia is as much hanging out, drinking shakes and scoffing banana pancakes as it is travelling. Starting in the south-east, Lombok has the Gili Islands, three coral-fringed specks of paradise that are each packed with inexpensive guesthouses (*losmens*). Lombok's next door neighbour is Bali, a legendary destination where the crowds can reach legend-making proportions.

Kuta was Bali's original budget beach area, but it has long been appropriated by mid-range and top-end tourism. The rock-bottom places are harder to find, but while you may pay a little more than in some other parts of Indonesia, you get a lot more for your money. Budget travellers with time to kill tend to gravitate to Lovina or Candidasa, though the beaches themselves are not as good. Ubud, the central arts and crafts capital of Bali, is still popular, though it's no longer the village it once was.

In Java, sooner or later everyone ends up in Yogyakarta (pronounced 'Jogjakarta'). There's plenty to see in and out of town, and there are frequent cultural performances.

In Sumatra, the mountain retreat of Bukittingi is a popular stopover and Lagundi, on Nias Island, is a popular beach hang-out. But the jewel in Sumatra's crown is probably Lake Toba, a crater lake with an island almost the size of Singapore. Most budget accommodation (some of the cheapest in Indonesia) is on the island (Samosir) at Tuk Tuk.

Very few travellers linger in Singapore, but in Malaysia there are some popular places to hang out. On the west coast of Peninsular Malaysia, Melaka, a historical town, and Penang, with its wonderful old-world Chinatown, are popular spots. On the east coast is Tioman Island, arguably one of the most beautiful islands in South-East Asia. Kota Bharu is a laid-back town up near the Thai border – it is another place where travellers tend to linger, though when compared with other major South-East Asian attractions it's difficult to understand why.

Thailand is packed with popular places to hang out. The most popular of the southern islands are Ko Pha-Ngan, Ko Tao and Ko Samui – the last is very touristed nowadays. There are also popular island getaways on the east coast – Ko Samet and Ko Chang both attract large numbers of long-timers. In the north, border areas like Mae Hong Son and Mae Sai (which lies at the heart of the Golden Triangle) are also favoured. Chiang Mai is a big city these days and most travellers use it as a transit point.

In Indochina, Luang Phabang in Laos and Angkor in Cambodia have emerged as two places where travellers take long vacations.

Wildlife

Ecotourism is catching on in South-East Asia – animals are becoming more profitable alive. Still, South-East Asia's national parks are not all that well developed, and there is nothing like the game parks of Africa. The variety of fauna is astonishing, but not all that easy to see.

Thailand has the most extensive national park network, but accommodation and facilities are limited. At the same time, they are relatively untouristic and, if you have plenty of time and patience, they present good opportunities for exploring the countryside and seeking out wildlife.

Malaysia has excellent national parks and the best setup in South-East Asia for observing wildlife, but numbers of big game (elephants, tigers, rhinoceroses etc) are low and the chances of spotting them in the dense jungle are slim. Taman Negara National Park has a system of hides to view the animals, while over in Borneo the Kinabatangan River and Danum Valley in Sabah are rich in wildlife.

Borneo is also home to three of the world's four orang-utan rehabilitation centres (the other is in Sumatra). In Sabah, the Sepilok Centre is very well organised, but also becoming very touristy, while the Semenggok Centre in Sarawak is not as well organised and probably not tourist-oriented enough. Camp Leakey, in Central Kalimantan (Indonesian Borneo), is one of the best places to see orang-utans, although it is less accessible. Easiest to reach, and in a beautiful setting with plenty of budget accommodation, the Orang-Utan Rehabilitation Centre at Bukit Lawang in North Sumatra is the most popular.

Indonesia's best and most accessible national parks for wildlife are Gunung Leuser and Kerinci Seblat in Sumatra; Ujung Kulon and Baluran in Java; and of course there are those infamous 'dragons' on Komodo and nearby Rinca. Bali also has a national park, in the west, and Sulawesi's Lore Lindu park is rich in flora and fauna.

In the Philippines, Quezon National Park in South Luzon and the Mt Ilig-Mt Baco National Wildlife Sanctuary in Mindoro are worth a visit. Mt Kanlaon National Park on Negros is a major refuge for wildlife in the central Philippines, but visitor facilities are limited.

VISAS & DOCUMENTS
Passport

To enter many countries your passport must be valid for at least six months, even if you're only staying for a few days. It is probably best to have at least a year left on your passport if you are heading off on a trip around South-East Asia.

Make sure it has plenty of pages left for those stamp-happy Asian bureaucrats to do their bit too. On a long trip, it's surprising how quickly a passport can fill up. A new one is relatively easy to organise in most major South-East Asian cities, but the processing may cause delays to your trip. Some nationalities (Americans for example) can simply have an extra, concertina-style, section added when their passport gets full.

Visas

Visas are a stamp in your passport that permit you to enter a country and stay for a specified period of time. Visa regulations have been loosening up in South-East Asia over recent years: they are available for most nationalities on arrival in Indonesia, Singapore, Malaysia, Brunei, Thailand, Cambodia and Hong Kong, but are still required for Myanmar, Vietnam and Laos.

As far as possible, get your visas as you go rather than all at once before you leave home: first, they often expire after a certain number of days; second, it is often easier and cheaper to get them in neighbouring countries than it is from far away. Visas for Myanmar, Laos and Vietnam are readily available in Bangkok and Hong Kong.

Visa regulations vary from country to country. In some cases, for example, extensions are near impossible, in others a mere formality. See the Visas sections under the individual countries in this book for further information. And remember the most important rule: treat visits to embassies, consulates and borders as formal occasions and dress up for them.

Photocopies

A sensible security precaution is to keep photocopies of essential documents separate from the documents themselves. You should do this with the data pages of your passport, birth certificate, credit cards, airline tickets and any other important documents you're carrying (education records etc). Best of all, leave a copy of this information with someone at home too.

While you're compiling that information, add the serial numbers of your travellers' cheques and US$50 or more as emergency cash. Keep all this emergency material totally separate from your passport, cheques and other cash.

Onward Tickets

In some countries in South-East Asia (Indonesia, for example) you are required to have an onward ticket out of the country before you can obtain a visa to enter. In practice, however, as long as you look fairly respectable, it's unlikely that your tickets will be checked. The best insurance against being turned away is to buy the cheapest ticket out of the country and cash it in later.

Travel Insurance

A travel insurance policy to cover theft, loss and medical problems is a wise idea. There is a wide variety of policies and your travel agent will have recommendations. Some policies offer lower and higher medical expenses options, but the higher one is chiefly for countries which have extremely high medical costs, like the USA. Check the small print:

- Some policies specifically exclude 'dangerous activities', which can include scuba diving, motorcycling and even trekking. If such activities are on your agenda, you don't want that sort of policy. A locally acquired motorcycle licence may not be valid under your policy.
- You may prefer a policy which pays doctors or hospitals direct rather than you having to pay on the spot and claim later. If you have to claim later make sure you keep all documentation. Some policies ask you to call back (reverse charges) to a centre in your home country where an immediate assessment of your problem is made.
- Check if the policy covers ambulances or an emergency flight home. If you have to stretch out you will need two seats and somebody has to pay for them.

Driving Licence & Permits

There are parts of South-East Asia where car and motorbike hire are options for getting around. Malaysia is a good country to drive a car in, and in parts of Thailand and Indonesia motorcycle hire is popular. If you are planning to do any driving, apply for an international driver's licence before you leave your home country – they are inexpensive and valid for one year.

Hostel Card

The YHA (Hostelling International) has only a handful of hostels in South-East Asia, and as budget accommodation is usually provided by guesthouses, a hostel card is not essential. A hostel card will get you a small discount in the few hostels available in Hong Kong, Thailand, Malaysia, Indonesia, the Philippines and Brunei, but hostels are only slightly cheaper than guesthouse accommodation. Some YHA hostels are supposedly only for members, but a student card will often get you in.

Student & Youth Cards

The International Student Identity Card (ISIC), a plastic ID-style card with a photograph, is the official student card to have. The problem in South-East Asia nowadays is that there are so many fakes floating around it is next to useless. Discounted international air tickets and so on are available to all and sundry providing you shop at the right agencies. A student card will occasionally get you discounts on domestic flights and entry to attractions. If you are eligible for an authentic student card, by all means get one and bring it with you – just don't expect too much of it.

Seniors' Cards

Generally seniors' cards won't be particularly useful in South-East Asia, but it's worth asking for discounts on domestic flights (the Philippines, for example, offers such discounts).

International Health Card

You will only need an international health card if you are arriving in South-East Asia from areas with yellow fever, such as Africa and South America.

EMBASSIES

Most travellers should have no need to contact their embassy while in South-East Asia. However, some embassies in Cambodia appreciate their nationals registering with them, particularly if they are planning a trip upcountry. See the Cambodia chapter for more details and check with your embassy if you go there.

CUSTOMS

Customs regulations vary little around the region. A dim view is taken of drugs and arms – the death sentence or a lengthy stay in prison are common measures taken to discourage travellers sneaking drugs across borders. Check the Customs sections of the countries in this book for duty-free allowances.

MONEY
Costs

South-East Asia is not the bargain it once was. Top-end travellers can spend as much per day in some parts of the region as they would in any other popular tourist destination around the world. Off the beaten track, however, in places like Indonesia, north-east Thailand, Laos, Cambodia and Vietnam, budget travel is still possible. And even the flourishing megacities of Asia generally have their crash-pad ghettoes, such as Bangkok's infamous Kao Sarn Rd.

Your budget is dependent upon how you live and travel. If you're moving fast and living it up in the big cities, your day-to-day living costs are going to skyrocket. On the other hand, if you stick to the less touristed parts of the region and travel at a relaxed pace, it's still possible to keep costs down to US$10 to US$20 per day in most South-East Asia countries.

See the chart below for a comparison of prices between western and South-East Asian countries.

Carrying Money

Obviously you don't want to have all your money swiped from your back pocket. Find somewhere safe to store it. The pouches that buckle around the waist are not good places to store large amounts of money, but a money belt or pouch that fits inside your clothes *is* and some travellers even have pouches sewn inside their clothes. Another option is take a pair of nylon stockings, fold one leg inside the other and tie it around your waist (inside your clothes of course) with your valuables positioned at the small of your back.

As already mentioned, it's sensible to keep a small emergency stash – say US$50 – separately from the bulk of your funds.

Cash

Nothing beats cash for convenience...or risk. If you lose it, it's gone forever – very few travel insurers will come to your rescue. However, it is a good idea to take some cash with you. Often, it is much easier to change just a few dollars (when leaving a country for example) in cash rather than cheques – and more economical.

Cash is also very handy when banks are closed, or nonexistent. Even in remote villages it seems everyone knows what the greenback is worth, and you can often find someone who will accept US dollars in an emergency.

Travellers' Cheques

American Express or Thomas Cook travellers' cheques are probably the best to carry because they are widely accepted and have 'instant replacement' policies. Amex has offices in most of the major cities. The main idea of carrying travellers' cheques rather than cash is the protection they offer from theft, although it doesn't do a lot of good if you have to go back home to get the refund. Remember that 'instant replacement' may not be exactly instantaneous, although overall most people seem to be pretty satisfied with the service.

Keeping a record of the cheque numbers and the initial purchase details is vitally important. Without this you may well find that 'instant' is a very long time indeed. If you're going to really out-of-the-way places, it may be worth taking a couple of different brands of travellers' cheques since banks may not always accept all varieties. Once again, take well-known brands.

Take nearly all the cheques in large denominations, say US$100s. It's only at the very end of a stay that you may want to change a US$20 or US$10 cheque just to get you through the last day or two. A number of institutions charge a per-cheque service fee, so changing US$100 in 20s can end up five times as expensive as a single US$100 cheque. In many cases, the exchange rate for travellers' cheques is better than the exchange rate for cash.

ATMs & Credit Cards

More and more 'budget travellers' are carrying credit cards these days. They may be useless for day-to-day travel expenses in South-East Asia, but they come in useful for major purchases, like airline tickets.

Credit cards also allow you to draw cash over the counter at selected banks, and if you have a personal identification number (PIN), you can also make cash withdrawals at automatic teller machines (ATMs) in the more developed countries of the region. In these countries it is also possible to access overseas savings accounts through ATMs – check with your bank at home before you leave.

Credit cards are a convenient way to carry your money: your money isn't tied up in travellers' cheques in a currency that is diving; you don't pay commission charges or transaction fees; and the exchange rates are often better than those offered by local banks for cash or travellers' cheques. The disadvantages are that interest is charged, unless your account is always in the black, and credit limits can be too limited. Not all banks in South-East Asia will give cash advances on a credit card, and it can be difficult outside major cities. Don't rely on a credit card in Indochina or Myanmar.

It is not a good idea to rely exclusively on credit cards for accessing money; carry travellers' cheques or cash as a backup. Nobody wants to be short of cash only to see 'Funds unavailable – contact your bank' flash up on an ATM when their bank is thousands of miles away.

Visa is generally more widely accepted in the region, but you shouldn't have any problems with MasterCard, and American Express has a large network of offices. A combination of two or three cards is better still.

Finally, always check purchases and receipts when you buy something with a credit card, and against accounts when you get home. Credit card fraud, especially in Bangkok, is not unknown.

Cheques & Giro

In some parts of South-East Asia, it is possible to cash Eurocheques or personal cheques with the appropriate identification, but this can't be counted on. Dutch travellers with a Dutch post office account can conveniently obtain cash from Indonesian post offices. These *girobetaalkaarten* are useful in the many Indonesian towns where there is no bank.

International Transfers

It is possible to instruct your bank at home to transfer money (assuming you've got it) to a bank overseas where you can collect it. You need to specify the bank and its address. If you're unsure which local bank is best to use, you can ask your bank at home.

A telegraphic transfer is the quickest way to send money – it should reach you in a couple of days. By mail allow at least two weeks. When it gets there, it will most likely be converted into local currency – you can take it as it is or buy travellers' cheques. Singapore and Hong Kong are easily the best countries included in this book to transfer money to. Malaysia and Thailand are not bad either, but even Indonesia and the Philippines are far easier than countries further west like India and Pakistan, where money transfers seem to drop into a bottomless pit, sometimes never to be seen again.

Currency Exchange

Currency exchange is generally straightforward throughout the region. Myanmar is an exception, enforcing extortionate official exchange rates that bear little relation to the value of the local currency. In Vietnam, Laos and Cambodia you needn't exchange money at all if you have a supply of US dollars cash.

If you are going to bring a supply of cash for your travels in South-East Asia, make it US dollars.

Black Market

You can travel through much of South-East Asia nowadays and never have to use the black market to change money – in most countries there isn't one. Myanmar has a thriving black market, mainly in US dollars and duty-free items. In Indochina the US dollar is a generally accepted currency – changing it for local currency is something that almost anyone with access to a cash register can do. See the relevant country chapters for more details.

Tipping & Bargaining

Tipping is not usually expected in South-East Asia. In Hong Kong and Singapore a tip may sometimes be expected, and the same is true of heavily touristed parts of Thailand. Elsewhere there should be no need, unless you are staying in an upmarket accommodation where international rules apply.

You may not need to tip, but you will certainly have to bargain. Haggling over prices is the rule outside supermarkets and department stores, where prices are fixed. If you buy anything in a market, at a street stall or even in a souvenir shop, some bargaining is called for. Remember to keep it friendly – if you think you're being ripped off, walk away and shop somewhere else.

POST & COMMUNICATIONS
Post

Postal services are generally reliable across the region. Even Cambodia has overhauled its postal system and can now be counted on to get letters and parcels to their destinations. Of course it's always better to leave important mail and parcels for the big Asian centres like Bangkok, Singapore, Hong Kong and Jakarta.

There's always an element of risk in sending parcels home by sea, though as a rule

they eventually reach their destinations. If it's something of value to you, it's worth considering air freight – better still, register the parcel.

Inquire at the post office before you bring in a parcel, because there may be special wrapping requirements or it may have to be inspected (as in Indonesia) before being wrapped.

Poste Restante

Poste restante is widely available throughout the region and is the best way of receiving mail. American Express has client mail services. Some travellers use hotels as poste restante services – sometimes this works, sometimes it doesn't. Nowadays, very few embassies will hold mail for their people – they'll just forward it to poste restante. When getting people to write to you, ask them to leave plenty of time for mail to arrive and to print your name very clearly. Underlining the surname also helps.

International Calls

The international phone system varies from country to country across South-East Asia, but it is generally easy to make international calls these days. Many guesthouses can organise direct-dial or reverse-charge calls. In Singapore, Malaysia, Cambodia and Hong Kong international card phones are also widely available. Check the individual country chapters for more details.

Fax

Fax services are widely available in most countries across the region. Try to avoid the business centres in upmarket hotels – tariffs of 30% and upwards are often levied on faxes and international calls.

Email

Despite growing numbers of Internet users across South-East Asia, access is still difficult if you are just travelling through. If you are on a budget, you can basically forget getting online – budget hotels will not provide access, nor will post offices. Check with your server for local access numbers before you set out.

BOOKS
Lonely Planet

A guidebook which covers an area as vast as South-East Asia can only hope to scratch the surface. For more detailed information on a specific area or country, refer to the large range of travel survival kits produced by Lonely Planet. These are updated regularly and provide useful maps and a wealth of information for travellers.

The titles to look for are:

Bali & Lombok – travel survival kit
Cambodia – travel survival kit
Hong Kong, Macau & Guangzhou – travel survival kit
Indonesia – travel survival kit
Java – travel survival kit
Laos – travel survival kit
Malaysia, Singapore & Brunei – travel survival kit
Myanmar (Burma) – travel survival kit
North-East Asia on a shoestring
Philippines – travel survival kit
Thailand – travel survival kit
Vietnam – travel survival kit

Look also for the following city guides:

Bangkok city guide
Ho Chi Minh City (Saigon) city guide
Hong Kong city guide
Jakarta city guide
Singapore city guide

Phrasebooks

Also of interest to travellers in South-East Asia are Lonely Planet's range of phrasebooks, which includes:

Burmese phrasebook
Cantonese phrasebook
Indonesian phrasebook
Lao phrasebook
Malay phrasebook
Mandarin phrasebook
Pilipino phrasebook
Thai phrasebook
Thai Hill Tribes phrasebook
Vietnamese phrasebook

NEWSPAPERS & MAGAZINES

Each of the countries of South-East Asia has its own English language dailies. They vary in quality and are sometimes not available away from the major tourist centres.

International newspapers and magazines are also available in the major regional centres. The newspapers you are most likely to come across are the *International Herald Tribune*, the *Asian Times* and the *Asia Wall Street Journal*, probably in that order. In some places you will come across three-or four-days-old British, European and Australian dailies. French dailies are widely available in Indochina.

On the magazine front, *Time* and *Newsweek* are the big ones, but *The Economist* also makes regular appearances on newsstands. *Asiaweek*, *Far Eastern Economic Review* and *Asia Inc* are Hong Kong productions with good coverage of regional news.

RADIO & TV

A short-wave radio is not a bad idea if you like to keep up with world events. Satellite TV is extremely popular across the region, and can be seen in restaurants, airport lounges and mid-range to top-end hotels. Popular English-language channels are CNN (American international news service), BBC (British news, not available in Hong Kong), HBO (movie channel), Star TV (three channels – sports, popular entertainment and Chinese) and MTV.

PHOTOGRAPHY & VIDEO
Photography

You'll run through plenty of film in South-East Asia, and in Singapore and Hong Kong it's fairly cheap. Film is readily available elsewhere (Malaysia, Thailand and Indonesia, for example), but slide film is often difficult to obtain.

Cameras are also cheap in Singapore and Hong Kong, where the choice of camera equipment is staggering. If you have any difficulties these are also the places to have your camera attended to.

When taking photos in the region compensate for the intensity of the light – for a few hours before and after midday the height of the sun will tend to make pictures very washed out. Try to photograph early or late in the day. There will also be plenty of occasions when you'll want a flash, either for indoor shots or in jungle locations where the amount of light that filters through can be surprisingly low.

Video

Properly used, a video camera can give a fascinating record of your holiday. As well as videoing the obvious things – sunsets, spectacular views – remember to record some of the ordinary everyday details of life in the country. Often the most interesting things occur when you're actually intent on filming something else. Remember too that, unlike still photography, video 'flows' – so, for example, you can shoot scenes of countryside rolling past the train window.

Video cameras these days have amazingly sensitive microphones and you might be surprised by how much sound is picked up. This can also be a problem if there is a lot of ambient noise – filming by the side of a busy road might seem OK when you do it, but viewing it back home might simply give you a deafening cacophony of traffic noise. Two good rules for beginners are: try to film in long takes, and don't move the camera around too much – otherwise, your video could well make your viewers seasick! If your camera has a stabiliser you can take good footage while travelling on various means of transport, even on bumpy roads.

Finally, remember to follow the same rules regarding people's sensitivities as for still photography – having a video camera shoved in their face is probably even more annoying and offensive for locals than a still camera. Always ask permission first.

Photographing People

Always try to make contact with people before you photograph them. Often a smile will do the trick. For portraits, it is best to ask politely. Don't stick cameras in people's faces indiscriminately.

Airport Security

X-ray machines that claim to be film-safe generally are. You are advised to have very sensitive film (1000 ASA and above) checked by hand. Most professionals insist that all their film is checked by hand, and in some cases will take the extra precaution of using a lead-lined bag. For the average traveller these are unnecessary precautions.

TIME

Almost all of South-East Asia is either seven or eight hours ahead of GMT/UTC (Greenwich Mean Time/Universal Time Coordinated).

Malaysia, Brunei, Singapore, Hong Kong, Macau and the Philippines are all eight hours ahead of GMT. Thus, when it's noon in Kuala Lumpur, it's 8 pm the previous day in Los Angeles, 11 pm the previous day in New York, 4 am in London and 2 pm in Sydney.

Thailand, Vietnam, Cambodia and Laos are seven hours ahead of GMT/UTC. When it is noon in Bangkok, it is 9 pm the previous day in Los Angeles, midnight in New York, 5 am in London and 3 pm in Sydney.

Myanmar is six and a half hours ahead of GMT/UTC, half an hour behind Bangkok time. When it is noon in Yangon, it is 9.30 pm the previous day in Los Angeles, 12.30 am in New York, 5.30 am in London and 3.30 pm in Sydney.

There are three time zones in Indonesia: Sumatra, Java and west and central Kalimantan are on West Indonesian Time, which is seven hours ahead of GMT/UTC; Bali, Nusa Tenggara, south and east Kalimantan and Sulawesi are on Central Indonesian Time, which is eight hours ahead of GMT/UTC; and Irian Jaya and Maluku are on East Indonesian Time, which is nine hours ahead of GMT/UTC. Thus, and allowing for variations caused by daylight saving, when it is noon in Jakarta, it is 9 pm the previous day in Los Angeles, midnight in New York, 5 am in London, 1 pm in Ujung Pandang, 2 pm in Jayapura and 3 pm in Sydney.

Make allowances for daylight saving time in the various countries.

ELECTRICITY

If you want to bring your ghetto blaster, notebook computer or hair drier, try to make sure that it can handle different voltages and cycles, and bring socket adaptors. Better still, make sure that it also runs on batteries.

The going voltage is 220V at 50 Hz (cycles), except for the Philippines, which is 220V at 60 Hz. Countries that used to have 110V have made the switch, but you may still occasionally come across 110V in Indonesia, the Philippines and Indochina. Looking at the shape of the outlet on the wall gives no clue as to what voltage is flowing through the wires, so try to find a light bulb or appliance with the voltage written on it. The best advice, however, is to ask before you plug in your appliances. Some have built-in 110/220V switches, and 240V appliances will happily run on 220V.

Reliability of supply is in direct relation to the affluence of the country. Myanmar, the Philippines and Indochina have frequent blackouts and Indonesia is generally reliable but not always; elsewhere you shouldn't have any problems.

Plugs & Sockets

It's best to be prepared for anything. Malaysia and Singapore use the flat three-pin type as used in the UK. Most other countries use the round two-pin type as found in Europe. Exceptions are the Philippines, which uses the flat, vertical, two-pin plug used in the USA, and Hong Kong, which has its own round three-pin socket. Outlets in Indochina generally take European plugs, but some outlets take the US flat-pin type. Buy socket adaptors before you leave – they can be difficult to find in Asia.

WEIGHTS & MEASURES

The metric system is used across South-East Asia. Refer to the conversion table on the inside back cover of this book if you have problems with metric measurements.

LAUNDRY

Getting your laundry done in South-East Asia is never a problem. Guesthouses and hotels provide inexpensive laundry services.

WOMEN TRAVELLERS

South-East Asia is generally a fairly safe region for women to travel in. In some places, the widespread myth of the easy virtue of western women is still taken as fact, but most of urban South-East Asia has become more sophisticated over recent years and this is less a problem than it once was.

Attitudes to Women

South-East Asia is not the Middle East. Women play an active role in day to day public life. Providing you dress appropriately and interact respectfully with the locals you too will be treated with respect. Bear in mind, however, that solo travel is an alien concept for many South-East Asians, particularly if carried out by a woman. It's always a good idea to have a companion.

While most of Indonesia and Malaysia is Muslim, it is not of the fundamentalist variety – you will not be stoned by religious zealots for baring an ankle. Nevertheless, women travellers can experience some difficulty in Sumatra, along the east coast of Malaysia and in the southern Philippines, so extra care should be taken there. Respectful dressing is certainly necessary – beach wear should be reserved for the beach and basically the less skin you expose the better. South-East Asia is not the sort of place where veils are required, however.

Safety Precautions

Attitude can be as important as what you wear. Never respond to come-ons or rude comments. Completely ignoring them is always best. A haughty attitude can work wonders!

A husband (which means any male partner) or children also confer respectability, although the husband doesn't have to be present. Some women travellers wear a wedding ring simply for the impression it makes. The imaginary husband doesn't even have to be left at home – who is to say you're not meeting him that very day?

Some precautions are simply the same for any traveller, male or female, but women should take extra care not to find themselves alone on empty beaches, down dark streets or in other situations where help might not be available.

Be deeply suspicious of any holes in the walls of cheap hotels, especially in showers. In some parts of the region cheap hotels often double as brothels; if you find yourself in one of these, turning the haughty attitude up a notch may help. However, as often as not it's no problem: some people may be there because it's a brothel, but it will be recognised that you're there because it's a cheap hotel. Nevertheless, you should take care, especially at night, and if you're uncomfortable move to another hotel.

Solo women travellers, just like solo males, should be wary when strangers are unexpectedly friendly. See the note about theft in the following Dangers & Annoyances section.

GAY & LESBIAN TRAVELLERS

In general, gay men are more accepted in South-East Asia than gay women. Public displays of affection, heterosexual or homosexual, are frowned upon across the region. It would pay to be discrete, if not obsessively so, but your private sexual conduct will not attract the attention of authorities in South-East Asia unless it involves children – the abuse of whom is a problem in some parts of the region.

DISABLED TRAVELLERS

Travellers with serious disabilities are unlikely to find South-East Asia very user friendly. Even the more sophisticated cities, such as Hong Kong and Singapore, are very much push-and-shove places. In general, care of the disabled is left to close family members and throughout the region it is unrealistic to expect much in the way of public amenities.

TRAVEL WITH CHILDREN

South-East Asia is a good place to travel with children. They'll be fussed over and looked after wherever you go, and kids are perfect ice-breakers – you'll get to meet far more locals if you have the children along. For more details on how to get the most out of your trip, pick up a copy of Lonely Planet's *Travel with Children*.

DANGERS & ANNOYANCES
Theft

Theft is not the problem that many people imagine it to be in South-East Asia. To be sure, if you wander around with money hanging out of your back pocket or with your bag open, you can expect things to go missing. But with a small amount of common sense and routine caution there's no reason why you should have anything stolen on your travels. The most important things to guard are your passport, certain documents, tickets and money. It's best to always carry these in a money belt or a sturdy leather pouch next to your skin.

Theft in South-East Asia is usually carried out by stealth. Be alert to the possible presence of snatch thieves, who will whisk a camera or a bag off your shoulder. Don't store valuables in easily accessible places. Violent theft is very rare but occurs from time to time – usually late at night and after the victim has been drinking. Be careful walking alone late at night and don't fall asleep in taxis. Feel free to relax a little in affluent cities like Hong Kong, Singapore and Kuala Lumpur.

Always be diplomatically suspicious of overfriendly locals. Don't accept gifts of food and drinks from someone you don't know. In Thailand, thieves have been known to use drugged food and drinks to knock travellers out and get at their belongings.

Finally, don't let paranoia ruin your trip. With just a few sensible precautions most travellers make their way across the region without incident.

Scams

Most scams assume you're either very gullible or very stupid – if you have your wits about you, there's no reason to become a victim of one.

Two perennial scams are airline-ticket rackets and gemstones (buy here cheap, sell at home for huge profits). It seems obvious, but it's not a good idea to fork out wads of cash for an airline ticket to an 'agency' that operates from a kitchen table – it's always better to spend a little more and buy from an established operator. As for gemstones, if there really were vast amounts of money to be made by selling them back home, there would be queues outside Bangkok jewellery shops.

There are any number of scams, but they all revolve around the unlikely scenario of a local presenting you with an opportunity to save or make lots of money. Gambling rackets, 'losing' travellers' cheques, guaranteeing loans – they're all scams on which unfortunate or foolish travellers have lost their shirts.

Drugs

The risks associated with drug use have grown to the point where, in most parts of the region, you won't even see joints being passed around. These days, even a little harmless grass can cause a great deal of trouble. To get mixed up with anything heavier would be to court a long jail sentence or, in some places, the death penalty. There are enough foreign travellers languishing in South-East Asian jails as it is; don't add to their numbers.

The days of paying off a few cops and making a speedy exit from the country have disappeared. Even easy-going Bali now has a jail just down the road from Kuta Beach where a number of travellers are enjoying the tropical climate much longer than they intended. In Indonesia, you can actually end up behind bars because your travel companions had dope and you didn't report them.

Other places can be a whole lot worse. A spell in a Thai prison is nobody's idea of a pleasant way to pass the time, while in Malaysia and Singapore, a prison spell may be supplemented with a beating with the *rotan*. In those countries simple possession can have you dangling from a rope, as two Australians discovered in 1986. On a per capita basis, the Malaysians execute far more people for drug-related offences (and with far less publicity) than the Americans do for murder.

Don't bother bringing drugs home with you either. Back home in the west you may not get hanged for possession, but with all those South-East Asian visa stamps there's a good chance customs officials will take a good look at your luggage.

ACTIVITIES
Trekking

Trekking in South-East Asia doesn't take on the same proportions as in Nepal, but plenty of good treks are possible, particularly jungle hikes. Most visitors at least hike up a mountain or volcano somewhere in their travels – this inevitably involves a shivering, predawn climb to catch the sunrise.

Trekking in the hill tribe regions of Thailand features on many travellers' itineraries. It's no longer a unique experience, but despite mass tourism many still find it rewarding. Shop around in Chiang Mai for a trek. Most last from three to seven days and may include rafting and elephant rides. Treks can also be organised in Chiang Rai, Mae Hong Son and other northern centres.

One of Malaysia's highlights is its national parks, and Taman Negara National Park has some excellent walks. Some good treks can also be organised in East Malaysia, particularly in Sarawak, at Gunung Mulu, and around Bario for the more adventurous. No trip to Sabah is complete without visiting the towering summit of Mt Kinabalu, a relatively easy two day climb.

In Indonesia, Sumatra has some good jungle treks, particularly in Gunung Leuser National Park, and it is easy to organise treks in Berastagi or Bukit Lawang. Java has some good walks in the national parks, but is noted more for its volcanic peaks: Gunung Merapi can be a taxing climb, while spectacular Gunung Bromo is more of a stroll. Batur and Agung volcanoes, on Bali, are popular day trips, or try Gunung Rinjani on neighbouring Lombok for an excellent three day hike. Indonesia's outer regions, particularly Irian

Jaya and Sulawesi, present plenty of more adventurous jungle trekking opportunities.

In the Philippines, Mt Mayon is a 'must climb', although recent eruptions have made it more difficult; this is also the case with Mt Pinatubo, another very active volcano. You can arrange walks around Banaue in North Luzon and Quezon National Park.

In Vietnam, Tam Dao has some of the best walks.

Surfing

Indonesia is the big surfing destination in Asia, and for years surfers have been carting their boards to isolated outposts of the archipelago in search of long, deserted waves. Ulu Watu in Bali, Grajagan in Java and Nias in Sumatra are famous surfing destinations, but there is surf right along the southern coast of the inner islands – from Sumatra through to Sumbawa, Sumba and across to Irian Jaya.

It is probably only a matter of time before new areas are opened up to surfing. Perhaps the famous surfing scene from *Apocalypse Now* will inspire a new invasion of Vietnam.

Diving & Snorkelling

South-East Asia is an underwater paradise that presents countless opportunities for diving and snorkelling. Indonesia, Malaysia and Thailand have the best facilities, and many easily-accessible reefs, but the Philippines and even Vietnam also have some diving spots.

Many beach resorts rent out masks, snorkels and fins, and novices will require little outlay. But if you intend to do a lot of snorkelling it is worth bringing your own equipment: rental gear is not always of good quality and it soon becomes more economical to buy rather than rent. You don't have to hire boats or venture to far-flung islands to find good snorkelling – Lovina Beach (Bali) and the Gili Islands (Lombok) in Indonesia; Tioman and the Perhentian Islands on Malaysia's east coast; and Ko Pha-Ngan in Thailand are all popular beach resorts with easily accessible snorkelling.

Diving is generally cheap in South-East Asia and there are some very good operators

around. However, it isn't always the best place to get a diving certificate because fewer operators are qualified to offer diving courses and those that do are not always of the highest standard. It is usually better to get a certificate before arriving, eg diving courses in Cairns, Australia, are often of high quality and cheaper than in South-East Asia.

Indonesia offers extensive opportunities for diving: Bali has some excellent dives and, because it is the main tourist area, there are plenty of operators; there are countless small islands and reefs between Labuanbajo, in Flores, and Komodo; Flores, Timor and Maluku all have good diving; and the 'sea gardens' of Sulawesi, particularly around Manado, are legendary.

There is some diving on the west coast of the Malaysian peninsula, but it is better on the east coast, where the islands of Tioman, Kapas, Redang and the Perhentians are just some of the possibilities. Some of the best diving in Malaysia is found in Borneo; Sabah, in particular, has excellent diving and very professional dive outfits. Sipadan Island and its amazing wall is the most famous (and expensive) dive site.

In Thailand, Pattaya is crammed with dive shops and is popular because of its easy access and proximity to Bangkok. Phuket is the next most popular and presents the best diving opportunities on plenty of nearby islands, including Ao Phang-Nga and the world-famous Similan and Surin Islands, in the Andaman Sea. Chumpon Province, just north of Surat Thani, has a dozen or so islands with undisturbed reefs.

Unfortunately, many of the coral reefs in South-East Asia are under threat. Dynamite fishing has been a major culprit: explosives are dropped into the water to stun fish, and then it is an easy matter to scoop up the catch from the surface. In the process the delicate coral is devastated. Other threats to the reefs include silting, caused by deforestation, overdevelopment in tourist areas and coral harvesting (live coral for board room fish tanks can bring big money). Moves are afoot to establish marine parks throughout the region, but it may be a case of too little too late.

WORK

Asia may be on an economic roll, but most of the region is still not quite affluent enough to provide jobs for itinerant westerners. Jobs are more forthcoming in North-East Asia – Korea, Japan and Taiwan – but even there the market is shrinking.

Hong Kong is the only place covered by this book that attracts large number of foreigners looking for work. Options range from teaching English (difficult to get in Hong Kong) to bar work (the preferred option for unskilled newcomers). Wages are poor relative to Hong Kong's very high standard of living. In mid-1997 Hong Kong will revert to mainland Chinese rule – whether foreign workers will still be so welcome there afterwards is anyone's guess.

Elsewhere around South-East Asia jobs are sometimes available teaching English. Wages are generally poor (unless you are properly qualified), but will at least cover your living expenses.

The other stand-by of the traveller is buying and selling. Unless you're highly motivated, able to order in bulk and have contacts in retail outlets at home, you are not realistically going to make much money out of this. Buyers who purchase collectables or gems are experts (if they are making any money at it).

ACCOMMODATION

South-East Asia is crammed with hotels, and it is very unusual to have problems finding somewhere to stay. The exception to this rule is at peak tourist periods, such as Christmas, when popular destinations like Bali, and Ko Samui and Phuket in Thailand, get packed out. Keep away from the big name destinations at busy times of the year.

All the major attractions on the South-East Asian circuit have inexpensive guesthouse (losmen in Indonesia) accommodation, but off the beaten track you may find yourself staying in Chinese hotels where prices verge on mid-range.

If you stick to the travellers' circuit, you should be able to keep accommodation costs down to US$5 to US$10 per day for a double.

In expensive destinations, such as Hong Kong, Singapore, Brunei and Kuala Lumpur, you will have to pay more or stay in a dorm.

There is often a hotel booking desk at international airports, although they often do not cover the lower strata of hotels. Some airports (like Bangkok's) are better than others (like Singapore's) for this game. Otherwise, you'll generally find hotels clustered near bus and train stations – always good places to start hunting. Check your room and the bathroom before you agree to take it. If the sheets don't look clean, ask to have them changed right away.

If you think a hotel is too expensive, ask if they have anything cheaper. A very important point to remember in Chinese hotels is that a 'single' room usually has a double bed while a 'double' has two beds. A couple can always request a single room. Many cheaper hotels throughout the region only supply one sheet on the bed; if you want a top sheet (useful for keeping mosquitoes away) you must supply your own.

FOOD

In general, food in South-East Asia is healthy. A good rule of thumb is to glance at the restaurant or food stall and the people running it – if it looks clean and they look healthy, then chances are the food will be OK too.

Be wary of salads and other uncooked food – it's no good avoiding the water if you then eat fruit or vegetables that have been washed in that unhealthy water. Cooked food that has been allowed to go cold can also be dangerous.

In general, you should have few problems and, in places like Singapore, you can usually eat from street stalls with impunity. Of course, you'll also find Coke and other hygienically pure western delights. McDonald's is spreading its tentacles through the region too and you'll find branches in Hong Kong, Macau, Malaysia, the Philippines, Singapore and Thailand. KFC has spread its influence even more widely.

Despite the pleasures of the local cuisine, some travellers feel there are benefits to be had by preparing their own food. This requires carrying cooking gear and a gas cooker (replacement cylinders are available in most places in the region), but you can save money this way and also eat well.

Fruit

Fruit can be one of the special taste treats of South-East Asian travel. Apart from all those mundane bananas, pineapples and coconuts, there is a host of fruits that will do wonderful things to your taste buds.

Durian – the most infamous fruit of the region, the durian is a large green fruit with a hard spiny exterior. Crack it open to reveal the biggest stink imaginable! Drains blocked up? No, it's just the durian season. If you can hold your nose and eat at the same time, you might actually learn to love them. The Chinese regard them as an aphrodisiac.

Jeruk – the all-purpose term for citrus fruit. There are many kinds available, including the huge *jeruk muntis* or *jerunga*, known in the west as a *pomelo*. It's larger than a grapefruit and has very thick skin, but tastes sweeter – more like an orange.

Mangosteen – the small purple-brown mangosteen cracks open to reveal tasty white segments with a very fine flavour. Queen Victoria once offered a reward to anyone able to transport a mangosteen back to England while still edible.

Nangka – an enormous yellow-green fruit that can weigh over 20 kg. Inside are hundreds of individual bright yellow segments. Also called jackfruit, the taste is distinctive and the texture slightly rubbery.

Rambutan – a bright red fruit covered in soft, hairy spines, the name means 'hairy'. Break it open to reveal a delicious, white, lychee-like fruit inside.

Salak – found chiefly in Indonesia, the salak is immediately recognisable because of its brown 'snakeskin' covering. Peel the skin off to reveal segments that taste like a cross between an apple and a walnut. Bali salaks are much nicer than any others.

Starfruit – called belimbing in Indonesia and Malaysia, the name is obvious when you see a slice – it's star shaped. It tastes cool, crisp and watery.

Zurzat – also spelt sirsak, and known in the west as soursop, a warty green skin covers a thirst-quenching interior with a slight lemonish taste. They are ripe when they feel squishy.

Other – the *sawo* looks like a potato and tastes like a pear. *Jambu* is pear shaped but has a radish-like crispy texture and a pink, shiny colour. *Papaya*, or *paw paw*, has a sweet, yellow pulp.

DRINKS
Nonalcoholic Drinks

It's rarely safe to drink tap water in South-East Asia – Hong Kong and Singapore are exceptions. It's a good idea to be careful with ice too, at least in budget eateries.

One of the great pleasures of dropping into the more touristed parts of South-East Asia (Bali, the southern beach retreats of Thailand etc) is the wide range of shakes and fruit juices. Canned and bottled drinks are also available everywhere – there's no escaping Coke, even if you trek days into the interior of Kalimantan.

Alcoholic Drinks

Beer is available nearly everywhere (Brunei is the odd one out), but prices vary dramatically from place to place. If such things are important to you, the Philippines has the cheapest beer prices, and Cambodia follows not far behind. In Thailand and Malaysia beer is a luxury item.

Wine drinkers will be disappointed by South-East Asia. Unless you go upmarket you're unlikely to come across it in restaurants, though inexpensive eastern European wines are available in Indochina.

Most countries in the region also have their local firewaters – see the country chapters for more details.

Getting There & Away

Step one is to get to Asia and, in these days of intense competition between the airlines, there are plenty of opportunities to find cheap tickets to a variety of 'gateway' cities. You have virtually no choice apart from flying, though – regular shipping services to South-East Asia are just about nonexistent and China-Vietnam and China-Laos are the only overland options.

AIR

The major Asian gateways for cheap flights are Singapore, Bangkok and Hong Kong. They are all good places to fly to and good places to fly from. Penang is another good place to shop for tickets.

Cheap tickets are available in two distinct categories – official and unofficial. Official ones are advance purchase tickets, budget fares, Apex, super-Apex or whatever other promotional devices airlines can think of to get 'bums on seats'.

Unofficial tickets are simply discounted tickets which the airlines release through selected travel agents. Don't go looking for discounted tickets straight from the airlines – they are only available through travel agents. Generally, you can find discounted tickets at prices as low as, or lower than, the Apex or budget tickets; there is no advance-purchase requirement nor should there be any cancellation penalty, although individual travel agents may institute their own cancellation charges.

It is necessary to exercise a little caution with discounted tickets. For example, make sure 'OK' on the ticket really means you have a confirmed seat. Phone the airline and reconfirm; it's better to find out immediately if the agent has made a firm booking.

Buying Tickets

Plane tickets will probably be the most expensive items in your budget, and buying them can be an intimidating business. There is likely to be a multitude of airlines and travel agents hoping to separate you from your money, and it is always worth putting aside a few hours to research the state of the market.

Start early: some of the cheapest tickets have to be bought months in advance and popular flights can sell out quickly. Talk to other recent travellers – they may be able to stop you making some of the same old mistakes. Look at the ads in newspapers and magazines (not forgetting the press of the ethnic group whose country you plan to visit), consult reference books and watch for special offers.

Phone several travel agents for bargains. (Airlines can supply information on routes and timetables, but, except during inter-airline wars, they do not supply the cheapest tickets.) Find out the fare, the route, the duration of the journey and any restrictions on the ticket. Then sit back and decide which is best for you.

You may discover that those impossibly cheap flights are 'fully booked, but we have another one that costs a bit more...' Or, the flight is on an airline notorious for its poor safety standards and leaves you in the world's least favourite airport in mid-journey for 14 hours. Or, they claim only to have the last two seats available for that country for the whole of July, which they will hold for you for a maximum of two hours. Don't panic – keep ringing around.

Use the fares quoted in this book as a guide only. They are approximate and based on the rates advertised by travel agents at the time of writing. Quoted air fares do not necessarily constitute a recommendation for the carrier.

If you are travelling from the UK or USA, you will probably find that the cheapest flights are being advertised by obscure bucket shops whose names haven't yet reached the telephone directory. Many such firms are honest and solvent, but there are a few rogues who will take your money and disappear, to reopen elsewhere a month or two later under a new name.

If you feel suspicious about a firm, don't give them all the money at once – leave a deposit of 20% or so and pay the balance when you get the ticket. If they insist on cash in advance, go somewhere else. And once you have the ticket, ring the airline to confirm that you are actually booked onto the flight.

You may decide to pay more than the rock-bottom fare by opting for the safety of a better known travel agent. Firms such as STA Travel, who has offices worldwide, Council Travel in the USA and Travel CUTS in Canada are not going to disappear overnight, leaving you clutching a receipt for a nonexistent ticket, and they offer good prices to most destinations.

Once you have your ticket write its number down, together with the flight number and other details, and keep this information somewhere separate and safe. If the ticket is lost or stolen, this will help you get a replacement.

It's sensible to buy travel insurance as early as possible. If you buy it the week before you fly, you may find, for example, that you're not covered for delays to your flight caused by industrial action.

Round-the-World Tickets & Circle Pacific Fares

Round-the-World (RTW) tickets have become very popular in the last few years. The airline RTW tickets are often real bargains, and can work out no more expensive or even cheaper than an ordinary return ticket. Prices start from about £850, A$1900 or US$1400.

The official airline RTW tickets are usually put together by a combination of two airlines and permit you to fly anywhere you want on their route systems, so long as you do not backtrack. Other restrictions are that you (usually) must book the first sector in advance and cancellation penalties then apply. There may be restrictions on how many stops you are permitted. Usually the tickets are valid for a period of between 90

days and a year. An alternative type of RTW ticket is one where a travel agency combines a number of discounted tickets.

Circle Pacific tickets use a combination of airlines to circle the Pacific – combining Australia, New Zealand, North America and Asia. As with RTW tickets, there are advance purchase restrictions and limits to how many stopovers you can make. These fares are likely to be around 15% cheaper than Round-the-World tickets.

North America

Intense competition between Asian airlines on the US west coast and Vancouver has resulted in ticket discounting.

The *New York Times*, the *Chicago Tribune*, the *LA Times*, the *San Francisco Examiner*, the *Vancouver Sun* and the *Toronto Globe & Mail* all produce weekly travel sections in which you'll find any number of travel agents' ads. Student travel specialists Council Travel and Student Travel Network have offices in major US cities, while Travel CUTS has outlets throughout Canada. For discounted fares and ticketing, also contact CIEE or STA Travel offices in the USA.

The magazine *Travel Unlimited* (PO Box 1058, Allston, Mass 02134, USA) publishes details of the cheapest air fares and courier possibilities for destinations all over the world from the USA.

From the US west coast, fares to Singapore, Bangkok or Hong Kong cost around US$700/1000 one way/return, while Bali flights cost from US$650/1100 in the low season (outside summer and Christmas). Flights to Malaysia are about US$800 one way. An interesting way to reach Indonesia is Garuda's Los Angeles-Honolulu-Biak-Denpasar flight for around US$700 one way, US$1200 return. There are plenty of competitive fares offered to Indonesia from the USA.

From Kuala Lumpur, in Malaysia, you can fly to the US west coast for RM1100. From Singapore, one-way fares to the US west coast are around S$900 direct or with a stop in Manila. If you shop around the travel agents in Manila, you should be able get tickets to the US west coast for US$370 to US$450. There are always special multi-stop deals on offer, such as Singapore-Jakarta-Sydney-Noumea-Auckland-Papeete-Los Angeles for S$1550. From Bangkok, one-way flights to Los Angeles or San Francisco cost from US$400 to US$500.

Australia & New Zealand

Since there are far fewer airlines flying to and from Australia and New Zealand than there are to and from Europe and North America, you won't find the same wide range of fares. Nevertheless, bargains can still be found with a little shopping around. STA Travel and Flight Centre offices are major dealers in cheap air fares. Check them for starters or simply scan the ads in newspaper travel sections.

Regular excursion return fares from New Zealand and Australia usually have a low and a high season. The high season normally only applies for a limited time over the December-January school holiday period. There are also 'special fares', usually operated by airlines which are not regulars over that route, or which take a more roundabout route.

Return fares from Melbourne and Sydney include: Singapore, A$750 to A$1000; Kuala Lumpur, A$1000 to A$1100; Bangkok, A$799 to A$1050; Hong Kong, A$950 to A$1200; and Manila, A$850 to A$1200. Logically it should be cheaper to fly to Denpasar (Bali), but its popularity as a holiday destination means that fares are around A$850 to A$1100, and the maximum stay is usually only 90 days. Low fares quoted here are for specials available through travel agents and restrictions usually apply; high fares are for more flexible tickets of six to 12 months' duration.

The cheapest flights to Asia are from Darwin and Perth. The Merpati flight from Darwin to Kupang (on the Indonesian island of Timor) costs A$198/330 one way/return (around A$50 more in the high season) and is an economical and interesting way out of the country. Merpati also flies from Darwin

to Ambon in Maluku for A$225/385. Other low-season fares from Darwin or Perth include Denpasar A$400/630 one way/return, Singapore or Kuala Lumpur A$400/670, Bangkok A$400/780, Manila A$500/880 and Brunei A$380/700.

From Auckland, you can get return flights to Denpasar for around NZ$1200 and to Bangkok for around NZ$1250. The Singapore run has the most competition, with flights from NZ$1150 return or only NZ$650 one way.

From Penang in Malaysia, you can get one-way fares to Sydney from as little as RM900; Perth is about RM800 one way. From Singapore, fares to Australia include Sydney or Melbourne for S$500 one way, or Perth for S$400 one way, S$500 return. From Bangkok, fares to Sydney/Melbourne are available for around US$399.

The UK & Continental Europe

Ticket discounting has long been established in the UK and it's wide open – the various agents advertise their fares and there's nothing under the counter about it at all.

Trailfinders, in West London, produces a lavishly illustrated brochure which includes air fare details. Look for ads in the listings magazine *Time Out* and the Sunday papers. Also look out for free magazines, such as *TNT* and *Southern Cross*, which are widely available in London. Start by looking outside the main railway stations.

The Globetrotters Club (BCM Roving, London WC1N 3XX) publishes a newsletter called *Globe* which covers obscure destinations and can help in finding travelling companions.

A couple of excellent agents to try are Trailfinders and STA Travel. Trailfinders is at 194 Kensington High St, London W8 (☎ (0171) 938-3939) and at 46 Earl's Court Rd (☎ (0171) 938-3366). STA is at 74 Old Brompton Rd, London W7 (☎ (0171) 581-1022) and at Clifton House, 117 Euston Rd (☎ (0171) 388-2261).

On the Continent, Amsterdam and Antwerp are among the best places for buying airline tickets. WATS, Keyserlei 44,

Antwerp, Belgium, has been recommended. In Amsterdam, NBBS is a popular travel agent.

Many of the cheapest fares from Europe to South-East Asia are offered by Eastern European carriers. Garuda Indonesia is also an active fare cutter and you can find all sorts of interesting routes to Jakarta or all the way to Australia with stopovers in Indonesia.

Rock-bottom fares (low season) from London to South-East Asia for one way/return include Bangkok, £305/£540; Singapore, £216/£399; Jakarta, £299/£439; Denpasar, £332/£587; Manila, £265/£529; and Hong Kong, £299/£479. From London to Malaysia, you're looking at UK£220/£400 return. Flights from London to Australia or New Zealand with stopovers in South-East Asia are available from around £400 one way. You can get a London-Australia return ticket with a stopover in Jakarta or Bali, Singapore or Bangkok for around £950.

To fly to London from Penang in Malaysia, fares start at around RM830 with the less popular airlines such as Aeroflot. From Singapore, fares to London or other European destinations cost from S$550 one way with the East European airlines, and from S$620 one way with the better airlines. From Bangkok, fares to London cost about US$623.

LAND
China
The only land borders between South-East Asia and the rest of Asia are the frontier that Myanmar shares with India, and the Chinese border with Myanmar, Laos and Vietnam. For decades they have been closed to foreign tourists, but at last it is possible to travel overland between China and Vietnam and China and Laos.

China-Vietnam border crossings are at Hekou-Lao Cai and at Pingxiang-Dong Dang, on the rail line between Beijing and Hanoi. A special visa is required to enter Vietnam from China – it is not difficult to get but costs extra. There are no special requirements for entering China.

You can cross into Laos from Yunnan Province in China at Boten in Luang Nam Tha Province in Laos if you have a Lao visa.

The border crossing from Riuli in China to Mu-se in Myanmar, currently open to group tours from China, may possibly open up to independent travellers. However, it is unlikely you will be able to exit Myanmar at this point.

SEA
No regular ships or ferries connect South-East Asia with destinations outside the region. Proposals to reopen the old Madras-Penang ferry surface from time to time, and rumours about the opening of a Darwin-Kupang ferry service are perpetual, but as yet flying is still the only way to cover these runs.

Some cargo ships from Europe and the US take passengers and stop in South-East Asia, but though this may be a romantic way to see the world, it is much more expensive than flying. The other option is to get hired as crew for private boats to Indonesia, or tag along and pay for your keep. This is certainly possible from Darwin, especially at the time of the Darwin-Ambon yacht race if you are an experienced sailor.

Getting Around

AIR

All sorts of ticket bargains around the region are available to you once you arrive in South-East Asia. These inter-Asia fares are widely available, although Bangkok, Singapore, Penang and Hong Kong are the major ticket discounting centres.

A little caution is necessary when looking for tickets in Asia. First of all, shop around – a wise move anywhere, of course. Secondly,

don't believe everything you are told – ticket agents in Penang (Malaysia) are very fond of telling people that tickets there are cheaper than in Bangkok or Singapore or wherever. In actual fact, they are often much the same price anywhere; if there is any difference it's likely to be in the favour of the originating city. For example, you're unlikely to find a Bangkok to Kathmandu ticket cheaper in Penang than in Bangkok. Or a Penang to

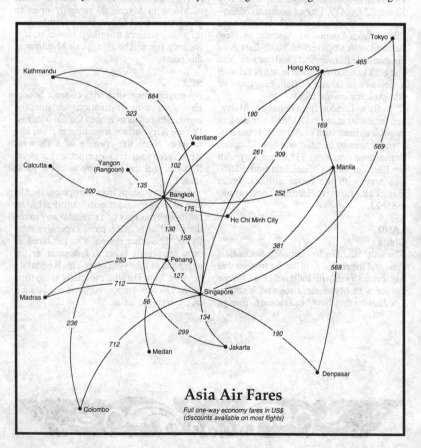

Asia Air Fares

Full one-way economy fares in US$
(discounts available on most flights)

Hong Kong ticket cheaper in Singapore than in Penang.

Most important of all, be very careful that you get what you want before handing over money and that the ticket is precisely what you pay for. Over the years, we have had many letters from people complaining that they were done by various agents.

Favourite tricks include tickets with very limited periods of validity when you have been told they are valid all year round. Or, you could find a ticket is marked 'OK', indicating that you have a seat reservation, when no reservation has been made. Also, you could find that an airline will not accept your ticket for a subsequent sector of your travels.

Take care, but don't get too uptight about it – most agents are reliable. People who buy tickets from 'agents' who operate from coffee-bar tables are asking for trouble. And remember to reconfirm. It doesn't hurt to reconfirm the moment you get your ticket, and that is the most certain way of finding out if the 'OK' on your ticket really is OK.

Most airports in South-East Asia charge a departure tax, so make sure you have that final necessary bit of local currency left.

Approximate inter-Asia fares are shown in the chart in this section.

Student Travel

There are student travel offices in most South-East Asian capitals, most of them associated in some way with STA Travel. In Asia, student fares rarely have an edge over simple discount fares (available at all agencies), but at least STA is a reliable operator.

Other services they can provide include local tours and accommodation bookings. Usually the hotels they deal with are somewhat upmarket and even with discounts they're outside the usual budget travellers' range. If you're a real student, they can also provide student cards.

OVERLANDING IN SOUTH-EAST ASIA

With all the water in the way, 'overlanding' through South-East Asia seems a misnomer. However, if by the term overlanding you mean travelling from place to place by local transport with the minimum use of aircraft, then South-East Asia offers enormous scope.

Indonesia & Singapore

If you want to trek right through Indonesia from the Australian end, the logical starting point is Kupang in Timor. There are regular flights from Darwin in Australia's Northern Territory to Kupang. From Kupang, you could work your way through the amazing and varied islands of Nusa Tenggara. Along the way you could climb to see the multi-coloured lakes of Keli Mutu in Flores, see the dragons of Komodo and pause at the wonderful Gili Islands off Lombok.

From Bali, after you've explored that magical island, the next stage is to hop on a bus to Surabaya, usually an overnight trip. On the way to Surabaya, it's worth stopping off to climb the extraordinary Gunung Bromo in Java. From Surabaya, you can continue to Yogyakarta, the cultural heartland of Java and Indonesia.

On from Yogya, you can catch a train or bus to Jakarta, although if you have time, there are interesting stops en route at, for example, the Dieng Plateau, Pangandaran, Bandung and Bogor.

At Jakarta, you may be forced to make a decision. If your visa is running short – and unfortunately present visa limitations make it virtually impossible to explore Indonesia in one bite – you have to leave. If you're in that situation head to Singapore, from where you can then re-enter Indonesia and start again. There's no need to return to Jakarta though.

From Singapore ferries operate to Batam and Bintan islands in the Riau Archipelago, and from there speed boats go to Pekanbaru in Sumatra. If you're not embroiled in visa problems back in Jakarta, you could continue by bus or train, and then by ferry, to Sumatra.

Travel in southern Sumatra involves long bus trips to get to the north, so many people opt instead for the regular ship or flight from Jakarta to Padang. After Padang, the road through Sumatra continues north through delightful Bukittinggi, with perhaps a side trip to Nias Island and then a well-earned rest at relaxing Lake Toba.

Finally, you exit Sumatra by taking the ferry or flying from Medan to Penang in Malaysia. An alternative to this route would be to go from Singapore up to Penang and enter Sumatra at Medan and then do the trip through Sumatra in reverse, finally exiting to Jakarta or to the Riau Archipelago and/or Singapore.

And of course, there are other Indonesian islands to the north and east, including Kalimantan (the southern half or Borneo), wonderful Sulawesi, the Maluku Islands and Irian Jaya. To Sulawesi, Pelni passenger ships go from Java, Lombok, Sumbawa and Flores. It is then possible to fly from Manado in northern Sulawesi to the Philippines, or you can take a boat from Sulawesi to Kalimantan and then cross overland to East Malaysia (only Pontianak to Kuching is visa-free).

Malaysia & Thailand

Assuming you've followed the traditional path up through Indonesia, you're now in Penang, and after enjoying yourself there you can head south to the hill stations like the Cameron Highlands, to Pulau Pangkor, to modern Kuala Lumpur, to historic Melaka and, finally, arrive at Singapore. Then you can head up the east coast and sample Malaysia's beaches and offshore islands. Travel in Malaysia is just about the most hassle-free of anywhere in Asia. There are excellent train and bus services, and very economical share-taxis; even the hitching is easy.

The north Bornean states – Malaysia's Sabah and Sarawak, and the independent kingdom of Brunei – are most easily visited from Singapore or Peninsular Malaysia, because connections between north Borneo and Kalimantan are limited. You can fly from Sabah direct to Manila or Hong Kong.

There are a variety of ways of crossing to Thailand from Malaysia, but the usual routes are to take a taxi or train from Penang to Hat Yai if you're on the west coast, or simply to walk across the border from Rantau Panjang to Sungai Kolok on the east coast.

From Hat Yai, the major city in the south of Thailand, you can continue by bus to Phuket, a resort island with superb beaches. Then continue north to Surat Thani and the equally beautiful islands of Ko Samui, Ko Pha-Ngan and Ko Tao. Finally, you reach hyperactive Bangkok and decide where to head next.

For most travellers, that decision will be to continue north to Chiang Mai – the second city of Thailand and another great travellers' centre. On the way, you could pause to explore the ancient cities of Ayuthaya and Sukhothai. From Chiang Mai, you can make treks into the colourful hill tribe areas or you can loop back to Bangkok through the north-east region. Bangkok is more than just the sin city of South-East Asia, it's also a centre for cheap airline tickets, so the next question is where to fly to – east or west.

Myanmar (Burma) & West

Since you can now get 28-day visas for Myanmar, it's a bit less of a rush around the attractions of that unusual country. Yangon (Rangoon) is the only entry point and you can visit Myanmar as a foray from Bangkok, or use Myanmar as a stepping stone between South-East Asia and West Asia. If the latter is your intention, then it's time to pack *South-East Asia on a shoestring* away and pick up other Lonely Planet guides on Bangladesh, India, Nepal and beyond.

Vietnam, Laos & Cambodia

This area of South-East Asia, often referred to as Indochina, has opened its doors to foreign travellers, but options for entering the area are still fairly limited. More border crossings should open, but as yet the only regular overland crossings are Thailand-Laos, China-Vietnam, China-Laos and Vietnam-Cambodia.

The main option is still to fly. To Vietnam there are a number of flights to and from Ho Chi Minh City's Tan Son Nhut or Hanoi's Noi Bai airports. Bangkok is the cheapest and most popular gateway.

The main overland option from Thailand is to enter Laos via the Nong Khai crossing near Vientiane. See the Laos chapter for other border crossings. With the possible exception of the Lao Bao exit point, you can still only fly between Laos and Vietnam. No border crossings are permitted between Laos and Cambodia, but buses run regularly between Phnom Penh in Cambodia and Vietnam's Ho Chi Minh City.

The popular way to reach Vietnam from China is via the border at Dong Dang or Lao Cai. You can also enter Laos from China at Boten. Travellers have reported other ways of reaching Indochina, notably by boat from Thailand to Cambodia via Ko Kong island, but these options are illegal and dangerous.

The most cost-effective way to tour Indochina is to take a flight from Bangkok to Phnom Penh or Ho Chi Minh City, then travel through Cambodia and up through Vietnam to the north. Then continue to China or fly from Hanoi to Laos. From Laos you can continue back overland into Thailand.

Hong Kong & East

From Hong Kong, the frenetic city-state and gateway to China, you've got a choice of heading further east or west (in which case you'll need Lonely Planet's *North-East Asia on a shoestring* for China, Japan, Korea and Taiwan), turning south for Vietnam or flying to the Philippines. Travelling across China to the far west then down into Pakistan via the Karakoram Highway from Kashgar, or into Nepal via Lhasa, are adventurous routes.

Philippines

Manila is overwhelmingly the gateway to the Philippines, but there is an interesting short flight between Davao in Mindanao and Manado in Sulawesi (Indonesia). It is also possible to fly directly from Singapore to Cebu.

From Manila you can head north to the rice terraces and beaches of north Luzon, and south to the Mayon volcano and other attractions of south Luzon. Or, island-hop through the tightly clustered Visayas.

Eventually, you can hop back to Manila and decide where to go next – on to Australia or further afield. A good loop through the region includes travelling from Australia to Indonesia, Singapore, Malaysia, Thailand, Indochina, Hong Kong, Philippines and, finally, back to Australia. But, of course, there are lots of other possibilities.

BUS

Bus travel can be absurdly comfortable, certainly by the standards further west in Asia, but there are always opportunities for crowded, bone-shaking rides shared with chickens, goats and all sorts of local produce.

Air-con luxury buses are widespread in Malaysia and Thailand (where they really are gigantic). In Indonesia air-con buses cover the main runs from north Sumatra right though to Flores, and the Philippines also has a number of air-con services. A host of cheaper, regular buses of a variety of standards cover the major and minor routes; minibuses also operate and sometimes provide luxury services.

Regular buses tend to be cheap and frequent, but are often crowded and leg room is at a premium. They are usually fine for short to medium hops.

TRAIN

The main train services are to be found in Thailand, Malaysia, Vietnam, Myanmar and on Java, in Indonesia. Buses are generally more convenient, more frequent, and often faster and cheaper, but the trains are still worth considering. Standards can vary enormously. In Thailand and Malaysia trains are very comfortable and a good alternative to the buses. The International Express runs between Thailand and Malaysia. Some of the crowded economy trains in Java are best avoided, but other services are excellent and cheap. Myanmar and Vietnam have dilapidated trains, but even they can be better than the dilapidated buses. Cambodia's rail service is off-limits to foreigners.

Rail passes are offered in some countries, but unless you are travelling quickly and extensively by train, they are often not economic.

See the individual country chapters for a full rundown of rail services.

CAR & MOTORCYCLE

Of course, you could hit the road with your own transport, but you really cannot go too far in South-East Asia: it's not like former days, when entire continents could be crossed overland. You could always buy a motorbike in Singapore, but once you've ridden it through Malaysia and Thailand you've come to the end of the road. Land borders to Myanmar are firmly shut, so the idea of crossing Burma and heading across Asia to Europe is just a dream.

Remember too that many places (including Thailand and Indonesia) require a carnet – an expensive customs document which guarantees that you will later remove the vehicle from their country.

If you must have your own wheels, it's better to hire them when necessary. Car hire is becoming much more readily available in the region. Malaysia is like most countries in the west when it comes to car hire, and you can also easily hire cars in Indonesia and Thailand. Motorbikes can be hired in many places in Malaysia and Thailand, and, of course, in Bali and other parts of Indonesia.

BICYCLE

Cycling is a cheap, convenient, healthy, environmentally sound and above all fun way of travelling. You can hire bicycles for day tripping in most tourist centres, including Bali, Penang, Chiang Mai and Bagan (Myanmar), but they don't rent bicycles for long-distance travel. Top quality bicycles and components can be bought in major cities like Singapore, but generally 10-speed bikes and fittings are hard to find – and impossible in places like Vietnam. Bring your own.

Before you leave home, go over your bike with a fine-toothed comb and fill your repair kit with every imaginable spare. As with cars and motorbikes, you won't necessarily be able to buy that crucial gizmo for your machine when it breaks down somewhere in the back of beyond as the sun sets. A basic kit starts with Allen keys, spoke key, tyre levers and a small Swiss army knife.

Bicycles can travel by air. You can take them to pieces and put them in a bike bag or box, but it's much simpler to wheel your bike to the check-in desk, where it should be treated as a piece of baggage. You may have to remove the pedals and turn the handlebars sideways so that it takes up less space in the aircraft's hold; check all this with the airline well in advance, preferably before you pay for your ticket.

Thailand is a good destination for bicycle touring and an increasing number of travellers take their bicycles and continue through to Malaysia and Singapore. Road conditions are good enough for touring bikes in most places, but mountain bikes are recommended for forays off the beaten track, or for travel further afield in South-East Asia. Vietnam is a great place to take a (mountain) bicycle – traffic is relatively light, buses take bikes and the entire coastal route is feasible, give or take a few potholes and hills. Indonesia is a more difficult proposition: distances in Sumatra, congested roads in Java, hills in Bali and poor road conditions in the outer islands all conspire against it – although they don't deter a steady stream of dedicated cyclists.

HITCHING

Hitching is never entirely safe in any country in the world and we don't recommend it. Travellers who decide to hitch should understand that they are taking a small but potentially serious risk. People who do choose to hitch will be safer if they travel in pairs and let someone know where they are planning to go.

BOAT

Ferry

Because many South-East Asian countries are separated by water, you'll unavoidably have to spend more on transport than you would in other parts of Asia. However, some of these trips can be great experiences. There are not a lot of inter-country shipping services – most are between Indonesia and

Malaysia or Singapore – although those that are available are often very interesting.

Indonesia and the Philippines are paradise if you love sea travel. Both countries have extensive ferry/passenger ship services.

Yacht

With a little effort, it's often possible to get yacht rides from various places in the region. Very often, yacht owners are also travellers and they often need an extra crew member or two. Willingness to give it a try is often more important than experience and all it may cost you is a contribution to the food kitty. Check out anywhere that yachts pass through, or towns with western-style yacht clubs.

On our first visit to Australia Maureen and I managed to get a yacht ride from Bali to Exmouth in Western Australia. Over the years we've had letters from people who've managed to get rides from Singapore, Penang, Phuket and (like us) Benoa in Bali.

Tony Wheeler

Brunei Darussalam

Brunei is a tiny Islamic sultanate lying in the north-eastern corner of Sarawak. Indeed, at just 5765 sq km, Brunei is one of the smallest countries in the world. Its vast oil reserves also make it one of the wealthiest.

Brunei is a very expensive place to visit, and most travellers only see it fleetingly en route between the Malaysian states of Sabah and Sarawak. While the lavish architecture of the capital Bandar Seri Begawan (known as Bandar or BSB) is not without interest, Brunei is like a rule-bound Islamic Singapore, with prohibitions on alcohol and girls and boys holding hands (among other things). In its defence, however, the locals are among the friendliest people you'll meet anywhere.

Facts about Brunei

HISTORY
In the 15th and 16th centuries Brunei was a considerable local power, its rule extending throughout Borneo and into the Philippines. Raja Brooke and the British put an end to all that.

A series of 'treaties' was forced onto the sultan by Raja Brooke, whittling the country away until finally, in 1890, the country was actually divided in half. In 1929 oil was discovered. That windfall allowed Brunei to flourish with no income tax, pensions for all, magnificent and pointless architecture and perhaps the highest public consumption of cars in South-East Asia.

In early 1984 the sultan, the 29th of his line, led his country somewhat reluctantly into complete independence from Britain. He celebrated by building a US$350 million palace and giving the country its current name, which means 'Abode of Peace'.

Brunei is the most Islamic country in South-East Asia. In 1991 the sale of alcohol was banned, stricter dress codes have been introduced, and in 1992 Melayu Islam Beraja (MIB), the national ideology stressing Malay culture, Islam and monarchy, became a compulsory subject in schools. Still, there are signs that change is afoot. A government committee recently recommended constitutional changes that would allow for an elected parliament. This a sign, perhaps, that even the sultan is aware that, as an absolute Islamic monarchy, Brunei is out of step with its neighbours.

GEOGRAPHY
Brunei consists of two areas separated by the Limbang District of Sarawak. The western part of Brunei contains the main towns: Bandar Seri Begawan (the capital), the oil town of Seria and the commercial town of Kuala Belait. The eastern part of the country, Temburong District, is much less developed. Brunei is mainly jungle, and approximately 75% of the country is covered by forest.

CLIMATE
Brunei is warm to hot year-round with heavy rainfall that peaks from September to January. See the Bandar Seri Begawan climate chart in the Appendix.

GOVERNMENT
Brunei is a monarchy, and the sultan appoints ministers to assist him in governing the

country. The sultan is both prime minister and defence minister. Two of the sultan's brothers are also ministers. The only democratic elections ever held were in 1962 and resulted in an attempted coup.

ECONOMY

Oil! The country is virtually dependent on the stuff, although some economic diversification plans are now being instituted for that fearsome day when the pump runs dry. Still, the prospect of an oil-less Brunei is still a long way off. Brunei has increased its oil production in the 90s, and new fields have been discovered. Brunei is also one of the world's largest exporters of liquefied natural gas. A small amount of rubber is also exported. Around 80% of the country's food requirements have to be imported.

POPULATION & PEOPLE

The total population of Brunei is about 260,000 and is composed of Malays (69%),

Chinese (18%), Indians and around 14,000 Iban, Lun Bawang and other tribal people of the interior. There are also around 20,000 expatriate workers from Europe and elsewhere in Asia.

ARTS

Traditional arts have all but disappeared in modern Brunei. In its heyday the sultanate was a source of brassware in the form of gongs, cannons and household vessels (such as kettles and betel containers) that were prized throughout Borneo and beyond. The lost wax technique used to cast bronze declined with the fortunes of the Brunei sultanate. Brunei's silversmiths were also celebrated. *Jong sarat* sarongs, using gold thread, are still prized for ceremonial occasions and the weaving art has survived.

SOCIETY & CONDUCT
Traditional Culture

Bruneians are mostly Malay, and customs,

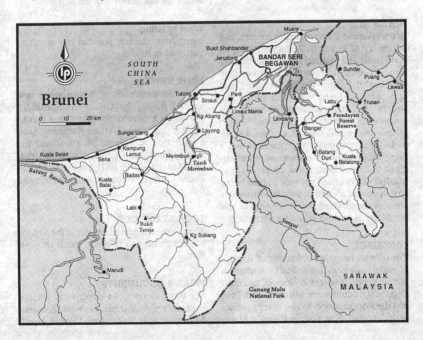

beliefs and pastimes are very similar if not identical to those of the Malays of Peninsular Malaysia. *Adat*, or customary law, governs many of the ceremonies in Brunei, particularly royal ceremonies and state occasions. There is even a government department of Adat Istiadat, which is responsible for preserving ceremony and advising on protocol, dress and heraldry.

Dos & Don'ts

The usual Asian customs apply: only the right hand should be used for offering or passing something; pointing with the forefinger is rude and should be done with the thumb; beckoning someone is done with an open hand with the fingers waving downwards. Offering pork or alcohol to Muslims not only may cause offence – it is tempting them to break the law. Eating shellfish and smoking are tolerated but not considered the done thing. Before entering a mosque or a house, remove your shoes.

RELIGION

Brunei is quite a strict Muslim country, and a Ministry of Religious Affairs has been set up to foster and promote Islam. The ministry also has special officers who investigate breaches of Islamic law by Muslims, and apparently government men prowl the streets after dark looking for unmarried couples standing or sitting too close to each other. Getting nailed for this crime, known as *khalwat*, can mean imprisonment and a fine. The constitution does allow other religions to be practised in the country – non-Muslim visitors need not worry about being spat upon and abused as infidels. Bruneians are very friendly and hospitable people, and not all are as zealous as their government.

LANGUAGE

The official language is Malay but English is widely spoken. Jawi, Malay written in Arabic script, is taught in schools, and most signs in the country are written in both Jawi and the Roman script. Malay is very similar to Indonesian. See Lonely Planet's *Malay*

phrasebook or *Indonesian phrasebook* and the Language sections in the Malaysia and Indonesia chapters of this book.

Facts for the Visitor

PLANNING
When to Go

It's difficult to imagine anyone planning their South-East Asia trip around Brunei. There's no need to anyway. Brunei's tropical climate has year-round warm weather, though you can expect occasional heavy downpours, particularly between September and January.

Maps

Explore Brunei is the government tourist guide, which has a good map of Bandar Seri Begawan. It's available at some travel agents and at the tourist office at the airport.

What to Bring

Apart from alcohol, you can buy anything you need in Brunei.

HIGHLIGHTS

The main attractions of Brunei are in and around BSB. The Omar Ali Saifuddin Mosque is a remarkable sight. Other worthwhile sights around BSB are Kampung Ayer, a collection of villages on stilts, and the Brunei Museum. The Temburong District, just 45 minutes from BSB, has the Peradayan Forest Reserve, which has walking trails and fine views.

TOURIST OFFICES

There's an information counter at the airport, but otherwise you're pretty much on your own.

VISAS & DOCUMENTS

For visits of up to 14 days, visas are not necessary for citizens of New Zealand, Norway, France, Switzerland, Canada, Japan,

Thailand, the Philippines, Indonesia, the Netherlands, Luxembourg, Belgium, Germany, Sweden, South Korea and the Republic of the Maldives. British, Malaysian and Singaporean citizens do not require visas for visits of 30 days or less.

All other nationalities, including British overseas citizens and British dependent territories citizens, must have visas to visit Brunei. Brunei embassies overseas have been known to give incorrect advice, so you should double-check if your nationality is not listed above and you are told that you do not require a visa to enter the country.

If entering from Sarawak or Sabah, there's no fuss on arrival and a one week stay is more or less automatic. If you ask you can usually get two weeks. What you'd do with them is another thing.

EMBASSIES
Brunei Embassies
Embassies include:

Australia
    16 Bulwarra Close, O'Malley, Canberra, ACT 2606 (☎ (06) 290-1801)
France
    No 4, Rue Logelbach, Paris 75017 (☎ 01 44 42 67 47)
Germany
    No 18 Kaiser Karl Rinc, 5300 Bonn (☎ (0228) 672-044)
UK
    19/20 Belgrave Square, London SW1X 8PG (☎ (0171) 581-0521)
USA
    Watergate Building, Suite 300, 2600 Virginia Ave NW, Washington, DC 20037 (☎ (202) 342-0159)

See the other chapters in this book for Bruneian embassies in those countries.

Foreign Embassies in Brunei
Countries with diplomatic representation in BSB include:

Australia
    4th floor, Teck Guan Plaza, Jalan Sultan (☎ 229435)

France
    301-306, Kompleks Jalan Sultan, Jalan Sultan (☎ 220960)
Germany
    6th floor, UNF Building, Jalan Sultan (☎ 225547)
Indonesia
    Lot 4498, Sungai Hanching Baru, Jalan Muara (☎ 330180)
Malaysia
    473 Kampong Pelambayan, Jalan Kota Batu (☎ 228410)
Philippines
    Badiah Complex, Jalan Tutong (☎ 241465)
Thailand
    1 Simpang 52-86-16 (☎ 448331)
UK
    Hongkong Bank Building, Jalan Sultan (☎ 229435)
USA
    3rd floor, Teck Guan Plaza, Jalan Sultan (☎ 229670)

CUSTOMS
Persons over 17 years of age may bring in 200 cigarettes or 250g of tobacco duty-free, and non-Muslims may import two bottles of liquor and 12 cans of beer, which must be declared upon arrival.

The importation of drugs carries the death penalty.

MONEY
Costs
Brunei's accommodation is fiercely expensive. Transport within the country and food are comparable to prices in the rest of East Malaysia, ie more expensive than Peninsular Malaysia but not outrageously expensive.

Currency
The official currency is the Brunei dollar (B$), but Singapore dollars are exchanged at the same value and can also be used. There's about a 40% difference between the Brunei dollar and the Malaysian ringgit. Banks give around 10% less for cash than they do for travellers' cheques.

Brunei uses 1c, 5c, 20c and 50c coins, and notes in denominations of B$1, B$5, B$10, B$50, B$100, B$500 and B$1000.

Currency Exchange

Exchange rates are as follows:

Australia	A$1	=	B$1.12
Canada	C$1	=	B$1.03
France	FF10	=	B$2.74
Germany	DM1	=	B$0.93
Hong Kong	HK$1	=	B$0.18
Japan	¥100	=	B$1.28
Malaysia	RM1	=	B$0.56
New Zealand	NZ$1	=	B$0.99
UK	UK£1	=	B$2.20
USA	US$1	=	B$1.41

POST & COMMUNICATIONS

Post offices are open from 7.45 am to 4.30 pm daily except Friday and Sunday. Friday opening hours are from 8 to 11 am and from 2 to 4.30 pm. Air-mail postcards to Malaysia and Singapore cost 30c; to all other countries they're 60c.

Telecom offices sell phone cards in denominations of B$10, B$20, B$50 and B$100, and these can be used in public booths to make international calls. Faxes can be sent from the Telecom office or from the big hotels, such as the Sheraton, which has a good business centre.

To make international calls from Brunei, the international access code is 01.

To call Brunei from outside the country, the country code is 673.

BOOKS

By God's Will – A Portrait of the Sultan of Brunei by Lord Chalfront is a measured look at the sultan and Brunei. *Brunei Darussalam, A Guide* is an excellent glossy publication that will be of use for those planning a long stay in Brunei.

NEWSPAPERS & MAGAZINES

The *Borneo Bulletin*, published in Kuala Belait, is the country's only daily newspaper. Malaysian and Singaporean newspapers are available, as are some foreign magazines, such as *Time*, *Newsweek* and *Asiaweek*.

RADIO & TV

Brunei has two radio channels transmitting on both the medium wave and FM bands.

One is a Malay channel, while the other transmits in English, Chinese and Gurkhali. English transmission times are from 6.30 to 8.30 am, 11 am to 2 pm and 8 to 10 pm.

Brunei is very proud of the fact that in 1975 it was the first country in the region to introduce colour TV. TV is broadcast on channel 5 for most of the country, while Belait District receives transmission on channel 8. Malaysian TV can also be received.

Five times a day, during Muslim prayer times, the radio and TV transmit the muezzin's call nationally.

ELECTRICITY

Electricity supplies are dependable and run at 220-240V and 50 Hz. Plugs are of the three-square-pin type, as used in Malaysia and Singapore.

WEIGHTS & MEASURES

Like almost everywhere else in the world, Brunei uses the metric system.

LAUNDRY

It would be cheaper to leave your laundry for Sabah or Sarawak. Laundry services are available at Brunei hotels but are expensive.

HEALTH

Brunei has high standards of hygiene and is generally a very healthy country. The tap water is safe to drink and malaria has been eliminated. The usual health precautions should be taken, especially in regards to heat exhaustion and dehydration.

The Hart Medical Clinic (☎ 225531), at 47 Jalan Sultan, is a clinic close to the centre of the capital, Bandar Seri Begawan. The RIPAS hospital just north of Jalan Tutong is a fully equipped, modern hospital.

WOMEN TRAVELLERS

Brunei is a very safe country to travel in. Muslim women are required to cover up from head to toe, with only the face and hands exposed, but allowances are made for non-Muslim women. The large expat population also means that many Bruneians are used to western ways. Nevertheless, dress should be conservative and not revealing. Bare shoulders and short dresses are inappropriate.

BUSINESS HOURS
Government offices are open from 7.45 am to 12.15 pm and 1.30 to 4.30 pm, Monday to Thursday and Saturday. Private offices are generally open from 9 am to 5 pm Monday to Friday, and from 9 am to noon on Saturday, while banks are open from 9 am to 3 pm during the week and from 9 to 11 am on Saturday. Shops open around 9 am, and in the big shopping areas, such as Jalan Tutong and Gadong, shops stay open until 9 or 9.30 pm. Most shops in the downtown area are closed by 6 pm.

PUBLIC HOLIDAYS & SPECIAL EVENTS
As in Malaysia, the dates of most religious festivals are not fixed, as they are based on the Islamic calendar. Fixed holidays are:

New Year's Day
1 January
National Day
23 February
Anniversary of the Royal Brunei Armed Forces
31 May
Sultan's Birthday
15 July
Christmas Day
25 December

Variable holidays include:

Chinese New Year
January or February
Isra Dan Mi'Raj
February
Awal Ramadan (1st day of Ramadan)
March
Anniversary of the Revelation of the Koran
April
Hari Raya Aidilfitri (end of Ramadan)
April
Hari Raya Haji
June
First Day of Hijrah
July
Hari Moulud (Prophet's Birthday)
July or August

ACCOMMODATION
The accommodation situation in Brunei is unlike any other country in South-East Asia. There is just one budget option (in BSB). It is sometimes full and sometimes the management turn away foreigners they don't like the look of (males with long hair are unlikely to find a room). All other accommodation is provided by expensive mid-range and top-end hotels.

FOOD
Like Malaysia, Brunei has an interesting mix of Malay and Chinese food. See the Food section of the Malaysia chapter for information on the local cuisine.

DRINKS
Nonalcoholic Drinks
Again, see the Drinks section of the Malaysia chapter for more information on local drinks. Brunei is a modern place, and all the international soft-drink labels can be found there.

Alcoholic Drinks
Just kidding. Brunei is strictly BYO.

Getting There & Away

AIR
Royal Brunei Airlines has direct flights from Bandar Seri Begawan to Darwin, Perth, Bali, Jakarta, Singapore, Kuala Lumpur, Kuching, Manila, Taipei, Hong Kong and Abu Dhabi. Malaysia Airlines, Singapore Airlines, Thai Airways International and Philippine Airlines also cover the routes to their home countries. Royal Brunei Airlines has flights continuing on to London, Frankfurt and Jeddah. Being a Muslim airline, Royal Brunei does not serve alcohol on its flights.

Malaysia
To Kuching the air fare is B$236 (RM250 from Kuching), Kota Kinabalu B$78 (RM83 from KK) and Kuala Lumpur B$399 (RM441 from KL). Because of the difference in exchange rates, it is around 40% cheaper to fly to Brunei from Malaysia than vice versa.

Singapore

The standard economy fare to Singapore is B\$377 one way (S\$377 from Singapore) or 30 day return excursion fares are available for B\$514 (S\$514). Discounts are not usually available on these flights.

Around South-East Asia

Published one-way fares to other South-East Asian destinations are Bali (B\$457), Jakarta (B\$574), Manila (B\$444) and Hong Kong (B\$666). On flights where Royal Brunei has competition, discounting of up to 20% is available if tickets are bought through a travel agent. To Bangkok the discounted fare is around B\$380 and to Manila B\$360.

Departure Tax

The departure tax is B\$5 to Malaysia and Singapore and B\$12 to all other destinations.

LAND

The main overland route is via bus from Miri in Sarawak. See the Bandar Seri Begawan Getting There & Away section for details. It is relatively easy to travel overland between Limbang in Sarawak and Bangar in the eastern part of Brunei, though a boat to Bandar Seri Begawan is the usual method. Overland travel between Lawas (Sarawak) and Bangar is difficult and expensive. See under Limbang and Lawas in the Sarawak section of the Malaysia chapter for details on these border crossings.

SEA

Boats connect Bandar Seri Begawan to Lawas and Limbang in Sarawak, and Labuan Island, from where boats go to Sabah. See the Bandar Seri Begawan Getting There & Away section for details.

Getting Around

Transport around Brunei, for those poor unfortunates who don't have a Volvo or a BMW, is by bus or minibus. The public transport system is infrequent and unreliable – there are no fixed schedules and buses leave when full. Buses on the main highway between Bandar Seri Begawan and Kuala Belait are fairly regular, but you may be in for a long wait on other routes. Hitchhikers are such a novelty that the chances of getting a lift are good.

Bandar Seri Begawan

The capital, Bandar Seri Begawan (often called BSB or Bandar), is the only town of any size and really one of the few places to go in the country. It's neat, very clean, modern and just a little boring. Islam and oil money are BSB's defining characteristics. Arabic script graces the street signs, domes and minarets dot the skyline. Most visitors find themselves scratching for something to do after a couple of days.

Orientation

The centre of BSB lies north of the Brunei River and is so compact that it can be explored in about an hour. It's a remarkably easy city to circumnavigate.

Information

Tourist Offices The tourist information booth at the airport is next to useless. Pick up a copy of *Explore Brunei* while you're there.

Money The Hongkong Bank in the centre of town is one of the most efficient places to change money.

Post & Communications The post office is on the corner of Jalan Sultan and Jalan Elizabeth Dua. It is open from 7.45 am to 4.30 pm daily except Friday and Sunday. Next door is a telephone office where you can make local and international calls and send faxes.

The area code for BSB is 02.

Travel Agencies The Teck Guan Plaza complex has a few travel agencies, including Ken Travel (☎ 223127) on the 1st floor,

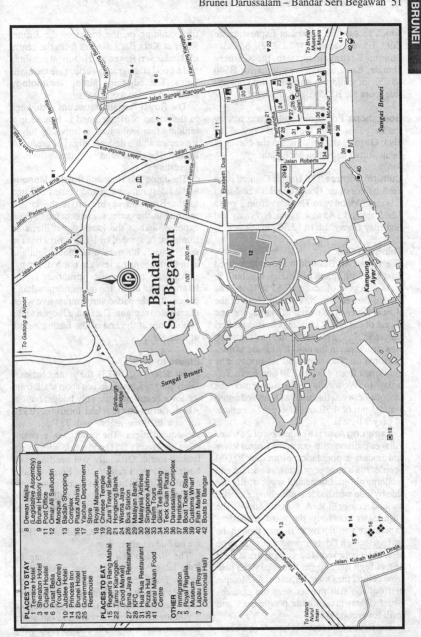

Bandar Seri Begawan

0   100   200 m

To Gadong & Airport

To Brunei Museum & Muara

Sungai Brunei

Kampung Ayer

Sungai Brunei

Edinburgh Bridge

To Istana Nurul Iman

To Bangar

Jalan Kubah Makam Diraja

Jalan Tutong

PLACES TO STAY
1   Terrace Hotel
3   Sheraton Hotel
4   Capital Hostel
6   Pusat Belia
    (Youth Centre)
10 Jubilee Hotel
14 Princess Inn
23 Brunei Hotel
25 Government
    Resthouse

PLACES TO EAT
15 Regent's Rang Mahal
22 Tamu Kiangggeh
    (Food Market)
27 Isma Jaya Restaurant
28 KFC
31 Hua Hua Restaurant
35 Pizza Hut
41 Gerai Makan Food
    Centre

OTHER
2   Immigration
5   Royal Regalia
    Museum
7   Lapau (Royal
    Ceremonial Hall)

8   Dewan Majlis
    (Legislative Assembly)
9   Brunei History Centre
11 Post Office
12 Omar Ali Saifuddin
    Mosque
13 Badi'ah Shopping
    Complex
16 Plaza Athirah
17 Yaohan Department
    Store
18 Royal Mausoleum
19 Chinese Temple
20 Zura Travel Service
21 Hongkong Bank
24 Wisma Jaya
26 Bus Station
29 Malaysia Airlines
30 Malaysia Bank
32 Singapore Airlines
33 Hotel Jaya
34 Gick Tee Building
36 Teck Guan Plaza
37 Darussalam Complex
38 Harrisons
39 Boat Ticket Stalls
40 Customs Wharf
42 Fish Market
    Boats to Bangar

which acts as the American Express agent. Zura Travel Service (☎ 225812), on Jalan Sungei Kianggeh next to the Chinese Temple, has afternoon city tours for B$40 (B$20 for children) and morning countryside tours for B$55 (B$25 children).

Bookshops For books and magazines try the Best Eastern on the ground floor of the Teck Guan Plaza building, on the corner of Jalan Sultan and Jalan McArthur.

Cultural Centres The British Council is on the 5th floor of the Hongkong Bank building. It is open Monday to Thursday from 8 am to 12.15 pm and 1.45 to 4.30 pm, on Friday and Saturday from 8 am to 12.30 pm.

Things to See
The **Omar Ali Saifuddin Mosque**, named after the 28th sultan of Brunei, was built in 1958 at a cost of about US$5 million. The golden-domed structure stands close to the Brunei River in its own artificial lagoon and is one of the tallest buildings in Bandar Seri Begawan. It's also one of the most impressive structures in the east. It's closed to non-Muslims on Thursday, and on Friday it is only open from 4.30 to 5.30 pm. From Saturday to Wednesday you may enter the mosque between the hours of 8 am and noon, 1 and 3 pm or 4.30 and 5.30 pm (ie outside of prayer times).

Kampung Ayer is a collection of 28 water villages built on stilts out in the Brunei River and houses a population of around 30,000 people. It's a strange mixture of ancient and modern; old traditions and ways of life are side by side with modern plumbing, electricity and colour TV. A visit to one of the villages is probably the most rewarding experience you'll have in Brunei, though the garbage which floats around them has to be seen to be believed. The villages are at their best at high tide. To get there, take the path from behind the Omar Ali Saifuddin Mosque or from the fish market near the customs wharf. Water taxis shuttle people back and forth for around B$1.

The **Brunei Museum** is housed in a beautiful building on the banks of the Brunei River at Kota Batu, six km from the centre of Bandar Seri Begawan. Historical treasures and a good ethnography section are the highlights. The adjoining **Malay Technology Museum** is also worth a visit.

The **Royal Regalia Museum** is devoted to the sultan of Brunei, and is housed in a building that looks like an imposing tub of ice cream with a delicate whorl of cream on the top. The coronation exhibits are the most interesting.

The **Jame'Asr Hassanil Bolkiah Mosque** is the latest minaretted and domed addition to the Bruneian skyline. It is the largest mosque in the country, constructed at great expense, and as the local tourist literature trumpets, 'a symbol of Islam's firm hold in the country'. It's quite a fabulous sight and is in Gadong, just a few km north of town.

Another photogenic attraction is the **Istana Nurul Iman**, the magnificent sultan's palace. It looks particularly impressive when illuminated at night. The *istana* is open to the public only at the end of the fasting month of Ramadan.

Places to Stay
Pusat Belia (☎ 229423), the youth centre on Jalan Sungai Kianggeh, is a short walk from the town centre. It is the only budget option. A bed in an air-con four bed dorm costs B$10 for one to three nights and B$5 for each subsequent night. The centre has a swimming pool (entry B$1) and a cafe with a very limited menu. Officially you need a youth hostel or student card to stay. Entry without a card is at the discretion of the manager, who may make things difficult and will probably tell you to come back in a few hours if he doesn't like the look of you. Some males with long hair have been turned away. There are no budget alternatives.

The *Bradoo Inn* (☎ 336723), Simpang 130, Jalan Sungei Akar, has much better rooms for B$50 or B$60/70 for singles/doubles with attached bath. It is out near the airport and a long way from anywhere, but if you are flying into Brunei and out again the next day it is worth considering. Ring them and they will pick you up from the airport, which will save you an expensive cab fare. The *Capital Hostel* (☎ 223561), off Jalan Tasek Lama just behind the Pusat Belia, has faded rooms costing from B$70 to B$138 with air-con, TV and fridge. The restaurant and bar downstairs serve reasonably priced meals and western breakfasts.

The *Terrace Hotel* (☎ 243554), on Jalan Tasek Lama, was formerly known as Ang's Hotel, and by Bruneian standards is an economical mid-range option. Discounts are frequently available; posted rates are B$82/92 for singles/doubles. Deluxe rooms range up to B$138. A 10% service charge applies. The hotel has its own restaurant and is fully air-conditioned.

Places to Eat
The *Gerai Makan* food centre on the riverfront just over the canal from the customs wharf is a good place to eat, although, as is the case all over BSB, not much happens in the evenings. For takeaway food, try the *Tamu Kianggeh market* or, in the evenings only, the food stalls that spring up behind the Chinese temple, opposite the post office. Satay, barbecued fish, chicken wings and kueh melayu (sweet pancakes filled with peanuts, raisins and sugar) are all available here.

The main street, Jalan Sultan, is the best place to look for cheap restaurants. *Isma Jaya Restaurant* has rice and curry meals for around B$3, and a few doors down the *Sin Tai Pong* has chicken and rice for B$2.50. The *Hua Hua Restaurant* nearby is a little more expensive, but the food is very good and it has a wide range of dishes. The *Carnation Country Bake Corner*, on the corner of Jalan McArthur and Jalan Sultan, is good for cakes.

Western fast food is not particularly cheap in Brunei. There are branches of *KFC* and *Pizza Hut* (takeaway only) in the city centre, but the real fast-food centre is in Gadong, five km out of the city, where you'll find a *McDonald's*, *Pizza Hut*, *Swenson's* and a *Sugar Bun*. The Pizza Hut has a good salad bar and Swenson's is the pick of these for a good meal.

Gadong also has a number of other restaurants, including some good Indian restaurants, such as *Fathul Razak Restaurant*, where you can get an enormous murtabak for just B$4.

Getting There & Away
Air Airline offices or general sales agents in Bandar Seri Begawan include:

British Airways (GSA)
    Harrisons, corner of Jalan Kianggeh & Jalan McArthur (☎ 243911)
Malaysia Airlines
    144 Jalan Pemancha (☎ 224141)
Philippine Airlines
    1st floor, Wisma Hajjah Fatimah Building, Jalan Sultan (☎ 222970)
Royal Brunei Airlines
    RBA Plaza, Jalan Sultan (☎ 242222)
Singapore Airlines
    49-50 Jalan Sultan (☎ 227253)
Thai Airways International
    51 Jalan Sultan (☎ 242991)

Bus Brunei's main highway links BSB with Sarawak via Seria and Kuala Belait. Getting to Limbang (Sarawak) by road is difficult but not impossible. The road to Lawas in Sabah stops at the border, after which you have to walk over a hill – it's best to travel to Sabah by boat. The BSB bus station is on Jalan Cator, beneath the Multistorey Carpark (that's what it's officially known as). Buses are infrequent and unscheduled. Private minibuses are the easiest way to get to Miri in Sarawak. Try the Miri-Sibu Express driver (☎ 225002). The fare is B$25.

Boat All international boats leave from the dock at the end of Jalan Roberts, where Brunei immigration formalities are taken care of. There are regular *ekspres* boats for Limbang (B$10, 30 minutes). For Labuan, there are numerous high-speed ferry services daily (B$20, 1½ hours). There is an express boat daily to Lawas (B$15, two hours).

Getting Around
The Airport Minibuses with the sign 'Lapangan Terbang Antarabangsa' (International Airport) do the eight km run out to the

airport approximately every 15 minutes. They cost B$1. Taxis cost around B$20.

Bus Local bus services are hit or miss. Generally they leave only when they are full, which often means a long wait. The bus station is beneath the Multistorey Carpark on Jalan Cator.

Taxi Taxis are metered, expensive and hard to find.

Water Taxi Water taxis, popularly known as flying coffins, are most easily caught near the customs wharf or the Tamu Kianggeh food market. Fares start at 50c and go up to B$2, but expect to pay much higher charter rates. To charter a boat for a tour of Kampung Ayer and the river shouldn't cost more than B$20 per hour, or less if you bargain hard.

Around Bandar Seri Begawan

The main landmass of Brunei in the western part of the country is quite small, and any destination is only a few hours drive from the capital. The countryside has a lot of pristine forest, with waterfalls and reserves that make pleasant day trips, but a car is essential to reach most of them. There are a few other points of interest – decent beaches, some more impressive istanas, longhouses etc – but because of the unreliability of the buses, the problem is getting to them.

MUARA
Muara is a container port and of no interest to travellers, but Muara Beach, two km from town, is a popular weekend retreat. Other beaches around Muara include Meragang Beach and Serasa Beach.

The bus from Bandar Seri Begawan to Muara town takes about 40 minutes and costs B$2. The beach is about a one km walk from the roundabout as you enter town.

JERUDONG
Jerudong is where the sultan indulges in his favourite pastime, polo. The main attraction is **Jerudong Playground**, a massive new amusement park. It has a wide range of rides, and is probably a great place to take the kids. At the time of writing, everything was free. Close by is **Jerudong Beach**. This whole area is difficult to explore without your own car. Buses to Seria pass through.

KUALA BELAIT
The last town before Malaysia, Kuala Belait is the place to get buses for Miri in Sarawak. It's not completely without interest, but hardly anyone lingers here. The best place to change money is at the Hongkong Bank opposite the bus station.

The area code for Kuala Belait is 03.

Places to Stay
The *Government Rest House* (☎ 334288) charges around B$12 but it's very unlikely you will be allowed to stay. The only alternatives are ridiculously expensive. The cheapest is the *Sentosa Hotel* (☎ 334341), at 92 Jalan McKerron; it charges B$98.

Getting There & Away
Five buses a day leave for Miri in Sarawak. The fare is B$9.

TEMBURONG DISTRICT
Temburong District is the eastern slice of Brunei, surrounded by Sarawak. This quiet backwater, rarely visited by travellers, is reached by boat from BSB and can be visited as a day trip. Much of the district is virgin rainforest.

Bangar, a sleepy town on the banks of the Temburong River, is the district centre. It has a mosque, but not much else. **Batang Duri** is an Iban longhouse on the Temburong River, 17 km south of Bangar. Two km before Batang Duri is the **Taman Batang Duri**, a park and small zoo with civets, monkeys, otters and birds.

Kuala Belalong Field Studies Centre is a scientific research centre in the Batu Apoi

Forest Reserve, a large area of primary rainforest that covers most of southern Temburong. It is primarily for scientists and school groups, though interested overseas visitors can stay at the centre. Bookings must be made through the biology department of the Universiti Brunei Darussalam (☎ 02-427001). It's not cheap.

The **Peradayan Forest Reserve** contains the peaks of Bukit Patoi and Bukit Peradayan, which can be reached along a walking trail – bring water and food for the walk. The one hour walk through rainforest to Bukit Patoi provides some fine views. It starts at the park entrance, 15 km from Bangar. Most walkers descend back along the trail, but it is possible to continue over the other side of the summit and around to Bukit Peradayan. This trail is harder, less distinct and takes two hours.

Places to Stay
It may be possible to stay at the *Government Rest House* in Bangar. The cost is B$12 per night. It is opposite the mosque.

Getting There & Away
Regular boats to Bangar leave from the wharf near the Gerai Makan food centre in BSB. They cost B$7 and take 45 minutes.

Getting Around
The only way to get around is by taxi. The private taxis usually work out cheaper – with a little negotiation. Returning to Batang Duri should cost B$20. For the Peradayan Forest Reserve and the walk to Bukit Patoi, taxis also charge B$20 to drop you off and pick you up at an arranged time. Hitching generally involves long waits.

Cambodia

Modern day Cambodia is the successor-state of the mighty Khmer Empire, which during the Angkorian period (9th to 14th centuries) ruled much of what is now Vietnam, Laos and Thailand. The remains of this empire can be seen in the fabled temples of Angkor. These stunning monuments, surrounded by dense jungle, are easily accessible by boat or by plane from Phnom Penh.

Cambodia is still recovering from two decades of warfare and violence, including almost four years (1975-79) of rule by the genocidal Khmer Rouge, who killed as many as two million of Cambodia's seven million people and systematically sought to obliterate the country's pre-revolutionary culture. The Khmer Rouge are a lingering problem. Travel in many remote parts of the country still remains dangerous. Most travellers sensibly restrict their visit to Angkor, Phnom Penh and, less frequently, Sihanoukville.

Facts about Cambodia

HISTORY

From the 1st to the 6th centuries, much of present day Cambodia was part of the kingdom of Funan, whose prosperity was due in large part to its position on the great trade route between China and India.

The Angkorian era, known for its brilliant achievements in architecture and sculpture, was begun by Jayavarman II around the year 800. During his rule, a new state religion establishing the Khmer ruler as a *devaraja* (god-king) was instituted. Vast irrigation systems facilitated intensive cultivation of the land around Angkor and allowed the Khmers to maintain a densely populated, highly centralised state.

For 90 years, from 1863, the French controlled Cambodia as an adjunct to their colonial interests in Vietnam. Independence was declared in 1953. For 15 years King Norodom

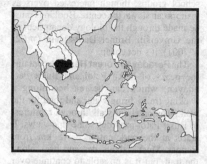

Sihanouk (later prince, prime minister and chief-of-state, and now king again) dominated Cambodian politics. But, alienating both the left and the right with his erratic and repressive policies, he was overthrown by the army in 1970 and fled to China.

From 1969 Cambodia was drawn into the Vietnam conflict. The USA secretly commenced carpet-bombing suspected Communist base camps in Cambodia and, shortly after the 1970 coup, American and South Vietnamese troops invaded the country to root out Vietnamese Communist forces. They failed. But the invasion did push Cambodia's indigenous rebels, the Khmer Rouge ('Red Khmer' in French), into the country's interior. Savage fighting soon engulfed the entire country, ending only when Phnom Penh fell to the Khmer Rouge on 17 April 1975, two weeks before the fall of Saigon.

Upon taking Phnom Penh, the Khmer Rouge, under leader Pol Pot, implemented one of the most radical, brutal restructurings of a society ever attempted. Its goal was the transformation of Cambodia into a Maoist, peasant-dominated, agrarian cooperative.

During the next four years, hundreds of thousands of Cambodians, including the vast majority of the country's educated people, were relocated into the countryside, tortured to death or executed. Thousands of people were branded as 'parasites' and systematically killed solely because they spoke a foreign language or wore spectacles. Hundreds of thousands more died of mistreatment, malnourishment and disease. At least one million, perhaps two million, Cambodians died between 1975 and 1979 as the result of the policies of the Khmer Rouge government.

At the end of 1978, Vietnam invaded Cambodia and overthrew the Khmer Rouge, who fled westward to the jungles on both sides of the border with Thailand. They maintained a guerrilla war through the late 1970s and throughout the 1980s, armed and financed by China and Thailand (and with indirect US support), against the Vietnamese-backed government in Phnom Penh.

In mid-1993 the UN administered elections in Cambodia. A constitution was drawn up and passed, and Norodom Sihanouk was made king. The present government is a coalition of the United Front for an Independent, Neutral and Free Cambodia (FUNCINPEC), led by Prince Norodom Ranariddh, and the Cambodian People's Party, led by Hun Sen. Cambodia has two prime ministers.

Despite much talk of forming a coalition with the Cambodian government, the Khmer Rouge remain outside the political process and a threat to the stability of the country.

GEOGRAPHY

Cambodia covers an area of 181,035 sq km, which is a bit over half the size of Italy or Vietnam. The country is dominated by two topographical features: the Mekong River and the Tonlé Sap (Great Lake). There are three main mountainous regions: in the south-west (the Elephant and Cardamom mountains), along the northern border with Thailand (the Dangkrek Mountains) and in the country's north-eastern corner (the Eastern Highlands).

The Tonlé Sap is linked to the Mekong at Phnom Penh by a 100-km-long channel sometimes called the Tonlé Sap River. From mid-May to early October (the rainy season), the level of the Mekong rises, backing up the Tonlé Sap River and causing it to flow north-westward into the Tonlé Sap. During this period, the Tonlé Sap swells from around 3000 sq km to over 7500 sq km. As the water level of the Mekong falls during the dry season, the Tonlé Sap River reverses its flow, and the waters of the lake drain back into the Mekong. This extraordinary process makes the Tonlé Sap one of the world's richest sources of freshwater fish.

CLIMATE

The climate of Cambodia is governed by two monsoons, which set the rhythm of rural life. The cool, dry, north-eastern monsoon, which carries little rain, occurs from around November to March. From April or May to early October, the south-western monsoon brings strong winds, high humidity and heavy rains. But even during the wet season, it rarely rains in the morning – most precipitation falls in the afternoons, and even then, only sporadically.

See the Phnom Penh climate chart in the Appendix.

GOVERNMENT

Cambodia is a constitutional monarchy. In 1996 it was governed by a precarious alliance of forces that included the Cambodian People's Party (CPP), the remnants of the former Vietnam-backed government, and FUNCINPEC, led by Prince Norodom Ranariddh. Norodom Sihanouk is king. The Khmer Rouge remain outside the political process. Elections are scheduled for 1998.

ECONOMY

Cambodia is one of the poorest countries in Asia – 80% of the population is employed in agriculture. All fuel and most raw materials, capital equipment and consumer goods must be imported. In recent years the country's main export has shifted from rubber to timber, which accounts for around half of Cambodia's export earnings. Other economic mainstays are the transshipment of gold and cigarettes, and wide-ranging foreign aid projects.

CAMBODIA

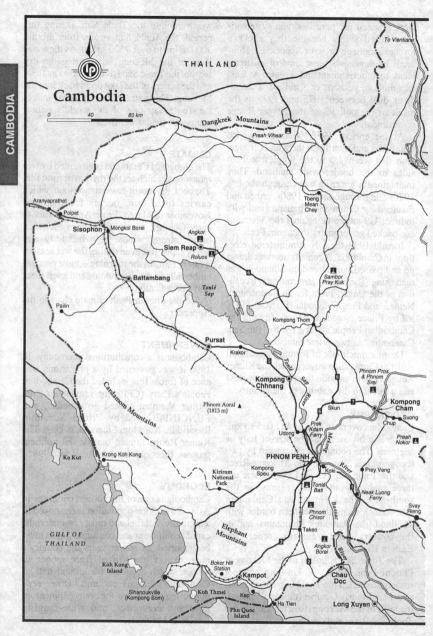

CAMBODIA

Cambodia

0   40   80 km

THAILAND

To Vientiane

Dangkrek Mountains

Preah Vihear

Aranyaprathet

Poipet

Sisophon   Mongkol Borei

Tbeng Mean Chey

Angkor

Siem Reap

Roluos

Battambang

Tonlé Sap

Pailin

Sambor Prey Kuk

Kompong Thom

Pursat

Krakor

Tonlé Sap River

Kompong Chhnang

Cardamom Mountains

Phnom Aoral (1813 m)

Phnom Pros & Phnom Srei

Kompong Cham

Skun   Chup

Suong

Prek Kdam Ferry

Udong

Mekong River

Preah Nokor

Ko Kut

Krong Koh Kong

PHNOM PENH

Koki   Prey Veng

Kompong Speu

Kirirom National Park

Tonlé Bati

Neak Luong Ferry

Svay Rieng

GULF OF THAILAND

Elephant Mountains

Phnom Chisor

Takeo

Angkor Borei

Bassac River

Koh Kong Island

Bokor Hill Station

Kampot

Chau Doc

Sihanoukville (Kompong Som)

Koh Thmei

Kep   Ha Tien

Long Xuyen

Phu Quoc Island

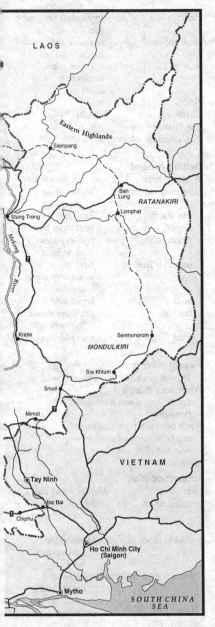

POPULATION & PEOPLE

In July 1995 the population of Cambodia was estimated to be 10.4 million. Infant mortality rates are the highest in the region at 120 per 1000. Women account for 54% of the population.

Official statistics put 96% of the Cambodian population as ethnic-Khmers (ethnic-Cambodians), making the country the most homogeneous in South-East Asia. In actual fact, however, there are probably much larger numbers of Vietnamese in Cambodia than the government cares to admit.

The most important minority group in Cambodia are the ethnic-Chinese, who, until 1975, controlled the country's economy and who, with the help of overseas Chinese investment, are once again a powerful economic force within Cambodia. Official estimates put their numbers at around 50,000; unofficially there may be as many as 400,000. Cambodia's Cham Muslims (Khmer Islam) officially number some 200,000, though this is another figure that may be an underestimation – some observers claim half a million. They suffered vicious persecution between 1975 and 1979 and a large part of their community was exterminated.

Cambodia's diverse ethnolinguistic minorities (hill tribes), who live up in the country's mountainous regions, number around 60,000 to 70,000.

ARTS

Khmer architecture reached its zenith during the Angkorian era. Some of the finest examples of architecture from this period are Angkor Wat and the structures of Angkor Thom. Many of the finest works of Khmer sculpture are on display at the National Museum in Phnom Penh. Cambodia's highly stylised classical dance, adapted from Angkor dances (and similar to Thai dances derived from the same source), is performed to the accompaniment of an orchestra and choral narration. There are sometimes opportunities to see classical Khmer dance in Phnom Penh and in Siem Reap (Angkor).

SOCIETY & CONDUCT

The Khmers are among the easiest people to get along with in all of South-East Asia. Like the Thais, they greet each other with a bow, the hands meeting in prayer. As is the case elsewhere around South-East Asia you should beckon with the palm facing downwards and should refrain from patting children (or anyone else) on the head.

Proper etiquette in *wats* (pagodas) is mostly a matter of common sense. A few tips:

- Don't wear shorts or tank tops.
- Take off your hat when entering the grounds of the wat.
- Take off your shoes before going into the *vihara* (sanctuary).
- If you sit down in front of the dais (the platform on which the Buddhas are placed), sit with your feet to the side rather than in the lotus position.
- Never point your finger – or, heaven forbid, the soles of your feet! – towards a figure of the Buddha (or towards human beings either).

RELIGION

Hinayana Buddhism is the dominant religion in Cambodia and was the state religion until 1975. It was reinstated as the state religion in the late 1980s. Between 1975 and 1979, the vast majority of Cambodia's Buddhist monks were murdered by the Khmer Rouge, who also destroyed virtually all of the country's 3000 wats. The 1990s have seen the restoration of many of the wats and mosques of Cambodia, and monks with alm bowls are once again a common sight.

LANGUAGE

Cambodia's official language is Khmer. For most westerners, writing and pronouncing this language proves confusing and difficult. For over a century, the second language of choice among educated Cambodians was French, which is still spoken by many people who grew up before the 1970s. English has recently surged in popularity.

Basics

Excuse me.	*suom tous*
Good night.	*rear trei suor sdei*
Goodbye.	*lear heouy*

Hello.	*joom reab suor/suor sdei*
How are you?	*tau neak sok sapbaiy jea te?*
Very well.	*sok touk jea thomada te*
Please.	*suom*
No.	*te*
Thank you.	*ar kun*
Yes. (used by men)	*bat*
Yes. (used by women)	*jas*

Getting Around

Where is a/the ...?	*tau ... nouv eir na?*
railway station	*sathani rout phleoung*
bus station	*ben lan*
airport	*veal youn huos*
ticket office	*kanleng luok suombuot*
tourist office	*kariyaleiy samrap puok tesajor*
boat	*kopal/tuok*
bus	*lan thom deouk monuos*
train	*rout phleoung*

I want a ticket to ...
khjoom junh ban suombuot teou ...
When does it depart?
tau ke jeng domneur moung ponmann?
When does it arrive here/there?
tau ke teou/mouk doul moung ponmaan?

Accommodation

I want a ...	*khjoom joung ban ...*
single room	*bantuop kre samrap mouy neak*
double room	*bantuop kre samrap pee neak*
room with a bathtub	*bantuop deil meen thlang gnout teouk*
bed	*kre mouy*

How much is a room?
*chnoul mouy bantuop tleiy
ponmaan?*

Health & Emergencies

Please call ...   *suom jouy hao ...*
  an ambulance   *lan peit*
  a doctor   *krou peit*
  the police   *police*
  a dentist   *peit thmenh*

It's an emergency.
nees jea pheap ason
I'm allergic to penicillin.
*khjoom min trouv theat neoung
thanam peneecilleen*

Numbers

1	*mouy*
2	*pee*
3	*bei*
4	*boun*
5	*bram*
6	*bram-mouy*
7	*bram-pee*
8	*bram-bei*
9	*bran-boun*
10	*duop*
11	*duop-mouy*
12	*duop-pee*
20	*maphei*
21	*maphei-mouy*
30	*samseb*
40	*sairseb*
100	*mouy-rouy*
500	*bram-rouy*
1000	*mouy-paun*
10,000	*mouy-meoun*

Facts for the Visitor

PLANNING

When to Go

Cambodia can be visited any time of year, though the ideal months are December and January. At this time of year humidity levels are relatively low and there is little likelihood of rain. From early February, temperatures start to rise until the hottest month, April, in which temperatures can reach 38°C. Sometime in April or early May the south-west monsoon brings rain and cooler weather. The wet season, which lasts from April to October, need not be a bad time to visit Cambodia. Angkor, for example, is surrounded by lush foliage and the moats are full of water at this time of year.

Maps

Tourist maps of Cambodia and Phnom Penh are available in Phnom Penh and Siem Reap, though they are fairly poor. The Periplus *Cambodia Travel Map* at a scale of 1:1,100,000 is probably the best around and is available in Phnom Penh and Bangkok bookshops. Nelles' *Vietnam, Laos & Cambodia* map at 1:1,500,000 scale is another good map of the country.

What to Bring

The usual rules apply: bring as little as possible. Phnom Penh is surprisingly well stocked with travel provisions, so if you have forgotten or lost anything it should be possible to replace it there.

HIGHLIGHTS

Due to security risks and the arduous nature of travel in Cambodia, travel options around the country are still limited. Before planning any 'adventurous' trips upcountry, it is essential that you check on the security situation with your embassy and/or with Non-Governmental Organisations (NGOs) in Phnom Penh. Cambodia is still in a state of civil war. Risks that backfire could have repercussions not just for you individually but also for the whole travel industry in Cambodia.

The standard itinerary for most travellers is: fly to Phnom Penh; from there fly or travel by boat to Angkor. A small number of travellers make their way to Sihanoukville, a beach retreat.

TOURIST OFFICES

Cambodia only has a handful of tourist offices, and these have little to offer the independent traveller. See the Phnom Penh and the Siem Reap sections for information on tourist offices there. Cambodia has no tourist offices abroad and it is unlikely that Cambodian embassies will be of much assistance in planning a trip.

VISAS & DOCUMENTS
Visas
Most nationalities receive a one month visa on arrival at Pochentong airport. The cost is US$20 and one passport-size photo is required.

Travellers arriving overland from Ho Chi Minh City (Saigon) will have to obtain a visa before they arrive, but these are easy to get in Vietnam nowadays.

Visa Extensions Visa extensions can usually be granted in Phnom Penh. Theoretically, extensions are simply a matter of having the cash to hand, but in practice they can sometimes be difficult to obtain. One passport-size photograph is required for visa extensions; one week costs US$20; one month US$30; three months US$60; six months US$100; and one year US$150.

Other Documents
Passport-size photographs are readily obtainable in Phnom Penh. If you are thinking of applying for work with NGOs in Phnom Penh, you should bring copies of your educational certificates and work references with you.

EMBASSIES
Cambodian Embassies
Embassies include:

Australia
    5 Canterbury Court, Deakin, Canberra, ACT 2600 (☎ (06) 273-1053)
France
    11, Ave Charles Floquet, Paris 75007 (☎ 01 40 65 04 70)
Germany
    Consulate: Arnold Zweing Strasse, 1013189 Berlin (☎ (030) 555165)

USA
    4500 16th St, Washington, DC 20011 (☎ (202) 726-7742)
    Consulate: 53-69 Alderton St, Rego Park, New York 11374 (☎ (212) 830-3770)

See the other chapters in this book for Cambodian embassies in those countries.

Foreign Embassies in Cambodia
Some of the embassies in Phnom Penh are as follows:

Australia
    11 254 St (☎ 426000/1; fax 426003)
Canada
    c/o Australian Embassy (see above)
China
    156 Mao Tse Toung Blvd (☎ 426271; fax 426972)
France
    1 Monivong Blvd (☎ 430021)
Germany
    76-78 214 St (☎ 426381; fax 427746)
Indonesia
    179 51 St (☎ 426148; fax 426571)
Laos
    15-17 Mao Tse Toung Blvd (☎ 426441; fax 427454)
Malaysia
    161 51 St (☎ 426176; fax 426004)
Philippines
    33 294 St (☎ 428048; fax 428592)
Thailand
    4 Monivong Blvd (☎ 426124)
USA
    27 240 St (☎ 426436; fax 426437)
UK
    27-29 75 St (☎ 427124; fax 428295)
Vietnam
    436 Monivong Blvd (☎ 810694)

CUSTOMS
If Cambodia has customs allowances, it is keeping close-lipped about them. A 'reasonable amount' of duty-free items are allowed into the country. Travellers arriving by air might bear in mind that alcohol and cigarettes sell at duty-free (and lower) prices on the streets of Phnom Penh – a carton of Marlboro costs just US$7!

Like any other country, Cambodia does not allow travellers to import weapons, explosives or narcotics.

MONEY
Costs
Budget travellers who have arrived from Vietnam will find that accommodation rates are cheaper in Cambodia but that food is slightly more expensive.

Rock-bottom travellers can probably manage Phnom Penh on around US$10 a day. Accommodation can be as cheap as US$2 to US$3 in Phnom Penh and Siem Reap (elsewhere, you will be looking at a minimum of US$5). It is generally possible to eat fairly well for US$2 to US$3, less if you eat local dishes and live off inexpensive soups and noodles (though you drastically increase the risk of spending your Cambodia trip in search of a toilet).

Visitors to Angkor will have to factor in the cost of entrance fees, which now seem to have finally settled down at US$20 for one day, US$40 for three days and US$60 for one week. An additional expense out at Angkor is the government ruling against travellers visiting the ruins without a guide. A guide with a motorbike will cost a minimum of US$6 per day.

Currency
Cambodia's currency is the riel, abbreviated here by a lower-case 'r' written after the sum. From around 200r to the US dollar in mid-1989 the riel has plummeted in value and now seems to have settled at around 2500r to the dollar. The riel comes in notes with the following values: 100, 200, 500, 1000, 2000, 5000, 10,000, 20,000, 50,000 and 100,000. Coins in denominations of 100, 200 and 500 have also been issued but these are rarely seen.

Cambodia's second currency is the US dollar, which is accepted everywhere and by everyone, though your change may arrive in riel.

Currency Exchange
Currency exchange rates are as follows:

Australia	A$1	=	1821r
Canada	C$1	=	1683r
France	FF10	=	4472r
Germany	DM1	=	1513r
Japan	¥100	=	2082r
New Zealand	NZ$1	=	1611r
Thailand	100B	=	9056r
UK	UK£1	=	3589r
USA	US$1	=	2300r

Changing Money
In the interests of making life as simple as possible, organise a supply of US dollars before you arrive in Cambodia. If you have cash in another major currency, you will be able to change it without any hassle in Phnom Penh or Siem Reap. The same goes for travellers' cheques. The Cambodian Commercial Bank is the best bank in Phnom Penh and Siem Reap for changing money. A commission of 2% is charged.

Black Market
There is no longer a black market in Cambodia. Exchange rates on the street are the same as those offered by the banks.

Tipping & Bargaining
Tipping is not expected in Cambodia, but as is the case anywhere if you meet with exceptional service or out-of-the-way kindness a tip is always greatly appreciated. Salaries remain extremely low in Cambodia.

Bargaining is the rule in markets, when hiring vehicles and sometimes even when taking a room. The Khmers are not the ruthless hagglers that the Thais and Vietnamese can be. A smile goes a long way.

POST & COMMUNICATIONS
Post is now routed by air through Bangkok, which makes Cambodia's postal services much more reliable than they once were. Telephone connections with the outside world have also improved immensely, though they are not cheap.

Postal Rates
Postal rates are listed in the Phnom Penh GPO. A 10g air mail letter to anywhere in the world costs 1500r, while a 100g letter costs 4800r to anywhere in Asia, 5400r to Australia, 5600r to Europe and 7100r to the USA.

CAMBODIA

CAMBODIA

Parcel rates are 18,000r for 500g within Asia, 20,600r to Australia, 21,800 to Europe and 29,400r to the USA. There is a 2000r fee to send items by registered mail – it is well worth it.

Letters and parcels sent further afield than Asia can take up to two or three weeks to reach their destination.

Receiving Mail

The Phnom Penh GPO has a poste restante box at the far left-hand end of the post counter. Basically anybody can pick up your mail, so it is not a good idea to have anything valuable sent there.

Telephone

Most hotels in Phnom Penh will allow you to make local calls free of charge. International calls can be made on the Telstra public phones, which are available in Phnom Penh and Siem Reap. Phone cards are available in denominations of US$2, US$5, US$20, US$50 and US$100. International phone rates are very expensive.

Numbers starting with 015, 017 and 018 are cellular phone numbers.

To make international calls from Cambodia, the international access code is 00.

To call Cambodia from outside the country, the country code is 855.

Fax & Email

If possible, save your faxes for somewhere else. They can cost as much as US$6 a page in Cambodia. At the time of writing, the information superhighway bypassed Cambodia, and short-term visitors were basically forced to access their Internet accounts via international calls. This is likely to change in the near future.

BOOKS

Travellers with an earnest archaeological bent heading out to Angkor are advised to pick up a copy of *Angkor – An Introduction to the Temples* (Odyssey) by Dawn Rooney. Also recommended is the pocket-size *Angkor – Heart of an Empire* (New Horizons) by Bruno Dagens. The classic travel

book is Norman Lewis' *A Dragon Apparent*, now available from Picador in the *Norman Lewis Omnibus*, a collection of three books recounting Lewis' travels in Indochina.

Angkor: An Introduction (Oxford University Press) by George Coedes gives excellent background information on Angkorian Khmer civilisation. You might also look for Malcolm MacDonald's *Angkor & the Khmers* (Oxford University Press).

The best widely available history of Cambodia is David P Chandler's *A History of Cambodia*. It is available in Cambodia and Bangkok, and published by Silkworm Press.

NEWSPAPERS & MAGAZINES

The *Cambodia Daily* appears at newsstands and restaurants from Monday to Friday. It costs just 1000r. The *Cambodge Soir* is a French paper that comes out twice weekly. The *Phnom Penh Post* is a biweekly newspaper that provides a very good overview of events in Cambodia. It also has a lift-out map of Phnom Penh with restaurants and business services. It costs 2000r and deserves your support.

The *Bangkok Post* and the *Nation* are Thai English-language dailies that are widely available in Phnom Penh, usually by mid-afternoon on the day of publication. *The Economist, Far Eastern Economic Review, Asia Week, Time, Newsweek* and others are readily obtained at bookshops around Phnom Penh.

RADIO & TV

Unless you have a shortwave radio, there is not a great deal of interest on Cambodian airwaves. Most of the mid-range hotels in Phnom Penh have satellite TV reception nowadays, which means that you should have access to the BBC World Service, CNN, Star TV, Channel V (regional answer to MTV) and possibly even the Australian ABC. Without satellite reception, you are restricted to Channel 2 (which is French).

PHOTOGRAPHY

Print film and processing are cheap in Cambodia. A roll of 100 ASA Kodak Gold (36 exposures), for example, costs US$2.50, or US$3.50 for 400 ASA. Konika film is cheaper again. The cheapest places for fast printing are the Konika photolabs, which can be found all over Cambodia. The Konika shops generally charge US$4 for 36 standard prints. Kodak photolabs are more expensive at US$6.

The only slide film available at the time of writing was Ektachrome Elite (100 ASA), which cost US$5 for a roll of 36 exposures. Do not process slide film in Cambodia.

ELECTRICITY

Electricity in Phnom Penh and most of the rest of Cambodia is 220V, 50 Hz. Power is in short supply in Cambodia, however, and power cuts are frequent. Most mid-range and top-end hotels and restaurants have their own generators.

Electric power sockets are generally of the round two-pin variety. Three-pin plug adaptors can be bought at the markets in Phnom Penh.

LAUNDRY

Laundry is never a problem in Cambodia. All hotels provide a laundry service and, unless you are holed up in some top-end joint where they charge you to switch on the lights, it is either free or very cheap.

WEIGHTS & MEASURES

Cambodia uses the metric system. For those unaccustomed to this system, there is a metric/imperial conversion chart inside the back cover of this book.

HEALTH

Your health is at more risk in Cambodia than it is in most other parts of South-East Asia. Medical services are also poor for the most part. In the event of a medical emergency, you will probably need to get to Bangkok. At the very least, it will be necessary to get to Phnom Penh.

The SOS International Medical Centre (☎ (015) 962914), 83 Mao Tse Toung Blvd, is one of the best medical services in Phnom Penh. Office hours are from 9 am to 5 pm

Monday to Friday, 9 am to noon Saturday. SOS also has a 24 hour emergency service (☎ (015) 912765) and can organise evacuation to Bangkok.

For dental problems, go to the European Medical Clinic (☎ (018) 812055), at 195 Norodom Blvd. Office hours are 8 am to noon and 2.30 to 6 pm Monday to Friday, 8 am to 1 pm Saturday.

See the Health section in the Appendix. Note that opisthorchiasis (liver flukes) may be contracted by swimming in the southern reaches of the Mekong River.

TOILETS

Although the occasional squat toilet turns up here and there, the general rule (particularly in hotels) is the sit-down variety. Public toilets are nonexistent.

WOMEN TRAVELLERS

As far as Cambodia can be described as safe, women will generally find the country to be a hassle-free place to travel in. Foreign women are unlikely to be particularly targeted by the attentions of local men, but at the same time it pays to be careful. As is the case anywhere in the world, walking or riding a bike alone late at night is risky; and if you are planning a trip off the beaten trail it would be best to find a travel companion.

Khmer women dress fairly conservatively, and it's best to follow suit, particularly when visiting wats. In general, long-sleeved shirts and long trousers or skirts are preferred.

DISABLED TRAVELLERS

Depending on your disability, Cambodia is not going to be an easy country to get around in. Local labour at least is inexpensive, which means that you can hire a guide for around US$10 a day or less. But on the whole it will probably be difficult: the roads are bad, many hotels are without lifts, and touring the country's major attraction, Angkor, would be near impossible. Travellers with major disabilities would be advised to look into a tour.

SENIOR TRAVELLERS

Senior travellers will not be eligible for anything in the way of discounts in Cambodia – all foreigners are rich as far as Cambodians are concerned.

TRAVEL WITH CHILDREN

Travellers visiting Cambodia with children should pick up a copy of Lonely Planet's *Travel with Children*. If you are just planning a visit to Angkor and Phnom Penh, there should be no problems. More adventurous travel in Cambodia with children is not recommended.

USEFUL ORGANISATIONS

Cambodia hosts a huge number of NGOs. The best way to find out who exactly is represented in Cambodia is to call in to the Cooperation Committee for Cambodia (CCC) (☎ 426009), at 35 178 St, Phnom Penh. This organisation has a handy list of all NGOs, both Cambodian and international.

DANGERS & ANNOYANCES
Security

Sadly the civil war drags on in Cambodia. In the last few years several foreign visitors have been killed in Cambodia. Do not take unnecessary risks.

Always make a point of checking on the latest security situation before making a trip that you know not many travellers undertake. Moreover, do not rely only on information provided by locals – they often undertake dangerous trips as a matter of necessity and have no way of assessing the risks for a foreigner.

Undetonated Mines, Mortars & Bombs

Never, ever touch any rockets, artillery shells, mortars, mines, bombs or other war material you may come across. In Vietnam most of this sort of stuff is 15 or more years old, but in Cambodia it may have landed there or been laid as recently as the previous night. The most heavily mined part of the country is the Battambang area, but mines are a problem all over Cambodia. In short:

do not stray from well-marked paths under any circumstances, even around the monuments of Angkor.

Snakes

Visitors to Angkor and other overgrown archaeological sites should beware of snakes, including the small but deadly light-green Hanuman snake.

Theft & Street Crime

Given the number of guns about in Cambodia, there is less armed theft than you might suppose. Still, motorcycle theft is a problem in Phnom Penh. There is no need to be overly paranoid, just cautious. Driving alone late at night is probably not a good idea.

Pickpocketing and theft by stealth is more of a problem in Vietnam and Thailand than it is in Cambodia. Again, though, it pays to be careful. Don't make the job of potential thieves any easier by putting your passport and wads of cash in your back pocket.

LEGAL MATTERS

Contrary to popular belief, marijuana is not legal in Cambodia. It's probably only a matter of time before the Cambodian police turn busting foreigners into a lucrative sideline.

Moral grounds alone should be enough to deter foreigners from seeking underage sexual partners in Cambodia. Paedophiles are treated as criminals by the authorities and several have served or are serving jail sentences as a result.

BUSINESS HOURS

Government offices, which are open Monday to Saturday, theoretically begin the working day at 7 or 7.30 am, breaking for a siesta from 11 or 11.30 am to 2 or 2.30 pm and ending the day at 5.30 pm. However, it is a safe bet that few people will be around early in the morning or after 4 or 4.30 pm.

Banking hours tend to vary according to the bank, but you can reckon on core hours of 8.30 am to 3.30 pm. The Foreign Trade Bank is open from 7.30 to 11.30 am on Saturdays.

PUBLIC HOLIDAYS & SPECIAL EVENTS

The festivals of Cambodia take place according to the lunar calendar, so the dates vary from year to year.

Chaul Chnam
  Held in mid-April, this is a three day celebration of Khmer New Year; Khmers make offerings at wats, clean out their homes and exchange gifts of new clothes.

Chat Preah Nengka
  Held in mid to late May, this is the Royal Ploughing ceremony, a ritual agricultural festival led by the royal family.

International Workers Day
  1 May

P'chum Ben
  Held in late September, this is a kind of all souls day, when respects are paid to the dead through offerings made at wats.

HM the King's Birthday
  30 October to 1 November

Bon Om Tuk
  Held in early November, this celebrates the reversal of the current of the Tonlé Sap River (with the onset of the dry season, water backed up in the Tonlé Sap lake begins to empty into the Mekong – in the wet season the reverse is the case).

Independence Day
  9 November

The Chinese inhabitants of Cambodia celebrate their New Year in late January or early to mid-February – for the Vietnamese, this is Tet.

ACTIVITIES

Tourism in Cambodia is still in its infancy and as yet there is little in the way of activities besides sightseeing. Snorkelling and diving are available in Sihanoukville.

WORK

Jobs are available in Phnom Penh and elsewhere around Cambodia. The obvious categories are English/French teaching work and volunteer work with one of the many NGOs operating in the country. For information about work opportunities with the NGOs call into the CCC (see Useful Organisations above), which has a noticeboard for positions vacant and may also be able to give advice on where to look.

Other places to look for work include the Classifieds sections of the *Phnom Penh Post* and the *Cambodia Daily*. The Foreign Correspondents' Club (FCC) in Phnom Penh has a noticeboard with job postings, as does Bert's Books & Guesthouse.

Do not expect to make a lot of money working in Cambodia. But if you want to learn more about the country and help the locals to get the place up and running again, it may well be a very worthwhile experience.

ACCOMMODATION

There is a reasonably wide range of accommodation options in Phnom Penh and in Siem Reap nowadays. Elsewhere around Cambodia, options are still fairly limited.

Budget hostels only exist in Phnom Penh, Siem Reap and Sihanoukville. Costs hover around US$3 for a bed, slightly more in Sihanoukville, where there is little competition. In other parts of Cambodia, the standard rate for the cheapest hotels is US$5 – in many places this will be the standard rate for all hotels in town.

In Phnom Penh and Siem Reap, which see a steady flow of traffic, hotels start to improve significantly once you start spending more than US$10. For US$15 or less it is usually possible to find an air-con room with satellite TV and attached bathroom.

FOOD

Cambodian food is closely related to the cuisines of neighbouring Thailand and Laos and, to a lesser extent, Vietnam, but there are some distinct local dishes. The overall consensus is that Khmer cooking is like Thai without the spices.

Phnom Penh is far and away the best place to try Khmer cuisine, though Siem Reap also has some good restaurants. In Phnom Penh you also have the choice of excellent Thai, Vietnamese, Chinese, French and Mediterranean cooking.

Rice is the principal staple and the Battambang region is the country's rice bowl. Most Cambodian dishes are cooked in a wok, known locally as a *chhnang khteak*.

CAMBODIA

DRINKS

All the famous international brands of soft drinks are available in Cambodia. Locally produced mineral water is available at 500r per bottle.

Coffee is sold in most restaurants. It is either served black or *café au lait* – with generous dollops of condensed milk, which makes it very sweet. Chinese-style tea is popular and in many Khmer and Chinese restaurants a pot of it will automatically appear as soon as you sit down.

The local beer is Angkor, which is produced by an Australian joint venture in Sihanoukville. Other brands include Heineken, Tiger, San Miguel, Carlsberg, VB, Foster's and Grolsch. Beer sells for around US$1.30 a can in restaurants.

In Phnom Penh, foreign wines and spirits are sold at very reasonable prices. The local spirits are best avoided, though some expats say that Sra Special, a local whisky-like concoction, is not bad. At around 1000r a bottle it's a cheap route to oblivion.

ENTERTAINMENT
Cinemas

Cinemas are best avoided. Even if you can understand the proceedings, Cambodia's cinemas tend to be scruffy, hot and sometimes dangerously overcrowded.

Discos

Phnom Penh is the place for disco nightlife. There are several clubs that see a good mix of locals and expats. Nightlife in Phnom Penh tends to not get going until fairly late – an 11 pm start seems to be the popular thing to do, after a leisurely meal and some drinks at a bar.

Nightclubs

Outside Phnom Penh, nightlife is dominated by the 'dancing restaurant'. These are basically 'hostess clubs' aimed at men, though it's unlikely that a foreign woman accompanied by a foreign man would have any trouble in these places.

Traditional Dance

Public performances of Khmer traditional dance are few and far between. Phnom Penh and Siem Reap the most likely places to find them. Check in the local English-language newspapers for news of upcoming events.

Pubs/Bars

Again, Phnom Penh is the place for pubs and bars. Elsewhere around Cambodia, drinking takes place in market areas, in restaurants and in 'dancing restaurants'.

SPECTATOR SPORTS

Sports events are held from time to time at the Olympic Stadium in Phnom Penh. Thai boxing is popular in Cambodia and can be interesting to watch. Check the local English-language newspapers for news of events at the stadium.

THINGS TO BUY

The checked cotton scarves everyone wears on their heads, around their necks or, if bathing, around their midriffs are known as *kramas*. Fancier coloured versions are made of silk or a silk-cotton blend. Some of the finest cotton kramas come from the Kompong Cham area.

For information on where in Phnom Penh to find antiques, silver items, jewellery, gems, colourful cloth for sarongs and *hols* (variegated silk shirts), woodcarvings, papier-mâché masks, stone copies of ancient Khmer art, brass figurines and oil paintings, see Things to Buy in the Phnom Penh section.

Also see the Phnom Penh section for information on buying craft items produced by Cambodian mine victims, handicapped and women's groups. The proceeds go to good causes, and the products themselves are very fine.

Getting There & Away

AIR

As yet, Cambodia is connected only by air to most other South-East Asian countries.

CAMBODIA

Thailand

Flights to Phnom Penh from Bangkok are available with Thai Airways International and Royal Air Cambodge. There is not much in the way of discounting available on these flights, but it may be worth shopping around a little. Royal Air Cambodge is the cheaper of the two at around US$120/220 one way/return. Thai Airways flights cost around US$140/280.

Hong Kong

Dragonair and Royal Air Cambodge fly between Hong Kong and Phnom Penh. Royal Air Cambodge is the cheaper of the two, with flights at US$190/300 one way/return. Dragonair costs US$210/310. There is no discounting on flights to and from Hong Kong, so it makes little difference who you buy your ticket from.

Singapore

Silk Air and Royal Air Cambodge have flights from Singapore to Phnom Penh. Royal Air Cambodge tickets cost around US$210/300 one way/return, while Silk Air flights are around US$210/360.

Malaysia

Flights between Kuala Lumpur and Phnom Penh are offered by Malaysia Airlines and Royal Air Cambodge. One-way flights with both airlines are around US$200. Return flights are around US$310 with Royal Air Cambodge and US$360 with Malaysia Airlines.

Vietnam

Vietnam Airlines does the short hop from Ho Chi Minh City to Phnom Penh for US$70/130 one way/return; Royal Air Cambodge costs US$65/110. Royal Air Cambodge is probably the better airline.

Laos

Daily flights between Vientiane and Phnom Penh cost US$150/300 one way/return.

Departure Tax

There is a departure tax of US$15 on all international flights out of Cambodia.

LAND

Vietnam

The only fully functioning land crossing in or out of Cambodia is at Moc Bai in Vietnam. The trip by bus or by taxi between Phnom Penh and Ho Chi Minh City should only take five to six hours, but delays are frequent. See Getting There & Away in the Phnom Penh section for details.

Thailand

There are no official land crossings between Thailand and Cambodia. A small trickle of adventurous travellers have made their way between Trat in Thailand and Koh Kong in Cambodia. This border crossing is not officially open to foreign travellers and the journey is dangerous. It is not recommended.

The border crossing between Aranyaprathet in eastern Thailand and Poipet in western Cambodia is extremely dangerous due to Khmer Rouge activity in this part of Cambodia. If you hear that this border has become safe to cross, it would be wise to confirm it with your embassy.

Getting Around

AIR

Royal Air Cambodge has flights to limited destinations around Cambodia. Angkor is well serviced and it is usually possible to get on a flight at short notice. But demand for flights to other destinations around the country often exceeds supply; it is not always easy to get seats.

There are seven flights a day from Phnom Penh to Siem Reap (Angkor); the cost is US$55/110 one way/return. For Battambang, there are five flights a week; the cost is US$45/90 one way/return. Flights to Ratanakiri are scheduled five times a week; the cost is US$55/100. Other destinations are Sihanoukville (four times a week) for

US$40/70; Koh Kong (four times a week) for US$50/100; Stung Treng (three times a week) for US$45/90 and Mondolkiri (twice a week) for US$50/100.

The airport tax for domestic flights was US$4 at the time of writing but was reportedly poised to rise to US$5.

BUS

Bus services in Cambodia are slow, crowded and limited to only a few destinations. For security reasons they are best avoided. A modern air-con bus service runs between Phnom Penh and Sihanoukville, and more are expected on this route. Most embassies advise against using it.

TRAIN

Cambodia's rail network is off limits to foreign travellers. It is a very dangerous way to travel due to frequent Khmer Rouge attacks.

TAXI

Long-distance taxis are widely available for hire in Cambodia nowadays. For major destinations you can hire them individually or pay for a seat and wait for other passengers to turn up.

MOTORCYCLE

Motorbikes are available for rent in Phnom Penh. Costs are US$4 per day and upwards depending on the bike. The cheapest models are 100cc Hondas. Bear in mind that medical facilities are less than adequate in Cambodia and that the driving is erratic. A bike can be useful for visiting out-of-town attractions in the Phnom Penh area. Cross-country biking is dangerous.

BOAT

Passenger boat services ply the Mekong as far north as Stung Treng, but the most popular services with foreigners are those that run between Phnom Penh and Siem Reap. The new express services do the trip in as little as four hours. They are, however, dangerously overcrowded and occasionally the target of attacks by fishing people.

For information on ferry services to/from Phnom Penh, see Getting There & Away in the Phnom Penh section.

LOCAL TRANSPORT
Bus

The only real local bus services running in Cambodia are those in Phnom Penh. For the most part, buses are not yet a practical way of getting around.

Taxi

The taxi situation has been steadily improving in Cambodia over the last few years. Whereas taxi hire was once only available through government ministries, there are now many private operators working throughout Cambodia. Even in Phnom Penh, however, you'll be hard pressed to find a taxi for short hops.

Moto

The moto is generally a 100cc Honda. The drivers almost universally wear a blue cap. They are a quick, if somewhat dangerous, way of making short hops around towns and cities. Prices range from 500r to US$1, depending on the distance you travel. Moto drivers assume you know the cost of a trip and prices are rarely agreed before starting.

Cyclo

As in Vietnam and Laos, the samlor or *cyclo* is a quick, cheap way to get around Cambodia's urban areas. In Phnom Penh, cyclo drivers can either be flagged down on main thoroughfares or found hanging out around marketplaces and major hotels. In Phnom Penh and elsewhere around Cambodia the cyclo driver is fast being pushed out of business by the moto.

Remorque-Kang & Remorque-Moto

The *remorque-kang* is a trailer pulled by a bicycle; a trailer hitched to a motorbike is called a *remorque-moto*. Both are used to transport people and goods, especially in rural areas. They are not seen so much nowadays in urban Cambodia.

Phnom Penh

Phnom Penh, capital of Cambodia for much of the period since the mid-15th century (when Angkor was abandoned), is situated at the confluence of the Mekong, the Bassac and the Tonlé Sap rivers. Once considered the loveliest of the French-built cities of Indochina, Phnom Penh's charm is fast succumbing to a construction boom but is still evident in parts of town.

Orientation

The Tonlé Sap and Bassac rivers define the eastern extent of town. The centre of town is roughly the area around the New Market (also known as the Central Market), an area with plenty of hotels.

The major thoroughfares run north-south. They are Monivong Blvd (the main commercial drag), Norodom Blvd (mainly administrative) and Samdech Sothearos Blvd (in front of the Royal Palace). The main east-west arteries are Pochentong Blvd in the north, Preah Sihanouk Blvd, which runs past the Victory Monument, and Mao Tse Toung Blvd, in the far south of town.

Besides the main boulevards are hundreds of numbered streets. In most cases, odd-numbered streets run more or less north-south (usually parallel to Monivong Blvd), with the numbers rising as you move from east to west. Even-numbered streets run in an east-west direction and their numbers rise as you move from north to south.

Maps Local maps of Phnom Penh, touted around the restaurants by children, are generally poor. The biweekly *Phnom Penh Post* includes a map with regularly updated listings. The *Cambodia Travel Map* published by Periplus is available at the Cambodiana Hotel bookshop and includes a large fold-out map of Phnom Penh at a scale of 1:17,000 – many of the items included are either out of date or incorrectly placed on the map.

Information

Tourist Offices The head office of Phnom Penh Tourism is across from Wat Ounalom at the oblique intersection of Samdech Sothearos Blvd and Sisowath Quay. The office is officially open from 7 to 11 am and from 2 to 5 pm. It's a sleepy place with nothing in the way of useful information; for the most part it restricts its activities to running the *Lotus D'Or* sightseeing boat.

The Ministry of Tourism (☎ 426876) is in a white, two storey building on the western corner of Monivong Blvd and 232 St. Inside chaos prevails.

Money The best bank for changing money and obtaining credit card advances is the Cambodian Commercial Bank, on the corner of Pochentong St and Monivong Blvd. It takes most travellers' cheques and can also organise credit card advances for Master-Card, JCB and Visa. A limit of US$2000 is imposed on cash advances, but there is no charge. Most other banks around town only deal with Visa and charge 2% commission.

Travellers' cheques can also be changed at the Foreign Trade Bank, at 24 Norodom Blvd, and next door at the Bangkok Bank. The Banque Indosuez, at 77 Norodom Blvd, is another place that changes travellers' cheques. Both the Diamond and Cambodiana Hotels have exchange counters, but they are only available for guests.

Post The GPO is just east of Wat Phnom on 13 St. It is open from 6.30 am to 9 pm daily. The GPO offers postal services as well as domestic and international telegraph and telephone links.

Telephone The best way to dial locally or internationally is with the Telstra card phones that are scattered around town. Cards are available at the Telstra office (☎ 426022), 58 Norodom Blvd, and at the FCC and other outlets.

The Phnom Penh area code is 23.

Fax Many of the mid-range hotels and all of the top-end hotels around town have fax

CAMBODIA

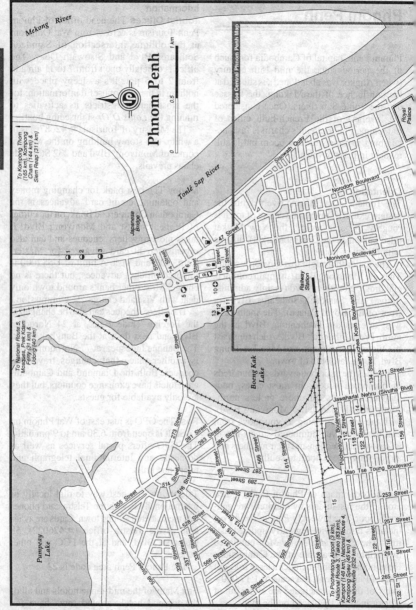

Mekong River

To Kompong Thom
(165 km), Kompong
Cham (144 km) &
Siem Reap (311 km)

Phnom Penh

1 km

0.5

0

See Central Phnom Penh Map

Royal Palace

Sisowath Quay

Norodom Boulevard

Monivong Boulevard

Tonlé Sap River

Japanese Bridge

47 Street
74 Street
72 Street
80 Street
84 Street
86 Street

Railway Station

Boeng Kak Lake

To National Route 5,
Mosques, Prek Kdam
Ferry (31 km) &
Udong (40 km)

70 Street

Kampuchea Krom Boulevard

211 Street

134 Street

Jawaharlal Nehru (Sivutha Blvd)

273 Street
281 Street
283 Street
285 Street
566 Street
614 Street

Pochentong Boulevard
112 Street
118 Street
122 Street

156 Street

Mao Tse Toung Boulevard

253 Street

51A
528 Street
287 Street
289 Street
291 Street
516 Street

355 Street
339 Street
337 Street
335 Street
528 Street
313 Street
317 Street
592 Street
608 Street
122 Street

257 Street

261 Street

265 Street

132 St

16

15

To Pochentong Airport (3 km),
National Route 3, Takeo (83 km),
Kampot (148 km), National Route 4,
Kompong Speu (45 km) &
Sihanoukville (232 km)

Pumpeay Lake

1
2
3
4
5
6
7
8
9
10
11
12
13
14

CAMBODIA

To National Route 1,
Koki Beach (10 km),
Svay Rieng (110 km)
& Ho Chi Minh City
(Saigon) (220 km)

To National Route 2,
Takmau, Tonle Bati (35 km),
Phnom Chisor (55 km)
& Takeo (777 km)

Bassac River

Vietnam
(Monivong)
Bridge

River

Boeng
Tompun
Lake

To the Killing Fields
of Choeung Ek

PLACES TO STAY
6 Bayon Hotel
8 Holiday International Hotel
18 Borei Thmei Hotel
19 Vimean Suor Hotel
26 Sydney International Hotel
27 Royal Phnom Penh Hotel

PLACES TO EAT
12 Restaurant Raksmey
Boeng Kak
13 Buong Thong Restaurant
14 Ly Lay Restaurant
16 La Casa Restaurant
32 Hua Nam Restaurant

OTHER
1 Golden Sea Express
   (Express Boats)
2 Slow Boats to Kratie
3 Siem Reap & Kratie
   Heiwa Shipping
   (Express Boats)
4 School of Fine Arts
5 French Embassy
7 Tabou Bar

9 British Embassy
10 Calmette Hospital
11 International Mosque
15 Phnom Penh University
17 Buses to Ho Chi
   Minh City (Saigon)
20 Danjkor Market
21 Martini Bar
22 Tuol Sleng Museum
23 Magic Circus Cafe-Theatre
25 Access Medical Services
26 Russian Embassy
28 European Medical Clinic
29 Wat Than Handicrafts
30 Royal Air Cambodge
31 Lao Embassy
33 SOS International Medical
   Centre
34 Wat Tuol Tom Pong
35 Chinese Embassy
36 Tuol Tom Pong
   (Russian) Market
37 Vietnamese Embassy
38 Cham Kar Mon Palace
39 Taxis to Ho Chi
   Minh City (Saigon)

services. Sending faxes from Phnom Penh is expensive, and it generally costs money to receive them too. The FCC has a business centre where faxes can be sent and received.

Travel Agencies The area near the Pacific Hotel on Monivong Blvd has a few budget travel agencies, including Pich Tourist Co (☎ 246585), which also has a reasonable bookshop.

One of the most reliable outfits in town is Diethelm Travel (☎ 426648), at 8 Samdech Sothearos Blvd, behind the FCC. Diethelm also has offices in Siem Reap, Bangkok and Ho Chi Minh City, making it a good agency to book regional flights and tours. Another popular agency is East West Tours (☎ 427118), at 84 Samdech Sothearos Blvd, just south of the Regency Park Hotel. Transpeed Travel (☎ 427366), at 19 106 St in the same building as Thai Airways, is another good option for flight bookings.

Bookshops Bert's Books, at 79 Sisowath Quay in the guesthouse of the same name, is the best place in town for browsing. For new books and magazines, the bookshop on the ground floor of the Cambodiana Hotel is one of the best stocked in town. It has a very good selection of French newspapers, magazines and books, as well as a modest selection of English coffee-table publications, novels and weeklies such as *Far Eastern Economic Review*, *The Economist*, *Time*, *Newsweek* and *Asiaweek*.

Bookazine, at 228 Monivong Blvd, has a reasonable selection of Penguins, magazines and a good range of books on Cambodia. The International Stationery & Book Centre is mainly devoted to dictionaries, but it also stocks some locally produced maps.

Libraries The National Library, on 92 St near Wat Phnom, is in a delightful old building but only has a small selection of reading material for foreign visitors. Most of the books were destroyed during the Pol Pot era. Opening hours are from 8 to 11 am and 2 to 5 pm.

Cultural Centres French speakers should call into the French Cultural Centre on 184 St (near the corner of Monivong Blvd). It has a good range of reading material. The Reading Room at the US Embassy is geared towards Khmer students looking to study in the USA.

Hash House Harriers A good opportunity to meet local expats is via the Hash House Harriers, usually referred to simply as 'the Hash'. A weekly run/walk takes place every Sunday. Participants meet in front of the railway station at 2.45 pm, and entry is US$5; the entry fee includes refreshments at the end.

Laundry Most of the hotels around town offer very reasonably priced laundry services – in some cases free.

Medical Services See Health in the earlier Facts for the Visitor section for information on Phnom Penh's medical facilities.

Dangers & Annoyances Phnom Penh is not as dangerous as many people imagine, but it is still important to take care. Armed theft is on the increase. It is not sensible to ride a motorbike alone late at night.

Those out clubbing in the evenings can expect to be stopped at checkpoints from time to time. Ostensibly, police checkpoints are there to check for firearms, but occasionally foreigners will be nabbed for a cigarette or a dollar. You are under no obligation to fork out.

The restaurant areas of Phnom Penh (particularly places with outdoor seating) are infested with beggars. Generally, however, there is little in the way of push and shove. If you give to beggars, do as the locals do and keep the denominations small – this way, hopefully, foreigners will not become special targets of begging.

Wat Phnom
Set on top of a 27-metre-high, tree-covered knoll, Wat Phnom was once visible from all over the city, and still makes for a good

landmark. According to legend, the first pagoda on this site was erected in 1373 to house four Buddha statues deposited here by the waters of the Mekong and discovered by a woman named Penh (thus the name Phnom Penh, the Hill of Penh).

Royal Palace

Phnom Penh's Royal Palace is the official residence of King Norodom Sihanouk, and is seldom open to the public. It is only possible to view the Silver Pagoda.

Silver Pagoda

The spectacular Silver Pagoda is so named because the floor is covered with over 5000 silver tiles weighing one kg each. It is also known as Wat Preah Keo (Pagoda of the Emerald Buddha). The Emerald Buddha, which is presumably made of baccarat crystal, sits on a gilt pedestal high atop the dais. In front of the dais stands a life-size Buddha made of solid gold and decorated with 9584 diamonds, the largest of which weighs 25 carats.

The Silver Pagoda is open to the public daily from 8 to 11 am and from 2 to 5 pm. The entry fee is US$2. There is an additional US$2 charge to bring a still camera into the complex; movie or video cameras cost US$5. Photography is not permitted inside the pagoda itself.

National Museum

The National Museum of Cambodia is housed in a graceful terracotta structure of traditional design (built 1917-20) just north of the Royal Palace. It is open Tuesday to Sunday from 8 to 11 am and 2 to 5 pm. The entry fee for foreigners is US$2, and English and French-speaking guides are available. Photography is prohibited inside.

The National Museum exhibits numerous masterpieces of Khmer art, artisanship and sculpture dating from the pre-Angkor period of Funan and Chenla (4th to 9th centuries AD), the Indravarman period (9th and 10th centuries), the classical Angkor period (10th to 14th centuries) and the post-Angkor period (after the 14th century).

Tuol Sleng Museum

In 1975 Tuol Svay Prey High School was taken over by Pol Pot's security forces and turned into a prison known as Security Prison 21 (S-21). It soon became the largest such centre of detention and torture in the country. Almost all the people held at S-21 were later taken to the extermination camp at Choeung Ek to be executed. Detainees who died during torture were buried in mass graves in the prison grounds. During the first part of 1977, S-21 claimed an average of 100 victims per day.

S-21 has been turned into the Tuol Sleng Museum, which is a testament to the crimes of the Khmer Rouge. The museum is open daily from 7 to 11.30 am and 2 to 5.30 pm; entry is US$2.

Wat Ounalom

Wat Ounalom, headquarters of the Cambodian Buddhist patriarchate, is on the southwestern corner of the intersection of Samdech Sothearos Blvd and 154 St (across from Phnom Penh Tourism).

Under Pol Pot, the complex, which was founded in 1443 and includes 44 structures, was heavily damaged and its extensive library destroyed. Today the wat is once again returning to prominence as a centre for Buddhist training (for local monks).

Other Wats

Other wats in Phnom Penh worth visiting include **Wat Lang Ka**, which is on the southern side of Preah Sihanouk Blvd just west of the Victory Monument; **Wat Koh**, which is on the eastern side of Monivong Blvd between 174 and 178 Sts; and **Wat Moha Montrei**, which is one block east of the Olympic Market on the southern side of Preah Sihanouk Blvd between 163 and 173 Sts.

English St

This is a cluster of private language schools that teach English (and some French). It is one block west of the National Museum on 184 St between Norodom Blvd and the back part of the Royal Palace compound. Between 5 and 7 pm, the whole area is filled with students who see learning English as the key to making it in postwar Cambodia. This is a good place to meet local young people.

Victory Monument

The Victory Monument, which is at the intersection of Norodom and Sihanouk Blvds, was built in 1958 as the Independence Monument. It is now a memorial to Cambodia's war dead (or at least those the present government considers worthy of remembering).

Places to Stay

Budget accommodation is scattered around town. The longest running, though by no means the best, is the *Capital Guesthouse* (☎ 364104), on 182 St not far from O Russei Market. The owners have expanded operations into two adjacent buildings under the names *Happy Guesthouse* and *Capital II* – the latter is almost exclusively the domain of Japanese travellers. Basic singles/doubles (no bathroom, often no window) are US$3/4, while rooms with bathroom cost US$5/6.

There are some more wholesome alternatives to the Capital not far away. *Narin's*

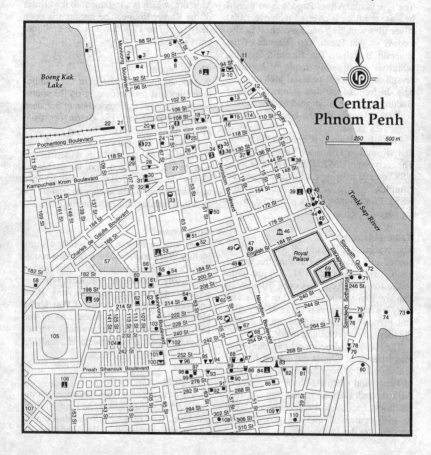

Central Phnom Penh

Boeng Kak Lake

Tonlé Sap River

Royal Palace

Guesthouse is probably the pick of the pack. It's a clean, family-run place that provides excellent meals. The guesthouse is at 50 125 St, and has an overflow annex a few doors down. Clean rooms with windows and shared bathroom cost US$3 for a single, US$5 for a double. The annex also has a double with bathroom for US$6, but it's very rarely free.

Around the corner from the Capital on 111 St is the family-run *Seng Sokhom House*. It's a friendly place with a pleasant veranda area. Rooms cost US$5 with bathroom and US$3 without. Elsewhere around town, the two most popular spots are Bert's Books & Guesthouse and Cloud Nine (formerly known as No 9 Guesthouse). *Cloud Nine*

PLACES TO STAY
1 Cloud Nine Guesthouse
4 Le Royal Hotel
5 Sharaton Cambodia Hotel
9 Wat Phnom Hotel
12 Bert's Guesthouse
15 Last Home Guesthouse
16 Cathay Hotel
24 Fortune Hotel
29 Monoram Hotel
30 Asie Hotel
31 Singapore Hotel
32 Diamond Hotel
38 Hotel Indochine
51 Lotus Guesthouse
58 Sangkor Hotel
60 Capital Guesthouse
61 Hong Kong Hotel
62 No 20 Guesthouse
74 Sofitel Cambodiana Hotel
75 Bophar Toep Hotel
81 Hotel Shinwa
85 Rama Inn
90 Golden Gate Hotel
91 Goldiana Hotel
92 Amara Hotel
99 Tokyo Hotel
104 Narin's Guesthouse

PLACES TO EAT
2 Chez Lipp Restaurant
7 Il Padrino Restaurant
11 Tonlé Sap Restaurant
18 Le Cuistot
20 Happy Neth Pizza
21 Indian Restaurant
26 Cathouse Tavern
28 Mamak's Corner & Kababeesh Restaurants
41 Wagon Wheel Restaurant
42 Pon Lok Restaurant
56 King's Bar
67 Baggio's Pizza
78 Chiang Mai Restaurant
79 Saigon House & EID Restaurants

82 The Mex
93 Phnom Kiev Restaurant
94 California II Restaurant
95 King of King's Restaurant
96 Singapore Chicken Rice & Cordon Bleue Restaurants
102 Royal India Restaurant
109 Ban Thai Restaurant

OTHER
3 Seven Seven Supermarket & Café
6 National Library
8 Wat Phnom
10 GPO
12 Bert's Books
13 Thai Airways & Dragonair
14 Old Market (Psar Char)
17 NCDP Handicrafts
19 Canadia Bank
22 Railway Station
23 Cambodian Commercial Bank
25 Thai Farmers' Bank
27 New Market (Central Market)
33 Local (City) Bus Station
34 Maybank
35 Foreign Trade Bank of Cambodia
36 Bangkok Bank
37 Sharky's (Disco)
39 Wat Ounalom
40 Phnom Penh Tourism
43 Diethelm Travel
44 Foreign Correspondent's Club of Cambodia (FCC)
45 UNESCO
46 National Museum
47 Banque Indosuez
48 Immigration (Direction des Étrangers) Bureau

49 Japanese Embassy
50 Heart of Darkness Bar
52 Cooperation Committee for Cambodia (CCC)
53 Wat Koh
54 French Cultural Centre
55 Ministry of Culture
57 O Russei Market
59 Wat Sampao Meas
61 Lucky! Lucky! (Motorbike Rental)
63 International Stationery & Book Centre
64 Bangkok Airways
65 Le Saint Tropez (Disco)
66 US Embassy
68 Australian Embassy
69 Silver Pagoda
70 National Assembly Building
71 Foreign Ministry
72 Chatomuk Theatre
73 Naga Floating Casino
76 East-West Tours
77 Cambodia-Vietnam Monument
80 Cambo Fun Park
83 Victory Monument
84 Wat Lang Ka
86 Irish Rover Pub
87 Vietnam Airlines
88 Fire Club (Disco)
89 Cactus
97 Ettamogah Pub
98 Lucky Supermarket
100 Post & Telecommunications Office
101 Suntan Foodmart
103 Ministry of Tourism
105 Olympic Stadium
106 Wat Moha Montrei
107 Olympic Market
108 Khemara Handicrafts
110 Prayuvong Buddha Factories

Guesthouse has a great location on the Boeng Kak Lake, and there's a wooden pavilion area with hammocks on the lake itself. The food here is very good, with some excellent curries courtesy of the Tamil-Malaysian management. It's advisable that you check any valuables in with management here if you stay – the rooms are not particularly secure. Dorm accommodation costs US$2. The nearby *No 10 Guesthouse* takes the overflow from Cloud Nine when it's full.

Bert of *Bert's Books & Guesthouse* (☎ 916411) runs a tighter ship than Cloud Nine. Downstairs is a wonderfully cluttered second-hand bookshop; upstairs there are 15 rooms and a couple of veranda areas that provide views of the Tonlé Sap River. There is a continuous supply of coffee, soft drinks and beer, and meals are provided in the evening on a rickety bamboo awning if you book ahead. Rooms cost US$6 with bathroom and US$3.50 without.

A new arrival on the guesthouse scene is the *Last Home* (☎ 724917), a German-run place at 47 108 St. Last Home has a bit of a crash-pad atmosphere, but will no doubt improve if the place takes off. A mattress on the floor of a high-ceilinged room costs US$2, singles cost US$4.50 and spacious doubles are US$5; bathroom facilities are communal.

Going up a notch in comfort and price, the *Lotus Guesthouse* (☎ 362409), on the corner of 63 and 172 Sts, has rooms with attached bathroom (no hot water) for US$10.

On the waterfront, at the corner of 144 St, is the *Hotel Indochine* (☎ 427292), a very friendly place with spacious air-con singles/doubles with attached bathroom for US$10/12. Given its prime location, this place will probably get the renovation treatment at some stage, but for the moment it is very good value.

The *Cathay Hotel* (☎ 427178) has been around for a while, and is popular with resident journalists and photographers. Air-con rooms on the 1st and 2nd floors cost US$20, while those prepared to puff their way up several flights of stairs get the same rooms

for US$15 on the 3rd and 4th floors (this is a common situation in Phnom Penh).

Not far from the Cathay, at 2 67 St, is the *Fortune Hotel* (☎ 428216). It does a steady business with regular visitors to Phnom Penh and seems to have cleaned up its once slightly seedy image. Singles/doubles cost US$15.

A favourite with long-termers is the *Golden Gate Hotel* (☎ 427618). Unfortunately it is not unusual for this extremely friendly Chinese-run hotel to be full – it's a good idea to ring ahead and book. The Golden Gate has a downstairs restaurant, verandas, areas to sit down with magazines provided; the rooms are spotless, air-con and fitted with satellite TV and mini-bars; and there is a free laundry service. Costs are US$15/17 for a single/double. It is close to the corner of 51 and 278 Sts.

If the Golden Gate is full, the *Tokyo Hotel* (☎ 722247) is not far away at 13 278 St. It is good value with rooms at US$15.

The *Tai Seng Hotel* (☎ 427220), at 56 Monivong Blvd, has a good location just east of Wat Phnom and is heavily promoted by the tourist office at Pochentong airport. Rooms here cost US$25, or US$20 on the higher floors – some of these have good views of the Boeng Kak Lake.

Places to Eat

The *Capitol Restaurant*, beneath the Capitol Guesthouse, is still the best place to catch up on travellers' gossip and down an inexpensive meal. The food is nothing to write home about and you'll be racing with the flies to see who finishes it first, but it's a popular place all the same.

Khmer Scattered around town are numerous Khmer restaurants that offer alfresco dining in the evenings. These places rarely have English signs and are as much about drinking beer as about eating, but they're lively places for an inexpensive meal. On the corner of 214 St and Monivong Blvd is a popular restaurant with a US$2.50 all-you-can-eat soup deal. The southern end of 51 St, just down from Baggio's Pizza, also has a couple of similar restaurants.

Beside the Boeng Kak Lake are a couple of long-runners that are still going strong. The *Restaurant Raksmey Boeng Kak*, the southernmost of the two, is built out over the lake and can turn out a delicious meal for less than US$5. Try the excellent duck soup or other traditional Cambodian dishes. The other lakeside restaurant is the *Buong Thong Restaurant*.

For inexpensive Khmer food with a Gallic touch, head down to the *Phnom Kiev Restaurant* on Sihanouk Blvd. The restaurant has a popular garden area out front, and it does good salads and some excellent beef dishes.

Australian No-frills Ozzie pub grub is available at the *Ettamogah Pub* on Sihanouk Blvd, next door to the Lucky Supermarket. The Ettamogah is open from very early in the morning until around midnight. The fish & chips and hamburgers are among the best in town.

Continental The *FCC*, on Sisowath Quay, has a restaurant and bar on its 3rd floor with fabulous views of the Tonlé Sap river on one side and the National Museum on the other. With great views, good music and a friendly crowd of regulars, the FCC is probably the best place to have that splash-out meal.

The best pizza in town can be had at *Baggio's Pizza*, on 51 St near the intersection of Sihanouk Blvd. Small pizzas (a meal for one) start at around US$5.

Happy Herb's, on Sisowath Quay between Ponlok and Wagon Wheels restaurants, is as close as you get to a Phnom Penh institution. If you want your pizza to leave you with a grin for the rest of the day (or evening), tell the waiter you want it 'happy' – those in pursuit of oblivion should request 'very happy'.

Indian & Malaysian There are some surprisingly good Indian restaurants in Phnom Penh. *Kababeesh*, on 128 St, just around the corner from the Singapore Hotel, is one of the best. Check out the US$2.50 all-you-can-

eat lunch buffet. Vegetarian and northern-style tandoori dishes are also available at very reasonable prices. Next door, look out for *Mamak's Corner*, a good place for an early morning roti chanai and a kopi susu. It's possible to eat well here for around US$3.

Mexican Mexican fast food is available at *The Mex*, on the corner of Sihanouk and Norodom Blvds. It has both takeaways and inexpensive sit-down meals. You can fill yourself up with a massive burrito for US$2.50.

Thai & Vietnamese Just east of the Victory Monument on Samdech Sotheros Blvd is *EID* (generally pronounced 'eed'). It's a small place and very basic, but it has arguably the best Thai food in town. Most dishes range from US$2 to US$4. Almost next door is *Saigon House*, a Vietnamese restaurant with prices that won't break the budget.

Self-Catering Baguettes are widely available around town, and usually cost from 200r to 500r. For something to eat with them, Phnom Penh's supermarkets are remarkably well stocked with goodies. For around US$3 to US$4 you can pick up treats such as pastrami, salami, gouda cheese, camembert and brie, among other things.

The best of the Phnom Penh supermarkets are the *Lucky Supermarket*, at 160 Sihanouk Blvd, and the *Seven Seven Supermarket,* at 13 90 St. Other good supermarkets include the *Sunrise Superstore*, opposite the northeast corner of the New Market, the *Suntan Foodmart* at 477 Monivong Blvd and the *Bayon Market* at 133 Monivong Blvd.

Entertainment

For entertainment news, check the latest issue of the *Phnom Penh Post* or the Friday edition of the *Cambodia Daily*.

Traditional dance may be held at the *Chatomuk Theatre*, just north of the Cambodiana Hotel. At the time of writing it was closed for repairs, but when it reopens it should hold performances of traditional dance by the National Royal Dance group every Friday and Saturday night.

The *Magic Circus Cafe-Theatre*, at 111 360 St, has traditional song and dance on Saturday nights at 8 pm. On Sundays at 5 pm, circus performances are held also. Tickets are US$2, and drinks and food are available.

Bars Undoubtedly the most popular early evening drinking spot is the *FCC*, on Sisowath Quay. Draught Angkor beer costs just US$1, and other drinks are reasonably inexpensive. The *Irish Rover*, on the corner of 51 St and Sihanouk Blvd, is another good spot for an early evening drink. Just up the road are *Cactus*, a French bar, and *Ettamogah Pub*, an Australian bar – both are popular and serve meals too.

The most popular late night haunt in town is *Heart of Darkness*. It's on 51 St, south of the New Market. The Heart, as locals call it, is generally deserted before 9.30 pm but often packed after midnight. Most drinks are US$1 or not much more, and the music is probably the best in town. The pool table at the back is the preserve of local Phnom Penh residents – newcomers are not particularly welcome.

Finally, if you're up in the Boeng Kak Lake area (or are staying at Cloud Nine Guesthouse), you might want to pop into the French-run *M-D Bar*.

Things to Buy

The New Market has four wings filled with shops selling gold and silver jewellery, antique coins, fake name-brand watches and other such items. For souvenir shopping the best place is Tuol Tom Pong Market, in the south of town.

The National Centre for Disabled Persons (NCDP) has a shop called NCDP Handicrafts at 3 Norodom Blvd. Articles on sale include silk and leather bags, slippers, kramas, shirts, wallets, purses and notebooks. The standards of artisanship are very high. Prices for some of the items tend to be expensive but there are also a lot of reasonably priced items too. Along similar lines is the handicraft shop at Wat Than.

Monivong Rd is the best place for photo supplies. One hour printing is cheapest at the Konika shops.

Getting There & Away

Air The Royal Air Cambodge booking office (☎ 428055) is at 206 Norodom Blvd. Opening hours are 7 to 11 am and 2 to 5 pm Monday to Saturday. It is generally possible to get flights at short notice to Siem Reap, but for other destinations it is wise to book well in advance.

Lao Aviation (☎ 426563) has two flights a week to Vientiane and can also organise Lao visas for US$25. The office is at 58 Sihanouk Blvd, and is open from 8 to 11.30 am and from 2 to 5 pm Monday to Saturday.

Vietnam Airlines (☎ 364460) has daily flights to Ho Chi Minh City, and can also issue Vietnam visas (US$50 for a five day service). The office is on Sihanouk Blvd, near the corner of 51 St. Opening hours are from 8 to 11.30 am and from 2 to 5 pm Monday to Saturday.

Bangkok Airways (☎ 426707), at 61 214 St, is presently only good for booking flights from Bangkok to Koh Samui, but flights between Bangkok and Phnom Penh may be re-established.

Other airlines around town are:

Air France
    Office 11, Cambodiana Hotel (☎ 426426)
Dragonair
    19, 106 St (☎ 427652)
Malaysia Airlines
    Diamond Hotel, 182 Monivong Blvd (☎ 426588)
Silk Air
    Pailin Hotel, Monivong Blvd (☎ 364747)
Thai Airways International
    19 106 St (☎ 427429)

Bus It is not recommended that foreigners travel around Cambodia by bus. Check with your embassy or with Phnom Penh-based NGOs for the latest on security.

The GST passenger bus service from Phnom Penh to Sihanoukville uses air-con Daewoo buses for the four to five hour run. At the time of writing, most embassies recommended that travellers fly to Sihanoukville, but the bus service (and others are planned) was popular all the same. Again, check with local authorities for the latest information on this road. Tickets cost US$5, and buses leave at 7 am and 1 pm.

Ho Chi Minh City There is a daily (except Sundays) air-con bus service to Ho Chi Minh City which leaves at 6 am from the Ho Chi Minh bus station on the corner of 211 and 182 Sts. The office is open from 5 to 10 am, and tickets cost US$12. There may also be a pack-'em-in service for US$5. Again, this is a service that most embassies will tell you not to use but is nevertheless popular.

Train Foreign travellers are not allowed to purchase train tickets. Travel by train in Cambodia is very dangerous.

Taxi Taxis to Sihanoukville and Kompong Chang leave from the local city bus station area just south of the New Market. They charge US$4 a head and cram six passengers into their vehicles. It's not a pleasant way to travel, and again most embassies advise against it.

Taxis to Ho Chi Minh City cost US$25 to charter and leave from the east side of the Monivong Bridge in the south of town.

It is also possible to hire taxis on a per-day basis. Rates start at US$25 for around Phnom Penh and for nearby destinations, and then go up according to distance. The Capital Guesthouse can also arrange taxi hire to popular destinations around Phnom Penh at reasonable rates.

Boat The most popular boat services are those to Siem Reap. Slow services take around 24 hours, while express services take just four or five hours to reach Siem Reap. These boats are subject to dangerous overcrowding, and often have nothing in the way of safety gear. It's safest to sit on the roof of the express boats.

Slow boats to Siem Reap leave on an irregular basis, so you will need to ask ahead for the next departure. The cost is US$6. Buy a hammock at the New Market and stock up on food and drinks for the trip.

Express boats to Siem Reap cost US$25. Heiwa Shipping and Golden Sea Express both have daily services at 7 am, arriving at 1 pm. There are a number of other operators using smaller boats to do the trip.

Slow boats to Kratie (on the Mekong) leave every four or five days and take two days and one night to complete the trip. Tickets cost US$6. It is possible to stop in Kompong Cham, but you would then have to continue by express boat or wait a long time before the next slow boat happened along. Heiwa Shipping has daily express boats from Phnom Penh to Kompong Cham (US$6) and Kratie (US$14). Boats leave at 7 am and arrive in Kratie at noon. Golden Sea Express runs an identical service every second day.

From Kratie to Stung Treng you will probably have to travel by slow boat. There are sometimes slow-boat services from Phnom Penh to Stung Treng, but they are very infrequent. There are no express services from Phnom Penh to Stung Treng.

Getting Around
The Airport Pochentong international airport is seven km west of central Phnom Penh via Pochentong Blvd. Official taxis cost US$10, but you can negotiate a taxi for US$5 to US$8. A moto will cost US$1 per passenger.

Bus Phnom Penh has a fledgling bus network, but figuring out where the buses go and when is a matter of fearful difficulty. The city bus terminus is just south of the New Market, at the north-east end of Charles de Gaulle Blvd. The green and white buses were donated by the Paris metropolitan government. You will need the help of someone who speaks Khmer in order to figure out where any bus goes. Alternatively you might just hop on one and see where you end up. Ticket prices are very inexpensive.

Motorcycle There are numerous motorbike hire places around town. Bear in mind that motorbike theft is a big problem in Phnom Penh, and if yours gets stolen you will be liable. One of the best places for motorbike hire is Lucky! Lucky! on Monivong Blvd next to the Hong Kong Hotel. A 100cc Honda costs US$4 per day or US$25 per week; 250cc bikes cost US$7 per day, and there are even a couple of 800cc jobs for US$25 per day. The Capital Guesthouse has some beat up 100cc Hondas for US$5 per day.

Moto The moto is usually a 100cc Honda. They are easily recognised by the blue-peaked caps favoured by the drivers. In areas frequented by foreigners (the Cambodiana, the FCC, the Capital Guesthouse etc) moto drivers generally speak English and sometimes a little French. Elsewhere around town it can be difficult to find anyone who understands where you want to go. Theoretically a short trip on a moto costs 500r, but most drivers demand a flat 1000r for destinations around town. Prices are rarely negotiated in advance – hop on and give the driver 1000r at the end of the trip.

Bicycle It is possible to hire bicycles at the Capital Guesthouse, but take a look at the traffic conditions before venturing forth on one.

Cyclo Cyclos are still common on the streets of Phnom Penh but have lost a lot of business to the moto drivers. Costs are generally 500r for a short trip, 1000r for longer ones.

Around Phnom Penh

KILLING FIELDS OF CHOEUNG EK

Between 1975 and December 1978, about 17,000 men, women and children (including nine westerners), detained and tortured at S-21 prison (now Tuol Sleng Museum), were transported to the extermination camp of Choeung Ek to be executed. They were bludgeoned to death to avoid wasting precious bullets.

The remains of 8985 people, many of whom were found bound and blindfolded, were exhumed in 1980 from mass graves in this one-time longan orchard. Some 43 of the 129 communal graves here have been left untouched. Fragments of human bone and bits of cloth are scattered around the disinterred pits. Over 8000 skulls, arranged by sex and age, are visible behind the clear glass panels of the Memorial Stupa, which was erected in 1988.

Getting There & Away
The Killing Fields of Choeung Ek are 15 km south-west of downtown Phnom Penh. The Capitol Guesthouse has a taxi service for US$4 for one person and U$10 for five people.

UDONG
Udong, 40 km north of Phnom Penh, is not a major attraction, but is a pleasant day trip from Phnom Penh for those with plenty of time. It served as the capital of Cambodia under several sovereigns between 1618 and 1866. **Phnom Udong**, a bit south of the old capital, consists of two hills joined by a ridge. There are good views of the Cambodian countryside and its innumerable sugar palm trees. The larger hill, **Phnom Preah Reach Throap** (Hill of the Royal Fortune), is so named because a 16th century Khmer monarch is said to have hidden the national treasury here during a war with the Thais.

The most impressive structure on Phnom Preah Reach Throap is **Vihear Preah Ath Roes**, or Vihara of the 18 Cubit Buddha. The vihara and the nine metre Buddha, dedicated in 1911 by King Sisowath, were blown up by the Khmer Rouge in 1977.

At the north-western extremity of the hill stand three large **stupas**. The first one you come to is the final resting place of King Monivong (ruled 1927-41).

Getting There & Away
The best way to get out to Udong is to hire a taxi with some other travellers for US$20 return. Taxis are available at the Capitol Guesthouse and at other hotels in Phnom Penh.

TONLÉ BATI

South of Phnom Penh, the laterite **Ta Prohm Temple** was built by King Jayavarman VII (ruled 1181-1201) on the site of a 6th century Khmer shrine. The main sanctuary consists of five chambers. In each is a statue or linga (or what is left of them after the destruction wrought by the Khmer Rouge). The site is open all day, every day. A Khmer-speaking guide can be hired for around US$1 a day.

About 300 metres north-west of Ta Prohm Temple, a long, narrow peninsula juts into the Bati River. On Sunday, it is packed with picnickers and vendors selling food, drink and fruit.

Getting There & Away

Ta Prohm Temple is 2½ km off national highway 2. Taxis taking up to four people are available at the Capitol Guesthouse for US$5 per head.

PHNOM CHISOR

There is a spectacular view of the surrounding countryside from the top of Phnom Chisor. The main temple, which stands at the eastern side of the hilltop, was constructed in the 11th century of laterite and brick. The carved lintels are made of sandstone. On the plain to the east of Phnom Chisor are two other Khmer temples, **Sen Thmol** (at the bottom of Phnom Chisor) and **Sen Ravang** (further east), and the former sacred pond of **Tonlé Om**.

Getting There & Away

Phnom Chisor is around 55 km south of Phnom Penh and can easily be combined with a trip to Tonlé Bati. Taxi hire for both destinations should be US$25 for the day.

Angkor

The world-famous temples of Angkor, built between seven and 11 centuries ago when the Khmer civilisation was at the height of its extraordinary creativity, constitute one of humanity's most magnificent architectural achievements. From Angkor, the kings of the Khmer Empire ruled over a vast territory that extended from the tip of what is now southern Vietnam northward to Yunnan in China, and from Vietnam westward to the Bay of Bengal.

The 100 or so temples constitute the sacred skeleton of a much larger and spectacular administrative and religious centre whose houses, public buildings and palaces were constructed out of wood – now long decayed – because the right to dwell in structures of brick or stone was reserved for the gods.

SIEM REAP

The town of Siem Reap is only a few km from the temples of Angkor and serves as a base for visits to the monuments. The name Siem Reap (pronounced 'see-EM ree-EP') means 'Siamese Defeated'.

Siem Reap is 6.4 km south of Angkor Wat and 9.7 km south of the Bayon.

Information

Tourist Office The Angkor office of Cambodia Tourism is in a new white structure opposite the Grand Hotel. There's a sign saying 'tourist information' but you will be very lucky to find the staff here awake unless you come in on a prepaid tour and they're expecting you.

For the most part, budget and mid-range travellers in Angkor get their travel information from other travellers or from their guesthouses.

Fees Visitors now have a choice of a one day pass (US$20), a three day pass (US$40) or a one week pass US$60. This gives you access to all the monuments of Angkor besides Banteay Srei, which is subject to separate rules due to security problems.

Passes are organised by your 'guide', which for most travellers is their moto or taxi driver.

Money There are two banks where you can change money in Siem Reap. The Cambodian Commercial Bank is open from 8 am to

CAMBODIA

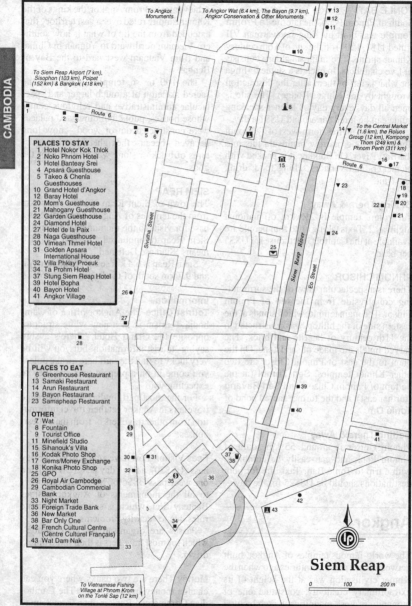

To Angkor
Monuments

To Angkor Wat (6.4 km), The Bayon (9.7 km),
Angkor Conservation & Other Monuments

▼ 13
■ 12
● 11

■ 10

To Siem Reap Airport (7 km),
Sisophon (103 km), Poipet
(152 km) & Bangkok (418 km)

❶ 9

■ 8

Route 6

To the Central Market
(1.6 km), the Roluos
Group (12 km), Kompong
Thom (249 km) &
Phnom Penh (311 km)

14 ▼

7

Route 6

16 ● ● 17

15

● 18
▼ 19
■ 20
■ 21

23 ▼

22 ■

24 ■

PLACES TO STAY
1 Hotel Nokor Kok Thlok
2 Noko Phnom Hotel
3 Hotel Banteay Srei
4 Apsara Guesthouse
5 Takeo & Chenla
   Guesthouses
10 Grand Hotel d'Angkor
12 Baray Hotel
20 Mom's Guesthouse
21 Mahogany Guesthouse
22 Garden Guesthouse
24 Diamond Hotel
27 Hotel de la Paix
28 Naga Guesthouse
30 Vimean Thmei Hotel
31 Golden Apsara
   International House
32 Villa Phkay Proeuk
34 Ta Prohm Hotel
37 Stung Siem Reap Hotel
39 Hotel Bopha
40 Bayon Hotel
41 Angkor Village

26 ●

27 ●

■ 28

Sivutha Street

Siem Reap River

Eo Street

25 ✉

PLACES TO EAT
6 Greenhouse Restaurant
13 Samaki Restaurant
14 Arun Restaurant
19 Bayon Restaurant
23 Samapheap Restaurant

OTHER
7 Wat
8 Fountain
9 Tourist Office
11 Minefield Studio
15 Sihanouk's Villa
16 Kodak Photo Shop
17 Gems/Money Exchange
18 Konika Photo Shop
25 GPO
26 Royal Air Cambodge
29 Cambodian Commercial
   Bank
33 Night Market
35 Foreign Trade Bank
36 New Market
38 Bar Only One
42 French Cultural Centre
   (Centre Culturel Français)
43 Wat Dam Nak

❾ 29

● 39

■ 40

41 ■

30 ■ ■ 31

32 ■

35
❾

37
38

36

42 ●

34
▼

43 ▲

33

To Vietnamese Fishing
Village at Phnom Krom
on the Tonlé Sap (12 km)

Siem Reap

0   100   200 m

3.30 pm Monday to Friday, and changes travellers' cheques at 2% commission. Cash advances (with a limit of US$2000) are available for MasterCard, JCB and Visa. No commission is charged for cash advances.

The Foreign Trade Bank is open from 7.30 am to 4 pm Monday to Friday, and from 7.30 to 11.30 am on Saturday. It also charges a 2% commission for changing travellers' cheques. It cannot provide advances on credit cards.

Post & Communications The post office is along the river 400 metres south of the Grand Hotel d'Angkor. It would probably be best to save your post for Phnom Penh or Bangkok.

Nowadays, making international calls from Siem Reap is as simple as from Phnom Penh. There are several Telstra public phone booths around town, including one outside the Cambodia Tourism office. You can buy cards at the tourism office if there's anyone there; otherwise try one of the hotels around town.

The Siem Reap area code is 23.

Dangers Siem Reap itself is perfectly safe to stroll around, even by night. Out at the temples, however, stick to clearly marked trails. There are still mines lurking out there. It is also not recommended that you visit remote sites alone – indeed the local authorities forbid it. There is a serious risk of armed robbery or perhaps even kidnapping in remote areas.

Places to Stay
The cheapest guesthouse in town is the *Naga Guesthouse*, around the corner from the Hotel de la Paix. Rooms cost as little as US$1, and doubles are available from US$2 to US$3. Its popularity makes it something of a circus at times. If you want some peace and quiet look elsewhere.

East of the Siem Reap River, just off national highway 6, is a cluster of long-running guesthouses that are more intimate and relaxed places to be than the Naga. *Mom's Guesthouse*, next door to the Bayon Restaurant, has been around for quite a while and is overseen by the ever-fussing mum herself. Singles are US$5 and doubles are US$6.

Mahogany Guesthouse is just a couple of doors up from Mom's and is the most popular place in this part of town. It's a large two storey building with a veranda area for socialising. Singles cost US$4, while doubles are US$5 to US$6 depending on the room. Across the road is the *Garden Guesthouse*, which also has singles/doubles at US$5/6. There are a couple of rooms with bathrooms for US$8. The Garden is popular with French travellers.

The other budget section of town is the area just west of the Greenhouse Restaurant on national highway 6. Pick of the pack is probably the *Apsara Guesthouse*, a big operation. The rooms are spacious and there's a leafy restaurant area in the garden. Singles cost US$3, while doubles cost US$5, or US$7 with bathroom.

The *Takeo Guesthouse* is popular with Japanese travellers and has rooms for US$4, or US$6 with bathroom. Next door is the *Chenla Guesthouse*, a clean family-run place with kitchen facilities. It charges US$2 per bed or US$5 for doubles with attached bathroom. The *Golden Apsara International House* (☎ 57537) is highly recommended. It's a wonderfully hospitable villa with verandas and a pleasant family atmosphere. Fan rooms with attached bathroom start at US$10, while air-con singles/doubles cost US$15/20. Doubles with hot-water showers cost US$25. It is wise to make a reservation, as the Golden Apsara is often full.

Across the road from the Golden Apsara are a couple more villa-style hotels. The *Villa Phkay Proeuk* (☎ (015) 919548) has fan singles/doubles for US$5/10 and air-con doubles at US$15. There are a couple of air-con triples, and these are a good deal at US$20. The *Vimean Thmei Hotel* (☎ 57494) is a similar kind of outfit, with fan rooms at US$10 and air-con singles/doubles at US$15/20.

Places to Eat
The most popular place in town is the *Bayon Restaurant*, next door to Mom's Guesthouse,

just off national highway 6. It has a pleasant garden setting and the food is consistently excellent – try the curry chicken in baby coconut.

The *Samapheap Restaurant* is close by, next to the river. It has a Thai atmosphere – complete with twinkling fairy lights at night – and the food is a mixture of Khmer, Thai and generic western. North of Samapheap and also beside the river is the *Arun Restaurant*, an inexpensive Khmer restaurant. It's probably the most popular budget restaurant in town.

The *Greenhouse* is on the corner of Sivutha St and national highway 6. It has a good atmosphere and is the only restaurant in town that sells red and white wine by the glass. It has a good mix of Thai and Khmer standards on the menu.

Getting There & Away
Air Flights between Phnom Penh and Siem Reap cost US$55 one way, or US$110 return. It is possible to book your return flight in Siem Reap. The Royal Air Cambodge office in Siem Reap is south of the De la Paix Hotel on Sivutha St and opening hours are from 6.45 to 11.30 am and 1 to 6 pm daily (yes, no holidays). The office is not computerised so your choice of flight is recorded and confirmed the next day, when you can pay and pick up your ticket.

Boat See the Phnom Penh Getting There & Away section for information about the kinds of ferries running between Siem Reap and Phnom Penh and their costs.

Ferries from Siem Reap back to Phnom Penh leave from Phnom Krom, 11 km south of Siem Reap. A moto out here costs US$1. Most of the guesthouses in town sell ferry tickets.

Getting Around
The Airport Many of the hotels and even some of the guesthouses in Siem Reap have a free airport pick-up service. The seven km ride from the airport on the back of a moto costs US$1. Taxis are also usually available at US$3 to US$5.

Minibus & Taxi Most of the hotels and guesthouses can organise taxi hire to see Angkor. The going rate is US$20 to US$25. Minibuses are available from Angkor Tourism or from Cambodia Travel & Tours (☎ (015) 918-609) in the south of town. A 12 seat minibus costs US$40 per day, a 22 seat minibus US$80 per day.

Motorcycle & Moto Motorcycles are no longer available for hire. The government now demands that tourists visiting Angkor travel with a 'qualified guide', which in practice means that you are compelled to hire a motorbike or a car with a driver.

Motos are available at daily rates of between US$6 and US$8. Most of the moto drivers are understandably unwilling to carry more than one passenger. It's not fair on the drivers to demand that they do.

The average cost for a short trip from one destination to another within town is 500r.

Bicycle & Cyclo
Some of the guesthouses around town hire out bicycles.

You can get around Siem Reap itself in the town's unique and rather uncomfortable cyclos, which are essentially standard bicycles with a two seat trailer in hitch. You can reach anywhere in town for 500r.

TEMPLES OF ANGKOR
Between the 9th and the 13th centuries, a succession of Khmer kings who ruled from Angkor utilised the vast wealth and huge labour force of their empire to carry out a series of monumental construction projects. Intended to glorify both the kings and their capitals, a number were built in the vicinity of Siem Reap.

The 'lost city' of Angkor became the centre of intense European popular and scholarly interest after the publication in the 1860s of *Le Tour du Monde*, an account by the French naturalist Henri Mouhot of his voyages. A group of talented and dedicated archaeologists and philologists, mostly French, soon undertook a comprehensive programme of research.

Under the aegis of the Ecole Française d'Extrême Orient, they made an arduous effort – begun in 1908 and interrupted at the beginning of the 1970s by the war – to clear away the jungle vegetation that was breaking apart the monuments and to rebuild the damaged structures, restoring them to something approaching their original grandeur.

The three most magnificent temples at Angkor are the Bayon, which faces east and is best visited in the early morning; Ta Prohm, which is overgrown by the jungle; and Angkor Wat, the only monument here facing westward and at its finest in the late afternoon.

If you've got the time, all these monuments are well worth several visits each. Angkor's major sites can be seen without undue pressure in three full days of touring.

Angkor Thom
The fortified city of Angkor Thom, some 10 sq km in extent, was built in its present form by Angkor's greatest builder, Jayavarman VII, who came to power in the 12th century just after the disastrous sacking of the previous Khmer capital, centred on the Baphuon, by the Chams.

The city has five monumental gates, one each in the north, west and south walls and two in the east wall.

The Bayon The most outstanding feature of the Bayon, which was built by Jayavarman VII in the exact centre of the city of Angkor Thom, is the eerie and unsettling third level, with its icily smiling, gargantuan faces of Avalokitesvara. Almost as extraordinary are the Bayon's 1200 metres of bas-reliefs, incorporating over 11,000 figures. The famous carvings on the outer wall of the first level depict vivid scenes of life in 12th century Cambodia.

The Baphuon The Baphuon, a pyramidal representation of Mt Meru, is 200 metres north-west of the Bayon. It was constructed by Udayadityavarman II (reigned 1050-66) at the centre of his city, the third built at Angkor.

The decor of the Baphuon, including the door frames, lintels and octagonal columns, is particularly fine. On the western side of the temple, the retaining wall of the second level was fashioned – apparently in the 15th century – into a reclining Buddha 40 metres in length.

Terrace of Elephants The 350-metre-long Terrace of Elephants was used as a giant reviewing stand for public ceremonies and served as a base for the king's grand audience hall. The middle section of the retaining wall is decorated with human-size garudas (mythical human-birds) and lions. Towards either end are the two parts of the famous Parade of Elephants.

Terrace of the Leper King The Terrace of the Leper King, just north of the Terrace of Elephants, is a platform seven metres in height on top of which stands a nude (though sexless) statue (actually a copy). The figure, possibly of Shiva, is believed by the locals to be of Yasovarman, a Khmer ruler whom legend says died of leprosy.

The front retaining walls are decorated with five or so tiers of meticulously executed carvings of seated *apsaras* (shapely dancing women).

On the southern side of the Terrace of the Leper King (facing the Terrace of Elephants) is the entry to a long, narrow trench excavated by archaeologists. This passageway follows the front wall of an earlier terrace that was covered up when the present structure was built. The figures look as fresh as if they had been carved yesterday.

Angkor Wat
Angkor Wat, with its soaring towers and extraordinary bas-reliefs, is considered by many to be one of the most inspired and spectacular monuments ever conceived by the human mind. It was built by Suryavarman II (reigned 1112-52) to honour Vishnu (with whom he, as god-king, was identified) and for use as his funerary temple. The central temple complex consists of three storeys, each of which encloses a square

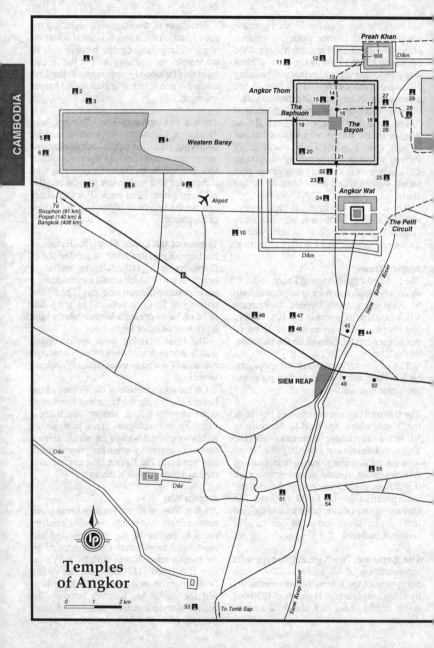

Temples
of Angkor

0   1   2 km

To Sisophon (91 km),
Poipet (140 km) &
Bangkok (406 km)

Western Baray

Airport

Dikes

Siem Reap River

Preah Khan

Dikes

Angkor Thom

The Baphuon

The Bayon

Angkor Wat

The Petit Circuit

Dikes

SIEM REAP

Dike

Dike

Siem Reap River

To Tonlé Sap

CAMBODIA

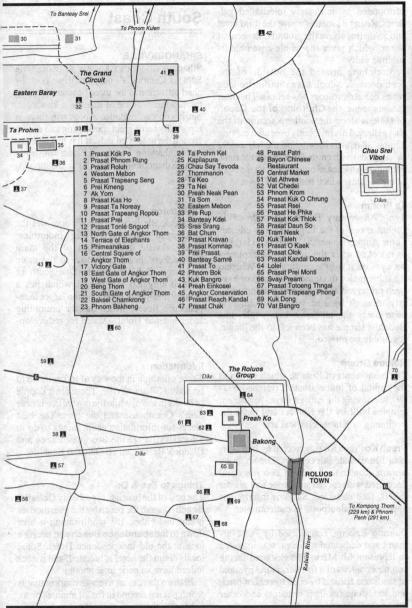

1 Prasat Kok Po	24 Ta Prohm Kel	48 Prasat Patri
2 Prasat Phnom Rung	25 Kapilapura	49 Bayon Chinese
3 Prasat Roluh	26 Chau Say Tevoda	Restaurant
4 Western Mebon	27 Thommanon	50 Central Market
5 Prasat Trapeang Seng	28 Ta Keo	51 Vat Athvea
6 Prei Kmeng	29 Ta Nei	52 Vat Chedei
7 Ak Yom	30 Preah Neak Pean	53 Phnom Krom
8 Prasat Kas Ho	31 Ta Som	54 Prasat Kuk O Chrung
9 Prasat Ta Noreay	32 Eastern Mebon	55 Prasat Rsei
10 Prasat Trapeang Ropou	33 Pre Rup	56 Prasat He Phka
11 Prasat Prei	34 Banteay Kdei	57 Prasat Kok Thlok
12 Prasat Tonlé Snguot	35 Sras Srang	58 Prasat Daun So
13 North Gate of Angkor Thom	36 Bat Chum	59 Tram Neak
14 Terrace of Elephants	37 Prasat Kravan	60 Kuk Taleh
15 Phimeanakas	38 Prasat Komnap	61 Prasat O Kaek
16 Central Square of	39 Prei Prasat	62 Prasat Olok
Angkor Thom	40 Banteay Samré	63 Prasat Kandal Doeum
17 Victory Gate	41 Prasat To	64 Lolei
18 East Gate of Angkor Thom	42 Phnom Bok	65 Prasat Prei Monti
19 West Gate of Angkor Thom	43 Kuk Bangro	66 Svay Pream
20 Beng Thom	44 Preah Einkosei	67 Prasat Totoeng Thngai
21 South Gate of Angkor Thom	45 Angkor Conservation	68 Prasat Trapeang Phong
22 Baksei Chamkrong	46 Prasat Reach Kandal	69 Kuk Dong
23 Phnom Bakheng	47 Prasat Chak	70 Vat Bangro

surrounded by intricately interlinked galleries. Rising 31 metres above the third level and 55 metres above the ground is the central tower, which gives the whole ensemble its sublime unity.

Stretching around the outside of the central temple complex is an 800-metre-long series of extraordinary bas-reliefs. The most famous scene, the **Churning of the Ocean of Milk**, is along the southern section of the east gallery. This brilliantly executed carving depicts 88 *asuras* (devils) on the left and 92 *devas* (gods) with crested helmets on the right, churning up the sea in order to extract the elixir of immortality, which both groups covet.

Ta Prohm

The 17th century Buddhist temple of Ta Prohm is one of the largest Khmer edifices of the Angkorian period. It has been left just as it looked when the first French explorers set eyes on it over a century ago. Whereas the other major monuments of Angkor have been preserved and made suitable for scholarly research by a massive programme to clear away the all-devouring jungle, this Buddhist temple has been left to the jungle. It is not to be missed.

Roluos Group

The monuments of Roluos, which served as the capital of Indravarman I (reigned 877-89), are among the earliest large, permanent temples built by the Khmers and mark the beginning of Khmer classical art.

Preah Ko Preah Ko was erected by Indravarman I in the late 9th century. The six brick *prasats* (towers), aligned in two rows and decorated with carved sandstone and plaster reliefs, face eastward. Sanskrit inscriptions appear on the doorposts of each temple.

Bakong Bakong, constructed by Indravarman I and dedicated to Shiva, was intended to represent Mt Meru. The eastward-facing complex consists of a five tier central pyramid of sandstone flanked by eight towers of brick and sandstone (or their remains) and other minor sanctuaries.

South Coast

SIHANOUKVILLE

Sihanoukville (also known as Kompong Som) is Cambodia's only maritime port. Its chief attraction is the three beaches that ring the headland. None of them is a knockout, but if you can organise a boat trip there is reportedly some great snorkelling and diving around the nearby islands. If it is just beaches and sunbathing you are looking for, however, Sihanoukville may be a disappointment.

Orientation

Sihanoukville is not a small place, and the best way to get around is to hire a motorbike. Sihanoukville itself is east of the main backpackers' beach and close to the more mid-range Ochatial Beach. Due south of town is tiny Ko Pos beach, which has a solitary mid-range hotel, and the larger Independence Beach, which has the crumbling Independence Hotel – slated for redevelopment.

Information

There's nothing in the way of information to be had in Sihanoukville. There are a couple of banks in town, while the post office is near Sam's Guesthouse and the port. The best places for information about things to do in Sihanoukville are the two guesthouses and Claude's Restaurant on Ochatial Beach.

Things to See & Do

The best of the beaches is probably **Ochatial Beach**, though the beach by the guesthouses is not bad either. It's worth taking a bike down to **Independence Beach** and taking a look at the old Independence Hotel. Some locals claim the hotel is haunted, and it does indeed have an eerie look about it.

In town there is an average **market** that is worth poking around in for 20 minutes or so. Otherwise the town, though not an unpleasant place, is pretty much devoid of attractions.

Sam's Guesthouse and Claude's Restaurant both have **snorkelling** gear for hire. Claude's also has a boat and can organise **diving trips** for experienced divers. The cost for a dive is US$35 with one tank of oxygen. Even if you are not a diver, you might want to call into Claude's and see if he has any boat trips planned. A day trip to nearby islands costs US$20 per head – for an extra US$7 per head, Claude puts on a seafood lunch with drinks. Sam's Guesthouse also has plans to set up boat trips.

Places to Stay & Eat

The budget accommodation is a couple of km west of town, south of the port area. *Sam's Guesthouse* has a pleasant restaurant with excellent food and six basic rooms in a longhouse setup. Costs are US$5 for one person, US$6 for two.

The *Mealichenda Guesthouse* is up on the hill above Sam's. It's a friendly place with an inexpensive restaurant and is very popular with backpackers. Rooms cost US$3.

If you're looking for some peace and quiet, and slightly higher levels of comfort, the *Koh Pos Hotel* is a good option. It has its

1 Railway Station
2 Post Office
3 Mealichenda Guesthouse
4 Sam's Guesthouse
5 Koh Pos Hotel
6 Independence Hotel
7 Kampuchea Hotel
8 Sarana Guesthouse
9 Angkor Arms Pub & Koh Tas Hotel
10 Sorya Hotel
11 Pet's Place
12 Market
13 Canadia Bank
14 Sokha Hotel
15 Cobra Hotel
16 Crystal Hotel
17 Seaside Hotel
18 Claude's Restaurant

Port

To Phnom Penh

To Airport & Phnom Penh

GULF OF THAILAND

Independence Beach

Sokha Beach

Ochatial Beach

Sihanoukville

0   0.5   1 km

own small stretch of beach and a beachfront restaurant with great sunset views. Rates are posted at US$15 for a big air-con double with attached bathroom, but midweek it's usually possible to haggle the price down to US$10.

The *Independence Hotel* might shut down at any time for renovations, but at the time of writing it was still hiring out decrepit rooms for US$5. Some travellers love the place, but it's a little isolated and you may be the only person staying there.

For a splash-out meal, *Claude's* at Ochatial Beach is the place to go. Claude, the French-Vietnamese owner, is a friendly chap and very knowledgeable about the area. The restaurant has a pleasant garden setting and the food is excellent. Hotel accommodation at Ochatial Beach starts at US$15.

Getting There & Away

The official embassy position on Sihanoukville is that travellers should fly there. It would be worth checking to see whether this is still the case.

Air Flights from Phnom Penh are scheduled four times a week and cost US$40 one way, US$70 return. There is a Royal Air Cambodge office in Sihanoukville close to the GST bus office.

Bus Air-con buses from Phnom Penh to Sihanoukville cost US$5 and leave from the New Market area twice daily at 7 am and 1 pm. The buses are air-con Korean numbers, and fairly comfortable. If you do decide to use this service, take the early morning service. Buses back to Phnom Penh leave at the same times and depart from the GST office in the centre of town. Other bus services are expected to start up in the near future. Buses take around three to four hours.

Taxi Taxis from Phnom Penh to Sihanoukville leave from the area just to the east of the Dusit Hotel near the New Market. They cost US$25, or US$4 per head. Those paying US$4 for a ride will find themselves doing the trip at terrifying speeds in very crowded conditions.

Getting Around

The Airport The airport is around 10 km out of town on national highway 4. A moto into town will probably cost around US$2, while taxis (if there are any) will probably cost US$5. Some haggling may be required.

Motorcycle Ask around at the guesthouses about motorbike hire. Sam's Guesthouse can generally organise something for around US$5 per day.

Moto Apart from hiring your own bike, the only way to get around Sihanoukville is by moto. There aren't that many of them around, and in the evenings you may end up waiting by the roadside for quite a long time before one happens along. Most long-distance trips (from Sam's Guesthouse to Claude's Restaurant, for example) cost US$1, while short hops cost 1000r.

Hong Kong

The prime gateway to the rest of China, Hong Kong is a curious anomaly. It's an energetic paragon of the virtues of capitalism in what is officially the largest Communist country in the world. Currently a British colony, Hong Kong will be handed back to China on 1 July, 1997.

Facts about Hong Kong

HISTORY
Hong Kong must stand as one of the more successful results of dope running. The dope was opium and the runners were backed by the British government. European trade with China goes back over 400 years. As the trade mushroomed during the 18th century and European demand for Chinese tea and silk grew, the balance of trade became more and more unfavourable to the Europeans – until they started to run opium into the country.

China, alarmed at this turn of events, attempted to throw the foreign devils out. The war of words ended when British gunboats were sent in. There were only two of them, but they managed to demolish a Chinese fleet of 29 ships. The ensuing First Opium War went much the same way and, at its close in 1842, the island of Hong Kong was ceded to the British.

Following the Second Opium War in 1860, Britain took possession of the Kowloon Peninsula. Finally, in 1898, a 99 year lease was granted for the New Territories. What would happen after the lease ended in 1997 was the subject of considerable speculation. Although the British supposedly had possession of Hong Kong Island and the Kowloon Peninsula for all eternity, it was pretty clear that if they handed back the New Territories, China would want the rest as well.

In late 1984 an agreement was reached allowing China to take over the entire colony in 1997 – but Hong Kong's unique free enterprise economy would be maintained for at least 50 years. Hong Kong will become a Special Administrative Region (SAR) of China and the official slogan is 'one country, two systems'.

China has repeatedly reassured Hong Kong's population that 'nothing will change', but few believe this. China's public anti-British tantrums have done much to undermine confidence in Hong Kong. Well aware of China's previous record of broken promises and harsh political repression, Hong Kongers are emigrating in droves.

GEOGRAPHY
Hong Kong's 1070 sq km is divided into four main areas – Kowloon, Hong Kong Island, the New Territories and the Outlying Islands.

Hong Kong Island is the economic heart of the colony but covers only 7% of Hong Kong's land area. Kowloon is the densely populated peninsula to the north – the southern tip of the Kowloon Peninsula is Tsimshatsui, where hordes of tourists congregate. The New Territories, which include the outlying islands, occupy 91% of Hong Kong's land area and much remains surprisingly rural and charming.

CLIMATE
Although it never gets below freezing, Hong Kong is certainly colder than South-East

Asian capitals like Bangkok, Singapore, Jakarta and Manila. More than a few travellers have arrived in the dead of winter wearing shorts and T-shirts and barely survived the experience! Summer is hot and humid, and thunderstorms often force visitors to scamper for cover. From June to October, Hong Kong is occasionally hit by typhoons. Autumn is the most pleasant time of the year.

See the Hong Kong climate chart in the Appendix.

GOVERNMENT & POLITICS

Heading Hong Kong's colonial administration is a governor (always British) who presides over meetings of both an Executive Council (EXCO) and a Legislative Council (LEGCO), whose members are mostly Chinese.

An election in 1995 saw many pro-democracy candidates elected to seats in LEGCO – the 'pro-Beijing' candidates fared poorly. China (which opposed the election to begin with) responded by threatening to dismiss democratically elected representatives to LEGCO and replace them with appointees approved by Beijing. Furthermore, Beijing has decided to scrap Hong Kong's Bill of Rights. No one really knows what sort of government will exist in post-1997 Hong Kong, but it's fair to guess that Hong Kong will cease to be a British colony and become a Chinese one.

ECONOMY

Hong Kong continues to prosper, even though nervousness about 1997 has caused much capital to flee to safe havens overseas. Trade with both the west and China has always been the cornerstone of the Hong Kong economy. Service industries such as banking, insurance, telecommunications and tourism now employ 75% of Hong Kong residents. All the polluting sweatshop factories have moved just across the border to China.

Part of the reason for Hong Kong's prosperity is that it is a capitalist's dream: it has lax controls and a maximum tax rate of 15%.

POPULATION & PEOPLE

Hong Kong is currently home to 6.2 million people, most of them squeezed on to Hong Kong Island, Kowloon and the so-called 'new towns' in the New Territories.

About 98% of Hong Kong's population is ethnic Chinese, most of whom have their origins in China's Guangdong Province.

EDUCATION

Hong Kong's education system closely follows the British model and achieves a literacy rate of 90%. Competition becomes fierce at the university level – only about 5% of students who sit for university entrance exams actually gain admission. This is less of a problem for wealthy families, who simply send their children abroad to study.

ARTS

Dance

Celebrations in Chinatowns throughout the world have made the 'lion dance' almost synonymous with Chinese culture. Actually, there is no reason why it should be so – lions are not indigenous to China. Nevertheless, Chinese festivals – which are never sombre affairs – usually include a lion dance.

Music

Hong Kong's home-grown variety of music consists of soft rock love melodies. The songs are sung in Cantonese and are collectively known as 'Canto-Pop'. Most Chinese find western-style hard rock, heavy metal and punk too harsh and grating.

Theatre

Chinese Opera Few festivals are complete without an opera performance. There are probably more than 500 opera performers in Hong Kong and opera troupes from China make regular appearances.

Puppets Puppets are the oldest of the Chinese theatre arts. You can see rod, glove, string and shadow puppets. The most likely place to see performances are on TV – live shows are somewhat rare these days.

SOCIETY & CONDUCT
Traditional Culture
Tai-chi This form of slow motion shadow boxing is traditionally performed at dawn. Parks are the place to see it: the most popular venue is Victoria Park in Causeway Bay, but others include the Zoological and Botanic Gardens in Central and Kowloon Park in Tsimshatsui.

Martial Arts China is famous for *kungfu* (more correctly spelled 'gongfu'). Kungfu differs from tai-chi in that the former is performed at much higher speed and with the intention of doing bodily harm. Kungfu also often employs weapons.

Qigong Kungfu meditation, known as *qigong*, is used both for self-defence and as a form of traditional Chinese medicine. *Qi* represents life's vital energy. Qigong practitioners claim to perform various miraculous acts, such as driving nails through boards with their fingers and curing terminally ill patients with a few waves of the hands. You're most likely to see it in the movies.

Dos & Don'ts
Clothing Hong Kong is cosmopolitan – they've seen it all, so you can get away with wearing almost anything. Revealing clothing is OK – shorts, miniskirts and bikinis (at the beach only) are common. However, nude bathing at beaches is a definite no-no.

Although Hong Kongers are usually tolerant when it comes to dress, there is one exception – thongs (flip-flop sandals). Thongs are OK to wear in hotel rooms or maybe the corridor of your hotel, but not in its lobby and most definitely not outdoors (except around a swimming pool or beach). Many restaurants and hotels will not let you in the door if you're wearing thongs.

Killer Chopsticks Leaving chopsticks sticking vertically into a bowl of rice or noodles is a bad omen: they resemble incense sticks in a bowl of ashes–a symbol of death.

Colour Codes Every colour symbolises something to the Chinese, and red is normally a happy colour. However, a grand exception is made for red ink. Messages written in red convey anger, hostility or unfriendliness. If you want to give someone your address or telephone number, write in any colour but red.

If invited to a wedding, you are expected to give a gift of money placed in a *red* envelope. Do not put it in a white envelope, as white is the colour of death.

RELIGION
In Chinese religion as it's now practised, Taoism, Confucianism and Buddhism have become inextricably entwined. Ancestor worship and ancient animist beliefs have also been incorporated into the religious milieu. Foreign influence has been heavy in Hong Kong, which explains why 9% of the population are Christians.

LANGUAGE
Cantonese is the most common Chinese dialect spoken in Hong Kong. Mandarin Chinese, or *putonghua*, is the official language in China and about half the people in Hong Kong can also understand it.

Although English is widely spoken in Hong Kong, it is on the decline. With 1997 approaching, those educated in English have the easiest time emigrating and are taking advantage of this fact.

Cantonese is difficult for *gwailos* (which literally means 'foreign devils') because it's tonal – the meaning varies with the tone. Few gwailos gain fluency, but here are a few phrases to have a go with:

Basics
Hello, how are you?	*nei hou ma?*
Good morning.	*jou san*
Goodbye.	*joi gin*
Thank you.	*m goi*
You're welcome.	*m sai haak hei*
I'm sorry/Excuse me.	*deui m jyu*
How much is it?	*gei siu chin?*
too expensive	*taai gwaige*
Waiter, the bill.	*fogei, maai daan*

HONG KONG

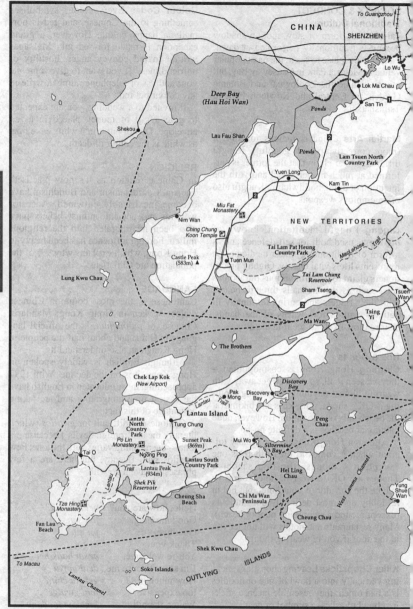

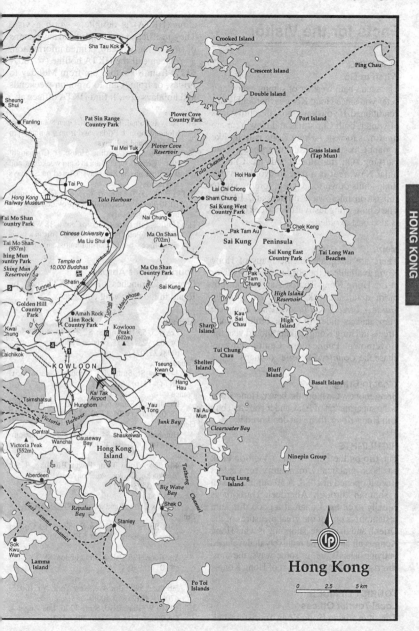

HONG KONG

Hong Kong

0   2.5   5 km

Facts for the Visitor

PLANNING
When to Go

The sauna-bath weather of summer shouldn't deter you since Hong Kong is thoroughly air-conditioned. If you don't mind the chill winds of winter, both Christmas and New Year are fun times to visit – Hong Kong is lit up like a giant Christmas tree and everybody is out partying. On the other hand, the Chinese lunar New Year is a time to avoid – everything shuts down for a week, forcing you to subsist on microwave dinners at 7 Eleven. The Ching Ming festival (first week of April) is also best avoided.

Maps

There are adequate freebie maps of Hong Kong available at the airport upon arrival, or at the Hong Kong Tourist Association. For more details, check out the *Hong Kong Guide – Streets & Places*. It has complete maps and an index of all the buildings and streets in Hong Kong. Hikers should visit the Government Publications Centre and purchase the *Countryside* series of maps.

What to Bring

Bring money, the more the better. Hong Kong is the supermarket of Asia, and if you can't buy it in Hong Kong, then you don't need it.

HIGHLIGHTS

The trip on the Peak Tram to Victoria Peak has been practically mandatory for visitors since it opened in 1888. A 30 minute ride on a sampan through Aberdeen Harbour is equally exciting. Lunch at a good dim sum restaurant is one of the great pleasures of the Orient, and of course, shopping is what Hong Kong is all about. The relatively undeveloped outlying islands are, in some ways, the most surprising and enjoyable part of Hong Kong.

TOURIST OFFICES
Local Tourist Offices

The enterprising Hong Kong Tourist Associ-ation (HKTA) is definitely worth a visit. They're efficient and helpful and have reams of free, or fairly cheap, printed information.

You can call the HKTA hotline (☎ 2807-6177) from 8 am to 6 pm from Monday to Friday, or from 9 am to 5 pm on weekends and holidays. You'll find HKTA offices at:

Star Ferry Terminal, Tsimshatsui. Open 8 am to 6 pm Monday through Friday, and from 9 am to 5 pm weekends and holidays.

Shop 8, Basement, Jardine House, 1 Connaught Place, Central. Open 9 am to 6 pm weekdays, and 9 am to 1 pm on Saturdays. Closed on Sundays and holidays.

Buffer Hall, Kai Tak airport, Kowloon. Open 8 am to 10.30 pm daily. Information is provided for arriving passengers only.

Head Office, 11th floor, Citicorp Centre, 18 Whitfield Rd, North Point (☎ (2807-6543). This is a business office – not for normal tourist inquiries.

Tourist Offices Abroad

Overseas branches of the HKTA can be found in the following countries:

Australia
  Level 5, 55 Harrington St, The Rocks, Sydney (☎ (02) 9251-2855, outside Sydney (008) 251071)
Canada
  347 Bay St, Suite 909, Toronto, Ontario M5H 2R7 (☎ (416) 366-2389)
France
  Escalier C, 8ème étage, 53 rue Francois 1er, 75008, Paris (☎ 01 47 20 39 54)
Germany
  Humboldt Strasse 94, D-60318 Frankfurt-am-Main (☎ (069) 959-1290)
Japan
  4th floor, Toho Twin Tower Building, 1-5-2 Yurakucho, Chiyoda-ku, Tokyo 100 (☎ (03) 3503-0731)
New Zealand
  PO Box 2120, Auckland (☎ (09) 575-2707)
Singapore
  13th floor, 13-08 Ocean Building, 10 Collyer Quay, Singapore 0104 (☎ 532-3668)
UK
  5th floor, 125 Pall Mall, London SW1Y 5EA (☎ (0171) 930-4775)
USA
  5th floor, 590 Fifth Ave, New York, NY 10036-4706 (☎ (212) 869-5008)
  10940 Wilshire Blvd, Suite 1220, Los Angeles, CA 90024-3915 (☎ (310) 208-4582)

VISAS & DOCUMENTS

Visas

Most visitors to Hong Kong do not need a visa. British passport holders are permitted to stay visa-free for 12 months; citizens of all Western European nations – plus Canada, Australia and New Zealand – can stay for three months; and citizens of the USA and most other countries get one month. Visas are still required for Eastern Europeans and all Communist countries (including the rest of China).

But beware – these visa regulations will almost certainly be changed after 1 July 1997. Western nationalities will probably not require a visa for a short visit, but it seems most unlikely that UK citizens will continue to get a 12 month visa-free stay. China remains silent on the issue, but our best guess is that foreigners will not be allowed to stay over one month unless they have a work permit.

Visa Extensions For visa extensions, inquire at the Immigration Department (☎ 2824-6111), 2nd floor, Wanchai Tower Two, 7 Gloucester Rd, Wanchai. In general, they do not like to grant extensions unless there are special circumstances, such as cancelled flights, illness, registration in a legitimate course of study, legal employment or marriage to a local.

Other Documents

Visitors and residents are advised to carry identification at all times in Hong Kong. It needn't be a passport – anything with a photo on it will do. This is because the immigration authorities do frequent spot checks to catch illegal workers and those who overstay their visas. If you have no ID, you could find yourself being 'rounded up'.

CONSULATES

Hong Kong is a good place to pick up visas if you're travelling further afield. Just some of the numerous foreign consulates include:

Australia
   23rd & 24th floors, Harbour Centre, 25 Harbour Rd, Wanchai (☎ 2827-8881)

Canada
   11th-14th floors, One Exchange Square, 8 Connaught Place, Central (☎ 2810-4321)
China
   Visa Office of the Ministry of Foreign Affairs, 5th floor, Lower Block, 26 Harbour Rd, Wanchai (☎ 2827-1881)
France
   26th floor, Tower Two, Admiralty Centre, 18 Harcourt Rd, Admiralty (☎ 2529-4351)
Germany
   21st floor, United Centre, 95 Queensway, Admiralty (☎ 2529-8855)
Indonesia
   6-8 Keswick St & 127 Leighton Rd, Causeway Bay (☎ 2890-4421)
Japan
   Exchange Square, 8 Connaught Place, Central (☎ 2522-1184)
Malaysia
   24th floor, Malaysia Building, 50 Gloucester Rd, Wanchai, (☎ 2527-0921)
Myanmar (Burma)
   Room 2421-2425, Sung Hung Kai Centre, 30 Harbour Rd, Wanchai (☎ 2827-7929)
New Zealand
   Room 3414, Jardine House, 1 Connaught Place, Central (☎ 2525-5044)
Philippines
   Room 603, United Centre, 95 Queensway, Admiralty (☎ 2866-8738)
Singapore
   Room 901, Tower One, Admiralty Centre, 18 Harcourt Rd, Admiralty (☎ 2527-2212)
Thailand
   8th floor, Fairmont House, 8 Cotton Tree Drive, Central (☎ 2521-6481)
UK
   c/o Overseas Visa Section, Hong Kong Immigration Department, 2nd floor, Wanchai Tower Two, 7 Gloucester Rd, Wanchai (☎ 2824-6111)
USA
   26 Garden Rd, Central (☎ 2523-9011)

CUSTOMS

High taxes are applied to tobacco, alcohol, petrol and motor vehicles, but almost everything else can be imported duty-free and hassle-free. The duty-free allowance for visitors is 200 cigarettes (or 50 cigars or 250g tobacco) and one litre of alcohol.

MONEY

Costs

Hong Kong is not only the most expensive city in this book, it's the second most expensive city in the world (only Tokyo is pricier). Nevertheless, there are ways to limit the damage. If you stay in dormitories, eat budget meals and resist the urge to shop, you can survive (barely) on under HK$200 per day. However, most travellers will spend more.

Currency

The unit of currency is the Hong Kong dollar (HK$), divided into 100 cents. Bills are issued in denominations of $10, $20, $50, $100, $500 and $1000. Coins are issued in denominations of $5, $2, $1, 50 cents, 20 cents and 10 cents.

Currency Exchange

Exchange rates are as follows:

Australia	A$1	=	HK$6.10
Canada	C$1	=	HK$5.66
China	Y$1	=	HK$0.92
France	FF10	=	HK$14.97
Germany	DM1	=	HK$5.15
Japan	¥100	=	HK$6.98
New Zealand	NZ$1	=	HK$5.41
UK	UK£1	=	HK$12.09
USA	US$1	=	HK$7.73

Changing Money

Hong Kong has no exchange controls – locals and foreigners can send large quantities of money in or out as they please with no restrictions, and even play the local stock market while they're at it. In fact, Hong Kong is the financial centre of Asia simply because it is so unregulated. Whether or not China will interfere with this financial freedom after 1997 is the big question that keeps bankers awake at night.

All major and many minor foreign currencies can be exchanged. Foreigners can open bank accounts in various currencies (or in gold!), and international telegraphic transfers are fast and efficient. International credit cards are readily accepted.

Banks theoretically give the best exchange rates, but they tack on a HK$50 service charge for each transaction. You'd have to change over US$200 at a time to make this worthwhile. Streetside moneychangers in tourist areas (the various Chequepoint outlets are best known) give relatively poor rates, though you can often bargain a discount on a large transaction. The moneychangers inside Chungking Mansions give the best rates, but not the moneychangers nearest the main entrance. Exchange rates are posted, and the best way to know if you're getting a good deal is to look at the spread (the difference between the buy and sell rates). A large spread means that you're getting a bad deal. Some comparative exchange rates at the time of writing (for US$1): Chequepoint, HK$7.05; Chequepoint after bargaining, HK$7.40; airport moneychangers, HK$7.30; hotel desks, HK$7.40; Hang Seng Bank if you change US$200, HK$7.45; Hang Seng Bank if you change US$1000, HK$7.65; Chungking Mansions moneychangers, HK$7.70.

Bank hours are from 9 am to 4 pm Monday to Friday, and from 9 am to noon or 1 pm on Saturday. Chequepoint operates 24 hours a day. Chungking Mansions moneychangers are open daily from approximately 9 am to 9 pm.

Tipping & Bargaining

In general, tipping is not expected in Hong Kong. A 10% service charge is usually added to restaurant bills in upmarket establishments, and this is a mandatory 'tip'. In taxis you should round the fare up to the nearest HK$0.50 or dollar.

You should always be wary of shops which do not put price tags on their merchandise. If you shop for cameras, electronics and other big ticket items in the Tsimshatsui tourist zone, bargaining is essential – you won't see price tags because the shops try to charge double (or more). However, bargaining is *not* the norm in Hong Kong. It's only normal in places where the tourists congregate. Out in the suburban shopping malls or the street markets of Mongkok and Shamshuipo, everything has a price tag and there is little scope for bargaining.

POST & COMMUNICATIONS
Postal Rates
Domestic letters and postcards under 30g cost HK$1 to mail.

For international mail, the Hong Kong postal service divides the world into two distinct zones. (Aerogrammes are HK$1.90 to anywhere in the world.) Zone 1 is China, Japan, Taiwan, South Korea, South-East Asia, Indonesia and India. Zone 2 is everything else. The rates are as follows:

Letters & Postcards	*Zone 1*	*Zone 2*
first 10g	HK$1.90	HK$2.40
each additional 10g	HK$1.00	HK$1.10

Printed Matter		
first 10g	HK$1.30	HK$1.80
each additional 10g	HK$0.60	HK$0.80

Sending Mail
On the Hong Kong Island side, the GPO is on your right as you alight from the Star Ferry. On the Kowloon side, one of the most convenient post offices is at 10 Middle Rd, east of the Ambassador Hotel and Nathan Rd, Tsimshatsui (this one has a stamp vending machine outside, a big convenience after hours). Another good post office (and less crowded) is in the basement of the Albion Plaza, 2-6 Granville Rd, just off Nathan Rd, Tsimshatsui. All major post offices are open Monday to Friday from 8 am to 6 pm and Saturday from 8 am to 2 pm. They are closed on Sunday and public holidays.

Receiving Mail
The GPO is on Hong Kong Island adjacent to the Star Ferry Terminal. If you want letters to go to the Kowloon side, they should be addressed to Poste Restante, 10 Middle Rd, Tsimshatsui, Kowloon.

Telephone
If you want to call overseas, it's cheapest to use an IDD (international direct dialling) telephone. You can place an IDD call from most phone boxes, but you'll need stacks of coins. A better alternative is to buy a phone card, which comes in denominations of HK$50, HK$100 or HK$250. Every 7 Eleven store in Hong Kong has an IDD phone and sells the requisite phone cards. You can also find card phones at a Hong Kong Telecom office. There's a Hong Kong Telecom at 10 Middle Rd in Tsimshatsui and another in the basement of Century Place at D'Aguilar and Wellington in Central (Lan Kwai Fong area).

To make an IDD call from Hong Kong, first dial 001, then the country code, area code and number.

When calling Hong Kong from abroad, the country code is 852.

For calls to countries that do not have IDD service, you can call from a Hong Kong Telecom office – first pay a deposit and they will hook you up (minimum three minutes) and give you your change after the call is completed.

The general emergency phone number for ambulance, fire and police is 999. You can dial this without a coin.

Fax, Telegraph & Email
Fax and telegraph services can be taken care of at Hong Kong Telecom. Many hotels and even hostels have fax machines and will allow you to both send and receive for a reasonable service charge.

Hong Kong is one of the most wired cities in cyberspace and competition keeps the cost for Email services low. If you've got an account with CompuServe, you can connect by dialling their node (☎ 3002-8332). For members of America Online, there is an Aol-Globalnet access number for Hong Kong (☎ 2519-9040). If you're a resident of Hong Kong and wish to surf the Internet, some providers of this service include: Asia-Online (☎ 2837-8888), Hong Kong Supernet (☎ 2358-7924) and Hong Kong Internet & Gateway Services (☎ 2527-4888).

Cyber-surfers may want to visit Kublai's Cyber Diner (☎ 2529-9117), 3rd floor, One Capital Place, 18 Luard Rd, Wanchai.

BOOKS
Lonely Planet
For an in-depth exploration of this fascinating city, see Lonely Planet's *Hong Kong city*

guide. For more on the surrounding area, look for *Hong Kong, Macau & Guangzhou – travel survival kit* and, for those venturing further afield, *China – travel survival kit*.

General

The government's annual reports are entitled *Hong Kong 1995, Hong Kong 1996* etc. In addition to the excellent photographs, the text is a gold mine of information.

A cynical antidote to the government's upbeat version of events is *The Other Hong Kong Report* (Chinese University Press).

History and Politics

Maurice Collis' *Foreign Mud* (Faber & Faber, UK, 1946) tells the sordid story of the Opium Wars. Novels to dip into include the readable *Tai-pan* by James Clavell, which is (very) loosely based on the Jardine-Matheson conglomerate in its early days. Richard Mason's *The World of Suzie Wong* is also interesting – after all, she was Hong Kong's best known citizen.

FILMS

Hong Kong produces far more films than all the rest of China, and many are exported to various Chinese communities around the globe. The sound track is usually in Cantonese or Mandarin, but English subtitles are almost always provided. Unfortunately, Hong Kong's movie producers specialise in blood-splattered kungfu spectaculars which offer little in the way of plot. However, there are always a few prize movies among all the rubbish – Hong Kong's movie studios do occasionally come up with a hilarious comedy or gripping romance story.

NEWSPAPERS & MAGAZINES

Hong Kong is Asia's news media capital, the home of such staid publications as the *Asian Wall Street Journal* and the *Far Eastern Economic Review*. Hong Kong also produces two English-language newspapers for the local market – the *South China Morning Post* and the *Hong Kong Standard*.

The big guillotine hanging over Hong Kong's news media heads is China's take-over in mid-1997. Most observers are pessimistic that China will eventually impose some sort of censorship on the currently free-wheeling press. Many Asian news organisation are said to have contingency plans to bolt to Singapore, Bangkok or wherever if China gets heavy-handed.

RADIO & TV

The most popular English-language radio stations are Radio 3 (AM 567 kHz), Radio 4 (classical music, FM 97.6 to 98.9 MHz), Commercial Radio (AM 864 kHz), Metro News (AM 1044 kHz), Hit Radio (FM 99.7 MHz), FM Select (FM 104 MHz), BBC World Service (AM 675 kHz, 4 am to 12.15 am). The English-language newspapers publish a daily guide to radio programmes.

TV broadcasts are only in the morning and evening during weekdays. On weekends and holidays, programmes run all day. There are two local stations which broadcast in English. Hong Kong's satellite-based Star TV is well known throughout Asia.

PHOTOGRAPHY & VIDEO

Almost everything you could possibly need in the way of film, cameras and video equipment is available in Hong Kong. Stanley St on Hong Kong Island is the place to look for reputable camera stores. Try not to buy anything in the rip-off Tsimshatsui neighbourhood.

For security reasons (terrorism?), you cannot take photographs of the runways at the airport or of the security procedures (x-ray machines, metal detectors, machine gun-toting airport police etc).

ELECTRICITY

The standard is 220V, 50Hz. Older electric outlets are designed to accommodate three round prongs, while newer buildings are wired with three square pins of the British design.

LAUNDRY

There is no need to hide your dirty laundry as there are plenty of places in Hong Kong which will clean it cheaply. Prices are typically

HK$30 for three kg. For dry-cleaning needs, you can try the chain store with the unforgettable name of Clean Living.

WEIGHTS & MEASURES

The international metric system is in official use in Hong Kong. In practice, traditional Chinese weights and measures are still common.

If you want to shop in the local markets, become familiar with Chinese units of weight. Fruits and vegetables are often sold by the *catty*, which is equivalent to about 600g. Small items like tea and herbs are sold by the *leung*, which is equivalent to 37.5g. There are exactly 16 leung to the catty.

HEALTH

Except for getting high blood pressure from the heart-attack pace of living, a visit to Hong Kong poses no unusual health problems.

Medical Services

There are some excellent private hospitals in Hong Kong, but their prices reflect the fact that they must operate at a profit. Some of the better private hospitals include:

Adventist Hospital
    40 Stubbs Rd, Wanchai, Hong Kong Island
    (☎ 2574-6211)
Baptist Hospital
    222 Waterloo Rd, Kowloon Tong (☎ 2337-4141)
Canossa Hospital
    1 Old Peak Rd, Mid-Levels, Hong Kong Island
    (☎ 2522-2181)
Grantham Hospital
    125 Wong Chuk Hang Rd, Deep Water Bay,
    Hong Kong Island (☎ 2554-6471)
Hong Kong Central Hospital
    1B Lower Albert Rd, Central, Hong Kong Island
    (☎ 2522-3141)
Matilda & War Memorial Hospital
    41 Mt Kellett Rd, The Peak, Hong Kong Island
    (☎ 2849-6301)
St Paul's Hospital
    2 Eastern Hospital Rd, Causeway Bay, Hong
    Kong Island (☎ 2890-6008)

Public hospitals are cheaper, though foreigners pay more than Hong Kong residents. Public hospitals include:

Queen Elizabeth Hospital
    Wylie Rd, Yaumatei, Kowloon (☎ 2710-2111)
Princess Margaret Hospital
    Lai Chi Kok, Kowloon (☎ 2310-3111)
Queen Mary Hospital
    Pokfulam Rd, Hong Kong Island (☎ 2819-2111)
Prince of Wales Hospital
    30-32 Ngan Shing St, Shatin, New Territories
    (☎ 2636-2211)

TOILETS

You need strong kidneys to visit Hong Kong – the city should be ashamed of its lack of public toilets. Even big shopping malls usually lock their 'public' toilets – these are only for the use of employees who work in the building. Subway stations do *not* have public toilets. If you need to use the toilet, your best bet is to look for a fast-food restaurant.

USEFUL ORGANISATIONS

The Hong Kong Information Services Department (☎ 2842-8777) is on the Ground, 1st, 4th, 5th and 6th floors of Beaconsfield House, 4 Queen's Rd, Central. They can answer specific questions or direct you to other government agencies that can handle your inquiry. It's best to try the HKTA before resorting to the Information Services Department.

Since the likelihood of getting ripped off by shopkeepers is high, it's good to know about the Hong Kong Consumer Council (☎ 2736-3322). The main office is in China Hong Kong City, Canton Rd, Tsimshatsui. It has a complaints and advice hot line (☎ 2736-3636) and an Advice Centre (☎ 2541-1422) at 38 Pier Rd, Central.

DANGERS & ANNOYANCES

Hong Kong is a reasonably safe place to walk around at night, but you should be as alert to trouble as you would in any big city. Pickpocketing can occur wherever there are crowds.

Most mugging victims tend to be local Chinese – after all, they have more money than many westerners. The best precaution is simply to look poor.

A bigger problem exists with con games, mostly perpetrated by Filipino expats living in Chungking Mansions. Be particularly wary of being invited up to someone's flat on some innocuous pretext and then being talked into playing a 'practice' card game.

LEGAL MATTERS

Like most countries in the region, Hong Kong takes a tough line on drug use (although there is no capital punishment, as in Malaysia or Singapore).

If you get ripped off by robbers (not sleazy shop merchants), you can obtain a loss report for insurance purposes at the Central Police Station, 10 Hollywood Rd (at Pottinger St) in Central. There are always English-speaking staff here.

Know any government officials you want to get rid of? Call the Report Centre of the Independent Commission Against Corruption (☎ 2526-6366).

BUSINESS HOURS

Office hours are Monday through Friday from 9 am to 5 pm, and on Saturday from 9 am to noon. Lunch hour is from 1 pm to 2 pm and many offices simply shut down and lock the door at this time. Banks are open Monday through Friday from 9 am to 4.30 pm and do not close for lunch – on Saturday they are open from 9 am to 12.30 pm.

Stores and restaurants that cater to the tourist trade keep longer hours, but almost nothing opens before 9 am. Even tourist-related businesses shut down by 9 or 10 pm.

PUBLIC HOLIDAYS & SPECIAL EVENTS

Public holidays include:

New Year
The first week day in January is a public holiday.
Lunar New Year
For the rest of this century, the Chinese lunar New Year falls on these dates: 7 February 1997, 28 January 1998, 16 February 1999 and 5 February 2000.
Easter
This is a three-day public holiday starting from Good Friday and running through Easter Sunday.
Ching Ming
This is held during the first week in April and is a time for the Chinese to worship at their ancestors' tombs.

Dragon Boat Festival
There are international races held in Victoria Harbour. This lunar holiday will fall on the following dates: 9 June 1997, 28 June 1998, 18 June 1999 and 6 June 2000.
Liberation Day
The last Monday in August, this public holiday commemorates the liberation of Hong Kong from Japan after World War II. The preceding Saturday is also a public holiday.
Mid-Autumn Festival
The major lunar holiday will be celebrated on the following dates: 16 September 1997, 5 October 1998, 24 September 1999 and 12 September 2000.
Christmas & Boxing Day
Christmas (25 December) and the day after (Boxing Day) are, of course, public holidays.

The Tin Hau festival, while not a public holiday, is one of Hong Kong's most colourful celebrations. This lunar festival will be held on the following dates: 29 April 1997, 19 April 1998, 8 May 1999 and 27 April 2000.

ACTIVITIES

If you'd like a morning jog with spectacular views, nothing beats the path around Victoria Peak on Harlech and Lugard Rds. Part of this is a 'fitness trail' with various exercise machines (parallel bars and the like).

If you like easy runs followed by beer and good company, consider joining Hash House Harriers (☎ 2376-2299), 3rd floor, 74 Chung Hom Kok Rd, Stanley, Hong Kong Island.

Anyone who is serious about sports should contact the South China Athletic Association (☎ 2577-6932), 88 Caroline Hill Rd, Causeway Bay, Hong Kong Island. The SCAA has numerous indoor facilities for bowling, tennis, squash, ping pong, gymnastics, fencing, yoga, judo, karate, billiards and dancing. Outdoor activities include golf and there is also a women's activities section. Membership is very cheap and a discounted short-term membership is available for visitors.

Another excellent place you can contact is the Hong Kong Amateur Athletic Association (☎ 2574-6845), Room 913, Queen Elizabeth Stadium, 18 Oi Kwan Rd, Wanchai. All sorts of sports clubs have activities here or hold members meetings.

WORK

There is plenty of work available at reasonable pay – the big problem is getting a work visa. While UK citizens and registered British subjects can work legally in Hong Kong without visa hassles, this will surely change when China takes over. It's a fair guess to say that things will get tougher for foreign workers in the near future.

ACCOMMODATION

Prices are rising to absurd levels. There are a couple of YHA dormitories which charge only HK$25 to HK$50 per bed, but most are very inconveniently located. You'll need a YHA card to stay at any of the hostels. If you arrive in Hong Kong without a YHA card and wish to join, the annual membership fee is HK$80 for Hong Kong residents (HK$150 for non-residents). The local YHA representative is Hong Kong Youth Hostels Association (☎ 2788-1638), Room 225, Block 19, Shek Kip Mei Estate, Kowloon. They can sell you a booklet showing the location of all the hostels.

Guesthouses are the salvation for most budget travellers. Some guesthouses (not many) have dormitories where beds go for HK$80 to HK$100, with discounts for long-term (one week or more) rentals. Private rooms the size of closets are available for as little as HK$150 but you can easily spend twice that. It definitely pays for two people to share a room, as this costs little or no extra. Rentals are about 20% cheaper if you pay by the week, but stay one night first to make sure the room is acceptable – noisy neighbours and rats may not be obvious at first glance.

A 'mid-range' Hong Kong hotel would be anything priced between HK$400 and HK$1000, but even these are becoming rare.

At mid-range and top-end hotels, you can get sizeable discounts (up to 30%) by booking through some travel agencies. One such place is Traveller Services (☎ 2375-2222), but a few other agents do it as well.

For information on exactly where to stay in Hong Kong, see the Places to Stay section later in this chapter.

Getting There & Away

AIR

Hong Kong is a good place to buy discounted air tickets, but watch out! There are a few real swindlers in the travel business. The most common trick is a request for a non-refundable deposit on an air ticket: you pay a deposit for the booking, but when you go to pick up the tickets they say the flight is no longer available. However, another flight will be available at a higher price – sometimes 50% more!

It is best not to pay a deposit. Rather, pay for the ticket in full and get a receipt clearly showing that there is no balance due, and that the full amount is refundable if no ticket is issued. Tickets are normally issued the next day after booking; you must pick up the real cheapie tickets (actually group tickets) yourself at the airport from a 'tour leader' (whom you will never see again once you've got the ticket). One caution: when you get the ticket from the tour leader, check it carefully, because errors occasionally occur. For example, you may be issued a ticket on which the return portion is valid for only 60 days although you paid for a ticket valid for one year.

Some budget fares available in Hong Kong follow, but note that these are discounted fares and will have various restrictions upon their use:

Destination	One Way (US$)	Return (US$)
Auckland	574	898
Bangkok	155	220
Beijing	267	532
Frankfurt	375	725
Guangzhou	57	114
Ho Chi Minh City	294	589
Honolulu	376	727
Jakarta	227	415
Kuala Lumpur	188	314
London	375	725
Manila	115	193
New York	496	870
Phnom Penh	272	532
San Francisco	428	675
Seoul	201	272

Destination	One Way (US$)	Return (US$)
Singapore	216	275
Sydney	570	825
Taipei	127	214
Tokyo	279	487
Vancouver	392	678
Yangon (Rangoon)	367	735

Airlines

You need to reconfirm your onward or return fight if you break your trip in Hong Kong.

Air France
   Room 2104, Alexandra House, 7 Des Voeux Rd, Central (Res ☎ 2524-8145, Info 2769-6662)
Air India
   10th floor, Gloucester Tower, 11 Pedder St, Central (Res ☎ 2522-1176, Info 2769-8571)
Air New Zealand
   Suite 902, Three Exchange Square, 8 Connaught Place, Central (Res ☎ 2524-9041, Info 2769-6046)
Alitalia
   Room 2101, Hutchison House, 10 Harcourt Rd, Central (Res ☎ 2523-7047, Info 2769-7417)
Ansett Australia
   Alexandra House, 7 Des Voeux Rd, Central (Res ☎ 2527-7883, Info 2769-6046)
Asiana Airlines
   Gloucester Tower, 11 Pedder St, Central (Res ☎ 2523-8585, Info 2769-7113)
British Airways
   30th floor, Alexandra House, 7 Des Voeux Rd, Central (Res ☎ 2868-0303, Info 2868-0768)
CAAC (Civil Aviation Administration of China)
   Ground floor, 17 Queen's Rd, Central (☎ 2840-1199)
Canadian Airlines International
   Ground floor, Swire House, Connaught Rd & Pedder St, Central (Res ☎ 2868-3123, Info 2769-7113)
Cathay Pacific
   Sheraton Hotel, 20 Nathan Rd, Tsimshatsui (Res ☎ 2747-1888, Info 2747-1234)
China Airlines (Taiwan)
   Ground floor, St George's Building, Ice House St & Connaught Rd, Central (Res ☎ 2868-2299, Info 2843-9800)
Dragonair
   12th floor, Tower Six, China Hong Kong City, 33 Canton Rd, Tsimshatsui (Res ☎ 2590-1188, Info 2769-7727)
Garuda Indonesia
   2nd floor, Sing Pao Centre, 8 Queen's Rd, Central (Res ☎ 2840-0000, Info 2769-6681)
Gulf Air
   Room 2508, Caroline Centre, 28 Yun Ping Rd, Causeway Bay (Res ☎ 2882-2892, Info 2769-8337)

Japan Airlines
   Harbour View Holiday Inn, Mody Rd, Tsimshatsui East (Res ☎ 2523-0081, Info 2769-6524)
KLM-Royal Dutch Airlines
   Room 701-5, Jardine House, 1 Connaught Place, Central (Res ☎ 2822-8111, Info 2822-8118)
Malaysia Airlines
   Room 1306, Prince's Building, Chater Rd & Ice House St, Central (Res ☎ 2521-8181, Info 2769-7967)
Northwest Airlines
   29th floor, Alexandra House, 7 Des Voeux Rd, Central, Central (☎ 2810-4288)
Philippine Airlines
   Room 603, West Tower, Bond Centre, Central (☎ 2524-9216)
Qantas Airways
   Room 1422, Swire House, Connaught Rd & Pedder St, Central (Res ☎ 2524-2101, Info 2525-6206)
Singapore Airlines
   United Centre, 95 Queensway, Admiralty (Res ☎ 2520-2233, Info 2769-6387)
Thai Airways International
   Shop 105-6, Omni, The Hongkong Hotel, 3 Canton Rd, Tsimshatsui (Res ☎ 2529-5601, Info 2769-7421)
United Airlines
   Ground floor, Empire Centre, Mody Rd, Tsimshatsui East (Res ☎ 2810-4888, Info 2769-7279)
Vietnam Airlines
   c/o Cathay Pacific Airlines, Ground floor, Swire House, Connaught Rd & Pedder St, Central
   Sheraton Hotel, 20 Nathan Rd, Tsimshatsui (Res ☎ 2810-6680, Info 2747-1234)
Virgin Atlantic
   Lippo Tower, 89 Queensway, Admiralty (☎ 2532-6060)

Travel Agencies

Some agencies we've personally tried and found to offer competitive prices include:

Phoenix Services
   Room B, 6th floor, Milton Mansion, 96 Nathan Rd, Tsimshatsui (☎ 2722-7378)
Shoestring Travel
   Flat A, 4th floor, Alpha House, 27-33 Nathan Rd, Tsimshatsui (☎ 2723-2306)
Traveller Services
   Room 1012, Silvercord Tower One, Haiphong & Canton Rds, Tsimshatsui (☎ 2375-2222)

Departure Tax

The airport departure tax is HK$100.

LAND

Shenzhen is the city just across the border from Hong Kong. The border checkpoint is open daily from 6 am to midnight. The easiest way to reach the border crossing is to take the Kowloon-Canton Railway (KCR) to the last station (Lo Wu).

SEA

Luxury cruise liners frequently visit Hong Kong, though this option is basically for elderly millionaires. For those of more humble means, there are economical boats between Hong Kong and several other Chinese cities. Most popular are the boats to Macau (see the Macau chapter in this book for details). Also worth considering are boats to Guangzhou, Shanghai and Haikou (Hainan Island). Tickets and schedules for these boats can be obtained from the pier at China Hong Kong City, 33 Canton Rd, Tsimshatsui, or from China Travel Service (☎ 2721-1331), 27 Nathan Rd, Tsimshatsui.

If departing by ship to Macau or China, the departure tax is HK$26, but it's included in the price of the ticket.

Getting Around

THE AIRPORT

The Airbus (airport bus) services are very convenient. There are five services – A1 to Tsimshatsui (HK$12.30); A2 to Wanchai, Central and the Macau Ferry Terminal (HK$17); A3 to Causeway Bay (HK$17); A5 to Tai Koo Shing (HK$17); and A7 to Kowloon Tong MTR station (HK$6.50). The buses operate every 15 to 20 minutes, from 7.40 am to midnight, and depart from right outside the arrivals area. There's plenty of luggage space on board and they go past most major hotels.

The A1 service to Tsimshatsui in Kowloon goes down Nathan Rd right in front of Chungking Mansions, then turns around at the Star Ferry Terminal and heads back, making numerous stops en route. An Airbus

brochure with a map showing the bus routes is available at the departure area.

BUS

Before setting out to travel anywhere by bus, ensure you have a pocket full of small change – the exact fare normally must be deposited in a cash box and nobody has change. There are plenty of buses, with fares starting from HK$1 and going up to HK$30.60 for the fancy City Buses, which take you to the New Territories.

Most services stop around 11 pm or midnight, but bus Nos 121 and 122 are Cross Harbour Recreation Routes, which operate through the Cross-Harbour Tunnel every 15 minutes from 12.45 to 5 am. Bus No 121 runs from the Macau Ferry Terminal on Hong Kong Island, through the tunnel to Chatham Rd in Tsimshatsui East, and then continues on to Choi Hung on the east side of the airport.

Bus No 122 runs from North Point on Hong Kong Island, through the tunnel to Chatham Rd in Tsimshatsui East, and continues on to the northern part of Nathan Rd and on to Laichikok in the north-west part of Kowloon.

MINIBUS & MAXICAB

Small red and yellow minibuses supplement the regular bus services. They cost HK$2 to HK$7 and you pay as you exit. They generally don't run such regular routes, but you can get on or off almost anywhere.

Maxicabs are just like minibuses except they are green and yellow and run regular routes. Two popular ones are from the car park in front of the Star Ferry Terminal in Central to Ocean Park or from HMS *Tamar* (east of the Star Ferry) to the Peak. Fares are between HK$1 and HK$8 and you pay as you enter.

MASS TRANSIT RAILWAY

The MTR operates from Central across the harbour and up along Kowloon Peninsula. The ticket machines do not give change (get it from the ticket windows) and single-journey tickets are valid only for the day they are purchased. Once you go past the turnstile, you must complete the journey within 90 minutes or the ticket becomes invalid. The MTR operates from 6 am to 1 am.

If you use the MTR frequently, it's very useful to buy a Common Stored Value Ticket for HK$70, HK$100 or HK$200. These tickets remain valid for nine months. The Tourist Souvenir Ticket is a rip-off at HK$25 because it gives you only HK$20 worth of fares!

Smoking, eating or drinking are not allowed in the MTR stations or on the trains (makes you wonder about all those Maxim's Cake Shops in the stations). The fine for eating or drinking is HK$1000, while smoking will set you back HK$2000. Busking, selling and soliciting are forbidden. There are no toilets in the MTR stations.

KOWLOON-CANTON RAILWAY
The KCR runs from Hunghom station in Kowloon to Lo Wu, where you can walk across the border into Shenzhen. Apart from being a launch pad into China, the KCR is also an excellent alternative to buses for getting into the New Territories.

The Common Stored Value Tickets which are used on the MTR are valid on the KCR too, but not for Lo Wu station, which requires a separate ticket.

TRAM
There is just one major tram line, running from east-west along the northern side of Hong Kong Island, plus a spur route off to Happy Valley. As well as being ridiculously picturesque and fun to travel on, the tram is quite a bargain at HK$1.20 for any distance. You pay as you get off. Some trams don't run the full length of the line, but you can just get on any tram that comes by. They pass frequently and there always seem to be half a dozen trams in sight.

TRAVELATOR
A series of moving walkways and escalators climbs the hillside in Central from Con-

naught Rd to Conduit Rd in the Mid-Levels. This futuristic transport system has been dubbed the 'travelator'. It's slow but non-polluting, and best of all it's free.

LIGHT RAIL TRANSIT
The LRT only operates on routes in the western part of the New Territories, in and around Tuen Mun. Fares are HK$3.20 to HK$4.70.

TAXI
On Hong Kong Island and Kowloon, the flag fall is HK$13, and then HK$1.10 for every 0.2 km. In the New Territories, flag fall is HK$11, thereafter HK$1 for every 0.2 km. There is a luggage fee of HK$5 per bag but not all drivers insist on this.

If you go through either the Cross-Harbour Tunnel or Eastern Harbour Tunnel, you'll be charged an extra HK$20. The toll is only HK$10, but the driver is allowed to assume that he won't get a fare back so you have to pay.

Taxis cannot pick up or put down passengers where there's a yellow line painted on the kerb.

BOAT
With such a scenic harbour, commuting by ferry is one of the great pleasures of Hong Kong. You have a wide choice of boats, though the one most familiar to tourists is the Star Ferry.

Star Ferry
There are three routes on the Star Ferry, but by far the most popular one shuttles between Tsimshatsui and Central. The boats cost a mere HK$1.40 (lower deck) or HK$1.70 (upper deck), except for the Hunghom ferry, which is HK$1.70 and HK$2, respectively. The schedule for all three ferries is as follows:

Tsimshatsui – Central, every five to 10 minutes from 6.30 am until 11.30 pm
Tsimshatsui – Wanchai, every 10 to 20 minutes from 7.30 to 10.50 pm

Hunghom – Central, every 12 to 20 minutes (every 20 minutes on Sundays & holidays) from 7 am to 7.20 pm

Hoverferries

These run mostly on routes to the New Territories and occasionally to the Outlying Islands. Some routes include:

Tsimshatsui East – Central (Queen's Pier), every 20 minutes from 8 am to 8 pm

Tsuen Wan – Central, every 20 minutes from 7.20 am to 5.20 pm

Tuen Mun – Central, every 10 to 20 minutes from 6.45 am to 7.40 pm

Small Boats

A *kaido* is a small to medium-sized ferry which can make short runs on the open sea. Few kaido routes operate on regular schedules, preferring to adjust supply according to demand. There is a rough schedule on popular runs like the trip between Aberdeen and Lamma Island. Kaidos run most frequently on weekends and holidays, when everyone tries to get away from it all.

A *sampan* is a motorised launch which can only accommodate a few people. A sampan is too small to be considered seaworthy, but can safely zip you around typhoon shelters like Aberdeen Harbour.

Bigger than a sampan, but smaller than a kaido, is a *walla walla*. These operate as water taxis on Victoria Harbour. Most of the customers are sailors living on ships anchored in the harbour.

Outlying Island Ferries

The HKTA can supply you with schedules for these ferries. Fares are higher on weekends and holidays and the boats can get crowded. From Central, most ferries go from the Outlying Island piers west of the Star Ferry Terminals.

ORGANISED TOURS

There are dozens of these, including boat tours. All can be booked through the HKTA, travel agents, large tourist hotels or directly from the tour company.

Things to See & Do

KOWLOON

Kowloon, the peninsula jutting out towards Hong Kong Island, is packed with shops, hotels, bars, restaurants, nightclubs and tourists. Nathan Rd, the main drag of Kowloon, has plenty of all. Start your exploration from Kowloon's southern tip, the tourist ghetto known as Tsimshatsui. Adjacent to the Star Ferry Terminal is the **Cultural Centre**. Just next door is the **Hong Kong Museum of Art**. Both are closed on Thursday, otherwise operating hours are weekdays and Saturday from 10 am to 6 pm, and Sunday and holidays from 1 to 6 pm.

Adjacent to the preceding is the **Space Museum**, which has several exhibition halls and a Space Theatre (planetarium). Opening times for the exhibition halls are weekdays (except Tuesday) from 1 to 9 pm, and from 10 am to 9 pm on weekends and holidays. The Space Theatre has about seven shows each day (except Tuesday), some in English and some in Cantonese, but headphone translations are available for all shows. Check times with the museum.

The lower end of Nathan Rd is known as the **Golden Mile**, which refers to both the price of real estate here and also its ability to suck money out of tourist pockets. If you continue north up Nathan Rd you reach the tightly packed Chinese business districts of Yaumatei and Mongkok.

Hidden behind Yue Hwa's Park Lane Store on Nathan Rd is **Kowloon Park**, which every year seems to become less like a park and more like an amusement park. The swimming pool is perhaps the park's finest attribute – it's even equipped with waterfalls.

The **Museum of History** is in Kowloon Park near the Haiphong Rd entrance. It covers all of Hong Kong's existence from prehistoric times (about 6000 years ago, give or take a few) to the present and contains a large collection of old photographs. The museum is open Monday to Thursday and

HONG KONG

HONG KONG

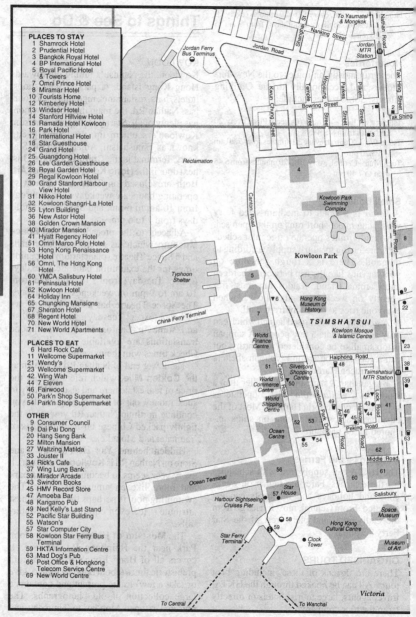

PLACES TO STAY
1 Shamrock Hotel
2 Prudential Hotel
3 Bangkok Royal Hotel
4 BP International Hotel
5 Royal Pacific Hotel
   & Towers
7 Omni Prince Hotel
9 Miramar Hotel
10 Tourists Home
12 Kimberley Hotel
13 Windsor Hotel
14 Stanford Hillview Hotel
15 Ramada Hotel Kowloon
16 Park Hotel
17 International Hotel
18 Star Guesthouse
24 Grand Hotel
25 Guangdong Hotel
26 Lee Garden Guesthouse
28 Royal Garden Hotel
29 Regal Kowloon Hotel
30 Grand Stanford Harbour
    View Hotel
31 Nikko Hotel
32 Kowloon Shangri-La Hotel
35 Lyton Building
36 New Astor Hotel
38 Golden Crown Mansion
40 Mirador Mansion
41 Hyatt Regency Hotel
51 Omni Marco Polo Hotel
53 Hong Kong Renaissance
    Hotel
56 Omni, The Hong Kong
    Hotel
60 YMCA Salisbury Hotel
61 Peninsula Hotel
63 Kowloon Hotel
64 Holiday Inn
65 Chungking Mansions
67 Sheraton Hotel
68 Regent Hotel
70 New World Hotel
71 New World Apartments

PLACES TO EAT
6 Hard Rock Cafe
11 Wellcome Supermarket
21 Wendy's
23 Wellcome Supermarket
42 Wing Wah
44 7 Eleven
46 Fairwood
50 Park'n Shop Supermarket
54 Park'n Shop Supermarket

OTHER
9 Consumer Council
19 Dai Pai Dong
20 Hang Seng Bank
22 Milton Mansion
27 Waltzing Matilda
33 Jouster II
34 Rick's Cafe
37 Wing Lung Bank
39 Mirador Arcade
43 Swindon Books
45 HMV Record Store
47 Amoeba Bar
48 Kangaroo Pub
49 Ned Kelly's Last Stand
52 Pacific Star Building
55 Watson's
57 Star Computer City
58 Kowloon Star Ferry Bus
    Terminal
59 HKTA Information Centre
63 Mad Dog's Pub
66 Post Office & Hongkong
    Telecom Service Centre
69 New World Centre

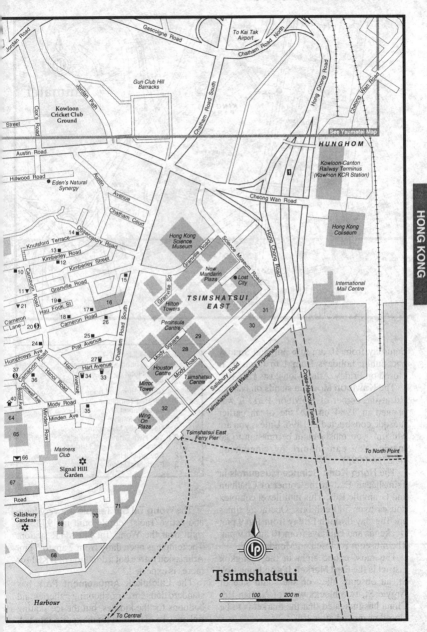

HONG KONG

See Yaumatei Map

HUNGHOM

Gascoigne Road

To Kai Tak Airport

Chatham Road North

Jordan Road

Gun Club Hill Barracks

Kowloon Cricket Club Ground

Cox's Road

Street

Jordan Path

Chatham Road South

Hong Chong Road

Cheong Wan Road

Austin Road

Kowloon-Canton Railway Terminus (Kowloon KCR Station)

1

Hillwood Road

Eden's Natural Synergy

Austin Avenue

Chatham Court

Cheong Wan Road

Hong Kong Coliseum

Observatory Road

14

Knutsford Terrace

13

Kimberley Road

12

Kimberley Street

10

Cameron Road

Granville Road

Hong Kong Science Museum

Science Museum Road

New Mandarin Plaza

Lost City

International Mail Centre

Granville Rd

TSIMSHATSUI EAST

11

21

19

Hau Fook St

17

16

15

Hilton Towers

Peninsula Centre

31

18

Cameron Road

26

30

Cameron Lane

20

24

25

Prat Avenue

29

Mody Square

28

Humphreys Ave

Hanoi Road

Hart Avenue

27

34

33

Houston Centre

Mody Road

Carnarvon Road

37

Bristol Ave

Cromwell Ave

Mirror Tower

Tsimshatsui Centre

Salisbury Road

Tsimshatsui East Waterfront Promenade

Cross-Harbour Tunnel

40

Mody Road

Minden Ave

35

32

Wing On Plaza

64

65

Tsimshatsui East Ferry Pier

To North Point

66

Mariners Club

Signal Hill Garden

67

Salisbury Gardens

69

70

71

68

Tsimshatsui

0   100   200 m

Harbour

To Central

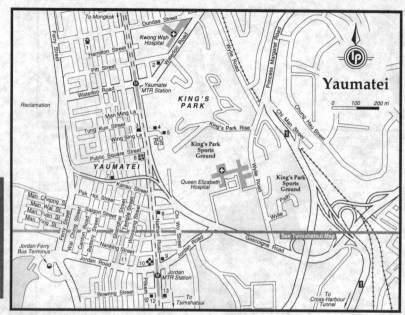

Saturday from 10 am to 6 pm, and Sunday and public holidays from 1 to 6 pm. It is closed on Friday. Admission costs HK$10.

The **Kowloon Mosque** stands on Nathan Rd at the corner of Kowloon Park. It was opened in 1984 on the site of an earlier mosque constructed in 1896. Unless you are Muslim, you must obtain permission to go inside. You can inquire by ringing up (☎ 2724-0095).

The **Hong Kong Science Museum** is in Tsimshatsui East at the corner of Chatham and Granville Rds. This multilevel complex houses over 500 exhibits. Operating times are Tuesday through Friday from 1 to 9 pm; weekends and holidays from 10 am to 9 pm. The museum is closed on Monday.

The most exotic sight in the Mongkok district is the **Bird Market**. It's on Hong Lok St, an obscure alley on the south side of Argyle St, two blocks west of Nathan Rd. China has indicated that the market is to be closed or moved after 1997.

The **Wong Tai Sin Temple** is a very large and active Taoist temple built in 1973. It's right near the Wong Tai Sin MTR station. The temple is open daily from 7 am to 5 pm. Admission is free but a donation of HK$1 (or more) is expected.

The **Laichikok Amusement Park** has standard dodgem cars, shooting galleries and balloons for the kiddies, but the ice skating rink may be of interest for the sports-minded.

There is a theatre within the park's grounds that has Chinese opera performances. The park's operating hours are: Monday to Friday from noon to 9.30 pm, and from 10 am to 9.30 pm on weekends and holidays. From the Kowloon Star Ferry Terminal take bus No 6A, which terminates near the park. Otherwise, it's a 15 minute walk from the Mei Foo MTR station. Admission is HK$15.

Adjacent to the Laichikok Amusement Park is the **Sung Dynasty Village**, which is hyped as an authentic replica of a Chinese village from 10 centuries ago. The village is open from 10 am to 8.30 pm daily. Admission costs HK$120. It drops to HK$80 on weekends and public holidays between 12.30 and 5 pm.

HONG KONG ISLAND

The north and south sides of the island have very different characters. The north side is an urban jungle, while much of the south is still surprisingly rural (but developing fast). The central part of the island is mountainous and protected from further development by a country park.

North Side

Central is the bustling business centre of Hong Kong. A free shuttle bus from the Star Ferry Terminal brings you to the lower station of the famous Peak Tram on Garden Rd. The tram terminates at the top of **Victoria Peak**, and the ride costs HK$14 one way or HK$21 return. It's worth repeating the peak trip at night. Don't just admire the view from the top: wander up Mt Austin Rd to **Victoria Peak Garden** or take the more leisurely stroll around Lugard and Harlech Rds – together they make a complete circuit of the peak. You can walk right down to Aberdeen on the south side of the island or you can try Old Peak Rd for a few km return to Central. The more energetic may want to walk the **Hong Kong Trail**, which runs along the top of the mountainous spine of Hong Kong Island from the Peak to Big Wave Bay.

There are many pleasant walks and views in the **Zoological & Botanic Gardens** on Robinson Rd overlooking Central. Entry is free to the **Fung Ping Shan Museum** in Hong Kong University (closed Sunday).

Hong Kong Park is just behind the city's second tallest skyscraper, the Bank of China. It's an unusual park, not at all natural but beautiful in its own weird way. Within the park is the **Flagstaff House Museum**, the oldest western-style building still standing in Hong Kong. Inside, you'll find a Chinese tea ware collection. Admission is free.

The **Hillside Escalator Link** is a mode of transport that has become a tourist attraction. The 800 metre moving walkway (known as a 'travelator') runs from the harbour alongside the Central Market and up to the Mid-Levels.

West of Central in the Sheung Wan district is appropriately named **Ladder St**, which climbs steeply. At the junction of Ladder St and Hollywood Rd is **Man Mo Temple**, the oldest temple in Hong Kong. A bit further north, near the Macau Ferry Terminal, is the indoor **Western Market**, a four storey red brick building built in 1906 and now fully renovated.

At the Western Market you can hop on Hong Kong's delightfully ancient double-decker trams, which will take you eastwards to Wanchai, Causeway Bay and Happy Valley.

Just east of Central is **Wanchai**, known for its raucous nightlife but relatively dull in the daytime. One thing worth seeing is the **Arts Centre** on Harbour Rd. The **Pao Sui Loong Galleries** are on the 4th and 5th floors of the centre, and international and local exhibitions with an emphasis on contemporary art are held year-round

Wanchai's **Police Museum**, 27 Coombe Rd, relates the history of the Royal Hong Kong Police Force. Opening hours are Wednesday to Sunday, 9 am to 5 pm, and Tuesday from 2 to 5 pm. It's closed on Monday and admission is free.

The **Hong Kong Convention & Exhibition Centre** is an enormous building on the harbour and boasts the world's largest 'glass curtain' – a window seven storeys high. Just be glad you don't have to wash it. You can ride the escalator to the seventh floor for a superb harbour view.

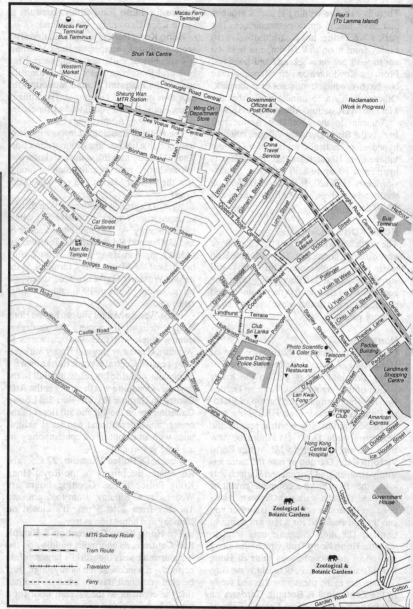

Pier 1
(To Lamma Island)

Macau Ferry
Terminal

Macau Ferry
Terminal
Bus Terminus

Shun Tak Centre

New Market Street

Western
Market

Wing Lok Street

Connaught Road Central

Sheung Wan
MTR Station

Government
Offices &
Post Office

Reclamation
(Work in Progress)

Wing Lok Street

Des Voeux Road Central

Wing On
Department
Store

Bonham Strand

Man Wa Lane

China Travel
Service

Pier Road

Bonham Strand

Wing Wo Street

Wing Kut Street

Gilman's Bazaar

Gilman

Connaught Road Central

Queen's Road West

Lok Ku Road

Cleverly Street

Burd Street

Hillier Street

Queen's Road Central

Lung Street

Bus
Terminal

Harbour

Cat Street
Galleries

Gough Street

Wellington Street

Central
Market

Street

Des Voeux Road Central

Square Street

Kui In Fong

Upper Lascar Row

Hollywood Road

Man Mo
Temple

Ladder Street

Bridges Street

Aberdeen Street

Graham Street

Cochrane Street

Queen Victoria

Pottinger

Li Yuen St West

Li Yuen St East

Chiu Lung Street

Street

Caine Road

Staunton Street

Lyndhurst
Terrace

Club
Sri Lanka

Pottinger St

Stanley Street

Queen's Road Central

Theatre Lane

Padder Building

Padder Street

Seymour Road

Castle Road

Peel Street

Shelley Street

Elgin Street

Hollywood Road

Photo Scientific
& Color Six

Telecom

D'Aguilar Street

Wyndham Street

Landmark
Shopping
Centre

Robinson Road

Old Bailey Street

Central District
Police Station

Ashoka
Restaurant

Lan Kwai
Fong

Fringe
Club

Zetland Street

American
Express

Duddell Street

Ice House Street

Caine Road

Mosque Street

Conduit Road

Hong Kong
Central
Hospital

Zoological &
Botanic Gardens

Albany Road

Upper Albert Road

Government
House

Zoological &
Botanic Gardens

Garden Road

Cotton

MTR Subway Route

Tram Route

Travelator

Ferry

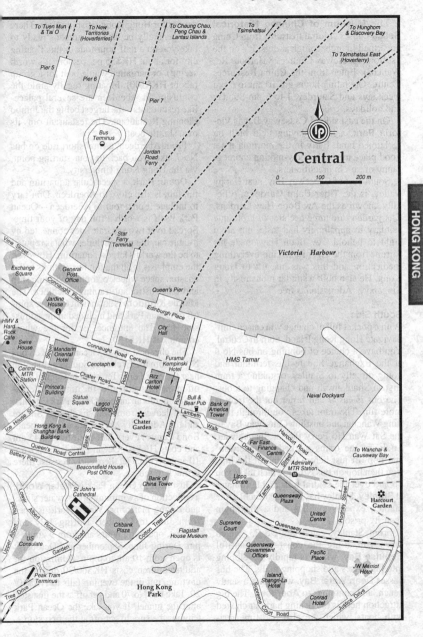

To Tuen Mun & Tai O

To New Territories (Hoverferries)

To Cheung Chau, Peng Chau & Lantau Islands

To Tsimshatsui

To Hunghom & Discovery Bay

To Tsimshatsui East (Hoverferry)

Pier 5

Pier 6

Pier 7

Bus Terminus

Jordan Road Ferry

Central

0   100   200 m

Victoria Harbour

Star Ferry Terminal

View Street

Exchange Square

General Post Office

Connaught Place

Jardine House

Queen's Pier

Edinburgh Place

HMV & Hard Rock Cafe

Swire House

Mandarin Oriental Hotel

Connaught Road Central

City Hall

Furama Kempinski Hotel

HMS Tamar

Central MTR Station

Chater Road

Ritz Carlton Hotel

Prince's Building

Statue Square

Cenotaph

Ice House Street

Ice House St

Legco Building

Bull & Bear Pub

Bank of America Tower

Lambeth Walk

Naval Dockyard

Hong Kong & Shanghai Bank Building

Jackson Road

Murray Road

Chater Garden

Bank St

Queen's Road Central

Battery Path

Harcourt Road

Far East Finance Centre

Drake Street

Tamar Street

Admiralty MTR Station

To Wanchai & Causeway Bay

Beaconsfield House Post Office

Bank of China Tower

Lippo Centre

Queensway Plaza

Rodney Street

Harcourt Garden

St John's Cathedral

Cotton Tree Drive

United Centre

Queensway

Citibank Plaza

Flagstaff House Museum

Supreme Court

US Consulate

Upper Albert Road

Lower Albert Road

Garden Road

Queensway Government Offices

Pacific Place

Tamar Street

JW Marriot Hotel

Peak Tram Terminus

Tree Drive

Hong Kong Park

Island Shangri-La Hotel

Conrad Hotel

Supreme Court Road

Justice Drive

The **Museum of Chinese Historical Relics** houses cultural treasures from China unearthed in archaeological digs. It's on the 1st floor, Causeway Centre, 28 Harbour Rd, Wanchai. Enter from the China Resources Centre. Operating hours are 10 am to 6 pm weekdays and Saturday, 1 to 6 pm Sunday and holidays.

On the east side of Causeway Bay is **Victoria Park**, a large playing field built on reclaimed land. Early in the morning it's a good place to see the slow-motion choreography of tai-chi practitioners.

South east of Causeway Bay, near Happy Valley, is the **Tiger Balm Gardens**, officially known as the Aw Boon Haw Gardens. The gardens are three hectares of grotesque statuary in appallingly bad taste, but are a sight to behold. Aw Boon Haw made his fortune from the Tiger Balm cure-everything medication and this was his gift to Hong Kong. He also built a similar monstrosity in Singapore. Admission is free.

South Side

With a pocket full of change you can circumnavigate Hong Kong Island. Start in Central. You have a choice of hopping on bus No 6 at the Exchange Square bus terminal and going directly to Stanley, or taking a tram first to Shaukeiwan and changing to a bus. The bus is easier and faster but the tram is more fun. The tram takes you through hustling Wanchai and bustling Causeway Bay to the Sai Wan Ho Ferry Pier at Shaukeiwan. Look for the trams marked 'Shaukeiwan' and hop off just before the end of the line. You then hop on bus No 14, which takes you up and over the central hills and terminates at **Stanley**. Stanley has a decent beach, a fine market, expensive villas and a maximum security prison.

From Stanley, catch bus No 73, which takes you along the coast via beautiful **Repulse Bay**, which is rapidly developing into high-rises and shopping malls. The bus passes **Deep Water Bay**, which has a sandy beach, and continues to **Aberdeen**. The big attraction here is the fishing harbour choked with boats, which are also part-time residences for Hong Kong's fishing fleet. There will generally be several sampans ready to take you on a half-hour tour of this floating city for about HK$35 per person (it's worth seeing), or bargain a whole boat for a group (about HK$100). Floating regally amid the confusion in Aberdeen are several palace-like restaurants – the largest being the Jumbo Floating Restaurant. The restaurant runs its own shuttle boat.

From Aberdeen, a final short ride on bus No 7 takes you back to your starting point, via the Hong Kong University.

Ocean Park, a spectacular aquarium and fun fair, is also close to Aberdeen. Don't try to include it on a tour to Aberdeen – Ocean Park itself is worth a full day of your time. Spread over two separate sites connected by a cable car, the park includes what is reputed to be the world's largest aquarium. However, the emphasis is on the fun fair, with its roller coaster, space wheel, octopus, swinging ship and other astronaut-training machines. The **Middle Kingdom** is an ancient Chinese spin-off of Ocean Park and included in the admission fee. The entrance fee for the whole complex is HK$130.

The cheapest way to Ocean Park is on bus No 70 from the Exchange Square bus station near the Star Ferry Terminal in Central – get off at the first stop after the tunnel. Alternatively, there's an air-con Ocean Park Citybus, which leaves from both Exchange Square and the Admiralty MTR station (underneath Bond Centre) every half-hour from 8.45 am and costs HK$10. Ocean Park is open from 10 am to 6 pm. Get there early because there is much to see.

Just next to Ocean Park is **Water World**, a collection of swimming pools, water slides and diving platforms. Water World is open from June to October. During July and August, operating hours are from 9 am to 9 pm. During June, September and October it is open from 10 am to 6 pm. Admission for adults/children costs HK$60/30 during the daytime, but in the evening falls to HK$40/20. Take bus No 70 and get off at the first stop after the tunnel. If you take the Ocean Park Citybus, be sure to get off at the first stop.

Shek O, on the south-east coast, has one of the best beaches on Hong Kong Island. To get there, take the MTR or tram to Shaukeiwan, and from Shaukeiwan take bus No 9 to the last stop.

NEW TERRITORIES

You can explore most of the New Territories by bus and train in one very busy day, assuming that you don't take time out for hiking or swimming (both worthwhile and recommended activities).

You start out by taking the MTR to the last stop at **Tsuen Wan**. The main attraction here is the **Yuen Yuen Institute**, a Taoist temple complex, and the adjacent Buddhist **Western Monastery**. You reach the institute by taking minibus No 81 from Shiu Wo St, which is two blocks south of the MTR station. Alternatively, it is not expensive to take a taxi.

Chuk Lam Sim Yuen is another large monastery in the hills north of Tsuen Wan. The instructions for getting there are almost the same as for the Yuen Yuen Institute. Find Shiu Wo St and take maxicab No 85.

At Tsuen Wan you have an option. You can continue west to Tuen Mun, or north to **Tai Mo Shan** (elevation 957 metres), Hong Kong's highest peak. To reach Tai Mo Shan, take bus No 51 from the Tsuen Wan MTR station – the bus stop is on the overpass that goes over the roof of the station, or you can also pick it up at the Tsuen Wan ferry pier. The bus heads up Route Twisk (Twisk is derived from Tsuen Wan Into Shek Kong). Get off at the top of the pass, from where it's uphill on foot. You walk on a road but it's unlikely you'll encounter traffic. The path is part of the **MacLehose Trail**, which is 100 km long. The trail runs from Tuen Mun in the west to the Sai Kung Peninsula in the east, and to walk its entire length would take several days.

If you choose not to visit Tai Mo Shan, from Tsuen Wan take bus No 60M or 68M to the bustling town of **Tuen Mun**. Here you can visit Hong Kong's largest shopping mall, the Tuen Mun Town Centre. From here, hop on the Light Rail Transit (LRT) system to reach **Ching Chung Koon**, a temple complex on the north side of Tuen Mun.

You then get back on the LRT and head to Yuen Long. From here, take bus No 54, 64K or 74K to the nearby walled villages at **Kam Tin**. These villages with their single stout entrances are said to date from the 16th century. There are several walled villages at Kam Tin, but **Kat Hing Wai** is most accessible. Drop about HK$5 into the donation box by the entrance and wander the narrow little lanes. The old Hakka women in traditional gear must be paid before you can photograph them.

The town of Sheung Shui is about eight km east on bus No 77K. Here you can hop on the Kowloon-Canton Railway (KCR) and go one stop south to **Fanling**. The main attraction in this town is the **Fung Ying Sin Kwun Temple**, a Taoist temple for the dead.

At Fanling, get on the KCR and head to Tai Po Market station. From here, you can walk 10 to 15 minutes to the **Hong Kong Railway Museum**. You can get back on the KCR and go south to the Chinese University, where there's an **art gallery** at the Institute of Chinese Studies. Admission is free.

The KCR will bring you to **Shatin**, a lively, bustling city where you can visit the huge **Shatin Town Centre** – one of Hong Kong's biggest shopping malls. From here you can climb to the **Temple of 10,000 Buddhas** (which actually has over 12,000).

All this should fill your day, but there are other places to visit in the New Territories. The **Sai Kung Peninsula** is one of the least spoilt areas in the New Territories – great for hiking and you can get from village to village on boats in the Tolo Harbour. Also, the best beaches in the New Territories are around the Sai Kung Peninsula, including **Clearwater Bay**.

OUTLYING ISLANDS

There are 235 islands dotting the waters around Hong Kong, but only four have bedroom communities and are thus readily accessible by ferry. While very tranquil during the week, the islands pack out on weekends and holidays. Cars are prohibited

HONG KONG

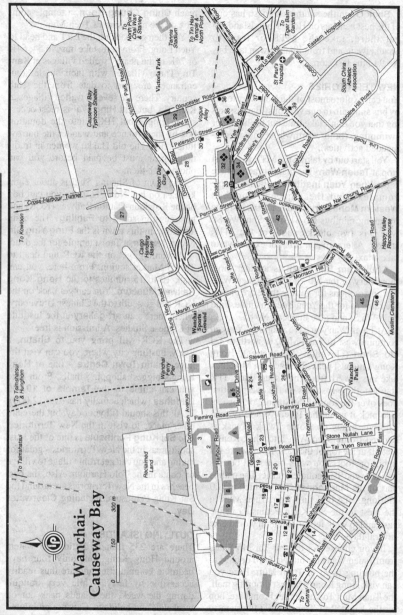

Wanchai-
Causeway Bay

on all of the islands except Lantau, and even there vehicle ownership is very restricted.

Cheung Chau

This dumb-bell-shaped island has a large community of western residents who enjoy the slow pace of island life and relatively low rents. Were it not for the Chinese signs and people, you might think you were in some Greek island village.

The town sprawls across the narrow neck connecting the two ends of the island. The bay on the west side (where the ferry lands) has an exotic collection of fishing boats, much like Aberdeen on Hong Kong Island. The east side of the island is where you'll find **Tung Wan Beach**, Cheung Chau's longest. There are a few tiny but remote beaches that you can reach by foot, and at the southern tip of the island is the hideaway cave of notorious pirate Cheung Po Tsai.

Lamma Island

This is the second largest of the outlying islands and the one closest to the city. Lamma has good beaches and a very relaxed pace on weekdays, but on weekends it's mobbed like anywhere else. There are two main communities here, Yung Shue Wan in the north and Sok Kwu Wan in the south. Both have a ferry service to Central.

Lantau Island

This is the largest of the islands and the most sparsely populated – it's almost twice the size of Hong Kong Island but the population is only 30,000. You could easily spend a couple of days exploring the mountainous walking trails and enjoying uncrowded beaches.

Mui Wo (Silvermine Bay) is the major arrival point for ferries. As you exit the ferry, to your right is the road leading to the beach. It passes several eateries and hotels along the way.

From Mui Wo, most visitors board bus No 2 to **Ngong Ping**, a plateau region 500 metres above sea level in the western part of the island. It's here that you'll find the impressive **Po Lin Monastery**. It's a relatively recent construction and almost as much a tourist attraction as a religious centre. Just outside the monastery is the world's largest outdoor Buddha statue. It's possible to have a vegetarian lunch at the monastery dining hall and you can spend the night here. The main reason to stay overnight is to launch a sunrise expedition to climb Lantau Peak (elevation 934 metres).

HONG KONG

PLACES TO STAY		PLACES TO EAT			
1	Grand Hyatt Hotel	23	Oliver's Super	20	Neptune Disco II
3	New World Harbour		Sandwiches	21	New Makati
	View Hotel			22	Wanchai MTR Station
8	Harbour View	**OTHER**		24	Wanchai Police
	International House	2	Hong Kong	26	British Council
12	Empire Hotel		Convention &	27	Royal Hong Kong
13	Wesley Hotel		Exhibition Centre		Yacht Club
15	New Harbour Hotel	4	Australian High	29	Daimaru Household
17	Wharney Hotel		Commission		Square
19	Luk Kwok Hotel	5	China Resources	32	Sogo Department
25	Century Hotel		Centre (Visas for		Store
28	Excelsior Hotel		China)	33	Causeway Bay MTR
30	Wang Fat Hostel	6	Central Plaza		Station
31	Noble Hostel	7	Immigration	34	Mitsukoshi
37	Regal Hong Kong		Department		Department Store
	Hotel	9	Hong Kong Arts	35	Matsuzakaya
38	New Cathay Hotel		Centre		Department Store
39	Leishun Court	10	The Wanch	36	HMV CD Store
40	Phoenix Apartments	11	Post & Telecom Office	42	Times Square
41	Emerald House	14	Cosmos Books	45	Queen Elizabeth
43	South Pacific Hotel	16	Neptune Disco		Stadium
44	Charterhouse Hotel	18	Joe Bananas	46	New China News
					Agency

Another place to visit is **Tai O**, a village at the west end of the island, which can be reached by bus No 1.

The two-km-long **Cheung Sha Wan** on Lantau Island is Hong Kong's longest beach. You'll have it to yourself on weekdays, but forget it on weekends.

To get a taste of abominations to come, you should probably visit **Discovery Bay** in the north-east part of the island. This is a very upscale housing development, complete with high-rises, shopping mall, yacht club and golf course. Jet-powered ferries run from Discovery Bay to Central every 20 minutes, but there are no places to stay and tourism is actively discouraged. The main reason for visiting isn't to see Discovery Bay, but to walk for one hour southwards along the coastline to find the **Trappist Haven Monastery**. Walking about another 1½ hours from there over a dangerously slippery trail brings you out to Mui Wo, from where you can get ferries back to Central.

Peng Chau

This is the smallest outlying island that is readily accessible. It's also the most traditionally Chinese, with narrow alleys, an outdoor meat and vegetable market and a very tiny gwailo community. The **Tin Hau Temple** was originally built in 1792. A climb to the top of **Finger Hill** (elevation 95 metres) will reward you with a view of the entire island and nearby Lantau.

Places to Stay

KOWLOON
Guesthouses

Chungking Mansions is the bottom-end accommodation ghetto of Hong Kong. It's a huge, high-rise dump at 30 Nathan Rd, in the heart of Tsimshatsui, with approximately 80 guesthouses. It's divided into five blocks labelled A through E, each with its own derelict lift. If you stand around the lobby with your backpack, chances are the touts

from the guesthouses will find you before you find them.

With few exceptions, there is little difference in prices for private rooms, but dormitories are of course significantly cheaper. The price range for a private room is roughly HK$150 to HK$250, while dorm beds go for about HK$50 to HK$80. Places in Chungking Mansions offering dorm beds include:

Friendship Travellers Hostel, B Block, 6th floor (☎ 2311-0797)
Kamal Dormitory , B Block, 6th floor (☎ 2739-3301)
New World Hostel, A Block, 6th floor (☎ 2723-6352)
Splendid Asia Guesthouse, B Block, 4th floor
Super Guest House, A Block, 12th floor (☎ 2723-4817)
Travellers' Hostel, A Block, 16th floor (☎ 2368-7710)
United Guesthouse, A Block, 17th floor

You can avoid the stigma of staying in Chungking Mansions by checking out *Mirador Arcade* at 58 Nathan Rd. There are numerous guesthouses here. Those with dormitories include:

Blue Lagoon Guesthouse, 3rd floor, Flat F2 (☎ 2721-0346)
City Guesthouse, 9th floor (☎ 2724-2612)
Garden Hostel, 3rd floor, Flat F4 (☎ 2721-8567)
London Guesthouse, 13th floor, Flat F2 (☎ 2369-0919)
Mini Hotel, 7th floor, Flat F2 (☎ 2367-2551)
New Garden, 13th floor (☎ 2311-2523)

An excellent guesthouse in Mirador Arcade which does not have dorms is *Man Hing Lung* (☎ 2722-0678), 14th floor, Flat F2. All rooms come equipped with private bath, air conditioning and TV – doubles cost HK$300 to HK$360. If you arrive by yourself and want a roommate, the management can put you in with another traveller – thus cutting the bill in half.

Also in Mirador and deserving a plug is *Ajit Guesthouse* (☎ 2369-1201), 12th floor, Flat F3. This friendly place has clean rooms for HK$150 to HK$200.

Golden Crown Mansion at 66-70 Nathan Rd, Tsimshatsui, has just two guesthouses, both on the 5th floor. *Golden Crown Guesthouse* (☎ 2369-1782) has dormitory beds for

HK$80; singles start at HK$200 and doubles at HK$280. But before you stay, take a look at neighbouring *Wahtat Travel & Trading Co* (☎ 2366-9495) – there are super-clean singles/doubles here for HK$250/300.

New Lucky Mansions, 300 Nathan Rd (entrance on Jordan Rd), Yaumatei, is in a better neighbourhood than most of the other guesthouses. Spread between the 3rd and 14th floors are nine guesthouses with rooms costing from HK$170 to HK$450. There are no dorms.

The *STB Hostel* (☎ 2710-9199), 2nd floor, Great Eastern Mansion, 255-261 Reclamation St, Mongkok, is run by the Student Travel Bureau. Dorm beds are HK$100. There are pricier doubles costing HK$400 to HK$450, and triples for HK$450 to HK$560.

Back in Tsimshatsui, the *Star Guesthouse* (☎ 2723-8951), 6th floor at 21 Cameron Rd, is immaculately clean. *Lee Garden Guesthouse* (☎ 2367-2284) is on the 8th floor, D Block, 36 Cameron Rd, close to Chatham Rd. Both guesthouses are run by the same owner, the charismatic Charlie Chan. Rooms with shared bath are HK$260 to HK$300, and with private bath they jump to HK$320 to HK$400.

The Lyton Building, 32-40 Mody Rd, has two decent guesthouses but neither is cheap. *Lyton House Inn* (☎ 2367-3791) is on the 6th floor of Block 2, and costs HK$400 for a double. *Frank's Mody House* (☎ 2724-4113), on the 7th floor of Block 4, has doubles for HK$350 to HK$550.

Tourists Home (☎ 2311-2622) is on the 6th floor, G Block, Champagne Court, 16 Kimberley Rd. Doubles are from HK$300 to HK$350. All rooms have an attached private bath.

Hotels

The small number of mid-range hotels in Kowloon includes the following:

Bangkok Royal, 2-12 Pilkem St, Yaumatei (Jordan MTR station) (☎ 2735-9181); 70 rooms, singles HK$420 to HK$600, doubles & twins HK$500 to HK$680

Booth Lodge, 11 Wing Sing Lane, Yaumatei (☎ 2771-9266); 54 rooms, doubles HK$500 to HK$800 – run by the Salvation Army

Caritas Bianchi Lodge, 4 Cliff Rd, Yaumatei (☎ 2388-1111); singles HK$590, doubles HK$690

Caritas Lodge, 134 Boundary St, Mongkok (near Prince Edward MTR station) (☎ 2339-3777); singles/doubles HK$450/520

Eaton, 380 Nathan Rd, Yaumatei (Jordan MTR station) (☎ 2782-1818); 392 rooms, doubles & twins HK$770 to HK$1650

Imperial, 30-34 Nathan Rd, Tsimshatsui (☎ 2366-2201); 215 rooms, singles HK$700 to HK$1150, doubles & twins HK$800 to HK$1250

International, 33 Cameron Rd, Tsimshatsui (☎ 2366-3381); 89 rooms, singles HK$430 to HK$750, twins HK$560 to HK$950

King's Hotel, 473 Nathan Rd, Yaumatei (☎ 2780-1281); 72 rooms, singles HK$410 to HK$430, doubles & twins HK$520 to HK$550

Nathan, 378 Nathan Rd, Yaumatei (☎ 2388-5141); 186 rooms, doubles & twins HK$880 to HK$950

Shamrock, 223 Nathan Rd, Yaumatei (☎ 2735-2271); 148 rooms, singles HK$520 to HK$850, doubles & twins HK$600 to HK$950

YMCA International House, 23 Waterloo Rd, Yaumatei (☎ 2771-9111); 333 rooms, singles HK$270 to HK$300, twins HK$720 to HK$930

Salisbury YMCA, 41 Salisbury Rd, Tsimshatsui (☎ 2369-2211); singles HK$730, doubles & twins HK$860 to HK$1060

YWCA. Badly located near Pui Ching Rd and Waterloo Rd in Mongkok (☎ 2713-9211). Its official address is 5 Man Fuk Rd and it's up a hill behind a Caltex petrol station. There are 169 rooms for women only: singles HK$300 to HK$500, doubles & twins HK$600 to HK$650.

HONG KONG ISLAND
Hostels

Ma Wui Hall (☎ 2817-5715) on top of Mt Davis on Hong Kong Island offers stunning views. Although it's a good hour's journey from Central, travellers say it's 'almost worth it'. Before embarking on the trek, ring up first to be sure a bed is available. To get there, take bus No 5B or 47 to the 5B terminus at Felix Villas on Victoria Rd. Walk back 100 metres and look for the YHA sign. You've then got a 20 to 30 minute climb up the hill! Don't confuse Mt Davis Path with Mt Davis Rd! There are 112 beds here and the nightly cost is HK$50. You need a YHA card (which can be purchased at the hostel) and it's open from 7am to 11 pm.

Guesthouses

Noble Hostel (☎ 2576-6148) at Flat A3, 17th floor, 27 Paterson St, Causeway Bay, is surely one of the best guesthouses in Hong Kong. Singles/doubles with shared bath are HK$230/320. With private bath it's HK$360/420. It's located in the Great George Building, just above the Daimaru Department Store.

Also at 27 Paterson St is *Kai Woo Hung Wan Co* (☎ 2890-5813). It's on the 11th floor in Flat A1, and offers good singles/doubles for HK$380/400.

Yet one more hostel at 27 Paterson St is *Wonderful Well* (☎ 2577-1278, 9480-6481), which is on the 4th floor in Flat A5. This wonderful accommodation owes much of its appeal to the charming Angela Hui, who runs the place. Superb double rooms cost HK$380.

In the same building but at a different entrance is the enormous *Wang Fat Hostel* (☎ 2895-1015) on the 3rd floor, Flat A2, 47 Paterson St. Rooms with shared/private bath are HK$280/380.

The *Phoenix Apartments*, 70 Lee Garden Hill Rd, Causeway Bay, has a number of elegant and reasonably priced guesthouses. The catch here is that most are short-time hotels, where rooms are rented by the hour. One hotel proudly advertises 'Avoidance of Publicity & Reasonable Rates'. Nevertheless, rooms are available for overnighters and, as long as they've changed the sheets recently, it's not a bad place to stay.

Nearby is *Emerald House* (☎ 2577-2368), 1st floor, 44 Leighton Rd, where clean doubles with private bath and round beds (no kidding) are HK$380. Enter the building from Leighton Lane just around the corner.

Leishun Court at 116 Leighton Rd, Causeway Bay, is another relatively cheap option, though the building appears a bit tattered: *Fuji House* (☎ 2577-9406), on the 1st floor, is reasonable at HK$290 for a room with private bath; on the 2nd floor are the *Sam Yu Apartment* and *VIP House*.

Hotels

There are even fewer mid-range hotels available on Hong Kong Island than in Kowloon.

Check with travel agents for discounts. Some places to check out include:

Emerald, 152 Connaught Rd West, Sheung Wan (☎ 2546-8111); 316 rooms, singles HK$500, doubles & twins HK$600 to HK$800
Harbour, 116-122 Gloucester Rd, Wanchai (☎ 2507-2702); 200 rooms, singles HK$500 to HK$800, doubles & twins HK$680 to HK$950
YMCA – Harbour View International, 4 Harbour Rd, Wanchai (☎ 2802-1111); 320 rooms, doubles & twins HK$620 to HK$850
YWCA – Garden View International, 1 MacDonnell Rd, Central (☎ 2877-3737); 130 rooms, doubles & twins HK$693 to HK$814

OUTLYING ISLANDS
Cheung Chau

There is a solid line-up of booths offering flats for rent opposite the ferry pier. Small flats for two persons begin at HK$300, but at least double on weekends and holidays.

Cheung Chau has one, upmarket, place to stay: the *Warwick Hotel* (☎ 2981-0081) with 70 rooms. Doubles cost HK$780 on a weekday and HK$1180 on weekends.

Lamma Island

There are several places to stay in Yung Shue Wan. Right by the Yung Shue Wan ferry pier is the *Man Lai Wah Hotel* (☎ 2982-0220), where doubles cost HK$350 on weekdays, rising to HK$700 on weekends. *Lamma Vacation House* (☎ 2982-0427) is at 29 Main St and offers coffin-sized rooms for HK$150 or cushier flats for HK$300 – prices double on weekends.

On nearby Hung Shing Ye beach is *Concerto Inn* (☎ 2982-1668), an upmarket place with rooms for HK$680 to HK$880.

Lantau Island

As you exit the ferry in Mui Wo, turn right and head towards the beach. Here you'll find several hotels with a sea view. The line-up of places to stay includes *Sea House* (☎ 2984-7757), which has rather dumpy-looking rooms starting at HK$300 on weekdays, HK$500 on weekends. One of the best deals around is the *Mui Wo Inn* (☎ 2984-1916); doubles are from HK$300 to HK$400 on weekdays and HK$550 to HK$700 on week-ends. Top of the line is the *Silvermine Beach Hotel* (☎ 2984-8295), which has doubles from HK$820 to HK$1200.

There are two places to stay in Ngong Ping. The *Tea Garden Hotel* (☎ 2985-5161) has some truly grotty single rooms with shared bath for HK$170 on weekdays; slightly better doubles cost HK$200. A better deal is the nearby *S G Davis Youth Hostel* (☎ 2985-5610; 48 beds), which costs HK$25, although a YHA card is required. The youth hostel also has a campsite for 20 tents.

Places to Eat

Hong Kong offers incredible variety when it comes to food, but finding a cheap place to eat is no picnic. Budget travellers may have to resort frequently to McDonald's – one of the cheapest restaurants in Hong Kong. Supermarkets offer the cheapest food if you have a place to cook or can get by with sand-wiches, fruit and yoghurt. Some convenience stores have microwave ovens, allowing a limited amount of no-frills self-catering.

No matter what your budget, you should try *dim sum* at least once. It is a uniquely Cantonese dish served only for breakfast or lunch (never dinner). Dim sum delicacies are normally steamed in a small bamboo basket. The baskets are stacked up on pushcarts and rolled around the dining room. No menu is needed – you choose whatever you like from the carts. Typically, each basket contains four identical pieces and you pay by the number of baskets you order, so four people is an ideal number for a dim sum meal.

In Cantonese restaurants tea is often served free of charge, or at most you'll pay HK$1 for a big pot which can be refilled indefinitely. On the other hand, coffee is seldom available, except in western restau-rants or coffee shops, and is never free. Chinese firewater gets the thumbs down from most westerners, but Chinese beer is quite all right. Imported drinks of all sorts are readily available.

KOWLOON

If you want to eat before 9 am, you may well have to make your own breakfast. After 9 am, you have the following options:

Breakfast

The window of the *Wing Wah Restaurant* is always filled with great- looking cakes and pastries. It's at 21A Lock Rd, near Swindon's Books and the Hyatt Regency. Either take it away or sit down with some coffee. Prices are very reasonable. Inexpensive Chinese food is also served and there is an English menu – a rare treat in a Hong Kong budget Chinese cafe.

Deep in the bowels of *every* MTR station you can find a *Maxim's Cake Shop*. The cakes and pastries look irresistible, but don't sink your teeth into the creamy delights until you're back on the street, as it is prohibited to eat or drink anything in the MTR stations or on the trains – there's a HK$1000 fine if you do.

There is a chain of bakeries around Hong Kong with the name *St Honoré Cake Shop*; there's no English sign on their stores, but you'll soon recognise their ideogram. You can find them at 12 Cameron Rd and 8 Canton Rd in Tsimshatsui.

If you're up early before the aforemen-tioned places open, 7 Eleven operates 24 hours and does good coffee, packaged breads and microwave cuisine.

American

Planet Hollywood, 3 Canton Rd, claims to be 'the galaxy's ultimate dining experience'. The food is good, if expensive, but what really distinguishes this place is the knock-out decor. The T-shirts make a good souvenir.

Dan Ryan's Chicago Grill, Shop 200, Ocean Terminal, Harbour City, Canton Rd, Tsimshatsui, is a trendy spot with prices to match.

Chinese – Dim Sum

This is normally served from around 11 am to 3 pm, but a few places have it available for breakfast. Nothing in Hong Kong is dirt cheap, but the following places have reasonable prices:

Canton Court, Guangdong Hotel, 18 Prat Ave, Tsimshatsui; dim sum served from 7 am to 4 pm

Eastern Palace, 3rd floor, Omni, The Hongkong Hotel, Shopping Arcade, Harbour City, Canton Rd, Tsimshatsui; dim sum served from 11.30 am to 3 pm

Harbour View Seafood, 3rd floor, Tsimshatsui Centre, 66 Mody Rd, Tsimshatsui East; dim sum served from 11 am to 5 pm

New Home, 19-20 Hanoi Rd, Tsimshatsui; dim sum served from 7 am to 4.30 pm

North China Peking Seafood, 2nd floor, Polly Commercial Building, 21-23 Prat Ave, Tsimshatsui; dim sum served from 11 am to 3 pm

Orchard Court, 1st & 2nd floors, Ma's Mansion, 37 Hankow Rd, Tsimshatsui; dim sum served from 11 am to 5 pm

Chinese – Street Stalls
The cheapest place to enjoy authentic Chinese cuisine is the *Temple St Night Market* in Yaumatei. It starts at about 8 pm and begins to fade at 11 pm. There are also plenty of mainstream indoor restaurants with variable prices.

Fast Food
Oliver's is on the ground floor of Hong Kong Pacific Centre, 28 Hankow Rd, and in the basement at 100 Nathan Rd. It's a great place for breakfast – inexpensive bacon, eggs and toast. The sandwiches are equally excellent, though it gets crowded at lunch time.

McDonald's occupies key strategic locations in Tsimshatsui. Late night restaurants are amazingly scarce in Hong Kong, so it's useful to know that two McDonald's in Tsimshatsui operate 24 hours a day: at 21A Granville Rd and at 12 Peking Rd. There is also a McDonald's at 2 Cameron Rd, and another in Star House, just opposite the Star Ferry Terminal.

Domino's Pizza (☎ 2765-0683), Yue Sun Mansion, Hunghom, does not have a restaurant where you can sit down to eat. Rather, pizzas are delivered to your door within 30 minutes of phoning in your order.

Other fast-food outlets in Kowloon include:

Café de Coral, Mezzanine floor, Albion Plaza, 2-6 Granville Rd, Tsimshatsui; 16 Carnarvon Rd, Tsimshatsui

Fairwood Fast Food, 6 Ashley Rd, Tsimshatsui; Basement Two, Silvercord Shopping Centre, Haiphong & Canton Rds, Tsimshatsui

Hardee's, Arcade of Regent Hotel, south of Salisbury Rd at the very southern tip of Tsimshatsui

Jack in the Box, G60-83, Tsimshatsui Centre, 66 Mody Rd, Tsimshatsui East

Ka Ka Lok Fast Food Shop, 55A Carnarvon Rd, Tsimshatsui; 16A Ashley Rd, but enter from Ichang St, Tsimshatsui

KFC, 2 Cameron Rd, Tsimshatsui; 241 Nathan Rd, Yaumatei

Pizza Hut, Lower Basement, Silvercord Shopping Centre, Haiphong & Canton Rds, Tsimshatsui; Shop 008, Ocean Terminal, Harbour City, Canton Rd, Tsimshatsui

Spaghetti House, 57 Peking Rd; 38 Haiphong Rd, Tsimshatsui

Wendy's, Basement, Albion Plaza, 2-6 Granville Rd, just off Nathan Rd, Tsimshatsui

Indian
The greatest concentration of cheap Indian restaurants is in Chungking Mansions on Nathan Rd. Despite the grotty appearance of the entrance to the Mansions, many of the restaurants are surprisingly plush inside. A meal of curried chicken and rice, or curry with chapatis and dhal, will cost around HK$30 per person.

Start your search for Indian food on the ground floor of the arcade. The bottom of the market belongs to *Kashmir Fast Food* and *Lahore Fast Food*. These open early, so you can have curry, chapatis and heartburn for breakfast. Consider this bottom-end Indian dining.

Up on the mezzanine floor is *Nepal Fast Food* – connoisseurs of budget Indian fast food say this is one of the best.

Upstairs in Chungking Mansions are many other places with better food and a more pleasant atmosphere. Prices are still low, with set meals from HK$35 or so. Some good ones are:

Delhi Club, 3rd floor, the best in C Block

Kashmir Club, A Block, 3rd floor; highly rated and even offers free home delivery

Khyber Pass Club Mess, E Block, 7th floor; looks decent

Mumtaj Mahal Club, C Block, 12th floor
Nanak Mess, A Block, 11th floor, Flat A4
Royal Club Mess, D Block, 5th floor; Indian and vegetarian food
Taj Mahal Club Mess, B Block, 3rd floor; excellent

Vegetarian

Bodhi, Ground floor, 56 Cameron Rd, Tsimshatsui, is one of Hong Kong's biggest vegetarian restaurants with branches at 36 Jordan Rd, Yaumatei, and 1st floor, 32-34 Lock Rd (you can also enter at 81 Nathan Rd), Tsimshatsui. Dim sum is dished out from 11 am to 5 pm.

Also excellent is *Pak Bo Vegetarian Kitchen*, 106 Austin Rd, Tsimshatsui. Another to try is *Fat Siu Lam*, 2-3 Cheong Lok St, Yaumatei

Self-Catering

If you're looking for the best in cheese, bread and other imported delicacies, check out the delicatessen at *Oliver's* on the ground floor of Ocean Centre on Canton Rd. Another branch is on the ground floor of the Tung Ying Building, Granville Rd (at Nathan Rd).

A health food store with great bread and sandwiches is *Eden's Natural Synergy* (☎ 2368-0725), Ground floor, 28 Hillwood Rd, Tsimshatsui.

Numerous supermarkets are scattered about. A few to look for include:

Park'n Shop
South-west corner of Peking Rd & Kowloon Park Drive, Tsimshatsui
Basement Two, Silvercord Shopping Centre, Haiphong & Canton Rds, Tsimshatsui
Wellcome
Inside the Dairy Farm Creamery (ice-cream parlour), 74-78 Nathan Rd, Tsimshatsui
North-west corner of Granville and Carnarvon Rds, Tsimshatsui

HONG KONG ISLAND

The place to go for eats and late-night revelry is the neighbourhood known as *Lan Kwai Fong*. However, it's such a conglomeration of pubs and all-night parties that it's covered in the Entertainment section.

Breakfast

To save time and money, food windows adjacent to the Star Ferry Terminal open shortly after 6 am. They serve standard commuter breakfasts, consisting of bread, rolls and coffee, with no place to sit except on the ferry itself. As you face the ferry entrance, off to the right is a *Maxim's* fast-food outlet, which also has no seats.

Chinese – Dim Sum

All of the following places are in the middle to lower price range:

Luk Yu Tea House, 26 Stanley St, Central; dim sum served from 7 am to 6 pm
Tai Woo, 15-19 Wellington St, Central; dim sum served from 10 am to 5 pm
Zen Chinese Cuisine, Lower ground floor, The Mall, Pacific Place, 88 Queensway, Admiralty; dim sum served from 11.30 am to 3 pm

Fast Food

Domino's Pizza (☎ 2521-1300), 9 Glenealy, Central, has no restaurant facilities but delivers to any address within a two km radius.

Famous fast-food chains have the following outlets in Central:

Café de Coral, 10 Stanley St; 18 Jubilee St; and 88 Queen's Rd
Fairwood, Ananda Tower, 57-59 Connaught Rd
Hardee's, Grand Building, 15 Des Voeux Rd; and Regent Centre
KFC, 6 D'Aguilar St; and Pacific Place, 88 Queensway
Maxim's, Swire House, Connaught Rd & Pedder St
McDonald's, 38-44 D'Aguilar St; Basement, Yu To Sang Building, 37 Queen's Rd; Sanwa Building, 30-32 Connaught Rd; and Shop 124, Level One, The Mall, Pacific Place, 88 Queensway
Pizza Hut, B38, Basement One, Edinburgh Tower, The Landmark, 11 Queen's Rd

Indian

The ever-popular *Ashoka* is at 57 Wyndham St. Just next door, in the basement at 57 Wyndham St, is the excellent *Village Indian Restaurant*.

Greenlands, 64 Wellington St, is another superb Indian restaurant offering all-you-can-eat buffets.

Club Sri Lanka in the basement of 17 Hollywood Rd (almost at the Wyndham St end) has great Sri Lankan curries. Their fixed price all-you-can-eat deal is a bargain compared with most Hong Kong eateries.

Self-Catering

An excellent health food store is *Healthgate* (☎ 2545-2286), 8th floor, Hung Tak Building, 106 Des Voeux Rd, Central.

For imported delicacies, check out *Oliver's Super Sandwiches*, with three locations: Shop 104, Two Exchange Square, 8 Connaught Place; Shop 201-205, Prince's Building, Chater Rd & Ice House St; and Shop 8, Lower ground floor, The Mall, Pacific Place, 88 Queensway, Admiralty.

Entertainment

PUBS, BARS & DISCOS
Kowloon

Rick's Cafe (☎ 2367-2939), Basement, 4 Hart Ave, is popular with the backpacker set.

Jouster II (☎ 2723-0022), Shops A&B, Hart Ave Court, 19-23 Hart Ave, Tsimshatsui, is a fun multistorey place with wild decor. Normal hours are noon to 3 am except on Sundays, when it's from 6 pm to 2 am. Happy hour is anytime before 9 pm.

Ned Kelly's Last Stand (☎ 2376-0562), 11A Ashley Rd, open 11 am to 2 am, became famous as a real Australian pub complete with meat pies. Now it is known mainly for its Dixieland jazz and Aussie folk bands.

Amoeba Bar (☎ 2376-0389), 22 Ashley Rd, Tsimshatsui, has local new wave music live from around 9 pm and doesn't close until about 6 am.

The *Kangaroo Pub* (☎ 2312-0083), 1st & 2nd floors, 35 Haiphong Rd, Tsimshatsui, is an Aussie pub in the true tradition. This place does a good Sunday brunch.

Mad Dog's Pub (☎ 2301-2222), Basement, 32 Nathan Rd, is a popular Aussie-style pub. From Monday through Thursday it's open from 7 am until 2 am, but from Friday through Sunday it's 24 hour service.

The *Hard Rock Cafe* has two locations in Tsimshatsui – one at 100 Canton Rd and the other inside the Star Ferry Terminal.

Hong Kong Island

Lan Kwai Fong Running off D'Aguilar St in Central is a narrow L-shaped alley closed to cars. This is Lan Kwai Fong, and along with neighbouring streets and alleys is Hong Kong's No 1 eating, drinking, dancing and partying venue. Prices range from moderate to outrageous.

Club 64 (☎ 2523-2801), 12-14 Wing Wah Lane, D'Aguilar St, is an old favourite, although the authorities no longer permit customers to sit outdoors.

As you face the entrance of Club 64, off to your left are some stairs (outside the building, not inside). Follow them up to a terrace to find *Le Jardin Club* (☎ 2526-2717), 10 Wing Wah Lane. This is an excellent place to drink, relax and socialise.

Facing Club 64 again, look to your right to find *Bon Appetit* (☎ 2525-3553), a Vietnamese restaurant serving moderately priced meals.

While *glasnost* is already yesterday's buzzword, you can still find it at *Yelt's Inn* (☎ 2524-7796), 42 D'Aguilar St. This place boasts Russian vodka, a bubbly party atmosphere and extremely loud music.

If it's fine Lebanese food, beer and rock music you crave, what better place to find it than in *Beirut* (☎ 2804-6611)? It's at 27 D'Aguilar St.

If you prefer Europe to the Middle East, visit *Berlin* (☎ 2530-3093), 19 Lan Kwai Fong. This place features loud disco music with members of the audience invited to sing along – think of it as disco karaoke.

Post 97 (☎ 2810-9333), 9 Lan Kwai Fong, is a very comfortable eating and drinking spot. During the daytime it's more of a coffee shop where you can sit for hours to take advantage of the excellent rack of western magazines and newspapers. It can pack out at night, when the lights are dimmed to discourage reading.

Next door in the same building and under the same management is *1997* (☎ 2810-9333), known for really fine Mediterranean food. Prices are mid-range.

Graffiti (☎ 2521-2202), 17 Lan Kwai Fong, is a very posh and trendy restaurant and bar, but high drink prices don't seem to have hurt business.

The *California Entertainment Building* is at the corner of Lan Kwai Fong and D'Aguilar St. There are numerous places to eat here at varying price levels, but it tends to be upmarket. Note that the building has two blocks with two separate entrances, so if you don't find a place mentioned in this book be sure to check out the other block.

The *California* (☎ 2521-1345), in the California Entertainment Building, is perhaps the most expensive bar mentioned in this book. It's a restaurant by day, open from noon to 1 am, but there's disco dancing and a cover charge Wednesday through Sunday nights from 5 pm onwards.

The *Jazz Club* (☎ 2845-8477), 2nd floor, California Entertainment Building, has a great atmosphere. Bands playing blues and reggae are a feature here, as well as friendly management and customers. Beer is reasonable at HK$40 a pint, but a cover charge is tacked on for special performances – sometimes up to HK$250 (half-price for members).

DD II (☎ 2524-8809) is short for 'disco disco'. This trendy place is in the California Entertainment Building. It's open from 9.30 pm until 3.30 am.

The *Cactus Club* (☎ 2525-6732), 13 Lan Kwai Fong, does passable Mexican food. It seems like more of a pub than a restaurant, with top-grade beer and tequila imported from Mexico. Their mescal, brewed from the peyote cactus, is pretty strong stuff – it tastes like it still has the needles in it.

Schnurrbart (☎ 2523-4700) at 29 D'Aguilar St, Lan Kwai Fong, is a Bavarian-style pub. There are a couple of other German pubs on either side.

Central Just outside of Lan Kwai Fong is *Fringe Club* (☎ 2521-7251), 2 Lower Albert Rd. It's an excellent pub known for cheap beer and an avant-garde atmosphere. Live music is provided nightly by various local folk and rock musicians.

The legendary *Hard Rock Cafe* (☎ 2377-8168), Swire House, Connaught Rd & Pedder St, Central, does its happy hour from 3 to 7 pm.

The *Bull & Bear* (☎ 2525-7436), Ground floor, Hutchison House, 10 Harcourt Rd, Central, is a British-style pub and gets pretty lively in the evenings. It is open from 8 am to 10.30 am, and again from 11 am to midnight.

Wanchai Most of the action concentrates around the intersection of Luard and Jaffe Rds.

Joe Bananas (☎ 2529-1811), 23 Luard Rd, Wanchai, has become a trendy disco nightspot and has no admission charge, but you may have to queue to get in. Happy hour is from 11 am until 9 pm (except Sunday) and the place stays open until around 5 am.

Neptune Disco (☎ 2528-3808), Basement, 54-62 Lockhart Rd, is pure disco and heavy metal from 4 pm until 5 am. To say this place is popular is an understatement. To survive the night, spend the previous week doing aerobic exercises and bring your dancing shoes and ear plugs.

To accommodate the spillover crowd, there is now *Neptune Disco II* (☎ 2865-2238), 98-108 Jaffe Rd. This place has live bands and a weekend cover charge of HK$80.

New Makati (☎ 2866-3928) at 100 Lockhart Rd is a Filipino fun-rage party place which became an instant hit with westerners.

JJ's (☎ 2588-1234 ext 7323), Grand Hyatt Hotel, 1 Harbour Rd, Wanchai, is known for its rhythm & blues bands. There is a cover charge after 9 pm.

At 54 Jaffe Rd just west of Fenwick Rd is *The Wanch* (☎ 2861-1621). It stands in sharp contrast to the more usual Wanchai scene of hard rock and disco. This is a very pleasant little folk-music pub with beer and wine at low prices, but it can pack out.

SPECTATOR SPORTS

The Chinese aren't real big on rugby, but many expats are. The biggest match of the year – the Cathay Pacific-Hongkong Bank Seven-A-Side Rugby Tournament – is held in early March or late April.

Both Chinese and foreigners are soccer

enthusiasts. Regular matches are played at Hong Kong Stadium at So Kan Po, about 300 metres due east of the horse race track at Happy Valley, on Hong Kong Island.

Things to Buy

It's very easy in Hong Kong to decide suddenly that you need all sorts of consumer goods you don't really need at all. Try not to let the flashy stores tempt you into an uncontrollable buying binge. The fact is that Hong Kong is not all that cheap, although the great advantage of shopping here is that you can find anything you want in a compact area.

The HKTA advises tourists to shop where they see the HKTA red logo on display. This means that the shop is an 'ordinary member' of the HKTA. From our experience, many of the 'ordinary members' charge high prices for rude service, while many non-members are quite all right.

The worst neighbourhood for shopping happens to be the place where most tourists shop. Tsimshatsui, the tourist ghetto of Kowloon, is where you are most likely to be cheated. Notice that none of the cameras or other big ticket items have price tags. This is *not* common practice elsewhere in Hong Kong. If you go out to the Chinese neighbourhoods where the locals shop, you'll find price tags on everything.

Clothing is the best buy in Hong Kong. All the cheap stuff comes from China and most is decent quality, but check zippers and stitching carefully – there is some real junk around. You'll find the cheapest buys at the street markets at Tong Choi St in Mongkok and Apliu St in Shamshuipo. Another good place for cut-rate clothes is the mezzanine floor of Chungking Mansions (not the ground floor). Better quality stuff is found in Tsimshatsui on the eastern end of Granville Rd. Two Chinese chain stores with Italian names, Giordano's and Bossini, offer quality clothing at reasonable prices.

Yue Hwa Chinese Products at 301 Nathan Rd, Yaumatei (corner of Nathan and Jordan Rds) is a good place to pick up everyday consumer goods. It's also one of the best places to get eyeglasses made.

The Golden Shopping Centre, Basement, 146-152 Fuk Wah St, Shamshuipo, has the cheapest collection of desktop computers – be sure to check out the adjacent annex. Another good place to explore is Mongkok Computer Centre at Nelson and Fa Yuen Sts in Mongkok. For laptop computers, the best shopping centre in Kowloon is Star Computer City in Ocean Terminal, Tsimshatsui. On Hong Kong Island, the main computer centre is Hong Kong Cumputer Centre at 298 Hennessy Rd.

If it's a camera you need, don't even waste your time on Nathan Rd in Tsimshatsui. Photo Scientific (☎ 2522-1903), 6 Stanley St, Central, is the favourite of Hong Kong's resident professional photographers. But if you're in a hurry and want to buy in Tsimshatsui, the best seems to be Kimberley Camera Company (☎ 2721-2308), Champagne Court, 16 Kimberley Rd.

Apliu St in Shamshuipo has the best collection of electronics shops selling Walkmans, CD players and the like.

HMV (☎ 2302-0122) at 12 Peking Rd in Tsimshatsui has the largest collection of CDs in Hong Kong, and prices are reasonable. There is another branch on the 10th floor of Windsor House, Great George St, Causeway Bay. KPS is also a good chain store for discounted CDs and tapes. There are branches around the city – most convenient is the shop in the basement of the Silvercord Shopping Centre at Haiphong & Canton Rds in Tsimshatsui. Tower Records (☎ 2506-0811), 7th floor, Shop 701, Times Square, Matheson St, Causeway Bay, also has a good CD collection.

Flying Ball Bicycle Shop (☎ 2381-5919), 201 Tung Choi St (near Prince Edward MTR station), Mongkok, is the best bike shop in Asia.

Hong Kong is a good place to pick up a decent backpack, sleeping bag, tent and other gear for hiking, camping and travelling. Mongkok is by far the best neighbourhood to look for this stuff, though there are a couple of odd places in nearby Yaumatei. Some places worth checking out include:

Grade VI Alpine Equipment
  115 Woosung St, Yaumatei (☎ 2782-0202)
Mountaineer Supermarket
  395 Portland St, Mongkok (☎ 2397-0585)
Rose Sports Goods
  39 Fa Yuen St, Mongkok (☎ 2781-1809)
Tang Fai Kee Military
  248 Reclamation St, Mongkok (☎ 2385-5169)
Three Military Equipment Company
  83 Sai Yee St, Mongkok (☎ 2395-5234)

Hong Kong is one of the best places in Asia to pick up books in English, though this may change in the post-1997 era if China imposes

heavy-handed censorship. Until then, it's worth checking the following shops:

Cosmos Books Ltd
  30 Johnston Rd, Wanchai (☎ 2528-3605)
Government Publications Centre
  Government Offices Building, Queensway, Admiralty
South China Morning Post Bookshop
  Star Ferry Terminal, Central
Swindon Books
  13 Lock Rd, Tsimshatsui
Times Books
  Basement, Golden Crown Court, corner Carnarvon & Nathan Rds, Tsimshatsui

Finally, if you want to see a good shopping mall where the locals go, visit Cityplaza in Quarry Bay. Take the MTR to the Tai Koo station.

Indonesia

Indonesia is a long chain of tropical islands offering a mixture of cultures, people, scenery, prospects, problems and aspirations unmatched in South-East Asia. For the budget traveller, Indonesia is a kaleidoscope of cheap food, adventurous travel and every sort of attraction – the tropical paradise of Bali, the untouched wilderness of Sumatra, the historical monuments of Yogyakarta, with the overcrowding of Jakarta thrown in to leaven the mix.

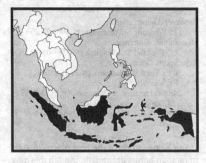

Facts about Indonesia

HISTORY

The earliest inhabitants of the Indonesian Archipelago date back to *Pithecanthropus erectus*, or Java Man, one of the earliest human ancestors that migrated via land bridges to Java at least half a million years ago. The people of Indonesia today are of Malay origin, closely related to the peoples of Malaysia and the Philippines, and are descendants of much later migrations from South-East Asia that began around 4000 BC.

Trade brought Hinduism and Buddhism from India as early as the 4th century AD and by the end of the 7th century, small trading posts had grown to become powerful kingdoms in Java and Sumatra. The Buddhist Sriwijaya Empire ruled southern Sumatra and much of the Malay peninsula for six centuries while the Hindu Mataram kingdom presided over Central Java. The two developed side by side as both rivals and partners and Mataram went on to raise inspiring monuments like Borobudur.

Mataram mysteriously declined and power shifted to East Java, where the Majapahit Empire rose to become the last great Hindu kingdom. Founded in the 13th century, it reached its peak under Prime Minister Gajah Mada and ruled Java, Bali and the island of Madura, off Java's north coast, although it

also claimed suzerainty over a vast area of the archipelago.

The spread of Islam into the archipelago spelt the end of the Majapahits – satellite kingdoms took on the new religion and declared themselves independent of the Majapahits. But by the time Islam reached Java, it was less orthodox than in the Middle East and became infused with Javanese mysticism. The Majapahits retreated to Bali in the 15th century to found a flourishing culture while Java split into separate sultanates.

By the 15th century, a strong Muslim empire had developed with its centre at Melaka (Malacca) on the Malay peninsula, but in 1511 it fell to the Portuguese and the period of European influence in the archipelago began. The Portuguese were soon displaced by the Dutch, who began to take over Indonesia in the early 1600s. A British attempt to oust the Dutch in 1619 failed – Melaka fell to the Dutch in 1641 and by 1700 they dominated most of Indonesia by virtue of their supremacy at sea and their control of the trade routes and some important ports. By the middle of the 18th century, all of Java was under their control.

The Napoleonic Wars led to a temporary British takeover between 1811 and 1816 in response to the French occupation of Holland and Java came under the command of Sir Stamford Raffles. Indonesia was eventually handed back to the Dutch after the cessation of the wars, and an agreement made whereby the English evacuated their settlements in Indonesia in return for the Dutch leaving India and the Malay peninsula.

While the Europeans may have settled their differences, the Indonesians were of a different mind – for five years from 1825 onwards the Dutch had to put down a revolt led by the Javanese Prince Diponegoro. It was not until the early 20th century that the Dutch brought the whole of the archipelago – including Aceh and Bali – under control.

Although Dutch rule softened, dissatisfaction still simmered and a strong nationalist movement – whose foremost leader was Soekarno – developed despite Dutch attempts to suppress it. The Japanese occupied the archipelago during WWII. After their defeat, Soekarno declared independence on 17 August 1945, but the Dutch returned and tried to take back control of their old territories. For four bitter years up to 1949, the Indonesians fought an intermittent war with the Dutch, who in the end were forced to recognise Indonesia's independence.

Weakened by the prolonged struggle, the transition to independence did not come easily. The first 10 years of independence saw Indonesian politicians preoccupied with their own political games until, in 1957, President Soekarno put an end to the impasse by declaring Guided Democracy with army backing and investing more power in himself. Soekarno proved to be less adept as a nation builder than as a revolutionary leader. Grandiose building projects, the planned 'socialisation' of the economy and the senseless Confrontation with Malaysia led to internal dissension and a steady deterioration of the national economy.

As events came to a head, there was an attempted coup in 1965 led by an officer of Soekarno's palace guard, and six of Indonesia's top army generals were killed. The coup was suppressed by the Indonesian army under the leadership of General Soeharto. The reasons for the coup are unclear but it was passed off as an attempt by the Communists to seize power and hundreds of thousands of Communists, suspected Communists and sympathisers were killed or imprisoned. Soeharto eventually pushed Soekarno out of power and took over the presidency. In stark contrast to the turbulent Soekarno years,

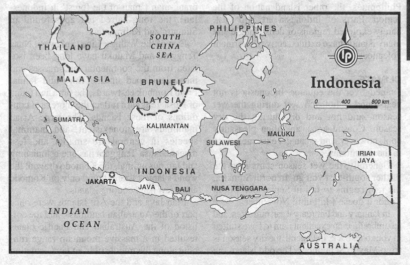

things have, on the whole, been more stable under Soeharto.

The invasion of Portuguese Timor, in 1975, stands as much to the world's discredit as Indonesia's, and it was surely no coincidence that then US secretary of state, Henry Kissinger, left Jakarta the day before the invasion. Recently, Indonesia has shown signs of coming to grips with its internal economic problems and some of the worse excesses have been curbed, though the Dili massacre in 1991 severely embarrassed Indonesia's international standing.

For many years the economy relied on large oil exports and other substantial natural resources. Despite graft and corruption being very much a way of life, the economy is growing dramatically with new foreign investment and industrialisation. The main political question facing Indonesia is who will succeed the aging Soeharto and what changes will eventuate. Despite growing calls for democracy, the armed forces remain a major political force.

GEOGRAPHY

Indonesia has an area of 1.9 million sq km scattered over about 13,700 islands. It is a far less compact mass of islands than the nearby Philippines, the other island nation of the region. Parts of Indonesia are still vast, barely explored regions of dense jungle and many islands have extinct, active or dormant volcanoes.

CLIMATE

Draped over the equator, Indonesia is hot year-round – hot and wet during the wet season, and hot and dry during the dry season. Coastal areas are often pleasantly cool, however, and it can get extremely cold in the mountains.

Generally, the wet season starts later the further south-east you go. In north Sumatra, the rain begins to fall in September, but in Timor it doesn't fall until November.

In January and February it can rain often, and an umbrella is an excellent item to have stuffed in your backpack. In general, the dry season is from May to September. The odd islands out are those of Maluku (the Moluccas), where the wet season is from May to September.

See the regional sections in this chapter and the Jakarta climate chart in the Appendix for more details.

FLORA & FAUNA

Indonesia has one of the world's richest natural environments, harbouring an incredible diversity of plant and animal species. The British naturalist Alfred Wallace first classified the Indonesian islands into two zones: a western, Asian ecological zone and an eastern, Australian zone. The 'Wallace Line' dividing these two zones runs between Kalimantan and Sulawesi and south through the straits between Bali and Lombok. Later scientists have further expanded on this classification to show distinct breaks between the ecologies of Sulawesi and Maluku, and further between Maluku and Irian Jaya.

West of the Wallace Line, Sumatra, Java, Kalimantan and Bali were once linked to the Asian mainland, and as a result some large Asian land animals, including elephants, tigers, rhinoceroses and leopards, still survive in some areas, and the dense rainforests and abundant flora of Asia are in evidence. Perhaps the most famous animal is the orang-utan ('man of the forest' in Indonesian), the long-haired red apes found in Sumatra and Kalimantan.

East of the Wallace Line, Sulawesi, Nusa Tenggara and Maluku have long been isolated from the continental land masses and have developed unique flora and fauna. From Lombok eastwards, the flora and fauna of Nusa Tenggara reflect the more arid conditions of these islands. The large Asian mammals are nonexistent, and mammal species in general are smaller and less diverse. Nusa Tenggara has one astonishing and famous animal, the Komodo dragon, the world's largest lizard, found only on Komodo and a few neighbouring islands.

Irian Jaya and the Aru Islands were once part of the Australian landmass, and the collision of the Australian and Pacific plates resulted in a massive mountain range running along the middle of Irian Jaya, isolating a number of unique environments, although the fauna throughout is closely related to Australia. Irian Jaya has kangaroos, marsupial mice, bandicoots, ring-tailed possums, crocodiles and frilled lizards – all marsupials found in Australia.

GOVERNMENT & POLITICS

Executive power rests with the president. Officially, the highest authority lies with the People's Consultative Congress (MPR), which elects the president every five years. The congress is made up of all members of the elected House of Representatives (which rarely meets), and presidential appointees from various interest groups, most notably the armed forces. Real power lies with the ruling party, Golkar, where the army is a major player, while the real business of government is handled by the president and ministers appointed by and responsible only to the president.

Democracy is largely a veneer, and the only opposition political parties allowed are the Muslim United Development Party (PPP) and the Indonesian Democratic Party (PDI). The PDI, led by Soekarno's daughter, Megawati Soekarnoputri, has growing popular support and is the focus for democratic aspirations. So much so, that the government sponsored a split in the party by promoting alternative leadership, resulting in riots in Jakarta in 1996 and threats of greater crackdowns on the nascent democracy movement.

The state philosophy is Pancasila (Five Principles), the sole philosophical base for all political, social and religious organisations. The five principles are Faith in God, Humanity, Nationalism, Representative Government and Social Justice. Though it has been used as an excuse for government authoritarianism, it also ensures religious and social tolerance in multi-ethnic Indonesia.

ECONOMY

With foreign-investment approvals averaging around US$1 billion per week, Indonesia's industrial base is rapidly growing and the economy is booming. Indonesia also has good oil reserves and large mineral resources, but while the lot of the average Indonesian is gradually improving, life is still very hard for the majority and average per capita income is only US$650 per year.

The country has a conspicuously wealthy elite, particularly in the main cities of Java where most of the new investment is flooding in, but most Indonesians still survive in a rural subsistence economy. Widespread corruption and inefficiency are ever present, and the problems of overpopulation and the strain on resources remain the greatest stumbling blocks to development.

POPULATION & PEOPLE

Indonesia is the fourth most populous country in the world. The population is just under 200 million and fully 60% are crammed into just 7% of the nation's land area – the island of Java. The people are of the Malay race, although there are many different groupings and a vast number of local dialects. There are distinct cultural differences between islands, and even within islands, making Indonesia the most culturally diverse nation in South-East Asia.

SOCIETY & CONDUCT

Indonesia has a diverse mix of cultures rather than a single one, but the effects of mass education, mass media and a policy of government-orchestrated nationalism have created a very definite Indonesian national culture.

'Keeping face' is important to Indonesians and they are generally extremely courteous – criticisms are not spoken directly and they will usually agree with what you say rather than offend.

Indonesians will accept any lack of clothing on the part of poor people who cannot afford them; but for westerners, thongs (flip-flops), bathing costumes, shorts or strapless tops are considered impolite except perhaps around places like Kuta in Bali. Elsewhere you have to look vaguely respectable. Women are better off dressing modestly – revealing tops are just asking for trouble. Short pants are marginally acceptable if they

INDONESIA

are the baggy type which almost reach the knees.

Permission should be requested to enter places of worship, particularly when ceremonies are in progress. Dress decently, and always remove footwear before entering a mosque. It is also customary to take shoes off before entering someone's house.

Asians resent being touched on the head, which is regarded as the seat of the soul and is therefore sacred.

When handing over or receiving things remember to use the right hand – the left hand is used as a substitute for toilet paper. To show great respect to a high-ranking or elderly person, hand something to them using both hands. Talking to someone with your hands on your hips is impolite and is considered a sign of contempt, anger or aggressiveness. Handshaking is customary for both men and women on introduction and greeting.

RELIGION

Nominally a Muslim nation, there is actually an amazing diversity of religions and a commendable degree of religious tolerance in Indonesia. From the time of the Dutch, pockets of Christianity have continued to exist on the islands of Timor and Flores, and in the Lake Toba region of north Sumatra and the Tanatoraja area of Sulawesi. At one time, Sumatra was predominantly Buddhist and Java was predominantly Hindu – this was before the spread of Islam and its eventual dominance of the region. The last remnants of Hinduism are found in Bali, though much of Muslim Java still follows Hindu tradition and thought.

LANGUAGE

Although there are a vast number of local languages and dialects in the country, Bahasa Indonesia, which is all but identical to Malay, is promoted as the one national language.

Like most languages, Indonesian has its simplified colloquial form and its more developed literate language. Indonesian is rated as one of the simplest languages in the world as there are no tenses or genders, and often one word can convey the meaning of a whole sentence. There are often no plurals, or it is only necessary to say the word twice – child is *anak*, and children are *anak anak*. Book is *buku* and books are *buku buku*. With other words, the context makes it clear that it's plural.

Indonesian can also be a delightfully poetic language with words like *matahari*, or 'sun', derived from *mata* (eye) and *hari* (day), so the sun is literally the eye of the day.

Lonely Planet's *Indonesian phrasebook* is a pocket-sized introduction to the language, intended to make getting by in Bahasa as easy as possible.

Basics

Good morning.	*Selamat pagi.*
Good day.	*Selamat siang.*
Good afternoon/ evening.	*Selamat sore.*
Good night.	*Selamat malam.*
Goodbye. (to person staying)	*Selamat tinggal.*
Goodbye. (to person going)	*Selamat jalan.*
How are you?	*Apa kabar?*
I'm fine.	*Kabar baik.*
Please.	*Silahkan.*
Thank you (very much).	*Terima kasih (banyak).*
Yes.	*Ya.*
No.	*Tidak.*
Excuse me.	*Maaf.*
I don't understand.	*Saya tidak mengerti.*
How much (price)?	*Berapa (harga)?*
expensive	*mahal*
What is this?	*Apa ini?*

Getting Around

How far?	*Berapa jauh?*
bus	*bis*
ship	*kapal*
train	*kereta api*
bus station	*setasiun bis/terminal*
ticket	*karcis*

I want to go to ...
 Saya mau pergi ke ...

What time does the ... leave/arrive?
Jam berapa ... berangkat/tiba?

Accommodation

guesthouse	*losmen*
bathroom	*kamar mandi*
key	*kunci*
bed	*tempat tidur*
toilet	*WC (way say)*
	/kamar kecil

Is there a room available?
Adakah kamar kosong?
Can I see the room?
Boleh saya melihat kamar?
one night/two nights
satu malam/dua malam

Around Town

Where is ...?	*Dimana ...?*
bank	*bank*
post office	*kantor pos*
tourist office	*dinas pariwisata*
here/there	*disini/disana*
left/right	*kiri/kanan*
near/far	*dekat/jauh*
straight ahead	*terus*

Time

When?	*Kapan?*
At what time ...?	*Jam berapa ...?*
open/close	*buka/tutup*
today	*hari ini*
tonight	*nanti malam*
tomorrow	*besok*
yesterday	*kemarin*

Numbers

½	*setengah*
1	*satu*
2	*dua*
3	*tiga*
4	*empat*
5	*lima*
6	*enam*
7	*tujuh*
8	*delapan*
9	*sembilan*
10	*sepuluh*

12	*duabelas*
20	*duapuluh*
21	*duapuluh satu*
30	*tigapuluh*
50	*limapuluh*
100	*seratus*
1000	*seribu*

Emergencies

Help!	*Tolong!*
doctor	*dokter*
police	*polisi*

Facts for the Visitor

PLANNING

When to Go

Though travel in the wet season is possible in most parts of Indonesia, it can be a definite deterrent to some activities and travel on mud-clogged roads in less developed areas is difficult. In general, the best time to visit Indonesia is in the dry season between May and September.

Maps

Locally produced maps are often surprisingly inaccurate. The Nelles Verlag map series covers Indonesia in a number of separate sheets, and they're usually quite good. Periplus also produces excellent maps to most of the archipelago and includes maps of the major cities. Both series are available in Indonesia and overseas.

HIGHLIGHTS

The most visited islands tend to be Sumatra, Java and Bali, and it is possible to see the main highlights of these three islands in one month, but that doesn't leave much time for relaxation.

Sumatra's main attractions are in the north between Medan and Padang. Spectacular Lake Toba is on most itineraries, and the Bukit Lawang orang-utan sanctuary is easily reached from Medan. The mountain town of Bukittinggi is the cultural heartland of the Minangkabau people and one of the main

INDONESIA

travellers' centres. Nias also gets a lot of visitors, drawn by both the ancient megalithic cultures and the surf.

In Java, the cultural city of Yogyakarta is the number one travellers' centre and a good base for exploring the awe-inspiring monuments of Borobudur and Prambanan. Nearby Solo is a quieter court city and repository of Javanese culture. Pangandaran is Java's beach resort, while the Gunung Bromo area is one of Indonesia's most spectacular volcanic landscapes. The big cities tend to be crowded and disorienting, but Bogor and Bandung have reminders of the Dutch presence. The bustling and increasingly modern capital of Jakarta still has the finest remnants of the Dutch era.

Bali has brilliant green terraced landscapes, fascinating Hindu culture and excellent facilities. Spectacular temples like Ulu Watu, Rambut Siwi and touristy Tanah Lot perch on cliffs over the sea, while hundreds of others come alive during colourful temple festivals. Kuta is Bali's most famous beach scene, but other resorts, such as Lovina, Candidasa and Sanur, also offer sun, sea, surf, snorkelling and/or socialising. Strange stone figures at Gunung Kawi date from the 11th century, while contemporary culture is best experienced at Ubud, where modern painting and carving thrive, along with traditional music and dance and the island's finest cuisine. Trekkers are attracted to the smoking caldera of Gunung Batur, with 3142 metre Gunung Agung an even bigger challenge.

Other Indonesian islands are not so inaccessible these days, though travel costs are often higher because flying becomes essential unless you have huge amounts of time. Nusa Tenggara and Sulawesi are easier to explore, while Maluku, Irian Jaya and Kalimantan are still unexplored territory for the vast majority of visitors to Indonesia but have plenty to offer.

Nusa Tenggara's main destination is Lombok, which gets a lot of the Bali overflow attracted by fine beaches, towering Gunung Rinjani and a more relaxed approach to tourism. The two most famous attractions of Nusa Tenggara are the fabulous dragons of Komodo and the spectacular coloured lakes of Keli Mutu on Flores. Scenic Flores also has traditional cultures to explore around Bajawa and decent beaches at Labuanbajo for relaxing. The island of Sumba has fascinating megalithic cultures, and Timor is as wild and as traditional as they come. Numerous other islands, volcanoes, beaches and some of the best diving in Indonesia can be found in Nusa Tenggara.

The colourful funerals of Tanatoraja are Sulawesi's best known attraction from June to August. The mountains of Tanatoraja are serenely beautiful, as are those of Central Sulawesi. Many hikers are venturing further afield to enjoy the island's natural beauty, as well as the unusual megaliths of the Bada Valley, south of Palu, and the unique wildlife of Sulawesi's many national parks. Sulawesi also has some superb beaches and coral reefs. The 'sea gardens' off Manado, particularly around Pulau Bunaken, offer some of the best snorkelling and diving in Indonesia, while the pristine reefs around the Togian Islands are an untouched tropical wonder.

The islands of Maluku are known for great beaches, diving and old forts. The main island of Ambon makes a good base and has beaches, hiking, diving and a superbly renovated fort. Nearby Saparua has tempting beaches and a fort, and undeveloped Seram has wonderful scenery, tough trekking and traditional cultures. To the north, Ternate has stunning volcanic scenery, black-sand beaches and even more forts. Close by, Halmahera has unspoiled beaches, crumbling forts, trekking, diving and WWII remnants. The highlight of Maluku, the Bandas, has it all: magnificent forts, the awesome Gunung Api volcano, and great diving and swimming. Further south, the Kai Islands have arguably the best beaches east of Bali.

The Baliem Valley, with its unique culture and trekking among stunning scenery, is the major tourist attraction in Irian Jaya. The other accessible traditional area, the Asmat region, is difficult and expensive to explore. Along the northern coast, Manokwari and Nabire are pleasant towns with a few islands and lakes to explore. Biak is a popular stopover with plenty of great diving spots, beaches and WWII remnants to explore around the island. Sentani, a better alternative to nearby Jayapura, is the place to explore the magnificent Sentani lake. Along the south coast, the delightful colonial town of Fak Fak is worth a detour.

Kalimantan is one of the least visited parts of Indonesia, mostly because its unique cultures, spectacular flora and unusual wildlife are well away from the ravages of development, and are expensive and time-consuming to reach. Balikpapan and its river life is the main tourist destination and a good place to start exploring this vast island. The orangutan rehabilitation centres are world-class attractions. The remote Kayan and Kenyah settlements in the Apokayan are worth a visit.

TOURIST OFFICES

The National Tourist Organisation of Indonesia produces a *Calendar of Events* for the entire country and a useful *Indonesia Travel Planner* book, which includes some good maps and helpful travel information. They're available from the Directorate General of Tourism office in Jakarta and at tourist offices overseas.

Otherwise, Indonesian tourist offices are generally poor, and often have limited or no literature or maps. The usefulness of individual tourist offices often depends on who works there and who you get to talk to.

Some of the regional tourist offices produce local information, or useful items such as festival calendars. Denpasar in Bali, and Jakarta, Bandung, Yogyakarta and Solo in Java have good tourist offices. Other good regional offices can be found in Bukittinggi and Padang in Sumatra, and Mataram in Lombok. There's also an excellent independent tourist office in Ubud in Bali. Outside of these areas, it often isn't worth the effort.

VISAS & DOCUMENTS

Visitors from most western countries can enter Indonesia without a visa, for a stay of up to 60 days, so long as they enter and exit through certain recognised airports or seaports. Officially (but not always in practice), you must have a ticket out of the country when you arrive. Officially (and almost certainly), you cannot extend your visa beyond 60 days. If you really intend to explore Indonesia in some depth, then 60 days is inadequate and you will have to exit the country and re-enter.

One possibility is to start from north Sumatra and travel down to Pekanbaru, then exit via Batam to Singapore for rest and refreshment. From there, you can start with a fresh 60 days and continue to Java and Bali, which still leaves Nusa Tenggara and the outer islands to worry about!

The 'ticket out' requirement seems to be less strictly enforced these days, and evidence of sufficient funds is sometimes acceptable in lieu – US$1000 seems to be the magic number. If you don't have it, dress as if you do; otherwise say you are only making a short visit – a 60 day entry permit is standard regardless of the length of stay. If you fly to Kupang (in Timor) from Darwin, Australia, or take the ferry to Batam from Singapore, it's unlikely that any great fuss will be made. In Kupang, they may ask to see a wad of travellers' cheques, but Batam is a breeze. Expect to flash your cash if arriving in Medan (in Sumatra) on the ferry from Penang (in Malaysia).

In Bali they may still ask to see a ticket but most Bali visitors are on short-stay package trips, so you're unlikely to be troubled. Jakarta can be a hassle. Some visitors have been forced to buy an onward ticket on the spot. The main problem is likely to be with airlines overseas, who may strictly enforce official requirements and not let you on flights to Indonesia without an onward ticket.

If you want a simple solution, the Malaysia Airlines flight between Medan and Penang is straightforward, reasonably cheap and can be refunded if you don't use it. The various flights between Jakarta and Singapore are also safe and cheap bets. See Getting There & Away later in this chapter for other short-hop international flights.

INDONESIA

The real problem with the visa-free entry system is for that tiny minority of travellers who plan to arrive or depart through an unrecognised 'gateway', such as Jayapura in Irian Jaya. If you fall into that category you have to get an Indonesian tourist visa before arriving, and visas are only valid for one month. Extensions on a one month visa are usually only for two weeks and cost around 50,000 rp.

The Indonesian government's list of recognised 'no visa' entry and exit points are the airports of Ambon, Bali, Balikpapan, Bandung, Batam, Biak, Jakarta, Manado, Mataram, Medan, Padang, Pekanbaru, Pontianak and Surabaya, and the seaports of Ambon, Batam, Belawan, Benoa, Jakarta, Padang Bai, Semarang, Surabaya, Tanjung Pinang and Manado. The only 'no visa' land crossing is at Entikong in West Kalimantan, between Pontianak and Kuching. The official list is rarely updated and does change, so if you're planning an odd entry or exit find out the latest story. Entering by air on a regular flight is usually not a problem, and the airline will be better informed than an Indonesian embassy. Entering or leaving Indonesia overland or by unusual sea routes usually requires a visa.

Finally, check your passport expiry date. Indonesia requires that your passport has six months of life left in it on your date of arrival.

EMBASSIES
Indonesian Embassies
Indonesian embassies include:

Australia
    8 Darwin Ave, Yarralumla, Canberra ACT 2600
    (☎ (06) 273-3222)
Canada
    287 Maclaren St, Ottawa, Ontario K2P OL9
    (☎ (613) 236-7403)
France
    47-49 Rue Cortambert, Paris 75116
    (☎ 01 45 03 07 60)
Germany
    2 Bernakasteler Strasse, 53175 Bonn
    (☎ (0228) 382-990)
India
    50A Chanakyapuri, New Delhi
    (☎ (011) 602348)

Japan
    5-9-2 Nighashi Qotanda, Shinagawa-ku, Tokyo
    (☎ (03) 3441-4201)
Netherlands
    8 Tobias Asserlaan, 2517 KC The Hague
    (☎ (70) 310-8100)
New Zealand
    70 Glen Rd, Kelburn, Wellington
    (☎ (04) 475 8697)
UK
    38 Grosvenor Square, London W1X 9AD
    (☎ (0171) 499-7661)
USA
    2020 Massachussetts Ave NW, Washington, DC
    20036 (☎ (202) 775-5200)

See the other chapters in this book for Indonesian embassies in those countries.

Foreign Embassies
Some of the foreign embassies in Jakarta include:

Australia
    Jalan Rasuna Said Kav C/15-16 (☎ 522-7111)
Brunei
    8th floor, Bank of Central Asia Building, Jalan
    Jenderal Sudirman Kav 22-23 (☎ 571-2180)
Cambodia
    4th floor, Panin Bank Plaza, 52 Palmerah Utara
    (☎ 548-3684)
India
    Jalan Rasuna Said S-1, Kuningan (☎ 520-4150)
Malaysia
    Jalan Rasuna Said Kav X/6/1 (☎ 522-4947)
Myanmar
    Jalan H Augus Salim 109 (☎ 314-0440)
Papua New Guinea
    6th floor, Panin Bank Centre, Jalan Jenderal
    Sudirman No 1 (☎ 712-5218)
Philippines
    Jalan Imam Bonjol 6-8 (☎ 314-9329)
Thailand
    Jalan Imam Bonjol 74 (☎ 390-4055)
Vietnam
    Jalan Teuku Umar 25 (☎ 310-0357)

CUSTOMS
Customs allows you to bring in a maximum of two litres of alcoholic beverages and 200 cigarettes or 50 cigars or 100 grams of tobacco. Bringing narcotics, arms and ammunition, cordless telephones, pornography, printed matter in Chinese characters and Chinese medicines into the country is prohibited.

Officially, cameras, computers, radios and the like should be declared upon arrival, but in effect customs officials rarely worry about how much gear tourists bring into the country – at least if you have a western face. Personal effects are not a problem.

MONEY
Costs

Indonesian costs are variable, depending on where you go. If you follow the well-beaten tourist track through Bali, Java and Sumatra, you may well find Indonesia one of the cheapest places in the region. Travellers' centres like Lake Toba, Yogyakarta and Bali are superb value for accommodation and food. Elsewhere transport costs rise, budget accommodation can be limited and prices are higher because competition is less. Sulawesi and Nusa Tenggara are cheap enough, but accommodation in Maluku and Irian Jaya can be two to three times higher, and transport costs in Kalimantan are high.

Fuel is cheap in Indonesia, so transport costs are also pleasantly low, particularly if you've got your own motorbike to travel around on. Fuel prices are pretty much the same throughout the country, and only in remote places (like the interior of Irian Jaya and Kalimantan) do prices skyrocket.

Credit Cards

Credit cards are accepted at big hotels, exclusive restaurants and shops. They are of limited use if travelling on a budget, but airline offices in the larger cities accept them and cash advances can be obtained over the counter at many banks in the main cities. Don't rely on them for cash in the more remote regions – in Java and Bali plenty of banks accept them, but elsewhere you may have to go to the provincial capital. Cash and travellers' cheques are far more convenient. In Bali and Java, Bank Bali and Lippobank offer cash advances through ATMs for MasterCard only.

Currency

The Indonesian rupiah is a floating currency, which steadily devalues against the US

dollar at about 3% per year. Many of the more expensive hotels in tourist areas quote prices in US dollars.

Currency Exchange

The official exchange rates are as follows:

Australia	A$1	=	1834 rp
Canada	C$1	=	1702 rp
France	FF10	=	4500 rp
Germany	DM1	=	1521 rp
Japan	¥100	=	2092 rp
Malaysia	M$1	=	925 rp
New Zealand	NZ$1	=	1621 rp
Singapore	S$1	=	1648 rp
UK	UK£1	=	3625 rp
USA	US$1	=	2319 rp

Changing Money

US dollars are easily the most widely accepted foreign currency and often have a better exchange rate than other currencies – this is especially so outside of Jakarta and the major tourist areas. If you're going to be in really remote regions, carry sufficient cash with you as banks may be scarce. Even those you do come across may only accept certain varieties of travellers' cheques – stick to the major companies. Dutch travellers can cash their giros (girobetaalkaarten) at all major post offices.

Exchange rates tend to vary a bit from bank to bank, so shop around. The rates also vary between cities. Jakarta and Bali have the best rates in Indonesia. Other main tourist destinations, such as Yogyakarta, and large regional cities have good rates but in some remote regions, the rate can be terrible or there may be no banks at all!

There are moneychangers in many locales and they're open longer hours and change money (cash or cheques) much faster than the banks. In places like Bali, they offer extremely competitive rates.

Tipping & Bargaining

Tipping is not a normal practice in Indonesia but is often expected for special service. Someone who carries your bag, guides you around a tourist attraction etc will naturally expect a tip.

INDONESIA

Bargaining is required in markets, for souvenirs and any tourist-oriented goods and for transport where prices are not fixed. It may even be required for everyday items, such as a bottle of water or a packet of cigarettes, especially from street hawkers in tourist areas such as Bali. Hotel prices are usually fixed but asking for a discount might bring a reduction, especially at the upper-end hotels.

Bargaining is a complex social game that Indonesians love to play well, and a necessary survival skill in a poor country. As with any social interaction, it is important to maintain equanimity. Remain good-humoured – shouting or aggressiveness will force the trader to lose face and push prices up. Above all, keep things in perspective. The 500 rp you may overpay for a *becak* (bicycle rickshaw) ride wouldn't buy a newspaper at home, but it is a meal for a poor becak driver.

POST & COMMUNICATIONS

The postal service in Indonesia is generally good and the poste restante service at Indonesian *kantor pos* (post offices) are reasonably efficient in the main tourist centres. Expected mail always seems to arrive, eventually.

Overseas parcels can be posted, insured and registered *(tercatat)* from a main post office but they'll usually want to have a look at the contents first, so there's not much point in making up a tidy parcel before you get there. If you are going on to Singapore, the postal service is more reliable and cheaper from there.

International calls are easy to make from private booths in Telkom offices and privately run Wartel (Warung Telekomunikasi). Reverse-charge calls can be made from Telkom offices free of charge, though private wartels usually charge for the first minute or don't offer the service at all. Many Telkom offices also have Direct Home Phones (press one button to get through to your home country operator) and they can also be found in international terminals at major airports and some big hotels.

Telkom offices usually have card phones outside where you can directly dial overseas calls, and a few big hotels have card phones in the lobby that offer this service. Otherwise, international calls cannot be made from public phones.

Local directory assistance is 108. The police emergency number is 110.

The international direct-dialling (IDD) code is 001.

To call Indonesia from outside the country, the country code is 62.

BOOKS

For more detailed information on Indonesia, look for the Lonely Planet guidebooks to *Indonesia*, *Bali & Lombok*, *Java* and *Jakarta*.

One of the better travelogues is *In Search of Conrad* by Gavin Young, who retraces Joseph Conrad's journeys by boat around Sumatra, Java, Kalimantan, Bali and Sulawesi. Or read Conrad's *Victory*, which is set in Indonesia.

Pramoedya Ananta Toer is Indonesia's most well known novelist and was jailed for criticism of the government. His famous quartet of novels set in the colonial era is *This Earth of Mankind*, *Child of All Nations*, *Footsteps* and *House of Glass*. Mochtar Lubis is another well-known Indonesian writer. His novel *Twilight in Djakarta* attacks corruption and the plight of the poor in Jakarta in the 1950s.

An excellent general history is *A History of Modern Indonesia* by MC Ricklefs. It covers Indonesian history from the rise of Islam, circa 1300, to the present.

Indonesia in Focus, edited by Peter Homan, Reimar Schefol, Vincent Dekker & Nico de Jonge, is a Dutch publication with numerous glossy photos and well-illustrated articles exploring Indonesia's rich ethnic diversity. Various books explore regional cultures in detail. *The Religion of Java* by Clifford Geertz is not only a classic book on Javanese religion, culture and values, but revolutionised the study of social anthropology.

Two good illustrated books on Indonesian fauna are *The Wildlife of Indonesia* by Kathy MacKinnon and *Wild Indonesia* by Tony & Jane Whitten. *The Malay Archipelago* by

Alfred Russel Wallace is the 1869 classic of this famous naturalist's wanderings throughout the Indonesian islands.

Art in Indonesia: Continuities and Change by Claire Holt is an excellent introduction to the arts of Indonesia. For an overall guide to Indonesian crafts, *Arts and Crafts of Indonesia* by Anne Richter is detailed and beautifully illustrated.

HEALTH

Being a tropical country with a low level of sanitation and a high level of ignorance, Indonesia is a fairly easy place to get ill. The climate provides a good breeding ground for malarial mosquitoes, but the biggest hazards come from contaminated food and water. You should not worry excessively. With some basic precautions and adequate information few travellers experience more than upset stomachs.

Drinking unboiled water is hazardous in Indonesia – most Indonesians also avoid it. Bottled water is available everywhere and many hotels and restaurants provide *air putih*, or boiled water, for guests. Take care with ice. Restaurants often provide hygienic, commercially prepared ice, and even roadside food stalls may buy commercial ice – then chop up it on the side of the road! The same warning applies to seafood, especially shellfish, which is really susceptible to contamination.

Indonesia is a malarial area, and malarial prophylactics and measures to avoid mosquito bites are recommended. Though the risk is low in the main cities and tourist areas, more remote areas are a higher risk.

See the Health section in the Appendix.

DANGERS & ANNOYANCES

Violent crime is very rare in Indonesia, but theft can be a problem. If you are mindful of your valuables and take precautions, the chances of being ripped off are small. A money belt worn under your clothes is the safest way to carry your passport, cash and travellers' cheques. Pickpockets are common and crowded bus and train stations are favourite haunts, as are major tourist areas.

Don't leave valuables unattended, and in crowded places hold your bag or day pack closely. Keep an eye on your luggage if it is put on the roof of a bus, but back-slashing or theft from bags next to you inside the bus is also a hazard. It is good insurance to have luggage that can be locked. Always lock your hotel room door and windows at night and whenever you go out. Don't leave valuables lying around in dorms or outside your room.

BUSINESS HOURS

Most government offices are open Monday to Friday from 7 am to 3 pm, with an extended lunch break for Friday prayers. Private business offices have staggered hours: Monday to Friday from 8 am to 4 pm or 9 am to 5 pm, with a break in the middle of the day. Some offices are also open on Saturday morning until noon. Banks are usually open Monday to Friday from 8 am to 3 or 4 pm. Some banks in major cities also open Saturday mornings, while others may have limited hours for foreign currency transactions, eg 8 am to 1 pm.

Shops tend to open about 8 am and stay open until around 9 pm. Sunday is a public holiday but some shops and many airline offices open for at least part of the day.

PUBLIC HOLIDAYS & SPECIAL EVENTS

Although some public holidays have a fixed date each year, the dates for many events vary each year depending on Muslim, Buddhist or Hindu calendars.

National public holidays are:

New Year's Day
    1 January
Lebaran (Idul Fitri)
    January or February
Saka New Year (Nyepi)
    March
Good Friday
    April
Idul Adha
    April
Ascension Day
    April
Muharram (Moslem New Year)
    May

INDONESIA

Waisak Day
   May
Mohammad's Birthday
   July
Independence Day
   17 August
Ascension of Mohammad
   December
Christmas Day
   25 December

Independence Day is the biggest event, with parades and celebrations held throughout the country. Lebaran marks the end of Ramadan and is a noisy celebration at the end of a month of gastric austerity. It is the major Muslim celebration of two days duration. Nyepi in Bali marks the New Year, and though it is preceded by festivals, all of Bali virtually closes.

With such a diversity of people in the archipelago there are many other local holidays, festivals and cultural events. On Sumba, for example, mock battles and jousting matches harking back to the era of internecine warfare are held in February and March. The Balinese have the Galungan Festival, during which time all the gods, including the supreme deity Sanghyang Widi, come down to earth to join in. In Tanatoraja, in Central Sulawesi, the end of the harvest season is the time for funeral ceremonies. In Java, Bersih Desa takes place at the time of the rice harvest – houses and gardens are cleaned, village roads and paths repaired.

A regional *Calendar of Events* is generally available from the appropriate regional tourist office. There's also an *Indonesia Calendar of Events* booklet which covers holidays and festivals throughout the archipelago. You should be able to pick up a copy from any of the overseas Indonesian Tourist Promotion Offices, or overseas Garuda Indonesia airline offices.

ACCOMMODATION

The government has largely been successful in making all accommodation use the term 'hotel' (hotels have to pay 10% government tax), but *losmen* and *penginapan* are other designations for cheap, rock-bottom hotels.

The word *wisma*, akin to guesthouse, is also worth watching out for.

Cheap hotels are usually very basic, rarely containing more than a bed and a small table. In compensation, a simple breakfast is often included and tea or coffee is usually provided gratis a couple of times a day. Traditional washing facilities consist of a *mandi*, a large water tank from which you scoop water with a dipper. Climbing into the tank is very bad form! Toilets may also be the traditional hole-in-the-floor variety but in places like Bali, showers and western sit-up toilets are now common. Don't expect hot water in budget places though.

Accommodation prices in Indonesia vary considerably – Yogyakarta and Lake Toba are much cheaper than elsewhere. Bali is slightly more expensive on the whole, but many Balinese hotels have pleasant gardens and huge breakfasts and you get much more for only a little extra. There are some really nice places around and finding rooms for US$4 to US$6 a night is often quite possible.

FOOD & DRINKS

A *rumah makan*, literally 'house to eat', is the cheaper equivalent of a *restoran*, but the dividing line is often hazy. Cheapest of all is a *warung*, a makeshift or permanent food stall, but again the food may be the same as in a rumah makan. With any roadside food it pays to be careful about hygiene. The *pasar* (market) is a good food source, especially the *pasar malam* (night market).

As with food in the rest of Asia, Indonesian food is heavily based on rice. *Nasi goreng* is the national dish: fried rice, with an egg on top in deluxe *(istimewa)* versions. *Nasi campur*, rice with whatever is available, is a warung favourite, often served cold. The two other real Indonesian dishes are *gado gado* and *sate*. Gado gado is a fresh salad with prawn crackers and peanut sauce. It tends to vary a lot, so if your first one isn't so special try again somewhere else. Sate are tiny kebabs served with a spicy peanut dip.

The Dutch feast *rijsttafel*, or rice table,

consists of rice served with everything imaginable – for gargantuan appetites only. Some big hotels still do a passable imitation. Indonesians are keen snackers, so you'll get plenty of *pisang goreng* (banana fritters), peanuts in palm sugar or shredded coconut cookies.

Padang food, from the Padang region in Sumatra, is popular throughout Indonesia. In a Padang restaurant, a bowl of rice is plonked in front of you, followed by a whole collection of small bowls of vegetables, meat, fish and eggs. Eat what you want and your bill is added up from the number of empty bowls. In Sumatra, food can be hot enough to burn your fingers. Spicy hot, that is.

Bottled water is available everywhere and many hotels and restaurants provide air putih (boiled water) for guests. The iced juice drinks can be good, but take care that the water/ice has been boiled or is bottled. Soft drinks are available everywhere.

Indonesian tea is fine and coffee is also good. Local beer is good – Bintang is Heineken-supervised and costs from around US$1.50 a bottle. Bali Brem rice wine is really potent, and the more you drink the nicer it tastes. *Es buah*, or *es campur*, is a strange concoction of fruit salad, jelly cubes, syrup, crushed rice and condensed milk. It tastes absolutely *enak* (delicious).

Food (makan)

beef	daging
chicken	ayam
crab	kepiting
egg	telur
fish	ikan
fried noodles	mie goreng
pork	babi
potatoes	kentang
prawns	udang
rice with odds & ends	nasi campur
fried rice	nasi goreng
white rice	nasi putih
soup	soto
vegetables	sayur
fried vegetables	cap cai

Drinks (minum)

beer	bir
coffee	kopi
cordial	stroop
drinking water	air minum
milk	susu
orange juice	air jeruk
tea with sugar	teh manis
plain tea	teh pahit

THINGS TO BUY

There are so many regional arts and crafts in Indonesia that they're dealt with under the regional sections. For an overview of the whole gamut of Indonesian crafts, pay a visit to the Sarinah department store or the art market of Pasar Seni at Ancol in Jakarta. They've got items from all over the archipelago. While you may not find all the most interesting products, you'll see enough for a good introduction to what is available.

Getting There & Away

AIR

Indonesia's two main international gateways are Denpasar in Bali and Jakarta in Java. Although Bali is by far Indonesia's major tourist attraction, the Indonesians limit the number of flights into Bali, so many visitors have to arrive in Jakarta and transfer there. Airport tax for international departures from these two airports is 25,000 rp.

Direct flights link Jakarta with all the capital cities in South-East Asia, and Bali is also well serviced with direct flights or flights via Jakarta. The cheapest and most popular are those between Indonesia and other cities in the region, outlined below.

Singapore

Singapore-Jakarta is one of the most popular flights. Many airlines service the route with fares as low as US$65 one way. To Bali costs around US$140.

Silk Air, the offshoot of Singapore Airlines, has a growing number of direct flights to regional Indonesian cities, including

INDONESIA

Manado and Ujung Pandang (Sulawesi); Solo (Java); and Pekanbaru, Padang and Medan (Sumatra). Sempati also flies Singapore-Manado direct. Merpati flies direct to Bandung, Pekanbaru and Pontianak from Singapore.

Malaysia

Popular connections include Penang-Medan for US$74. Numerous other flights go to Sumatran destinations from Kuala Lumpur, Penang and other Malaysian cities. One of the more interesting is the Penang-Banda Aceh flight with Pelangi Air. See the Sumatra Getting There & Away section for more details on Malaysia-Sumatra flights.

In Borneo, Malaysia Airlines flies between Pontianak in Kalimantan and Kuching in Sarawak, and Bouraq flies between Tarakan in Kalimantan and Tawau in Sabah. See the Kalimantan Getting There & Away section.

Philippines

Direct flights connect Manila with Jakarta and Bali, but the cheapest options are from Sulawesi. Bouraq has twice weekly flights from Manado to Davao for US$150.

Papua New Guinea

A lesser known route is the one between Irian Jaya and Papua New Guinea. From PNG, the Sunday flight with Air Niugini between Jayapura and Vanimo, just inside the PNG border, costs US$63. From Vanimo, there are connections to Port Moresby. If you are arriving from PNG, you must have an Indonesian (four week) tourist visa before you arrive in Jayapura – they are available in Vanimo and Port Moresby. PNG visas are available in Jayapura within 24 hours.

Australia

Bali is the main gateway with connections to all the main Australian cities. A few direct flights go to Jakarta, but most go via Bali. From Bali, the cheapest flights are to Darwin or Perth for around A$400, and Merpati also has a once weekly flight to Port Hedland in Western Australia. Cheapest of all are the Merpati flights from Darwin to Kupang in Timor for A$198 one way.

LAND

Only two countries – Malaysia and Papua New Guinea – have land borders with Indonesia. Regular buses run between the Malaysian city of Kuching in Sarawak and Pontianak in Kalimantan, and this is a visa-free entry point. The land border between Papua New Guinea and Irian Jaya is closed.

SEA

Most sea connections are between Malaysia and Sumatra (see Sumatra Getting There & Away for full details). The most popular ferry service is between Penang (Malaysia) and Medan (Sumatra), but ferries also connect Medan with Port Kelang and Lumut in Malaysia, and Dumai (Sumatra) with Melaka. Another alternative is to take a boat from Pasir Gudang (near Johor Bahru in Malaysia) to Batam, Bintan or Surabaya in Java (see the Malaysia Getting There & Away section).

From Singapore to Batam in Indonesia's Riau Archipelago is less than half an hour by ferry, and from Batam boats go through to Pekanbaru in Sumatra. Ferries also run between Singapore and nearby Bintan Island, from where passenger boats go on to Jakarta. See the Sumatra Getting There & Away section for more details.

Getting Around

AIR

Indonesia has a number of airlines flying to some pretty amazing places. The national airline, Garuda Indonesia, operates all the long-distance international connections and many major domestic routes using jet aircraft. Merpati is the country's main domestic carrier with the most extensive network covering just about everywhere. Merpati provides a reasonable service on the main runs, but in the back blocks flights are subject to frequent and unexplained cancellations. Garuda and Merpati were merged but are now independent.

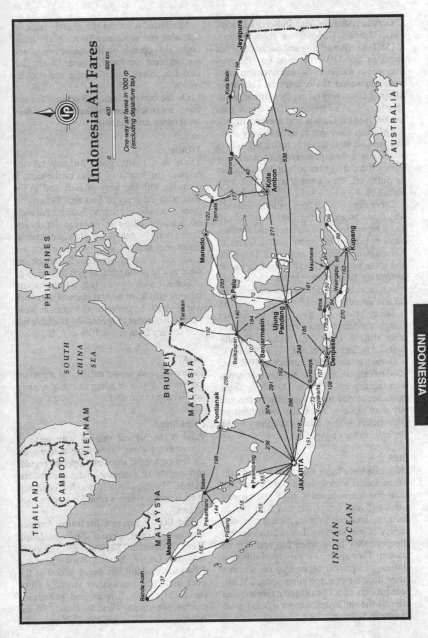

Indonesia Air Fares

One-way air fares in '000 rp
(excluding departure tax)

0   200   400   600 km

Garuda issues the Visit Indonesia Decade Pass. It costs US$300 for three sectors, US$500 for five sectors and each additional sector is US$110. You must buy the pass overseas or within 14 days of arrival in Indonesia, and enter the country on Garuda or Merpati. If arriving on another airline, a surcharge of US$50 applies. The Garuda pass can be used on Garuda and Merpati flights, but Merpati has plans to issue its own separate pass. If your travel is restricted to Java and Sumatra, these passes might not save any money but if flying out to Irian Jaya, Maluku or Sulawesi, they soon start to look very attractive.

Other domestic airlines include Sempati, which has an expanding fleet of jet aircraft and a reputation for efficiency and the best service. Bouraq has some useful flights to Kalimantan, Sulawesi and Nusa Tenggara, and some very old aircraft. Mandala has an interesting fleet of mostly vintage aircraft, which seem to spend their time stationary at Jakarta airport.

Ticket prices are fixed and all airlines charge the same fares. Merpati, and most other airlines, offer 25% discount for students up to 26 years of age.

Domestic air tickets attract a 10% tax, 1500 rp insurance and airport tax that varies with the airport – 5500 to 11,000 rp. These extras are almost always included when you buy your ticket – check the *small* print on your ticket – the main exception being domestic tickets bought overseas.

BUS

Indonesia has a huge variety of bus services – from trucks with wooden seats in the back to air-con deluxe buses with TV and karaoke – that will take you all the way from Bali to Sumatra. Java and Sumatra have the greatest variety of bus services. Local buses are the cheapest; they leave when full and stop on request. Then there is a variety of different classes and prices, depending on whether buses have air-con, reclining seats, TV, onboard toilets etc. The deluxe express buses often do the night runs, when traffic is lighter and travel is faster.

Minibuses often do the shorter runs. In Sumatra, and especially Java, deluxe minibuses also operate on the major routes and are the most comfortable buses of all. Bali also has tourist buses plying the popular routes.

On the other islands, the options for bus travel are much more limited and often only local buses are available.

TRAIN

There is a pretty good railway service running the length of Java. In the east, it connects with the ferry to Bali, and in the west with the ferry to Sumatra. Otherwise, there's just a bit of rail into Sumatra but most of that vast island is reserved for buses. Trains vary – there are slow, miserable, cheap ones and fast, comfortable, expensive ones, and some in between. So check out what you're getting before you pay.

Some major towns (eg Surabaya and Jakarta) also have several stations, so check where you'll be going to and from as well. Student discounts are generally available but tend to vary from about 10% to 25%.

BOAT

Indonesia is an island nation, so ships are important. If you're going to really explore you'll have to use them.

Pelni Ships

Pelni is the biggest shipper with services almost everywhere. They have modern, all air-con passenger ships and operate regular two-weekly or monthly routes around the islands. The ships usually stop for four hours in each port, so there's time for a quick look around.

The fleet comprises the ships *Kerinci, Kambuna, Rinjani, Umsini, Kelimutu, Lawit, Tidar, Tatamailau, Sirimau, Awu, Ciremai, Dobonso, Leuser, Binaiya, Bukit Raya* and *Tilongkabila.* More are being added to the fleet, and Pelni boats cover virtually all of the archipelago. Routes and schedules change every year. Pick up a copy of the latest schedule from any Pelni office.

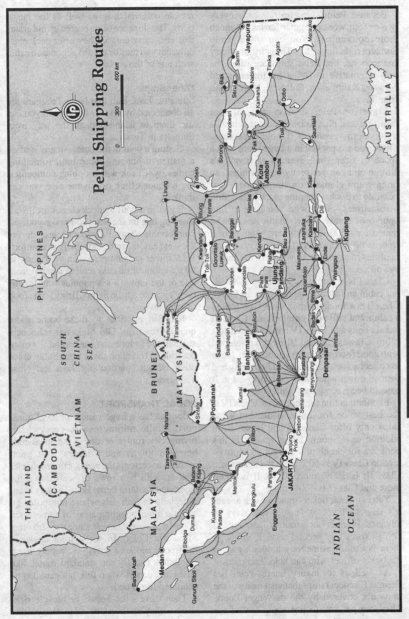

Because Pelni ships operate only every two or four weeks, regular ferries are much more convenient. You can travel from Sumatra right through to Timor by land/ferry connections, but Pelni ships are often the only alternative to flying for travel to and between Kalimantan, Sulawesi, Maluku and Irian Jaya.

Travel on Pelni ships consists of four cabin classes, plus Kelas Ekonomi, which is the modern version of the old deck class. There you are packed in a large room with a space to sleep; but, even in *ekonomi*, it's air-con and can get pretty cool at night, so bring warm clothes or a sleeping bag. It is possible to book a sleeping place in ekonomi – sometimes – otherwise you have to find your own empty space. Mattresses can be rented for 2500 rp and many boats have a 'tourist deck' upstairs. There are no locker facilities in ekonomi, so you have to keep an eye on your gear.

Class I is luxury-plus with only two beds per cabin and a price approaching air travel. Class II is a notch down in style, with four to a cabin, but still very comfortable. Class III has six beds and Class IV has eight beds to a cabin. Classes I, II and III have a restaurant with good food, while in ekonomi you queue to collect an unappetising meal on a tray and then sit down wherever you can to eat it. It pays to bring some food with you.

Ekonomi is fine for short trips. Class IV is the best value for longer hauls, but some ships only offer Classes I and II, or III, in addition to ekonomi. Prices quoted in this book are for ekonomi – as a rough approximation Class IV is 50% more than ekonomi, Class III is 100% more, Class II is 200% more and Class I is 400% more.

You can book tickets up to a week ahead; it's best to book at least a few days in advance. Pelni is not a tourist operation, so don't expect any special service, although there is usually somebody hidden away in the ticket offices who can help foreigners.

As well as its luxury liners, Pelni has Perintis (Pioneer) ships that visit many of the ports not covered by the passenger liners. They can get you to just about any of the remote outer islands, as well as the major ports. The ships are often beaten up old crates that also carry cargo. They offer deck class only, but you may be able to negotiate a cabin with one of the crew.

Other Ships

Sumatra, Java, Bali and Nusa Tenggara are all connected by regular ferries and you can use them to island-hop all the way from Sumatra to Timor.

Getting a boat in the outer islands is often a matter of hanging loose until something comes by. Check with shipping companies, the harbour office or anyone else you can think of.

If you're travelling deck class, unroll your sleeping bag on the deck and make yourself comfortable. Travelling deck class during the wet season can be extremely uncomfortable. Either get one person in your party to take a cabin or discuss renting a cabin from one of the crew (it's a popular way for the crew to make a little extra). Bring some food of your own.

It's also possible to make some more unusual sea trips. Old Makassar schooners still sail the Indonesian waters and it's often possible to travel on them from Sulawesi to other islands, particularly Java and Nusa Tenggara.

LOCAL TRANSPORT

Indonesia has a huge variety of local transport. Public minibuses are everywhere, plying city routes or doing the local runs between towns and villages. The great minibus ancestor is the *bemo*, a three wheeler pick-up with two rows of seats down the sides, and the term bemo is still widely used, especially in Bali. Elsewhere minibuses go under a mind-boggling array of names such as *opelet, mikrolet* or *colt*, since they are often Mitsubishi Colts. *Angkot* – from *angkutan* (transport) and *kota* (city) – is widely used. Minibuses usually run standard routes like buses and depart when full, but can also be chartered like a taxi.

Then there's the *becak*, or bicycle rickshaw – they're the same as in many other

Asian countries, but are only found in towns and cities. Increasingly, they are being banned from the central areas of major cities. The *bajaj*, a three wheeler powered by a noisy two-stroke engine, is only found in Jakarta. They're identical to what is known in India as an autorickshaw. In quieter towns, you may find *dokar* and *andong* – a horse or pony cart with two or four wheels respectively.

In Bali, Yogyakarta and many other centres you can also hire bicycles or motorbikes. Many towns, of course, have taxis (they even use their meters these days in the big cities in Java). You can also hire cheap drive-yourself cars in Bali. Then there are all sorts of oddities: you can hire horses in some places.

Java

Indonesia's most populous island presents vivid contrasts of wealth and squalor, majestic open country and crowded filthy cities, quiet rural scenes and bustling modern traffic. For the traveller, it has everything from live volcanoes to inspiring 1000-year-old monuments.

Java is a long, narrow island conveniently divided into three sections – West, Central and East Java.

West Java, also known as Sunda, is predominantly Islamic, and it surrounds the capital, Jakarta. The most visited places, other than Jakarta, are Bogor, Bandung and the relaxing beach centre of Pangandaran.

Central Java is the centre for much of the island's early culture. Two great Hindu/Buddhist dynasties centred here constructed the immense Borobudur temple and the complex of temples at Prambanan. Later, the rise of Islam carried sultans to power and their palaces, or *kratons*, at Yogyakarta and Solo (Surakarta) can be visited. This is a region for dance drama, or *wayang orang*, *gamelan* orchestras and *wayang kulit*, leather shadow puppet performances.

Finally, there is East Java, the area most likely to be rushed through in the haste to get to Bali. The major city here is the important port of Surabaya. Although East Java's attractions include the ruins at Trowulan and the temples around Malang, the main interest in the region is natural rather than manmade: the settings of the many hill stations and the superb Gunung Bromo volcano.

Most people travelling through Java follow the well-worn route of Jakarta-Bogor-Bandung-Pangandaran-Yogyakarta-Solo-Surabaya-Bali, with short diversions or day trips from points along that route. Many only stop at Jakarta and Yogyakarta! There are also a number of interesting towns along the north coast, but they attract few visitors.

History

The history of human habitation in Java extends back over half a million years when 'Java Man' lived along the banks of Bengawan Solo River in Central Java. Waves of migrants followed, coming down through South-East Asia to inhabit the island.

Hinduism and Buddhism first appeared in small coastal trading posts in West Java as early as the 4th century AD. Around the beginning of the 8th century, King Sanjaya founded the first major Hindu kingdom of Mataram, which controlled much of Central Java.

Sanjaya's kingdom was followed by a Buddhist interlude under the Sailendra Dynasty, when work began (probably around 780 AD) on Borobudur. Hinduism continued to exist alongside Buddhism and the massive Hindu Prambanan complex was built and consecrated around 856. Hinduism and Buddhism often fused into one religion in Java.

Mataram mysteriously collapsed and its great monuments were abandoned. No great kingdoms were recorded until the rise of civilisation in the Brantas Valley in East Java in the 11th century. King Airlangga was a legendary king who, until his death in 1049, fought to bring much of East Java under his control and extended Javanese influence to Bali.

INDONESIA

Early in the 13th century, the kingdom of Singosari rose to prominence and expanded its power until its last king, Kertanegara, was murdered in a rebellion in 1292.

Kertanegara's son-in-law and successor, Wijaya, then established the Majapahit Empire, the greatest empire of the Hindu-Javanese period. Under Hayam Wuruk (ruled 1350-89) the Majapahit Empire claimed sovereignty over much of the Indonesian archipelago. Hayam Wuruk's strongman prime minister, Gajah Mada, was responsible for many of Majapahit's territorial conquests.

After the death of Hayam Wuruk, Majapahit declined and coastal principalities began to adopt Islam and break away from Majapahit rule. The 15th and 16th centuries saw the rise of new Islamic kingdoms such as Demak, Cirebon and Banten along the north coast.

Demak finally conquered Majapahit, and by the end of the 16th century, a new Muslim kingdom in Central Java assumed the name of Mataram, in memory of the glorious past kingdom of Central Java. The new Mataram went on to control central and eastern Java, and it was the greatest power in Indonesia when the Dutch arrived.

From the start, the Dutch looked to Java as the centre of their colony, establishing a post at Batavia and then conquering the port of Banten in the west. The Dutch East India Company (VOC) successfully repelled Mataram, then began to spread its influence into the interior. The Dutch, while never directly at war, were only too keen to lend their military services to opposing principalities in return for land concessions.

Mataram was racked by internecine war until the Dutch resolved the conflict by splitting it into the principalities of Surakarta (Solo) and Yogyakarta. Through divide and rule, the Dutch slowly acquired much of Java before the Dutch government dissolved the VOC and assumed direct control in 1799.

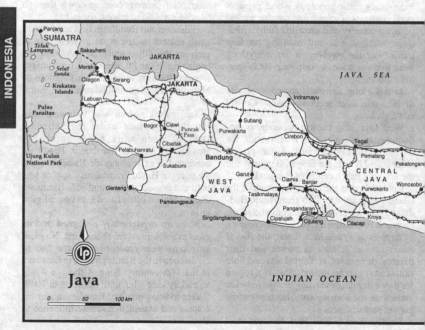

Java

The company was bankrupt and the colonial government set about making the colony, particularly Java, pay for itself through plantations. This brought great hardship to the peasantry, which supported Prince Diponegoro's Java War from 1825 to 1830. The Dutch held the cities but were at sea against Diponegoro's guerilla tactics in the countryside. Dutch military might eventually prevailed and Diponegoro was treacherously lured into negotiations in Magelang and then exiled to Sulawesi. Thousands were dead and Dutch control over Java was complete.

Java, with its vast human resources and Dutch colonial investment, very much dominated Indonesia. Though the mineral and natural resources of the other islands began to overshadow Java in economic importance, Java was the most developed island and sucked in the greatest resources. This is still the case in modern Indonesia, and often causes resentment in the other provinces.

Things to Buy

Yogyakarta is the main centre for crafts in Java, with a wide variety from Java and other parts of Indonesia. Jakarta is the place to find things from all over the archipelago but shopping is more spread out and prices can be high.

Batik The art of batik is one of Indonesia's best known crafts. Batik is the craft of producing designs on material by covering part of it with wax and then dyeing it. When the wax is scraped or melted off, an undyed patch is left. Repeated waxing and dyeing can produce colourful and complex designs. Batik pieces can be made by a hand-blocked process known as *batik cap*, in which a copper stamp is used to apply the wax, or they can be hand drawn *(batik tulis)* using a wax-filled pen known as a *canting*.

Batik can be bought as pieces of material, cushion covers, T-shirts, dresses, dinner sets and paintings. An easy check for quality is to

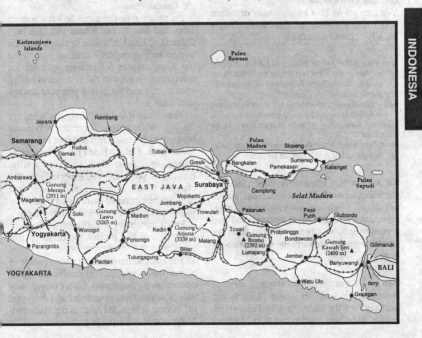

INDONESIA

simply turn the item over to ensure the design is of equal colour strength on both sides of the material – that makes it batik and not just printed material. Solo, Yogyakarta and Pekalongan are the major batik centres.

Other Crafts Silverwork can be found in the Kota Gede area, a few km south-east of Yogyakarta. Wayang puppets can be found all over Java. Leather wayang kulit are made in Yogyakarta, while wooden wayang golek puppets are a speciality of West Java. Leatherwork in Yogyakarta is cheap and the quality is usually good. Cane craft can be found in Yogyakarta and other areas but is difficult to transport. Javanese woodcarvers produce some fabulous work, mostly carved furniture at Jepara. Pottery is made everywhere – Kasongan near Yogyakarta and Kelampok near Purwokerto are major centres.

Getting There & Away

You can get to Java by a number of means and from a variety of directions. People usually come to Java from:

Sumatra – either by the Padang to Jakarta shipping service or the short trip across the Selat Sunda (Sunda Strait) from Bakauheni in Sumatra to Merak in Java.
Bali – take the very short ferry trip from Gilimanuk in Bali to Banyuwangi at the eastern end of Java.
Sulawesi, Kalimantan, Maluku or Irian Jaya – by air or sea.
From Singapore – see the Getting There & Away section earlier in this chapter for details.

Air Jakarta is a reasonably good place for shopping around for international airline tickets, although it is not as good as Singapore. Jakarta is the main international and domestic hub, with connections to all of the archipelago. Surabaya is the other main air hub.

Sea Java is a major hub for shipping services from other Indonesian islands. Jakarta and Surabaya are the main ports for Pelni ships. For details on how to get to Java from Malaysia

or Singapore, see the Getting There & Away section earlier in this chapter.

Getting Around

Air There's no real need to fly around Java, unless you're in a hurry or have money to burn – there's so much road transport available. If you do decide to take to the air, you will get some spectacular views of Java's many mountains and volcanoes.

Fares include Jakarta to Yogyakarta for 162,100 rp and Jakarta to Surabaya for 229,200 rp.

Bus Daytime bus travel is often slow and nerve-racking. It is probably just as bad for your nerves at night (if you are awake), but at least travel is much faster. Trains are often better for the long hauls, but bus departures are much more frequent. In some places, there are good reasons for taking the bus, as on the scenic Jakarta to Bandung trip over the Puncak Pass.

As with trains, there can be variations in fares and bus types. Where the fare isn't ticketed or fixed, it's wise to check the fare with other passengers – minibus drivers are the worst culprits for jacking up fares for foreigners. Beware of the practice of taking your money and not giving you your change until later.

The cheapest and most frequent buses are the big public buses. There are also *patas* buses, which are air-con services that make fewer stops. Deluxe buses run on important routes, usually at night to avoid traffic. Beware of your luggage, especially on the cheaper buses. Some travellers have had bags slashed or small items lifted when they weren't looking, or when they fell asleep.

Small minibuses, usually called colts or angkots, run the shorter routes more frequently.

The easiest, most comfortable version of all are the deluxe air-con minibuses which operate on the major runs. Called *travel*, they will pick you up at your hotel and drop you off at your designated hotel at the other end. Many hotels can arrange pick-up.

Train Choose your trains for comfort, speed and destination. Trains range from cheap, slow trains to reasonably cheap fast trains, very expensive expresses and squalid all ekonomi-class cattle trains. The schedules change frequently and although departures may be punctual, arrivals will be late for most services and very late for others.

In Jakarta and Surabaya in particular there are several stations, some of them far more convenient than others. Bear this in mind when choosing your trains. Ekonomi trains are slow, usually run over schedule and can be horribly crowded. *Bisnis* trains are a better option and seating is guaranteed.

Student discounts are generally available, but not for the expensive express trains. Try going straight to the stationmaster for speedier ticketing, and to get tickets even when, officially, the train is booked out. Remember, once again, that fares for the same journey and in the same class will vary widely from train to train.

Local Transport Around towns in Java, there are buses, taxis, colts, becaks and some very peculiar and purely local ways of getting from A to B.

JAKARTA

Jakarta has undergone a huge transformation in recent years. New freeways, office towers, luxury hotels and shopping malls have replaced much of the squalor and Jakarta has the appearance of a modern Asian boom city – at least in parts. Away from the glossy central business district, it still has its fair share of grime, crime and poverty. This sprawling capital of nine million people is the centre of power and wealth in Indonesia but it is also a vortex that sucks in the poor, often providing little more than the hope of hard work for low pay.

Despite its traffic snarls and overcrowding, Jakarta has a lot to offer. Apart from a few interesting museums and a collection of grotesque public monuments, there is some fine old Dutch architecture and, at the old schooner dock, you can see the most impressive reminder of the age of sailing ships to be found anywhere in the world.

The Dutch took Jakarta and renamed it Batavia back in 1619, when it became the centre of the Dutch empire in Indonesia. The name reverted to Jakarta after the Japanese occupation, and Soekarno declared Indonesia's independence from his Jakarta home in 1945.

Orientation

Jakarta sprawls 25 km from the docks to the southern suburbs. Soekarno's towering national monument (Monas) in Merdeka Square is an excellent central landmark. North of the monument is the older part of Jakarta, including the Chinatown area of Glodok, the old Dutch area of Kota, then the waterfront and the old harbour of Sunda Kelapa. The modern harbour, Tanjung Priok, is several km along the coast to the east. The more modern part of Jakarta is to the south of the monument.

Jalan Thamrin is the main north-south street of the new city and this wide boulevard has Jakarta's big hotels, banks and the Sarinah department store. A couple of blocks east along Jalan Kebon Sirih is Jalan Jaksa, the cheap accommodation centre of Jakarta.

Information

Tourist Office The very helpful Jakarta tourist information office (☎ 314-2067) is in the Jakarta Theatre building on Jalan Thamrin. It is open Monday to Friday from 8 am to 5 pm, Saturday from 8 am to 1 pm. They also have a desk at the airport.

Money Jakarta is crawling with banks offering the best exchange rates in Indonesia, though it pays to shop around. Banks offer better rates than moneychangers.

Most banks are open Monday to Friday from 8 am to 4 pm, and Saturday from 8 to 11.30 am. Handy banks to Jalan Jaksa are the Lippobank and Bank Duta on Jalan Kebon Sirih. In the Plaza Indonesia, the BDNI bank on the 1st level of the Sogo department store is open from 10 am to 9 pm, and offers OK rates. Downstairs, the Bank Internasional

Central Jakarta

0   250   500 m

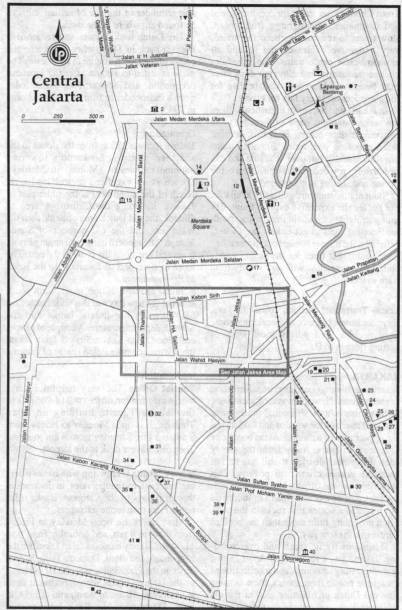

Jalan Medan Merdeka Utara

Merdeka Square

Jalan Medan Merdeka Selatan

Jalan Kebon Sirih

Jalan Wahid Hasyim

See Jalan Jaksa Area Map

Jalan Kebon Kacang Raya

Jalan Sultan Syahrir

Jalan Prof Moham Yamin SH

Jalan Imam Bonjol

Jalan Diponegoro

INDONESIA

Indonesia, Plaza Indonesia LB 17-18, also keeps extended hours and has better rates.

Almost all banks give credit card cash advances over the counter. Bank Internasional Indonesia ATMs (on Jalan Thamrin and in the Plaza Indonesia) allow cash advances on Visa and MasterCard. Bank Bali and Lippobank ATMs give cash advances on MasterCard.

Post & Communications The main post office, with its efficient poste restante service, is behind Jalan Pos Utara, to the north-east of Monas. It is open Monday to Friday from 8 am to 8 pm, and on weekends from 8.30 am to 4 pm. It's a good half-hour walk from the city centre or you can take a No 12 bus from Jalan Thamrin.

International phone calls can be made from the 24 hour phone office in the Jakarta Theatre building, next to the tourist office. The RTQ Warparpostal, Jalan Jaksa 25, is convenient.

The area code for Jakarta is 021.

Bookshops Singapore's Times Bookshop in the Plaza Indonesia shopping centre on Jalan Thamrin has the best range of books in English. The main Indonesian book chains, Gramedia and Gunung Agung, are well stocked and have stores all over the city.

Kota (Old Batavia)

The heart of the old Dutch city is the old town square, Taman Fatahillah, where you'll find Indonesia's best and oldest Dutch architecture. Take a P11 or P10 bus from Jalan Thamrin.

Facing the open cobbled square is the old City Hall, dating from 1710, now the **Jakarta History Museum**, with furniture and paintings from Dutch colonial life. The city hall was also the main prison compound of Batavia – in the basement there are cells and 'water prisons' where often more than 300 people were kept. Admission to the museum is 1000 rp. It's open every day except Monday from 9 am to 3 pm (Friday to 2.30 pm and Saturday to 12.30 pm).

The old Portuguese cannon **Si Jagur**, or Mr Fertility, opposite the museum, was believed to be a cure for barrenness because of its suggestive clenched fist with protruding thumb. Women offered flowers to the cannon and sat astride it in the hope of bearing children.

Across the square on Jalan Pintu Besar Utara, the **Wayang Museum** has a good display of puppets from Indonesia and other parts of Asia. Wayang golek or wayang kulit is performed every Sunday from 10 am to 1.30 pm. Admission and opening hours are the same as the Jakarta History Museum.

INDONESIA

PLACES TO STAY		
8	Borobudur Inter-Continental Hotel	
18	Hotel Aryaduta	
19	Sofyan Hotel Betawi	
20	Gondia Internationa Guest House	
21	Hotel Menteng I	
24	Sofyan Hotel Cikini	
26	Yannie International Guest House	
27	Karya II Hotel	
29	Hotel Menteng II	
30	Hotel Marcopolo	
31	President Hotel	
34	Grand Hyatt Jakarta Hotel	
35	Hotel Indonesia	
36	Mandarin Oriental Jakarta Hotel	
41	Kartika Plaza Hotel	

42	Shangri-La Hotel

PLACES TO EAT	
1	Seafood Night Market
25	Raden Kuring Restaurant
28	Oasis Bar & Restaurant
38	Tamnak Thai Restaurant
39	Gandy Steakhouse

OTHER	
2	Presidential Palace
3	Istiqlal Mosque
4	Catholic Cathedral
5	Mai Post Office
6	Free Irian Monument
7	Mahkamah Agung & Ministry of Finance Building

9	Gedung Pancasila
10	Bharata Theatre
11	Emanuel Church
12	Gambir Railway Station
13	National Monument (Monas)
14	Entrance to Monas
15	National Museum
16	Tanamur Disco
17	US Embassy
22	Immigration Office
23	Taman Ismael Marzuki (TIM)
32	Bank Internasional Indonesia
33	Pasar Tanah Abang
37	British Embassy
40	Adam Malik Museum

Jakarta Bay

Sunda Kelapa

1	Phinisi Cafe
2	Banda Kelapa Cafe
3	Luar Batang Mosque
4	Museum Bahari
5	Watchtower
6	VOC Shipyards
7	Chicken Market Bridge
8	Omni Batavia Hotel
9	Toko Merah
10	Wayang Museum
11	Cafe Batavia
12	Balai Seni Rupa
13	Jakarta History Museum
14	Gereja Sion

Sunda Kelapa & Kota

0   150   300 m

INDONESIA

The **Balai Seni Rupa** (Fine Art Museum), on the east side of the square, has a small gallery of modern Indonesian paintings and a collection of ceramics. It is closed on Monday.

Nearby, at Jalan Pangeran Jayakarta 1, **Gereja Sion** is the oldest remaining church in Jakarta. It was built in 1695 outside the old city walls for the 'black Portuguese' who were brought to Batavia as slaves and given their freedom if they joined the Dutch Reformed Church.

From Taman Fatahillah, you can walk along the Kali Besar canal to the old harbour of Sunda Kelapa. More fine old Dutch architecture lines the canal, including the **Toko Merah**, formerly the home of Governor-General van Imhoff. Further north, the last remaining Dutch drawbridge, the **Chicken Market Bridge**, spans the Kali Besar.

To the south of Kota, **Glodok** was the old Chinatown of Batavia. It is now a centre of trade and entertainment but, behind the new Glodok shopping plazas, the lanes off Jalan Pancoran are still crammed with narrow crooked houses, small shops, temples and market stalls.

Sunda Kelapa

This is one of Jakarta's finest sights. The old Dutch port has more sailing ships, the magnificent Buginese Macassar schooners, than you ever thought existed. Sunda Kelapa is a hot but easy walk from Taman Fatahillah or take the unique local transport – a ride on a 'kiddie seat' on the back of a pushbike.

Admission to the harbour is 1000 rp. Old men will take you in row boats around the schooners for about 3000 rp.

The early morning fish market, **Pasar Ikan**, is close by. In the same area, one of the old Dutch East India Company warehouses has been turned into the **Museum Bahari** (Maritime Museum). Admission is 1000 rp and it's open every day except Monday. The old **watchtower** near the bridge has good views of the harbour.

Monuments

Inspired tastelessness best describes the plentiful supply of monuments Soekarno left to Jakarta – all in the Russian 'heroes of socialism' style.

Monas (Monumen Nasional), the giant column in Merdeka Square topped with a gold flame, is the most dramatic. It's open every day from 8 am to 5 pm. Admission is 500 rp to the **National History Museum** in the base, or 3000 rp for both the museum and the lift to the top. The museum tells the history of Indonesia's independence struggle in 48 dramatic, overstated dioramas. The lift zips you up for superb views across Jakarta, but the queues are very long on weekends and holidays.

Monas has been dubbed 'Soekarno's last erection' and all the other monuments have also acquired descriptive nicknames. The gentleman at Kebayoran holding the flaming dish is the 'Pizza Man' and the Free Irian Monument at Lapangan Banteng, showing a muscular gent breaking the chains of colonialism, is the 'Howzat Man'.

Indonesian National Museum

Situated on the western side of Merdeka Square, this is one of the most interesting museums in South-East Asia. There are excellent displays of pottery and ancient Hindu statuary, a huge ethnic map of Indonesia and an equally big relief map on which you can pick out all those volcanoes you have climbed.

It's open daily (except Monday) from 8.30 am to 2.30 pm (Friday to 11.30 am and Saturday to 1.30 pm). Conducted tours, in a number of languages, are organised by the Indonesian Heritage Society (☎ 360551, ext 22).

Taman Mini Indonesia Indah

This is one more of those 'whole country in one park' collections which every South-East Asian country seems to have acquired. Catch a bus to Taman Mini from the Kampung Rambutan bus station, a ride of about 1.5 km. It's open from 8 am to 5 pm daily (the houses close at 4 pm). Admission is 2000 rp and the exhibits include 27 traditional houses for the 27 provinces of Indonesia and a lagoon 'map' where you can row around the islands of Indonesia.

Allow 1½ hours to get there and three hours to look around. It's pretty good value. On Sunday morning there are free cultural performances in most regional houses and a monthly calendar of various events is available at the tourist information office.

Taman Impian Jaya Ancol

Ancol 'Dreamland' is on the bayfront between Kota and Tanjung Priok harbour. This huge amusement complex has an oceanarium, an amazing swimming pool complex, an Indonesian Disneyland and the excellent Pasar Seni Art Market with its numerous small shops and sidewalk cafes. Admission to Ancol is 2500 rp on weekdays, 3000 rp on weekends – extra for the attractions.

The big drawcard is Dunia Fantasi (Fantasy World), closely modelled on Disneyland, although it's much smaller. It is really quite good if you've got children. Admission (including entry to Ancol) is 21,500 rp on weekdays, 26,000 rp on weekends. Dunia Fantasi is open Monday to Saturday from 2 to 9 pm, Sundays and holidays from 10 am to 9 pm.

Most visitors find the Pasar Seni of most interest. No extra entry fee applies and it is open from 10 am to 10 pm.

To get there, take a No 60 or 22 bus from Pasar Senin, or a bus to Kota and then bus No 64 and 65 or a M15 minibus.

INDONESIA

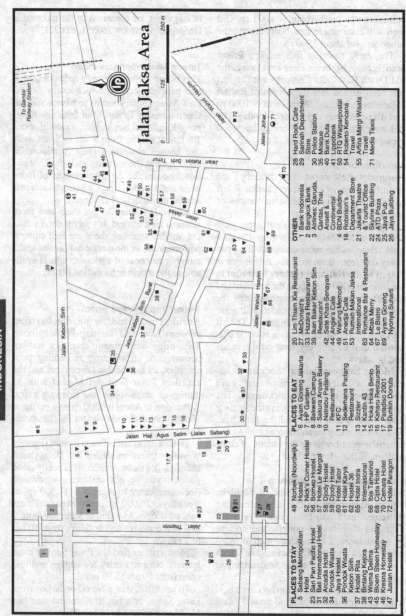

Jalan Jaksa Area

To Gambir Railway Station

0   125   250 m

PLACES TO STAY
5   Sabang Metropolitan Hotel
23 Sari Pan Pacific Hotel
31 Bali International Hotel
32 Arcadia Hotel
34 Pondok Wisata
36 Pondok Wisata Kebon Sirih
37 Hotel Rita
38 Bintang Kejora
43 Bisma Delima
45 Bloom Steak Homestay
46 Kresna Homestay
47 Justran Hostel
48 Norbek (Noordwijk)
52 Nick's Corner Hostel
56 Borno Hostel
57 Hotel Le Margot
58 Djody Hostel
59 Djody Hotel
60 Hotel Tator
61 Hotel Karya
62 Hostel 36
65 Hotel Indra
        Internasional
66 Ibis Tamarind
70 Cipta Hotel
71 Convention 2001
72 Hotel Paragon

PLACES TO EAT
6   Ayam Goreng Jakarta
7   HP Café
8   Bakwan Campur
9   Sakura Anpan Bakery
10 Natrabu Padang Restaurant
11 KFC
12 Sederhana Padang Restaraunt
13 Sizzler
14 Kantin 43
15 Hoka Hoka Bento
17 Kaharu Restaurant
18 Padiso 2001
19 Dunkin Donuts
20 Lim Thiam Kie Restaurant
27 McDonald's
33 Hazara Restaurant
39 Restaurant Kebon Sirih
42 Sate Khas Senayan
44 Angie's Cafe
49 Warung Memori
51 Anedja Cafe
53 Rumah Makan Jaksa Internasional
63 Romance Bar & Restaurant
64 Mbak Merry
67 Le Bistro
69 Ayam Goreng Nyonya Suharti

OTHER
1   Bank Indonesia
2   Bangkok Bank
3   Airlines: Garuda, Qantas, Thai, Ansett & Continental
4   BDN Building
18 Robinson's Department Store
21 Jakarta Theatre & Tourist Office
22 Skyline Building
24 ATD Plaza
25 Jaya Pub
26 Jaya Building
28 Hard Rock Cafe
29 Sarinah Department Store
30 Police Station
35 Mosque
40 Bank Duta
41 Lippobank
50 RTQ Warparpostal
54 Roberto Kencana Travel
55 Arfina Margi Wisata Travel
71 Media Taxis

Other Attractions

To the north of Merdeka Square you'll see the gleaming white **Presidential Palace**. To the north-east is the vast **Istiqlal Mosque**, the largest mosque in South-East Asia.

The **Ragunan Zoo**, in the Pasar Minggu District south of the city, has Komodo dragons, orang-utans and other interesting Indonesian wildlife. The **Jalan Surabaya** market stalls sell antiques, and at Jalan Pramuka there is a **bird market**.

Of Jakarta's many museums one of the most interesting is the **Textile Museum** at Jalan Satsuit Tubun 4, west of the National Museum. It has a large collection of fabrics from all over Indonesia plus looms, batik-making tools and so on.

Places to Stay – bottom end

Jakarta's cheap accommodation is almost all centred on Jalan Jaksa, a small street centrally located in the newer part of Jakarta, a few blocks over from Jakarta's main drag, Jalan Thamrin.

Once, *Wisma Delima*, Jalan Jaksa 5, was the only cheap place to stay. Now there are lots of alternatives and Wisma Delima is still popular but quieter. Dorm beds are 7500 rp (6500 rp for HI members), or small but spotless doubles are 15,000 rp. Food and cold drinks are available, as is good travel information.

The *Norbek (Noordwijk) Hostel* (☎ 330392) is across Jalan Jaksa at No 14. It's a dark rabbit warren with plywood walls, but friendly and well run. Fan rooms start at 9000/12,000 rp, from 25,000 rp with air-con and 30,000 rp with attached bathroom. Down a small alleyway nearby, the *Jusran Hostel* is a smaller, quiet place. Basic plywood rooms cost 17,500 rp with fan.

Nick's Corner Hostel (☎ 314-1988) at No 16 is a classier, fully air-con place with mock granite everywhere. A bed costs 8000 rp in immaculate, if somewhat cramped, dorms. Rooms with fan cost 20,000 to 37,000 rp, and rooms with bathroom cost 47,000 and 65,000 rp.

The *Djody Hostel*, Jalan Jaksa 27, is another old stand-by. Spartan rooms with shared mandi cost 15,000/22,000 rp. A few doors further up is the related *Djody Hotel* (☎ 315-1404) at No 35, which is a notch above the pack. Simple rooms without bath cost 16,000/27,000 rp. Rooms with air-con and bathroom cost 45,000 to 50,000 rp.

The newly renovated *Hotel Tator* (☎ 323940), Jalan Jaksa 37, is a definite step above the others in quality. Rooms cost 27,500/42,500 rp with fan, or 50,000 and 55,000 rp with air-con and telephone.

More places can be found in the small streets running off Jalan Jaksa. The *Kresna Homestay* (☎ 325403), at 175 Gang I, and the *Bloem Steen Homestay* next door at No 173, are two smaller places. They're a bit cramped, but reasonable value for Jakarta. The friendly Kresna has rooms for 15,000/20,000 rp without/with mandi; the Bloem Steen has rooms from 15,000 rp.

At Kebon Sirih Barat 35, running west off Jalan Jaksa, *Borneo Hostel* (☎ 320095) is popular, well run and friendly and has a lively cafe/bar. Well-kept rooms cost 25,000 rp and 30,000 rp, or 35,000 rp with mandi. The annex next door is under different management and badly in need of maintenance. Other reasonable places dotted along this lane include the *Bintang Kejora* (☎ 323878), at No 52, and the *Hostel Rita*.

Places to Stay – middle

Most places in this category add 21% tax and service to the quoted rates. Discounts are readily available at the more expensive hotels.

Hotel Le Margot (☎ 391-3830), Jalan Jaksa 15, is a small, new hotel with plain but comfortable rooms, reasonably priced at US$35 (including tax and service).

Jalan Wahid Hasyim has a string of mid-range hotels. The *Cemara Hotel* (☎ 314-9985), on the corner of Jalan Cemara, has rooms for US$60 and US$70. The new *Hotel Paragon* (☎ 391-7070), Jalan Wahid Hasyim 29, is strangely designed like a multistorey motel but has immaculate singles/doubles for US$60/70.

The good-value *Sabang Metropolitan Hotel* (☎ 373933), Jalan Haji Agus Salim 11, is an older high-rise with a pool. Rooms cost US$55/70 to US$80/95, less with discount.

Another enclave of hotels is just south-east of the city centre in Cikini. The homey *Gondia International Guest House* (☎ 390-9221), Jalan Gondia Kecil 22, has air-con rooms around a garden for US$37.50/42.50. The popular *Yannie International Guest House* (☎ 314-0012), Jalan Raden Saleh Raya 35, has spotless rooms for US$35/40. The big *Hotel Marcopolo* (☎ 230-1777), Jalan Teuku Cik Ditiro 19, has a pool and is at the top of this range. It is good value at 139,000 rp a single or double.

The cheapest hotel near the airport is the *Hotel Bandara Jakarta* (☎ 619-1964), Jalan Jurumudi Km 2.5, Cengkareng. There's nothing fancy about it – air-con rooms with bath start at US$35/48.50. They usually have a representative at the airport hotel booths, offering free transport and discounts.

Places to Eat

Jakarta has the best range of restaurants in Indonesia, with food from all over the archipelago and all over the world.

Popular places along Jalan Jaksa, all dishing out the standard travellers' menu, include *Angie's Cafe, Warung Memori* and *Anedja Cafe*. The *Rumah Makan Jaksa International* at No 16-18, next to Nick's, changes name every year but still tops the popularity polls and gets very lively in the main tourist season. *Romance Bar & Restaurant*, Jalan Jaksa 40, is the fanciest restaurant in the street with air-con, a varied menu and a small bar.

At Jalan Kebon Sirih 31A, on the corner of Jalan Jaksa, *Sate Khas Senayan* is air-con and more expensive but the food is good and the sate superb.

For real Indonesian food at a rock-bottom price, there are lots of *night stalls* along Jalan Kebon Sirih and Jalan Wahid Hasyim. Some are of dubious cleanliness, so inspect them first.

The next street west of Jalan Jaksa, Jalan Haji Agus Salim, has a string of cheap to mid-range restaurants. Though it was renamed years ago, everyone still knows it by its former

name – Jalan Sabang – and it is famed as the sate capital of Indonesia. Dozens of sate hawkers set up on the street in the evening and the pungent smoke from their charcoal braziers fills the air. Most business is takeaway, but benches are scattered along the street if you want to eat it there.

Restaurants on this stretch include *Natrabu*. If you only try Padang food once in your whole stay in Indonesia, then this is an excellent place to do it. For standard Chinese fare, the *Lim Thiam Kie* is at No 49, or down an alley a little further north, the *Paradiso 2001* is an interesting little Chinese vegetarian restaurant. Other more expensive restaurants range from *Sizzler*, for chain-food grills, to the *HP Garden*, serving Chinese steamboat.

For more fast food, the Jakarta Theatre building on Jalan Thamrin has *Pizza Hut*. On the ground floor, the *Green Pub*, a popular expat hang-out, has Mexican food and live music at night. Of course, you can have a big mac in Jakarta. Indonesia's first *McDonald's* is at the front of the Sarinah department store on Jalan Thamrin. *Sarinah* also has a supermarket and an expensive but good food-stall area in the basement. For more upmarket western food, the Sarinah building also houses *American Chili's Bar & Grill* for American grills and Tex Mex, or the *Hard Rock Cafe* here also does good grills.

The Plaza Indonesia further down Jalan Thamrin has plenty of other mall-based eateries, including the *Cira Food Court* on the 3rd level, with a range of excellent Asian and western food stalls.

Entertainment

The Jakarta cultural centre, *Taman Ismael Marzuki*, or TIM, at Jalan Cikini Raya 73, hosts all kinds of top-class cultural performances – western and Indonesian. Events are listed in the TIM monthly programme available from the tourist information office.

At 8.15 pm every evening, except Monday and Thursday, wayang orang can be seen at the *Bharata Theatre*, Jalan Kalilio 15 near the Pasar Senen. *Ketoprak* (Javanese folk theatre) performances take place here on Monday and Thursday evenings.

The *Wayang Museum*, on Jalan Pintu Besar Utara in Kota, stages wayang kulit or wayang golek every Sunday, and *Taman Mini* has regular cultural performances.

Jakarta has plenty of nightlife. It's the most sophisticated, broad-minded and corrupt city in Indonesia with nightlife to match. Jakarta's nightclubs have been hit by an ecstasy craze. Loopholes in the law have meant that penalties for use of the drug were surprisingly lenient, but the government is now cracking down.

On Jalan Thamrin, the Sarinah building houses the ever-popular *Hard Rock Cafe* and, across the road nearby, the *Jaya Pub* is a long-running rock'n'roll place. *Planet Hollywood*, south of the city centre on Jalan Gatot Subroto, is the latest 'in' spot for moneyed Jakartans.

Cafe Batavia on Taman Fatahillah gets some excellent imported bands and is open 24 hours. *O'Reileys* in the Grand Hyatt Jakarta Hotel on Jalan Thamrin is another upmarket bar that gets some good bands.

Many of the big hotels house smart discos, and the Glodok area, Jakarta's Chinatown, has an interesting collection. *Stardust* on Jalan Hayam Wuruk next to the Jayakarta Tower Hotel is very popular with young Chinese and is the original disco in the area, but it now has lots of competition. Nearby, in the backstreets around the Glodok Plaza, unprepossessing entrances and grotty lifts lead to some amazingly sophisticated clubs. *Terminal 1* has three floors of bar girls, karaoke, bands and a disco. The Kanto Pub here attracts an ecstatic crowd. *Zodiac* is the biggest and has a huge pumping dance floor. The 9th floor disco of *Sydney 2000* has impressive decor and a dazzling laser show.

Jakarta's most infamous disco is *Tanamur* at Jalan Tanah Abang Timur 14. This long-running institution is jammed nightly with gyrating revellers of every race, creed and sexual proclivity, and innumerable ladies of the night.

Getting There & Away

Jakarta is the main travel hub for Indonesia, with ships and flights to destinations all over

the archipelago. Buses depart for destinations throughout Java and for Bali and Sumatra. Trains are a convenient alternative for many destinations on Java.

Air Most flights go from Soekarno-Hatta international airport although a handful of domestic flights (eg to Bandung, Bandar Lampung, Cilacap) use the more central Halim airport. Airport tax is 25,000 rp on international flights (payable at check-in) and 11,000 rp on domestic flights (usually included in the ticket price).

The domestic airline offices are dotted around the city. Garuda has several offices, including one in the BDN building (☎ 230-0925), Jalan Thamrin 5, and another in the Hotel Indonesia (☎ 320-0568) on Jalan Thamrin. Merpati (☎ 424-3608) is at Jalan Angkasa 2, and Bouraq (☎ 629-5364) is at Jalan Angkasa 1-3, both in Kemayoran. Sempati has several offices, including one at the Hotel Indonesia (☎ 320008). Mandala (☎ 424-6100) is at Jalan Garuda No 79, out near the Pelni office. Travel agents also sell domestic tickets.

For international flights, agents on Jalan Jaksa are a good place to start looking. Indo Shangrila Travel (☎ 632703), Jalan Gajah Mada 219G, in Glodok, is a long-running discounter and specialises in student fares.

Jakarta is no discount centre, but some reasonably priced tickets can be found. The most popular is the short hop to Singapore, costing as little as US$65 with Pakistan International Airlines or Gulf Air. Other typical one-way/return fares are: Bangkok US$200/370, Penang US$200/370, Hong Kong US$310/510, London US$510/820, Los Angeles US$570/1100, Perth US$290/380 and Sydney US$440/630.

Bus Jakarta has four main bus stations, all well out of the centre.

Kalideres, 15 km west of the city centre, has frequent buses throughout the day to destinations west of Jakarta such as Merak, Serang and Labuan.

The Kampung Rambutan terminal, 18 km south of the city, primarily handles buses to destinations south and south-east of Jakarta such as Bogor, Bandung and Tasikmalaya. The trains to Bogor and Bandung are a better alternative.

Pulo Gadung, 12 km east of the city centre, has buses to Cirebon, Central and East Java, Sumatra and Bali. Buses to Yogya leave throughout the day from 8 am to 6 pm, with the deluxe night buses leaving around 3 to 6 pm. This is also the main terminal for Sumatran buses, which leave between 10 am and 3 pm.

Lebak Bulus, 16 km south of the city, handles many of the long-distance deluxe buses to Yogya, Surabaya and Bali. Most departures are late afternoon or evening.

So many buses leave that you can usually just front up at the terminal, though it pays to book for deluxe buses and during busy holiday periods. Travel agents on Jalan Jaksa sell tickets and usually include transport to the terminal. Their prices are a lot higher but save a lot of hassle.

Minibus Door-to-door *travel* minibuses are not such a good option in Jakarta because it can take hours to pick up or drop passengers in the traffic jams. Some travel agents book them, but you may have to go to a depot on the outskirts.

Arfina Margi Wisata (☎ 315-5908), at Jalan Kebon Sirih Barat 39, just off Jalan Jaksa near the Borneo Hostel, has convenient buses to Pangandaran (32,000 rp) from Jalan Jaksa on Tuesday, Thursday and Saturday. Jalan Jaksa travel agents also have direct minibuses to Yogya (35,000 rp) and bus tours to Padang (Sumatra).

Train Jakarta has a number of train stations. The most convenient and most important is Gambir, on the eastern side of Merdeka Square, a 15 minute walk from Jalan Jaksa. Gambir handles mostly express trains to Bogor, Bandung, Yogyakarta, Solo, Semarang and Surabaya. Most Gambir trains also stop at Kota, the station in the old city area in the north. The Pasar Senen station, to the east, has mostly ekonomi trains to eastern desti-

nations. Tanah Abang, to the west, has a couple of slow trains to Merak.

Trains in Java are often subject to delays, but from Jakarta the train stations are much more central than the bus stations and trains don't have to battle the Jakarta traffic jams.

For longer hauls, the express trains are far preferable to the ekonomi trains, and most have cheaper bisnis class in addition to air-con *eksekutif* class. For most express trains, tickets can be bought in advance, either at the station, or some travel agents arrange tickets for a premium.

On arrival at Gambir station, taxis cost a minimum of 7000 rp from the taxi booking desk. A cheaper alternative is to go out the front to the main road and hail down a bajaj, which will cost at least 2000 rp to Jalan Jaksa, after bargaining.

Bogor Trains to Bogor (900 rp; 1½ hours) leave every 20 minutes or so from Gambir and Kota. Trains can be horribly crowded during rush hour, but otherwise provide a good service. Best of all are the bisnis trains (2500 rp; one hour) leaving at 7.30, 8.15, 10.35 am, and 2.20 and 4.25 pm.

Bandung The efficient and comfortable *Parahyangan* service departs to Bandung (15,000 rp bisnis; three hours) roughly every hour between 5 am and 9.30 pm from Gambir station. The new, more luxurious *Argogede* departs at 10 am and 6 pm, and costs 30,000 rp in eksekutif class.

Cirebon Most trains that run along the north coast, and those to Yogya, go through Cirebon. One of the best services is the *Cirebon Ekspres* departing Gambir station at 7 and 9.45 am, and 4.30 pm. It costs 15,000 rp bisnis, 23,000 rp in eksekutif and takes 3½ hours.

Yogyakarta & Solo The *Fajar Utama Yogya* (23,000 rp bisnis; nine hours) departs Gambir at 6.10 am, and the *Senja Utama Yogya* (25,000 rp bisnis) departs at 7.20 and 8.40 pm. The *Senja Utama Solo* is the best option to Solo (28,000 rp bisnis; 10½ hours) and it also stops in Yogyakarta. Expect overruns on the scheduled journey times.

Surabaya Trains to Surabaya either take the shorter northern route via Semarang or the longer southern route via Yogyakarta. Express trains range from the *Jayabaya Utama* (33,000 rp; 12 hours) to the luxurious *Argobromo* (100,000 rp; nine hours).

Boat See the Indonesia Getting Around section for information on the Pelni shipping services which operate on a regular two week schedule to ports all over the archipelago. Most ships go through Jakarta (Tanjung Priok harbour). Pelni ships all arrive at (and depart from) Pelabuhan Satu (Dock No 1) at Tanjung Priok, 13 km from the centre of the city. Take the grey Himpunan bus No 81 from Jalan Thamrin, opposite the Sarinah building; allow at least an hour. A taxi will cost around 9000 rp.

The Pelni ticketing office (☎ 421-1921) is at Jalan Angkasa No 18, north-east of the centre, or buy through Pelni agents, who charge a small premium but are much more convenient – try Menara Buana Surya (☎ 314-2464), in the Tedja Buana building, Jalan Menteng Raya 29, about half a km east of Jalan Jaksa.

Ships go from Jakarta to Tanjung Pinang in the Riau Archipelago, from where it is just a short ferry ride to Singapore. As well as the Pelni boats, the MV *Samudera Jaya* leaves Jakarta every Saturday and does the trip in 18 hours for 80,000 rp. Bookings can be made through travel agents or at PT Admiral Lines, 21 Jalan Raya Pelabuhan, right on Tanjung Priok harbour.

Getting Around
The Airport Soekarno-Hatta is 35 km west of the city at Cengkareng. Allow an hour to get there, longer during peak hours.

There's a good Damri bus service (4000 rp) every 30 minutes from 3 am to 7 pm between the airport and Gambir railway station (close to Jalan Jaksa) in central Jakarta.

Alternatively, a metered taxi costs about 30,000 to 35,000 rp, including the 2300 rp

airport service charge and the 6500 rp toll road charges, paid on top of the metered fare. Catch cabs from taxi ranks outside the terminal, and avoid offers of 'transport' from unregistered taxis. Some Jalan Jaksa hostels offer minibuses to the airport, but are no bargain if they don't use the toll road.

Bus Jakarta has a large network of city buses. Ordinary buses cost 400 rp, express (Patas) buses cost 700 rp and air-con Patas buses cost 1800 rp. Jakarta's crowded buses have their fair share of pickpockets and bag slashers. The more expensive buses are generally safer, as well as being more comfortable.

In addition to the big buses, mikrolets and other minibuses operate in some areas. Jakarta still has some Morris bemos, the original three wheelers.

The tourist office has information on buses around Jakarta. Some of the useful buses that operate along central Jalan Thamrin include:

No 81 – Blok M to Kota, Ancol and Tanjung Priok
P11, P10 (air-con) – Kampung Rambutan to Kota
P1 – Blok M to Kota
P7A – Pulo Gadung to Kalideres via Jalan Juanda

Taxi The taxis in Jakarta are modern, well kept, and have air-con and working meters (usually). The first km costs 1500 rp, then 550 rp for each additional km. Taxis expect, if not demand, a tip. It is customary to round the fare up to the nearest 1000 rp for good service. Bluebird Taxis have a good reputation.

Local Transport Bajaj are nothing less than Indian autorickshaws – three wheelers that carry two passengers (three at a squeeze) and are powered by noisy two-stroke engines. A short ride of a couple of km will cost 2000 rp but bajaj are not allowed along Jalan Thamrin.

Becaks have long since disappeared from Jakarta, but around the historic Kota area, you can get around on bicycles with padded 'kiddy carriers' on the back.

INDONESIA

PULAU SERIBU

Pulau Seribu, or Thousand Islands, starts a few km out in the Bay of Jakarta. Though only a short boat ride from Jakarta, the islands have some of the finest white sand beaches in Java. A dozen of the islands have resorts, which are comfortable but not as luxurious as the price tag suggests – US$75 to US$130 per day. The Jakarta tourist information office (☎ 314-2067) has details on the islands.

Many of the islands can be visited on day trips. The closer islands such as **Pulau Bidadari** and **Pulau Ayer** are popular day trip destinations. The further you go from the coast, the clearer the waters become and the more expensive the resorts.

Getting There & Away

Most resorts have daily boats from Jakarta's Ancol Marina for guests and day-trippers, usually leaving around 8 or 9 am and returning around 3 pm. The resorts provide speedboats, and even the furthest islands take only a little over two hours. A day trip to Bidadari costs 30,000 rp, while day trips to the other resorts start at US$25.

MERAK

Merak is a small, unexceptional port town at the western end of Java from where the ferry crosses to Sumatra. If you have to spend the night, the *Hotel Anda* and the *Hotel Robinson* next door are a couple of cheap hotels over the railway line from the bus station.

Getting There & Away

Buses for Merak (3000 rp; three hours) depart frequently from the Kalideres bus station in Jakarta. Much slower trains leave at 6 am and 2 pm from the Tanah Abang railway station.

Ferries between Merak and Bakauheni in Sumatra leave every 36 minutes round the clock. The trip takes 1½ hours and costs 1500 rp in deck class, 2600 rp in 1st class. The new 'Superjet' service (6000 rp; 30 minutes) leaves every 30 minutes from 8.40 am to 4.50 pm.

BANTEN

En route to Merak from Jakarta, Serang marks the turn-off for the historic town of Banten, where the bedraggled Dutch first set foot on Java in 1596. In the 16th and 17th centuries, the wealthy sultanate of Banten had the most important and magnificent trading port on the spice routes, but it's hardly splendid now.

There's not a lot to see around this small coastal village but Banten has an interesting mosque, the **Mesjid Agung**, and a great white lighthouse of a minaret which was designed by a Chinese Muslim in the early 17th century. The old palaces are now in ruins and the Dutch **Speelwijk Fortress**, built in 1682, is equally decayed.

WEST COAST

Java's west coast, facing the Selat Sunda (Sunda Strait) between Labuan and Merak, has good beaches at **Anyer**, **Karang Bolong** and **Carita**, which attract the Jakarta crowds on weekends.

Carita, eight km north of Labuan, has the only vaguely cheap accommodation and is a good base for visits to **Krakatau**, about 50 km from Carita and Labuan. Boat hire to the site of the world's biggest volcanic explosion will cost at least US$50 per person for four people, around US$35 for nine or more. Operators will pool interested people to share a boat, but it may take a few days to find enough people. It is cheaper and closer from Kalianda in Sumatra.

Carita is also the place to organise a trip to Ujung Kulon National Park (see below).

Places to Stay

Eight km north of Labuan in Carita – opposite the huge, intrusive Lippo resort – is the popular *Rakata Hostel* (☎ 81171). Bright rooms with bathroom for 35,000 and 65,000 rp are no bargain but a reasonable deal in expensive Carita. A good restaurant is attached, and the hostel runs tours to Ujung Kulon and Krakatau.

Further north, the *Hotel Wira Carita* (☎ 81116) has a swimming pool and simple rooms from 45,000 rp. Around the nine km mark, the friendly *Pondok Pandawa* (☎ 82193) has a good beach but overpriced rooms for 50,000 rp.

Nearby, the *Carita Baka Baka* (☎ 81126) also has a good beach and a pleasant restaurant. Very good rooms with shower cost 48,000 rp (60,000 rp when it's busy).

Further north, the *Badak Hitam* (Black Rhino; ☎ 81072) is a budget favourite undergoing renovation. Tours to Krakatau and Ujung Kulon are organised. Next door, the *Sunset View* (☎ 81075) has clean rooms with mandi from 20,000 rp, the cheapest in Carita. Next along, the *Ratih Homestay* (☎ 81137) has spartan rooms for 25,000 rp, or 35,000 rp with mandi – try bargaining.

Getting There & Away
Buses go hourly from the Kalideres bus station in Jakarta to Labuan (3100 rp; 3½ hours), and colts run from Labuan to Carita (500 rp). Anyer, Carita and Labuan can also be reached from Merak. First take a bus to Cilegon and then other buses along the coast road.

UJUNG KULON NATIONAL PARK
This park is home both to the near-extinct Javan rhinoceros and the near-extinct Javan rainforest. It's Java's best national park, with fine beaches, snorkelling and hiking. Accommodation costs US$10/15 for singles/doubles at Tamanjaya, which is accessible by rough road. The most popular but expensive places to stay are on the islands of Handeuleum (US$15/25) and Peucang (from US$30).

The Labuan PHPA (Indonesian national park service) office, about two km from the centre of town on the road to Carita, handles park permits but accommodation is run by Wanawisata Alamhayati (☎ 81217), closer to Labuan on the same road. They sometimes have a boat to the park for US$45 per person, but you will usually have to charter a boat for US$175. A cheaper alternative is to take a colt from Labuan south to Sumur (4000 rp; four hours) and then try to find a motorcycle *ojek* to Tamanjaya, but this is a tedious route

and takes you to the less interesting part of the park.

Given the expense of reaching the park, tours from Carita start to look attractive. All-inclusive four-day/three-night tours start at US$150 for a minimum of four people. Accommodation is in tents.

BOGOR
Bogor, 60 km south of Jakarta, stands at a height of only 290 metres but is appreciably cooler than the capital, although visitors in the wet season should bear in mind the town's nickname: the City of Rain. Bogor has probably the highest annual rainfall in Java and is credited with 322 thunderstorms a year.

Information
Bogor's tourist office (☎ 325701), Jalan Merak 1, is way north of the town and provides little information anyway. A small branch is at the entrance to the gardens. Jalan Ir H Juanda has plenty of banks for changing money, such as the BNI bank.

The area code for Bogor is 0251.

Things to See & Do
The **Kebun Raya** are huge botanical gardens in the centre of Bogor, which is just 60 km south of Jakarta. Stamford Raffles founded the gardens in 1817, during the British interregnum, and they have a huge collection of tropical plants. A monument to Raffles' wife, Olivia, is near the main entrance. The gardens are open from 8 am to 5 pm every day. Admission is 2000 rp, or only 1000 rp on crowded Sundays and public holidays.

The **Presidential Palace** (Istana Bogor), built by the Dutch and much favoured by Soekarno (Soeharto has ignored it), stands beside the gardens and deer graze on its lawns. The palace is not normally open to the public but tours can be arranged through the tourist office.

Near the garden entrance, the **Zoological Museum** exhibits a blue whale skeleton, and if you have ever heard about the island of Flores having a rat problem, one glance at the showcase stuffed with the Flores version

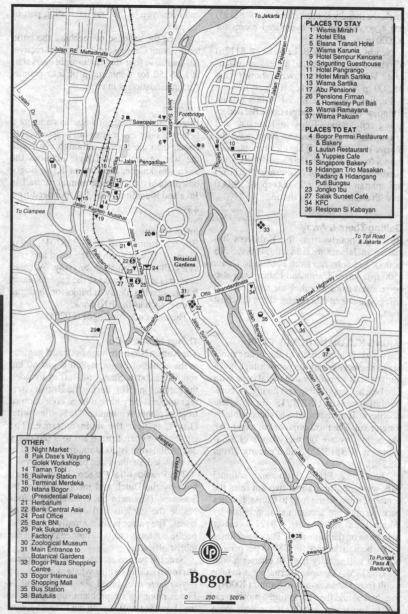

To Jakarta

Jalan RE Mattadinata

Jalan Dr. Semeru

Jalan Jend Sudirman

Sawojajar

Footbridge

Jalan Pajajaran

Jalan Raya Pajajaran

Jalan Pengadilan

Jalan Dewi Sartika

To Ciampea

Jalan Kapten Muslihat

Jalan Paledang

Jalan Ir H Juanda

Botanical Gardens

To Toll Road & Jakarta

Jl Otto Iskandardinata

Jagorawi Highway

Jl Empang

Jalan Suryakencana

Jalan Bangka

Sungai Cisadane

Jalan Pahlawan

To Puncak Pass & Bandung

Jalan Raya Pajajaran

Jalan Siliwangi

Jalan Batutulis

Lawang

Guntang

Bogor

0   250   500 m

PLACES TO STAY
1 Wisma Mirah I
2 Hotel Efita
5 Elsana Transit Hotel
7 Wisma Karunia
9 Hotel Sempur Kencana
10 Srigunting Guesthouse
11 Hotel Pangrango
12 Hotel Mirah Sartika
13 Wisma Sartika
17 Abu Pensione
26 Pensione Firman
     & Homestay Puri Bali
28 Wisma Ramayana
37 Wisma Pakuan

PLACES TO EAT
4 Bogor Permai Restaurant
     & Bakery
6 Lautan Restaurant
     & Yuppies Cafe
15 Singapore Bakery
19 Hidangan Trio Masakan
     Padang & Hidangang
     Puti Bungsu
23 Jongko Ibu
27 Salak Sunset Café
34 KFC
36 Restoran Si Kabayan

OTHER
3 Night Market
8 Pak Dase's Wayang
     Golek Workshop
14 Taman Topi
16 Railway Station
18 Terminal Merdeka
20 Istana Bogor
     (Presidential Palace)
21 Herbarium
22 Bank Central Asia
24 Post Office
25 Bank BNI
29 Pak Sukarna's Gong
     Factory
30 Zoological Museum
31 Main Entrance to
     Botanical Gardens
32 Bogor Plaza Shopping
     Centre
33 Bogor Internusa
     Shopping Mall
35 Bus Station
38 Batutulis

of Indonesian rats will explain why. Admission to the museum is 400 rp and it's open from 8 am to 4 pm daily.

Places to Stay

Bogor has a good selection of family-run places which make staying in Bogor a real pleasure, if a little expensive.

Abu Pensione (☎ 322893), near the railway station at Jalan Mayor Oking 15, is clean, attractive and well set up for travel services. It overlooks the river and has a good restaurant. It is moving upmarket and has a variety of rooms starting at 20,000 rp without bath and from 25,000 rp with bath, up to 45,000 rp with hot water. On the other side of the railway station, the *Wisma Sartika* (☎ 323747), Jalan Dewi Sartika 4D, is convenient and well run. Small and dark singles start at 11,000 rp, or better doubles with shower cost 25,000 to 35,000 rp. Breakfast is included.

Just across from the gardens at Jalan Ir H Juanda 54 is the very colonial *Wisma Ramayana* (☎ 320364). Doubles from 19,000 rp without bath are average, but the rooms with bath, from 33,000 to 43,000 rp, have style. Breakfast is included.

Round the corner at Jalan Paledang 48, the friendly *Pensione Firman* (☎ 323246) is a budget favourite and the cheapest around with dorm beds at 6000 rp and rooms from 14,000 rp with shared bathroom and from 20,000 rp with bath, all including breakfast. The *Homestay Puri Bali* (☎ 317498), next door at No 50, is a quiet place with an attractive garden but is becoming run down. Rooms cost 15,000/20,000 rp with bath.

North of the botanical gardens, the *Wisma Karunia* (☎ 323411), Jalan Sempur 33-35, is a little out of the way but quiet and reasonably priced at 17,500 rp for doubles with shared bath, and from 25,000 to 35,000 rp for rooms with private bath.

Places to Eat

Cheap eats can be found at the *night market* on Jalan Dewi Sartika.

A good restaurant for Sundanese food is the *Jongko Ibu* opposite the post office at

Jalan Ir H Juanda 36. Prices are moderate and you can dine buffet-style and try a number of dishes. *Restoran Si Kabayan*, Jalan Bina Marga I No 2, is one of Bogor's most pleasant Sundanese restaurants, with individual bamboo huts arranged around an attractive garden.

The *Salak Sunset Café*, Jalan Paledang 38, is a chic but cheap little place with river views. Standard Indonesian and western dishes are featured.

Getting There & Away

Bus Buses from Jakarta (1200/2500 rp air-con) depart every 10 minutes or so from the Kampung Rambutan terminal. The trip takes only a little over half an hour via the Jagorawi Highway toll road, but double that time from Kampung Rambutan to central Jakarta.

Buses depart frequently from Bogor to Bandung (3000 to 5000 rp; three hours). On weekends, buses are not allowed to go via the scenic Puncak Pass (it gets very crowded) and have to travel via Sukabumi (3300/5500 rp; four hours). Air-con, door-to-door minibuses also go to Bandung for 12,500 rp.

Train Trains to Jakarta leave roughly every 20 minutes until 8.20 pm and take about 1½ hours. They cost 900 rp to Gambir station or 1000 rp to Kota. The best services are the bisnis trains (2500 rp) at 6.25, 7.05 and 9.30 am, and 1.10 and 2.30 pm.

Getting Around

Angkots (300 rp) shuttle around town, particularly between the bus and railway station, in an anticlockwise loop around the gardens. Becaks are banned from the main road encircling the gardens.

BOGOR TO BANDUNG

There are a number of sprawling resort towns and tea plantations on the way up and over the beautiful **Puncak Pass**, between Bogor and Bandung – a very scenic bus trip. The area is a very popular escape from Jakarta on weekends, when the traffic jams are horrendous. Accommodation tends to be

INDONESIA

expensive, though budget places can be found in Cisarua on the Bogor side of the pass, or Cibodas and Cipanas on the other side.

On the way up to the Puncak summit from Bogor, you can stop at the **Gunung Mas Tea Plantation** or for a meal at the Rindu Alam Restaurant right near the top of the pass. **Taman Safari Indonesia**, just east of Cisarua, is a drive-in 'safari park'.

At **Cibodas**, just over the Puncak Pass, there is a cooler, high-altitude extension of the Bogor botanical gardens. The gardens are four km off the main road, 500 rp by angkot from Cipanas. From here, you can climb **Gunung Gede**, a volcano peak offering fine views of the surrounding area. The PHPA office opposite the entrance to the gardens issues permits and has good maps of the route. The walk takes all day, so an early start (usually around 2 am) is essential.

Places to Stay

The excellent *Kopo Hostel* (☎ 254296) at Jalan Raya Puncak 557 in Cisarua is on the main Bogor-Bandung road. It has its own garden, dorm beds for 8000 rp and rooms from 21,000 rp; Hostelling International (HI) members get a small discount and breakfast is included.

In Cibodas village, 500 metres before the gardens, *Freddy's Homestay* (☎ 515473) is a great option. Bright, cleans rooms are 15,000 and 20,000 rp, or the dorm is 10,000 rp – all with shared mandi but breakfast is included. Meals are available and good information is provided. The *Pondok Pemuda Cibodas* (☎ 512807), near the Cibodas PHPA office, caters mostly to school groups and has large dorms costing 5000 rp per person.

In Cipanas, the *Villa Cipanas Indah* (☎ 512513), Jalan Tengah 8, has rooms for 20,000 and 30,000 rp with hot water. Good information and guides are on offer.

Getting There & Away

You can get up to the towns on the pass by taking a colt, or any Bandung bus from Bogor.

PELABUHANRATU

From Bogor, you can continue south-west of the small town of Cibadak to Pelabuhanratu, a popular coastal resort where swimming, surfing and walking are possible. There are rocky cliffs, caves and gorges to explore and a fine beach, but the sea here is treacherous and signs warn swimmers away.

The area code for Pelabuhanratu is 0266.

Places to Stay

Pelabuhanratu is very crowded on weekends and it's expensive. In the town, *Hotel Laut Kidul*, 148 Jalan Siliwangi, and *Wisma Karang Nara*, 82 Jalan Siliwangi, both have basic rooms from 15,000 rp.

The best places to stay are on the beach, starting about two km from town. *Buana Ayu* (☎ 41111) has good rooms from 60,000 rp, and the seafood restaurant has fine sea views. Further around the headland, the *Bayu Amrta* (☎ 41031), run by the same proprietor, has rooms from 30,000 rp. Eight km out, Cimaja, the surfing beach, has a few basic hotels, and more upscale places are scattered along the coast all the way to Cisolok, 15 km west of Pelabuhanratu.

Getting There & Away

Local buses run throughout the day from Bogor (2000 rp; three hours). From Bandung first take a bus to Sukabumi and then another to Pelabuhanratu.

BANDUNG

Bandung is Indonesia's third largest city and the capital of West Java, the homeland of the Sundanese people. It's a bustling city on the move, a centre for learning and Indonesia's new high-tech industries, but its 750 metre altitude makes it cool and comfortable, and the leafy northern part of town is home to some of Indonesia's finest Dutch architecture.

The surrounding highlands are dotted with hot springs and volcanoes, the most notable being Tangkuban Perahu.

Information

The very helpful Visitor Information Centre (☎ 420-6644) at the *alun alun*, the main square on Jalan Asia Afrika, is open Monday to Saturday from 9 am to 5 pm. The railway station also has a tourist office booth.

The Golden Megah Corp moneychanger, Jalan Otista 180, changes cash and travellers' cheques at good rates and is open Monday to Friday from 8.30 am to 4.30 pm, Saturday to 2 pm.

The area code for Bandung is 022.

Museums

Bandung was famous as the venue for the Afro-Asian conference, when Soekarno, Chou Enlai, Ho Chi Minh, Nasser and other Third World figureheads met in 1955. The **Freedom building** (Gedung Merdeka), on Jalan Asia Afrika, has the full story.

At Jalan Diponegoro 57, in the northern part of the city, the **Geological Museum** (Museum Geologi) has some interesting exhibits including relief maps and volcano models.

Other museums include the **Army Museum** (Museum Mandala Wangsit) on Jalan Lembong, with its grim and explicit photographs of the Darul Islam rebellion. The **West Java Cultural Museum** is south-west of the city centre on Jalan Otto Iskandardinata (Jalan Otista for short). It is closed Monday.

Jeans St

Bandung is a centre for clothing manufacture and shops on a km-long strip of Jalan Cihampelas compete for the most outrageous shopfronts and decor. It's definitely worth seeing, and the jeans and T-shirts are cheap.

Other Attractions

Bandung is noted for its fine Dutch art deco architecture. The **Savoy Homann Hotel** and the **Grand Hotel Preanger**, both on Jalan Asia Afrika, are worth a look. Also take a look at the magnificent **Gedung Sate** near the Geological Museum, the regional government building, so-called because it's topped by what looks like a sate stick.

Bandung's ITB, or **Institute of Technology**, is one of the most important universities in Indonesia – it's on the north side of the city

– and also has some fine examples of Indo-European architecture. On Jalan Taman Sari, close to the ITB, Bandung's **zoo** has open park space and a wide variety of Indonesian bird life. Most Sundays, traditional **rambutting fights** are held at Cilimus, near Terminal Ledeng to the north of the city.

Places to Stay

Jalan Kebonjati, near the railway station and the city centre, is the place to head for. The *By Moritz* (☎ 420-7264), Kompleks Luxor Permai 35, Jalan Kebonjati, is a well-managed travellers' guesthouse with a good restaurant. Dorm beds cost 8000 rp and spotless singles/doubles/triples are 12,500/17,000/25,000 rp. Breakfast is included.

Le Yossie Homestay (☎ 420-5453), 53 Jalan Kebonjati, is not quite as immaculate but is also good. A dorm bed costs 7000 rp per person, and singles/doubles are 10,000/13,500 rp. The rooms are light, free tea and coffee are provided and there is a downstairs cafe.

Bandung's original guesthouse, *Losmen Sakardana* (☎ 420-9897), is down a little alley beside the Hotel Melati I at No 50/7B. Basic but well-kept rooms are 8000/12,000 rp. *Sakardana Homestay* (☎ 421-8553), Gang Babakan 55-7/B, further along the alley, is its more popular copy. It's friendly and has a good upstairs restaurant. Now in new premises, the plywood rooms are still basic, but clean and cheap enough at 10,000/13,000/17,000 rp, or 7000 rp for a dorm bed.

Jalan Kebonjati also has a few hotels. *Hotel Surabaya* (☎ 444133), at No 71, is a run-down old hotel with plenty of colonial ambience. Spartan rooms range from 11,500/20,000 up to 45,000 rp for rooms with bath in the 'renovated' section, but these are only marginally better.

North of the railway station, the *Hotel Patradissa* (☎ 420-6680), at Jalan H Moch Iskat 8, has clean, modern rooms with bath. Small singles/doubles are 15,000/20,000 rp, while better doubles with hot water showers start at 35,000 rp. A number of other hotels are nearby.

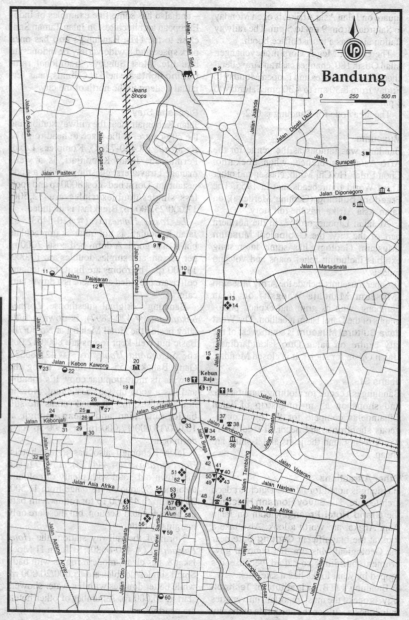

Hotel Patradissa II (☎ 420-2645), Jalan Pasirkaliki 12, just around the corner from Jalan Kebonjati, has small but spotless rooms with attached bathroom and hot water showers for 30,000 rp, including breakfast. A good deal.

Places to Eat

Bandung has plenty of tempting restaurants including an appetising *night market*, directly across from the Visitor Information Centre. On Jalan Gardujati, opposite the Hotel Trio, there is a string of lively night-time warungs and a selection of *Chinese restaurants*. Cheap, if slightly grotty, warungs can be found directly in front of the railway station, facing Jalan Kebonjati.

Jalan Braga, the fancy shopping street of Bandung, has all sorts of interesting places. The centrepiece is the *Braga Permai*, with its open-air cafe, at No 74. It's a more expensive restaurant but cheaper meals are available and the ice cream is superb. Other places on Jalan Braga include the *Canary Bakery* for fast food, the *Sumber Hidangan* bakery and the *French Bakery* for a snack or light meal, croissants or Danish pastries.

The *Sindang Reret Restaurant*, Jalan Naripan 9, just around the corner from Jalan Braga, has good, if slightly expensive, Sundanese food, and is noted for its Saturday-night cultural performances.

Just south of the alun alun, at Jalan Dewi Sartika 7A, the *Warung Nasi Mang Udju* has cheap Sundanese food, eaten with the fingers, like nasi padang.

Entertainment

Bandung is the cultural centre of West Java and a good place to see Sundanese arts. All-night wayang golek puppet performances are held every other Saturday night at *Rumentang Siang*, Jalan Baranangsiang 1, near Pasar Kosambi on Jalan Ahmad Yani.

	PLACES TO STAY		
3	Wisma Asri		
10	Bumi Sakinah		
13	Wisma Remaja		
19	Hotel Guntur		
21	Hotel Patradissa		
24	Hotel Patradissa II		
25	Sakardana Homestay		
28	Losmen Sakardana		
29	Le Yossie Homestay		
30	Hotel Surabaya		
31	By Moritz		
32	Kramatdjati Buses Hotel Trio		
37	Hotel Panghegar		
44	Grand Hotel Preanger		
47	Savoy Homann Hotel		

	PLACES TO EAT
9	Tojoyo
23	Rumah Makan Mandarin
27	Warungs & Restaurants
35	Braga Permai Cafe
40	Sindang Reret Restaurant
41	Canary Bakery
42	French Bakery

49	Rumah Makan Tenda Biru
50	Braga Restaurant & Pub
52	Night Market Warungs
59	Warung Nasi Mang Udju

	OTHER
1	Zoo
2	ITB (Bandung Institute of Technology)
4	Museum Geologi (Geological Museum)
5	Museum Pos dan Giro
6	Gedung Sate (Regional Government Building)
7	Galael Supermarket
8	Flower Market
11	Bandung Cepat Buses
12	Bouraq Office
14	Plaza Bandung Indah Shopping Mall
15	City Hall (Kantor Walikota)
16	Catholic Church
17	Bank Indonesia

18	Bethel Church
20	Governor's Residence
22	4848 Taxis
26	Railway Station
33	4848 Taxis
34	North Sea Bar
36	Museum Mandala Wangsit (Army Museum)
38	Telkom
39	Rumentang Siang
43	Sarinah Department Store
45	Merpati Office
46	Wartel
48	Gedung Merdeka (Freedom Building)
51	Ramayana Department Store & Supermarket
53	Bank BRI
54	Main Post Office
55	Golden Megah Corp Moneychanger
56	King's Department Store
57	Visitor Information Centre
58	Palaguna Shopping Centre
60	Kebun Kelapa Angkot Station

INDONESIA

You can also catch a scaled-down exhibition with a meal every Saturday night at the *Sindang Reret Restaurant* (see Places to Eat).

Jaipongan dancing is held at the *Langen Setra* club, Jalan Otista 541A, and at *Fajar Parahiyangan*, Jalan Dalem Kaum, near the river. While owing much to traditional dance, Jaipongan is a modern social dance and hostesses dance primarily to entertain male clients.

Angklung performances take place at Pak Ujo's *Saung Angklung* (Bamboo Workshop), Jalan Padasuka 118, and you can see the instruments being made. Performances are 12,500 rp and appeal mostly to tour groups. There are a number of other places around the city to see wayang, Sundanese dance, gamelan playing and *pencak silat*, an Indonesian martial art.

Jalan Braga is a good place in the evening for less cultural pursuits, and has a string of expensive discos, plus the *North Sea Bar*, a relaxed bar popular with expats. *Polo* on the 11th floor of the BRI building on Jalan Asia Afrika, is a chic disco and an ecstasy hangout. Further out, north-west of the centre at Jalan Dr Junjunan 164, *Laga Pub* is a convivial expat hang-out that gets some good bands.

Getting There & Away
Air Sempati, Bouraq and Merpati fly from Bandung to Jakarta for 67,000 rp. Merpati also flies direct to Yogyakarta (96,000 rp), Palembang (Sumatra), Semarang, Surabaya and Singapore.

Bus The Leuwi Panjang bus terminal, five km south of the city centre on Jalan Soekarno-Hatta, has buses to the west to places like Bogor (3000 to 5000 rp; 3½ hours), Sukabumi (2300 rp; three hours) and Jakarta's Kampung Rambutan terminal (3500 to 7500 rp; 4½ hours). Buses to Bogor are not allowed to take the scenic Puncak Pass route on weekends. Door-to-door minibuses also go to Bogor (12,500 rp) via Puncak.

Buses to the east leave from the Cicaheum bus station, on the eastern outskirts of the city. Normal/air-con buses go to Cirebon (2700/5100 rp; 3½ hours), Garut (1400 rp; two hours), Tasikmalaya (2500/3500 rp; four hours) and Yogya (10,800 to 21,500 rp; 12 hours). Most departures to Yogya leave around 3 to 7 pm.

For Pangandaran, a few direct buses go from Cicaheum, otherwise take a bus to Tasikmalaya or Banjar and then another to Pangandaran. A door-to-door taxi service is provided by 4848 Taxi, and Sari Harum (☎ 771447) has less cramped, air-con minibuses (15,000 rp, five hours).

For luxury night buses to major Javanese cities and Bali, conveniently located companies include Bandung Cepat (☎ 431333), Jalan Doktor Cipto 5.

Train The Bandung-Jakarta *Parahyangan* is the main service with departures to Jakarta's Gambir station roughly every hour from 4 am to 8.30 pm. Slower trains pass through midmorning for Jakarta's Pasar Senen station. The *Argogede* luxury service departs at 6.30 am and 2.30 pm.

Several daily trains also operate between Yogyakarta and Bandung. The journey takes about nine to 10 hours and the fare varies from around 9000 rp in ekonomi, and from 14,000 rp in bisnis. Trains to Surabaya include the *Badra Surya* (10,000 rp ekonomi) and the express *Mutiara Selatan* (28,000 rp bisnis).

Getting Around
Bandung's airport is four km north-west of the city centre, about 4000 rp by taxi. In Bandung, bemos are called angkots. They cost 250 to 500 rp around town (400 rp for most destinations) and depart from the terminal outside the railway station or from the bus stations. Big Damri city buses Nos 9 and 11 run from west to east down Jalan Asia Afrika to Cicaheum.

Metered taxis are common in Bandung. As in other cities, the becaks are being relegated to the backstreets and are no longer seen in great numbers.

TANGKUBAN PERAHU AREA

Tangkuban Perahu (overturned perahu, ie boat) is a huge volcanic crater 30 km north of Bandung. Legend tells of a god challenged to build a huge boat during a single night. His opponent, on seeing that he would probably complete this impossible task, brought the sun up early and the boat builder turned his nearly completed boat over in a fit of anger.

Tangkuban Perahu is quite spectacular, but as cars can drive right to the top, it attracts a huge number of visitors and is very commercial – car parks, restaurants, hawkers, an information centre and an admission fee. To get there, take a Subang-bound minibus (2000 rp) from Bandung's train station, which goes via Lembang to the park entrance, and then a minibus to the top (1500 rp). Weekends and mornings are the best time for finding other passengers to share, otherwise you can walk the 4.5 km to the top. An excellent side trail, away from most of the madding crowd, leads through the jungle via the Domas crater area of steaming and bubbling geysers. The trail is much easier to walk, and easier to find, coming down from the crater rather than going up.

There are hot springs at **Ciater**, a few km beyond the Tangkuban Perahu entrance point, and at **Maribaya**, five km beyond Lembang. Ciater has the better hot springs for a swim on a cold, rainy day but both are commercialised.

You can extend your Tangkuban Perahu trip by walking from the bottom end of the gardens at Maribaya down through a brilliant river gorge (there's a good track) to **Dago**, an exclusive residential suburb of Bandung with a famous teahouse. Allow about two hours for the walk to Dago. It's a good spot to watch the city light up and you can then get back into the city on the local bemos, which run to/from the train station in Bandung.

BANDUNG TO PANGANDARAN

Garut, 63 km south-east of Bandung, is just a service town for the surrounding agricultural valley, but the area has a number of attractions. The small hot springs resort of **Cipanas**, on the outskirts of town six km to the north-west, makes an ideal base to explore the area.

There are volcanoes and mountains to climb, including **Gunung Guntur**, which towers above Cipanas. **Gunung Papandayan**, 28 km south-west, is the main volcanic attraction – take a minibus to Cisurupan (1000 rp) and then an ojek (2500 rp) from the turn-off. You can walk to the bubbling sulphurous crater of Papandayan – take care – and the peak is two hours further on. Papandayan is not as impressive as Tangkuban Perahu but far less touristed.

Near Leles, 10 km north of Garut, **Candi Cankuang** is a rare 8th century Hindu temple lying at the edge of a small lake. This is a very popular stop for tour buses. Take a No 10 angkot to Leles, then it is four km by andong to the lake. Boats across the lake are 15,000 rp per person.

Places to Stay

Garut has hotels, but Cipanas is much more attractive and has a dozen hotels strung along Jalan Raya Cipanas, the resort's single road. All rooms have large baths with water piped in from the hot springs – pamper yourself after a hard day's trekking.

Cipanas hotels include the basic *Pondok Kurnia Artha*, which has dark rooms for 15,000 rp. The *Hotel Tirta Merta* is cheerier and has singles/doubles from 17,500/22,500 rp. Both hotels charge 5000 rp more on weekends.

PANGANDARAN

The fishing village of Pangandaran lies on a narrow, bulbous peninsula with broad sandy beaches that sweep back along the mainland. At the end of the peninsula is the Pangandaran National Park.

Pangandaran has black-sand beaches and dangerous swimming (except for the more sheltered southern end of the west beach), but despite these drawbacks it is Java's number one beach resort. It is one of the most relaxing and friendly places in Java to hang out, the living is cheap, and apart from the

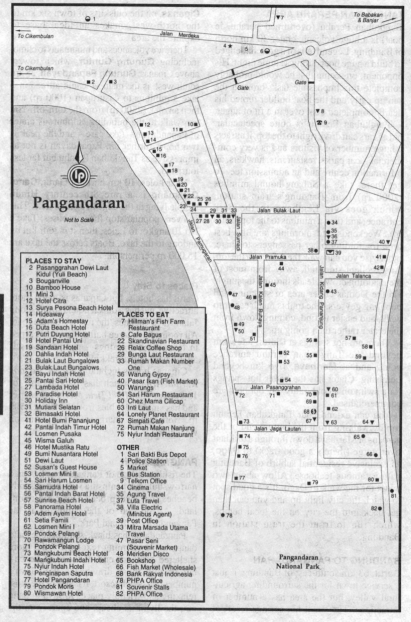

Pangandaran

Not to Scale

PLACES TO STAY
2 Pasanggrahan Dewi Laut Kidul (Yuli Beach)
3 Bouganville
10 Bamboo House
11 Mini 3
12 Hotel Citra
13 Surya Pesona Beach Hotel
14 Hideaway
15 Adam's Homestay
16 Duta Beach Hotel
17 Putri Duyung Hotel
18 Hotel Pantai Uni
19 Sandaan Hotel
20 Dahlia Indah Hotel
21 Bulak Laut Bungalows
23 Bulak Laut Bungalows
24 Bayu Indah Hotel
27 Pantai Sari Hotel
27 Lambada Hotel
30 Paradise Hotel
30 Holiday Inn
31 Mutiara Selatan
32 Bimasakti Hotel
41 Hotel Bumi Pananjung
42 Pantai Indah Timur Hotel
44 Losmen Pusaka
46 Wisma Galuh
46 Hotel Mustika Ratu
49 Bumi Nusantara Hotel
51 Dewi Laut
52 Susan's Guest House
53 Losmen Mini II
54 Sari Harum Losmen
55 Samudra Hotel
56 Pantai Indah Barat Hotel
57 Sunrise Beach Hotel
58 Panorama Hotel
59 Adem Ayem Hotel
61 Setia Famili
62 Losmen Mini I
69 Pondok Pelangi
70 Pondok Pelangi
71 Rawamangun Lodge
73 Mangkubumi Beach Hotel
74 Mangkubumi Indah Hotel
75 Nyiur Indah Hotel
76 Penginapan Saputra
77 Hotel Pangandaran
79 Pondok Moris
80 Wismawan Hotel

PLACES TO EAT
7 Hillman's Fish Farm Restaurant
8 Cafe Bagus
22 Skandinavian Restaurant
26 Relax Coffee Shop
29 Bunga Laut Restaurant
33 Rumah Makan Number One
36 Warung Gypsy
40 Pasar Ikan (Fish Market)
50 Warungs
54 Sari Harum Restaurant
60 Chez Mama Cilicap
63 Inti Laut
64 Lonely Planet Restaurant
67 Simpati Cafe
72 Rumah Makan Nanjung
75 Nyiur Indah Restaurant

OTHER
1 Sari Bakti Bus Depot
4 Police Station
5 Market
6 Bus Station
9 Telkom Office
34 Cinema
35 Agung Travel
37 Luta Travel
38 Villa Electric (Minibus Agent)
39 Post Office
43 Mitra Marsada Utama Travel
47 Pasar Seni (Souvenir Market)
48 Meridien Disco
65 Bookshop
66 Fish Market (Wholesale)
68 Bank Rakyat Indonesia
78 PHPA Office
81 Souvenir Stalls
82 PHPA Office

Pangandaran National Park

beach, there are walks in the national park and other nearby attractions.

Pangandaran is a busy resort on weekends and is positively swarming with local visitors during holiday periods, when prices soar. At other times it is still just an overgrown fishing village and a relaxing place to take a break from travel.

Information

A once-only 1000 rp fee is charged when entering Pangandaran. Entry to the national park is another 1250 rp. The Bank Rakyat Indonesia on Jalan Kidang Pananjung changes most currencies and major brands of travellers' cheques at poor rates.

The area code for Pangandaran is 0265.

Organised Tours

A host of good-value tours are offered to destinations around Pangandaran. They include the excellent Green Canyon boat trip for 30,000 rp, but the canyon is now clogged with an armada of boats on weekends. Various other informative tours visit cottage industries and take in anything of any remote interest near Pangandaran.

Places to Stay

Most of Pangandaran's cheapest hotels are around the main street at the southern end of town.

Losmen Mini I on Jalan Kidang Pananjung is clean, convenient and popular. Singles/doubles with mandi cost 8500/12,500 rp, including breakfast. Across the road, the *Rawamangun Lodge* is very basic but clean, welcoming and cheap at 7500/10,000 rp.

On Jalan Kalen Buhaya is *Losmen Mini II* with rooms for 8000 rp, or 15,000 rp for more substantial rooms with attached mandi, including breakfast.

On the eastern beach, the *Panorama Hotel* (☎ 639218) straddles the bottom end and mid-range. Pleasant veranda rooms facing the sea cost 25,000 rp with bathroom.

While the southern end of town has more of a village atmosphere, the northern end around Jalan Bulak Laut is Pangandaran's

Riviera, popular with Europeans. Most places tend to be mid-range, but Bulak Laut has some good budget places as well.

The popular *Holiday Inn* (☎ 639285), Jalan Bulak Laut 50, is one of the cheapest. Rooms cost 7000/10,000 rp, or rooms with attached mandi are 15,000 rp. Next door at No 49, *Mutiara Selatan* (☎ 639416) is also good value. Rooms with porch and attached bathroom cost 15,000 rp, including breakfast.

Closer to the beach, the popular *Pantai Sari Hotel* (☎ 639175) has a good restaurant. Doubles with fan and mandi cost 15,000 rp, or air-con rooms cost 25,000 rp. The quality varies considerably, as does the price, depending on the season and the length of stay.

Bamboo House (☎ 639419) is to the north and away from the beach, but this small, family-run place is well worth considering. Attractive singles/doubles with mandi cost 10,000/15,000 rp including breakfast.

For something more upmarket, *Bulak Laut Bungalows* (☎ 639377), on the corner of Jalan Pamugaran and Bulak Laut, has attractive bungalows, most with their own sitting rooms, for 25,000 and 30,000 rp, including breakfast. At Jalan Bulak Laut 45, the new *Bimasakti Hotel* (☎ 639194) has a restaurant, small pool and immaculate rooms for 66,000 and 88,000 rp (more on weekends). *Sandaan Hotel* (☎ 639165) has plain fan rooms with shower costing 35,000 and 50,000 rp, or more luxurious air-con rooms are 80,000 rp, including breakfast. The main attractions are the small swimming pool and the good restaurant.

Further up, the delightful *Adam's Homestay* (☎ 639164) has eclectic architecture, a bookshop, good cappuccinos and a small pool. Large rooms cost from 29,000/35,000 rp, up to 125,000 rp for a luxury two bedroom bungalow.

Around Pangandaran The quiet beaches outside Pangandaran are increasingly popular places to hang out and relax, especially when Pangandaran is crowded during the main holiday periods. Most of the following guesthouses are run by westerners who have settled in Pangandaran, and are on the ball with information and services.

Cikembulan, four km along the beach road to the west, has a small enclave of guesthouses. *Delta Gecko* has a wide variety of bamboo and wood bungalows. A dorm bed costs 7500 rp, singles 10,000 rp, doubles with mandi from 15,000 rp, all including breakfast and free bicycles. It has a restaurant, lots of information and a cultural/BBQ night once a week. Next door, the smaller *Losmen Kelapa Nunggal* has new, spotless rooms with bathroom for 12,500/15,000 rp. About half a km back towards Pangandaran on the beach road, *Tono Homestay* is a friendly, cosy place where good rooms with mandi cost 20,000 rp.

Four km east of Pangandaran in Babakan, *Laguna Beach Bungalows* (☎ 639761) offers stylish mid-range bungalows facing the beach for 45,000 rp, dropping to 35,000 rp per day for stays of more than two days. Ring for pick-up.

Places to Eat

Restaurants are also in plentiful supply in Pangandaran, and the fish is often superb. Usually, you pick your fish and the price is dependent on weight.

The basic *Simpati Cafe* is often packed because its prices are so reasonable; it serves excellent fruit salads, gado gado and a variety of grilled fish. Over the road, the *Inti Laut* restaurant specialises in superb grilled fish and seafood. The nearby *Lonely Planet Restaurant* (no relation!) is on the grotty side but the seafood is cheaper and very good.

Chez Mama Cilacap, at Jalan Kidang Pananjung 187, is one of Pangandaran's best restaurants with an extensive menu, moderate prices, fresh fish and icy fruit juices.

On the west beach at the southern end, the no frills *Rumah Makan Nanjung* has good cheap seafood and they really know how to barbecue fish. Next to the Bumi Nusantara Hotel at the southern end of Jalan Pamugaran is a warung area with cheap Indonesian dishes and sea breezes.

On Jalan Bulak Laut, the *Pantai Sari*

Hotel has a popular restaurant with Indonesian dishes, reasonable western fare and fish. The *Holiday Inn* has a typical travellers' menu, is cheap and the breakfasts are good. Further back from the beach *Rumah Makan Number One* has a mixed menu, moderate prices and some style.

In addition to the restaurants, the excellent *Pasar Ikan* (fish market) on the east beach sells fresh fish and a selection of good warungs serve seafood according to weight.

Getting There & Away

Bus & Train Local buses run from Pangandaran's bus station to Tasikmalaya (3500 rp; three hours), Ciamis (3500 rp; 2½ hours), Banjar (2500 rp; 1½ hours) and Kalipucang (500 rp; 40 minutes). Buses also run along the west coast as far as Cijulang (750 rp; 40 minutes).

Express buses to Bandung (7000 rp; six hours) and Bogor (11,500 rp; nine hours) leave from the bus company depots about two km west of Pangandaran along Jalan Merdeka. Travel agents sell tickets for a premium but include transport to the depots.

Agents also sell tickets to Jakarta, but buses normally stop in Bekasi, 22 km east of the capital. The easiest way to reach Jakarta is by the Mitra Marsada Utama (☎ 639733) bus that picks up in Pangandaran and goes right to Jalan Jaksa for 28,000 rp. The most comfortable way to Bandung is with the Sari Harum door-to-door minibus for 14,000 rp.

Travel east is usually via the Kalipucang-Cilacap ferry (see Boat below). Otherwise take a bus to Banjar, then another bus to Purwokerto for onward buses to Yogya or Wonosobo. You can take the train from Banjar, but ekonomi services heading east are crowded and slow and it is hard to get a seat. Heading to Bandung and Jakarta by train the *Galuh* originates in Banjar, leaving at 6 am.

Boat The most popular way to reach Yogyakarta is via the interesting backwater trip between Cilacap and Kalipucang. This starts with a 17 km bus trip east from Pangandaran to Kalipucang. From Kalipucang the ferry travels across the wide expanse of Segara Anakan and along the waterway sheltered by the island of Nusa Kambangan. It's a fascinating trip, hopping from village to village in a rickety 25 metre wooden boat. Though popular with tourists it's still very much a local service. It takes four hours to Cilacap and costs 1300 rp. The last boats leaves at 1 pm. From the Cilacap jetty you can get a becak and then a bemo to the Cilacap bus station, and then a bus to Yogyakarta.

The trip is made very easy by the door-to-door services between Pangandaran and Yogyakarta that will drop you at the ferry and pick you up on the other side for 15,000 rp, including the ferry ticket. All up the journey takes about eight hours.

AROUND PANGANDARAN

By hired motorbike you can tour right along the scenic west coast road to **Cipatujah**, 74 km south of Tasikmalaya. Of the many beaches, **Batu Karas**, 42 km from Pangandaran and 10 km off the highway, is the best and has surfing and safe swimming around a sheltered headland. Accommodation, favoured by surfers, includes the *Melati Indah*, which is good value and has well-kept rooms for 15,000 and 20,000 rp. *Alana's Bungalows* has bamboo decor, surf culture and rooms for 15,000 and 30,000 rp with mandi. Batu Karas can be reached from Pangandaran by taking a bus to Cijulang (750 rp) and then an ojek for 1000 rp.

Near the turn-off to Batu Karas, boats on the river take tours up the emerald green river to **Green Canyon**, usually organised out of Pangandaran.

CIREBON

Cirebon, midway between Jakarta and Semarang, gets few visitors yet has interesting Javanese and Sundanese influences, and two kratons (palaces) in the manner of Yogya and Solo. It is also a centre for batik, and is famed for its seafood.

The area code for Cirebon is 0231.

Things to See

In the south of the city, the **Kraton Kesepuhan** was built in 1527 and its architecture and interior are a curious blend of Sundanese, Javanese, Islamic, Chinese and Dutch styles. It is has a number of old artefacts and the impressive Kereta Singabarong, a 17th century gilded coach. Entry is 1000 rp and it is open daily from 8 am to 4 pm. The less important **Kraton Kanoman**, dating from 1681, is sadly neglected but also worth a visit. It's approached through the colourful Pasar Kanoman outdoor market.

Four km south-west of town is the **Gua Sunyaragi**, a bizarre 'cave' pleasure palace honeycombed with chambers, doors and staircases leading nowhere. The **Tomb of Sunan Gunungjati** is another of the town's claims to fame – he was one of the nine *walis* (holy men) who spread Islam through Java. His tomb attracts pilgrims from all over Java.

Cirebon is famed for its distinctive batik, particularly from the nearby village of **Trusmi** (try Ibu Masina's).

Places to Stay

A little expensive, but worth the extra, the *Hotel Asia* (☎ 202183), Jalan Kalibaru Selatan 15, is a well-kept old Dutch-Indonesian inn. It's a 15 minute walk or 1500 rp by becak from the railway station. Rooms with shared mandi cost 15,000 and 18,000 rp, 27,000 to 32,000 rp with mandi and fan, all including breakfast.

Inexpensive hotels can be found opposite the railway station. Very basic rooms can be had in the *Penginapan Budi Asih* and *Penginapan Lesana* for 10,000 rp. The *Hotel Setia* (☎ 207270), Jalan Inspeksi PJKA 1222, is much better but expensive at 20,000 rp a double with mandi.

Jalan Siliwangi is the main drag for hotels. At No 66, the *Hotel Famili* (☎ 207935) is another basic place with singles/doubles from 12,500/17,000 rp. The *Hotel Cordova* (☎ 204677) at No 87 has older, tatty rooms for 12,500 rp, or 17,500 rp with mandi; renovated rooms with air-con and hot water are a good buy at 30,000 to 60,000 rp. In the centre of town on Jalan Siliwangi the *Hotel*

INDONESIA

Damai at No 130 and the *Losmen Semarang*, next door at No 132, are cheap but uninspiring hotels.

The *Hotel Grand* (☎ 208867), at Jalan Siliwangi 98, is a pleasantly old-fashioned place with worn rooms from 43,000 to 63,000 rp.

Places to Eat

Nasi lengko, a rice dish with bean sprouts, tahu, tempe, fried onion and cucumber, is a local speciality. *Rumah Makan Jatibarang*, on the corner of Jalan Karanggetas and Jalan Kalibaru Selatan, is a good place for this dish. Nearby on Jalan Karanggetas is the clean and reasonable *Kopyor Restaurant*. Good warungs serving seafood, ayam goreng and sate can be found along Jalan Kalibaru Selatan between the Asia and Niaga hotels.

Seafood restaurants along Jalan Bahagia include the well-known *Maxim's* at No 45-47. *Restoran Pujaneka* at Jalan Siliwangi 105 is a mid-range, buffet-style eatery with Sundanese and Cirebon specialities as well as western dishes.

Getting There & Away

The bus station is four km south-west of the centre of town. Regular local buses run between Cirebon and Jakarta (5500 rp; five hours), Bandung (2600 rp; 3½ hours), Pekalongan (3000 rp; four hours), Semarang (5000 rp; seven hours), Yogya (7500 rp; nine hours) and other destinations. Less frequent air-con buses run to all major cities.

The ACC Kopyor 4848 office (☎ 204343), Jalan Karanggetas 7, next door to the Kopyor Restaurant, has door-to-door minibuses to Bandung (10,000 rp), Semarang (15,000 rp), Yogya (15,000 rp) and Cilacap (9000 rp).

Cirebon is on the railway line from Jakarta for both Surabaya in the north and Yogyakarta in the south, so there are frequent trains. To Jakarta's Gambir station, the *Cirebon Ekspres* (15,000 rp bisnis; 3½ hours) departs Cirebon at 5.50 am, and 12.50 and 3.30 pm.

Pelni's KM *Sirimau* stops in Cirebon on its zigzagging course between Pontianak and Banjarmasin in Kalimantan.

YOGYAKARTA

The most popular city in Indonesia, Yogya is easy-going, economical and, as a centre for Javanese culture, offers plenty of attractions.

Yogyakarta was founded in 1755 when the declining Mataram kingdom fragmented under growing Dutch intervention. Prince Mangkubumi, the brother of the Susuhunan of Surakarta, was granted the territory of Yogyakarta and took the title of 'sultan'. From 1825 to 1830, the great Indonesian hero, Prince Diponegoro, led a bitter revolt against the Dutch in the Yogya area. In this century, Yogya was again a centre of resistance to the Dutch and after WWII was the capital of the revolution until independence was eventually won. Today, Yogya is not only the cultural and artistic centre of Java, but a major university town crammed with prestigious institutions.

Although Yogyakarta is spelt with a Y, it's pronounced with a J. Asking for 'Yogya' will get you blank stares – it's pronounced 'Jogja'.

Orientation

It is easy to find your way around Yogya. Jalan Malioboro, named after the Duke of Marlborough, is the main road and runs straight down (north-south) from the railway station. Most of the shops are along this street and most of the cheap accommodation places are just off it, in the Sosrowijayan enclave, near the railway line. There's a second enclave, principally of mid-range places, around Jalan Prawirotaman, just south of the Dalem Pujokusuman Theatre.

The Kraton, or Palace, is the centre of the intriguing area of old Yogya, where you will also find the Water Palace and numerous batik galleries.

Information

Tourist Office The helpful tourist information office (☎ 566000), Jalan Malioboro 16, is open Monday to Friday from 8 am to 7.30 pm, Saturday to noon. The railway station and the airport also have tourist office counters.

Post & Communications The main post office is on Jalan Senopati at the bottom of Jalan Malioboro and is open Monday to Friday from 8 am to 8 pm, and until 5 pm on Saturday.

The Telkom office, one km east of Jalan Malioboro on Jalan Yos Sudarso, is open 24 hours and has Home Country Direct phones. Convenient wartels are those behind the post office at Jalan Trikora 2 and opposite the railway station at Jalan Pasar Kembang 29.

The area code for Yogyakarta is 0274.

Money The BNI bank, Jalan Trikora 1 opposite the post office, is efficient and has good rates for most currencies, or try the BCA bank on Jalan Mangkubumi. Moneychangers are numerous and keep extended hours but rates are worse than the banks. PT Baruman Abadi, in the Natour Garuda Hotel, is one moneychanger that gives excellent rates.

Dangers & Annoyances Yogya has its fair share of thieves – of the break into your room, snatch your bag, steal your bicycle and pick your pocket varieties. The Prambanan and Borobudur buses are reputed to be favourites for pickpockets.

Batik salesman, posing as guides or simply instant friends, can be a pain, especially around the Taman Sari. Shake them off unless you want to endure the inevitable hard sell at a batik gallery.

Kraton
In the heart of the old city the huge palace of the sultans of Yogya is effectively the centre of a small walled-in city within a city. Over 25,000 people live within the greater Kraton compound, which contains its own market, shops, batik and silver cottage industries, schools and mosques. The palace is guarded by elderly gentlemen in traditional costume and a guide shows you around its sumptuous pavilions and halls. The 1500 rp admission includes the guided tour. The kraton is open from 8 am to 2 pm daily, except Friday, when it closes at 1 pm. It is closed on national and kraton holidays.

The inner court, with its 'male' and 'female' stairways to the entrance, has a museum dedicated to Hamengkubuwono IX, the current sultan's father. In the inner pavilion between 10 am to noon you can see gamelan on Mondays and Tuesdays, wayang golek on Wednesdays, classical dance on Thursdays and Sundays, wayang kulit Saturdays and Mojopait folk singing on Fridays.

Taman Sari & Bird Market
The Taman Sari, or Water Palace, was a complex of canals, pools and palaces built within the Kraton between 1758 and 1765. Damaged first by Diponegoro's Java War and then further by an earthquake, it is today a mass of ruins, crowded with small houses and batik galleries. The main bathing pools have been restored. Admission is 500 rp to the restored area, open daily from 9 am to 3 pm.

On the edge of the site is the interesting Pasar Ngasem bird market.

Museums
Close to the Kraton, on the north-western corner of Kraton Square, the **Sono-Budoyo Museum** has a first-rate collection of Javanese arts, including wayang kulit puppets, topeng masks, kris and batik, and the outside courtyard is packed with Hindu statuary. It's open from 8 am to 2.30 pm daily except Monday. Entry is 250 rp.

Between the kraton entrance and the Sono-Budoyo Museum in the palace square, the **Museum Kereta Kraton** holds some opulent chariots of the sultans. It's open from 8 am to 4 pm daily and admission is 250 rp.

Up until his death in 1990, Affandi, Indonesia's internationally best known artist, lived and worked at his home, now the **Affandi Museum**, five km from the centre of town overlooking the river on Jalan Solo. His impressionist works, paintings by his daughter Kartika and other artists are exhibited. The museum is open from 8 am to 3 pm and entry costs 1300 rp.

Yogya has plenty of other museums, usually dedicated to some independence hero or military escapade. Dating from 1765,

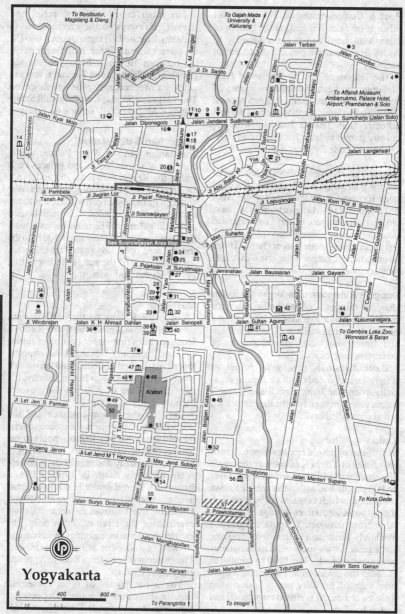

To Borobudur,
Magelang & Dieng

To Gajah Mada
University &
Kaliurang

Jalan Terban

Jalan Colombo

Jalan Magelang

Jalan J W Monginsidi

Jalan A M Sangaji

Jl Dr Sarjito

Jalan Simanjuntak

Jalan Cik Ditiro

Jalan Rahayu Samiono

● 3

● 4

To Affandi Museum,
Ambarrukmo, Palace Hotel,
Airport, Prambanan & Solo

Jalan Kyai Mojo

● 13

Jalan Diponegoro

11 10 9 8
1 11 10 9 8

7

● 6

5

Jl Suryo

Jalan Urip Sumoharjo (Jalan Solo)

Jl Cokroaminoto

14

15

16

17
18
19

20

Jalan P Mangkubumi

Yos

● 21

Jalan Langensari

Jl Abu Bakar Ali

Jl Dr Wahidin Sudirohusodo

Jl Pembela
Tanah Air

Jl Jlagran Lor

Jl Pasar Kembang

Jl Sosrowijayan

See Sosrowijayan Area Map

Jalan Mataram

Jl Malioboro

Jalan Joyonegaran

Jl Mas Suharto

Jalan Lempuyangan

Jalan Kom Pol B Suprapto

Jalan Dr Sutomo

Jalan Mawar

Jalan Gondosuli

Jalan Cokroaminoto

Jalan Let Jen Suprapto

22

26

24
25
23

Jl Pajeksan

Jl Suryatmajan

Jalan Jeminahan

Jalan Bausasran

Jalan Gayam

27

Jalan Bhayangkara

28
29
30

31

Jl A Yani

32

Jl Mayor Suryotomo

Jalan Gajahmada

42

Jalan Suryopranoto

44

Jl Cendana

34

35

Jl Wirobrajan

Jalan K H Ahmad Dahlan

36

33

38
39

40

Jalan Senopati

Jalan Sultan Agung

41

Jalan Kusumanegara

To Gembira Loka Zoo,
Wonosari & Baran

37

43

Jalan Wahid Hasyim

47

48 ● 46

Jl Ngasem

Kraton

45

Jalan Brigjen Katamso

Jalan Taman Siswa

Jl Let Jen S Parman

49

50

51

Jl Taman

52

Jalan Sugeng Jeroni

Jl Let Jend M T Haryono

Jl May Jend Sutoyo

Jalan Kol Sugiyono

Jalan Menteri Supeno

58

To Kota Gede

Jalan Parijatan

54

Jalan Suryo Diningratan

Jalan Tirtodipuran

55

56

Jl Prawirotaman

57

Jalan Sisonamanganjaja

Jalan Soroeulen

53

Jalan Mangkuyudan

Jalan Jogo Karyan

Jalan Manukan

Jalan Tritunggai

Jalan Soro Genan

Yogyakarta

0   400   800 m

To Parangtritis

To Imogiri

INDONESIA

Benteng Vredeburg is the old Dutch fort opposite the post office. Now restored, it houses a museum with dull dioramas showing the history of the independence movement, but the fort architecture is worth a look. Opening hours are 8.30 am to 2.30 pm; closed Mondays. Admission is 200 rp.

Of the other museums, fans of Prince Diponegoro might appreciate the **Museum Sasana Wiratama**, also known as the Monumen Diponegoro. A motley collection of the prince's belongings and other exhibits are kept in this small museum built at the site of his former Yogya residence. The museum is open from 8 am to 1 pm daily.

Other Sights

The smaller **Pakualaman Kraton**, on Jalan Sultan Agung, is also open to visitors and has a small museum, a *pendopo* (open-sided pavilion) which can hold a full gamelan orchestra (performances are held every fifth Sunday) and a curious colonial house with fine cast-iron work. The kraton is open Tuesday, Thursday and Sunday from 9.30 am to 1.30 pm.

The main street of **Kota Gede**, five km south-east of Yogya, is the silverwork centre of Yogya. This is a must for those after silver jewellery or ornaments, and the sacred **grave** of Senopati, the first king of Mataram, can also be seen.

Yogya's **Gembira Loka Zoo** is a spacious but sad affair about three km east of the centre.

Places to Stay

Accommodation in Yogya is remarkably good value and there is a superb choice. It's certainly the best city in Java for places to stay. There are two particularly popular enclaves – the central Sosrowijayan area for the really cheap places and the Prawirotaman area, a couple of km south of the Kraton, for mid-range hotels.

Sosrowijayan Area South of the railway line between Jalan Pasar Kembang and Jalan

INDONESIA

Sosrowijayan, the narrow alleyways of Gang Sosrowijayan I and II have most of the cheap accommodation and popular eating places. More good places to stay are in other small gangs in this area. Despite mass tourism, the gangs are quiet and still have a kampung feel to them.

Gang Sosrowijayan I has some very basic places that cost as little as 4000/6000 rp for singles/doubles, but they are dingy and cater mostly to locals. At the north end, the *Losmen Sastrowihadi* and *Losmen Beta* are in this category. A bit further along is the *Losmen Superman*, behind the restaurant of the same name. Light, clean rooms with shared mandi are 7000 rp, or the rooms with mandi for 10,000 rp are darker but have interesting rock garden bathrooms. *New Superman's*, further south, also has good rooms a couple of doors from the restaurant.

Next along is the *Sari Homestay*, where bright rooms built around a courtyard cost 10,000/12,000 rp with mandi. Just around the corner, the popular *Losmen Lucy* has good rooms with mandi for 10,000 rp.

On Gang Sosrowijayan II, the *Hotel Bagus* is a passable cheap place. Clean rooms with fan cost 5000/6500 rp and 6000/8000 rp. Further south, the *Gandhi Losmen*, in its own garden, has very basic rooms but is friendly and geared to travellers. They don't come much cheaper at 4000 rp per person.

There are a host of small losmen in the small alleys off Gang II, most of them in a similar rock-bottom price range. *Hotel Selekta* is popular and friendly. It's roomier and lighter than most. Rooms with mandi cost 10,000 rp, including breakfast. Nearby is the new *Monica Hotel* (☎ 580598), a small, flash hotel among the cheapies. Opening rates of 16,000 rp for rooms with mandi are very good value. Of the other cheap losmen along this alley, the *Utar Pension* is the best.

Between Gang I and Gang II, the friendly *Dewi Homestay* has more style, with a garden, a cafe and antiques in the sitting area. Unfortunately the rooms with shared mandi for 8500 rp are less impressive, though those with mandi for 12,500 rp are better.

On Jalan Sosrowijayan, between Gang I and Malioboro, is the security-conscious *Aziatic*, an old Dutch-style hotel. Large but run-down doubles are 10,000 rp. Across the road, the larger *Hotel Indonesia* (☎ 587659), Jalan Sosrowijayan 9, is one of the better options. It is well run and has open courtyard areas. Good-sized rooms start at 6000 rp; rooms with mandi cost 9000, 12,500 and 15,000 rp.

At the western end of Jalan Sosrowijayan, 100 metres down an alley, another favourite is the friendly *Ella Homestay* (☎ 582219), Gang Sosrodipuran GT I/487. It's good value with rooms from 6500/10,000 rp; upstairs rooms with mandi for 16,000 rp are of hotel standard.

Sosrowijayan also has plenty of good mid-range places. On Jalan Pasar Kembang, opposite the railway, the *Asia-Afrika* (☎ 566219) at No 21 has a pool and an attractive garden cafe. Prices range from 16,000/22,000 rp, to 50,000/57,000 rp for air-con rooms with hot water showers. The *Hotel Mendut* (☎ 563435) at No 49 and the *Batik Palace Hotel* (☎ 563824) at No 29 are similar.

Jalan Sosrowijayan also has some good mid-range hotels. At No 49, *Oryza Hotel* (☎ 512495) is a renovated villa. Pleasant rooms with shared mandi cost 17,500 rp and rooms with private bath cost 20,000 to 37,500 rp. At No 78, the very friendly *Hotel Karunia* (☎ 565057) is a cheaper alternative with a good rooftop restaurant. Rooms cost 11,000/13,000 rp to 30,000 rp, all plus 10%. Next door at No 76, the *Bladok Restaurant & Losmen* (☎ 560452) is also good value and has a better class of rooms for 20,000/22,500 rp and 32,000/35,000 rp. The restaurant is very good.

Jalan Dagen, one street further south from Jalan Sosrowijayan, is another mid-range enclave. The stylish, well-kept *Peti Mas* (☎ 561938), Jalan Dagen 37, is the favourite here. It has a pool and an attractive garden restaurant. Rooms cost from US$17/19 to US$37.50/40. The *Hotel Batik Yogyakarta II* (☎ 561828), in a quiet back alley north of Jalan Dagen, has spacious grounds and a large pool. Air-con rooms cost US$26/31, bungalows from US$32/38.

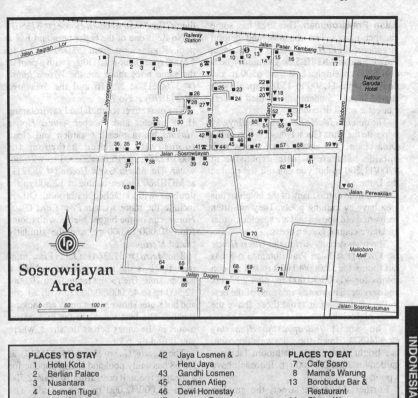

Sosrowijayan
Area

0   50   100 m

INDONESIA

PLACES TO STAY			
1	Hotel Kota	42	Jaya Losmen &
2	Berlian Palace		Heru Jaya
3	Nusantara	43	Gandhi Losmen
4	Losmen Tugu	45	Losmen Atiep
5	Hotel Mendut	46	Dewi Homestay
9	Batik Palace Hotel	47	Losmen Rama
10	Hotel Asia-Afrika	48	Losmen Happy Inn
11	Hotel Ratna	49	Hotel Jogja
15	Kencana Hotel	50	New Superman's
16	Trim Guest House		Losmen
17	Hotel Trim	53	Losmen Lucy
19	Sari Homestay	54	105 Homestay
21	Losmen Beta	56	Lima Losmen
22	Losmen Sastrowihadi	57	Hotel Kartika
23	Supriyanto Inn	58	Hotel Aziatic
24	Losmen Setia Kawan	61	Marina Palace Hotel
25	Hotel Bagus	62	Hotel Indonesia
26	Losmen Setia	63	Ella Homestay
29	Isty Losmen	64	Puntodewo Guest
30	Utar Pension		House
31	Dewi II	65	Wisma Nendra
32	Hotel Selekta	66	Kombokarno Hotel
33	Monica Hotel	67	Peti Mas
35	Hotel Karunia	68	Blue Safir Hotel
36	Yogya Inn	69	Lilik Guest House
37	Oryza Hotel	70	Hotel Batik
39	Wisma Gambira		Yogyakarta II
40	Bakti Kasih	71	Wisma Perdada
		72	Sri Wibowo Hotel

PLACES TO EAT	
7	Cafe Sosro
8	Mama's Warung
13	Borobudur Bar &
	Restaurant
14	Cheap Warungs
18	Superman's
	Restaurant &
	Losmen
20	N&N
27	Anna's Restaurant
28	Budarti
34	Bladok Restaurant &
	Losmen
38	Caterina Restaurant
44	Restoran Tanjung
51	New Superman's
	Restaurant
52	Eko Restaurant
55	Bu Sis
59	Prada Cafe
60	Legian Restaurant

OTHER

6	Wartel
12	PT Haji La Tunrung
	Moneychanger
41	Warpostal

Jalan Prawirotaman This area has some cheaper places, like the neat and helpful *Vagabond Youth Hostel* (☎ 371207) at Jalan Prawirotaman MG III/589. Dormitory beds cost 6000 rp, singles cost from 6500 rp and doubles from 11,500 to 15,000 rp, all with shared mandi. Student and HI card holders can get a small discount.

The quiet *Didi's Hostel*, down an alleyway opposite the Duta Guest House, is part of the Duta chain. The small, clean rooms with outside bath are a little expensive at 9200/11,500 rp but you can use the pool at the Duta.

For a little extra, many of the hotels in this area have swimming pools. They are often converted old houses that are spacious, quiet and have central garden areas.

The high-density *Airlangga Guest House* (☎ 378044) at Jalan Prawirotaman 6-8 has fan rooms for 35,000/40,000 rp and air-con rooms for 40,000/50,000 rp, plus 20% tax and service. The rooms are some of the best in Prawirotaman but avoid those above the noisy nightclub.

The small *Indraprastha Homestay* (☎ 374087), down the alleyway opposite, has bright rooms with bathroom facing a garden for 20,000/25,000 rp. It doesn't have a pool.

Further down the street, the smaller *Prambanan Guest House* (☎ 376167) at No 14 is a newer place with a pool, attractive garden and very comfortable rooms from 25,000/37,500 rp, to 74,000 rp for large doubles with air-con.

At No 26, the big, often crowded *Duta Guest House* (☎ 372064) is one of the more luxurious places, favoured by European tour groups. The gardens and pool are very inviting. Rooms cost from 28,000/35,000 rp to 81,000/92,000 rp.

The popular and good-value *Rose Guest House* (☎ 377991) at No 28 has a larger than normal pool and a restaurant next to it. Rooms cost 12,500/15,000 rp with shared mandi, from 15,000/20,000 rp to 45,000/50,000 rp with mandi.

A lot of the guesthouses in the old villas are pleasant enough but the rooms can be dingy. The *Sumaryo Guest House* (☎ 373507) at No 22 is one of the better ones and has a pool. Rooms cost from 20,000 rp, up to 52,000 rp with air-con. Others with a pool in the same price range are the *Wisma Indah* (☎ 376021) at No 16 and the *Sriwijaya* (☎ 371870) at No 7.

The next street south, Jalan Prawirotaman II, is quieter and cheaper. *Guest House Makuta* has a pleasant garden and clean rooms with attached bathroom for 9000/12,000 rp, 16,000/25,000 rp with hot water. The *Muria Guest House* (☎ 387211) at MGIII/600 is reasonable at 12,500 rp for doubles with attached bathroom. Others include the more spartan *Post Card Guest House*, run by the bigger Metro, with rooms from 10,000/15,000 rp, and the similarly priced *Merapi*.

The *Metro* (☎ 372364) at Jalan Prawirotaman II 71 is the most popular and has a garden area. The rooms range from 10,000/12,500 rp to 45,000/50,000 rp with air-con and hot water showers, but many are looking shabby. The best value are the mid-priced rooms in the annex across the street, where you'll find the pool.

The *Agung Guest House* (☎ 375512) at No 68 has a tiny pool and is also popular for a cheaper room. It costs from 10,000/12,500 rp to 35,000/42,000 rp with air-con. The *Delta Homestay* (☎ 378092) at No 597A is good value. It has a small pool and good rooms for 11,500/18,400 rp, 27,600/32,200 rp with bathroom or 39,100/43,700 with air-con.

Places to Eat

Sosrowijayan Area This area is overrun with cheap eating houses featuring western breakfasts and snacks, as well as Indonesian dishes, and no travellers' menu is complete without fruit salads and banana pancakes.

A whole host of good warungs line Jalan Pasar Kembang, beside the railway line, but *Mama's* is definitely number one in the evenings. On Jalan Pasar Kembang at No 17, *Borobudur Bar & Restaurant* has average fare at high prices, but they have unlimited cold beer and bands later in the evening.

Gang Sosrowijayan I is a favourite hunting ground for cheap eats. The famous *Superman's* is one of the original purveyors of banana pancakes and has been around for decades. These days its offshoot, *New Superman's*, a bit further down Gang I, is more switched-on, with better music and decor, and good apple pie. The *Eko Restaurant* has cheap steaks and the no-frills *N & N* is very popular for its low prices. For the cheapest eats on Gang I, head to the little cluster of wall-hugging warungs at the station end.

Gang II also has some good, cheap places. *Anna's* is very popular, while the *Cafe Sosro* has the best decor but average food. The *Heru Jaya* at the Jaya Losmen has French grills along with Indonesian dishes. *Budarti* is a cheap family-run rumah makan down a side alley.

Jalan Sosrowijayan has a number of good restaurants. *Caterina* at No 41 has a varied menu, good food at low prices and you can dine sitting on mats at the back. *Bladok Restaurant*, opposite at No 76, is a classier little place with predominantly European food. On the corner of Jalan Malioboro, the more expensive *Prada Cafe* has authentic Italian food.

Jalan Malioboro After 10 pm, *food stalls* replace the souvenir stands on Jalan Malioboro and you can take a seat on the woven mats along the pavement. Most of them serve the speciality of Yogya – nasi gudeg (rice with young jackfruit cooked in coconut milk).

On the corner of Jalan Malioboro and Jalan Perwakilan, the more exclusive *Legian Restaurant* is hidden away upstairs. It's very classy and they do a great claypot gudeg ayam (chicken with jackfruit). The western dishes are less inspiring.

That big intrusion on Jalan Malioboro – Malioboro Mall – is not complete without fast food, and *McDonald's* takes pride of place in this monument to western consumerism. The mall has some reasonable cafes inside and the top floor has a so-so food stall area.

Two good little cafes further down are the *Cherry Cafe*, upstairs at Jalan Jenderal A Yani 57 next to the Tatiana Batik shop, and *Griya Dahar Timur*, Jalan Jenderal A Yani 57.

Jalan Prawirotaman The area has a host of mid-range restaurants of fairly average standard. *Tante Lies*, also known as *Warung Java Timur*, at the Jalan Parangtritis intersection is a cheaper, very popular alternative with Central and East Javanese dishes.

Via Via, Jalan Prawirotaman 24B, is an excellent Belgian-run travellers' cafe and meeting spot. As well as providing good food that includes a daily changing menu of Indonesian dishes, they organise a variety of activities.

Hanoman's Forest Restaurant features Indonesian and western cuisine, but the main attraction is the classical Javanese dance or wayang shows each night.

Entertainment

Yogya is an excellent place to see traditional Javanese performing arts. The tourist information office can advise you of what's on, or check in the tourist newspapers. The *Kraton* has daily gamelan, dance or wayang rehearsals. Performances also take place in hotels, restaurants and a variety of performing arts centres.

Wayang kulit can be seen virtually every night of the week. The *Agastya Art Institute* has 3 pm performances every day except Saturday. The *Sono-Budoyo Museum* has performances at 8 pm every evening except Monday. Every second Saturday, all-night performances are held at the southern square (Sasono Hinggil) of the Kraton area.

Wayang golek plays are performed at the *Agastya Art Institute* on Saturday afternoon and there is a daily Nitour performance, except on Sunday. Wayang orang or wayang wong are Javanese dance dramas, and these can also be seen at a variety of venues.

The most famous dance performance is the great Ramayana ballet at Prambanan (see the Around Yogyakarta section). Excellent shortened performances of the Ramayana ballet are also held at the *Purawisata Theatre*

INDONESIA

at the THR, Jalan Katamso, every night from 8 to 10 pm. Another fine troupe performs at *Dalem Pujokusuman* at Jalan Katamso 45 every Monday, Wednesday and Friday from 8 to 10 pm.

Things to Buy

Yogya is a noted batik centre, but other craft industries in and around Yogya include silver, leather, pottery and wayang puppets. Even if you don't intend to buy, galleries and workshops are open free of charge for visitors to observe traditional Javanese crafts in action.

Jalan Malioboro is one great long colourful bazaar of souvenir shops and stalls offering a wide selection of cheap cotton clothes, leatherwork, batik bags, topeng masks and wayang golek puppets. Prices are the cheapest here, depending on your bargaining skills.

On Jalan A Yani (the continuation of Jalan Malioboro), the Terang Bulan shop at No 108 and Batik Keris at No 71 are fixed-price and have a good range of batik. Mirota Batik at No 9 is a good shop to get an idea of prices for general handicrafts as well as batik. Malioboro's labyrinthine market, Pasar Beringharjo, is always worth a browse, especially for cheap batik and textiles.

Yogya has dozens of batik art galleries. Prices are high at the better known galleries, and ridiculously cheap at the mass production galleries, most of which are found around the Taman Sari (Water Palace). Try to avoid the touts and 'guides' who follow you – you'll end up paying commission on anything you buy. Yogya is crawling with batik sellers and many scams are tried. A time-honoured ploy is the tale about a huge ASEAN exhibition in Singapore which will empty the city of batik and today is your last chance to buy!

Another major area to shop is Jalan Tirtodipuran, the continuation of Jalan Prawirotaman. A string of expensive batik factories, galleries and art shops sell furniture, antiques and curios. Antiques are often instantly aged and prices can be ridiculously high here. Many of the batik workshops here,

such as Batik Indah, Jalan Tirtodipuran 6A, give free guided tours of the batik process.

Silverwork can be found all over town, but the best area to shop is in the silver village of Kota Gede, on the eastern outskirts of Yogya. Fine filigree work is a Yogya speciality but many styles and designs are available. You can get a guided tour of the process at the large factories such as Tom's Silver and MD, with no obligation to buy at their high prices.

Kasongan, the potters' village seven km south-west of Yogya, produces an astonishing array of pottery, mostly large figurines and pots.

Getting There & Away

Air Garuda (π 514400), Merpati (π 514272), Sempati (π 511612) and Mandala (π 589521) all service Yogya. Flights include Jakarta (158,000 rp), Denpasar (147,000 rp), Surabaya (80,000 rp) and Bandung (97,000 rp).

Bus Yogya's Umbulharjo bus station is four km south-east of the city centre. Ordinary/air-con buses include: Solo (1500/2500 rp; two hours), Semarang (3000/5000 rp; 3½ hours), Cilacap (4500/7000 rp; five hours), Bandung (10,800/21,500 rp; 12 hours, Jakarta (13,000/21,000 rp; 12 hours), Surabaya (7500/13,000 rp; eight hours), Probolinggo (9000/15,000 rp; nine hours) and Denpasar (16,000/27,000 rp; 16 hours).

For the long hauls, tickets for the big luxury buses can be bought at the bus station, or it's more expensive but less hassle to check fares and departures with the ticket agents along Jalans Mangkubumi, Sosrowijayan and Prawirotaman. These agents can also arrange pick-up from your hotel. Direct minibuses to Pangandaran (17,500 rp air-con) and Gunung Bromo (25,000 rp non air-con) can also be arranged.

From the main bus station, buses also operate regularly to towns in the immediate area: Borobudur (1200 rp; 1½ hours), Parangtritis (1200 rp; one hour) and Kaliurang (600 rp; one hour). For Prambanan (500 rp) take the yellow Pemuda bus. For Imogiri (500 rp; 40 minutes) take a colt or the Abadi bus No 5 to Panggang and tell the conductor to let you off at the *makam* (graves). Buses to Imogiri and Parangtritis can also be caught on Jalan Sisingamangaraja at the end of Jalan Prawirotaman. You can catch the Borobudur bus going north along Jalan Magelang at the Pingit bus stop.

From the Terban sub-terminal to the north of the centre on Jalan Simanjuntak, colts go to Kaliurang (850 rp) and Solo (2000 rp) passing the airport en route.

Minibus Door-to-door minibuses run to all major cities from Yogya. Most will pick up from hotels in Yogya, but not for the short runs like Solo, in which case you have to go to the depots, most of which are on Jalan Diponegoro. Minibuses go to Solo (5000 rp), Jakarta (35,000 rp), Malang and Surabaya (20,000 rp), Cilacap (7500 rp), Semarang (6000 rp), Wonosobo (5000 rp), Bandung (25,000 rp) and numerous other destinations.

Train Yogya's Tugu railway station is conveniently central.

Better express services to/from Jakarta are the *Fajar Utama Yogya* day trains and *Senja Utama Yogya* night services, which go via Cirebon. Both cost from 23,000 rp in bisnis class to 55,000 rp in air-con eksekutif, and take around 8½ hours. Slower, crowded ekonomi trains depart from Jakarta's Pasar Senen station: the *Gaya Baru Malam Selatan* and *Matamaja*, or the better *Empujeva*, which leaves Pasar Senen at 3.55 pm.

There are more than half a dozen trains a day between Yogya and Surabaya. The *Mutiara Selatan* (25,000 rp bisnis; five hours) is a good express service, and the *Argopuro* (4500 rp; seven hours) is a good ekonomi service leaving Yogya at 7.30 am.

The quickest and most convenient way to get to Solo is on the *Prambanan Ekspres* (2000 rp; one hour) departing at 9 am and 3.15 pm.

Getting Around
The Airport Taxis from the airport to Yogya, 10 km away, cost around 7000 rp. From the main road, only 200 metres from the terminal,

you can get a colt to Yogya's Terban colt terminal or a bus to the bus terminal.

Bus Bis Kotas are bright orange minibuses operating on 17 set routes around the city for a flat 400 rp fare. All terminate at the bus station. Bus No 2 operates runs from Jalan Parangtritis, past Jalan Prawirotaman, to Jalan Mataram, one block from Jalan Malioboro. For Kota Gede, take bus No 4 from Jalan Malioboro or bus No 8 from the bus terminal.

Local Transport Bicycles and motorbikes can be hired cheaply but lock them up very securely. There's an enormous supply of becaks that pester you for a ride. Furious bargaining is usually required. Count on 1000 rp for a short trip. Jalan Prawirotaman to Jalan Malioboro should cost no more than 2000 rp. Horse-drawn andongs cost about the same. Metered taxis are readily available.

AROUND YOGYAKARTA
Yogya's, indeed Java's, biggest drawcards are the complex of Prambanan and the huge Buddhist centre at Borobudur, but a number of other interesting places can be visited outside the city.

Prambanan
The biggest Hindu temple complex in Java, Prambanan is 17 km east from Yogya on the Solo road. Though some 50 temple sites have been discovered in and around Prambanan, the main temples are all in the tourist complex fronting the village on the highway.

The largest of these, the **Shiva temple**, soars 47 metres high and is lavishly carved. The statue of Shiva stands in the central chamber and statues of the goddess Durga, Shiva's elephant-headed son Ganesh and Agastya the teacher stand in the other chapels of the upper part of the temple. The Shiva temple is flanked by the Vishnu and Brahma temples, the latter carrying further scenes from the *Ramayana*. In the small central temple, opposite the Shiva temple, stands a fine statue of the bull Nandi, Shiva's mount.

Built in the 9th century AD, possibly 50 years after Borobudur, the complex at Prambanan was abandoned soon after its completion when the old Mataram kingdom mysteriously declined. Many of the temples had collapsed by the last century and not until 1937 was any form of reconstruction attempted. Other temple ruins can be found close to Prambanan and on the road back to Yogya.

There is a 5000 rp admission charge to the temple complex. This includes camera fees and a guided tour (if you are prepared to wait to join a large enough group) in most major languages. The temple enclosure is open daily from 6 am to 6 pm, with last admission at 5.15 pm.

If you are here at the right time don't miss the great Ramayana ballet performance. The ballet is performed over four successive nights, twice each month of the dry season, from May to October, leading up to the full moon. Prambanan's Trimurti Theatre has performances throughout the year on Tuesday, Wednesday and Thursday nights from 7.30 pm.

Getting There & Away From Yogya, take the yellow Pemuda bus (500 rp; 30 minutes) from the main bus station, or a Solo colt from

Around Yogyakarta

0   15   30 km

INDIAN OCEAN

the Terban sub-terminal. A bicycle is an ideal way to explore all the temples in the area via the backroads.

Borobudur

Ranking with Bagan and Angkor Wat as one of the greatest South-East Asian Buddhist monuments, Borobudur is an enormous construction covering a hill 42 km from Yogya. With the decline of Buddhism, Borobudur was abandoned and only rediscovered in 1814 when Raffles governed Java.

The temple consists of six square bases topped by three circular ones and it was constructed roughly contemporaneously with Prambanan in the early part of the 9th century AD.

Over the centuries, the supporting hill became waterlogged and the whole immense stone mass started to subside at a variety of angles. A US$25 million restoration project returned it to its former glory.

Nearly 1500 narrative panels on the terraces illustrate Buddhist teachings and tales while 432 Buddha images sit in chambers on the terraces. On the upper circular terraces there are latticed stupas which contain 72 more Buddha images.

The **Mendut Temple**, three km east of Borobudur, has a magnificent statue of Buddha seated with two disciples. He is three metres high and sits with both feet on the ground, rather than in the usual lotus position. It has been suggested that this image was originally intended to top Borobudur but proved impossible to raise to the summit.

The temple site is open from 6 am to 5.15 pm and admission is 5000 rp, including a guide (in most major foreign languages), camera fees and entry to the museum.

Places to Stay & Eat The small village of Borobudur has quite a selection of accommodation. The welcoming, well-run *Lotus Guest House* (☎ 88281), on the east side of the temple near the main parking area, has singles/doubles with mandi for 7500/10,000 rp up to 20,000 rp, including breakfast. It has a good cafe, information on things to do in the area and bicycles for rent.

One km from the temple, the flash *Pondok Tinggal Hostel* (☎ 88245) has bamboo-style rooms for 33,000 to 125,000 rp, or a bed in the spotless, often empty dorms costs 7500 rp. The plush *Manohara Hotel* (☎ 88131) is right in the monument grounds.

Getting There & Away From Yogya take a direct bus (1200 rp; 1½ hours) via Muntilan. It's a fine walk to Mendut and the smaller Pawon Temple, otherwise a bus or bemo is 300 rp to hop from one temple to the next, or you could hire a becak.

Kaliurang, Selo & Gunung Merapi

Kaliurang is a pleasant mountain resort on the slopes of Gunung Merapi, 26 km north of Yogya. There are great views of the mountains, lovely walks, waterfalls and a rather chilly swimming pool. It's pleasant to feel the crisp mountain air after the sweaty heat of the plains.

Gunung Merapi is one of Java's most dangerous volcanoes and has erupted numerous times. The last major eruption was on 22 November 1994, when 69 people were killed. Since then, Merapi continues to rumble and spew lava down its flank. The once popular climb from Kaliurang is now off-limits but it is possible to climb to a viewpoint to see the lava flows – a spectacular sight. You can only go with a qualified guide – contact the owner of Vogels for information and advice (see Places to Stay).

It is possible, and easier, to climb Merapi from **Selo** on the north side but you cannot see the lava flows.

Places to Stay In Kaliurang, *Vogels Hostel* (☎ 895208), Jalan Astamulya 76, has deservedly been the travellers' favourite for years. There is a variety of rooms to suit most tastes and budgets, starting at 3500 rp in the dorm. Doubles range from 6000 rp, up to good mid-range bungalows at the back with bath for only 22,000 rp. HI card holders get a small discount. It has a good, cheap restaurant and this is the place to arrange treks to Merapi and other good walks.

The nearby *Christian Hostel* is a Vogels offshoot. New, spotless rooms with mandi provide excellent accommodation for 12,500 rp (10,000 rp for HI members). The rooftop sitting area has views of Merapi and the lava flow. Kaliurang has over 100 other places to stay.

In Selo, *Pak Auto* has simple accommodation for 5000 rp per person and arranges guides. The *Losmen Jaya & Restaurant* and *Hotel Agung Merapi* also have basic rooms.

Getting There & Away From Yogya take a Magelang bus to Blabak and then a colt or bus to Selo. Direct Solo-Magelang buses pass Selo.

Imogiri

The royal cemetery of the sultans of Mataram lies 20 km south-east from Yogya at Imogiri, high on a hillside at the top of 345 steps. Imogiri is a sacred site and many local people visit to pay their respects at the royal graves, especially that of the great Sultan Agung.

It's an interesting place to visit but you are expected to follow the strict etiquette of the kraton rules. All visitors have to sign the Visitor's Book, pay a small donation and hire traditional Javanese dress before they enter the graveyard.

The main tombs are only open from 10 am to 1 pm on Monday and from 1.30 to 4 pm on Friday and Sunday, and there is no objection to visitors joining the pilgrims then.

Parangtritis

The best known of the beaches south of Yogya, Parangtritis is 27 km away. It is a scruffy local resort that is packed on weekends and the currents and undertows can be dangerous. Still, accommodation is cheap, you can take long and lonely walks (on weekdays) along the beach and over the sand dunes, and there are interesting caves to visit.

Parangtritis is a centre for the worship of Nyai Loro Kidul, the queen of the South Seas. Her mystical union with the sultans of Yogya and Solo requires regular offerings. Parangtritis attracts all sorts of mystics and meditators.

Places to Stay & Eat Cheap, basic losmen are everywhere. On the main street/promenade, *Hotel Widodo* is the best cheap option with rooms for 15,000 rp, including breakfast and free tea and coffee. It has a good little restaurant and tours along the coast are offered. Their more basic offshoot is behind the main drag with rooms from 5000 rp per person. The *Agung Garden* also caters to travellers but no longer seems to care. Crumbling rooms cost 10,000 to 35,000 rp with air-con. Other reasonable places are the *Wisma Lukita*, which has rooms with mandi for 10,000 rp, and the *Budi Inn*.

Getting There & Away From Yogya, it's 1200 rp and one hour from the bus terminal, and this includes the entry fee. The last bus back to Yogya leaves at 5.30 pm.

Bandungan & Gedung Songo

Between Yogya and Semarang, Bandungan is a pleasant enough hill resort, but the main reason to visit is to see the nearby Gedung Songo (Nine Buildings, in Javanese). This collection of small Hindu temples on the slopes of Gunung Ungaran is not the most awe-inspiring in Java, but the views from the hilltop setting are magnificent.

The town of Ambarawa, on the main central route, is the turn-off point for Bandungan. The **Ambarawa Railway Station Museum** has a collection of ancient steam locomotives built between 1891 and 1928, including a 1902 cog locomotive still in working order.

Places to Stay Bandungan has dozens of losmen and more expensive hotels. The *Daruki* and *Tiga Dara* are basic but acceptable places with rooms from 10,000 rp. The *Pura Mandira Karya* (☎ 91454) is a notch up in quality and has rooms from 12,000 to 17,500 rp. Some have hot water. The friendly *Kusuma Madya Inn* (☎ 91136) has comfortable rooms with mandi from 15,000 to 50,000 rp.

Getting There & Away Buses run directly from Semarang to Bandungan, or coming from Yogya, get down in Ambarawa and then take a colt to Bandungan. From Bandungan's bustling marketplace, catch a colt for the three km to the turn-off to the temples. From the turn-off, take a motorcycle ojek for the final three km to Gedung Songo (1000 rp). All of the temples can be visited on foot in an hour.

WONOSOBO

Wonosobo is the main gateway to the Dieng Plateau, otherwise it is a forgettable place.

The tourist office (☎ 21194) at Jalan Kartini 3 is helpful. The BNI bank on Jalan A Yani changes cash and travellers' cheques at passable rates.

The area code for Wonosobo is 0286.

Places to Stay & Eat

Wisma Duta Homestay (☎ 21674), Jalan Rumah Sakit 3, is the best budget option. Comfortable, bright rooms with mandi cost 12,500 rp, including breakfast. Also good, the small *Citra Homestay* (☎ 21880), Jalan Angkatan 45, has rooms with shared bathroom for 15,000 rp. Wonosobo has plenty of other cheap, uninspiring losmen.

If you can't be bothered heading into town, the mid-range *Hotel Dewi* (☎ 21813), Jalan A Yani 90A, right opposite the bus station, has good rooms for 10,000 to 30,000 rp. The *Hotel Nirwana* (☎ 21066) at Jalan Resimen 18 No 34 is secure, quiet and friendly. Comfortable rooms cost 40,000 rp with hot shower, or 70,000 rp for large family rooms. Rates are inflated, but a substantial breakfast is included.

The *Dieng Restaurant*, Jalan Kawedanan 29, has excellent buffet-style food and information on Dieng. The *Asia* two doors down has good Chinese food.

Getting There & Away

From Yogya take a bus to Magelang (1100 rp; one hour) and then another to Wonosobo (1400 rp; two hours). Rahayu Travel (☎ 21217) has door-to-door minibuses to/from Yogya for 5500 rp per person. Other travel agency minibuses go to Semarang, Purwokerto and Jakarta.

The bus terminal is two km south of the town centre (300 rp by angkot; 500 rp by andong). Hourly buses go to Semarang (2500 rp; four hours) via Secang and Ambarawa (1700 rp; three hours). For Cilacap, first take a bus to Purwokerto (2400 rp; three hours). Leave around 6 am to catch the ferry to Kalipucang and on to Pangandaran.

Buses to Dieng leave from Terminal Dieng, half a km west of the town centre.

DIENG PLATEAU

About 130 km from Yogya, this 2000-metre-high plateau has some interesting temples, beautiful scenery, good walks and (at night) freezing temperatures. Come prepared for the night-time cold, Dieng's basic losmen and unexciting food, and you'll probably find it interesting.

Dieng is the collapsed remnant of an ancient crater. On the swampy plain in front of the village are five Hindu/Buddhist temples that form the **Arjuna Complex**. These temples are thought to be the oldest in Java, predating Borobudur and Prambanan. Though historically important, they are small, squat and plain. Other temples scattered around include **Candi Bima**, to the south, and the small site **museum** contains statues and sculpture from the temples.

The plateau's natural attractions of mineral lakes, steaming craters and other quiet places are the main reason to visit. From the village, you can do a loop walk that takes in beautiful **Telaga Warna** (Coloured Lake) and **Kawah Sikidang**, a volcanic crater with steaming vents and frantically bubbling mud ponds. You can see all the main sights, including the temples, on foot in a morning or afternoon. Other volcanic areas and lakes lie further afield.

The walk to Sembungan, reputed to be the highest village in Java at 2300 metres, to see the sunrise from the hill one km from the village is a popular activity. Start at 4 am to reach the top 1½ hours later. The Dieng Plateau Homestay and Losmen Bu Jono both offer guides for 5000 rp per person.

Places to Stay & Eat

Dieng has a handful of spartan hotels. The *Dieng Plateau Homestay* and the *Losmen Bu Jono* next door are the best options. Both charge 7500/10,000 rp for basic singles/doubles with shared mandi, and they both have cafes, information on Dieng and offer guides.

Other options include the *Hotel Asri*, which has reasonable rooms, and the overpriced *Hotel Gunung Mas*.

Getting There & Away

Frequent buses to Dieng (1000 rp; 1½ hours) leave from Wonosobo throughout the day and continue on to Batur, on Bali. From Batur infrequent buses run to Pekalongan (1600 rp; four hours) on the steep, bad road.

SOLO

Situated between Yogya and Surabaya, Solo (or Surakarta) was for a time the capital of the Mataram kingdom. The sultanate had shifted its capital several times from Kota Gede to Plered, and then to Kartasura. The court of Kartasura was devastated by fighting in 1742 and the capital was moved east to the small village of Sala on the Bengawan Solo River.

Solo competes with its sister city Yogya as a centre of Javanese culture. It has two royal palaces, is a major batik centre and its schools of dance, music and wayang are as highly regarded as Yogya's. In fact, it has almost all of Yogya's attractions, without the tourist hordes.

Information

The helpful tourist office (☎ 711435), Jalan Slamet Riyadi 275, is open from 8 am to 5 pm. The tourist office also has a helpful stand at the bus station.

The area code for Solo is 0271.

Kratons

The Susuhunan of Mataram, Pakubuwono II, finally moved from Kartasura into his new palace, the **Kraton Surakarta**, in 1745. A visit to the museum here is particularly interesting, especially with one of the English-speaking

PLACES TO STAY	PLACES TO EAT	15	Radya Pustaka
1 Hotel Agas International	7 Adem Ayam Restaurant	21	Museum Garuda (Lippobank
3 Hotel Jayakarta	8 Swensen's & KFC		Building)
5 Sahid Sala Hotel	16 Pujosari	24	Pasar Triwindu
9 Solo Inn	18 Cipta Rasa Restaurant	25	Kraton Mangkunegara
10 Hotel Putri Ayu	19 Tio Ciu 99	36	SMKI School
11 Riyadi Palace Hotel	26 Jalan Teuku Umar	38	Nirwana Disco
12 Ramayana Guest House		Warungs	39	Pasar Gede
17 Hotel Dana	27 American Donut Bakery	40	Telkom Office
20 Java Homestay	28 Warung Baru	41	Main Post Office
22 Hotel Cakra	29 News Cafe	42	Adpura Kencana Monument
23 Wisata Indah	31 Cafe Gamelan	43	Matahari Department Store
30 Hotel Central	35 Pringgondani	
32 Solo Homestay	48 Kasuma Sari Restaurant	44	Balai Agung
33 Kusuma Sahid Prince Hotel	51 New Holland Bakery	45	BC Bank
34 Griyadi Sahid Kusuma	52 Kantin Bahagia	46	Mesjid Agung
37 Hotel Trio	62 Kafe Solo	50	Wartel
47 Mama Homestay		55	Batik Keris
49 Hotel Kota	**OTHER**	58	Taxi Stand
53 Relax Homestay	2 Balapan Railway Station	59	Singosaren Plaza
54 Cendana Homestay & Warung Biru	4 RRI Radio Station	60	Batik Danarhadi
56 Paradise Guest House	6 Toko Bedoyo Srimpi	61	Legenda Disco
57 Westerners	13 Sriwedari Amusement Park	64	Vihara Rahayu Chinese Temple
63 Happy Homestay	14 Tourist Office	65	Pasar Klewer
		66	Kraton Surakarta
		67	Kraton Museum

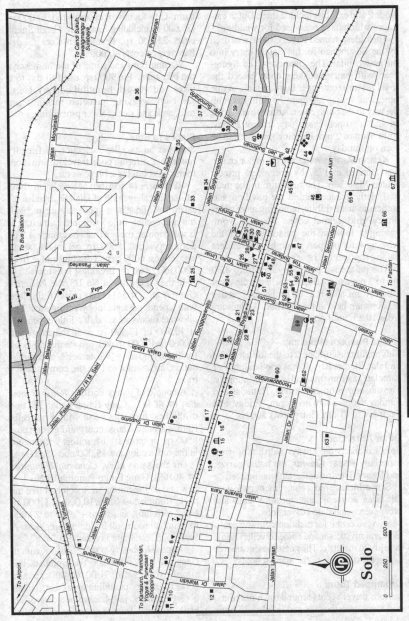

Solo

INDONESIA

0   250   500 m

To Airport

To Bus Station

To Candi Sukuh,
Tawangmangu &
Surabaya

To Kartasuro, Prambanan,
Yogya & Purwosari
Shopping Plaza

To Pacitan

guides, and exhibits include three Dutch carriages which have been used for weddings.

The oldest, named Kiyai Grudo, was used by the Susuhunan for his stately entry into the new capital. The giant pop-eyed figurehead with hairy whiskers once graced the royal *perahu* (outrigger boat), which, at one time, was able to navigate the Solo River all the way to the north coast. Admission is 1000 rp and it's open every day, except Friday, from 8 am to 2 pm. Dancing practice can be seen on Sunday.

Kraton Mangkunegaran, the minor kraton, was founded in 1757 by a dissident prince, Raden Mas Said. The museum, in the main hall of the palace behind the pavilion, has some unusual exhibits, including an extraordinary gold genital cover. It's also worth having a look in the palace shop at the wayang kulit puppets made by the resident dalang (puppet operator).

The palace is open every day from 8.30 am to 2 pm except Sunday, when it closes at 1 pm. Admission is 1500 rp. Dance practice sessions are held at the pavilion Wednesday from 10 am until noon.

Radya Pustaka Museum

This small museum, next to the tourist office on Jalan Slamet Riyadi, has good exhibits of gamelan instruments and wayang puppets. The museum is open Tuesday, Thursday and Sunday from 8 am to 1 pm, Friday and Saturday to 11 am. Entry costs 500 rp.

Other Attractions

Solo's markets are always worth a browse, especially **Pasar Klewer**, the batik market, and **Pasar Triwindu**, the antique market.

Sriwedari is Solo's amusement park with fair rides, souvenir and sideshow stalls and other somewhat dated diversions.

Solo is a centre for traditional Javanese religion and mysticism and some travellers come here just to meditate. The guesthouses can steer you in the direction of the many schools.

Organised Tours

Various travel agents around town run tours, and many guesthouses and hotels will book them. City tours will cost around 20,000 rp (25,000 rp including Sangiran), Candi Sukuh costs 25,000 rp, Prambanan-Kota Gede-Parangtritis costs 40,000 rp.

Warung Baru and some of the homestays run bike tours. For 9000 rp, one full-day tour takes you through beautiful countryside to see batik weaving, gamelan making, and tofu, arak and rice-cracker processing.

Places to Stay

Solo has an excellent selection of friendly homestays offering good travel information, tours, bus bookings, bicycles etc.

Westerners (☎ 633106) at Kemlayan Kidul 11, the first alley north of Jalan Secoyudan off Jalan Yos Sudarso, is spotlessly clean, well run and secure. Solo's original homestay, it is still popular, though it can be cramped. The dormitory costs 5000 rp per night, small singles cost 6000 rp and doubles range from 7000 to 12,000 rp. Breakfast is extra.

In the same alley at No 1/3, the *Paradise Guest House* (☎ 54111) is a classy little place with a pendopo-style lobby/sitting area. The all-white rooms are good, if a little expensive, at 10,500 to 17,500 rp with shared mandi, 25,000 to 40,000 rp with private mandi. Look for the sign offering 'Westerner's' accommodation, an attempt to lure the competition's trade.

A couple of gangs north is *Relax Homestay* (☎ 46417), Gang Empu Sedah 28, one of the best homestays and with a bar/cafe. Rooms around a large courtyard garden cost 8500 rp, or more stylish rooms with mandi in the old section are 15,000 and 25,000 rp.

Off the same alley, *Cendana Homestay* (☎ 46169), Gang Empu Panuluh III No 4, is new and so the rooms are a notch above the pack. Rooms cost 7500/10,000 rp (1000 rp extra with fan), and from 15,000 to 20,000 rp with bathroom, all including breakfast. A very good restaurant is attached.

Mama Homestay (☎ 52248), Kauman Gang III, also off Jalan Yos Sudarso, has simple rooms for 7000/10,000 rp and 8000/10,000 rp, including breakfast. This is a very friendly, laid-back place and offers batik courses. *Solo Homestay*, in an alley near Warung Baru, also has batik courses for 8500 rp per day, and many of the guests stay here just for the courses. It's friendly, if a little dingy, and rooms cost 7000/10,000 rp.

Away from the main guesthouse enclave, but still central, is *Java Homestay*, Jalan Jawa 11. The rooms, from 7000 to 12,500 rp including breakfast, can be gloomy, but this friendly place is new, so it tries harder.

Further out, *Atmo Witatan* (☎ 54538), Jalan Sidikoro 42, is another new place with just a few attractive rooms for 10,000/15,000 rp with outside mandi. It is one block south of the Museum Vreteburg at the kraton.

The small *Happy Homestay* (☎ 57149), Gang Karagan 12, off Jalan Honggowongso (look for the sign), has tiny but comfortable singles for 6000 rp or larger doubles for 10,000 rp.

Solo has dozens of hotels, but they tend to be anonymous places. The long-running *Hotel Kota* (☎ 632841), Jalan Slamet Riyadi 125, is a two storey place built around a courtyard. Rooms cost from 8000/12,000 rp to 15,000/20,000 rp with mandi. At Jalan Ahmad Dahlan 32 is the open and airy *Hotel Central* (☎ 712814). It has some fine art deco woodwork, but not a lot else. The rooms, all without bath, are 7500 rp for doubles.

The well-maintained *Hotel Putri Ayu* (☎ 711812), Jalan Slamet Riyadi 331, is edging into the mid-range. Rooms cost 27,000 rp with mandi, 42,000 rp with air-con. *Ramayana Guest House* (☎ 712814), Jalan Dr Wahidin 22, is an attractive house with a garden and stylish dining/lobby area. Doubles with bath cost 25,000 to 50,000 rp, plus 21%. Conveniently located, the *Hotel Dana* (☎ 711976), Jalan Slamet Riyadi 286, is an old colonial hotel with luxurious, renovated rooms for 85,000 and 109,000 rp.

Places to Eat

Solo is famous for its all-night warungs serving local specialities such as nasi liwet, rice with chicken and coconut milk. Another local speciality is srabi, the small rice puddings served up on a crispy pancake with banana, chocolate or jackfruit on top.

Pujosari is a good selection of warungs next to the museum and tourist office in the Sriwedari Park area. The *Lezat*, open 24 hours, and the Chinese *Oriental* are two favourites here.

Jalan Ahmad Dahlan is the centre for budget travellers' eateries. At No 23, the most popular travellers' meeting place is the long-running *Warung Baru* for substantial breakfasts and Indonesian and western fare at most reasonable prices. Across the street, *News Cafe* is a cheap restaurant and bar, a good place for a late drink. Further down at No 28, the friendly *Cafe Gamelan* is the main competition to Warung Baru for the travellers' trade. It has a varied menu of Indonesian and western dishes.

Close to most of the homestays, *Kantin Bahagia* is a pleasant little restaurant with bamboo decor, cheap Indonesian food and cheap beer. Some of the homestays themselves have good restaurants. The *Warung Biru* at the Cendana Homestay has good food and vegetarian meals, and the cafe at the Relax Homestay is also popular.

For Javanese food try *Adem Ayam*, Jalan Slamet Riyadi 342, or *Pringgondani*, north of the river at Jalan Sultan Sahrir 79. *Kusama Sari*, on the corner of Jalan Slamet Riyadi and Jalan Yos Sudarso, has seductive air-con, good hot platter grills and ice creams.

Entertainment

Solo is an excellent place to see traditional Javanese performing arts. The tourist office has details

The Sriwedari Theatre at the *Sriwedari Amusement Park*, Jalan Slamet Riyadi, boasts one of the most famous wayang orang troupes in Java, which performs from 8.15 to 10.15 pm Monday to Thursday, and 8.15 to 11.15 pm on Saturdays.

Radio Republik Indonesia (RRI), Jalan Abdul Rahman Saleh 51, has all-night wayang kulit shows on the third Saturday of every month from 9 pm, and other regular performances.

Both *kratons* also have traditional Javanese dance practice: Wednesday from 10 am to noon at the Pura Mangkunegara, and

Sunday morning and afternoon performances at the Kraton Surakarta.

You can see dance practice every morning except Sunday at the *STSI* (Sekolah Tinggi Seni Indonesia), the arts academy in the north-east of the city, and at *SMKI*, the high school for the performing arts on Jalan Kepatihan Wetan.

Things to Buy

Solo is Indonesia's main batik centre and most of the large batik outlets – Batik Keris, Batik Semar and Batik Danarhadi – are based here, with showrooms in the centre of the city. You can see the batik process at the big Batik Keris factory in Lawiyan, west of the city. Pasar Klewer, near Kraton Surakarta, is the cheapest place to buy batik if you know your stuff.

Pasar Triwindu on Jalan Diponegoro is Solo's famous antique market. Bargain hard and be aware that many of the 'antik' are newly aged. Kris and other souvenirs can be purchased from street vendors at the eastside alun alun to the north of the Kraton Surakarta. Vendors at Sriwedari also sell souvenirs. At the Balai Agung, on the north side of the alun alun, you can see high-quality wayang kulit puppets being made and gamelan sets are for sale.

Getting There & Away

Air The airport is 10 km north-west of the city centre; 10,000 rp by taxi or take a bus to Kartosuro and then another to the airport. Garuda and Sempati have direct flights to Jakarta, while Merpati flies to Bandung. Silk Air flies directly to Singapore.

Bus The main Tirtonadi bus station is just north of the railway station, three km from the centre of town. Frequent buses go to Prambanan (1000 rp; 1½ hours), Yogya (1400 rp; two hours), Semarang (2100/3600 rp air-con; 2½ hours), Bandung (11,000/19,000 rp) and Jakarta (14,000/25,000 rp). Going east and south, buses include those to Tawangmangu (900 rp; one hour), Pacitan (2600 rp; four hours), Blitar (5300 rp; six hours), Surabaya (7500/13,000 rp air-con; six hours), Malang (7600/13,000 rp; eight hours) and Probolinggo (7500 rp; eight hours).

Near the main bus station, the Gilingan minibus station has door-to-door minibuses to nearly as many destinations as the buses. Homestays and travel agents also sell tickets. Bromo Express, Jalan Slamet Riyadi 201, has a minibus service to Ngadisari (for Gunung Bromo) for a hefty 25,000 rp non-air-con or 35,000 rp air-con.

Train Solo is on the main Jakarta-Yogya-Surabaya train line. For Yogya, the efficient *Prambanan Ekspres* (2000 rp bisnis; one hour) departs at 7 am and 1 pm. For Jakarta, good trains include the express *Senja Utama* (28,000 rp bisnis; 10½ hours) departing at 6 pm. For Bandung, the *Senja Mataram* (20,000 rp bisnis; nine hours) departs at 8.15 pm.

To Surabaya, the *Argopuro* (4500 rp; six hours) is a reasonable and less-crowded ekonomi train departing at 9 am.

Getting Around

A becak from the railway station or bus station into the town centre is around 1500 rp, a taxi 5000 rp. The orange minibus No 06 costs 300 rp to Jalan Slamet Riyadi.

The city double-decker buses run between Kartasura in the west and Palur in the east, directly along Jalan Slamet Riyadi, and cost a flat fare of 300 rp. Bicycles can be hired from the homestays.

AROUND SOLO
Sangiran

Prehistoric Java Man fossils were discovered at Sangiran, 15 km north of Solo, and there is a small museum with fossil exhibits including some amazing 'mammoth' bones and tusks.

They are still finding things and if you wander up the road past the museum and have a look in some of the exposed banks you may find shells or fossil bones and crabs. To get there take a bus to Kalijambe (500 rp) and it's a four km walk from there (1000 rp by ojek).

Candi Sukuh,
Tawangmangu & Sarangan

Candi Sukuh is a fascinating temple on the slopes of Gunung Lawu, 36 km east of Solo. Dating from the 15th century, it was one of the last Hindu temples to be built on Java and has a curious Inca-like look. Take a bus to Karangpandan (700 rp), then a Kemuning minibus to the turn-off to Candi Sukuh (500 rp). On market days the bus goes right to the temple; otherwise it's a two km uphill walk to the site. It is about 1½ hours travelling by bus in total but it's worth it for the superb views and atmosphere. About 10 km further up the mountain is Candi Ceto, a simpler temple built in the same style.

Tawangmangu, a straggling mountain resort about a 1½ hour ride out of Solo, has an impressive waterfall (the Grojogan Sewu). It is incredibly crowded on weekends – go during the week. You can catch a bus from Karangpandan or it's possible to walk to Tawangmangu from Candi Sukuh, a pleasant 2½ hour stroll along a narrow paved road, and from Tawangmangu you can bus back to Solo for 900 rp.

Just over the border in East Java, 18 km past Tawangmangu (2000 rp by colt), Sarangan is a cooler and more attractive hill resort built around a crater lake. The lake has boating and there are nearby walks. Sacred Gunung Lawu (3265 metres) can be climbed from Cemoro Sewu, on the Tawangmangu road five km from Sarangan.

Places to Stay In Tawangmangu, the *Pak Amat Losmen* is right by the bus station. Rooms with enclosed verandas are good value at 9000 rp, though the attached mandis could do with a good scrub. Prices and quality increase as you head up the hill. The *Pondok Garuda* (☎ 97239) has good rooms to suit most budgets, from 8000 to 60,000 rp.

Sarangan is a more expensive resort. *Penginapan Nusantara* is basic and expensive at 25,000 rp a room, but in a good position near the lake. The colonial *Hotel Sarangan* (☎ 98022) has singles/doubles with sitting rooms and open fire places from 60,000/75,000 rp.

Pacitan

On the south coast, the small town of Pacitan has a fine beach, **Pantai Ria Teleng**, three km from the town. Pacitan has cheap hotels, but the only one on the beach is the excellent *Happy Bay Beach Bungalows* (☎ 81474), with attractive singles/doubles with bathroom for 15,000/20,000 rp or private bungalows for 27,500 rp.

Direct buses run to/from Solo (2600 rp; four hours).

SEMARANG

This large north coast port city is the capital of Central Java, about 120 km north of Yogya. It is primarily just a stopover if you're venturing along the north coast.

Information

The city tourist office (☎ 414332) is on the 1st floor of the Plaza Simpang Lima, on the city's main square. It is open every day from 9 am to 4 pm.

The area code for Semarang is 024.

Things to See

The **Sam Po Kong Temple** (better known as Gedung Batu, or Stone Building), in the south-west of the city, is dedicated to Admiral Cheng Ho – a famous Muslim eunuch of the Ming Dynasty who led many expeditions from China to South-East Asia in the early 15th century. He is particularly revered in Melaka (Malaysia), and the Chinese temple in Semarang is the largest in Indonesia, honoured by both Chinese Buddhists and Muslims. To get to Gedung Batu, take Damri bus No 2 from Jalan Pemuda to Karang Ayu, and then get a Daihatsu from there to the temple.

Semarang's old city has a sprinkling of buildings from the Dutch colonial era. On Jalan Let Jen Suprapto, south of Tawang railway station, the 1753 **Gereja Blenduk** church has a huge dome and baroque organ. Numerous old warehouses are nearby. The **Tay Kak Sie Temple** is one of Indonesia's finest Chinese temples on Gang Lombok, off Jalan Pekojan in Semarang's old Chinatown.

INDONESIA

Puri Maerakoco is Semarang's version of Jakarta's Taman Mini, with traditional houses representing all of Central Java's *kabupaten* (regencies). It is well done and the houses have small displays of crafts and information on points of interest in the regency. It is open daily from 7 am to 6 pm, and entry is 1000 rp, 1500 rp on Sundays. It is out near the airport, and not accessible by public transport.

Places to Stay

The popular, well-maintained *Hotel Oewa Asia* (☎ 542547), Jalan Kol Sugiono 12, is the best bet close to the centre. It is 15 minutes walk from Tawang railway station (1500 rp by becak). Large rooms with fan and mandi cost 20,000 rp, or darker air-con rooms cost 27,500 rp.

Another colonial hotel is the pleasant *Raden Patah* (☎ 511328), Jalan Jend Suprapto 48. It is further from the centre but close to the railway station. Spartan but good-value rooms cost 10,000 rp, or 16,000 rp with mandi and fan.

If these two are full, and you can speak some Indonesian, Jalan Imam Bonjol near the Hotel Oewa Asia has a number of options. The seedy *Hotel Singapore* (☎ 543757), at No 12, has no-frills rooms with shared mandis for 12,500 rp. The similarly priced *Losmen Arjuna* (☎ 544186) at No 51 is much better but nearly always full. The *Hotel Rahayu* (☎ 542532) at No 35 has decent rooms with mandi from 17,500 rp, or from 32,500 rp with air-con.

The Chinese-run *Hotel Nendra Yakti* (☎ 542538) at Gang Pinggir 68 is in the interesting Chinatown area and has a better class of room with fan and mandi for 21,000 to 24,000 rp. Air-con rooms cost 45,000 rp.

Places to Eat

The *Toko Oen*, Jalan Pemuda 52, is not to be missed. This large, old-fashioned tearoom maintains its genteel colonial atmosphere and has an Indonesian, Chinese and European menu, good grills and a great selection of ice creams.

Jalan Gajah Mada has some good Chinese restaurants. Try *Rumah Makan Tio Cio*, opposite the Telemoyo Hotel, a popular place with reasonably priced seafood. At Jalan Gajah Mada 37A, *Depot Naga* is a scrupulously clean, open-sided cafe.

At night all life seems to revolve around the Simpang Lima, Semarang's answer to Times Square. Dozens of warungs cluster around the southern side, and the big malls on the north edge are the place for fast food, including a *McDonald's* in the Ciputra Mall.

Entertainment

The *Ngesti Pandowo Theatre* at Jalan Pemuda 116 has wayang orang performances every night from 9 pm to midnight, except Mondays, when ketoprak is performed. *RRI* on Jalan A Yani puts on wayang kulit shows on the first Saturday of the month. The *TBRS amusement park* on Jalan Sriwijaya, Tegalwareng, has wayang kulit every Thursday Wage (one of the five days of the Javanese calendar) and ketoprak every Monday Wage of the Javanese calendar.

Getting There & Away

From the airport, six km west of town, there are direct flights to Bandung, Jakarta, Surabaya and various cities in Kalimantan.

Semarang's Terboyo bus terminal is four km east of town, just off the road to Kudus. Buses include: Yogya (2500 rp; three hours), Solo (2100 rp; 2½ hours, Wonosobo (2500 rp; four hours), Pekalongan (2100 rp; three hours), Cirebon (4900 rp; six hours), Kudus (1200 rp; one hour) and Surabaya (7000 rp; nine hours). Luxury, air-con buses also do most of these runs.

For express minibuses try the Rahayu agent (☎ 543935), Jalan Haryono 9, or Nusantara Indah next door. Minibuses go to Solo, Yogya, Kudus, Wonosobo, Pekalongan, Surabaya and other destinations.

Semarang is on the main Jakarta-Cirebon-Surabaya train route and there are frequent services operating to and from these cities. Tawang is the main railway station.

PEKALONGAN

On the north coast between Semarang and Cirebon, Pekalongan is known as Kota Batik (Batik City) and its batiks are some of the most sought-after in Indonesia. Few travellers pause here but it is a must for batik freaks and has a fairly dull **batik museum**.

The area code for Pekalongan is 0285.

Places to Stay

Pekalongan has decent budget hotels directly opposite the railway station on Jalan Gajah Mada. The best is the friendly and very clean *Hotel Gajah Mada* (☎ 22185) at No 11 with doubles for 8500/9500 rp, or 12,000 rp with mandi. In the centre of town, Pekalongan's best budget-to-moderate bet is the *Hotel Hayam Wuruk* (☎ 22823) at Jalan Hayam Wuruk 152-154. Rooms cost from 22,000/29,000 rp to 42,000/49,000 rp. Breakfast is included.

Getting There & Away

Pekalongan's bus station is about four km south-east of the centre of town, 300 rp by colt or 1500 rp by becak. Frequent buses run along the north coast to Cirebon (via Tegal) and Semarang, and south-east to Wonosobo. The railway station is central.

KUDUS

An important Islamic centre, Kudus is north-east of Semarang near the north coast. The **Al-Manar Mosque** in the centre of the old town dates from 1549. Kudus is also a noted centre for *kretek* (clove-flavoured cigarette) manufacture. You can visit factories, and there is an interesting **Kretek Museum**.

The area code for Kudus is 0291.

Places to Stay & Eat

The central *Hotel Slamet* (☎ 37579), Jalan Jenderal Sudirman 63, is a rambling old place with spartan rooms from 8000 rp. The *Hotel Notasari Permai* (☎ 37245), Jalan Kepodang 12, is a good mid-range hotel with a swimming pool. Rooms with mandi start at 23,000 rp including breakfast; air-con rooms start at 42,500 rp.

The *Rumah Makan Hijau*, Jalan A Yani 1, near the Plasa Kudus shopping centre, is

cheap, and good for Indonesian food and supercool fruit juices. The *Hotel Notasari Permai* has a good restaurant and the *Garuda*, Jalan Jenderal Sudirman 1, has good Chinese food.

Getting There & Away

The bus station is four km south of town, 300 rp by minibus, 2500 rp by becak. Buses go to Semarang (1200 rp; one hour), Surabaya (5500 rp) and Solo (4400 rp; 3½ hours). Buses to Jepara (800 rp; 45 minutes) leave from the Jetak sub-terminal, four km west of town (300 rp by purple minibus).

AROUND KUDUS

The town of **Mayong**, 12 km north-west of Kudus on the road to Jepara, was the home of Raden Ajeng Kartini, a noted Indonesian writer who died in 1904. **Jepara** is the centre for Java's best traditional woodcarvers. **Pantai Bandengan**, eight km north-east of Jepara, has a surprisingly good beach and cheap accommodation.

SURABAYA

The capital of East Java, Surabaya is a major port and the second largest city in Indonesia. For most visitors, it is merely a transit point on the way to or from Bali or Sulawesi. It has an interesting old city and if you thrive on big cities, then you'll find teeming Surabaya certainly lively.

Information

The tourist office (☎ 532-4499) at Jalan Pemuda 118 is open Monday to Saturday from 9 am to 5 pm.

There are plenty of banks around including a Bank Ekspor Impor office on Jalan Pemuda. The main post office is on Jalan Kebon Rojo. The easiest place to make telephone calls is at the wartel in Tunjungan Plaza.

The area code for Surabaya is 031.

Things to See

The old part of town to the north is the most interesting. The streets around **Jembatan Merah** have some fine old Dutch architecture,

INDONESIA

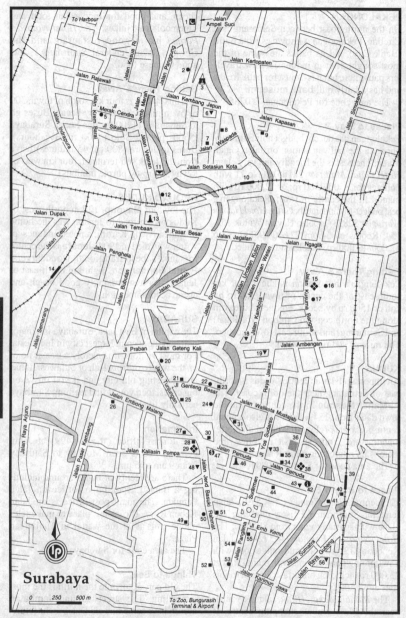

Surabaya

0   250   500 m

To Zoo, Bungurasih
Terminal & Airport

and from here you wander across to China-town. **Pasar Pabean** is a sprawling, dark market worth a wander, and the interesting 300-year-old **Kong Co Kong Tik Cun Ong** temple has wayang performances on the full moon. **Mesjid Ampel**, in the heart of the Arab Quarter, is the most sacred mosque in Surabaya and pilgrims chant and offer rose petal offerings to Sunan Ampel, one of the *wali songo* (nine saints) who brought Islam to Java. The mosque is approached through Jalan Ampel Suci, a narrow, covered bazaar. Plenty of Makassar schooners can be seen at the **Kali Mas wharf**.

The Surabaya **zoo** has a large collection of animals and is well maintained by Indonesian standards. It has a couple of big dazed and aging Komodo dragons. Admission is 1500 rp and it is open 7 am to 4 pm. The zoo is four km south of the centre of town – take any bus heading down Jalan Panglima Sudirman. The small **MPU Tantular Museum** has interesting archaeological exhibits and is across the road from the zoo.

Close to the town centre is the **THR amusement park**, usually dead but worth a visit on Thursday evenings when transvestites perform *dangdut* music.

Places to Stay

The *Bamboe Denn* (☎ 534-0333), Jalan Ketabang Kali 6A, a 20 minute walk from Gubeng railway station, is a Surabaya institution and has been the number one travellers' centre in Surabaya for over 20 years. Beds in the large dorm are 5500 rp and a few, tiny singles/doubles are 6500/12,500 rp.

Apart from the Bamboe Denn, Surabaya doesn't have a great choice of cheap, central accommodation. Across the river from the Bamboe Denn on Jalan Genteng Besar, the *Hotel Paviljoen* (☎ 534-3449) is in an old colonial house at No 94. Renovated rooms with mandi are of mid-range standard and a good deal at 27,500 rp, or 35,000 rp with air-con, including breakfast.

The *Hotel Gubeng* (☎ 534-1603) at Jalan Sumatra 18 is close to the Gubeng station if you can't be bothered going any further. Basic rooms cost 25,500 rp, or 30,500 rp with mandi.

Well north of the town centre, near the Kota railway station, *Hotel Ganefo* (☎ 364880), Jalan Kapasan 169-171, is a spacious old hotel. Very simple rooms don't match the lobby and cost 30,000 rp with shared mandi. Rooms in the new section with mandi, air-con,

INDONESIA

PLACES TO STAY			
7	Hotel Semut	54	Elmi Hotel
8	Hotel Irian	55	Tanjung Hotel
9	Hotel Ganefo		
21	Hotel Paviljoen	**PLACES TO EAT**	
23	Weta Hotel	6	Kiet Wan Kie
25	Hotel Majapahit	18	Soto Ambengan
26	Westin Hotel	19	Cafe Venezia
27	Sheraton Hotel	33	Zangrandi Ice Cream
28	Hotel Tunjungan		Palace
30	Natour Simpang	43	Turin
31	Bamboe Denn	45	Granada Modern
34	Garden Palace Hotel		Bakery
35	Garden Hotel	48	Galael Supermarket,
37	Radisson Plaza		KFC & Swensen's
	Suite Hotel	56	Kuningan Seafood
40	Sahid Surabaya		
	Hotel	**OTHER**	
41	Hotel Gubeng	1	Mesjid Ampel
44	Hotel Remaja	2	Pasar Pabean
49	Cendana Hotel	3	Kong Co Kong Tik
51	Ramayana Hotel		Cun Ong
52	Hyatt Regency	4	Jembatan Merah
	Surabaya	5	Gedung PTP XXII
		10	Kota Railway Station

11	Post Office
12	Pelni Office
13	Tugu Pahlawan
14	Pasar Turi
	Railway Station
15	Surabaya Mall
16	TH Amusemen
	Park
17	Taman Remaja
20	Garuda Office
22	Genteng Market
24	Andhika Plaza
29	Tunjungan Plaza
32	Governor's
	Residence
36	World Trade Centre
38	Plaza Surabaya
39	Gubeng Railway
	Station
42	Tourist Office
46	Joko Dolog
47	Bank Duta
50	Minibus Agents
53	Bouraq Office

TV and phone are 50,000 rp. In the same area, another hotel with some colonial style is the *Hotel Irian* (☎ 20953), Jalan Samudra 16, which has doubles for 15,000 to 20,000 rp with shared mandi.

Places to Eat

For cheap eats, the *Genteng Market* on Jalan Genteng Besar, just across the river from the Bamboe Denn, has good night warungs. Most other eats in the city centre are expensive and found in the shopping malls.

The ground floor of the Plaza Surabaya has the *Food Plaza* with a range of restaurants with Korean, Cantonese and Indonesian food, and western fast food. The best deal is the *Food Bazaar* on the 4th floor with a large variety of moderately priced stalls.

The Tunjungan Plaza is similarly well stocked with restaurants and fast-food outlets, starting with a *McDonald's* and *KFC* on the ground floor. The 4th level has the *Mon Cheri* ice cream parlour, the Chinese *New Singapore* and the cheaper *Es Teler 77*.

At Jalan Yos Sudarso 15, the *Zangrandi Ice Cream Palace* is an old establishment ice cream parlour with planters chairs and low tables.

Getting There & Away

Air Surabaya is an important hub for domestic flights. There are direct flights to Jakarta (227,000 rp), Denpasar (116,000 rp), Yogyakarta (82,000 rp), Banjarmasin (171,000 rp) and Ujung Pandang (257,000 rp), with numerous other connections.

Bus Most buses operate from Surabaya's main Bungurasih bus station, 10 km south of the city centre. Buses along the north coast and to Semarang depart from the Terminal Oso Wilangun, 10 km west of the city.

Normal/air-con buses from Bungurasih include: Pandaan (1000 rp; one hour), Malang (1800/3000 rp; two hours), Blitar (3600/2800 rp; four hours), Probolinggo (2100/3500 rp; two hours), Banyuwangi (6500/11,500 rp; six hours), Bondowoso (5000/8500 rp; 4½ hours), Solo (7000/ 12,500 rp; 6½ hours) and Yogya (7500/13,000 rp;

eight hours). Buses also operate from this terminal to Pulau Madura.

Luxury buses from Bungurasih also do the long hauls to Solo, Yogya, Bandung, Bogor and further afield. Most are night buses leaving in the late afternoon/early evening. Bookings can be made at Bungurasih, or travel agents in the centre of town sell tickets with a fair mark up. The most convenient bus agents are those on Jalan Basuki Rahmat. Intercity buses are not allowed to enter the city so you will have to go to Bungurasih to catch your bus.

From Terminal Oso Wilangun buses go to north coast destinations such as Gresik (500 rp), Tuban (2400 rp), Kudus (5500 rp) and Semarang (7000 rp; 13,000 air-con).

Train Trains from Jakarta, taking the northern route via Semarang, arrive at the Pasar Turi station. Trains taking the southern route via Yogya, and trains from Banyuwangi and Malang, arrive at Gubeng and most carry on to Kota.

The trip from Jakarta takes nine to 17 hours, although in practice the slower ekonomi trains can take even longer. Fares vary from 13,500 rp in ekonomi class, to 33,000 rp in bisnis and 100,000 rp on the luxury *Argobromo*. The cheapest are the ekonomi services like the *Gaya Baru Malam Utara* (12 hours) on the northern route or the *Gaya Baru Malam Selatan* (16 hours) on the southern route.

Trains to or from Solo (4½ to six hours) and Yogyakarta (5½ to seven hours) cost from 4500 rp in ekonomi, from 17,000 rp in bisnis. The train is faster and cheaper than the buses. The 8.45 am *Purbaya* and the faster 1.45 pm *Argopura* are good ekonomi services.

Apart from services to the main cities, there are six trains per day to Malang (two hours) and these continue to Blitar. The *Mutiara* goes to Banyuwangi (4500 rp ekonomi/9000 rp bisnis; seven hours) at 8 am and 10 pm, and the ekonomi *Argopuro* departs at 2.10 pm. All go via Probolinggo.

Boat Surabaya is an important port and a major travel hub for ships to the other islands.

Popular Pelni connections are those to Sulawesi, with at least five Pelni ships doing the Surabaya-Ujung Pandang run, and to Kalimantan with ships to Pontianak, Kumai, Banjarmasin, Balikpapan, Batu Licin and Sampit. See the Indonesia Getting Around section earlier in this chapter for Pelni route details. Ekonomi fares include: Ujung Pandang 65,000 rp, Lembar 40,000 rp, Banjarmasin 46,000 rp and Balikpapan 103,000 rp.

The Pelni ticket office at Jalan Pahlawan 112 is open Monday to Friday from 9 am to 3 pm, and on weekends, if there are ship departures, from 9 am to noon. Ships depart from Tanjung Perak harbour – bus P1 or C will get you there.

Ferries to Kamal on Madura (550 rp; 30 minutes) leave every half hour from Tanjung Perak.

Kalla Lines (☎ 335801), Jalan Perak Timur 158, has a passenger ship once every fortnight to Pasir Gudang (150,000 rp; 60 hours), just outside Johor Bahru in Malaysia.

Getting Around

The Airport Taxis from the Juanda airport (15 km) operate on a coupon system and cost 12,000 rp to the city centre. The Damri airport bus drops off in the city centre and costs 2000 rp, but departures are not frequent.

Local Transport Surabaya has plenty of air-con metered taxis and flag fall is 1300 rp. Typical fares from central Surabaya include the Pelni office for 4500 rp, the harbour for 8000 rp and Bamboe Denn to Gubeng station for 3500 rp. Becaks are useful for local transport and there are plenty of them around town. Bemos are labelled A, B, C etc and all charge a standard 350 rp. Patas (express) buses are labelled P and charge a fixed 500 rp fare.

AROUND SURABAYA

Trowulan

Scattered around Trowulan, 60 km south-west from Surabaya on the Solo road, are the remains of the capital of the ancient Majapahit Empire, the last great Hindu kingdom to rule

on Java until the Muslims drove them out to Bali in the early 1500s.

One km from the main Surabaya-Solo highway, the **Trowulan Museum** houses superb examples of Majapahit sculpture and pottery from throughout East Java. The museum is open from 7 am to 4 pm; closed Monday and public holidays. Reconstructed temples are scattered around the museum, some within walking distance, though you need to hire a becak to see them all.

Tretes

This hill resort, 55 km south of Surabaya, is a cool break if you have to kill time in Surabaya. Its main claim to fame is as a red-light resort, but it has walks around town and hiking to Gunung Welirang (seven hours to the top with a night camping on the mountain).

On the way to Tretes, **Pandaan**, 40 km south of Surabaya, is home to the open-air Candra Wilwatikta Theatre. East Javanese classical dance, a poor cousin of Prambanan's Ramayana ballet, is held here once a month during the dry season from June to October.

Places to Stay & Eat Tretes and adjoining Prigen have plenty of accommodation, most of it overpriced. This is principally a local resort where few foreigners are seen. On the main road near the Natour Bath Hotel, *Mess Garuda* is a reasonable place with rooms for 15,000 rp during the week. The *Wisma Semeru Indah* (☎ 81701), Jalan Semeru 7, is below the main shopping area and has over-priced rooms from 32,000 rp.

MADURA

Only half an hour from Surabaya by ferry, the relatively untouristic island of Madura has fine beaches and picturesque remote countryside. Coming up from Bali, Madura is also accessible by daily ferry from Jangkar, north of Banyuwangi, to Kalianget on the island's eastern tip – you could make a trip through Madura and exit from Kamal to Surabaya.

Madura is a flat and rugged island, much of it dry and sometimes barren, and it's a

INDONESIA

contrast to Java in both landscape and life-style. Cattle raising is important, rather than rice growing. The production of salt is another major industry – much of Indonesia's supply comes from the vast salt tracts around Kalianget.

During the dry season, particularly in August and September, Madura is famed for its colourful **bull races**, the *kerapan sapi*, which climax with the finals held at Pamekasan. The bulls are harnessed in pairs, two teams compete at a time and they're raced along a 120 metre course in a special stadium. Races don't last long – the bulls can do nine seconds over 100 metres, faster than the men's world track record. Bull races for tourists are sometimes staged at the Bangkalan Stadium, and race practice is held throughout the year in Bangkalan, Pamekasan and Sumenep, but dates are not fixed. The tourist office in Surabaya can supply details of where and when the bull races will be held.

There are a number of interesting places to visit around the island. Near the village of Arasbaya, 28 km north of Bangkalan, **Air Mata** is the old royal cemetery of the Cakraningrat family, with beautiful views across the terraced hills.

The south coast road to Pamekasan, 100 km east of Kamal where the ferry docks, has fields of immaculately groomed cattle, small fishing villages and a sea of rainbow-coloured perahus. **Pamekasan**, the capital of Madura, comes alive in the bull racing season, but is quiet the rest of the year. **Camplong**, about 15 km short of Pamekasan, has a reasonable beach and calm water.

Sumenep is an old and attractive town, 53 km north-east of Pamekasan. This more refined, royal town is the most interesting town on Madura and the best base for exploring the eastern part of the island. You can see Sumenep's 18th century mosque, and the kraton with its water palace and interesting museum. **Asta Tinggi**, the royal cemetery, is only about three km from the town centre.

The tourist literature raves above Madura's beaches, but nobody else does. Still they are worth a visit for a swim if you are spending any length of time in Sumenep. **Slopeng**, 21 km from Sumenep, has yellow sand dunes and palm trees. **Lombang**, 30 km from Sumenep near the eastern tip of the island, is similar.

Places to Stay

In Pamekasan, opposite the alun alun, the run-down *Hotel Garuda* (☎ 22589), Jalan Mesigit 1, has pokey rooms for 4400 rp and big, old rooms with mandi for 9900 to 22,000 rp. Nearby, *Hotel Trunojoyo* (☎ 22181), Jalan Trunojoyo 48, is better. Rooms are 6000 rp, or 15,000 rp with mandi, 20,000 to 35,000 rp with air-con. *Hotel Ramayana* (☎ 22406), Jalan Niaga 55, is the best in town. Rooms with shared mandi cost 7500 rp, bright rooms with mandi are 15,000 rp, and air-con rooms start at 30,000 rp.

In Sumenep, *Hotel Wijaya I* (☎ 21433), Jalan Trunojoyo 45-47, is the best bet. Good clean rooms cost 7000 and 8000 rp without mandi, 10,000 and 12,000 rp with mandi, and 22,000 to 60,000 rp with air-con. The sister *Hotel Wijaya II* (☎ 62532) nearby is also good. The cheapest option is the basic *Hotel Damai* on Jalan Sudirman where rooms cost 8000 rp.

Bangkalan has a selection of hotels and Camplong has mid-range bungalows on the beach, but there is not a lot of reason to stay at either.

Getting There & Away

It's only half an hour by ferry from Surabaya to Kamal, the harbour town in Madura. From the ferry terminal in Kamal you can take a bus or colt to other main towns, including Bangkalan (600 rp; 30 minutes), Pamekasan (2500 rp; 2½ hours) and Sumenep (3500 rp; five hours). Buses also run from Sumenep right through to Surabaya, Malang and Bali.

There is also a ferry between Kalianget and Jangkar, near Asembagus in the very north-east of Java. Ferries leave Kalianget at 8 am Thursday to Saturday, returning from Jangkar the same days at 2 pm. The ferry costs 5500 rp and takes four hours.

MALANG

Malang is a small, pleasant city on the alternative 'back route' between Yogyakarta and Bali. The countryside on this run is particularly beautiful and Malang has just enough altitude to take the edge off the heat. It's a clean city with a well-planned square, and the central area of town is studded with parks, tree-lined streets and old Dutch architecture.

Every Sunday morning at the Taman Rekreasi Senaputra on Jalan Kahuripan, *kuda lumping* 'horse trance' dancers ride cane horses and perform masochistic acts without harm.

The area code for Malang is 0341.

Places to Stay

The most popular hotel is the *Hotel Helios* (☎ 362741), Jalan Pattimura 37, with rooms from 14,000 to 35,000 rp. It's clean, comfortable and all rooms have balconies overlooking the garden. Good travel information, bus bookings and tours are provided. Near the Hotel Helios, the *Hotel Palem II* (☎ 25129), Jalan Thamrin 15, has clean rooms with mandi for 19,500 to 27,500 rp.

In the lively central area, the rambling *Hotel Riche* (☎ 24560) is well placed near the Toko Oen restaurant at Jalan Basuki Rachmat 1, but the rooms are dingy and cost 17,500 rp, or from 19,000 rp with mandi. Other central hotels are the uninspiring *Hotel Santosa* (☎ 23889), in the thick of things at Jalan Agus Salim 24, with rooms from 22,000 rp; a better option is the *Hotel Tosari* (☎ 26945), Jalan Achmad Dahlan 31, with bare but very clean rooms for 16,000 rp, and from 24,000 rp with mandi.

Places to Eat

The anachronistic colonial *Toko Oen* is opposite the Sarinah department store. Relax and read a newspaper while being served by waiters in white sarongs and black *peci* hats. It has Chinese and western dishes plus good Indonesian food and home-made ice cream.

For cheap and varied eats, head for Jalan Agus Salim. The Chinese *Gloria Restaurant* at No 23 specialises in noodles. Closer to the alun alun, *Rumah Makan Agung* has excellent savoury murtabak and chicken biryani. The *Food Centre*, sandwiched between the Mitra department store and the Gajah Mada Plaza, has excellent hawker dishes.

Getting There & Away

Malang has three bus terminals. Arjosari, five km north of town, is the main bus station with buses to northern route destinations such as Surabaya (1800 rp; two hours), Probolinggo (2100 rp; 2½ hours) and Banyuwangi (6800 rp; seven hours), as well as Denpasar (9000 rp; 10 hours). Air-con express buses also cover these routes, and to Yogya and Solo. Mikrolets run from Arjosari to nearby villages such as Singosari (500 rp) and Tumpang (600 rp).

Terminal Gadang is five km south of the town centre and has buses along the southern routes to destinations such as Blitar (1800 rp; two hours). Terminal Landungsari, five km north-west of the city, has buses to the western destinations such as Kediri and Madiun and mikrolets to Batu (500 rp; 30 minutes).

Travel agents book luxury buses and door-to-door minibuses. The Hotel Helios and the travel agent at the Toko Oen make bookings and offer tours to Gunung Bromo and other destinations.

Ekonomi trains run from Surabaya to Blitar via Malang, or the *Patas* express train on this route provides a good service and costs 3000 rp to Surabaya or Blitar.

AROUND MALANG
Temples

Close to Malang are interesting temples dedicated to the kings of the Singosari Dynasty (1222-92 AD), the precursors of the Majapahit Empire. **Candi Singosari** is 12 km north of Malang (the temple is 500 metres west of the main highway). **Candi Jago** is at Tumpang, 18 km from Malang, and then seven km south is **Candi Kidal** in the small village of Kidal. To Singosari, take a green mikrolet from Malang's Arjosari terminal. To Candi Jago take a white mikrolet from Arjosari. Infrequent colts run from Tumpang Market to Candi Kidal.

Batu

On the slopes of Gunung Arjuna, 15 km north-west of Malang, Batu is one of Java's most attractive hill resorts. There is not a lot to do in Batu, but the mountain scenery is superb, the climate delightfully cool and a number of side trips can be made. **Songgoriti**, three km west of Batu, and **Selekta**, five km north, are adjoining resorts. Five km south-west of Songgoriti are the **Cubanrondo Falls** and past Selekta is the **Air Panas Cangar**, hot springs high in the mountains, surrounded by forest and mist.

Places to Stay Most hotels in Batu are scattered along Jalan Panglima Sudirman, the main road running west from the town centre. Most are mid-range but the friendly *Hotel Kawi* (☎ 591139) at No 19, 400 metres from the central plaza, has passable rooms for 7500 rp, or 15,000 rp with mandi (with cold water).

Prices and standards increase as you proceed up the hill. A better bet for a room with bathroom is the cosy *Hotel Ragil Kuning* (☎ 593051), half a km further west, which costs 20,000 rp. *Hotel Perdana* (☎ 591104) at No 101 is a good mid-range hotel. Rooms with shower and hot water cost 25,000 rp, or large, newer rooms at the back cost 40,000 rp.

BLITAR

Blitar is a small town on the Malang to Kediri road. You can travel this back route to Solo via Blitar and the beach at Pacitan. The extensive **Panataran Temple Complex**, 16 km north of Blitar, is the most impressive Majapahit ruins in East Java and can easily be reached by minibus from Blitar bus station. Two km north of the town centre on the way to Panataran is **Soekarno's grave**. The former president was buried here, against his wishes, as far from the capital as possible. The grave attracts pilgrims, and Soekarno is worshipped like a saint.

Places to Stay

The best hotel is the *Hotel Sri Lestari* (☎ 81766) at Jalan Merdeka 173, a few hundred metres from the bus station. It has a variety of rooms from 8000 to 98,000 rp.

GUNUNG BROMO

Gunung Bromo is an active volcano lying at the centre of the Tengger Massif, a spectacular volcanic landscape and one of the most impressive sights in Indonesia. The massive Tengger crater stretches 10 km across and its steep walls plunge down to a vast, flat sea of lava sand. From the crater floor emerges the smoking peak of Gunung Bromo (2392 metres), the spiritual centre of the highlands. This desolate landscape has a strange end-of-the-world feeling, particularly at sunrise, the favoured time to climb to the rim of Bromo's crater.

Often the whole area is simply referred to as 'Mt Bromo', but Bromo is only one of three mountains within the caldera of the ancient Tengger volcano, and it is flanked by the peaks of Batok (2440 metres) and Kursi (2581 metres). Further south the whole supernatural moonscape is overseen by Gunung Semeru (3676 metres), the highest mountain in Java and the most active volcano in these highlands. The whole area has been incorporated into the **Bromo-Tengger-Semeru National Park**.

A visit to this fantastic volcano is easy to fit in between Bali and Surabaya. The usual jumping-off point for Bromo is the town of Probolinggo on the main Surabaya to Banyuwangi road. From there, you head to Ngadisari or Cemoro Lawang, high on the Tengger crater.

Get up at 4.30 am or earlier for an easy stroll across to Bromo. By the time you've crossed the lava plain from Cemoro Lawang and started to climb up Bromo (246 steps, one traveller reported) it should be fairly light. Bromo itself is not one of the great volcanoes of Indonesia – it is the whole landscape that is breathtaking – but from the top you'll get fantastic views down into the smoking crater and of the sun sailing up over the outer crater. In the wet season, the dawn and the clouds often arrive simultaneously so at that time of year you might just as well stay in bed and stroll across later in the day.

Though Probolinggo is the usual approach, Bromo can also be reached via Tosari from the north-west and Ngadas from the south-west.

Tours come via Tosari because 4WD vehicles can drive all the way to the base of Gunung Bromo. The main traffic via Tosari, however, is minibus tours via a paved road to the top of **Gunung Penanjakan** (2770 metres) to see the dawn from there. The superb views right across Bromo and the Tengger crater to smoking Gunung Semeru are unsurpassed. Gunung Penanjakan can also be reached from Cemoro Lawang: on foot (one hour) or by chartered jeep along the road to the 'Penanjakan II' viewpoint, itself a spectacular vantage point, but it's worth taking the walking trail behind this viewing area one hour more up to Penanjakan proper.

From Malang, it is possible to travel by mikrolet to Tumpang, and then by another mikrolet to Gubug Klakah, from where you walk 12 km to Ngadas. From Ngadas it is two km to Jemplang at the crater rim, and then three hours on foot (12 km) across the floor of the Tengger crater to Gunung Bromo and on to Cemoro Lawang. Alternatively, from Ngadas it is an 8.5 km walk to Rano Pani, where Pak Tasrep runs a homestay and can help organise a climb of Gunung Semeru. It is a full day's walk from Rano Pani to Arcopodo, the camp site on the mountain, and you must be equipped for freezing conditions. The rugged ascent is usually done at 2 am the following morning to reach the peak before sunrise.

In January or February, the big annual Kesada festival is held by the local Hindu community when offerings are made to appease Bromo.

Places to Stay & Eat
Ngadisari From Probolinggo, it's 42 km to Ngadisari, where *Yoschi's Guest House* (☎ 23387), just outside Ngadisari village, is an excellent place to stay. This attractive, friendly inn has singles from 6000 rp, doubles from 7000 to 17,500 rp and comfort-able family cottages. It has a good restaurant and offers tours and cheap transport to Bromo. A short walk away, the *Bromo Home Stay* (☎ 23484) has comfortable rooms with mandi from 15,000 rp.

Cemoro Lawang Cemoro Lawang, three km from Ngadisari at the lip of the Tengger crater, is right at the start of the walk to Bromo and so is the most popular place to stay.

Cafe Lava Hostel (☎ 23458) is the number one travellers' place. Singles/doubles cost 6000/8000 rp or a dorm bed is 4000 rp. Rooms and shared mandis are basic but the hostel is cheap, convivial and has an excellent restaurant. Their fancier *Lava View Lodge* is along a side road from the bus terminal and right at the edge of crater with great views and good rooms with bathroom for 15,000/20,000 rp.

One hundred metres past the Cafe Lava, the *Hotel Bromo Permai I* (☎ 23459) is the best hotel. It has a restaurant and bar. Rooms with shared mandi cost from 13,500 rp, and with attached bathroom and hot water from 46,500 to 88,500 rp.

The *Cemara Indah Hotel* (☎ 23457) is also on the lip of the crater with fantastic views and an excellent, airy restaurant. The large dormitory costs 4000 rp and very spartan rooms are 7000/10,000 rp. Comfortable rooms with bathroom and hot water cost 37,500 and 50,000 rp.

Probolinggo On the highway between Surabaya and Banyuwangi, this is the jumping-off point for Gunung Bromo. The town has plenty of hotels if you get stuck.

The *Hotel Bromo Permai* (☎ (0335) 22256), Jalan Panglima Sudirman 237, is the most popular travellers' hotel and has comfortable, clean rooms from 8700 rp, to 29,000 rp with air-con. It is on the main road close to the centre of town at the eastern end.

Hotel Ratna (☎ (0335) 21597) further west at Jalan Panglima Sudirman 16 is one of the best in town. Good economy rooms cost 8000 and 9000 rp, or rooms with bath range from 22,500 to 50,000 rp with air-con.

The *Hotel Tampiarto Plaza* (☎ (0335) 21280), Jalan Suroyo 16, is the best hotel in town, but only just. It has a swimming pool and comfortable rooms from 11,000 to 110,000 rp.

Getting There & Away

Probolinggo's bus terminal is five km west of town on the road to Bromo – catch a yellow angkot from the main street or the railway station for 500 rp. Buses include: Surabaya (2100/3500 rp air-con; two hours), Malang (2200/3800 rp; 2½ hours) and Banyuwangi (4400/7000 rp; five hours). Deluxe buses to Yogya or Denpasar take eight hours and cost around 20,000 rp. Be wary of rip-off 'tourist office' bus agents at the bus station and general misinformation.

Bison minibuses from the terminal go to Cemoro Lawang (2500 rp; two hours) via Ngadisari (2000 rp; 1½ hours) until around 5 or 6 pm, as late as 9 pm in the main August tourist season. To charter a jeep will cost 25,000 rp to Ngadisari, and 30,000 rp to Cemoro Lawang. At Ngadisari you pay the 2100 rp entry fee to the national park.

The bisnis-class *Mutiara* and ekonomi *Argopuro* trains between Surabaya and Banyuwangi stop at Probolinggo's station, 1.5 km north of the centre of town.

Travel agents in Solo and Yogya sell direct minibus tickets to Bromo for 25,000 rp, or 35,000 rp air-con, but these only go as far as the Bromo Home Stay in Ngadisari. Two-day/one-night tours from Solo and Yogya cost around 80,000 rp or from Bali they cost from 100,000 rp.

PASIR PUTIH

Roughly halfway between Probolinggo and Banyuwangi, on the north coast highway, this is East Java's most popular seaside resort and is mobbed on weekends by sun'n'sand worshippers from Surabaya. It has picturesque outrigger boats and safe swimming, but its name (*pasir putih* means 'white sand') is a misnomer – the sand is more grey than white.

This quite ordinary beach would make a pleasant enough stopover if the grubby

hotels weren't so overpriced. The *Hotel Sido Muncul* (☎ 91352) is at least clean and has rooms from 15,000 rp, or 25,000 to 60,000 rp with mandi.

BALURAN NATIONAL PARK

This park is in a dry pocket on the coast between Pasir Putih and Banyuwangi. The parklands surround the solitary hump of Gunung Baluran (1247 metres) and contain extensive dry savanna grassland threaded by stony-bedded streams and coastal mangrove. The park headquarters (☎ 61650) are right on the highway, so this drive-in park is one of the most visited on Java.

Accommodation is at Bekol, 12 km into the park, and at Bama, three km east of Bekol on a decent beach. Rooms start at 6000 rp, and you should bring your own food.

BANYUWANGI

Banyuwangi is the last stop on the eastern tip of Java before Bali, but the actual ferry departure point is eight km north of the town at **Ketapang**. You may find yourself in this lazy backwater on the way to Kawah Ijen or the national parks to the south.

The Banyuwangi tourist office is in the centre of town at Jalan Diponegoro 2, and a helpful branch kiosk is at the ferry terminal in Ketapang, open daily from 8 am to 7 pm. The PHPA office (☎ 241119) is at Jalan A Yani 108, two km south of the town centre.

Places to Stay

The *Hotel Baru* (☎ 21369), Jalan MT Haryono 82-84, is a popular choice. Singles/doubles with mandi start at 9500/10,600 rp, or with air-con from 25,600/27,000 rp. Nearby *Hotel Slamet* (☎ 24675), next to the old railway station at Jalan Wahid Hasyim 96, is another friendly place with a restaurant. Singles/doubles with mandi start at 10,000/12,000 rp and range up to the new rooms for 35,000 rp with air-con.

For something better, the *Hotel Pinang Sari* (☎ 23266) at Jalan Basuki Rachmat 116 is a few hundred metres north of the Blambangan bemo terminal. It has a very attractive garden and a restaurant. Rooms with bath and balcony cost 12,000 to 18,000 rp, or with air-con from 43,000 to 80,000 rp.

Getting There & Away

Ferries to Bali leave from the ferry terminal at Ketapang, eight km north of Banyuwangi, at least every hour around the clock. The train station, a few hundred metres north of the ferry terminal, has departures to Surabaya via Probolinggo.

The main bus station, Terminal Seri Tanjung, is three km north of the ferry terminal, and has frequent buses along the northern route to Probolinggo, Surabaya and just about everywhere else including Yogya. Terminal Brawijaya (or Karang Ente) is four km south of Banyuwangi and has buses along the southern route to Jember.

Yellow 'Lin' bemos (400 rp) run between the bus and ferry terminals and train station, terminating at the Blambangan bemo terminal in the centre of town.

AROUND BANYUWANGI

The Banyuwangi area has some of Java's most remote, unspoilt and spectacular scenery, but facilities and public transport are all but nonexistent.

The main reason to stop in Banyuwangi is to visit **Kawah Ijen** (Ijen Crater), a spectacular volcanic crater lake west of Banyuwangi, ringed by volcanic cones. From Banyuwangi, take a bemo to Sasak Perot, then a colt to Jambu. It is then 17 km on foot along the road to the PHPA post at Paltuding, from where the trail to Kawah Ijen begins. Alternatively, the tourist office at Ketapang can arrange a jeep for 100,000 rp return to Pos Paltuding. From Pos Paltuding, walk one hour along a steep well-worn path to the vulcanology post, and then another half hour to the crater. From Bondowoso in the west, cars can drive all the way to Pos Paltuding, but irregular public transport only goes as far as Sempol, 18 km away.

Alas Purwo National Park occupies the remote Blambangan peninsula at the south-eastern tip of Java. On Grajagan Bay, it is most famous for its world-renowned surf beach at Plengkung, otherwise known as 'G-Land' to the surfing fraternity. You can stay at the PHPA post at Trianggulasi. Plengkung, 12 km away on foot, is the preserve of surfing tours organised out of Bali.

Meru Betiri National Park, on the south coast between Jember and Banyuwangi, receives few visitors because access is difficult. The major attraction is the protected **Sukamade** (Turtle Beach), where turtles come to lay their eggs. The *Wisma Sukamade* has very basic accommodation for 11,000 rp. Like Alas Purwo, public transport into the park is by public truck – if you are lucky, otherwise be prepared for a long walk.

Bali

To westerners, Bali has been both a tropical paradise and an example of the destructive effects of tourism. It has a rich culture, beautiful landscapes and coastline, a small bustling capital, several interesting towns, and hundreds of rural villages, where most Balinese live. The most conspicuous effects of tourism are confined to a few areas, and it's not hard to find fascinating places where tourists are a novelty. Balinese dancing, music, visual arts and architecture are unique and accessible to visitors. Religion is central to Balinese life, and the temples, festivals and offerings are ubiquitous.

History

Bali was populated before the Bronze Age commenced there about 300 BC, but the earliest records are stone inscriptions from around the 9th century AD. By that time rice was grown with a complex irrigation system, and there were the beginnings of a rich culture. Hindu influences from Java grew from the reign of King Airlangga (1019-42) – the rock-cut memorials of Gunung Kawi are a legacy of 11th century links to Java.

The great Majapahit Empire, and its legendary chief minister, Gajah Mada, conquered Bali in 1343. As Islam spread in Java, the Majapahit court progressively moved to Bali, making its final exodus, with priests,

INDONESIA

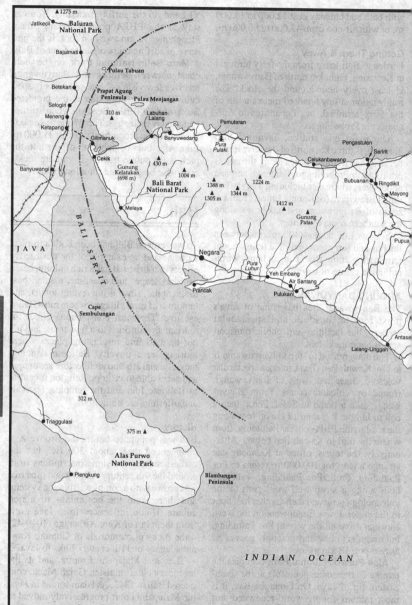

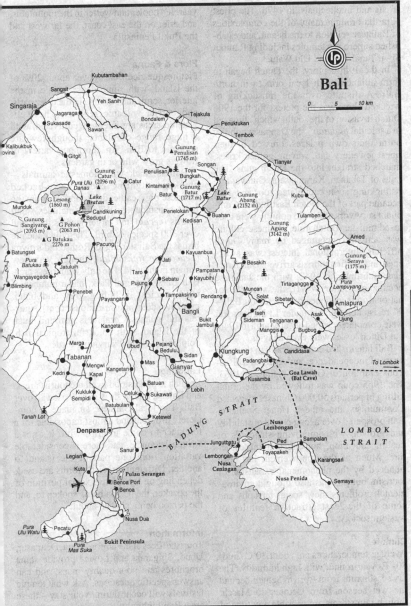

Bali

0   5   10 km

To Lombok

INDONESIA

Kubutambahan
Sangsit
Singaraja
Jagaraga
Sukasade
Sawan
Yeh Sanih
Kalibukbuk
Lovina
Gitgit
Bondalem
Tejakula
Penuktukan
Tembok
Tianyar
Gunung Penulisan (1745 m)
Penulisan
Songan
Toya Bungkah
Pura Ulu Danau
Gunung Catur (2096 m)
Catur
Kintamani
Batur
Gunung Batur (1717 m)
Lake Batur
Gunung Abang (2152 m)
Kubu
Tulamben
Lake Bratan
G Lesong (1860 m)
Candikuning
Bedugul
Penelokan
Kedisan
Buahan
Munduk
Gunung Sangiyang (2093 m)
G Pohon (2063 m)
G Batukau 2276 m
Pacung
Amed
Culik
Gunung Seraya (1175 m)
Gunung Agung (3142 m)
Batungsel
Pura Batukau
Jatuluih
Penebel
Payangan
Kayuanbua
Jati
Taro
Sebatu
Pujung
Tampaksiring
Besakih
Pampatan
Kayubihi
Rendang
Muncan
Selat
Pura Lempuyang
Tirtagangga
Sibetan
Asak
Ujung
Amlapura
Wangayegede
Blimbing
Bangli
Bukit Jambul
Iseh
Sideman
Tenganan
Manggis
Bugbug
Kangetan
Marga
Tabanan
Mengwi
Kangetan
Kapal
Kedri
Ubud
Pejang
Bedulu
Mas
Sidan
Gianyar
Klungkung
Padangbai
Candidasa
Kukluk
Sempidi
Celuk
Batuan
Sukawati
Lebih
Batubulan
Ketewel
Kusamba
Goa Lawah (Bat Cave)
BADUNG STRAIT
Tanah Lot
Denpasar
Sanur
Jungutbatu
Nusa Lembongan
Ped
Sampalan
LOMBOK STRAIT
Legian
Kuta
Lembongan
Toyapakeh
Karangsari
Nusa Ceningan
Pulau Serangan
Benoa Port
Benoa
Nusa Penida
Semaya
Pura Ulu Watu
Pecatu
Nusa Dua
Pura Mas Suka
Bukit Peninsula

artists and intellectuals, in 1478. The priest Nirartha brought many of the complexities of Balinese religion to the island, and established superb sea temples including Rambut Siwi, Tanah Lot and Ulu Watu.

In the 19th century, the Dutch began to form alliances with local princes in north Bali. A dispute over the ransacking of wrecked ships was the pretext for the 1906 Dutch invasion of the south, which climaxed in a suicidal *puputan* – the Denpasar nobility burnt their own palaces, dressed in their finest jewellery and, waving golden krises, marched straight into the Dutch guns. The rajas of Tabanan, Karangasem, Gianyar and Klungkung soon capitulated too, and Bali became part of the Dutch East Indies. Compliant survivors of the old nobility were used to administer Dutch rule. Balinese culture was actually encouraged by many Dutch officials, international interest was awakened and the first tourists arrived. Dutch rule ended abruptly in 1942, with the Japanese occupation. After WWII, the struggle for national independence was fierce on Bali – 94 resistance fighters under Lt Ngurah Rai were completely wiped out at Marga in 1946, but Dutch losses were even heavier.

Bali languished economically in the early years of independence, and suffered a disastrous eruption of Gunung Agung in 1963. The 1965 coup was followed by the brutal killing of perhaps 50,000 Chinese, suspected Communists and others. Under Soeharto, Bali prospered over a long period of stability and growth, with improving standards of health, education, housing and infrastructure. Much of the improvement has been financed by the phenomenal expansion of tourism, but this has also brought environmental problems, new social tensions and some of the least attractive features of western society.

Climate
Average temperatures are about 30°C (mid-80s°F) year-round, with high humidity. The dry season runs from April to September and the wet season from October to March, though rain storms are possible any time of year. It's cooler and wetter in the mountains, and drier on the east coast, the far west and the Bukit Peninsula.

Flora & Fauna
Picturesque rice fields cover about 20% of the island, with some dense jungle in the interior, scrub and savanna in the drier parts, and barren volcanic regions. The well-watered areas are intensely cultivated, with a huge range of plants, though few are endemic to Bali. An enormous variety of flowers grow wild or in gardens.

Bali is thick with domestic animals – chickens, fighting cocks, sway-backed Balinese pigs, cattle, ducks and dogs are the most conspicuous. Wildlife includes small lizards *(cecak)* and larger geckos, bats and over 300 species of bird. The only endemic bird is the Bali starling, or Rothschild's myna *(Leucopsar rothschildi)*, though very few remain in the wild. The only wilderness area, Bali Barat National Park, has a number of wild species, including grey and black monkeys, deer, *muncak* (mouse deer), squirrels and iguanas. Coral reefs surround much of the island, with colourful tropical fish, dolphins and a few surviving turtles.

Language
English is understood in all the tourist areas, and Bahasa Indonesia is widely used all over Bali. The local Balinese language is completely different and almost impossible for a foreigner to come to grips with. It's not a written language, and there is considerable variation from one part of the island to another. Different linguistic forms are used, depending on the relative social position of the speaker, the person being spoken to, and the person being spoken about.

Information
Tourist offices at the airport, Kuta, Denpasar, Ubud, Singaraja and Lovina provide some brochures and poor-quality maps, and can answer specific questions. Ask what temple festivals will occur during your stay – these are a Bali highlight.

Moneychangers are everywhere in tourist areas, and some banks give credit-card advances. You can travel for under US$10 per day, but it's easy to spend much more.

Kuta and Ubud are convenient addresses for poste restante mail. Private and Telkom wartels are widespread.

Dangers & Annoyances
Violent crime is uncommon, but there is some bag snatching, pickpocketing (especially on bemos) and theft from losmen rooms. Touts and hawkers can be a major annoyance, and overcharging can border on the criminal.

There's no drug scene – ignore any offers on the street. Magic mushrooms (oong) appear at certain times of the year, but for legal and psychological reasons they can't be recommended.

Activities
Bali is famous for its surf, and visiting surfers will easily find all the information and equipment they need in Kuta Beach. Most of the breaks are around the southern beaches, the Bukit Peninsula and the small neighbouring island of Nusa Lembongan.

The main sites for scuba diving are near Candidasa, on the shipwreck at Tulamben, and around Menjangan Island off the northwest coast. Diving operations based at Sanur, Lovina, Candidasa and Tulamben arrange day trips from about US$50, including two dives, transport and equipment. Check the credentials of the operation carefully – the best ones have PADI-accredited dive masters and instructors.

Trekkers can enjoy pleasant strolls through gorgeous rice fields around Ubud, day trips in the Bali Barat National Park, sunrise climbs around the Gunung Batur volcano and the demanding ascent of 3142 metre Gunung Agung.

Well-publicised white-water rafting trips are also popular, along with touristy activities like bungie jumping and paintball games.

Things to Buy
Popular purchases include woodcarvings, leather goods, paintings, silverwork, clothing, carved coconut shells, bone work, temple umbrellas, kites, model boats, bronze castings, stone statues, musical instruments, cassettes and coffee-table books. There are some wonderful things to buy, but shop around, because there's a lot of junk too, and initial asking-prices can be exorbitant.

Getting There & Away
Air Denpasar is a major international gateway. Reconfirm tickets because flights out of Bali are often full. Most of the airlines have offices at the airport and in the Grand Bali Beach Hotel, Sanur.

Air France	–	☎ 287734
Air New Zealand	–	☎ 756170
Ansett Australia	–	☎ 289636
Cathay Pacific Airways	–	☎ 286001
China Airlines	–	☎ 757298
Continental	–	☎ 752106
Garuda Indonesia	–	☎ 235169;
reconfirmation	227825, 222788 or 234606	
Japan Airlines	–	☎ 287577
KLM-Royal Dutch Airlines	–	☎ 756126
Korean Air	–	☎ 289402
Lufthansa Airlines	–	☎ 286952
Malaysia Airlines	–	☎ 285071
Qantas Airways	–	☎ 288331
Singapore Airlines	–	☎ 287940
Thai Airways International	–	☎ 288141

Domestic carriers which link Bali to other Indonesian islands have offices in Denpasar.

Bouraq	–	☎ 223564
Merpati	–	☎ 235358
Sempati	–	☎ 237343 (open 24 hours every day)

Some sample Merpati fares from Denpasar are: Surabaya (96,000 rp), Yogyakarta (127,000 rp) and Jakarta (239,000 rp) on Java; Mataram (43,000 rp) on Lombok; Bima (153,000 rp) on Sumbawa; Maumere (235,000 rp) on Flores; Waingapu (208,000 rp) on Sumba; and Kupang (244,000 rp) and Dili (301,000 rp) on Timor. It is cheaper to fly to Ujung Pandang (167,000 rp) on Sulawesi from Bali than from Java. Add 10% tax and 11,000 rp departure tax to these fares.

INDONESIA

Bus Direct air-con buses go every morning and evening to destinations in Java, including Surabaya (22,400 rp; 10 to 12 hours), Yogyakarta (41,500 rp; 15 to 16 hours) and even Jakarta (62,900 rp; 26 to 30 hours). The main departure point is Denpasar's Ubung bus terminal, where the companies are based and you can get the cheapest tickets. Many agents in Kuta sell tickets – transport to Ubung will cost extra. There are also Surabaya buses direct to/from Singaraja and Padangbai. The Bali-Java ferry is included in the ticket price.

Boat Ferries to/from Java go every half to one hour between the ports of Gilimanuk (Bali) and Ketapang (East Java, a few km north of Banyuwangi) for 1000 rp one way.

To Lombok's Lembar harbour, there are ferries every two hours from Padangbai (5000 rp ekonomi), and two fast-boat services a day on the *Mabua Ekspres* (☎ 72370) from Benoa (from US$13.50).

Four Pelni ships stop at Benoa on their loops through the archipelago: *Kelimutu*, *Awu*, *Tilongkabila* and *Dobonsolo*. The Pelni office (☎ 238962; fax 228962) is at Jalan Pelabuhan Benoa in Benoa Port.

Getting Around

The Airport There's a taxi counter at the airport where you buy a fixed-price ticket – 6500 rp to the southern end of Kuta; 8500 rp to Legian; 11,000 rp to Denpasar. Walk east out of the airport car park for a few hundred metres and you'll be on the route of the public bemo, which goes to Kuta for 500 rp or so.

Bemo Bemos are the minibuses which provide public transport on Bali. They're cheap and fun, but can be inconvenient. Every town has a bemo terminal, or at least a bemo stop. Denpasar is the hub of the system, and it has four main terminals; Singaraja has three. You may have to transit one or more of these terminals to get from one part of Bali to another. On longer routes, larger minibuses and full-size buses operate from the same terminals.

For local trips, it's around 500 rp for a short trip and 800 rp for five km – watch how much other passengers are paying. It's impossible to be precise about bemo fares – regular passengers on a route pay the bottom price and anyone else may be charged more. There may be a different price for different directions on the same route. They charge extra if you have a large bag. The bemo won't leave till it's full and may take a very roundabout route.

The Denpasar terminals and some of their destinations and approximate fares are:

Tegal
The terminal for Bali's southern peninsula has bemos to: Kuta, Legian and Sanur (blue bemo) (700 rp); the airport (800 rp); Nusa Dua (1000 rp); Ulu Watu (2000 rp); Batubulan terminal (700 rp); Ubung terminal (600 rp); and Kereneng terminal (600 rp).
Ubung
The terminal for the north and west of Bali, and also the main terminal for destinations in Java, has bemos to: Kediri (1000 rp); Mengwi (900 rp); Tabanan (1200 rp); Negara (3500 rp); Singaraja (3500 rp); Gilimanuk (4500 rp); Bedugul (3500 rp); Tegal terminal (600 rp); Kereneng terminal (500 rp); and Batubulan terminal (700 rp).
Batubulan
This terminal is actually several km north-east of Denpasar, and it serves destinations in the east and central area of Bali: Ubud (1500 rp); Gianyar (1000 rp); Tampaksiring, Klungkung and Bangli (1200 rp); Padangbai (2000 rp); Candidasa (2200 rp); Amlapura (3000 rp); and Kintamani (2000 rp).
Sanglah
This terminal, near the market at the south end of Diponegoro, has bemos to Suwung and Benoa Port (600 rp).
Kereneng
This is mainly an urban transfer terminal, with bemos to Sanur (600 rp), Tegal (600 rp), Ubung (500 rp) and Batubulan (600 rp).
Wangaya
This small terminal on the north side of town has bemos for Sangeh Monkey Forest, Pelaga and Petang.

Charters In tourist areas, white minibuses are available for charter – for a trip, by the hour or by the day. The cost depends on time and distance; figure on 60,000 rp per day, and allow more for long trips. Outside tourist areas you can charter unlicensed bemos for lower rates, but petrol is extra and the driver won't speak English. For longer charters, you should buy the driver some nasi campur and a bottle of water when you stop for a break.

Tourist Shuttle Bus Direct shuttle buses run between the main tourist areas on Bali, with connections to Java, Lombok and Sumbawa. They are faster, more convenient and more expensive than public bemos and buses, but much cheaper than car rental or chartered transport. Perama is the most established operator. Typical fares from Kuta are: Padangbai and Candidasa, 10,000 rp; Ubud, 7500 rp; Lovina, 12,500 rp; Mataram (Lombok), 20,000 rp. Distances are short, but travel times depend on traffic and the number of stops.

Taxi Metered taxis are available in Kuta, Denpasar and Sanur. Praja taxis (☎ 289090) are blue and yellow and cost 900 rp to start, 900 rp for the first km or part thereof, then around 50 rp per 100 metres. Bali taxis (☎ 701111) charge similar fares, with a minimum of 2500 rp. They won't pick up passengers in streets where minibus drivers hustle for charter business.

Car The most popular rental vehicle is the little Suzuki mini-jeep (Jimny), which typically costs from 35,000 to 40,000 rp a day, including insurance. Negotiate a cheaper rate for a week. A Kijang, which seats six in some comfort, costs from 65,000 rp for one day. Get an international driver's licence before you leave home – there are steep fines for unlicensed driving, and insurance may be invalidated. Driving is hazardous, and a car intrudes on the environment and isolates you from it. Parking can be difficult, and costs 200 to 500 rp in a town or near a tourist attraction. Cops find pretexts to extract on-the-spot fines.

Motorcycle Motorbikes cost 8000 to 12,000 rp per day, negotiable according to length of rental and the quality of the bike. They're more fun, more convenient and less intrusive than cars, but even more dangerous – only for experienced riders. Check the machine first, and ride sensibly. If your international driver's licence isn't endorsed for motorbikes, you'll have to get a one month Balinese visitors' licence at the police station in Denpasar. The bike owner will help; the process is easy but takes a whole morning and costs around 60,000 rp. Helmets are compulsory.

Bicycle Bicycles rent for around 5000 rp per day, but less for longer periods. They're handy transport in towns, and an ideal way to explore the countryside. Most are multi-gear mountain bikes. If uphill stretches are too arduous, it's possible to put your bike on a bemo, but they can charge a lot for the service.

Organised Tours Tours can be good value if time is short, or for places like Besakih, where public transport is difficult. Day tours cost from around 20,000 rp, but the price varies widely depending on the quality of the tour company, and where you buy the ticket. Ask around for a good operator – some tours are hard-sell shopping trips.

DENPASAR

The capital of both Bali and its own municipal district, Denpasar (population 370,000) has good shopping, government offices, universities, temples, mosques and churches. It has retained some tree-lined streets and pleasant gardens, despite increased traffic, noise and congestion.

Orientation

The main street starts as Jalan Gajah Mada in the west, becomes Jalan Surapati in the centre, then Jalan Hayam Wuruk and finally Jalan Raya Sanur in the east. Confusing one-way traffic restrictions and parking problems make it a bad place to drive – take taxis, bemos or walk.

Information

The Denpasar tourist office (☎ 234569) is on Jalan Surapati 7, just north of the Bali

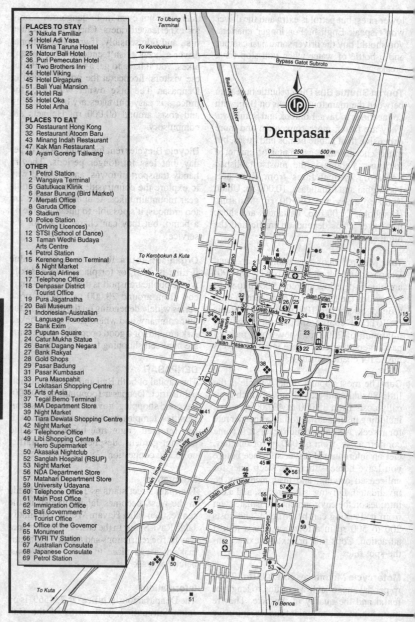

PLACES TO STAY
3   Nakula Familiar
4   Hotel Adi Yasa
11 Wisma Taruna Hostel
25 Natour Bali Hotel
36 Puri Pemecutan Hotel
41 Two Brothers Inn
44 Hotel Viking
45 Hotel Dirgapura
51 Bali Yuai Mansion
54 Hotel Rai
55 Hotel Oka
58 Hotel Artha

PLACES TO EAT
30 Restaurant Hong Kong
32 Restaurant Atoom Baru
43 Minang Indah Restaurant
47 Kak Man Restaurant
48 Ayam Goreng Taliwang

OTHER
1   Petrol Station
2   Wangaya Terminal
5   Gatutkaca Klinik
6   Pasar Burung (Bird Market)
7   Merpati Office
8   Garuda Office
9   Stadium
10 Police Station
    (Driving Licences)
12 STSI (School of Dance)
13 Taman Wedhi Budaya
    Arts Centre
14 Petrol Station
15 Kereneng Bemo Terminal
    & Night Market
16 Bouraq Airlines
17 Telephone Office
18 Denpasar District
    Tourist Office
19 Pura Jagatnatha
20 Bali Museum
21 Indonesian-Australian
    Language Foundation
22 Bank Exim
23 Puputan Square
24 Catur Mukha Statue
26 Bank Dagang Negara
27 Bank Rakyat
28 Gold Shops
29 Pasar Badung
31 Pasar Kumbasari
33 Pura Maospahit
34 Lokitasari Shopping Centre
35 Arts of Asia
37 Tegal Bemo Terminal
38 MA Department Store
39 Night Market
40 Tiara Dewata Shopping Centre
42 Night Market
46 Telephone Office
49 Libi Shopping Centre &
    Hero Supermarket
50 Akasaka Nightclub
52 Sanglah Hospital (RSUP)
53 Night Market
56 NDA Department Store
57 Matahari Department Store
59 University Udayana
60 Telephone Office
61 Main Post Office
62 Immigration Office
63 Bali Government
    Tourist Office
64 Office of the Governor
65 Monument
66 TVRI TV Station
67 Australian Consulate
68 Japanese Consulate
69 Petrol Station

Denpasar

To Tohpati,
Batubulan
& Sanur

To Tohpati,
Batubulan
& Sanur

Jalan Supratman

Abian Kapas

Jalan Nusa Indah

11

12

13

Jalan Hayam Wuruk

Kedaton

14

Jalan Hajar Dewantara

66

64

Jalan Dr Kusumah Atmaja

63

Jalan Tjut Nyah Dln

60 61 62

65

Jalan Moh Yamin

Jalan Raya Puputan

67

69

Renon

68

To Sanur &
Sidakarya

Museum. It has a calendar of events, an OK map and information on using Bali's bemo system. The office is open Monday to Thursday from 8 am to 2 pm, Friday to 11 am. Banks are mostly along Gajah Mada.

Telkom has a wartel at Jalan Teuku Umar 6, near the Jalan Diponegoro intersection, and there are several private wartels.

The main Denpasar post office, with a poste restante service, is inconveniently located in the Renon District, south-east of the centre. The immigration office (☎ 227828) is at Jalan Panjaitan 4, just around the corner, and is open Monday to Thursday from 8 am to 2 pm, Friday to 11 am.

RSUP Sanglah (☎ 223868) is the main hospital. It's in the southern part of town, and the best place in Bali for urgent medical care.

Denpasar, and all of south Bali, is in the 0361 area code.

Consulates The Australian consulate (☎ 235092) in Denpasar also serves citizens of other Commonwealth countries. There are honorary consuls for France (☎ 233555), Germany (☎ 288535), Netherlands (☎ 751-517), Norway and Denmark (☎ 235098), Sweden and Finland (☎ 288407/8), Switzerland (☎ 751735) and the USA (☎ 233605).

Things to See
The **museum** (open from 8 am to 5 pm, Friday to 3.30 pm, closed Monday) has some interesting exhibits of traditional tools and crafts, masks and costumes from all over Bali. Opposite the museum, **Puputan Square**, with its heroic Catur Mukha statue, is a meeting place in the evening. It commemorates the suicidal stand against the Dutch. The two most important **temples** are Pura Jagatnatha, the state temple next to the museum, and the 14th century Pura Maospahit.

On the east side of town, **Taman Budaya Arts Centre** (☎ 222776), exhibits paintings, crafts and carvings and has regular music and dance performances, especially during the arts festival in June and July.

INDONESIA

Places to Stay

There are plenty of places to stay, mostly aimed at business travellers and domestic tourists. *Adi Yasa* (☎ 222679), at Jalan Nakula 23B, is a venerable, standard budget losmen, with adequate rooms at 12,500/17,000 rp for singles/doubles with shared mandi, 15,000/20,000 rp with private bathroom; breakfast is included. On the other side of the street, *Nakula Familiar* (☎ 226446) is new, not spacious, but clean, friendly and inexpensive. Near the Tegal bemo terminal, *Two Brothers Losmen* (☎ 222704), in a gang off Jalan Imam Bonjol, is another old standard, asking 13,000/18,000 rp for an ordinary room with shared bathroom.

Bali Yuai Mansion (☎ 228850), at Jalan Satelit 22, in Sanglah, is a tidy place with a very helpful owner, and clean, comfortable rooms from 10,000/15,000 rp – phone first and they may pick you up. *Hotel Viking* (☎ 223992) at Jalan Diponegoro 120 has economy rooms from 15,000 rp for singles, and other rooms with air-con, TV and phone for up to 50,000 rp. There are other mid-range, business-traveller places in the area.

Places to Eat

Several places along Jalan Teuku Umar serve real Balinese food; Padang and Lombok-style food is also available, as well as the Indonesian standards. Chinese places on or near Gajah Mada include the *Hong Kong* and the *Atoom Baru*; main courses are from 4000 to 9000 rp. You'll find excellent and cheap *food stalls* near the markets and bemo terminals, especially in the evenings. The food court in the *Tiara Dewata* shopping centre is very clean, and has a good selection of typical street-stall food. The rooftop eateries at *NDA* are also good. For a splurge, try the old-fashioned dining room at the *Natour Bali Hotel*, where a fine rijstaffel costs 10,500 rp.

Things to Buy

Pasar Badung, one of the main markets, has a fascinating range of food, clothing, crafts and ceremonial accessories. A little southeast, the area called Kampung Arab has shops with gold jewellery, batik, ikat and other fabrics. Kumbasari is another market/shopping centre, with handicrafts, fabrics and gold work. Matahari and the New Dewata Ayu (NDA) are the best of the new department stores.

Getting There & Away

See the Bali Getting Around section for details of the bus and bemo network centred in Denpasar.

Getting Around

Bemos shuttling between the main terminals take various routes around town (500 to 700 rp for most trips), but it's hard to know which ones go where. Ask at the terminals.

KUTA & LEGIAN

Kuta is the biggest tourist area on Bali, and the closest place to the airport. It's great for cheap accommodation, food, shopping, surf, sunsets and partying; and there is a Balinese community here, beneath the brash, commercialised surface.

The beach is wide and white, with fine surf, though the currents and tides can be very dangerous. Beach-selling is restricted to the upper part of the beach; close to the water you can sunbathe in peace. Inland from the beach is a network of roads and tiny gangs with hundreds of hotels, losmen, restaurants, bars and shops. Legian is the next beach north of Kuta, but the developments have merged. Legian merges into Seminyak, further north, where a lot of long-term visitors stay. South of Kuta, Tuban extends down to the airport, with more tourist development along the beach. Kuta is moving upmarket – the beery, boisterous nightlife remains, but there are more sophisticated alternatives. Shopping is the big growth area.

Orientation

Restaurants, bars, travel agents, banks, moneychangers and shops line Jalan Legian, the main road which runs south from Seminyak to Kuta. More tourist businesses and most of the cheap places to stay are on the lanes between Jalan Legian and the beach. Bemo Corner is at the southern end of Jalan

Legian, at the intersection with Jalan Pantai Kuta. Many of the roads have one-way traffic.

Information

Tourist Office The Badung District tourist office (☎ 751419), Jalan Bakung Sari 1, is open daily except Sunday from 8 am to 6 pm. The Bali government tourist information service (☎ 753540), in a new building on Jalan Benesari, is open daily except Sunday from 8 am to 2 pm. Both have some printed information, and will tell you when and where temple festivals are being held.

Money The numerous moneychangers are faster than banks, open longer hours and give just as good a rate. Some banks will do money transfers and credit card advances. ATMs at the airport and in Legian give cash on Visa and Cirrus cards, if they're working.

Post & Communications The main post office is on a small backroad near the night market, with a sort-it-yourself poste restante service. There is also a postal agent on Jalan Legian, and another on Jalan Melasti. There are numerous wartels for long-distance and international calls. Most permit reverse-charge

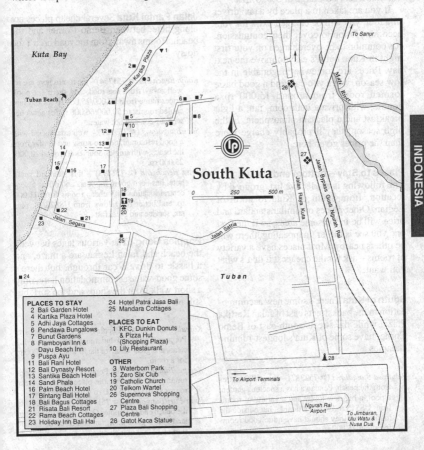

South Kuta

0   250   500 m

PLACES TO STAY
2 Bali Garden Hotel
4 Kartika Plaza Hotel
5 Adhi Jaya Cottages
6 Pendawa Bungalows
7 Bunut Gardens
8 Flamboyan Inn & Dayu Beach Inn
9 Puspa Ayu
11 Bali Rani Hotel
12 Bali Dynasty Resort
13 Santika Beach Hotel
14 Sandi Phala
16 Palm Beach Hotel
17 Bintang Bali Hotel
18 Bali Bagus Resort
21 Risata Bali Resort
22 Rama Beach Cottages
23 Holiday Inn Bali Hai

24 Hotel Patra Jasa Bali
25 Mandara Cottages

PLACES TO EAT
1 KFC, Dunkin Donuts & Pizza Hut (Shopping Plaza)
10 Lily Restaurant

OTHER
3 Waterbom Park
15 Zero Six Club
19 Catholic Church
20 Telkom Wartel
26 Supernova Shopping Centre
27 Plaza Bali Shopping Centre
28 Gatot Kaca Statue

To Sanur

Kuta Bay

Tuban Beach

Jalan Karna Plaza

Mati River

Jalan Bypass Gusti Ngurah Rai

Jalan Raya Kuta

Jalan Segara

Jalan Satria

Tuban

To Airport Terminals

Ngurah Rai Airport

To Jimbaran, Ulu Watu & Nusa Dua

calls for a fee, and have fax services. The Kambodja wartel in Kuta Square may have an Internet connection working.

Places to Stay

Kuta and Legian have hundreds of places to stay. The most expensive hotels are along the beachfront. Mid-range places are mostly on the bigger roads between Jalan Legian and the beach, with the cheapest losmen on the smaller lanes in between. There's a 10% tax on all accommodation, usually included in the price, but more expensive places add it on, plus a service charge of 5% to 15%.

If you are taken to a place by a taxi driver or a tout, you will be charged extra for your accommodation to cover their commission. It's common to be overcharged on your first night in Kuta, but it's easy to move the next day. Prices are somewhat negotiable in the low season, when you can find a good basic losmen room from around 15,000 rp a double, with private bathroom, fan, a light breakfast and a pleasant atmosphere. In the high season, they'll probably charge more than the prices given here.

Places to Stay – bottom end

The following is a selective list, grouped by location, from south of Kuta to north of Legian. Other places of similar standard and price will be in the same areas, so if the first one you see is full or unappealing, there will be others nearby. Most places have a variety of rooms – ask for the cheapest if that's what you want.

South of Kuta There's some new accommodation in the backstreets east of Jalan Kartika Plaza, while the streets south-east of Bemo Corner have some of Kuta's longest-running cheapies.

Pendawa Bungalows (☎ 752387) – about 400 metres from the beach, Pendawa has a spacious garden, a pool, a big new lobby and a variety of rooms from US$15 to US$45 a double, but outside the high season they should have quite good rooms for about 25,000 rp.

Bamboo Inn (☎ 751935) – this traditional little losmen is in a gang south of Jalan Bakung Sari, on the southern edge of central Kuta but far enough away to be quiet. It's some distance from the beach but close to restaurants and bars. OK rooms cost from 15,000 rp including breakfast.

Jesen's Inn II (☎ 752647) & *Zet Inn* (☎ 753135) – these are pleasant little places in the same gang as the Bamboo Inn, with double rooms at around 20,000 rp.

Anom Dewi Youth Hostel (☎ 752292) – close to Bemo Corner, this is a cheap but well-run youth-hostel-affiliated losmen with standard rooms at 12,000/17,000 rp, superior rooms at 14,000/20,000 rp. There's a 5000 rp high-season supplement and a 2000 rp discount for HI members.

Jalan Pantai Kuta Several cheap places are along here, between Bemo Corner and the beach. Rooms away from the road aren't too noisy.

Kodja Beach Inn (☎ 751754) – the rooms here are set well away from the road, and there's a pool; prices range from 20,000/25,000 rp for old fan-cooled rooms, to 50,000/66,000 rp for new ones with air-con and hot water.

Suci Bungalows (☎ 753761) – well established with a good restaurant, not too noisy and not far from the beach, with singles/doubles at around 20,000/25,000 rp.

Yulia Beach Inn (☎ 751893) – this standard small hotel has been going for years and offers a very central location with cheap rooms from 11,000 rp, and better bungalows from US$23/28, plus tax, service and breakfast.

Poppies Gang I The various lanes between the beach and Jalan Legian are a maze, and a hassle to drive a car through, but there's some good-value accommodation here, only a short walk from the shops and the surf, but still nice and quiet.

Komala Indah I – in Poppies Gang right opposite Poppies Cottages I but much more basic. It's clean, and great value for the location at 12,000 rp for a room.

Kempu Taman Ayu – off Poppies Gang, this long-running and friendly little place has nice, cheap rooms at 10,000/15,000 rp without breakfast.

Kuta Puri Bungalows (☎ 751903) – well located at the beach end of Poppies Gang, on a large plot of land with a good pool; fan-cooled cottages here start at 32,000 rp including tax and breakfast.

Rita's House – in a gang going north of Poppies Gang, this popular little losmen is not fancy, but good value at 12,000/15,000 rp.

Rempan Accommodation (☎ 753150) – squeezed between the buildings behind Rita's, this three storey building has plain but clean rooms from 13,000/17,000 rp.

Berlian Inn (☎ 751701) – further up the same gang, with good rooms from 17,000/23,000 rp including breakfast, this is good value in a central location.

Sorga Cottages (☎ 751897) – there are quite a few rooms and a swimming pool squeezed onto this site, but it's a quiet location and inexpensive at 19,000/25,000 rp, or 36,000/46,000 rp with air-con; the open meals area upstairs is a very pleasant bonus.

Bali Sandy Cottages (☎ 753344) – secluded in one of the last coconut plantations left in Kuta, close to the beach and Poppies Gang II, the rooms here are pretty nice too, from only 25,000 rp.

Puri Ayodia Inn – this small and very standard losmen is in a quiet but convenient location and has rooms for just 10,000/12,000 rp.

Sari Bali Bungalows (☎ 753065) – nice bungalows in a spacious garden with a good pool, from 26,000/30,000 rp; up to 60,000 rp with air-con.

Jus Edith – a basic place, but very cheap with rooms from 8000/12,000 rp.

Ronta Bungalows (☎ 754246) – good, clean budget accommodation, with a nice garden, central location and rooms at 12,000/17,000 rp for a single/double.

Poppies Gang II There are plenty of cheap places to stay here, and the gang running north, Poppies Gang II Utara (north), is about the best place to look for rock-bottom accommodation.

Palm Gardens Homestay (☎ 752198) – a neat and clean place on Poppies Gang II, good value from 20,000/25,000 rp, and popular with surfers.

Bali Dwipa (☎ 751446), *Bali Indah* (☎ 752509), *Bali Duta Wisata* (☎ 753534) & *Losmen Cempaka* (☎ 754744) – on Poppies Gang II Utara, these multistorey concrete blocks don't have much character or comfort, but they're central, and cheap at around 12,000 rp for a double.

Suka Beach Inn (☎ 752793) – a popular place in the same bottom-end part of Poppies Gang II Utara, with good rooms in a garden setting for around 12,000 rp.

Meka Jaya (☎ 754487), *Bendesa* (☎ 751358) & *Beneyasa Beach Inn* – further north on Poppies Gang II Utara, these losmen have cheap rooms, also facing gardens, from 10,000/15,000 rp.

Legian Cheap accommodation in Legian tends to be north of Jalan Padma – look on the side streets and back lanes.

Sayang Beach Lodging (☎ 751249) – tucked away on a lane south of Jalan Melasti, handy to the beach and not too far from the action. It has a small pool, and a variety of rooms from small, basic ones at US$6/8, up to larger air-con ones at US$25/30.

Puri Tanah Lot Cottages (☎ 752281) – on the same lane, the cheaper rooms here, from 17,500/25,000 rp, are pretty nice too.

Legian Mas Beach Inn (☎ 755334) – a little further up towards Melasti, this simple losmen is in a quiet location, with clean rooms from 10,000/12,000 rp.

Ady's Inn (☎ 753445) – off a small street north of Jalan Melasti, this is basic accommodation in a pleasantly overgrown garden. It's nice, friendly and cheap with quite good rooms at 10,000/15,000 rp, but breakfast is extra.

Legian Beach Bungalows (☎ 751087) – in the centre of Legian on busy Jalan Padma, there are friendly staff here, and OK rooms from 20,000 rp to 25,000 rp, set well back from the street.

Puri Damai Cottages (☎ 751965) – also on Jalan Padma, this is a traditional budget losmen with singles/doubles from 10,000/15,000 rp, and a lot more character than many of the newer places.

North Legian & Seminyak Development here is quite spread out, and there's no public transport so getting around can be difficult. But there are places within an easy walk of both the beach and the facilities on Jalan Legian.

Three Brothers Inn (☎ 751566) – a long-standing and popular place off Jalan Legian, with rooms scattered round a gorgeous garden – the newer rooms have less character than the originals. There's a nice pool, and some rooms are good for families. Prices run from 27,000 rp to 69,000 rp, plus 10% tax.

Sinar Indah (☎ 755905) – on the small road between Jalan Padma and Jalan Pura Bagus Taruna, this standard-style losmen is handy to the beach and asks 25,000 rp for a double room without breakfast; they also have bigger rooms with kitchen facilities.

Sinar Beach Cottages (☎ 751404) – in the same area, this quiet and pleasant little place asks 20,000 rp for rooms set around the garden.

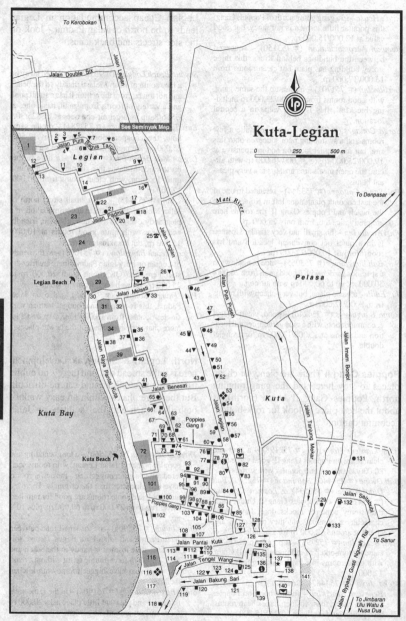

Kuta-Legian

PLACES TO STAY

1	Jayakarta Hotel
6	Sari Yasai Beach Inn & Hotel Baleka
10	Sinar Beach Cottages & Adika Sari Bungalows
12	Puri Tantra Beach Bungalows
13	Bali Niksoma Inn & Bali Kelapa Hotel
14	Sinar Indah & Bali Sani Hotel
15	Three Brothers Inn
17	Puri Damai Cottages
18	Legian Beach Bungalows
22	Garden View Cottages
23	Bali Padma Hotel
24	Bali Mandira Cottages
27	Ady's Inn
29	Legian Beach Hotel
31	Bali Intan Legian
34	Kul Kul Resort
35	Legian Mas Beach Inn
36	Puri Tanah Lo Cottages
37	Camplung Mas
38	Bruna Beach Hotel
39	Kuta Jaya Cottage
40	Sayang Beach Lodging
41	Kuta Bungalows
62	Bali Dwipa, Bali Indah & Losmen Cempaka
63	Bendesa I & Bendesa II
64	Meka Jaya
67	Suka Beach Inn
69	Kuta Suci Bungalows
71	The Bounty Hotel
72	Sahid Bali Seaside Hotel
73	Poppies Cottages II
74	Palm Gardens Homestay
75	Bali Sandy Cottages
77	Ronta Bungalows
78	Jus Edith
86	Komala Indah I
89	Kempu Taman Ayu
90	Puri Ayodia Inn
91	Suji Bungalows
92	Sari Bali Bungalows
93	Sorga Cottages
94	Arena & Mimpi Bungalows
95	Berlian Inn
96	Rita's House & Rempan Accommodation
100	Kuta Puri Bungalows
101	Kuta Segara Caria
102	Aneka Beach Bungalows
104	La Walon Bungalows
106	Poppies Cottages I
107	Budi Beach Inn
108	Kodja Beach Inn
110	Ida Beach Inn
111	Asana Santhi Homestay (Willy I)
112	Suci Bungalows
113	Yulia Beach Inn
115	Natour Kuta Beac Hotel
118	Melasti Hotel & Karthi Inn
120	Ramayana Seaside Cottages
134	Anom Dewi Youth Hostel
139	Bamboo Inn, Zet Inn & Jesen's Inn II

PLACES TO EAT

2	Topi Koki Restaurant
3	Swiss Restaurant
4	Sawasdee Thai Restaurant
5	Twice Cafe
7	Rum Jungle Road Bar & Restaurant
8	Bamboo Palace Restaurant
9	Glory Bar & Restaurant
11	Poco Loco Mexican Restaurant
16	Warung Kopi
20	Rama Garden Restaurant
26	Do Drop Inn
30	Karang Mas Restaurant
32	Restaurant Puri Bali Indah & Legian Garden Restaurant
33	Orchid Garden Restaurant
44	Aroma's Cafe
47	Yanies
49	Gemini Restaurant
50	Mama's German Restaurant
52	Mama Luccia Italian Restaurant
53	McDonald's
56	Mama's German Restaurant
60	Batu Bulong Restaurant
61	Twice Pub
66	Brasil Bali Restaurant
68	The Corner Restaurant
70	Nana's Swedish Restaurant
80	Mini Restaurant
83	Indah Sari Seafood
85	Poppies Restaurant
87	TJs
88	Bambo Corner
97	Nusa Indah Bar & Restaurant
98	Kedin Restaurant
99	Tree House Restaurant
103	Kempu Cafe
105	Fat Yogi's Wood Fired Pizza Restaurant
109	Lenny's Restaurant
119	Singasana Restaurant
121	Agun Korea House Restaurant
122	Dayu I
123	Nagasari Restaurant
127	Made's Warung
128	Sushi Bar Nelayan
133	KFC

OTHER

19	Bali Rock
21	Joni Sunken Bar & Restaurant
25	Wartel
28	Postal Agency
42	Government Tourist Information
43	Bookshop
45	The Bounty
46	Peanuts
48	Legian Mall & ATM
51	001 Club
53	Matahari Department Store, Timezone & Cinema
54	Jonathon Silver Gallery
55	Norm's Sport Bar
57	Yusef's Silver
58	SC (Sari Club)
59	Rudy's Art & Antiques
65	Australian Bungy Jump
76	Tubes Bar
79	BDI Bank
81	Kuta Postal Agency
82	Hard Rock Cafe
84	Perama Office
114	Matahari Department Store
116	Kuta Square Shopping Centre
117	Kuta Art Market
121	Supermarket
123	Wartel
124	Kul Kul Music
125	The Pub
126	Bemo Corner
129	Duty-Free Store
130	Fuji Image Plaza
131	KCB Tours & Travel & Dutch Consulate
132	Petrol Station
133	Galeal Supermarket
135	Casablanca Bar
136	Badung Tourist Information & Sulawesi Tourist Office
137	Police Station
138	Chinese Temple
140	Post Office
141	Night Market (Pasar Senggol)

INDONESIA

LG Beach Club Hotel (☎ 751060) – not very professionally run, but with a great location on a spacious lot behind the beachfront restaurants; the rooms start at 33,000 rp, but some are a bit run down.

Mesari Beach Inn (☎ 751401) – one of the few budget places up in Seminyak, off Jalan Dhyana Pura behind the stables, with single/double rooms for 17,000/20,000 rp, and bungalows at around 315,000 rp per week.

Places to Stay – middle

There are a great many mid-range hotels, from US$25 to US$55 plus tax and service, but the published rate is always negotiable, up to 50% off in the low season. Kuta is a good place for the budget traveller to indulge in something better for a night or two. The following are some of the best-value places, listed from south to north:

La Walon Bungalows (☎ 752463) – on Poppies Gang I, La Walon has a pool and some budget rooms with verandas, open-air bathrooms and ceiling fans from US$21/24; air-con rooms cost US$5 more.

Poppies Cottages II – this is the original Poppies (despite the name), and not as fancy as Poppies I. There are only a few cottages, but they're attractive and reasonably priced at US$23/28. Guests can use the pool at Poppies I.

The Bounty Hotel (☎ 753030) – very central on Poppies Gang II, this is a nice-looking place with a distinctive black-tiled pool. The published rates start at US$90 (including tax and service), but they discount heavily in the off season, to as little as US$35, including free passes to some well-known nightspots.

Kuta Bungalows (☎ 754393) – these bungalows, on Jalan Benesari, are a bit stark, but the pool, garden and general ambience are very nice. Normal price is US$35/40, but maybe US$25 in the low season.

Puri Tantra Beach Bungalows (☎ 753195) – the six traditional-style bungalows here provide some of the most tasteful accommodation in Bali, for US$40; they're often full.

Places to Eat

If you want to eat cheaply, try the *food carts* near Legian beach, or the *warungs* at the night market. Dozens of tourist restaurants have the standard Indonesian items (nasi goreng, nasi campur etc), as well as hamburgers, jaffles, spaghetti and salads (costing between 2000 and 4500 rp at most places). A good pizza, seafood or steak dish will cost between 10,000 and 15,000 rp.

For fancier food, you'll find French, German, Italian, Japanese, Korean, Mexican and Swiss restaurants. Wine is expensive, but some places have Australian wine by the glass for around 4000 rp. Beer goes well with most meals and is a fair index of prices – in cheap places a large beer is around 4500 rp; in expensive places it costs from 6000 rp.

On Bakung Sari, standard tourist restaurants include *Dayu I* and *Nagasari*. The supermarket here has many western-style food items, for snacks and to supplement losmen breakfasts. Along Jalan Pantai Kuta, near Bemo Corner, popular *Made's Warung* is an open-fronted place which is good for people-watching – the food is excellent, though a touch expensive. The *Suci Restaurant*, on the south side of Pantai Kuta, is good value with delicious fruit drinks.

Poppies Gang I, the tiny lane between Jalan Legian and the beach, is named for *Poppies*, one of the oldest and most popular restaurants in Kuta. The garden setting and the atmosphere are delightful, and the food is consistent, but pricey and not particularly imaginative. A few steps west is *TJ's*, a deservedly popular Mexican restaurant, with a good ambience and main courses from 9000 to 16,000 rp. Further down Poppies Gang, heading towards the beach, there are several good eateries. *Bamboo Corner* has a good selection of Chinese and Indonesian dishes for around 5000 rp. *Nusa Indah Bar & Restaurant* is recommended by locals, while the inexpensive *Kempu Cafe* has some fine vegetarian dishes. The *Tree House Restaurant* does an excellent American breakfast for 4200 rp.

On the beach, where Jalan Pantai Kuta turns north, *Warung PKK* is good for basic, inexpensive food and cold beer while you watch the sunset. Other kiosks along the beach serve drinks and snacks, at slightly higher prices than you'd pay in town.

Busy Jalan Legian is thick with restaurants. Just north of Bemo Corner is the *Sushi Bar Nelayan*, with sushi for 2000 to 5000 rp, and sashimi from around 12,000 rp. Continue north towards Legian, and you reach the *Mini Restaurant*, a huge place despite the name, but busy, serving good straightforward food at low prices. The *Sari Club Restaurant* is similar in style, price and quality. On the east side of the road, *Indah Sari* is a big seafood place, and quite expensive though the service and the food are of variable standard.

Around the corner, Poppies Gang II has a lot of budget restaurants where a good meal and a big beer will be under 10,000 rp. They include the popular *Batu Bulong*, *Nana's*

Swedish Restaurant, the *Twice Pub* and the *Corner Restaurant*. Many of these have laser video movies at night, which can detract from the ambience and the service. The gang going north has sprouted several good, cheap eateries to satisfy those staying in the cheap hotels nearby.

Continue north on Jalan Legian, where *Mama's German Restaurant* has pretty authentic German food with main courses for around 8000 rp. (Mama has a second restaurant further north.) The *Gemini* is an open-roofed place with surprisingly good Indonesian and Chinese food, despite its bare

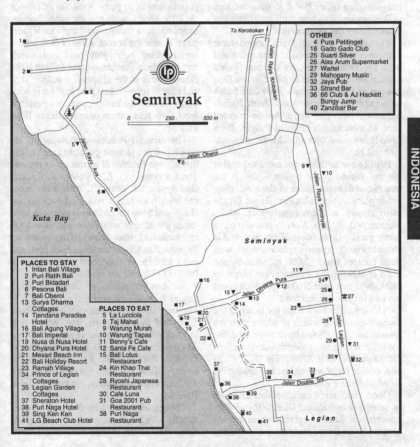

Seminyak

To Kerobokan

Kuta Bay

Seminyak

Legian

OTHER
4 Pura Petitinget
18 Gado Gado Club
25 Suarti Silver
26 Alas Arum Supermarket
27 Wartel
29 Mahogany Music
32 Strand Bar
33 Jaya Pub
36 66 Club & AJ Hackett Bungy Jump
40 Zanzibar Bar

PLACES TO STAY
1 Intan Bali Village
2 Puri Ratih Bali
3 Puri Bidadari
6 Pesona Bali
7 Bali Oberoi
13 Surya Dharma Cottages
14 Tjendana Paradise Hotel
16 Bali Agung Village
17 Bali Imperial
19 Nusa di Nusa Hotel
20 Dhyana Pura Hotel
21 Mesari Beach Inn
22 Bali Holiday Resort
23 Ramah Village
34 Prince of Legian Cottages
35 Legian Garden Cottages
37 Sheraton Hotel
38 Puri Naga Hotel
39 Sing Ken Ken
41 LG Beach Club Hotel

PLACES TO EAT
5 La Lucciola
8 Taj Mahal
9 Warung Murah
10 Warung Tapas
11 Benny's Cafe
12 Santa Fe Cafe
15 Bali Lotus Restaurant
24 Kin Khao Thai Restaurant
28 Ryoshi Japanese Restaurant
30 Cafe Luna
31 Goa 2001 Pub Restaurant
38 Puri Naga Restaurant

INDONESIA

and basic appearance. The prices are pleasantly basic too, which accounts for its steady popularity. Across the road is *Aroma's Cafe*, a mid-priced restaurant with great vegetarian food and a delightful setting.

A little further north, and just off Jalan Legian, *Yanie's* has tasty burgers, pizzas and steaks as well as Indonesian standards. It's inexpensive, is open till late and has a good, fun atmosphere. Continuing north to the heart of Legian, you'll come to *Warung Kopi*, which is well regarded for its varied menu of European, Asian and vegetarian dishes, breakfasts and tempting desserts. The long-standing *Glory Bar & Restaurant* does a Wednesday Balinese buffet, offering a chance to try the local cuisine.

The streets west of Jalan Legian have numerous mid-range tourist restaurants and bars. On Jalan Melasti are the big *Orchid Garden Restaurant*, the *Legian Garden Restaurant* and the *Restaurant Puri Bali Indah* with excellent Chinese food. Jalan Padma has similar places, as well as Aussie-oriented bars. In a backstreet north of Padma, *Poco Loco* is a popular, upmarket Mexican restaurant and bar.

Further north, things get more expensive but the standards are higher – this is the trendy end of town. Some of the most interesting places are on Jalan Pura Bagus Taruna (also known as Rum Jungle Rd). At its western end, the *Topi Koki Restaurant* has a pretty good go at la cuisine Française, and is about the most expensive place around, with main courses from 12,000 rp, wine by the glass at 8000 rp – a full meal for two with drinks will cost over 50,000 rp, which is not too bad for fine French food.

A little further back from the beach is the *Swiss Restaurant*, which is adjacent to the Swiss consul so should have some credibility. Other restaurants along this street include the *Sawasdee Thai Restaurant*, *Yudi Pizza* and, nearer to Jalan Legian, the distinctive *Bamboo Palace Restaurant*.

Good, though not cheap, places to eat up in Seminyak include the *Goa 2001 Pub Restaurant*, on Jalan Legian, where trendy expats choose from a multicultural menu and

a long list of fancy drinks. Further north are the *Ryoshi* Japanese restaurant, *Kin Khao* for Thai food, some trendy tapas bars, and even an Indonesian restaurant, the inexpensive *Warung Murah*. On a beach track past the Oberoi, *La Lucciato* is an Italian place with food that people rave about, and prices which aren't excessive.

Entertainment

Most bars are free, and often have special drink promotions and 'happy hours' between 6 and 9 pm – the biggest concentration of bars is on Jalan Legian. One of the most popular places to party is the *Sari Club* (or 'SC' for short), with a giant video screen, dance music, a young crowd and lots of local guys. Round the corner is *Tubes Bar*, where surfers drink beer, play pool and watch surfing videos. Further up Jalan Legian is the *Bounty*, built in the shape of a sailing ship and easy to spot – it gets people in early with a two-for-one drinks deal, provides passable food, then packs them onto the dance floor till 2 am.

The original Peanuts club is being redeveloped as a shopping centre (a sign of the times!), but *Peanuts II* carries on its reputation (or notoriety). Also known as Kacang (Indonesian for 'peanut'), it has a big outer bar with pool tables and loud rock music (free), and a big dance floor inside with loud dance music (free until midnight, then 5000 rp, including one drink). The infamous Peanuts Pub Crawl includes transport and entry to three or four local watering holes (☎ 751333 for all the sordid details).

Some other places to check on Jalan Legian include *Lips*, a slightly sleazy C&W bar, the *001 Club*, a self-proclaimed Rage Spot, and *Norm's Sports Bar*, which is a long-established Aussie favourite. Other down-under drinking places on Jalan Padma are *Bali Rock* and the *Bali Aussie*. In the south of Kuta, *The Pub*, one of Kuta's original bars, and *Casablanca*, are both on Jalan Buni Sari.

The best reggae venue is *Bruna*, facing the beach, which gets some hot local bands doing good covers of reggae classics. There's a roomy dance floor and the crowd is enthu-siastic – it's popular with Japanese.

More upmarket venues, attracting older customers, include the glossy *Hard Rock Cafe* on Jalan Legian, with live music, free entry and pricey drinks. Nearby is the new *Studebaker Club*, which is similar in style. *Zero Six*, near the beach down in Tuban, sometimes offers the unusual combination of rock bands and Balinese dancing.

The real social scene is centred up north in Seminyak, starting with drinks and/or dinner at the *Goa 2001 Pub Restaurant*. Alternatively, the *Jaya Pub* is a place for an older crowd to enjoy relaxed music and con-versation, while the street-side tables at *Luna Cafe* are a place to be seen. Later on, but *never* before 1 am, the action shifts to the beachside *66 Club* (pronounced 'double six'), or the chic *Gado Gado*; they both have a cover charge (8000 to 12,000 rp) which includes one drink. At quiet times, only one of these will open on a given night. Both places have open-air dance floors, and attract a trendy, affluent crowd of tourists, expats and Indonesians, with quite a few gays and the occasional, expensive bar girl.

Getting There & Away
Many travel agencies sell sightseeing tours to Balinese dances, craft centres and other attractions, as well as tickets for buses to Java, Lombok and Sumbawa, and for the regular tourist shuttle buses to Ubud (7500 rp), Lovina (12,500 rp), Padangbai (10,000 rp), Candidasa and other tourist centres on Bali. Perama (☎ 751551) is near the southern end of Jalan Legian, but there are several other shuttle bus operations.

Public bemos do a route from Denpasar's Tegal terminal to the airport via Kuta and Legian, and the easiest place to catch one is at the Jalan Raya Kuta intersection, 50 metres east of Bemo Corner. For most destinations on Bali you have to go via Tegal plus one of the other Denpasar bus/bemo terminals.

Many travel agents sell air tickets and reconfirm flights. Bali's not a great place for cheap air fares, but KCB Tours, on the Denpasar road, has the best deals. The

Garuda office (☎ 751179) is in the Natour Kuta Beach Hotel.

Getting Around
It's hard to get around Kuta and Legian by public transport. The only bemo route goes west and north on Jalan Pantai Kuta, east on Melasti and south on Jalan Legian. In theory it costs about 300 rp. In practice bemos are reluctant to pick up tourists – the guys with minibuses for charter are trying to monopo-lise the transport business, and discourage both public bemos and metered taxis from taking passengers. Bemos are scarce from late afternoon onwards.

BUKIT PENINSULA
The southern peninsula, known as Bukit (Hill) is dry and quite sparsely populated, but slated for major tourism development. Just south of the airport, **Jimbaran Bay** is a superb crescent of white sand and blue sea, with a colourful fishing fleet and a few luxury hotels. Beachside restaurants do won-derful barbecued seafood here every evening, for around 12,000 rp. Near the beach, *Nelayan Jimbaran Cafe & Homestay* (☎ 702253) has small, clean, but pricey, rooms, at 50,000/60,000 rp. East of the main road, *Puri Indra Prasta* bungalows asks 35,000 rp for very ordinary accommodation.

A sealed road goes south from Jimbaran to **Ulu Watu**, where an important temple perches at the tip of the peninsula, and sheer cliffs drop into the sea. Just before the temple car park, there's a sign to **Pantai Suluban** (Suluban Beach), famous for its great surf. Other surf breaks are at **Oalangan**, **Bingin**, **Padang** and **Nyang Nyang**, some of which have secluded little beaches. Guys on motor-bikes will take you to the more isolated ones, where there are usually warungs but no places to stay.

Nusa Dua
Nusa Dua is Bali's most expensive beach resort – a luxury enclave for tourists who want to experience Bali in very small and sanitised doses, if at all. There's a ritzy shopping centre,

and a consistent right-hand surf break on the reef.

The nearest thing to budget accommodation is *Pondok Lamun* (☎ 771983), run by the Hotel & Tourism Training Institute, with mediocre air-con rooms for 50,000 rp. Go north to Benoa village for better value.

Benoa

Labuhan Benoa, the wide but shallow bay east of the airport, is one of Bali's main harbours. Benoa is actually in two parts. **Benoa Port**, with a wharf and some offices (including Pelni's), is on the north side, with a two-km-long causeway connecting it to the main Kuta-Sanur road. The *Mabua Ekspres* boat to Lombok leaves here at 8 am and 2.30 pm. Tourist excursion boats also operate from Benoa Port, and private yachts anchor here.

On the south side of the bay, **Benoa village** is at the tip of Tanjung Benoa. This peninsula has watersport activities, and is sprouting upper mid-range hotels and some reasonable restaurants. For cheap accommodation, try *Homestay Hasam*, with singles from 25,0000 rp, or *Rasa Sayang Beach Inn* (☎ 771643), which is friendly, clean and great value at 20,000/25,000 rp for fan-cooled rooms, 32,000/40,000 rp with air-con.

SANUR

Sanur is an upmarket resort for package tourists after sea, sand and sun. The water is safe for kids, but very shallow at low tide. There's sometimes excellent surf on the reef. The main road, Jalan Danau Toba-Jalan Danau Tamblingan, runs parallel to the beach, and has restaurants, shops, travel agencies, moneychangers and other facilities. American Express and most airlines have offices in the big Grand Bali Beach Hotel at the northern end of town. Nearby is the former home of prewar Belgian artist Le Mayeur, now a **museum**.

Places to Stay

The few low-budget places are away from the beach, mostly at the northern end of town. Side by side on Jalan Segara, west of the main road, are three cheapies – the *Hotel Sanur-Indah*, *Hotel Taman Sari* and *Hotel Rani* (☎ 288578). They have rooms from around 15,000/20,000 rp, to 55,000 rp with air-con and hot water. At the northern end of Sanur Beach, the *Ananda Hotel* (☎ 288327) is neat and clean with rooms from 25,000/30,000 rp. The *Watering Hole* (☎ 288289), opposite the Grand Bali Beach Hotel entrance, is friendly and well run with good food, a bar and rooms from 25,000 rp.

Three basic homestays, the *Yulia*, the *Luisa* and the *Coca*, are at the northern end of Jalan Danau Toba, behind shops at numbers 38, 40 and 42. Clean, simple rooms with private mandi go for around 25,000 rp per night. Further south, on a side street west of the main road, *Wirasana* (☎ 288632) is cheap at 20,000/40,000 rp. On a side road to the beach, *Werdha Pura* (☎ 288171) is a government-run 'beach cottage prototype', with bargain single/double rooms at 35,000/60,000 rp. More mid-range places on the main road include the *Laghawa Beach Inn* (☎ 288494), *Swastika Bungalows* (☎ 288699) and *Hotel Ramayana* (☎ 288429), all with pools and non-air-con rooms at around US$30.

Places to Eat

For cheap, authentic Indonesian food, try the rumah makans on the Bypass road, the warungs at the night market and the food carts and stalls at the northern end of the beach. Good tourist restaurants, with main courses around 6000 rp, include (from north to south), the *Watering Hole*, *Borneo Restaurant*, *Swastika Garden Restaurant* and *Donald's Cafe & Bakery*, but there are plenty of others. For vegetarian/health food, try *Santai Restaurant* or *Cafe Batu Jimbar*, both slightly pricier. *Warung Jawa Barat* has inexpensive Indonesian food, and plenty of vegetarian options. More expensive are the better Japanese, Thai and seafood restaurants. *Restoran Segara Agung*, at the Sanur Beach Market, is a mid-range place right on the beach.

UBUD

In the hills north of Denpasar, Ubud is the centre of 'cultural tourism' on Bali. Recently it has developed as fast as the beach resorts, and now has traffic problems in the centre and urban sprawl on the edges. It's still a wonderful place to see Balinese arts, handicrafts, dance and music, and it has the best restaurants in Bali.

Orientation & Information

Ubud now encompasses the neighbouring villages of Campuan, Penestanan, Padangtegal, Peliatan and Pengosekan, but the centre is at the intersection of Jalan Raya and Monkey Forest Rd, where you'll find the royal palace and the handicraft market. The friendly and helpful tourist office (Bina Wisata) is on Jalan Raya a few doors to the west. There are numerous moneychangers, a small post office (with poste restante) and a few wartels.

Things to See & Do

The **Puri Lukisan Museum**, in the middle of town, displays fine examples of all schools of Balinese art. The superb **Museum Neka**, in Campuan, has modern Balinese art and fine pieces by western artists who have worked in Bali (both museums are open daily; 2000 rp). There are many commercial galleries, but Neka Gallery on Jalan Raya, Agung Rai Gallery in Peliatan and Rudana in Teges are some of the largest and most important.

The home of the late Gusti Nyoman Lempad, a pioneering Balinese artist, is also a gallery, and worth a visit. Antonio Blanco's home is also open to visitors (2500 rp), and the man himself will try to impress with his 'artiness'. The home of Walter Spies, an influential German artist from the 1930s, is now one of the rooms at the Campuan Hotel. The work of Dutch painter Han Snel can be seen in his restaurant.

The **Monkey Forest** in Ubud's south has monkeys which provide entertainment, demand peanuts, and snatch purses, cameras and sunglasses. Other interesting **walks** are: east to Pejeng, across picturesque ravines; north to Petulu, where herons roost at dusk; and west to Sayan, with views over the Ayung River gorge. The best map for walks is Travel Treasure's *Ubud Surroundings*.

Places to Stay

Ubud has many small homestays, where a simple, clean room in a pretty garden will cost around 10,000 to 12,000 rp, with private bathroom and a light breakfast. Many mid-range places are even nicer, often well decorated with local artwork, and perhaps with a view of rice fields or a garden. Tax of 10% is added to the cost of a room, and fancier places add 5% to 10% more for service. Some accommodation is rented by the week, and includes cooking facilities.

Central Ubud & Monkey Forest Road

Close to the top of Monkey Forest Rd, near the market, is *Canderi's* (also Candri's or Tjanderi's), a typical losmen in a traditional family compound, with singles/doubles at 12,000/15,000 rp. A little further south is *Gayatri*, also in a charming family compound, and well priced at 10,000 rp.

Jalan Arjuna, the small street off the west side of Monkey Forest Rd, has the OK *Anom Bungalows*, at 10,000/14,000 rp. *Igna 2 Accommodation* is further back in the rice fields, and only 10,000/12,000 rp. There are other secluded but central little homestays around here. Oka Wati's *Sunset Bungalows* (☎ 96386) is a long-standing mid-range place which still has a rice paddy in view. Rooms range from US$28/33 to US$50/55, and there's a swimming pool and a romantic restaurant.

Mid-range places near the centre include *Mumbul Inn* (☎ 975364), near the Puri Lukisan Museum. It still has some simple rooms at 30,000 rp, but mostly it's around US$30 and very pleasant. *Hotel Puri Saren Agung* (☎ 975957) is part of the home of Ubud's old royal family. It's not signposted as a hotel, but walk into the courtyard and inquire – a bungalow with Balinese antiques, a big veranda and a full breakfast costs from US$45 to US$60.

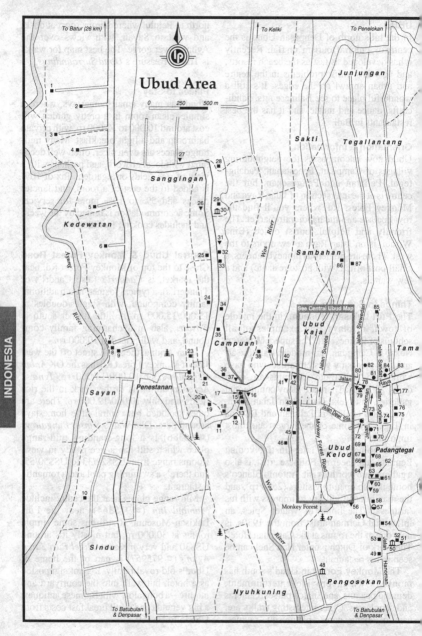

Ubud Area

0   250   500 m

To Batur (26 km)

To Keliki

To Penelokan

Junjungan

Sakti

Tegallantang

Sanggingan

Kedewatan

Sambahan

Ayung River

Wos River

Campuan

See Central Ubud Map

Ubud Kaja

Tama

Sayan

Penestanan

Ubud Kelod

Padangtegal

Monkey Forest Road

Sindu

Monkey Forest

Jalan Hanoman

Nyuhkuning

Pengosekan

To Batubulan
& Denpasar

To Batubulan
& Denpasar

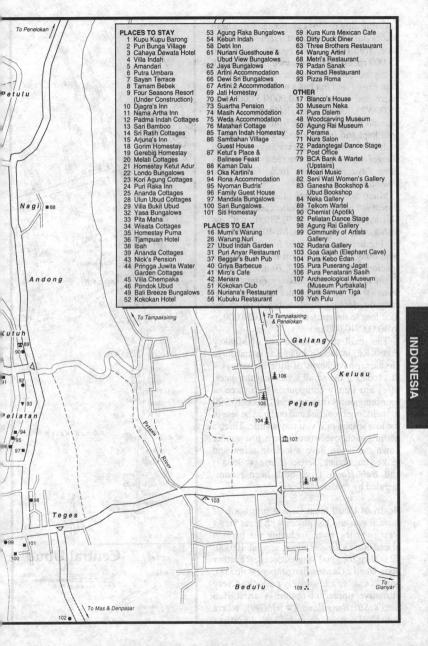

PLACES TO STAY
1 Kupu Kupu Barong
2 Puri Bunga Village
3 Cahaya Dewata Hotel
4 Villa Indah
5 Amandari
6 Putra Umbara
7 Sayan Terrace
8 Tamam Bebek
9 Four Seasons Resort
  (Under Construction)
10 Djagra's Inn
11 Nama Artha Inn
12 Padma Indah Cottages
13 Sari Bamboo
14 Sri Ratih Cottages
15 Arjuna's Inn
18 Gorim Homestay
19 Gerebig Homestay
20 Melati Cottages
21 Homestay Ketut Adur
22 Londo Bungalows
23 Kori Agung Cottages
24 Puri Raka Inn
25 Ananda Cottages
28 Ulun Ubud Cottages
29 Villa Bukit Ubud
32 Yasa Bungalows
33 Pita Maha
34 Wisata Cottages
35 Homestay Puma
36 Tjampuan Hotel
38 Ibah
39 Ananda Cottages
43 Nick's Pension
44 Pringga Juwita Water
  Garden Cottages
45 Villa Chempaka
46 Pondok Ubud
49 Bali Breeze Bungalows
52 Kokokan Hotel

53 Agung Raka Bungalows
54 Kebun Indah
58 Detri Inn
61 Nuriani Guesthouse &
  Ubud View Bungalows
62 Jaya Bungalows
65 Artini Accommodation
66 Dewi Sri Bungalows
67 Artini 2 Accommodation
69 Jati Homestay
70 Dwi Ari
73 Suartha Pension
74 Masih Accommodation
75 Weda Accommodation
76 Matahari Cottage
85 Taman Indah Homestay
86 Sambahan Village
  Guest House
87 Ketut's Place &
  Balinese Feast
88 Kaman Dalu
91 Oka Kartini's
94 Rona Accommodation
95 Nyoman Budris'
96 Family Guest House
97 Mandala Bungalows
100 Sari Bungalows
101 Siti Homestay

PLACES TO EAT
16 Murni's Warung
26 Warung Nuri
27 Ubud Indah Garden
31 Puri Anyar Restaurant
37 Beggar's Bush Pub
40 Griya Barbecue
41 Miro's Cafe
42 Menara
51 Kokokan Club
55 Nuriana's Restaurant
56 Kubuku Restaurant

59 Kura Kura Mexican Cafe
60 Dirty Duck Diner
63 Three Brothers Restaurant
64 Warung Artini
68 Metri's Restaurant
78 Padan Sanak
80 Nomad Restaurant
93 Pizza Roma

OTHER
17 Blanco's House
30 Museum Neka
47 Pura Dalem
48 Woodcarving Museum
50 Agung Rai Museum
57 Perama
71 Nurs Salon
72 Padangtegal Dance Stage
77 Post Office
79 BCA Bank & Wartel
  (Upstairs)
81 Moari Music
82 Seni Wati Women's Gallery
83 Ganesha Bookshop &
  Ubud Bookshop
84 Neka Gallery
89 Telkom Wartel
90 Chemist (Apotik)
92 Peliatan Dance Stage
98 Agung Rai Gallery
99 Community of Artists
  Gallery
102 Rudana Gallery
103 Goa Gajah (Elephant Cave)
104 Pura Kebo Edan
105 Pura Puserang Jagat
106 Pura Penataran Sasih
107 Archaeological Museum
  (Museum Purbakala)
108 Pura Samuan Tiga
109 Yeh Pulu

INDONESIA

Going down Monkey Forest Rd, cheap places include *Pandawa Homestay*, with nice, traditional-style rooms at 10,000/15,000 rp, and *Igna Accommodation*. South of the football field, the very clean and well-kept *Frog Pond Inn* has a welcoming atmosphere and costs from 10,000/15,000 rp to 15,000/25,000 rp a single/double. Nearby *Mandia Bungalows*, back from the street, are well kept and friendly, at 25,000/30,000 rp, with hot water. The inexpensive *Pramesti Bungalows* have also been recommended, as have *Jaya Bungalows*, *Bella House* and *Ibunda Inn*.

Many new mid-range places on Monkey Forest Rd are dull and featureless, but *Puri Garden Bungalows* (☎ 975395), with its lush garden, is delightful, for 40,000/50,000 rp. Further south is *Ubud Inn* (☎ 975071), with bungalows and rooms dotted around a spacious garden and pool, from US$30/40. Right at the bottom, *Monkey Forest Hideaway* (☎ 975354) has some rooms romantically overlooking the forest, and others far too close to the road, from 15,000/20,000 rp to 30,000/40,000 rp.

The small streets to the east of Monkey Forest Rd, including Jalan Karna and Jalan Goutama, have heaps of little homestays – just look for the small signs near the gates. Most are family compounds with three or four bungalows from around 12,000/15,000 rp including breakfast and tax; maybe less in the low season or if you stay awhile. There's nothing to choose between them, just wander down the lanes, have a look in a few and make your choice. *Seroni House* (☎ 96357) and *Bali House* have both been recommended by readers.

North of Ubud Jalan Kajang runs north of Jalan Raya, and has places with great views west over the river, including the bargain priced *Roja's Homestay*, at around 10,000/12,000 rp for good singles/doubles. Further up is *Gusti's Garden Bungalows* (☎ 96311), with hot water and a lovely outlook. A very attractive upmarket option is artist Han Snel's *Siti Bungalows* (☎ 975699), where individual cottages decorated with the artist's

Central Ubud

0   100   200 m

Approximate Scale

own work cost from US$50 to US$60 a night.

Jalan Suweta has the *Suci Inn* (☎ 975304), across from the banyan tree, a straightforward losmen with simple rooms from 12,000/15,000 rp. The rooms look out onto the central garden, and it's a friendly, relaxed place that's quiet yet very central. Further north,

in Sambahan, is *Ketut's Place* (☎ 96246), with rooms in a family compound from 15,000/20,000 rp for singles/doubles in the front, to 25,000/35,000 rp for cottages at the back. Nearby *Sambahan Village Guest House* is another good one.

Beyond the north end of Jalan Sandat, a walk in the rice fields brings you to *Taman*

PLACES TO STAY
1 Gusti's Garden Bungalows
2 Arjana Accommodation
3 Shanti's Homestay
5 Siti Bungalows
6 Suci Inn
7 Roja's Homestay
10 Mumbul Inn
12 Puri Saraswati Cottages
21 Pondok Wisata Sudharsana
31 Anom Bungalows
33 Happy Inn
34 Canderi's Losmen
35 Yuni's House
37 Wayan Karya Homestay
38 Shana Homestay
39 Wena Homestay
40 Nirvana Pension
41 Dewi Putra House
42 Sayong's House
43 Sania's House
44 Wija House
45 Bali House
46 Ning's House
47 Devi House
50 Merta House
51 Seroni House
52 Sudartha House
53 Gandra House
54 Pandawa Homestay
56 Gayatri Accommodation
60 Igna Accommodation
61 Puri Muwa Bungalows
62 Alit's House
64 Suarsena House
65 Oka Wati's Sunset Bungalows
68 Igna 2 Accommodation
70 Bendi's Accommodation
72 Wahyu Bungalows
74 Esty's House
75 Sidya Homestay
76 Ramasita Pension

80 Accommodation Kerta
83 Karyawan Accommodation
85 Frog Pond Inn
86 Pramesti Bungalows
87 Mandia Bungalows
88 Ubud Village Hotel
91 Pertiwi Bungalows
92 Puri Garden Bungalow
93 Rice Paddy Bungalows
94 Sri Bungalows
95 Nani House (Karsi Homestay)
96 Villa Rasa Sayang
97 Jati 3 Bungalows & Putih Accommodation
100 Jaya Bungalows
101 Ibunda Inn
102 Ubud Bungalows
104 Dewi Ayu Accommodation
105 Ubud Terrace Bungalows
107 Sagitarius Inn
108 Fibra Inn
109 Ubud Inn
110 Lempung Accommodation
111 Pande Permai Bungalows
112 Monkey Forest Hideaway
113 Hotel Champlung Sari

PLACES TO EAT
4 Han Snel's Garden Restaurant
11 Mumbul's Cafe
13 Lotus Cafe
17 Coconut's Cafe
18 Momoya Japanese Restaurant
22 Restaurant Puri Pusaka
27 Ary's Warung
28 Ryoshi Japanese Restaurant

30 Casa Luna
32 Satri's Warung
34 Canderi's Warung
36 Seroni's Warung
48 Tutmac Cafe
49 Bamboo Restaurant
55 Gayatri Restaurant
63 Ayu's Kitchen
66 Lillies Garden Restaurant
67 Oka Wati's Warung
69 Beji's Cafe
71 Bendi's Restaurant
73 Do Drop In Cafe
77 Cafe Bali
78 Ibu Rai Restaurant
81 Yogyakarta Cafe
82 Dian Restaurant
89 Coco Restaurant
90 Cafe Wayan
98 Mendra's Cafe
99 Jaya Cafe
106 Ubud Restaurant

OTHER
8 Puri Lukisan Museum
9 Wartel
14 Pura Taman Saraswati
15 Pura Desa Ubud
16 Bemo Stop
19 Pura Merajan Agung
20 Palace & Hotel Puri Saren Agung
23 Gusti Nyoman Lempad's House
24 Bemo Stop
25 Tourist Office (Bina Wisata)
26 Ary's Bookshop
29 Supermarket
57 Postal Agency
58 Ibu Rai Gallery
59 Bookshop
79 Bead & Bali
84 Batik Workshop & Crackpot Coffee Shop
103 Meditation Shop
114 Parking

INDONESIA

Indah Homestay, with just three secluded rooms at 12,000 rp.

South-East of Ubud In Padangtegal, on Jalan Hanoman, *Jati Homestay* and *Suartha Pension* are small, cheap, basic homestays. *Nuriani Guesthouse* (☎ 975346), just off to the east side in the rice fields, costs 20,000 to 25,000 rp a double. Nearby *Ubud View* (☎ 974164) has similar prices, and a similar attractive outlook.

Further east is Peliatan, where Jalan Tebesaya has some possibilities, including the popular *Rona Accommodation* (☎ 96229), a very nice place with rooms from around 15,000 rp, and very helpful management. A few doors south is *Nyoman Budri*, for only 10,000/12,000 rp, and the *Family Guest House* (☎ 974054), another well-recommended place with a pretty garden and rooms for 15,000/20,000 rp.

At the south end of Jalan Peliatan, a sign points right to the *Sari Bungalows* (☎ 975541), just 100 metres or so away. It's family-run, in a pleasantly quiet location, and very good value with singles/doubles from 8000/10,000 rp, including a 'big breakfast'. Nearby is the pleasant *Siti Homestay*, with a garden and rooms at 10,000/15,000 rp, and also *Nyoman Astana Bungalows* and *Mandra Cottages*.

West of Ubud Heading west on Jalan Raya you pass Jalan Bisma on the left, with a few places to stay – the cheapest is *Pondok Ubud*, which is pretty good value for 7000/10,000 rp, including breakfast. Nearby, *Nick's Pension* has a restaurant and pool in front, with comfortable rooms set much further back, overlooking a lush river valley; they're good value for 45,000 rp.

Follow the main road to Campuan, cross the suspension bridge, and take the steep road uphill on the left to Penestanan, a quiet but arty area. Along this road you'll find the attractive *Arjuna's Inn*, with rooms at 15,000 to 20,000 rp, and also *Sari Bamboo* (☎ 975597), with rooms at 20,000 rp, and two storey bungalows, ideal for families, at 30,000 rp.

There are more places further back into the rice fields – you have to walk to get to them. Ones near the road include *Gerebig*, *Gorim*, *Reka* and *Made Jagi*. Others are more easily reached by climbing the stairs west of the Campuan road, and following the sign boards. Places to look for include *Siddharta*, *Danau*, *Pugur* and *Londo*. Asking prices are from around 20,000/25,000 rp for smaller singles/doubles, to around 40,000 rp per night for a larger bungalow. Many people stay much longer and negotiate a much lower rate. In the low season, a nice bungalow should rent for 80,000 to 100,000 rp per week, perhaps more with a kitchen.

Further west is Sayan, with great views over the Ayung River; one of the few cheap places here is *Putra Umbara*, with rooms for 30,000 rp. *Sayan Terrace* (☎ 975384) has a brilliant view and attractive rooms for US$25, or bungalows at US$35. Nearby, *Taman Bebek Villas* (☎ 976533) and *Djagra's Inn* (☎ 974343) have similar views and prices.

Places to Eat
Ubud's many restaurants offer the best and most interesting food on the island. Well-prepared Indonesian and Balinese food is available, and a great selection of international dishes. The very best places might cost 20,000 to 30,000 rp, but you can get very fine food for less than half that price.

Jalan Raya has some of the longest-running restaurants, like *Lotus Cafe*, which is pricey but still trendy and a lovely spot for a light meal or a snack. *Mumbul's Cafe*, on the same side, is small with friendly service, excellent food and a children's menu. *Ary's Warung* has moved steadily upmarket, but it still serves a wide variety of excellent food, including vegetarian dishes and wholemeal sandwiches. A new Japanese restaurant, *Ryoshi*, has sashimi from 7000 to 12,000 rp. On the other side of the road is *Casa Luna* (☎ 96283), with a superb multicultural menu, and the big *Menara Restaurant*, which does a good Balinese banquet. *Miro's Cafe* is another top place to eat, with

Indonesian and vegetarian main courses from about 5000 to 8000 rp.

In Campuan, *Murni's Warung* is an old Ubud favourite in a beautiful setting over the river, though it's a little expensive. Further west, *Beggar's Bush* is a British-style pub serving pub-style food, popular with expats.

On the eastern end of Jalan Raya, *Nomad Restaurant* does standard Indonesian and Chinese dishes (4000 to 9000 rp), and it stays open later for drinks. Further east is *Padang Sanak*, where the padang food is very inexpensive.

Book into *Ketut's Place* (☎ 975304), a km north up Jalan Suweta, for a superb and sociable Balinese feast (20,000 rp).

Monkey Forest Road has many budget possibilities, including (from north to south) *Satri's Warung*, an inexpensive place with good food, *Canderi's Warung*, with Indonesian, western and vegetarian dishes, and *Bendi's*, with Balinese specialities. Further south, *Cafe Wayan* (☎ 975447) is more expensive but has some of the best food in town, and delightful open-air tables at the back. The side street on the north side of the football field, Jalan Bima, has some new places like the *Bamboo Restaurant*, and *Tutmac*, with about the best coffee in Ubud.

East of Monkey Forest Rd, *Seroni's Warung*, on Jalan Karna, has top food at bottom-end prices, as does *Metri's*, on Jalan Hanoman.

Entertainment
The main entertainment in Ubud is *Balinese dancing*. Though most performances are for tourist entertainment, the dances show a high degree of skill and are wonderfully presented. Entry is about 6000 rp; see the tourist office for information. Restaurants like *Menara* and *Yogyakarta Cafe* run video movies, which are becoming popular. *Casa Luna* sometimes has a kids' session at 4.00 pm.

Getting There & Away
Bemos from the Batubulan bus terminal, outside Denpasar, are 1500 rp. They stop right in the middle of town. Other bemos go to/from here to nearby villages like Kedewaten,

Pejeng, Bedelu, Mas, Sakah and Blahbatuh (around 500 rp). To get a bemo to southern or western Bali, go via Batubulan and one of the other Denpasar terminals. For bemos to eastern or northern Bali, go first to Gianyar.

Tourist shuttle buses go directly to other tourist areas: Sanur, Kuta, the airport, Padangbai, Candidasa or Kintamani cost 7500 rp; to Singaraja or Lovina it's 12,500 rp. The Perama depot (☎ 96316) is way down south towards Pengosekan. Some companies pick up closer to town – try the one at the Nomad Restaurant.

You can rent a bicycle (5000 rp for a day, cheaper for longer), motorbike (10,000 to 12,000 rp) or car (from 38,000 rp per day, including insurance).

AROUND UBUD
Two km along the main road to Gianyar is the heavily touristic **Goa Gajah**, or elephant cave, discovered in the 1920s and believed to have been a Buddhist hermitage. Nearby is **Yeh Pulu** with its carved bas-relief. Go a couple of km north to the **Pura Penataran Sasih**, a temple with a huge bronze drum said to be 2000 years old. A legend tells of it falling to earth as the Moon of Pejeng.

Off to the eastern side of the Gianyar road, near Tampaksiring, **Gunung Kawi** is a group of large stone memorials cut into cliffs on either side of a picturesque river valley. Believed to date from the 11th century, it's one of the most impressive sights in Bali, for its size, unusual style and lovely setting.

A bit further north, in the shadow of the Soekarno-era presidential palace, is the holy spring and temple of **Tirta Empul**. An inscription dates the spring from 926 AD. There are fine carvings and Garudas on the courtyard buildings.

BESAKIH
Nearly 1000 metres up the side of mighty Gunung Agung, this is Bali's mother temple. It's big, majestically located and very well kept. Your contribution is 600 rp per car to park, 1100 rp to enter, 2000 rp to rent a temple sash and sarong, plus 1000 rp for a camera or 2500 rp for a video camera. You

can also pay for a guide, but you don't need one. There are actually many temples here, but their inner courtyards are all closed to visitors. There are regular bemos from Klungkung.

From Besakih you can climb to the top of Gunung Agung in around six hours. Take a guide and start very early. Guides can be contacted through the tourist information office by the car park, and charge around 60,000 rp. The *Lembah Arca*, about five km below Besakih, is a convenient place to stay for an early start; from 15,000/20,000 rp.

DENPASAR TO KLUNGKUNG

The traffic is heavy from Denpasar to Klungkung, but then becomes much lighter. There are some things to see in the main towns, and interesting detours to the coast and the mountains.

In **Gianyar**, the capital of Gianyar regency, there are weaving workshops, where workers dye threads and weave sarongs. You are welcome to visit, and of course to buy.

Halfway up the slope to Penelokan, is **Bangli**, usually reached from Gianyar, but also accessible by a very pretty road from near Rendang. Bangli has two fine temples, Pura Kehen, with a massive banyan tree, and Pura Dalem Penunggekan, a temple of the dead with some gruesome sculpture panels along the front. You can stay at the *Artha Sastra Inn*, a faded former palace, with rooms from 10,000/12,000 rp; *Losmen Dharmaputra*, a dismal youth-hostel affiliate which charges 7000 rp for a grotty room; or the new *Bangli Inn* (☎ (0366) 91419), from 15,00/20,000 rp. They're all in the north-east corner of town near the bemo stop.

KLUNGKUNG

Once the centre of an important Balinese kingdom, Klungkung (about 42 km north-east of Denpasar and officially named Semarapura) is noted for its **water palace** and the adjacent **Kherta Ghosa**, or Hall of Justice. Disputes that could not be settled locally were brought here, and the accused could study lurid paintings on the roof of wrongdoers suffering in the afterlife. There's

a mildly interesting museum here too. Entry to the complex costs 2000 rp. It's just west of the shopping strip.

The *Hotel Ramayana Lojo* (☎ (0366) 21044), east of town on the Candidasa road, is pleasant, with a good restaurant and quite OK rooms for 20,000/25,000 rp.

Frequent bemos to/from Batubulan terminal cost 1200 rp. There's no regular tourist shuttle here, but Perama buses will stop on request. Lots of organised tours visit Kherta Ghosa.

NUSA PENIDA AREA

Nusa Penida is the largest of three islands which comprise the administrative area of Nusa Penida within Klungkung District. Nusa Penida itself currently has few visitors and few facilities, and tiny Nusa Ceningan is sparsely inhabited. Nusa Lembongan, to the north-west, attracts visitors for its surf and seclusion.

Nusa Penida

The hilly island of Nusa Penida (population 45,000) was once used as a place of banishment for criminals from the Klungkung kingdom. **Sampalan**, the somnolent main town, is on the north coast. *Losmen Made* is a basic but friendly place to stay, charging about 12,000/15,000 rp. *Pemda*, opposite the police station, 200 metres to the east, is mainly for visiting officials and is slightly dearer.

Fast, twin-engine fibreglass boats run between Padangbai and Buyuk harbour, Sampalan. The trip takes less than an hour and costs 5000 rp. Boats also cross from Kusamba, heavily loaded with supplies; they're much slower. A boat from Nusa Lembongan can drop you on the beach at **Toyapakeh**, where you can stay at *Losmen Terang*.

Nusa Lembongan

The offshore coral reef is where the surf breaks, and it protects the arc of white beach. Incoming boats beach at **Jungutbatu**, or a little further north-east where most of the accommodation is. The most conspicuous place is the two storey *Main Ski Restaurant*

& Cottages, right on the beach, with good food, a great view and rooms from 10,000/ 15,000 rp. *Agung's Lembongan Lodge*, *Nusa Lembongan Bungalows* and *Ta Chi* are similar.

Boats to Nusa Lembongan cost 15,000 rp per person, and leave from the north end of Sanur Beach, where there's a ticket office. The boats leave early, 8.30 am at the latest, and take at least 1½ hours. The trip can be very rough. Local boats go between Jungutbatu and Nusa Penida, particularly on market days.

PADANGBAI

The port town of Padangbai, east of Klung-kung, is on a perfect bay two km off the main road. Frequent ferries to Lombok leave from here, and visiting cruise ships anchor off-shore. West of Padangbai, near the fishing village of Kusamba, sea salt is extracted by evaporation from hundreds of shallow wooden troughs. Also nearby is **Goa Lawah**, where thousands of bats line the cave behind the temple. It's not very interesting and the smell is overpowering.

Places to Stay & Eat

There are several pleasant places to stay on the beachfront. *Rai Beach Inn* (☎ (0363) 41385) has two-storey cottages at 27,500 rp, and standard single storey rooms with bath at 22,000 rp. The *Kerti Beach Inn* and the *Padangbai Beach Inn* (☎ (0363) 41517) both have basic rooms facing the sea from about 12,000/15,000 rp. At the far end of the beach, *Topi Restaurant & Inn* has small, plain rooms at 9000/12,000 rp, and a dorm for 3000 rp per person. In the town, there's the neat and tidy *Homestay Dharma*, at 15,000/20,000 rp. *Pantai Ayu Homestay* (☎ (0363) 41396) is back from the beach but friendly; rooms cost from 10,000/15,000 rp.

On the beachfront, *Pantai Ayu Restaurant* is popular, but the others are also good and cheap. *Marco's* serves a good pizza. It's worth walking up the beach to *Topi Restaurant*, with its sand-floor dining area, colour-ful menu and reasonable prices. The *Ozone Cafe* in town is an evening gathering place.

Getting There & Away

Ferries to Lombok's Lembar harbour leave every two hours – see the Bali Getting There & Away section for details. Buses meet the ferry and go straight to Denpasar. Orange bemos go to Candidasa and Amlapura, while blue ones go to Klungkung – they're more frequent in the morning. The Perama office (☎ (0363) 41419) is at the Dona Cafe in the main street.

Direct buses go right through to Surabaya and Yogya in Java, for slightly more than the fares from Denpasar; you'll find the buses in the parking area near the pier, and the touts will find you.

The fast, fibreglass boats to Nusa Penida (5000 rp) leave from the beach near the eastern corner of the car park next to the pier.

BALINA BEACH

About 11 km along the main road from the Padangbai turn-off, Balina Beach is a quiet stretch of coast. It has acquired its first large hotel, and is losing its nice beach to erosion.

Places to Stay

The comfortable *Balina Beach Bungalows* (☎ (0363) 41002) have their own diving operation, a pool and rates from US$30/40, but they discount heavily if they're quiet. The *Puri Buitan* (☎ (0363) 41021), on the opposite side of the access road, is less attrac-tive. Two *homestays*, about 200 metres to the east along the beach, have bungalows at about 16,000/20,000 rp in the low season.

TENGANAN

North-west of Candidasa, about five km from the main road, is Tenganan, a Bali Aga village with walled homes, a symmetrical layout and unique crafts. The Bali Aga were the original inhabitants of Bali, before the arrival of the Hindu Javanese. It's a charming place, if a bit commercialised, and it has some fascinating festivals. Get a lift from the main road by motorbike (about 1000 rp). Alternatively, it's a good walk from Can-didasa. A donation is requested as you enter.

INDONESIA

CANDIDASA

Candidasa changed from a quiet fishing village to a new beach resort during the 1980s. In the process its coral reef was dug up to make lime for concrete, which resulted in the beach being completely eroded away. Large, T-shaped concrete breakwaters have been constructed to save what little is left, and these now provide some nice little bathing areas if the tide is right. The main drag is almost overbuilt, but some visitors still like Candidasa – it's quieter than Kuta, cheaper than Sanur, and a good base from which to explore East Bali or do scuba trips.

Information

All the tourist facilities are along the main street, including moneychangers, travel agents, postal agents, bookshops and car rental places. You can make phone calls from the Kubu Bali Restaurant.

The area code for Candidasa is 0363.

Places to Stay

Starting at the Denpasar side, *Sari Jaya Seaside Cottage*, *Pelangi*, *Tarura* and *Flamboyant* are on the beach side of the road just before town. They all charge about 10,000/

15,000 rp for singles/doubles and offer adequate accommodation within walking distance of Candidasa's restaurant row. On the right, about 200 metres past the Tenganan turn-off, *Homestay Geringsing* (☎ 41084) has attractive cottages clustered in a quiet garden, from 9000/12,000 rp, or 15,000 rp for a beachfront position – very good for the price. Continuing east, the *Puri Bali* (☎ 41063) has simple, clean and well-kept rooms for 9000/12,000 rp including breakfast, and the cheap rooms at *Wiratha Bungalows* (☎ 41973) are also good value at 9000/15,000 rp, or 5000 rp more with beach frontage.

Also on the beach side, *Puri Pandan Bungalows* (☎ 41541) ask from US$10/12 for singles/doubles with breakfast, but give a 30% discount in the low season. The popular, rock-bottom *Homestay Lilaberata*, for 10,000/12,000 rp, has a good location, squat toilets and chickens in the garden. *Pondok Bamboo* (☎ 41354) is a little fancier, with double rooms from 25,000 to 35,000 rp, and a restaurant overlooking the ocean.

Homestay Ida (☎ 41096), close to the lagoon, is spacious, with airy bamboo cottages in a grassy coconut plantation. Smaller rooms are 17,500/20,000 rp, larger ones

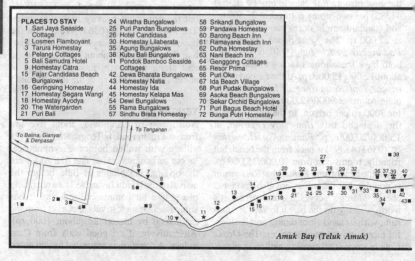

PLACES TO STAY		
1 Sari Jaya Seaside Cottage	24 Wiratha Bungalows	58 Srikandi Bungalows
2 Losmen Flamboyant	25 Puri Pandan Bungalows	59 Pandawa Homestay
3 Tarura Homestay	26 Hotel Candidasa	60 Barong Beach Inn
4 Pelangi Cottages	30 Homestay Lilaberata	61 Ramayana Beach Inn
5 Bali Samudra Hotel	35 Agung Bungalows	62 Dutha Homestay
9 Homestay Catra	38 Kubu Bali Bungalows	63 Nani Beach Inn
15 Fajar Candidasa Beach Bungalows	41 Pondok Bamboo Seaside Cottages	64 Genggong Cottages
16 Geringsing Homestay	42 Dewa Bharata Bungalows	65 Resor Prima
17 Homestay Segara Wangi	43 Homestay Natia	66 Puri Oka
18 Homestay Ayodya	44 Homestay Ida	67 Ida Beach Village
20 The Watergarden	45 Homestay Kelapa Mas	68 Puri Pudak Bungalows
21 Puri Bali	54 Dewi Bungalows	69 Asoka Beach Bungalows
	55 Rama Bungalows	70 Sekar Orchid Bungalows
	57 Sindhu Brata Homestay	71 Puri Bagus Beach Hotel
		72 Bunga Putri Homestay

To Balina, Gianyar & Denpasar

↑ To Tenganan

Amuk Bay (Teluk Amuk)

25,000 rp, and family rooms with a mezzanine level are 40,000 rp, including breakfast and tax. *Homestay Kelapa Mas* (☎ 41947), next door, is also well kept and spacious, with a range of rooms from around 20,000/25,000 rp – the seafront rooms are particularly well situated.

East of the lagoon there are some small losmen near the beach, including the friendly *Dewi Bungalows*, *Rama Bungalows* (☎ 41778) and the *Sindhu Brata Homestay* (☎ 41825) – all have rooms from around 15,000/20,000 rp. Nearby *Pandawa Homestay* is a bit cheaper, at 12,000/15,000 rp.

The main road to Amlapura swings away from the coast, and a small track branches off to some more places to stay, facing onto what's left of the beach. They're quiet, but some way from the shops and restaurants. Low-budget options include the *Barong Beach Inn* (☎ 41137), *Ramayana Beach Inn* and *Nani Beach Inn*, all with basic rooms from around 10,000/15,000 rp, as well as more expensive rooms. Going east, the next place is *Genggong Cottages* (☎ 41105), nicely situated by the sea, with a variety of clean and comfortable rooms from 15,000/20,000 rp to 25,000/30,000 rp. Right at the

end of the beach, the *Bunga Putri Homestay* (☎ 41140) has a great coastal view and rooms from 15,000/20,000 rp to 25,000 rp. It has a new restaurant, but there's nothing else nearby.

Good-value, mid-range places include *Fajar Candidasa* (☎ 41539), which is well located with a pool, and pleasant rooms, somewhat crowded together, from US$25/30. In the centre of the strip, *Hotel Candidasa* (☎ 41536) is a three storey hotel crammed onto its site, but the rooms are quite good, from US$35/45 for air-con singles/doubles, including a substantial breakfast. *Dewa Bharata Bungalows* has a pool, bar, restaurant and good-value rooms from US$25/30 with air-con.

One unusual, quality place is *The Watergarden* (☎ 41540), where tasteful rooms overlook fish-filled ponds amid a jungle garden. Another is *Kubu Bali Bungalows* (☎ 41532), where beautifully finished individual bungalows, streams and a pool are landscaped into a steep hillside with views out to sea. It's worth the climb, and the US$45/50 low-season price tag.

Places to Eat

The food in Candidasa is pretty good, particularly the fresh seafood, with main courses

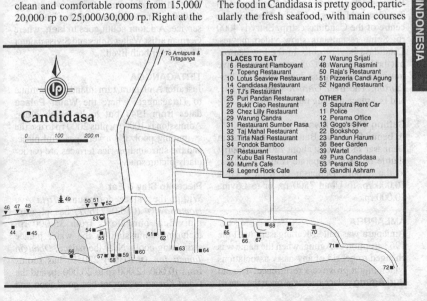

PLACES TO EAT		47 Warung Srijati
6 Restaurant Flamboyant		48 Warung Rasmini
7 Topeng Restaurant		50 Raja's Restaurant
10 Lotus Seaview Restaurant		51 Pizzeria Candi Agung
14 Candidasa Restaurant		52 Ngandi Restaurant
19 TJ's Restaurant		
25 Puri Pandan Restaurant		**OTHER**
27 Bukit Ciao Restaurant		8 Saputra Rent Car
28 Chez Lilly Restaurant		11 Police
29 Warung Candra		12 Perama Office
31 Restaurant Sumber Rasa		13 Gogo's Silver
32 Taj Mahal Restaurant		22 Bookshop
33 Tirta Nadi Restaurant		23 Pandun Harum
34 Pondok Bamboo		36 Beer Garden
Restaurant		39 Wartel
37 Kubu Bali Restaurant		49 Pura Candidasa
40 Murni's Cafe		53 Perama Stop
46 Legend Rock Cafe		56 Gandhi Ashram

Candidasa

To Amlapura & Tirtagangga

0   100   200 m

INDONESIA

from 5000 to 10,000 rp at most of the tourist eateries. Restaurants are dotted along the main road, starting at the Denpasar end with *Lotus Seaview*, an upmarket tourist restaurant with a wonderful outlook. *TJ's* is related to TJ's Mexican restaurant in Kuta, though it's not quite as good. *Bukit Ciao Restaurant*, behind the Pandan Harum dance stage, serves first-class Italian food, and *Chez Lilly* has some imaginative offerings. *Warung Candra* and *Taj Mahal* both do reasonably good Indian dishes at reasonable prices. The beachside restaurant at the *Puri Pandan* does Balinese feasts, and has better than average Chinese and seafood dishes.

Kubu Bali Restaurant is a big place with a busy open kitchen out front, where mid-priced Indonesian and Chinese dishes are turned out with energy and panache. For cheaper eating, try *Warung Srijati* and *Warung Rasmini*. Just beyond the lagoon, the *Pizzeria Candi Agung* does a good pizza, while *Raja's* has burgers, pasta and other western and Indonesian standards.

Entertainment
Balinese dances are staged at 9 pm on Tuesday and Friday at *Pandan Harum*, in the centre of the Candidasa strip. Entry is 4000 rp. Some restaurants show video movies. Candidasa is very quiet in the low season, but the *Legend Rock Cafe* sometimes has live music and dancing, as does *Tirta Nadi Restaurant*. The *Beer Garden* stays open late, and is a place to hang out.

Getting There & Away
A bemo from the Batubulan terminal in Denpasar should cost about 2200 rp. Tourist shuttle buses also operate from Candidasa; to the airport, Denpasar or Kuta it costs 10,000 rp, to Ubud 7500 rp, or to Lovina 20,000 rp.

AMLAPURA
Amlapura was called Karangasem until the 1963 eruption of Agung, when the name was changed to get rid of any nasty associations which might provoke a recurrence! The old **Puri Agung** palace here was once the seat of

the old Raja of Karangasem. You can see its faded glory for 1500 rp. The ruins of the **Ujung Palace** are uninspiring, but nicely located near the coast about three km south of town.

Homestay Lahar Mas (☎ (0363) 21345), on the left as you come into town, is basic, but friendly and quite OK, with rooms at 12,500/15,000 rp for singles/doubles.

Regular buses go to/from Denpasar (3000 rp; 80 km), with less frequent connections around the east coast to Singaraja.

AMLAPURA TO RENDANG
From Amlapura, you can follow the slopes of Gunung Agung through some very scenic countryside to Rendang. It's easy with your own transport, but time-consuming by bemo. You can stay at the homey *Homestay Lila*, three km from Amlapura, for 12,000/15,000 rp. About 15 km from Amlapura, a turn-off goes to Putung, right at the top of the ridge, with a fabulous view over the south coast. *Pondok Bukit Putung* (☎ (0366) 23039) has pricey bungalows from US$18/20, but it's a good stop for lunch. You can also stay near Selat at *Pondok Puri Agung*, which asks 40,000 rp for a very nice room, but has erratic service. A detour south goes to **Iseh**, where German artist Walter Spies and Swiss painter Theo Meier both lived.

TIRTAGANGGA
Just after Amlapura, turn inland and continue to Tirtagangga, where the **Water Palace** dates from 1947 but looks much older. Admission is 1000 rp, plus 2000 rp to use the swimming pool. It's a very peaceful place, and the surrounding rice terraces are particularly picturesque.

Places to Stay & Eat
Within the palace compound, *Tirta Ayu Homestay* (☎ (0363) 21697) has pleasant individual bungalows from 35,000 rp, including admission to the water palace swimming pools. Near the palace, *Dhangin Taman Inn* (☎ (0363) 22059) has rooms from 10,000/12,000 rp to 20,000 rp, and the *Good Karma* restaurant has good food and

music. Across the road from the palace, the *Rijasa Homestay* is a small, simple place with clean single/double rooms at 12,000/15,000 rp.

Kusuma Jaya Inn, the 'Homestay on the Hill', 300 metres beyond the water palace and up the steep steps, has a fine view over the rice paddies and rooms from 15,000/20,000 rp. Another 600 metres brings you to the steps of *Prima Bamboo Homestay*, also with a great outlook and rooms at 12,000/16,000 rp.

TULAMBEN & AMED

North beyond Tirtagangga the road descends through some spectacular terraced rice fields to the coast. Head north to reach Tulamben, where the wreck of the USS *Liberty* is a major attraction for divers and snorkellers, and where there are bungalows from around 15,000/20,000 rp. Continue around the good-quality coast road for about 70 km to reach Singaraja.

Alternatively, after descending from Tirtagangga you can branch east at Culik to some delightfully isolated accommodation on the coast near Amed, including *Vienna Beach Bungalows* and *Good Karma*, which both have rooms from around 25,000 rp. Bemos come from Culik in the morning (1000 rp), or take an ojek for 2000 rp. Try to arrive early.

The road continues round the south-east peninsula, with narrow, winding switchbacks, but it's scenic and quite passable right round to Ujung and Amlapura.

SOUTH-WEST BALI

North of Seminyak, the road doesn't follow the coast, but you can detour to beaches at **Petingan** (on the fringe of the Kuta-Legian development), **Berewa** (with some nice hotels) and **Canggu** (with a famous surf break).

From Denpasar's Ubung terminal, buses and bemos go west to Tabanan (1200 rp), Negara (3500 rp) and Gilimanuk (4500 rp). Turn north off the main road to **Mengwi**, where there's an impressive royal water palace and temple. About 10 km further north is the monkey forest and temple of **Sangeh** – watch out, as the monkeys will snatch anything they can. South of the main road, **Tanah Lot** is a temple spectacularly balanced on a rocky islet. It's probably the most photographed temple in Bali, particularly at sunset; it's also horrifically touristy.

The completely untouristed town of **Tabanan** is the capital of Tabanan District. It's in the heart of the fertile south Bali rice belt, and a centre for dancing and gamelan music. **Krambitan**, south-west of Tabanan, has a royal palace, and you can stay nearby at *Bee Bees* in Tibubiyu – it's well off the beaten track.

About 16 km beyond Tabanan, the main road swings south to the coast but doesn't actually follow it. Numerous side roads lead to villages with black-sand beaches, some beautiful scenery and very little tourist development. **Lalang-Linggah** is a getaway-from-it-all place where you can stay at the *Balian Beach Club*, overlooking the river and surrounded by coconut plantations. Most rooms are slightly worn, from 34,000 to 60,000 rp, and a few are even cheaper.

The turn-off to the **Medewi** surfing point is just west of Pulukan village – there's a large sign on the main road. *Hotel Pantai Medewi* is mostly mid-range, but has a few very ordinary rooms at 25,000 rp. A bit further west, *Tinjayya Bungalows* costs 20,000 to 25,000 rp, with some small rooms at 15,000 rp.

The beautiful temple of **Rambut Siwi** is just south of the main road, high on a clifftop overlooking the sea. It's definitely worth a stop.

Bullock races are held at **Negara** between July and October each year, but otherwise it's a quiet town. There are a few losmen on the main street – *Wira Pada* (☎ (0365) 41161) is the best value, from 10,000/12,500 rp.

Off the main road about seven km north of Melaya, **Blimbingsari** and **Palasari** are (respectively) the main Protestant and Catholic communities on Bali, each with an impressive church.

Right at the western end of the island, **Gilimanuk** is the port for ferries to and from Java (1000 rp per person). There's a bus

INDONESIA

terminal behind the market on the main street, about a km from the dock. There are several cheap, basic losmen along the main road, including *Nirwana* and *Lestari*. Only 200 metres from the port, and well to the east of the main drag, *Nusantara II* is a bit quieter, with small, bare rooms from 12,000 rp.

GUNUNG BATUR AREA

Lake Batur and the volcanic cones of Gunung Batur are contained in a huge bowl-shaped caldera. It's one of Bali's natural wonders and a great area for trekking. Unfortunately, it's also an area where visitors are often hassled by persistent hawkers, would-be guides and outright rip-offs. The entry ticket to the Batur area is 1100 rp, plus 800 rp for a car, 1000 rp for a camera and 2500 rp for a video camera.

Around the Crater Rim

From the south, **Penelokan** is the first place you'll come to on the rim of the caldera. There's a brilliant view if it's clear, but be prepared for wet, cold and cloudy conditions and aggressive souvenir selling. A steep side road winds down to Kedisan on the shore of the lake. Almost opposite the turn-off, the tourist information office, Yayasa Bintang Danu (☎ (0366) 23370), has useful information about transport, trekking and so on – check with them before you're taken in by one of the local hustlers. Further around the rim are a wartel, post office and bank.

Lakeview Restaurant & Homestay (☎ (0366) 51464) has brilliant views and asks US$7.50 for very small 'economy' rooms and US$30 for family rooms. The big restaurants around the rim provide buffet-style lunches for the tour groups which arrive by the busload. The smaller restaurants and warungs are better value.

Further north-west is the town of **Batur**, which merges into **Kintamani**, the main town on the rim of the caldera. The original town of Batur, down in the crater, was engulfed in the 1926 eruption. Batur was rebuilt up on the caldera rim, along with its important temple. The *Hotel Miranda*, at 7000 to 10,000 rp for basic rooms with breakfast, has a friendly atmosphere and helpful owners.

Just beyond Kintamani is **Penulisan**, the site of the highest temple in Bali and the Bali TV relay-station tower. The road descends from here through misty villages to Kubutambahan, on the north coast.

Perama buses stop at the Gunung Sari restaurant, about two km west of the Kedisan turn-off, and they will help arrange transport down to the lakeside. Orange public bemos go round the rim regularly (200 rp), while others go down to Kedisan (500 rp) and Toyah Bungkah (1000 rp), every half hour in the morning, hourly in the afternoon. Chartered transport to Toyah Bungkah is 25,000 rp.

Around Lake Batur

Down at the lakeside is Kedisan, from where you can take a boat across to Trunyan, or follow the quaint little road winding round to Toyah Bungkah. This road continues through the old village of Songan to the north-eastern rim of the crater, while another rough road goes right around Gunung Batur, through amazing 'flows' of solidified black lava.

Kedisan Turning left at the bottom of the hill you come to *Segara Bungalows* (☎ (0366) 51136), with basic rooms from 8000/10,000 rp, and better rooms up to 25,000 rp. A bit further on is the *Surya Homestay* (☎ (0366) 51139), which also has a variety of rooms from 10,000 to 25,000 rp. Turn right and you'll go through the village and past lakeside market gardens to **Buahan**, where *Baruna Cottages* (☎ (0366) 51221) has a restaurant and reasonable rooms from 10,000/12,000 rp.

Trunyan There's very little to see in this Bali Aga village – a few remaining old-style buildings, an old temple and an enormous banyan tree. Beyond Trunyan is the cemetery, where bodies are laid out in bamboo cages to decompose. It's a pretty morbid tourist trap. To get there, take a boat from the jetty near the middle of Kedisan, where there is a ticket office and a fenced car park.

There's a fixed price for a boat and guide for a round-trip from Kedisan to Trunyan, the cemetery, Toyah Bungkah and back – 38,100 rp with two or three people; 44,100 rp with seven. You could also walk about three km to Trunyan from Buahan.

Toyah Bungkah This small settlement, also called Tirtha, is named for its hot springs (Tirtha and Toyah both mean Holy Water). They charge 1000 rp just to enter the village. The hot springs are channelled into a concrete bathing pool (1000 rp), which is not very well kept but relaxing after a climb up the volcano. For reliable trekking information, go to the office at Arlina Bungalows or to Jero Wijaya Tours, *before* you agree to anything with a would-be guide. They can also arrange charter transport to Ubud and other tourist centres.

There are several cheap accommodation options, none particularly attractive. Check the room first and discuss the price if it seems excessive. *Arlina Bungalows* (☎ (0366) 51165) is better than average. *Nyoman Pangus* is OK, at 10,000/15,000 rp, and *Tirta Yastra* is cheap and near the lake. *Lakeside Cottages* (☎ (0366) 51249) is new and comfortable, at 20,000/25,000 rp, or 50,000 rp with hot water. The big new *Puri Bening Hotel* is almost luxurious, but expensive. Assorted warungs and restaurants share similar menus and prices – fresh fish from the lake is a local speciality.

Climbing Batur

There are routes up Gunung Batur (1717 metres) from Toyah Bungkah, Songan, Kedisan and Kintamani. Try to reach the top for sunrise, a magnificent sight, and take a longer route down to explore the various volcanic cones. Mist can obscure the view later in the day. The easiest route is from the north-east, starting near Songan, but it's a hassle to get to the trailhead and parking there is not secure. From Toyah Bungkah, start from the ticket office at the entrance to the village, go up past the temple and keep climbing. Allow about two hours to reach the top.

There can be major hassles from guys who ask outrageous amounts to guide you up Batur – don't pay more than 20,000 rp, and don't pay it all in advance. If you have a torch (flashlight) and a reasonable sense of direction, you won't need a guide at all. Some guides will cook eggs or bananas in the hot fissures near the summit, but please don't let them leave litter. Warungs at the top sell coffee and snacks, and kids sell soft drinks – agree on the price first.

LAKE BRATAN AREA

Next to pretty Lake Bratan, **Bedugul** is on the most direct route between Denpasar and the north coast. Three km north of Bedugul at **Candikuning**, the picturesque temple of Pura Ulu Danau stands on an island near the lakeshore.

Upmarket watersports, such as waterskiing and parasailing, are available in the **Taman Rekreasi** (Leisure Park) at the southern end of the lake – entry and parking costs 500 rp. The cool and attractive **Botanical Gardens** (entry 500 rp) are on the slopes of Gunung Pohon, and there are colourful market gardens around.

Budget accommodation here is poor value. *Hotel Ashram* (☎ (0368) 22439), right by the lake, charges 15,000 rp for an ordinary room with shared bathroom; better rooms are from 30,000 to 70,000 rp. *Lila Graha* (☎ (0368) 21446), up a steep drive from the lakeside road, has good views and reasonable rooms for 30,000/35,000 rp, but it's slightly sleazy. *Strawbali*, near the Taman Rekreasi entrance, is just OK, but no bargain at 20,000/25,000 rp for a plain room.

The *Ulun Danau Restaurant*, near the temple, does a 12,000 rp buffet lunch, and it's the stop for Perama (☎ (0368) 21191). Bemos between Singaraja and Denpasar (Ubung terminal) will drop you at Bedugul.

OTHER MOUNTAIN ROUTES

South-west of Lake Bratan is Gunung Batukau, with the remote temple **Pura Luhur** perched on its slopes. The road from there east to Pacung has wonderful panoramas.

INDONESIA

Interesting trips can be made to the west round Lake Buyan and Lake Tamblingan and to Munduk, where you can stay at the stylish *Puri Lumbung* (☎ (0362) 92810) for US$43/50, or at old-fashioned *losmen* for 20,000 rp. The road continues through to Seririt on the north coast.

Another scenic road winds up from the south, through Blimbing and Pupuan to Seririt. Even less travelled is the route from near Pulukan on the south coast, climbing through spice-growing country and picturesque paddy fields until it joins the road at Pupuan.

SINGARAJA

Singaraja is Bali's principal north-coast town, and the capital of Buleleng District. Its colonial-era port has closed, but it is still a thriving town (95,000) with a substantial student population, some broad tree-lined streets and quite a few old Dutch buildings.

The helpful tourist office (☎ (0362) 25141) is at 23 Jalan Veteran, on the southeast side of town, open every morning but Sunday. The post office and a Telkom wartel are near each other on Jalan Imam Bonjol.

Places to Stay & Eat

Hotels mainly cater to Indonesian business travellers. *Hotel Sentral* (☎ (0362) 21896), on Jalan Achmad Yani, is well run, with basic singles/doubles from 8000/12,000 rp, and there are similar hotels along the same street. *Wijaya Hotel* (☎ (0362) 21915), a few hundred metres from the Banyualit bus terminal on the east side of Jalan Sudirman, is the most comfortable place, with standard rooms from 12,000/14,000 rp.

There are several places to eat on Jalan Achmad Yani, including the *Restaurant Gandhi*, a popular Chinese place, and the *Restaurant Segar II*, across the road. *Cafeteria Koka* is popular with local students.

Getting There & Away

Singaraja has three bus terminals – Banyualit in the west, Penarukan about three km to the east, and Sukasada south of town. Local bemos between the terminals cost around

400 rp. Minibuses to Denpasar (Ubung terminal) via Bedugul leave every half hour from Sukasada terminal (3500 rp). Buses from Banyualit terminal go to Gilimanuk, and to Surabaya on Java.

EAST OF SINGARAJA

There are a number of places of interest just to the east of Singaraja. The soft local stone has allowed temple sculptors to produce some extravagantly whimsical scenes. **Pura Beji** at Sangsit, on the coast side of the main road, has a whole Disneyland of demons and snakes on its front panels. **Jagaraga temple**, a few km inland, features vintage cars, a steamship and even an aerial dogfight between early aircraft. About a km east of the Kintamani turn-off, the **Pura Maduwe Karang**, on the coast side of the road, has the famous relief of a gentleman riding a bicycle with flower-petal wheels.

Fifteen km east of Singaraja, at **Yeh Sanih** (also called Air Sanih), cool freshwater springs are channelled into a fine **swimming pool** (entry 400 rp; children 200 rp). *Bungalow Puri Sanih*, in the springs complex, has doubles from 15,000 rp, but it isn't very good. *Puri Rena*, up the hillside on the southern side of the road, has better rooms from 10,000/15,000 rp. Be careful of your belongings in Yeh Sanih. Another km east, *Tara Beach Bungalows* is basic, but with a beautiful beach frontage and cheap at 12,000/15,000 rp.

LOVINA BEACHES

To the west of Singaraja is a string of coastal villages which have become a popular budget beach resort collectively known as Lovina. The beaches are black volcanic sand, and a reef keeps the water calm and is good for snorkelling. Boats take tourists out to see dolphins cavorting in the sea at sunrise.

It's a good base for day trips to temples and craft centres on Singaraja, to nearby waterfalls and for dive trips to Pulau Menjangan.

Orientation & Information

Accommodation is spread over seven km of the coast, but the main focus is at Kalibukbuk, 10.5 km from Singaraja, where there's a helpful tourist office, restaurants, shops, bars, a wartel, postal agent and bank.

The area code for all Lovina is 0362.

Places to Stay

Most of Lovina's cheap accommodation is clustered on side roads to the beach. In August, rooms fill up and prices are higher, sometimes even double. Tax of 10% is added in more expensive places.

Singaraja to Anturan The first bunch of budget places is at Pantai Happy, where *Happy Beach Inn* is in fact a cheerful place, with very good food and rooms from 8000 to 15,000 rp. Nearby, *Puri Bedahulu* (☎ 41731) is right on the beach and has Balinese features and comfortable rooms from 20,000 rp (with fan) to 35,000 rp (with air-con). Further inland, *Permai Beach Bungalows* (☎ 41471) has basic rooms from 10,000 rp. *Happy Beach Bungalows* is quite a long way from the beach, and trying to cash in on the popularity of the original Happy Beach Inn.

Bali Taman Beach Hotel (☎ 41126) fronts the main road but extends down to the beach, with all the mid-range comforts from US$25/30. Tucked in behind, *Sri Homestay* is a cheap place with small rooms but a brilliant beachfront location.

Anturan The scruffy fishing village of Anturan now has an excess of accommodation – rooms are crowded together, touts can be aggressive and the sea water is not as clean as it should be. *Gede Homestay* is the friendliest place here, with good meals, and rooms from 10,000 to 25,000 rp. Other options include *Mandhara Cottages*, from 10,000 to 30,000 rp, and the slightly upmarket *Simon Seaside Cottages* at 25,000/30,000 rp, but much more in the high season. On the main road, *Hotel Perama* (☎ 41161) has basic rooms from 8000/ 10,000 rp.

Anturan to Kalibukbuk The next turn-off goes down to the *Lila Cita*, right on the beachfront, where plain, clean rooms cost around 10,000/15,000 rp – a little more for upstairs rooms with perfect sea views. It's a great location and the staff are helpful.

The next side road to the beach has quite a few places, including the pleasant *Kali Bukbuk Hotel* (☎ 41701), from 15,000/ 20,000 rp. Back a bit from the beach, *Banyualit Beach Inn* (☎ 25889) has fan-cooled doubles at 30,000 rp, air-con cottages at 65,000 rp, and a range of options in between – it's well run, with a pool and gardens, and very good value. Other places here, with rooms around 12,000/15,000 rp, include *Yudhistra Inn*, *Ray II*, *Awangga Inn* and *Hotel Janur*.

Kalibukbuk Approaching the 'centre' of Lovina you'll find *Ayodya Accommodation*, in a big old Balinese house with basic rooms from 8000 rp. You sit and eat outside, where it's very pleasant in the evening, despite some traffic noise.

The track beside Ayodya goes down to the beach past *Rambutan Cottages* (☎ 41388), where beautifully finished rooms cost from 30,000/35,000 rp (5000 rp more in the peak season). They have a swimming pool set in a pretty garden, and a spacious restaurant with excellent food. Next along is the *Puri Bali Bungalows* with comfortable good-value accommodation at 12,000/15,000 rp.

Closer to the beach, the superclean and well-run *Rini Hotel* (☎ 41386) has a selection of rooms from 15,000/20,000 rp in the low season, and a good restaurant. Opposite Rini is the long-standing *Astina Cottages*, in a garden setting with rooms from 10,000/ 12,000 rp, or 15,000/20,000 rp with private bath (5000 rp more in the peak season). *Bayu Kartika Beach Bungalows* (☎ 41055) is a new establishment facing the beach, with cottages from 20,000/25,000 rp, but prices are bound to rise.

The next turn-off, officially called Jalan Bina Ria, goes past some bars and restaurants to the beach. At the end of this road is the driveway to the rambling *Nirwana*

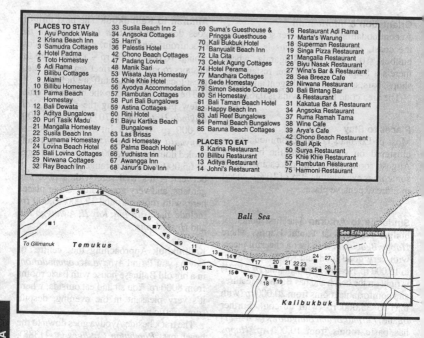

PLACES TO STAY		
1 Ayu Pondok Wisita	33 Susila Beach Inn 2	69 Suma's Guesthouse &
2 Krisna Beach Inn	34 Angsoka Cottages	Pringga Guesthouse
3 Samudra Cottages	35 Harri's	70 Kali Bukbuk Hotel
4 Hotel Padma	36 Palestis Hotel	71 Banyualit Beach Inn
5 Toto Homestay	42 Chono Beach Cottages	72 Lila Cita
6 Adi Rama	47 Padang Lovina	73 Celuk Agung Cottages
7 Billibu Cottages	48 Manik Sari	74 Hotel Perama
9 Miami	53 Wisata Jaya Homestay	77 Mandhara Cottages
10 Billibu Homestay	55 Khie Khie Hotel	78 Gede Homestay
11 Parma Beach	56 Ayodya Accommodation	79 Simon Seaside Cottages
Homestay	57 Rambutan Cottages	80 Sri Homestay
12 Bali Dewata	58 Puri Bali Bungalows	81 Bali Taman Beach Hotel
13 Aditya Bungalows	59 Astina Cottages	82 Happy Beach Inn
20 Puri Tasik Madu	60 Rini Hotel	83 Jati Reef Bungalows
21 Mangalla Homestay	63 Bayu Kartika Beach	84 Permai Beach Bungalows
22 Susila Beach Inn	Bungalows	85 Baruna Beach Cottages
23 Purnama Homestay	63 Las Brisas	
24 Lovina Beach Hotel	64 Adi Homestay	PLACES TO EAT
25 Bali Lovina Cottages	65 Palma Beach Hotel	8 Karina Restaurant
29 Nirwana Cottages	66 Yudhistra Inn	10 Billibu Restaurant
32 Ray Beach Inn	67 Awangga Inn	13 Aditya Restaurant
	68 Janur's Dive Inn	14 Johni's Restaurant

16 Restaurant Adi Rama		
17 Marta's Warung		
18 Superman Restaurant		
19 Singa Pizza Restaurant		
21 Mangalla Restaurant		
26 Biyu Nasak Restaurant		
27 Wina's Bar & Restaurant		
28 Sea Breeze Cafe		
29 Nirwana Restaurant		
30 Bali Bintang Bar		
& Restaurant		
31 Kakatua Bar & Restaurant		
34 Angsoka Restaurant		
37 Ruma Ramah Tama		
38 Wine Cafe		
39 Arya's Cafe		
42 Chono Beach Restaurant		
45 Bali Apik		
50 Surya Restaurant		
55 Khie Khie Restaurant		
57 Rambutan Restaurant		
75 Harmoni Restaurant		

(☎ 41288), on a large slab of beachfront property. The rooms are pretty good, from 10,000/15,000 rp for singles/doubles, to 45,000 rp for comfortable family cottages; in the high season this rises to 20,000 and 60,000 rp – it's a bit impersonal, but the location is the best. Another side track goes to *Angsoka Cottages* (☎ 41841), which has a pool and a couple of rooms at 25,000 rp or less, but most are more expensive – from 35,000 to 70,000 rp. *Susila Beach Inn 2*, on the same track as Angsoka, is a very small, friendly, family losmen with basic cheap rooms from about 8000 rp.

On Jalan Bina Ria itself, *Palestis Hotel* (☎ 41035) is colourfully decorated, with quite good rooms for only 15,000 rp in the low season. A small side road next to Palestis leads to some other cheap places, like *Harri's*, *Manik Sari* and *Padang Lovina* – central and quite OK for around 12,500/15,000 rp.

Back on the main road there's a string of cheaper places with low-season prices from

about 8000 rp. They include the *Purnama Homestay*, *Mangalla Homestay* and *Susila Beach Inn*, which are all grouped together on the north side of the road. Try for a room away from the traffic noise. *Lovina Beach Hotel* (☎ 41473) has rooms in a garden running down to the beach – pretty basic ones are 17,000 rp; better ones are up to 50,000 rp with air-con and hot water. *Puri Tasik Madu* (☎ 41376) costs 12,000 rp for downstairs rooms, 15,000 rp upstairs, and is friendly and close to the beach.

West of Kalibukbuk *Aditya Bungalows & Restaurant* (☎ 41059) is a big mid-range place with beach frontage, pool, shops and a variety of rooms with TV, phone and fridge, from US$20 to US$60. *Parma Beach Homestay* has cottages from 15,000/20,000 rp, also in a garden extending down to the beach. *Bali Dewata*, on the south side of the road, is a basic but clean and friendly place for 10,000/12,000 rp.

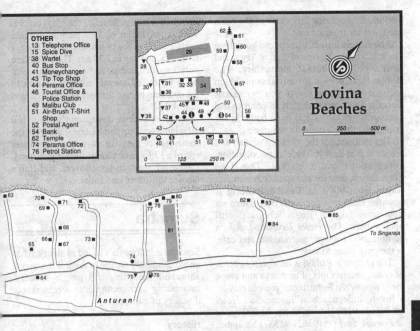

OTHER
13 Telephone Office
15 Spice Dive
38 Wartel
40 Bus Stop
41 Moneychanger
43 Tip Top Shop
44 Perama Office
46 Tourist Office &
   Police Station
49 Malibu Club
51 Air-Brush T-Shirt
   Shop
52 Postal Agent
54 Bank
62 Temple
74 Perama Office
76 Petrol Station

Lovina
Beaches

Anturan

To Singaraja

INDONESIA

Right on the beach, but close to the road, *Toto Homestay* has very basic rooms at 10,000 rp a double, and a questionable reputation. It's at the end of town, but there are even more places along the road going west. *Hotel Padma* (☎ 41140) is new, near the road and may be noisy, but until it's better known the rooms are cheap for a mid-range hotel, at 20,000 to 60,000 rp. *Samudra Cottages* (☎ 41571) is also new, with spotless rooms from 25,000 rp, but may be more when the pool has water in it. *Krisna Beach Inn* is next, at 15,000 rp, followed by *Agus*, and probably more to follow.

Places to Eat

Most of the places to stay have restaurants and snack bars. Many restaurants are also bars, especially later at night. With all these, plus a handful of warungs, there are dozens of places to eat and drink. In central Kalibukbuk, *Arya's Cafe*, *Ruma Ramah Tama*, *Kakatua* and the *Sea Breeze Cafe* are current

local favourites. Going west on the main road, there's *Wine Cafe*, *Biyu Nasak*, the *Singa Pizza Restaurant* and *Superman's*. You'll do well just looking around and eating anywhere that takes your fancy. The *Malibu Club* does meals too, but it's mainly a bar, with live music and local beach boys.

Getting There & Away

By public transport from south Bali, go first to Singaraja then take a bemo west to Lovina (600 rp). Buses between Singaraja, Gilimanuk and Surabaya stop at Lovina – ☎ 22696 to arrange a pick-up, so you don't have to go into Singaraja first. Lovina is well served with tourist shuttles – Perama has an office in Anturan (☎ 41161) and another in Kalibukbuk (☎ 41104).

NORTH-WEST COAST

West of Lovina the main road follows the north coast. Daybreak Waterfall, or **Singsing Air**

Terjun, is about one km south of the main road, not far from Lovina.

About eight km on, a steep road goes three km south to the village of Banjar Tega, and Bali's only **Buddhist monastery**. The **Banjar Hot Springs** are only a couple of km west of the monastery if you cut across directly. The water is slightly sulphurous and pleasantly hot – it's 450 rp to bathe in the pools, and there's a good restaurant.

The junction for the road to Pulukan and the south is at **Seririt**. There's a petrol station, some shops and a market. The *Hotel Singarasari*, near the bus and bemo stop, has rooms from 9000 rp. **Celukanbawang** is now the main port for north Bali. There's a new terminal, but Bugis schooners still anchor here. The *Hotel Drupadi Indah*, a combination losmen, cinema, bar and cafe, is the only place to stay.

The temple at **Pulaki** is on a pretty stretch of coast, and has lots of monkeys and grape vines nearby. At **Pemuteran** you can stay by a lovely little beach at *Taman Sari Hotel* (☎ (0362) 92623) from about 40,000 rp, or at *Pondok Sari* (☎ (0362) 92337) for somewhat more.

BALI BARAT NATIONAL PARK

Taman Nasional Bali Barat (West Bali National Park) covers nearly 80,000 hectares of western Bali, with the adjacent coastal waters and coral reef. There's a visitors' centre at Cekik, near Gilimanuk, and limited facilities at Labuhan Lalang. A 2500 rp day ticket allows you to stop in the park, but you don't have to pay any entrance fees just to drive through.

The foreshore area at Labuhan Lalang has a pleasant white-sand beach and a couple of warungs. There's a jetty for boats to tiny **Pulau Menjangan** (Deer Island), which has about the best diving in Bali. Arrange a diving trip in Lovina – it's a long way from the southern resorts. For sightseeing or snorkelling, a four hour boat excursion is 36,000 rp for a boat with up to 10 people.

For **jungle treks** you must be accompanied by a guide, which can be arranged at Labuhan Lalang, ideally the day before. With a maximum of four people, a guide costs 20,000 rp for two hours, 60,000 rp for six hours, starting at 7.30 am. The guides are very knowledgeable, and can usually point out a variety of animals and birds. Treks in the southern part of the park can be arranged in Cekik.

At Teluk Terima, **Jayaprana's grave** is a 10 minute walk up some stone stairs from the south side of the road. Jayaprana, the foster son of a 17th century king, and his girlfriend, Layonsari, were ill-fated lovers, and Bali's answer to Romeo and Juliet.

Sumatra

Sumatra is Indonesia's island of plenty. It has an extraordinary wealth of natural resources, abundant wildlife, wild jungle scenery, astonishing architecture and a remarkable diversity of cultures.

History

Knowledge of Sumatra's pre-Islamic history is extremely sketchy. Mounds of stone tools and shells unearthed north of Medan show that hunter gatherers were living along the Selat Melaka 13,000 years ago, but otherwise there is little evidence of human activity until the appearance about 2000 years ago of a megalithic culture in the mountains of western Sumatra. The most notable remains are in the Pasemah Highlands near Lahat. A separate megalithic cult developed at about the same time on the island of Nias.

Sumatra had little contact with the outside world until the emergence of the kingdom of Sriwijaya as a regional power at the end of the 7th century. Presumed to have been based near the modern city of Palembang, Sriwijayan power was based on control of the Selat Melaka, the main trade route between India and China. At its peak in the 11th century, it controlled a huge slab of South-East Asia covering most of Sumatra, the Malay peninsula, southern Thailand and Cambodia. Sriwijayan influence collapsed after it was conquered by the south Indian king Ravendra Choladewa in 1025. For the next 200 years, the void was partly filled by Sriwijaya's main regional rival, the Jambi-based kingdom of Malayu.

After Malayu was defeated by a Javanese expedition in 1278, the focus of power moved north to a cluster of Islamic sultanates on the east coast of the modern province of Aceh. These sultanates began life as ports servicing trade through the Selat Melaka. Many of the traders were Muslims from Gujarat (west India), and the animist locals were soon persuaded to adopt the faith of their visitors – giving Islam its first foothold in the Indonesian archipelago.

As well as a religion, these traders also provided the island with its modern name. Until this time, the island was generally referred to as Lesser Java. The name Sumatra is derived from Samudra, meaning 'ocean' in Sanskrit. Samudra was a small port near modern Lhokseumawe that became the most powerful of the sultanates. As Samudran influence spread around the coast of Sumatra and beyond, the name gradually came to refer to the island as a whole. Marco Polo spent five months in Samudra in 1292, corrupting the name to Sumatra in his report.

After the Portuguese occupied Melaka (on the Malay peninsula) in 1511 and began harassing Samudra and its neighbours, Aceh took over as the main power on Sumatra. Based close to modern Banda Aceh at the strategic northern tip of Sumatra, it carried the fight to the Portuguese and carved out a substantial territory of its own, covering much of northern Sumatra as well as large chunks of the Malay peninsula. Acehnese power peaked until Sultan Iskandar Muda at the beginning of the 17th century.

One thing Dutch traders had going for them when they began their probing into Sumatra was that they weren't Catholics (like the Portuguese). Apart from the occasional demonstration of their firepower, the Dutch made little effort to impose themselves militarily on Sumatra until the post-Napoleonic War phase of their empire building.

They began their Sumatran campaign with the capture of Palembang in 1825 and worked their way steadily north before running into trouble against Aceh. The Acehnese turned back the first Dutch attack in 1873 but succumbed to massive assault two years later. They then took to the jungles for a guerrilla struggle that lasted until 1903.

The Dutch were booted out of Aceh in 1942 immediately before the Japanese WWII occupation, and did not attempt to return during their brief effort to reclaim their empire after the war.

Sumatra provided several key figures in the independence struggle, including future vice president Mohammed Hatta and the first prime minister, Sutan Syahrir. It also provided the new nation with its fair share of problems. First up were the staunchly Muslim Acehnese, who rebelled against being lumped together with the Christian Bataks in the newly created province of North Sumatra and declared an independent Islamic republic in 1953. Aceh didn't return to the fold until 1961, when it was given special provincial status.

The Sumatran rebellion of 1958-61 posed a much greater threat. Much debate surrounds the true objectives of the rebels when they declared their rival Revolutionary Government of the Republic of Indonesia (PRRI) in Bukittinggi on 15 February 1958. While many local grievances were involved, the main argument with Jakarta concerned the Communist Party's growing influence with President Soekarno. Some have suggested that the rebels had no intention of fighting, and that the Bukittinggi declaration was intended as an ultimatum to Soekarno to back away from the Communists.

The central government showed no interest in negotiations and moved quickly to smash the rebellion, capturing the key cities of Medan and Palembang within a month. By mid-1958 Jakarta had regained control of all the major towns, but the rebels fought on in the mountains of south Sumatra for another three years until a general amnesty was granted as part of a peace settlement.

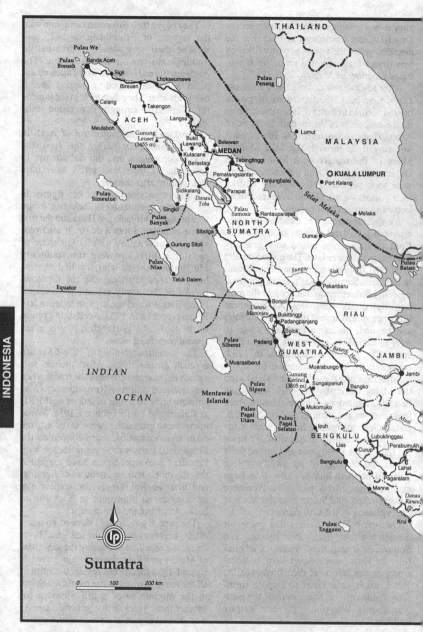

Sumatra

0   100   200 km

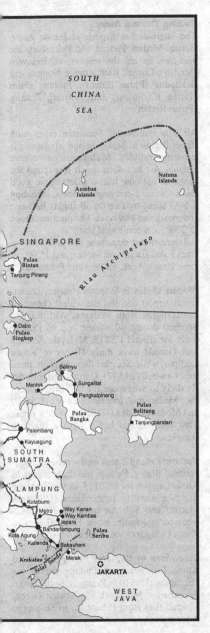

SOUTH
CHINA
SEA

Natuna
Islands

Anmbas
Islands

SINGAPORE

Pulau
Bintan

Tanjung Pinang

Riau Archipelago

Dabo
Pulau
Singkep

Belinyu

Mentok   Sungailiat

Pangkalpinang

Pulau
Bangka

Pulau
Belitung

Tanjungpandan

Palembang

Kayuagung

SOUTH
SUMATRA

LAMPUNG

Kotabumi

Metro   Way Kanan
Way Kambas

Jepara

Bandarlampung   Pulau
Seribu

Kota Agung

Kalianda   Bakauheni

Krakatau   Selat Sunda   Merak

JAKARTA

WEST
JAVA

Geography

Stretching nearly 2000 km and covering an area of 473,607 sq km, Sumatra is the sixth largest island in the world. The island is divided neatly in two by the equator just north of Bukittinggi.

The main feature is the Bukit Barisan mountains, which run most of the length of the west coast, merging with the highlands around Lake Toba and central Aceh in the north. Many of the peaks are over 3000 metres (the highest is Gunung Kerinci at 3805 metres). Spread along the range are almost 100 volcanoes, 15 of them active. The mountains form the island's backbone, dropping steeply to the sea on the west coast but sloping gently to the east. The eastern third of the island is low-lying, giving way to vast areas of swampland and estuarine mangrove forest bordering the shallow Selat Melaka. It's traversed by numerous wide, muddy, meandering rivers, the biggest being the Batang Hari, Siak and Musi.

The string of islands off the west coast, including Nias and the Mentawai Islands, are geologically older than the rest of Sumatra.

Climate

Sitting astride the equator, Sumatra's climate is about as tropical as tropical gets. Daytime temperatures seldom fail to reach 30°C on the coast, but fortunately most of the popular travellers' spots are in the mountains where the weather is appreciably cooler. Places like Berastagi, Bukittinggi and Danau Toba get cool enough at night to warrant a blanket.

The time to visit Sumatra is during the dry season, which runs from May to September. June and July are the best months. The timing of the wet season is hard to predict. In the north, the rain starts in October, and December/January are the wettest months; in the south, the rains start in November, peaking in January/February. Bengkulu and West Sumatra are the wettest places, with average rainfall approaching 3500 mm.

Flora & Fauna

Large areas of Sumatra's original rainforest have been cleared for plantations, but some

INDONESIA

impressive tracts of forest remain – particularly around Gunung Leuser National Park in the north and Kerinci Seblat National Park in the central west.

The extraordinary *Rafflesia arnoldii*, the world's largest flower, is found in pockets throughout the Bukit Barisan – most notably near Bukittinggi – between August and November.

Sumatra's forests are home to a range of rare and endangered species, including the two-horned Sumatran rhino, the Sumatran tiger and the honey bear. Gunung Leuser National Park is one of the last strongholds of the orang-utan, with more than 5000 living in the wild. The rehabilitation centre at Bukit Lawang is one place where you can be sure of seeing one.

Economy

Sumatra is enormously rich in natural resources and generates the lion's share of Indonesia's export income. The biggest earners are oil and natural gas. The fields around the towns of Jambi, Palembang and Pekanbaru produce three-quarters of Indonesia's oil. Lhokseumawe, on the east coast of Aceh, is the centre of the natural gas industry.

Rubber and palm oil are the next biggest income earners. Timber is another heavily exploited resource, and the forests of the eastern Sumatran lowland are disappearing rapidly into an assortment of pulp mills and plywood factories. Other crops include tea, coffee, cocoa beans and tobacco. Sumatra was noted as a source of prized black pepper by the Chinese more than a thousand years ago, and pepper remains a major crop in southern Sumatra.

People

Sumatra is the second most populous island in the archipelago with 40 million people. Population density is, however, but a fraction of Bali or Java. Continuing transmigration from these two islands has added to the remarkably diverse ethnic and cultural mix.

Getting There & Away

The international airports at Banda Aceh, Batam, Medan, Padang and Pekanbaru are visa-free, as are the seaports of Belawan (Medan); Dumai; Batu Ampar, Nongsa and Sekupang (Pulau Batam); Tanjung Balai (Pulau Karimun); and Tanjung Pinang (Pulau Bintan).

Air The number of Sumatran cities with direct flights to Malaysia and Singapore is growing rapidly. Malaysian newcomer Pelangi Air has done much to expand the range of options. It also offers some good deals for (card-carrying) students, including a 50% stand-by fare on all flights between Indonesia and Malaysia. The discount drops to 25% for a confirmed seat.

International departure tax is 20,000 rp from Pulau Batam and Medan, and 15,000 rp from Banda Aceh, Padang and Pekanbaru.

Medan Medan is Sumatra's major international airport and has the widest choice of destinations. Both Malaysia Airlines and Sempati do the 40 minute hop to Penang daily for around US$75. Malaysia Airlines and Garuda have daily flights to Kuala Lumpur, while Sempati flies the route three times a week (all $77). Garuda and Silk Air fly daily to Singapore for US$140. Pelangi flies Medan-Ipoh four times a week (US$70) and Medan-Melaka (US$104) twice a week. Thai International has a weekly flight to Bangkok.

Padang Padang is also well served for international flights. Pelangi has daily flights to Kuala Lumpur for US$123, as well as three flights a week to Johor Bahru (US$104). Merpati and Silk Air have three flights a week to Singapore, while Sempati flies to Kuala Lumpur twice a week.

Elsewhere in Sumatra Pelangi flights to Kuala Lumpur from Padang travel via Pekanbaru (US$107). Pelangi also flies from Pekanbaru to Melaka (US$60) twice a week. Merpati flies from Pekanbaru to Singapore twice a week.

The latest international option to open up is the Pelangi Air route from Banda Aceh to Kuala Lumpur (US$134), via Penang (US$107).

Sumatra to Java Garuda has direct flights to Jakarta from Batam (284,900 rp) and Medan (414,700 rp), and from Banda Aceh (539,000 rp) via Medan. Merpati has direct flights daily to Jakarta from most other major Sumatran cities, including Bengkulu (192,500 rp), Padang (300,300 rp) and Palembang (171,000 rp). It also flies daily from Palembang to Bandung (179,300 rp).

Boat The express ferries between Penang in Malaysia and Medan's port of Belawan are the most popular way to travel. The route between Singapore and Pekanbaru via Batam is an interesting alternative.

Belawan to Penang The hi-speed ferries *Ekspres Selasa* and *Ekspres Bahagia* take about four hours to do the run across the Selat Melaka. Between them, there are departures from Medan every day except Monday for 95,000 rp and from Penang every day except Sunday for RM110. The fares from Belawan include port tax (7500 rp) and bus transport from Medan. Children pay half fare.

Belawan to Port Kelang & Lumut There are ferries from Belawan to Port Kelang, near Kuala Lumpur, at 11 am on Monday and Wednesday. The trip takes six hours and costs 114,000 rp. The boats return at 10 am on Tuesday and Thursday (RM120).

There are ferries from Belawan to Lumut (200 km south of Penang) on Tuesday and Saturday at 2 pm, returning on Wednesday and Sunday at 9 am. Fares are the same as for Penang-Medan.

Singapore to Sumatra via Batam The island of Batam, part of Indonesia's Riau Archipelago, lies just 45 minutes south of Singapore by ferry and is a good stepping stone to the Sumatran mainland. It is also the cheapest way of getting to Sumatra, providing you don't get stuck overnight. Batam's hotels are outrageously overpriced by Indonesian standards.

Ferries shuttle constantly between Singapore's World Trade Centre and Batam's visa-free port of Sekupang from 7 am to 6 pm (S$18; 30,000 rp from Sekupang). The trip takes about 40 minutes. You go through immigration at Sekupang, turn right out of the terminal and walk through the hole in the fence to the domestic ferry terminal. There you will find a row of ticket offices offering speedboat connections to a long list of mainland towns and to other islands. Pekanbaru is the most popular option. In theory, the journey involves a four hour speedboat trip to the mainland bus/ferry terminal of Tanjung Buton, followed by a three hour bus trip. In practice, the trip can take up to nine hours. Fares for the combined ticket start at 35,000 rp. Pekanbaru is about 5½ hours by bus from Bukittinggi. The boat to Tanjung Buton goes via Tanjung Balai on Pulau Karimun and Selat Panjang on Pulau Tebingtinggi (15,000 rp), but there's no reason to stop.

There is also a daily service to Jambi (56,000 rp), made up of a seven hour boat trip to Kuala Tunkal and a two hour bus ride.

Jakarta to Sumatra Pelni has ships from Jakarta to a number of Sumatran ports. The Jakarta-Padang-Gunung Sitoli-Sibolga-Padang-Jakarta route serviced by the KM *Lawit* is the one most used by travellers. The boat leaves Jakarta for Padang (81,500 rp ekonomi; 41 hours) every second Wednesday, returning from Padang every second Sunday.

There are also boats to Medan every Saturday, returning on Tuesday, and to Bintan every Thursday, returning on Sunday.

Merak to Bakauheni Ferries operate 24 hours a day between Merak on Java and Bakauheni at the southern tip of Sumatra. They leave every 36 minutes, so there's never long to wait. The trip across the narrow Selat Sunda takes 1½ hours. You're better off travelling deck class (1500 rp) and enjoying the breeze than sitting in the smoke-filled

1st class lounge (2600 rp). If you travel by bus between Jakarta and destinations in Sumatra, the price of the ferry is included in your ticket.

There's also a new 'Superjet' service that does the crossing in 30 minutes for 6000 rp. They leave Bakauheni every 70 minutes from 8.40 am to 4.50 pm.

Getting Around

Air An hour on a plane is a very attractive alternative to countless hours on a bus. Merpati has a comprehensive network of services between Sumatra's major cities. Sample fares include Bengkulu to Palembang for 101,200 rp, Palembang to Padang for 179,300 rp, Padang to Medan for 172,700 rp and Medan to Banda Aceh for 145,200 rp. SMAC flies to some of the remoter destinations that Merpati doesn't bother with. It has daily flights from Medan to Gunung Sitoli on Nias for 131,300 rp.

Bus Bus is the most popular way to get around. The old travellers' tales of hours of bone-shaking horror on appalling roads are fading into history – on the main roads, at least. A lot of money has been spent on improving the island's roads in the last 10 years. If you stick to the Trans-Sumatran Highway and other major roads, the big air-con buses and tourist coaches make travel a breeze. The best express air-con buses have reclining seats, toilets, video and even karaoke. The only problem is that many of them do night runs, so you miss out on the scenery. The non air-con buses are in many cases just older versions of the air-con buses. They rattle more, the air-con no longer works and they can get very crowded, but they are fine for short trips.

There are numerous bus companies covering the main routes and prices vary greatly, depending on the level of comfort. Tickets can be bought direct from the bus company or from an agent. Agents usually charge about 10% more, but they are generally more convenient. In some towns, they are the only places to buy tickets. It can pay to shop around, especially in the main tourist areas where agent charges can be excessive.

Many travellers take the convenient 'tourist' buses that do the Bukit Lawang-Berastagi-Parapat-Bukittinggi run. You may feel like you're in a tour group at times, and 'tourist' doesn't necessarily mean comfortable – but they do take some scenic routes that normal buses don't cover. They also pick up and drop off at hotels, travel during the day so you can see the scenery, and stop at points of interest on the way. The cost and journey times are about the same as for air-con buses.

Travel on the backroads is a different story. Progress can still be grindingly slow, uncomfortable and thoroughly exhausting, particularly during the wet season when bridges are washed away and the roads develop huge potholes.

Train Sumatra has a very limited rail network. The only useful service runs from Bandarlampung in the south to Palembang, and then on to Lubuklinggau. There are also passenger trains from Medan to Pematangsiantar, Rantauparapat and Tanjungbalai.

BAKAUHENI

Bakauheni, at Sumatra's southern tip, is the terminal for ferries from Java. There are ferries between Bakauheni and Merak in Java every 36 minutes, 24 hours a day. They take 1½ hours and cost 1500 rp deck class.

There are frequent buses from right outside the terminal building for the 90 km trip to Bandarlampung (1700 rp). If you're planning to stay in Bandarlampung, it's worth paying 5000 rp for a seat in a share taxi which will take you to the hotel of your choice.

BANDARLAMPUNG

Bandarlampung is the fourth biggest city in Sumatra with a population of about 600,000. The city was formed by a merger of the old towns of Telukbetung (coastal) and Tanjungkarang (inland). When Krakatau erupted in 1883, almost half its 36,000 victims were claimed by the 30-metre-high tidal wave that funnelled up the Bay of Lampung and devastated Telukbetung.

Orientation & Information

Most places of importance to travellers are in Tanjungkarang, including cheap hotels, the railway station and the bus station. The centre of Tanjungkarang is the roundabout at the junction of Jalans Teuku Umar, Kotaraja and Raden Intan. The regional tourist office (☎ 51900) is right on the roundabout at Jalan Kotaraja 12. Several of the staff speak English. The bus station is several km north of town along Jalan Teuku Umar, which leads to the Trans-Sumatran Highway. The railway station is on Jalan Kotaraja, 200 metres from the roundabout. The Telkom office (with Home Direct phone) is on Jalan Kartini, the southern extension of Jalan Teuku Umar. The main post office is a long way from the city centre at Jalan Kh Dahlan.

The area code for Bandarlampung is 0721.

Krakatau Monument

A large steel maritime buoy that was washed out of the Bay of Lampung by the post-Krakatau tidal wave has been turned into a monument where it came to rest on a hillside overlooking Telukbetung. It's a sobering thought that everything below this point was wiped out by the wall of water. The buoy now stands in a shady small park off Jalan Veteran, guarded by a concrete rhino.

Places to Stay

The best of an uninspiring bunch of bottom-end places is the *Hotel Cilimaya*, close to the city centre on Jalan Imam Bonjol. It has very basic singles/doubles for 5000/10,000 rp, and rooms with fan for 10,000/15,000 rp. The *Hotel Gunungsari* is a rock-bottom place on Jalan Kotaraja between the tourist office and the railway, with doubles for 8000 rp.

The *Hotel Garding* (☎ 55512) is a step up from these. Doubles with fan are 15,000 rp, and air-con doubles start at 32,000 rp. The hotel is signposted off Jalan Teuku Umar between the roundabout and Jalan Imam Bonjol.

Places to Eat

The best food in Bandarlampung is to be found at the *Pasar Mambo* night markets in Telukbetung, at the junction of Jalans Supratman and Malahayati. A taxi ride from Tanjungkarang costs about 3500 rp. There are smaller night markets in Tanjungkarang on Jalan Kartini and next to the cinema complex on Jalan Imam Bonjol. The *Sari Bundo* and the *Bedagang I* are a couple of good Padang restaurants on Jalan Imam Bonjol.

Getting There & Away

Air Merpati operates five flights a day between Jakarta and Bandarlampung (91,300 rp) and two a week to Palembang (88,200 rp). The Merpati office is at Jalan Kartini 90 (☎ 63419).

Bus Rajabasa bus station is one of the busiest in Sumatra. There's a constant flow of departures, 24 hours a day, both south to Jakarta and north to all parts of Sumatra. There are buses to Palembang (15,000 rp; 10 hours) and Bengkulu (from 17,500 rp; 16 hours), but most people heading north go to Bukittinggi, a 22 hour haul that costs from 30,000 rp ekonomi to 70,000 rp air-con. The trip to Jakarta takes eight hours and tickets range from 12,000 to 22,500 rp (air-con), which includes the price of the ferry between Bakauheni and Merak.

Train There are three services a day each way between Bandarlampung and Palembang, leaving at 8.30 and 10 am, and 9 pm in both directions. The 8.30 am and 9 pm trains have bisnis (18,000 rp) and eksekutif (28,000 rp) class only and take 6½ hours, while the 10 am 'market' trains have ekonomi class only (4500 rp) and take an hour longer.

Taxi Share taxis offer a door-to-door service between Bandarlampung and Bakauheni (5000 rp), Jakarta (30,000 rp) and Palembang (25,000 rp). For Bakauheni, try Taxi 4545 (☎ 52264); for Jakarta or Palembang, try Taxi Dinasty (☎ 45674).

INDONESIA

Getting Around

Taxis charge a standard 16,000 rp for the 22 km ride from the airport to town. There are frequent opelets between Tanjungkarang railway station and Rajabasa bus station (300 rp).

KALIANDA

It's possible to arrange boat trips out to **Krakatau** from the small coastal town of **Kalianda**, 30 km north of Bakauheni. The *Hotel Beringin* (☎ (0727) 2008) has good doubles with mandi for 9900 rp and can organise boats. It costs 160,000 rp to charter a small boat for up to eight people, or 200,000 rp for a larger craft.

Getting There & Away

There are opelets to Kalianda from Bakauheni (1700 rp) and buses from Bandarlampung (also 1700 rp).

WAY KAMBAS

Local tourist authorities are keen to promote the attractions of **Way Kambas National Park**, but the soccer-playing elephants of the **elephant training centre** appeal more to domestic tourists than to foreign visitors. The tourist office in Bandarlampung can organise **elephant rides** if you give them a day's notice. An hour's ride costs 20,000 rp, which is quite long enough for the average bum. There's a small *guesthouse* at Way Kambas with basic doubles for 25,000 rp, and there are food stalls during the day. You'll have to bring food if you're staying the night. A permit to enter the park costs 2550 rp, payable at the entrance.

Getting There & Away

The hourly buses from Bandarlampung's Rajabasa bus station to Way Jepara (3500 rp; 2½ hours) go past the turn-off to the park, marked by an archway in the village of Rajabasalama. Here you will be approached by local lads on motorbikes wanting 8000 rp to take you remaining the 14 km. Aim to arrive before 5 pm.

PALEMBANG

Standing on the Musi River, only 50 km upstream from the sea, Palembang is a huge, hot, heavily polluted industrial city of about 1.5 million people – the second biggest city in Sumatra. There are two oil refineries and a huge fertiliser plant, and plans to build the largest pulp mill in the southern hemisphere. Palembang is presumed to have been the capital of the great Sriwijayan Empire, which dominated the region a thousand years ago, but few relics of this era have been found. Today it is the capital of the province of South Sumatra, but there is little to attract tourists.

Orientation & Information

The city is split in half by the Musi River and sprawls along both banks. The two halves of the city are connected by the Ampera Bridge (Jembatan Ampera). A hotchpotch of wooden houses on stilts crowd both banks, but the south side, known as Ulu, is where the majority of people live.

The 'better half', Ilir, is on the north bank. It has most of the government offices, shops, hotels and the wealthy residential districts. Jalan Sudirman is the main street, running right to the bridge. The Palembang city tourist office (☎ 358450) is at the Museum Sultan Machmud Badaruddin II, off Jalan Sudirman near the bridge. The South Sumatran provincial tourist office (☎ 357348) is among the government offices on Jalan POM IX.

There are branches of all the major banks. The best is the Bank of Central Asia on Jalan Kapitan Rivai. The nearby Bank Rakyat Indonesia also has reasonable rates. The BNI bank is on Jalan Sudirman. Outside banking hours, the major hotels are the best bet. The post office and Telkom office are side by side on Jalan Merdeka.

The area code for Palembang is 0711.

Things to See

There is very little to see in Palembang. There's a colourful **floating market** on the Musi River next to the main market, **Pasar 16 Ilir**. You can check out the lifestyle of

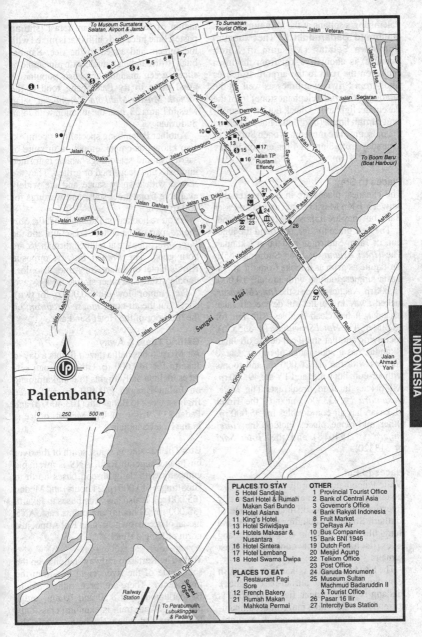

Palembang

0   250   500 m

INDONESIA

PLACES TO STAY
5   Hotel Sandjaja
6   Sari Hotel & Rumah
    Makan Sari Bundo
9   Hotel Asiana
11 King's Hotel
13 Hotel Sriwidjaya
14 Hotels Makasar &
    Nusantara
16 Hotel Sintera
17 Hotel Lembang
18 Hotel Swarna Dwipa

PLACES TO EAT
7   Restaurant Pagi
    Sore
12 French Bakery
21 Rumah Makan
    Mahkota Permai

OTHER
1   Provincial Tourist Office
2   Bank of Central Asia
3   Governor's Office
4   Bank Rakyat Indonesia
8   Fruit Market
9   DeRaya Air
10 Bus Companies
15 Bank BNI 1946
19 Dutch Fort
20 Mesjid Agung
22 Telkom Office
23 Post Office
24 Garuda Monument
25 Museum Sultan
    Machmud Badaruddin II
    & Tourist Office
26 Pasar 16 Ilir
27 Intercity Bus Station

Palembang's sultans at the **Museum Sultan Machmud Badaruddin II**. The **Museum Sumatera Selatan** (Museum of South Sumatra) is about five km from the town centre on the road to the airport. It houses finds from Sriwijayan times as well as the famous *batu gajah* (elephant stone) from the Pasemah Highlands. Check out the magnificent **rumah limas** (traditional house) behind the museum. The museum is open Sunday to Thursday from 8 am to 4 pm and on Friday from 8 to 11 am.

Places to Stay

The cheapest places are in the market area between Jalan Mesjid Lama and Jalan Pasar Baru, but they are impossible to recommend.

The best place to look is around the junction of Jalan Sudirman and Jalan Iskandar. The *Hotel Asiana*, at Jalan Sudirman 45E, isn't quite as grim as it looks from the street. Basic singles/doubles with fan are 10,000/ 15,000 rp. A better choice is the *Hotel Makasar*, tucked away in a quiet cul de sac off Jalan Iskandar. It has clean doubles with fan for 15,000 rp. The *Hotel Sriwidjaja* (☎ 355555), occupying another small cul de sac off Jalan Iskandar, has a wide range of rooms. Large doubles with fan are 20,000 rp, and rooms with air-con, hot water and TV are 49,000 rp. All prices include breakfast. The *Hotel Nusantara* (☎ 353306), next to the Hotel Makasar, has air-con doubles for 35,000 rp. Other mid-range places include the *Hotel Sintera* (☎ 354618) and the *Hotel Sari* (☎ 313320).

Places to Eat

While Palembang is hardly a name to make the taste buds tingle in anticipation, the city gives its name to the distinctive cuisine of southern Sumatra (including Lampung and Bengkulu) in the same way that Padang gives its name to the cooking of West Sumatra.

The best known dish is ikan brengkes (fish served with a spicy durian-based sauce). Pindang is a spicy, clear, fish soup. Food is normally served with a range of accompaniments. The main one is tempoyak, a combi-

nation of fermented durian, terasi (shrimp paste), lime juice and chilli that is mixed with the fingers and added to the rice. Sambal buah (fruit sambals), made with pineapple or sliced green mangos, are also popular. A good place to try Palembang food is the *Rumah Makan Mahkota Permai*, at Jalan Mesjid Lama 33, near the junction with Jalan Sudirman.

Another Palembang speciality is pempek, also known as empek-empek, a mixture of sago, fish and seasonings which is formed into balls and deep-fried or grilled. They are served with a spicy sauce and are widely available from street stalls and warungs for 250 rp each.

If you're hooked on Padang food, the *Sari Bundo*, part of the Hotel Sari set-up, and the *Pagi Sore*, opposite at Jalan Sudirman 96, are both good. The *French Bakery*, opposite King's Hotel on Jalan Kol Atmo, also does noodle dishes and other simple meals.

For a minor blow-out (20,000 rp for two), check out the air-con *Chinese restaurant* on the top floor of the Hotel Sandjaja.

Getting There & Away

Air Merpati has half a dozen flights a day to Jakarta for 149,600 rp. Other Merpati services include daily flights to Pangkalpinang on Pulau Bangka (70,400 rp) and three flights a week to Bengkulu (103,400 rp) and Padang (179,300 rp). The Merpati office is in the Hotel Sandjaja.

Bus The bus station is just south of the river on Jalan Pangeran Ratu. ANS is a reliable company with daily air-con buses north to Bukittinggi (40,000 rp; 24 hours) and Medan (65,000 rp). It also has daily buses to Jakarta (38,000 rp; 20 hours) and points east. ANS has an office in town on Jalan Kol Atmo, just north of King's Hotel.

Train The Kertapati railway station is on the south side of the river, eight km from the town centre. There are three trains a day to Bandarlampung, at 8.30 and 10 am, and 9 pm. The 10 am train is ekonomi class only (4500 rp) and takes 7½ hours, while the other services have only bisnis (18,000 rp) and eksekutif class (28,000 rp) and take an hour less. There are also three trains to Lubuklinggau, at 8 and 10.30 am, and 8 pm, which stop at Lahat (for the Pasemah Highlands). It's four hours to Lahat and seven to Lubuklinggau, but the fares are the same: 4500 rp in ekonomi (10.30 am service only), 12,000 rp in bisnis and 22,000 rp in eksekutif.

Boat There are 'jetfoil' services from Palembang's Boom Baru jetty to Mentok on Pulau Bangka daily at 7.30 and 9.30 am. The journey takes about 3½ hours and the fare is 25,000 rp.

Getting Around
Sultan Badaruddin II airport is 12 km north of town and taxis cost a standard 10,000 rp. Opelets around town cost a standard 300 rp. There is no city centre opelet station. They leave from around the huge roundabout at the junction of Jalan Sudirman and Jalan Merdeka.

PASEMAH HIGHLANDS
The highlands, tucked away in the foothills of the Bukit Barisan west of Lahat, are famous for the mysterious **megalithic monuments** that dot the landscape. The stones have been dated back about 2000 years, but little else is known about them or the civilisation that carved them. The museums of Palembang and Jakarta now house the pick of the stones. The best of those remaining are around the village of **Pagaralam**, where the *Hotel Mirasa* (☎ (0730) 21266) is a good place to base yourself. There's a range of doubles from 15,000 rp, and the owner can organise transport to the sites. The hotel is on the edge of town on Jalan Mayor Ruslan, about two km from the bus station.

Getting There & Away
The nearest major town is Lahat, on the Trans-Sumatran Highway nine hours from Bandarlampung and 12 hours from Padang. Lahat is also a stop on the railway line between Palembang and Lubuklinggau.

There are regular buses between Lahat and Pagaralam (1800 rp; two hours).

JAMBI
Jambi is a busy port city on the banks of the Batang Hari river. There's not much reason to come here. It's a long way from anywhere of interest, and the only attraction of any consequence is the ancient temple complex at Muara Jambi, 25 km downstream.

Orientation & Information
Jambi sprawls over a wide area. Most of the banks, hotels and restaurants are in the old city centre area by the port. The main post office is opposite the river on Jalan Sultan Thaha. The tourist office (☎ 25330) is about five km from the port among the government buildings on Jalan Basuki Rachmat – out beyond the bus station on Jalan M Yamin. Mayang Tour & Travel (☎ 25450) is an efficient travel agency at Jalan Mattaher 27.

The area code for Jambi is 0741.

Places to Stay & Eat
The cheap hotels are in the market streets by the port. They are rock-bottom, survival-only places. The *Hotel Sumatra*, at Jalan Kartini 26, has doubles for 10,000 rp and looks marginally the least uninviting. If you can afford it, step up a notch to somewhere like the *Hotel Pinang* (☎ 23969), 100 metres from the river at Jalan Dr Sutomo 9. It has clean doubles with fan for 21,000 rp, and air-con rooms for 42,000 rp. New hotels seem to be sprouting everywhere. The *Hotel Jambi Raya* (☎ 34971) is a comfortable mid-range place tucked away on Jalan Camar, off Jalan Gatot Subroto. It has air-con doubles starting at 65,000 rp, plus tax. The two star *Hotel Abadi* (☎ 25600), at Jalan Gatot Subroto 92, is the best place in town – which isn't saying much.

There's a reasonable choice of *food stalls* at the small night market on Jalan Sultan Iskandar Muda. The market is opposite the well-stocked *Mandala Supermarket*. *Saimen Perancis* is an excellent bakery on Jalan Mattaher that also does meals. The *Simpang*

INDONESIA

Raya, at Jalan Mattaher 22, and the *Safari*, at Jalan Veteran 29, do good Padang food.

Getting There & Away
Air Merpati has two direct flights a day to Jakarta (207,900 rp). Merpati has an office at the Hotel Abadi.

Bus Jambi is not on the Trans-Sumatran Highway, but there are good sealed roads linking the city to Palembang in the south, to Pekanbaru in the north and to the highway at Muarabungo and Saralungun. Intercity services use the Simpang Kawat bus station on Jalan M Yamin.

There are frequent buses to Palembang, from 6000 to 13,000 rp depending on the level of comfort, and to Padang (from 15,000 rp; 10 hours). Ratu Intan Permata (☎ 60234), near the bus station on Jalan M Yamin, has door-to-door services to Pekanbaru (27,500 rp; eight hours).

Boat Ratu Intan Permata (see Bus above) operates connecting services from Jambi to the coastal town of Kuala Tungkal (6000 rp; two hours), from where there's a daily speedboat service to Pulau Batam (50,000 rp; seven hours).

MUARA JAMBI
The huge temple complex at Muara Jambi ranks as one of Sumatra's most important archaeological sites. It is thought to have been the capital of the Malayu kingdom, although some historians have speculated that the Sriwijayans also ruled from here. Four of the nine temples uncovered so far have been 'restored', but surprisingly little seems to be known about the site. The earliest temples are thought to have been built in the 7th century, but most date from the 11th century.

Getting There & Away
The temples are 25 km downstream from Jambi on the Batang Hari river. The easiest way to get there is to charter a taxi from Jambi – reckon on paying about 30,000 rp for the return trip plus two hours waiting

time. On Sunday, there are lots of boats from Jambi charging 6000 rp return, or you can pay 45,000 rp to charter a boat.

BENGKULU
Bengkulu was the setting for a fairly half-hearted British attempt to challenge Dutch control of the Indonesian spice trade. The British arrived in Bengkulu, or Bencoolen as they called it, in 1685 and lingered until 1824 when it was traded for Melaka and a Dutch guarantee to leave the British alone on the Malay peninsula and Singapore. Stamford Raffles ruled the remote colony from 1818 until the transfer to Dutch rule.

Modern Bengkulu is a relaxed town of about 60,000, but there's not much to do and few travellers bother to make the detour off the Trans-Sumatran Highway.

Orientation & Information
Although Bengkulu is right by the sea, it only really touches it near Fort Marlborough. The coast around here is surprisingly quiet and rural only a km or so from the city centre. Jalan Suprapto and the nearby Pasar Minggu Besar are the modern town centre, separated from the old town area around Fort Marlborough by the long, straight Jalan Ahmad Yani/Jalan Sudirman.

The tourist office (☎ 21272) is inconveniently situated to the south of town at Jalan Pembangunan 14. There's not much material in English other than a couple of glossy brochures, but the staff are friendly. The post office and telephone office are opposite the Pasar Barukoto, near the fort.

The area code for Bengkulu is 0736.

Things to See
The British ruled their remote colony from **Fort Marlborough**, a curiously unimpressive piece of military architecture built between 1714 and 1719. Opponents clearly weren't that impressed either, and the fort fell both times it was attacked. The old British gravestones at the entrance make poignant reading.

The Dutch decided that Bengkulu was perfect as a place of exile for Soekarno, and the future president lived here from 1938 until the Japanese arrived in 1941. The small villa where he lived on Jalan Soekarno-Hatta is maintained as a **museum**. There are a few faded photos, the wardrobe where his clothes used to hang and, not to be missed, Bung's trusty bicycle.

Soekarno, who was an architect, designed the **Mesjid Jamik** mosque at the junction of Jalan Sudirman and Jalan Suprapto during his stay. It is commonly known as the Bung Karno mosque.

Bengkulu's main beach, **Pantai Panjang**, hardly rates as an attraction – it's long, grey, featureless and unsafe for swimming.

Places to Stay

The area around Fort Marlborough is the best place to look. As in most major towns in Sumatra, the cheap hotels are a dismal lot. The *Losmen Samudera*, opposite the fort entrance on Jalan Benteng, does at least have location going for it. It's an old place with lots of character, but the rooms are extremely basic and there are no fans – essential in steamy Bengkulu. It charges 3500 rp per person. *Wisma Rafflesia* (☎ 21650), at Jalan Ahmad Yani 924, has slightly better doubles for 10,000 rp.

The *Wisma Balai Buntar* (☎ 21254), near the fort at Jalan Khadijah 122, is the best value in town. It's a fine old Dutch villa with huge air-con singles/doubles for 20,500/27,500 rp, including breakfast. The place is run by a very friendly former Indonesia army colonel who speaks excellent English. A lot of travellers stay here and the colonel is a great source of information about Bengkulu.

The *Asia Hotel* (☎ 21901), at Jalan Ahmad Yani 922, is a clean place with a range of air-con rooms from 30,500 rp.

Places to Eat

The *Rumah Makan Srikandi*, opposite the Asia Hotel on Jalan Ahmad Yani, does excellent southern Sumatran food very cheaply. Locals rate the *Rumah Makan Si Kabayan*, at Jalan Sudirman 51, as the best restaurant in town. It serves Sundanese food. Seafood fans should head straight to the wonderful

Warung Makan Laut Dedi, opposite the Si Kabayan. It does a huge bowl of chilli crab for 6000 rp. The *Gandhi Bakery*, on Jalan Suprapto, has a fine selection of ice creams as well as cakes.

Getting There & Away

Air Merpati has two direct flights a day to Jakarta (188,100 rp) and three a week to Palembang (101,200 rp). The Merpati office (☎ 42337) is in the Hotel Samudera Dwinka at Jalan Sudirman 246.

Bus Terminal Panorama, the long-distance bus station, is several km east of town. Most services continue to the various company depots in town, otherwise a mikrolet to town costs 300 rp.

Several companies have offices on Jalan MR Haryono. Putra Rafflesia (☎ 21811), at No 57, and Bengkulu Indah (☎ 22640), at No 14, both have a wide range of destinations. Fares include Padang for 17,500 rp (22,500 rp air-con) and Jakarta for 30,500 rp (up to 55,000 rp deluxe). Sriwijaya Express, at Jalan Bali 36, runs buses up the coast to Mukomuko (7500 rp) and to the Kerinci valley for 12,000 rp.

Getting Around

Airport cabs charge a standard 10,000 rp to town. The airport is 200 metres from the main road south and there are regular bemos to town for 300 rp. Tell the driver you want to go to the *benteng* (fort).

KERINCI

Kerinci is a cool mountain valley tucked away high in the Bukit Barisan south of Padang. The setting is dominated by the towering peak of Gunung Kerinci, an active volcano and Sumatra's highest mountain at 3805 metres. Picturesque Danau Kerinci is nestled at the southern end of the valley, and the Sungai Kerinci waters the rich farmland in between.

The valley supports a population of almost 300,000, scattered around 200-odd villages. The main town and transport hub is Sungaipenuh. Culturally, Kerinci has much in common with West Sumatra. The people are strict Muslims and have a similar matrilineal social structure.

More than 100 people were killed when an earthquake measuring seven on the Richter Scale rocked the valley in October 1995. Sungaipenuh suffered little damage. Gungung Kerinci last erupted in 1934.

Things to See & Do

The valley is surrounded by **Kerinci Seblat National Park**, which protects almost 1.5 million hectares of prime equatorial rainforest. It's one of the last strongholds of the **Sumatran tiger** and **Sumatran rhinoceros**. Facilities in the park are poor, and most travellers visit on tours organised in Bukittinggi. If you're planning to visit the park, you'll need to pick up a permit (1500 rp) from the PHPA office (☎ 21692) in Sungaipenuh.

It's a tough two day climb to the summit of **Gunung Kerinci** from the village of **Kersik Tua**, 43 km from Sungaipenuh. There's a camp site at 3000 metres where most climbers spend the night. The route to the top is clearly defined, but it's advisable to take a guide. There are **cave paintings** in the **Kasah Cave** on the lower slopes five km from Kersik Tua.

Stone carvings dotted around the villages south of Danau Kerinci show that the area supported a sizeable settlement in megalithic times. The best known of these stone monuments is the **Batu Gong** (gong stone) in the village of Muak, 25 km from Sungaipenuh. It is thought to have been carved 2000 years ago.

Places to Stay & Eat

There are half a dozen hotels in Sungaipenuh. The best place for travellers is the *Hotel Matahari* (☎ 21061) on Jalan Basuki Rachmat, with clean doubles for 7000 rp. It has a useful map and transport information. The *Hotel Yani* (☎ 21409), at Jalan Muradi 1, has singles/doubles for 11,000/16,500 rp, including breakfast. There's good Padang food at the *Minang Soto* restaurant next door. The *Dendeng Batokok* restaurant, also on

Jalan Muradi, is named after the local speciality – charcoal-grilled strips of smoked beef.

There are a couple of small homestays in Kersik Tua.

Getting There & Away

The closest major city to Sungaipenuh is Padang, a journey of 246 km via the coast road (7500 rp; six hours). There are also frequent buses east to Bangko (4500 rp; four hours) on the Trans-Sumatran Highway.

Getting Around

You can get almost anywhere in the valley from the bus station in Sungaipenuh Market.

PADANG

Few people stay long in Padang, a sprawling, steamy coastal city of 700,000. It is the capital of West Sumatra province, home of the Minangkabau people. No ethnic group in Sumatra maintains its cultural traditions more proudly than the Minangkabau. They are staunch Muslims, yet their society remains matrilineal – the eldest female is the head of the family and property is inherited through the female line. The most obvious sign that you are in Minangkabau country is the spectacular peaked roofs of the houses, shaped like buffalo horns.

Orientation & Information

The city centre is quite compact and easy to negotiate. Most places of importance are within easy striking distance of the main street, Jalan M Yamin, which runs inland from the coast road to the junction with Jalan Azizcham. The bus terminal, the opelet terminal and central market are all on the northern side of Jalan M Yamin, and the post office is on Jalan Azizcham.

There are two helpful tourist offices: the West Sumatran tourist office at Jalan Sudirman 43, and the regional office further north at Jalan Khatib Sulaiman 22 (take an opelet along Jalan Sudirman). Both are open Monday to Thursday from 8 am to 2 pm, Friday to 11 am and Saturday to 12.30 pm.

All the major Indonesian banks are to be found around the city centre. The Bank of

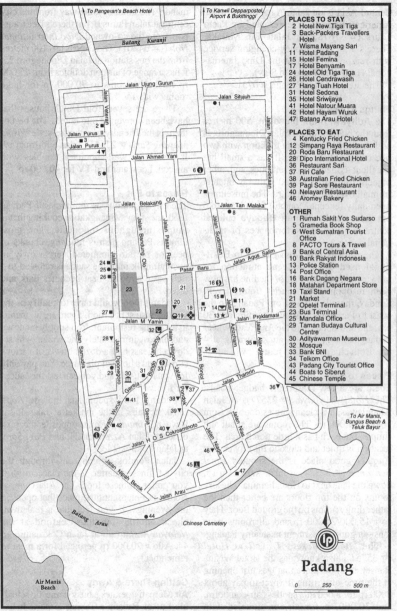

INDONESIA

Padang

0   250   500 m

Central Asia is on Jalan Agus Salim, while American Express is represented by Pacto Tours (☎ 37678) on Jalan Tan Malaka. There's a 24 hour money-changing service with reasonable rates at the Dipo International Hotel (see Places to Stay).

The area code for Padang is 0751.

Things to See & Do

The **Adityawarman Museum**, 500 metres from the bus station on Jalan Diponegoro, is built in the Minangkabau tradition with two rice barns out the front. It has a small but excellent collection of antiques and other objects of historical and cultural interest from all over West Sumatra. The museum is open daily (except Monday) from 8 am to 6 pm. The nearby **Taman Budaya** cultural centre has regular performances of traditional dance.

The **railway line** from Padang to Bukittinggi used to be quite an attraction for railway enthusiasts. Part of the line has now been re-opened for tourist trains. Every Sunday, there is a train from Padang up the coast to Pariaman at 8 am, returning at 2.30 pm, and another train to the Anai Valley, near Padangpanjang, at 8.45 am, returning at 4 pm. Both charge 6000 rp return.

Places to Stay

There are a few reasonable budget hotels. The *Hotel Sriwijaya* (☎ 23577), at Jalan Alanglawas, has clean singles/doubles from 10,000/15,000 rp. The rooms are small and simple, but each has a little porch area. The location is quiet and close to the city centre. Another good place is the spotless *Hotel Benyamin* (☎ 22324) at Jalan Azizcham 15, down the lane next to Hotel Femina. The airy rooms on the top floors are better than the rather dingy rooms on the ground floor. They cost 15,000/24,000 rp and all rooms have fans – a good investment in steamy Padang.

The *Back-Packers Travellers Hotel* (☎ 35751), also known as the Hotel Wisma Ransel, is a new place that was just opening at the time of writing. Expect to pay about 8000 rp for a bed in a spotless air-con dorm, and 30,000 rp for air-con doubles with

mandi. The hotel is some way from the city centre at Jalan Purus II, but there's free transport from the co-owned *Dipo International Hotel* (☎ 34261). The Dipo is just 100 metres from the bus station at Jalan Diponegoro 25. It has a range of air-con doubles from 45,000 rp for basic rooms to 70,000 rp for huge rooms with TV.

There are several old Dutch houses that have been converted into hotels. The best of them is the friendly guesthouse-style *Wisma Mayang Sari* (☎ 22647), Jalan Sudirman 19. It has clean, well-appointed doubles with air-con, hot water and TV for 40,000 rp.

Places to Eat

The city is famous as the home of Padang food, the spicy Minangkabau cooking that is found throughout Indonesia. The most famous Padang dish is *rendang*, chunks of beef or buffalo simmered very slowly in coconut milk until the sauce is reduced to a rich paste and the meat becomes dark and dried.

Padang food would have to qualify as the world's fastest fast food. There are no menus in a Padang restaurant. You simply sit down and almost immediately the waiter will set down at least half a dozen bowls of various curries and a bowl of plain rice. You pay only for what you eat, and you can test the sauces for free.

Padang food specialists include *Roda Baru*, upstairs in the market at Jalan Pasar Raya 6; *Simpang Raya*, opposite the post office at Jalan Azizcham 24; and *Pagi Sore*, at Jalan Pondok 143.

Jalan Pondok, which runs through the city's Chinese quarter, is the place to go if you prefer Chinese food. The *Riri Cafe*, at No 86, is a pleasant little place that opens in the evenings. If you feel like a real treat, check out the fabulous seafood at the *Nelayan Restaurant* at Jalan Cokroaminoto 44. Allow 20,000 rp per head for a meal to remember.

Getting There & Away

Air Merpati operates a busy domestic schedule out of Padang's Tabing airport. It has three flights a day to Jakarta (298,100 rp), daily flights to Batam (151,800 rp) and Medan (172,700) and three a week to Palembang (179,300 rp). Sempati flies twice a day to Jakarta and four times a week to Pekanbaru (72,600 rp). Mandala also has daily flights to Jakarta, while SMAC flies to Gunung Sitoli on Pulau Nias every Wednesday.

Merpati, Pelangi Air and SMAC are all based at the Hotel Natour Muara (☎ 38103), Jalan Gereja 34, while Sempati (☎ 51612) is based at Pangeran's Beach Hotel, Jalan Ir Juanda. Mandala (☎ 32773) is at Jalan Pemuda 29A. Silk Air (☎ 38120) has an office at the Hotel Hayam Waruk.

Bus Padang's bus station is conveniently central. Every north-south bus comes through here, so there are loads of options. There are frequent buses to Bukittinggi (2000 rp; two hours). You can get all the way to Jakarta in 30 hours for 45,000 rp, or 70,000 rp air-con. Fares to Parapat (for Danau Toba) and Medan are the same, ranging from 25,000 rp without air-con, to 45,000 rp for the best services. Other destinations include Bengkulu (18,000 rp), Sibolga (15,000 rp) and Sungaipenuh (7500 rp).

Boat The Pelni ship *Lawit* calls at Padang's port of Teluk Bayur every second Friday en route to Gunung Sitoli (36,500/100,500 rp in ekonomi/1st class). It stops again every second Sunday on the way south to Jakarta (81,500/230,500 rp), Semarang and Pontianak. The Pelni office (☎ 33624) is at Teluk Bayur, but you can buy tickets from the travel agency at the Dipo International Hotel.

Boats to Pulau Siberut leave from the harbour on the Batang Arau, just south of Padang's city centre. See the Mentawai Islands section for more details.

Getting Around
The Airport Padang's Tabing airport is nine km north of the centre on the Bukittinggi road. Airport taxis charge a standard 10,000 rp for the ride into town. The budget alternative is to walk from the airport terminal to the main road and catch any opelet into town

for 300 rp. Heading to the airport, city bus (biskota) 14A is the best one to get.

Local Transport There are numerous opelets and mikrolets around town, operating out of the Pasar Raya terminal off Jalan M Yamin. The standard fare is 300 rp. There's a taxi stand beside the market building on the corner of Jalan M Yamin.

AROUND PADANG
Air Manis
The fishing village of Air Manis is four km from Padang, just south of the Muara River. You can get there by opelet, but a more interesting route is to take a perahu across the river from where the boats to Siberut leave. There's a Chinese cemetery which overlooks the town, and then it's a one km walk to Air Manis. According to local mythology, the rock at the end of the beach is the remains of Malin Kundang (a man who was turned into stone when he rejected his mother after making a fortune) and his boat. There are opelets from Air Manis back to Padang for 500 rp.

Beaches
There are some good beaches on the coast around Padang. **Pantai Bungus**, 22 km south of Padang, remains a popular spot despite the huge plywood mill that dominates the northern end. The southern end is palm-fringed and postcard-pretty. *Losmen Carlos* (☎ (0751) 30353) is a laid-back place to hang out for a few days. It has basic singles/doubles for 6000/10,000 rp, and rooms with mandi for 10,000/15,000 rp. Carlos organises snorkelling trips to nearby islands and has information on other local attractions. There are regular opelets from Padang for 700 rp.

Pasir Jambak, 15 km north of town, is the best of several beaches north of Padang. You can stay at *Uncle Jack's Homestay* for 12,500 rp with meals. Jack can organise snorkelling trips to nearby Pulau Sawo. Opelet No 423 will get you to Pasir Jambak for 500 rp.

INDONESIA

MENTAWAI ISLANDS

The Mentawais are a remote chain of islands about 100 km west of Padang. The largest island, Siberut, is home to most of the Mentawais' population of 30,000. The other islands – Sipora, Pagai Utara and Pagai Selatan – are sparsely populated and seldom visited.

After being left quietly on their own for thousands of years, change is coming at an alarming rate. Trekking has become big business on Siberut, with a steady stream of travellers heading out into the jungles to catch a glimpse of a primitive culture that is fast disappearing. The villagers, their bodies covered with ritual tattoos and wearing little but loin clothes and decorative bands and rings, are a photogenic lot who have found tour groups to be a good source of income. Tourism is, however, but a minor development alongside logging and transmigration.

The islands have some unusual endemic wildlife, including the *siamang kerdil* (dwarf black gibbon). Chloroquine-resistant malaria is a problem.

Information

Siberut's port of Muarasiberut is the only town of any consequence. It has shops where you can stock up on provisions, as well as the only losmen, *Syahruddin's Home Stay*. There's also a post office and a wartel office.

If you're planning on organising your own way around the islands, you can hire guides in Muarasiberut. The tourist offices in Padang have more information about the islands. Permits for the islands are issued on landing in Muarasiberut and cost 2000 rp.

Organised Tours

Most travellers take the easy option of joining an organised tour. It is also the cheap option in view of the costs involved in chartering boats on your own. The best place to shop for tours is Bukittinggi, where they are promoted in every coffee shop, losmen and travel agency. You can pay anything from US$150 to US$700 for a 10 day tour, depending on the level of comfort. Seven-day tours (US$125) are also available, but

are not good value given that they involve three days in transit.

Tour prices include guide service and accommodation (in village huts), food (usually prepared by the guide), local transport and transport to and from the island.

May is supposedly the driest month and theoretically a good time to go, but you can expect heavy rain at any time of the year. The treks usually include plenty of mud slogging, river crossings and battles with indigenous insects, so it's definitely not a casual hiking experience. Tours are often cancelled in June and July when the seas are too rough for safe sailing.

Getting There & Away

There are boats to Muarasiberut from Padang's Muara River harbour four times a week. PT Rusco Lines (☎ 21941), Jalan Batang Arau 31, has boats from Padang on Monday and Wednesday, returning on Tuesday and Thursday. The fares are 11,000/16,000 rp for deck/cabin class. The PT Rusco office is to the right through the alleyway next to Elia English Course, opposite the port gates. Mentawai Indah (☎ 28200), Jalan Batang Arau 88, has boats from Padang on Thursday and Saturday, returning on Friday and Sunday. All boats leave at 8 pm and the journey takes 10 to 12 hours.

PADANG TO BUKITTINGGI

There's some magnificent scenery on the 90 km trip from Padang to the hill town of Bukittinggi, thanks to a combination of rich volcanic soil and ample rainfall. The road climbs through vast patchworks of rice paddy and pockets of lush tropical rainforest. Looming in the background are the peaks of the Merapi and Singgalang volcanoes – each over 3000 metres.

Along the way is the **Lembah Anai Nature Reserve**, notable for its waterfalls, orchids and giant rafflesia flowers. The main town along the way is **Padangpanjang**, 19 km from Bukittinggi. It has a conservatorium of Minangkabau culture and a good Monday market. A road leads south-east from Padangpanjang to **Danau Singkarak**, bigger than Danau Maninjau but still un-discovered by tourists.

BUKITTINGGI

This cool, easy-going mountain town is one of the most popular travellers' centres in Sumatra. It's easy to spend a week here checking out the town and surrounding attractions. Lying 930 metres above sea level, it can get quite cold at night. South of town lie three majestic mountains – Merapi, Singgalang and the more distant Sago.

Bukittinggi was a Dutch stronghold during the Padri Wars (1821-37), and it was here that Sumatran rebels declared their rival government in 1958. Today it is a centre for Minangkabau culture, as well as being a busy market town with a small university. The town is sometimes referred to as Kota Jam Gadang (Big Clock Town), after its best known landmark, the Minangkabau-style clock tower that overlooks the large market square.

Orientation

The town centre is conveniently compact. Most of the cheap hotels, restaurants and travel agencies are at the northern (bottom) end of the main street, Jalan Ahmad Yani. The clock tower and markets are at the top end. Jalan Sudirman runs south from the clock tower to the post office and bus station.

The area code for Bukittinggi is 0752.

Information

Tourist Office The tourist office is beside the market car park, overlooked by the clock tower. The staff are friendly and helpful, although they don't have much other than the standard leaflets and brochures. It's open Monday to Thursday from 8 am to 2 pm, Friday to 11 am and Saturday to 12.30 pm.

Money The BNI bank, next to the overhead bridge on Jalan Ahmad Yani, is the best place. You can also change money at Bank Rakyat Indonesia, near the clock tower. After hours, you can change money at places like Toko Eka, on Jalan Minangkabau, in the market.

Things to See & Do

Bukittinggi's large and colourful **market** is crammed with stalls of fruit and vegetables, clothing and handicrafts. Market days are Wednesday and Saturday.

Apart from the defensive moat and a few rusting cannons, not much remains of Bukittinggi's old **Fort de Kock**, built during the Padri Wars by the Dutch. It does, however, provide fine views over the town and surrounding countryside from its hilltop position.

A footbridge leads from the fort over Jalan Ahmad Yani to Taman Bundokandung, site of the museum and zoo. The **museum** is a fine example of Minangkabau architecture with its two rice barns at the front. It has a good collection of Minangkabau historical and cultural exhibits. The **zoo** is reportedly a disgrace.

Panorama Park, on the southern edge of the town, overlooks the deep **Sianok Canyon**. Inside the park is an extensive grid of **caves** built by the Japanese during WWII using slave labour.

Organised Tours

Almost every hotel, coffee shop and travel agency offers tours of the district. They range from trips to the bullfighting and full-day tours of the area's attractions to activity tours like mountain climbing and pig hunting.

Places to Stay

Bukittinggi's budget hotels are a pretty charmless lot, but they're certainly cheap. Most are close together at the bottom of Jalan Ahmad Yani. The friendly *Bamboo Homestay* has dorm beds for 4000 rp and doubles with shared mandi for 8000 rp. You will have no trouble finding doubles with shared mandi for 7000 rp at places like *Murni*, the decrepit-looking *Rajawali* and the *Wisma Tiga Balai*. The *Singgalang Hotel* (☎ 21576), next to the BNI bank, is a popular place with doubles for 8000 rp.

Many travellers head for the relative seclusion of the *Hotel Tropic* (☎ 23207), a quiet place down the steps on Jalan Pemuda. Singles/doubles are 8000/10,000 rp with

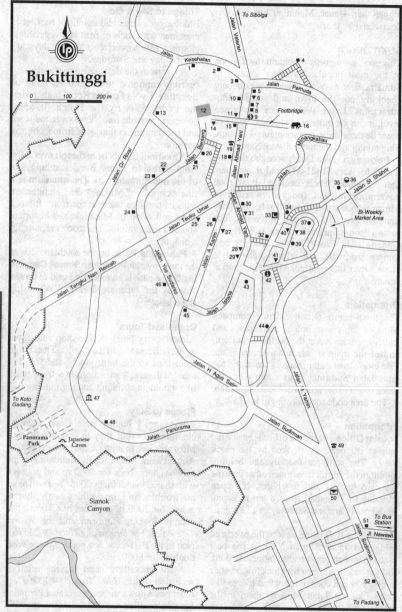

Bukittinggi

0   100   200 m

shared mandi, 9000/12,000 rp with your own. The *Merdeka Homestay* (☎ 21253), at the corner of Jalan Dr Rivai and Jalan Yos Sudarso, is a solid old Dutch house with large singles/doubles for 10,000/12,500 rp.

There are several good places on the road to Fort de Kock. The quiet *Suwarni Guesthouse* occupies another old Dutch house and has doubles for 10,000 rp. The nearby *Wisma Bukittinggi* has a wide choice of rooms from small singles for 6000 rp to large doubles with a view of Gunung Singgalang for 15,000 rp.

The comfortable *Benteng Hotel* (☎ 21115), close to the fort, has singles/doubles from 40,000/45,000 rp. All rooms have baths, hot water and TV.

Places to Eat

The restaurants among the cheap hotels on Jalan Ahmad Yani feature all the favourite travellers' fare. There are half a dozen different ways to have your breakfast egg as well as various pancakes, muesli, fruit salad and buffalo yoghurt.

The most popular places to hang out are the *Three Tables Coffee House* and the *Rendezvous Coffee Shop* at the bottom end of the street. Both are also good places to pick up information, although you'll have to deal with all the guides who stop by to offer their services. The Rendezvous also has a Home Country Direct phone. The pace is a bit slower at the quiet *Canyon Coffee Shop* on Jalan Teuku Umar.

Many travellers reckon the best food in town is to be found at the *Restaurant Sari*, near the fort on Jalan Benteng. The menu is predominantly Chinese, with a good selection of juices. Other places to eat Chinese are the *Selecta* at Jalan Ahmad Yani 3, and the long-running *Mona Lisa*, down the street at No 58.

Naturally enough, Padang food is plentiful. The best places are around the market. The *Roda Group* and *Simpang Raya* are big names in the nasi padang business with branches all over Sumatra. Each has two branches in the market. The Simpang Raya also has menus, unusual in Padang restaurants.

A number of places, including the western-oriented coffee houses, serve the local speciality, dadiah campur, a tasty mixture of oats, coconut, fruit, molasses and buffalo yoghurt.

INDONESIA

PLACES TO STAY		**52**	Hotel Bagindo		**16**	Museum &
1	Hotel Denai					Zoo
2	Marmy Hotel		**PLACES TO EAT**		18	Mitra Wisata
3	Sri Kandi Hotel	6	Three Tables &			Tours & Travel
4	Hotel Tropic		Rendezvous		19	Wartel
5	Rajawali Hotel		Coffee Shops		32	Toko Eka
7	Bamboo Homestay	11	The Cool Cave		33	Mosque
8	Singgalang Hotel	14	Family Restaurant		34	Gloria Cinema
10	Hotels Murni	22	Restaurant Sari		35	Pasar Bawah
	& Nirwana	25	Canyon Coffee Shop		36	Opelet Station
13	Merdeka Homestay	27	ASEAN Restaurant		37	Pasar Wisata
15	Hotel Yany	28	Selecta Restaurant		39	Pasar Atas
17	Wisma Tiga Balai	29	KFC		42	Tourist Office
20	Benteng Hotel	31	Mona Lisa Restaurant			& Small Post
21	Suwarni Guesthouse	38	Roda Group			Office
23	Mountain View		Restaurant		43	Clock Tower
	Guesthouse	40	Simpang Raya		44	Medan Nan
24	Wisma Bukittinggi		Restaurant			Baliduang
26	Hotel Surya	41	Simpang Raya			(Dance
30	Gangga Hotel		Restaurant			Performances)
45	Novotel Bukittinggi				47	Military Museum
46	Hotel Sari		**OTHER**		49	Telkom Office
48	Minang Hotel	9	BNI Bank		50	Post Office
51	Dymen's Hotel	12	Fort de Kock			

Entertainment

There are performances of Minangkabau dance/theatre every night in a hall on the road linking Jalan Sudirman and Jalan M Yamin. The shows start at 8.30 pm and cost 7500 rp.

Things to Buy

There are several interesting antique shops and craft shops in the market streets near the clock tower.

Getting There & Away

The Aur Kuning bus station is about two km south of the town centre, but easily reached by opelet. There are heaps of buses south to Padang (2000 rp; two hours), as well as frequent services east to Pekanbaru (7000 rp; five hours).

All buses travelling the Trans-Sumatran Highway stop at Bukittinggi. Heading south, you can catch a bus right through to Jakarta for 35,000 rp, or 60,000 rp air-con. There are a few buses to Bengkulu, Jambi and Palembang, but most services leave from Padang.

The road north to Sibolga and Parapat is twisting and narrow for much of the way. Regular buses take about 11 hours to Sibolga (12,000 rp), 18 hours to Parapat (23,000 rp) and 22 hours through to Medan (25,000 rp). The express air-con buses cut hours off the journey to Parapat by bypassing Sibolga. They cost about 10,000 rp more. The tourist office has a list of bus companies and ticket prices. Ticket prices vary quite a lot between travel agencies, so shop around. You can also buy tickets at the bus station.

Tourist buses leave for Parapat every morning at 7.30 am and cost 27,000 rp. Tickets can be booked at a number of places in town. The bus picks up from some hotels and travel agencies that sell tickets. The buses stop just outside Bonjol at the equator, site of a tacky monument and several stalls selling 'I Crossed The Equator' T-shirts and other souvenirs.

If you're arriving in Bukittinggi from the north (Parapat) or east (Pekanbaru), get off the bus near the town centre to save the hassle of an opelet ride back from the bus station.

Getting Around

Opelets around Bukittinggi cost 250 rp for three wheelers or 300 rp for the four wheel variety. The four wheelers run to the bus station. A *bendi* (horsecart) costs from 1500 rp depending on the distance.

AROUND BUKITTINGGI

The village of **Koto Gadang**, known for its silverwork, is an hour's walk south-east of Bukittinggi through the Sianok Canyon. Turn left at the bottom of the road just before the canyon and keep going – *don't* cross the bridge.

The 1500-metre-long cave at **Ngalau Kamanga**, 15 km north-east of Bukittinggi, was used as a base for guerrilla attacks against the Dutch in the late 19th and early 20th centuries. The cave is dripping with stalactites and stalagmites and has a small, clear lake.

The bustling small town of **Batu Sangkar**, 41 km south-east of Bukittinggi, lies at the heart of traditional Minangkabau country. The massive **Rumah Gadang Payarugung** at the small village of Silinduang Bulan, five km north of Batu Sangkar, is a smaller replica of the original palace of the area's rulers. The original adorns Indonesia's 100 rp coin.

There are plenty of more modest examples of traditional architecture in the surrounding villages, particularly at **Belimbing**, 10 km south of Batu Sangkar.

There is a **rafflesia sanctuary** about 16 km north of Bukittinggi near the village of Palupuh. A sign in the village indicates the path to the sanctuary. The rafflesia normally blooms between August and November. The tourist office in Bukittinggi can tell you if there are blooms around.

DANAU MANINJAU

Maninjau, 38 km west of Bukittinggi, is another of Sumatra's beautiful mountain crater lakes. The final descent to the lake on the road from Bukittinggi is unforgettable. The road twists and turns through 44 numbered hairpin bends in quick succession, and offers stunning views over the shimmering blue lake and surrounding hills. At 500 metres above sea level, the air is pleasantly cool. The lake is 17 km long, eight km wide and 480 metres deep in places. The place is well set up for travellers, but remains relatively unspoiled.

Orientation & Information
The only village of any size is also called Maninjau. Most people arrive from Bukittinggi, and the bus stop is at the crossroads where the Bukittinggi road meets the main street. The post office and telephone office are nearby. The Bank Rakyat Indonesia will change US dollars only – either cash or travellers' cheques.

The area code for Maninjau is 0752.

Things to See & Do
Hanging out by the lake is the reason most people come to Maninjau. The waters are considerably warmer – and cleaner – than at Lake Toba, so it's a good place for swimming. Some of the guesthouses hire/lend dugout canoes or inflated truck inner tubes.

Many people cannot resist the lure of the road that circles the lake. It's a solid six hours by bicycle or 2½ hours by motorbike – both of which can be rented in Maninjau. The road is fairly flat, but almost three-quarters of the 70 km is on unsealed road. There are also some good walks. Fit people only should attempt the strenuous three hour hike from the lake to **Sakura Hill** and **Lawang Top**, which have excellent views of the lake and the surrounding area. It's much easier to do this hike in reverse, catching a Bukittinggi-bound bus as far as **Matur** and climbing Lawang Top from there before walking down to the lake.

Places to Stay & Eat
There are more than 20 guesthouses to choose from as well as a couple of upmarket hotels. Most guesthouses operate their own restaurants.

There are a several places to stay in the village. The spotless *Pillie Homestay* (☎ 61048), 200 metres from the bus stop, charges 6000/10,000 rp for singles/doubles. The nearby *Amai Cheap* (☎ 61054) is a bizarre old Dutch colonial house with a huge balcony and rooms from 5000 to 7000 rp.

Most of the guesthouses are by the lakeside north of the village. The *Riak Danau*, *Feby's* and the *Beach Guesthouse* are three popular places right by the lake after about 500 metres. They all have singles/doubles for 5000/8000 rp.

New places are springing up all the time. If you want to rest up in a bit more style, the *Hotel Tandirih* (☎ 61253) has comfortable modern rooms with hot water and TV for 50,000 rp. The flashest place is the *Hotel Pasir Panjang Permai* (☎ 61022), which has doubles from 75,000 rp.

The long-running *Three Tables Coffee House* in Maninjau village has Padang food as well as travellers' fare. *Café 44* is a restaurant and party spot on the lakeside, reached down a path next to the Panururan Homestay about 600 metres north of the village.

Entertainment
If you want to be entertained while you eat, check out the *Maninjau View Coffee House* 500 metres north of the village, where you'll find regular cultural shows in the evenings. The 5000 rp entry fee includes a snack and a drink. The restaurant at the nearby *Alam Maninjau Guest House* has displays of Minangkabau dance on Friday nights.

Getting There & Away
There are buses between Maninjau and Bukittinggi every hour for 1000 rp. The journey takes almost an hour. There are two direct buses a day to Padang (3500 rp; 2½ hours) which go via the coast.

Getting Around
There are several places renting mountain bikes for about 6000 rp a day, and motorbikes for 25,000 rp.

PEKANBARU
Before American engineers struck oil in the area shortly before WWII, Pekanbaru was little more than a sleepy river port on the Sungai Siak river. Today, it is Indonesia's oil capital, a bustling modern city of more than

500,000 people. There's little reason for travellers to stop here, and most treat it as no more than an overnight stop on the route between Singapore and Bukittinggi.

Orientation & Information

The main street of Pekanbaru is Jalan Sudirman. Almost everything of importance to travellers – banks, hotels and offices – can be found here or close by. Speedboats leave from the wharf at the end of Jalan Sudirman, while the bus station is at the other end of town on Jalan Nangka, off Jalan Sudirman.

The tourist office (☎ 31562) is a long way from the city centre at Jalan Merbabu 16. The Bank of Central Asia, at Jalan Sudirman 448, is the best place to change money.

The area code for Pekanbaru is 0761.

Things to See & Do

Few people hang around Pekanbaru for long enough to do anything other than buy a ticket out. Not a bad idea, really, but if you've got time to burn there's always the **Museum Negeri Riau** and the neighbouring **Riau Cultural Park** towards the airport on Jalan Sudirman. They are open from 8 am until 2 pm Sunday to Thursday, 8 am until 11 pm on Friday. The **Balai Adat Daerah Riau**, on Jalan Diponegoro, has displays of traditional Malay culture and is open the same hours.

Places to Stay & Eat

Most people head straight to *Poppie's Homestay* (☎ 33863), an excellent place a few minutes walk from the bus station on Jalan Cempedak II. There are doubles for 10,000 rp and dorm beds for 3500 rp, and a small restaurant serving basic meals. The owner speaks good English and can arrange boat tickets to Batam. To get there from the bus station, cross Jalan Nangka and head up Jalan Taskurun. Take the second street on the left (Jalan Kuini), and Jalan Cempedak II is the first street on the right. If you are coming from the port, phone for a free pick-up.

The alternative is *Tommy's Place*, 400 metres from the bus station on Gang Nantongga, next to Jalan Nangka 53. Tommy charges 4000 rp per person and can also arrange tickets for the Batam boats. From the bus station, turn right and Gang Nantongga is the second gang on the right side, opposite the Bank Buana. Walk down and ask for Tommy's, which is tucked away on the right after about 50 metres.

The *Hotel Anom* (☎ 30863), on the corner of Jalan Sudirman and Jalan Gatot Subrato, has reasonable rooms set around a courtyard. Air-con doubles with mandi start at 35,000 rp.

There are innumerable cheap places to eat along Jalan Sudirman, particularly in the evening around the market at the junction with Jalan Imam Bonjol. The *New Holland Bakery*, at Jalan Sudirman 153, has a fine selection of cakes and pastries as well as hamburgers and ice cream. It also does fresh fruit juices.

Getting There & Away

Air Simpang Tiga is one of the busiest airports in Sumatra. It is also a visa-free entry point. Pelangi Air and Sempati both fly to Kuala Lumpur for US$107; Pelangi also flies to Melaka for US$60. Merpati and Silk Air fly to Singapore for US$102.

Merpati also has direct flights to Jakarta, Batam, Medan and Pangkalpinang. Kota Piring Kencana Travel (☎ 21382), Jalan Sisingamangaraja 3, is a good place to buy tickets.

Bus Bukittinggi is the main destination and there are frequent departures from the bus station on Jalan Nangka. The 240 km trip takes about five hours and tickets cost from 7000 rp.

Boat Agencies all around town sell tickets for the boats to Batam. It's possible to go all the way by boat, leaving from the port at the end of Jalan Sudirman, but most tickets involve a combination of bus and ferry. There is not a lot of difference between the speedboat services, though the prices vary from around 35,000 to 37,500 rp. The journey takes about nine hours, reaching Batam at about 5 pm – just in time to catch a ferry to Singapore.

Getting Around

Airport cabs charge 10,000 rp for the 12 km trip into town. It's a one km walk to the main road if you want to catch an opelet (300 rp) into town.

DUMAI

Most of Pekanbaru's oil exits through the port of Dumai, 158 km to the north. Unless you're a fan of oil loading facilities, there's no point in coming here. It is, however, a visa-free entry point with ferry links to the Malaysian port of Melaka. The ferries leave Dumai (105,500 rp) on Thursday and Sunday, and Melaka (RM120) on Monday and Friday.

SIBOLGA

It's hard to find a traveller with a good word to say about Sibolga, a drab little port about 10 hours north of Bukittinggi. It's the departure point for boats to Nias, which is the only reason people come here.

Orientation & Information

There are two harbours, and the town centre lies midway between the two. Boats to Nias leave from the harbour at the end of Jalan Horas. You can change money at the BNI bank at the beach end of Jalan Katamso.

Bangun, who runs the small tourist information service (☎ 21734) at Jalan Horas 78, specialises in dealing with westerners who want to spend as little time in town as possible. He sells tickets for the tourist minibuses and for the boats to Nias, and takes travellers to the boats.

The area code for Sibolga is 0631.

Places to Stay & Eat

If you need to stay the night, you'll be doing yourself a favour by avoiding the budget hotels in the town centre. They are generally dirty and/or unfriendly. The better cheapies are along Jalan Horas near the port. Both the *Hotel Karya Samudra*, at No 134, and *Losmen Bando Kanduang* have rooms for 5000 rp.

The best place to head is the *Hotel Pasar Baru* (☎ 22167), a clean place on the corner

of Jalans Imam Bonjol and Raja Junjungan. It charges 6000 rp per person for rooms with fan, and 30,000 rp for air-con doubles. There's Chinese food at the restaurant downstairs. The *Ikan Bakar Siang Malam*, near the BNI bank at Jalan Katamso 45, serves delicious grilled fish for lunch and dinner – just as the name suggests. Reckon on about 6500 rp per head, including rice and vegetables.

Getting There & Away

Bus Sibolga is a bit of a backwater as far as bus services are concerned. The express buses that travel the Trans-Sumatran Highway bypass Sibolga by taking a shortcut inland between the towns of Taratung and Padangsidempuan. There are still plenty of buses, but the going is painfully slow. Typical fares and journey times from Sibolga are: Bukittinggi (12,000 rp; 12 hours); Medan (11,000 rp; 11 hours); and Parapat (7000 rp; six hours).

All this makes the door-to-door tourist minibuses an attractive option. There are six a day to Medan (15,000 rp; nine hours), via Parapat (12,500 rp; five hours). There are also daily minibuses to Bukittinggi (20,000 rp) and Padang (25,000 rp).

Boat Ferries to Nias leave from the harbour at the end of Jalan Horas. There are boats to both Gunung Sitoli and Teluk Dalam at 8 pm every night except Sunday. The fares are 9700/19,700 rp for deck/cabin class to Gunung Sitoli, and 12,500/17,500 rp to Teluk Dalam.

The Pelni boat *Lawit* travels from Gunung Sitoli to Sibolga every second Saturday, and continues to Padang and Jakarta.

Getting Around

Tales of woe about rip-offs by becak drivers are a dime a dozen, and surfers weighed down with bags and boards are the favourite targets. It is essential to agree on the fare and destination before you start – and bargain hard. Becaks theoretically cost about 1500 rp for most distances in town.

INDONESIA

NIAS ISLAND

Nias is an island almost the size of Bali 125 km off the west coast of Sumatra. Magnificent beaches and a legendary surfing break combine with an ancient megalithic culture and unique customs to make it one of Sumatra's most exotic destinations.

It still takes quite an effort to get to Nias, but it's no longer off the beaten track. Lagundri Bay is now part of the world professional surfing circuit, and there's talk of more resorts to follow in the footsteps of the swank Sorake Beach Resort.

Chloroquine-resistant malaria has been reported on Nias so take appropriate precautions.

Orientation & Information

Gunung Sitoli, in the north, is the island's biggest town. The only airport is nearby. There is a small tourist information office (☎ 21545) at Jalan Soekarno 6.

Most of the interesting places are in the south and that's where most travellers head. Teluk Dalam is the port and main town of the south, but there no reason to linger any longer than it takes to organise transport to Lagundri, 13 km away.

Changing money is no longer the hassle it once was. Branches of the BPDSU bank in Gunung Sitoli and Teluk Dalam both offer respectable rates for US dollars, cash and travellers' cheques.

Area codes are 0639 for Gunung Sitoli, and 0630 for Teluk Dalam and Lagundri.

Things to See & Do

The perfect horseshoe bay at **Lagundri** is the reason most people come to Nias. The surf break is at the mouth of the bay off **Sorake Beach**. It stages a leg of the World Qualifying Series in June/July, when some of the best young talent in the southern hemisphere is on display. The surf is at its best from June to October. For the rest of the year, the waves are perfect for beginners. Boards can be hired from the Nias Surf Club for 5000 rp per day. There is good swimming at the back of the bay on **Lagundri Beach**.

Lagundri is also a good base for visits to the traditional villages of the south. **Bawomataluo**, perched on a hill about 400 metres above sea level, is the most famous of them. Unfortunately, the place is on every tourist itinerary and villagers have learned to view foreigners as money jars waiting to be emptied. The houses are arranged along two main stone-paved avenues which meet opposite the impressive chief's house, thought to be the oldest and largest on Nias. Outside the houses are *daro daro*, stone seats for the spirits of the dead. The village is the setting for the **lompat batu** (stone jumping) featured on Indonesia's 1000 rp note. Bawomataluo can be reached by public bus from Teluk Dalam (1500 rp).

The villages of **Botohili** and **Hilimaeta** are both within easy walking distance of Lagundri. In the middle of Hilimaeta stands a two-metre-high stone penis.

Local legend has it that all Niassans are descended from six gods who came to earth around **Gomo** in the central southern highlands. Menhirs (standing stones) and stone carvings show that Gomo was an important site in megalithic times. The most spectacular examples are at **Tundrumbaho**, five km from Gomo. Getting there is hard work. There's no public transport, and the 'road' ends at Gomo. The last leg to Tundrumbaho involves a tough five km uphill slog through the steamy jungle.

There are easier places to visit, including the much photographed cluster of statues at **Olayama**, 50 km from Gunung Sitoli on the way to Teluk Dalam. The statues are just 300 metres from the road and are clearly signposted.

Gunung Sitoli is deadly dull, but there are some fine examples of northern Niassan architecture at the nearby villages of **Sihireo Siwahili** and **Tumori**. Sihireo Siwahili is smaller but easier to get to. Opelets from Gunung Sitoli to Hilidu can drop you at the turn-off (500 rp), leaving a walk of about 200 metres.

Places to Stay & Eat

Gunung Sitoli Most travellers head for the *Wisma Soliga* (☎ 21815), four km south of town. It's clean, spacious and has a good restaurant that specialises in seafood. It has a choice of rooms ranging from doubles with mandi and fan for 15,000 rp to air-con doubles for 35,000 rp. The manager can organise tickets and transport.

The hotels in town are nothing to get excited about. The *Hotel Wisata* (☎ 21858), opposite the parade ground, has doubles with fan for 12,500 rp, and air-con doubles with mandi for 27,500 rp. The nearby *Hotel Gomo* (☎ 21926), with its corrugated-iron model of a northern Niassan house on the roof, has doubles with mandi and fan for 15,000 rp and

air-con doubles from 30,000 rp. There are lots of small restaurants along the main streets. The *Bintang Terang* turns out a decent serve of fried noodles for 3000 rp, while the *Nasional* is the pick of the nasi padang places. Both are on Jalan Sirao.

Lagundri The bay is ringed by dozens of places to stay. You can take your pick of everything from basic palm-thatch huts to resort-style luxury.

Every form of accommodation comes with its own restaurant. Some losmen offer ridiculously cheap lodging (1000 rp a night)

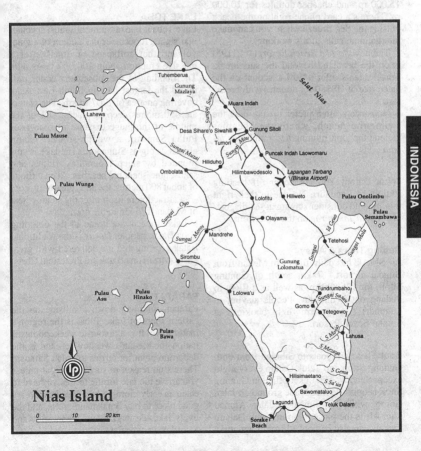

INDONESIA

Nias Island

0   10   20 km

just to get customers for their restaurants. Owners get very peeved if people eat elsewhere. It's worth paying a bit more to be a free agent. It's also worth paying a bit more for the extra security – petty theft is a growing problem.

The most popular cheapies are those closest to the surf break, such as *Olayama* and *Sun Beach*. The *Damai*, tucked around the corner to the west of the headland, offers comparative seclusion.

The *Sea Breeze* (☎ 21224), close to the judging tower, is a bit more upmarket. It has decent doubles with mandi and fan for 15,000 rp, and cheaper doubles for 10,000 rp. There's a card phone right on the beach outside the Sea Breeze where you can make international calls (if it's working).

The new *Sorake Beach Resort* (☎ 21195) is on the headland beyond the surf break. Travel agents offer a 50% discount on the listed rate of US$80 for doubles with breakfast.

Nonsurfers often prefer to stay near the swimming beach, where the cheapies include the long-running *Risky* and *Magdalena*.

Teluk Dalam You are better off heading straight to Lagundri. No one in their right mind would consider staying at the disgusting *Wisma Jamburae* on the waterfront.

Getting There & Away
Air SMAC has daily flights to Medan from Binaka airport, 17 km south of Gunung Sitoli, for 125,800 rp, as well as a flight to Padang on Wednesday. People staying in Lagundri can confirm flight bookings at Sorake Beach Resort.

Boat There are boats to Sibolga from both Gunung Sitoli and Teluk Dalam every night except Sunday. The ticket office in Gunung Sitoli is opposite the parade ground on Jalan Gomo, while PT Simeuleu, Jalan Ahmad Yani 41, is the place to go in Teluk Dalam. Tickets can also be booked from Lagundri.

Getting Around
The Airport SMAC operates a minibus between Binaka airport and Gunung Sitoli for 3000 rp.

Gunung Sitoli to Teluk Dalam There are regular buses between Gunung Sitoli and Teluk Dalam. The fare is 7500 rp and the journey takes about four hours. The buses can drop you at the turn-off to Lagundri.

Teluk Dalam to Lagundri Lagundri is about 12 km from Teluk Dalam: 1500 rp by truck or bemo or 2500 rp by motorbike.

LAKE TOBA
Lake Toba is one of Sumatra's most spectacular sights. It occupies the caldera of a giant volcano that collapsed on itself after a massive eruption about 100,000 years ago. The flooding of the subsequent crater produced the largest lake in South-East Asia, covering an area of 1707 sq km. The waters are 450 metres deep in places. Out of the middle of this huge expanse of blue rises Pulau Samosir, a wedge-shaped island almost as big as Singapore. The lake is surrounded by steep mountains, ridges and sandy, pine-sheltered beaches. At an altitude of about 800 metres, the air is pleasantly cool – an attraction in itself after the steamy heat of Medan, 176 km to the north.

Lake Toba is the home of the outgoing Toba Batak people. *Horas* is the traditional Batak greeting and it's delivered with great gusto. Most Toba Batak are Protestant Christians.

PARAPAT
Parapat, tumbling down a hillside on the eastern shore of Lake Toba, is the region's major town. It is a favourite weekend destination for Medan's wealthy set, and is the departure point for ferries to Pulau Samosir. There's no reason to stay in Parapat unless you arrive too late for the ferries, or have to catch an early morning bus. It is, however, a good place to buy Batak handicrafts, and the lively lakeside markets on Wednesday and Saturday are worth a visit.

Orientation & Information

Parapat is divided into two parts. The first part you'll encounter is the cluster of restaurants and shops on the Trans-Sumatran Highway, known as Jalan Sisingamangaraja through town. The town centre is down by the lakeside marketplace, known as Tiga Raja, about 1.5 km away. The two are linked by Jalan Pulau Samosir, which becomes Jalan Haranggaol for the final stretch down to the lake. There is a small tourist office on Jalan Pulau Samosir near the highway.

You can change money at the BNI bank on the highway or at Sejahtera Bank Umum,

next door to the Toba Hotel on Jalan Pulau Samosir. Rates are poor for currencies other than US dollars, but better than you'll find on Samosir.

The area code for Parapat is 0625.

Places to Stay

There are dozens of places to stay scattered around the hillside between the highway and the lake. Most are mid-range hotels catering for visitors from Medan.

Travel agent *Andilo Nancy* has singles/doubles for 5000/7500 rp above its office by the ferry dock, and more rooms next to its

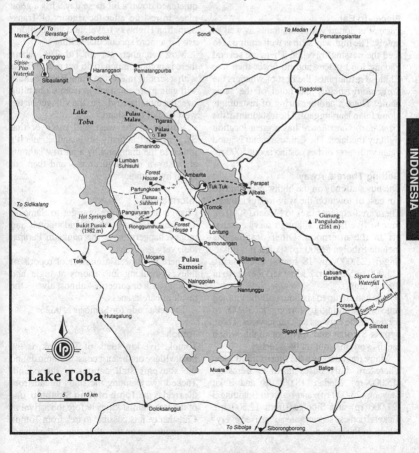

Lake Toba

0   5   10 km

INDONESIA

office at the bus station. There are several places on Jalan Haranggaol just uphill from the market. The *Penginapan Melati* (☎ 21174), at No 37, has clean singles/doubles for 7500/10,000 rp. You'll find similar prices at the *Pago Pago Inn*, at No 50, but the rooms are not as flash as the smart bamboo lobby.

Wisma Gurning is a simple, friendly place right by the lakeside with doubles for 10,000 rp. It's on the street to the left of the ferry dock as you face the lake. The *Trogadero Guesthouse* (☎ 41148), Jalan Harrangaol 112, is a step up from these with small bungalows for 15,000 rp.

Places to Eat
Parapat is dotted with restaurants as well as hotels. The highway strip is well equipped to feed the passing traveller. There are several Padang food places and no fewer than five Chinese restaurants, the best of which is the *Singgalang*, below the hotel of the same name. There's another string of restaurants along Jalan Harranggaol. The restaurant at the *Trogadero Guesthouse* has a great location right by the lake. The Chinese menu is good value with most dishes costing about 5000 rp.

Getting There & Away
The bus station is on the highway about two km east of town on the way to Bukittinggi. There are frequent buses to Medan (4000 rp; four to five hours), although services taper off in the afternoon. Other destinations include Sibolga (7000 rp; six hours), Bukittinggi (23,000 rp; 18 hours) and Padang (25,000 rp; 20 hours). Most services leave in the morning.

You can cut up to six hours off the journey time to Bukittinggi by forking out 30,000 rp for one of the express air-con services. These bypass Sibolga and travel at night, which means you miss out on the scenery.

Many travellers use the tourist minibuses. There are daily buses north to Berastagi (15,000 rp), Medan (18,000 rp) and Bukit Lawang (23,000 rp), and south to Bukittinggi (27,000 rp) and Sibolga (from 12,500 rp). Tickets for these services are advertised everywhere in Parapat and on Samosir.

Getting to Berastagi by public bus is a real hassle. It involves changing buses at Pematangsiantar and Kabanjahe, and can take up to six hours.

Getting Around
Opelets shuttle constantly between the ferry dock and the bus station (250 rp).

PULAU SAMOSIR
Samosir has long been Sumatra's premier attraction for foreign travellers, although it acquired a bad reputation for hustling in the late 1980s and early 1990s. Things have quietened down a bit these days. It's a good place to rest up after the rigours of Trans-Sumatran Highway travel, and you couldn't ask for a more spectacular setting.

Most foreigners stay in Tuk Tuk, where there is nothing much to do but relax. Those with a serious interest in Toba Batak culture will gain more satisfaction from scrambling over the mountain ridge to the villages on the west side of the island.

Visitors to the west will discover that Samosir isn't actually an island at all. It's linked to the mainland by a narrow isthmus at the town of Pangururan – and then cut again by a canal.

Information
Change money before you get to Samosir. The rates offered by the island's hotels and moneychangers make the banks in Parapat look very generous.

There have been a number of reports of thieves sneaking into rooms at night and stealing cash or cameras – almost always the result of carelessness.

The area code for Samosir is 0625.

Tomok
Tomok, five km south of Tuk Tuk, is the main village on the east coast of Samosir and the souvenir stall capital of the island. Tucked away among the stalls inland from the road is the **Tomb of King Sidabatu**, one of the last animist kings before the arrival of Christianity. It is possible to trek from Tomok to Pangururan on the other side of the island.

Tuk Tuk

This once small village has expanded into a string of hotels and restaurants stretching right around the peninsula. Horn-shaped Batak roofs are plonked on many of the new concrete-block hotels, but otherwise traditional Batak culture is not much in evidence. Still, the living is easy and very cheap, and Tuk Tuk is a pleasant base from which to visit the rest of the island.

Ambarita

A couple of km north of the Tuk Tuk Peninsula, Ambarita has a group of **stone chairs** where important matters and disputes were once settled. Guides will spin you a yarn about how serious wrongdoers were led to a further group of stone furnishings in an adjoining courtyard and decapitated.

Simanindo & Pangururan

The fine old **king's house** at Simanindo, on the northern tip of the island, has been restored and turned into a museum. The adjoining replica of a traditional village compound stages **Batak dance** at 10.30 and 11.45 am every day except Sunday, when the only show is at 11.45 am. Entry is 3000 rp.

Pangururan is the biggest town on the island, but it has nothing of interest. There are **hot springs** on the mainland five km away.

Trekking

There are a couple of treks across the island that are popular with the energetic. Both are well trodden and have a range of accommodation options, so you can proceed at your own pace. Gokhon Library, at Tuk Tuk, has information about the treks.

Most people opt for the short trek from Ambarita to Pangururan. The path starts opposite the bank in Ambarita. Keep walking straight at the escarpment and take the path to the right of the graveyard. The climb to the top is hard and steep, taking about 2½ hours. The path then leads to the village of Partungkoan (also called Dolok), where there you can stay at *Jenny's Guesthouse* or at *John's Losmen*. From Partungkoan,

it takes about five hours to walk to Pangururan via Danau Sidihoni. You can, of course, avoid the initial steep climb by doing the trek in reverse.

A longer version of the trek starts from Tomok. It's 13 km from Tomok to Pasanggrahan (Forest House 1), where you can stay if you wish. From here, you can walk along the escarpment to Partungkoan.

Places to Stay & Eat

Samosir has some of the best-value accommodation in Indonesia. Losmen have moved steadily upmarket over the years, and most places offer a range of rooms. The majority tend to be of the concrete-box variety, but you can still find a good-sized, clean box, usually with attached mandi, for 3000/5000 rp for singles/doubles.

Every losmen or hotel comes with a restaurant, but there are few surprises around – and very little difference in prices. The restaurants are good earners, and some places get pretty cranky if you don't eat where you stay.

Tuk Tuk This is where the vast majority of people stay. The shoreline is packed solid with hotels and losmen of every shape and size, almost all adorned with traditional horned-shaped roofs. There is such a choice of places that the best advice is to wander around until you find something that suits.

Starting in the south, the first stop for the ferries is near the *Bagus Bay* (☎ 41482). It has large doubles in part-stone, Batak-style houses for 10,000 rp, and a good restaurant which has a display of traditional dance every Monday and Saturday, and folk music on Wednesday. Next door is *Tabo Vegetarian Restaurant & Bakery*, with fresh wholemeal bread every day and a range of tasty burgers and snacks. It also has a couple of well-appointed bungalows for 15,000 rp. Uphill from Tabo is *Linda's*, a popular budget place run by the energetic Linda. Doubles are 6000 rp.

Second stop for the ferries is the long-running *Carolina's* (☎ 41520), easily the most stylish place on the island. Its older bungalows are from 12,500 rp – for 25,000 rp you get hot water as well. Carolina's also has a range of modern doubles for 40,000 rp and family units for 100,000 rp. Beyond Carolina's is the first of Samosir's new breed of package hotels, the *Silintong 1*. Next door is *Rumba Homestay* with clean singles/doubles by the lake for 4000/6000 rp. Its *Pizzeria Rumba* is a popular meeting spot at night. Further north, the restaurant at *Bernard's* turns out consistently good food.

Romlan (☎ 41557) is a secluded place set on its own small headland with a private jetty. It has basic rooms for 3000/5000 rp and better doubles for 7500 rp. Beyond Romlan is a cluster of big, package-type hotels, including the giant *Toledo Inn*. Among them are a couple of good mid-range places: *Samosir Cottages* (☎ 41050) and *Anju Cottages* (☎ 41348). Both have rooms for 5000/8000 rp, as well as larger new rooms with hot water from 15,000 rp. Nearby is *Leo's Bar & Restaurant*, advertising the cheapest cold beer on the island.

The north-west coast of the peninsula beyond the Toledo Inn is occupied by a string of budget places. *Tony's* (☎ 41209) has quiet rooms right by the lake from 4000/5000 rp, and doubles with hot water for 10,000 rp.

There are half a dozen more places dotted along the road to Ambarita. *Tuktuk Timbul* is a great spot for people who want to get away from it all. There's a range of rooms from 4000 to 10,000 rp.

Ambarita If you find Tuk Tuk a bit hectic, there are some quiet guesthouses on the lakeside north of Ambarita. They include *Barbara's* (☎ 41230), where you'll find a good swimming beach and rooms from 5000 to 15,000 rp.

If you really are serious about getting away from it all, *Le Shangri-La* is the place, six km past Ambarita (300 rp on a Simanindo-bound bus). Clean Batak-style bungalows front a sandy beach and cost 4000/6000 rp. You can get there from

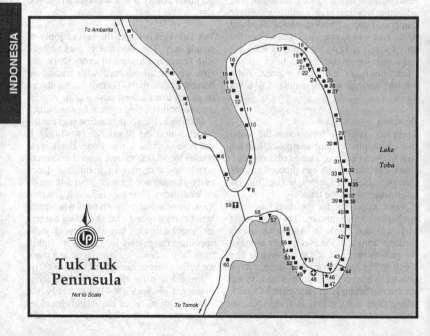

To Ambarita

Lake Toba

Tuk Tuk Peninsula

Not to Scale

To Tomok

INDONESIA

Parapat on ferries operated by the Nasional cooperative.

Tomok Few people stay in Tomok, although there are plenty of restaurants and warungs here for day-trippers who come across on the ferry from Parapat. *Roy's Restaurant*, on the main street, has accommodation on the edge of town for 3000 rp per person.

Pangururan *Mr Barat Acomodation* (☎ 20053), right in the middle of town at Jalan Sisinga-mangaraja 2/4, has extremely basic rooms for 4000 rp per person and a restaurant with a tourist menu. The nearby *Hotel Wisata Samosir* (☎ 20050) is a better bet. It has clean but spartan economy rooms for 6000 rp per person, as well as better doubles from 20,000 rp.

Getting There & Away

Bus See the Parapat section for information on bus travel to and from Lake Toba. There are daily buses from Pangururan to Berastagi (5500 rp; four hours) at 8 and 9 am and 3 pm.

Ferry There is a constant flow of ferries between Parapat and various destinations on Samosir. Ferries between Parapat and Tuk Tuk operate roughly every hour. The last ferry to Samosir leaves at about 5.30 pm, and the last one back is at about 4.30 pm. The fare is 1000 rp one way. Some ferries serve only a certain part of Tuk Tuk, so check at Parapat and you will be pointed to the appropriate boat. Tell them where you want to get off on Samosir when you pay your fare, or sing out when your hotel comes around – you'll be dropped off at the doorstep or nearby. When leaving for Parapat, just stand out on your hotel jetty and wave a ferry down.

Some ferries to Tuk Tuk continue to Ambarita, but four or five boats a day go direct from Parapat. There are also hourly ferries from Parapat to Tomok for 500 rp. Car ferries to Tomok leave from Ajibata, just south of Parapat.

Every Monday at 7.30 am there's a ferry from Ambarita to Haranggaol (3000 rp; 2½ hours). There are buses from Haranggaol to Kabanjahe (for Berastagi).

Getting Around

It is possible to get right around the island – with the exception of Tuk Tuk – by public transport. There are regular mini-buses between Tomok and Ambarita (500 rp), continuing to Simanindo (1000 rp) and

PLACES TO STAY			
1	Tuktuk Timbal	31	Rodeo
2	Mas	32	Hotel Silintong 2
3	Nina's	33	Rudy's
4	Sony	34	Hotel Sumber Polo
5	Yogi		Mas
6	Christina's	35	Romlan
7	Ho-l'e	36	Marroan
9	Antonius	37	Hisar's
10	Murni	38	Bernard's
11	Laster Jony	39	Lenny's
12	Sibayak	40	Matahari's
13	Tony's	41	Merlyn
14	Abadi's	43	Rumba Homestay
15	Caribien	44	Hotel Silintong 1
17	Toledo Inn	47	Carolina's
21	Dewi's	50	Mafir
23	Samosir Cottages	52	Vandu
24	Anju Cottages	53	Elsina
26	Popy's	54	Horas
27	Endy's	55	Dumasari
28	Lekjon	56	Linda's
29	Toledo 2	58	Bagus Bay
30	Ambaroba Resort Hotel	60	Smiley's

PLACES TO EAT	
8	Romlan's Beer Garden
16	Reggae Restaurant
18	Anju Restaurant
19	Leo's Bar & Restaurant
20	Tarian Vegetarian Restaurant
22	Baruna Restaurant
31	France Restaurant
42	Franky's Restaurant
45	Many Toba Restaurant
49	Juwita's Restaurant
51	Roy's Pub
57	Tabo Vegetarian Restaurant

OTHER	
25	Gokhon Library
46	Police Station
48	Health Centre
59	Church

INDONESIA

Panguraran (1750 rp). Services dry up after 3 pm.

You can rent motorbikes in Tuk Tuk for between 15,000 and 20,000 rp a day. They come with a free tank of petrol, but no insurance – so take care. There are lots of stories about travellers who have been handed outrageous repair bills. Bicycles cost from 4000 rp a day for a rattler to 8000 rp for a flash mountain bike.

BERASTAGI (BRASTAGI)

Berastagi is a picturesque hill town in the Karo Highlands, only 70 km from Medan on the backroad to Lake Toba. At an altitude of 1300 metres, the climate is deliciously cool after the heat of Medan. The setting is dominated by two volcanoes: Gunung Sinabung to the west and the smoking Gunung Sibayak to the north.

Few towns in Sumatra are better set up for travellers, although the town itself is not wildly exciting. Most people use Berastagi as a base for trekking and other adventure activities. Architecture buffs can enjoy trips to nearby traditional villages.

Orientation & Information

Berastagi is essentially a one street town spread along Jalan Veteran. The tourist office, by the memorial in the centre of town, is friendly and well set up, but the best source of travellers' information is the notice boards at the Wisma Sibayak.

You can change US dollars, cash and travellers' cheques, at the Bank Rakyat Indonesia at the bottom end of Jalan Veteran. You can change other currencies at any of the several moneychangers, but the rates are terrible.

The area code for Berastagi is 0628.

Things to See & Do

Many people come to Berastagi to climb **Gunung Sibayak** (2172 metres), probably the most accessible of Indonesia's volcanoes. The walk takes about three hours if you start from town. You need good walking boots because the path is steep in places and slippery year-round. It can be cold at the top,

so bring something warm to wear as well as food, drink and a torch (in case you get caught out after dark). The guest books at Wisma Sibayak have more information about this climb, including numerous warnings about the dangers of sudden weather changes. People are strongly advised not to tackle the climb alone. A lone Danish traveller died on the mountain in July 1995 after getting lost in a storm and falling.

The town is crawling with guides for treks along the well-trodden trails through **Gunung Leuser National Park** to Bukit Lawang. Prices start at 30,000 rp per day for a three-day/two-night trip, staying at villages along the way.

Golfers can get a game at Hotel Bukit Kubu (☎ 20832), an old Dutch guesthouse just north of town on Jalan Sempurna. Green fees are 10,000 rp for the nine par-three holes and you can hire a set of clubs for 12,500 rp.

Places to Stay

The *Wisma Sibayak* (☎ 20953), at the bottom end of the main street, is one of the best-run travellers' places in the country. It has dorm beds for 3000 rp and small singles/doubles for 5000/7000 rp as well as larger rooms for 12,000 rp. It's packed with travellers and the guest books are full of useful and amusing information about sightseeing, festivals, transport, walks, climbs and other things to do in the area. The Sibayak's back-up place is *Losmen Sibayak Guesthouse* in the middle of town on Jalan Veteran.

There are several reasonable places at the top end of town. The *Ginsata Hotel*, at Jalan Veteran 79, has clean doubles with shower for 10,000 rp. Just around the corner is the *Ginsata Guest House*, a pleasant old timber building with singles/doubles from 3500/5000 rp. The *Crispo Inn* (☎ 91023), at Jalan Veteran 3, has doubles for 5000 rp, or 10,000 rp with hot shower and breakfast.

Places to Eat

Most of the budget hotels also operate restaurants. The restaurant at the *Wisma Sibayak* is fast and efficient and serves good food, while the Torong Inn's *Jane & Tarzan*

Coffee Shop also turns out typical travellers' fare. The *Europah Restaurant*, at Jalan Veteran 48G, does good cheap Chinese food.

The colourful fruit market is near the memorial. Passionfruit is a local speciality – the purple-skinned marquisa asam manis make delicious drinks.

Getting There & Away

Berastagi's bus station is on Jalan Veteran. There are frequent buses from Berastagi to Medan (1400 rp; two hours).

Getting to Parapat by public bus is a hassle (see the Parapat Getting There & Away section). The easy option is to catch one of the tourist buses making the Bukit Lawang-Parapat run. Berastagi is the midpoint and buses stop for lunch in both directions, leaving at about 1 pm. It costs 15,000 rp to both Bukit Lawang and Parapat.

PLACES TO STAY
2 Rose Garden Hotel
3 Rudang Hotel
4 Hotel Bukit Kubu
6 Demerel Guesthouse
7 Wisma Ikut
10 Crispo Inn
13 Ginsata Hotel
14 Ginsata Guest House
15 Losmen TS Lingga
16 Losmen Trimurty
17 Merpati Inn
21 Torong Inn
24 Losmen Sibayak Guesthouse
31 Wisma Sibayak

PLACES TO EAT
11 Rendezvous Restaurant
22 Asia Restaurant
25 Europah Restaurant

OTHER
1 Peceren Traditional Longhouse
5 Power Station
8 Petrol Station
9 Fruit Market
12 Memorial
18 Tourist Office
19 Telephone Office
20 Post Office
23 Public Health Centre
26 Bank Rakyat Indonesia
27 Ria Cinema
28 Market
29 Bus & Opelet Station
30 Mini Market

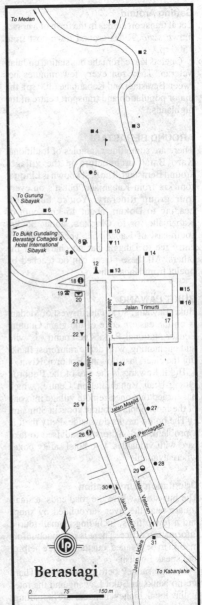

Berastagi

Getting Around

Local transport comes in the form of a horse-drawn *sado*. Rides around town cost from 1500 rp.

Opelets leave from the bus station on Jalan Veteran. They run every few minutes between Berastagi and Kabanjahe (300 rp), the major population and transport centre of the highlands.

AROUND BERASTAGI

There are some fine examples of traditional Karo Batak architecture in the villages around Berastagi. The best known is **Lingga**, four km from Kabanjahe, but it's on every tour group itinerary. You're better off heading to **Dokan**, about 15 km south of Kabanjahe, or to **Cingkes**, about 35 km south-east of Kabanjahe. There's a 300 rp entry fee to Lingga, but no charge for the others. All these places can be reached by opelet from Kabanjahe.

BUKIT LAWANG

Bukit Lawang, 80 km north-west of Medan, is on the eastern edge of the giant Gunung Leuser National Park. The country is wild and enchanting, with dense rainforest flanking the clear, fast-flowing Bohorok River.

Bukit Lawang is the site of the Bohorok Orang-Utan Rehabilitation Centre, which has turned this once-remote village into one of the most popular tourist spots in Sumatra.

The boom has its downside. Petty theft is a problem, and visitors are advised to take care with valuables. Use hotel safety boxes where available.

Orientation & Information

The bus stops where the road ends: a small square near the river surrounded by shops and a few offices, including a small tourist information office. There is not much information to be gleaned, but the staff are helpful and speak English.

Change money before you arrive. There are no banks in Bukit Lawang and the rates at the local moneychangers are appalling. There is no post office, but you can buy stamps at the shops and there are post boxes. There is a small Telkom office by the river.

The area code for Bukit Lawang is 061.

Things to See & Do

The **Bohorok Orang-Utan Rehabilitation Centre** was set up by the World Wide Fund for Nature (WWF) in 1973 to help these fascinating creatures readjust to the wild after captivity. That was the original intention. These days, the tourist industry that has grown up around the centre would be devastated if the animals actually learned to fend for themselves and failed to front for the cameras.

The orang-utans can be seen every day at a jungle feeding platform in the national park. Before you set off, get a permit from the national parks office in Bukit Lawang – open from 7 am every day. The permit is valid for two days and costs 4000 rp plus 500 rp insurance. In theory, only 40 permits are issued each day, but numbers seem to swell at weekends. The feeding site is 30 minutes walk from the office in town, including a free crossing of the Bohorok River in a dugout canoe. The path into the national park from the river crossing can get very muddy.

Feeding times are from 8 to 9 am and from 3 to 4 pm. These are the only times visitors are allowed to enter the national park other than with a guide or an organised trek.

The cages by the Losmen PHPA are used to keep new arrivals in quarantine and sick animals under observation.

Occasionally, orang-utans can be seen by the river opposite the Jungle Inn and Losmen Bohorok River, where they come down to check out the tourists.

The **Bukit Lawang Visitor Centre**, opposite the bus stop, has good displays of the park's flora and fauna and a section to explain the orang-utan rehabilitation programme.

A lot of people use Bukit Lawang as a base for **trekking**. Almost every losmen advertises trekking, and half the losmen workers seem to be guides – without whom you are not allowed into the park. They offer a range of treks around Bukit Lawang as well as three and five-day walks to Berastagi. Around Bukit Lawang, expect to pay 25,000 rp for a day trek, and 30,000 per day for treks that involve camping out. Prices include meals, guide fees and the cost of the permit to enter the park.

Many of the losmen rent out inflated truck inner tubes which can be used to ride the rapids of the Bohorok River, a pastime known as **tubing**. The Back to Nature Guesthouse offers **whitewater rafting** for 75,000 rp per day.

Places to Stay & Eat

Bukit Lawang has a string of good, cheap losmen spread out along the river and most have associated restaurants. Accommodation is concentrated in two main areas: along the riverbank opposite the town and upstream along the path to the orang-utan feeding site.

The best budget accommodation is upstream near the canoe crossing, about 15 minutes walk from town. This is also the best spot to go swimming. The *Jungle Inn*, with its creative carpentry and incredibly relaxed style, is very popular. It has very basic doubles for 5000 rp as well as rooms with balconies overhanging the river for 15,000 rp.

Some of the Jungle Inn's neighbours offer better value. The *Losmen Bohorok River* has rooms on the riverbank for 7000 rp, while the nearby *Sinar Guesthouse* and *Back to Nature Guesthouse* each charge 5000 rp. *Farina Guesthouse*, opposite the camping ground, is good value with large, clean doubles for 6000 rp.

The downstream accommodation is dominated by the *Wisma Bukit Lawang Cottages* (☎ 545061) and the *Wisma Leuser Sibayak* (☎ 550576), two large bungalow complexes offering a range of rooms. The Sibayak has some cheapies for 5000 rp as well as comfortable modern rooms by the river for 25,000 rp, while Bukit Lawang Cottages charges 7500 rp to 20,000 rp. Both also have good restaurants. You can make international calls from the card phone at Bukit Lawang Cottages.

Getting There & Away

There are direct buses to Medan's Pinang Baris bus station every half hour between 5.30 am and 6 pm. The 96 km journey takes three hours and costs 1500 rp. A chartered taxi to Medan costs 75,000 rp.

As elsewhere, the tourist minibuses are heavily promoted. They leave early in the morning for Medan (10,000 rp), Berastagi (15,000 rp) and Lake Toba (25,000 rp).

MEDAN

Medan is the capital of the province of North Sumatra and the third largest city in Indonesia with a population approaching two million. It's a sprawling, steamy city with little to recommend it apart from shopping and some good restaurants. Most people's abiding memory of Medan is of battered old motorcycle becaks belching fumes into the already heavily polluted air. Most treat the city strictly as an entry and exit point.

Orientation

Finding your way around Medan presents few problems, although the traffic can be horrendous. Most places of importance are on or around the main street, Jalan Ahmad Yani, which runs north-south through the city centre. South of the city centre, it becomes Jalan Pemuda and then Jalan Katamso; to the north, it becomes Jalan Soekarno-Hatta and then Jalan Yos Sudarso.

Travellers arriving in Medan from Parapat and points south will find themselves deposited at the giant Amplas bus station, 6.5 km from town on Jalan Sisingamangaraja (often written as SM Raja). It runs into the city centre parallel to Jalan Katamso.

Information

Tourist Office The North Sumatran tourist office (☎ 538101) is at Jalan Ahmad Yani 107. The staff here are friendly and speak good English. It's open from Monday to Thursday from 7.30 am to 4.15 pm, on Friday to noon. There is a small information office at the international arrival terminal at the airport.

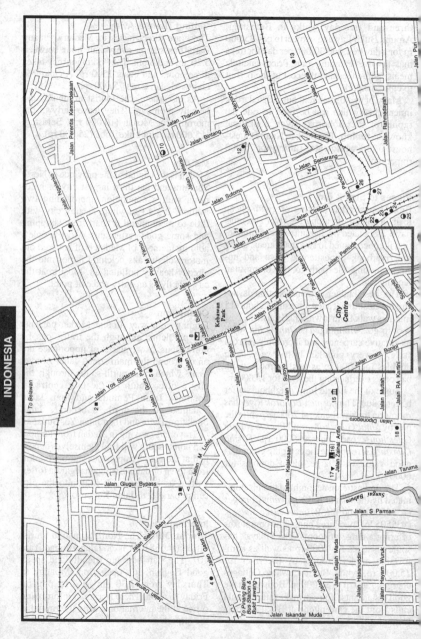

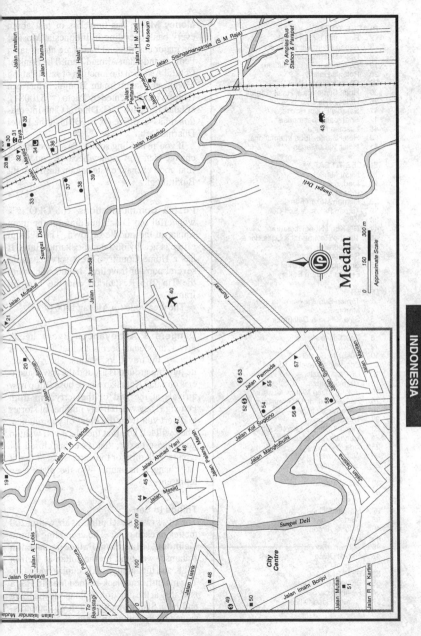

PLACES TO STAY
2   Emerald Garden Hotel
3   Asean International Hotel
7   Hotel Dharma Deli
19 Penginapan Taipan Nabaru
20 Polonia Hotel
28 Garuda Plaza Hotel
30 Hotel Sumatera & Hotel Garuda
36 Hotel Zakia
41 Sarah's Guest House
42 Shahibah Guesthouse
48 Losmen Irama
50 Hotel Danau Toba International
51 Hotel Tiara Medan

PLACES TO EAT
14 Night Market
17 Medan Bakery
21 Pizza Hut
29 Rumah Makan Famili
32 Taman Rekreasi Seri Deli
39 KFC
44 G's Koh I Noor Restaurant
46 Tip Top Restaurant & Lyn's Bar &
    Restaurant
55 Restaurant Agung
56 Brastagi Fruits Market
57 France Modern Bakery

OTHER
1   Taman Budaya
4   Medan Fair
5   Sinar Plaza & Deli Plaza
6   Telkom Office
8   Post Office
9   Railway Station
10 Buses to Singkil
11 Edelweiss Travel
12 Olympia Plaza
13 Thamrin Plaza
15 Bukit Barisan Military Museum
16 Parisada Hindu Dharma Temple
18 Governor's Office
22 Trophy Tours
23 Pacto & Selasa Ekspres Office
24 Mandala & Bouraq Offices
25 Inda Taxi
26 Water Tower
27 Gelora Plaza
31 Wartel
33 Istana Maimoon
34 Mesjid Raya
35 ALS Office
37 Merpati Office
38 Wartel
40 Polonia Airport
43 Zoo
45 Souvenir Shops
47 Tourist Office
49 Bank of Central Asia
52 Bank BNI 1946
53 Banks SBU & Duta
54 Pelni Office
58 Garuda Head Office

Money Medan has branches of just about every bank operating in Indonesia. Most of the major commercial banks are along Jalan Pemuda and Jalan Ahmad Yani. The Bank of Central Asia is at the junction of Jalan Palang Merah and Jalan Imam Bonjol. American Express is represented by Pacto (☎ 510081), at Jalan Katamso 35G. Diner's Club International has an office (☎ 513331) at the Hotel Dharma Deli.

If you're heading south, it's a good idea to change plenty of money because you won't find good exchange rates again until you hit Bukittinggi.

Post & Communications The GPO is a wonderful old Dutch building on the main square in the middle of town. The Telkom office is nearby on Jalan Soekarno-Hatta. It has a Home Country Direct service, as do several popular travellers' haunts, including the Tip Top Restaurant and the Losmen Irama.

The area code for Medan is 061.

Dangers & Annoyances Every becak driver in Medan seems to tout for one or other of the travellers' haunts. Their favourite hunting ground is around the travel agencies on Jalan Katamso where buses drop new arrivals at the end of the ferry trip from Penang. They will tell any number of stories to divert you from the hotel of your choice. They will tell you that the place you want to go to doesn't exist; that it's either closed for repairs, full, dirty or too expensive; or that it has changed its name – to the place they represent.

Things to See
The city's two finest buildings are within 200 metres of each other. The crumbling **Istana Maimoon** (Maimoon Palace), on Jalan Katamso, was built by the sultan of Deli in 1888, and the family still occupies one wing. The magnificent black-domed **Mesjid Raya** is nearby at the junction of Jalan Mesjid Raya and Jalan Sisingamangaraja. It was commissioned by the sultan in 1906.

The **Museum of North Sumatra** is south of the city on Jalan HM Joni. It has good displays of North Sumatran culture and history. It's open Tuesday to Sunday from 8.30 am to noon and from 1 to 5 pm, admission 200 rp.

Cultural performances are staged at **Taman Budaya** on Jalan Perintis Kemerdekaan. The tourist office has a list of what's on. Don't bother visiting Medan's depressing **Taman Margasawata Zoo**, south of the city on Jalan SM Raja, or the run-down **crocodile farm** at Asam Kumbang.

Places to Stay

Medan's cheapies are a grim lot. The *Losmen Irama* (☎ 326416), in a little alley at Jalan Palang Merah 1125, gets a lot of travellers despite having some of the city's grottiest rooms and laziest staff. Its sole virtue is its proximity to the city centre. It also has a Home Country Direct phone for international calls. It charges 5000 rp per person, but you'll need to fork out another 2500 rp for a fan to have any chance of getting to sleep.

The *Penginapan Taipan Nabaru* (☎ 512155) occupies an old timber house on the banks of the Sungai Deli at Jalan Hang Tuah 6. It's a quiet place with dorms for 3000 rp and doubles with shared bath for 6500 rp, but a long way off the beaten track.

The best travellers' places are south of the city centre off Jalan SM Raja. The *Hotel Zakia* (☎ 722413), right next to the Mesjid Raya on Jalan Sipiso-Piso, is a friendly family-run place with a choice of rooms. It has dorm beds for 6000 rp, doubles with fan for 12,500 rp and doubles with bathroom and fan for 15,000 rp. Prices include a breakfast of roti and coffee.

Further south, tucked away at Jalan Pertama 10, is *Sarah's Guest House* (☎ 743783). It has doubles with fan for 10,000 rp and doubles with bathroom for 15,000 rp.

Further north on Jalan SM Raja is a string of uninspiring mid-range places such as the *Dhaksina Hotel* (☎ 324561) at No 20, and the *Hotel Sumatera* (☎ 24973) at No 21, where you'll get an air-con double for about 35,000 rp.

Places to Eat

One of Medan's saving graces is Jalan Semarang, east of the railway line between Jalan Pandu and Jalan Bandung. By day it's just a grubby side street, but come nightfall it's jam-packed with food stalls offering great Chinese food.

The *Taman Rekreasi Seri Deli*, across the road from the Mesjid Raya, is a slightly upmarket approach to food stall eating. You just sit down and waitresses bring round a menu that allows you to choose from the offerings of about 20 stalls.

The *Tip Top Restaurant*, at Jalan Ahmad Yani 92, is not the cheapest place in town, but it's an old favourite with foreign visitors. It's a pleasant spot, in spite of the continuous traffic jam outside. It serves European and Chinese food as well as Padang food. It also has a Home Country Direct phone.

There are much better places to eat Padang food than the Tip Top. Try the *Restaurant Agung* at Jalan Pemuda 40, or the *Rumah Makan Famili* at Jalan SM Raja 21B.

Vegetarians looking for something other than gado gado should check out *G's Koh I Noor*, a family-run Indian restaurant at Jalan Mesjid 21.

If you're hanging out for some junk food, there are *KFCs* on the corner of Jalan Juanda and Jalan Katamso and at Deli Plaza. *Pizza Hut* (☎ 519956), on the corner of Jalan Multatuli and Jalan Suprapto, offers free delivery to your home or hotel.

Brastagi Fruits Market – an upmarket, air-con shop rather than a market – has a great selection of local and imported tropical fruit. It's close to the city centre on Jalan Sugiono.

Things to Buy

Medan has a number of interesting arts and crafts shops, particularly along Jalan Ahmad Yani. Try Toko Asli at No 62, Toko Rufino at No 56 or Toko Bali Arts at No 68. They all have a good selection of antique weaving, Dutch pottery, carvings and other pieces.

Getting There & Away

Medan is Sumatra's main international arrival and departure point.

Air There are daily international flights from Medan to Singapore, Kuala Lumpur and Penang, as well as a weekly direct service to Bangkok on Saturdays. See the Sumatra Getting There & Away section for details.

There are numerous direct flights to Jakarta (414,700 rp). Garuda alone does the trip five times a day. It also flies twice a day to Banda Aceh (145,200 rp) and direct to Denpasar (559,800 rp) three times a week. Merpati has daily flights to Padang (173,800 rp).

SMAC flies from Medan to Gunung Sitoli (131,300 rp) on Nias Island at least once a day.

Bus There are two main bus stations. Buses to Parapat, Bukittinggi and other points south leave from the huge Amplas terminal, 6.5 km south of the city centre along Jalan SM Raja. The best companies for long-distance travel south are ALS and ANS. Their offices are in a separate building behind the main block. They charge similar fares – 30,000 rp for air-con services to Bukittinggi, or 45,000 rp for the deluxe buses. ALS also has a booking office in town at Jalan Amaliun 2, 150 metres from the Mesjid Raya. Almost any opelet heading south on Jalan SM Raja will get you to Amplas.

Buses to the north leave from Pinang Baris bus station, 10 km west of the city centre on Jalan Gatot Subroto. There are buses to both Bukit Lawang (1500 rp; three hours) and Berastagi (1400 rp; two hours) every half hour between 5.30 am and 6 pm. There are also frequent buses to Banda Aceh. The journey takes anything up to 13 hours in daytime, but the express night buses do the trip in about nine hours. Fares range from 19,000 rp for public buses to 40,000 rp for the latest luxury buses with reclining seats.

There are lots of opelets to Pinang Baris along Jalan Gatot Subroto. A taxi from the city centre costs about 6500 rp.

SMJ Travel (☎ 720652), opposite the junction of Jalan SM Raja and Jalan Sipiso-Piso, has five minibuses a day to Parapat and Sibolga. A seat costs 15,000 rp, regardless of how far you go, including hotel pick-up.

Taxi There are several long-distance taxi operators in Medan. Inda Taxi (☎ 516615), Jalan Katamso 60, has share taxis to Parapat (18,000 rp) and Sibolga (20,000 rp). Hotels can arrange charter taxis for four people to places like Berastagi (65,000 rp) and Bukit Lawang (75,000 rp).

Boat The hi-speed ferries to Penang can be booked at the agents on Jalan Brigjen Katamso. The *Ekspres Selasa* (☎ 514888), Jalan Katamso 35C, leaves on Wednesday and Friday at 2 pm and on Sunday at 2 pm. Pacto (☎ 510081), Jalan Brigjen Katamso 35G, handles tickets for the *Ekspres Bahagia*, which leaves on Tuesday, Thursday and Saturday at 10 am. Both services cost 95,000 rp, which includes the bus to Medan's port of Belawan.

Pelni has boats to Jakarta and points further east every Monday (116,500 rp deck class; 45 hours). The Indonesia Getting Around section earlier in this chapter has details of Pelni routes. The Pelni office (☎ 518899) in Medan is at Jalan Sugiono 5.

Getting Around

The Airport Airport taxis (which operate on a coupon system) charge a standard 8000 rp to the city. You'll pay half that if you can find a regular, metered cab.

Local Transport Medan's cabs are a good way of getting around. Flag fall is 1150 rp and fares work out at about 700 rp per km, which is a good deal less than you'll pay if you use the pedal-powered becaks that hang out around the travellers' places.

There are numerous tales of woe involving becak riders and demands for outrageous amounts of money, almost always as a result of breaking the golden rule of becak travel: agree on the fare beforehand. Reckon on paying about 1500 rp per km – which means that most journeys around the city centre should cost no more than 3000 rp.

Opelets are the main form of public transport. They cost 300 rp, although you may be asked to pay double if you have a large backpack. Just stand by the roadside and call out your destination.

BANDA ACEH

Banda Aceh, right at the northern tip of Sumatra, is the capital of Aceh province. Fiercely independent and devoutly Islamic, Aceh was once a powerful state in its own right and later held out against the Dutch longer than almost anywhere else in the archipelago. After independence, the Acehnese took exception to being incorporated into the province of North Sumatra and declared their own Islamic republic (1953-61). Today the Acehnese are kept on side by a deal which gives them autonomy in religious, cultural and educational matters.

Orientation & Information

Banda Aceh is split in two by the Krueng Aceh river. The city's best known landmark, the magnificent Mesjid Raya Baiturrahman (Great Mosque), lies on the southern side. Behind the mosque is the huge Pasar Aceh central market, and adjoining the market is the main opelet station.

The city north of the river is centred on the junction of Jalan Ahmad Yani and Jalan Khairil Anwar. There are lots of hotels and restaurants in this area. The tourist office (☎ 23692) is nearby at Jalan Chik Kuta Karang 3, just around the corner from the post office on Jalan Teuku Angkasah. The best place to change money is the Bank of Central Asia at Jalan Panglima Polem 38-40.

The area code for Banda Aceh is 0651.

Things to See & Do

With its brilliant white walls and liquorice-black domes, the **Mesjid Raya Baiturrahman** is a truly dazzling sight on a sunny day. The first section of the mosque was built by the Dutch in 1879 as a conciliatory gesture towards the Acehnese after the original had been burnt down. Further domes and minarets have been added at regular intervals.

Non-Muslims are not allowed to enter any part of the mosque.

For a contrast in architectural styles, check out the **Gunongan** on Jalan Teuku Umar, near the clock tower. It was built by Sultan Iskandar Muda (ruled 1607-36) as a gift for his wife, a Malayan princess, and was intended as a private playground and bathing place.

The **Museum Negeri Aceh** on Jalan Alauddin Mahmudsyah houses a collection of weapons, household furnishings, ceremonial costumes, everyday clothing, gold jewellery and books. In the same compound is the **Rumah Aceh**, a fine example of traditional architecture.

The **fish market** on Jalan Sisingamangaraja is one of the most striking and lively in Sumatra.

Places to Stay

There are no bargains to be found in Banda Aceh. You're better off staying clear of the losmen along Jalan Khairil Anwar. Places like the *Aceh Barat* and the *Losmen Palembang* look interesting, but seem to have no interest in foreign guests.

You'll be made much more welcome at *Losmen Raya* (☎ 21427), an old Dutch building 500 metres from the Mesjid Raya at Jalan Ujong Rimba 30. It has doubles with fan for 12,500 rp and with private bathroom for 15,000 rp. Rates include breakfast. If it's full, try the similarly priced *Hotel Sri Budaya* (☎ 21751), nearby on Jalan Prof A Majid Ibrahim III 5E. It also has a few air-con doubles for 30,000 rp.

If you're looking at spending a bit more money, the best bet is the *Hotel Medan* (☎ 21501), Jalan Ahmad Yani 15. It looks nothing special, but it has clean, comfortable air-con doubles with TV for 45,000 rp.

Places to Eat

The table-filled square at the junction of Jalan Ahmad Yani and Jalan Khairil Anwar is the setting for Banda Aceh's lively night food market, known as the *Rek*. If there's nothing here that takes your fancy, the *Restoran New Tropicana*, Jalan Ahmad Yani 90-92, does upmarket Chinese and seafood.

INDONESIA

If you're staying south of the river, the place to go is the *Taman Sari Rindang*, opposite the Hotel Kuala Tripa. It's a cafe-style place that's very popular with Banda Aceh's young crowd in the evenings. Most meals are under 5000 rp.

Getting There & Away

Air Pelangi Air has three flights a week from Banda Aceh to Penang (US$107) and Kuala Lumpur (US$134). Pelangi's office (☎ 21705) is at Jalan Nyak Arief 163. Garuda has two flights a day from Banda Aceh to Medan (141,900 rp). The Garuda office is at the Hotel Sultan (☎ 22469).

Bus The main bus station is the Terminal Bus Seutui at the southern approach to town on Jalan Teuku Umar. The express services run at night, take about nine hours and cost from 30,000 rp. Kurnia and PMTOH are both good, and both have offices in town on Jalan Mohammed Jam (near the mosque) where you can book. PMTOH is at No 58 and Kurnia is at No 68.

Heading down the west coast, PMTOH and Aceh Barat run buses from Banda Aceh to Calang (6500 rp; four hours), Meulaboh (8000 rp; five hours) and Tapaktuan (16,000 rp; 11 hours). From Tapaktuan, it's possible to continue to Sidikalang, and then complete a loop of northern Sumatra to Medan via Berastagi.

Getting Around

Airport taxis charge a standard 15,000 rp for the 16 km ride into town, and 36,000 rp to Krueng Raya (for Pulau We).

Opelets (known locally as *labi-labi*) are the main form of transport around town and cost 300 rp. There are also motorised becaks, which require the usual hard bargaining before you set off.

PULAU WE

This beautiful little island just north of Banda Aceh is the main reason most travellers come to Aceh. It has some magnificent palm-fringed beaches, good snorkelling and a rugged, jungle-covered interior.

Picking the best time to visit is a bit of a lottery. Rain is never far away – different winds seem to bring rain from different directions. You can, however, be fairly sure that it will rain constantly from November until early January. July is supposedly the driest month.

Malaria has been reported on the island.

Orientation & Information

There are only 24,000 people on the island, most of them in the main town and port of Sabang. For most people, Sabang is no more than an overnight stop on the way to the beaches at Gapang and Iboih. The Stingray Dive Centre (☎ 21265) on the corner of Jalan Teuku Umar and Jalan Perdagangan, doubles as a tourist office. The post office is on Jalan Perdagangan, and the telephone office is next door, open 24 hours. It has a Home Country Direct phone.

The area code for Sabang is 0652.

Things to See & Do

The most popular beach is at **Iboih**, the destination for most of the tourists coming to the island. Opposite Iboih, 100 metres offshore (10,000 rp return by boat), is **Pulau Rubiah**, a densely forested island surrounded by spectacular coral reefs known as the **Sea Garden**. It is a favourite snorkelling and diving spot. The Stingray Dive Centre hires out equipment as well as organising trips to a range of diving locations.

Gapang Beach, around the headland from Iboih, is good for swimming and there are fewer tourists.

Places to Stay & Eat

Sabang has a couple of reasonable places to stay. Both the *Losmen Irma* (☎ 21148), at Jalan Teuku Umar 3, and *Losmen Pulau Jaya* (☎ 21344), further up the street at No 17-25, are well set up for travellers. The Pulau Jaya is marginally the better of the two with basic singles/doubles for 4000/7500 rp and large doubles with bathroom for 20,500 rp. *Harry's Cafe*, downstairs from the Losmen Irma, has a range of pancakes and breakfast goodies. There are a couple of good Chinese restaurants on Jalan Perdagangan. The *Dynasty*, at No 54, also serves cold beer.

Accommodation at Iboih is in the form of numerous palm-thatch bungalows costing 3000/5000 rp for singles/doubles. Each group of bungalows has its own restaurant.

Getting There & Away
Ferries to Pulau We leave from Krueng Raya, 33 km east of Banda Aceh. There are regular bemos (No 1) from the central market in Banda Aceh (1500 rp; 45 minutes). Ferries leave Krueng Raya daily at 3 pm, returning at 9 am the next morning. The voyage takes two hours and costs 4250 rp deck class.

Passengers will be reassured to find that the ferry brought in to replace the ill-fated KM *Gurita* is equipped with such basics as life jackets. As many as 250 people, including two foreign tourists, drowned when the *Gurita* capsized and sank on January 19, 1996.

Getting Around
The ferries to Pulau We arrive at the port of Balohan, from where there are bemos for the 15 minute ride to Sabang (1500 rp). There are pick-up trucks from Sabang to Gapang and Iboih every day at 10.30 am and 6 pm, returning at 7 am and 4 pm. They cost 2000 rp and leave from outside the Stingray Dive Centre in Sabang.

The island has a good road network and motorcycles are the ideal way to get around if you want to see a bit of the island. They can be rented from Harry's Cafe in Sabang.

PULAU BANYAK
The Banyaks ('many' islands) are a cluster of 99 islands, most of them uninhabited, about 30 km west of the Acehnese port of Singkil. A few years ago, the islands were right off the beaten track; these days they are flavour of the moment and everybody seems to be heading there.

Malaria has been reported on the islands, so take suitable precautions.

Orientation & Information
The village of Desa Pulau Balai on Pulau Balai is where boats from the mainland will deposit you. It is the only settlement of any consequence – it even has electricity in the evenings. It also has a post office and a telegram office, but there is nowhere to change money. The Nanda restaurant, close to where the boats dock, has information about accommodation and boats to other islands.

Things to See & Do
The setting is perfect for hanging out. The islands are ringed by pristine palm-fringed **beaches**, and there is excellent **snorkelling** on the surrounding coral reefs. **Diving** can be organised at the Point Bungalows on Pulau Palambak Besar. There is good **trekking** through the virgin jungles of the largest island, Pulau Tuangku.

Conservationists are campaigning to save the **turtles** of Pulau Bangkaru from poachers. Green turtles can be seen year-round, and giant leatherback turtles in January and February. A group called the Turtle Foundation organises three-day trips to Bangkaru for small groups. They cost 100,000 rp, including food and accommodation, and leave every Saturday. Tours should be booked in Desa Pulau Balai on arrival.

Places to Stay & Eat
New places are opening up all the time, and there are now half a dozen islands with accommodation – mostly in small, palm-thatch bungalows by the beach. Every place has its own kitchen, usually charging about 6000 rp for three set meals. Fish, rice and vegetables feature prominently.

Few people bother to stick around on Pulau Balai, although there are several places to stay. *Daer's Retreat* has basic singles/doubles for 3000/5000 rp, or 6000/8000 rp with private bathroom.

The most popular destination is Pulau Palambak Besar, which has three good places. The biggest is the aptly named *The Point*, which charges 4000/6000 rp for singles /doubles. The nine rooms make it one of the few places large enough to offer a choice in its restaurant. It also has a generator, which means cold drinks. *Bina Jaya Bungalows* and *Pondok Asmara Palambak*, known as PAP, are the other options.

There's also accommodation on Pulau Panjang *(Jasa Baru)*, Pulau Rangit Besar *(Coco's)* and Pulau Ujung Batu *(Jambu Kolong Cottages)*. Visitors to Pulau Tuangku can stay with the Lukman family at the health centre for 2500 rp per person.

Getting There & Away

There are regular boats to Pulau Balai from the mainland ports of Singkil (5500 rp; four hours) and Teluk Jamin (10,000 rp; six hours). Boats leave Singkil at 8 am on Monday, Thursday and Friday, and Teluk Jamin at 9.30 am on Tuesday and Wednesday.

Singkil is a remote port at the mouth of the Sungai Alas. There are direct minibuses to Singkil (15,000 rp; eight hours) from Medan every day at 11 am. They leave from outside the Singkil Raya restaurant, behind Olympia Plaza on Jalan Bintang. There are several cheap losmen in Singkil.

Teluk Jamin is a tiny port village about 70 km south of Tapaktuan. There are buses to Tapaktuan from Medan (Pinang Baris bus station) and from Banda Aceh. You can spend the night in town and catch an early bus to Teluk Jamin the next morning.

Getting Around

Boats to the various beach bungalows can be arranged through the Nanda restaurant on Pulau Balai. Sample fares include 3500 rp to Pulau Rangit Besar and 5000 rp to Pulau Palambak Besar.

Riau Archipelago

Stretching south from Singapore are the islands of the Riau Archipelago, scattered like confetti over the South China Sea. There are as many islands, locals say, as there are grains in a cup of pepper (3214 islands in all, more than 700 of them uninhabited and many of them unnamed).

Tanjung Pinang, on Pulau Bintan, is the traditional capital of the islands, but much attention is focused these days on Pulau Batam, which is rapidly being developed as an industrial extension of Singapore.

Both Batam and Bintan have ferry links to Singapore and are visa-free entry/exit points, making them convenient stepping stones to the rest of Indonesia. Furthermore, you do not have to show an onward or return ticket on entry. If they ask for one, you can always buy a ferry ticket back to Singapore for less than US$10.

BATAM

Nowhere in Indonesia is the pace of development more rapid than on Pulau Batam. Until the island was declared a free-trade zone in 1989, it was a backwater comprising little more than the shanties of Nagoya and a few coastal villages.

Several years of frantic construction later, Batam is almost unrecognisable. There are a number of expensive golf resorts on the north coast, but for the most part there's a distinct frontier town atmosphere to the place, with high prices, ugly construction sites and no reason to pause any longer than it takes to catch a boat out. Batam has now largely usurped neighbouring Bintan's traditional role as the transport hub of the Riau islands. The seaports of Batu Ampar, Nongsa and Sekupang and Hang Nadim airport are all visa-free entry and exit points.

Orientation

Most travellers arrive on Batam by boat from Singapore to the port of Sekupang. After you clear immigration, there are counters for money exchange, taxis and hotels. It's a minute's walk to the domestic ferry terminal, from where there are speedboats to numerous other Sumatran destinations. Ferries to Bintan leave from Telaga Panggur in the south-east.

Information

The Batam Tourist Promotion Board (☎ (0778) 322852) has a small office outside the international terminal at Sekupang. There's a money exchange counter at the Sekupang ferry building, but the rates are better in

Nagoya, where all the major banks are based. Singapore dollars are as acceptable as Indonesian rupiah.

Places to Stay

Budget accommodation on Batam is some of the worst in Indonesia, and another argument for not sticking around. There is a line of utterly rock-bottom places about a km out of town at Blok C, Jalan Teuku Umar. The *Minang Jaya* is the best of a bad bunch with bare, partitioned singles/doubles for 10,000 rp. The *Wisma Chendra Wisata*, on nearby Jalan Sriwijaya, is marginally better, with singles for 15,000 rp.

Mid-range accommodation is similarly uninspiring and overpriced. Prices are quoted in Singapore dollars, and it's a struggle to find a double for under S$60. The *Horizona* (☎ (0778) 457111) has singles/doubles for S$45/60 and is centrally located on Jalan S Rahman.

Places to Eat

Restaurants on Batam are expensive, much like everything else, but there are some good seafood places. The best eating in Nagoya is found at the night food stalls along Jalan Raja Ali Haji or at the big and raucous *Pujasera Nagoya* food centre.

Getting There & Away

Air The brand-new airport at Hang Nadim is international in name only. At this stage, there are no international flights.

Garuda, Sempati and Bouraq all have daily direct flights to Jakarta (231,500 rp). Sempati and Bouraq also have daily flights to Medan (193,000 rp). Merpati destinations include Padang, Palembang, Pangkalpinang (on Pulau Bangka), Pekanbaru and Pontianak (on Kalimantan).

Boat There are numerous services to Singapore as well as daily links to the Sumatran mainland.

Singapore Ferries shuttle constantly between Singapore's World Trade Centre and Sekupang. The trip takes 40 minutes and costs S$18 from Singapore, or 30,000 rp from Sekupang.

There are less frequent services from the World Trade Centre to Batu Ampar and Nongsa.

Pulau Bintan Speedboats to Tanjung Pinang on neighbouring Pulau Bintan leave from Telaga Panggur, 30 km south-east of Nagoya. There's a steady flow of departures from 8 am to 5.15 pm. The trip takes 45 minutes and costs 10,000 rp one way, plus 1000 rp port tax.

Elsewhere in Indonesia The main reason travellers come to Batam is to catch an onward boat to Pekanbaru on the Sumatran mainland. Boats leave from the domestic wharf at Sekupang, 100 metres south of the international terminal. The trip to Pekanbaru involves a four hour boat trip to Tanjung Buton on the Sumatran mainland, travelling via Selat Panjang (on Pulau Tebingtinggi), followed by a three hour bus ride. The combined ticket costs about 35,000 rp. There is no point in breaking the journey en route. Selat Penjang is a grotty, bustling, oversized water village with a strong Chinese influence, while Tanjung Buton is just a bus/ferry terminal. There are no services to Pekanbaru after 10 am, so you'll need to make an early start if you're coming from Singapore.

Other destinations from Sekupang include: Pulau Karimun (13,000 rp); Pulau Kundur (15,000 rp); Dumai (35,000 rp); and Kuala Tungkal on the Jambi coast (50,000 rp).

Getting Around

Fixed-fare taxis operate from the ports of Sekupang and Telaga Panggur as well as from the airport. Sample fares from Sekupang include Nagoya for 12,000 rp and Telaga Panggur for 18,000 rp.

There is a token bus service between Nagoya and Sekupang for 600 rp, but most people use the share taxis that cruise the island: just stand by the roadside and call out your destination to passing cabs. Sample fares from Sekupang include 1000 rp to Nagoya and 5000 rp to Telaga Panggur. You will need to make it clear that you are paying for a seat, not the whole taxi.

PULAU BINTAN

Bintan is twice as large as Batam and many times more interesting. Singapore development is very low-key on Bintan with the exception of a cluster of golf resorts on the north coast around Laboi. The main attractions are the old town of Tanjung Pinang (a visa-free entry/exit point), nearby Penyenget Island and the relatively untouched beaches of the east coast.

Tanjung Pinang

After development-mad Batam, Tanjung Pinang comes as a very pleasant surprise. It may be the largest town in the Riau Archipelago – being the modern administrative centre – but it retains much of its old-time charm, particularly the picturesque, stilted section of the town that juts over the sea around Jalan Plantar II. The harbour sees a constant stream of shipping of every shape and size, varying from tiny sampans to large freighters.

Information There's no point in trekking two km around the coast to the new regional tourist office. They haven't got even a brochure, yet alone anything useful like a map. Bong's Homestay (see Places to Stay) is a much better source of information. The best place to change money is the Bank of Central Asia on Jalan Temiang.

The post office is near the harbour on the main street, Jalan Merdeka. International phone calls can be made from the wartel office on Jalan Hangtuah.

The area code for Tanjung Pinang is 0771.

Things to See The old stilted part of town around **Jalan Plantar II** is well worth a wander. To get there, turn left at the colourful **fruit market** at the northern end of Jalan Merdeka.

Senggarang is a fascinating village just across the harbour from Tanjung Pinang. The star attraction is an old Chinese temple held together by the roots of a huge banyan tree that has grown up through it.

The temple is to the left at the end of the pier, coming by boat from Tanjung Pinang. Half a km along the waterfront is a big square with three Chinese temples, side-by-side. Boats to Senggarang leave from the end of Jalan Plantar II.

You can charter a sampan to take you up the **Sungai Ular** (Snake River) through the mangroves to see the Chinese Temple with its gory murals of the trials and tortures of hell.

Places to Stay Don't believe a word you're told by the hotel touts at the ferry dock, who will try to persuade you that popular travellers' places don't exist. Tanjung Pinang has some good budget accommodation. Lorong Bintan II, a small alley between Jalan Bintan and Jalan Yusuf Khahar in the centre of town, is the place to look. The popular *Bong's Homestay* at No 20 has dorm beds for 5000 rp and doubles for 10,000 rp, including breakfast. *Johnny's Homestay*, next door at No 22, acts as an overflow. *Rommel Homestay* (☎ 21081), on the corner of Lorong Bintan II and Jalan Yusuf Khahar, has beds in dingy dorms for 4000 rp.

The *Hotel Surya* (☎ 21811), on Jalan Bintan, has clean, simple singles/doubles with fan for 14,000/18,000 rp. The *Wisma Riau* (☎ 21023) and the *Sampurna Inn* (☎ 21555), side-by-side on Jalan Yusuf Khahar, have air-con rooms with TV for 40,000 rp.

Places to Eat Tanjung Pinang has a superb *night market* which sets up in the bus station on Jalan Teuku Umar. The grilled seafood is particularly good. During the day, there are several pleasant coffee shops with outdoor eating areas in front of the basketball stadium on Jalan Teuku Umar; try *Flipper* or *Sunkist*. There are some good Padang food places along Jalan Plantar II where you can get a tasty fish curry for 1500 rp, or jackfruit curry (kare nangka) for 800 rp.

Pulau Penyenget Tiny Penyenget Island, a short hop across the harbour from Tanjung Pinang, was once the capital of the Riau rajas. It is believed to have been given to Raja Riau-Lingga VI in 1805 by his brother-in-law, Sultan Mahmud, as a wedding present. The place is littered with reminders of its past and there are ruins and graveyards wherever you walk. There are frequent boats to the island from Bintan's main pier for 1000 rp per person. There's a 500 rp entry charge on weekends.

Beaches The best beaches are along the east coast, where there is also good snorkelling outside the November to March monsoon period. Getting there can be a battle, but there is a choice of accommodation at the main beach, **Pantai Trikora**. There are buses to Trikora for 2500 rp from the bus station in Tanjung Pinang, otherwise it's 20,000 rp for a taxi.

Places to Stay *Yasin's Guesthouse* (☎ 26770), at the Km 36 marker near the village of Teluk Bakau, is a laid-back place with half a dozen simple palm huts right on the beach. It charges 17,000 rp per person per day, including three meals. *Bukit Berbunga Cottages*, right next door, has very similar accommodation. It charges 16,000/27,000 rp for singles/doubles, including breakfast.

Getting There & Away
Air Bintan's airport has taken something of a back seat following the upgrading of Batam. Merpati no longer flies out of Bintan, but Sempati has daily direct flights to Jakarta (287,000 rp) and SMAC flies to remote spots like Ranai (241,300 rp) on Pulau Natuna Besar.

Boat Although most of the boats to mainland Riau now operate from neighbouring Batam, Tanjung Pinang retains its traditional role as the hub of Riau's interisland shipping as well as having links to Singapore and Malaysia. Most services leave from the main pier at the southern end of Jalan Merdeka, but check when you buy your ticket. New Oriental Tours & Travel, Jalan Merdeka 61, is a reliable ticket agent.

Singapore There are three boats a day direct to Singapore's World Trade Centre wharf for 49,000 rp.

Malaysia There are two boats a day to Johor Bahru for 48,500 rp.

Pulau Batam There are regular speedboats from Tanjung Pinang's main pier to Telaga Panggur on Batam (10,000 rp; 45 minutes), as well as three boats a day direct to Sekupang (12,000 rp; 1½ hours).

Elsewhere in Sumatra There are two fast boats a day to Tanjung Balai on Pulau Karimun (21,000 rp; 2½ hours), and two a day to Dabo on Pulau Singkep (21,000 rp; four hours). There's a daily express service to Pekanbaru (51,000 rp), which involves changing boats on Batam. There are also occasional slow boats up the Sungai Siak to Pekanbaru for 31,000 rp.

Jakarta Pelni offers two ways of getting to Jakarta. Either the KM *Rinjani* or KM *Umsini* sails from the port of Kijang, in the south-eastern corner of the island, every Monday. The journey takes 28 hours and costs 38,000 rp deck class.

The alternative is the MV *Samudera Jaya*, which leaves Tanjung Pinang every Thursday and does the trip in 18 hours for 80,000 rp. The Pelni office (☎ 21513) in Tanjung Pinang is at Jalan Ketapang 8.

Getting Around
Taxis charge a standard 15,000 rp for the 17 km run from the airport to Tanjung Pinang. Buses and share taxis to other parts of Bintan leave from the bus and taxi station on Jalan Teuku Umar.

PULAU SINGKEP
Few travellers make the trip south from Bintan to Pulau Singkep, the third largest island in the archipelago. The place has become even more of a backwater since the closure of the huge tin mines that provided most of the island's jobs. Much of the former

INDONESIA

population has now gone elsewhere in search of work.

Getting There & Away
The boat trip from Tanjung Pinang crosses the equator and passes several shimmering islands on the way. Boats dock at the northern port Sunggai Buluh, from where there are buses to Dabo. Daily ferries run to Daik on Pulau Lingga.

There's also a weekly boat from Dabo to Jambi. Several shops in Dabo act as ticket agencies. SMAC flies from Dabo to Batam, Jambi and Pekanbaru.

Dabo
Dabo is the main town on the island, shaded by lush trees and gardens and clustered around a central park. A large **mosque** dominates the skyline. **Batu Bedua**, not far out of town, is a white-sand beach fringed with palms. It's a good place to spend a few hours. The fish and vegetable **markets**, near the harbour, are interesting and Jalan Pasar Lamar is a good browsing and shopping area.

Information The Bank Dagang Negara reportedly offers respectable rates for US dollars.

The post office is on Jalan Pahlawan and there is also an overseas telephone office about three km out of town on the road to Sunggai Buluh.

Places to Stay & Eat *Wisma Sri Indah*, on Jalan Perusahaan, has rooms from 15,000 rp. It's spotlessly clean and has a comfortable sitting room. Similar places are the *Wisma Gapura Singkep*, on the opposite side of the street and a bit north, and *Wisma Sederhana*. Some travellers have reported very good deals at the smartest place in town, the *Hotel Wisma Singkep*, which overlooks the town.

You can eat at the *markets* behind Wisma Sri Indah or try any of the *warungs* on Jalan Pasar Lama and Jalan Merdeka. Food stalls and warungs pop up all over the place at night.

Nusa Tenggara

Nusa Tenggara refers to the string of islands which starts to the east of Bali and ends with Timor. Some of the most spectacular attractions of Indonesia can be found in Nusa

Nusa Tenggara

Tenggara – Gunung Rinjani on Lombok, the dragons of Komodo, the immense stone tombs of Sumba and the coloured volcanic lakes of Keli Mutu on Flores.

Although a steady stream of travellers passes through, until recently the lack of transport confined most of them to a limited route. There are now more opportunities for off-the-beaten-track explorations, and the lack of tourists in these places will mean that your reception will be more natural. It does create one problem, though: you will sometimes be the centre of attention, attracting an entourage of children in a small village, all programmed to yell 'hello mister' until either they or you collapse from exhaustion.

You need at least a month to get a reasonable look around the whole chain.

Getting There & Away

Denpasar in Bali is the usual jumping-off point for the islands of Nusa Tenggara – you can go by ferry, hydrofoil or plane across to Lombok, or fly to one of the other islands. Flights from Nusa Tenggara terminate in Bali or Surabaya (Java), with same-day connections on to other parts of Indonesia.

Merpati flies twice a week between Kupang in Timor and Darwin in Australia's Northern Territory. This is an excellent way to travel to Indonesia from Australia. You can then island-hop through Nusa Tenggara to Bali without having to backtrack, as you would on a return trip into the islands from Bali.

Regular ferries run between all the islands and Nusa Tenggara is serviced by the Pelni ships *Lambelo*, *Dobonsolo*, *Binaiya* and *Tilongkabila*.

Getting Around

Air Most flights in Nusa Tenggara are handled by Merpati, although Sempati and Bouraq also have services. Merpati's theme song – 'It's Merpati and I'll Fly If I Want To' – comes true in Nusa Tenggara. Short flights are subject to cancellation, and bookings are not always reliable. Mataram, Kupang and Maumere are the main air hubs and the most reliable places to get a flight.

Boat Regular vehicle/passenger ferries connect all the main islands, thus making a loop through the islands from Bali and back fairly easy. Pelni also has regular connections.

INDONESIA

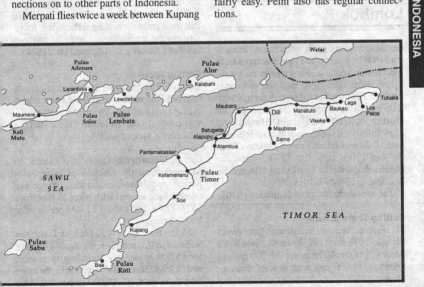

Bus On the islands travel is by bus. Air-con express coaches run right across Lombok and Sumbawa, but elsewhere small buses with limited legroom are crammed with passengers and all manner of produce. They constantly stop to drop off and pick up passengers, and if buses are not full, they will endlessly loop around town searching for passengers until they are full. The main highways are now paved, but narrow and usually winding. Don't underestimate journey times – a trip of only 100 km may take three hours or more – and don't overestimate your endurance abilities.

Most buses leave early in the morning, so be prepared for early starts.

Car & Motorcycle A motorbike is an ideal way to explore Nusa Tenggara, but outside Lombok, hiring a motorbike is not always easy, so you really need to bring your own.

Cars with driver can be hired, but outside Lombok, asking rates are outrageous. You'll do well if you can get a car with driver for under 100,000 rp per day.

Lombok

Lombok has one main urban area, tranquil countryside, uncrowded beaches and a truly spectacular volcano. Senggigi is an established resort, and basic facilities exist in a few other places, but otherwise there's very little tourist development. Most people are Muslim, but 10% are Balinese Hindus, and a few follow the indigenous Wektu Telu religion. Balinese princes ruled Lombok from the mid-1700s until the 1890s, when the Dutch sided with the Sasaks and defeated the Balinese in bloody battles.

The area code for all of Lombok is 0364.

Getting There & Away
Air Merpati, Sempati and Bouraq have direct flights to Bima (132,400 rp), Sumbawa Besar (73,000 rp), Denpasar (56,500 rp) and Jakarta (311,000 rp), with onward connections.

Bus Direct buses from Sweta terminal go to Sumbawa destinations including Sumbawa Besar (10,000 rp; five hours; four daily) and Bima (26,000 rp; 12 hours; three daily). Other destinations are Taliwang, Dompu and Sape. You can buy tickets from agents, but they're cheaper at the terminal.

Tourist shuttle buses go to Lembar, Mataram, Senggigi, the Gili Islands, Labuhan Lombok and Kuta Beach on Lombok from various tourist centres on Bali, and also connect to Java and Sumbawa. A Perama ticket from south Bali to Mataram or Senggigi is 20,000 rp, including the ferry. From Mataram to Bima is 28,000 rp.

Boat Passenger ferries go every two hours between Lombok's Lembar harbour and Padangbai on Bali (5500 rp ekonomi; at least four hours). The *Mabua Ekspres* fast catamaran goes between Lembar and Bali's Benoa Port (US$13.50 ekonomi; 2½ hours), leaving Benoa at 8 am and 2.30 pm, and leaving Lembar at 11.30 am and 5.30 pm. Ferries to Poto Tano on Sumbawa depart hourly from Labuhan Lombok (2300 rp; about 1½ hours).

Pelni ships *Kelimutu*, *Sirimau* and *Awu* call at Lembar on their scheduled loops through the archipelago. The Pelni office is at Jalan Industri 1 in Ampenan (☎ 21604).

Getting Around
Bemo & Bus There are several terminals on Lombok, the main one at Sweta and others at Praya and Kopang. Away from main roads, you have to take a *cidomo* (horse cart), a motorcycle ojek or walk.

Car & Motorcycle On Jalan Gelantik in Mataram, near the junction of Jalan Selaparang and Jalan Hasanuddin, motorbike owners hang around with bikes to rent from 15,000 rp a day, maybe 12,000 per day for longer periods.

Metro Rent Car (☎ 32146), at Jalan Yos Sudarso in Ampenan, rents Suzuki Jimnys for 45,000 rp per day including insurance, with a US$250 excess. If you rent for more than three days, it's 40,000 rp per day. Also

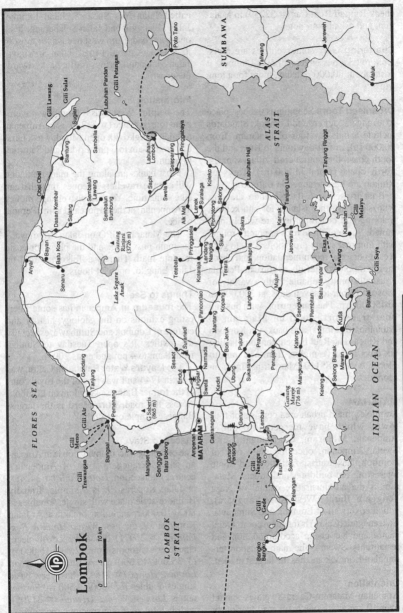

Lombok

0 5 10 km

FLORES SEA

LOMBOK STRAIT

INDIAN OCEAN

ALAS STRAIT

SUMBAWA

Poto Tano
Taliwang
Jereweh
Maluk

Gili Lawang
Gili Sulat
Gili Petangan
Labuhan Pandan
Sugian
Sambelia
Belanting
Obel Obel
Dasan Kembar
Sajang
Senaru
Batu Koq
Bayan
Anyar
Gondang
Tanjung
Pemenang
Bangsal
Gili Air
Gili Meno
Gili Trawangan
Mangset
Senggigi
Batu Bolong

Sembalun Lawang
Sembalun Bumbung
Gunung Rinjani (3726 m)
Lake Segara Anak

Labuhan Lombok
Selaparang
Pringgabaya
Sapit
Swela
Labuhan Haji
Tanjung Ringgit

Alk Mel
Lenek
Suralaga
Pringgasela
Pohgotong
Lendang Nangka
Sikur
Kotaraja
Terara
Tetebatu
Sakra
Koleko
Sokong
Janapria
Mujur
Keruak
Jerowaru
Tanjung Luar
Gili Melayu
Batu Nampar
Batujai
Ekas
Awang
Gili Saya

Pancordao
Kopang
Langko
Sengkol
Rembitan
Kuta
Mantang
Bon Jeruk
Pujung
Praya
Sade
Kateng
Selong Blanak
Mawan

Sesaot
Narmada
Surabadi
Ubung
Sukarara
Penujak
Mangkung
Keleng

Endut
Lingsar
Swela
Kediri
Gerung
Lembar
Gunung Mareje (716 m)

Ampenan
MATARAM
Cakranegara
G Saberis (865 m)
Gunung Pensong

Gili Nanggu
Taun
Sekotong
Pelangan
Gili Gede
Bangko Bangko

INDONESIA

check Rinjani Rent Car (☎ 32259) in Mataram, and ask at your hotel.

Chartering Only some vehicles are registered to take passengers all over Lombok; it costs about 60,000 rp a day, more for a long trip.

Organised Tours Senggigi is the best place to arrange a tour around Lombok. Standards include a half-day tour of Mataram (from 20,000 rp), or full-day tours to Kuta and the south coast, the central craft villages, or the north coast (from 35,000 rp). Treks on Rinjani are best arranged in Batu Koq.

Boat trips to see the Komodo dragons, with stops at other islands for snorkelling, trekking and beach parties, are widely promoted. Some of these trips are pretty rough, with minimal safety provisions – try to get a recent personal recommendation, and check the operation as carefully as you can. Perama is usually pretty reliable, with a variety of trips from four to seven days, at 200,000 rp to 450,000 rp. The longer trips, with bus and boat transport, go from Mataram to Labuanbajo (Flores) and back, via Komodo and Rinca. The Reef Expedition tour, lasting six days and five nights, from Mataram to Flores, costs US$110. Many trips finish on Flores.

MATARAM
Lombok's main urban area consists of four towns which have merged into one – Ampenan, Mataram, Cakranegara and Sweta. Ampenan, once the main port of Lombok, has tourist facilities and some interesting old buildings and streets. Mataram is the administrative capital of Nusa Tenggara Barat (West Nusa Tenggara), which covers all of Lombok and Sumbawa. Cakranegara (Cakra) is the main commercial centre and has cheap accommodation and restaurants. Sweta is the main transport terminal of Lombok and has the largest market.

Orientation
Ampenan-Mataram-Cakra-Sweta is spread over 10 km along one main road, variously

called Jalan Yos Sudarso, Jalan Langko, Jalan Pejanggik and Jalan Selaparang. It's a one-way road, from west to east, for most of its length. A parallel road, Jalan Sriwijaya-Jalan Majapahit, brings traffic back towards the coast.

Information
The helpful West Nusa Tenggara government tourist office (☎ 31730) is in Ampenan at Jalan Langko 70, open Monday to Thursday from 8 am to 3 pm, Friday and Saturday to noon.

Most banks are along the main road, and will change travellers' cheques, though it can take some time. You can also change money in Ampenan, at the airport and at the Perama office.

The Mataram GPO on Jalan Sriwijaya is the main post office and the place for poste restante mail. There's a Telkom wartel on Jalan Langko, open 24 hours.

Things to See
The **museum** in Ampenan has some interesting exhibits on the geology, history and culture of Lombok and Sumbawa, especially the textiles. It's open Tuesday to Sunday from 8 am to 4 pm and costs 200 rp.

The **Mayura Water Palace**, in Cakra, was built in 1744 and was part of the royal court of the former Balinese kingdom on Lombok. Across the road, **Pura Meru** is the largest Balinese temple on Lombok.

Places to Stay
The best budget accommodation is in Ampenan and Cakranegara. East of Ampenan's central intersection, *Hotel Zahir* (☎ 34248), at Jalan Koperasi 9, is a simple, friendly Balinese-style place with singles/ doubles at 8000/10,000 rp including breakfast. At Jalan Koperasi 19, the new *Wisata Hotel & Restaurant* (☎ 26971) has a choice of clean, characterless rooms from 12,000/ 15,000 rp to 35,000/40,000 rp. A little further on *Losmen Horas* (☎ 31695) has very basic singles/doubles for 9000/12,500 rp. Further out is *Losmen Wisma Triguna* (☎ 31705), with helpful staff and spacious rooms from

10,000/13,000 rp. Nearby *Losmen Angi Mammire* is cheap but OK. Just west of central Ampenan, *Losmen Pabean* (☎ 21758) has basic rooms at 5000/7500 rp with shared mandi.

At Jalan Pejanggik 64 in Mataram, next to the Perama office, *Hotel Kertajoga* (☎ 21775) is nothing special, but good value, with fan-cooled rooms at 15,000/18,500 rp, or 20,500/25,500 rp with air-con.

In Cakranegara, there are mid-range business traveller hotels on Jalan Pejanggik, including *Selaparang Hotel* (☎ 32670) and *Mataram Hotel* (☎ 23411), with rooms from around 25,000 rp, or 45,000 rp with air-con. Just south of the main drag, at Jalan Maktal 15, *Hotel & Restaurant Shanti Puri* (☎ 32649) has comfortable rooms from 15,000/20,000 rp. In the blocks around here are a number of Balinese-style losmen, like the *Oka* (☎ 22406), *Adiyuna* (☎ 25946) and the friendly *Losmen Ayu* (☎ 21761), with cheap rooms from about 10,000 rp a double.

If you want some comfort, the *Puri Indah* (☎ 37633) on Jalan Sriwijaya has a restaurant, pool and good rooms from 25,000 rp, or 35,000 rp with air-con.

Places to Eat

Ampenan has several Indonesian and Chinese restaurants including the popular *Cirebon*, at Jalan Yos Sudarso 113, and the *Pabean*, next door. A little further west, *Rainbow Cafe* is an inexpensive, friendly little place with reggae-inspired decor. *Poppy Nice Cafe*, on Jalan Koperasi, is as appealing as its name, with a good range of dishes. On the road to Senggigi, *Flamboyan Restaurant* is more expensive, with excellent Indonesian and seafood. Further up, *Pizzeria Cafe Alberto* (☎ 36781) has authentic cucina Italiana.

In Mataram, *Taman Griya* is a pleasant open-air place on Jalan Pejanggik, popular for its ice cream. *Denny Bersaudra*, just north of the main road, specialises in Sasak-style food.

Close to the losmen in Cakra, two cheap Chinese places are the *Friendship Cafe*, on Jalan Panca Usaha, and *Aroma*, on a side street beside the Mataram Hotel; a stir-fried meat and/or vegetable dish costs 3000 to 4000 rp. The conspicuous *KFC* is popular with affluent locals, while *Sekawan Depot Es*, across the road, has cold drinks downstairs and a seafood and Chinese restaurant upstairs. Around the corner on Jalan Hasanuddin a few places have Padang and Sasak food. There are also some bakeries around here, and plenty of cheap, spicy food at the market.

Things to Buy

Ampenan has interesting craft and 'antique' shops, with some good stuff at the Lombok Handicraft Centre at Sayang Sayang, and very authentic products at Sweta Market. To see the dyeing and weaving of traditional ikat, go to Selamat Riady or Rinjani Hand Woven; they both have fine fabrics for sale. The Lombok Pottery Centre is in Ampenan and sells some of the best earthenware products.

Getting There & Away

See the Lombok Getting There & Away section for details of flights and ferry services to and from Lombok. The Merpati office (☎ 23762) in Ampenan, at Jalan Yos Sudarso 6, also handles bookings and inquiries for Garuda flights. Sempati (☎ 21612) is in the Cilinaya shopping centre in Mataram, and Bouraq (☎ 27333) is at the Selaparang Hotel. Perama (☎ 35936) is at Jalan Pejanggik 66.

From Sweta, bemos go to Lembar (700 rp), Praya (700 rp), Masbagik (1300 rp), Labuhan Lombok (2000 rp), Senggigi (600 rp), Pemanang (for the Gili Islands; 900 rp) and Bayan (2300 rp). The terminal in Ampenan serves destinations to the north, and may be more convenient for Senggigi, Pemanang and Bayan.

Getting Around

Frequent No 7 bemos come by the airport, and go to the Ampenan bemo terminal. Yellow bemos shuttle up and down the two main routes between the Ampenan terminal at one end and the Sweta terminal at the

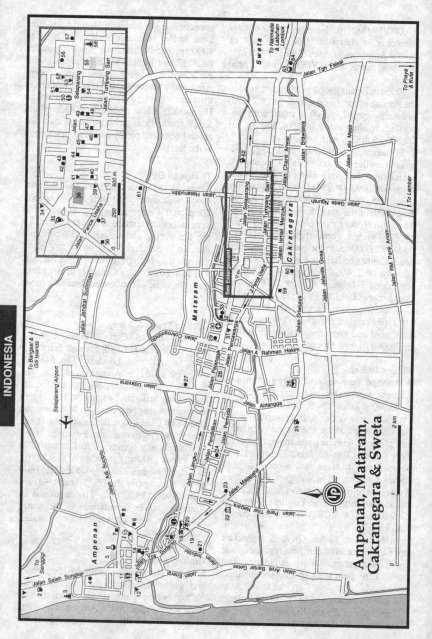

Ampenan, Mataram,
Cakranegara & Sweta

PLACES TO STAY			
7	Losmen Angi Mammire	14	Wisata Restaurant
8	Losmen Wisma Triguna	31	Taman Griya Restaurant
9	Losmen Horas	34	Denny Bersaudra Restaurant
14	Hotel Zahir & Wisata Hotel	39	Friendship Cafe
16	Nitour Hotel & Restaurant	41	Aroma Chinese Restaurant
32	Hotel Kertajoga	52	Rumah Makan Madya
36	Hotel Granada	53	KFC
37	Hotel Lombok Raya	54	Sekawan Depot Es
40	Oka Homestay		
43	Selaparang Hotel		**OTHER**
44	Mataram Hotel	2	Petrol Station
45	Hotel & Restaurant Shanti Puri	3	Pura Segara Temple
46	Losmen Ayu	4	Antique Shops
47	Adiyuna Homestay	5	Ampenan Market
48	Astiti Guest House	6	Ampenan Bemo Terminal
59	Graha Ayu	11	Moneychangers
60	Puri Indah Hotel	15	Antique Shops
		17	Tourist Office
	PLACES TO EAT	18	Wartel
1	Pizzeria Cafe Alberto	19	Post Office
10	Poppy Nice Cafe	20	Police
12	Rainbow Cafe	21	Pelni Office
13	Pabean & Cirebon Restaurants	22	Museum
		23	Lombok Pottery Centre

24	Mataram University
25	Petrol Station
26	GPO (Poste Restante)
27	Immigration Office
28	Main Square (Lampangan Mataram)
29	Governor's Office
30	Hospital
33	Perama Office
35	Petrol Station
38	Cilinaya Shopping Centre
42	Rinjani Hand Woven
49	Merpati Office
50	Bank Ekspor-Impor
51	Motorbike Rental
55	Market
56	Selamat Riady
57	Mayura Water Palace
58	Pura Meru Temple
61	Lombok Handicraft Centre
62	Petrol Station
63	Sweta Bus/Bemo Terminal
64	Sweta Market

other. The fare is a standard 300 rp regardless of distance. You can rent good bicycles for about 5000 rp a day from near the Cirebon Restaurant.

SENGGIGI BEACH

On a series of sweeping bays, between three and 12 km north of Ampenan, Senggigi is the most developed tourist area on Lombok. Senggigi has experienced a lot of new development in the last few years, and there are plans to promote more three and four-star hotels, though some projects seem to be stalled pending a new influx of investment. The beach is the main attraction, but there are some signs of erosion. There's some snorkelling, and beautiful sunsets over the Selat Lombok (Lombok Strait).

All the facilities are here – restaurants, bars, travel agents, photoprocessors, moneychangers, souvenir shops and a range of budget, mid-range and top-end accommodation. There's also a Telkom wartel, postal agent and a supermarket.

Places to Stay

There are a few low-budget places, but expect steep price hikes in the tourist season. *Pondok Senggigi* (☎ 93273) advertises rooms at 20,000 rp, but most of them cost from US$15/20 for singles/doubles, plus 15.5% for tax and service. Rooms face a pleasant garden, and there's a new pool and a popular restaurant. *Pondok Sederhana* (☎ 93040), a little north-west, has quite good rooms, some with views, for 20,000/25,000 rp. On the beach side of the road, *Lina Cottages* (☎ 93237) is central, friendly and good value at 25,000/35,000 rp, and its restaurant has a good reputation. Next door, *Dharma Hotel* has rooms and cottages in an open field by the beach for 15,000/20,000 to 30,000 rp.

Small places away from the beach are quiet and less expensive. *Bumi Aditya*, on a grassy slope up behind Pondok Melati Dua, has small bamboo bungalows which are clean, and somehow appealing, from 10,000 to 15,000 rp. *Astiti Guesthouse*, behind Pondok Wisata Rinjani, is less spacious, with

INDONESIA

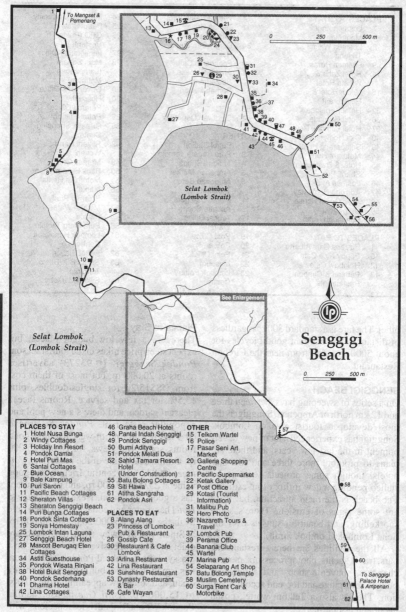

Senggigi Beach

Selat Lombok
(Lombok Strait)

Selat Lombok
(Lombok Strait)

Selat Lombok
(Lombok Strait)

See Enlargement

To Mangset &
Pemenang

To Senggigi
Palace Hotel
& Ampenan

0   250   500 m

0   250   500 m

0   250   500 m

PLACES TO STAY
1 Hotel Nusa Bunga
2 Windy Cottages
3 Holiday Inn Resort
4 Pondok Damai
5 Hotel Puri Mas
6 Santai Cottages
7 Blue Ocean
9 Bale Kampung
10 Puri Saron
11 Pacific Beach Cottages
12 Sheraton Villas
13 Sheraton Senggigi Beach
17 Puri Bunga Cottages
18 Pondok Sinta Cottages
19 Sonya Homestay
25 Lombok Intan Laguna
27 Senggigi Beach Hotel
28 Mascot Berugaq Elen
    Cottages
34 Astiti Guesthouse
35 Pondok Wisata Rinjani
38 Hotel Bukit Senggigi
40 Pondok Sederhana
41 Dharma Hotel
42 Lina Cottages

46 Graha Beach Hotel
48 Pantai Indah Senggigi
49 Pondok Senggigi
50 Bumi Aditya
51 Pondok Melati Dua
52 Sahid Tamara Resort
    Hotel
    (Under Construction)
55 Batu Bolong Cottages
59 Siti Hawa
61 Atitha Sangraha
62 Pondok Asri

PLACES TO EAT
8 Alang Alang
23 Princess of Lombok
    Pub & Restaurant
26 Gossip Cafe
30 Restaurant & Cafe
    Lombok
33 Arlina Restaurant
42 Lina Restaurant
43 Sunshine Restaurant
53 Dynasty Restaurant
    & Bar
56 Cafe Wayan

OTHER
15 Telkom Wartel
16 Police
17 Pasar Seni Art
    Market
20 Galleria Shopping
    Centre
21 Pacific Supermarket
22 Ketak Gallery
24 Post Office
29 Kotasi (Tourist
    Information)
31 Malibu Pub
32 Hero Photo
36 Nazareth Tours &
    Travel
37 Lombok Pub
39 Perama Office
44 Banana Club
45 Wartel
47 Marina Pub
54 Selaparang Art Shop
57 Batu Bolong Temple
58 Muslim Cemetery
60 Surga Rent Car &
    Motorbike

ordinary rooms round a small courtyard for 10,000/15,000 rp; friendly local guys hang around here.

Further up the main road, on the left, *Sonya Homestay* (☎ 63447) is a basic, family-run losmen with small rooms for 10,000/12,000 rp. Close by, *Pondok Sinta Cottages* is the same price, in slightly more spacious surroundings.

A couple of km further (100 rp on a bemo), and off to the east in Kampung Krandangan, *Bale Kampung* is billed as a backpackers place and has dorm beds at 6000 rp, rooms at 10,000 and 12,000 rp. They serve cheap food, and give good info about local attractions. Further north, in Mangset, *Santai Cottages* (☎ 93038) has a homely atmosphere, a library and book exchange, and serves traditional meals in a pleasant pavilion. Most of the cottages cost around 30,000 rp, but there are some cheaper rooms.

Pondok Damai (☎ 93019) and *Windy Cottages* (☎ 93191) are out by themselves five or six km north of Senggigi. They charge 30,000 to 35,000 rp for their most standard rooms.

Well south of the Senggigi strip, *Siti Hawa* (☎ 93414) is a funky little family-run homestay fronting a fantastic beach. A few, very small, very basic bamboo cottages cost 9000/10,000 rp.

Places to Eat

Most of the places to stay have their own restaurants, but there are other eating places along the main road in the centre of the strip. Local warungs seem to have been priced out of the real estate market, but you'll find a few food carts down near the beach.

Pondok Senggigi is the old favourite Senggigi stand-by, though it's not the cheapest (nasi goreng is around 3000 rp), but still popular from breakfast time until late at night. *Lina Cottages Restaurant* is also popular, with a big menu of very tasty dishes. It's a little cheaper, and has a great location by the beach. Nearby, *Sunshine Restaurant* has slightly westernised Chinese food – standard dishes are about 5000 rp, seafood specials run to 9000 rp. *Princess of Lombok*

serves slightly pricey Mexican food in its upstairs dining area. *Arlina* is also central, OK and reasonably priced. In the craft market, *Kafe Alberto* does pasta, pizza and barbecued seafood – a bit better, and a bit pricier, than the standard tourist fare.

Cafe Wayan (☎ 93098), south of the centre, is related to its namesake in Ubud, which should be recommendation enough. It will pick up in the Senggigi area if you call first.

Entertainment

Pondok Senggigi, *Banana Club* and *Marina Pub* host local bands doing rock and reggae with an Indonesian flavour. In the busy season, they can all get crowded with tourists and young locals, but at other times there's not much action. *Lombok Pub* and *Princess of Lombok* can be quite sociable.

Getting There & Away

Public bemos from Ampenan to Senggigi cost 450 rp, more if you are going to the northern end of the strip. Koprasi, the transport cooperative, will help with charter or rental vehicles. Perama (☎ 93007) and other shuttle companies have good connections to Senggigi. Sunshine Tours (☎ 930329) arranges boats direct to Gili Trawangan (7500 rp).

NARMADA, LINGSAR & SURANADI

About 10 km east of Cakra, **Narmada** is a landscaped hill and lake, laid out as a stylised, miniature replica of Gunung Rinjani and its lake, constructed for a king who could no longer make the pilgrimage up Rinjani. It's a nice place to spend a few hours, but crowded on weekends. They charge for admission, and also to use the swimming pool. There are frequent bemos from Sweta; the gardens are 100 metres south of the road.

A few km north-west of Narmada is **Lingsar**, a large temple complex catering for the Bali-Hindu, Islam and Wektu Telu religions. Buy hard-boiled eggs to feed to the holy eels in the Wektu Telu Temple. The temples are a short walk south of the main road.

INDONESIA

East of Lingsar, **Suranadi** has one of the holiest temples on Lombok. There are holy eels here too, which also appear for hard-boiled eggs. The Dutch-built *Suranadi Hotel* asks US$25 for the cheapest rooms, but you can use the spring-fed swimming pools for 1500 rp. Nearby *Pondok Surya* is basic but cheap, at 10,000/12,000 rp, and has wonderful food.

LEMBAR

Lembar, 22 km south of Ampenan, is Lombok's main port. The Bali ferries dock here, and there are regular buses and bemos between Lembar and Sweta during the day. There's a ferry office, and a canteen where you can buy snacks and drinks while waiting for the ferry. The only place to stay, the inexpensive *Serumbum Indah* (☎ 37153), is about two km north of the harbour on the main road.

SUKARARA

Just 25 km south-east of Mataram, Sukarara is one of the traditional weaving centres of Lombok. You can watch women weaving ikat and songket (hand-woven silver or gold-threaded cloth) and look at the colourful fabrics for sale. Catch a bemo from Sweta to Praya (700 rp), but get off at Puyung, about five km before Praya. From Puyung, take a cidomo to Sukarara (about 250 rp).

PRAYA TO KUTA

There are several Sasak villages south of Praya, though the number of traditional buildings is diminishing. Penujak is a centre for Lombok pottery and well worth a stop. Sade is a tourist-oriented 'traditional' village; Rembitan is more authentic and more interesting.

KUTA BEACH

Lombok's Kuta Beach is a magnificent stretch of sand with hills rising around it, though it's too dry for palm trees and lush greenery. There are some basic beach bunga-lows here, and big plans to develop the coast with four and five-star hotels. At the annual

nyale fishing celebration, which usually falls in February-March, Indonesians flock to Kuta.

You can change money at Anda Cottages, make phone calls at Matahari, and book Perama buses at Wisma Segara Anak (see below).

Places to Stay & Eat

Kuta's accommodation is mostly along the beachfront road east of the village. Most places have shoddy bamboo boxes, from 8000 to 10,000 rp a double with breakfast, but there are some slightly bigger, better and more expensive rooms. They all have limited leases and will have to close to make way for classier developments.

From the west, after the police station, you come to *Rambutan*, *Wisma Segara Anak* (☎ 54834), with a restaurant, *Pondok Sekar Kuning*, where upstairs rooms have a view, and *Anda Cottages* (☎ 54836), the original place at Kuta, with a garden and a good restaurant.

A bit further along is *Rinjani Agung Beach Bungalows* (☎ 54849), and *Cockatoo Cottages & Restaurant* (☎ 54830) is the last place along the beach.

Matahari Inn (☎ 54832), on the road to Mawan, is somewhat better, clean and good value from 10,000/15,000 rp to 30,000/40,000 rp.

Getting There & Away

On public transport, go first to Praya. From there, a few bemos run direct to Kuta, but you'll probably have to change at Sengkol. Shuttle buses are about 10,000 rp from Mataram or Senggigi, and much quicker.

AROUND KUTA

A good road goes five km east to **Tanjung Aan**, where there are two superb beaches – all of the beachfront land has been bought up for fancy tourist resorts.

West of Kuta, a scenic road goes past Are Goleng, Mawan and **Selong Blanak**, all with beautiful bays and perfect white beaches. You'll need your own transport. The only accommodation is at *Selong*

Blanak Cottages, a few km north of the coast on the road to Praya, and very nice from 20,000 rp. West of Selong Blanak, the road is passable to Pengantap, and extremely difficult beyond there to Blongas.

KOTARAJA AREA
The villages of **Kotaraja** and **Loyok** in eastern Lombok are renowned for their handicrafts, particularly basketware and plaited mats. You may also come across intricate metal jewellery, vases, caskets and other decorative objects. The area is cooler than the lowlands, and a great place to walk through rice fields, jungle and unspoilt villages.

Tetebatu is a mountain retreat on the southern slopes of Gunung Rinjani, seven km north of Kotaraja. The area is becoming popular with visitors, with lots of new accommodation. **Lendang Nangka**, about seven km east of Kotaraja, is an interesting Sasak village and a good base from which to explore the surrounding area. **Pringgasela**, three km north-east of there, is a centre for weaving blankets and sarongs.

Places to Stay & Eat
Wisma Soedjono in Tetebatu has a variety of single/double rooms and bungalows from around 15,000 to 45,000 rp. *Diwi Enjeni*, in the rice fields on the right as you come in from the south, is simple but nice, with rooms at 6000/10,000 rp. Other bungalows, like *Mekar Sari*, *Pondok Tetebatu*, *Green Ory*, *Hakiki* and *Rambutan Garden*, are sprouting in the rice fields around here.

At Lendang Nangka, you can stay with Hadji Radiah, the local primary school teacher who speaks good English and is a mine of information on the area. It costs 10,000/15,000 rp per day for a simple room with three excellent meals. There's also *Pondok Wira*, west of the village, *Pondok Bambu* to the north and *Akmal Homestay* in Pringgasela.

Getting There & Away
Take a bemo from Sweta to Pomotong (about 1200 rp) or Masbagik (1300 rp) and then head north by cidomo (500 rp), or on the back of a motorbike.

EAST COAST
The east coast is sparsely populated, with few tourist facilities. There's a nearly deserted beach bungalow at **Labuhan Haji**, the former harbour, and a pungent fishing port at **Tanjung Luar**.

The beach at Transad, 14 km north of Labuhan Lombok, is popular with locals on Sunday and holidays, and there's basic accommodation at *Gili Lampu Cottages*. Further north, *Siola Cottages*, near the sea at **Labuhan Pandan**, are attractive and secluded, at 15,000/25,000 rp. From here you can charter a boat out to explore the uninhabited offshore islands.

Labuhan Lombok
This is the port for ferries to Sumbawa, visible across the strait in clear weather. Look around the houses on stilts near the old port, or climb the hill on the south side of the harbour. *Losmen Munawar*, on the road round to the ferry port, is simple but quite OK at 5000/10,000 rp.

Getting There & Away There are regular buses between Labuhan Lombok and Sweta (2000 rp; about two hours). The ferries to/from Poto Tano on Sumbawa use the port about three km away on the north side of the harbour – take a bemo for 300 rp. Ferries depart about every hour (2300 rp; about 1½ hours) from 6 am to 10 pm. There are food stalls and a wartel at the port, and you can get water for the hot boat trip.

NORTH COAST
A sealed road runs right around the north coast, and there are public bemos on the route. With your own transport, it's easier to make side trips to several waterfalls, and to visit the fascinating traditional village of Segenter. At Bayan, branch south to Batu Koq and Senaru for access to Gunung Rinjani (see below). You can also detour to **Sembalun Lawang** and **Sembalun Bumbung**, on the eastern slopes of Rinjani.

GUNUNG RINJANI

Gunung Rinjani is the highest mountain in Lombok and the third highest in Indonesia. It has a huge half-moon shaped crater with a large green lake, hot springs and a number of smaller volcanic cones. Gunung Baru, the perfectly shaped cone in the centre of the lake, erupted in 1994. The view from the rim is stunning – it takes in the amazing crater, the whole north coast of Lombok, and Gunung Agung on Bali. From the very top you can see all of Lombok and half of Sumbawa as well. Rinjani is sacred to both Sasaks and Balinese, and many make pilgrimages here – it can get crowded. In the wet season the paths are slippery and dangerous.

The most frequently used route up Rinjani is from Senaru, on the northern slopes, reached via Bayan and Batu Koq. There are a number of places to stay along the road up to Senaru. They're nothing fancy, but cheap at around 7500/10,000 rp, and some have great views. Most can provide information, supplies and equipment, and arrange trekking guides and porters. Equipment rental is around 15,000 rp for a sleeping bag, tent, stove and cooking gear.

The most common trek is to climb from Senaru to Pos III (2100 metres) on the first day, which takes about 4½ hours of steep walking. Most people camp there and climb to the rim (2600 metres) for sunrise the next morning – this climb takes around 1½ to two hours. From there you descend into the crater and walk around to the hot springs (2010 metres), which takes about two hours on a very exposed track. The hot springs are a place to relax and camp for the second night, before returning all the way to Senaru the next day. The whole trip takes three full days – and probably another day to recover.

To get to the actual summit of Rinjani takes at least four days from Senaru. Two hours walk east from the hot springs, a track branches off to the summit. From this junction (Pelawangan II, at about 2400 metres), it's a difficult three or four hour climb over loose ground to the top (3726 metres).

Another option is to traverse the whole mountain by continuing east from the hot springs for about seven hours to Sembalun Lawang on the eastern slopes of Rinjani. Losmen in Senaru might be able to arrange for a bemo to pick you up there, or spend a night at Sembalun Lawang and return by bemo the following day.

If you start from Senaru at midnight, it's possible to get to the rim for sunrise, and return the same day. You can also traverse east around the rim for two hours to Gunung Senkerang Jaya (2904 metres), which gives a magnificent view to the east.

Getting There & Away

Several buses a day go from Sweta to Bayan (2300 rp; three hours), the first leaving around 9 am; some continue to Batu Koq. On the eastern side, there is transport in the morning from Sembalun Lawang to the north-coast road. The road south from Sembalun Bumbung is not drivable, but it's a wonderful walk to Sapit, which has a great place to stay, and infrequent transport to Pringgabaya and Labuhan Lombok.

GILI ISLANDS

Off the north-west coast of Lombok are three small coral-fringed islands – Gili Air, Gili Meno and Gili Trawangan – known as the Gili Islands by the thousands of visitors who come here for the very simple pleasures of sun, snorkelling and socialising. The islands have some small shops, wartels, moneychangers and 'pubs', but no hawkers and no motor vehicles. Reefseekers Pro Dive (☎ 34387), on Gili Air, is an excellent diving operation, as are Blue Marlin (☎ 32424), Albatross (☎ 30134) and Blue Coral (☎ 34497) on Trawangan.

To some extent, each island has developed its own character. Gili Air is the closest to the mainland, with homestays dotted among the palm trees – it's the prettiest and the most suitable for families. Gili Meno, the middle island, has the smallest population and the fewest tourists – it's the place to play Robinson Crusoe. Trawangan is the largest island, with the most visitors, the most facilities and a reputation as the party island.

There are proposals for upmarket resorts on the Gili Islands, even a golf course. These plans are not supported by many islanders, who have done well with low-budget tourism on their leased land. In 1992 some bungalows on Trawangan were forcibly relocated, leaving the northern part of the island rather desolate, while the rebuilt facilities further south are distinctly lacking in charm. There is no sign of any grandiose development, yet.

Please note that topless (for women) or nude sunbathing is offensive to the local people, and skimpy clothing is not appreciated away from the beaches.

Places to Stay & Eat

The quality of accommodation is improving, and a greater variety is available now, but there are still lots of places where you stay in a plain little bamboo bungalow, with a thatched roof, a small veranda and a concrete bathroom block out the back. Prices start at around 8000/10,000 rp for singles/doubles in the low season. In the busy seasons (July, August and around Christmas) they ask a lot more – maybe double the prices given here.

Most basic losmen provide a light breakfast, and most will also do dinner, typically with simple, local food. Restaurants are becoming more tourist oriented, especially on Trawangan – fresh seafood can be excellent.

Gili Air Accommodation is scattered round the coast, mostly in basic bungalows charging the standard rates (8000/10,000 rp with breakfast). Most are simple but attractive, and very similar – pick one in a location you like, or one that's been recommended by another traveller.

About the cheapest is *Anjani Bungalows*, for 5000/7000 rp; it's quite OK, but not attractively located. *Coconut Cottages* (☎ 35365) is better than the average, and charges 12,000/15,000 rp for standard bamboo bungalows, or 30,000 rp for very nice new ones. They serve great food, including some Sasak specialities. *Pondok Gili Air* has some standard rooms at 8800/13,200 rp,

plus better bungalows at 20,000/25,000 rp. Their menu includes vegetarian dishes and homemade yoghurt.

Gili Indah (☎ 36341) is the biggest place on Gili Air, with pleasant rooms from 20,000 rp, or a spacious, private pavilion for 45,000 rp. It also has the Perama office, a wartel and moneychanger. Up at the north end of the island, *Hotel Gili Air* (formerly Han's Bungalows; ☎ 34435) is another upmarket option, with a great-looking restaurant and well-finished bungalows from 55,000/66,000 rp to 77,000/88,000 rp.

Apart from eating at your losmen, or at the places mentioned above, you could also try *Il Pirata*, a reasonably priced Italian restaurant, open for dinner only. It's the place that looks like a pirate ship. *The Legend* and *Go Go* are both places to eat, and also venues for the island's limited nightlife.

Gili Meno The accommodation here is mostly on the east beach, with several places which are pretty upmarket by Gili standards. Good bottom-end places include *Pondok Meno* and *Malia's Child*, both at around 10,000/15,000 rp, but considerably more in the high season.

Zoraya Pavilion (☎ 33801) has interesting rooms from US$10/12 to US$30/32 for singles/doubles, and offers watersports and a tennis court. *Casablanca* (☎ 33847) is back from the beach, with rooms from US$10/12 to US$45, but it's not particularly appealing, even with its tiny swimming pool. *Gazebo Hotel* (☎ 35795) has tastefully decorated Bali-style bungalows, comfortably spaced among the coconut trees. It costs US$47/59 for bed & breakfast. Anyone can change cash or travellers' cheques here, make phone calls or eat in the fancy balcony restaurant.

Kontiki (☎ 32824) has good value rooms at 12,000/15,000 rp, and more expensive ones too. *Bouganvil Resor* (☎ 27435) is a new mid-range hotel with swimming pool, air-con, and rates from US$45 and rising.

Brenda's Place, the beachfront restaurant at Mallia's Child, is one of the best places to eat, and does a tasty pizza. *Kontiki* has pretty

INDONESIA

good food, in a big breezy pavilion, while *Good Heart*, on the other side of the island, is a pleasant place to pause on a round-island trek, and has a great view at sunset. Don't expect snappy service or wild nightlife anywhere on Gili Meno.

Gili Trawangan Most of the tourist facilities are concentrated near the beach in the southern part of the island. Old-style bamboo places in this area include *Halim Bungalows* and *Sagittarius*, from 8000/10,000 rp for singles/doubles in the low season, but increasing dramatically when it's busy. Newer

places, like *Danau Hijau Bungalows* and *Fantasi*, ask about 12,000/15,000 rp. *Pak Majid*, *Melati* and *Borobudur* are better quality, from 20,000 to 35,000 rp, but without much character. Behind the main drag are some really basic options, like *Pretty Peace* and *Alex Homestay*, where a room will cost as little as 6000 rp with a shared bathroom.

At the north end of the island, *Nusa Tiga* and *Coral Beach* are right by the beach, wonderfully isolated, dirt cheap, but a bit run down. The south coast doesn't have nice beaches, but there's secluded, cheap and ade-

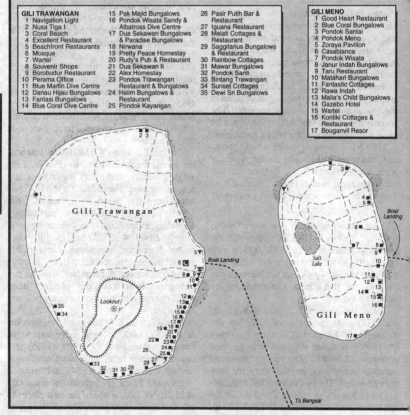

GILI TRAWANGAN
1. Navigation Light
2. Nusa Tiga I
3. Coral Beach
4. Excellent Restaurant
5. Beachfront Restaurants
6. Mosque
7. Wartel
8. Souvenir Shops
9. Borobudur Restaurant
10. Perama Office
11. Blue Marlin Dive Centre
12. Danau Hijau Bungalows
13. Fantasi Bungalows
14. Blue Coral Dive Centre

15. Pak Majid Bungalows
16. Pondok Wisata Sandy & Albatross Dive Centre
17. Dua Sekawan Bungalows & Paradise Bungalows
18. Nirwana
19. Pretty Peace Homestay
20. Rudy's Pub & Restaurant
21. Dua Sekawan II
22. Alex Homestay
23. Pondok Trawangan Restaurant & Bungalows
24. Halim Bungalows & Restaurant
25. Pondok Kayangan

26. Pasir Putih Bar & Restaurant
27. Iguana Restaurant
28. Melati Cottages & Restaurant
29. Saggitarius Bungalows & Restaurant
30. Rainbow Cottages
31. Mawar Bungalows
32. Pondok Santi
33. Bintang Trawangan
34. Sunset Cottages
35. Dewi Sri Bungalows

GILI MENO
1. Good Heart Restaurant
2. Blue Coral Bungalows
3. Pondok Santai
4. Pondok Meno
5. Zoraya Pavilion
6. Casablanca
7. Pondok Wisata
8. Janur Indah Bungalows
9. Taru Restaurant
10. Matahari Bungalows
11. Fantastic Cottages
12. Rawa Indah
13. Malia's Child Bungalows
14. Gazebo Hotel
15. Wartel
16. Kontiki Cottages & Restaurant
17. Bouganvil Resor

Gili Trawangan

Lookout

Boat Landing

Gili Meno

Salt Lake

Boat Landing

To Bangsal

quate accommodation at places like *Mawar* and *Bintang Trawangan*. *Pondok Santi* is a nice one, for 17,500/20,000 rp. Right round on the west side, *Dewi Sri* is a tidy place, well away from everything, and pretty good value from 8000/10,000 rp.

Borobudur is a popular restaurant, with a typical menu and prices – a great tuna steak costs 5000 rp, plus 2000 rp for salad. Mie or nasi goreng will cost under 2000 rp. *Trawangan*, *Blue Marlin* and *Rainbow* are other popular restaurants. *Iguana* is also good, with some Sasak-style food, seafood specials and the best beef burgers on the

island. During the day, there's a bunch of simple eateries by the beach just north of the boat landing.

The bigger restaurants in the tourist strip are more like bars in the evening. A few show video movies, which do nothing for conviviality. Party nights alternate between *Trawangan*, *Rainbow*, *Iguana* and the *Excellent*, with music, dancing, much drinking and the odd mushroom. The highlight of Trawangan's social calendar is the full moon beach party, where a fixed price of about 8000 rp gets you your first drink, food and music.

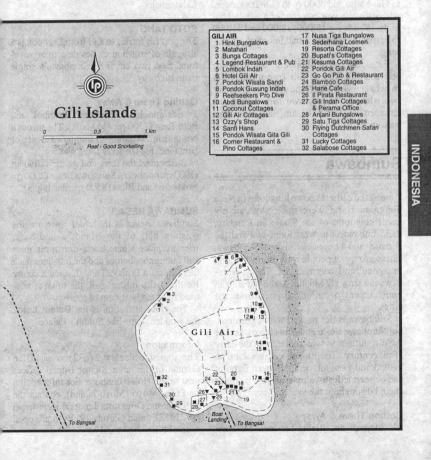

GILI AIR
1 Hink Bungalows
2 Matahari
3 Bunga Cottages
4 Legend Restaurant & Pub
5 Lombok Indah
6 Hotel Gili Air
7 Pondok Wisata Sandi
8 Pondok Gusung Indah
9 Reefseekers Pro Dive
10 Abdi Bungalows
11 Coconut Cottages
12 Gili Air Cottages
13 Ozzy's Shop
14 Sanfi Hans
15 Pondok Wisata Gita Gili
16 Corner Restaurant & Pino Cottages
17 Nusa Tiga Bungalows
18 Sederhana Losmen
19 Resorta Cottages
20 Bupati's Cottages
21 Kesuma Cottages
22 Pondok Gili Air
23 Go Go Pub & Restaurant
24 Bamboo Cottages
25 Harie Cafe
26 Il Pirata Restaurant
27 Gili Indah Cottages & Perama Office
28 Anjani Bungalows
29 Satu Tiga Cottages
30 Flying Dutchmen Safari Cottages
31 Lucky Cottages
32 Salabose Cottages

Gili Islands

0   0.5   1 km

Reef - Good Snorkelling

Gili Air

Boat Landing

To Bangsal   To Bangsal

INDONESIA

Getting There & Away

From Ampenan or the airport, take a bemo to Pemenang (600 rp) – you may have to change at Rembiga. From Pemenang it's a 250 rp cidomo ride to the harbour at Bangsal. Tourist shuttle buses go to Bangsal from Mataram, Senggigi (5000 rp) and elsewhere.

Boat tickets are 1200 rp to Gili Air, 1500 rp to Gili Meno and 1600 rp to Gili Trawangan. It's a matter of waiting until there's a full boatload (15 people), or paying the extra fares between you. Try to get to Bangsal by 9.30 am.

A scheduled boat service leaves at 10 am and 4 pm, costing 3000 rp to Gili Air, 3500 rp to Gili Meno and 4000 rp to Gili Trawangan. Alternatively, you can charter a whole boat to the islands for 15,000, 18,000 and 21,000 rp respectively, with a maximum of 10 passengers.

Fares for 'island-hopping' are 4000 rp between Gili Air and Gili Trawangan; 3000 rp between Gili Meno and either of the other two islands. They do two runs a day, one between 8.30 and 10 am, and the other between 2.30 and 4 pm.

Sumbawa

Among the earliest known kingdoms in Nusa Tenggara Barat were the comparatively small kingdoms of the Sasaks in Lombok, the Sumbawans in west Sumbawa and the Bimans and Dompuese in east Sumbawa. These groups of people were animists living in agricultural communities. Today, Sumbawa is a strongly Muslim island but with an undercurrent of animism away from the cities.

Sumbawa is not packed with attractions, but Sumbawa Besar and Bima have traces of the old sultanates, which date from the early 18th century. Traditional villages can be visited and Lombok or Sumbawan fighting can be seen at festival times. Horse racing is staged throughout the year.

Getting There & Away

Air Merpati has flights between Mataram and Sumbawa Besar (70,800 rp) but Bima is the main hub with direct flights to Bajawa, Ende, Labuanbajo, Ruteng (all in Flores), Mataram and Tambulaka (Sumba). Connecting flights include Denpasar and Kupang.

Boat Ferries from Poto Tano depart for Lombok every hour. In the east, Sape is the departure point for ferries to Komodo and Flores, every day except Friday.

Pelni's KM *Binaiya* stops in Bima on its loop through Nusa Tenggara every two weeks, and the KM *Tilongkabila* goes from Bima to Ujung Pandang in Sulawesi via Labuanbajo.

POTO TANO

The port for ferries to and from Lombok is a straggle of stilt houses beside a mangrove-lined bay, two km from Sumbawa's single main highway.

Getting There & Away

Ferries run hourly between Lombok and Poto Tano (2300 rp; 1½ hours). The through buses from Mataram to Sumbawa Besar or Bima include the ferry fare.

Buses meet the ferry and go to: Taliwang (1000 rp; one hour), Sumbawa Besar (2000 rp; two hours) and Bima (8500 rp; nine hours).

SUMBAWA BESAR

Sumbawa Besar is the chief town on the western half of the island, a laid-back, friendly place where horse-drawn cidomos still outnumber bemos and the mosques pack them in on a Friday. Though once a centre for the 'hello mister' cult, the town is now used to a steady stream of tourists.

The chief attraction is the **Dalam Loka**, the wooden, barn-like Sultan's Palace.

Information

The tourist office (☎ 21632) is on Jalan Garuda in the large Kantor Bupati offices next to the Hotel Tambora. For information on Pulau Moyo (Moyo Island), contact the PHPA at the Direktorat Jenderal Kehutanan (☎ 21358), Jalan Garuda 12. Both are open normal office hours only.

Bank Danaman changes a wide variety of currencies and gives credit card cash advances, or try the BNI bank at Jalan Kartini 10.

The area code for Sumbawa Besar is 0371.

Places to Stay

Right on the doorstep of the sultan's palace, the *Losmen Garoto* (☎ 22062) at Jalan Batu Pasak 48 has tiny singles/doubles for 3500/6000 rp or larger rooms with mandi cost 6000/10,000 rp. The *Losmen Taqdeer* (☎ 21987), down a residential lane off Jalan Kamboja near the old bus terminal on Jalan Diponegoro, is a clean little establishment with rooms from 6000 rp.

Other cheap hotels are clustered along Jalan Hasanuddin close to the mosque and a 4.30 am wake-up call. Experience indigenous culture at its loudest. *Losmen Saudara* (☎ 21528) or the less clean *Losmen Tunas* (☎ 21212) both have rooms for around 5000/7500 rp. The *Hotel Suci* (☎ 21589) has large double rooms with private mandi around a neat courtyard for 15,000 rp.

The *Hotel Tambora* (☎ 21555), just off Jalan Garuda on Jalan Kebayan, is an excellent mid-range hotel and worth the extra. Rooms, all with attached bath, range from 8250/11,000 rp to 77,000/93,000 rp for deluxe rooms. The hotel has plenty of information, a good restaurant and makes bus bookings.

Places to Eat

Warungs set up in front of the stadium on Jalan Yos Sudarso in the evenings and sell soto ayam, sate, bakso and other cheap Madurese fare. The *Rukun Jaya*, on Jalan Hasanuddin close to many of the hotels, is a small restaurant with cheap food. *Rumah Makan Mushin*, Jalan Wahidin 31, is a spotless little cafe with simple but very tasty Lombok/Taliwang dishes.

Sumbawa Besar has two very good Chinese restaurants: the *Aneka Rasa Jaya* at Jalan Hasanuddin 14 and the *Puspa Warna* at Jalan Kartini 16. The *Hotel Tambora* has a pleasant restaurant and a varied menu.

Getting There & Away

Air Merpati (☎ 21416), Jalan Kebayan 2A, flies to Mataram and on to Denpasar and Surabaya.

Bus The main long-distance bus station is the new Karang Dima terminal, 5.5 km west of town on the highway. Buses include: Sape (7500 rp; 7½ hours), Bima (6000 rp; six hours), Dompu (5000 rp; 4½ hours), Taliwang (2500 rp; three hours) and Poto Tano (2000 rp; two hours). Some morning buses to Bima leave from the Brang Bara terminal on Jalan Kaharuddin, closer to the centre, and afternoon through buses stop at the old terminal on Jalan Diponegoro in the centre of town. The long-distance deluxe buses from Mataram to Sape are preferable to the more numerous old rattlers.

Boat Pelni's KM *Tatamailau* stops every two weeks at the small port of Badas, seven km west of Sumbawa Besar, on its loop through the eastern islands. The Pelni office is at Labuhan Sumbawa, the town's fishing port three km west of town.

Getting Around

Sumbawa Besar is small and you can walk around much of it with ease. Bemos operate on a flat rate of 250 rp per person including to the airport, bus station, post office or to Labuhan Sumbawa.

PULAU MOYO

Two-thirds of Pulau Moyo, three km off Sumbawa's north coast, is a reserve noted for its excellent snorkelling and abundant fish. The boat tours between Lombok and Flores usually stop here on the north side of the island, or the less interesting southern side can be reached by chartering a boat (10,000 rp one way) from Aik Bari, half an hour north of Sumbawa Besar. The PHPA is helpful for arranging a visit.

HUU

Sumbawa's south coast has some beautiful beaches and good surf. Huu, south of

Dompu, is Sumbawa's surfing mecca. *Mona Lisa* and *Intan Lestari* are two of the cheaper hotels with accommodation from 10,000 rp per person.

Getting to Huu by public transport is a real hassle. From Dompu's Ginte bus terminal take a bemo (250 rp) to the central market, then a cidomo (250 rp per person) to the Lepardi bus terminal, then an infrequent bus to Rasabau (750 rp; 1½ hours) and finally a crowded bemo to the beach. Most visitors come by chartered taxi from Bima airport.

BIMA

This is Sumbawa's main port and the major centre on the eastern end of the island. It's really just a stop on the way through Sumbawa, and there's nothing much to see or do. The only notable attraction of Bima is the large former **sultan's palace**, now a museum open 7 am to 5 pm. Guides will attach themselves to you and offer minimal insight but expect a large donation – a few hundred rupiah should suffice. The Jalan Flores **night market** is worth a wander.

Information

The tourist information office (☎ 44331) is next to the Kantor Bupati on Jalan Soekarno-Hatta about two km east of the town centre.

The Bank Rakyat Indonesia on Jalan Sumbawa changes foreign currency and travellers' cheques, as does the BNI bank on Jalan Sultan Hasanuddin.

The area code for Bima is 0374.

Places to Stay & Eat

Bima is compact and most hotels are in the middle of town.

The long-popular *Hotel Lila Graha* (☎ 42740), Jalan Lombok 20, is a 10 minute walk from the central bus station. It has an excellent restaurant but ordinary rooms for 8000/11,500 rp, or 13,500/16,500 rp with mandi. Breakfast is included. Just next door is the dingy but cheap *Losmen Pelangi* (☎ 42878). Boxy double rooms are 6000 rp per person with shared mandi, or 7500 rp with private mandi.

A good option is the friendly *Wisma Komodo* (☎ 42070) on Jalan Sultan Ibrahim, which has long been popular with travellers. Good-value doubles are 7500 rp, or 12,500 rp with mandi.

The cheapest place in town is the seedy *Losmen Kartini* (☎ 42072) at Jalan Pasar 11. They rent more than just rooms, but you can stay there for 4000 rp per person.

Restaurant Lila Graha, attached to the hotel of the same name, has a long menu and good food. Also on Jalan Lombok *Rumah Makan Sembilan Sembilan* specialises in fried chicken and has other good Chinese and Indonesian dishes. The night market has stalls selling sate, curry, gado gado, rice creations and interesting snacks.

Getting There & Away

Air The Merpati office (☎ 42697) is at Jalan Soekarno-Hatta No 60, east of the town centre. Direct flights go between Bima and Denpasar, Bajawa, Ende, Labuanbajo, Mataram, Maumere, Ruteng and Tambulaka, with connections to points further afield.

Bus Buses to destinations west of Bima depart from Bima's central bus station, just 10 minutes walk from the centre of town. Day buses to Sumbawa Besar cost 6000 rp. The numerous express night-bus agents near the bus station sell tickets for air-con buses to Sumbawa Besar (12,500 rp; six hours) and Mataram (22,000 rp; 11 hours). Buses to Mataram leave around 7.30 pm.

Buses to Sape (1100 rp; two hours) depart from Kumbe in Raba, a 20 minute bemo ride (250 rp) east of Bima, but they can't be relied upon to meet the early-morning ferry to Flores and Komodo. The big buses coming though Bima from Surabaya at 4 am can pick up from the hotels and take you through to Sape for 2000 rp, if you arrange it the night before at the bus station. A chartered bemo to Sape costs around 25,000 rp.

Boat The Pelni office (☎ 35402) is at Jalan Martadinata 73, near the Losmen Kartini. Pelni's KM *Binaiya* stops in Bima on its loop through Nusa Tenggara every two weeks, and the KM *Tilongkabila* goes from Bima to Ujung Pandang in Sulawesi via Labuanbajo.

Getting Around
Bima has plenty of bemos and dokars for short trips. Both cost 250 rp per person. Bima's airport is 16 km out of town; bemos are cheap but infrequent while taxis cost 10,000 rp.

SAPE
Sape is a pleasant enough little town but the only reason to visit is to catch the ferry to Komodo and Flores from Pelabuhan Sape, three km from Sape.

The PHPA office for Komodo information is two km from the town towards Pelabuhan Sape.

Places to Stay & Eat
Losmen Mutiara, nestled just outside the entrance to the port, is the most convenient. Rooms with shared mandi cost 7500/10,000 rp. In town, *Losmen Friendship* lives up to its name. Clean doubles with shared mandi cost 8000 rp (10,000 rp with private mandi). Two cheaper, more basic places are the *Losmen Ratna Sari* and the *Losmen Give* with rooms from 6000 rp.

Getting There & Away
Bus Buses go to Sape (1100 rp; two hours) from the Kumbe bus station in Bima-Raba. Buses to Bima meet the ferry from Komodo and Labuanbajo, and you can pick up the air-con express buses all the way to Mataram or even through to Surabaya.

Boat The car/passenger ferries to Labuanbajo (11,500 rp) on Flores, stopping at Komodo (10,000 rp) on the way, leave at 8 am every day except Friday from Pelabuhan Sape. Ferries have been known to break down and be out of action for weeks. Check schedules in Bima. The duration of the crossing varies with the tides and weather, but allow five to seven hours to Komodo, eight to 10 hours to Labuanbajo.

Komodo & Rinca

Komodo is a hilly, dry, desolate island sandwiched between Flores and Sumbawa. Its big attraction is lizards – four-metre, 130-kg lizards, appropriately known as Komodo dragons. The best time to see dragons is from June to September, in the dry season, when they come to the watering holes. The only village on the island is **Kampung Komodo**, a fishing village on the east coast of the island and worth a look. Also on the coast, a half-hour walk from the village, is **Loh Liang**, the site of the PHPA tourist camp.

Some people prefer to visit Rinca because it is closer to the Flores coast and less visited. Dragon-spotting is less organised and the chances of seeing them less certain. The PHPA also has a tourist camp on Rinca at **Loh Buaya**.

Permits for Komodo are issued at the PHPA camp at Loh Liang, or on Rinca at Loh Buaya. Permits cost 2000 rp per person.

Dragon-Spotting
Banu Nggulung, the most accessible place to see dragons, has been set up like a little theatre. The PHPA guides will take you to this dried up river bed about a half-hour walk from Loh Liang. The dragons used to flock here for a free feed of goat provided by tourist groups, but this gruesome ritual has been discontinued. Spotting dragons is no longer guaranteed, but a few of these fabulous beasties are almost always in attendance.

A guide costs 3000 rp, or 1000 rp per person for groups of more than three. The PHPA prefers to organise fixed times and take large groups, though smaller groups are less like a zoo.

Around Komodo
While most visitors only stay overnight to see the dragons at Banu Nggulung, Komodo has plenty of other activities.

You can climb to Gunung Ara for expansive views across the island. A guide costs

INDONESIA

20,000 rp for a maximum of five people and the trip takes 3½ hours return. Longer walks are to Poreng Valley and Loh Sabita. The half-hour walk along the beach to Kampung Komodo can be done without a guide.

Wild pigs are commonly seen, often close to the camp, and the Komodo dragons occasionally wander into the PHPA camp, but they avoid the kampung because there are too many people. Snakes inhabit the island and signs are posted as a warning.

Good snorkelling can be found at **Pantai Merah** (Red Beach) and the small island of **Pulau Lasa** near Kampung Komodo. Boats can be hired, as can a snorkel and mask from the PHPA, but if you want to go snorkelling it's best to bring your own equipment.

Places to Stay & Eat
The PHPA camp at Loh Liang is a collection of large, spacious, clean wooden cabins on stilts. Each cabin has four or five rooms and singles/doubles cost 10,000/15,000 rp. During the peak tourist season around July/August the rooms may be full but the PHPA will rustle up mattresses to sleep on. Accommodation on Rinca is similar and costs the same.

The camp restaurant is limited to below-average mie goreng and nasi goreng, plus expensive beverages. Bring some supplies or stock up in Kampung Komodo.

Getting There & Away
The ferries between Labuanbajo in Flores and Pelabuhan Sape on Sumbawa stop at Komodo. The ferries cannot dock at Loh Liang and stop about one km out to sea, from where small boats transfer you to Komodo for 1500 rp.

Boat tours can be arranged to Komodo and Rinca from Labuanbajo.

Flores

One of the most beautiful islands in Indonesia, Flores is an astounding string of active and extinct volcanoes. The name is Portu-

guese for 'Flowers', as the Portuguese were the first Europeans to colonise the island. They eventually sold it to the Dutch. Flores is 95% Catholic, the church dominates every tiny village and only in the ports will you find any number of Muslims.

The main attraction is the coloured volcanic lakes of Keli Mutu near Moni. Labuanbajo is a popular place to kick back for few days and has decent beaches. Bajawa has become something of a travellers' centre and is the place to visit nearby traditional villages.

Getting There & Away
Air Maumere is the best place for getting to or from Flores by air. Book well in advance for flights from other towns in Flores and always reconfirm. Ende, Labuanbajo and Bajawa only accommodate small aircraft, so seating is limited.

Bouraq connects Maumere with Denpasar in Bali (271,000 rp) and Kupang in Timor (101,600 rp). Merpati also connects Maumere with Bima in Sumbawa, and Kupang. It also connects Bajawa, Labuanbajo and Ruteng with Bima, and Ende with Kupang.

Boat Regular ferries connect Labuanbajo in western Flores with Komodo and Sumbawa. From Larantuka in eastern Flores ferries go to Kupang and the eastern islands of the Solor and Alor archipelagos. From Ende regular boats go to Waingapu in Sumba and to Kupang.

Pelni's KM *Tatamailau* calls at Labuanbajo and Larantuka on its way between Surabaya and Dili (Timor), Maluku and Irian Jaya. The KM *Binaiya* travels Bali-Lembar-Bima-Labuanbajo-Waingapu-Ende-Kupang-Kalabahi-Dili-Maumere and then to Sulawesi. The KM *Tilongkabila* stops at Labuanbajo before continuing on to Sulawesi.

Getting Around
Air Merpati has flights from Labuanbajo to Ende and Ruteng, and between Bajawa and Ende.

Bus The Trans-Flores Highway loops and tumbles nearly 700 scenic km from Labuanbajo to Larantuka. The highway connects all the major centres and the road is surfaced virtually all the way. Travel is now much easier and more reliable, but still exhausting. Travel in the wet season can be problematic, especially off the highway when vehicles on the unsealed roads get bogged; a trip that might take hours in the dry season can take days.

Public buses run regularly between all the major towns. They are cheap, leave when full (sometimes very full) and stop at all stations. Tickets can usually be bought the day before departure from agents or from the drivers. The big air-con luxury buses you'll find on Sumatra or Java don't exist on Flores. The highway is too narrow and winding to accommodate big buses, and the road would quickly turn any 'delux' bus into 'ekonomi'. Open-sided trucks with wooden seats also cover the local runs.

LABUANBAJO

This fishing village at the extreme western end of Flores is a jumping-off point for Komodo. If you've got a few days to while away, then Labuanbajo is a pleasant enough village to do it in. It's a pretty place with a harbour sheltered by several small islands. There are reasonable beaches just outside town, such as Waicicu, good snorkelling and a host of tours on offer.

Information

The Bank Rakyat Indonesia is open Monday to Friday from 7 am to 3 pm. For currencies other than US dollars, expect a very poor exchange rate. The PHPA office is a five minute walk along the airport road from the Hotel Wisata. The Telkom office is just beyond it, and the tourist office (☎ 41170), open normal office hours, is behind the Telkom office.

The area code for Labuanbajo is 0385.

Organised Tours

Labuanbajo has a host of boat tours to Komodo, Rinca and further afield. A two day tour, sleeping overnight on the boat, to Komodo, Rinca and Kalong (Bat Island)

costs around 50,000 rp per person on a fishing boat that takes eight people. Many hotels can arrange boats for day trips to Komodo or to Pulau Sabolo, which has good snorkelling.

Popular boat tours run to Lombok via Komodo, Rinca and then along the north coast of Sumbawa, stopping at Pulau Moyo before continuing on to Lombok. Fares are typically around US$95 to US$115 for a five or six day trip, though the last day may be at uninteresting Labuhan Lombok. Shop around and find out exactly what is included – entrance fees, equipment, bus transfers to Mataram, what sort of food is served, sleeping arrangements (always on the boat but check the cabin) etc.

Places to Stay

The *Mutiara Beach Hotel* (☎ 41039) has harbour views and very basic singles/doubles cost 5000/8000 rp, or dark rooms with mandi cost 6000/12,000 rp. The well-appointed *Bajo Beach Hotel* (☎ 41009) across the road is more upmarket. Rooms start at 4000/7000 rp, or those with mandi, from 7000/10,000 rp to 12,500/17,500 rp, are much better.

The popular *Gardena Hotel* has a hilltop position above the main road. Simple bungalows around a garden cost 6000/8500 rp to 8000/12,500 rp.

A good, new place with a young management that tries hard is the *Mitra Hotel* (☎ 41003). Very clean rooms cost 6000/8000 rp, or 10,000/12,500 rp with mandi.

The well-run *Hotel Wisata* (☎ 41020) competes with the Bajo Beach as the best hotel in the town. Rooms cost 10,000/12,500 rp to 15,000/20,000 rp.

Labuanbajo also has a number of small homestays. The best is *Chez Felix*, run by a friendly family that speaks good English. Singles/doubles are 6000/8000 rp, or 8000/12,500 rp to 10,000/15,000 rp with mandi. Nearby is the quiet *Sony Homestay*, with a nice hilltop view. Basic but clean singles/doubles with private bath are 5000/7500 rp.

A number of beach hotels can be found outside the town. Most are reached by boat

– free for guests. The *Weicucu Beach Hotel*, a 20 minute boat ride north of Labuanbajo, has long been a popular budget option because of its price – 7500 rp per person for a basic bamboo bungalow or 10,000 rp with attached mandi, including all meals – but prices are set to double.

Other expensive options include the *Batu Gosok Lodge* (☎ 41030), a half-hour boat ride from town, and the *New Bajo Beach Hotel* (☎ 41047), 2.5 km by road south of town.

Kanawa Island Bungalows on Kanawa Island, one hour by boat from Labuanbajo, has simple bungalow accommodation costing 12,500/17,500 rp. *Nuca Lala Bungalows* on Pungu Island, a half-hour boat ride from Labuanbajo, is a new place with good bungalows for 15,000 rp a double.

Places to Eat
Labuanbajo has a few good restaurants specialising in seafood at reasonable prices. Pick of the crop is the *Borobudur*, more expensive than most but worth it. It has excellent fish, prawns, a few Thai dishes, steaks and even schnitzel.

The *Dewata* and the *Sunset* restaurants are also good. The Bajo Beach, Gardena and Wisata hotels all have good restaurants.

Getting There & Away
Air Merpati has direct flights between Labuanbajo and Ende (116,000 rp), Ruteng (53,000 rp) and Bima (61,000 rp), with connections on to Mataram (184,700 rp), Denpasar (229,800 rp) and further afield.

The airfield is 2.5 km from the town and hotels can arrange a taxi (5000 rp). The Merpati office is between Labuanbajo and the airport, about 1.5 km from the town.

Bus Buses to Ruteng (4000 rp; four hours) leave at 7.30 am and around 4 pm when the ferry arrives from Sape and Komodo. Buses to Bajawa (10,000 rp; 10 hours) leave at 6.30 am and a bus also usually meets the ferry. The Damri bus to Ende (15,000 rp; 14 hours) meets the ferry if you are desperate to get to

Keli Mutu in a hurry and are well stocked with pain killers!

Boat The ferry from Labuanbajo to Komodo (4000 rp; three hours) and Sape (11,500 rp; five to seven hours) leaves at 8 am every day except Friday.

Pelni's KM *Tatamailau* calls at Labuanbajo on its way from Banyuwangi and Badas and goes on to Larantuka, Dili and Maluku, then returns. The KM *Tilongkabila* runs direct to Ujung Pandang in Sulawesi every two weeks.

RUTENG
Ruteng is basically just another stop on the way through Flores. For spectacular views of the rice paddies and terraced slopes of the hills and valleys to the north, climb the hill to the north of Ruteng early in the morning. **Gunung Ranaka**, an active volcano that erupted in 1989, is just outside town. An overgrown road leads to the top but you cannot walk to the still-active crater.

Information
The BNI bank on Jalan Kartini and the Bank Rakyat Indonesia on Jalan Yos Sudarso handle foreign exchange. The post office is at Jalan Baruk 6.

The area code for Ruteng is 0384.

Places to Stay & Eat
The *Hotel Sindha* (☎ 21197) on Jalan Yos Sudarso is central and a good option. Rooms with outside mandi for 7000/10,000 rp are bright, roomy and better value than those with mandi for 15,000/20,000 rp. More luxurious rooms cost 20,000/24,000 rp to 40,000 rp. The attached restaurant serves good Chinese food.

Wisma Agung 11 (☎ 21835), behind Toko Agung on Jalan Motang Rua, is basic but clean and right in the town centre. Economy rooms cost 7500/10,000 rp, or rooms with mandi are 12,500/15,000 rp.

Hotel Manggarai (☎ 21008) on Jalan Adi Sucipto is close to the centre. Rooms with outside mandi go for 8000/10,000 rp, or with mandi cost 10,000/15,000 rp.

Hotel Karya, on Jalan Motang Rua, is the cheapest place in town at 5000 rp per person, but it's very dark and often 'full'.

Wisma Agung I (☎ 21080), Jalan Waeces 10, is the best hotel in town but it is a 15 minute walk from the centre. Pleasant economy rooms are 7000/10,000 rp or renovated rooms with bathroom are 15,000/20,000 rp to 25,000/30,000 rp.

Ruteng has some good Chinese restaurants, including the *Rumah Makan Dunia Baru* on Jalan Yos Sudarso and the *Restaurant Merlin* on Jalan Kartini. On Jalan Motang Rua, the cosy and friendly *Bamboo Den* next to the Hotel Karya has fried chicken, sate and other dishes.

Getting There & Away
Air Merpati (☎ 21197) is out in the rice paddies, about a 10 minute walk from the centre of town. It has direct flights to Labuanbajo, Bima and Kupang with onward connections from those centres.

Bus Buses to Labuanbajo (4000 rp; four hours), Bajawa (4500 rp; five hours) and Ende (8500 rp; eight hours) leave around 7.30 am. There are noon buses to Bajawa and Labuanbajo, and the Agogo bus to Ende leaves at 5 pm.

BAJAWA
Bajawa, a little town nestled in the hills, is the centre for the Ngada people of the Bajawa Plateau area. Coming in on the road from Ruteng, you'll see the great volcanic **Gunung Inerie** – a spectacular sight in the setting sun. Nearby is **Gunung Wolobobor**, an extinct volcano with the top half shaved off.

Bajawa is a pleasant enough place for a short stop, but the main attraction is the surrounding Ngada villages. **Bena**, 19 km north of Bajawa, is one of the most traditional and interesting villages. It has also had the greatest exposure to tourism and visitors' fees are expected. **Soa** has an interesting Thursday market, while **Langa**, **Boawae**, **Wogo** and **Ogi** are other villages worth vis-

iting. Guides hang out at the hotels and arrange good trips for 20,000 rp per person.

The area has many traditional houses and *ngadhu*, basically a carved pole supporting a conical thatched roof, rather like a large umbrella. Ngadhu are a male symbol used in ancestor worship, and to guard against sickness and preserve fertility – both human and agricultural. The female counterpart of this all-round 'tree of life' is the *bhaga*, a structure that looks something like a miniature thatched-roof house.

The area code for Bajawa is 0384.

Places to Stay & Eat
The *Hotel Korina* (☎ 21162) at Jalan Ahmad Yani 81 is one of the better places, with friendly and efficient staff. Rooms cost 7000 rp; 10,000 and 15,000 rp with mandi. Nearby, *Homestay Sunflower* (☎ 21236), on a small path off Jalan Ahmad Yani, has long been popular but is looking a little run down. Small and dark singles/doubles cost 6000/8000 rp, or 7000/10,000 rp with attached mandi.

The small *Hotel Ariesta* (☎ 21292) on Jalan Diponegoro is bright, clean and a good choice. Rooms cost 15,000/20,000 rp with mandi or 10,000 rp with outside mandi.

The family-run *Elizabeth Hotel* (☎ 21223) on Jalan Inerie is a fair hike from the centre of town but worth the effort. Spotless, bright rooms cost from 6500/10,000 rp to 15,000/20,000 rp with shower. Nearby, the *Stela Sasandy* (☎ 21198) just off Jalan Soekarno-Hatta is a small, new place with rooms for 7000/12,500 rp, and 10,000/20,000 rp with mandi.

Hotel Dam (☎ 21145) is a quiet and delightful little place near the church, run by a friendly family. Rooms with attached bath cost 15,000 rp.

A group of hotels can be found close to the centre of town, just west of the market. The *Hotel Anggrek* (☎ 21172) on Jalan Letjend Haryono has clean rooms with mandi for 10,000/15,000 rp and a good restaurant. The largest hotel is *Hotel Kembang* (☎ 21072) on Jalan Marta Dinata with well-appointed

INDONESIA

double rooms with bath for 22,500 and 25,000 rp.

Bottom of the barrel, the *Hotel Kencana*, Jalan Palapa 7, is grungy but friendly and they don't come any cheaper at 3000/6000 rp with mandi.

The popular *Restoran Carmellya* is a cosy travellers' restaurant on Jalan Ahmad Yani, just across from the Hotel Korina. *Rumah Makan Wisata*, near the market, is similar and has a varied menu. The friendly *Rumah Makan Kasih Bahagia*, near the market on Jalan Ahmad Yani, has cold beer and inexpensive food.

Getting There & Away

Air Merpati flies from Bajawa to Bima and Ende, with onward connections. The Merpati office (☎ 21051) is opposite the Bajawa Market.

Bus The long-distance bus station is three km outside of town near the highway – 300 rp by bemo. The bus to Labuanbajo (10,000 rp; 10 hours) leaves around 7 am. More frequent buses go to Ruteng (5000 rp; five hours). Buses to Ende (5000 rp; five hours) leave at 7 am and noon, and there is a through bus to Moni. Most hotels arrange bus tickets.

For surrounding villages, small buses and trucks leave from the market.

RIUNG

Riung, on the coast north of Bajawa, has beaches and giant iguanas – not quite Komodo dragons, but impressive beasts nonetheless and more colourful. The offshore reserve of **Pulau Tujuh Belas** (Seventeen Islands) offers excellent snorkelling. Riung has a number of basic homestays, including the *Nur Iklas*, *Liberti*, *Madona* and *Tamri Beach*, all costing around 10,000 rp per person including all meals. On the road into town, the *Missionaries* has the best rooms for 25,000 rp.

The direct road from Bajawa to Riung is now complete, making access much easier, and buses do the trip in 2½ hours. A direct bus from Ende leaves at 6 am.

ENDE

Dominated by the volcanic cones of Gunung Meja and Gunung Iya, the capital of Flores is a hot and dusty town – it's easy to see why the Dutch exiled Soekarno here in the 1930s. You can visit the house he lived in, but otherwise Ende is primarily a stopover to catch buses or the boat to Sumba. Trips to nearby villages are worthwhile if you are stuck for something to do. Ende has its own distinctive style of ikat weaving, and examples of Jopu, Nggela and Wolonjita weaving can also be found in the main street market near the waterfront.

Information

The Bank Rakyat Indonesia is in the same building as the Dwi Putri Hotel, on Jalan KH Dewantara.

Places to Stay & Eat

Out near the airport, *Hotel Ikhlas* (☎ 21695) on Jalan Jenderal Ahmad Yani is in a 'klas' of its own – friendly and on the ball with travel information. Clean, basic singles/ doubles cost 3500/6000 rp with shared mandi. Rooms with mandi and fan are 7000/10,000 rp to 10,000/15,000 rp. Good, cheap western and Indonesian food is available. Next door, the spacious and airy *Hotel Safari* (☎ 21499) has friendly staff and a restaurant. Rooms cost 10,000/15,000 rp with mandi, up to 35,000/40,000 rp with air-con.

The small *Hotel Amica* (☎ 21683), Jalan Garuda 39, is a good budget hotel. Rooms with mandi cost 10,000/15,000 rp. The young manager speaks excellent English and can fill you in on excursions around Ende.

The *Hotel Flores* (☎ 21075) at Jalan Sudirman 28 has a range of good rooms, from 10,000/15,000 rp to 16,500/22,500 rp with mandi. There's a small restaurant as well.

The large and spotless *Hotel Dwi Putri* (☎ 21685) on Jalan KH Dewantara is the best in town. Rooms cost 20,000/25,000 rp to 40,000/50,000 rp.

The quiet *Hotel Wisata* (☎ 21368), on Jalan Keli Mutu, is another more upmarket hotel and reasonably priced. Large, new rooms at the back cost 15,000/20,000 rp with mandi. Huge air-con rooms are 30,000/40,000 rp to 45,000/60,000 rp.

The market area has the biggest concentration of rumah makan, including the *Bundo Kandung* for Padang food and the next door *Istana Bambu*, one of Ende's best restaurants with a long menu of Indonesian, Chinese and seafood dishes.

Getting There & Away

Air Merpati (☎ 21355) is on Jalan Nangka, a 15 minute walk from the airstrip. From Ende direct flights go to Bajawa, Bima, Kupang and Labuanbajo.

Bus Buses to the east leave from Terminal Wolowana, four km from town. Buses to Moni (2000 rp; two hours) depart between 6 am and 2 pm, or take a Wolowaru bus. Buses to Maumere (6000 rp; five hours) leave around 8 am and 5 pm. Maumere buses will drop you in Moni but charge for the full fare to Maumere. A bus to Nggela leaves at 7 am and a through bus to Larantuka leaves at 8 am.

Buses to the west leave from Terminal Ndao, two km north of town on the beach road. Bus departures are: Bajawa (5000 rp; five hours) at 7 and 11 am, Ruteng (10,000 rp; 10 hours) at 7.30 am, Labuanbajo (15,000 rp; 14 hours) at 7 am and Riung (4000 rp; four hours).

Boat Ships dock at Pelabuhan Ipi, the main port, 2.5 km from the town. The ferry from Kupang to Ende (17,000 rp; 16 hours) departs on Mondays, and leaves Ende on Tuesdays at 2 pm for Waingapu (12,000 rp; 10 hours) on Sumba, then continues to Sabu and returns. Ende to Kupang departures are at 2 pm on Saturdays.

Pelni's KM *Binaiya* stops in Ende every two weeks as it comes in from Waingapu (15,500 rp ekonomi; seven hours) and continues on to Kupang in Timor (22,500 rp; 10 hours). It runs in the reverse direction one week later.

Getting Around

Bemo fares around town are a flat 400 rp, including the airport, bus stations and Pelabuhan Ipi.

KELI MUTU

This extinct volcano is the most fantastic sight on Flores and one of Nusa Tenggara's main attractions. The crater has three lakes – the largest is light turquoise, the one next to it olive green, and the third one black. Chemicals in the soil account for this weird colour scheme and it changes with time (the green lake was previously a deep maroon/brown). Colours can also change in the rainy season, when they may be less spectacular.

The best time to see Keli Mutu is in the early morning as clouds usually settle later on and you need strong sunlight to bring out the colours of the lakes. On a really bad day – or if you get to the top too late in the day – the clouds will have rolled in and you won't be able to see anything at all.

Getting There & Away

Most visitors base themselves in Moni, the village at the foot of the volcano, and make their way up to the top at 4 am by truck or minibus arranged by the hotels for 3000 rp per person. You can set out at 2 am and walk the 13 km to the top in three to four hours, arriving in time for the sunrise. The truck goes down the mountain at 7 am, but many walk back in about two hours.

The park entry post, halfway up the road, charges 1500 rp entry fee. Coming down, there's a shortcut from just beside the entry post which comes out by the hot springs and waterfall. It's fine going down but would be difficult to find, in the dark, on your way up.

MONI

Moni (Mone) is a little village and mission on the Ende to Maumere road at the base of Keli Mutu. It is cooler than the lowlands, scenic and a good place for walks. About two km before Moni, on the Ende side, is the turn-off to the top of Keli Mutu.

Moni's Monday **market** is a major local event and attracts a large and colourful crowd. Traditional dance performances are held every evening at the rumah adat near the market and cost 2500 rp.

Places to Stay & Eat

Moni is a popular stop for a few days and has a collection of basic, cheap homestays clustered together along the road through town. The correct price – fixed by the government for all homestays – is 5000 rp per person or 7500 rp per person in a room with attached mandi, plus 10% tax. Breakfast is included. In quiet periods, price wars have seen rates drop to ridiculous levels – as little as 3000 rp per person, 10,000 rp or less for a double with mandi.

Along the main road opposite the market, *Homestay Daniel* is clean and tidy. *Homestay Amina Moe* is the most aggressive discounter, and also has a few rooms with mandi. Next along, *Homestay Sao Lelegana John* is a notch up in standards and has larger rooms with basin and attached mandi. *Homestay Friendly* is another more substantial place with a good aspect and better than average rooms, with and without mandi. *Homestay Maria*, just behind it, has rooms with attached mandi and veranda. *Homestay Amina Moe II*, just off the main road, is the most basic of all but is usually heavily discounted.

More homestays are clustered about five minutes walk along the road to Ende. They tend to be quieter and less cramped. *Sylvester* has cheap, simple rooms while *Lovely Rose* has better rooms with mandi and a decent restaurant. *Nusa Bunga*, *Regal Jaya* and *Lestari* are other reasonable places nearby and *Hidayai* is further up the road.

On the Ende road 1.5 km from Moni, the most upmarket place is the *Sao Ria Wisata*. Bungalows with mandi perched on the hillside are the best in Moni, but overpriced at 20,000 and 25,000 rp.

Most of the homestays provide simple buffet meals. The *Lovely Rose*, *Restaurant Moni Indah* and *Nusa Bunga* are good, cheap restaurants with local and western dishes. The *Ankermi Pub & Restaurant* is a switched-on place and the most popular in town.

Getting There & Away

Moni is 52 km north-east of Ende and 96 km west of Maumere. For Ende (2000 rp; two hours), buses start at around 7 am. Other buses comes through from Maumere or Wolowaru to Ende until about noon. Late buses come through at around 9 pm. Many buses and trucks leave on Monday market day.

For Maumere (5000 rp; four hours) the first buses from Ende start coming though at around 9 or 10 am and then later in the evening around 7 pm.

As most of the buses stop in Moni mid-route they can be crowded and it's first-come, first-served for a seat. Some of the homestays make 'bookings', which usually means they will just hail a bus down for you.

WOLOWARU AREA

Wolowaru is an oversized village 13 km from Moni on the road to Maumere. From Wolowaru, a road leads to the coast and the villages of **Jopu**, **Wolonjita** and **Nggela**. Beautiful and intricately woven sarongs and shawls can be found in these and other small villages. The villages are an interesting and pleasant walk from Wolowaru, so long as you avoid the heat of the day. The volcano-studded skyline is beautiful and near Nggela, perched on a clifftop, there are fine views of the ocean. Nggela has a number of traditional houses but the town's chief attraction is the stunning weaving.

Wolowaru has two losmen. In Nggela, the *Homestay Nggela Permai* costs 5500 per person.

Getting There & Away

Buses based in Wolowaru go to Maumere, Ende and Moni in the morning, and the through buses all stop in Wolowaru at the Rumah Makan Jawa Timur.

A paved road leads all the way from Moni to Nggela via Wolowaru, Jopu and Wolonjita. A bus runs from Ende to Nggela at 7 am, otherwise walk from Wolowaru. At Wolowaru, a road leads off to Jopu, four km away, and on to Wolonjita, a further four km. From Wolonjita, the road drops downhill to Nggela – about an hour's walk. You can easily get from Wolowaru to Nggela and back in a day, even if you have to walk.

MAUMERE

Maumere is a medium-size port on the north-east coast and a stopover on the route between Ende and Larantuka. This is still an important mission centre and the Maumere area also has strong ikat-weaving traditions. In December 1992, Maumere was devastated by the earthquakes that hit Flores and the ensuing 20-metre-high tsunami killed thousands. Most of Maumere has been rebuilt.

Maumere itself has no attractions. On Jalan Pasar Baru Timur, the Harapan Jaya Art shop has an excellent selection of ikat cloth.

Information

The tourist office (☎ 21652) is on Jalan Wairklau. The BNI bank on Jalan Soekarno-Hatta is the best place to change money, and the Bank Rakyat Indonesia also handles foreign exchange.

The post office is next to the soccer field on Jalan Pos, and the Telkom office is further south from the town centre on Jalan Soekarno-Hatta.

The area code for Maumere is 0382.

Places to Stay

The popular *Hotel Senja Wair Bubak* (☎ 21498) on Jalan Komodor Yos Sudarso, near the waterfront, has a travel agent and like many hotels offers tours, motorbike and car rental. Nondescript singles/doubles with shared mandi cost 6600/12,100 rp, or the rooms with mandi for 8800/15,400 rp to 27,500/36,300 rp are much better.

Nearby, the small and friendly *Hotel Jaya* (☎ 21292), Jalan Hasanuddin 26, is a good buy and has rooms with fan and mandi for 10,000/15,000 rp.

The *Gardena Hotel* (☎ 21489) on Jalan Pattirangga is quite central and has clean, if uninspiring, rooms for 10,000/15,000 rp with mandi, 25,000/30,000 rp with air-con.

The friendly *Veranus Homestay* (☎ 21464) has a couple of decrepit rooms for 3000/5000 rp. It could be good if the damage from the earthquake is ever repaired.

A little far from the town centre but close to the west bus terminal, the well-run *Hotel*

Wini Rai (☎ 21388), Jalan Gajah Mada 50, has good mid-range rooms with mandi for 22,000/27,500 rp or 36,000/42,000 rp with air-con, and a few basic rooms for 8250/13,750 rp.

Other hotels include the Muslim-run *Hotel Bogor II* (☎ 21137) on Jalan Slamet Riyadi, near the port. It has rooms with mandi for 10,000/15,000 rp but is undergoing renovation. It is better than the seedy *Hotel Bogor I* opposite.

Places to Eat

The best place to hunt out a restaurant is Jalan Pasar Baru Barat, the main street running down to the waterfront. The *Sarina Restaurant* has Chinese food and does good squid. The *Stevani Pub & Restaurant* has small huts dotted around in a garden setting. It's a pleasant place to sit with a drink, and western and Indonesian dishes are served.

The *Bamboo Den* near the Hotel Wini Rai has cheap Indonesian food, good fish and cold beer.

Getting There & Away

Air Maumere's airport handles bigger aircraft and is the best place on Flores for flights to and from other islands. Bouraq and Merpati fly to Kupang (101,000 rp) and Bali (235,000 rp). Merpati flies via Bima (Sumbawa) en route to Bali. Bouraq's office (☎ 21467) is on Jalan Nong Meak. Merpati (☎ 21342) is at Jalan Don Thomas 18.

Bus Buses and bemos east to Larantuka (5000 rp; four hours), Geliting, Waiara, Ipir and Wodong leave from the Lokaria (or Timur) terminal, about three km east of town. Buses west to Moni (4000 rp; 3½ hours), Ende (6000 rp; five hours), Sikka and Ladalero leave from the Ende (or Barat) terminal, 1.5 km south-west of town.

Buses often endlessly do the rounds of the town searching for passengers. Hotels can arrange pick-up. Ende buses leave at 8 am and 5 pm. For Moni, take an Ende bus. Buses to Larantuka leave throughout the day.

INDONESIA

Boat Pelni's KM *Binaiya* sails to and from Ujung Pandang in Sulawesi (41,500 rp; 23 hours) and Dili (39,500 rp; 18 hours). The Pelni office is on Jalan Slamet Riyadi, next to Losmen Bogor II.

Getting Around

The airport is three km from the town centre, off the Maumere to Larantuka road – 6000 rp by taxi, or chartered bemo. Bemos around town and to the bus terminals cost 400 rp.

AROUND MAUMERE

Just off the Larantuka road, 13 km east of Maumere, **Waiara** has scuba diving, but the reefs were damaged by the 1992 earthquake. The two places to stay at Waiara Beach have diving facilities. *Flores Sao Resort* (☎ 21555) caters mostly to tour groups and rooms start at US$30/40. A day dive package costs US$80. The *Sea World Club* (☎ 21570) is a cheaper alternative with rooms from 40,000 rp.

The village of **Sikka**, an hour by bus from Maumere, has its own distinctive style of weaving. **Ladalero**, about 24 km from Maumere, is a major Catholic seminary and has a museum with ikat and artefacts from all over Indonesia.

Wodong village, 28 km east of Maumere, is on the Maumere-Larantuka road. The excellent, well-run *Flores Froggies*, run by a French couple, is a popular spot by a reasonable beach. Lovely bamboo beachside huts cost 8000/16,000 rp and the French bread is a winner.

LARANTUKA

This little port nestles at the base of a high hill at the eastern end of Flores. From here, you can see the islands of Solor and Adonara across the narrow strait. It is primarily a place to catch ferries.

The BNI bank and Bank Rakyat Indonesia both change money.

Places to Stay & Eat

The family-run *Hotel Rulies* (☎ 21198) at Jalan Yos Sudarso 44 has the best setup. Clean singles/doubles with shared bath cost 10,000/16,000 rp and food is available. Next

door, the *Hotel Tresna* (☎ 21072) is a reasonable place catering mainly to business travellers. Rooms cost 8000 rp a double or 15,000/25,000 rp with mandi.

The *Hotel Sederhana* right in the middle of town has cheap rooms for 5000 rp but may be 'full'.

The *Hotel Fortuna I* (☎ 21140), two km north-east of town at Jalan Diponegoro 171 near the Telkom office, has dreary rooms for 5000/10,000 rp, or much better fan rooms cost 11,000/16,500 rp. *Hotel Fortuna II*, directly across the road, is its more upmarket offshoot.

Eating possibilities are limited, but a few warungs set up in the evening along Jalan Niaga. *Rumah Makan Nirwana* on Jalan Niaga is a decent Chinese restaurant and the best in town. Nearby, the small and welcoming *Virgo Cafe* has fish & chips in addition to the usual nasi and mie meals.

Getting There & Away

Air The Merpati agent's house is at Jalan Diponegoro 64, opposite the cathedral. One flight a week does a Kupang-Larantuka-Lewoleba (Lembata)-Kupang loop but is often cancelled.

Bus Regular buses run between Maumere and Larantuka (5000 rp; four hours). The main bus terminal is five km west of the town (300 rp by bemo), but you can pick buses up in the centre of town. Coming into town, buses can drop you at or near your hotel, though the bemo drivers may insist that you get down and catch a bemo from the terminal.

Boat Ferries to Kupang (14,000 rp; 14 hours) depart Monday and Friday at 2 pm from Waibulan, four km south-west of Larantuka (300 rp by bemo). Ferries can be crowded, so board early to get a seat. Take some food and water.

The car-and-passenger ferry to Adonara, Lembata and Alor also leaves from Waibulan on Tuesday, Thursday and Sunday at 7 am. More convenient, smaller boats to Adonara, Solor and Lembata leave from the pier in the centre of town. They run twice a day to

Lewoleba (3000 rp; four hours) on Lembata at around 8 am and 1 pm, stopping at Waiwerang (on Adonara) on the way. A boat goes once a week to Lamalera (5000 rp; seven hours) on Friday at 9 am.

Pelni's KM *Tatamailau* calls at Larantuka on its way between Labuanbajo and Dili.

Solor & Alor Archipelagos

This chain of volcanic, mountainous islands separated by swift, narrow straits is reached by ferry from Larantuka. The Solor Archipelago consists of the islands of Adonara, Solor and Lembata, the main island of interest where the traditional whaling village of Lamalera can be visited.

Lying between Lembata and Timor are the islands of Pantar and Alor, the main islands of the Alor Archipelago.

LEMBATA
The terrain of Lembata Island in the Solor Archipelago is strongly reminiscent of Australia, the palm trees of the coast giving way to gum trees in the hills. Fine ikat comes from villages on the slopes of Ili Api.

Lewoleba
Despite the ominous smoking of Ili Api volcano in the background, the chief settlement on Lembata is a relaxed little town. A few large government buildings and a Telkom office are all that distinguish it from any other scruffy village. Lewoleba's banks do not change money.

Stay at the *Hotel Rejeki I*, opposite the market in the middle of town. Singles/doubles with outside mandi cost 6500/12,000 rp, and the hotel serves the only decent food in town.

Getting There & Away Merpati, in the Hotel Rejeki I, has once weekly flights from Larantuka to Lewoleba and on to Kupang (maybe).

Passenger ferries to Larantuka leave around 8 am and 1 pm. It is a spectacular journey through the islands past smoking volcanoes.

Ferries to Kalabahi (Alor) depart Lewoleba on Tuesday, Thursday and Sunday at 11 am. They stop for the night in eastern Lembata at Belauring (4500 rp; four hours), which has a losmen or you can sleep on the deck of the boat. At 7 am the next morning the ferry continues on to Kalabahi (9000 rp; nine hours) via Baranusa on Pantar. Bring food and water.

The main road across the island is sealed and regular mikrolets and buses run to destinations around Lewoleba including Waipukang, Loang and Puor (for Lamalera).

Lamalera
On the south coast, Lamalera is a whaling village where the villagers still hunt whales using small rowboats and hand-thrown harpoons. During the whaling season, from May to October, you may see the catch being brought back to the village and hacked up. The village receives a steady trickle of tourists, and you can even go out on a hunt in one of the boats for 15,000 rp. Lamalera has a number of homestays costing 7500 rp per person, including meals.

Getting There & Away The boat from Lewoleba to Lamalera (3500 rp; six hours) leaves after the Monday night market (any time between 1 and 5 am). From Larantuka, a boat leaves on Friday at 9 am.

Otherwise take a bemo from Lewoleba to Puor, from where it's a three hour walk, mostly downhill. Buses also go to Bota, an alternative approach, but it is then a harder four hour walk. Bring plenty of water.

ALOR
Famed for its highly prized *moko*, bronze drums found mysteriously buried all over the island, Alor is a rugged, scenic island. Travel was once so difficult and the people so isolated, that some 50 tribes spoke almost as many different languages. Head-hunting was practised up until the 1950s. A road now

rings the island, but tourism is still undeveloped. Traditional villages, such as **Takpala**, 13 km east of Kalabahi, can be visited. The island has excellent diving, though this is best arranged in Kupang.

Kalabahi
Kalabahi is the chief town on Alor, at the end of a long, narrow and spectacular palm-fringed bay. This slow-moving Christian settlement is a pleasant enough place to wait for a ferry. The BNI bank on Jalan Soedomo and the Bank Rakyat Indonesia change cash and travellers' cheques.

Places to Stay The central *Hotel Adi Dharma* (☎ 21049), Jalan Martadinata 12, has great harbour views and good rooms from 10,000 rp a double. The nearby *Hotel Melati* (☎ 21073) is similarly priced. Out near the bus terminal, *Hotel Pelangi Indah* (☎ 21251), Jalan Diponegoro 100, has a good restaurant and the best rooms in town, starting at 15,000/20,000 rp with mandi.

Getting There & Away Merpati flies from Kupang to Kalabahi (113,500 rp) and back daily except Friday.

The ferry to Kupang (16,500 rp; about 16 hours) leaves on Tuesday and Thursday at 2 pm. On Sunday at 10 pm a ferry runs to Atapupu (8000 rp; eight hours) on Timor. A regular ferry to Dili is planned.

Ferries to Lewoleba and Larantuka via Solor leave Sunday, Tuesday and Thursday at 7 am. They stop overnight at Belauring on Lembata.

The Pelni ship *Binaiya* calls in at Kalabahi on its route between Dili and Kupang. Slow, uncomfortable Pelni cargo ships also regularly run from Kalabahi to Dili and Kupang and take passengers.

Timor

Kupang, the 'big city' of Nusa Tenggara, gets a steady stream of travellers passing through on the way to Australia. Outside of Kupang,

Timor is one of the most traditional regions of Indonesia, but sees few tourists. Dominated by the scenic central mountains, this large, rugged and dry island is home to a wide variety of cultures. Despite the dominance of Christianity, animism is very much in evidence, and large parts of the island have had little contact with Indonesian national culture.

Timor is divided into West Timor and East Timor. Almost all visitors go only to West Timor, because of East Timor's reputation as one of the world's hot spots. However, East Timor is not a war zone, and it is safe and easy to travel to Dili, the capital. You can go right through to Tutuala, East Timor's most easterly point.

History
The Portuguese were the first Europeans to land in Timor, in the early 16th century. The Dutch occupied Kupang in the middle of the 17th century and after a lengthy conflict, the Portuguese finally withdrew to the eastern half of the island in the middle of the 18th century. When Indonesia became independent in 1949, the Dutch half of Timor became part of the new republic but the Portuguese still retained the eastern half.

On 25 April 1974, there was a military coup in Portugal and the new government set about discarding the Portuguese colonial empire. Within a few weeks of the coup, three major political parties had been formed in East Timor. After the UDT attempted to seize power in August 1975, a brief civil war between the rival parties, Fretilin and UDT, saw Fretilin come out on top.

However, Indonesia opposed the formation of an independent East Timor and leftist Fretilin raised the spectre of Communism in Indonesian eyes. On 7 December 1975, Indonesia launched a full-scale invasion of the former colony, just one day after US Secretary of State Henry Kissinger had cleared out of Indonesia after a brief visit – presumably having put the US seal of approval on the invasion.

By all accounts, the Indonesian invasion was brutal. Fretilin fought a guerrilla war with marked success in the first two or three years but after that began to weaken considerably. The cost to the Timorese people was horrific, many dying through starvation or disease due to the disruption of food and medical supplies. By 1989, Indonesia had things firmly under control and opened East Timor to tourism, but on 12 November 1991 army troops opened fire on protestors at the Dili cemetery, once again alerting the world to East Timor's plight.

Today, the army well and truly controls East Timor, and armed resistance has been pacified. Life for the East Timorese now goes on much as normal – as much as it can under the watchful eye of the security forces that remain in large numbers.

Getting There & Away
Air Merpati, Sempati and Bouraq all fly to Kupang from other parts of Nusa Tenggara and Indonesia. A good way to explore Nusa Tenggara is to fly directly from Bali to Kupang and then island-hop back.

Merpati has a twice weekly service between Darwin in Australia and Kupang. See the Indonesia Getting There & Away section for more details. This is a terrific way of getting to Indonesia; the flight is popular but usually not heavily booked. Kupang is on the no-visa-required entry list.

Boat The Perum ASDP ferry company, based in Kupang, has car/passenger ferries throughout Nusa Tenggara. One ferry operates Kupang-Larantuka (Flores)-Lewoleba (Solor)-Kalabahi (Alor) and returns twice a week. Another runs twice a week been Kupang and Kalabahi. Another useful ferry runs Kupang-Ende (Flores)-Waingapu (Sumba)-Sabu and returns every week. Other ferries operate to the island of Roti.

Pelni's KM *Dobonsolo* and KM *Binaiya* both stop in Kupang. Perintis cargo line also takes passengers and operates ships to many other destinations in the region.

Getting Around
The main highway is surfaced all the way from Kupang to Dili, though the buses are of the cramped and crowded version found throughout Nusa Tenggara. Away from the highway, many of the roads are in bad condition.

KUPANG
Kupang is the biggest city on the island and capital of the province of Nusa Tenggara Timur. It's a small city, but compared with the sedate little towns on Flores and Sumbawa, Kupang is a booming metropolis. It's not a bad place to hang around – Captain Bligh did, after his *Bounty* misadventures.

Kupang's **Museum NTT**, open every day from 8 am to 3 pm, is worth a look.

Information
Tourist Office The Kupang tourist office, open government hours only, is out in the sticks near the Walikota bemo terminal.

Money Kupang is the best place to change money in Nusa Tenggara outside Mataram on Lombok. The Bank Dagang Negara, Jalan Urip Sumohardjo 16, is central and most other banks usually have good rates. If you want a cash advance on Visa or MasterCard, get it here. The currency exchange office at Kupang airport is open when flights arrive from Darwin.

Post & Communications Poste restante mail goes to the central post office, Kantor Pos Besar, at Jalan Palapa 1. A branch post office is at Jalan Soekarno 29. The Telkom office is at Jalan Urip Sumohardjo 11.

The area code for Kupang is 0391.

Tour & Dive Operators
Many fascinating traditional villages can be visited on Timor, but Indonesian, let alone English, is often not spoken so a local guide is necessary. Guides will find you, and start at around 20,000 rp per day. Big tour companies include Pitoby Tours (☎ 32700), Jalan Jenderal Sudirman 118.

Nusa Tenggara has some of Indonesia's best diving, and Kupang is a good place to arrange diving trips. Graeme and Donovan Whitford (☎ 21154; fax 24833), two Australian dive

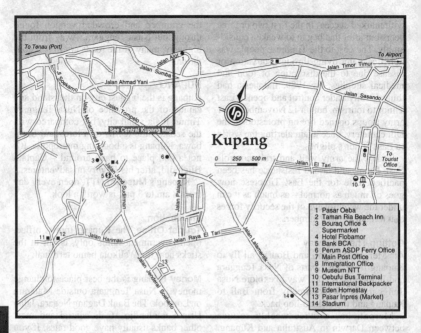

Kupang

0   250   500 m

1 Pasar Oeba
2 Taman Ria Beach Inn
3 Bourag Office &
   Supermarket
4 Hotel Flobamor
5 Bank BCA
6 Perum ASDP Ferry Office
7 Main Post Office
8 Immigration Office
9 Museum NTT
10 Oebufu Bus Terminal
11 International Backpacker
12 Eden Homestay
13 Pasar Inpres (Market)
14 Stadium

INDONESIA

masters based in Kupang, arrange dives to Alor, Dili, Labuanbajo and Komodo.

Places to Stay

Accommodation in Kupang is spread out, but the efficient bemo system makes everywhere easily accessible.

Two popular budget options, despite their distance from town (take bemo No 3), are in a quiet area on Jalan Kencil. *Eden Homestay* (☎ 21931) at No 6 is opposite a shady freshwater pool, the local swimming spot. Bungalows are very basic but very cheap at 3000 rp per person. This friendly place offers meals and cheap tours. *International Backpacker* at Jalan Kencil 37B is one street away. Dormitories and small rooms are more substantial and also cost 3000 rp person. This is another friendly place that also has meals and tours.

Closer to town at Jalan Sumatera 8, *L'Avalon* (☎ 32278) is Kupang's other main backpackers' place. It's a laid-back place

good for information on touring Timor. Well-kept four and six-bed dorms cost 4000 rp per person or the double room costs 10,000 rp.

The *Taman Ria Beach Inn* (☎ 31320), Jalan Timor Timur 69, is on the beachfront about three km from Terminal Kota Kupang (catch a No 10 bemo) and gets a steady trade off the plane from Darwin. The beach is pleasant enough and the restaurant is good. Singles/doubles with mandi and fan are 15,500/21,000 rp and they also rent on a dorm basis at 7500 rp.

Fateleu Homestay (☎ 31374) at Jalan Gunung Fateleu 1 is a friendly place close to the city centre. Basic rooms cost 8000/ 12,500 rp with fan and shared bath; rooms with private mandi are better but expensive at 16,000/21,500 rp.

The central *Hotel Setia* (☎ 23291), Jalan Kosasih 13, used to be full with bookings from the Darwin hostels but it has changed management and is now less popular. Nevertheless it is clean and tidy with rooms for

8000/16,000 rp, or 10,000/20,000 rp with mandi.

Along the waterfront on Jalan Sumatera, a short bemo ride from Terminal Kota Kupang, the *Timor Beach Hotel* (☎ 31651) has a good restaurant with panoramic sea views. Rooms around an elongated courtyard are a little dark but good value at 12,500/17,000 rp with fan and mandi. Aircon rooms go for 24,500/30,000 rp.

Places to Eat
Around the Terminal, *Restaurant Lima Jaya Raya*, Jalan Soekarno 15, has Chinese and Indonesian food, and a loud and sweaty nightclub upstairs. Across the road, at Jalan Ikan Paus 3, the *Happy Cafe* is a bright place serving cheap Chinese and Indonesian food.

Visiting Darwinites like to hang out at *Teddy's Bar*, Jalan Ikan Tongkol 1-3, for meat pie & chips. The expensive food is compensated by sea views and cold beer. The nearby *Pantai Laut Restaurant* has seafood

and other dishes, and is a better bet than the grotty *Restaurant Karang Mas* further along at Jalan Siliwangi 88.

Depot Makan Tanjung on Jalan Kosasih has good, cheap Chinese food, and the *Depot Mini* on Jalan Jenderal Ahmad Yani is a spotless restaurant with similar fare.

Getting There & Away
Air Merpati (☎ 33833), Jalan Kosasih 2, has direct flights to Denpasar (244,000 rp), Dili (95,000 rp), Waingapu (171,000 rp), Maumere (101,000 rp), Kalabahi (111,500 rp), Larantuka, Ruteng, Ende and Roti.

Bouraq (☎ 21421), Jalan Sudirman 20, has direct flights to Waingapu and Maumere, with onward connections. Sempati (☎ 31612), at the Hotel Marina, Jalan Ahmad Yani 79, has direct flights to Dili and Surabaya.

Merpati also flies between Darwin (Australia) on Wednesday and Saturday. From Kupang the fare is US$150 one way – shop around the travel agents. You won't be

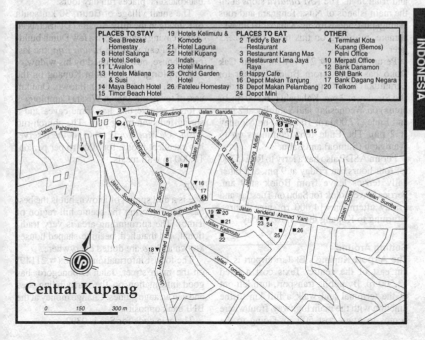

PLACES TO STAY
1 Sea Breezes Homestay
8 Hotel Salunga
9 Hotel Setia
11 L'Avalon
13 Hotels Maliana & Susi
14 Maya Beach Hotel
15 Timor Beach Hotel
19 Hotels Kelimutu & Komodo
21 Hotel Laguna
22 Hotel Kupang Indah
23 Hotel Marina
25 Orchid Garden Hotel
26 Fateleu Homestay

PLACES TO EAT
2 Teddy's Bar & Restaurant
3 Restaurant Karang Mas
5 Restaurant Lima Jaya Raya
6 Happy Cafe
16 Depot Makan Tanjung
18 Depot Makan Pelambang
24 Depot Mini

OTHER
4 Terminal Kota Kupang (Bemos)
7 Pelni Office
10 Merpati Office
12 Bank Danamon
13 BNI Bank
17 Bank Dagang Negara
20 Telkom

INDONESIA

Central Kupang

0   150   300 m

Jalan Siliwangi Jalan Garuda Jalan Sumatera
Jalan Pahlawan
Jalan Merpati
Jalan Kosasih
Jalan G Lakaan
Jalan Gunung Mutis
Jalan Soekarno
Jalan Eltari
Jalan Urip Sumohardjo
Jalan Flores
Jalan Sumba
Jalan Jenderal Ahmad Yani
Jalan Kelimutu
Jalan Mohammed Hatta
Jalan Tompelo

allowed on the plane without an Australian visa – obtainable in Denpasar or Jakarta, not in Kupang.

Bus Long-distance buses depart from the Oebufu terminal out near the museum – take a No 10 bemo. Departures include: Soe (4250 rp; three hours), Niki Niki (5250 rp; 3½ hours), Kefamenanu (7500 rp; 5½ hours), Atambua (10,500 rp; eight hours) and Dili (15,500 rp; 12 hours). Bemos to villages around Kupang go from the central terminal, Kota Kupang.

Boat Pelni passenger ships leave from Tenau, 10 km west of Kupang (400 rp by bemo No 12). Ferries leave from Bolok, 13 km west of Kupang (550 rp by bemo No 13).

Pelni (☎ 22646) is at Jalan Pahlawan 3, near the waterfront. Pelni's KM *Dobonsolo* runs directly between Banyuwangi (Java) and Kupang and on to Dili, Ambon (Maluku) and Irian Jaya. The KM *Binaiya* stops at all the main islands of Nusa Tenggara and runs Waingapu-Ende-Kupang-Kalabahi-Dili-M aumere, returning on this route two weeks later.

Perum ASDP (☎ 21140) on Jalan Cak Doko has ferries from Bolok harbour to: Larantuka (14,000 rp; 14 hours) on Thursday and Sunday at 2 pm, Kalabahi (16,500 rp; 16 hours) on Wednesday and Saturday at 2 pm, and Ende (17,000 rp; 16 hours) on Monday at 2 pm. The Ende ferry continues on to Waingapu (Sumba) and Sabu.

Perum ASDP also has a ferry to Roti (5700 rp; four hours) on Friday at 9 pm, and other daily ferries leave from Bolok at 9 am. Ferries leave Bolok for Sabu on Tuesday and Friday afternoon (14,000 rp; nine hours), returning to Kupang the following day.

Getting Around
The Airport Kupang's El Tari airport is 15 km east of the centre. Taxis cost a fixed 12,500 rp. By public transport, turn left out of the terminal and walk a full km to the junction with the main highway, from where bemos to town cost 500 rp. Going to the airport take bemo No 14 or 15 to the junction and then walk.

Bemo Kupang's bemo terminal is at the waterfront, on the corner of Jalan Soekarno and Jalan Siliwangi. Around town, bemos cost a standard 400 rp and are fast, efficient, brightly painted and incredibly noisy – drivers like the bass turned up high and a multispeaker stereo system is de rigueur.

AROUND KUPANG
Past the airport, about 18 km east of town, **Baumata** has a swimming pool and caves with stalactites and stalagmites.

The beaches around town are unappealing but **Pantai Lasiana**, 10 km east of town, is a half-decent stretch of sand and popular on weekends. **Tablolong**, 15 km west of Kupang, has a better beach. The small islands of **Pulau Semau** and **Pulau Kera** just off the coast are more interesting, and the backpackers' places run day tours.

The small village of **Baun**, 30 km south of Kupang in the hilly Amarasi District, is an ikat-weaving centre, with a few Dutch buildings. You can visit the *rumah raja*, the last raja's house, now occupied by his widow.

Camplong, 46 km from Kupang on the Soe road, is a cool, quiet hill town. One km east of town, the Taman Wisata Camplong is a forest reserve that has some caves and a spring-fed swimming pool. The church-run *Wisma Oe Mat Honis* (☎ 6), at the reserve, has excellent rooms for 5000 rp per person, 15,000 rp with meals.

SOE
Soe is a dull sprawl of a town, but is the best base for exploring the scenic hill region of Timor. The surrounding area is very traditional, and thatched, beehive-shaped houses known as *lopo* are dotted everywhere.

The tourist information centre (☎ 21149) on the main street, Jalan Diponegoro, has good information on the surrounding area and can arrange guides. Change money at the BNI bank opposite.

The area code for Soe is 0392.

Places to Stay

The travellers' favourite is the *Hotel Anda* (☎ 21323), Jalan Kartini 5. This would have to be the most eccentric losmen in Indonesia, starting with the gaudy statuary and dazzling paint job at the front, and at the back is a huge, home-made replica of a warship. Rooms with shared mandi cost 5000 rp per person. They are basic, but rooms in the ship are cute. Pak Yohannes is a wonderful host, speaks English, Dutch and German, and is a wealth of knowledge on the area.

If this is full, the *Hotel Cahaya* (☎ 21087), next door, has clean rooms with mandi for 7500/15,000 rp.

Soe has a few mid-range hotels. The *Hotel Bahagia 1* (☎ 21015), Jalan Diponegoro 72, is the best and has rooms with outside mandi for 20,000 rp, or singles/doubles with mandi cost 22,000/25,000 rp.

Getting There & Away

The Haumeni bus terminal is four km west of town (400 rp by bemo). Regular buses run from Soe to Kupang (4250 rp; three hours), Kefamenanu (3000 rp; 2½ hours) and Oinlasi (2500 rp; 1½ hours), while bemos cover Niki Niki (1000 rp) and Kapan (800 rp).

AROUND SOE

On market days in the towns, villagers come from miles around, many in traditional dress. As well as everyday goods, ikat weaving and crafts can be found. The Tuesday market at **Oinlasi**, 51 km from Soe, is one of the largest, or the Wednesday market at **Niki Niki**, 34 km east of Soe, is just as lively and easier to reach.

The main attraction around Soe is **Boti**, a traditional village presided over by a self-styled *raja* (king). Christianity never penetrated here, and the raja maintains strict adherence to *adat* (tradition). The village is used to tourists, and even gets the occasional tour bus. Buses run to Oinlasi, from where it is 12 km on foot along a bad road to Boti. It is best to take a guide who speaks the local dialect. You can stay overnight for a donation.

North of Soe are the **Oehala Waterfall**, the cool hill town of **Kapan**, and **Fatumasi**, surrounded by highland forest and traditional villages.

KEFAMENANU

Kefamenanu is a forgettable (and forgotten) place – just a through town on the way to East Timor. **Temkessi**, 50 km north-east of Kefa, is an interesting but isolated traditional village.

If you stop, the friendly *Losmen Soko Windu* has simple rooms for 7500 rp. The much fancier *Hotel Ariesta* has rooms from 16,000 rp.

ATAMBUA

Atambua is the major town and resting place on the overland Dili-Kupang route. Nearby, **Atapupu** is a major port, where a ferry runs to Kalabahi (Alor) on Mondays at 10 am.

Accommodation ranges from the grungy *Losmen Sahabat*, Jalan Merdeka 7, with rooms from 8000/16,000 rp, to the sparkling *Hotel Intan* (☎ 21343), Jalan Merdeka 12, with rooms from 15,000/23,000 rp.

DILI

The capital of the East Timor is a pleasant, lazy city – the most attractive in Nusa Tenggara. It has a number of reminders of Portugal, such as the villas on the beach road and the **Mercado Municipal**, the old Portuguese market. Near the waterfront is the **Integration Monument**, which has a Timorese rapturously breaking his chains of colonial bondage.

This strongly Catholic city has plenty of churches, and at the eastern end of the bay at **Cape Fatucama**, a massive, new statue of Christ occupies the hilltop headland. It is styled after Rio de Janiero's Christ the Redeemer and there are magnificent views from the hilltop. Some decent beaches, such as Areia Branca (White Sands) are nearby.

Information

The tourist office (☎ 21350), west of the Mercado Municipal on Jalan Kaikoli, is helpful and has maps and brochures.

Toko Dili, a souvenir shop near the Telkom office, has maps.

INDONESIA

Places to Stay

Head for the friendly, well-run *Villa Harmonia* (☎ 23595), three km east of town on the way to the Becora bus terminal. The manager speaks excellent English and this is the best place for travel information. Singles/doubles with outside mandi cost 10,000/14,000 rp. Food and drinks are available.

The other vaguely cheap options are usually 'full'. *Wisma Taufiq* (☎ 21934) on Jalan Americo Thomas costs 11,000/18,000 rp, or 16,000/22,000 rp with mandi. The *Basmery Indah* (☎ 22151) on Jalan Estrade de Balide, opposite the University of Timor Timur, has large but run-down rooms with mandi from 16,000 rp.

Everyone will direct you the *Hotel Tourismo* (☎ 22029) on the waterfront, on Jalan Avenida Marechal Carmona. It has a delightful garden eating area and a hint of colonial charm. Good mid-range rooms are reasonably priced for Dili: 25,000/30,000 rp and 35,000/45,000 rp with fan and shower; from 45,000/55,000 rp with air-con.

Nearby, *Hotel Dili* (☎ 21871), Jalan Avenida Sada Bandeira 25, is deserted most of the time, but the large rooms for 25,000 and 30,000 rp are clean and have their own sitting areas.

Dili has a few other expensive, dull hotels.

Places to Eat

Dili has a good range of restaurants, and Portuguese food is a real treat.

For cheap eats, the *Rumah Makan Mona Lisa* on Jalan Alberqueque has Javanese food, and *Rumah Makan Seroja* on Jalan Avenida Aldeia has nasi/mie dishes.

Dili's best Portuguese restaurant is the moderately priced *Massau* on the eastern edge of town, a fair hike from the centre. The excellent food is best appreciated with a bottle of Portuguese wine brought with you – only 20,000 rp a bottle in Dili's Chinese shops.

The *Hotel Tourismo* has one of the best restaurants in town, serving Chinese, Indonesian and Portuguese dishes in a lovely garden setting.

Getting There & Away

Air Merpati (☎ 21088) has daily direct flights to Bali, and a Wednesday flight to Kupang. Sempati (☎ 23144) has three flights a week to Kupang (95,000 rp) and on to Surabaya.

Bus Coming into East Timor on the bus from West Timor, Indonesians are required to show their identity cards at police checkpoints along the way, but they don't seem to bother with foreigners. There is usually one army checkpoint before Dili where the bus jockey will take your passport to be inspected.

Terminal Tasitolo, to the west of town past the airport, has buses to the west, such as Atambua (5000 rp; 3½ hours) and Kupang (15,500 rp; 12 hours). Tickets can be bought in advance from agents opposite the Mercado Municipal.

Buses east to Baukau (4000 rp; three hours), Los Palos (7000 rp; seven hours) and Vikeke (6000 rp; seven hours) leave from Terminal Becora, four km east of town. Buses and bemos to Maubisse (3000 rp; three hours) and Suai (8000 rp; 10 hours) leave from the Balide Terminal, one km south of town. Most buses leave before 8 am.

Boat The Pelni office (☎ 21415), Jalan Sebastian de Costa 1, is on the road to the airport near the centre. The KM *Binaiya* travels from Kupang to Kalabahi then Dili and on to Maumere and Ujung Pandang. The KM *Dobonsolo* travels from Kupang to Dili and on to Ambon in Maluku. The KM *Tatamailau* comes from Larantuka to Dili and continues on to southern Maluku and Irian Jaya, and then reverses its route. A regular ferry is scheduled to start operation to Kalabahi, and Pelni's Perintis cargo ships also have some interesting routes.

Getting Around

Dili's Comoro airport is five km west of the town; the standard taxi fare is 5000 rp. Buses A or B (200 rp) stop on the main road outside the airport and they also go to Terminal

Tasitolo. From Terminal Tasitolo, mikrolet No I (300 rp) and bus D (200 rp) run to the Villa Harmonia and Terminal Becora, through the centre of town.

Dili's beat up taxis cost a flat 1000 rp around town.

AROUND DILI

Dili gets a steady trickle of visitors, but outside of Dili a foreigner is still a rare sight. Though East Timor is open to tourists, facilities are limited and you will usually have to register with the police on arrival and exit when staying in the towns. The army also sets up checkpoints where you have to show your passport.

The checks are merely a formality, but East Timor does attract some visitors with an activist bent. If you want to help the East Timorese, enjoy the attractions and spend your much-needed dollars, but be careful about delving into politics. The worst that can happen to you is that you'll be deported for being a journalist without the correct visa, but you risk getting your hosts into trouble.

The old hill towns make a delightful break from the heat of the coast, and the government has started renovating the fine old Portuguese resthouses, which now cost 25,000 rp. From Dili, the easiest hill town to reach is **Maubisse**, sitting high in rugged mountains, surrounded by spectacular scenery. Accommodation is in the government guesthouse or the *Losmen Udiana* costs 5000 rp.

Baukau, the second largest town in East Timor, is a charmingly run-down old colonial town. It has many old Portuguese buildings, of which the Mercado Municipal is the most impressive. In pre-invasion times, it was the site of the international airport (now a military airbase). The altitude makes it pleasantly cool and the **beaches**, five km sharply downhill from the town, are breathtakingly beautiful. The Portuguese-built *Hotel Flamboyant* is the only place to stay, and costs 20,000 rp per person. It may have been special once, but now nothing seems to work.

From Baukau you can continue on to **Los**

Palos, the main plateau town of the Lautem regency. The traditional, high-pitched Fataluku houses in the area are a symbol for all East Timor and grace every tourist brochure. The *Losmen Pui Horo Jaya* (otherwise known as the Losmen Verrisimo) is the place to stay and costs 6000 rp. You can hire guides in Los Palos to explore the surrounding countryside. The pretty village of **Rasa**, on the main road 11 km from Los Palos, is easily reached by bemo (500 rp) and has a number of traditional houses.

From Los Palos, early morning buses go along a bad road to **Tutuala** (2000 rp; two hours), on the eastern tip of the island. Tutuala is perched on cliffs high above the sea. The government resthouse here has breathtaking views along the coast. A road down the cliffs to the pretty beach leads to caves that house ancient, primitive paintings.

Roti & Sabu

Roti (also spelled Rote) is the southernmost island in Indonesia, and has linguistic ties with nearby Timor. Further west, Sabu (also spelled Sawu) has closer linguistic and cultural ties to Sumba. These small dry islands are seldom visited, but a steady trickle of visitors make it to Roti, which is fairly easily accessed from Kupang.

As is often the case with obscure Indonesian islands, it is surfers that have 'discovered' Roti and opened it up to tourism. Nemberala on the west coast is the surf centre with cheap losmen costing 8000 rp with meals, or the *Nemberala Beach Hotel* is more upmarket. You can also stay in the main town of Baa. Sabu also has a few homestays in the main settlement of Seba.

Getting There & Away

Merpati flies Kupang-Roti-Sabu-Roti-Kupang on Fridays (maybe). Kupang to Roti costs 46,000 rp and Kupang-Sabu costs 95,000 rp.

See the Kupang Getting There & Away section for details on ferries to Sabu and Roti. A weekly ferry also runs between Sabu and Sumba. On Roti, the ferry docks at Pantai Baru, from where waiting buses will take you to Baa (2000 rp; 1½ hours). Direct buses to Nemberala (5000 rp; 4½ hours) sometimes meet the ferry, otherwise you'll have to go to Baa and arrange transport from there.

Sumba

This dry island, one of the most interesting in the Nusa Tenggara group, is noted for its large, decorated stone tombs and traditional houses. Composed of various linguistic groups, the small warring tribes that inhabited Sumba produced Indonesia's finest horses, used in warfare, and honoured their kings with huge burial stones. Great slabs of rock, weighing up to 70 tonnes, were transported across the countryside by a procession of people and buffalo. These tombs and stone carvings grace many villages.

Though Christianity has made inroads, Sumba's isolation has helped preserve one of the country's most bizarre animist cultures. Sumba is also famous for its ikat blankets with their interesting motifs, including skulls hanging from trees, horse riders, crocodiles, dragons, lions, chickens, monkeys and deer.

Getting There & Away
Air Flights operate from Bali, Flores, Timor and Sumbawa to the main centres of Tambulaka (the airport for Waikabubak) and Waingapu. Merpati operates a Denpasar-Bima-Tambulaka-Waingapu-Kupang route, while Bouraq flies Denpasar-Waingapu-Kupang.

Boat Pelni's KM Binaiya operates through Nusa Tenggara every two weeks and sails from Padang Bai (Bali) to Lembar, Bima, Waingapu, Ende (Flores), Kupang (Timor), Kalabahi, Dili, Ujung Pandang (Sulawesi), and return. The weekly Kupang-Ende-Waingapu-Sabu and return ferry is the most popular way to reach Sumba.

WAINGAPU
Waingapu is just the main town on Sumba, but is a good place for day-tripping to the interesting villages in the surrounding area.

Orientation & Information
Waingapu has two centres: the older, northern one focuses on the harbour; the southern one is around the main market and bus station, about one km inland. The BNI bank is on Jalan Ampera near the market, and the Bank Rakyat Indonesia is on Jalan Ahmad Yani.

The area code for Waingapu is 0386.

Places to Stay & Eat
On Jalan Kartini, the very popular *Hotel Permata*, otherwise known as Ali's, is handy if arriving by ferry. Large rooms with attached mandi are 4500 rp per person, meals are available and good information is provided.

If the Permata is full, the *Hotel Lima Saudara* (☎ 21083) at Jalan Wanggameti 2 is the nearest cheap hotel, but it's a dive. Rooms with mandi and midget-sized beds are 8800/17,000 rp.

The other hotels are in the new part of town near the bus station. The *Hotel Elvin* (☎ 22097) at Jalan Ahmad Yani 73 is well run, with a good restaurant and large rooms. A few basic rooms without mandi cost 7000/12,500 rp but most rooms are newly renovated with mandi for 12,500/17,500 rp, 27,500/35,000 rp with air-con.

The popular *Hotel Sandle Wood* (☎ 21199) on Jalan WJ Lalaimantik is close to the bus terminal. It has an attractive garden and art shop. Small, run-down rooms with outside mandi cost 11,000/16,500 rp. Much better rooms with mandi cost 16,500/22,000 rp and air-con rooms are 27,500/38,500 rp.

The *Hotel Merlin* (☎ 21300) on Jalan Panjaitan has better service and is the top hotel in town. Rooms start at 16,500/22,000 rp, with shower, intercom and comfy beds. The 4th floor restaurant has great views, and the hotel has an art shop attached.

On the same street as the Sandle Wood is the quiet *Hotel Kaliuda* (☎ 21264). Rooms with shared bath are 10,000 rp, or 16,000 rp with attached bath.

The Merlin and Elvin hotels have good restaurants, otherwise Waingapu is not over-endowed with good eateries. The *Rumah Makan Mini Indah*, Jalan Ahmad Yani 27, is a simple place but has very tasty food.

Getting There & Away

Air Merpati (☎ 21329), Jalan Ahmad Yani 73, and Bouraq (☎ 21363), Jalan Yos Sudarso 57, between them have direct flights to/from Bima (99,500 rp), Kupang (169,000 rp), Tambulaka (Waikabubak; 66,500 rp) and Denpasar (208,000 rp).

Bus Buses to Waikabubak (4500 rp; five hours) depart around 7 am, noon and 3 pm. The hotels will book tickets, or go to one of the bus agents opposite the bus station. Buses also head south-east to Melolo, Rende and Baing.

Boat The Perum ASDP ferry from Kupang departs Ende on Tuesdays at 2 pm for Waingapu (12,000 rp; 10 hours) and then continues on to Sabu (13,500 rp; nine hours) on Wednesdays at 2 pm. It returns from Sabu on Thursdays and sails from Waingapu to Ende on Fridays at 2 pm, continuing on to Kupang the next day.

Pelni's KM *Binaiya* calls in every two weeks at a special dock at the other end of the harbour – a bemo to this pier is 300 rp per person. From Waingapu it runs to/from Ende or Bima.

Getting Around

Bemos from the town centre to the airport, six km out, cost 300 rp while a chartered bemo will be about 3000 rp. There are regular bemos to villages around Waingapu.

AROUND WAINGAPU

A number of the traditional villages in the south-east can be visited from Waingapu. The stone ancestor tombs are impressive and the area produces some of Sumba's best ikat. The villagers are quite used to tourists. Almost every village has a visitors' book,

and a donation of 1000 rp or so is expected. Ikat for sale will appear.

Melolo, a nothing village on the main road 62 km south-east of Waingapu, is easily reached by bus and the *Losmen Hermindo* has rooms for 6000 rp per person if you want to do more than day-trip from Waingapu. From Melolo infrequent bemos run to nearby traditional villages.

Seven km from Melolo, at **Rende**, the former raja's tomb is a massive stone slab construction, one of Sumba's largest tombs. The village has good ikat and many traditional houses.

Umabara & Pau, four km from Melolo, have several traditional Sumba houses and tombs. These villages are a 20 minute walk from the main road – the turn-off is two km north-east of Melolo.

Some 70 km from Waingapu, **Kaliuda** has some of Sumba's best ikat. To get there, take a bus heading to Baing from Waingapu or Melolo and get off at Ngalu – Kaliuda is about a three km walk from there.

There's good surf between May and August at **Kalala**, about two km from Baing off the main road from Melolo. An Australian has set up bungalow accommodation along the wide, white-sand beach, costing 30,000 rp per person. Buses from Melolo run to Baing.

WAIKABUBAK

Waikabubak is a neat little town with many traditional houses and old graves carved with buffalo-horn motifs. One of the spectacular attractions of western Sumba is the *Pasola*, or mock battle ritual, held near Waikabubak each year. It's a kind of jousting match on horseback. The Pasola Festival is held at the villages of Lamboya and Koda in February, and at Wanokaka and Gaura in March.

The BNI bank on Jalan A Yani changes most major currencies at good rates. The tourist office is on Jalan Teratai on the eastern outskirts of town.

The area code for Waikabubak is 0387.

Places to Stay

The *Hotel Aloha* (☎ 21024) is a popular budget choice. It has good food and information on western Sumba. Clean singles/doubles with shared bath cost 6600/ 8800 rp, or 11,000/ 13,750 rp with private bath.

Just around the corner, at Jalan Pemuda 4, the *Hotel Manandang* (☎ 21197) is the best in town. It has a variety of rooms around the garden and a good restaurant. Large, spotless rooms are 11,000/16,000 rp, or rooms with bathroom range from 20,000/25,000 rp to 40,000/45,000 rp. Prices exclude 10% tax.

The cheapest in town is the *Hotel Pelita* (☎ 21104) on Jalan Ahmad Yani. Dingy rooms are 5000/8000 rp, or better rooms with mandi at the back are 10,000/15,000 rp.

The *Hotel Artha* (☎ 21112) on Jalan Veteran is a quiet, relatively new place. The rooms around the courtyard garden start at 17,500 rp with mandi.

Getting There & Away

The Merpati agent (☎ 21051) is at Jalan Ahmad Yani 11. The airport is at Tambulaka, 42 km north. The flights between Waingapu and Bima stop at Tambulaka, but it is not always easy to get a seat.

The bus terminal is central. Buses run to Waingapu (4500 rp; five hours) at 8 am, noon and 3.30 pm, and throughout the day to Anakalang (700 rp; 40 minutes) and Waikelo (1500 rp; 1½ hours). Less frequent and less certain minibuses and trucks run to other villages.

Getting Around

The Bumi Indah goes to the airstrip at Tambulaka for 2000 rp, but is not always reliable. Otherwise, a taxi costs a whopping 45,000 rp.

The bigger hotels, such as the Hotel Manandang, rent cars. Ask around about renting a motorbike.

AROUND WAIKABUBAK

At **Anakalang**, 22 km east of Waikabubak, some large tombs are right beside the highway, though the more interesting villages are south of town past the market. **Kabonduk** has some fine tombs, and then it is a pleasant 15 minute walk across the fields and up the hill to **Matakakeri** and the original

ancestral village for the area, **Lai Tarung**, which has impressive tombs and great views. Lai Tarung is the site of the Purung Takadonga Ratu – a festival honouring the ancestors, held every year around June.

Directly south of Waikabubak is the Wanokaka District, a centre for the Pasola festival in March. **Waigali** and **Praigoli** are interesting traditional villages. The south coast has some fine beaches, particularly **Rua** and **Pantai Morosi**. The *Homestay Mete Bulu*, 1.5 km from Pantai Morosi, reached on foot, has rooms for 15,000 rp.

More good beaches are found in the north, near **Waikelo**. Newa, a couple of km from Waikelo, has a new hotel.

On the west coast, the coastal village of **Pero** has accommodation at the *Homestay Story* for 12,000 rp per person. It makes a good base for visiting nearby villages. Occasional buses run from Waikabubak to Pero, otherwise take a bus to Waitabula and another to Pero.

Kalimantan

Kalimantan, the southern two-thirds of the island of Borneo, is a vast, jungle-covered wilderness – or at least it was: the loggers and miners are making serious inroads into the region. Apart from the area around Pontianak and the region from Samarinda to Banjarmasin there are few roads. The boats and ferries of the numerous rivers and waterways are the chief form of long-distance transport, although there are also plenty of flight connections.

Some of the coastal cities have their own remarkable attractions – the canals of Banjarmasin and the fiery orange sunsets over Pontianak, for example. On the whole, however, it is the native Dayak tribes of the inland areas that are the main reason for coming to Kalimantan. Unfortunately, access to such tribes is becoming increasingly expensive, often prohibitively so for the budget traveller.

Getting There & Away

East Malaysia Despite the long land border with the East Malaysian states of Sabah and Sarawak, options for crossing between the two countries are limited. The only real options are by air or land between Kuching in Sarawak and Pontianak, and by air or sea between Tawau in Sabah and Tarakan.

MAS has flights twice a week between Pontianak and Kuching, or a daily express bus does the trip in about 10 hours. See the Pontianak section for details. Both the land crossing at Entikong and Pontianak airport are visa-free ports these days.

Bouraq flies from Tarakan to Tawau, or boats run between Tarakan and Nunukan, and from Nunukan regular boats go to/from Tawau. Tarakan is not a visa-free entry/exit point and an Indonesian visa is required for arrival by air or sea. See the Tarakan section for details of this route.

Indonesian visas can be easily obtained at the consulates in Kuching, Kota Kinabalu or Tawau. Most nationalities do not require a visa to enter Malaysia.

Other Parts of Indonesia Kalimantan has a variety of air and sea connections with other places in Indonesia.

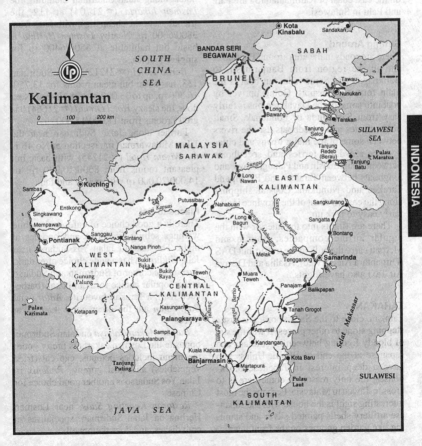

Air Bouraq, Merpati, Garuda and Sempati all fly into Kalimantan. Flights are abundant and can usually be obtained at the last minute if need be.

Boat There are shipping connections to Java and to Sulawesi, both with Pelni and other shipping companies. Most of Pelni's ships stop at Kalimantan somewhere along their routes. See the introductory Indonesia Getting Around section for details of Pelni ships and the routes they take.

There are also regular ships from the ports on the east coast of Kalimantan to Pare Pare and Palu in Sulawesi.

Getting Around

There are roads in the area around Pontianak and in the region from Banjarmasin to Balikpapan and Samarinda, but boat is the main form of transport. Going upriver by boat into some of the Dayak regions is fairly easy from Samarinda or Pontianak. Small boats, ferries and speedboats use the rivers between some of the major towns and cities – there are daily ferries and speedboats between Banjarmasin and Palangkaraya, and longboats between Tarakan and Berau, and Tarakan and Nunukan. Coastal shipping along the eastern coast of the province is also fairly easy to pick up.

There are flights into the interior with the regular airline companies. Bouraq and Merpati carry the bulk of the traffic, but DAS (Dirgantara Air Service), Asahia and Deraya Air Taxi also have flights.

TARAKAN

Tarakan, close to the Sabah border, is just a stepping stone to other places. It was the site of bloody fighting between Australians and Japanese at the end of WWII. Unless you have a deep interest in Japanese blockhouses, the only reason to come here is to cross to Tawau in Malaysia. Perhaps the most interesting sight is the house with old Japanese artillery shells painted silver and standing like garden gnomes on the front lawn.

Information

The Bank Dagang Negara on Jalan Yos Sudarso will change some standard travellers' cheques and major currencies.

The area code for Tarakan is 0551.

Places to Stay

Hotel Taufiq (☎ 21347), Jalan Yos Sudarso 26, is a huge rambling place near the main mosque. It is basic but affordable at 8000/9000 rp, 14,500/17,500 rp with mandi, or 28,500/ 29,750 rp with air-con.

There's a line of cheap and mid-range hotels along Jalan Sudirman including the *Losmen Jakarta* (☎ 21704) at 112, the friendliest of the cheap digs, with rates from 3800/6600 rp. Nearby *Losmen Herlina* is basic but habitable at 5500/6400 rp for singles/doubles.

Barito Hotel (☎ 21212), Jalan Sudirman 133, has basic but clean rooms for 13,750/16,500 rp, up to 33,000 rp with air-con. Next door, the sleazy *Hotel Orchid* (☎ 21664) has grotty rooms from 11,000/15,000 rp.

Further along Jalan Sudirman near the Jalan Mulawarman intersection at No 46 is the *Wisata Hotel* (☎ 21245) with basic but pleasant rooms from 8500/10,900 rp, or 14,000/20,000 rp with mandi and fan.

Places to Eat

There is a good choice of cafes and mobile warungs selling fried rice and noodles at night. The lane off Jalan Yos Sudarso near Jalan Sudirman has a wide choice after dark. *Turi* on the corner of Sudirman and Sudarso is the popular choice for ikan bakar (barbecued fish), a Tarakan favourite. *Antara* and *Bagi Alam* are the other good ikan bakar places.

Rumah Makan Cahaya on Jalan Sudirman opposite the Losmen Jakarta is pretty good; the menu includes octopus, cap cai (fried vegetables) and nasi goreng. *Phoenix* in Jalan Yos Sudarso is another good choice for Chinese.

Restoran Kepeting Saos, near Losmen Herlina on Jalan Sudirman, specialises in crab dishes, and does them well.

Getting There & Away

Air Sempati, Bouraq, DAS or Merpati fly to Tarakan from Balikpapan or Samarinda. All airline flights from Tarakan to Balikpapan connect with onward flights across Indonesia and internationally.

In Tarakan, Sempati (☎ 21870) is in the Tarakan Plaza on Jalan Yos Sudarso. Merpati (☎ 21911) is at Jalan Yos Sudarso 10. Bouraq (☎ 21248) is at Jalan Yos Sudarso 9B, across from the Tarakan Theatre. DAS (☎ 51612), at Jalan Sudirman 9, has useful flights inland, as does MAF (☎ 51011), the missionary airline in the tax building at Jalan Sudirman 133.

Boat The Pelni office is at the main port – take a colt almost to the end of Jalan Yos Sudarso. The Pelni ship *Tidar* calls into Tarakan on its regular Pantoloan-Balikpapan-Pare Pare-Surabaya run. There's another Pelni boat, the *Leuser*, which goes straight from Toli-Toli to Nunukan and Tawau.

Malaysia For boats on to Tawau in the east Malaysian state of Sabah, go to Pelabuhan Tarakan. Longboats leave daily at around 9 am and arrive in Nunukan 12 hours later for 15,000 rp per person. In Nunukan you can catch a speedboat to Tawau for 21,000 rp – it takes about four hours. You can also spend the night at the *Losmen Nunukan* for 5000 rp and get a speedboat the next day.

There is an Indonesian immigration office in Nunukan where you must finalise your paperwork. Note that if you got a two month tourist visa on arrival in Indonesia, you will need an exit permit from the immigration office in Jakarta. If you have a one month tourist visa before coming to Indonesia, Nunukan can stamp your passport without an exit permit from Jakarta. Some travellers report an easy exit via this route, but most get turned back.

Getting Around

The Airport Taxis (3000 rp) or chartered bemos (1000 rp) are your only option from town to the airport (five km) for those dawn flights. At all other times, bemos pass the terminal gate about 200 metres from the terminal, and can get you to and from town in 10 minutes for 300 rp.

Colt Transport around town is by colt, which cuts a circular route via Jalan Sudirman and Jalan Yos Sudarso. A 300 rp flat rate gets you anywhere.

SAMARINDA

Just as Balikpapan, not far to the south, has grown around the oil industry, Samarinda is sustained by timber. It's another trading port on one of Kalimantan's mighty rivers, and is a good place to arrange trips up the Sungai Mahakam – budget travellers should base themselves here rather than Balikpapan.

Orientation & Information

Samarinda lies along the northern bank of the Sungai Mahakam. The centre of town is the enormous mosque on the riverfront. Running east along the riverfront is Jalan Yos Sudarso and to the west is Jalan Gajah Mada. Most of the offices and hotels are in these two streets or in the streets behind them.

The tourist office (Kantor Parawisata) is just off Jalan Kesuma Bangsa at Jalan Al Suryani 1.

The Bank Dagang Negara on Jalan Mulawarman changes cash and travellers' cheques.

The area code for Samarinda is 0541.

Places to Stay

The *Hotel Hidayah II* (☎ 41712), Jalan Hahlid 25, is central, spartan but clean. Singles/doubles start from 17,500/22,500 rp, or 20,000/25,000 rp with mandi. Rates include a small breakfast. The *Hotel Hidayah I* (☎ 31210), on Jalan Temenggung, is cheaper: singles/doubles with mandi cost 18,150/21,175 rp, air-con doubles from 40,000 rp. Next door, the *Aida* (☎ 42572) is a good place to be based. It has a coffee shop veranda area and singles/doubles for 19,000/22,000 rp, and air-con rooms from 38,000 rp. Between them these three hotels get to host most of the budget travellers who make it into town.

The *Hotel Andhika* (☎ 42358), Jalan Agus Salim 37, has noisy, stuffy economy singles/doubles from 19,000/22,990 rp. Next door is The *Hotel Maharani* (☎ 49995), where basic singles/doubles cost 15,000/20,000 rp.

The *Wisma Pirus* (☎ 21873) is on Jalan Pirus, a quiet street. Stuffy rooms in the old wing start from 20,000 rp, while air-con rooms in the new wing range from 60,000 rp. The *Hotel Hayani* (☎ 42653) across the street at No 31 is also good, with doubles ranging from 22,990 to 54,540 rp.

Hotel Mesir (☎ 42624), Jalan Sudirman 57, is an unfriendly larger cheapie with rooms from 15,000 to 20,000 rp. This place is best avoided except as a last resort.

Places to Eat

Samarinda's chief gastronomic wonder is the udang galah (giant river prawns) found in the local warung. The Citra Niaga *hawker centre* off Jalan Niaga, a block or two east of the mosque, is a pleasant pedestrian precinct with an excellent range of seafood, padang, sate, noodle and rice dishes, fruit juices and warm beer. Establish prices in advance.

At the *Mesra Indah shopping centre* close to the Hotel Hidayah on Jalan Hahlid are two decent food centres and, upstairs overlooking the street, an ice cream parlour.

If you like sticky pastries, try the *Sweet Home Bakery*, at Jalan Sudirman 8, west of Jalan Pirus on the left. For the best kueh outside Banjarmasin, try the *warung* opposite Mesra Indah, which has a fabulous selection including custard star cakes. Alternatively, there is a tempe stall in the lane behind Mesra Indah.

Those desperate for a fast-food fix should head over to the new *KFC* on Jalan Mutawarman.

Getting There & Away

Air DAS (☎ 35250), Jalan Gatot Subroto 92, has heavily subsidised and heavily booked flights to the interior – you will need to book at least a month in advance.

Merpati (☎ 43385), Garuda, Sempati and Bouraq are all at Jalan Sudirman 20, and can be contacted on the same telephone number. Merpati and Bouraq have flights to Berau,

Tarakan (198,000 rp) and Balikpapan (56,000 rp).

Bus From Samarinda you can head west to Tenggarong or south to Balikpapan. The long-distance bus station is adjacent to the riverboat terminal, on the west side of the river a couple of km upstream from the bridge. Bemos run between the centre of town and the bus station for 500 rp. There are daily buses to Tenggarong (1700 rp; one hour) and to Balikpapan (3000 rp, 4000 rp air-con; two hours) along well-surfaced roads.

Boat Pelni (☎ 41402) is at Jalan Sudarso 40-56; or ask at the nearby Terminal Penumpang Kapal Laut Samarinda and the Direktorat Jenderal Perhubungan Laut – both on Jalan Sudarso. The *Leuser* does a fortnightly run from here to Toli-Toli and Nunukan, and south to Pare Pare, Batulicin and Surabaya. Ekonomi fares are 92,000 rp to Nunukan, 81,000 rp to Tarakan and 49,000 rp to Toli-Toli.

There are many non-Pelni boats from Samarinda to other ports along the Kalimantan coast, including weekly boats to Berau (aka Tanjung Redeb; 28,000 to 45,000 rp; about 36 hours) and occasionally to Tarakan. If you can't get a ship to Tarakan, then take one as far as Berau. From there it's easy to get a boat to Tarakan.

For information on what leaves when, check with the harbourmaster at the Adpel office, on the corner of Jalan Sudarso and Jalan Nakhoda.

Riverboat Boats up the Mahakam leave from the Sungai Kunjang ferry terminal south-west of the town centre. To get there take a green city minibus A (called taxi A) west on Jalan Gajah Mada, and ask for 'feri'. The regular fare is 500 rp but if you get in an empty taxi they may try to make you charter – insist on *harga biasa* (the usual price).

A boat to Tenggarong takes four hours, to Melak one day and a night (10,000 rp), and to Long Bagun two days and a night (conditions permitting). Most boats have a sleeping deck upstairs, which costs extra, and warungs downstairs.

Getting Around

The airport is in the northern suburbs – it costs 8000 rp from the taxi counter into the centre of town. Alternatively, walk 100 metres down to Jalan Gatot Subroto, turn left and catch a reddish-brown colt – a taxi B – all the way to the waterfront (400 rp).

TENGGARONG

Situated 39 km west of Samarinda, this little riverside town is noted for its **Sultan's Palace**, built by the Dutch in 1936 and now used as a museum.

Places to Stay

Down on the waterfront there are two places right on the boat dock. The *Penginapan Zaranah I* has rooms for 5000 rp. The *Warung & Penginapan Anda* costs 7500 rp. If you're looking for a little more comfort, try the *Anda II*, which has basic economy rooms at 11,000/13,750 rp, standard rooms with mandi for 18,150/22,000 rp and air-con deluxe rooms at 33,000/38,500 rp. The nearby *Rumah Makan Penginapa Diana* is a good budget option, with large rooms from 10,000/15,000 rp.

Getting There & Away

Boats to Tenggarong from Samarinda take three hours. The simpler option is to take a colt, which takes just one hour and costs 1700 rp. The colt pulls into the Petugas station on the outskirts of Tenggarong. From here you have to get a taxi kota (another colt) into the centre of Tenggarong for 300 rp.

Motorcycle taxis will also take you into town for 500 rp. City taxis run between 7 am and 6 pm. It takes about 10 minutes to get from Petugas station to Pasar Tepian Pandan, where you get off for the boat dock, palace and tourist office.

UP THE SUNGAI MAHAKAM

Samarinda is probably the best jumping-off point for visits to the Dayak tribes of East Kalimantan. Some of these places are easily

reached on the regular longboats that ply the Sungai Mahakam from Samarinda and Tenggarong all the way to Long Bagun, 396 km upriver. Many of the towns and villages have a budget hotel or two or a longhouse where travellers can stay – the standard price everywhere is 5000 rp per person.

Most people head upriver to **Tanjung Isuy** on the shores of Danau Jempang. Activity focuses on the Taman Jamrot Lamin, a longhouse vacated in the late 1970s and rebuilt by the provincial government as a craft centre and tourist hostel. Group tourists flock here for performances of Kenyah, Kayan and Banuaq dancing – commercial but lively, rhythmic and loads of fun for the whole town. Accommodation is provided by the *Taman Jamrot Lamin*, on Jalan Indonesia Australia, for 5000 rp. The *Penginapan Beringan* has rooms for the same price.

Nearby **Mancong** has another slightly touristy longhouse (built by the government in 1987), where it is possible to stay. To get to Danau Jempang, take a longboat from Samarinda to Muara Muntai (5000 rp; 13 hours) first and spend the night there before getting a boat to Tanjung Isuy (4000 rp; four hours).

Melak, 325 km from Samarinda, is famous for its 5000 acre Kersid Luwai Orchid Reserve, 16 km from Melak by jeep or ojek charter. The *Rahmat Abadi* is the best place to stay. In nearby **Eheng**, some 200 Banuaq Dayak reside in Eheng's 65 metre longhouse. You can walk there, or rent a jeep or ojek from Melak. Longboats from Samarinda to Melak (8000 rp; 24 hours) leave at 9 am.

Long Iram, 409 km from Samarinda, is the end of the line if the river is low. Long Iram has become a sort of backwater boom town as a result of gold mining, and accommodation is more expensive. From Tering, near Long Iram, it may be possible to hitch to Tanjung Balai and on to Muara Tewah, from where longboats ply the Barito River to Banjarmasin. Long Iram is 33 hours by longboat from Samarinda (10,000 rp).

Further upriver are more longhouses between **Datah Bilang** and **Muara Merak**, including the Bahau, Kenyah and Punan settlements. The end of the line for regular longboat services is **Long Bagun**, or **Long Apari** if the conditions are right. The journey from Samarinda can take three days (with an overnight in Long Iram) and the fare is from 15,000 to 20,000 rp.

If you want to start your trip from the top, DAS flies to **Data Dawai** four times a week, an airstrip near Long Lunuk, for 53,000 rp – you will need to book weeks, perhaps months in advance. From there you can work your way downriver back to Samarinda, or trek overland to the Apokayan Highlands.

BALIKPAPAN

Best avoided by budget travellers, Balikpapan is an air-conditioned boom town that has got rich on oil money. It's far from an unpleasant place, sporting some of the best food and undoubtedly the liveliest nightlife in Kalimantan; yet it's simply not cheap and offers very little to see.

Information

There's a small tourist office at the airport, but other than that you're on your own. The BNI bank on Jalan Pengeran Antasari and its branch at the airport will change major travellers' cheques and cash currencies.

The area code for Balikpapan is 0542.

Places to Stay

Travellers flying in to Balikpapan from elsewhere in Indonesia are in for a shock. Accommodation is expensive – if possible take a bus (two hours) to Samarinda, where you will find much better value for money.

The *Hotel Aida* (☎ 21006), inconveniently located out of town on Jalan Yani, has airless singles/doubles from 12,000/18,000 rp and air-con rooms at 38,000 rp. Close by, the *Hotel Murni* has rooms from 18,000/22,000 rp and looks OK, but get a room at the back away from the main road.

The *Penginapan Royal*, near the Pasar Baru, is at the start of the airport road near the Jalan Ahmad Yani corner. It's a grim place and it's unlikely you'll get a room here. Rooms start from 8500 rp.

One other option is the very central *Hotel Gajah Mada* (☎ 34634), Jalan Sudirman 14, where economy rooms are 22,500/27,500 rp, and standard ones are 45,000/50,000 rp; all with private mandi. The terrace off the 2nd floor overlooks the sea. Unfortunately this hotel is often full. Elsewhere around town, room rates start at around 50,000 rp and upwards.

Places to Eat

Balikpapan has some excellent restaurants. For Padang seafood, try the *Restaurant Masakan Padang Simpang Raya* next to the Hotel Murni. The *Restaurant Salero For Padang Minang* at Jalan Ahmad Yani 12B is similarly priced, as is the *Restaurant Sinar Minang* on Jalan Sudirman.

If you're budgeting and you just want a quick snack, there is plenty of inexpensive Indonesian-style Chinese fare around town. One of the best areas is the string of restaurants, including *Frielanda*, opposite the Mirama Hotel (Jalan Pranoto).

Finally, for a splurge, *Bondy's*, on Jalan Ahmad Yani, offers seafood and hearty serves of western fare in an open courtyard. The seafood is much better than the steaks.

Getting There & Away

Air Garuda (☎ 22300), Jalan Ahmad Yani 14, is diagonally opposite the Hotel Benakutai. Sempati (☎ 31612) is in the Hotel Benakutai, Merpati (☎ 24477) is at Jalan Sudirman 22 and Bouraq (☎ 23117) has an office next to Hotel Budiman.

Balikpapan's airport is the busiest in Kalimantan and there are frequent flights to major destinations within Kalimantan and around the rest of Indonesia.

Bus Buses to Samarinda (3000 rp, 4000 rp air-con; two hours) depart from a bus stand in the north of the city accessible by a No 2 or 3 bemo for 700 rp (it's a long way out). Buy your ticket on the bus or at the station.

Buses to Banjarmasin (16,000 rp, 22,000 rp air-con; 12 hours) depart from the bus terminal on the opposite side of the harbour to the city. To get there, take a colt from the

Rapak bus terminal to the pier on Jalan Mangunsidi. Charter a speedboat to take you to the other side (the speedboat drivers will mob you). It costs 1500 rp per person, or around 5000 rp to charter, and takes 10 minutes. Alternatively, a motorised longboat costs 1000 rp and takes 25 minutes.

Boat The Pelni liners *Kambuna*, *Umsini* and *Tidar* call in fortnightly, connecting Balikpapan to Tarakan, Pantoloan, Ujung Pandang, Surabaya and beyond.

In Balikpapan the Pelni office (☎ 21402) is at Jalan Yos Sudarso 76. For regular ships to Surabaya try PT Elang Raya Abadi for the MV *Hafag* services to Ujung Pandang (35,000 to 68,000 rp), or Surabaya (55,000 to 90,000 rp). Alternatively, try PT Ling Jaya Shipping (☎ 21577) at Jalan Yos Sudarso 40 and PT Sudi Jaya Agung (☎ 21956) at Jalan Pelabuhan 39. Fares are around 35,000 rp.

A recently added service is the *Paradipta Darma*, which leave three times a week for Mamuju in south Sulawesi. The eight hour trip costs 22,000 rp in ekonomi.

Getting Around
A taxi from Seppingan airport is 11,000 rp, less from town.

Bemos cost 350 rp to anywhere around town. They do circular routes around the main streets from the Rapak terminal at the end of Jalan Panjaitan. Guys with motorbikes also hang around the Rapak terminal and will take you anywhere as a pillion passenger.

BANJARMASIN
At first glance it might not look like much, but get out on the canals of Banjarmasin and it quickly becomes one of most stunning cities in Indonesia. With its maze of waterways and other nearby attractions, Banjarmasin is the only city in Kalimantan worth lingering in.

Orientation & Information
Although Banjarmasin is quite a big place, almost everything you'll need is packed into a very small area in the region of Jalan Pasar Baru.

The best place for travel information is the Borneo Homestay (see Places to Stay). The South Kalimantan tourist office at Jalan Panjaitan 3, near the mosque, can also be very helpful and arranges guides for trekking in the province.

The Bank Dagang Negara, next to the Telkom office on Jalan Lambung Mangkurat, has the best rates for travellers' cheques but insists on seeing your purchase agreement.

The area code for Banjarmasin is 0511.

Mesjid Raya Sabilal Muhtadin
In the middle of Banjarmasin is this giant mosque, with its copper-coloured flying saucer-shaped dome and minarets with lids and spires. The interior is striking. Visitors must pay a small fee to enter.

Boat Trips
Banjarmasin's two premier attractions are its canals and its floating market. As locals will point out, the latter is one of the few left in Asia that has not been turned into a tourist trap. It's possible to tour the waterways of Banjarmasin in a motorised canoe *(klotok)* for 5000 rp per hour. Ask around the wharf near the junction of Jalan Lambung Mangkurat and Jalan Pasar Baru. Borneo Homestay runs inexpensive tours of the floating market and canals that get rave reviews from travellers.

It's worth taking a boat to the river islands of **Pulau Kaget** and **Pulau Kembang**. It takes four to five hours to visit Pulau Kaget, 12 km from town, where you can see the famous proboscis, or long-nosed, monkeys. The much closer Pulau Kembang has an old Chinese temple that's home to hundreds of long-tailed macaques. For these islands, you'd best forget the klotoks and hire a speedboat from the pier at the end of Jalan Pos.

Places to Stay
The *Borneo Homestay* (☎ 57545; fax 57515), in an alley just off Jalan Pos, is a good information centre and excellent place

INDONESIA

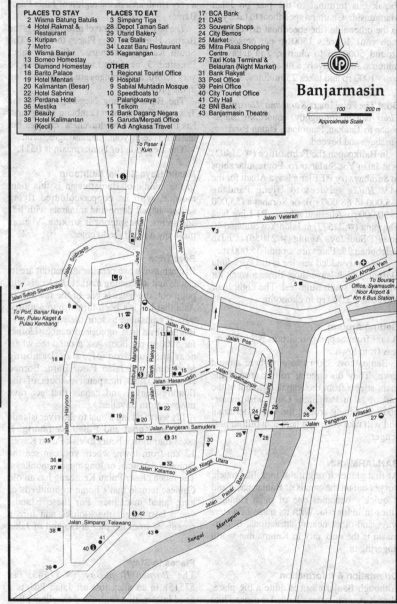

Banjarmasin

PLACES TO STAY
2 Wisma Batung Batulis
4 Hotel Rakmat & Restaurant
5 Kuripan
7 Metro
8 Wisma Banjar
13 Borneo Homestay
17 Diamond Homestay
18 Barito Palace
19 Hotel Mentari
20 Kalimantan (Besar)
22 Hotel Sabrina
32 Perdana Hotel
36 Mestika
37 Beauty
38 Hotel Kalimantan (Kecil)

PLACES TO EAT
3 Simpang Tiga
28 Depot Taman Sari
29 Utarid Bakery
30 Tea Stalls
34 Lezat Baru Restaurant
35 Kaganangan

OTHER
1 Regional Tourist Office
6 Hospital
9 Sabilal Muhtadin Mosque
10 Speedboats to Palangkaraya
11 Telkom
12 Bank Dagang Negara
15 Garuda/Merpati Office
16 Adi Angkasa Travel
17 BCA Bank
21 DAS
23 Souvenir Shops
24 City Bemos
25 Market
26 Mitra Plaza Shopping Centre
27 Taxi Kota Terminal & Belauran (Night Market)
31 Bank Rakyat
33 Post Office
39 Pelni Office
40 City Tourist Office
41 City Hall
42 BNI Bank
43 Banjarmasin Theatre

0   100   200 m
Approximate Scale

To Pasar Kuin

Jalan Veteran

Jalan Sudirman

Jalan Tendean

Jalan Subrapto

Jalan Ahmad Yani

To Bouraq Office, Syamsudin Noor Airport & Km 6 Bus Station

Jalan Sutoyo Siswomiharjo

To Port, Banjar Raya Pier, Pulau Kaget & Pulau Kembang

Jalan Pos

Jalan Pos

Jalan Mangkurat

Jalan Lambung Mangkurat

Bank Rakyat

Jalan Hasanuddin

Jalan Sudimampir

Jalan Ujung Murung

Jalan Haryono

Jalan Pangeran Samudera

Jalan Pangeran Antasari

Jalan Niaga Utara

Jalan Katamso

Jalan Pasar Baru

Jalan Simpang Telawang

Sungai Martapura

to be based. The owner, Johan, speaks English and knows South and Central Kalimantan well. There is a bar and rooftop lounging area overlooking the river upstairs. Single rooms without fan cost 7500 rp, with fan 10,000 rp, and with private mandi 20,000 rp.

The *Diamond Homestay* (☎ 50055), on the next alley, is another friendly budget option. It is run by terrific staff at the moneychanger next door. Ring the bell above the door at the homestay on Jalan Simpang Hasanuddin or knock on the blue shutters at No 58. This pleasant place charges 12,000/18,000 rp for singles/doubles.

Just over the iron bridge, the *Hotel Rakmat* (☎ 54429) at Jalan Ahmad Yani 9 is sizeable, with a friendly manager. Singles/doubles cost from 10,500/17,500 rp with shared mandi and no fan. The *Hotel Kalimantan* on Jalan Haryono near Jalan Telawang (not to be confused with the luxury hotel of the same name) has singles/doubles for 9000/15,000 rp.

The popular *Wisma Banjar* (☎ 53561), 100 metres from the mosque, on Jalan Suprapto 5, is a slightly more expensive option. Rooms range from 12,500 rp, to 25,000 rp with air-con.

For something a little more mid-range, the comfortable *Hotel Sabrina* (☎ 54442), Jalan Bank Rakyat 21, has singles/doubles for 20,000/25,000 rp with fan, and 32,000/38,000 rp with air-con and TV. If it's full, you'll probably be directed to the nearby *Perdana Hotel* (☎ 68029), Jalan Katamso 3. The Perdana has economy singles for 31,500 rp, doubles with fan for 37,000 rp, and air-con doubles for 48,000 rp.

Places to Eat
Banjarmasin's excellent array of kueh (cake) includes deep-fried breads, some with delicious fillings, and sticky banana rice cakes – a cheap but tasty option for breakfast at the tea stalls. Stuff yourself for 300 to 400 rp or even less at the canoe warung at the floating markets. Other breakfast fare includes nasi kuning (a local rice and chicken dish) from the *Warung Makan Rakmat* next door to the Rakmat Hotel on Jalan Ahmad Yani; it's open between 6 and 10 am. Across the street

is a no-name warung that serves cheap and tasty soto banjar, another local speciality.

A local speciality is ayam panggang (chicken roasted and served in sweet soy), but fish and freshwater cray hold pride of place in Banjar cuisine. There is a string of eateries along Jalan Pangeran Samudera; try the *Kaganangan* at No 30 for local dishes. As with most regional cuisine, you only pay for what you eat. The *Lezat Baru* on the same street is reckoned to have the best Chinese food in town – it's not expensive.

If you're on a tight budget or want a taste of street culture, eat at the tea stalls along Jalan Niaga Utara between Jalan Katamso and Jalan Pangeran Samudera near Pasar Baru. There is a friendly *tea stall* next to the Jalan Ahmad Yani bridge and another at Jalan Simpang Hasanuddin.

Getting There & Away
Air Garuda/Merpati (☎ 54203), at Jalan Hasanuddin 31, is open Monday to Thursday from 7 am to 4 pm, Friday from 7 am to noon and 2 to 4 pm, Saturday from 7 am to 1 pm and Sunday and holidays from 9 am to noon. Bouraq (☎ 52445) is inconveniently situated at an office four km from the centre on Jalan Ahmad Yani 343. DAS (☎ 52902), Jalan Hasanuddin 6, Blok 4, is across the road from Garuda.

Adi Angkasa Travel at Jalan Hasanuddin 27 is a good place to buy air tickets and offers some discounts.

Bus Buses and colts depart frequently from the Km 6 terminal for Martapura and Banjarbaru (1600 rp). Night buses to Balikpapan (16,000 rp, or 22,000 rp air-con) leave daily between 4 and 4.30 pm and arrive in Panajam, across the river from Balikpapan, about 12 hours later. From there, take a speedboat across the river – the cost should be included in your bus ticket.

Boat Ships leave for Surabaya twice a week (16 hours) and Semarang once a week (20 hours). The ships dock at Trisakti pisini harbour. To get there take a bemo from the taxi kota terminal on Jalan Pangeran Samudera for

400 rp. The bemo will take you past the harbourmaster's and ticket offices.

The harbourmaster's office (☎ 54775) is on Jalan Barito Hilir at Trisakti. Opposite is a line of shops with several agencies for boat tickets to Surabaya, but Pelni fares are cheapest from the Pelni counter inside. It's also possible to book tickets at Borneo Homestay. Pelni fares from Banjarmasin to Surabaya range from 50,000 rp in ekonomi class, 103,000 rp 2nd class and 136,000 rp 1st class. Fares to Semarang are 58,000 rp ekonomi class, 118,000 2nd class and 156,000 rp 1st class.

Heading inland, speedboats to Palangkaraya leave from a dock at the mosque end of Jalan Pos. From Banjarmasin to Palangkaraya is 27,000 rp and there are boats daily. River ferries (bis airs) to Palangkaraya depart from the Banjar Raya pier on the Sungai Barito, and cost 7500 rp.

Long-distance bis air which journey up the Barito leave from the river taxi terminal near the Banjar Raya fish market. To get there take a yellow colt (400 rp) to the end of Jalan Sutoyo Siswomiharjo west of the city centre. The end of the route is the town of Muara Teweh in Central Kalimantan, 56 hours away and costing only 17,500 rp. The tariff includes the price of a bed.

Getting Around

The Airport The airport is 26 km out of town on the road to Banjarbaru. Getting there by public transport is a hassle and involves a 1.5 km walk. Take a bemo from Jalan Pasar Baru to the Km 6 terminal, and then catch a Martapura-bound colt. Get off at the branch road leading to the airport and start walking. Alternatively, a taxi all the way to the airport will cost you around 12,500 rp.

Local Transport Bemos congregate at the junction of Jalan Samudera and Jalan Pasar Baru and they cost from 400 rp to various destinations around town, including the Km 6 terminal for long-distance buses.

Banjarmasin becak and bajaj drivers ask hefty prices and are hard to bargain with. Guys with motorbikes, who hang around Pasar Baru and Km 6, will take you wherever you want to go.

BANJARBARU

This town, on the road from Banjarmasin to Martapura, has an interesting **museum** with a collection of Banjar and Dayak artefacts along with statues excavated from ancient Hindu temples in Kalimantan. The museum is open from 8 am to 1 pm, closes earlier on Friday and is closed all day Monday. From Banjarmasin take a colt to Matapura and ask to be dropped off at Banjarbaru.

MARTAPURA

The large market at Martapura is at its busiest on Fridays. It is a photographer's paradise – colourfully dressed Banjar women haggle over a cornucopia of exotic snacks and fruit, among other things. A visit to Martapura can easily be combined with a visit to the diamond mines at Cempaka – unfortunately the mines do not operate on Fridays (which is why the market is busy).

A section of the market sells uncut gems, silver jewellery and trading beads – the choice, both strung and unstrung, is excellent. Be prepared to bargain determinedly. The diamond-polishing factory and shop are also worth a look. Do not think about spending too much money on diamonds unless you know what you are doing.

Frequent colts leave from the Km 6 terminal in Banjarmasin. The fare is 1100 rp and it takes about 45 minutes along a good surfaced road.

CEMPAKA

The diamond fields of Cempaka, 43 km south of Banjarmasin, are a fascinating excursion. The miners labour in muddy holes – often up to their necks in water – sifting for gold, diamonds, agates. Note that the mines are closed on Fridays.

Take a Banjarmasin-Martapura bemo, and ask to get off at the huge roundabout just past Banjarbaru (1600 rp). From here take a green taxi to 'Alur' (500 rp), and walk the last 500 metres from the main road to the diamond digs. Bemos leave infrequently from Martapura;

otherwise charter a bemo from Martapura bus station. The round-trip costs 7500 rp. Borneo Homestay, in Banjarmasin, offers economical tours to Cempaka.

PONTIANAK

Pontianak is a sprawling equatorial city that sits astride the confluence of the Landak and Kapuas Kecil rivers. Like Banjarmasin, it really needs to be seen from its canals to be appreciated. Even so, Pontianak is not set to win any awards on the 'Asian destinations' front, and most travellers get out as quickly as possible.

If you're stuck for something to do, take an early evening stroll over the Kapuas Bridge for sweeping urban views and brilliant orange sunsets that make Bali sunsets look ordinary.

Orientation & Information

The commercial centre of Pontianak is in the north of town, close to the bank of the Sungai Kapuas. Most of the banks can be found along Jalan Rahadi Usman, particularly in the area close to the city passenger ferry.

The Kalimantan Barat tourist office is way out at Jalan Ahmad Sood 25 (☎ 36172). It has fine intentions but lousy maps and little English. Staff at the big hotels and private travel agencies often offer better advice.

The area code for Pontianak is 0561.

Mesjid Abdurrakhman

This 18th century royal mosque was built by Syarif Adbul Rahman, sultan of Pontianak from 1771 to 1808. Built in the Malay style, it's an impressive structure with a high, square-tiered roof. It's a short canoe trip (500 to 700 rp for a charter or 200 rp per person in a shared canoe) across the Sungai Landak from the pisini harbour.

Behind the royal mosque is the sultan's former palace, **Istana Kadriyah**. Now a museum, it displays a collection of the royal family's personal effects.

Museum Negeri Pontianak

Near Tanjungpura University, this national museum contains a very good collection of *tempayan*, or South-East Asian water containers, from Thailand, China and Borneo. There are also Dayak exhibits that illustrate the tribal cultures of West Kalimantan.

Equator Monument

If you're really stuck for something to do, this monument is to the north of the city centre across the river. Equator monument models are wonderfully kitsch souvenirs.

Places to Stay

Don't expect any bargains in Pontianak. The best budget beds are at the *Wisma Patria* (☎ 36063) at Jalan Merdeka Timur 497. Clean singles/doubles cost from 16,000 rp with fan and mandi, 25,000 rp with air-con. Another reasonably good budget option (by Pontianak standards) is the *Berlian Hotel* (☎ 32092), which has fan-cooled doubles with shared bathroom for 15,000 rp. Rooms with bathroom are 25,000 rp, while air-con rooms cost 35,000 rp.

Backing on to the river opposite the Kapuas Indah bemo terminal is the grim *Hotel Wijaya Kusuma* (☎ 32547), at Jalan Kapten Marsan 51-53. It has barely habitable economy rooms from 25,000 rp. Smaller and cleaner is the *Hotel Istana Pinangmerah* just next door. Singles/doubles start at 25,000 rp; there are larger air-con rooms for 32,500 rp and VIP triples at 37,500 rp.

The new *Hotel Central* (☎ 37444), Jalan Merdeka Timur 232, is friendly and has rooms with air-con, TV and hot water mandi from 36,000 to 44,000 rp. The rooms suffer from their proximity to two busy roads.

The *Hotel Khatulistiwa* (☎ 36773), Jalan Diponegoro 151, is a sprawling place with grubby economy rooms for 22,000 rp. There are rooms with air-con and TV from 27,500 rp. The *Orien Hotel* (☎ 32650) is in the south of town on Jalan Tanjungpura. It's a good mid-range place; rooms with fan, video and bath are 34,000 rp, and 42,000 to 54,000 rp with air-con.

Places to Eat

The local coffee is excellent, and there are numerous warung kopi around town. The

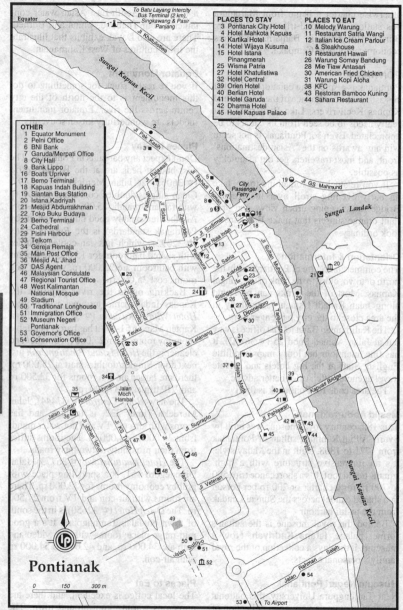

To Batu Layang Intercity
Bus Terminal (2 km),
Singkawang & Pasir
Panjang

Equator

Jl Khatulistiwa

Sungai Kapuas Kecil

PLACES TO STAY
3 Pontianak City Hotel
4 Hotel Mahkota Kapuas
5 Kartika Hotel
14 Hotel Wijaya Kusuma
15 Hotel Istana
   Pinangmerah
25 Wisma Patria
27 Hotel Khatulistiwa
32 Hotel Central
39 Orien Hotel
40 Berlian Hotel
41 Hotel Garuda
42 Dharma Hotel
45 Hotel Kapuas Palace

PLACES TO EAT
10 Melody Warung
11 Restaurant Satria Wangi
12 Italian Ice Cream Parlour
   & Steakhouse
13 Restaurant Hawaii
26 Warung Somay Bandung
28 Mie Tiaw Antasari
30 American Fried Chicken
31 Warung Kopi Aloha
38 KFC
43 Restoran Bamboo Kuning
44 Sahara Restaurant

OTHER
1 Equator Monument
2 Pelni Office
6 BNI Bank
7 Garuda/Merpati Office
8 City Hall
9 Bank Lippo
16 Boats Upriver
17 Bemo Terminal
18 Kapuas Indah Building
19 Siantan Bus Station
20 Istana Kadriyah
21 Mesjid Abdurrakhman
22 Toko Buku Budaya
24 Bemo Terminal
29 Cathedral
33 Pisini Harbour
33 Telkom
34 Gereja Remaja
35 Main Post Office
36 Mesjid AL Jihad
37 DAS Agent
47 Malaysian Consulate
47 Regional Tourist Office
48 West Kalimantan
   National Mosque
49 Stadium
50 'Traditional' Longhouse
51 Immigration Office
52 Museum Negeri
   Pontianak
53 Governor's Office
54 Conservation Office

Jl Pak Kasih

Jl Rajawali

Jl Fatimah

Jl Rahadi Usman

Jl Sidas

Jl Zainudin

Jl Sudirman

City
Passenger
Ferry

Jl GS Mahmund

Sungai Landak

Pasar Nusa Indah

Jl Jen Urip

Jl Patimura

Jl Satria

Jl Sultan Muhammed

Jl Juanda

Jl Mendora Timur
(Jl Cokroaminoto)

Sisingamangaraja

Jl Diponegoro

Jl Tanjungpura

Jl Teuku

Jl K.H A Dahlan

Jl Lelanang

Jl Gajah Mada

Kapuas Bridge

Jalan
Moch
Hambal

Jalan Sultan Abdur Rakhman

Jl Johan Idrus

Jl KS Tubun

Jl Suprapto

Jl Pahlawan

Jl Imam Bonjol

Sungai Kapuas Kecil

Jl Veteran

Jl Jen Ahmad Yani

Jalan
Sutoyo

Jalan Rahman Saleh

Pontianak

0   150   300 m

To Airport

INDONESIA

best place to seek them out is in the centre of town on the side streets between Jalan Tanjungpura and Jalan Pattimura. The *Warung Kopi Aloha* is a good place for coffee and snacks.

The clean little *Somay Bandung*, in the theatre complex on Jalan Sisingamangaraja near Jalan Pattimura, serves delicious Chinese-style bubur ayam (sweet rice porridge with chicken) and the house speciality, somay, a tasty concoction of potatoes, tofu, hard-boiled egg and peanut sauce, for 1300 rp. It also serves good ice drinks.

For good warung food, the Kapuas Indah station has a good selection, but this area tends to get smelly when it rains. Try the night warung on Jalan Sudirman and Jalan Diponegoro for goat sate and steaming plates of rice noodles, crab, prawns, fish, vegetables – all fried up in a wok for 2000 rp.

Pontianak has a big Chinese population and excellent Chinese food. The speciality of *Mie Tiaw Antasari* on Jalan Antasari 72 is its fabulous beef mie tiaw (fried or rapid boiled noodles). It also offers tasty bihun (beef noodle dish, fried or boiled), bakso (meatball soup) and yellow noodles. There are several similar-style restaurants in nearby Jalan Diponegoro, including the *Mie Tiau Sam* at No 63 with its popular bakso, beef and bean noodle soup.

Getting There & Away

Air Garuda/Merpati (☎ 34142) is at Jalan Rahadi Usman 8A; DAS (☎ 32313) is at Jalan Veteran Baru Blok B/1; Bouraq (☎ 37261) is at Jalan Pahlawan 3A; and Deraya (☎ 32835) is at the airport.

It's worth noting that Pontianak is better connected with the rest of Indonesia than it is with destinations around Kalimantan. Getting a flight at short notice to Banjarmasin is not always easy.

Bus Pontianak's intercity bus terminal is Batu Layang, north-west of town. Take a ferry to Siantan (150 rp) and a white bemo to Batu Layang (350 rp). From there you can catch buses north along the coast to Singkawang (4000 rp; 3½ hours) and Sambas

(6000 rp), inland to Sanggau (7000 rp) or Sintang (10,000 to 13,000 rp), or over to Pemangkat (7000 rp), Tebas (6000 rp) and Kartiasa (7000 rp). Singkawang buses leave throughout the day. Others are less frequent, but the mornings are busiest.

For the longer hauls to Kuching (30,000 rp; 8½ hours), most of the mid-range hotels in Pontianak can arrange bookings – try to book at least a day ahead.

Boat There are five Pelni ships that regularly connect Pontianak with Jakarta: the fortnightly *Lawit, Sirimau, Binaiya* and *Bukitraya*, and the monthly *Tatamailau*. The Pelni office is on Jalan Pak Kasih at the Pelabuhan Laut Dwikora. Ticket sales are only in the mornings.

For other ships ask at the entrance to the port adjacent to the Pelni office. At least two non-Pelni cargo ships also take passengers on the Pontianak-Jakarta run daily for around 30,000 rp, but you might have to sleep on deck. Travellers have reported miserable conditions and long delays on some of these ships.

There are six daily jet boats to Ketapang (36,000 rp; six hours). This is more like a plane trip than a boat. The coastal boat leaves from just downstream of the Siantan car ferry.

Riverboats up Sungai Kapuas leave from behind the Kapuas Indah station near the Hotel Wijaya Kusuma. Some, like the houseboat bandungs, leave from the pisini harbour near the end of Jalan Sultan Muhammed.

Getting Around

The Airport A counter at the airport sells tickets for taxis into town (15,000 rp). Alternatively, walk down the road in front of the station building to the main road in Pontianak and from there you should be able to get a bemo for 500 rp. It is a half-hour drive from the airport to the Kapuas Indah station. Ticketing agencies in Pontianak can organise lifts to the airport for 5000 rp.

Local Transport There are two main bemo stations in the middle of the city – the Kapuas terminal near the waterfront and the other on Jalan Sisingamangaraja. Taxis can be found next to the Garuda office.

SINGKAWANG

This predominantly Chinese town's main attraction is nearby **Pasir Panjang**, a beach with clean white sand and calm water, 12 km south of Singkawang. Singkawang has plenty of hotels, and Pasir Panjang too has a couple of places to stay – prices are high.

From Pontianak, catch the City Passenger Ferry (150 rp) to Pontianak's Siantan bus terminal, and then take a white colt (350 rp) from there to the Batu Layang terminal, a few km past the equator monument. Opelets to Singkawang (5400 rp; 3½ hours) leave throughout the day. There is no longer a main depot in Singkawang, so let your driver know where you want to get off. When leaving town, you will find buses outside Rumah Makan Asun, Rumah Makan Aheng or along Jalan Niaga.

To get to Pasir Panjang from Singkawang, take a bemo from Toko Olimpik on the corner of Jalan Suman Bajang and Jalan Sintut (700 rp; 15 to 20 minutes) and get out at the Taman Pasir Panjang gate, or at the warung 200 metres further on. From there, you'll have a 500 metre walk to the beach.

Sulawesi

The funeral festivals of Tanatoraja in the south-western peninsula are Sulawesi's best known attraction. This beautiful highland region and its festive culture is all that many visitors get to see. But as the island's rapidly improving transport infrastructure opens access to once-isolated areas, more travellers are venturing north to see the unusual Bada Valley megaliths south of Palu, the stunning coral reefs of the Togian Islands and the marine parks around the northern capital of Manado, and the unique wildlife of Sulawesi's network of national parks.

Getting There & Away

Air Most international connections are via Jakarta and Denpasar, but Singapore's regional carrier, Silk Air, has direct flights from Singapore to Ujung Pandang (US$174) and Manado (US$260), and Malaysia Airlines now links Kuala Lumpur with Ujung Pandang (US$174). The Philippines city of Davao is serviced by Bouraq flights to and from Manado twice a week (US$150), and Garuda was planning a direct service between Manado and Japan. Manado and Ujung Pandang are approved gateways for visa-free tourists.

Garuda, Merpati, Sempati, Bouraq and Mandala all service domestic routes to Sulawesi, with most connections via Ujung Pandang.

Boat Ujung Pandang is a major hub for Indonesia's national ferry network and most Pelni ships stop there, giving travellers cheap and easy access to most other major centres in the archipelago. A number of other Sulawesi ports are serviced by Pelni. See the Indonesia Getting Around section for route details.

The trip from the Javanese port of Surabaya to Ujung Pandang takes less than 24 hours. Then it's a couple of days more around to Bitung (the port for Manado), with several stops in between. Road transport in Sulawesi is often faster, but the ferries tend to be more comfortable.

When looking for ships in any of the ports, check with the Pelni office first and then check around other shipping agents, and ask around the port. A really interesting trip would be by Makassar schooner – ask at Paotere harbour in Ujung Pandang about schooners carrying goods to Surabaya, Kalimantan or Nusa Tenggara. Fares depend on negotiation, as well as your capacity to entertain with stories and songs.

UJUNG PANDANG

Ujung Pandang is Sulawesi's largest and liveliest city. The Muslim Bugis are the dominant group in Ujung Pandang and the city is best known as the home of their magnificent

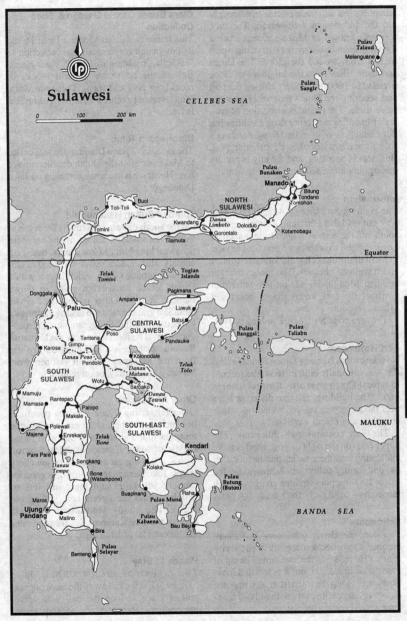

Sulawesi

0   100   200 km

CELEBES SEA

Pulau
Talaud
Melanguane

Pulau
Sangir

Pulau
Bunaken
Manado

Bitung
Tondano
Tomohon

NORTH
SULAWESI

Buol

Toli-Toli

Tomini

Kwandang

Danau
Limboto

Doloduo

Kotamobagu

Gorontalo

Tilamuta

Equator

Teluk
Tomini

Togian
Islands

Donggala

Palu

Ampana

Pagimana

Luwuk

Batui

Pulau
Banggai

Pulau
Taliabu

CENTRAL
SULAWESI

Poso

Tentena

Gimpu

Pandauke

Karosa

Danau Poso

Kolonodale

Pendolo

Danau
Matano

Teluk
Tolo

Wotu

Soroako

Danau
Towuti

SOUTH
SULAWESI

Mamuju

Rantepao

Palopo

MALUKU

Mamasa

Makale

Majene

Polewali

Enrekang

SOUTH-EAST
SULAWESI

Teluk
Bone

Kendari

Pare Pare

Sengkang

Kolaka

Danau
Tempe

Bone
(Watampone)

Pulau
Butung
(Buton)

Maros

Buapinang

Raha

Ujung
Pandang

Malino

Pulau Muna

BANDA   SEA

Bira

Pulau
Kabaena

Bau Bau

Benteng

Pulau
Selayar

INDONESIA

schooners that still trade extensively throughout the Indonesian archipelago. The city, formerly known as Makassar, was once a thriving cosmopolitan port drawing spice traders from around the globe. The Dutch and their allies from the kingdom of Bone invaded in 1660, effectively closing the port and securing the Dutch monopoly over the spice trade. The recent construction of container handling and other dock facilities has done much to rejuvenate Ujung Pandang's role as eastern Indonesia's premier port. Business is booming, and the city is rapidly undergoing unprecedented development.

Information

The main tourist office (☎ 443355) is a long way out on Jalan Pettarani, a street heading south off the airport road. Hostels such as Legends tend to offer more practical advice.

Most of the banks handle foreign currency and travellers' cheques. The moneychanger at Jalan Monginsidi 42, on the waterfront north of the fort, keeps longer hours and offers competitive rates.

The area code for Ujung Pandang is 0411.

Fort Rotterdam

Now known as Benteng Ujung Pandang, this fort was originally built in 1634, then rebuilt in typical Dutch style after their takeover in 1667. The buildings fell into disrepair but a restoration project has renovated the whole complex, apart from a wall or two.

The fort contains two museums. The larger one (on the right as you enter) is more interesting and the smaller one has a rather sad and scruffy collection. Admission to the fort is 1000 rp, plus separate charges to both museums – open daily from 8 am to 4 pm.

Schooners

You can see Bugis schooners at Paotere harbour, a long becak ride north from the city centre. There is not the awesome line-up of Pasar Ikan in Jakarta, but it is worth a look. Elsewhere along the waterfront, you may see *balolang*, large outriggers with sails, or *lepa-lepa*, smaller outrigger canoes.

Clara Bundt Orchid Garden & Shell Collection

This house is at Jalan Mochtar Lufti 15 and its compound contains a large collection of seashells, including dozens of giant clams. Behind the house are several blocks of orchids in pots and trays. These are world famous among orchid specialists. Admission is free.

Diponegoro Tomb

The Javanese Prince Diponegoro was exiled to Makassar after the Dutch double-crossed him. His grave is in a small cemetery on Jalan Diponegoro.

Tomb of Sultan Hasanuddin

On the south-eastern outskirts is the tomb of Sultan Hasanuddin, leader of the southern Sulawesi kingdom of Gowa in the mid-17th century. Hasanuddin resisted a bloody campaign to subdue Gowa which began with a Dutch attack on foreign ships in Gowa harbour in 1660. Other remnants of Gowa include a graveyard at the nearby **Katangka Mosque**, and the Sungguminasa Palace – once a royal residence but now the **Museum Ballalompoa**. It is a half-hour, 350 rp trip from the Makassar Mall. It is open from Monday to Saturday, or on request.

Other Attractions

Other interesting Ujung Pandang peculiarities include the brilliantly ornate **Chinese temples** found along Jalan Sulawesi in the middle of town. Check out **Jalan Sombu Opu** – it has a great collection of jewellery shops. Toko Kerajinam, at No 20, is good for touristy souvenirs and there are lots of people around the streets here selling old coins. The gaudy **Monument Mandala** obelisk south of Karebosi Square celebrates the 'liberation' of Irian Jaya.

Places to Stay

The *Legends Hostel* (☎ 328203), Jalan Jampea 5G, is far and away the most popular budget place and on the ball with travel information. Dorm beds cost 5500 rp, rooms

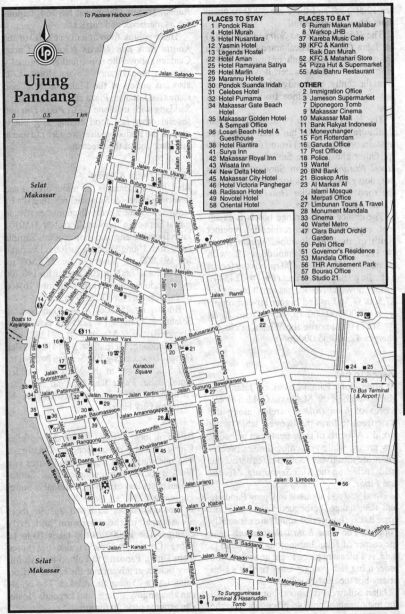

Ujung Pandang

0   0.5   1 km

Selat Makassar

To Paotere Harbour →

Jalan Sabutung

Jalan Satando

Jalan Tarakan

Jalan Hatta

Jalan Nusantara

Jalan Kalimantan

Jalan Caddi

Jalan Salemo

Jalan Seram Ujung

Jalan Butung

Jalan Irian

Jalan Serappo

Jalan Banda

Jalan Sangir

Jalan Mohammadi Yah

Jalan Akademis

Jalan Diponegoro

Jalan Lembeh

Jalan Martadinata

Jalan Nusantara

Jalan Sulawesi

Jalan Lampeta

Jalan Timor

Jalan Bali

Jalan Sumbah

Jalan Hasyim

Jalan Cokroaminoto

Jalan Ramli

Jalan Serui Sama

Jalan Mesjid Raya

Boats to Kayangan

Jalan Ujung Pandang

Jalan Ahmad Yani

Jalan Balaikota

Jalan Kajaolalido

Karebosi Square

Jalan Bulusaraung

Jalan Cerekang

Jalan Slamet Riyadi

Jalan Supratman

Jalan Lompobattang

Jalan Pattimura

Jalan Thamrin

Jalan Kartini

Jalan Gunung Bawakaraeng

Jalan Gn Latimojong

Jalan Baumassepe

Jalan Amannagappa

Jalan G Merapi

Jalan G Meratus

Jalan Lompobattang

Jalan Ranggong

Jalan Incenurdin

Jalan Sudirman

Jalan Veteran Selatan

Jalan Khairilanwar

Jalan Mochtar Lutfi

Jalan Sawerigading

Losari Beach

Jl Somba Opu

Jl Penghibur

Jl Daeng Tompo

Jalan Datumusengemi

Jalan Toampanua

Jalan Sibula

Jalan Lariang

Jalan S Limboto

To Bus Terminal & Airport

Jalan Lamadukkeleng

Jalan Kenari

Jalan Dr

Jalan G Klabat

Jalan G Nona

Jalan Sarif Alqadri

Jalan Ratulangi

Jalan S Saddang

Jalan Abubakar Lambogo

Jalan Monginsidi

Selat Makassar

Jalan Arifrate

To Sungguminasa Terminal & Hasanuddin Tomb

PLACES TO STAY
1   Pondok Rias
4   Hotel Murah
5   Hotel Nusantara
12 Yasmin Hotel
13 Legends Hostel
22 Hotel Aman
25 Hotel Ramayana Satrya
26 Hotel Marlin
29 Marannu Hotels
30 Pondok Suanda Indah
31 Celebes Hotel
32 Hotel Purnama
34 Makassar Gate Beach Hotel
35 Makassar Golden Hotel & Sempati Office
36 Losari Beach Hotel & Guesthouse
38 Hotel Riantira
41 Surya Inn
42 Makassar Royal Inn
43 Wisata Inn
44 New Delta Hotel
45 Makassar City Hotel
46 Hotel Victoria Panghegar
48 Radisson Hotel
49 Novotel Hotel
58 Oriental Hotel

PLACES TO EAT
6   Rumah Makan Malabar
8   Warkop JHB
37 Kareba Music Cafe
39 KFC & Kantin
    Baik Dan Murah
52 KFC & Matahari Store
54 Pizza Hut & Supermarket
55 Asia Bahru Restaurant

OTHER
2   Immigration Office
3   Jameson Supermarket
7   Diponegoro Tomb
9   Makassar Cinema
10 Makassar Mall
11 Bank Rakyat Indonesia
14 Moneychanger
15 Fort Rotterdam
16 Garuda Office
17 Post Office
18 Police
19 Wartel
20 BNI Bank
21 Bioskop Artis
23 Al Markas Al
    Islami Mosque
24 Merpati Office
27 Limbunan Tours & Travel
28 Monument Mandala
33 Cinema
40 Wartel Metro
47 Clara Bundt Orchid Garden
50 Pelni Office
51 Governor's Residence
53 Mandala Office
56 THR Amusement Park
57 Bourag Office
59 Studio 21

INDONESIA

are 12,500 rp, and there are 3000 rp crash mats when all else is full.

The *Hotel Ramayana Satrya* (☎ 442478) on Jalan Gunung Bawakaraeng has rooms from 15,000 rp with bath, or from 25,000 rp with air-con and hot water. It is a fair way from the centre, but handy for the Panaikang bus terminal, and bemos from the airport pass by.

The *Hotel Purnama* (☎ 323830) at Jalan Pattimura 3 has basic but clean rooms (the upstairs ones are better) from 16,500/22,000 rp. Other cheapies are far less impressive. *Hotel Nusantara*, Jalan Sarappo 103, has hot, noisy sweat boxes for 7000 rp. Across the road is the similar *Hotel Murah* with 'boxes' from 10,000 rp.

The choice of mid-range hotels is excellent, especially in the residential precinct south of the fort. *Pondok Suanda Indah* (☎ 312857), Jalan Hasanuddin 12, with rooms from 42,350/48,400 rp, has the feel of a classic guesthouse. *Wisata Inn* (☎ 324344), further down at No 36, has small rooms for 27,500/37,500 rp and bigger air-con rooms from 50,000/60,000 rp. *New Delta Hotel* (☎ 312711), opposite the Wisata at No 43, charges 42,500/55,000 rp.

Places to Eat

At night along Pantai Losari, on Jalan Penghibur south of the Makassar Golden Hotel, scores of *food trolleys* stretch along the waterfront to form the 'longest table in the world'. All sorts of tasty treats can be had at low prices, while you enjoy the sea breeze. There are also lively rooftop cafes across the road, including the *Kios Semarang*, *Minasa* and *Fajar*.

Good seafood abounds in Ujung Pandang and ikan bakar (barbecued fish) and cumi cumi bakar (barbecued squid) are especially popular. The *Asia Bahru Restaurant*, near the corner of Jalan Latimojong and Jalan G Sala, is a pleasant place to eat and when you order a big fish you get a *big* fish! It's a bit pricey but the quality is high.

Jalan Sulawesi is a good hunting ground for restaurants – notable places include the *Rumah Makan Malabar* at No 264, famous for its martabak and curries.

There is junk food aplenty at *KFC* or the *Kantin Baik dan Murah* (Good & Cheap Canteen) above the supermarket diagonally opposite the Marannu Tower Hotel. *KFC* also has outlets at the Makassar Mall and shares the Latanete Plaza precinct on Jalan S Saddang with its clone *CFC*, *Pizza Hut* and several other fast food chains. Big hotels such as the Radisson offer western cuisine at the other end of the spectrum.

Getting There & Away

Air Ujung Pandang is the major arrival and departure point for Sulawesi whether it's by air or sea. Some agents discount heavily, so start at Limbunan Tours and Travel (☎ 315010), Jalan Bawakaraeng, and shop around. Sample fares from Ujung Pandang include: Denpasar for 191,800 rp, Surabaya for 254,500 rp, Ambon for 277,600 rp, Balikpapan for 190,700 rp, Manado for 296,300 rp, Palu for 176,400 rp and Kendari for 117,000 rp.

Bouraq (☎ 452506) is at Jalan Veteran Selatan 1; Garuda (☎ 322543) is at Jalan Slamet Riyadi 6; Mandala (☎ 324288) is at Jalan Saddang; Merpati (☎ 24114) is at Jalan Gunung Bawakaraeng 109; Sempati (☎ 324116) and Silk Air are in the Makassar Golden Hotel, Jalan Pasar Ikan 50; and Malaysia Airlines (☎ 331888) has an office at the Marannu City Hotel.

Bus For most people, the next stop after Ujung Pandang is Rantepao in Tanatoraja. The bus station for north-bound buses is a few km out on the main airport road. South-bound buses leave from the terminal at Sungguminasa.

Tanatoraja buses leave at 8 am, plus there are several in the afternoon and early evening. The 10,000 rp trip takes 10 to 12 hours. Liman (☎ 315851) also has buses from Ujung Pandang to Palopo and Malili. Buy tickets in advance at the Liman office, Jalan Laiya 25 near the market. The hotels can also arrange tickets, and Legends Hostel can arrange pick-up for guests.

INDONESIA

Boat Pelni (☎ 331393), Jalan Sudirman 38, has nine modern liners making regular stops here. Ekonomi fares from Ujung Pandang include: Lembar (on Lombok) for 43,500 rp, Surabaya for 65,000 rp, Ambon for 88,500 rp, Balikpapan for 46,000 rp, Bitung for 131,000 rp, Pantoloan for 70,000 rp and Kendari for 52,000 rp.

Getting Around

The Airport Pete-petes (bemos) from Makassar Mall to Ujung Pandang's Hasanuddin airport (22 km out of town) run via Terminal Daya for 1000 rp. From the airport, walk 500 metres to the main road for a pete-pete to the city. Taxi coupons from the airport to the city centre cost 14,300 rp, or pay 10,000 to 12,000 rp using the meter. Groups can charter minibuses parked opposite the arrivals area for around 10,000 rp, a good option for those rushing to meet 8 am buses to Tanatoraja.

Local Transport Ujung Pandang is too hot to do much walking – you'll need becaks and pete-petes. The main pete-pete station is at Makassar Mall and the standard fare is 300 rp, or 400 rp to the suburbs. Big old Damri buses take you any distance for 250 rp. Becak drivers kerb-crawl for custom and are hard bargainers – the shortest fare costs 500 rp. Some enterprising drivers offer menus of tours around town at set prices. Taxis run on argo-meters – 1500 rp will get you three to four km.

AROUND UJUNG PANDANG

The **Bantimurung reserve**, 41 km from Ujung Pandang, is noted for its waterfall and eroded and overgrown rocky pinnacles and cliffs. There are also caves so bring a torch. It makes a pleasant day's retreat from Ujung Pandang and is noted for the numerous beautiful butterflies. Avoid Sundays, which are very crowded.

To get to Bantimurung, take a Patas bus from in front of Ujung Pandang's BRI bank. The trip takes a bit over an hour. If you can't find a direct bus then take one to Maros

(1000 rp; one hour) and another from there (500 rp; 30 minutes).

A few km before Bantimurung is the turn-off for the **Leang Leang Caves**, noted for their prehistoric paintings. To get there take a pete-pete (250 rp) from Maros to the Taman Purbakala Leang-Leang turn-off on the Bone road, then walk the last couple of km.

SOUTH COAST

South Sulawesi's south coast is remarkably barren compared with the peninsula's rich agricultural hinterland. The climate is drier, and boat-building and fishing are the main activities. **Bulukumba** and **Tanah Beru Tanah Beru** are famous for their traditional boat building. Bulukumba is also the port for the Pulau Selayar ferry when the May-July currents close Bira's jetty.

Bira

Bira's white-sand beaches draw travellers off the tourist trail, but Bira has neither the beauty nor the comfort of Bali's beach resorts. There is swimming, snorkelling, fishing and dolphin-watching (if you can find them), but most people peg out a shady corner of the long west beach and drift off with a book. Facilities are basic, the food is functional and the beach often disappears under feral tides. Nearby Marumasa is a centre for traditional boat building.

Places to Stay

Riswan Guesthouse is a Bugis house on a rise looking out to sea. Singles with shared bath cost 14,000 rp, including meals. *Riswan Bungalows* all face the main road, and cost 13,500/17,000 rp including breakfast. If you need to hire a snorkel, mask and fins (7500 rp), negotiate these with the room price.

Bira View Inn has Bugis-style cottages on a cliff overlooking the bay for 35,000/45,000 rp. *Anda Bungalows'* gritty thatched-roof cottages cost 8000/10,000 rp, *Bira Beach Hotel* (☎ (0413) 81515) has doubles for 45,000 rp and *Hotel Sapolohe* next door has a beautiful Bugis-style house with rooms from 40,000 rp.

INDONESIA

Getting There & Away

From Ujung Pandang's Sungguminasa terminal there are kijangs (4WD taxis) that go the full 195 km direct to Bira for 7000 rp, but most terminate at Bulukumba (5000 rp). Crowded bemos complete the trip to Tanah Beru (25 km; 1200 rp), then to Bira (18 km; 700 rp). Bemos between Bira and Bira Beach cost 200 rp.

Ferries from Bira to Pamatata harbour on Pulau Selayar (4000 rp) depart from the East Beach jetty at 2 pm daily. When the seasonal currents bring waves to Bira, usually between May and July, the ferry service switches to Bulukumba.

BONE (WATAMPONE)

Bone is a modern, pretty town set in a rich agricultural area. Its former palace is now the **Museum Lapawawoi** (open daily from 8 am to 2 pm), which houses one of Indonesia's most interesting regional collections. The harbour of Bajoe is a busy centre of commerce, five km (500 rp) from Bone, and the stepping-off point for daily ferries to South-East Sulawesi.

Places to Stay

Most accommodation is central, comfortable and clean. *Wisma Bola Ridie* on Jalan Merdeka has small rooms from 10,000 rp, as does *Wisma Merdeka* next door at No 4. *Losmen National*, Jalan Mesjid Raya 86, near the mosque, costs 7500/15,000 rp, and *Wisma Tirta Kencana* (☎ 21838), close to the bus terminal, has modern rooms with king-size beds from 15,000 rp.

Getting There & Away

Bus & Bemo Bone can be reached by bus from Ujung Pandang, a pretty ride through mountainous country (5000 rp; six hours). There are bemos from Bulukumba for 4000 rp, and buses through to Rantepao (usually via Soppeng) cost 9000 rp.

Boat Three ferries ply the route between Bone and Kolaka in South-East Sulawesi. They leave Bajoe late afternoon and early evening for the eight hour journey across the

gulf. Fares are 10,300/8500/6800 rp in 1st/2nd/3rd class, or you can book a combined bus/boat ticket direct to Kendari.

PARE PARE

Pare Pare is a bustling seaport – a mini Ujung Pandang – but without the obnoxious traffic. For the most part, however, it's just a place to hang around in as you await a boat to Kalimantan or northern Sulawesi.

The area code for Pare Pare is 0421.

Places to Stay & Eat

The *Hotel Gandaria* (☎ 21093) at Jalan Baumassepe 171 is clean, comfortable and friendly with singles from 15,000 rp. *Hotel Gemini* (☎ 21754) at Jalan Baumassepe 451 has small rooms from 6500 rp, and rooms with mandi for 8500 rp. *Tanty Hotel* (☎ 21378), Jalan Sultan Hasanuddin 5, has basic rooms from 10,000 rp.

Restaurant Asia has Chinese food, including excellent but pricey seafood, from 8000 to 14,000 rp. *Warung Sedap*, next door to the Asia, serves barbecued fish.

Getting There & Away

Bus The bus fare from Ujung Pandang is 6000 rp. From Pare Pare, most travellers head north-east to Rantepao (four to five hours), but there are also excellent roads inland to Sengkang (2500 rp; two hours) or north to Mamasa or around the coast to Majene and Mamuju. Avoid the bus station several km south of the city – it is much easier to just hail the buses as they fly through town.

Boat The main reason to come to Pare Pare is to catch a ship to Kalimantan, or along the coast to Pantoloan (the port of Palu). Pelni (☎ 21017), at Jalan Andicammi 130, is the best place to start. The harbourmaster's office is near the waterfront on Jalan Andicammi, and several shipping companies have their offices here.

TANATORAJA

Tanatoraja is about 320 km north of Ujung Pandang. It's a high, mountainous area with beautiful scenery and a fascinating culture. The Toraja have embraced Christianity, but retain strong pre-Christian traditions, including complex death rituals.

The first thing that strikes you in Tanatoraja is the traditional houses, shaped like buffalo horns (an animal of great mythical and economic importance to the Toraja) with the roof rearing up at front and rear. The houses are remarkably similar to the Batak houses of Lake Toba in Sumatra and are always aligned north-south with small rice barns facing them.

A number of villages in the region are still composed entirely of these traditional houses but most have corrugated-iron roofs. The beams and supports of the Torajan houses are cut so that they all slot together neatly and the whole house is painted and carved with chicken and buffalo motifs – buffalo skulls often decorate the front, symbolising the wealth and prestige of the owners.

The burial customs of the Toraja are unique. They generally have two funerals – one immediately after the death and then an elaborate second funeral after sufficient time has elapsed to make the complex preparations and raise the necessary cash. Because they believe you can take it with you, the dead generally go well equipped to their graves. Since this led to grave plundering, the Toraja started to secrete their dead in caves (of which there are plenty around) or in hacked-out niches in rocky cliff faces. The coffins go deep inside, and sitting in balconies on rock-faces you can see the *tau tau*, or life-size carved wooden effigies of the dead.

The funeral ceremonies are the main tourist attraction. The more important the deceased, the more buffalo that must be sacrificed: one for a commoner, and then four, eight, 12 or 24 as you move up the social scale. Pigs are also sacrificed. Animals ain't cheap either. A medium-sized buffalo costs several million rp – size, fatness, colour and good horns all push the price up. At a funeral, dress respectfully and don't plonk yourself in the areas designated for families and guests.

The middle of the year, at the end of the rice harvest from around May onwards, is ceremony time in Tanatoraja; included are funerals, house and harvest ceremonies. All may involve feasting and dancing, often buffalo fights, and Torajan *sisemba* fighting, where the combatants kick each other. Various people around Rantepao will take you to ceremonies for a negotiable price. It's a good way of finding out what's going on – if they speak enough English or if you speak enough Indonesian you will be able to get an explanation of what's happening.

Makale (the capital) and Rantepao (the largest town) are the two main centres of Tanatoraja. Bemos link the surrounding villages but many roads are terrible and walking is a better way of getting around. All the interesting places are scattered around the lush green country surrounding Rantepao – you've got to get out and explore.

Rantepao

Rantepao has few sights of its own, but provides a comfortable base for trips to the countryside. Every six days there is a livestock market at the main market north-east of town. This is the prime social event for everyone in the valley, and is not to be missed.

Information The tourist office is in the central square. The staff are helpful and have the dates of forthcoming ceremonies. There are also several useful private agencies, such as JET, along the main street.

The Bank Rakyat Indonesia is opposite the Bank Danamon on the main street but the rates aren't as good as in Ujung Pandang. The best rates are from the authorised moneychanger in the Hotel Indra.

The post office, across from the Bank Rakyat Indonesia, has a poste restante service. The telephone office next door is open 24 hours.

Places to Stay The height of the tourist season is July and August, when tour groups arrive in plague proportions and hotel prices skyrocket. Rantepao has dozens of good-value,

INDONESIA

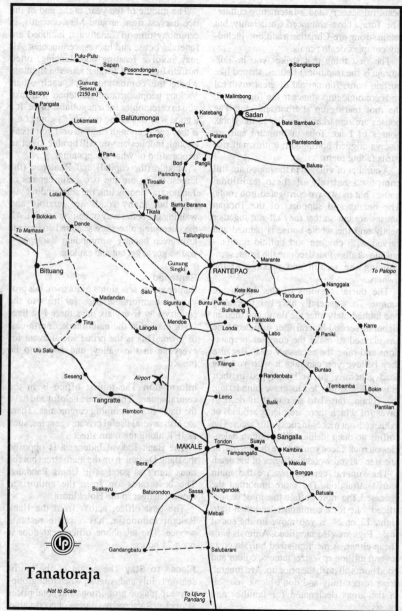

Tanatoraja

Not to Scale

clean and usually comfortable hotels – plus many homes open their doors to visitors during the high season.

Ceria Homestay, Jalan Monginsidi, is a clean, basic losmen with bed and breakfast from 5000 rp. Just across the bridge, *Wisma Rosa* (☎ 21075), Jalan Sadan 28, charges 10,000/12,000 rp including breakfast, and herds of backpackers mob the *Wisma Malita* (☎ 21011), Jalan Suloara 110, which has basic rooms from 10,000/12,000 rp. The nearby *Mace Homestay* (☎ 21852), Jalan Tenko Saturu 4, is set in a pretty garden with four rooms for 12,500 rp in the low season.

Wisma Wisata (☎ 21746), Jalan Monginsidi 40, and *Wisma Surya* (☎ 21312) are neighbours which back onto the river. Both charge 10,000/15,000 rp. *Wisma Maria* (☎ 21165), Jalan Ratulangi, is central and clean with rooms from 10,000/15,000 rp, but the staff tend to be aloof. Much more hospitable is the *Wisma Monika* (☎ 21216) across the road, with rooms from 15,000 to 20,000 rp with breakfast.

Further south at No 62 is *Wisma Martini* (☎ 21240), tattered but friendly with rooms from 7500/10,000 rp. *Wisma Nirmala* (☎ 21319), Jalan Andi Mapanyuki, is relatively quiet and has rooms for 15,000/17,500 rp.

Wisma Rantepao (☎ 21397) is central, with reasonable rooms ranging from 10,000 to 25,000 rp. The *Rapa Homestay* (☎ 21517) on Jalan Pembangunan has two rooms for 10,000 to 15,000 rp. *Rainbow Homestay*, almost opposite at No 11A, has modern rooms for 15,000/20,000 rp. *Homestay Padatindo*, a few doors down, has 10,000 rp rooms.

Losmen Flora (☎ 21586), right next to a mosque, is basic but cheap with 5000 rp singles. A few km north of town, restaurateur Pak Bitty runs *Homestay Chez Dodeng* at the village of Tallunglipu, with rooms from around 10,000 rp.

For a little mid-range class, try *Wisma Te Bass* (☎ 21415), an old but pleasant place run by a couple – the husband speaks English and the wife speaks Dutch. Rooms are 15,000/20,000 rp, or 25,000 rp in the high season.

Wisma Irama (☎ 21371) at Jalan Abdul Gani 16 has a large garden – its rooms start at 20,000/25,000 rp. *Wisma Monton* (☎ 21675; fax 21665) at Jalan Abdul Gani 14A, in an alley behind the Irama, starts at 20,000 rp. The capable manager speaks English.

Less conveniently located but recommended are the *Pison Hotel* (☎ 21344), Jalan Pong Tiku 8, with rooms from 15,000/27,500 rp, and the marginally cheaper *Pia's Poppies* (☎ 21121) across the lane at No 27A.

Places to Eat Many of the eateries around Rantepao serve Torajan food. A local speciality is pa'piong, a mix of meat (usually pork or chicken) and leaf vegetables smoked over a low flame for hours. Order a couple of hours in advance and enjoy it with black rice.

Smaller, unmarked warung along Jalan Andi Mapanyuki and Jalan Suloara offer first-class barbecued fish for considerably less than the restaurants. It's best to go with a local rather than barging in uninvited. So too the many *balok* (palm wine) bars around town, which welcome foreigners, but not in big numbers.

Kiosk Mambo, Jalan Ratulangi, serves Indonesian and Torajan food but is also great for western breakfasts. Nearby *Hotel Indra I* has an upmarket Indonesian and Torajan restaurant – the chicken pa'piong is especially recommended. The classy restaurants at the *Pia's Poppies* and *Pison* hotels serve Torajan food. The former also dishes up continental breakfasts, yoghurt, juices and other goodies, but expect very slow service.

Rumah Makan Rima I, Jalan Mapanyuki, has generous serves of Indonesian fare and the best banana pancakes. Pak Bitty's *Chez Dodeng*, Jalan Emi Saelan, is a Rantepao landmark serving basic warung fare.

River Cafe is a professional outfit a few km north of town with huge serves of Indonesian and other fare, including rich, tasty Mexican dishes. The breezy dining deck overlooks small rapids and a river flat where men spend hours washing and grooming their buffalo. There are crafts and antiques in the gallery next door.

Getting There & Away The airport is near Makale, 25 km south of Rantepao. Merpati

INDONESIA

(☎ 21485), Jalan Pao Pura, flies daily from Ujung Pandang and twice on Sunday. The fare is 106,000 rp. Be prepared for delays and always reconfirm flights – staff often double-book.

Bus & Bemo In Rantepao the bus company offices are clustered in the centre of town. The main companies on the Rantepao-Ujung Pandang route are Litha, Liman and Alam Indah. Departures are typically at 7, 10 and 11 am, and 1, 6 and 9 pm. The trip to Ujung Pandang (330 km) costs 10,000 rp (13,000 rp for the Alam Indah executive bus with air-con and legroom). Pare Pare to Rantepao takes four to five hours and costs 6000 rp.

Litha, Alam Indah, Damri and other buses heading north to Tentena, Poso and Palu tend to leave Rantepao at 10 am. Fares to Pendolo (10 hours), Tentena (12 hours) and Poso (13 hours) are all 20,000 rp. To Palu (20 hours), it's 25,000 rp.

Bemos run down to the coastal city of Palopo (4500 rp; two hours). There are daily buses from Rantepao to Soroako on Lake Matano, leaving at about 10 am from the Rantepao bus terminal (8000 rp; 10 hours).

Getting Around Central Rantepao is small and easy to walk around. Becaks start at 500 rp.

Kijangs (4WD taxis) opposite the post office run almost continuously from Rantepao south to Makale (500 rp) and you can get off at the signs for Londa (400 rp), Tilanga (400 rp) or Lemo (400 rp) and walk. From Jalan Diponegoro there are frequent bemos east towards Palopo for the sights in that direction, and bemos north to Lempo (near Batutumonga) start from Jalan Monginsidi. Others leave from Jalan Tappang and the bridge – to Sadan costs 800 rp. Almost all services stop at 6 pm.

Motorbikes can be rented from the main street tour agencies for 10,000 to 20,000 rp per day. It can be cheaper for a group to charter a bemo or a 4WD. If trekking, take a water bottle, something to eat, a torch in case you end up walking at night, and an umbrella or raincoat.

AROUND RANTEPAO

The following places – the distance in km from Rantepao is shown – are all within fairly easy reach on day trips. If you make longer trips and stay overnight in private homes along the way, please pay your way with money or gifts. Guides aren't necessary – the Torajans are friendly and used to tourists, and it's great to escape on your own into the beautiful countryside around Rantepao.

South of Rantepao

Karasbik (one km) Karasbik is on the outskirts of Rantepao, just off the road leading to Makale. The traditional-style houses here are arranged in a square. Apparently the complex was erected some years ago for a single funeral.

Singki (one km) You can climb this small hill just outside Rantepao for a panoramic view over the surrounding area.

Kete Kesu (six km) Just off the main road, south of Rantepao, this traditional village is reputed for its woodcarving. On the cliff face behind the village are some cave graves and some very old hanging graves – the rotting coffins are suspended from an overhang.

Sullukang (seven km) Off to the side of the main road in this village there's a derelict shack on a rocky outcrop which contains several derelict tau tau, almost buried under the foliage. There's also *rante* here – large stone slabs planted in the ground – one of them about four metres high.

Londa (six km) Two km off the Rantepao to Makale road, this is a very extensive burial cave, with a number of coffins containing bones and skulls. Kids hang around outside renting their oil lamps for 3000 rp (you could try bargaining but they're not very amenable to it) to guide you around. Unless you've got a strong torch, you really do need a guide with a lamp.

Tilanga (nine km) There are several cold and hot springs in the Toraja area, and this natural cold water pool is very pretty. It's an attractive walk along the muddy trails and through the rice paddies from Tilanga to Lemo – keep asking for directions along the way.

Lemo (11 km) This is probably the most interesting burial area in Tanatoraja. The sheer rock-face has a whole series of balconies carved out for tau tau. The biggest balcony has a dozen figures – like spectators at a sports event. One tall tau tau stands on a slightly depressed section of floor so he can fit in. There would be even more if they weren't in such demand by unscrupulous antique dealers.

It's a good idea to go early in the morning so you get the sun on the rows of figures – by 9 am their heads are in the shadows. A bemo from Rantepao will drop you off at the road leading up to Lemo, from where it's a 15 minute walk.

Siguntu (seven km) Siguntu, a traditional village situated on a slight rise off to the west of the main road, is a pleasant walk from Rantepao. The walk from Rantepao via Singki and Siguntu to the main road at Alang Alang near the Londa burial site is pleasant.

East of Rantepao
Marante (six km) This very fine traditional village is only a few metres off the road east to Palopo.

Nanggala (16 km) In the same direction (and rather further off the Palopo road) is this traditional village with a particularly grandiose traditional house with a whole fleet – 14 in all – of rice barns. Bemos from Rantepao take you straight there for 500 rp, or they might just drop you off on the main road, and then it's a 1.5 km walk.

North & North-West of Rantepao
Palawa (nine km) This traditional village a km or two north of Pangli has tongkonan houses and rice barns.

Sadan (13 km) Sadan is a weaving centre further to the north. Bemos go there from Rantepao along a shocking road. The women here have established a tourist market where they sell their weaving.

Batutumonga (23 km) From Batutumonga you can see a large part of Tanatoraja. The views are even more stunning from the summit of **Gunung Sesean**, a 2150 metre peak towering above the village. Most bemos stop at Lempo, which is an easy walk from Batutumonga. Guesthouses include *Mama Siska's* at 15,000 rp per head for dinner, bed and breakfast; *Londoruden Homestay* and its amazing views for 20,000 rp; and *Mama Rina's* for 14,000 rp.

The return hike to Rantepao is an easy hike down the slopes to **Pana**, with its ancient hanging graves among bamboo, and a few baby graves in nearby trees. Pass by tiny villages with towering tongkonan, see women pounding rice, men scrubbing their beloved buffalo and children splashing happily in pools. The path ends at **Tikala**, from where there are regular bemos to Rantepao.

Lokomata (26 km) There are more cave graves and more beautiful scenery at Lokomata, just a few km past Batutumonga.

Other Villages
At **Pangli** (seven km) are house graves; **Bori** (eight km) is a funeral ceremony site; and **Pangala** (35 km) is a traditional village. One of the most popular **treks** is from Bittuang (58 km) to Mamasa in the west.

MAKALE
Makale provides refuge from tourist-heavy Rantepao. On Sundays, the town echoes with the singing from local churches, which seem to be on every hilltop. Makale has the same bus connections to other parts of Sulawesi as Rantepao.

Places to Stay & Eat
There are simple but clean places near the town centre. *Wisma Bungin* (☎ 22255), Jalan Pongtiku 35, has airy rooms for 10,000 rp and Bungin's neighbour, *Wisma Yani Randanan*

INDONESIA

(☎ 22409), Jalan Nusantara 3, is good value at 15,000 rp.

Losmen Indra (☎ 22022), Jalan Merdeka 11, is clean and friendly. Its rooms with shared bath are 10,000 rp. *Losmen Merry* (☎ 22013), above a shop, charges 5000 rp a head.

A disadvantage of Makale is the lack of restaurants. There are several cheap *noodle shops* on Jalan Merdeka near the mosque but little else.

PENDOLO

A road bears eastwards from Rantepao to Soroako on the shores of Lake Matano in Central Sulawesi. Midway along this road is the village of Wotu, where the Trans-Sulawesi Highway veers north to the small village of Pendolo on the southern bank of beautiful **Lake Poso**.

The lake and its lovely beaches are the main attractions. You can swim, take boat rides or go for walks. There are daily ferries across the lake to Tentena on the northern side at 8 am for 2000 rp.

Places to Stay & Eat

The *Pondok Wisata Masamba* and the *Pondok Wisata Victory* both overlook the beach adjacent to the jetty and have small rooms from 7500 rp. Their food is good and the prices reasonable. *Homestay Petezza*, Jalan Pelabuhan 216, a couple of doors up from the Victory, is also good value at 7500 rp per head.

The *Mulia Hotel*, about a km out, has comfortable rooms for 25,000 to 35,000 rp, and plenty of fairy tales about the other losmen. Don't believe them. The helpful folk at *Pendolo Cottages*, near the Mulia, have rooms for 15,000/17,500 rp including breakfast.

TENTENA

This lakeside village lacks Pendolo's fine beaches but has plenty of other attractions including the nearby **Salopa Waterfalls**, set amid unspoilt forest west of Tentena. Take a bemo to Tonusu (750 rp), then walk the last three km. There is a sunken gully of steaming

white water on the Poso River at **Sulewana**, 12 km north of Tentena. Take a bemo to Watunoncu, then walk three km west.

Tentena is host to the undisputed highlight of Central Sulawesi's social calendar, the annual **Lake Poso Festival** in late August, a colourful celebration of culture with dancing, song, traditional sports and other activities.

Places to Stay

The *Losmen Victory* (☎ 21392) on Jalan Diponegoro 18 has spotless rooms for 15,000 to 25,000 rp. The *Pamona Indah* (☎ 21245), adjacent to the lakeside jetty, has economy rooms from 12,000 rp, and across the bridge the *Pondok Wisma Ue'Data* (☎ 21222) is a delightful place with a cafe – rooms from 20,000 rp.

The *Hotel Wasantara* (☎ 21345) by the lake is large and cheery. Room rates range from 16,000 rp. *Natural Cottages* (☎ /fax 21356), Jalan Yani 32, is also by the lake with rooms from 10,000/16,500 rp.

Getting There & Away

Buses make the run to Poso for 2500 rp in about two hours. Set out early. Buses to Kolonodale (152 km; 8000 rp) originate in Poso, but seats can be reserved through Ebony Visitor Information Centre for a 3000 rp booking fee.

LORE LINDU NATIONAL PARK

Tentena is the starting point for treks west to Lore Lindu National Park and through to Palu. The main attraction is ancient megalithic relics, mostly in the Bada, Besoa and Napu valleys. It's a wonderful area for trekking – the park is rich in exotic plant and animal life.

It's best to travel as light as possible. From Tonusu, walk two days west to **Bomba**, and get a local guide to help you find the Bomba, Bada and impressive Sepe megaliths (10,000 to 15,000 rp per day). There are more megaliths around **Gintu**, and homestay accommodation at both villages. The walk on to Palu will take you via Tuare, Moa and **Gimpu**, which all have homestay accommodation.

From Gimpu to Palu there are five buses a day, starting at 7.30 am and taking three to six hours (4000 rp).

Guides from Tentena and Palu cost around 40,000 rp a day, plus expenses. They provide shortcuts, tips and alternatives – well worth considering.

POSO

Although it's Central Sulawesi's second largest city, Poso's main attractions are its banks which change foreign currency. There are beaches out of town: **Pantai Madale**, a snorkelling spot five km to the east (350 rp by bemo), the white-sand **Pantai Matako** 25 km east (1000 rp) and **Pantai Toini** seven km west (500 rp). Further west (40 km), **Maranda** has a small waterfall, a hot water spring and a swimming spot (1500 rp). The ebony carving is first-class – check it out at **Lembomawo**, across a footbridge four km south of Poso.

Information

One of Sulawesi's few informative tourist information services (☎ 21211) is at Jalan Sudirman, behind the telephone exchange.

Poso is the last chance for Togian or Tentena-bound travellers to change travellers' cheques. The BNI bank on Jalan Yos Sudarso is open Monday to Friday from 8 am to 4 pm.

Places to Stay & Eat

The guesthouse being built over the water at the *Warung Lalango Jaya*, near the dock, has an unbeatable location. Hopefully the prices will match its modest standard. Poso's other hotels tend to be cheap and functional, such as *Hotel Kalimantan* (☎ 21420), Jalan Haji Agus Salim 14, at 8500/14,500 rp; *Hotel Alamanda* (☎ 21333), Jalan Bali 1, at 5000 rp per head; and *Losmen Alugoro* (☎ 21336), Jalan Sumatera 20, from 5000/7000 rp. *Penginapan Sulawesi* (☎ 21294), on the corner of Jalan Haji Agus Salim and Jalan Imam Bonjol, has singles for 4000 rp – tiny, but clean.

Warung Lalango Jaya near the dock on Jalan Yos Sudarso is reasonably priced and

has unbeatable views of the harbour. *Restaurant Depot Anugrah* (☎ 21586) has good cheap Chinese-Indonesian food near the bus offices along Jalan Sumatera.

Getting There & Away

Bus & Bemo There are regular buses from Poso to Tentena (2500 rp). For buses to Palu (8500 rp; six hours) try Jawa Indah (☎ 21560) or the other bus offices along Jalan Sumatera. There are daily buses to Kolonodale (10,000 rp) and Ampana (5500 rp).

Boat Ferry connections to Gorontalo via the Togians vary according to the season and the number of boats on the route. Check the tourist information office for details.

PALU

Set in a rain shadow for most of the year, Palu is one of the driest places in Indonesia with less than 600 mm of rain a year. Outside of the narrow Palu Valley the pattern changes dramatically. Despite perfect swimming weather, the beaches are lousy. Head to Donggala instead (see below).

Information

The regional tourist office, on Jalan Raja Moili, has maps of the city and hiking suggestions. Office hours are 7.30 am until 2 pm.

At *Ebony Tours & Travel* (☎ 26260), Jalan Setia Budi 21, a woman from more remote parts of Central Sulawesi, Jeng, speaks good English and can advise on trekking through Lore Lindu and beyond.

The area code for Palu is 0451.

Places to Stay & Eat

Central and cheerful is *Purnama Raya Hotel* (☎ 23646), Jalan Wahidin 4, with rooms for 9000/15,000 rp. There is also *Hotel Karsam* (☎ 21776), Jalan Suharso 15, for 8000/15,000 rp; the noisy *Hotel Pasifik*, Jalan Gajah Mada 130, from 6000 rp; and *Taurus Hotel* (☎ 21567) at Jalan Hasanuddin 36 at 8800/15,000 rp.

Not so central, but good value, is the *Andalas Hotel* (☎ 22332) at Jalan Adin Saleh 50 with rooms for 10,000 rp.

Jalan Hasanuddin II is a busy alley with many places to eat, including *Milano Ice Cream* (☎ 23857) and the *Restaurant New Oriental* (☎ 23275) across the lane. Just around the corner on Jalan Wahidin, *Golden Bakery* has row upon row of confected pastries and cakes. More substantial fare is available from the Ramayana, further along Jalan Wahidin, which serves all sorts of dishes from the huge hot woks out front.

Getting There & Away

Air Merpati (☎ 21271) at Jalan Monginsidi 71 has the broadest network and oldest planes, with direct flights to Toli-Toli (137,900 rp), Luwuk (152,200 rp), Gorontalo (140,000 rp) and Ujung Pandang (176,400 rp). Merpati's busy agent (☎ 21295) at Jalan Hasanuddin 33 keeps extended hours.

Bouraq (☎ 21195), Jalan Juanda 87, offers flights west to Balikpapan and Banjarmasin, or east to Gorontalo, Manado and the Philippines. Sempati (☎ 21612), at the Central Hotel, Jalan Kartini 6, has flights to Ujung Pandang and beyond. Garuda (☎ 21095) has an office at the airport.

Bus Buses to Poso, Palopo, Rantepao, Gorontalo and Manado all leave from the Inpres station. Palu to Gorontalo takes a day and costs 22,500 rp. At Masomba station you can get buses to inland cities. Jawa Indah buses to Poso (8500 rp; six hours) depart from the company's Jalan Hasanuddin office (opposite the Merpati agent).

Boat There are three ports near Palu. Pelni and other large vessels dock at Pantoloan, north-east of Palu. Smaller ships dock at Donggala north-west of Palu, or at Wani, two km past Pantoloan.

Pelni (☎ 21696) has an office at Jalan Kartini 96, and another at Pantoloan opposite the road to the wharf. The offices of the other shipping companies are at the various ports. Three modern Pelni boats now call at Pantoloan, with frequent connection to East Kalimantan and other parts of Sulawesi.

Getting Around

Palu's Mutiara airport is seven km from town, not far past the post office – take a bemo (2000 rp; 10 minutes) or taxi (5000 rp).

Transport around town is by bemo – 350 rp gets you anywhere. Routes are flexible so flag down one that looks like it is going your way and state a landmark near your destination. Terminal Buru has 4WD kijangs to Donggala for 1500 rp, or 4000 to 6000 rp to charter all the way to the beach at Tanjung Karang.

DONGGALA

Donggala was once an important town until its harbour silted up and the ships switched to the harbours on the other side of the bay. Its main attractions now are sun, sand and coral reefs at **Tanjung Karang** north of town. The reef off the Prince John Dive Resort is a delight for snorkellers and beginner divers. **Towale**, 12 km south-west of Donggala, is another excellent swimming and snorkelling spot.

Places to Stay

Prince John Dive Resort offers simple, clean accommodation from 25,000 to 45,000 rp a head, including meals. *Natural Cottages* (☎ 21235) is an excellent spot on the tip of the peninsula, just past the dive resort. Its cottages cost 15,000 rp, including meals. The downside is that Prince John refuses to rent any of its diving gear to Natural's guests.

Getting There & Away

From Palu you can catch a 'taksi Donggala' for 1500 rp; the ride takes 40 minutes. It's another 20 minutes on foot to the beach. Alternatively, you could charter to Tanjung Karang beach for 4000 to 6000 rp.

AMPANA

Ampana is the stepping-off point for ferries and chartered boats to the Togian Islands. If you need to stay over, try *Losmen Irama*, Jalan Kartini 11, about 200 metres west of the market, from 6000 rp per person. *Penginapan Rejeki* (☎ 21274) at Jalan Talatako 45 has pleasant singles for 5000 rp, and

Penginapan Mekar, Jalan Kartini 5, is the cheapest, at 4500 rp for old singles.

Getting There & Away

Bus Ampana is on the main road from Poso (5500 rp; five hours) to Luwuk (eight hours from Ampana).

Boat The ferry from Poso chugs on to Gorontalo via the Togian ports of Wakai, Katupat and Dolong. Boats drop in and out of service, so check with locals along the way for updates. Another route to Gorontalo is by bus to Pagimana (7000 rp) and by ferry from there (see the Gorontalo section). There are smaller public boats from Ampana to Bomba (2500 rp; three hours) or to Wakai (2000 to 3000 rp) every day.

TOGIAN ISLANDS

This remarkably diverse archipelago of coral and volcanic isles is the only place in Indonesia where you can find all three major reef environments – atoll, barrier and fringing reefs – in one location. There are few beaches, but the colour and movement in these reefs make up for a lifetime of beaches.

Getting Around

Transport within the Togians is a chronic problem. Regardless of where you stay, you need boats to get there and away, and to reach swimming and snorkelling spots. A convenient (but not cheap) solution is to try to charter a boat from Ampana for a few days. A cheaper and more flexible option is to base yourself on an island and do short snorkelling and whale-watching excursions from there.

The cheapest way between islands is to look out for cargo boats. A boat going from Wakai to Dolong can drop passengers at Katupat or Pulau Malenge for around 3000 rp. Otherwise you might need to spend 40,000 to 50,000 rp on a charter.

Bomba

This tiny outpost at the south-eastern end of Pulau Batu Daka has nearby reefs and two places to stay: *Pak Ismail's* homestay accommodation in the village for 10,000 rp including meals, and Pak Amah's *Island Homestay*, a pleasant place on stilts adjacent to a speck of rock a few hundred metres offshore – also 10,000 rp a day.

Wakai

Wakai has a port, two fine hotels and some well-stocked general stores, but no beaches. The friendly and very capable Tante Yani runs *Wakai Cottages*, charging 16,500/30,000 rp including three excellent meals. The *Togian Islands Hotel* is an airy weatherboard hotel built over the water near Wakai jetty. Prices range from 7500 to 50,000 rp, not including meals.

Both the hotel and Wakai Cottages have basic huts on a sandy beach at **Pulau Kadiri**, both for 15,000 rp a day. The seclusion, beach and adjacent snorkelling make up for what you lose in creature comforts. The boat to Kadiri will cost 2500 rp, and you can arrange excursions to atoll reefs to the north for around 25,000 rp a day.

Katupat

A relaxed village on Togian Island, Katupat is also the closest port to the atoll reefs. Stay at *Losmen Bolilanga Indah* adjacent to Katupat's main jetty for 15,000 rp a head, or at the far more congenial *Losmen Indah Tongkabu* on nearby Tongkabu Island, which offers friendly homestay accommodation for 11,000 rp including meals.

Malenge

Pulau Malenge is a nature reserve, also close to the atoll reefs. The *Malenge Indah Losmen* near the pier charges 10,000 rp a night, including plenty of food. Day trips to the atoll lagoons cost around 20,000 rp, but you will need your own snorkelling gear.

GORONTALO

The port of Gorontalo has the feel of a large, friendly country town and features some of the best preserved colonial houses in Sulawesi. On the outskirts of town are two fortresses, **Otanaha Fort**, on a hill at Lekobalo overlooking Danau Limboto, and another on the shore of the lake. The **Lombongo** hot springs are 17 km from Gorontalo, at the western edge of Dumoga Bone National Park. There is a good swimming hole near a waterfall about three km past the springs.

Places to Stay & Eat
Melati Hotel (☎ 21853), Jalan Gajah Mada 33, is a lovely old place facing the Nani Wartabone square. Alex Velberg has opened this former harbourmaster's house to guests for 10,000/15,000 rp a night. Om Alex's advice in English, Dutch or Indonesian is accurate and free.

Hotel Saronde (☎ 21735), Jalan Walanda Maramis 17, just across the square, has rooms from 13,200/19,000 rp, and *Penginapan Teluk Kau* at Jalan Parman 42 has large rooms for 6600/13,000 rp.

The local delicacy is milu siram, a corn soup with grated coconut, fish, salt, chilli and lime. Look for it at stalls and warung along Jalan Pertiwi at night.

Brantas Bakery on Jalan Sultan Hasanuddin, opposite the main mosque, is a depot of delights and the *Boulavard* has a varied selection of fish and Chinese food.

Getting There & Away
Air Merpati (☎ 21736) is in the Hotel Wisata at Jalan 23 Januari 19; Bouraq (☎ 21070) is at Jalan Ahmad Yani 34 next to the BNI bank. Both have frequent connections to Manado and Palu.

Bus The main bus station is three km north of town. There are direct buses to Palu (22,500 rp), Poso (32,500 rp) and Tentena (40,000 rp) in Central Sulawesi, one day away. Buses to Manado take 10 hours on small, crowded buses (13,000 rp), air-con buses (17,500 rp) or top-of-the-range Tomohon Indah buses (30,000 rp). Paris Express buses to Kotamobagu cost 10,000 rp.

Boat Pelni's KM *Tilongkabila* is the most comfortable way to get to Bitung (near Manado – ekonomi fare is 25,000 rp) or to Luwuk and beyond. Pelni (☎ 20419), Jalan 23 Januari 31, also has an office at the port

in Kwandang, which is a stop for the KM *Umsini*.

PT ASDP (Persero) runs a ferry from Gorontalo to Pagimana every second day. Tickets cost 10,000 rp, plus 25,000 rp if you want a cabin. Connecting buses in Pagimana go straight to Luwuk or Ampana.

Getting Around
A shared Merpati and Bouraq bus goes from town to the airport 32 km away for 5000 rp per person. Mikrolets direct from the port to the main bus terminal cost 1500 rp per person. Allow plenty of time to get to a departing ferry.

Try a horse-drawn bendi around town – 300 rp will get you almost anywhere. For longer routes take mikrolets (bemos) from the terminal opposite the central market.

DUMOGA BONE NATIONAL PARK
About 50 km west of Kotamobagu, Dumoga Bone is a 300,000 hectare national park at the headwaters of the Sungai Dumoga. It was established to protect large irrigation projects downstream from flooding, silting and poor water quality, and now provides invaluable refuge for cuscus, maleo and countless other bird species. You should at least get to see colourful flora, plenty of hornbills, macaques and tiny tarsier.

Trekking
The main entrance to the park is from the east via Doloduo. Go to the ranger station at nearby Kosinggolan to purchase a 1000 rp permit to enter the park, and contract rangers there for 15,000 rp per excursion, or 45,000 rp for overnight trips. Stay at *Ibu Niko Homestay* in Kosinggolan for 20,000 rp a night, including meals; at the cheaper homestay near the dam for 7500 rp, excluding meals; or hike nine km through the jungle to Toraut, and put up at the ranger's lodge for 30,000 rp a head, plus 3000 to 7500 rp for meals. While not cheap, this option is very convenient for dawn treks.

Getting There & Away
There are buses directly from Manado's

Malalayang station to Doloduo for 6500 rp, and frequent connections from Kotamobagu.

MANADO
The Minahasan city of Manado is the capital of North Sulawesi, a strongly Christian region with historically close ties to the Netherlands. Many older people in this tidy, prosperous city speak fluent Dutch, Dutch ships are often crewed by Minahasans, and affluent Minahasans send their children to Dutch universities. Manado provides a good base to explore the region's interesting hinterland, and it is only an hour by motorboat to the brilliant coral reefs off Bunaken Island.

Orientation
Mikrolets from every direction loop around Pasar 45, a block of shops, fruit stands and department stores in the heart of town. The market backs on to Jalan Sam Ratulangi, the main road running south, where you will find upmarket restaurants, hotels and supermarkets. Pasar Jengki fish market, north of the centre, is the main launching place for boats to Bunaken Island.

Information
Tourist Offices Mikrolets marked '17 Aug Wanea' from Pasar 45 will get you to the North Sulawesi tourism office (☎ 64299) on Jalan 17 Agustus. More convenient is the information and booking centre at the Bunaken Souvenir Shop at Jalan Sam Ratulangi 178.

The area code for Manado is 0431.

Immigration The immigration office (☎ 63491) is near the tourist office on Jalan 17 Agustus, and the Philippines has a consulate general (☎ 62365; fax 55316) at Jalan Lumimuut 8.

Special Events
Festivals include the Tai Pei Kong festival at Ban Hiah Kong temple in February; the Pengucapan Syukur (Minahasan Thanksgiving Day) in June/August; the Bunaken Festival in July; the Anniversary of Manado on 14 July; traditional horse races in the second week of August; and the anniversary of North Sulawesi province on 23 September.

Places to Stay
Smiling Hostel (☎ 68463), Jalan Rumambi 7, is cheerful, central and spotlessly clean. There is a comfortable rooftop cafe and advice aplenty from the staff, other travellers and books of tips. Dorm beds cost 5500 rp, and basic singles start at 7500 rp.

The friendly *Rex Hotel* (☎ 51136), Jalan Sugiono 3, is modern and clean, from 9000/15,000 rp a night. *Manado Bersehati Hotel* (☎ 55022), Jalan Sudirman 1, is a Minahasan-style house set about 20 metres off the main road with rooms for 8500/14,000 rp.

An old favourite with travellers is *Crown Losmen* (☎ 66277), Jalan Hasanuddin 28, with rooms from 6000/10,000 rp. The marginally cheaper *Jakarta Jaya* (☎ 64330) is across the road.

Manado Homestay (☎ 60298), Wanea Lingkungan III, Komplex Diklat Rike, is less conveniently located, but compensates with comfort, information, tours and rooms from 25,000 rp per night. To get there, take a 'Teling' mikrolet from Pasar 45 and ask to get off at Komplex Diklat.

Places to Eat
Manado is a mecca for adventurous diners. Regional delights include spicy kawaok (fried 'forest rat'), tough, gamy rintek wuuk (spicy dog meat), lawang pangang (stewed bat), the tender and tasty freshwater ikan mas (gold fish) and tinutuan (vegetable porridge).

Tinoor Jaya, south of the Matahari store on Jalan Sam Ratulangi, is one of the few restaurants in Manado serving regional cuisine. But to eat really well, stop at the row of restaurants in the Lokon foothills, just before Tomohon, south of Manado. The food at *Tinoor Indah* and the *Pemandangan* is as incredible as the spectacular views over Manado. The drinks of choice are saguer, a very quaffable fermented sago wine, and Cap Tikus (literally 'rat brand'), the generic name for distilled saguer.

The esplanade near Pasar 45 attracts a good selection of night warung selling cheap

Indonesian food. For fresh hot seafood, try the *Ria Rio* at Jalan Sudirman 5, or the *Raja Oci* up the road. The *Surabaya* on Jalan Sarapung has a long, varied menu, and the *Xanadu* is for smartly dressed diners on that special night out.

The ubiquitous *KFC* is above the Gelael supermarket on Jalan Sudirman, with a smaller outlet next to the Matahari supermarket and department store opposite the post office. There's also a *CFC* outlet above the Jumbo supermarket behind Pasar 45.

Entertainment
Music is a way of life for the Minahasans. They love jazz and there are always small concerts and backroom gigs, so ask around. There are plenty of discos – *Hot Gossip* next to the Benteng cinema attracts the young crowd; go late.

Cinema options include *Studio 21* at the southern end of Jalan Sam Ratulangi – it's modern, cold and tends to have more recent releases. Check the local *Manado Post* daily for screening details.

Getting There & Away
Air Like Ujung Pandang, there are huge discrepancies between airlines' listed prices and the discounts some agents are prepared to offer. Start at Limbunan (☎ 52009), Jalan Sam Ratulangi 159, or Pola Pelita Express (☎ 60009), Jalan Sam Ratulangi 113, and shop around.

Garuda (☎ 51544) is at Jalan Diponegoro 15, Merpati (☎ 64027) is near Paal 2, Bouraq (☎ 62757) is at Jalan Serapung 27B, Sempati (☎ 51612) is at the Kawanua City Hotel and Mandala is at the southern end of Jalan Sam Ratulangi.

Useful connections include Bouraq's twice weekly flights to Davao in the Philippines (US$150 – try for discounts), direct flights to Singapore on Silk Air (US$260), flights to Gorontalo and Palu by Bouraq and Merpati, and daily flights to Ujung Pandang by all the big domestic carriers.

Bus Bus fares to Gorontalo (10 hours) range from 13,000 to 30,000 rp – the mid-range

17,500 rp older air-con buses are the best. Buses go around the gulf to Palu for 37,500 rp, and all the way to Ujung Pandang for 70,000 rp – if you can tolerate the three day haul. Allow for delays during wet weather. These and the Kotamobagu-bound buses (5500 rp) all leave from the Malalayang bus terminal south of Manado.

Boat Pelni (☎ 62844), at Jalan Sam Ratulangi 7, is open Monday to Friday from 8 am to 2 pm. It has several large boats calling at the deep-water port of Bitung, near Manado, plus there are smaller ferries out of Manado itself. They tend to call at ports along the coast, go north to Tahuna (Pulau Sangihe) and Lirung (Talaud Islands) or over to Ternate and Ambon.

From Bitung, ekonomi fares on the KM *Kerinci* include 79,500 rp to Ambon and 131,000 rp to Ujung Pandang. Ekonomi fares on the KM *Ciremai* include Ternate 39,000 rp, Banggai 36,000 rp and Bau Bau 107,000 rp. The KM *Kambuna* sails west to Toli Toli 49,500 rp (ekonomi), and the KM *Tilongkabila* stops include Gorontalo 26,500 rp, Luwuk 46,000 rp and Kolonodale 62,500 rp.

Getting Around
The Airport Mikrolets from Sam Ratulangi airport go to Paal-2 (350 rp), where you change to another to Pasar 45 (250 rp) or elsewhere in the city. Taxis from the airport to the city (13 km) cost 6000 to 7500 rp.

Local Transport Transport around town is by mikrolet for a flat fare of 250 rp. Destinations are shown on a card in the front windscreen. There are various bus stations around town for destinations outside Manado – get to any of them from Pasar 45.

AROUND MANADO
Bunaken Island
Get your feet wet and float over some of the world's most spectacular and accessible coral drop-offs, caves and valleys. You can buy snorkelling gear from sport shops in Manado, such as Toko Akbar Ali on the western boundary of Pasar 45, or hire well-

worn masks and snorkels from places along the beaches on Bunaken. Boats to Bunaken (2500 rp) depart from near Manado's fish market.

The going rate for dive excursions around Bunaken and nearby islands is around US$50 for two dives in the low season, and US$65 in the June-July high season. This is an option for experienced divers. *Nusantara Diving Centre*, or NDC (☎ 63988; fax 63707), on Molas Beach, Manado, its neighbour *Baracuda Diving Resort* (☎ 62033; fax 64848), and *Murex* (☎ 66280), Jalan Sudirman 28, Manado, cater for beginners, but not very well. Bunaken-based operators include Ronny at *MDC*, near Daniel's Homestay.

Places to Stay & Eat Hastily built homestays crowd Liang Beach in the west, and there are places on the quieter, less crowded Pangalisang Beach near Bunaken village.

Pantai Pangalisang *Daniel's Homestay* is the biggest, most popular place with beds from 17,500 rp, including meals. *Lorenzo Cottage* next door is smaller, with cottages for 17,500 rp per person including meals (20,000 rp in the high season). *Doris Homestay* at the far end of the beach is simple and relaxing – 15,000 rp, including meals.

Pantai Liang The popularity of the coral drop-off 100 metres offshore created a building boom along this beach. None are designed to last.

Papa Boa's and his neighbours at the far end of the beach charge 20,000 rp per person, including meals. A little south is *Nelson's*, run by a pushy character, with rooms from 15,000 rp. The next in line, *Yani*, is clean and comfortable at 15,000 rp, and *Bastiona Cottages* is the classiest option – by Bunaken standards – at 40,000 rp per head. Try to negotiate prices.

Ibu Konda's and *Rusli's* are the best of the rest, both charging 15,000 rp. *Yulin*, set apart on its own little stretch of sand, also has simple rooms for 15,000 rp.

Other Attractions

At **Airmadidi**, or 'Boiling Water', you'll find *waruga*, odd little pre-Christian tombs. Corpses were buried in a squatting position with gold, porcelain and household articles – most have been plundered by now. A group of these tombs is at Sawangan, a 15 minute walk from Airmadidi bemo station.

During the Japanese occupation of Indonesia in WWII, caves were cut into the hills surrounding Manado to act as air-raid shelters, quarters and storage space for supplies. One group of caves is three km out of **Kawangkoan** on the road to Kiawa. More impressive Japanese caves are just outside **Tondano**, past Airmadidi.

About five km from Kawangkoan, close to Desa Pinabetengan, **Watu Pinabetengan** is a stone carved with vague outlines and is said to be the meeting place for the chiefs of the Minahasan tribes.

TOMOHON

Minahasa's extraordinary cuisine is served in a string of restaurants on a cliff overlooking Manado, just a few km before Tomohon (see Manado's Places to Eat section).

Tomohon has a **vulcanology centre** which monitors and advises on the safety of active volcanoes in the area. Seek advice before tackling Gunung Soputan, Lokon or Mahawu. It also has information and spectacular photographs of other volcanoes.

Between Tomohon and Lahendong, there's the extensive **Lahendong hot springs**. Also near Lahendong is **Danau Linow**, a small highly sulphurous lake. It is possible to hike from here via small footpaths to **Danau Tondano**, seven km east.

Place to Stay

Happy Flower Homestay at the foot of Gunung Lokon is justifiably applauded by all who stay. This simple but delightful refuge costs 7500/9000 rp for singles, or 13,500 rp for doubles, including breakfast. From Manado, take a Tomohon-bound bus and get out at 'Gereja Pniel' a few km before Tomohon. Take the path opposite the church, walk 300 metres, cross a stream and look for

INDONESIA

the homestay tucked away in trees to the right of the path.

BITUNG

Bitung is the chief port of Minahasa and lies to the east of Manado. Despite its spectacular setting, the town is not very attractive. The Pelni office (☎ 21167) is in the harbour compound.

Places to Stay & Eat

The *Samudra Jaya* (☎ 21333), Jalan Sam Ratulangi 2, is cheap and central, with rooms from 15,000 rp including breakfast. *Penginapan Sansarino* near the main market has rooms for 15,000 rp and a downstairs restaurant.

A few km north of Bitung is the *Kunkungan Bay Resort*, a swank dive resort amid coconut plantations on a secluded bay. There is helpful staff, an American dive master and excellent diving. Packages, including accommodation and meals, cost around US$170.

Getting There & Away

Bitung is 50 km from Manado. Mikrolets depart regularly from Manado's Paal-2 terminal (1000 rp; one hour). The mikrolet drops you off at the Mapalus terminal just outside Bitung, where you catch another mikrolet into town (300 rp; 10 minutes).

TANGKOKO BATUANGAS DUA SAUDARA

Tangkoko is one of the most impressive and accessible nature reserves in Indonesia. Situated 30 km from Bitung, it is home to black apes, anoas, babirusa and maleo birds, among others. This national park, an amalgam of several reserves, also includes the coastline and coral gardens offshore.

The easiest way to Batuputih, the main entrance to Tangkoko, is by jeep from the Girian (one hour), a terminus on the main Manado to Bitung road. Stay with *Mama Ruus* for 20,000 rp including three meals, or at the ranger-run accommodation just inside the park for 15,000 rp. Neither will be a highlight of your travels, but both are con-

veniently placed for the 5 am rise needed to see the wildlife – the real reason for staying here. To enter the park you need a permit from the PHPA office, plus 10,000 rp for guides to point the way.

Maluku (Moluccas)

The islands of Maluku are the fabled spice islands to the west of Irian Jaya. Spices, once unique to the islands previously known as the Moluccas, attracted European traders and colonialists hundreds of years ago. Maluku has over 1000 islands, most of which are uninhabited. Visitors to Maluku usually go to Ambon, the provincial capital, the delightful Banda Islands, or Ternate and Tidore, two adjacent islands off western Halmahera. More remote islands are difficult to get to, but are often worth the effort.

Climate

Timing a visit to Maluku is a bit different from the rest of Indonesia. The dry season is from October to April, and the wet season from May to September, although there are slight variations among the islands. Try to avoid the wet season, but also be prepared for some rain at any time of the year.

Flora & Fauna

The Manusela National Park on Pulau Seram has unique species of parrots, including the brightly coloured *nuri* (often kept as pets), and cockatoos. Another national reserve on the Aru Islands has the flightless cassowary, and the shy bird of paradise, or *cenderawasih*. In remote parts of Pulau Seram, south-east Maluku and Pulau Halmahera, you may see a long-nosed bandicoot, a Timor deer or a miniature version of a kangaroo. Pulau Bacan is famous for its tail-less monkeys.

Some of the vast forests are home to unique species of butterflies, and huge orchids. The nutmeg – that little tree that has caused so much strife in the past – is still cultivated in parts of Ambon and Saparua islands, and the Bandas.

Activities

Skin diving is spectacular, particularly around the Bandas, Pulau Ambon and the neighbouring islands of Seram, Saparua and Nusa Laut. The interior of most islands is mountainous, offering unlimited trekking opportunities, particularly on Halmahera and Seram islands; and there are volcanoes to climb in the Bandas and on Pulau Ternate. For some of the prettiest beaches in Indonesia head to the southern Kai Islands.

Getting There & Away

Air The capital of the province – Kota Ambon on Pulau Ambon – is connected daily by air to all parts of Indonesia mainly by Merpati, but also by Bouraq, Mandala and Sempati. Flights also operate between Manado, in northern Sulawesi, and Ternate and Mangole (Sula Islands).

Boat Pelni liners (and many other boats) link Maluku with the rest of Indonesia. The *Kerinci* links Ambon and Ternate with Bitung (north Sulawesi) and Bau Bau (south Sulawesi), and goes on to Java; the *Dobonsolo*

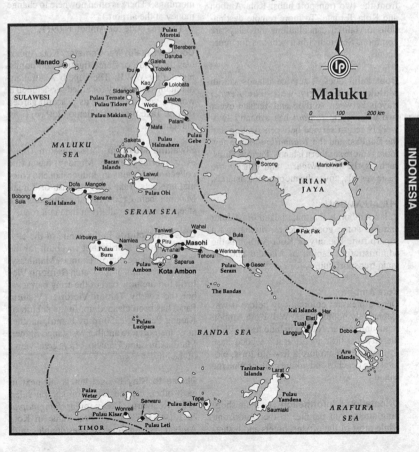

INDONESIA

connects Ambon with Sorong (Irian Jaya), Dili (East Timor) and Java; the *Rinjani* has a great route from Ambon to the Bandas, Tual (Kai Islands) and Fak Fak (Irian Jaya) and back, and then on to Bau Bau and Java; the *Tatamailau* links southern Maluku with Nusa Tenggara and Irian Jaya; and the *Ciremai* goes from Ternate to Bitung and Sorong, as well as other ports in Irian Jaya and Java.

Getting Around

Air Merpati has an extensive network of flights around Maluku, all of which start from the two transport hubs: Kota Ambon and Kota Ternate. To more remote destinations in Maluku, cancellations and delays are common. See individual sections for more details.

Boat Pelni doesn't service islands within Maluku particularly well. The *Kerinci* travels between Ambon and Ternate every two weeks; the *Rinjani* has a handy two-weekly return service between Ambon and the Bandas; and the *Tatamailau* joins a few more remote southern islands. Perintis ships, such as the KM *Nagura*, and other more basic vessels, cover the more remote islands.

PULAU AMBON

Pulau Ambon is the main island of Maluku and has some good beaches, diving and a superb fort. The city of Kota Ambon is the administrative capital of Maluku and the main transport hub.

Kota Ambon

Once a pleasant colonial city before it was extensively bombed in WWII, Kota Ambon is not unlike many others in Indonesia. While the city has little to offer, it's a good base from which to explore a few old forts, picturesque beaches and hiking trails around the island.

Orientation & Information The main shopping streets run parallel to the waterfront, while most of the offices, hotels and restau-rants are along, or near, Jalans Sultan Hairun, Raya Pattimura and AM Sangaji.

The helpful tourist office (☎ 52471), on the ground floor of the governor's office (enter from Jalan Sultan Hairun), is open weekdays from 7.30 am to 4.30 pm. The post office is on Jalan Raya Pattimura, and the Telkom office is a becak ride away on Jalan Dr JB Sitanala.

Ambon is the only place (other than Ternate) in Maluku to change money. The best banks are Bank Exim, on Jalan Raya Pattimura, and the Bank of Central Asia, on Jalan Sultan Hairun – both are open weekday mornings. (There is often nowhere to change money at the airport.)

The area code for Ambon is 0911.

Commonwealth War Cemetery Kota Ambon was the centre of fierce fighting and bombing during WWII. The superb Australian-maintained cemetery for allied servicemen is worth a visit if only for its peaceful garden setting. Take the Tantui bemo (250 rp) from the terminal.

Siwalima Museum This museum (open every morning, except Monday) has a fine collection of Malukan, Indonesian and colonial artefacts. Take the Amahusu or Taman Makmur bemo (300 rp); the museum is a steep 10 minute walk from the main road.

Other Attractions In the centre of the city, the **Pattimura Monument** was built for the local resistance hero, Thomas Matulessy. The few remains of the Dutch **Benteng Victoria** fort are now part of the army barracks, but the nearby **Taman Victoria** (Victoria Park) has been cleaned up. In the suburb of Karang Panjang (250 rp by bemo), another huge memorial to another resistance fighter, Martha Christina Tiahahu, offers great views of the city.

Places to Stay Budget hotels, all next to each other, can be found on central Jalan Wim Reawaru. The popular *Penginapan Beta* (☎ 53463) is the best value in Kota Ambon – clean, quiet singles/doubles with mandi cost 14,000/21,000 rp. Next door, the *Hotel Transit Rezfanny* (☎ 42300) has rooms without mandi for 14,000 rp, but is nothing special. *Hotel Hero* (☎ 42978) is a shiny new place with air-con, hot water and TV from 40,000 rp a room. The quiet *Baliwerti Hotel* (☎ 55996) is of a similar standard and price as the Hero.

Hotel Elenoor (☎ 52834), Jalan Anthony Rhebok 30, has rooms for 22,000/32,000 rp, with mandi and some charm. Almost next door, *Hotel Gamalama* (☎ 53724) is also good value for 13,200/19,250 rp, with mandi. Get there early; it is often full.

At Jalan Ahmad Yani 12, *Wisma Game* (☎ 53525) with rooms from 13,000/19,500 rp without mandi continues to be popular; and the central *Hotel Sumber Asia* (☎ 56587), near the terminal on Jalan Pala, has a good range of rooms starting at 17,500 rp. In the 'Muslim sector', a little south-west of the main mosque, several good places such as the quiet *Wisma Jaya* (☎ 41545) and *Hotel Abdulalie* (☎ 52057) have rooms from 17,000 rp.

See the Around Pulau Ambon section for some good alternatives around the island.

Places to Eat During the evening, the side-walk of Jalan AM Sangaji is lined with ladies selling huge plates of nasi campur for around 1000 rp. Tiny warungs congregate around the terminal, port and near the Hotel Sumber Asia.

Halim's Restaurant on Jalan Sultan Hairun is always popular, and often too busy. Good Chinese food costs around 7500 rp a dish, and the beer is ice-cold for the regular Australian clientele. Next door, the *Tip Top Restaurant* and *Restaurant Sakura* are also good, cheaper and quieter. *Restoran Amboina*, on Jalan AY Patty, is recommended for its good meals, ice creams and cakes. *Yang-Yang* on Jalan Wim Reawaru has a nice setting, with meals, such as baked fish, from around 5000 rp.

The Ambon Plaza has a *KFC* and the eatery on the 3rd floor of the Matahari department store serves Asian meals (from 3000 to 5000 rp). Probably the best food

(meals from 7000 to 10,000 rp) and service is at the *Sangranii*, opposite the main mosque.

Getting There & Away Merpati (☎ 52481), Jalan Ahmad Yani 19, has flights to every corner of Maluku. There are regular local flights to Bandaneira (102,700 rp), Ternate (201,700 rp) and Langgur (224,800 rp) in the Kai Islands; daily flights to the Irian Jayan hubs of Biak (276,600 rp) and Sorong (145,600 rp); and daily flights to Ujung Pandang (277,500 rp), with connections to other places such as Kupang, Jakarta and Denpasar.

Sempati (☎ 51612), Jalan AM Sangaji 46C, flies direct to Surabaya (494,300 rp) every day. Mandala (☎ 42551), Jalan AY Patty 21, flies to Ujung Pandang and on to Jakarta every day. Bouraq (☎ 52314), Jalan Mutiara 9A, goes to Ternate daily (and twice a week on to Manado), and regularly to Langgur.

Boat See the Maluku Getting There & Away and Getting Around sections for details on boats to/from Ambon. The Pelni office (☎ 52049) is in the main harbour complex. Smaller boats to just about every island around Maluku leave from a harbour at the end of Jalan Pala. A board outside the harbour shows what's going where and when.

Getting Around Pattimura airport is 36 km from the city, on the other side of the bay. A taxi officially costs 20,000 rp; less if you bargain with the driver in the car park. The cheapest and shortest way is by bemo from outside the airport to Poka (350 rp), then by frequent ferry (250 rp) to Galala, then another bemo (250 rp) to the Mardika terminal. A good option is the comfortable DAMRI bus (3500 rp), which may be in the airport car park. Allow an hour for all forms of transport.

Local Transport Bemos for Kota Ambon and places near the city leave from the chaotic Mardika terminal, along the water-front. Buses to places further away on Pulau

INDONESIA

Ambon, and to Pulau Seram, leave from the Batu Merah terminal, a little further north-east of Mardika.

The city is small enough to walk around, or a becak costs about 1000 rp. (Becaks can only stop around the Wisata Hotel, and don't go all the way to the bemo or bus terminals.) Local bemos stop at designated places around the city.

AROUND PULAU AMBON
Diving
Pulau Ambon, and many nearby islands, offers exciting diving opportunities virtually all year round (roughest between April and June). One or two travel agencies in Kota Ambon offer some diving hire and trips, but easily the best place is the Ambon Dive Centre (☎ 55685), opposite the entrance to the Namalatu beach.

Hila
Hila's strategic position on the north coast has resulted in a long and fascinating pre-colonial and colonial history. Originally built by the Portuguese in 1512, then taken over by the Dutch East India Company (VOC) in the early 17th century, the magnificently restored **Benteng Amsterdam** fort in Hila is the best of its kind in Maluku. A few minutes walk away are the **Wapauwe mosque** (built in 1414), and the quaint **Immanuel Church** (built in 1580, but extensively restored since). Direct buses (1300 rp; one hour – more regular early in the morning) leave from the Batu Merah terminal.

Beaches
A lovely beach not far from the city is **Natsepa**. There are a few restaurants and places to stay – the best is right on the beach: *Bungalow Vaneysa* (☎ 61451). Take the Passo or Suli bemo (1000 rp). In the north-east, **Liang** and nearby **Hunimua** have many secluded beaches but nowhere to stay. **Amahusu** isn't really a beach but is famous as the finishing point for the annual Darwin to Ambon Yacht Race.

The best beaches are south of the city, at **Namalatu**, and nearby at **Latuhalat**. Both are easily accessible from Kota Ambon by direct bemo (600 rp) and have great snorkelling. At Latuhalat, there are two resorts – *Santai Beach Resort* and *Lelisa Beach Resort* – with nice bungalows from 60,000 rp, and the new, and already popular, *Homestay Europa*, with homely singles/doubles for 25,000/30,000 rp.

Soya Atas
Close to the city (400 rp by bemo), the tiny village of Soya Atas has an old church. Follow the narrow, obvious trail for 20 minutes to the top of Sirimau hill for great views of the island. From the top, trails lead down to villages on the south coast.

PULAU SERAM
Maluku's second largest island (17,151 sq km), Seram is mountainous and heavily forested. In the middle, **Manusela National Park** is renowned for its wildlife, rugged terrain and traditional Alfuro people. With a guide, and plenty of determination and luck, you can trek across the island and through the park, from the northern village of Wahai (where there are two losmen) to Tehoru (also two losmen) in the south. But this is a *very rough* five to seven day trip.

Masohi is the administrative centre, while nearby **Amahai** is the location of the airport and port. Along the main road in Masohi, Jalan Abdullah Soulissa, *Hotel Sri Lestari* (☎ 21178) is comfortable and has good singles/doubles for 20,000/25,000 rp, and *Penginapan Nusantara* (☎ 21339) is OK but overpriced at 18,150/22,000 rp – more with mandi. For 13,750 rp a person, *Penginapan Nusa Ina* (☎ 21221), just east of the market, is the best value. The market has plenty of good places to eat. The *Rumah Makan Sate Surabaya*, next to the Sri Lestari, is the best place in town.

Merpati flies twice a week from Amahai to Ambon for 54,400 rp and to Bandaneira, but these flights have a habit of being cancelled. Between Kota Ambon and Pulau Seram, there are several daily bus/ferry/bus packages to Masohi, Saleman in the north, and other more remote destinations. Quicker, but dearer, is the daily superjet boat (11,000 rp) between Tulehu, on Pulau Ambon, and Amahai.

PULAU SAPARUA

Pulau Saparua, still an important centre for nutmeg production and of historical importance in Malukan history, is a gorgeous little island close to Ambon. There are plenty of diving, swimming and trekking opportunities, a pottery centre at **Ouw** in the south and loads of unhurried, friendly people.

You could day-trip from Kota Ambon, but it's better to stay a day or two in Kota Saparua's only losmen – the *Penginapan Lease Indah* (☎ 21040), which costs from 10,000 rp per person, more for mandi and air-con. Nearby, **Benteng Duurstede** fort (built in 1676) sits majestically in the harbour, and there's an interesting museum next door.

Daily speedboats and ferries from Hurnala, on Pulau Ambon, go to Haria, only 10 minutes by bemo from Kota Saparua.

BANDA ISLANDS

The Bandas are an irresistible cluster of islands south-east of Ambon. Various European colonial powers fought for centuries over Banda's spices, and have left a number of forts and colonial houses. With some stunning island and volcanic scenery, and diving, the Bandas are an increasingly popular place to spend some time. Bandaneira, the main village in the Bandas, is situated on the most populous island, Pulau Neira.

Bandaneira

Information Thankfully, the Bandas are still not geared towards mass tourism. Bandaneira has no bank, so stock up on rupiah in Ambon. The tourist information counter at the airport is often closed. The post office, near Benteng Nassau, is quaint but often closed, while the incongruously large Telkom office, a becak ride away from hotels, never closes.

The area code for Bandaneira is 0910.

Museums & Houses Bandaneira has a number of delightfully restored colonial buildings. The **Rumah Budaya Museum** has a small collection of cannons, old coins, modern paintings and Portuguese helmets. Nearby, the residence occupied by British Captain Christopher Cole, who wrestled the Bandas from the Dutch in 1810, is often closed.

Two homes once occupied by independence heroes, Mohammed Hatta and Sutan Syahrir, have been well restored, and include a lot of memorabilia about their lives. Also worth a look is the Dutch VOC **Governor's Palace**, on the waterfront, and the **Dutch Church** (built in 1680).

Forts Built by the VOC in 1611, the imposing **Benteng Belgica** stands above Bandaneira and offers staggering views of Gunung Api. The fort (and its small museum) is a great place to clamber around, and to envisage former colonial times. Below, **Benteng Nassau**, built by the Dutch in 1609 (on the stone foundations laid, but later abandoned, by the Portuguese in 1529) is still in need of some restoration.

Diving The Bandas offer some extraordinary scuba and skin diving. You can hire snorkelling equipment, boats and guides from a few hotels such as the Branta, Matahari and Flamboyan (we've had reports of unreliable scuba gear from the Hotel Maulana). Ask around at these and other hotels about any boats visiting diving sites or other islands – there is nothing organised on a regular basis.

Places to Stay & Eat The best places to stay are the homestays in Bandaneira, which charge from 17,500 rp per person, including three good meals. The best are the friendly *Rosmina* (☎ 21145) on Jalan Kujali; the *Matahari*, just off Jalan Pelabuhan; and *Likes*, further up the street, which both have magnificent sea views. Good value in the range of 22,000 to 35,000 rp per room including meals – or more with air-con – are the *Flamboyan Guest House* (☎ 21233) and *Branta Penginapan* (☎ 21068), both on Jalan Syahrir, and the *Penginapan Delfika* (☎ 21027) on Jalan Gereja Tua.

INDONESIA

There are some reasonable places to eat, including a couple of ice cream parlours, along Jalan Pelabuhan, but you're best off with an accommodation package which includes meals.

Getting There & Away Several times a week, Merpati flies to Ambon and less frequently to Amahai on Pulau Seram. Planes are necessarily small (the airport is being extended) and flights can be cancelled and are often overbooked, so confirm, and then reconfirm. The Merpati office (☎ 21040) is on Jalan Pelabuhan.

Every two weeks, the Pelni liner *Rinjani* does a handy trip during the day between Ambon and Bandaneira, and on to south-east Maluku and Irian Jaya, and back again. Other smaller, less comfortable boats, such as the Perintis ship KM *Iweri*, infrequently link Bandaneira with Ambon, and with the Irian Jayan coast.

Getting Around Bandaneira and Pulau Neira are easy to walk around, although there are a handful of becaks. From the airport, take a free hotel or Merpati bemo, a public bemo, or even walk for about 15 minutes to your hotel. All sorts of longboats, speedboats and canoes can be rented from the fish market area.

Other Islands

Gunung Api Only a short canoe trip from Bandaneira, this volatile volcano has some wonderful diving around its shores. You can also climb 666 metres to the top in a couple of hours. It can be a tough scramble towards the top, but the views (especially at sunrise and when the tiny Merpati plane is landing) are worth the effort. You don't need a guide; your boatman will show you where to start.

Pulau Banda Besar From the fish market, regular boats go to Lonthoir, the main village on Big Banda Island. Walks along the coast from Lonthoir will take you through pretty villages and still-operating nutmeg plantations. The steep steps in the village lead (after you ask for some directions) to the 17th century **Benteng Hollandia**. This disappointing fort was almost completely destroyed by an earthquake but still offers great views.

Pulau Ai A couple of daily boats connect Bandaneira to relaxed Pulau Ai, with its deserted beaches and crumbling forts. There are also several good, cheap losmen – the best is *Homestay Weltevreden*, which costs from 12,500 rp per person including meals.

SOUTH-EAST MALUKU

Probably the most forgotten in Indonesia, the islands of southern Maluku are dispersed across the sea between Timor and Irian Jaya. The three main groups, all south-east of Banda, are Kai, Aru and Tanimbar, and there are several other very undeveloped island groups further south.

The Kais boast some of the best beaches you will ever see. The twin city of Tual and Langgur is the capital of the district, and has a good range of accommodation – the best are *Rosemgen II* and *Linda Mas Guest House*. Saumlaki is the main town in the Tanimbars, which have little to offer. The best place to stay in Saumlaki is *Penginapan Harapan Indah*. The Arus are very undeveloped and offer almost no facilities for visitors.

Regular flights from Ambon to Langgur (224,800 rp) on Merpati and Bouraq make the Kais the focal point of the islands. Merpati also flies from Ambon to Dobo (Aru) and to Saumlaki. The Pelni liner *Tatamailau* joins these islands with each other and with the Irian Jayan coast, and three Perintis ships travel every few weeks in the area.

PULAU TERNATE & TIDORE

These islands were one of the first places where the Portuguese (in 1511) and, later, the Dutch established themselves in Maluku. Once bitter rivals, the two islands are littered with the ruins of old European forts, great beaches and beautiful scenery. With good air and boat connections to Manado, in northern

Sulawesi, Ternate is an ideal place to stop over before heading to Ambon or Irian Jaya.

Kota Ternate

Orientation & Information
A lot of places in Kota Ternate are on, or just parallel to, the main street, Jalan Pahlawan Revolusi, which stretches from the Ternate port in the south to the bemo terminal and market. The tourist office (☎ 22646), open from 8.30 am to 4 pm Monday to Saturday, is in the governor's office, on Jalan Pahlawan Revolusi. Also on this street are Bank Exim and Bank Danamon for changing money, the post office and, next door, the Telkom office.

The area code for Ternate is 0921.

Kedaton Sultan
Built around 1250, the Sultan's Palace lies just back from Jalan Sultan Baballuh, the road leading to the airport. It's now a museum containing an absorbing collection of Portuguese cannons, Dutch helmets and armour, and memorabilia of the past sultans. The best time to find it open is weekday mornings.

Benteng Oranye
Opposite the bemo terminal, this fort was built by the Dutch in 1607 on top of an undated Malay fortress. It hasn't been restored, but a walk around gives you a good idea of its former opulence.

Places to Stay
The cheapest places – from 5000 to 10,000 rp per person – are around the entrance to the Ternate port but they're often dreadful. The best of this lot are the penginapans *Permata* and *Keluarga* (☎ 22250). Along Jalan Salim Fabanyo, the family-run but noisy *Wisma Sejahtera* (☎ 21139) is popular at 15,000/20,000 rp for singles/doubles with mandi. On the same street, the *Wisma Nusantara* (☎ 21086) costs 20,000 rp for a room with mandi.

On Jalan Bosoiri, the central *Hotel Indah* (☎ 21334) is good value with rooms from 21,000/30,000 rp. The Dutch-built *Hotel Merdeka* (☎ 21120), on Jalan Monunutu, is quiet and clean from 17,500 rp per person. The *Hotel El Shinta* (☎ 21050), on Jalan

Pahlawan Revolusi, has a range of rooms starting at 22,000/33,000 rp including meals.

Places to Eat
Several cheap Padang restaurants huddle around the Ternate port, and warungs spring up every night around the Merpati office (but these may move when a new shopping centre nearby is completed). On Jalan Pahlawan Revolusi, the *Gamalama Restaurant* is good and cheap – nasi ikan for around 1300 rp. On the same street, the *Restoran Garuda* is popular, with a good selection from 3000 to 5000 rp a plate, but beware of the booming karaoke. Nearby, *Bonanza Cafe* has the best fruit drinks and cakes in Maluku. Worth a 10 minute walk north of the terminal, *Bambu Kuring* has an attractive setting and very good, reasonably priced meals from 5000 to 6000 rp.

Getting There & Away
Ternate is the hub for northern Maluku. Merpati flies almost daily to Ambon, infrequently to centres on Pulau Halmahera, and, conveniently, to Manado (125,800 rp) at least once a day. The Merpati office (☎ 21651) is on Jalan Bosoiri 81.

Every day, Bouraq (☎ 21288), Jalan Ahmad Yani 131, also connects Ternate with Ambon and Manado.

Boat
Every two weeks, the Pelni liner *Ciremai* links Ternate with Bitung (northern Sulawesi) and with Sorong (Irian Jaya), and the *Kerinci* goes to Bitung and Ambon. Perintis and other regular boats go to Pulau Halmahera, Pulau Bacan, Ambon and Sulawesi – information is posted around the various ports.

The ports can be a little confusing. Two ports, only a few hundred metres apart at Bastiong, a few km south of Kota Ternate, have ferries and speedboats to Tidore, Halmahera and the Bacan Islands. Another larger port in Kota Ternate caters for Pelni liners, and larger boats to Sulawesi and Ambon.

Getting Around
The airport is close to Kota Ternate. You can get a taxi for 5000 rp, or walk down to the main road from the

terminal and catch a bemo for 250 rp. The city is small enough to walk around, or for a change why not take a horse and cart, known as a bendi?

Around Pulau Ternate

There are plenty of places to visit around the island during day trips from the city on public transport, or by chartering a bemo for about 8000 rp per hour.

Forts Built in 1512 by the Portuguese, and restored by the Dutch in 1610, **Benteng Tolucco** is one of the better forts on the island. Ask the lady next door to let you in. The fort is just off the road to the airport. Near Bastiong, the 1540 Portuguese **Benteng Kayuh Merah** has recently been restored, and consequently has lost a lot of its charm. Still, the setting is pretty, and it's worth a look.

Lakes & Beaches Not far from Takome in the west is **Danau Tolire Besar** (not the scruffy, nearby Danau Tolire Kecil), a stunning, deep volcanic lake (550 rp by bemo). A trail from the main road leads to the lake, which is believed to have crocodiles, and even the wreckage of a WWII plane. Closer to Kota Ternate, **Danau Laguna** is also beautiful, but there's a wall around it and the gate is often locked.

The beaches are mostly black (volcanic) sand. The best are at **Sulamadaha** (where there is one losmen), picturesque **Pulau Maitara** (a very short boat trip from Rum, on Pulau Tidore) and **Afetaduma**.

Gunung Api Gamalama Completely dominating the island, Gamalama volcano has erupted fiercely many times over the centuries, most recently in late 1994. With a guide (ask at the tourist office or Hotel Merdeka) and some effort, you can trek to the top in a few hours. Masses of lava from a 1737 eruption lie just off the main road, not far from the airport, in an area known as **Batu Angus**.

Pulau Tidore

Pulau Tidore, the centre of the Central Halmahera District, is less appealing than Pulau Ternate and doesn't have the facilities of its more developed neighbour, but is worth a day trip from Kota Ternate.

In or around **Soa Siu**, the capital of Tidore, there are some hot springs, nice beaches, an interesting market and **Gunung Kiematubu**, which can be climbed or explored. Between Rum and Soa Siu are the compelling but decrepit **Benteng Tohula**, and the engaging (but often closed) **Sultan's Memorial Museum.** Soa Siu has a couple of losmen, but there is no need to stay there.

Speedboats (1000 rp) go every few minutes, and other boats less often, between Bastiong and Rum in northern Tidore. From Rum, regular bemos go to Soa Siu (1000 rp).

PULAU HALMAHERA

Dominating Ternate and Tidore islands is the rugged island of Halmahera. Most of the southern part remains undeveloped, except for **Pulau Bacan**. Bacan, a congenial little island with the fascinating **Benteng Barnevald** fort, is well connected by boat to Ternate, and has a few losmen – the best is *Pondok Indah*.

From Ternate, it's easy to get ferries and other boats to various parts of northern Halmahera, especially to **Sidangoli**, which has two losmen. From Sidangoli, buses go along the western road to **Jailolo** (with a losmen) up to Ibu; and along the rough, eastern road through dusty **Kao**, once a Japanese WWII headquarters (and where there is a losmen) and Tobelo. **Tobelo** has several good places to stay, such as the *Hotel Pantai Indah* and *Penginapan Alfa Mas*. It's an agreeable place from which to explore nearby volcanic lakes, such as **Danau Duma**, mountains and beaches.

Pulau Morotai is three hours by daily ferry from Tobelo. Another important Allied WWII headquarters, Morotai is very relaxed and offers plenty of WWII remnants and beaches. The only losmen is *Penginapan Panber*.

Irian Jaya

Irian Jaya, the Indonesian side of the island of New Guinea, was only acquired from the Dutch in 1963. Since it had no racial or historical connection with the other Indonesian islands, some interesting arm-bending had to be conducted to get the Dutch to hand it over. Indonesian mining and transmigration have not gone unopposed by some Irianese, particularly the independence movement known as the Free Papua Organisation (OPM), which still engages in some rebellious activities against the Indonesian government.

Irian Jaya is over 400,000 sq km of mostly impenetrable forest and mountains (some permanently snow-capped) with up to 250 designated cultural sub-groups speaking around 500 different languages. It is one of the few areas in the Asia-Pacific region where traditional cultures still survive (but only just). Almost all visitors head to the Baliem Valley – the only part of the interior generally accessible to tourism – with a side trip to Biak and/or Jayapura, but Irian Jaya has a lot more to offer.

Climate
Generally, the driest – and best – time to visit is from May to October, although it can rain anywhere, anytime. Strong winds and rain are usual along the north coast from November to March. Along some of the south coast, however, it can be wild and woolly from April to October, but this is the dry season in Merauke. The best time for the Baliem Valley is March to August, when the days are drier and cooler, but the nights are usually cold all year around.

Flora & Fauna
Seventy-five per cent of Irian Jaya is dense forest in which a unique range of flora and fauna flourishes. Species of the *cenderawasih*, or bird of paradise, still inhabit the remote areas of the Bird's Head Peninsula and Pulau Yapen, and around the southern coastal regions there are large cassowaries and storks. Bandicoots and possums live in many forest regions, and around Merauke wallabies are not uncommon.

The forests have nearly 3000 types of orchids, but don't get too close because there are also plenty of poisonous snakes and 800 species of spiders. Mangroves and the vital sago palm cover a lot of the coast while eucalypts abound in the south-east. With some effort, you can visit national parks in northern Pulau Biak, between Agats and Nabire, and near Merauke.

Permits
Currently, you can visit Jayapura, Sentani, Sorong and Biak without a *surat jalan*, or travel permit, but for other areas, such as Merauke, Agats and the Asmat region, Manokwari and Nabire, as well as Wamena and the Baliem Valley, you will need one. A surat jalan can easily be obtained at major police stations; it's particularly straightforward in Jayapura, Sentani and Biak. You need two photographs (black & white will do); there is often an 'administration fee' of about 2000 rp; and it should be issued on the same day. Alternatively, your travel agent or hotel can easily arrange it for an extra charge. Don't forget to list on the document every place you will, and may, go, and take some photocopies to hand out when you report to the relevant district police stations or check into your hotel.

Certain parts of Irian Jaya remain off-limits to foreigners, namely the Paniai lake region, anywhere near the PNG border, Gunung Trikora and most parts of the interior.

Activities
Not surprisingly, most activities for visitors centre on Irian Jaya's mountains, people and coast. Biak and Yapen islands boast some astonishing coral and fish but the diving industry is in its infancy. The best time for diving is from April to September.

Trekking is the best way to really see the countryside and traditional lifestyles. The Baliem Valley is generally the only place in

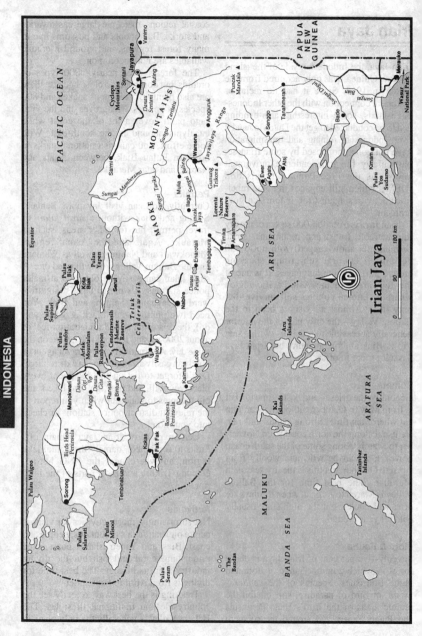

Irian Jaya

the interior where trekking is allowed, but it's also permissible, and worthwhile, around the Arfak mountains near Manokwari, and the flood plains north of Merauke. Organised birdwatching tours are increasingly popular in the Bird's Head Peninsula and Pulau Yapen.

Getting There & Away

Air Unless you have a lot of time, flying is the only way to travel. The transport centres for Irian Jaya are Sorong, Biak and Jayapura, so you may spend some time in these places waiting for a connection.

Many travellers just get on a flight to Biak and/or Jayapura, but there are several more interesting ways of getting into Irian Jaya. These include a Pelni boat or plane from Sorong to the delightful colonial town of Fak Fak, from where there is a flight to Biak and Jayapura through Nabire; or a Pelni boat to Merauke, stopping off at several ports including Fak Fak and Agats (in the Asmat region), and flying from Merauke to Jayapura.

Garuda reportedly plans to re-introduce stopovers at Biak on its Los Angeles-Jakarta flight, but don't count on it.

PNG The only way into Papua New Guinea is to fly from Jayapura to Vanimo (every Sunday; US$63), just inside the PNG border, and on to Port Moresby (US$359). International departure tax from Jayapura is 14,500 rp.

Boat The sheer size of Irian Jaya, and the increasing number of transmigrants, means there are good Pelni connections with Maluku and the rest of Indonesia. The *Rinjani* has an interesting connection to Fak Fak from Ambon, through Bandaneira and Tual (south-east Maluku), and also goes to Java and Sulawesi; the *Tatamailau* covers all of Irian Jaya, and also connects it with south-east Maluku and Nusa Tenggara; the *Ciremai* connects all of the northern coast of Irian Jaya with Ternate (northern Maluku) and ports in Sulawesi and Java; and the *Dobonsolo* links the Irian Jayan north coast with Ambon, Nusa Tenggara and Java.

Getting Around

Air Merpati is the main carrier throughout Irian Jaya. Sorong is the hub for north-west Irian Jaya; Biak for the Cenderawasih Bay region and for connections to Jayapura; Jayapura for the Baliem Valley; and Merauke for the far south. Except for the regular and popular Merauke-Jayapura-Biak-Sorong route, most planes are tiny Twin-Otters, which are sometimes cancelled or delayed for any number of reasons.

Other possible alternatives are the missionary services, MAF (Mission Aviation Fellowship) and AMA (Associated Missions Aviation), which will take tourists if they have the room and have some notice. Cargo planes, such as Airfast, Trigana and SMAC, will take passengers between Jayapura and Wamena.

Boat Both coasts are well covered by two regular, comfortable Pelni liners. The *Tatamailau* meanders along both coasts as far as Jayapura and Merauke every four weeks, stopping off at every major town; and the *Dobonsolo* does a two-weekly trip along the northern coast. Less comfortable and regular boats, such as the Perintis KM *Ilosangi*, also travel between Jayapura, Sorong and Merauke every three weeks, and back again.

JAYAPURA & SENTANI

Once known as Kota Bahru, Hollandia and Soekarnopura, Jayapura is the capital and major town of Irian Jaya. Deliberately built by the Dutch next to the border of the former German New Guinea, Jayapura is an uninteresting modern Indonesian city, although it has a nice harbour setting.

Sentani, next to the airport (36 km from Jayapura), and near the shores of the magnificent lake Danau Sentani, is quieter, cooler and more convenient than Jayapura. Sentani has just about all the facilities you may need, so many people prefer to stay there. Jayapura and Sentani have a lot to offer, so try to stay a few days on your way to or from the Baliem Valley.

INDONESIA

Orientation

Just about everything you will need in Jayapura is confined to Jalan Ahmad Yani, and, parallel to it, Jalan Percetakan. Sentani is compact, with a lot of facilities on Jalan Kemiri Sentani Kota, the main road to Jayapura.

Information

The useful tourist office (☎ 33381, ext 2441), open weekdays from 7 am to 3 pm, is a bemo ride away from Jayapura, in the governor's office on Jalan Soa Siu Dok II. The best bank to change money is Bank Exim, which has branches on Jalan Ahmad Yani in Jayapura, and on the main road in Sentani.

In Jayapura, the post office and adjacent Telkom office are along the waterfront. In Sentani, the post office is on the main road, Telkom just behind it. The police stations in Sentani, at the entrance to the airport, and in Jayapura, on Jalan Ahmad Yani, are easy places to get that all-important surat jalan for the Baliem Valley.

Several good travel agencies can arrange local diving and sightseeing trips, as well as tours to the Baliem Valley and Asmat region:

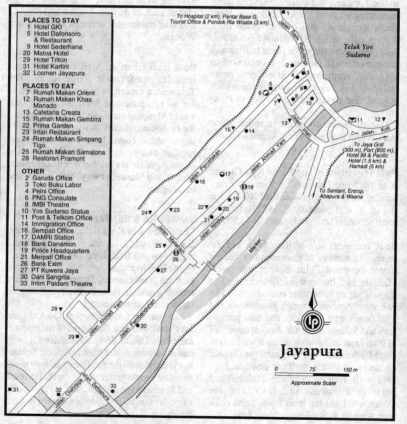

PLACES TO STAY
1 Hotel GKI
5 Hotel Dafonsoro & Restaurant
9 Hotel Sederhana
20 Matoa Hotel
29 Hotel Triton
31 Hotel Kartini
32 Losmen Jayapura

PLACES TO EAT
7 Rumah Makan Orient
12 Rumah Makan Khas Manado
13 Cafetaria Creata
15 Rumah Makan Gembira
22 Prima Garden
23 Intan Restaurant
24 Rumah Makan Simpang Tigo
25 Rumah Makan Samalona
28 Restoran Pramont

OTHER
2 Garuda Office
3 Toko Buku Labor
4 Pelni Office
6 PNG Consulate
8 IMBI Theatre
10 Yos Sudarso Statue
11 Post & Telkom Office
14 Immigration Office
16 Sempati Office
17 DAMRI Station
18 Bank Danamon
19 Police Headquarters
21 Merpati Office
26 Bank Exim
27 PT Kuwera Jaya
30 Dani Sangrila
33 Intim Paldam Theatre

To Hospital (2 km), Pantai Base G,
Tourist Office & Pondok Ria Wisata (3 km)

Teluk Yos
Sudarso

To Jaya Grill
(300 m), Port (800 m),
Hotel 99 & Pacific
Hotel (1.5 km) &
Hamadi (5 km)

To Sentani, Entrop,
Abepura & Waena

Jayapura

0   75   150 m

Approximate Scale

Dani Sangrila Tours & Travel
Jalan Pembangunan 19, Jayapura (☎ 31060)
Best Tours & Travel
Jalan Raya Sentani (the main road), Sentani (☎ 91861)
PT Kuwera Jaya
Jalan Ahmad Yani 39, Jayapura – especially good for diving and flights to PNG (☎ 31583)

The area code for Jayapura and Sentani is 0967.

PNG Consulate The PNG consulate (☎ 31250), open weekdays from 8 am to 4 pm, is currently at Jalan Percetakan 28. All foreigners need a visa to enter PNG. They take a day to issue, and you will need a ticket out of PNG, one photo and 20,000 rp.

Danau Sentani

This magnificent lake is worth a visit to Sentani in itself. You will see the 9630 hectare lake and its 19 islands as you fly in, and while travelling along the Sentani-Jayapura road. Renting a boat around the lake can be difficult – try at Yahim or Yabaso harbours or, easier but dearer, at the Yougwa (see below). For breathtaking views, take a bemo up Gunung Ifar to the **Tugu Mac-Arthur** statue. Alternatively, walk past the Hotel Mansapur Rani for an easy hour to the lake's shore. The *Pondok Wisata Yougwa* (☎ 71570) has rooms with no frills (or views) right on the lake, for 30,000 rp.

Museums

Along the Sentani-Abepura bemo route, three places are worth a look. The **Museum Negeri** has a small, but very good, collection of Irianese artefacts. Next door, the **Taman Budaya** (Cultural Park) is full of tacky and forlorn 'traditional houses' but it's free, so why not have a quick look? In the grounds of the University, the **Museum Loka Budaya** is particularly good for its assortment of Asmat carvings.

Beaches

Pantai Hamadi was the site of an American amphibious landing in 1944. The beach is nice, and there are rusting WWII wrecks and a statue nearby. The town has a bustling market, and several places to stay. Bemos to Hamadi leave every second or so (300 rp) from Jayapura.

Pantai Base G, known locally as Tanjung Ria, is another famous WWII site. The beach is a 15 minute walk from where the regular bemo (400 rp) drops you off. Good beaches and diving around **Depapre** are also accessible by bemo from Sentani.

Places to Stay

Jayapura The bottom of the price barrel belongs to *Losmen Jayapura* (☎ 33216), Jalan Olahraga 4, where poor singles/doubles, some with attached bath, start from 9600/14,400 rp. Far better is *Hotel Kartini* (☎ 31557), over the bridge at the top of Jalan Ahmad Yani, where rooms cost from 17,600/26,400 rp, more for private mandi. *Hotel Sederhana* (☎ 31561), Jalan Halmahera 2, is central. Clean rooms cost 25,300 rp, more with air-con.

Hotel GKI (☎ 33574) is a short walk up Jalan Sam Ratulangi. It has a pleasant outdoor sitting area, but the rooms, without mandis, for 20,400/33,000 rp are a bit dingy. Past the port, and on the way to Hamadi, *Hotel 99* (☎ 35689) and *Pacific Hotel* (☎ 35427), for around 25,000 rp a room, have a great location, but not the views you would expect. There are also places to stay in Hamadi.

Sentani The popular *Hotel Ratna* (☎ 91435), on the main road, has rooms with mandi for 30,000/40,000 rp. Just over the road, the *Hotel Minang Jaya* (☎ 91067) provides good local information and rooms from 24,000/35,200 rp with shared mandi. One of the best, the *Hotel Mansapur Rani* (☎ 91219), just around the corner from the airport, has rooms for 22,000/30,250 rp with private veranda and mandi.

In the middle range, the *Hotel Semeru* (☎ 91447), near the airport entrance, is the best at 46,750 rp per room with air-con.

Places to Eat

Jayapura Night warungs can be found near the Pelni office, along Jalan Ahmad Yani and around the waterfront. Along Jalan Percetakan, rumah makans *Gembira* and *Simpang Tigo* are simple (around 3000 rp a meal) and good, as is the restaurant in the *Hotel Dafonsoro* for choice. A little better, but dearer, is the *Restoran Hawaii*, under the IMBI Theatre. For the same views as the expensive *Jaya Grill*, *Rumah Makan Khas Manado*, on the way to the port, is recommended. Opposite the Merpati office, the *Prima Garden* is *the* place for Irianese coffee and cakes.

Sentani *Restoran Mickey* remains one of the most popular places in town, with meals from 3500 rp, and cold beer. Nearby, rumah makans *Maduratna* and *Aurina* serve great baked fish and rice meals from around 3000 to 5000 rp. The *Yougwa Restaurant*, on the Sentani-Abepura road, is definitely worth a visit for the views of Danau Sentani and the good, reasonably priced food.

Getting There & Away

Air Merpati flies daily to Biak (131,400 rp) and Merauke (185,300 rp), regularly to Nabire (157,800 rp) and at least twice a day to Wamena (77,500 rp). Merpati (☎ 33111) is at Jalan Ahmad Yani 15, Jayapura. Its office in Sentani (☎ 91314), on the main road, also handles bookings and confirmations.

For the same prices as Merpati, Garuda (☎ 36217) flies to Biak, Ujung Pandang and on to Jakarta, and Sempati (☎ 31612) goes to Ujung Pandang, Manado and Jakarta. Both their offices are on Jalan Percetakan, Jayapura.

If the Merpati flight to Wamena is full, or cancelled, try missionary flights run by AMA and MAF, which may take passengers, or the cargo services Airfast, Trigana and SMAC, which will do so. Their offices are around the airport or on the main road in Sentani.

Boat Jayapura is the start and finish for north coast runs by Pelni liners *Tatamailau* (every four weeks) and *Ciremai* and *Dobonsolo* (every two weeks). They go along the north coast as far as Sorong, and then on to major ports in Nusa Tenggara, Sulawesi, Java and Maluku. (The *Tatamailau* also heads down to Merauke.) Travelling by boat is an interesting way to quickly see a few places along the northern coast, such as Nabire, Manokwari and Biak. The Pelni office (☎ 21270) is on Jalan Halmahera, Jayapura, near the waterfront.

Getting Around

Sentani airport is 36 km from Jayapura. It's a hefty 25,000 rp by taxi from the airport to Jayapura. Try sharing a taxi with other equally stunned passengers, or take bemos. You can easily walk to your hotel in Sentani or take a 5000 rp taxi.

It takes three bemos, and an hour, to get from Sentani to Jayapura. From Sentani, take one to Abepura terminal (800 rp), then to Entrop terminal (400 rp) and then to Jayapura (350 rp). Bemos to most places leave every few seconds from around the streets of Jayapura; every minute or so from around the streets of Sentani.

PULAU BIAK

Pulau Biak, an important part of the battle for the Pacific in WWII, has numerous remnants of those horrific days, and is also a major Indonesian naval base. The island is small and has several attractions, although transport is limited in the north. The only major town, Kota Biak, and particularly the seaside villages of Bosnik and Korim, were heavily damaged by an earthquake and subsequent tidal wave in early 1996.

Kota Biak

Orientation & Information Kota Biak is a fairly compact town. A lot of what you need is along Jalans Ahmad Yani, Sudirman and Imam Bonjol, all of which meet at the Bank Exim building. This bank, and the nearby Bank Bumi Daya, will change money.

The main post office, the 24 hour Telkom office and the helpful tourist office (☎ 21663; open weekdays from 7.30 am to 3 pm) are a bemo ride away on the road to the airport. The police station on Jalan Diponegoro is an easy place to get permits for the region and for the Baliem Valley.

The area code for Biak is 0961.

Museum Cenderawasih On Jalan Sisingamangaraja, 10 minutes walk east of the Hotel Maju, this museum has a mildly interesting stockpile of regional Indonesian artefacts and some WWII memorabilia. Ask someone around the back of the museum to open up for you.

Places to Stay The cheapest are the *Hotel Solo* (☎ 21397) on Jalan Monginsidi, where singles/doubles with paper-thin walls cost 14,500/25,000 rp; and the rambling and inconvenient *Hotel Sinar Kayu* (☎ 22137), on Jalan Sisingamangaraja, for 12,000 rp per person. *Hotel Maju* (☎ 21841), on Jalan Imam Bonjol, is good value with rooms from 19,400/30,250 rp with mandi – ask for quieter rooms at the back.

Hotel Mapia (☎ 21383), Jalan Ahmad Yani 23, continues to be popular but is really decaying badly; rooms start at 13,915/21,780 rp, more for air-con and mandi. In the middle range, the *Basana Inn* (☎ 22281), virtually opposite the Maju, is about the best at 37,900/48,000 rp with welcome air-con and hot water.

Either side of the airport are two places that are good value as they include meals. To the west, the huge *Hotel Irian* (☎ 21939) has an agreeable lawn area to sit and admire the sea views; and to the east, the new *Airport Beach Hotel* (☎ 21496) is clean, quiet and has good service. Both charge from around 33,000/54,000 rp with fan and mandi.

Places to Eat Kota Biak isn't blessed with the greatest range of places to eat. Warungs naturally congregate around the markets and the bemo/bus terminal. On Jalan Imam Bonjol, the *Rumah Makan Jakarta* and *Restaurant 99* serve good, but a little overpriced, meals – Indonesian food costs from 3000 to 4000 rp; seafood twice as much. Better are the badly signed *Cinta Rosa* (open evenings only), near the Hotel Mapia, where baked fish meals cost 2700 rp, and, over the road, the *Restoran Cleopatra*. Opposite the Pelni office, on Jalan Sudirman, the *Nirwana* serves wonderful cold fruit drinks and cakes.

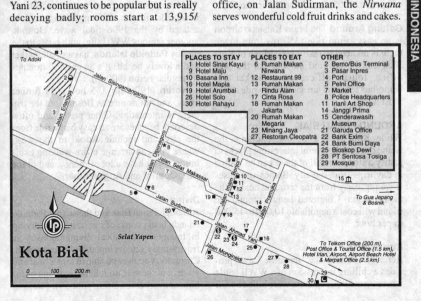

PLACES TO STAY	PLACES TO EAT	OTHER
1 Hotel Sinar Kayu	6 Rumah Makan	2 Bemo/Bus Terminal
9 Hotel Maju	Nirwana	3 Pasar Inpres
10 Basana Inn	12 Restaurant 99	4 Port
16 Hotel Mapia	13 Rumah Makan	5 Pelni Office
19 Hotel Arumbai	Rindu Alam	7 Market
26 Hotel Solo	17 Cinta Rosa	8 Police Headquarters
30 Hotel Rahayu	18 Rumah Makan	11 Iriani Art Shop
	Jakarta	14 Janggi Prima
	20 Rumah Makan	15 Cenderawasih
	Megaria	Museum
	23 Minang Jaya	21 Garuda Office
	27 Restoran Cleopatra	22 Bank Exim
		24 Bank Bumi Daya
		25 Bioskop Dewi
		28 PT Sentosa Tosiga
		29 Mosque

Kota Biak

To Adoki

Jalan Sisingamangaraja

Jalan Erlangga

Jalan Diponegoro

Jalan Selat Makassar

Jalan Sudirman

Jalan Imam Bonjol

Jalan Pramuka

Jalan Ahmad Yani

Jalan Monginsidi

Selat Yapen

15 🏛

To Gua Jepang & Bosnik

To Telkom Office (200 m), Post Office & Tourist Office (1.5 km), Hotel Irian, Airport, Airport Beach Hotel & Merpati Office (2.5 km)

0   100   200 m

Getting There & Away Biak is one of Irian Jaya's transport hubs, so many flights go through here. Merpati flies daily to Jayapura (131,400 rp) and Manokwari (108,200 rp); almost daily to Nabire (114,800 rp) and Ambon (277,600 rp); and a couple of times a week to nearby Serui (44,400 rp) on Pulau Yapen and tiny Pulau Numfor (62,000 rp). The perennially unhelpful and unreliable Merpati office (☎ 21213) is opposite the airport.

Garuda (☎ 21416), Jalan Sudirman 3, flies to Jayapura, Ujung Pandang and on to Jakarta. Garuda may re-introduce the stopover in Biak on its Los Angeles-Jakarta flight, but don't hold your breath.

Boat Pelni liners *Ciremai* and *Dobonsolo* (but not, surprisingly, the *Tatamailau*) stop in Biak and then go on to major ports in Java, Maluku, Nusa Tenggara and Sulawesi every two weeks. Other Perintis boats also regularly stop in Biak. If you have the time, a great way of coming to Irian Jaya is a leisurely boat trip to Biak, from where there are good connections elsewhere. The Pelni office (☎ 21065) is at Jalan Sudirman 37.

Getting Around The Frans Kaisiepo airport is an easy bemo ride (350 rp) from town; there is no need to take a taxi. Much of Kota Biak can be covered on foot but the post office, tourist office, main market and bemo/bus terminal are short bemo rides from most hotels.

AROUND PULAU BIAK

While Kota Biak isn't that exciting, the island does have several interesting places to justify a stopover. All of these can be visited in day trips from the city. Bemos and buses leave regularly from the terminal next to the main market. Chartered bemos around the island will cost a negotiable 10,000 to 15,000 rp per hour.

Gua Jepang

Actually a tunnel, the 'Japanese Cave' provides a chilling impression of a WWII battle where up to 5000 Japanese were killed by US bombs and fires. A museum next door has a fascinating array of WWII memorabilia. The easiest way to the cave is to take a bemo heading towards Bosnik, get off at Dennis Orchard Park (which is nothing to write home about) and walk a few hundred metres up the hill.

Wardo

The tiny village of Wardo, set in a pretty bay in the west, is definitely worth a visit. You can hire a boat and guide for an alluring ride along an overgrown jungle river to the **Wapsdori waterfalls.** Climb up a shaky ladder for a dip at the top. Bemos take an hour and cost 2200 rp.

Taman Burung dan Anggrek

On the way to Bosnik, the Bird and Orchid Park is worth a quick stop. It's about as close as you will probably get to a bird of paradise. You can also admire a double-eyed fig parrot and pink-spotted fruit dove, if you really want to.

Beaches

The island is littered with pretty beaches and beachside villages, although some were devastated by the 1996 tidal wave. **Bosnik**, another famous WWII site, with boats to the nearby **Padaido Islands**, has a small market and a lovely beach. It's an easy 30 minutes by regular bemo (900 rp).

Korim (1900 rp; 1½ hours) is further away, and not as nice as Bosnik, but the trip there is interesting. Other pretty, and often deserted, beaches are an easy bemo ride from the city, and include **Adoki** to the west, where you can arrange a fire-walking exhibition if you have a lot of money, and to the east, **Oparief** and **Anggaduber**.

Diving

Although Pulau Biak and the nearby Padaido Islands boast some of the best scuba diving in Indonesia, the local diving industry is frustratingly undeveloped and unorganised. Currently, you *may* be able to rent a boat and guide, but there is no reliable equipment for hire, or instructors. Bring your own gear, and ask around at the travel agencies Janggi Prima (☎ 22973), Jalan Pramuka 5, or Sentosa Tosiga (☎ 21398), opposite the Hotel Mapia; the Hotel Biak Beach, at Bosnik; or the tourist office. The best time to dive is between April and September.

TELUK CENDERAWASIH

Stretching from Manokwari to the far east of Pulau Yapen, and incorporating the Cenderawasih Marine Reserve, the Cenderawasih Bay region is easily the most underrated and undervisited part of Irian Jaya. With outstanding diving and trekking, wildlife, deserted beaches, isolated islands, traditional cultures and easy-going towns, the region's potential is, however, still hindered by limited transport and government prohibitions.

Manokwari

The first place in Irian Jaya to be inhabited by missionaries (in 1855), Manokwari is easy to get around and well connected, and nearby there's trekking in the Arfak Mountains, the Anggi Lakes and islands such as Pulau Rumberpon.

The area code for Manokwari is 0962.

In Manokwari itself, an easy five km walk takes you through the lush **Taman Gunung Meja** park, which has plenty of butterflies and a Japanese WWII memorial. A good beach, **Pasir Sen Babai**, is easy to get to, and a canoe trip to **Pulau Mansinam** is a real must.

A good of range of accommodation includes *Hotel Pusaka Sederhana* (☎ 21263), on Jalan Bandung, where comfortable singles/doubles cost about 15,000/20,000 rp with mandi; *Hotel Apose* (☎ 21369), opposite the Merpati office, from 15,000/20,000 rp without mandi; and the *Hotel Arfak* (☎ 21293), Jalan Brawijaya, for city views and decaying charm, from 30,000/36,000 rp.

At the top of Jalan Jenderal Sudirman, rumah makans *Hawai* and *Kebun Sirih* are pretty good; otherwise try some of the cheap places around the Hotel Pusaka and the terminal/market.

Merpati flies infrequently to Sorong (159,900 rp), and daily to Biak. Merpati (☎ 21133), on Jalan Kota Baru, is open in the morning and evening only. One of the three Pelni liners servicing the north coast stops in Manokwari at least every week.

Anggi Lakes

Set 2030 metres high in the Arfak Mountains, the twin lakes of Danau Gigi and Danau Gita offer exquisite scenery and wildlife, and excellent walking and swimming. From Manokwari, Merpati flies to Anggi twice a week (30,200 rp; 25 minutes). Alternatively, catch a regular bus to Ransiki (7000 rp; three hours) and ask at the district office for a guide to the lakes. From Ransiki the trek takes two or three days. You will need to bring all your own gear, and remember that it is always cold at night. At Anggi, you can stay at the home of the village head.

Pulau Yapen

This elongated, mountainous island south of Pulau Biak is home to various species of the *cenderawasih*. There's also great scuba and skin diving at nearby Pulau Arambai, but bring all your own gear. Yapen is pleasant enough, but suffers from limited facilities and has little to justify a detour.

The main town, Serui, has three losmen. The best, *Hotel Merpati* (☎ 31186), has singles/doubles for 27,000/45,000 rp including meals, and is also the location of the Merpati office (☎ 31620). Merpati flies daily to Biak (42,300 rp) only. The Pelni liner *Tatamailau* comes by about twice a month, and there are regular ferries to Biak.

Nabire

Nabire is a worthy stopover on the way to Biak, Jayapura or Wamena. It's a particularly pleasant town, with wide streets, and nearby beaches and islands to explore. And for some reason no one (yet) has learnt how to say 'hello mister'!

The area code for Nabire is 0964.

The best places to stay are *Hotel Nusantara* (☎ 21180) – which also houses the Merpati office (☎ 21591) – on Jalan Pemuda, for

16,800/24,000 rp, more with mandi and meals; and *Hotel Anggrek* (☎ 21066), on Jalan Pepera, for 17,500 rp per person without mandi or meals. Try the warungs on the waterfront for huge baked fish.

Merpati flies daily to Biak (114,800 rp), and to Jayapura (203,900 rp) almost every day. The flight from Nabire to Mulia, from where you can get a connection to Wamena, is an interesting entry into the Baliem Valley – if current government regulations allow.

The Lake Paniai region, which has as much potential as the Baliem Valley for experiencing unique scenery and culture, is still off limits, but this may change. If regulations allow, you can take a Merpati flight to Enarotali (60,900 rp).

BALIEM VALLEY

Easily the most popular destination in Irian Jaya, and the most accessible place in the interior, is the Baliem Valley, where the Dani people were only 'discovered' in 1938. While the Danis have adopted many modern conveniences, and the main town, Wamena, has some up-to-date facilities, the valley is one of the truly fascinating traditional areas still left in the world.

Even in Wamena, some Dani men still wear penis gourds and nothing else. As the evening falls, men stand with their arms folded across their chests to keep warm. You'll regularly see Dani women, dressed only in a grass skirt, carrying string bags from their heads, heavily loaded with vegetables, and even babies and valuable pigs.

The Danis maintain their polygamous marriage system – a man may have as many wives as he can afford. Brides have to be paid for in pigs and the man must give five or six pigs to the family of the wife. Grass skirts usually indicate that a woman is unmarried, although in some parts of the valley married women also wear them. One of the more unusual, but increasingly outdated, customs is for women to amputate part of their fingers when a close relative dies.

For several days every August, Wamena and nearby villages host a spectacular tourist festival with pig feasts, mock wars and traditional dancing.

Wamena

The main town in the Baliem Valley, Wamena is a neat, spread-out place. Although there's not much in the town itself, it's a good base from which to explore nearby villages and the countryside. Wamena is expensive compared with the rest of Indonesia but this is understandable as *everything* has to be flown in from Jayapura.

Orientation & Information While the focal point of town is the scruffy Pasar Nayak Market, a lot of what you will need is on, or near, Jalan Trikora. Bank Exim, and the incongruous Bank Rakyat Indonesia, both on Jalan Trikora, change money. The post office is on Jalan Timor, and the 24 hour Telkom office on Jalan Thamrin.

The new tourist office (☎ 31365), open from 8 am to 2 pm daily except Sunday, is at the top of Jalan Yos Sudarso. It's worth a walk or becak ride out there as soon as you arrive to get current information about trekking, guides, markets, festivals and so on.

The area code for Wamena is 0969.

Surat Jalan You *must* have a surat jalan, or travel permit, if you want to stay in Wamena and the Baliem Valley. You can't get one in Wamena but they're easy to obtain in Biak, Jayapura and Sentani. On the surat jalan, list every place you wish to visit, and take a few photocopies to give to regional police stations.

Your surat jalan will be stamped by the police on arrival and departure at the Wamena airport. You must also report to the local police if you stay outside of Wamena, eg at sub-district centres such as Jiwika and Kurima, but this is usually unnecessary if you're trekking to remote areas. Some more isolated places in the valley may be off limits; the police station on Jalan Safri Darwin in Wamena will fill you in on the current situation.

Travel Agencies Several good – and some not so good – travel agencies catering for trekking tours of the Baliem Valley have sprung up in Wamena, and in Jayapura and Sentani (see the Jayapura & Sentani section for details). In Wamena, the most reliable agencies are Best Tours & Travel (☎ 32101), Jalan Trikora, opposite Hotel Trendy; and, one of the first and best, Chandra Nusantara Tours & Travel (☎ 31293), Jalan Trikora 17.

Places to Stay *Hotel Syahrial Jaya* (☎ 31306), on Jalan Gatot Subroto, a five minute walk south of the airport, is the cheapest place in town, but is no longer great value at 20,000 rp per room. *Hotel Anggrek* (☎ 31242), on Jalan Ambon, is central and comfortable. Singles/ doubles cost 22,000/ 33,000 rp; more with mandi, and hot water is usually available to all guests.

Nayak Hotel (☎ 31067), directly opposite the airport, is noisy. Its large rooms with mandi cost from 35,000/45,000 rp. *Srikandi Hotel* (☎ 31367), Jalan Irian 16, is quiet, friendly and worth a try; rooms with an enormous bathroom are 30,000/35,000 rp. *Hotel Trendy* (☎ 31092), at the north end of Jalan Trikora, has a terrible name but good rooms (better at the front) for 27,000/33,000 rp.

There is very little value in the middle-to-top range; air-con isn't really needed, and most places don't even offer hot water. The best in this range (and one of the best in Irian Jaya) is the *Pondok Wisata Putri Dani* (☎ 31223), Jalan Irian 40. Spotless and very comfortable rooms cost 40,000 rp; 55,000 rp with mandi. The *Baliem Cottages* (☎ 31370), on Jalan Thamrin, has huge, quiet and modern 'Dani huts' from 45,000 rp.

See the Around the Baliem Valley section for cheap alternatives – mostly Dani-style huts – in villages near Wamena.

Places to Eat Other than a few Padang-style places around the market, most restaurants seem to serve the same sort of food for the same sort of price – ie 3000 to 5000 rp for Indonesian food, or 9000 to 10,000 rp a dish for chicken, or locally caught prawns or fish, with one of three different sauces.

The better places are the convenient *Rumah Makan Mas Budi*, on one side of the Hotel Trendy; on the other side, the *Rumah Makan Reski* has good 'Chainese' food; and *Kantin Bu Lies*, next to the airport, is good for simple Indonesian food. For a small splurge, and a bit of a walk up Jalan Yos Sudarso, the *Mentari Restoran* is definitely recommended.

Wamena is officially a 'dry area', so no alcohol is available. If you're desperate, some of the better hotels may be able to find something for you at an outrageous price.

Things to Buy Souvenir shops selling locally made items of varying quality have sprung up around the market and along Jalan Trikora. Alternatively, you can buy things in the villages or from the increasing number of sellers roaming the streets of Wamena. Naturally, bargaining is the order of the day, and in the villages bartering is also acceptable. If you cannot get to the Asmat region (and most people won't), Wamena is the place to pick up some quasi-authentic Asmat carvings.

Readily available souvenirs include string bags (a *noken*) from 4000 to 10,000 rp; intricate hand-woven bracelets; grass skirts (*jogal* or *thali*); necklaces of cowrie shells (*mikak*); the inevitable penis gourd (*horim*) from 1000 to 20,000 rp, depending on size(!) and materials; black stone axes for around 10,000 rp, far more for the better ones; and carved bows, arrows and spears from around 6000 rp.

Getting There & Away Merpati flies several times a day between Jayapura and Wamena (77,500 rp). Flights are often in heavy demand, so book early and reconfirm regularly. The Merpati office (☎ 31080) is at Jalan Trikora 41. If regulations allow, an interesting way into or out of Wamena is the twice weekly Merpati flight to Mulia, from where there is a connection to Nabire in the Cenderawasih Bay area.

Missionary services, MAF and AMA, have offices around the Wamena airport. They are useful for chartering planes to obscure places, but they're not really interested in being an alternative tourist airline.

A better alternative if the Merpati flight is

INDONESIA

full, or has been cancelled, is one of the cargo services. They are more expensive (but usually more reliable) than Merpati – around 82,000 rp from Wamena to Jayapura when the planes are empty, more for the other way. Airfast (☎ 31053), Trigana (☎ 31611) and SMAC (☎ 31567) have offices around the Wamena airport.

Getting Around Wamena is easy enough to walk around. Becaks for a very negotiable 500 to 1000 rp normally congregate around the market, but disappear at night and often, it seems, when it rains!

AROUND THE BALIEM VALLEY

Trekking is certainly the best way to see particular scenery, special ceremonies and more remote cultures. But if you do not have the time, money or inclination to trek, don't be put off coming to the Baliem Valley. With the increasing number of places to stay in the valley, and more transport along new and improving roads, many visitors will be able to see all the traditional people and customs, mummies, markets, scenery and wild pigs they want during day trips from Wamena, Jiwika and Kurima.

Trekking

This is great hiking country but travel light; trails are muddy and slippery. You often have to clamber over stone fences, ford streams and cross trenches and creeks on bridges made of rough wooden planks or a slippery log. Rivers are crossed by dugout canoes or rafts made of three logs loosely lashed together and pushed along with a pole.

It's normally cold at night, and it often rains, so bring warm clothes, an umbrella or jacket, and, if you're camping, a waterproof tent. You can buy food, water and a lot of cooking equipment in Wamena, although it will be expensive. Bring everything else with you.

Staying in village huts, or the homes of teachers or leading local families, should cost from 5000 to 10,000 rp per person per night, or your guide may be able to build makeshift wooden shelters. There are simple Dani-style huts and losmen in a few villages between Akima and Jiwika, as well as in Manda, Kurima and near Wosilimo.

Guides A real cutthroat guide industry has emerged in Wamena. Guides will latch onto you as soon as you arrive and, if you show any interest, they will never let go. Before committing yourself to a guide, decide if you really want to go trekking (as opposed to day-tripping from Wamena and other villages), ask other travellers and think about where you want to go and for how long.

Prices depend on where you go, for how long, how many in the group and your bargaining power. As a general rule, a good licensed guide will cost from about 20,000 to 30,000 rp per day and a porter around 10,000 rp.

Alternatively, the tourist office and the tourist information counter at the airport can arrange licensed (and probably cheaper) guides and porters for you. There are no proper maps of the Baliem Valley; some hotels sell a passable map, but don't rely on it for trekking.

Transport

Hopelessly overcrowded bemos go almost as far south as Kurima (1500 rp); as far north, on the western side of the valley, as Pyramid (3000 rp); and as far north on the eastern side as Manda (2500 rp). To go anywhere else, or to avoid these sardine cans on wheels, you can hire bemos from the terminal for a very negotiable 10,000 to 15,000 rp per hour.

Rafting

Rafting down the Sungai Baliem between August and November is now possible. Trips for five days or more from Manda to Kurima, staying in Dani homes along the way, cost from US$450 per person. Inquire at Dani Sangrila Tours & Travel in Jayapura.

Baliem Valley – Central & South

Virtually a 'suburb' of Wamena, **Wesaput** is an easy stroll across the runway. The only museum in the valley, the **Palimo Adat Museum**, with its limited collection of local artefacts, is at the end of the trail. On the way, the *Wio Silimo Tradisional Hotel* is one of the best Dani-style places around. It costs 20,000 rp per room.

Behind the museum, a long swinging bridge leads to **Pugima**, a flat one hour walk away. Pugima isn't that exciting, but the trail goes past some charming Dani villages and scenery. At the end of Jalan Yos Sudarso, **Sinatma** has charming walks around the Sungai Wamena, a market and a swinging bridge (broken at the time of our visit).

The road south passes through the village of **Hitigima**. An hour or so on foot from Hitigima (you will need to ask directions or take a guide) are some saltwater wells. The road south stops a few km short of **Kurima**, a good base in the south – the *Kuak Cottage* losmen is reasonable. From Kurima, there's more great trekking to places like **Hitugi**, a few hours away. A popular two or three day trek is Wamena-Kurima-Hitugi-Pugima-Wamena.

Baliem Valley – East

Near Pikhe, the northern road crosses the mighty Sungai Baliem and passes **Akima**, which is only notable for its mummy. Between Akima and Jiwika, an interesting, flat three to four hour walk, several Dani-style huts with Dani-style mandis and breakfast – all for 10,000 rp per person – have been built.

The better ones are: *Pondok Wisata Dani Homestay*, just south of Jiwika; *PW Tumagunem Indah* in Mulima village; and the very pleasant *Pondok Wisata Suroba Indah* in **Suroba**. Suroba, a serene village set 20 minutes off the main road, is worth a stop to admire the countryside and the intricate hanging bridges.

Jiwika (1000 rp by frequent bemo) is a good base. The comfortable *Lauk Inn* has simple rooms without mandi for 11,000 rp; the same sort of rooms with mandi are less value at 20,000/35,000 rp. An hour's scramble above the village are some salt wells, and there's a mummy nearby.

North of Jiwika, the **Gua Kotilola** caves are worth a look; ask to be dropped off because there is no sign. In **Wosilimo**, the

Gua Wikuda caves are more interesting. An hour's walk west of Wosilimo, **Danau Anegerak** lake has fish and some huts to stay in. From Wosilimo, a hiking trail continues to, and beyond, Pass Valley. Also popular is the one to two day trek from Wosilimo to Pyramid via Meagaima and Pummo.

Public transport continues north to **Manda**, where there are authentic (ie muddy) Dani-style huts and more pretty countryside. From Manda, treks start to the Wolo Valley.

Baliem Valley – West

There isn't a great deal on this side of the valley for trekking, but it's worth a bemo trip anyway as far as **Pyramid**, a graceful missionary village with churches, a theological college, an airstrip and a bustling weekly market. You may be able to stay at **Kimbim**, the nearby sub-district centre. Kimbim is a reasonable place, with some shops and the local police station.

From Pyramid, popular treks go to **Kelila** in the north and to **Pietriver** in the west. If trekking, take the trail along the Sungai Baliem from Kimbim to Pummo and on to Wamena through Muai, rather than the dull, direct Pyramid-Wamena road.

Danau Habbema

A popular two day trek from Wamena is to Habbema lake. There are two ways there: a trekking trail from Elagaima, through Ibele; or a vehicle path from Sinatma, through Walaek and along the Sungai Wamena. If trekking, you'll need to camp and bring everything. If you don't fancy this, a chartered return bemo will set you back about 120,000 rp.

SOUTH COAST

An underrated and underdeveloped part of Irian Jaya is the extensive southern coast stretching from Sorong to Merauke. Most of the coast is swamp, many of the smaller towns have limited facilities, and transportation is often infrequent and unreliable, but it's certainly worth the effort if you have the time and an adventurous streak.

Every four weeks, the Pelni liner *Tatamailau*

INDONESIA

goes up and down the south coast, with detours to south-east Maluku. Other more basic boats meander up and down the coast as well. You cannot travel the full length of the coast by air.

Sorong

Sorong is a spectacularly uninteresting oil, logging and administrative port. But it is the centre for regional air and sea transport, so you may be stuck here waiting for a connection.

The best places to stay, for around 20,000 rp per room, are the *Hotel Batanta* (☎ 21569), opposite the soccer ground, where rooms have a mandi and TV; and the *Hotel Indah* (☎ 21514), near the small boat harbour, has mandis and views. Baked fish and incredible sunsets can be enjoyed at, or places near, the *Hotel Irian Beach*.

Besides the *Tatamailau* to Merauke, Sorong is also the start of the northern coastal runs of the *Dobonsolo* and *Ciremai*. Merpati (☎ 21402), in the Hotel Grand Pacific, has daily flights to Ambon (145,600 rp) and Biak (178,600 rp), and regularly to Fak Fak (114,800 rp). Jefman airport is spectacularly but inconveniently located on Pulau Jefman. From the airport take a speedboat or longboat with everyone else; *to* the airport, check with Merpati for the ferry schedule.

Fak Fak

The first Dutch settlement on Irian Jaya, Fak Fak (it *is* pronounced *that* way) is a lovely colonial town and well worth a visit. Set along a sparkling bay, the main road, Jalan Izaak Telussa, on which most things are located, is reminiscent of a small European seaside village (except for the mosque, that is!).

The area code for Fak Fak is 0956.

Fak Fak's attractions are hindered by limited local transport, however. Nearby beaches, islands, waterfalls and amazing WWII remnants and rock paintings around **Kokas** will take some effort to reach. A boat ride to **Pulau Tubir Seram** is easy, and a must.

On Jalan Izaak Telussa, the *Hotel Marco Polo* (☎ 22228) has dorm-style beds for 18,000 rp, and the *Hotel Tembagapura* (☎ 22530) has good-value singles/doubles for 17,500/27,500 rp. The Tembagapura has the best restaurant, and warungs along the street above the main road serve huge, baked fish.

Fak Fak is connected by air as part of the almost daily, but sometimes unreliable, Twin-Otter Sorong-Fak Fak-Kaimana-Nabire route. The Merpati office (☎ 22130) is also on the main road. A two-weekly connection on the Pelni liner *Rinjani* with Bandaneira (Banda Islands) and Ambon make Fak Fak an interesting way into Irian Jaya; and every four weeks the *Tatamailau* sails by.

Asmat Region

The coastal area towards Merauke is known as the Asmat region, named after its indigenous people who are famous for their woodcarvings. The Asmat people are semi-nomadic, and their life naturally revolves around the rivers, which are subject to huge tides. To explore the area will take a great deal of time and money: Agats and the Asmat region are nowhere near as developed and accessible as Wamena and the Baliem Valley.

The main village is Agats. Built on wooden laneways above the water, Agats has no vehicles, one bank (which changes money), sporadic electricity, one restaurant and no telephones. There are only two places to stay; the better is the *Asmat Inn*, which charges about 15,000 rp per person. The **Museum Kebudayaan dan Kemajuan** has a small, authentic display of Asmat art. Travelling around the Asmat region from Agats will cost a whopping 200,000 rp or so per day for a 10 person longboat.

Agats is connected to the rest of the world by the *Tatamailau* about once a month. At the time of our visit, the Ewer airport (a boat ride from Agats) had been closed for eight months, with no sign of re-opening. If the airport does open again, infrequent Merpati flights go to Ewer from only Merauke.

Laos

Laos has been known from antiquity as Lan Xang, or Land of a Million Elephants, and by Indochina War-era journalists as the Land of a Million Irrelevants. It is one of the least developed and most enigmatic countries in Asia. With its 4.5 million inhabitants spread over more than 200,000 sq km, Laos has been spared the population pressures of neighbouring countries.

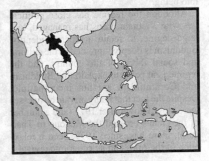

Facts about Laos

HISTORY

The country has long been occupied by migrating Thai-Kadais (an ethnolinguistic family that includes Shans, Siamese, Lao and many smaller tribes) and by Hmong-Mien hill tribes practising slash-and-burn cultivation (as they do to this day). The first Lao *meuang* (districts or principalities), however, were consolidated in the 13th century following the invasion of south-western China by Kublai Khan's Mongol hordes.

In the mid-14th century a Khmer-sponsored Lao warlord, Fa Ngum, formed his own kingdom, Lan Xang, out of a large coalition of meuangs around the town of Luang Prabang. Although the kingdom prospered in the 14th and 15th centuries, it came under increasing pressure from its neighbours and also suffered from internal divisions. In the 17th century it split up into three warring kingdoms centred on Luang Prabang, Wieng Chan (Vientiane) and Champasak.

By the end of the 18th century most of Laos came under Thai suzerainty but there was also pressure from the Vietnamese to pay tribute. Unable or unwilling to serve two masters, the country went to war with Siam in the 1820s. After this disastrous challenge, all three kingdoms fell under Thai control. Throughout the 19th century France was busy establishing French Indochina in the Vietnamese kingdoms of Tonkin and Annam. By 1893 the French and the Siamese had fashioned a series of treaties that put Lao territories under the protection of the French.

During WWII, the Japanese occupied Indochina and a Lao resistance group, Lao Issara, formed to prevent a return to French rule at war's end. The Franco-Laotian Treaty of 1953 granted full independence to Laos but conflict persisted between royalist, neutralist and Communist factions. The US bombing of the Ho Chi Minh Trail in eastern Laos commenced in 1964 and greatly escalated the conflict between the royalist Vientiane government and the Communist Pathet Lao.

Although the ground war in Laos was far less bloody than in Vietnam or Cambodia, the bombing of eastern Laos caused many casualties and, eventually, the displacement of most of the population of the eastern provinces, a process that went on until a ceasefire was negotiated in 1973. By this time, Laos had the dubious distinction of being the most bombed country in the history of warfare (the USA dropped more bombs on Laos between 1964 and 1973, on a per capita basis, than it did worldwide during WWII).

A coalition government was formed but, with the fall of Saigon in April 1975, it became clear which way the political wind

LAOS

was blowing and most of the rightists went into exile in France. In December 1975 the Lao People's Democratic Republic came into being.

Although the regime has close political ties with Vietnam, Laos has managed, to a large degree, to retain a separate identity. Buddhism is deeply ingrained in the cultural and social fabric of the country, and the regime is at pains to explain that Buddhism and Communism are not incompatible. Despite the fact that many private businesses were closed down after 1975 (and a number of merchants crossed the Mekong to Thailand), there has, since 1979, been a relaxation of the rules and an economic revival.

GEOGRAPHY

Laos covers 235,000 sq km and is bordered by Thailand, Cambodia, Vietnam, China and Myanmar (Burma). Over 70% of the country is mountains and plateaus, and two-thirds is forested.

Most of the population is settled along river valleys. The largest river, the Mekong, or Nam Khong, runs the entire length of the country. It provides fertile floodplains for agriculture and is the main transportation artery.

CLIMATE

The annual Asian monsoon cycle gives Laos two distinct seasons: May to October is wet and November to April is dry.

Average precipitation varies considerably according to latitude and altitude, with southern Laos getting the most rain overall. The peaks of the Annamite Chain receive the heaviest rainfall, over 300 cm annually.

The provinces of Luang Prabang, Sainyabuli and Xieng Khuang, for the most part, receive only 100 to 150 cm a year. Vientiane and Savannakhet get about 150 to 200 cm, as do Phongsali, Luang Nam Tha and Bokeo.

Temperatures vary according to altitude. In the Mekong River Valley (from Bokeo Province to Champasak Province), as in most of Thailand and Myanmar, the highest temperatures occur in March and April

(these temperatures approach 38°C, or 100°F) and the lowest occur in December and January (as low as 15°C, or 59°F).

In the mountains of Xieng Khuang, however, December/January temperatures can easily fall to 0°C, or 32°F, at night. In mountainous provinces of lesser elevation, temperatures may be a few degrees higher. During most of the rainy season, daytime temperatures average around 29°C (84°F) in the lowlands, and around 25°C (77°F) in mountain valleys.

See the Vientiane climate chart in the Appendix.

ECOLOGY & ENVIRONMENT

Although major disruptions were wreaked on the eastern section of the country along the Ho Chi Minh Trail (where herbicides and defoliants – not to mention bombs – were used in abundance during the war), Laos as a whole has one of the most pristine ecologies in mainland South-East Asia. Along with Cambodia, it is also the most understudied country in the region in terms of zoological and botanical research.

In 1993 the Lao government conferred legal protection upon 17 national biodiversity conservation areas (NBCAs), for a total of 24,600 sq km, or just over 10% of the country's land mass. Most of them are in southern Laos, which bears a higher percentage of natural forest cover than the north. The largest of the NBCAs, Nakai-Nam Theun, covers 3710 sq km and is home to the newly discovered Vu Quang ox.

As in many developing countries, one of the biggest obstacles facing environmental protection is corruption among those in charge of enforcing conservation regulations. Illegal timber felling and the smuggling of exotic wildlife species would decrease sharply if all officials were held accountable for their civil duties. Most Lao still lead their lives at or just above a subsistence level, consuming comparatively much less of their own natural resources than the people of any 'developed' country. The frugal country ranks 99th in the world with regard to per-capita energy consumption by the kg-oil-equivalent measure.

FLORA & FAUNA

According to the International Union for the Conservation of Nature & Natural Resources (IUCN), natural, unmanaged vegetation covers 85% of Laos. About half the country (47% to 56%, depending on which source you believe) bears natural forest cover. Of these woodlands about half can be classified as primary forest – a very high proportion in this day and age – while another 30% or so represents secondary growth. The country's

percentage of natural forest cover ranks 11th, ahead of Malaysia and just behind Indonesia.

Although the official export of timber is tightly controlled, no one really knows how much teak and other hardwoods may be being smuggled out of the country into China, Vietnam and Thailand. During the Indochina War, the Pathet Lao allowed the Chinese and Vietnamese to take as much timber as they wanted from the Liberated Zone (11 provinces in all) in return for building roads.

In addition to teak and Asian rosewood, the country's flora includes a toothsome

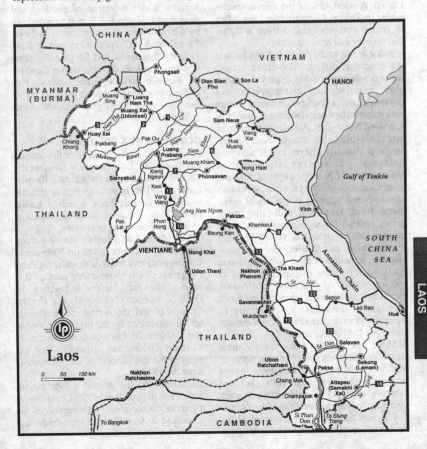

array of fruit trees (see the Food section in the Regional Facts for the Visitor chapter earlier in this book), bamboo (more species than any country outside Thailand and China) and an abundance of flowering species, including orchids. In the high plateaus of the Annamite Chain, extensive grasslands, or savanna, are common.

As in Cambodia, Vietnam, Myanmar and much of Thailand, most of the fauna in Laos belongs to the Indochinese zoogeographic realm (as opposed to the Sundaic domain found south of the Isthmus of Kra in southern Thailand or the Palearctic to the north in China). Around 45% of the animal species native to Thailand is shared by Laos, often in greater numbers because there is higher forest cover and fewer hunters.

Notable mammals found in Laos include the concolor gibbon, snub-nosed langur, lesser panda, raccoon dog, pygmy slow loris, giant muntjac, Lao marmoset rat and Owston's civet. Other species common to an area that overlaps neighbouring countries in mainland South-East Asia are a number of macaques (pig-tailed, stump-tailed, Assamese and rhesus), Phayre's leaf monkey, François' leaf monkey, Douc langur, Malayan and Chinese pangolin, Siamese hare, six species of flying squirrel, 10 species of non-flying squirrel, 10 species of civet, marbled cat, Javan and crab-eating mongoose, spotted linsang, leopard cat, Asian golden cat, bamboo rat, yellow-throated marten, lesser mouse deer, serow (a goat-antelope sometimes called Asian mountain goat), goral (another goat-antelope) and 69 species of bats. Around 3000 wild Asiatic elephants roam areas of open-canopy forest throughout the country, especially in Sainyabuli Province north-west of Vientiane and along the Nakai Plateau.

More rare are the endangered Asiatic jackal, Asiatic black bear, Malayan sun bear, Malayan tapir, barking deer, sambar (a type of deer), gaur, banteng (both gaur and bantengs are types of wild cattle), leopard, tiger, clouded leopard and Irrawaddy dolphin.

The most exciting regional zoological discovery of recent years has been the detection of a previously unknown mammal, the spindlehorn bovid – also known as the Vu Quang ox (*saola* in Vietnam, *nyang* in Laos) – a horned animal found in the Annamite Chain along the Lao-Vietnamese border.

A few Javan one-horned and/or Sumatran two-horned rhinos, probably extinct in neighbouring Thailand, are thought to survive in the Bolaven Plateau area of southern Laos. Sightings of kouprey, a wild cattle extinct elsewhere in South-East Asia, have been reported in Attapeu and Champasak provinces as recently as 1993.

The pristine forests and mountains of Laos harbour a rich selection of resident and migrating bird species. Surveys carried out by a British team of ornithologists in 1992-93 recorded 437 species, including eight globally threatened and 21 globally near-threatened species. Notable among these are the Siamese fireback, green peafowl, red-collared woodpecker, brown hornbill, tawny fish-owl, sarus crane, giant ibis and Asian golden weaver.

GOVERNMENT & POLITICS

Since 1975 the official name of the country has been the Lao People's Democratic Republic (Sathalanalat Pasathipatai Pasason Lao), or LPDR. Informally, it is acceptable to call the country Laos, which in Lao is Pathet Lao – *pathet*, from the Sanskrit *pradesha*, means land or country.

The ruling Lao People's Revolutionary Party (LPRP) is modelled on the Vietnamese Communist Party and is directed by the Party Congress, which meets every four or five years to elect party leaders. In practice, the Political Bureau (Politburo), the Central Committee and the Permanent Secretariat are all dominated by the Prime Minister of the Council of Government (currently Khamtay Siphandone), a position that has enjoyed the full support of the Vietnamese since the 1940s.

Interestingly, the country's constitution, which was only drafted in 1990, contains no reference to socialism with regard to the economy; it formalises private trade and fosters foreign investment.

The country is divided into 16 provinces (*khwaeng*) plus the prefecture of Vientiane. Below the province is the meuang, or district, which comprises two or more *tasseng* (subdistricts or cantons), which are in turn divided into *ban* (villages).

ECONOMY

Although rich in minerals, Laos has not yet exploited these resources. Major exports include hydroelectricity and forestry products. Most goods come via Thailand and the Mekong but a highway to Danang in Vietnam has now been completed.

Agriculture, fishing and forestry is carried out by 80% of the population. There is very little manufacturing and foreign aid makes up a large portion of the annual national budget. Much of the domestic trade occurs on the openly tolerated free market. Markets throughout Laos trade freely in untaxed goods smuggled in from Thailand (and elsewhere) and the changing of currency (mostly US dollars and Thai baht) at free market rates is quite open. Laos is still one of the poorest countries in the world, with an annual per capita income of about US$325.

POPULATION & PEOPLE

The population of Laos is 4.5 million and about half are lowland Lao, most of whom inhabit the Mekong River Valley. Of the remaining half, 10% to 20% are estimated to be tribal Thai (who live in upland river valleys), 20% to 30% are Lao Theung (lower mountain-dwellers mostly of proto-Malay or Mon-Khmer descent) and 10% to 20% are Lao Sung (Hmong or Mien hill tribes who live at higher altitudes).

EDUCATION

Laos' public school system is organised around five years at the *pathom* (primary) level beginning at age six, followed by three years of *mathayom* (middle) and three years of *udom* (high) school. In reality less than three years of formal education is the national norm, and most teachers themselves have spent less than five years in school.

The country has only two complete universities, Dong Dok University and Phaetsaat University, plus two technical colleges, all four of which are in Vientiane. Together they enrol a very small percentage of the school-age population.

Although the national literacy rate is 84%, if urban areas (representing only 15% of the population) aren't included, the reading rate drops to around 45%.

ARTS

Lao art and architecture can be unique and expressive, although limited in range. Most is religious in nature. This includes the pervasive image of Buddha and the *wat*, or temple/monastery. Distinctively Lao is the Calling for Rain Buddha, a standing image with a rocket-like shape. Wats in Luang Prabang feature *sim*, or chapels, with steep, low roofs much like the Lanna style in the north of Thailand. The typical Lao *thâat*, or stupa, is a four-sided, curvilinear, spire-like structure – the best national example is perhaps That Luang in Vientiane. Many other stupas show Thai or Sinhalese influence.

The upland folk crafts include gold and silversmithing among the Hmong and Mien tribes, and tribal Thai weaving (especially among the Thai Dam and Thai Lú). Classical music and dance have been all but lost in Laos. Traditional folk music is still quite popular, however, and usually features the *khaen*, or Lao pan-pipe. Modern Lao pop, derived from folk traditions, is also quite popular. In the Mekong River Valley, many Lao favour Thai music, which is heard over the radio and imported on cassette tapes.

SOCIETY & CONDUCT

Historically, traditional culture in Laos has been much influenced by various strains of Khmer, Vietnamese and Thai cultures which entered the territory during periods when Lao principalities were suzerains of these countries. As the lowland Lao and the various Thai tribes are all descended from a common ancestry, the similarities between Lao and Thai culture are strong.

LAOS

Many of the same standards of conduct which apply for Thailand also apply in Laos. Touching another person's head is taboo and so is the pointing of one's feet at another person or at a Buddha image. Strong displays of emotion are highly discouraged.

When greeting a Lao, the traditional gesture is the *phanom* or *wai*, a prayer-like placing together of the palms in front of the face or chest. Nowadays, the handshake is becoming more commonplace, for both men and women.

RELIGION

Most lowland Lao are Theravada Buddhists. Many Lao males choose to ordain as monks temporarily, typically spending anywhere from a week to three months at a wat. Monks are forbidden to promote *phíi* (spirit) worship, which has been officially banned in Laos along with *sāiyasaat* (folk magic). Although the worship of phíi is officially forbidden, it remains the dominant non-Buddhist belief system in the country. Even in Vientiane, Lao citizens openly perform the ceremony called *sukhwān* or *basi*, in which the 32 guardian spirits known as *khwān* are bound to the guest of honour by white strings tied around the wrists. Each of the 32 khwān are thought to be guardians over different organs in a person's body.

Outside the Mekong River Valley, the phíi cult is particularly strong among tribal Thai, especially the Black Thai (Thai Dam). Priests *(māw)* who are specially trained in the propitiation and exorcism of spirits preside at important Black Thai festivals and other ceremonies.

The Khamu and Hmong-Mien tribes also practise animism and the latter group combine ancestral worship. During the 1960s some Khamu participated in a 'cargo cult' that believed in the millennial arrival of a messianic figure who would bring them all the trappings of western civilisation. Some Hmong also follow a Christian version of the cargo cult in which they believe Jesus Christ will arrive in a jeep, dressed in combat fatigues. The Akha, Lisu and other Tibeto-Burman groups mix animism and ancestor

cults, except for the Lahu, who worship a supreme deity called Geusha.

LANGUAGE

The official language is Lao, as spoken and written in Vientiane. It's spoken with differing accents and with slightly differing vocabularies as you move from one part of the country to the next, especially in a north to south direction, but the Vientiane dialect is widely understood. Like Thai and Chinese, it's a mostly tonal language with simple grammar. The standard dialect makes use of six separate tones – the word *sao*, for example, can mean 'girl', 'morning', 'pillar' or '20' depending on the tone.

All dialects of Lao are closely related to languages spoken in Thailand, northern Myanmar and pockets of China's Yunnan Province. Standard Lao is close enough to standard Thai (as spoken in central Thailand) that, for native speakers, the two are mutually intelligible. French and English compete for status as the second language, with Russian a distant third. Generally speaking, older Lao will speak some French and younger Lao some English or Russian.

Basics

Greetings.	*sa-bāi-dịi*
No. (or not)	*baw*
Thank you.	*khàwp jại*
How are you?	*sa-bāi-dịi baw?*
(I'm) fine.	*(khàwy) sa-bāi-dịi*
It doesn't matter.	*baw pẹn nyāng*

Getting Around

(I) want to go to ...	*... yàak pại*
(I) want a ticket.	*yàak dâi pîi*
Where is the ...?	*... yuu sāi?*
bus	*lot bát or lot méh*
pedicab	*sāam-lâw*
boat	*heúa*
post office	*pại-sá-níi*
station	*sá-thāa-níi*

Accommodation

hotel	*hóhng háem*
room	*hàwng*

toilet	*hàwng nâam (rest room)/sùam (commode)*
bath/shower	*àap nâam*
Do you have ...?	*mǐi ... baw?*
How much?	*thao dǎi?*

Food

market	*talàat*
restaurant	*hâan ąahǎan*

(I) don't like it hot and spicy.
  baw mak phét
(I) only eat vegetarian food.
  khàwy kịn jẹh

Health & Emergencies

(I) need a doctor.	*tâwng-ką̄an mǎw*
hospital	*hóhng pha-yáa-ba̧an*
doctor	*thaan mǎw*
Help!	*suay dae!*
Stop!	*yút!*
I'm lost.	*khàwy puay*

Numbers

1	*neung*
2	*sǎwng*
3	*sǎam*
4	*sìi*
5	*hâa*
6	*hók*
7	*jét*
8	*páet*
9	*kâo*
10	*síp*
11	*síp-ét*
12	*síp-sąwng*
20	*sáo*
21	*sáo-ét*
30	*sǎam-síp*
40	*sìi-síp*
50	*hâa-síp*
100	*neung hâwy*
200	*sǎwng hâwy*
300	*sǎam hâwy*
1000	*neung phán*
10,000	*neung méun*

Facts for the Visitor

PLANNING
When to Go

The best overall time for visiting most of Laos is between November and February – during these months it rains least and is not too hot. If you plan on focusing on the mountainous northern provinces, the early rainy season – say May to July – is not bad either, as temperatures are moderate at higher elevations.

Extensive road travel in remote areas like Attapeu, Phongsali and Sainyabuli may be impossible during the main rainy season, July to October, when roads are often inundated or washed out for weeks, even months at a time. River travel makes a good alternative during these months.

Maps

Lonely Planet has a full-colour *Laos* travel atlas. It contains 48 pages and includes topographic shading, a 1:1,000,000 scale and the most up-to-date road and place naming scheme for Laos so far published anywhere. Travellers might find the travel atlases to the adjacent countries of Vietnam and Thailand handy also.

The National Geographic Service in Vientiane has produced a series of adequate maps of Laos and certain provincial capitals.

TOURIST OFFICES

The government-sponsored Lao National Tourism Authority (LNTA) was established in Vientiane in the late 1980s as the sole travel agency and tour operator in the country. Following the privatisation of the travel business in the early 90s, its function as a travel agency has declined substantially, although the office can still arrange tours and guides for travel around the country. Its private competitors (see Organised Tours in the Getting Around section later in this chapter) do a better job, however.

One of the LNTA's main functions these days seems to be arranging expensive tourist

LAOS

visa extensions; all applicants who visit the immigration department in Vientiane are now referred to the LNTA.

The LNTA office (☎ /fax 212013) is on Thanon Lan Xang opposite the Centre du Langue Française in Vientiane.

VISAS & DOCUMENTS

Most travellers to Laos enter on a 14 day tourist visa, which, at last report, is usually issued only through travel agencies authorised by the LNTA. Lao embassies will occasionally issue tourist visas directly to individuals but the only way to find out is to apply, as their decisions seem to be made on an individual basis (it's never automatic). Visas from embassies and consulates typically cost US$15 to 20, while if you go through an agency they start at US$40 and can reach over US$100. In some countries you may be required to book a package tour in order to get the visa.

In Thailand you can easily arrange Lao visas through travel agencies in Bangkok, Chiang Mai, Chiang Khong, Nong Khai, Ubon Ratchathani and Udon Thani. Costs range from 1500B to 2700B depending on the agency and on the speed of visa delivery. Generally speaking the cheaper services take up to five business days to issue a visa, while the more expensive services usually provide one within 24 hours or less.

At the new Lao consulate (☎ 223698, 221961) at 123 Photisan Road in Khon Kaen, Thailand, foreigners have successfully obtained 15-day tourist visas in three days time for 750B to 1000B, depending on nationality. Apparently this is an experimental programme, since the Lao embassy in Bangkok does not issue such visas directly.

Tourist visas are usually obtainable from Lao embassies in the capitals of the neighbouring countries of Cambodia (US$20) and Myanmar (US15). The Lao consulate in Kunming, China, issues Lao tourist visas for US$28.

The transit visa is the easiest visa to get but is the most restricted. It is intended for air stopovers in Vientiane for passengers travelling between two other countries. For example, it's common to request this type of visa when travelling between Hanoi and Bangkok. The visa is granted upon presentation of a confirmed ticket between the two destinations. The maximum length of stay for the transit visa is 10 days (some embassies and consulates offer only five to seven days) and no extension is allowed. No travel is permitted outside the town of Vientiane on this visa. The fee for this visa is usually US$10 to 12.

Persons with a professed investment interest in Laos can easily obtain business visas via Lao sponsors, valid for 30 days, directly from any Lao embassy.

Visa Extensions

Tourist visas issued through a travel agency abroad usually come with notes scribbled alongside them that limit the tourist visa holder to applying through a specified travel agent in Vientiane for visa extensions. If you obtained your tourist visa directly from a Lao embassy abroad, you should theoretically be able to extend your visa at any immigration office in Laos. In actual practice only a few offices – usually the more remote ones – will grant extensions. At the time of writing, the Luang Prabang immigration office was no longer granting tourist visa extensions; in Luang Nam Tha, Attapeu and several other of the more remote areas extensions were readily available. In some of these areas an extension is available even if your visa was arranged by a travel agency.

The cost of an extension is highly variable depending on the level of corruption at the particular agency or immigration office with which you're dealing. In Vientiane the immigration office was referring all applicants to the LNTA office on Thanon Lan Xang, where an extension could be arranged with an hour's worth of paperwork and a cost of US$3 a day. Some travel agencies were charging US$4 to US$5 per day. In the provinces the immigration offices usually charge US$1 a day, although some asked for more. Many travellers have reported being able to negotiate the extension fee downwards.

A second or even third extension of up to

15 days is possible from most sources, though some immigration offices upcountry have been known to baulk at the idea. If you anticipate needing to stay more than a month in Laos, you should investigate the possibility of obtaining a non-immigrant visa or a business visa.

The transit visa cannot be extended under any circumstances.

Overstaying Your Visa If you overstay your visa, you will have to pay a fine at the immigration checkpoint upon departure from Laos. The standard fine at the moment is US$5 for each day you've stayed beyond the visa's expiry date.

TRAVEL RESTRICTIONS

For nearly 20 years following the 1975 revolution, the Lao government required travel permits *(bại anuyâat dọen tháang* in Lao or *laissez passer* in French) for all travel outside Vientiane Prefecture. Both foreigners and Lao citizens were required to carry them. In March 1994 the permit system was abolished and foreigners are now theoretically free to travel throughout most of the country without any special permission other than a valid passport containing a valid visa.

Recent travel experience suggests that local permits may still be required in areas where there's considerable undetonated ordnance (eg the Ho Chi Minh Trail) and in 'sensitive' areas like Sainyabuli (insurgents, opium), Hua Phan (re-education camps, the Pathet Lao caves) and most of the new Saisombun Special Zone – what used to be eastern Vientiane Province at the borders of Luang Prabang, Xieng Khuang and Bolikhamsai provinces. The latter area is militarily insecure and is plagued by attacks on vehicles passing through; for more information see Dangers & Annoyances later in this section.

Some of the more 'remote' provinces like Sekong, Attapeu and Hua Phan are still run like independent fiefdoms by the local police, and in these areas travellers may occasionally come across officials who bar

entry. In such cases it's best simply to obey the orders of the police and head in the opposite direction; it's no use arguing with people who have the power to incarcerate you indefinitely without trial.

Checkpoints

The Lao government still has one major way of keeping track of your whereabouts. Each time you enter and leave a province – whether by land, air or water – you must stop at a customs or police office and get *jâeng khào* and *jâeng àwk* ('inform enter' and 'inform leave') rubber stamps on your departure card or on a slip of blank paper provided by the checkpoint officials. The police usually collect a charge for this service, anywhere from 100 to 1500 kip per chop.

Every airport in the country has a desk or booth where officials check arriving and departing passengers in and out of the province, so if you're flying it's easy to comply with regulations. For road and river travel there are very few controls in most places and local officials don't seem to care whether you're stamped in or not. In fact, it can be very difficult to locate anyone who will give you the necessary chops. A major exception is Luang Prabang, where there has recently been an all-out effort to 'capture' as many unstamped visitors as possible in order to collect a 3000 kip penalty. See the Luang Prabang section later in this chapter for details on how the police try to entrap visitors.

Failing to get stamped in or out seems to be a fairly minor offence in most places. The main risk is being sent back to a place you've already been. It's worth keeping abreast of the general trends regarding interprovincial stamps. As with visa extensions, it's an area that remains very fluid.

EMBASSIES
Lao Embassies

If you're going to Laos on a tourist visa, you most likely won't deal directly with any Lao embassy, since tour agencies handle all visa arrangements. To apply for a visa on your own, you can try one of these embassies:

Australia
    1 Dalman Crescent, O'Malley, Canberra, ACT 2606 (☎ (06) 286-4595)
China
    11 E 4th St, Sanlitun, Chao Yang, Beijing (☎ (010) 532-1224)
    Consulate: N 23 Haigeng Rd, Room 501, Kunming (☎ (0871) 414-1678)
USA
    2222 'S' St NW, Washington, DC 20006 (☎ (212) 667-0058)

See the other chapters in this book for Lao embassies in those countries.

Foreign Embassies in Laos

Seventy-five nations have diplomatic relations with Laos, of which around 25 maintain embassies and consulates in Vientiane (many of the remainder, for example Canada and the UK, are served by their embassies in Bangkok, Hanoi or Beijing). The addresses and telephone numbers of the principal consular offices are listed below and several of the more important ones (embassies that Lonely Planet readers are likely to visit) are indicated on the Vientiane map.

Australia
    Thanon Phonxai Noi (☎ 413610, 413805)
Cambodia
    Thanon Saphan Thong Neua (☎ 314952)
China
    Thanon Wat Nak Yai (☎ 315103)
Malaysia
    Thanon That Luang (☎ 414205)
Myanmar (Burma)
    Thanon Sok Pa Luang (☎ 314910)
Thailand
    Thanon Phon Kheng (☎ 214582, 214585)
USA
    Thanon That Dam (Bartholomie) (☎ 212580, 212581)
Vietnam
    Thanon That Luang (☎ 413400, 413409)

CUSTOMS

Customs inspections at ports of entry are very lax as long as you're not bringing in more than a moderate amount of luggage. You're not supposed to enter the country with more than 500 cigarettes or one litre of distilled spirits. All the usual prohibitions on drugs, weapons and pornography apply, otherwise you can bring in just about anything you want, including unlimited amounts of Lao and foreign currency.

MONEY
Costs

Except for the high rates travel agencies charge to arrange visas, Laos is a relatively inexpensive country to visit by most standards. Outside Vientiane basic local hotels and guesthouses typically charge 1000 to 2000 kip per bed, nicer places 5000 to 8000 kip. Tourist hotels start at US$25 a night.

The average meal in a Lao restaurant costs less than US$2 per person. A cup of coffee costs about US$0.21, a huge bowl of *fŏe* (rice noodles) around US$0.53 upcountry or US$0.75 in Vientiane and a litre of draught beer just US$0.70.

Bus transport averages around US$0.12 to US$0.28 per km depending on road conditions; the worse the road, the more expensive the ride. Flying cuts into your budget but over long hauls saves time and thus hotel and food costs. Sample fares: Vientiane to Luang Prabang US$46, Luang Prabang to Xieng Khuang US$31, Vientiane to Pakse US$95.

In Vientiane or Luang Prabang you can squeeze by for about US$10 a day if you stay in the cheaper guesthouses and eat local food; in remote areas where everything's less expensive you can whittle this figure down to around US$6 to US$8 a day.

Currency

The official national currency is the kip. Although only kip is legally negotiable in everyday transactions, in reality the people of Laos use three currencies for commerce: kip, Thai baht and US dollars.

Notes come in denominations of 1, 5, 10, 20, 50, 100, 500 and 1000 kip. Kip coins (aat) were once available but are being withdrawn from circulation since anything below one kip is virtually worthless.

Currency Exchange

Exchange rates include:

Australia	A$1	=	685 kip
Canada	C$1	=	674 kip
France	FF10	=	1879 kip
Germany	DM1	=	642 kip
Japan	¥100	=	893 kip
New Zealand	NZ$1	=	601 kip
Thailand	100B	=	3652 kip
UK	UK£1	=	1425 kip
USA	US$1	=	920 kip

Changing Money

With some exceptions the best exchange rates are available at banks rather than money-changers. At banks, travellers' cheques receive a slightly better exchange rate than cash. Banks in Vientiane can change UK pounds, German marks, Canadian, US and Australian dollars, French francs, Thai baht and Japanese yen only. Outside Vientiane most provincial banks will accept only US dollars or Thai baht.

The best overall exchange rate is generally offered by the Banque pour le Commerce Extérieur Lao (BCEL; Lao Foreign Trade Bank in English). Licensed moneychangers also maintain booths around Vientiane and at some border crossings. Without exception their rates and commissions are not as good as the exchange at BCEL or other banks; their only advantage is being open longer hours.

Outside Vientiane and Luang Prabang it can be difficult to change travellers' cheques; even at Wattay airport the moneychanger is sometimes short of kip (be sure to ask whether they can cover your cheque(s) before signing). Hence visitors are advised to carry plenty of cash outside Vientiane. If you plan to carry Thai baht and US dollars along for large purchases (as is the custom), be sure to arrange your cash stash in these currencies before you leave the capital. Even in Luang Prabang, the most touristed town in Laos after Vientiane, it is impossible to get anything but kip at the bank.

As part of the 'baht bloc' (along with Thailand and Cambodia), Laos relies most heavily on the Thai baht for the domestic cash economy. If you plan on making major transactions (eg over US$40 each) you can save luggage space by carrying most of your cash in baht, along with smaller amounts of kip and dollars. A workable plan would be to carry half your cash in Thai baht and a quarter each in kip and US dollars. But if you plan to make only small purchases (under US$40 per transaction) and you won't be travelling more than a few days, carry kip.

Credit Cards

Many hotels, upscale restaurants and gift shops in Vientiane accept Visa and Master-Card credit cards. A few also accept American Express; the national representative for Amex is Diethelm Travel Laos.

BCEL on Thanon Pangkham offers cash advances/withdrawals on MasterCard credit/debit cards for a 2% to 3% transaction fee depending on whether you take kip, baht or US dollars. For Visa, BCEL adds a further half percent commission. Thai banks in Vientiane charge more.

Outside of Vientiane credit cards are virtually useless.

Parallel Market Rates

Officially the kip is a free-floating currency but in reality higher rates than those offered by licensed banks are usually available from retail shops and non-licensed, freelance moneychangers in Vientiane. Typically these rates run about 20 to 25 kip more per dollar – with no commission – for crisp US$100 or B1000 notes.

Tipping & Bargaining

Tipping is not customary in Laos except in upscale Vientiane restaurants where 10% of the bill is appreciated – but only if a service charge hasn't already been added to the bill.

Anything bought in a market should be bargained for; in some shops prices are fixed while in others bargaining is expected (the only way to find out is to try). In general the Lao are gentle and very scrupulous in their bargaining practices. A fair price is usually arrived at quickly with little attempt to gouge

LAOS

the buyer (some tour operators are an exception to this rule).

Remember there's a fine line between bargaining and niggling – getting hot under the collar over 100 kip (about US$0.14) makes both seller and buyer lose face.

POST & COMMUNICATIONS
Post
Outgoing mail from Vientiane is fairly dependable and inexpensive but incoming mail is unreliable. Forget about mailing things from upcountry Laos. Local residents and expats who work outside Vientiane save their mail and pass it on to acquaintances who are going to Vientiane or Thailand.

Telephone
The domestic phone service is inefficient, with phones often unserviceable and lines down, especially in the rainy season.

International calls can be made only from Vientiane. IDD has recently become available at selected locations in Vientiane, including the Public Telephone Office on Thanon Setthathirat in Vientiane, which is open daily 7.30 am to 10 pm.

To make international calls from Laos, the international access code is 00.

To call Laos from outside the country, the country code is 856.

Fax, Telex & Telegraph
At the Public Telephone Office in Vientiane fax/telex/telegraph services are available daily from 7.30 am to 10 pm.

In provincial capitals fax, telex and telegraph services are handled at the GPO or at the separate telephone office, where such exists.

BOOKS
Lonely Planet's *Laos – travel survival kit* has more detailed information on Laos and is the only current guide to the country in English.

Some accounts of the country's recent pre-1989 history include *Contemporary Laos: Studies in the Politics & Society of the Lao People's Democratic Republic*, edited by Martin Stuart-Fox, and, by the same author, *Laos: Politics, Economics & Society*, which provides a better overview. More up-to-date is *Laos: Beyond the Revolution*, edited by Joseph Zasloff and Leonard Unger, a collection of essays on political and economic history to 1989. The 1991 *The Ravens: Pilots of the Secret War in Laos* by Christopher Robbins is a highly readable history of the US-directed secret air war.

Visitors interested in Lao weaving should have a look at Patricia Cheesman's *Lao Textiles: Ancient Symbols – Living Art*, which offers a thorough and well-illustrated explanation of the various weaving styles and techniques – old and new – found in Laos.

Atlas des ethnies et des sous-ethnies du Laos by Laurent Chazee, published in 1995 and sold in Bangkok and Vientiane, is based on ethnographic research accomplished between 1988 and 1994. This colour-illustrated book comes with a map tucked into a pocket in the back cover which diagrams the locations of 119 ethnic groups in Laos.

NEWSPAPERS & MAGAZINES
The *Vientiane Times* is a weekly English-language newspaper produced by the Ministry of Information & Culture. For the most part it's a business-oriented paper, with occasional articles on Lao culture and a short but useful list of ongoing cultural events and social activities in the capital. Since all the staff are government employees, the paper is careful not to print anything critical of the government or anyone in the government.

The government controls all distribution of the *Bangkok Post* and it is legally available only by subscription. Day-old issues of the *Post* can be purchased at Phimphone Mini-mart in Vientiane but the paper is rarely seen elsewhere in Laos except in government offices! Raintree Bookstore in Vientiane carries *Time, Asiaweek, Far Eastern Economic Review* and a few other news periodicals – but not the *Bangkok Post*.

RADIO & TV
Laos has one radio station, Lao National Radio. English-language news is broadcast

twice daily on LNR but most expats prefer the English-language news available from the usual short-wave radio programming. With a short-wave radio you can easily pick up BBC, VOA, Radio Australia, Stockholm Radio, Radio Manila, Radio France International and others with transmitters in South-East Asia.

Lao National Television sponsors two TV channels – 3 and 9 – which can only be received in the Mekong River Valley and are only broadcast from 7 to 11 pm nightly. Typical fare includes Lao-dubbed episodes of ALF and Roadrunner cartoons. Most Lao watch Thai television, which can be received anywhere in the Mekong River Valley. Thailand's channels 5 and 9 telecast a variety of English-language programmes.

Satellite TV setups can pick up transmissions from many Asian satellites.

PHOTOGRAPHY

Colour print film is readily available in larger towns like Vientiane, Savannakhet and Luang Prabang. Kodak Ektachrome and Fuji Sensia slide film is available at reasonable prices at a few photo shops in Vientiane. Outside Vientiane, slide film of any kind is rare. For black and white film or other types of slide film bring your own supply.

Military installations, soldiers or airports are not to be photographed. Some hill tribes have strong taboos against having their photos taken, so always ask first.

ELECTRICITY

Laos uses 220V AC circuitry; power outlets most commonly feature two-prong round or flat sockets. Bring adaptors and transformers as necessary for any appliances you're carrying. Adaptors for common European plugs are available at shops in Vientiane.

Blackouts are common during the rainy season, so it's a good idea to bring a torch (flashlight).

WEIGHTS & MEASURES

The international metric system is the official system for weights and measures in Laos. Shops, markets and highway signs for the most part conform to the system. In rural areas distances are occasionally quoted in *meun*; one meun is equivalent to 12 km. Gold and silver are sometimes weighed in *bàat*; one *bàat* is 15g.

HEALTH
Opisthorchiasis

Travellers in Laos should be on guard against liver flukes (opisthorchiasis). These are tiny worms that are occasionally present in freshwater fish in Laos. The main risk comes from eating raw or undercooked fish – in particular, avoid eating *pạa dạek*, which is fermented fish used as an accompaniment to rice.

A much less common way to contract liver flukes is by swimming in rivers – the only known area where this may happen is the Mekong River around Don Khong (Khong Island) in southern Laos, near the Cambodian border.

See the Health section in the Appendix for more information.

TOILETS & SHOWERS

In both design and custom, toilets and showers in Laos are much the same as in Thailand; see the relevant section in the Thailand chapter for descriptions.

WOMEN TRAVELLERS

Everyday incidents of sexual harassment are much less common in Laos than in virtually any other Asian country. Lonely Planet, in fact, has had no reports of any such incidents among visitors to Laos so far. In general, all visitors to Laos are treated with the utmost respect and courtesy.

Comparisons with Thailand are inevitable, and the two are rather similar with regard to women's social status. One major difference between the two countries is that prostitution is much less common in Laos, where it is a very serious criminal offence. While a Thai woman who wants to preserve a 'proper' image usually won't associate with foreign males for fear of being perceived as a prostitute, in Laos this is not the case (although a Lao woman generally isn't seen alone with any male in public unless married). But Lao women drink beer and *lào-láo* (rice liquor), something 'proper' Thai females rarely do (even in Bangkok).

Hence a foreign woman seen drinking in a cafe or restaurant isn't usually perceived as 'loose' or available as she might be in Thailand. This in turn means that there are generally fewer problems with uninvited male solicitations.

What *is* often perceived as improper or disrespectful behaviour by foreign females is the wearing of clothes that bare the thighs, shoulders or breasts. Long trousers and walking shorts (for men too), as well as skirts, are acceptable attire; tank tops, sleeveless blouses and short skirts or shorts are not.

GAY & LESBIAN TRAVELLERS

Lao culture is very tolerant of homosexuality, although there is not as prominent a gay/lesbian scene as in neighbouring Thailand. Public displays of affection – whether heterosexual or homosexual – are frowned upon.

DISABLED TRAVELLERS

With its lack of paved roads or footpaths (sidewalks) – even when present the latter are often uneven – Laos presents many physical obstacles for the mobility-impaired. Rarely do public buildings feature ramps or other access points for wheelchairs, nor do any hotels consistently make efforts to provide handicapped access. Hence you're pretty much left to your own resources. Public transport is particularly crowded and difficult, even for the fully ambulatory.

DANGERS & ANNOYANCES

Laos seems to be remarkably free of petty theft, at least in relation to visitors. Ordinary precautions, such as locking your hotel room door and keeping your valuables in a secured place, should of course be followed.

One known trouble spot is the area around Kasi on the Vientiane to Luang Prabang road. Anti-government rebels have been known to attack vehicles along this road with small arms, grenades and rocket-launchers.

In late 1995 two French travellers on a public bus from Luang Prabang to Kasi were wounded in such an attack.

Another section of road where there were frequent ambushes between 1993 and 1995 was the western portion of Route 7 in Xieng Khuang Province, between the road's westernmost terminus at Route 13 and its crossing over the Nam Ngum river near Muang Sui (east of Phonsavan). An Australian engineer was killed in this area in early 1995 and several Lao have also died in attacks. At the moment military checkpoints along this section of Route 7 turn back anyone travelling without military escort.

South of the aforementioned road is Saisombun Special Zone, a new administrative district which was definitely *not* safe at the time of writing. Carved out of eastern Vientiane, south-western Xieng Khuang and north-western Bolikhamsai provinces in 1994, this 7105 sq km district (larger than the province of Bokeo) is considered a 'troubled' area. Four UN Drug Control Programme staff – all Lao – died in an attack in this zone in 1994 and there have been some vicious attacks on local buses as well. The Lao government created the new zone with the intent of clearing up the guerrilla/bandit problem in the area and have stationed two military battalions here to accomplish the task.

Route 6 north of Pakxan through Saisombun Special Zone to just south of Muang Khun (Xieng Khuang Province) continues to be plagued with security problems. North of Muang Khun, all the way to Sam Neua in Hua Phan Province, this road is relatively safe.

BUSINESS HOURS

Government offices are generally open from 8 to 11 am and 2 to 5 pm. Shops and private businesses open and close a bit later, and either stay open during lunch or close for just an hour.

PUBLIC HOLIDAYS & SPECIAL EVENTS

The Lao Buddhist Era (BE) calendar figures year one as 638 BC (not 543 BC as in Thailand), which means that you must subtract

638 from the Lao calendar year to arrive at the Christian calendar familiar in the west (eg 1990 AD is 2628 BE according to the Lao Buddhist calendar).

Festivals in Lao are mostly linked to agricultural seasons or historic Buddhist holidays. The general word for festival in Lao is *bun* (or *boun*).

Magha Puja (*Makkha Bu-saa*, Full Moon)
February – This commemorates a speech given by Buddha to 1250 enlightened monks who came to hear him without prior summons. Chanting and offerings mark the festival, culminating in the candlelit circumambulation of wats throughout the country.

Vietnamese Tet & Chinese New Year
February – This is celebrated in Vientiane, Pakse and Savannakhet, with parties, deafening nonstop fireworks and visits to Vietnamese and Chinese temples. Chinese and Vietnamese-run businesses usually close for three days.

Pii Mai
The 15th, 16th and 17th of April are official public holidays – The lunar new year begins in mid-April and practically the entire country comes to a halt and celebrates. Houses are cleaned, people put on new clothes and Buddha images are washed with lustral water. Later the citizens take to the streets and dowse one another with water.

International Labour Day
1 May is a public holiday.

Visakha Bu-saa (*Visakha Puja*, Full Moon)
May – This falls on the 15th day of the 6th lunar month, which is considered the day of the Buddha's birth, enlightenment and *parinibbana*, or passing away. Activities are centred on the wat, with much chanting, sermonising and, at night, beautiful candlelit processions.

Bun Bang Fai (Rocket Festival)
May – This is a pre-Buddhist rain ceremony that is now celebrated alongside Visakha Puja in Laos and north-eastern Thailand. This can be one of the wildest festivals in the country, with plenty of music and dance (especially the irreverent *măw lám* performances), processions and general merrymaking, culminating in the firing of bamboo rockets into the sky.

Khao Phansaa (*Khao Watsa*, Full Moon)
July – This is the beginning of the traditional three-month 'rains retreat', during which Buddhist monks are expected to station themselves in a single monastery. This is also the traditional time of year for men to enter the monkhood temporarily, hence many ordinations take place.

Awk Phansaa (*Awk Watsa*, Full Moon)
October/November – This celebrates the end of the three-month rains retreat. Monks are allowed to leave the monasteries to travel and are presented with robes, alms-bowls and other requisites of the renunciative life.

Bun Nam (Water Festival)
October/November – Held in association with Awk Phansaa. Boat races are commonly held in towns located on rivers, such as Vientiane, Luang Prabang and Savannakhet.

That Luang Festival (Full Moon)
November – This takes place at Pha That Luang in Vientiane. Hundreds of monks assemble to receive alms and floral votives early in the morning on the first day of the festival. There is a colourful procession between Pha That Luang and Wat Si Muang. The celebration lasts a week and includes fireworks and music, culminating in a candlelit circumambulation (*wien thien*) of That Luang.

Lao National Day
2 December – This celebrates the 1975 victory of the proletariat over the monarchy with parades, speeches etc. It is a public holiday.

ACTIVITIES
Boating

The rivers and streams of Laos provide potential venues for all sorts of recreational boating, particularly rafting, canoeing and kayaking. No modern equipment exists, however, so it's strictly bring your own. Nor are there any regular bamboo-raft trips as in Thailand, though the country is prime territory for it.

As with bicycles, you shouldn't have any special customs difficulties in bringing your own small boat to Laos. Because of the difficulties of overland transport, however, the smaller and lighter your craft is, the more choices you'll have for places to paddle.

Cycling

The overall lack of vehicular traffic makes cycling an attractive proposition in Laos, although this advantage is somewhat offset by the general absence of roads in the first place. For any serious out-of-town cycling you're better off bringing your own bike, one that's geared to very rough road conditions. For obvious routes to avoid, see Dangers & Annoyances earlier in this section.

LAOS

Hiking & Trekking

Laos' mountainous, well-forested geography makes it a potentially ideal destination for people who like to walk in the outdoors. All 13 provinces have plenty of hiking possibilities, although the generally cautious nature of the authorities means that overnight trips that involve camping or staying in villages are viewed with suspicion. So far not a single travel agency in Laos has been granted permission to lead overnight treks in any of the tribal areas, though several have tried to arrange such itineraries.

Warning: In the eastern portions of the country towards the Vietnamese border – particularly in the provinces of Hua Phan, Xieng Khuang, Sekong and Attapeu – there are large areas contaminated by unexploded ordnance left behind by nearly 100 years of warfare. Travellers should exercise caution when considering off-road wilderness travel in these provinces. Never touch an object on the ground that may be an unexploded ordnance, no matter how old, crusty and defunct it may appear.

Provinces in Laos with the highest potential for relatively safe wilderness walking include Bokeo, Champasak, Khammuan, Luang Nam Tha, Luang Prabang and Vientiane. In particular the 17 newly designated National Biodiversity Conversation Areas (NBCAs) should yield rewarding territory for exploration (see Ecology & Environment in the previous Facts about Laos section).

COURSES
Language Study

Short-term courses in spoken and written Lao are available at the following study centres in Vientiane:

Centre de Langue Française
    Thanon Lane Xang (☎ 215764)
Lao-American Language Center
    152 Thanon Sisangvon, Ban Naxay (☎ 414321; fax 413760)
Mittaphap School
    Km 3 Tha Deua (☎ 313452)
Saysettha Language Centre
    Thanon Nong Bon, Ban Phonxai (☎ 414480)

Vientiane University College
    Thanon That Luang, opposite the Ministry of Foreign Affairs (☎ 414873; fax 414346)

Meditation Study

If you can speak Lao or Thai, or can arrange an interpreter, you may be able to study *vipassana* (insight meditation) with Ajaan Sali, the abbot of Wat Sok Pa Luang in south-east Vientiane. See under Wat Sok Pa Luang in the Vientiane section later in this chapter for more details.

WORK

With Laos' expanding economy and the quickening influx of aid organisations and foreign companies, the number of jobs available to foreigners increases slightly each year, although one can't count on finding employment immediately. By far the greatest number of available positions – as they occur – will be found in the nation's capital.

Possibilities include teaching English privately or at one of the several language centres in Vientiane, work which is currently paying around US$10 an hour. Certificates or degrees in English teaching aren't absolutely necessary, though they increase your chances of hire considerably.

If you possess a technical background or international volunteer experience, you might be able to find work with a UN-related programme or a nongovernmental organisation involved with foreign aid or technical assistance to Laos. For positions such as these, your best bet is to visit the Vientiane offices of each organisation and inquire about personnel needs and vacancies.

Once you have a sponsoring employer, a visa valid for working and residing in Laos is relatively easy to obtain.

ACCOMMODATION

Tourist hotels are typically priced in US dollars, while guesthouses and less expensive business hotels (common in Huay Xai, Luang Prabang, Savannakhet and Pakse) are priced in Thai baht or kip.

It is almost always cheaper to pay in the requested currency rather than let the hotel or guesthouse convert the price into another currency. If the price is quoted in kip, you'll do best to pay in kip; if priced in dollars, pay in dollars. Room rates in this chapter are given in the currency medium quoted by the particular establishment.

Outside the Mekong River Valley, most provincial capitals have only two or three basic hotels or guesthouses, although the number and quality of places to stay seems to be increasing every year. Vientiane has a few guesthouses now with rooms costing as little as US$5 or US$6 a night with shared toilet and bathing facilities. In the more far flung areas of the country rustic guesthouses with shared facilities cost only 1000 to 3000 kip (about US$1 to US$3) per night per person. Though oriented towards local guests, these guesthouses generally welcome foreigners.

Small business hotels in Luang Prabang, Muang Xai, Savannakhet and Pakse cost around US$5 to US$8 per night for simple double rooms. Hotel rooms in Vientiane, Luang Prabang, Savannakhet and Pakse offer private bathrooms and fans as standard features for around US$10 to 15 a night. Higher cost rooms have air-con, and sometimes hot water, for US$15 to 25. Hot water is hardly a necessity in lowland Laos (where it is most likely to be available), but would be nice in the mountains (where it's almost never available).

Large hotels oriented towards the Asian business and leisure traveller or the occasional western tour group are beginning to multiply in the larger cities. At these hotels, tariffs of US$25 to US$60 are common for rooms with air-con, hot water, TV and mini-refrigerator.

FOOD

Lao cuisine is very similar to Thai in many ways. Like Thai food, almost all dishes are cooked with fresh ingredients, including vegetables (phák), fish (pạa), chicken (kai), duck (pét), pork (mũu), beef (sìn ngúa) or water buffalo (sìn khwái). In Luang Prabang, dried water-buffalo skin (nãng khwái hàeng) is a popular ingredient in local dishes.

Food is salted with nâam pạa, a thin sauce of fermented anchovies (usually imported from Thailand) and pạa dạek, a coarser Lao preparation which has fermented freshwater fish, rice husks and rice 'dust' as its main ingredients. Common seasonings include the galingale root (khaa), ground peanuts (more often a condiment), hot chillies (màak phét), tamarind juice (nâam màak khãam), ginger (khíng) and coconut milk (nâam màak phâo). Chillies are sometimes served on the side in hot pepper sauces called jaew.

All meals are eaten with rice or noodles. Glutinous rice (khào nío) is the preferred variety, although ordinary white rice (khào jâo) is also common. Sticky rice is eaten with the hands – the general practice is to grab a small fistful from the woven container that sits on the table, then roll it into a ball and dip it into the various dishes. Khào jâo is eaten with a fork and spoon. Noodles may be eaten with fork and spoon or chopsticks. The most common noodles in Laos are fõe (flat rice noodles) and khào pûn (thin white wheat noodles).

The closest thing to a national dish is làap, a spicy beef, duck, fish or chicken salad made with fresh lime juice, mint leaves, onions and lots of chillies. It can be hot or mild depending on the cook.

In Vientiane, Luang Prabang and Savannakhet, French bread is a popular breakfast food. Sometimes it's eaten plain with kạa-fáe nóm hâwn (hot coffee with milk), sometimes it's eaten with eggs (khai) or in a baguette sandwich that contains Lao-style paté and vegetables. When they're fresh, Lao baguettes are superb. Croissants and other pastries are also available in the bakeries of Vientiane.

Bread (khào jịi)
baguette sandwich
   khào jịi pá-tê
croissants
   kwaa-song
plain bread (usually French-style)
   khào jịi

LAOS

Eggs (khai)

fried egg	khai dạo
hard-boiled egg	khai tôm
scrambled eggs	khai khùa
plain omelette	khai jẹun

Fish (pạa)

crisp-fried fish	jéun pạa
grilled fish	jị̀i pạa
steamed fish	nèung pạa
grilled prawns	pîng kûng

Noodles (fõemii)

rice noodle soup with vegetables and meat
 fõe nâam
same noodles served on plate with gravy
 làat nàa
fried noodles with soy sauce
 phát sáyûu
yellow wheat noodles in broth, with vegetables and meat
 mii nâam
same as mii nâam but without broth
 mii hàeng
white flour noodles, served with fish curry sauce
 khào pûn

Soups (kạeng)

mild soup with vegetables and pork
 kạeng jèut
same as above, with bean curd
 kạeng jèut tâo-hûu
fish and lemon grass soup with mushrooms
 tôm yám pạa
rice soup with fish/chicken
 khào pìak pạa/kai

Miscellaneous

spicy beef salad
 làap sìn
grilled chicken
 pîng kai
chicken fried with chillies
 kai phát màak phét
spicy chicken salad
 làap kai
roast duck
 óp pét

rice
 khào
fried rice
 khào phát
spicy green papaya salad
 tam-sòm or sòm màak-hung
cellophane noodle salad
 yám sèn lâwn
stir-fried vegetables
 phát phák

DRINKS

drinking water
 nâam deum
weak Chinese tea
 nâam sáa
hot Lao tea with sugar
 sáa dạm hâwn
hot Lao tea with milk and sugar
 sáa nóm hâwn
iced Lao tea with milk and sugar
 sáa yén
no sugar (command)
 baw sai nâam-tạan
hot Lao coffee with sugar
 kạa-fáe dạm
hot Lao coffee with milk and sugar
 kạa-fáe nóm hâwn
beer
 bịa
orange soda
 nâam máak kîang
plain milk
 nâam nóm
rice whiskey
 lào láo
yoghurt
 nóm sôm

ENTERTAINMENT
Music & Dancing

For most non-urban Laos local entertainment involves sitting around with friends over a few jiggers of lào láo, telling jokes or recounting the events of the day and singing *phéng phêun múang* (local Lao folk songs). Almost every provincial capital has a couple of dance halls – called 'discos' by the Lao in spite of the fact that they usually host live bands nightly and play no recorded music.

Food as well as beverages is always available at Lao dance halls, though most people drink rather than eat. The music is mostly Lao, though in the north and north-east you'll also hear Chinese and Vietnamese songs mixed into the night's repertoire. Dance styles in any given place vary from the traditional *lám wóng* to US country-style line dancing to wiggle-your-hips-and-dangle-your-fingertips pop styles – all in one night. You'll even see a foxtrot now and then.

Cinema & Video

The arrival of video in Laos has completely killed off local cinema save for one surviving cinema house in Vientiane. Video shops in the larger cities rent pirated versions of all the latest Chinese, Thai and western videos.

See the Vientiane Entertainment section later in this chapter for information on other film venues found only in the capital.

THINGS TO BUY

Laos is not a big country for shopping. Many of the handicrafts and arts available in Laos are easily obtainable in Thailand. Hill tribe crafts can be less expensive in Laos but only if you bargain. Like elsewhere in South-East Asia, bargaining is a local tradition, first introduced by Arab and Indian traders. Most shops now have fixed prices but you can still bargain for fabrics, carvings, antiques and jewellery.

Getting There & Away

AIR

Vientiane's Wattay airport is the only legal arrival or departure point for all foreign airline passengers.

Thailand

Bangkok Bangkok to Vientiane flights operate daily, alternating between Lao Aviation and Thai Airways International airlines. In each case the fare is US$100 one way, though specials as low as US$75 are occasionally available.

Chiang Mai Lao Aviation flies to and from Chiang Mai every Thursday and Sunday. The one hour flight costs US$70 each way.

Vietnam

Hanoi Direct flights between Hanoi and Vientiane leave four times weekly aboard Vietnam Airlines, twice weekly with Lao Aviation. Flights take approximately an hour and cost US$70 to US$90 one way.

Ho Chi Minh City (Saigon) Lao Aviation flies between Ho Chi Minh City and Vientiane every Friday for US$155 one way; the flight takes about three hours. Vietnam Airlines also has four Vientiane flights weekly to/from Ho Chi Minh City via Hanoi for the same fare. Either airline can issue tickets for the other.

Cambodia

Lao Aviation flies between Phnom Penh and Vientiane on Friday. The flight takes about 1½ hours and costs US$125 one way. Royal Air du Cambodge also flies from Phnom Penh to Vientiane once a week for the same fare. Either airline can issue tickets for the other.

China

Lao Aviation flies between Kunming and Vientiane every Sunday, while China Southern Airlines (CSA) does the job every Thursday. Both airlines usually charge US$100 one way but special fares as low as US$88 are occasionally available. Flights take 1 hour and 20 minutes. Lao Aviation and CSA can issue tickets for either airline on this route.

Singapore

Silk Air flies between Singapore and Vientiane twice weekly for US$337 each way.

Myanmar (Burma)

Lao Aviation flies from Vientiane to Yangon and back every Thursday. The flight usually costs US$150 one way (specials as low as US$128 are occasionally available) and takes 1¾ hours each way. Myanmar Airways

LAOS

International acts as the sales agent for Lao Aviation in Yangon.

Departure Tax

There is a US$5 departure tax.

LAND
Thailand

It is now legal for non-Thai foreigners to cross by land or river into Laos from Thailand at the following points: Chiang Khong (opposite Huay Xai); Chong Mek (near Pakse); Mukdahan (opposite Savannakhet); Nakhon Phanom (opposite Tha Khaek); and Nong Khai (the Thai-Lao Friendship Bridge near Vientiane).

Vietnam

Border officials at Lao Bao, a small town on the Lao-Vietnamese border near Sepon (directly east from Savannakhet) will permit visitors holding valid Lao visas to enter the country overland from Vietnam. In the reverse direction – from Laos to Vietnam – you'll need a visa from a Vietnamese embassy or consulate in Laos. For more information see Savannakhet's Getting There & Away section under Southern Laos later in this chapter.

China

From Mengla district in southern Yunnan Province in China it is legal to enter Laos via Boten, Luang Nam Tha Province, if you possess a valid Lao visa.

The Lao consulate in Kunming, China, issues both seven day transit and 15 day tourist visas. These cost US$28 and US$50 respectively and take three to five days to process. You must bring *four* photos and already have a visa from a third country (such as Thailand) stamped in your passport.

Other Countries

Laos also shares its land borders with Myanmar and Cambodia but, at present, no overland crossing points are usually open for foreigners.

Rumours persist that foreigners will soon be allowed to cross the border between Champasak Province in Laos and Stung Treng Province in Cambodia. Apparently some foreigners have actually managed to accomplish this crossing – most likely with the palms-up cooperation of the local border police – but according to Lao officials in Vientiane it's not yet kosher for everyday travel.

We've had similar reports – balanced by denials from the Lao government – regarding entry from Myanmar at the Lao town of Xieng Kok, on the Mekong River in Luang Nam Tha Province. Travellers who want to attempt either crossing will increase their chances of success if they arrive at the border with a valid visa.

Getting Around

AIR

Lao Aviation handles all domestic flights in Laos with Vientiane as the main hub. Following the 1994 abolition of the interprovincial travel permit system, you can now book Lao Aviation tickets yourself, without any sponsoring agency or special permit.

At the moment, Lao Aviation does not accept credit cards for domestic ticket purchases – all payments must be made in cash. Prices are quoted in US dollars but you can pay in kip. Depending on the current exchange rate, it may be cheaper to pay in kip.

The main aircraft used for Lao Aviation's domestic flights are the 15 passenger Chinese Y-12 and the 50 passenger Chinese Y-7, both copies of Russian Antonov aircraft with upgraded features. When Lao Aviation is short of Chinese planes, an old Antonov 24 may be pulled from retirement and used instead.

Luang Prabang airport is undergoing improvement and expansion so it will be able to field larger planes. Wattay international airport itself reportedly will be expanded with Singaporean assistance. There has also been talk of allowing a Thai company –

possibly Bangkok Airways – to supplement domestic flight schedules in Laos.

Lao Aviation (☎ 212058) has its main office on Thanon Pangkham, around the corner from the Lane Xang Hotel, in Vientiane.

Air Fares & Taxes

Air fares for Lao citizens are subsidised at less than half what a foreigner must pay. Children ages five to 12 are charged half the adult fare, infants pay only 10%.

The departure tax for domestic flights is 300 kip. Passengers must also pay immigra-tion officers at each domestic airport 100 kip for the privilege of checking in or out of the province each time they arrive or depart by air.

BUS

The road system in Laos remains very unde-veloped. At the time of writing Laos had 13,971 km of classified roads, most of which can charitably be termed 'in a deteriorated condition'. An estimated 25% are tarred; 34% are graded and sometimes covered with gravel; and the remaining 41% are ungraded dirt tracks. The roads around Vientiane

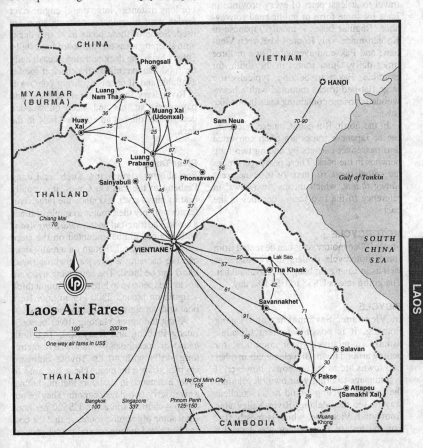

Laos Air Fares

One-way air fares in US$

Prefecture, as far out as Vang Vieng, are surfaced and adequate for just about any type of vehicle. Elsewhere in the country, unsurfaced roads are the rule. Since Laos is 70% mountains, even relatively short road trips involve incredibly long intervals (eg a typical 200 km upcountry trip takes around 10 to 18 hours to accomplish). A number of international aid projects promise to upgrade the current system and build new roads by the end of the decade.

The availability of interprovincial public transport has increased markedly since the last edition of this book. It is now possible to travel to at least parts of every province in Laos by some form of public road conveyance. Regular buses – mostly Japanese or Korean-made – ply Route 13 between Vientiane and Pakse an average of two or three times daily. Other routes in the south, for example, Pakse to Sekong, typically use large flat-bed trucks mounted with a heavy wooden carriage containing seats in bus-like rows.

In the north, Russian, Chinese, Vietnamese or Japanese trucks are often converted into passenger carriers by adding two long benches in the back. These passenger trucks are called *thàek-sìi* (taxi) or in some areas *sãwng-thâew*, which means 'two rows' in reference to the two facing benches in the back.

MOTORCYCLE

Small 100cc motorcycles can be rented from some motorcycle dealers in Vientiane, as well as in Luang Prabang and Savannakhet. The going rate is US$8 to US$10 a day.

BICYCLE

In Vientiane, Savannakhet and Luang Prabang, it is possible to rent bicycles, usually in relatively poor condition, for getting around town. Bicycle rentals in other Lao towns are as yet unknown, however. If you manage to bring your own bicycle into the country, cycling would be an excellent way to see the Mekong River Valley area from south Vientiane, which is mostly flat. For the rest of the country you'd need a

sturdy mountain bicycle. You should be able to register it with Lao customs upon entry.

BOAT

Rivers are the true highways and byways of Laos, the main thoroughfares being the Mekong, Nam Ou, Nam Khan, Nam Tha, Nam Ngum and Se Don. The Mekong River is the longest and most important water route and is navigable year-round between Huay Xai in the north and Vientiane.

River Ferries

For long distances, large diesel-engine river ferries with overnight accommodation are used. Some of these boats have two decks with sleeping areas and on-board food stalls. Others have one deck and stop occasionally for food. On overnight trips check if food is available and, if necessary, bring your own.

River ferry facilities are quite basic and passengers sit, eat and sleep on wooden decks. The toilet is an enclosed hole in the deck.

River Taxis

For shorter river trips, such as Luang Prabang to the Pak Ou Caves, it's usually best to hire a river taxi since the large river ferries only ply their routes a couple of times a week. The long-tail boats *(héua hãng nyáo)* with engines gimbal-mounted on the stern are the most typical, though for a really short trip (eg crossing a river) a rowboat *(héua phai)* can be hired. The héua hãng nyáo are not as inexpensive to hire as you might think – figure on around 2800 kip an hour for a boat with an eight to 10 person capacity.

Along the upper Mekong River between Luang Prabang and Huay Xai, Thai-built *héua wái* (speedboats) – shallow, five-metre-long skiffs with 40 hp Toyota outboard engines – are common. These are able to cover a distance in six hours that might take a river ferry two days or more. They're not cheap – charters run about US$20 per hour – but some ply regular routes so that the cost can be shared among several passengers.

LOCAL TRANSPORT
Taxi
Each of the three largest towns – Vientiane, Luang Prabang and Savannakhet – has a handful of car taxis that are used by foreign businesspeople and the occasional tourist. The only places you'll find these are at the airports (arrival times only) and in front of the larger hotels. These taxis can be hired by the trip, by the hour or by the day. Typical all-day rental costs are from US$20 to US$40. By the trip, you shouldn't pay more than US$0.50 per km.

Three-wheeled motorcycle taxis are also common in the larger towns as well as in some smaller ones. This type of vehicle can be called taxi (thàek-sii) or samlor (sǎam-lâw), meaning 'three wheels'. The larger ones made in Thailand are called jumbos (jamboh) and can hold four to six passengers. Fares are about 100 kip per km per vehicle but you must bargain to get the correct rate. They can go every place a regular taxi can, but they aren't usually hired for distances greater than 20 km.

Pedicabs
The bicycle samlor, once the mainstay of local transport for hire throughout urban Laos, has nearly become extinct. Bicycle samlor fares are about the same as for motorcycle taxis but are generally used only for distances less than two km. Bargaining is sometimes necessary to get the correct fare, though pedicab drivers seem to be more honest than the motorcycle taxi drivers.

ORGANISED TOURS
Around 25 agencies operate in Vientiane, some of which maintain branches in other cities, such as Luang Prabang, Pakse and Phonsavan. For the most part, each agency has a standard set of packages, ranging from two nights in Vientiane only to 14 days in Vientiane, Luang Prabang, the Plain of Jars (Xieng Khuang), Savannakhet, Salavan and Champasak. Some agencies advertise tours which they can't actually deliver, while better ones can go almost anywhere and can create custom itineraries.

Standard prices vary little from company to company; the main difference is linked to the number of people signing up for a package. Per-person rates drop – typically around US$50 to 100 per person – for each person added to the group. Costs for one person travelling solo can be as much as US$200 or more per day, while four to six persons travelling together can arrange packages for under US$50 per person per day. If you don't mind travelling with other people, ask if you can join a group already scheduled to depart – some agencies will allow this while others try to keep the groups as small as possible in order to collect the most loot.

It is also possible to bargain in some cases. Several readers have written to describe how they shopped around from agency to agency and were able to get at least a few tour operators to lower their asking rates.

In general, tours arranged by the Vientiane agencies are not bad value as far as package tours go. Except for the obvious inconvenience of having to put up with a group (although sometimes the group is as small as two to four people) and follow a guide around, the tours are generally well planned and genuinely informative. Guides are usually flexible when it comes to the itinerary, adding or deleting bits (within obvious time, distance and cost limits) according to your needs.

At each destination, the agencies arrange all accommodation (double occupancy) and a tour guide. In more expensive packages inter-country transport and meals are included. Prices for packages without meals are much lower, and eating out on your own is often more fun than eating pre-arranged hotel meals anyway.

Meals, where they are included, are plentiful if a bit on the bland side, but you can sometimes request local specialities. Or simply inform your guide that you want to eat real Lao food during the tour, not the ersatz version usually offered to westerners.

Unlike early China tours in which visitors were herded from factory to agricultural collective, Laos itineraries do not try to present visitors with a proletarian paradise – political rhetoric is in fact relatively absent from guide commentary.

Vientiane Tour Operators

The following are some reputable tour operators in Vientiane:

Aerocontact Asia
    29 Thanon Wat Xieng Nhun
    (☎ 216409; fax 414346)
Diethelm Travel Laos
    Namphu Square, Thanon Setthathirat, PO Box 2657 (☎ 215920; fax 217151)
Inter-Lao Tourisme
    Cnr of Thanons Pangkham and Setthathirat
    (☎ 214832; fax 216306)
Lane Xang Travel & Tour
    Thanon Pangkham, PO Box 4452
    (☎ 215804; fax 215777)
Lao Travel Service
    8/3 Thanon Lan Xang, PO Box 2553
    (☎ 216603; fax 216150)
Societé de Development Touristique (SODETOUR)
    16 Thanon Fa Ngum, PO Box 70
    (☎ 216314; fax 216313)
That Luang Tour
    28 Thanon Kamkhong, PO Box 3619
    (☎ 215809; fax 215346)

Vientiane

Originally one of the early Lao river-valley fiefdoms (meuang) that were consolidated around the time Europe was emerging from the Dark Ages, Vientiane sits on a bend in the Mekong River amid fertile alluvial plains. At times controlled by the Burmese, Siamese, Vietnamese and Khmers, it was made a capital city by the French in the late 19th century. Throughout the Indochina War years, royalists, neutralists and leftists vied for control of the city and, thereby, the country. Following the Communist takeover of 1975, it continued to serve as the seat of government.

It's one of the three classic Indochinese cities (including Ho Chi Minh City and Phnom Penh) that conjure up images of exotic Eurasian settings and has remained amazingly laid-back. Vientiane is actually pronounced 'Wieng Chan'.

Orientation

The city curves along a bend in the Mekong River with the central business district at the middle of the bend. Most of the government offices, hotels, restaurants and historic temples are in this district near the river.

Street signs are mostly written in Lao script only, although signs at major street intersections are also written in French. The French designations for street names vary (eg route, rue and avenue) but the Lao script always reads *thanōn* and it's always best just to avoid possible confusion and use the Lao word.

The main streets in the central district are Thanon Samsenthai, which is the main shopping area, Thanon Setthathirat, where several of the most famous temples are located, and Thanon Fa Ngum, which runs along the river. Branching off northward is Thanon Lan Xang, Vientiane's widest street.

The main portion of Thanon Lan Xang is a divided boulevard that leads past Talaat Sao to the Patuxai, or Victory Gate. After the Patuxai, it splits into two roads, Thanon Phon Kheng and Thanon That Luang. Thanon Phon Kheng leads to the Unknown Soldiers Memorial and the Lao People's Army Museum as well as the Thai embassy. Thanon That Luang leads to Pha That Luang in the north-east of central Vientiane, where there are also several embassies.

To the south-east is the mostly local residential district of Sisattanak and to the west is the similarly residential Sikhottabong.

Maps The *Vientiane Tourist Map*, published by the LNTA in 1993, is a fairly useable street map of the city featuring major sites and the mostly unlabelled locations of many hotels and public services. It's available at the National Geographic Service, Raintree Bookstore, Phimphone Minimart and several retail shops in the city.

Information

Tourist Office The Lao National Tourism Authority (LNTA) – also known as the Lao National Tourism Company or the National Lao Tourist Authority – has a new office on

Thanon Lan Xang between Talaat Sao and the Patuxai monument. This office (☎ /fax 212013) is little more than a thinly disguised travel agency, and one that is not very competitive with the private agencies in town in terms of price or service. As an information source on where to go, or even on official tourism policy, it is nearly worthless.

Money La Banque pour le Commerce Extérieur Lao (BCEL) at Thanons Pangkham and Fa Ngum, near Lao Aviation and the Lane Xang Hotel, has the best foreign exchange rate of any bank in Vientiane. It's open from 8.30 am to 4.30 pm Monday to Friday, and until 11 am Saturday. Other banks well equipped to handle foreign exchange include Bangkok Bank, Joint Development Bank, Siam Commercial Bank and Thai Military Bank.

Licensed money changing booths can also be found in Talaat Sao and in a few other locations around town. You can also change on the 'parallel market' at various shops in town for no commission or from the unofficial moneychangers hanging out on Thanon Lan Xang near Talaat Sao. The latter usually offer the best rates in Vientiane but it helps to be on your toes as far as knowing what the going rates are; count your money carefully.

Post The Post, Telephone and Telegraph (PTT) office is on the corner of Thanons Lan Xang and Khu Vieng, across from Talaat Sao. Business hours are from 8 am to 5 pm Monday to Saturday and until noon on Sunday.

Telephone The PTT office is only for calls within Laos. Overseas calls and fax transmissions can be arranged at the Public Telephone Office on Thanon Setthathirat. It's open daily from 7.30 am to 10 pm.

The area code for Vientiane is 21.

Bookshops Near the fountain on Thanon Pangkham (next to the Thai Airways International office), Raintree Bookstore stocks a selection of mostly used paperbacks, magazines and other periodicals.

The gift shop at the Lane Xang Hotel has a few books in English and rather expensive maps of Vientiane and Laos.

Laundry Most hotels and guesthouses offer laundry services (a few even include it with room charges). Several laundry and dry cleaning shops can be found in Vientiane's Chinatown area, especially along Thanon Heng Boun and Thanon Samsenthai just east of Thanon Chao Anou. Typical laundry rates run about 300 to 500 kip per piece, and one day service is usually available if you drop off your clothes in the morning.

Medical Services Medical facilities in Vientiane are quite limited. The two state hospitals, Setthathirat and Mahasot, operate on levels of skill and hygiene below that available in neighbouring Thailand. Mahasot Hospital operates a Diplomatic Clinic 'especially for foreigners' that is open 24 hours. In reality, few foreigners use this clinic.

The Australian Clinic (☎ 413603; after hours ☎ 312343), operated by the Australian embassy in Vientiane, can treat minor problems for rather steep fees. It's behind the Australian embassy, off Thanon Phonxai Noi, and is open Monday to Friday from 8.30 am to noon and 2 to 5 pm (except Wednesday, when it closes at noon and stays closed the rest of the day). It is on call 24 hours. It's staffed by registered nurses but isn't equipped to handle major medical emergencies. Private clinics in town charge rates that are less than half those charged at the Australian Clinic.

The 150 bed Hôpital de l'amitié (☎ /fax 413663) is a new centre for trauma and orthopaedics operated by the Association Médicale Franco Asiatique (AMFA) and is located at the site of the old Soviet Hospital, north of the city on the road to Tha Ngon. For emergencies you're supposed to be able to call ☎ 413306 for a radio-dispatched ambulance, but early tests of this procedure have found it lacking in verisimilitude. At night the hospital is closed and locked, with no staff on duty.

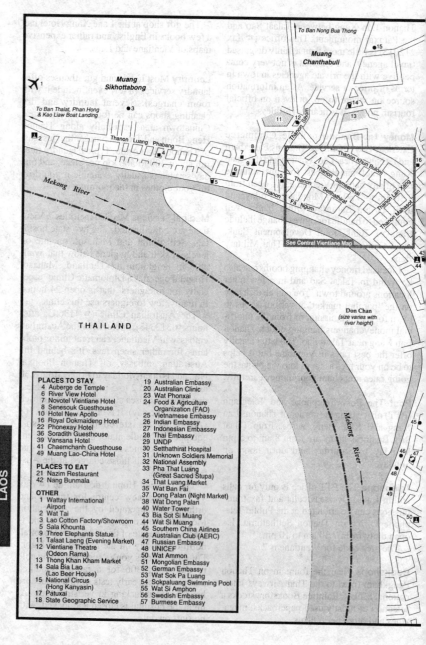

PLACES TO STAY
4 Auberge de Temple
6 River View Hotel
7 Novotel Vientiane Hotel
8 Senesouk Guesthouse
10 Hotel New Apollo
16 Royal Dokmaideng Hotel
22 Phonexay Hotel
36 Soradith Guesthouse
39 Vansana Hotel
41 Chaemchanh Guesthouse
49 Muang Lao-China Hotel

PLACES TO EAT
21 Nazim Restaurant
42 Nang Bunmala

OTHER
1 Wattay International
  Airport
2 Wat Tai
3 Lao Cotton Factory/Showroom
5 Sala Khounta
9 Three Elephants Statue
11 Talaat Laeng (Evening Market)
12 Vientiane Theatre
  (Odeon Rama)
13 Thong Khan Kham Market
14 Sala Bia Lao
  (Lao Beer House)
15 National Circus
  (Hong Kanyasin)
17 Patuxai
18 State Geographic Service

19 Australian Embassy
20 Australian Clinic
23 Wat Phonxai
24 Food & Agriculture
  Organization (FAO)
25 Vietnamese Embassy
26 Indian Embassy
27 Indonesian Embasssy
28 Thai Embassy
29 UNDP
30 Setthathirat Hospital
31 Unknown Soldiers Memorial
32 National Assembly
33 Pha That Luang
  (Great Sacred Stupa)
34 That Luang Market
35 Wat Ban Fai
37 Dong Palan (Night Market)
38 Wat Dong Palan
40 Water Tower
43 Bia Sot Si Muang
44 Wat Si Muang
45 Southern China Airlines
46 Australian Club (AERC)
47 Russian Embassy
48 UNICEF
50 Wat Ammon
51 Mongolian Embassy
52 German Embassy
53 Wat Sok Pa Luang
54 Sokpaluang Swimming Pool
55 Wat Si Amphon
56 Swedish Embassy
57 Burmese Embassy

Muang Sikhottabong

To Ban Thalat, Phan Hong
& Kao Liaw Boat Landing

Thanon Luang Phabang

Mekong River

THAILAND

To Ban Nong Bua Thong

Muang
Chanthabuli

Thanon Khun Bulom
Thanon Samsenthai
Thanon Setthathirat
Thanon Fa Ngum
Thanon Lan Xang
Thanon Mahasot
Thanon

See Central Vientiane Map

Don Chan
(size varies with
river height)

Mekong River

LAOS

To Tha Ngon

Muang
Saisettha

Thanon Phon Kheng

Thanon That Luang

Thanon Nong Bon

Thanon Sayiton

Thanon Khu Viang

Thanon Tha Deua

Muang
Sisattanak

Vientiane

0   0.5   1 km

To Buddha Park & Tha Deua

For medical emergencies that can't wait till Bangkok and can't be treated at one of the local or embassy clinics, you can arrange to have ambulances summoned from nearby Udon Thani or Khon Kaen in Thailand.

Emergency In an emergency, contact the police kiosk on Thanon Setthathirat.

Walking Tour
This walk takes you through the central area and past some of the lesser known wats in a leisurely two to 2½ hours. Start at the fountain on Thanon Pangkham and walk west on Setthathirat approximately 250 metres to **Wat Mixai** on your left. The sim is built in the Bangkok style, with a veranda that goes all the way around. The heavy gates, flanked by two *nyak*, or guardian giants, are also in Bangkok style.

Another 80 metres west and on the right-hand side of the street is **Wat Hai Sok**, with its impressive five tiered roof (nine if you count the lower terrace roofs). Opposite, and just a bit further on, is **Wat Ong Teu**, and past Thanon Chao Anou on the next block west and on the left again is **Wat In Paeng**. The sim of this latter wat is nicely decorated with stucco reliefs depicting various mythical characters from the Hindu *Ramayana* and *Mahabharata* epics, as coopted by Buddhism. Over the front veranda gable is an impressive wood and mosaic facade.

In the reverse direction, go back to Thanon Chao Anou, turn right (south) and walk until you meet Thanon Fa Ngum along the Mekong River. Just around the corner to the left is **Wat Chan**, a typically Lao temple with skilfully carved wooden panels on the rebuilt sim. Inside is a large bronze seated Buddha from the original temple on this site. In the courtyard are the remains of a stupa with a Buddha image in the Calling for Rain pose.

Continue east on Thanon Fa Ngum until you pass the Lane Xang Hotel on your left. Beyond the hotel a bit, turn left on Thanon Chantha Khumman and walk straight (northeast) about half a km (passing the Hotel Ekalath Metropole on your left) and you'll run into **That Dam**, the Black Stupa. Local

LAOS

mythology says the stupa is the abode of a dormant seven-headed dragon that came to life during the 1828 Siamese-Lao War and protected local citizens.

Pha That Luang

The Great Sacred Stupa is the most important national monument in Laos, a symbol of both the Buddhist religion and Lao sovereignty. The construction of the current monument began in 1566 and, in succeeding years, four wats were built around the stupa. Only two remain, Wat That Luang Tai to the south and Wat That Luang Neua to the north. The latter is the monastic residence of the Supreme Patriarch (Pha Sangkharat) of Lao Buddhism. In front of the entrance to the compound is a statue of King Setthathirat.

A high-walled cloister with tiny windows surrounds the 45 metre stupa. The base of the stupa is designed to be mounted by the faithful, with walkways around each level and connecting stairways.

Each level of the monument has different architectural features in which aspects of Buddhist doctrine are encoded – devout Buddhists are supposed to contemplate the meaning of these features as they circumambulate. The tall central stupa, which has a brick core that has been stuccoed over, is supported here by a bowl-shaped base which is reminiscent of India's first Buddhist stupa at Sanchi.

The cloister measures 85 metres on each side and contains various Buddha images. A display of historic sculpture, including not only classic Lao sculpture but also Khmer figures, is on either side of the front entrance (inside). Especially during the That Luang Festival (Bun That Luang) in November, worshippers stick balls of rice to the walls to pay respect to the spirit of King Setthathirat.

The grounds are open to visitors from 8 to 11.30 am and 2 to 4.30 pm Tuesday to Sunday. Admission is 200 kip per person. Pha That Luang is about four km north-east of the city centre at the end of Thanon That Luang. Any bus going north of Thanon Lan Xang will pass within a short walk from the compound.

If you happen to be in Vientiane in mid-November, don't miss the That Luang Festival, the city's biggest annual event.

Haw Pha Kaew

About 100 metres from Wat Si Saket along Thanon Setthathirat is a former royal temple of the Lao monarchy. It has been converted into a museum and is no longer a place of worship.

According to the Lao, the temple was originally built in 1565 by command of King Setthathirat, heir to the Lan Xang throne, in order to house the so-called Emerald Buddha. In Laos the name Pha Kaew means 'jewel Buddha image', although the image is actually made of a type of jade. The image was originally from northern Thailand's Lanna kingdom, but following a skirmish with the Lao in 1779 the Siamese recovered the Emerald Buddha and installed it in Bangkok's royal temple. Later, during the Siamese-Lao War of 1828, Haw Pha Kaew was razed.

The temple was rebuilt between 1936 and 1942 in a rather Bangkok-style rococo. Today, the veranda shelters some of the best examples of Buddhist sculpture in Laos. Included are a 6th to 9th century Dvaravati-style stone Buddha, several bronze standing and sitting Lao-style Buddhas and a collection of inscribed Lao and Mon stelae. Various royal requisites are also on display inside, along with some Khmer stelae, various wooden carvings (door panels, candlestands, lintels) and palm-leaf manuscripts.

Hours and admission for Haw Pha Kaew are the same as for Pha That Luang.

Wat Si Saket

This temple is near the Presidential Palace and is at the corner of Thanons Lan Xang and Setthathirat. Built in 1818, by King Anouvong (Chao Anou), it is the oldest temple in Vientiane – all the others were either built after Wat Si Saket or were rebuilt after destruction by the Siamese in 1828.

In spite of an overall Siamese architectural influence, Wat Si Saket has several unique features. The interior walls of the cloister are riddled with small niches that contain silver and ceramic Buddha images – over 2000 of them. Over 300 seated and standing Buddhas of varying sizes and materials (wood, stone and bronze) rest on long shelves below the niches, and most are sculpted or cast in the characteristic Lao style. Most of the images are from 16th to 19th century Vientiane but a few hail from 15th to 16th century Luang Prabang. A Khmer-style Naga Buddha, brought from a Khmer site at nearby Hat Sai Fong, is also on display.

The hours and admission are the same as for Pha That Luang and Haw Pha Kaew. A Lao guide who speaks French and English is usually on hand to describe the temple and answer questions – for free.

Wat Sok Pa Luang

The full name for this forest temple *(wat pạa)* in south Vientiane's Sisattanak district is Mahaphutthawongsa Pa Luang Pa Yai Wat. It's famous for its rustic herbal saunas, which are administered by eight precept nuns who reside at the temple. After the relaxing sauna, you can take tea while cooling off. Massages are also available. A donation is requested for sauna and massage services.

Wat Sok Pa Luang is also known for its course of instruction in vipassana, a type of Buddhist meditation that involves careful mind and body analysis. The abbot and teacher is Ajaan Sali Kantasilo, who was born in 1932 in Yasothon, Thailand. He accepts foreign students but only speaks Lao and Thai, so interested persons will have to arrange for an interpreter if they speak neither of these languages.

Taxi, jumbo and samlor drivers all know how to get to Wat Sok Pa Luang. The temple buildings are set back in the woods so all that is visible from the road is the tall ornamental gate.

Patuxai (Victory Monument)

This large monument, very reminiscent of the Arc de Triomphe in Paris, is known by a variety of names. Ironically, it was built in 1969 with US-purchased cement that was supposed to have been used for the construction of a new airport. Since it commemorates the Lao who had died in prerevolutionary wars, current Lao maps typically label it Old Monument (Ancien Monument in French, or Anusawali Kao in Lao) in order to draw attention to the newer Unknown Soldiers Memorial, erected since the Revolution.

The bas-relief on the sides and the temple-like ornamentation along the top and cornices are typically Lao. Beneath the arch is a small outdoor cafe with snacks. A stairway leads to the top of the monument, where you can look out over the city (there's a small entry fee to climb the stairs).

Lao Revolutionary Museum

Housed in a well-worn classical mansion on Thanon Samsenthai and originally built in 1925 as the French governor's residence, this museum opened in 1985. For the most part, the museum contains a collection of artefacts and photos from the Pathet Lao's lengthy struggle for power. Many of the displays consist of historic weaponry; some labels are in English as well as Lao.

Posted hours (which are not scrupulously followed) for the museum are from 8 to 11.30 am and 2 to 4.30 pm weekdays; entry is 200 kip.

Xieng Khuan

Often called Buddha Park (Suan Phut), this collection of slightly bizarre Buddhist and Hindu cement sculpture in a meadow by the side of the Mekong River lies 24 km south of the city centre off Thanon Tha Deua. Entry is 100 kip. A few vendors in the park offer fresh young coconuts, soft drinks, beer and Lao food.

Talaat Sao

Talaat Sao (Morning Market) is on the north-east corner of the intersection of Thanons Lan Xang and Khu Vieng. It actually runs all day, from about 6 am to 6 pm. The sprawling collection of stalls offer fabric, ready-made clothes, hardware, jewellery, electronic goods and just about anything else imaginable.

LAOS

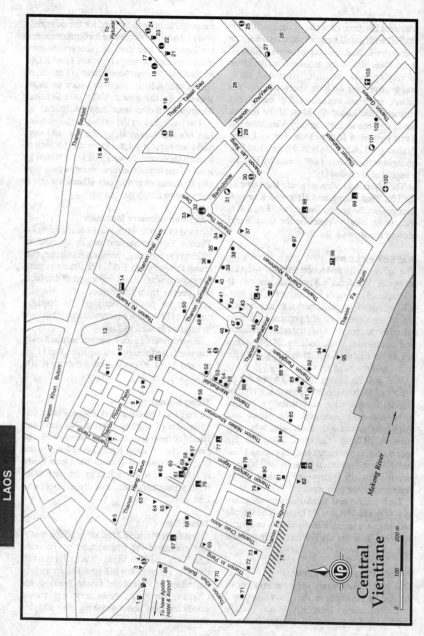

Central Vientiane

Mekong River

0   100   200 m

To New Apollo
Hotel & Airport

Other Markets

South-east of Talaat Sao, just across Thanon Mahasot (or Thanon Nong Bon, as it's labelled on some maps), is **Talaat Khua Din**, which offers fresh produce and fresh meats, tobacco and other smoking material, as well as flowers and other assorted goods.

A bigger fresh market is **Talaat Thong Khan Kham**, which is sometimes called the Evening Market since it was originally established to replace the old Evening Market in Ban Nong Duang (which burned down in 1987). Like Talaat Sao, it's open all day, but is best in the morning. It's the biggest market in Vientiane and has virtually everything. You'll find it north of the city centre in Ban

PLACES TO STAY		63	Le Chanthy	31	US Embassy
6	Anou Hotel		(Nang Janti)	32	That Dam
7	Vannasinh Guest	64	Sweet Home & Liang		(Black Stupa)
	House		Xiang Bakeries	34	Phimphone Market
9	Santisouk Guest House	65	Nai Xieng Chai Yene	38	Phimphone Minimart
11	Syri Guest House	69	Restaurant Le	39	Souvenir &
15	Saylomyen Guest		Vendôme		Handicraft Shops
	House	70	Nang Kham Bang	44	Mosque
16	Lani II Guest House	74	Night Vendors	45	Public Telephone
34	Hotel Ekalath	79	L Bistrot		Office
	Metropole	82	Mixay Café	46	Diethelm Travel
35	Asian Pavilion Hotel	88	Le Souriya	47	Fountain Circle
36	Hua Guo Guest House	95	Sukiyaki Bar &	51	Bank of Lao PDR
40	Lao Paris Hotel		Restaurant/Lao	52	IMF
41	Pangkham Guest		Restaurant	55	State Book Shop
	House			56	Lao Textiles
49	Settha Guest House	**OTHER**		57	Lane Xang Travel
50	Lao Hotel Plaza	1	Win West Pub	60	Samlo Pub
	(Under		(Bane Saysana)	61	Wat Hai Sok
	Construction)	2	Shell Petro Station	66	Russian Cultural
53	Phantavong Guest	4	Thai Military Bank		Centre
	House	5	Maningom	67	Wat In Paeng
54	MC&I Guest House		Supermarket	71	SODETOUR
62	Lani I Guest House	10	Lao Revolutionary	75	Wat Chan
68	Saysana Hotel		Museum	76	Wat Ong Teu
72	Phornthip Guest	12	Tennis Club de	77	Wat Mixai
	House		Vientiane	83	Haw Kang
73	Inter Hotel	13	National Stadium	85	The Art of Silk
78	Lao International	14	National Pool	86	Lao Air Booking
	Guest House	17	Centre du Langue	87	Inter-Lao Tourisme
80	Tai-Pan Hotel		Française	89	Raintree Bookstore
81	Mixai Guest House	18	Tourist Authority of	90	Thai International
84	Samsenthai Hotel		Thailand		(THAI)
94	Lane Xang Hotel	19	Immigration Office	91	La Banque pour le
		20	Bangkok Bank		Commerce
PLACES TO EAT		21	Crêperie-Pub Belle Ile		Extérieur Lao
3	Phikun Restaurant	22	Lao National Tourism		(BCEL Lao
8	Thai Food (Phikun)		Authorit (LNTA)		Foreign Trade
	Restaurant	23	Nightclub Vienglatry		Bank)
9	Santisouk	24	Thai Farmer's Bank	92	Lao Aviation
	Restaurant	25	Siam Commercial	93	National Library
33	Soukvimane Lao Food		Bank	96	Ha Kha (Presidential
37	Kua Lao	26	Khua Din Market		Palace)
42	The Taj Restaurant	27	Bus Terminal	97	Ministry of Foreign
43	Namphu & L'Opera	28	Talaat Sao (Morning		Affairs
	Restaurants		Market)	98	Wat Si Saket
48	Scandinavian	29	Post, Telephone &	99	Haw Pha Kaew
	Bakery/Restaurant		Telegraph office	100	Mahasot Hospital
	Le Provençal		(PTT)	101	French Embassy
58	Le Bayou	30	Siam Commercial	102	Le Club France
59	Restauran Sourchanh		Bank	103	Catholic Church

LAOS

Thong Khan Kham (Gold Bowl Fields Village), at the intersection of Thanons Khan Kham and Dong Miang.

Talaat That Luang is just a little southeast of Pha That Luang on Thanon Talaat That Luang. The speciality here is exotic foods, like snakes, that are favoured by the Vietnamese and Chinese.

Places to Stay

Vientiane has a choice of over 50 hotels and guesthouses, many of which cost over US$20 per night. Fortunately for budgeteers, during the last two years lower-priced rooms have begun opening up. Many hotels and guesthouses in Vientiane quote US dollar or Thai baht rates and some of the more expensive require payment in US currency despite the recent ban on all currencies other than kip.

Guesthouses The *Ministry of Culture & Information Guest House* (MC & I Guest House; formerly the SECP Guest House), at the corner of Thanons Manthatulat and Setthathirat, is still the cheapest place in town. Large, three-bed fan rooms cost US$3 per person a night, while two-bed air-con rooms are US$8/10 single/double. Toilet and shower facilities are shared. It's a bit dreary and smelly, and isn't particularly clean – guests often have to request a change of sheets or borrow a broom to sweep out their own rooms.

Just up Thanon Manthatulat from the MC & I Guest House, on a corner on the same side of the street, the private *Phantavong Guest House* (☎ 214738) offers 12 basic rooms for US$5/8 single/double with shared toilet and shower, US$10/15 with private bath and air-con.

Santisouk Guest House (☎ 215303), above the Restaurant Santisouk on Thanon Nokeo Kumman, has plain but clean rooms with wooden floors, high ceilings and shared bath for US$10 to US$12 depending on the size. The restaurant downstairs is a good breakfast spot.

The *Mixai Guest House* (☎ 216213; fax 215445), opposite the Mixay Cafe at 30/1

Thanon Fa Ngum, has simple, clean, air-con rooms with shared facilities for US$10/12 single/double.

A little out from the city centre, the quiet and friendly *Senesouk Guest House* (☎ 215567; fax 217449), behind the Novotel Vientiane off Thanon Luang Prabang (Km 2 Ban Khounta), costs US$8 with fan, and US$12 air-con for small to medium-size rooms with shared facilities.

Saylomyen Guest House (☎ 214246), a two storey shophouse-style place on Thanon Saylom, has eight simple, clean rooms for 200B with fan and cold-water shower, 300B with air-con and hot-water shower. There's some street noise in the front so take a room towards the back if you have a choice.

A new, centrally located place that bridges the gap between bottom and middle is the *Vannasinh Guest House* (☎ /fax 222020) at 51 Thanon Phnom Penh at the edge of Chinatown (a block north of Thanon Samsenthai). Large, clean rooms with high ceilings and fans cost US$8 to US$10 with shared toilet and shower, while similar rooms with air-con, private toilet and hot-water shower cost US$15 to US$20. There are also a couple of family units with two bedrooms and similar prices. Proprietors Somphone and Mayulee speak very good French and English.

A half block north of the fountain square, at 72/6 Thanon Pangkham, a narrow four storey building houses the new *Pangkham Guest House* (☎ 217053). Small rooms with fan and attached toilet and hot-water shower cost US$10, while similar rooms with air-con cost US$15. Slightly larger rooms are available for US$20. Rooms at the back are quieter than those which face Thanon Pangkham. The manager speaks good English.

Towards the river, the *Lao International Guest House* (☎ 216571) on Thanon François Nginn, north of the Tai-Pan Hotel, offers 11 rooms with varying prices. Bare rooms with fan and shared bath start at US$8, while rooms with attached bath on the same floor are US$10.

Three blocks west, tucked away on parallel Thanon In Paeng, is the similarly varied but better-designed *Phornthip Guest House*

(☎ 217239). Spacious, clean, basic rooms with bath and fan cost US$7/12 single/double, while air-con rooms go for US$12/16.

Hotels *Hotel Ekalath Metropole* (☎ 213420) on the corner of Thanons Samsenthai and Chantha Khumman has undergone at least three incarnations, starting with the pre-1975 Imperial Hotel. The latest version is basically a middle-price hotel, but a semi-attached annex contains cheap, plain fan rooms for US$6 to US$8 single and US$10 double with fan and shared cold-water shower, or US$12 single and US$14 double with fan and attached cold shower (but shared toilet).

Inter Hotel (☎ 215137) at the corner of Thanons Chao Anou and Fa Ngum is near the river. Rates here are US$12 to US$16 single/double, depending on the size of the room; all rooms come with air-con. Larger, two-room units with hot-water showers cost US$20. Formerly the Lao Chaleune Hotel, this hotel is well located and often full, although the rooms are nothing special. One definite drawback is the hotel's bar/disco, which when active causes the whole building to shake.

The *Samsenthai Hotel* at 15 Thanon Manthatulat near the river has gone downhill considerably over the last year or so and is not very clean any more – but at least the rates have dropped to match the standards. Rooms with fan and shared bath now go for US$6 single/double, while for US$12/15 you can get air-con and a private cold-water shower. The dimly lit, cavernous lobby is off-putting.

Places to Eat

Vientiane is good for eating possibilities, with a wide variety of cafes, street vendors, beer halls and restaurants offering everything from rice noodles to filet mignon. Nearly all fit well into a shoestring budget.

Breakfast Most of the hotels in Vientiane offer set 'American' breakfasts (two eggs, toast and ham or bacon) for 1000 to 3000 kip. Or you could get out on the streets and eat where the locals do. A popular breakfast is khào jìi pá-têh, a split French baguette stuffed with Lao-style paté (which is more like English or American luncheon meat than French paté) and various dressings.

Vendors who sell breakfast sandwiches also sell plain baguettes (khào jìi) – there are several regular bread vendors on Thanon Heng Boun and also in front of Talaat Sao. The fresh baguettes are usually gone by 8.30 am and what's left will be starting to harden.

Two side-by-side cafes on Thanon Chao Anou, *Liang Xiang Bakery House* and *Sweet Home Bakery*, sell passable croissants and other pastries in the morning, along with strong brewed coffee.

Lao For real Lao meals, try the *Dong Palan Night Market*, off Thanon Ban Fai (marked Thanon Dong Palan on some maps) and behind the Nong Chan ponds near the Lan Thong cinema. Vendors sell all the Lao standards, including làap (spicy salad) and pîng kai (grilled chicken).

The well-patronised *Mixay Cafe* is in a wooden building that's open on three sides and overlooks the Mekong River near the intersection of Thanons Fa Ngum and Nokeo Khumman. The menu is not very extensive, but the làap is very tasty and it has cold draught beer for 750 kip a litre. This is a great spot to watch the sun set over the Mekong River, with the Thai town of Si Chiangmai as the backdrop.

The *Vientiane Department Store* (part of Talaat Sao) has a small but excellent food centre with an extensive variety of Thai and Lao dishes for 500 to 1200 kip.

Thai With an increasing number of Thais visiting Vientiane for business and pleasure these days, it is no wonder that there are more Thai restaurants. On Thanon Samsenthai, just past the Lao Revolutionary Museum, is the *Phikun* (the English sign reads 'Thai Food') restaurant, which has all the Thai standards, including tôm yam kûng (shrimp and lemon grass soup) and kài phàt bai kàphrao (chicken fried in holy basil). Curries are good here – something you don't see

LAOS

much of in Lao cuisine. A second branch of the Phikun on Thanon Luang Prabang, near the Thai Military Bank just west of Thanon Khun Bulom, is now open.

Noodles, Chinese & Vietnamese Noodles of all kinds are very popular in Vientiane, especially along Thanon Heng Boun, the unofficial Chinatown. Basically, you can choose between fõe, a rice noodle that's popular throughout mainland South-East Asia (known as kuaythiaw or kwayteow in Thailand, Malaysia and Singapore), and mee, the traditional Chinese wheat noodle.

Le Chanthy (Nang Janti) Cuisine Vietnamienne, a small shop on Thanon Chao Anou, one door south of the corner of Thanons Chao Anou and Heng Boun, makes very good Lao-style khào pũn with a choice of three toppings – it's probably the best place in the city centre to try this dish. Janti also offers Vietnamese nãem neũang (barbecued pork meatballs) and yáw (spring rolls), usually sold in 'sets' *(sut)* with cold khào pũn, fresh lettuce leaves, mint, basil, various dipping sauces, sliced starfruit and sliced green plantain.

Indian *The Taj* on Thanon Pangkham opposite Nakhonluang Bank (just north of the fountain) has an extensive menu of well-prepared north Indian dishes, including tandoor, curries, vegetarian and many Indian breads. Service is good and the place is very clean, though prices are a bit high by Vientiane standards. The Taj also has a sizeable daily lunch buffet for 3800 kip and set evening dinners for 3700 to 4500 kip.

Cheaper Indian food can be found at *Nazim Restaurant* on Thanon Phonexay near the Aussie embassy and opposite the Phonexay Hotel. The extensive menu includes mostly North Indian dishes along with a few South Indian items, such as masala dosa and idli.

European Several commendable French and French-Lao restaurants can be found in Vientiane. Most are costly by local standards

but they are definitely better value than restaurants in Vientiane hotels.

One that is particularly good, as well as inexpensive, is the *Santisouk* (formerly a famous teahouse called Café La Pagode) on Thanon Nokeo Khumman, under the Santisouk Guest House. The cuisine is of the 'French grill' type and is quite tasty. A filling plate of steak or filet mignon – served on a sizzling platter – or filleted fish or roast chicken with roast potatoes and vegetables costs less than 3500 kip. Breakfasts are also very good.

Le Bistrot Snack Bar (☎ 215972), opposite the Tai-Pan Hotel on Thanon François Nginn, is owned by an older Lao couple who spent most of their lives in Paris. The fare includes good, relatively inexpensive French dishes, such as poulet provençal and boeuf bourguignon (both of which come with vegetables and potatoes or rice), along with a spicy salade chinoise made with bean-thread noodles and chicken, and a variety of couscous meals offered with chicken, mutton or merguez (spicy Moroccan lamb sausage). Don't let the sometimes empty dining room put you off – for some reason this place hasn't caught on yet (perhaps because service is a tad slow for the technocratic set) but it's good value.

Popular with techies, diplomats, UN staff, and other expats on large salaries is the intimate *Restaurant-Bar Namphu* (☎ 216248) on the Fountain Circle off Thanon Pangkham. The food and service are generally impeccable and the menu includes a number of German and Lao dishes as well as French – the popular blue-cheese hamburger adds an American touch; there's also a well-stocked bar. Prices average 9000 kip per entree, or roughly one-tenth Laos' annual per-capita income.

Le Bayou Bar Brasserie on Thanon Setthathirat, diagonally opposite Wat Ong Teu, is a simple but charming spot with a choice of seating in the air-con dining room or narrow beer garden alongside. Prices are very reasonable – among the lowest of any European restaurant outside the Santisouk and Le Bistrot – and the fare includes draught beer, breakfasts, pasta, pizza, sandwiches, fondue and brochettes. The various salads and fruit shakes are especially good.

Entertainment

Bars *Samlo Pub*, next door to Restaurant Sourichanh on Thanon Setthathirat (opposite Wat In Paeng), is a small, well-stocked bar that's popular with visitors and expats alike. Draught Beerlao is available on tap.

Other watering holes worth checking out include the tiny but well-serviced bar at *Restaurant-Bar Namphu*. On hot nights *Namphou Garden*, the collection of outdoor tables around the fountain, is also quite popular.

If you're looking for something with more of a local flavour, and less expensive than the expat bars, your best bet is one of the many bịa sót (draught beer) bars around town. These are usually nondescript rooms filled with wooden tables at the bottom of a shophouse – look for plastic jugs of beer on the tables. One of the better deals is *Bia Sot Si Meuang* at the south-eastern end of Thanon Samsenthai near Wat Si Muang. Bia Sot Si Meuang offers draught Beerlao at a mere 650 kip per litre, along with the bottled stuff for 800 kip per large bottle.

Sala Bia Lao (Lao Beer House), on Thong Kham Square near Talaat Thong Khan Kham, is a hipper beer bar decorated with Lao folk and old-west motifs; live Lao and Thai pop is featured from 5 pm to 1 am nightly.

Cinema Lao cinema houses have all but died out in the video shop tidal wave of recent years. A lone survivor, the *Odeon Rama* (also known as *Vientiane Theatre*, ☎ 214613) near Talaat Laeng in Ban Nong Duang, maintains a regular schedule of Thai, Chinese and western movies, all of which are dubbed in Lao by a live team of dubbers using three microphones.

The *Centre de Langue Française* (☎ 215764) on Thanon Lan Xang screens French films (subtitled in English) each Thursday at 7.15 pm. Admission is 700 kip and the screenings are open to the general public. Film titles for the following week are usually listed in the weekly *Vientiane Times* or you can call the centre for information.

Dancing Vientiane has at least six 'discos' with live music. Popular places include the *Nightclub Vienglatry* on Thanon Lan Xang, a bit north of Talaat Sao (and on the same side of the street), along with clubs attached to the *Anou*, *Saysana* and *Inter* hotels.

Things to Buy

Just about anything made in Laos is available for purchase in Vientiane, including hill tribe crafts, jewellery, traditional fabrics and carvings. The main shopping areas are Talaat Sao (including shops along Thanon Talaat Sao), west along Thanon Samsenthai (near the Hotel Ekalath Metropole) and on Thanon Pangkham.

Getting There & Away

Air Vientiane is the only legal port of entry into Laos for international flights.

Bus Bus travel beyond Vientiane Prefecture no longer requires any special travel permits. The main bus terminal, built with Japanese aid in 1990, stands next to Talaat Sao on Thanon Khu Vieng. A second terminal on Route 13 near Km 6 also has buses to the south, eg Tha Khaek, Savannakhet and Pakse. Fares and departure frequencies are the same.

If you plan to travel by interprovincial bus out of Vientiane, it's a good idea to visit the terminal the day before your anticipated departure to confirm departure times, which seem to change every few months. For some of the long-distance buses, such as Savan and Pakse, it may be possible to purchase tickets in advance.

Friendship Bridge The Thai-Lao Friendship Bridge is about 20 km from Vientiane. A car taxi costs 4000 kip and a jumbo motorcycle taxi should cost about 1000 kip, although many drivers will ask new arrivals from Thailand for 100B (which is what a car taxi should cost).

LAOS

Boat A single river route runs north to Luang Prabang along the Mekong River from Vientiane. Foreigners no longer need special permission to board these boats. Boat service to Luang Prabang has become more irregular following improvements to Route 13 north to Vang Vieng and Kasi; most Lao nowadays use road transport since it's faster and cheaper – even if it means risking a shootout around Kasi. The boat is much safer, although slower; if you can't fly to Luang Prabang, we recommend going by boat rather than bus – at least until the 'problem' around Kasi is worked out.

The ferry to Luang Prabang usually takes four or five days upriver, three or four days down, depending on type of boat, cargo load and river height. When the river is low, direct Vientiane-Luang Prabang service aboard the large, two deck ferries may be suspended and passengers must board smaller craft, changing boats at the halfway point in Pak Lai.

Luang Prabang ferries leave from the Kao Liaw Boat Landing (Tha Heua Kao Liaw), which is 7.7 km west of the Novotel Vientiane (3.5 km west of the fork in the road where Route 13 heads north) in Ban Kao Liaw. The usual departure time is between 8 and 9 am, and the maximum passenger load for most boats is 20 people. You should go to Kao Liaw the day before your intended departure to make sure a boat is going and to reserve deck space.

The Luang Prabang ferry makes several stops along the way. Passengers typically sleep on the boat, except in Pak Lai, where there are a couple of small guesthouses.

Destination	Fare (kip)
Huay La	2500
Sanakham	3500
Don Men	5000
Pak Lai	5300
Tha Deua	7000
Luang Prabang	12,000

Speedboats Faster boat service is available aboard six passenger *héua wái* (speedboats), which cost 15,000 kip per person to Pak Lai, 22,000 kip to Tha Deua and 30,000 kip to Luang Prabang. Count on a full day to reach Tha Deua or Luang Prabang, four or five hours for Pak Lai. To charter a speedboat you'd have to pay a fee equal to six passenger fares. Like the slower ferries, speedboats leave from the Kao Liaw Boat Landing.

Savannakhet Regular ferry service to Savannakhet has been cancelled, though in rare instances when Route 13 South is flooded (as it was in October 1995), service may be temporarily reinstated. If so, boats to Savan will leave from the old southern ferry pier at Km 4, Thanon Tha Deua.

Getting Around

Central Vientiane is entirely accessible on foot. For trips into neighbouring districts, however, you'll need vehicular support.

The Airport Taxis wait in front of the airport for passengers going into town. The going rate is 1000 kip for a motorcycle taxi, 2000 kip for a car taxi; drivers may ask for more (typically 100B). You would be better off catching a motorcycle taxi on the road in front of the airport, where the fare is only around 15B or about 500 kip. If you're heading further – say to eastern Vientiane past Wat Si Muang – you'll have to pay around 1500 kip for a jumbo, 2500 to 3000 kip for a car.

Bus There is a city bus system but it's not oriented towards central Chanthabuli, where most of the hotels, restaurants, sightseeing and shopping are located. Rather, it's for transport to outlying districts to the north, east and west of Chanthabuli. Fares for any distance within Vientiane Prefecture are low – about 200 kip for a 20 km ride.

Motorcycle Taxi The standard size holds two or three passengers. The larger jumbos have two short benches in the back and can hold four, five or even six passengers if the passengers are not too large. Hire charges are about the same as for pedicabs but, of course, they're much speedier. A jumbo driver will

LAOS

be glad to take passengers on journeys as short as half a km or as far as 20 km. Although the common asking fare for foreigners seems to be 1000 kip, the standard local fare for a chartered jumbo should be 400 to 500 kip for distances of two km or less; bargaining is mandatory.

Share jumbos which run regular routes around town (eg Thanon Luang Prabang to Thanon Setthathirat, or Thanon Lan Xang to That Luang) cost 200 kip per person; no bargaining is necessary.

Motorcycle Vientiane Motor, opposite the fountain on Thanon Setthathirat, rents 100cc motorcycles for US$8 to US$10 per day.

Pedicabs Recently, samlor (sãam-lâw) have almost become extinct. Charges are about 300 kip per km (but don't hire a samlor for any distance greater than two or three km).

Bicycle This is the most convenient and economical way to see Vientiane besides walking. Several guesthouses rent bikes on a regular basis for around 1000 kip per day. Kanchana Boutique opposite the Hotel Ekalath Metropole on Thanon That Dam also has a few bikes for rent.

AROUND VIENTIANE
Lao Pako

Lao Pako (☎ 216600), a rustic bamboo-thatch village on the Ngum River about 55 km north-east of Vientiane via Ban Somsamai, is a good spot to enjoy the Lao countryside without leaving Vientiane Province. Rates are 6000 kip in a dormitory and 15,000 to 20,000 kip for private bungalows with bath. All rooms are screened and come with mosquito nets but no electricity. There is also an open-air *sala* where you can sleep on the floor for 2000 kip a night. Activities include swimming, boating and hiking, and there are Lao-style buffet meals, weekend barbecues and monthly full-moon parties.

The best way to reach Lao Pako is to drive or take a 1½ hour bus trip to Somsamai (bus No 19 from Talaat Sao, 350 kip, three times daily at 6.30, 11 am and 3 pm) on the Nam Ngum river, where a local motorised canoe will take you on to the lodge, a 25 minute journey, for 1500 kip.

Ang Nam Ngum (Nam Ngum Reservoir)

Approximately 90 km north of Vientiane, Ang Nam Ngum is a huge artificial lake that was created by damming the Nam Ngum (Ngum River). A hydroelectric plant here generates most of the power used in the Vientiane Valley, as well as the power sold to Thailand via high-power wires over the Mekong River.

The lake is dotted with picturesque islands and a cruise is well worth arranging (7000 kip per hour for boats holding up to 20 passengers is the going rate). On the way to the lake you can stop in **Ban Ilai**, in the Muang Naxaithong district, known for a market with basketry, pottery and other daily utensils. Several other villages can be visited along the way.

Places to Stay Ang Nam Ngum can be visited on a day trip from Vientiane. Nam Ngum Tour Company operates a *floating hotel*, with large, clean rooms complete with private hot-water baths and air-con for 10,000 kip per night. The boat is fairly pleasant but rarely leaves the pier except when groups book the entire boat. The dock location is not particularly scenic because of the trashy lumber operations nearby.

A new *hotel* recently opened on Don Dok Khon Kham, an island only 10 minutes by boat from the harbour. This one costs 7000 kip single/double; food is available, but running water and electricity only come on in the evening. A shuttle boat to this island costs 1000 kip.

Getting There & Away From Talaat Sao, you can catch the 7 am bus all the way to Kheuan Nam Ngum (Nam Ngum Dam) for 500 kip. This trip takes three hours and proceeds along Route 13 through Ban Thalat. Taxis in Vientiane charge US$35 to US$40 return to the lake. If you hire one, ask the

LAOS

driver to take the more scenic Route 10 through Ban Keun; the trip is about the same distance as the trip via Ban Thalat. Or make a circle route to see both areas.

Vang Vieng

Surrounded by scenic karst topography, this small town about 70 km north of Phon Hong (160 km north of Vientiane) via Route 13 nestles in a bend in the Song River. Caverns and tunnels in the limestone are named and play small roles in local mythology – all are said to be inhabited by spirits.

The most famous of the Vang Vieng caves is **Tham Jang**, a large cavern that was used as a bunker in defence against marauding Chinese Ho (Jiin Haw) in the early 19th century. To find these caves, ask an angler or boatman along the river to show you the way – most will be glad to guide you to two or three caves for a few hundred kip. The section of the river where most of the caves are found is within walking distance (about two km south-west) of the town centre. Even if you don't plan on any cave exploration, a walk along the river can be rewarding.

Other than the Chinese-built cement factory just outside of town and a little-used airstrip between Route 13 and the town, Vang Vieng is well removed from modernisation.

Places to Stay Two guesthouses next to the bus terminal and market, *Phou Bane* and *Saynamsong*, offer basic but clean two-bed rooms for 2000 to 3000 kip per night with shared bath. *Vang Vieng Resort* (☎ 214743; radio phone 130440), slightly out of town but near the caves and river, features quiet, comfortable red-tiled cottages for US$15 per room.

Getting There & Away Route 13 is paved all the way to Vang Vieng. From Vientiane's Talaat Sao bus terminal catch bus No 1 at 7.30, 9.30 am or 1 pm. The fare is 1300 kip and the trip takes about 3½ hours.

Northern Laos

LUANG PRABANG

The Luang Prabang area was the site of early Thai-Lao meuangs that were established in the high river valleys along the Mekong River and its major tributaries, the Nam Khan, the Nam Ou and the Nam Seuang (Xeuang). The first Lao kingdom, Lan Xang, was consolidated here in 1353 by the Khmer-supported conqueror Fa Ngum. Luang Prabang remained the capital of Lan Xang until King Phothisarat moved the seat of administration to Vientiane in 1545.

Even after the Lan Xang period, Luang Prabang was considered the main source of monarchic power. When Lan Xang broke up following the death of King Suliya Vongsa in 1694, one of Suliya's grandsons established an independent kingdom in Luang Prabang that competed with the other kingdoms in Vientiane and Champasak. From then on, the Luang Prabang monarchy was so weak that it was forced to pay tribute at various times to the Siamese and the Vietnamese, and finally, in the early 20th century, to the French when Laos became a French protectorate.

The French allowed Laos to retain the Luang Prabang monarchy, however, as did the fledgling independent governments that followed, and it wasn't until the Vietnamese-backed Pathet Lao took over in 1975 that the monarchy was finally dissolved.

Today, Luang Prabang is a sleepy town of 16,000 inhabitants with a handful of historic temples and old French mansions in a beautiful mountain setting.

Orientation

The town sits at the confluence of the Mekong River and the Nam Khan. A large hill called Phu Si (sometimes spelt Phousy) dominates the town skyline at the upper end of a peninsula formed by the junction of the two rivers. Most of the historic temples are between Phu Si and the Mekong. The whole town can easily be covered, on foot, in a day or two.

Maps The LNTA and National Geographic Service released a good bilingual colour map of the city, *Louang Prabang Tourist Map*, in 1994 – it's available at the main tourist hotels for around US$2.

Information

Immigration Luang Prabang's immigration is the strictest in the country when it comes to officially checking in and out of the province. If you fly into the city, the *jâeng khào/jâeng àwk* procedure is efficiently taken care of at Luang Prabang airport as at most other Lao airports. If you arrive by road or boat, be sure to check in with immigration on the day of arrival if possible. Officials in Luang Prabang are quick to levy fines – in fact they do so with great gusto – if you delay the procedure for getting your permit checked.

There are small immigration police posts at the slow-boat and speedboat landings for those arriving by river, and one at the bus terminal as well. The main immigration office is on Thanon Wisunalat. Here you'll

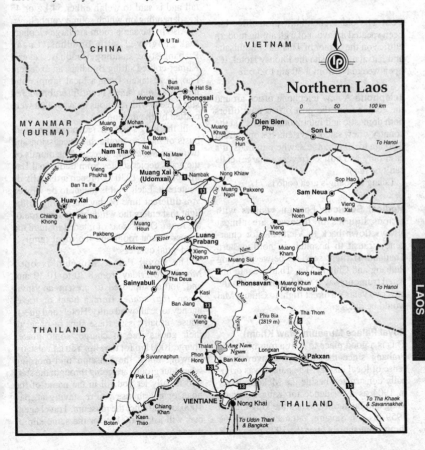

Northern Laos

0   50   100 km

LAOS

find a list of all the potential fines you must pay for neglecting to check in or for overstaying your visa; they are the highest in Laos and it's no use arguing that other provincial offices charge less.

Money Lane Xang Bank, 65 Thanon Phothisalat, will change Thai and US currency only – cash or travellers' cheques – for kip. The bank normally won't change in the other direction – kip for either baht or dollars – because of a claimed shortage of these currencies. The rate is a bit lower than in Vientiane.

Post The old French-built post office has been vacated in favour of a gleaming modern edifice on the corner of Thanons Phothisalat and Kitsalat, opposite the Phousy Hotel. It's open weekdays from 8.30 am to 5 pm.

Telephone A new telephone office around the corner from the post office now offers both domestic and international calls via the country's new satcom system. It's open from 7.30 am to 10 pm; as elsewhere in Laos, it's cash only and collect (reverse-charge) calls can't be made.

Luang Prabang's area code is 71.

Medical Services Foreign visitors with serious injuries or illnesses are almost always flown back to Vientiane for emergency transit to hospitals in north-eastern Thailand. If flight services between Luang Prabang and Chiang Mai, Thailand, are initiated (rumours say it will happen within the next two years), a direct flight to Chiang Mai would be quicker.

Royal Palace Museum (Haw Kham)

This is a good place to start a tour of Luang Prabang since the displays convey some sense of local history. The palace was originally constructed beside the Mekong River in 1904 as a residence for King Sisavang Vong and his family. When the king died in 1959 his son Savang Vattana inherited the throne, but shortly after the 1975 revolution

he and his family were exiled to northern Laos (never to be heard from again) and the palace was converted into a museum.

Various royal religious objects are on display in the large entry hall, as well as rare Buddhist sculpture from India, Cambodia and Laos. One memorable exhibit is a Luang Prabang-style standing Buddha, which is sculpted from marble and in the Contemplating the Bodhi Tree pose.

The right front corner room of the palace, which opens to the outside, contains the museum's most prized art, including the Pha Bang. This gold standing Buddha is 83 cm tall and is said to weigh either 54 kg or 43 kg, depending on which source you believe.

Also in the same room are large elephant tusks engraved with Buddhas, Luang Prabang-style standing Buddhas, several Khmer-crafted sitting Buddhas, an excellent Lao frieze taken from a local temple and three *saew mâi khán* – beautiful embroidered silk screens with religious imagery that were crafted by the queen.

In the king's former reception room are busts of the Lao monarchic succession and two large *Ramayana* screens. The murals on the walls depict scenes from traditional Lao life, painted in 1930 by French artist Alix de Fautereau. Each wall is meant to be viewed at a different time of day, according to the light that enters the windows on one side of the room. Other areas of interest include the former throne room and the royal family's residential quarters.

The Royal Palace Museum is open Monday to Friday from 8.30 to 10.30 am, and you're supposed to present an 'invitation' *(bai sanõe)* from a hotel or travel agency to be allowed entry. Hotels and guesthouses usually issue these slips of paper to their guests free of charge; some places charge 1000 kip for the slip. You can also try showing up at the museum mid-morning when tour groups are going through; the staff will usually let you fill in the name of the hotel or guesthouse you're staying at, pay 1000 kip and enter the museum. Travel agencies will ask 3000 kip for the same slip of paper.

Wat Xieng Thong

Near the northern tip of the peninsula formed by the Mekong and Nam Khan rivers is Luang Prabang's most magnificent temple, Wat Xieng Thong (Golden City Temple). It was built by King Setthathirat in 1560 and until 1975 remained under royal patronage. Like the royal palace, Wat Xieng Thong was placed within easy reach of the Mekong.

The sim represents classic Luang Prabang temple architecture, with roofs that sweep low to the ground (the same style is also found in northern Thailand). The rear wall of the sim features an impressive 'tree of life' mosaic set on a red background. Inside, richly decorated wooden columns support a ceiling that's vested with *dhammachakkas* (dharma wheels).

Near the compound's eastern gate stands the royal funeral chapel. Inside is an impressive 12-metre-high funeral chariot and various funeral urns for each member of the royal family. Gilt panels on the exterior of the chapel depict erotic episodes from the *Ramayana*.

Admission to Wat Xieng Thong is 250 kip.

Wat Wisunalat

This temple, also known as Wat Vixoun, is to the east of the town centre and was originally constructed in 1513, making it the oldest continually operating temple in Luang Prabang. It was rebuilt in 1898 following a fire two years earlier. The original was made of wood, and in the brick and stucco restoration, the builders attempted to make the balustraded windows of the sim appear to be fashioned from lathed wood (an old south Indian and Khmer contrivance that is uncommon in Lao architecture). Also unique is the front roof which slopes sideways over the terrace.

Inside the high-ceilinged sim is a collection of wooden Calling for Rain Buddhas and 15th to 16th century Luang Prabang *sima* (ordination stones). In front of the sim is That Pathum (Lotus Stupa) which was built in 1514. It's more commonly called That Mak Mo, or Watermelon Stupa, for its hemispherical shape.

Phu Si

The temples on the slopes of Phu Si are all of rather recent construction, but it's likely that other temples were previously located on this important hill site. None of the temples are that memorable, but the top of the hill affords an excellent view of the town.

On the lower slopes of the hill are **Wat Paa Huak** and **Wat Pha Phutthabaat**. To continue an ascent all the way to the summit of the hill you are required to pay a 500 kip admission fee, collected at the northern entrance near Wat Paa Huak. At the summit is **That Chomsi**, the starting point for a colourful Lao New Year procession held in mid-April. Behind this temple is a small cave shrine called **Wat Tham Phu Si**, or Wat Thammothayaram. On a nearby crest is an old Russian anti-aircraft cannon that children use as a makeshift merry-go-round.

Other Temples

Close to the Phousy Hotel and the GPO is **Wat Mai Suwannaphumaham** (New Temple), built in 1796 and at one time a residence of the Sangkharat, or Supreme Patriarch of the Lao Sangha. The front veranda is remarkable for its decorated columns and for the sumptuous gold relief panels on the doors that recount the legend of Vessantara (Pha Wet), the Buddha's penultimate incarnation, as well as scenes from the *Ramayana* and local village life. The Pha Bang, which is usually housed in Luang Prabang's National Museum, is put on public display at Wat Mai Suwannaphumaham during the Lao New Year celebrations.

Across the Mekong River from central Luang Prabang are several temples that aren't remarkable except for the pleasant rural settings. **Wat Tham Xieng Maen** is in a limestone cave almost directly across the river from Wat Xieng Thong. Many Buddha images from temples that have burned down or fallen into decay are kept here. Near Wat Tham are several other caves that are easily found and explored – bring along a torch (flashlight).

Tastefully restored **Wat Long Khun** is a little to the east of Wat Tham and features a nicely decorated portico of 1937 vintage, plus older sections from the 18th century. When the coronation of a Luang Prabang king was pending, it was customary for him to spend three days in retreat at Wat Long Khun before ascending the throne. Boats can be chartered from Luang Prabang's northern pier to Wat Long Khun for 3000 kip for a round trip or you can wait for the infrequent ferry boats which charge just 100 kip per passenger.

At the top of a hill above the previous two wats is peaceful **Wat Chom Phet**, where one can obtain an undisturbed view of the river.

A few km to the south-east of town is the recently constructed **Santi Jedi**, or Peace Pagoda. This large yellow stupa contains three levels inside plus an outside terrace near the top with a view of the surrounding plains. The interior walls are painted with all manner of Buddhist stories and moral admonitions.

Behind the That Luang Market in town is a modern Vietnamese-Lao Buddhist temple, **Wat Pha Baat Tai**.

Markets

Luang Prabang's main marketplace, **Talaat Dala**, stands at the intersection of Thanons

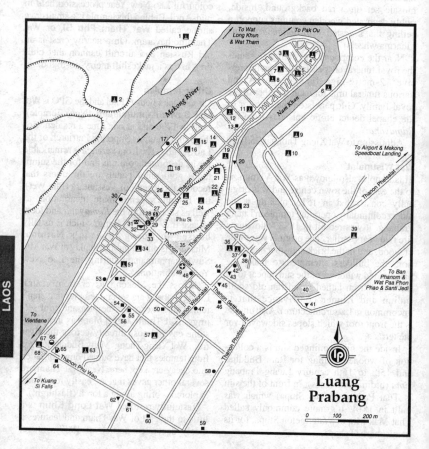

Luang Prabang

Kitsalat and Latsavong. Although not huge by Vientiane standards, it nonetheless features an impressive array of hardware, cookware, dried or preserved foodstuffs, textiles and handicrafts.

The main fresh market, **Talaat Sao**, is at the intersection of Thanons Phothisalat and Phu Wao near the river and Wat Pha Baat Tai. Also important for fresh produce is **Talaat Vieng Mai** at the north-eastern end of Thanon Photisan.

Places to Stay

Viengkeo Hotel (☎ 212271) on Thanon Setthathilat is a funky two storey house that has seven plain two and three-bed rooms with shared bath for 4200 kip per room. The staff and mostly local clientele are friendly and welcoming, but virtually no English or French is spoken. An upstairs veranda sitting area overlooks the street.

Around the corner near Wat Wisunalat is the basic but well-run *Rama Hotel* (☎ 212247), where large, clean doubles with fan and private cold-water bath cost 5000/7000 kip single/double a night.

Vannida Guest House (☎ 212374), 87/4 Thanon Noranarai, is a huge, atmospheric 80-year-old ex-colonial mansion in the quiet residential neighbourhood of Ban That Luang, a few blocks south-west of Talaat Dala. Simple rooms with unscreened windows cost US$8 single, US$10 double. Toilet and shower facilities are shared. Less than a block away, on the same side of the street in Ban That Luang, the *Boun Gning Guest House* (☎ 212274) offers rooms with screened windows in a modern house for US$6/8 single/double, with shared facilities.

Places to Eat

There are numerous small restaurants and cafes along Thanon Phothisarat near the Phousy Hotel, some of which specialise in làap. The *Young Koun Restaurant*, down the street from Wat Wisunalat, has Lao and Chinese food at fairly reasonable prices. Two or three doors up from the Young Koun – and more 'in' these days with visiting development players – is the equally good *Visoun Restaurant*, which serves mostly Chinese food. Both restaurants are open from early in

PLACES TO STAY		OTHER		27	Lane Xang Bank
13	Villa Santi	1	Wat Chom Phet	29	Luang Prabang
28	New Luang Prabang	2	Wat Xieng Maen		Tourism
	Hotel	3	Wat Xieng Thong	30	Long-distance Ferries
33	Hotel Phousy	4	Wat Pakkhan	31	Telephone Office
44	Rama Hotel	5	Wat Khili	32	Post Office
46	Viengkeo Hotel	6	Wat Sa-at	34	Wat Ho Siang
50	Champa-Lao Hotel	7	Wat Si Bun Heuang	35	Talaat Dala
52	Hotel	8	Wat Si Muang Khun	36	Wat Aham
	Souvannaphoum	9	Wat Paa Khaa	37	Wat Wisunalat
54	Vannida Guest House	10	Wat Phon Song	38	Lao Red Cross
55	Boun Gning Guest	11	Wat Saen	39	Wat Tao Hai
	House	12	Wat Nong	40	Talaat Vieng Mai
59	Phu Vao Hotel		Sikhunmuang	42	Immigration
60	Manoluck Hotel	14	Wat Paa Phai	47	Lao Aviation
61	Muangsua Hotel	15	Wat Xieng Muan	48	Lane Xang Travel
64	Silivongvanh Hotel	16	Wat Chum Khong	49	Provincial Hospital
		17	Boats to Pak Ou	51	Wat That
PLACES TO EAT		18	Royal Palace Museum	53	Provincial Office
20	Khem Karn Food	19	Wat Thammo	56	Air Lao
	Garden	21	Wat Pha Phutthabaat	57	Wat Manolom
41	Vieng Mai Restaurant	22	Wat Tham Phu Sì	58	Talaat Naviengkham
43	Visoun Restaurant	23	Wat Aphai	63	Wat That Luang
45	Young Koun	24	That Chomsi	65	Petrol Station
	Restaurant	25	Wat Paa Huak	66	Bus Terminal
62	Malee Lao Food	26	Wat Mai	67	Wat Pha Baat Tai
			Suwannaphumaham	68	Talaat Sao

LAOS

the morning till late at night and have fairly extensive bilingual menus.

Very good and authentic Lao food is available at *Malee Lao Food*, a rustic wooden eatery run by Malee Khevalat on Thanon Phu Wao.

Along the Mekong River are several small thatched-roof, open-air restaurants with passable Lao food. Khào pùn (thin wheat noodles topped with curry) is available from early morning till early afternoon at the back of the That Luang Market.

Luang Prabang's first independently owned falang (foreign) eatery, *Bar-Restaurant Duang Champa*, is housed in a white two storey colonial near the Nam Khan. The extensive menu includes set meals such as steak frites or poulet grillé et frites for a bargain 3000 to 3500 kip, along with ice cream, paté, sandwiches, a few Lao dishes and imported French wines by the glass or bottle.

Getting There & Away

Air Lao Aviation has daily flights from Vientiane to Luang Prabang. The flight takes only 40 minutes and the fare is US$46 one way. The Lao Aviation office is on Thanon Wisunalat, around the corner from the Viengkeo Hotel. There are four flights per week to/from Phonsavan (35 minutes, US$31) and three flights per week from Huay Xai (50 minutes, US$42), plus one or two flights per week to/from Luang Nam Tha (30 minutes, US$34) and Udomxai (35 minutes, US$25). Flight frequency to/from Luang Nam Tha and Udomxai depends largely on passenger load and availability of aircraft; the only way to find out for sure is to ask at Lao Aviation a day in advance of scheduled departures.

Bus & Truck It is possible but not recommended to travel by road out of Luang Prabang. Many of the roads are dangerous, both due to their poor condition and security problems from dissident groups.

Vientiane Luang Prabang can be reached via Route 13 from Vientiane (420 km) but until the road is completely graded and paved –

and until the security situation is improved – it's a trip for the foolhardy. So far the road is finished from Vientiane as far as Kasi, roughly two-thirds of the way. See Dangers & Annoyances in the earlier Facts for the Visitor section for important information on bandit/rebel attacks between Kasi and Luang Prabang.

Other Provinces Luang Prabang is linked with Udomxai Province by road via Nambak (Route 1) and Muang Xai to Luang Nam Tha Province (Route 2). It's also possible to reach Xieng Khuang via Route 7 (which continues east into northern Vietnam), but the road is high and beset with natural and political hazards.

Boat In Luang Prabang the main landing for long-distance Mekong River boats, at the north-west end of Thanon Kitsalat, is called Thaa Héua Méh.

Speedboats use a landing at Ban Don, six km north of Luang Prabang. A jumbo to Ban Don from Talaat Dala can be chartered for 1500 kip. From Ban Don into town foreigners are charged a standard 800 kip for a shared jumbo; to charter one you must pay 4800 kip.

Vientiane Several times a week cargo boats leave Vientiane's Kao Liaw Boat Landing on the Mekong River for the 430 km river trip to Luang Prabang. The duration of the voyage depends on river height, but is typically four or five days upriver, three or four days down. From Vientiane the fare is 12,000 kip per person.

For downriver (Vientiane-bound) journeys the local boat service charges foreigner's prices that are 50% higher than local fare (and 50% higher than those charged in Vientiane).

See under Getting There & Away in the Vientiane section earlier in this chapter for further information on this route.

Pakbeng & Huay Xai It's also possible to travel by boat along the Mekong River northwest to Pakbeng (160 km) on the Sainyabuli/

Udomxai border (for road trips north to Muang Xai) or all the way to Huay Xai (300 km) in Bokeo Province, both of which are now open to foreigners carrying the proper permits.

By slow river ferry the trip to Huay Xai takes two days with an overnight in Pakbeng. The passenger fare is 12,000 kip from Luang Prabang (9000 kip in the reverse direction), and only 6000 kip as far as Pakbeng (4000 kip reverse).

Faster and smaller speedboats reach Pakbeng in three hours, Huay Xai in six or seven. The inflated fares out of Luang Prabang are 13,500 kip and 27,000 kip respectively (9000 kip and 18,000 kip downriver until two-tier pricing fever catches on). If you want to share the cost of hiring a boat with other passengers it's best to show up at the northern pier the day before you want to leave and see what your prospects are. Then show up again around 6 am the morning of your intended departure to queue up. Speedboat fares are often quoted in Thai baht, though either kip or Thai baht (or US dollars) are acceptable payment.

Nong Khiaw & Muang Khua An alternate way to Luang Prabang from Muang Xai in Udomxai Province is via Nong Khiaw in northern Luang Prabang Province, which is about 127 km by road or along the Nam Ou river. The Nong Khiaw landing is sometimes referred to as Muang Ngoi, the village on the opposite bank of the Nam Ou, or as Nambak, a larger village to the west. Shared speedboats between Luang Prabang and Nong Khiaw cost 8000 kip upriver, 5200 kip downriver, and take around 2½ hours when the water is high enough; during the dry season some stretches of the upper Nam Ou can be treacherous and most pilots won't attempt the trip. From Nong Khiaw it's an hour west to Nambak by passenger truck.

Further upriver from Nong Khiaw are the riverbank villages of Muang Khua (205 km from Luang Prabang) and Hat Sa Neua (265 km), both jumping-off points for Phongsali Province excursions. Speedboats to Muang Khua cost 18,000 per person from Luang

Prabang (12,000 kip in the reverse direction) and take four to five hours. To Hat Sa Neua, a short truck ride from Phongsali's capital, speedboats cost 28,500 kip (18,000 kip reverse) and take up to six hours.

Once Route 13, north parallelling the Nam Ou between Luang Prabang and Nambak, is upgraded and paved, speedboat service along this route will most likely be discontinued.

Getting Around
The Airport Shared jumbos or mini-trucks charge a uniform 1000 kip per foreigner (less for Lao) from the airport into town; in the reverse direction you can usually charter an entire jumbo for the same price.

Local Transport Most of the town is accessible on foot. Jumbos and motor samlor charge around 200 kip per km, with a 300 kip minimum.

The Rama Hotel rents bicycles for 1000 kip per day.

AROUND LUANG PRABANG
Pak Ou Caves
About 25 km by boat from Luang Prabang along the Mekong River, at the mouth of the Nam Ou, are the famous Pak Ou Caves (Pak Ou means Mouth of the Ou). The two caves in the lower part of a limestone cliff are crammed with a variety of Buddha images, most of them classic Luang Prabang standing Buddhas.

On the way to Pak Ou, you can have the boatman stop at small villages on the banks of the Mekong, including one that specialises in the production of *lào láo*, distilled rice liquor.

Getting There & Away You can hire boats from the pier behind the Royal Palace Museum. A long-tail boat seating up to 10 passengers should cost about US$20 to US$25 for the day, including petrol. The trip takes one to 1½ hours one way, depending on the speed of the boat. If you stop at villages along the way, it will naturally take longer.

Kuang Si Falls

This beautiful spot 29 km south of Luang Prabang features a wide, multi-tiered waterfall tumbling over limestone formations into a series of cool, turquoise-green pools. The lower level of the falls has been turned into a public park with shelters and picnic tables, and vendors sell drinks and snacks. A trail ascends through the forest along the left side of the falls to a second tier which is more private (most visitors stay below) and has a pool large enough for swimming and splashing around.

Getting There & Away Guided tours to the falls booked through a local agency cost US$50 to US$60 and include transport and lunch at the falls. Freelance guides in Luang Prabang offer trips by car or motorcycle for US$12 to US$15.

Nong Khiaw (Muang Ngoi)

Anyone travelling by road or river from the capital to Phongsali, Hua Phan or Xieng Khuang provinces stands a good chance of spending some time in Nong Khiaw, a village on the banks of the Nam Ou in northern Luang Prabang Province. Route 1, which extends west to east from Muang Xai to Nam Noen (at the junction with Route 6 in Hua Phan Province), crosses the river here via a steel bridge.

The village is little more than a haphazard collection of palm thatch and bamboo shacks on the Nam Ou's west bank. Sometimes it's referred to as Muang Ngoi, which is actually the group of shacks on the east bank, and sometimes it's called Nambak, which is actually 23 km west of Nong Khiaw by road.

Places to Stay & Eat Near the bridge and river landing is an unnamed bamboo *guesthouse* with very basic three-bed rooms for 1000 kip per person or 2000 kip for the whole room. There's no running water or electricity; you must bathe using buckets of water carried from the river.

A couple of very simple outdoor *cafes* next to the parking area for passenger trucks offer fish soup, sticky rice and noodles.

Getting There & Away Japanese pickups travelling to Muang Xai leave Nong Khiaw roughly three times a day – around 8 to 9 am, 12.30 to 1 pm and 3 to 4 pm. The trip takes five hours and costs 4000 kip.

XIENG KHUANG PROVINCE

Along with Hua Phan Province, Xieng Khuang province was devastated by the war. Virtually every town and village in the province was bombed between 1964 and 1973. Flying into the province, one is struck at first by the awesome beauty of high green mountains, rugged karst formations and verdant valleys. But as the plane begins to descend, you notice how much of the province is pockmarked with bomb craters in which little or no vegetation grows.

The province's population of 170,000 is composed of lowland Lao, Thai Dam, Hmong and Phuan. The original capital city, Xieng Khuang, was almost totally bombed out, so the capital was moved to nearby Phonsavan (often spelt Phonsavanh) after the 1975 change of government. Not far from Phonsavan is the mysterious Plain of Jars (Thong Hai Hin).

The moderate altitude in central Xieng Khuang, including Phonsavan and the Plain of Jars, means an excellent year-round climate – not too hot in the hot season, not too cold in the cool season and not overly wet in the rainy season.

Phonsavan

There's not much to the new provincial capital – an airfield, a semipaved main street lined with tin-roofed shops, a market and a few government buildings. Local villagers bring war junk, found in their fields or in the forests, to scrap metal warehouses in town. The warehouses buy the scrap (eg bomb shards, parts of Chinese, Russian and US planes), then sell it to larger warehouses in Vientiane, who in turn sell it to the Thais.

Take care when walking in the fields around Phonsavan, as undetonated live bombs are not uncommon. The locals use bomb casings as pillars for new structures and as fenceposts. Muddy areas are sometimes dotted with pineapple bombs or bomb-lets *(bombi* in Lao), fist-sized explosives that are left over from cluster bombs dropped in the 1970s.

Places to Stay & Eat

Hay Hin Hotel, a simple wooden place on the main street near the market, has basic two-bed rooms with mosquito nets and shared cold-water bath for 2500 kip per night. Further east along the same street, the well-maintained *Dorgkhoune Guest House* offers nicer rooms with mosquito nets and better quality mattresses for 3000 kip single/double and 4000 kip triple with shared facilities, or 4000 kip single/double, 5000 kip triple with private shower and toilet.

Continuing east along the same street, the *Muong Phuan Hotel* has similar but more numerous rooms with attached bath for 5000 kip single/double. Those in the back annex are quietest. This hotel also has its own restaurant.

Back down towards the market are two more fair choices. The two storey *Vanhaloun Hotel* charges 4000 to 5000 kip for simple rooms with shared bath, 8000 kip for larger rooms with private shower and toilet. It's very clean and food can be arranged.

A couple of km south-west of the central area, towards the airport and the Plain of Jars (Site 1), the *Phu Doi Hotel* (formerly the Mittaphap Hotel) is housed in a two storey, V-shaped building opposite Aroun May Bank. Ordinary rooms with shared toilet and cold-water shower facilities are overpriced at 8000 kip; the three VIP rooms come with hot-water showers and good mattresses, overall better value at 15,000 kip.

The clean and well-run *Sangah (Sa-Nga) Restaurant* near the market and post office offers an extensive menu of Chinese, Thai and Lao food, including good yám, tôm yám, khào khùa and fõe, plus a few western food items. Some expats working in Phonsavan have been known to survive on a nightly diet of steak and chips here. Exactly opposite the Sangah, the friendly *Nang Phonkaew* serves the best fõe in town.

Getting There & Away

Planes fly to/from Vientiane once or twice daily (40 minutes, US$37) and to/from Luang Prabang thrice weekly (35 minutes, US$31). Delays are common on the latter flight. The Lao Aviation office (Phonsavan ☎ 103), a wooden shed off the main street in town, is open daily from 7 to 11 am and 1.30 to 3.30 pm; these hours are not strictly followed.

Potholed Route 1 carries passengers east across Udomxai and northern Luang Prabang till the road terminates at Route 7, where a change of buses at the village of Nam Noen continues southward to Phonsavan. It's best to break this journey up by spending the night in Nambak or Nong Khiaw (both in northern Luang Prabang) so that you can get an early start and make it straight from Nambak to Phonsavan in one day – a journey of about 12 hours, including a change of bus in Nam Noen. You're also more likely to find public transport in the early morning; afternoon buses are few and far between in this part of the country.

To/from Sam Neua, capital of Hua Phan Province, is a 12 hour, 238 km road trip to Phonsavan via Routes 6 and 7. You must change buses at the junction of Routes 6 and 1 (Nam Noen). Logistically, one of the best ways to do this trip is to fly to Sam Neua from Vientiane, then head south by road to Phonsavan. For details see under Sam Neua in the following Hua Phan Province section.

Plain of Jars

A few km south-east of Phonsavan is an area of rolling fields where huge jars of unknown origin are scattered about. The jars weigh an average of 600 kg to one tonne each, though the biggest of them weigh as much as six tonnes. They appear to have been fashioned from solid stone, but there is disagreement on this point.

Various theories (none proved conclusively as yet) have been advanced as to the functions of the stone jars: they were used as sarcophagi, as wine fermenters or for rice storage. Many of the smaller jars have been taken away by collectors, but there are still several hundred or so on the plain. In addition to the main site known as **Thong Hai Hin**, there are two other sites in the area which can be visited with the assistance of a guide, available through any guesthouse.

Tham Piu

In this cave, near the former village of Ban Nameun, nearly 400 villagers, many of them women and children, were killed by a single rocket (most likely from a Nomad T-28 fighter plane manned by a Royal Lao Air Force pilot) in 1969. The cave itself is not much to see, just a large cave in the side of a limestone cliff. It's the journey to Tham Piu that is the real attraction, since it passes several Hmong and Thai Dam villages along the way and involves a bit of hiking in the forest.

The cave is a few km beyond the small town of Muang Kham, which is 33 km east of Phonsavan on Route 7. Also in this area is a hot mineral spring (baw nâam hâwn) that feeds into a stream a few hundred metres off the road. You can sit in the stream right where the hot water combines with the cool stream water and 'adjust' the temperature by moving around.

Further east along the same road, 60 km from Phonsavan, is the market town of Nong Haet, only about 25 km short of the Vietnam border.

Getting There & Away To get to Tham Piu, you'd have to take a Nong Haet bus from Phonsavan and ask to be let out at the turn-off for Tham Piu. From the turn-off, start walking towards the limestone cliff north of the road until you're within a km of the cliff. At this point you have to plunge into the woods and make your way along a honeycomb of trails to the bottom of the cliff and then mount a steep, narrow trail that leads up to the mouth of the cave.

It is best to ask for directions from villagers along the way or you're liable to get lost. Better yet, find someone in Phonsavan who knows the way and invite them along for an afternoon hike. You might be able to hire a jeep and driver in town for around US$30 a day.

Muang Khun (Old Xieng Khuang)

Xieng Khuang's ancient capital was so ravaged in the 19th century by Chinese and Vietnamese invaders, then so heavily bombarded during the Indochina War, that it was almost completely abandoned by 1975. Twenty years after war's end the old capital is once again inhabited, though the original French colonial architecture has been replaced by a long row of plain wooden buildings, with slanted metal roofs, on either side of the dirt road from Phonsavan. Officially the town has been renamed Muang Khun. Many of the local residents are Phuan, Thai Dam or Thai Neua.

Several Buddhist temples built between the 16th and 19th centuries lie in unrestored ruins.

Places to Stay & Eat The town has one funky wooden *hotel* with rooms for 2000 kip. Near the market in the centre of town are a couple of noodle shops. *Raan Khai Foe* (an English sign reads 'Restaurant') opposite the market is the best choice for lunch.

Getting There & Away Four buses a day ply the bumpy, torturous 36 km route between Phonsavan and Xieng Khuang for 1000 kip per person.

HUA PHAN PROVINCE

The remote mountainous north-eastern province of Hua Phan is enclosed by Vietnam to the north, east and south-east, Xieng Khuang to the south-west and Luang Prabang to the west. Twenty-two ethnic groups make the province their home, predominantly Thai Khao, Thai Daeng, Thai Meuay, Thai Neua, Phu Noi, Hmong, Khamu, Yunnanese and Vietnamese. The Vietnamese influence is very strong as Sam Neua is closer to (and more accessible from) Hanoi than Vientiane; because the province falls on the eastern side of the Annamite Chain, Thai TV and radio broadcasts don't reach here either.

As a tourist attraction the province's main claim to fame is that Vieng Xai served as the headquarters for the Lao People's Party throughout most of the war years. Textiles in the 'Sam Neua' style – of tribal Thai origins – are another draw. The best textiles are said to come from the areas around Muang Xon and Sop Hao.

Sam Neua

Tucked away in a long narrow valley formed by the Nam Sam at about 1200 metres above sea level, Sam Neua is so far one of the country's least visited provincial capitals. Verdant hills, including pointy Phu Luang, overlook the town but other than the natural setting there's not a lot to write home about. District residents are mostly Lao, Vietnamese and Hmong, along with some Thai Dam, Thai Daeng and Thai Lü. For local residents, Sam Neua boasts what is perhaps the largest and fastest-growing **market** in the region. Consumer products from China and Vietnam line up alongside fresh produce and domestic goods.

Places to Stay & Eat Welcome to Laos' rat capital. *Lao Houng Hotel*, near the south end of a bridge spanning the Nam Sam near the market, is a crumbling Chinese/Vietnamese-style place built around a couple of courtyards by the Vietnamese in 1975 – though it looks much older due to the poor concrete engineering used. Ordinary rooms with two beds, mosquito nets, private shower and toilet cost 3500 kip, while suites with spacious sitting rooms and one large bed are 6500 kip. The hotel's major rat problem has rats running about in the ceiling in the middle of the night, sounding like children playing football on the roof.

Around the corner from Lao Houng on a perpendicular street up from the market, the *Dokmaidieng Guest House* is a three storey cube with fairly clean rooms with shared facilities for 1500 kip per bed. Rats, yes, but not as many as at the Lao Houng. Further on along the same road is the *Phou Loung Guest House*, a pleasant two storey place similar to the Dokmaidieng but with more atmosphere.

There are only two regular public eating establishments in town, both inside the market compound. For anything other than fŏe you must order in advance.

Getting There & Away Lao Aviation has scheduled flights between Vientiane and the renovated airport at Sam Neua thrice weekly (1¼ hours, US$67 one way). The Y-12 landing involves an impressive descent through the narrow Sam Neua valley.

Sam Neua can be reached by road from both Xieng Khuang and Udomxai provinces. Route 6 from Xieng Khuang is quite good by Lao standards between Phonsavan and Nam Noen, a small truck stop at the junction of Routes 6 and 1 just north of the Hua Phan Province border. It's usually necessary to change buses (actually large converted Russian or Chinese diesel trucks) in Nam Noen; each leg of the journey takes six hours and costs 2500 kip.

South-east of Sam Neua, Route 6 links with Route 1 from Nambak (Luang Prabang Province) and Muang Xai (Udomxai Province).

Vieng Xai

Originally called Thong Na Kai (Chicken Field) because of the abundance of wild junglefowl in the area, the postwar name for this former Pathet Lao revolutionary headquarters means City of Victory. The district sits in a striking valley of verdant hills and limestone cliffs riddled with caves, several of which were used to shelter Pathet Lao officers during the Indochina War.

The district capital itself is a small town that seems to be getting smaller as Sam Neua grows larger. The central market is a poor collection of vendors who can't afford transport to the provincial capital, 29 km away.

There are 102 known **caves** in the district, around a dozen with war history. The Vieng Xai caves are supposed to be open to the public as a revolutionary memorial and tourist attraction, but in everyday practice the local authorities thus far treat them as if they're some sort of military secret. Depending on the local mood, you may or may not be allowed to tour the caves.

Tham Thaan Kaysone, the office and residence of the Lao People's Party/Pathet Lao chief – who served as prime minister and president from 1975 till his 1992 death – extends 140 metres into a cliffside that was scaled by rope before steps were added. **Tham Thaan Souphanouvong** (called Tham Phaa Bong before the war) was deemed fit for royalty and housed Prince Souphanouvong, the so-called Red Prince.

Getting There & Away The 29 km journey from Sam Neua to Vieng Xai takes around 45 minutes by private vehicle or about an hour by public bus.

LUANG NAM THA PROVINCE

Bordered by Myanmar to the north-west, China to the north, Udomxai to the south and east and Bokeo to the south-west, Luang Nam Tha (Nam Tha for short) is a mountainous province with a high proportion of Lao Sung and other minorities. The province population includes Hmong, Iko (Akha), Mien, Samtao, Thai Daeng, Thai Lü, Thai Neua, Thai Khao, Thai Kalom, Khamu, Lamet, Lao Loum, Shan and Yunnanese. As in Udomxai the Chinese presence is increasing rapidly with the importation of skilled labour from Yunnan for construction and road work.

In the early 60s the western half of the province became a hotbed of CIA activity; much of the opium and heroin transported by Air America and other air services either originated in or came through Luang Nam Tha. Westerners still seem to carry a romance for Nam Tha and there is a higher than average number of World Bank, UN, NGO and commercial projects under way in the province.

Luang Nam Tha

Rising from the ashes of war, Luang Nam Tha's capital is expanding rapidly in its burgeoning role as trade entrepôt for commerce between China, Thailand and Laos. There are two town centres, one in the older, southern section of the district near the airfield and

boat landing, and a second seven km to the north where the highway comes in from Muang Sing, Boten and Udomxai. The main market is located in the latter section.

Places to Stay & Eat A no-name *Chinese guesthouse* near the market has rooms with hard mattresses, mosquito nets, shared toilet and bath for 1500 to 2000 kip per room.

About 300 metres north of the market, a dirt road leads east off the main street to 16 room *Oudomsin Hotel.* Basic three-bed rooms cost 2000 kip with shared shower and toilet, or 4000 kip with private facilities. Nicer two-bed rooms with private facilities cost 5000 kip. There are a restaurant and night club on the premises; once the latter shuts down around 11 pm, nights are quiet.

Houa Khong Hotel, right across from the airfield, features separate bungalows with two or three rooms per unit, some with private bath and fan, some with shared bath, for 3500 kip per person. The bungalows feature large sitting areas with rattan furniture. There's a restaurant on the premises.

Luang Kham Hotel, 150 metres before the turn-off to the airport on the left, offers 12 rooms with shared bath and no fan for 2000 kip per room, plus rooms with fan and private bath for 5000 kip. It's basically quite OK, though the rooms are a bit dark.

The *Luang Nam Tha Restaurant*, just a simple wooden place around the corner from the Chinese restaurant, serves OK Lao and Chinese fare. The proprietors give foreign customers a copy of the bilingual menu from the Sala Khem Kane Restaurant in Luang Prabang as a reference, although the two restaurants are unrelated. It's generally open from early morning till around 8 or 9 pm.

Getting There & Away Lao Aviation flies to Nam Tha from Vientiane thrice weekly (one hour and 10 minutes, US$80). Flights to/from Luang Prabang are supposed to depart twice weekly (35 minutes, US$34), but in reality the schedule varies with passenger demand. There are also occasional flights to/from Huay Xai (40 minutes, US$36).

Nam Tha can be reached by road via all-weather Route 2 from Muang Xai (117 km south-east) in four or five hours. Passenger trucks cost 3000 kip per person (40,000 kip charter) and leave in the early morning and early afternoon from either end. The main truck stop in Nam Tha stands in front of the market, not far from the post office and bank.

A side road north off Route 2 about two-thirds of the way to Nam Tha from Muang Xai leads directly to Boten on the Lao-Chinese border. Passenger trucks bound for Boten leave morning and afternoon from Nam Tha (1500 kip, two to three hours on a very poor road).

Muang Sing

Lying on the broad river plains of the Nam La north-west of the provincial capital, Muang Sing is a traditional Thai Lü cultural nexus as well as a trade centre for Lao Huay (Lenten), Iko, Hmong, Mien, Lolo and Yunnanese. The entire district numbers 22,500 inhabitants, making it the second most populous district in the province after Luang Nam Tha itself.

Among the buildings left standing from the French era is a 75-year-old brick and plaster garrison which once housed Moroccan and Senegalese troops. It's now used as a small Lao army outpost. One of the arms of the 'China Road' passes through Muang Sing on its way to Mengla, Yunnan, hence the area has come under much Chinese influence since the 1960s.

The main **market** at Muang Sing – called *talàat nyai* in Lao, *kaat long* in Thai Lü – was once the biggest opium market in the golden triangle, a function officially sanctioned by the French. Today it's a venue for fresh produce, meats, and food and clothing staples bought and sold by a polyglot crowd mainly consisting of Thai Lü, Thai Neua, Iko, Yunnanese, Shan, Hmong and Mien.

During the full moon of the 12th lunar month, which usually occurs sometime between late October and mid-November, all of Muang Sing and half the province turn out for the That Muang Sing Festival (Bụn Thâat Meúang Sǐng).

Places to Stay & Eat The *Singthong Hotel*, an atmospheric old two storey wooden hotel on the main street near the market, offers simple multi-bed rooms with mosquito nets for 2000 kip per bed for foreigners, 1500 kip for locals. *Singxai Hotel* is a newer concrete establishment behind the market with beds for 1500 to 2000 kip depending on the size of the room.

Aside from the restaurants at the two hotels, the only places to eat are a few simple *fŏe shops* along the main street and in the market.

Getting There & Away Two or three trucks a day ply between Nam Tha and Muang Sing, a journey of around two hours (1500 kip).

Boten

This village on the Chinese border in the north-eastern corner of Luang Nam Tha Province is a major exit point for Japanese cars being smuggled from Thailand to China via Laos. Other than the lines of parked cars, thick with dust, waiting to get into China, there's virtually nothing else to see here.

Now that Boten is a legal border crossing for all nationalities, and with the upgrading of the road to Luang Nam Tha, the village will probably grow into a town of sorts, complete with hotels and restaurants. At the moment a couple of noodle shops and a truck stop are the only services provided. Overnight facilities are available in Mengla on the Chinese side.

The Lao border crossing is open from 8 am to noon and 2 to 4 pm, while the Chinese crossing is open from 8 am to 5 pm.

A side road north off Route 2 about two-thirds of the way to Nam Tha from Muang Xai leads directly to Boten. Passenger trucks bound for Boten leave morning and afternoon from Nam Tha (1500 kip).

BOKEO PROVINCE

Laos' smallest and second-least-populous province, wedged between the Mekong River border with Thailand and Luang Nam Tha Province, was known as Hua Khong (Head of the Mekong) in earlier times; its current name means 'Gem Mine', a reference to sapphire deposits in Huay Xai district. The province borders Thailand and Myanmar, and is less than a hundred km from China, hence it's an important focus of the much-ballyhooed 'Economic Quadrangle', a four-nation trade zone envisioned mainly by corporate entities in Thailand and China.

Despite it's diminutive size Bokeo harbours 34 different ethnicities, the second-highest number of ethnic groups per province (after Luang Nam Tha) in the country. They include Lao Huay (Lenten), Khamu, Hmong, Iko (Akha), Mien, Kui, Phai, Lamet, Samtao, Tahoy, Shan, Phu Thai, Thai Dam, Thai Khao, Thai Daeng, Thai Lü, Phuan, Thai Nai, Ngo, Kalom, Phuvan, Musoe (Lahu) and Chinese. Bokeo is the only province with a significant population of Lahu, a hill tribe common in northern Myanmar and Thailand, and is the main provenance of the Lao Huay.

Huay Xai

Huay Xai today is a bustling riverside town whose main commercial district centres on the vehicle and passenger ferry landings for boats to Chiang Khong in Thailand. Many new shophouses are under construction along the main street, which curves along the base of a hill overlooking the river.

A set of naga stairs ascends this hillside to Shan-style, 1880 vintage **Wat Jawm Khao Manilat**, a thriving temple that overlooks the town and river.

Huay Xai is a valid border entry/exit point for any visitor regardless of nationality. You no longer need special permission to cross into Laos here, just a valid visa.

Places to Stay & Eat Up from the Mekong ferry landing is the well-run *Manilat Hotel*, with basic but clean rooms with fan and private bath for 6000 kip single/double. There's a very good, inexpensive restaurant downstairs.

The *Hotel Houei Sai*, nearby on the same side of the street, is similar in overall appearance and rates but significantly shabbier. Better is the three storey *Bokeo Hotel* opposite the other two hotels, where rooms with fan and bath are 6000 kip or 150B.

Cheap noodle and rice plates are available in an open-air shop next to the Bokeo Hotel.

Getting There & Away Flights between Huay Xai and Luang Prabang operate daily for US$42 each way and take 50 minutes. There are also weekly flights to/from Luang Nam Tha (US$36) and Udomxai (US$34).

This used to be a difficult road because of its poor surface, but upgrading is now under way. Passenger trucks to Luang Nam Tha, 217 km north-east, cost 8000 kip and currently take 10 hours under good road conditions, though during the rainy season it's often impassable. Once the upgrading and sealing project is completed, the road will be traversable year-round and buses should be able to make the trip in an estimated four to six hours (depending on number of stops).

The short ferry ride from Chiang Khong on the Thai side costs 20B each way. A Thai company has plans to construct a new bridge across the Mekong River from Chiang Khong to Huay Xai by late 1997. Once the bridge is completed, cross-river ferry services will most likely be replaced by a shuttle bus system as in Nong Khai.

Long-distance river ferries down the Mekong to Pakbeng and Luang Prabang cost 4000 kip and 8000 kip respectively. Speedboats to Pakbeng and Luang Prabang cost 300B to 400B and 600B to 800B (you can pay in kip or dollars but baht are preferred) respectively. In Huay Xai the landings for both the slow boat and speedboats are about two km south of the town centre, near the stadium and passenger truck terminal.

Southern Laos

Only two southern provinces, Savannakhet and Champasak, are regularly travelled by tourists. The Mekong River Valley, including the towns of Savannakhet (also known as Muang Khanthabuli), Salavan and Pakse, is mostly inhabited by lowland Lao. In many ways Southern Laos – especially along the Mekong River Valley – remains the most

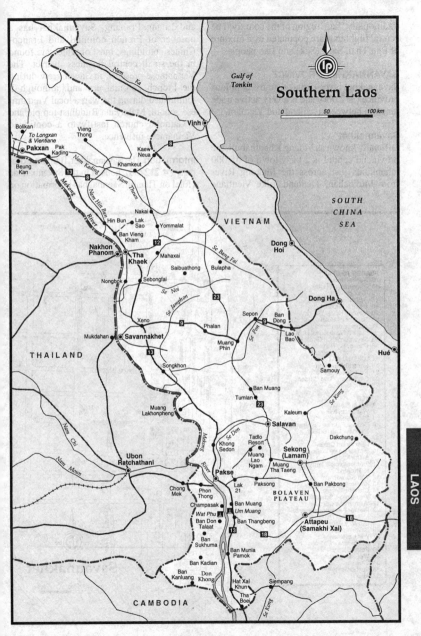

Southern Laos

traditionally 'Lao' region of the country. The central highlands are populated by a mixture of Phu Thai, Saek (Sek) and Lao peoples.

SAVANNAKHET PROVINCE

Savannakhet is the country's most populous province (312,000) and is a very active trade junction between Thailand and Vietnam.

Savannakhet

Officially known as Muang Khanthabuli, the provincial capital is a busy town of 45,000 inhabitants just across the Mekong River from Mukdahan, Thailand. Like Vientiane

and Luang Prabang, Savannakhet has a number of French colonial and Franco-Chinese buildings, most of which are found in the small central business district. The Vietnamese presence in Savan grew during the French colonial era and, although it diminished during the war, a local Vietnamese school, Mahayana Buddhist temple and a Catholic church testify to a continued Vietnamese influence.

Information The Savannakhet Tourism Company (☎ 212733), housed in the Savanbanhao Hotel on Thanon Saenna, has information on

PLACES TO STAY
3 Nanhai Hotel
5 Phonepaseut Hotel
8 Hoongtip Hotel
15 Savannbanhao Hotel
18 Savanh I Hotel
20 Mekong Hotel
23 Santyphab Hotel
31 Auberge du Paradis
(Sala Savanh Guest House)
33 Sayamungkhun Guest House
36 Phonevilay Hotel

PLACES TO EAT
19 Nang Khamweung
21 Four Seasons Restaurant
24 Savanhlaty Food Garden
28 Nang Iam Foe

OTHER
1 Petrol Station
2 Wat Chom Kaew
4 Petrol Station
6 Banque Pour Le Commerce
Extérieur Lao (BCEL)
7 Talaat Yai
9 Boat Ticket Office
10 Pier for Boats to Vientiane
& Tha Khaek
11 Pier for Vehicle Ferry
to Thailand
12 Wat Sainyaphum
13 Kouvoravong Statue
14 Chinese Temple
16 Vietnamese School
17 Vietnamese Consulate
22 Pier for Passenger Ferry to
Mukdahan (Thailand)
25 Lao May Bank
26 Savannakhet Chinese School
27 Wat Lattanalangsi
29 St Theresa's Catholic Church
30 Petrol Station
32 Wat Sainyamungkhun
34 Cinema
35 Post Office
37 Airport

Savannakhet

0   100   200 m

local attractions and can arrange tours to Sepon, the Ho Chi Minh Trail and other spots outside the city.

The area code for Savannakhet is 41.

Places to Stay & Eat Savan's cheaper hotels were once clustered in the older part of town towards the ferry piers. Only one is still in operation, the run-down *Santyphab Hotel* (☎ 212277) on Thanon Tha Dan, two blocks east of the main ferry pier. Basic rooms cost 3000/3500 kip single/double with fan or 5000 kip air-con, both with shared bath.

On the river in an old French colonial villa is the Vietnamese-owned *Mekong Hotel* (☎ 212249), with large, high-ceiling rooms, ceiling fans, air-con, tile floors and lots of wood panelling. The place seems deserted most of the time, except at night when the downstairs nightclub is filled with Vietnamese men and Vietnamese hostesses. Rates are 5000 kip single/double if you don't turn on the air-con, 7500 kip with air-con.

Consisting of four two-storey houses built around a series of courtyards, the *Savanbanhao Hotel* (☎ 212202) has the largest variety of rooms in town. Large single-bed rooms with air-con and shared hot-water shower cost 5000 kip, similar rooms with private hot-water shower cost 7700 kip and rooms with two beds and a one-channel black and white TV are 8700 kip. The mid-price rooms are very good value.

If you have an early bus to catch, or if you simply want to stay in the cheapest place in town, there's a *Vietnamese-owned motel* along one side of the bus terminal north of town with bare two and three-bed rooms for 800 kip per person.

In the central area are many small Chinese-Vietnamese restaurants, none of them particularly outstanding. A small night market called *Savanhlaty Food Garden*, towards the river from the church in the small town plaza, serves good, inexpensive Lao, Chinese and Thai food.

Getting There & Away Lao Aviation flies Chinese Y-7 turboprops to Savannakhet

daily at 7 am. Flights take an hour one way and cost US$61.

Two buses per day leave Vientiane's bus terminal for the 12 hour ride to Savannakhet. The fare is about 7000 kip. From Pakse the bus costs 2500 kip and takes six hours.

Thailand Catch a ferry to get to Mukdahan in Thailand. They cross the Mekong River between Savannakhet and Mukdahan frequently between 8.30 am and 5 pm weekdays, and 8.30 am to 12.30 pm Saturday. The cost is 30B each way.

It's now legal for foreigners to enter and exit the country via Savannakhet; no special permission is needed.

Lao Bao, Vietnam It is legal to enter or exit the country overland via Lao Bao on the Lao-Vietnamese border. From the Savan end, one bus a day goes to the border along unpaved Route 9 at 5 am, arriving around 5 pm, for 2800 kip. In the reverse direction the bus leaves around 7 am. The 100 km road is rough-going and buses tend to be very crowded. Road travel can be especially difficult during the rainy season from June to October.

There is also a cross-border bus that runs between Savannakhet and Danang in Vietnam. See the Getting There & Away section in the Vietnam chapter for more details.

If you don't already have a visa for Vietnam, you can obtain one at the Vietnamese consulate in Savannakhet or Pakse.

Getting Around Samlor fares are comparable to those in Vientiane, around 200 kip per km.

That Ing Hang

Thought to have been built in the mid-16th century (about the same time as Vientiane's Pha That Luang and north-eastern Thailand's That Phanom), this well-proportioned, nine metre thâat is the holiest religious edifice in southern Laos. The monument features three terraced bases topped by a traditional Lao stupa and a gold umbrella weighing 450g. A hollow chamber in the lower section contains an undistinguished collection of Buddha images (by religious custom, women are not permitted to enter the chamber).

On the full moon of February or March is the big That Ing Hang Festival featuring processions and fireworks.

Getting There & Away That Ing Hang is 12 km north of Savannakhet via Route 13, then three km east on a dirt road. Any north-bound bus passes this turn-off.

Sepon (Xepon) & the Ho Chi Minh Trail

The infamous Ho Chi Minh Trail – actually a complex network of dirt paths and gravel roads – runs parallel to the Lao-Vietnamese border beginning at a point directly east from Savannakhet.

Though mostly associated with the 1963-74 Indochina War, the road network was originally used by the Viet Minh against the French in the 50s as an infiltration route to the south. The trail's heaviest use occurred between 1966 and 1971 when over 600,000 North Vietnamese Army troops – along with 100 tonnes of provisions and a half-million tonnes of trucks, tanks, weapons and ordnance – passed along the route. At any one time around 25,000 North Vietnamese Army troops guarded the trail, which was honeycombed with underground barracks, fuel and motor repair depots and anti-aircraft emplacements.

The nearest town to the Ho Chi Minh Trail is Sepon (pop 5000), approximately 170 km east of Savannakhet via Route 9. Sepon was destroyed during the war and is now just another of the many makeshift wooden towns that mark the long-term bombing legacy of eastern Laos. From here the outer edges of the Ho Chi Minh Trail are another 15 to 20 km.

A short distance north or south along the trail a few ruined tanks and other war junk may be seen. Although there's plenty of debris around, much of it lies in the bush covered by undergrowth. Unless you're prepared to hike some distance from the road (you will need a guide because of the danger of unexploded ordnance), it's not worth going all the way out to Sepon.

Rustic accommodation is available in Sepon.

Getting There & Away The bus from Savan to the Vietnamese border stops in Sepon for 2000 kip. Savannakhet Tourism at the Savanbanhao Hotel can arrange car and driver for up to five passengers for about US$200.

SALAVAN PROVINCE

The big attraction in Salavan is the Bolaven Plateau, which actually straddles parts of Salavan, Sekong, Champasak and Attapeu provinces. On the Se Set (Xet) River (a tributary of the Se Don) are several waterfalls and traditional Lao villages. Like the Plain of Jars in Xieng Khuang Province, the Bolaven Plateau has an excellent climate. For more information, see the Champasak Province section below.

Among the province's approximately 256,000 inhabitants are a number of relatively obscure Mon-Khmer groups, including Ta-oy (Tahoy), Lavai, Alak, Laven, Katang, Ngai, Tong, Pako, Kanay, Katu and Kado. The provincial capital of Salavan was all but destroyed in the war. The rebuilt town is a collection of brick and wood buildings with a population of around 40,000.

Places to Stay & Eat

In the provincial capital, the government-owned *Saise Guest House* is in a compound about two km from the bus terminal. The three buildings in the compound feature rooms ranging in price from 2000 kip per bed with shared facilities to 8500 kip for rooms with two beds, fan and private facilities.

There are several *noodle shops* in the vicinity of the market, plus a small night market along a side street near the main market with pre-cooked Lao food.

Getting There & Away

Lao Aviation intermittently schedules flights to Salavan, stopping first at Savannakhet and continuing on to Pakse. When flights are operating, the fare is US$91 one way from Vientiane or US$37 from Savannakhet.

Service was suspended in 1995 to work on upgrading the US airstrip in Salavan and may resume in 1996 or 1997 with flights to/from Pakse only.

You can also get to Salavan by bus or truck from Pakse in Champasak Province.

CHAMPASAK PROVINCE

The Champasak area has a long history that began with Kambuja occupation during the Funan (a Chinese mispronunciation of Phanom) and Chenla empires between the 1st and 9th centuries AD. From the 10th to 13th centuries Champasak was part of the Cambodian Angkor Empire. Following the decline of Angkor between the 15th and late 17th centuries it was enfolded into the Lan Xang kingdom but then broke away to become an independent Lao kingdom at the beginning of the 18th century.

Champasak Province has a population of around 160,000 that includes lowland Lao, Khmer, Phu Thai and various Mon-Khmer groups. The province is well known for *mat-mii*, silks and cottons that are hand-woven of tie-dyed threads.

Pakse

Pakse is a relatively new town at the confluence of the Mekong and Se Don rivers that was founded in 1905 by the French as an administrative outpost. It is now the capital of Champasak Province (formerly three separate provinces – Champasak, Xedon and Sithandon) but has little of interest except the lively market.

Pakse is also the gateway for trips to the former royal capital of Champasak and the Angkor temple ruins of Wat Phu.

Information You can change Thai baht or US dollars (cash) for kip at the BCEL branch near the market and Pakse Hotel. It's open weekdays from 8.30 am to 3.30 pm, Saturday until 10 am.

The area code for Pakse is 31.

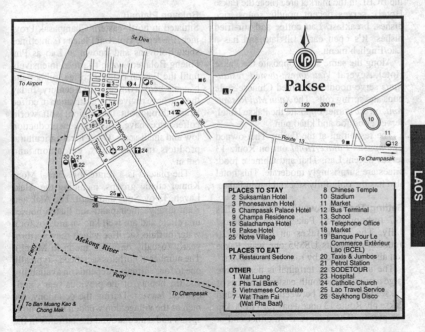

Pakse

PLACES TO STAY	OTHER
2 Suksamlan Hotel	1 Wat Luang
3 Phonesavanh Hotel	4 Pha Tai Bank
6 Champasak Palace Hotel	5 Vietnamese Consulate
9 Champa Residence	7 Wat Tham Fai
15 Salachampa Hotel	(Wat Pha Baat)
16 Pakse Hotel	8 Chinese Temple
25 Notre Village	10 Stadium
	11 Market
PLACES TO EAT	12 Bus Terminal
17 Restaurant Sedone	13 School
	14 Telephone Office
	18 Market
	19 Banque Pour Le Commerce Extérieur Lao (BCEL)
	20 Taxis & Jumbos
	21 Petrol Station
	22 SODETOUR
	23 Hospital
	24 Catholic Church
	25 Lao Travel Service
	26 Saykhong Disco

To Airport

Se Don

0   150   300 m

Route 13

To Champasak

To Champasak

Mekong River

To Champasak

Ferry

Ferry

To Ban Muang Kao & Chong Mek

LAOS

Places to Stay The *Phonsavanh Hotel*, on the main road crossing the Se Don from the west, has basic but clean two-bed rooms for 4000 kip and three-bed rooms for 6000 kip, both with shared bath. Near the central market the large *Pakse Hotel* has better rooms for 4400 to 8800 kip per night.

The clean and friendly *Suksamlan (Souksamlane) Hotel* (☎ 212002) in the same central area has decent air-con rooms with private cold-water bath for 9000/12,000 kip for a single/double. Many of the guests at the Suksamlan are Thais doing business in Pakse.

Notre Village (☎ 212503), a guesthouse owned by Lao Travel Service near the hospital, has five rooms for 5000 kip with shared bath, or 7000/10,000 kip single/double with air-con and private facilities. Notre Village may move to an old French mansion nearby on the river.

Places to Eat *Restaurant Sedone*, opposite the BCEL in the market area (near the Pakse Hotel), serves decent noodle soups, rice dishes, breakfast, Lao coffee and stir-fried dishes. It's open early till late and has a Lao/English menu.

Along the same street opposite the Pakse Hotel, several *Vietnamese-owned restaurants* serve noodles, steamed Chinese-style buns and spring rolls. The *Xuan Mai Restaurant*, on the corner opposite the Pakse Hotel, serves good fõe and khào pûn.

The restaurant at the flashy, Thai-owned *Champasak Palace Hotel* out on Route 13 serves decent Lao, Thai and Chinese food; prices are surprisingly moderate. This hotel also has the only fully stocked bar in Pakse.

Getting There & Away Lao Aviation flies Y-7 turboprops to Pakse from Vientiane daily. The flight takes an hour and 20 minutes, and costs US$95 one way. Pakse can also be reached by road from Salavan.

The intercity bus terminal is next to the large market on the south-eastern outskirts of Pakse. Direct buses between Vientiane and Pakse ply Route 13 once a day for 11,000 kip per person. These leave from either end at around 6 am and take a gruelling 16 to 18 hours. Two buses a day go to/from Savannakhet at around 5 and 10 am. These cost 3200 kip per person and take four to six hours.

Chong Mek, Thailand Ferries run back and forth between the pier at the junction of the Don and Mekong rivers and Ban Muang Kao on the west bank of the Mekong throughout the day. The regular ferry costs 200 kip per person or you can charter a boat across for 2000 kip.

From Ban Muang Kao to the Lao-Thai border you can queue up for a share taxi that carries six passengers for 1000 kip each or hire a whole taxi for 6000 kip (or 200B). The 40 km journey to the Lao side of the border takes about 45 minutes. At the border you simply check out through Lao immigration, walk across the line and check in on the Thai side. Passenger trucks on the Thai side are waiting to take passengers onward to Ubon Ratchathani via Phibun Mangsahan.

Bolaven Plateau

Situated in north-eastern Champasak Province, the fertile Bolaven Plateau (sometimes spelt Bolovens and known in Lao as Phu Phieng Bolaven) wasn't farmed intensively until the French planted coffee, rubber and bananas here in the early 20th century. Today the Lao have revived the cultivation of coffee beans throughout the region; soft world coffee prices have, however, kept production low and small-scale. Other local agricultural products include fruits, cardamom and rattan.

The plateau is a centre for several Mon-Khmer ethnic groups, including the Alak, Laven, Ta-oy, Suay and Katu. The Alak and Katu arrange their palm-and-thatch houses in a circle and are well known in Laos for a water buffalo sacrifice which they perform yearly (usually on a full moon in March). The number of buffalos sacrificed – typically one to four animals – depends on availability and the bounty of the previous year's agricultural harvest. During the ceremony, the men of the village don wooden masks, hoist spears and dance around the buffalos in the centre of the circle formed by their houses. See under Wat Phu Special Events below for further details.

Places to Stay *Tadlo Resort* (reservation number in Pakse (☎ 031) 212725), next to the Taat Lo waterfall on the Bolaven Plateau, is a modest complex of thatched bungalows of which several are owned by the government, while a few are privately owned and used by SODETOUR, a tour operator in Pakse. Simple 3rd class rooms with shared cold-water bath cost 5000 kip, while 2nd class rooms provide a private cold-water bath for 10,000 kip.

Getting There & Away Passenger trucks between Pakse and Salavan (passing the entrance to Tadlo Resort) cost 1500 kip per person and take about two hours. Tadlo Resort is 88 km north-east of Pakse and about 1.5 km east of the road to Salavan. The turn-off for Tadlo comes after Lao Ngam, about 30 km before Salavan; you should get off the bus at a bridge over the Se Set. Ask at the pharmacy near this stop for help with your bags if you can't make the 1.5 km walk.

Champasak

This small town of less than 20,000 on the west bank of the Mekong is a ghost of its former colonial self. An ambitious fountain circle in the middle of the red-dirt main street looks almost absurd, while either side of the street is lined with French colonial homes in various states of disrepair, along with a couple of noodle shops and a morning market.

Places to Stay & Eat The *Sala Wat Phou*, a reincarnation of the former Champasak Hotel, is housed in a renovated two storey building next to the provincial offices and near the market. Nine medium-sized rooms with high ceilings, air-con and hot water are priced at US$25/30 per single/double. Meals are available in the hotel dining room.

A large *fŏe shop* south of the traffic circle on the east side of the street also does rice dishes and offers cold beer.

Getting There & Away Ferries from Ban Muang on the eastern side of the Mekong River to Ban Phaphin on the western side (five km north of Champasak) run regularly throughout daylight hours for 200 kip per person. From Ban Phaphin a passenger truck to Champasak costs another 100 kip.

Wat Phu

This Angkor-period (10th to 13th centuries) Khmer temple site is on the lower slopes of Phu Pasak, about eight km south-west of the town of Champasak.

The site is divided into lower and upper parts and joined by a stairway. The lower part consists of two ruined palace buildings at the edge of a pond used for ritual ablutions. The upper section is the temple sanctuary itself, which once enclosed a large Shiva phallus. Some time later it was converted into a Buddhist temple but the original Hindu sculpture remains in the lintels, which feature various forms of Vishnu and Shiva as well as Kala, the Hindu god of time and death. The *naga* (dragon) stairway leading to the sanctuary is lined with *dok jampa* (plumeria), which is the Lao national tree. The upper platform affords a good view of the valley below.

Special Events Near Wat Phu is a large crocodile stone that may have been the site of the purported Chenla sacrifices. Each year, in June, the locals perform a ritual water buffalo sacrifice to the ruling earth spirit for Champasak, Chao Tengkham. The blood of the buffalo is offered to a local shaman who serves as a trance medium for the appearance of Chao Tengkham.

Another important local festival is Bun Wat Phu, when pilgrims from throughout southern Laos come to worship at Wat Phu in its Buddhist incarnation. The festival lasts three days and features Thai boxing matches, cockfights, music and dancing. It's held as part of Magha Puja (Makkha Bu-saa) at the full moon in February.

Getting There & Away Wat Phu is 46 km south from Pakse but only eight km from Champasak. To hire a taxi from Champasak,

LAOS

ask for Wat Phu or Muang Kao (Old City); the cost should be around 5000 to 6000 kip for the round trip, including waiting time at the site. You can also hop on a passenger truck or bus bound for Ban Samkha or Ban Don Talaat (200 kip) further south and ask to be let off at Wat Phu.

Si Phan Don (Four Thousand Islands)

During the rainy season this very scenic 50 km section of the Mekong River just north of the Cambodian border reaches a breadth of 14 km, the river's widest girth along its entire 4350 km journey from the Tibetan Plateau to the South China Sea. During the dry months between monsoons the river recedes to reveal hundreds (or thousands if you count every sandbar) of river islands and islets. The largest of the permanent islands are inhabited year-round and offer fascinating glimpses of tranquil river-oriented village life.

The French left behind a defunct short-line railway (the only railway ever built in Laos), a couple of river piers and a few colonial villas on the islands of Don Khong, Don Det and Don Khon. Other attractions include some impressive rapids and waterfalls where the Mekong riverbank suddenly drops in elevation at the Cambodian border, and a rare species of freshwater dolphin, the Irrawaddy dolphin.

Places to Stay Near the ferry landing and next door to Don Khong's largest noodle shop, *Done Khong Guest House* contains three simple but clean three-bed rooms with shared facilities for 7000 kip per room. Further north towards Ban Xieng Wang, *Souksan Guest House* offers seven cottages, each with two small rooms containing air-con and private cold-water bath for US$30. A separate building further back features dorm-style accommodation – basically just a mattress on the floor – for 2500 kip per bed. The Souksan has a very pleasant restaurant overlooking the river.

The *Auberge Sala Done Khong* in Muang Khong offers spacious, nicely decorated rooms in an old teak house for US$20 per

night with fan only, US$30 if you use the air-con. All rooms come with private toilet and hot-water showers. According to SODE-TOUR these rates may be raised to around US$45 soon. Rooms at the Sala Done Khong may be booked in advance through SODE-TOUR in Vientiane or Pakse.

The manager of the Auberge Sala Done Khong has double rooms in his own house – *Thongleuam's House* – for US$10. Toilet and bath facilities are shared.

Pakse's Lao Travel Service plans to building a new guesthouse 200 metres south of the town centre.

Places to Eat Don Khong is nationally famous for its lào láo, often cited as the smoothest in the country. It's available in the market or at any restaurant.

Near the Muang Khong pier are a couple of adequate *hâan kin dɛum* (eat-drink shops). A large *noodle shop* near the ferry landing also serves khào nĩaw and, with advance notice, khào jâo.

Souksan Guest House has a nice little wooden restaurant overhanging the river. Along the street that leads to the Souksan are several small *cafes* with fõe and Lao snacks.

Getting There & Away Though scheduled for twice a week, the Lao Aviation flight between Pakse and Don Khong actually only goes when at least six passengers make reservations. The fare is US$26 each way.

More reliably, there are one or two passenger trucks per day from Pakse to Hat Xai Khun, directly opposite Muang Khong on the east mainland shore of the Mekong River. The 1000 kip, six hour ride includes the short vehicle ferry ride across to Muang Khong.

There are rumours that the vehicle ferry crossing may move south to Ban Nokhok, opposite Ban Naa on Don Khong, to take advantage of a deeper channel and a slightly shorter distance between mainland and island. If this transpires, small boats will continue to operate from Hat Xai Khun.

During times of high water, ferry boats sail back and forth between Pakse and Don

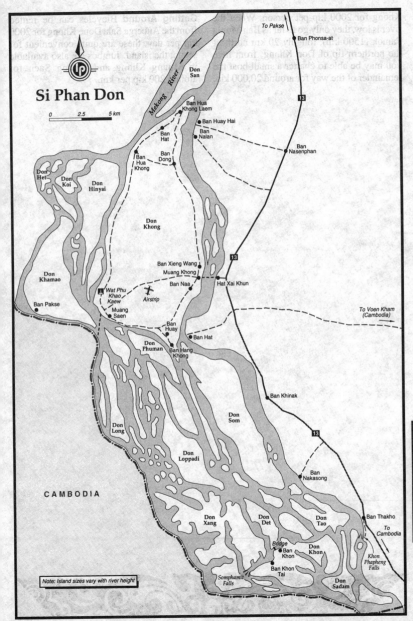

Si Phan Don

0   2.5   5 km

Mekong River

To Pakse

Ban Phonsa-at

Don San

Ban Hua Khong Laem

Ban Huay Hai

Ban Hat

Ban Nalan

Ban Dong

Ban Hua Khong

Ban Nasenphan

13

Don Het

Don Koi

Don Hinyai

Don Khong

Don Khamao

Ban Xieng Wang

Muang Khong

Ban Naa

Hat Xai Khun

13

Ban Pakse

Wat Phu Khao Kaew

Airstrip

Muang Saen

To Voen Kham (Cambodia)

Ban Huay

Ban Hat

Don Phuman

Ban Hang Khong

Ban Khinak

Don Som

13

Don Long

Don Loppadi

Ban Nakasong

CAMBODIA

Ban Thakho

To Cambodia

Don Xang

Don Det

Don Tao

Bridge

Ban Khon

Don Khon

Khon Phapheng Falls

Ban Khon Tai

Somphamit Falls

Don Sadam

Note: Island sizes vary with river height

LAOS

Khong for 2000 kip per person. When the river is low, they only go as far as Ban Munla Pamok (1500 kip), roughly 20 km north of the northern tip of Don Khong; from here you may be able to charter a small boat the remainder of the way for around 20,000 kip.

Getting Around Bicycles can be rented from the Auberge Sala Done Khong for 2000 kip per day; these are quite convenient for seeing the island. Jumbos are also available in Muang Khong and Muang Saen for around 200 kip per km.

Macau

Sixty km west of Hong Kong, on the other side of the Pearl River's mouth, is the oldest European settlement in the East – the tiny Portuguese territory of Macau. The lure of Macau's casino gaming tables has been so actively promoted that its other attractions are almost forgotten, but the history and attractions of Macau are rich and varied. In fact, much that can be said about Macau will not fit into this brief chapter.

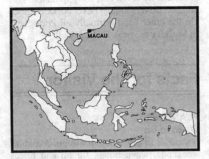

Facts about Macau

HISTORY

Portuguese galleons visited Macau in the early 1500s; in 1557, as a reward for clearing out a few pirates, China ceded the tiny enclave to the Portuguese.

For centuries it was the principal meeting point for trade with China. In the 19th century, European and American traders could operate in Guangzhou (just up the Pearl River) only during the trading season. They would then retreat to Macau during the off season.

When the Opium Wars erupted between the Chinese and the British, the Portuguese stood diplomatically to one side and Macau soon found itself the poor relation of more dynamic Hong Kong. Legalised gambling changed Macau's fortunes considerably.

GEOGRAPHY

Macau's 16 sq km consists of a peninsula joined to the Chinese mainland and the islands of Taipa and Coloane, which are joined by a causeway and linked to central Macau by two bridges.

CLIMATE

The weather in Macau is nearly identical to nearby Hong Kong. See the Hong Kong chapter for details.

GOVERNMENT & POLITICS

Macau is currently a territory of Portugal, led by an appointed governor and a partially elected legislative assembly. Macau is slated to be handed back to China in 1999 – two years after Hong Kong.

ECONOMY

Macau's current prosperity is given a big boost from the Chinese gambling urge, which every weekend sends hordes of Hong Kongers shuttling off to the casinos.

Prostitution is believed to be the second biggest profession, and certainly the oldest.

POPULATION & PEOPLE

Macau is home to approximately 400,000 souls. About 95% are Chinese, 3% are Portuguese and 2% are foreigners from various places employed in what is loosely called the 'entertainment industry'.

RELIGION

For the Chinese majority, Taoism and Buddhism are the dominant religions. However, nearly 500 years of Portuguese influence has definitely left an imprint, and the Catholic church is very strong in Macau. Many Chinese have been converted and you are likely to see Chinese nuns.

LANGUAGE

Portuguese may be the official language but Cantonese is the real one. Mandarin Chinese is spoken by about half the population. Bus and taxi drivers almost never speak English. On the other hand, virtually all Portuguese in Macau can speak English well.

Facts for the Visitor

PLANNING
When to Go

It's easier to say when *not* to go. Avoid *all* weekends, when hotels fill up and prices double. As in Hong Kong, avoid the Chinese New Year. But Christmas and the solar New Year (1 January) are good times to visit Macau.

Maps

The Macau Government Tourist Office hands out an excellent freebie map. The *Map of Macau & Zhuhai*, published by Universal Publications Ltd, is available from bookstores in Hong Kong and Macau.

TOURIST OFFICES
Local Tourist Offices

The Macau Government Tourist Office (MGTO) (☎ 315566) is well organised and extremely helpful. It's at Largo do Senado, Edificio Ritz No 9, next to the Leal Senado building in the square in the centre of Macau. It's open daily from 9 am to 6 pm.

Tourist Offices Abroad

Macau's overseas tourist representative offices, usually called the MTIB (Macau Tourist Information Bureau), are as follows:

Australia
    MTIB, 449 Darling St, Balmain, Sydney, NSW 2041 (☎ (02) 9555-7548, (008) 252448)
Canada
    MTIB, Suite 157, 10551 Shellbridge Way, Richmond, BC, V6X 2W9 (☎ (604) 231-9040)

France
    MTIB Consultant, Atlantic Associates, SARL, 52 Champs-Elysées, Paris 75008 (☎ 01 42 56 45 51)
Germany
    Macau Tourism Representative, Shafergasse 17, D-60313, Frankfurt-am-Main (☎ (069) 234094)
Hong Kong
    MGTO, Room 3704, Shun Tak Centre, 200 Connaught Rd (Macau Ferry Terminal) – closed for lunch from 1 to 2 pm (☎ 2540-8180)
Japan
    MTIB, 4th floor, Toho Twin Tower Building, 5-2 Yurakucho 1-chome, Chiyoda-ku, Tokyo 100 (☎ (03) 3501-5022)
Malaysia
    MTIB, 22 Jalan Imbi, Kuala Lumpur 55100 (☎ (03) 245-1418)
New Zealand
    MTIB, PO box 42-165, Orakei, Auckland 5 (☎ (09) 575-2700)
Philippines
    MTIB, 664 EDSA Extension, Pasay City, Metro Manila (☎ (02) 521-7178)
Singapore
    MTIB, 11-01A PIL Building, 140 Cecil St, Singapore 0106 (☎ (02) 225-0022)
Thailand
    MTIB, 150/5 Sukhumvit 20, Bangkok 10110, or GPO Box 1534, Bangkok 10501 (☎ (02) 258-1975)
UK
    MTIB, 6 Sherlock Mews, Paddington St, London WIM 3RH (☎ (0171) 224-3390)
USA
    MTIB, 3133 Lake Hollywood Drive, Los Angeles, CA, or PO Box 1860, Los Angeles, CA 90078 (☎ (213) 851-3402, (800) 331-7150)

VISAS & DOCUMENTS

For most visitors, all that's needed to enter Macau is a passport. Everyone gets at least a 20 day stay on arrival (90 days for Hong Kongers). Visas are not required for the following nationalities: Australia, Austria, Belgium, Brazil, Canada, Denmark, Finland, France, Germany, Greece, Hong Kong, India, Ireland, Italy, Japan, Luxembourg, Malaysia, Mexico, Netherlands, New Zealand, Norway, Philippines, Singapore, South Africa, South Korea, Spain, Sweden, Switzerland, Thailand, UK and USA.

All other nationalities must have a visa, which can be obtained on arrival in Macau. Visas cost M$205 for individuals, M$410 per family, M$102.50 for children under 12 and M$102.50 per person in a bona fide tour group (usually 10 persons minimum). People holding passports from countries which do not have diplomatic relations with Portugal must obtain visas from an overseas Portuguese consulate before entering Macau. An exception is made for Taiwanese, who can get visas on arrival for free despite their lack of diplomatic relations. The Portuguese consulate (☎ 2802-2585) in Hong Kong is at Harbour Centre, Harbour Rd, Wanchai.

Visa Extensions
After your 20 days are up, you can obtain a one month extension if you can come up with a convincing excuse (emergency poker game?). A second extension is not possible, though it's easy enough to go across the border to China and then come back again. The immigration office (☎ 577338) is on the 9th floor, Macau Chamber of Commerce Building, Rua de Xangai 175, which is one block to the north-east of the Beverly Plaza Hotel.

EMBASSIES
There are no embassies or consulates in Macau. If you need assistance for a lost passport etc, you must call your consulate in Hong Kong.

CUSTOMS
Like Hong Kong, Macau is a duty-free port and you can bring in or take out just about anything except drugs, weapons and bombs.

MONEY
Costs
As long as you don't go crazy at the blackjack tables or slot machines, Macau is cheaper than Hong Kong. Hotel rooms in Macau are a bargain (though not on weekends or holidays). It gets cheapest during the winter off-season. At the bottom end you can survive on M$200 a day, though you'll be a lot more comfortable if you can afford M$400.

Currency
Macau issues its own currency, the pataca, written as M$. The pataca is divided into 100 avos and is worth about 3% less than the HK dollar. HK dollars are accepted everywhere on a 1:1 basis with patacas, which means of course that you'll save a little by using patacas.

Although Hong Kong coins are acceptable in Macau, you'll need pataca coins to make calls at public telephones. Get rid of your patacas before departing Macau – they are hard to dispose of in Hong Kong, though you can change them at the Hang Seng Bank.

Changing Money
There is a convenient moneychanger at the Jetfoil Pier (where most tourists arrive) and at the China border. Banks are normally open on weekdays from 9 am to 4 pm, and on Saturday from 9 am until noon. If you need to change money when the banks are closed, major casinos (especially the Lisboa) can accommodate you 24 hours a day.

Tipping & Bargaining
Tipping is not customary, though hotel porters and waiters may have different ideas.

Most stores have fixed prices, but if you buy clothing, trinkets and other tourist paraphernalia from the street markets there is some scope for bargaining. On the other hand, if you buy from the ubiquitous pawn shops, bargain ruthlessly. Pawnbrokers are more than happy to charge whatever they can get away with – five times the going price for second-hand cameras and other goods is not unusual!

Taxes
Upmarket hotels hit you with a 10% service charge and 5% 'tourism tax'.

POST & COMMUNICATIONS
Postal Rates
Domestic letters cost M$1 for up to 20g. As for international mail, Macau divides the world into zones. Zone 1 is east Asia, including Korea, Taiwan etc. Zone 2 is everything

else. There are special rates for the rest of China and Portugal. Printed matter receives a discount of about 30% off the regular rates. Registration costs an extra M$12.

Sending Mail

Large hotels like the Lisboa also sell stamps and postcards and can post letters for you. Scattered around Macau are several red-coloured 'mini-post offices', which are basically machines that sell stamps.

Receiving Mail

Poste restante is at the GPO on Leal Senado. It's open from 9 am to 8 pm, Monday to Saturday.

Telephone

Companhia de Telecomunicações (CTM) runs the Macau telephone system and for the most part the service is good. However, public pay phones can be hard to find, being mostly concentrated around the Leal Senado. Most large hotels have one in the lobby, but you may have to stand in line to use it.

Local calls are free from a private or hotel telephone. At a public pay phone, local calls cost M$1 for five minutes. All pay phones permit international direct dialling (IDD). The procedure for dialling to Hong Kong is totally different from all other countries. You first dial 01 and then the number you want to call – you must *not* dial the country code.

The international access code for every country *except* Hong Kong is 00. To call Macau from abroad, the country code is 853.

Telephone cards from CTM are sold in denominations of M$50, M$100 and M$200. A lot of phones which accept these cards are found around Leal Senado, the Jetfoil Pier and at a few large hotels. You can also make a call from the telephone office at Largo do Senado, next to the GPO. The office is open from 8 am until midnight Monday through Saturday, and from 9 am until midnight on Sunday.

Some useful phone numbers in Macau include:

Emergency	☎ 999
Police	☎ 573333
Directory Assistance (Macau)	☎ 181
Directory Assistance (Hong Kong)	☎ 101
Time	☎ 140

Fax, Telegraph & Email

Unless you're staying at a hotel that has its own fax, the easiest way to send and receive fax is at the GPO (not the telephone office) on Leal Senado. You can receive a fax at this office (fax (853) 550117). The person sending the fax must put your name and hotel telephone on top of the message so the postal workers can find you.

The telephone office handles cables (telegrams).

Email services are not well developed in Macau. If you belong to a service like Compuserve or America Online, you'll have to call to Hong Kong. Residents of Macau can apply for an Internet account through the CTM telephone office on Avenida do Dr Rodrigo Rodrigues.

BOOKS
Lonely Planet

The section on Macau in *Hong Kong, Macau & Guangzhou – travel survival kit* has much more detailed information than contained herein. There is also a brief section on Macau in Lonely Planet's *Hong Kong city guide*.

General

There are several pictorial coffee-table books about Macau. One such book is simply called *Macau* and is by Jean-Yves Defay. Another, also called *Macau*, is by Leong Ka Tai and Shann Davies and is part of the Times Editions series.

A Macao Narrative (Oxford University Press) is by Austin Coates, a well-known Hong Kong magistrate, who also wrote *City of Broken Promises*.

NEWSPAPERS & MAGAZINES

Aside from the free monthly tourist newspaper *Macau Travel Talk*, no English newspapers or magazines are published in Macau. However, imported publications are readily available, including the Hong Kong newspapers.

RADIO & TV
There are no local English-language radio stations, but you should be able to pick up Hong Kong stations.

Teledifusão de Macau (TdM) is a government-run station which broadcasts on two channels. Shows are mainly in English and Portuguese, but with some Cantonese programmes. It's easy to pick up Hong Kong stations in Macau (but not vice versa). Hong Kong newspapers list Macau TV programmes. Satellite TV is available at many hotels.

PHOTOGRAPHY & VIDEO
You can find most types of film, cameras and accessories in Macau, and film processing is of a high standard. The best store in town for all photographic services is Foto Princesa (☎ 555959), Avenida do Infante D'Henrique 55-59, one block east of Rua da Praia Grande. This is also the best place to get visa photos made.

ELECTRICITY
It's 220V, 50 Hz. The electric outlets are the same as Hong Kong's older design, that is, three round pins.

LAUNDRY
Hidden in the alleys are many hole-in-the-wall laundry services that charge reasonable prices. The trick is finding them. Most of them display only Chinese characters on their advertisements.

Almost all hotels do laundry, but check prices first before handing over your clothes.

WEIGHTS & MEASURES
Macau uses the international metric system, but there are some local Chinese units of measure. See the Hong Kong chapter for details.

HEALTH
Macau poses no particular health problems. Just try not to have a heart attack if you hit the jackpot on the slot machines.

Medical Services
The Government Hospital (☎ 514499, 313731) is available for medical treatment.

TOILETS
Macau has far more public toilets per capita than Hong Kong. Good venues to find toilets include parks, temples, casinos, fast food restaurants, the Jetfoil Pier and shopping plazas.

TRAVEL WITH CHILDREN
On the third floor of the Hotel Lisboa is Children's World, where kids can play video games for hours while mum and dad lose their life savings at the blackjack tables.

DANGERS & ANNOYANCES
Pickpocketing can occur in crowded areas and Macau has a problem with residential burglaries, but violent crime is very rare.

BUSINESS HOURS
The operating hours for most government offices in Macau are Monday to Friday from 9 am to 1 pm and 2.30 to 5.45 pm. Private businesses keep longer hours and some casinos are open 24 hours a day.

Banks are normally open on weekdays from 9 am to 4 pm.

PUBLIC HOLIDAYS & SPECIAL EVENTS
Chinese in Macau celebrate the same religious festivals as their counterparts in Hong Kong, but there are several Catholic festivals and some Portuguese national holidays too. The tourist newspaper *Macau Travel Talk*, available from the MGTO, has a regular listing of events and festivals.

The biggest event of the year is no doubt the Macau Grand Prix, a two day event held on the third weekend in November. Accommodation can be very tight at that time.

ACTIVITIES
Future Bright Amusement Centre (☎ 989-2318) has Macau's only ice skating rink and is also a venue for bowling. It is on Praça Luis de Camões, just on the south side of Camões Grotto & Gardens.

MACAU

Up around the Guía Lighthouse is the best track for jogging. It's also the venue for early morning tai-chi exercises.

The Westin Resort on Coloane boasts a golf course. Hotels offering tennis facilities include the Hyatt Regency, Mandarin Oriental, New Century and Westin Resort, but there is also a public tennis court at Hac Sa Beach on Coloane.

Hash House Harriers hold various weekend jogs around Macau, with a drinking party thrown in at the end. Stop in at expat pubs such as Pyretu's and Talker to find out where the Hash is meeting.

There are two good swimming beaches on Coloane, Hac Sa and Cheoc Van. Cheoc Van Beach has a yacht club and Hac Sa has a horse riding stable. Hac Sa Beach also has a number of sea toys for rent, including windsurfers and water scooters. There's a hiking trail in the hills of Coloane (see the Coloane section later in this chapter). Bicycles are available for hire on Taipa Island only.

WORK

At least until 1999, Portuguese nationals are permitted to legally work in Macau. Most other non-Chinese nationalities are excluded, except for some 'foreign experts' (Filipina waitresses, Russian prostitutes etc), who earn dismal wages.

Getting There & Away

AIR
Airlines

Except for CAAC (the airline of China), all the airlines have offices inside the airport. For reservations and reconfirmation, you can contact the airlines at the following phone numbers:

Air Macau (☎ 898-3388)
Asiana Airlines (☎ 861400)
CAAC, TTS Travel Service (☎ 787877, 787-2501)
EVA Airways (☎ 861330)
Korean Air (☎ 861480)
Malaysia Airlines (☎ 886-1253, 787898)
Sabena Airlines (☎ 750412)

Singapore Airlines (☎ 861321, 711728)
TAP Air Portugal (☎ 898-2288, 713780)
Trans Asia Airways (☎ 862200, 701777)

Travel Agencies

Some useful agencies include:

Amigo Travel
    Ground floor of the new wing in the Hotel Lisboa
    (☎ 337333)
Hong Kong Student Travel (Macau) Ltd
    Rua do Campo 13 (☎ 311100)

Europe

Two airlines offer direct Macau-Europe service. TAP Air Portugal flies Macau-Lisbon and Sabena Airlines flies Macau-Brussels.

China

Air Macau connects Macau with Beijing, Shanghai and Xiamen. CAAC flies from Macau to Changsha, Chongqing, Dalian, Shenyang, Qingdao, Xi'an, Yantai and Wenzhou.

Hong Kong

For Hong Kongers in a hurry to lose their money, East Asia Airlines runs a helicopter service. Flying time from Hong Kong is 20 minutes at a cost of HK$1206 on weekdays, HK$1310 on weekends – quite an expense just to save the extra 30 minutes required by boat. There are up to 17 flights daily between 9.30 am and 10.30 pm. In Hong Kong, departures are from the ferry pier at Shun Tak Centre (☎ 2859-3359), 200 Connaught Rd, Sheung Wan; in Macau, departures are from the Jetfoil Pier (☎ 725939).

Korea

Asiana Airlines and Korean Air offer direct Macau-Seoul flights.

Singapore

Singapore Airlines and Malaysia Airlines have direct flights between Macau and Singapore.

Taiwan

You can fly from either Taipei or Kaohsiung

to Macau on EVA Airways, Trans Asia Airways or Air Macau. Round-trip tickets cost US$250.

Departure Tax
Airport departure tax is M$130.

LAND
Macau is an easy gateway into China. You simply take a bus to the border and walk across. Bus No 5 runs between Leal Senado and the Barrier Gate at the Macau-China border.

SEA
Hong Kong-Macau
The vast majority of visitors to Macau arrive and depart by boat from Hong Kong. There are departures about every 15 minutes during daylight hours, and every 30 minutes at night. The boats operate from 7 am to 4 am.

There are four basic types of vessels to choose from: jetfoils (jet-powered hydrofoils), foil-cats (jetfoil catamarans), catamarans and HK ferries (433-passenger, two-deck ferries). The journey takes 55 minutes on the jetfoils and foil-cats, 65 minutes by catamaran and 95 minutes on HK ferries.

Most of the boats depart from the huge Macau Ferry Terminal next to Shun Tak Centre at 200 Connaught Rd, Sheung Wan, Hong Kong Island – this is easily reached by MTR to the Sheung Wan station. A few boats also depart from the China-Hong Kong City ferry terminal on Canton Rd in Tsimshatsui.

On weekends and holidays, you'd be wise to book your return ticket in advance because the boats are sometimes full. Tickets can be purchased up to 28 days in advance in Hong Kong at the pier.

Most boats offer two classes (economy and first). The catamarans have a VIP cabin which seats up to six persons, and the cost per ticket is the same whether one or six persons occupy the cabin. Boat tickets cost M$4 less in Macau than in Hong Kong – the following prices are what you pay in Hong Kong:

Vessel	Weekday (HK$)	Weekend (HK$)	Night (HK$)
Catamaran	123/223/ 1336	134/234/ 1396	146/246/ 1476
Foil-cat	133/147	145/190	165/190
Ferry	111	126	144
Jetfoil	123/136	134/146	152/166

A boat departure tax of M$22 is included in the price of the ticket.

Getting Around

THE AIRPORT
Airport bus AP1 zips around Taipa, then crosses the bridge, stops at the Hotel Lisboa and some other hotels in the centre, and terminates at the Jetfoil Pier. The fare is M$5. Numerous taxis meet all incoming flights. The taxi fare is about M$30.

BUS
There are minibuses and large buses, and both offer air-con and frequent service. They operate from 7 am until midnight. Buses on the Macau Peninsula cost M$2, and Hong Kong coins are acceptable.

Arguably, the two most useful buses to travellers are Nos 3 and 3A, which run between the Jetfoil Pier and the central area near the GPO. No 3 also goes to the China border, as does No 5. There are numerous other routes, but these change so frequently that Macau's map makers have given up – most maps of the city do not show bus routes. Nevertheless, a detailed map (preferably bilingual) will be of some help in navigation.

Buses to Taipa are Nos 11, 26, 26A, 28A and 33; Nos 26 and 26A also go to Coloane Village and Cheoc Van and Hac Sa Beaches. No 38 is a race-day bus which goes to the Taipa Jockey Club one hour before the races. Buses to Taipa cost M$2.50, to Coloane Village it's M$3.20 and to Hac Sa Beach (on Coloane) it's M$4. Taipa-Hac Sa costs M$2.50 and Coloane-Hac Sa is M$1.70.

MACAU

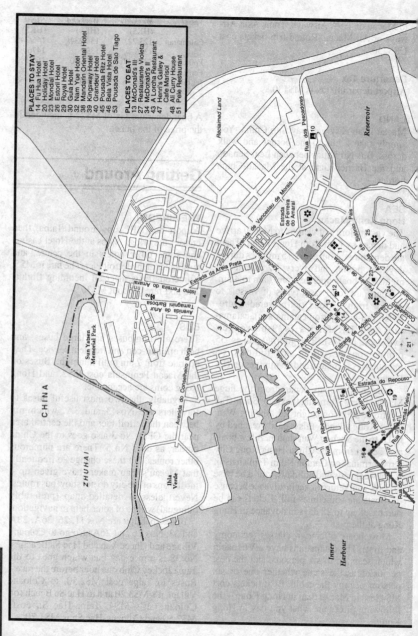

PLACES TO STAY
14 Fu Hua Hotel
20 Holiday Hotel
26 Mondial Hotel
28 Estoril Hotel
29 Royal Hotel
30 Guia Hotel
32 Nam Yue Hotel
38 Mandarin Oriental Hotel
39 Kingsway Hotel
40 Grandeur Hotel
45 Pousada Ritz Hotel
46 Bela Vista Hotel
53 Pousada de Sao Tiago

PLACES TO EAT
13 McDonald's III
27 Restaurante Violeta
34 McDonald's II
43 A Lorcha Restaurant
47 Henri's Galley &
   Cafe Marisol
48 Ali Curry House
51 Pele Restaurant

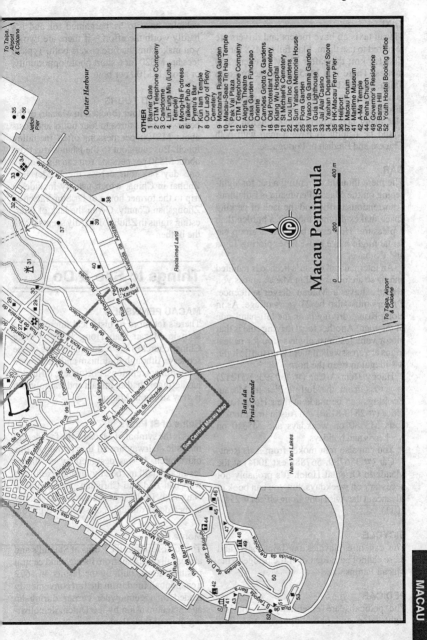

OTHER
1 Barrier Gate
2 CTM Telephone Company
3 Canidrome
4 Lin Fung Miu (Lotus Temple)
5 Mong-Ha Fortress
6 Talker Pub & Pyretu's Bar
7 Kun Iam Temple
8 Our Lady of Piety Cemetery
9 Montanha Russa Garden
10 Macau–Seac Tin Hau Temple
11 Pak Vai Plaza
12 ATM Telephone Company
13 Alegria Theatre
14 Casa Garden Fundaçao Oriente
17 Camões Grotto & Gardens
18 Old Protestant Cemetery
19 Kiang Wu Hospital
21 St Michael's Cemetery
23 Lou Lim Ioc Gardens
24 Sun Yatsen Memorial House
25 Casa Garden Fundaçao
28 Vasco da Gama Garden
31 Guia Lighthouse
33 Jai-Alai Casino
34 Yaohan Department Store
35 HK-Macau Ferry Pier
36 Heliport
37 Macau Forum
41 Maritime Museum
42 A-Ma Temple
44 Penha Church
49 Governor's Residence
50 Barra Hill
52 Youth Hostel Booking Office

Macau Peninsula

0   200   400 m

Outer Harbour

Jetfoil Pier

To Taipa, Airport & Coloane

Reclaimed Land

Baia da Praia Grande

Nam Van Lakes

To Taipa, Airport & Coloane

See Central Macau Map

Avenida da Amizade

Rua de Xangai

MACAU

TAXI

Macau taxis all have meters and drivers are required to use them. Flag fall is M$8 for the first 1.5 km; thereafter it's M$1 every 250 metres. There is a M$5 surcharge to go to Taipa, and M$10 to go to Coloane, but there is no surcharge on return trips. Taxis can be dispatched by radio if you ring up (☎ 519519). Not many taxi drivers speak English, so it would be helpful to have a map with both Chinese and English or Portuguese.

CAR

The mere thought of renting a car for sightseeing on the Macau Peninsula is ridiculous – horrendous traffic and the lack of parking space makes driving more of a burden than a pleasure. However, between a group car rental might make sense for exploring Taipa and Coloane.

An international driver's licence is required and these are not issued in Macau unless you already have a Macau driver's licence. Drivers must also be 21 years of age. As in Hong Kong, driving is on the left-hand side of the road. Another local driving rule is that motor vehicles must always stop for pedestrians at a crosswalk if there is no traffic light. It's illegal to beep the horn.

Happy Rent-A-Car (☎ 439393, 831212) is across from the Jetfoil Pier in Macau. Bookings can be made at their Hong Kong office (☎ 2540-8180). An Austin 'mini-moke' costs M$280 on weekdays and M$310 on weekends and holidays.

You can also rent mokes from Avis Rent-A-Car (☎ 336789, 567888 ext 3004) at the Mandarin Oriental Hotel. It's probably not necessary on weekdays, but you can book in advance at the Avis Hong Kong office (☎ 2541-2011).

BICYCLE

You can hire bicycles on Taipa only, and these cannot be ridden over the bridge to the Macau Peninsula.

PEDICAB

The pedicabs are essentially for touristy sightseeing and photo opportunities. The vehicles have to be bargained for and it's hardly worth the effort – if there are two of you make sure the fare covers both. Typical fees are M$20 for a short photo opportunity, or about M$100 per hour.

ORGANISED TOURS

A typical city tour (booked in Macau) of the peninsula takes three to four hours and costs about M$100 per person, often including lunch. Bus tours out to the islands run from about M$50 per person. You can also book a one day bus tour across the border into Zhuhai in China, which usually includes a trip to the former home of Dr Sun Yatsen in Zhongshan County. Given the lack of interesting sights in Zhuhai, it hardly seems worth the bother.

Things to See & Do

MACAU PENINSULA

There's far more of historical interest to be seen in Macau than Hong Kong. Unlike China, churches are a dominant part of the scenery. Although Buddhism and Taoism are the dominant religions, Portuguese influence has definitely had an impact and Catholicism is very strong in Macau.

Ruins of St Paul's

This is the symbol of Macau – the facade and majestic stairway are all that remain of this old church. It was designed by an Italian Jesuit and built in 1602 by Japanese refugees who had fled anti-Christian persecution in Nagasaki. In 1853 the church was totally burned down during a catastrophic typhoon.

Monte Fort

The fort overlooks the Ruins of St Paul's and almost all of Macau from its high and central position. It was built by the Jesuits. In 1622 a cannonball fired from the fort conveniently landed in a gunpowder carrier during an attempted invasion by the Dutch, demolishing most of their fleet.

Kun Iam Temple

This is the city's most historic temple. In the study are 18 wise men in a glass case – the one with the big nose is said to be Marco Polo. The 400-year-old temple is dedicated to Kun Iam, the queen of heaven and goddess of mercy.

Old Protestant Cemetery

Lord Churchill (one of Winston's ancestors) and the English artist George Chinnery are buried here, but far more interesting are the varied graves of missionaries and their families, traders and seamen, and the often detailed accounts of their lives and deaths. One US ship seems to have had half its crew 'fall from aloft' while in port.

Camões Grotto & Gardens

This serves as a memorial to Luis de Camões, the 16th century Portuguese poet who has become something of a local hero, though Macau's claim on him is not all that strong. He is said to have written his epic *Os Lusiadas* by the rocks here, but there is no firm evidence that he was ever in Macau. A bust of him is in the gardens, which provide a pleasant, cool and shady place. The gardens are popular with the local Chinese and you may see old men sitting here playing checkers.

Barrier Gate

This used to be of interest because you could stand 100 metres from it and claim that you'd seen into China. Now you can stand on the other side and claim you've seen Macau.

Leal Senado

Known in English as the Loyal Senate, this graceful building looks over the main town square and is the main administrative body for municipal affairs. At one time it was offered (and turned down) a monopoly on all Chinese trade! The building also houses the National Library.

Guía Fortress

This is the highest point on the Macau Peninsula and is topped with a lighthouse and 17th century chapel. The lighthouse is the oldest on the China coast, first lit up in 1865.

St Dominic's Church

Arguably the most beautiful church in Macau, this 17th century building has an impressive tiered altar. There is a small museum at the back, full of church regalia, images and paintings.

Lou Lim Ioc Gardens

These peaceful gardens with an ornate mansion (now the Pui Ching School) are a mixture of Chinese and European influences with huge shady trees, lotus ponds, pavilions, bamboo groves, grottoes and odd-shaped doorways.

A-Ma Temple

Macau means 'City of God' and takes its name from A-Ma-Gau, the Bay of A-Ma. A-Ma Temple (Ma Kok Miu), which dates from the Ming Dynasty, stands at the base of Penha Hill near the southern end of the peninsula. According to legend, A-Ma, goddess of seafarers, was supposed to have been a beautiful young woman whose presence on a Guangzhou-bound ship saved it from disaster. All the other ships of the fleet, whose rich owners had refused to give her passage, were destroyed in a storm. The boat people of Macau come here on a pilgrimage each year in April or May.

Macau Maritime Museum

There are a number of boats on exhibit, including a *lorcha*, a type of sailing cargo-vessel used on the Pearl River. The museum offers short cruises for M$15. The Maritime Museum is on the waterfront opposite the A-Ma Temple.

THE ISLANDS

Directly south of the mainland peninsula are the islands of Taipa and Coloane. Two bridges connect Taipa to the mainland, and a causeway connects Taipa and Coloane.

MACAU

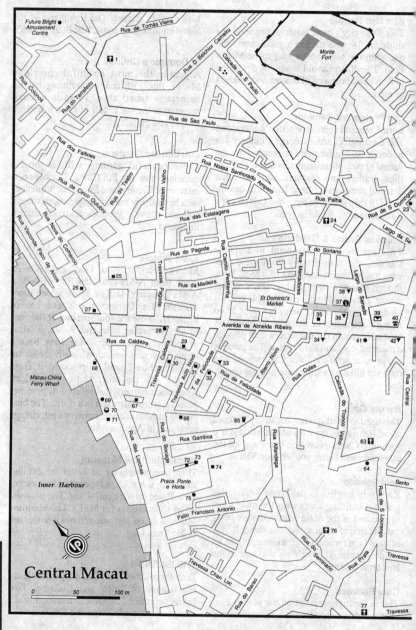

Future Bright
Amusement
Centre

Rua de Tomás Vieira

Monte
Fort

Rua Colonos

Rua do Terraféiro

Rua D Belchior Carneiro

Calçada de S Paulo

1

2

Rua de Sao Paulo

Rua dos Faitioes

Rua de Cinco Outubro

Rua do Teatro

Rua Nossa Senhora do Amparo

Rua Palha

Rua de S Domingos

23

Rua das Estalagens

24

Largo da Se

Rua Nova do Comercio

Rua Visconde Paço de Arcos

T Amazem Velho

Rua do Pagode

Rua Camilo Pessanha

Rua Mercadores

T do Soriano

Largo do Senado

25

26

Travessa Pagode

Rua da Madeira

St Dominic's
Market

38
37
35 36
39
40

27

28

Avenida de Almeida Ribeiro

34
41
42

Rua da Caldeira

29

Rua Áttero Novo

Rua Cules

68

Travessa Caldeira

30

Rua Auto Novo

T da Felicidade

31
32
33

Rua de Felicidade

Calçada do Tronco Velho

Rua Central

Macau-China
Ferry Wharf

69
70
71

67

66

65

63

Rua do Bocage

Rua Gamboa

Rua Allandega

64

Santo

Rua das Lorchas

72 73
74

Rua de S Lourenço

Inner Harbour

Praca Ponte
e Horta

75

Patio Francisco Antonio

76

Rua do Seminario

Rua Praia

Travessa

Central Macau

0   50   100 m

Travessa Chan Loc

Rua do Barao

77

Travessa

MACAU

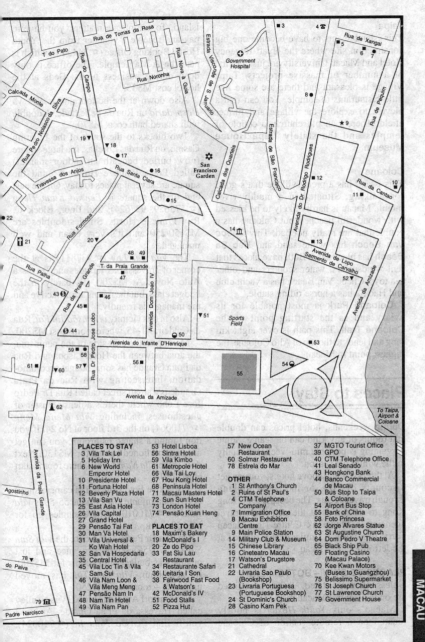

MACAU

Taipa

This island seems to have become one big construction site where the Hyatt Regency Hotel and Macau University are just the first of a number of massive projects. Taipa Village is pleasant and there are some fine little restaurants to sample. You can rent a bicycle to explore the village and further afield. There's an old church, a couple of temples and the stately **Taipa House Museum**.

Coloane

This island has a pretty village that's good for walking. Situated in a muddy river mouth, Macau is hardly likely to be blessed with wonderful beaches, but Coloane has a couple that are really not bad. Tiny **Cheoc Van Beach** has white sand and **Hac Sa Beach** has black sand. Both have places that rent windsurfers, water scooters and other sea toys. Cheoc Van Beach has a yacht club and Hac Sa has a horse riding stable.

Coloane Park is most notable for its aviary and as the starting point of the **Coloane Trail**. This path is over eight km long and leads to the top of Alto Coloane, the highest point in Macau.

Places to Stay

During weekends, hotel prices can double and rooms of any kind can be scarce. Some bargaining is possible mid-week, especially in the winter off-season.

At three-star and above hotels, you can get discounts of 20% or more by booking through travel agents. The best place in Hong Kong to do this is at the numerous travel agencies in Shun Tak Centre (the Macau Ferry Terminal). A similar deal is offered at the Jetfoil Pier in Macau.

PLACES TO STAY – BOTTOM END

Unless otherwise stated, all the places listed are on the Central Macau map.

Macau's only *Youth Hostel* is poorly located on a remote section of Coloane Island. To complicate matters, you have to pay and receive a voucher from the Youth Hostel Booking Office (☎ 344340), which is near the A-Ma Temple. The office is only open during business hours. Beds at the hostel cost M$35.

Also down at the bottom end is *San Va Hospedaria* on Rua de Felicidade. A double with shared bath costs M$70.

Two blocks to the south of the Floating Casino, on Rua das Lorchas, is a large square (now buried beneath an indoor market) called Praça Ponte e Horta. Around the square are several places to stay. On the east end of the square is *Pensão Kuan Heng* (☎ 573629, 937624), 2nd floor, Block C, Rua Ponte e Horta. Singles/doubles are M$150/250 and it's very clean and well managed.

The *Vila Tai Loy* (☎ 937811) is at the corner of Travessa das Virtudes and Travessa Auto Novo. At M$200, it's barely in the budget class, but the rooms are attractive and the manager is friendly.

Also in this vicinity is *Pensão Tai Fat*, Rua da Caldeira 41-45, where rooms cost M$200.

Moving to the east side of the peninsula, the area between the Hotel Lisboa and Rua da Praia Grande has some budget accommodation. Intersecting with Rua da Praia Grande is a small street called Rua Dr Pedro Jose Lobo where there's a dense cluster of guesthouses, including *Vila Meng Meng* (☎ 710064) on the 3rd floor at No 24. If you don't mind a shared bathroom, you can get an air-conditioned rooms for M$130. Next door is the *Vila Nam Loon*, where rooms start at M$150.

Just above Foto Princesa (a camera shop) at Avenida Infante D'Henrique 55-59 is *Vila Kimbo* (☎ 710010), where singles go for M$130 and up.

On Rua Dr Pedro Jose Lobo, the *Vila Sam Sui* (☎ 572256) seems very nice and just qualifies as budget with rooms for M$200. Its neighbour, *Vila Loc Tin*, has moved upmarket – rooms are M$250.

Running off Avenida D João IV is an alley called Travessa da Praia Grande. At No 3 you'll find *Pensão Nam In* (☎ 710024), where singles with shared bath are M$110, or M$230 for a pleasant double with private bath. On the opposite side of the alley is the *Nam Tin Hotel* (☎ 711212), which looks cheap but isn't – singles are M$330! *Vila Nam Pan* (☎ 572289) on the corner has also gotten too pricey, with singles for M$250, but try polite bargaining.

Behind the Hotel Lisboa on Avenida de Lopo Sarmento de Carvalho is a row of pawn shops and a couple of guesthouses. The *Vila San Vu* is friendly and has good rooms for M$200.

PLACES TO STAY – MIDDLE

For the sake of definition, a mid-range hotel in Macau is anything priced between M$200 and M$500.

A personal favourite is the excellent *East Asia Hotel* (☎ 922433), Rua da Madeira 1A. This is one of the city's classic colonial buildings – the outside maintains its traditional facade, but it's been fully remodelled on the inside. Spotlessly clean singles/twins are M$320/360 with private bath and fierce air-conditioning. The dim sum restaurant on the 2nd floor does outstanding breakfasts.

Almost next door to the East Asia Hotel is the *Vila Capital* (☎ 920154) at Rua Constantino Brito 3. Singles/twins are M$250/300.

The *Central Hotel* (☎ 373838) is centrally located at Avenida de Almeida Ribeiro 26-28, a short hop west of the GPO. Singles/doubles with private bath cost from M$250/300.

The *London Hotel* (☎ 937761) on Praça Ponte e Horta (two blocks south of the Floating Casino) has singles for M$230. Rooms are comfortable and clean.

A few doors to the south of the Floating Casino you'll find an alley called Travessa das Virtudes. On your left as you enter the alley is the *Hou Kong Hotel* (☎ 937555), which has doubles/twins for M$260/350. Its official address is Rua das Lorchas 1.

Just a block to the north of the Floating Casino, at Avenida de Almeida Ribeiro 146, is the *Grand Hotel* (☎ 921111), where singles/twins cost M$380/480.

One block to the east of the Floating Casino is a street called Travessa Caldeira, where

you'll find the *Man Va Hotel* (☎ 388655), whose official address is Rua da Caldeira 32. Doubles cost M$280, but this place is perpetually full.

In the same neighbourhood is the very clean and very friendly *Vila Universal* (☎ 573247) at Rua de Felicidade 73. The manager can speak good English and doubles/twins cost M$200/252.

Next door at Rua de Felicidade 71, close to Travessa Auto Novo, is *Ko Wah Hotel* (☎ 375599), which has doubles for M$202 to M$212. Reception is on the 4th floor – check out the ancient lift.

Just on the north side of the Floating Casino on Rua das Lorchas is the *Peninsula Hotel* (☎ 318899). Singles/twins are M$350/400. This hotel is large, clean and popular.

One more place to look around is the area north of the Hotel Lisboa on a street called Estrada de São Francisco. You have to climb a steep hill to get up this street, but the advantage is that the hotels have a little sea breeze and it's quiet.

At Estrada de São Francisco 2A is *Vila Tak Lei* (☎ 577484), where doubles go for M$300. However, with some bargaining you can shave off about M$50.

Stretching the definition of 'mid-range' is the *Macau Masters Hotel* (☎ 937572), Rua das Lorchas 162 (next to the Floating Casino). Doubles are M$440, twins M$550 to M$1000.

Also on the top end of the middle is *Guia Hotel* (☎ 513888) at Estrada do Eng Trigo 1-5 (see the Macau Peninsula map). Twins are priced from M$470 to M$600, triples are M$650 and suites cost M$750 to M$930.

The *Metropole* (☎ 388166) has a prime location at Rua da Praia Grande 63. Doubles are M$460, twins M$600 and suites M$1050 to M$1150.

The *Mondial Hotel* (☎ 566866) is on a side street called Rua de Antonio Basto, east side of Lou Lim Ioc Gardens (see the Macau Peninsula map). It's rather far from the centre but still not cheap. In the old wing doubles go for M$360 to M$480, and there are suites for M$850. In the new wing twins are M$580 to M$630 and suites cost M$1050 to M$2300.

Places to Eat

Given its cosmopolitan past, it's not surprising that the food is an exotic mixture of Portuguese and Chinese cooking. There is also a little influence from other European countries and Africa. The English-speaking waitresses are invariably from the Philippines.

The most famous local speciality is African chicken – chicken baked with peppers and chillies. Other specialities include *bacalhau*, which is cod, served baked, grilled, stewed or boiled. Sole, a tongue-shaped flatfish, is another Macanese delicacy. There's also ox tail and ox breast, rabbit prepared in various ways, and soups like *caldo verde* and *sopa a alentejana* made with vegetables, meat and olive oil. The Brazilian contribution is *feijoadas*, a stew made of beans, pork, potatoes, cabbage and spicy sausages. The contribution from the former Portuguese enclave of Goa on the west coast of India is spicy prawns.

The Portuguese influence is visible in the many fine imported Portuguese red and white wines, port and brandy. Mateus rosé is the most famous but bottles of red or white wine are even cheaper.

A long, lazy Portuguese meal with a carafe of red to wash it down is one of the most pleasant parts of a Macau visit. The menus are often in Portuguese, so a few useful words are *cozido* (stew), *cabrito* (kid), *cordeiro* (lamb), *carreiro* (mutton), *galinha* (chicken), *caraguejos* (crabs), *carne de vaca* (beef) and *peixe* (fish).

Another pleasure of Macau is to sit back in one of the many little cake shops *(pastelarias)* with a glass of *cha de limão* (lemon tea) and a plate of cakes – very genteel! These places are good for a cheap breakfast. People eat early in Macau – you can find the chairs being put away and that the chef has gone home around 9 pm.

Henri's Galley (☎ 556251) is on the waterfront at Avenida da República 4, on the south end of the Macau Peninsula. The adjacent *Ali Curry House* is also worth a visit.

For Portuguese and Macanese food which is both good and cheap, the *Estrela do Mar* (☎ 322074) at Travessa do Paiva 11, off the Rua da Praia Grande, is the place to go. So is the *Solmar* (☎ 574391), at Rua da Praia Grande 11. Both places are famous for African chicken and seafood.

Fat Siu Lau (☎ 573580) serves Portuguese and Chinese food. It's at Rua de Felicidade 64, once the old red-light Street of Happiness. The speciality is roast pigeon.

An excellent place is *Restaurante Safari* (☎ 322239) at Patio do Cotovelo 14, a tiny square off Avenida de Almeida Ribeiro across from the Central Hotel. It has good coffee-shop dishes as well as spicy chicken, steak and fried noodles.

Ze do Pipo (☎ 374047), Rua da Praia Grande 95A (near Rua do Campo) is a two storey splashy Portuguese restaurant with all the trimmings. Once you get past the mirrors and the marble, it's not a bad place to eat, but check the menu prices first.

Chinese-style yoghurt and milk shakes are dished up at *Leitaria I Son* (☎ 573638), next to the MGTO.

Lots of people hop over to Taipa Village for the excellent restaurants found there, though it's no longer cheap. One place to try is *Pinocchio's* (☎ 827128). Other popular Taipa Village restaurants include the very Portuguese *Restaurante Panda* (☎ 827338), *Galo Restaurant* (☎ 827318) and *O'Manuel* (☎ 827571).

At Hac Sa Beach on Coloane Island, *Fernando's* (☎ 882264) deserves honourable mention for some of the best food and nightlife in Macau. Fernando recommends the clams.

Entertainment

GAMBLING

Even if gambling holds no interest for you, it's fun to wander the casinos at night. The largest and most fun arena for losing money is the *Hotel Lisboa*. Cheating at gambling is a serious criminal offence, so don't even think about it.

There's also horse racing on Taipa Island at the *Jockey Club*. Dog races are held at the *Canidrome* (yes, they really call it that) at 8 pm on Tuesday, Thursday, Saturday and Sunday.

PUBS

There are two adjacent pubs that can claim to be the centre of Macau's nightlife. Both are near the Kun Iam Temple on the same street, Rua de Pedro Coutinho. At No 104 is *Talker Pub* (☎ 550153, 528975). Just next door at No 106 is *Pyretu's Bar* (☎ 581063). Most of Macau's pubs open around 8 pm, but don't get moving until after 9 pm and may not close until well after midnight.

A hot spot which is open only on Friday and Saturday nights is the *Jazz Club*, Rua Alabardas 9, near St Lawrence Church. Live music is normally performed here between 11 pm and 2 am.

There is a sedate pub of sorts inside the *Military Club*, which is known for its rustic atmosphere. Other notable pubs include:

Africa Pub, Rua de Xangai 153 (next to the immigration office) (☎ 786369)
Bar Da Guia, Mandarin Oriental Hotel (☎ 567888)
Casa Pub, Estrada de Cacilhas 25, R/C 4, Edificio Hoifu Garden (☎ 524220)
Kurrumba Bar, Rua do Tap Siac 21 (☎ 569752)
Oskar Pub, Holiday Inn Hotel (☎ 783333)

Panguiao Bar, Calçada do Gaio 14 (☎ 304620)
Paprika Bar, Rua de Ferreira do Amaral 34A (☎ 381799)
RJ Bistro, Rua da Formosa 29E R/C (☎ 339380)

SPECTATOR SPORTS

Spectator sports are best seen at the *Macau Forum* (near the Jetfoil Pier) and the *Taipa Stadium* (next to the Jockey Club on Taipa).

Things to Buy

Pawn shops are ubiquitous in Macau, and it is possible to get good deals on cameras, watches and jewellery, but you must be prepared to bargain without mercy. In Macau at least, the sordid reputation of pawnbrokers is well deserved!

The MGTO has a number of good souvenir items for sale at low prices. Some of the items to consider are Macau T-shirts, books, sets of postcards and other tourist paraphernalia.

St Dominic's Market, in the alley behind the Central Hotel, is a good place to pick up cheap clothing.

If you've got the habit, Macau is cheap for Portuguese wine, imported cigarettes, cigars and pipe tobacco. However, Hong Kong's customs agents only allow you to bring in one litre of wine and 50 cigarettes duty-free.

Malaysia

Travel in Malaysia is the easiest in South-East Asia, and its natural attractions and the historic cities of Penang and Melaka are popular destinations. Though not noted for traditional culture, Malaysia is a fascinating mix of exceptionally friendly people, ranging from the Malays, Chinese and Indians of Peninsular Malaysia to the diverse tribespeople of Sabah and Sarawak in East Malaysia.

Apart from its superb beaches, mountains and national parks, Malaysia is one of the most prosperous countries in South-East Asia. It is at the heart of the 'new Asia' and its rapidly increasing wealth and industrial development make it one of the most modern countries in the region.

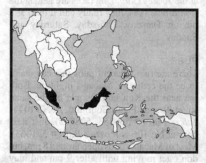

Facts about Malaysia

HISTORY

Little is known about prehistoric Malaysia, but around 10,000 years ago the aboriginal Malays – the Orang Asli – began to move down the peninsula from a probable starting point in south-western China.

In the early centuries of the Christian era, Malaya was known as far away as Europe. Ptolemy showed it on his early map with the label 'Golden Chersonese'. It spelt gold not only to the Romans but to others as well, for it wasn't long before Indian and Chinese traders arrived in search of that most valuable metal and Hindu mini-states sprang up along the great Malay rivers.

The Malay people were ethnically similar to the people of Sumatra, Java and even the Philippines, and from time to time various South-East Asian empires exerted control over all or parts of the Malay peninsula.

In 1405 the Chinese admiral Cheng Ho arrived in Melaka with greetings from the Son of Heaven (the emperor) and, more importantly, the promise of protection from the encroaching Siamese to the north. With this support from China, the power of Melaka extended to include most of the Malay peninsula.

At about the same time, Islam arrived in Melaka and soon spread through Malaya. Melaka's wealth and prosperity soon attracted European interest, and it was the Portuguese who first took over in 1511, followed by the Dutch in 1641 and, finally, the British in 1795.

For years, the British were only interested in Malaya for its seaports and to protect their trade routes, but the discovery of tin prompted them to move inland and take over the whole peninsula. Meanwhile, Charles Brooke, the 'white raja', and the North Borneo Company made similar British takeovers of Sarawak and Sabah respectively. The British, as was their custom, also brought in Chinese and Indians, an action which radically changed the country's racial mix.

Malaya achieved *merdeka* (independence) in 1957 but there followed a period of instability due to an internal Communist uprising and the external 'confrontation' with neighbouring Indonesia. In 1963 the north Borneo states of Sabah and Sarawak, along with Singapore, joined Malaya to create Malaysia.

Relations with Singapore soured almost immediately and, only two years later, Singapore withdrew from the Malaysian confederation. Soekarno's demise ended the disputes with Indonesia and the Communist threat has simply withered away to become a total anachronism in modern Malaysia.

In 1969 violent intercommunal riots broke out, particularly in Kuala Lumpur (KL), and hundreds of people were killed. The government moved to dissipate the tensions, which existed mainly between the Malays and the Chinese. Moves to give Malays a larger share of the economic pie have led to some resentment among the other racial groups but, overall, present-day Malaysian society is relatively peaceful and cooperative.

Elections in 1974 resulted in an overwhelming majority for the Barisan, or National Front, of which the United Malays National Organisation (UMNO) is the key party. All elections since then have seen power remain with the UMNO. Prime Minister Dr Mahathir Mohamad presides over an economically booming Malaysia and is keen to exert his influence on the world stage as a pan-Asian leader.

GEOGRAPHY

Malaysia consists of two distinct parts. Peninsular Malaysia is the long finger of land extending down from Asia, as if pointing towards Indonesia and Australia, and it accounts for about 40% of the country's area. Although most of the forests have been cleared over the years to make way for plantations of rubber trees and oil palms, there are still stands of virgin forest remaining, largely in the national park of Taman Negara.

The balance of the land area is made up of the states of Sabah and Sarawak, which occupy the northern segment of the island of Borneo. Here too, the forests have been cleared for agriculture and timber exports and the tracts of virgin rainforest are rapidly diminishing. Mt Kinabalu in Sabah is the highest peak in South-East Asia.

CLIMATE

Malaysia has a typically tropical climate – it's hot and humid year-round. The temperature rarely drops below 20°C (68°F), even at night, and usually climbs to 30°C (86°F) or more during the day.

Malaysia gets rain throughout the year, but the west coast of Peninsular Malaysia gets heavier rainfall from September to December. The east coast bears the full brunt of the monsoon rains from November to February, and Sarawak and Sabah are similarly affected. Throughout the region the humidity tends to hover around the 90% mark, but on the peninsula you can escape from the heat and humidity by retreating to the delightfully cool hill stations.

See the Kuala Lumpur climate chart in the Appendix.

FLORA & FAUNA

Malaysia is home to some of the most diverse flora and fauna in the world. Its ancient rainforests, the area's climatic stability, plentiful rainfall and tropical greenhouse heat have endowed Malaysia with a cornucopia of bizarre life forms.

In Peninsular Malaysia alone there are over 8000 species of flowering plants, including 2000 trees, 800 orchids and 200 palms. They include the world's tallest tropical tree species, the *tualang*, and the world's largest flower, the rafflesia, measuring up to one metre across.

Mammals include elephants, rhinos (very rare now), tapirs, tigers, leopards, honey bears, several kinds of deer, tempadau (forest cattle), various gibbons and monkeys (including, in Borneo, the orang-utan and the bizarre proboscis monkey), scaly anteaters (pangolins) and porcupines, to name a few.

The bird life features spectacular pheasants, the sacred hornbills and many groups of colourful birds, such as kingfishers, sunbirds, pittas, woodpeckers, trogons and barbets. Snakes include cobras (notably the spitting cobra, which shoots venom into the eyes of its prey), vipers, pythons and colourful tree snakes.

GOVERNMENT & POLITICS

Malaysia is a confederation of 13 states and the capital district of Kuala Lumpur. Nine of the peninsular states have sultans and every five years an election is held to determine which one will become the *yang di-pertuan agong*, or 'king' of Malaysia.

The states of Sabah and Sarawak in East Malaysia are slightly different from those of Peninsular Malaysia since they were separate colonies, not parts of Malaya, prior to independence. They still retain a greater degree of local administrative autonomy than the peninsular states.

The political system is a federal one, with each state having its own legislature, but power is concentrated in the national government. General elections are held every five years, but power is firmly in the hands of UMNO.

ECONOMY

Malaysia is traditionally one of the world's major suppliers of tin, natural rubber and palm oil. Rubber and oil palm plantations cover a large part of the peninsula. In East Malaysia the economy is based on timber and in Sarawak oil and pepper are major exports. With the decline of these traditional mainstays of the economy, Malaysia has successfully diversified into manufactured goods. The country is a major supplier of electronic components and equipment and, along with other goods such as textiles and footwear, manufactured goods now count for over half of all exports.

POPULATION & PEOPLE

Malaysia's population is currently around 19.5 million. The people of Malaysia come from a number of different ethnic groups – Malays, Chinese, Indians, the indigenous Orang Asli of the peninsula and the various tribes of Sarawak and Sabah.

It's reasonable to say that the Malays control the government while the Chinese have their fingers on the economic pulse. Approximately 85% of the population lives in Peninsular Malaysia and the remaining 15% in the much more lightly populated states of Sabah and Sarawak.

There are still small scattered groups of Orang Asli (Original People) in Peninsular Malaysia. Although most have given up their

nomadic or shifting-agriculture techniques and have been absorbed into modern Malay society, a few groups of Orang Asli still live in the forests.

Dayak is the term used for the non-Muslim people of Borneo. These people migrated to Borneo at times and along routes which are not clearly defined. It is estimated that there are more than 200 Dayak tribes in Borneo, the most important being the Iban and Bidayuh in Sarawak and the Kadazan in Sabah. Other smaller groups include the Kenyah, Kayan and Punan, whose lifestyle and habitat is rapidly disappearing.

SOCIETY & CONDUCT

As many Muslim countries have in the last decade, Malaysia has been going through a period of increasing concentration on religion and religious activity. It's certainly a world away from the sort of fundamentalism found in other parts of the world, but you still need to be aware of local sensibilities so as not to offend.

It's wise to be appropriately discreet in dress and behaviour, particularly on the stricter Muslim east coast of the peninsula. For women, topless bathing is definitely not acceptable and away from the beaches you should cover up as much as possible. For men, shorts are considered low class away from the beach, and bare torsos are not acceptable in the villages and towns.

RELIGION

The variety of religions found in Malaysia is a direct reflection of the diversity of races living there. Although Islam is the state religion of Malaysia, freedom of religion is guaranteed. The Malays are almost all Muslims and there are also some Indian Muslims. The Chinese are predominantly followers of Taoism and Buddhism, though some are Christians. The majority of the region's Indian population come from the south of India and are Hindu, though a sizeable percentage are Muslim.

Although Christianity has made no great inroads into Peninsular Malaysia, it has had a much greater impact upon East Malaysia, where many of the indigenous people have converted to Christianity, although others still follow their animist traditions.

LANGUAGE

The official language is Bahasa Malaysia, or Bahasa Melayu ('language of the Malays'). You can get along quite happily with English throughout Malaysia and, although it is not the official language, it is often still the linking language between the various ethnic groups, especially the middle class.

Other everyday languages include Chinese dialects like Hakka or Hokkien. The majority of the region's Indians speak Tamil, although there are also groups who speak Malayalam, Hindi or other Indian languages.

Bahasa Malaysia is virtually the same as Indonesian. See Lonely Planet's *Malay phrasebook* or, for an introduction to the language, see the Language section in the Indonesia chapter of this book.

Facts for the Visitor

PLANNING

When to Go

Rain occurs fairly evenly throughout the year, but travel is possible year-round. The exception is the east coast of the peninsula, which receives heavy rain from November to January, when many resorts close down and boat services stop.

Malaysia has many colourful festivals, such as Thaipusam, around January/February, but with such a wide ethnic diversity, celebrations are held throughout the year. During public holidays – especially Chinese New Year, Hari Raya and Christmas – transport is crowded and hotel prices rise in the resorts.

Maps

Mapping in Malaysia is generally poor. Tourist office maps are usually little more than sketch maps, but adequate for getting around. Good maps can be found for the main cities; Periplus and Nelles Verlag each produce a good series.

HIGHLIGHTS

Travel in Malaysia is easily divided between the peninsula and the Borneo states of Sabah and Sarawak. To get a good look at both halves of Malaysia will take at least a couple of months, but most visitors only go to the peninsula, and Borneo is almost another country.

A typical route through the west coast of the peninsula takes in Melaka, Kuala Lumpur and Penang, Malaysia's more historical and culturally interesting cities, with a diversion to the hill station of the Cameron Highlands. The east coast's attractions are beaches, including Tioman Island, Cherating and the Perhentian Islands. Most visitors find themselves in Kota Bharu on the east coast, and in the centre, Taman Negara National Park is a big drawcard.

Sarawak is famed for jungle and Dayak tribes, but the city of Kuching is one of the most pleasant in Malaysia. The national parks such as Bako, Niah Caves and Mulu are the main attractions, and a trip up the Rejang River takes you into the heart of Borneo. Sabah's main attraction is Mt Kinabalu, one of the world's easiest mountains to climb. You can see orang-utans at the Sepilok Orang-Utan Rehabilitation Centre, and the Turtle Islands National Park is a popular island retreat with turtles.

VISAS & DOCUMENTS

Passports must be valid for at least six months beyond the date of entry into Malaysia.

British Commonwealth citizens (except those from India, Bangladesh, Sri Lanka and Pakistan) and citizens of the Republic of Ireland, Switzerland, the Netherlands, San Marino and Liechtenstein do not require a visa to visit Malaysia.

Citizens of Austria, Belgium, Czech Republic, Denmark, Finland, Hungary, Germany, Iceland, Italy, Japan, Luxembourg, Norway, Slovak Republic, South Korea,

Sweden and the USA do not require a visa for a visit not exceeding three months.

Citizens of France, Greece, Poland and South Africa do not require a visa for a visit not exceeding one month. Most other nationalities are given a shorter stay period or require a visa.

Most nationalities are given a 30 day or 60 day permit on arrival. As a general rule, if you arrive by air you will be given 60 days automatically, though coming overland you may be given 30 days unless you specifically ask for a 60 day permit. It's then possible to get an extension at an immigration office in the country for a total stay of up to three months.

Sabah and Sarawak are treated like separate countries. Your passport will be checked again on arrival in each state and a new stay permit, usually for 30 days, is issued. Travelling directly from either Sabah or Sarawak back to Peninsular Malaysia, however, there are no formalities and you do not start a new entry period, so your 30 day permit from Sabah or Sarawak remains valid. Your initial 30 day permit can be extended, though extensions can be difficult to get in Sarawak.

Documents

A car can be hired on the production of a valid home licence with a photo. Officially an international driver's licence is not required, but is good to present to overly officious police.

A Hostelling International (YHA) card is of limited use, as only KL, Melaka and Port Dickson have HI hostels, though it can also be used to waive the small initial membership fee at some YMCAs and YWCAs.

An ISIC (international student identity card) is also of limited use. Most student discounts, such as on the trains, are only available for Malaysian students, but it can also be useful at hostels and flashing it occasionally brings discounts.

EMBASSIES
Malaysian Embassies

Malaysian embassies abroad include:

Australia
    7 Perth Ave, Yarralumla, Canberra ACT 2600
    (☎ (06) 273-1543)
Canada
    60 Boteler St, Ottawa, Ontario K1N 8Y7
    (☎ (613) 237-5182)
France
    2 bis rue Benouville, Paris 75116
    (☎ 01 45 53 11 83)
Germany
    Mittelstrasse 43, 5300 Bonn 2
    (☎ (0228) 37 68 03 06)
Japan
    20-16 Nanpeidai-cho, Shibuya-ku, Tokyo 150
    (☎ (03) 3476-3840)
New Zealand
    10 Washington Ave, Brooklyn, Wellington
    (☎ (04) 385-2439)
UK
    45 Belgrave Square, London SW1X 8QT
    (☎ (0171) 235-8033)
USA
    2401 Massachusetts Ave NW, Washington, DC
    20008 (☎ (202) 328-2700)

See the other chapters in this book for Malaysian embassies in those countries.

Foreign Embassies in Malaysia

Countries with embassies in Kuala Lumpur include:

Australia
    6 Jalan Yap Kwan Sweng (☎ 242-3122)
Brunei
    MBF Plaza, 172 Jalan Ampang (☎ 261-2800)
India
    Jalan Taman Duta (☎ 253-3510)
Indonesia
    233 Jalan Tun Razak (☎ 984-2011)
    Consulates:
    467 Jalan Burma, Penang (☎ (04) 282-4686)
    5A Pisang Rd, Kuching, Sarawak
    (☎ (082) 241734)
    Jalan Karamunsing, Kota Kinabalu, Sabah
    (☎ (088) 219110)
    Jalan Apas, Tawau, Sabah (☎ (089) 772052)
Laos
    Jalan Bellamy (☎ 248-3895)
Myanmar
    5 Jalan Taman U Thant (☎ 242-3863)
Philippines
    1 Jalan Changkat Kia Peng (☎ 248-4233)
Singapore
    209 Jalan Tun Razak (☎ 261-6277)

Sri Lanka
 2A Jalan Ampang Hilir (☎ 456-0917)
Thailand
 206 Jalan Ampang (☎ 248-8222)
 Consulates:
 1 Jalan Tunku Abdul Rahman, Penang
 (☎ (04) 282-8029)
 4426 Jalan Pengkalan Chepa, Kota Bharu
 (☎ (09) 744-0867)
Vietnam
 Vietnam House, 4 Pesiaran Stonor (☎ 248-4036)

Australia	A$1	=	RM1.99
Canada	C$1	=	RM1.84
France	FF10	=	RM4.87
Germany	DM1	=	RM1.65
Indonesia	Rp1000	=	RM1.08
Japan	¥100	=	RM2.26
New Zealand	NZ$1	=	RM1.75
Singapore	S$1	=	RM1.78
Thailand	100B	=	RM9.87
UK	UK£1	=	RM3.92
USA	US$1	=	RM2.51

CUSTOMS

The following dutiable items can be brought into Malaysia free of duty: one litre of alcohol, 225g of tobacco (200 cigarettes), souvenirs and gifts not exceeding RM200. Cameras, portable radios, perfume, cosmetics and watches do not attract duty.

The list of prohibited items is longer – the main thing to avoid is the importation of illicit drugs, which carries the death penalty in Malaysia.

MONEY
Costs

Malaysia is more expensive than other South-East Asian nations, although less so than Singapore. You get pretty much what you pay for – there are lots of hotels where a couple can get a quite decent room for around US$5, or guesthouses in the tourist centres offer dormitory beds for around US$2.50 as well as cheap rooms. Food at hawkers' centres is cheap and transport is also reasonable and efficient.

Currency

The local currency is the Malaysian ringgit (RM), which is divided into 100 sen. Notes in circulation are RM5, RM10, RM20, RM50, RM100, RM500 and RM1000; the coins in use are 1, 5, 10, 20 and 50 sen, and RM1. Old RM1 notes are occasionally seen and new RM2 and RM15 notes are coming into circulation.

Currency Exchange

The following table shows the exchange rates:

Changing Money

Banks are efficient and there are also plenty of moneychangers to be found in the main centres. Credit cards are widely accepted, and many ATMs accept Visa and MasterCard if your card has a PIN.

Tipping & Bargaining

Tipping is not normally done in Malaysia. The more expensive hotels and restaurants have a 10% service charge, while at the cheaper places tipping is not expected.

Bargaining is not usually required for everyday goods, unlike in some Asian countries. Always bargain for souvenirs, antiques and other tourist items, even if prices are displayed. Transport prices are fixed but negotiation is required for trishaws and unmetered taxis around town or for charter.

POST & COMMUNICATIONS

Malaysia has an efficient postal system and a reliable poste restante service at the major post offices. Most post offices are open daily from 8 am to 5 pm but closed on Sunday. Aerogrammes and postcards cost RM0.50 to any destination.

Telephone

There are good telephone communications throughout the country. You can make direct-dial long-distance calls between all major towns in Malaysia. Local calls cost 10 sen for three minutes.

Convenient card phones, Kadfon, are found all over the country and take plastic cards, though two telephone systems – Telekom and Uniphone – operate using different cards. Credit-card phones are also available. International calls can be direct-dialled from many public phone booths and from most Telekom offices. Reverse-charge international calls can easily be made from any phone by dialling the Home Country Direct numbers that are listed in the telephone book. Calls to Singapore are long-distance calls, not international calls.

For international direct dialling (IDD), dial 007, then the country code, area code and number.

Malaysia's country access code is 60, if you're dialling from overseas.

In Malaysia (010) and (011) are area codes for cellular phones.

BOOKS

There's a wide variety of books available in Malaysia, and a number of good bookshops in which to find them.

Kampong Boy by the cartoonist Lat provides a delightful introduction to Malay life.

An Analysis of Malay Magic by KM Endicott is a scholarly look at Malay folk religion and the importance of spirits and magic in the world view of Malays.

Chinese Beliefs & Practices in South-East Asia edited by Cheu Hock Tong is an excellent introduction to Chinese religion and society.

The Prime Minister, Dr Mahathir Mohamad, is a prolific writer. *The Malay Dilemma* and his latest offering, *The Voice of Asia*, are interesting polemics of racial stereotyping.

A Short History of Malaysia, Singapore & Brunei by C Mary Turnbull is straightforward and a good introductory volume on Malaysia's history. *A History of Malaysia* by Barbara Andaya and Leonard Watson is one of the best histories with a post-independence slant.

Vanishing World, the Ibans of Borneo by Leigh Wright has some beautiful colour photographs. Redmond O'Hanlon's *Into the Heart of Borneo* is a wonderfully funny tale of a jaunt through the jungles of northern Borneo. For Bornean wildlife, *A Field Guide to the Mammals of Borneo* by Junaidi Payne, Charles M Francis and Karen Phillipps is a must.

Malaysia has provided a fertile setting for novelists and Joseph Conrad's *The Shadow Line* and *Lord Jim* both use the region as a setting. Somerset Maugham also set many of his classic short stories in Malaya – look for the *Borneo Stories*. Paul Theroux's *The Consul's File* is based in the small town of Ayer Hitam. *The Long Day Wanes* is a reissue in one volume of Anthony Burgess' classic *Malayan Trilogy* – some of the finest English-language fiction set in South-East Asia.

NEWSPAPERS & MAGAZINES

Malaysia has newspapers in English, Malay, Chinese and Tamil. The *New Straits Times* is the main offering in English. Foreign magazines are widely available.

TV

Malaysia has two government TV channels, RTM 1 and 2, and two commercial stations. Programmes range from local productions in the various languages to imports from the USA and UK.

HEALTH

Malaysia enjoys good standards of health and cleanliness. The usual rules for healthy living in a tropical environment apply. The main problem to look out for is malaria in East Malaysia, so take those tablets or carry a net, or both.

For more information, see the Health section in the Appendix.

WOMEN TRAVELLERS

Foreign women travelling in Malaysia face no particular problems. The main point to bear in mind is that Malaysia is a Muslim country and modesty in dress is important. Though Malaysia is generally a very safe country, don't walk alone at night on empty beaches or poorly lit streets.

Many travellers – not just women – have reported the existence of small peepholes in the walls and doors of cheap hotels. Plug them up with tissue paper, ask for another room or move to another hotel. Remember that in some places cheap hotels are in fact brothels.

Tampons can be found in supermarkets in the main cities if you hunt around, but pads are more commonly available, so if you use tampons bring your own.

GAY & LESBIAN TRAVELLERS

Gay issues are swept under the carpet in Malaysia. Just as the government denied for many years that AIDS was a problem, the official attitude seems to be that, as a strongly Muslim country steeped in Asian values, homosexuality in Malaysia doesn't exist and it is a western aberration. Gay groups and venues are thin on the ground, except in the more cosmopolitan and liberal-minded cities such as KL.

DANGERS & ANNOYANCES

Malaysia is a relatively wealthy country and theft is not a major problem compared with other countries in the region, though of course the normal precautions should be taken. Violent crime is virtually unheard of.

As for drugs, the answer is simple – don't. Drug trafficking carries a mandatory death penalty, and being a foreigner will not save you from the gallows. A number of foreigners have been executed in Malaysia, some of them for possession of amazingly small quantities. In almost every village in Malaysia you will see anti-*dadah* (drugs) signs portraying a skull and cross-bones and a noose. No one can say they haven't been warned!

BUSINESS HOURS

Government offices are usually open Monday to Friday from around 8 am to 12.45 pm, and then again from 2 to 4.15 pm. On Friday the lunch break usually lasts from 12.15 to 2.45 pm. On Saturday morning the offices are open from 8 am to 12.45 pm. These hours vary slightly from state to state; on the east coast of the peninsula most government offices are closed on Friday.

Shop hours are also somewhat variable, although from 9.30 am to 7 pm is a good rule

of thumb. Major department stores, Chinese emporiums and some stores catering particularly to tourists are open until 9 or 10 pm seven days a week.

PUBLIC HOLIDAYS & SPECIAL EVENTS

Although some public holidays have a fixed annual date, the Hindus, Muslims and Chinese all follow a lunar calendar, which means the dates for many events vary each year.

National public holidays are:

New Year's Day
    1 January
Chinese New Year
    January or February
Hari Raya Puasa
    January or February
Hari Raya Haji
    April
Awal Muharam
    April or May
Labour Day
    1 May
Wesak Day
    April or May
King's Birthday
    1st Saturday in June
Birthday of the Prophet
    July
National Day
    31 August
Deepavali
    November
Christmas Day
    25 December

In addition, each state has its own public holidays to celebrate the birthdays of the sultans or other state-specific events, such as the Dayak harvest festivals in Sabah and Sarawak.

During school holidays, Hari Raya Puasa (the end of the fasting month) and Chinese New Year, accommodation may be difficult to obtain and transport can be fully booked.

Cultural Events

With so many cultures and religions there is quite an amazing number of occasions to celebrate in Malaysia. The most important and colourful are described here, and

MALAYSIA

Tourism Malaysia puts out a *Calendar of Events* with specific dates and venues of various festivals and parades.

The major Muslim annual events are connected with Ramadan, the 30 days during which Muslims cannot eat or drink from sunrise to sunset. Hari Raya Puasa marks the end of the month-long fast with three days of joyful celebration. This is the major holiday of the Muslim calendar.

Chinese New Year is the most important celebration for the Chinese community. Dragon dances and pedestrian parades mark the start of the new year. Families hold open house, unmarried relatives (especially children) receive *ang pows*, or money in red packets, businesses traditionally clear their debts and everybody wishes you a 'kong hee fatt choy' (a happy and prosperous new year). The Moon Cake Festival around September celebrates the overthrow of the Mongol warlords in ancient China with the eating of moon cakes and the lighting of colourful paper lanterns. The Festival of the Nine Emperor Gods involves nine days of Chinese operas, processions and other events honouring the nine emperor gods. In KL and Penang, in October or November, fire-walking ceremonies are held on the evening of the ninth day. The Dragon Boat Festival is celebrated around June with boat races in Penang.

Thaipusam is one of the most dramatic Hindu festivals, in which devotees honour Lord Subramaniam with acts of amazing masochism. Self-mutilating worshippers make the procession to the Batu Caves outside Kuala Lumpur, usually in January or February. The festival of Deepavali celebrates Rama's victory over the demon King Rawana with the Festival of Lights, where tiny oil lamps are lit outside Hindu homes. It is held in October.

If you are in Sarawak from 1 to 2 June, don't miss Gawai Dayak, the festival of the Dayaks to mark the end of the rice season. War dances, cockfights and blowpipe events all take place. National Day, 31 August, is celebrated throughout the country with parades and special events.

ACCOMMODATION

For the budget traveller, the best places to track down are traditional Chinese hotels, which are found in great numbers all over Malaysia. They're the mainstay of backpackers, and in Malaysia you can generally find a good room from RM12 to RM25. Chinese hotels are generally spartan – bare floors and just a bed, a couple of chairs, a table, a wardrobe and a sink. A gently swishing ceiling fan completes the picture.

Couples can sometimes economise by asking for a single, since in Chinese hotel language single means one double bed and double means two beds. Don't think this is being tight – in Chinese hotels you can pack as many into one room as you wish.

The main catch with these hotels is that they can sometimes be terribly noisy. Part of the noise comes from the street, as the hotels are often on main roads, but there's also the traditional dawn chorus of coughing, hacking and spitting, which has to be experienced to be believed. It's worst in the oldest hotels where the walls don't quite reach the ceiling but are meshed in at the top for ventilation.

Malaysia also has a variety of cheap local accommodation, usually at beach centres. These may be huts on the beach or guesthouses (private homes or rented houses divided by partition walls into a number of rooms). A dorm bed will cost RM6 to RM8, and hotel-style rooms can cost anywhere from RM12 to RM40 with air-con.

In Malaysia there's a 5% government tax that applies to all hotel rooms. On top of this there's a 10% service charge in the more expensive places. Cheap Malaysian hotels, however, generally quote a price inclusive of the 5% government tax.

FOOD

While travel in some parts of Asia can be as good as a session with Weightwatchers, Malaysia is quite the opposite. The food is simply terrific, the variety unbeatable and the costs pleasantly low. Whether you're looking for Chinese, Malay, Indian or Indonesian food, or even a hamburger, you'll find happiness!

Chinese Food

You'll find the full range of Chinese cuisine in Malaysia. If you're kicking round the backwoods of Sabah or Sarawak, however, Chinese food is likely to consist of little more than rice and vegetables.

Indian Food

Indian food is one of the region's greatest delights. Indeed, it's easier to find good Indian food in Malaysia than in India! You can roughly divide Indian food into southern, Muslim and northern: food from southern India tends to be hotter with the emphasis on vegetarian dishes, while Muslim food tends to be more subtle in its spicing and uses more meat. The rich Mogul dishes of northern India are not so common and are generally only found in more expensive restaurants.

A favourite Indian Muslim dish which is cheap, easy to find and of excellent standard is biryani. Served with a chicken or mutton curry, the dish takes its name from the saffron-coloured rice it is served with.

Malay, Indonesian & Nonya Food

Surprisingly, Malay food is not as easily found in Malaysia as Chinese or Indian food, although many Malay dishes, like satay, are everywhere.

Nonya cooking is a local variation on Chinese and Malay food. It uses Chinese ingredients, but employs local spices like chillies and coconut cream. Nonya cooking is essentially a home skill rather than a restaurant one – there are few places where you can find Nonya food. Laksa, a spicy coconut-based soup, is a classic Nonya dish that has been adopted by all Malaysians.

Other Cuisine

Western fast-food addicts will find that Ronald McDonald, the Colonel from Kentucky and A&W have all made inroads into the regional eating scene.

Tropical Fruit

Once you've tried rambutans, mangosteens, jackfruit and durians, how can you ever go back to boring old apples and oranges? Refer to the Food section in the Regional Facts for the Visitor chapter at the beginning of this book for all the info on these delights.

DRINKS

Life can be thirsty in Malaysia, so you'll be relieved to hear that drinks are excellent, economical and readily available. For a start, water can be drunk straight from the tap in most larger Malaysian cities.

Fruit juices are popular and very good. With the aid of a blender and crushed ice, delicious concoctions like watermelon juice can be whipped up in seconds. Old-fashioned sugar cane crushers, which look like grandma's old washing mangle, can still be seen in operation.

Halfway between a drink and a dessert are *es kacang* and *cendol*. An es or ais (ice) kacang is rather like an old-fashioned sno-cone, but the shaved ice is topped with syrups and condensed milk and it's all piled on top of a foundation of beans and jellies. It sounds gross and looks lurid but tastes terrific! Cendol consists of coconut milk with brown sugar syrup and greenish noodle-like things topped with shaved ice.

Other oddities? Well, the milky white drink in clear plastic bins sold by street drink sellers is soybean milk, which is also sold in a yoghurty form. Soybean milk is also available in soft drink bottles. Medicinal teas are a big deal with the health-minded Chinese.

Beer drinkers will probably find Anchor beer or Tiger beer to their taste, or locally brewed Carlsberg and Guinness are also popular. Alcohol is expensive and sometimes hard to find in the 'dry' east coast states.

Getting There & Away

AIR

The usual gateway to Malaysia is KL, although Penang also has international connections. Singapore is also a handy arrival point as it's just a short trip across the Causeway from Johor Bahru. Singapore also has more international connections and is therefore a better place to shop for tickets.

Penang is a major centre for cheap airline tickets. These days the better agents are usually OK, but beware of places which ask for big advance payments before they issue you with the tickets. Typical one-way fares being quoted out of Penang include: Medan RM140, Madras RM610, Phuket RM170, Bangkok RM350 and Hong Kong RM610. Other fares may involve flying from KL or even Bangkok.

Thailand

Malaysia Airlines (MAS) and Thai Airways International fly between Penang and Hat Yai, Phuket and Bangkok. You can fly from Penang to Bangkok for about RM350, more from KL. The fare from Penang to Phuket is RM170.

Indonesia

There are several interesting flight options from Indonesia to Malaysia. The short hop from Medan in Sumatra to Penang costs around US$60; from Penang it's RM140. There are also weekly flights between Kuching in Sarawak and Pontianak in Kalimantan, the Indonesian part of the island of Borneo, for RM177. Similarly at the eastern end of Borneo there is a weekly connection between Tawau in Sabah and Tarakan in Kalimantan. For Jakarta, the cheapest connections are from Singapore from as little as US$70, though MAS has competitively priced flights from Johor Bahru.

Singapore

It is much cheaper to fly from Malaysia to Singapore than in the reverse direction. See the Singapore chapter for details on flights to and from Singapore.

Other Places in Asia

From Hong Kong, the cheapest one-way flights to Malaysia cost around US$200. Philippine Airlines has flights via Manila to Kuala Lumpur and Kota Kinabalu for HK$1420/1620 one way and HK$2620/2820 return respectively. Dragonair and MAS also have flights to Kota Kinabalu, but they are expensive.

Although Indonesia and Thailand are the two 'normal' places to travel to or from, there are plenty of other possibilities, including India, Sri Lanka, Myanmar or the Philippines.

Departure Tax

Malaysia levies airport taxes on all its flights. It's RM40 on international flights, RM20 to Singapore and Brunei. If you buy your tickets in Malaysia, the departure tax is included in the price.

LAND

Thailand

The main border crossings are at Padang Besar (road or rail), Bukit Kayu Hitam (road) or Keroh-Betong (road) in the west, or at Rantau Panjang-Sungai Kolok in the east.

Road – West Coast Although there are border points at Padang Besar and Keroh, the usual crossing is via Bukit Kayu Hitam on the main north-south highway for Hat Yai. This crossing is made easy by the buses that run from Georgetown in Penang right through to Hat Yai for around RM30. Alternatively, take a bus from Alor Setar to the large border complex at Bukit Kayu Hitam, walk a few hundred metres to the Thai checkpost, and then take Thai buses and taxis to Sadao or Hat Yai.

The other alternative is to cross at Padang Besar, where it is an easy walk across. The train from Alor Setar all the way to Hat Yai is the easiest way to cross the border at this point. The only reason to go this way by road is if you're heading to/from Langkawi.

Road – East Coast The Thai border is at Rantau Panjang (Sungai Kolok on the Thai side), 1½ hours by bus from Kota Bharu. From Rantau Panjang walk across the border, and then it's about one km to the station, from where trains go to Hat Yai, Surat Thani and Bangkok.

Train The rail route into Thailand is on the Butterworth-Alor Setar-Hat Yai route, which crosses into Thailand at Padang Besar. You can take the International Express (all 2nd class) from Butterworth all the way to Bangkok with connections from Singapore and Kuala Lumpur. From Hat Yai there are frequent train and bus connections to other parts of Thailand. One train a day also goes from Alor Setar to Hat Yai.

Indonesia

A daily express bus (10 hours) runs between Pontianak in Kalimantan and Kuching in Sarawak. The bus crosses at the Tebedu-Entikong border, which is now a visa-free entry point into Indonesia.

Singapore

Most travellers enter or exit Singapore by the Causeway connecting Johor Bahru and Singapore Island. Frequent buses do the short run, and a number of long-distance buses operate from the regional centres in Malaysia direct to Singapore city. The Malaysian rail system also terminates in Singapore.

SEA
Thailand

Regular daily boats run between Langkawi in Malaysia and Satun in Thailand. There are customs and immigration posts here, so you can cross quite legally, although it's an unusual and rarely used entry/exit point. Make sure you get your passport stamped on entry.

In the main tourist season (around Christmas) yachts also operate irregularly between Langkawi and Phuket in Thailand, taking in Thai islands on the way for around US$200 per person.

Indonesia

Three main services connect Malaysia and Indonesia – Penang-Medan and Melaka-Dumai connecting Peninsular Malaysia with Sumatra, and Tawau-Tarakan connecting Sabah with Kalimantan in Borneo.

The very popular crossing between Penang and Medan is handled by two companies that, between them, have services six days a week.

The journey takes 4½ hours and costs RM110/90 in 1st/2nd class. The boats actually land in Belawan in Sumatra, and the journey to Medan is completed by bus (four hours, included in the price).

Twice daily high-speed ferries operate between Melaka and Dumai (RM80, 2½ hours) in Sumatra. Dumai is now a visa-free entry port into Indonesia for most nationalities.

Boats also operate most days from Tawau in Sabah to Nunukan in Kalimantan and then on to Tarakan in Kalimantan. This is not a recognised border crossing for visa-free entry so an Indonesian visa must be obtained in advance if entering or exiting this way.

Yet another possibility is to take a boat from Pasir Gudang, about 30 km from Johor Bahru. Boats go direct to Batam and Bintang in Indonesia's Riau Archipelago, and to Surabaya in Java. SS Holidays in Pasir Gudang is the main agent. A new duty-free complex and ferry terminal is under construction in Johor Bahru and when completed will have ferries to Singapore and the Riau Archipelago.

Singapore

The vast majority of people cross on the Causeway, either by train or by road, but a regular ferry crosses between North Changi (Singapore) and Tanjung Belungkor (Malaysia). It is mainly for Singaporeans holidaying at Desaru on the Malaysian coast. Small boats also ply between Pengerang in Johor and Changi Village in Singapore. See the Singapore chapter for details.

Getting Around

AIR

Malaysia Airlines (MAS) is the country's main domestic operator and has an extensive network linking the major regional centres on the peninsula, Sabah and Sarawak and the offshore islands of Tioman and Langkawi. Pelangi Air is a small regional airline that has useful services to Tioman, Langkawi, Pangkor and Melaka, among other destinations.

MALAYSIA

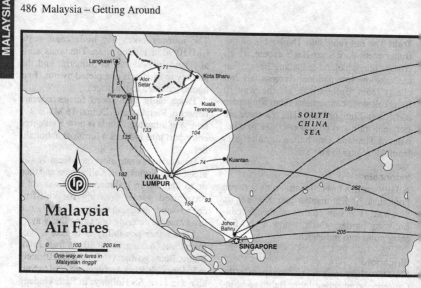

Langkawi

Alor
Setar

71

Kota Bharu

51

Penang

87

Kuala
Terengganu

104

104

SOUTH
CHINA
SEA

104

133

135

74

Kuantan

182

**KUALA
LUMPUR**

262

158

93

169

Johor
Bahru

205

SINGAPORE

Malaysia
Air Fares

0   100   200 km

One-way air fares in
Malaysian ringgit

The air fares chart above details some of the main regional routes and their fares in Malaysian dollars.

The main reason to catch flights within Malaysia is to travel between the peninsula and East Malaysia. You can save quite a few dollars if flying to Sarawak or Sabah by flying from Johor Bahru rather than Kuala Lumpur or Singapore. The regular economy fare is RM169 from Johor Bahru to Kuching against RM262 from KL and S$193 (RM205) from Singapore. To Kota Kinabalu, the respective fares are RM347, RM437 and S$391 (RM418). MAS has many other regional routes in Sarawak and Sabah.

MAS also has a number of special night flights and advance purchase fares. Seven day advance purchase one-way tickets/30 day advance purchase return tickets are available for the following flights:

Destination	Fare
JB to Kuching	RM144/305
JB to Kota Kinabalu	RM295/624
JB to Penang	RM150/318
KL to Kuching	RM227/425
KL to Kota Kinabalu	RM372/689
KL to Miri	RM359/679
KL to Labuan	RM372/656

BUS

Malaysia has an excellent bus system. There are public buses on local runs and a variety of privately operated buses on the longer trips. In larger towns there may be a number of bus stops – a main station or two, plus some of the private companies may operate directly from their own offices.

Buses are fast, economical and reasonably comfortable, and seats can be reserved. Many routes use air-con buses which usually cost just a few ringgit more than regular buses. They make midday travel a sweat-free activity, but beware – as one traveller put it, 'Malaysian air-conditioned buses are really meat lockers on wheels with just two settings: cold and suspended animation'.

TRAIN

Malaysia has a modern, comfortable and economical railway service, although there are basically only two railway lines. One runs from Singapore to Butterworth and continues on into Thailand. The other branches from this line at Gemas, south of KL, and runs through Kuala Lipis up to the north-east corner of the country near Kota Bharu.

Malaysia basically has three types of rail

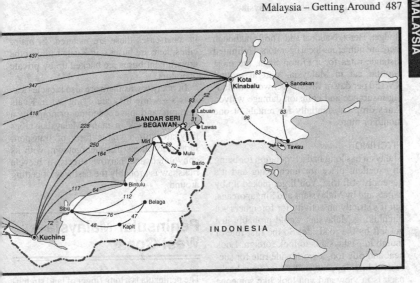

services – express, limited express and local trains. Express trains are air-con, generally 1st and 2nd class only, and on night trains there's a choice of sleepers or seats. Limited express trains may have 2nd and 3rd class only but some have 1st, 2nd and 3rd class with overnight sleepers. Express trains cost about 20% more than ordinary trains, are faster, only stop at main stations and in most respects are the ones to take. Book as far in advance as possible for the express trains.

The national railway company, Keretapi Tanah Melayu (KTM), offers a Tourist Railpass for 30 days for US$120 (children US$60) or 10 days (US$55; children US$28). You have to do a lot of train travel to make them worthwhile.

In Sabah there's also a small narrow-gauge line which can take you through the Padas River gorge from Tenom to Beaufort. It's a great trip and is well worth doing.

TAXI
Long-distance taxis make Malaysian travel, already easy and convenient even by the best Asian standards, a real breeze. In almost every town there will be a 'teksi' stand where the cars are lined up and ready to go to their various destinations. The taxis are ideal for groups of four, and are also available on a share basis. As soon as a full complement of four passengers turns up, off you go. Between major towns you have a reasonable chance of finding other passengers to share without having to wait too long, but otherwise you will have to charter a whole taxi at four times the single fare rate.

You can often get the taxis to pick you up or drop you off at your hotel. You can also take a taxi to other destinations at charter rates. Shared taxi fares generally work out at about twice the comparable bus fares.

CAR
Rent-a-car operations are well established in Malaysia. Basically, driving in Malaysia follows much the same rules as in Britain or Australia – cars are right-hand drive and you drive on the left side of the road. The roads are good and most drivers in Malaysia are relatively sane, safe and slow, though a fair few specialise in overtaking on blind corners and trusting in divine intervention.

Petrol costs are around RM1.15 a litre; diesel fuel costs RM0.65 per litre. Major rental operators in Malaysia include Avis,

Budget, Hertz, National and Thrifty, although there are numerous local operators. Unlimited distance rates for a Proton Saga, the most popular car in Malaysia, start at around RM150 per day or RM900 per week, including insurance and collision damage waiver. Rates drop substantially for rentals of one month or more.

HITCHING

Malaysia has long had a reputation for being an excellent place for hitchhiking and it's generally still true. You'll get picked up by expats and by Malaysians and Singaporeans, but it's strictly an activity for foreigners – a hitchhiking Malaysian would probably just get left by the roadside! So the first rule of thumb in Malaysia is to look foreign. Look neat and tidy too, a worldwide rule for successful hitching, but make sure your backpack is in view and you look like someone on their way around the country.

On the west coast of Malaysia, particularly on the busy Johor Bahru-Kuala Lumpur-Butterworth route, hitching is generally quite easy. On the east coast, traffic can often be quite light and there may be long waits between rides. Hitching in East Malaysia also depends on the traffic, although it's quite feasible.

Keep in mind that hitching is never entirely safe in any country in the world, and we don't recommend it. Travellers who decide to hitch should understand that they are taking a small but potentially serious risk. People who do choose to hitch will be safer if they travel in pairs and let someone know where they are planning to go.

BOAT

There are no services connecting the peninsula with East Malaysia. On a local level there are boats between the peninsula and offshore islands, and along the rivers of Sabah and Sarawak – see the relevant sections for full details.

LOCAL TRANSPORT

Local transport varies widely from place to place. Almost everywhere there are taxis and in most cases these are metered. In major cities there are buses – in Kuala Lumpur the government buses are backed up by private operators.

In many towns there are also bicycle rickshaws – while they are dying out in Kuala Lumpur and have become principally a tourist gimmick in many Malaysian cities they are still a viable form of transport. Indeed in places like Georgetown, with its convoluted and narrow streets, a bicycle rickshaw is probably the best way of getting around.

Peninsular Malaysia – West Coast

The peninsula is a long finger of land stretching down from the Thai border to Singapore, the tip of which is only 137 km north of the equator. It comprises 11 of the 13 states that make up Malaysia. On the western side of the peninsula, you'll find the major cities – oriental Penang, the bustling, modern capital of Kuala Lumpur, historic Melaka – and the restful hill stations.

The shining beaches of the east coast, Taman Negara National Park and the wild central mountains are covered in the Peninsular Malaysia – East Coast section later in this chapter. The following description starts with the capital, Kuala Lumpur, but otherwise follows the route from Johor Bahru, just across the Causeway from Singapore, and moves up the west coast to the Thai border.

KUALA LUMPUR

Malaysia's capital city is a curious blend of the old and the new. It's a modern and fast-moving city although the traffic never takes on the nightmare proportions of Bangkok. It has gleaming high-rise office blocks beside multilane highways, but the old colonial architecture still manages to stand out proudly.

It's also a blend of cultures – the Malay capital with a vibrant Chinatown, an Indian

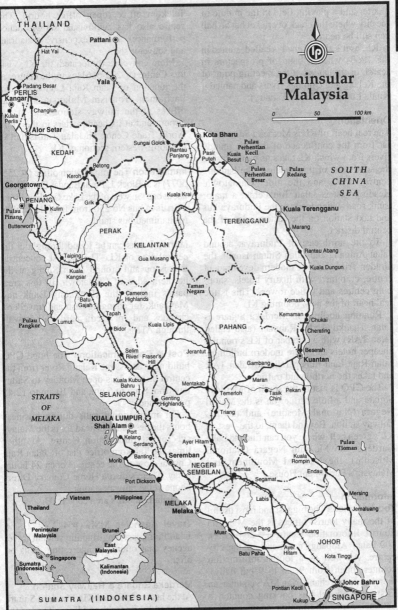

Peninsular Malaysia

0   50   100 km

THAILAND

Pattani

Hat Yai

Padang Besar

PERLIS

Kangar

Kuala Perlis

Changlun

Alor Setar

KEDAH

Tumpat

Sungai Golok

Rantau Panjang

Kota Bharu

Pasir Puteh

Kuala Besut

Pulau Perhentian Kecil

Pulau Perhentian Besar

Pulau Redang

SOUTH CHINA SEA

Betong

Keroh

Georgetown

PENANG

Pulau Pinang

Kulim

Butterworth

Grik

Kuala Krai

Kuala Terengganu

Marang

TERENGGANU

PERAK

KELANTAN

Rantau Abang

Taiping

Gua Musang

Kuala Dungun

Kuala Kangsar

Ipoh

Cameron Highlands

Taman Negara

Kemasik

Kemaman

Chukai

Batu Gajah

Tapah

Cherating

Pulau Pangkor

Lumut

Bidor

Kuala Lipis

PAHANG

Beserah

Kuantan

Selim River

Fraser's Hill

Jerantut

Gambang

Maran

Kuala Kubu Bahru

Mentakab

Temerloh

Tasik Chini

Pekan

SELANGOR

Genting Highlands

Triang

STRAITS OF MELAKA

KUALA LUMPUR

Shah Alam

Port Kelang

Serdang

Ayer Hitam

Pulau Tioman

Morib

Banting

Seremban

NEGERI SEMBILAN

Gemas

Kuala Rompin

Port Dickson

Segamat

Endau

MELAKA

Melaka

Labis

Mersing

Muar

Yong Peng

Jemaluang

Batu Pahat

Kluang

Ayer Hitam

JOHOR

Kota Tinggi

Pontian Kecil

Johor Bahru

Kukup

SINGAPORE

Thailand

Vietnam

Philippines

Peninsular Malaysia

Brunei

East Malaysia

Singapore

Sumatra (Indonesia)

Kalimantan (Indonesia)

SUMATRA (INDONESIA)

quarter and a playing field in the middle of the city where the crack of cricket bat on ball can still be heard.

KL, as it's almost always called, started in the 1860s when a band of prospectors in search of tin landed at the meeting point of the Kelang and Gombak rivers and named it Kuala Lumpur (Muddy Estuary).

Orientation

The real heart of KL is Merdeka Square, not far from the confluence of the two muddy rivers from which KL takes its name. Just to the south-east of this square is the banking centre of KL and the older Chinatown. Heading east is Jalan Tun Perak, a major trunk road which leads to the Puduraya bus and taxi station on the eastern edge of the central district.

To the north-east of Puduraya, around Jalan Ampang and Jalan Sultan Ismail, the Golden Triangle is the modern development centre, crammed with luxury hotels, shopping centres and office towers. This is the real heart of the new, booming KL.

Running north from Merdeka Square is Jalan Tuanku Abdul Rahman (also called Jalan TAR) with a number of KL's popular cheaper hotels and more modern buildings. Jalan Raja Laut runs parallel to Jalan TAR and takes the northbound traffic.

The GPO is just to the south of Merdeka Square and a little further on is the Masjid Negara (National Mosque) and the KL railway station. Beyond them, to the west, is KL's green belt, where you can find the Lake Gardens, the Muzium Negara (National Museum), the National Monument and Malaysia's Parliament House.

Information

Tourist Offices The biggest and most useful of the many tourist offices is the Malaysia Tourist Information Centre (☎ 264-3929), 109 Jalan Ampang, north-east of the city centre. As well as a tourist information counter (open from 9 am to 9 pm daily), there's a moneychanger, an MAS counter, an Ekspres Nasional bus booking counter, a national parks information counter and a Telekom office (open office hours). The centre also has audiovisual shows, dance performances and an expensive restaurant and souvenir shop.

More conveniently located, the KL Visitors Centre (☎ 293-6661) is in the centre, at the junction of Jalan Raja Laut and Jalan Parliamen. Tourism Malaysia also has offices at the railway station and at the airport, and at its headquarters in the Putra World Trade Centre on Jalan Tun Ismail in the north-western section of KL.

Immigration The immigration office (☎ 255-5077) is at Block 1, Pusat Bandar Damansara, about one km west of the Lake Gardens. Take a Sri Jaya bus No 250 from the Jalan Sultan Mohammed bus stand.

Money Banks can be found throughout the central area of KL. The biggest concentration is on and around Jalan Silang at the northern edge of Chinatown. In this area, banks include the Hongkong Bank and Maybank, for changing cash and travellers' cheques and for credit card withdrawals through ATMs.

Post & Communications The huge GPO building is across the Kelang River from the central district. It is open Monday to Saturday from 8 am to 6 pm, and 10 am to 12.45 pm on Sunday.

For international calls during business hours the best place to head for is the Malaysia Tourist Information Centre. At other times the Telekom office just off Jalan Raja Chulan close to the centre is open 24 hours a day. There's also a Home Country Direct phone at the railway station.

Kuala Lumpur's area code is 03.

Travel Agencies MSL (☎ 442-4722), 66 Jalan Putra, is a long-running student travel agency that often has interesting deals on offer.

Merdeka Square & Railway Station

At the heart of colonial KL, Merdeka Square is ringed by fine old buildings. The mock-

Tudor **Royal Selangor Club** was a social centre for KL's high society in the tin-rush days of the 1890s. Across the road is the impressive **Sultan Abdul Samad building**, designed by the British architect AC Norman and built between 1894 and 1897. Formerly the Secretariat building it is topped by a 43 metre clock tower. The old city hall is in a similar Moorish style, and now houses **Infokraf**, a dull exhibition centre for Malaysian handicrafts. Over the road, the **Kuala Lumpur Memorial Library**, once colonial administration offices, now houses a permanent exhibition on the history of the city.

To find a building full of eastern promise, head south to KL's magnificent **railway station**. Built in 1911, this delightful example of British colonial humour is a Moorish fantasy of spires, minarets, towers, cupolas and arches.

Across from this superb railway station is the equally wonderful **Malayan Railway Administration building**. Next door is the **National Art Gallery**, with changing exhibits, usually modern art, from around the world. The art gallery is housed in the once-gracious colonial Majestic Hotel.

Nearby is the modernistic **Masjid Negara** (National Mosque), one of the largest in South-East Asia, but the most delightful of all KL's mosques is the **Masjid Jamek**, or Friday Mosque. Built in 1909 at the confluence of the Kelang and Gombak rivers near Merdeka Square, this was the place where KL's founders first set foot in the town and where supplies were landed for the tin mines.

Chinatown

Just south of the Masjid Jamek are the teeming streets of KL's Chinatown. This crowded, colourful area is the usual melange of signs, shops, activity and noise. The central section of Jalan Petaling is a busy, interesting market selling souvenirs and other goods, at its liveliest in the evening.

The main point of interest in Chinatown is the **Central Market**. This refurbished Art Deco building is a centre for handicraft, antique and art sales. As well as shops, hawkers' centres, restaurants and bars, various rotating exhibits are on display and cultural shows are staged in the evenings.

Lake Gardens

These 60 hectare gardens form the green belt of KL, just west of the city centre. The central focus of the gardens is the lake of Tasik Perdana, where boats can be rented on weekends. The gardens contain a host of other attractions, open from 9 am to 6 pm. Entry to most is RM5, and a shuttle bus runs around the gardens. The large **Bird Park** has a large variety of South-East Asian and other birds. Nearby is the **Orchid Garden**, the adjoining **Hibiscus Garden** and the **Deer Park**. The **Butterfly Park** has a number of species in its landscaped enclosure, a butterfly museum and a cafe.

The massive **National Monument** overlooks the Lake Gardens from a hillside as does Malaysia's **Parliament House**.

Muzium Negara

At the southern end of the Lake Gardens and less than a km along Jalan Damansara from the railway station is the **Muzium Negara** (National Museum). It's full of unusual exhibits, such as the skull of an elephant which derailed a train! Another strange sight is an 'amok catcher', an ugly barbed device used to catch and hold a man who has run amok. Admission to the museum is RM1 and it is open daily from 9 am to 6 pm except on Friday, when it closes between noon and 2.45 pm.

Jalan Tuanku Abdul Rahman (Jalan TAR)

North from the city centre, Jalan TAR leads through an old section of the city, passing **Masjid Little India**. Detour along Jalan Masjid India, which is crammed with Indian shops and restaurants. Centred on the mosque, Little India has all the feel of a Middle-Eastern bazaar.

The **Chow Kit Market** is a Malay market, with a gaggle of roadside vendors lining Jalan TAR. On Saturday nights, Jalan TAR is closed to traffic and hosts the liveliest night market in the city.

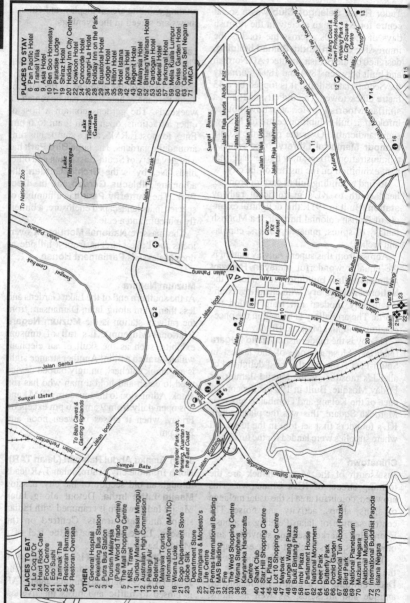

PLACES TO STAY
6 Pan Pacific Hotel
8 Transit Villa
9 Asia Hotel
10 Ben Soo Homestay
19 Paradise Lodge
19 Shiraz Hotel
20 Holiday Inn City Centre
22 Kowloon Hotel
24 Concorde Hotel
26 Shangri-La Hotel
28 Holiday Inn on the Park
29 Equatorial Hotel
34 Lodge Hotel
35 Hilton Hotel
39 Hotel Istana
42 Agora Hotel
43 Regent Hotel
50 Malaysia Hotel
53 Bintang Warisan Hotel
53 Cardogan Hotel
55 Federal Hotel
57 Parkroyal Hotel
59 Melia Kuala Lumpur
60 Swiss Garden Hotel
63 Carcosa Seri Negara
71 YMCA

PLACES TO EAT
14 Le Coq D'Or
24 Hard Rock Cafe
37 Food Centre
41 Edo Sushi
51 Tamnak Thai
54 Restoran Ramzan
56 Restoran Oversea

OTHER
1 General Hospital
2 Pekeliling Bus Station
3 Putra Station
4 Tourism Malaysia
5 The Mall Shopping Centre
   (Putra World Trade Centre)
7 MSL Travel
11 Sunday Market (Pasar Minggu)
12 Malaysia Tourist
   Information Centre (MATiC)
13 Australian High Commission
15 Pelangi Air
16 Betelnut
17 Malaysia Tourist
   Information Centre (MATiC)
18 Wisma Stephens
21 Sogo Department Store
23 Globe Silk
   Department Store
25 Brannigans & Modesto's
27 Life Centre
30 Pernas International Building
31 MAS Building
32 Fire
33 The Weld Shopping Centre
36 Wisma Stephens
38 Karyaneka Handicrafts
   Centre
40 Shark Club
44 Star Hill Shopping Centre
45 KL Plaza
46 Lot 10 Shopping Centre
47 Maybank
48 Sungei Wang Plaza
49 Bukit Bintang Plaza
52 Imbi Plaza
61 President House
62 National Monument
64 Deer Park
65 Butterfly Park
66 Orchid Garden
67 Memorial Tun Abdul Razak
68 Bird Park
69 National Planetarium
70 Muzium Negara
   (National Museum)
72 International Buddhist Pagoda
73 Istana Negara

Lake Titiwangsa Gardens

Lake Titiwangsa

To National Zoo

Jalan Pahang

Sungai Gombak

Sungai Untut

Sungai Batu

Jalan Sentul

To Batu Caves & Genting Highlands

To Templer Park, Ipoh, Penang & the East Coast, Kuantan & the East Coast

Jalan Tun Razak

Jalan Ipoh

Jalan Kuching

Jalan Sultan Salahuddin

Jalan Raja Muda Abdul Aziz

Sungai Bunus

Jalan Raja Mahmud

Jalan Raja Uda

Jalan Watson

Jalan Hamzah

Sungai Kelang

Chow Market

Jalan Sultan Ismail

Jalan Tuanku Abdul Rahman

Jalan TAR

Jalan Putra

Jalan Raja Laut

Jalan Pahang

Dang Wangi

To Ming Court & Crown Princess Hotels, Ampang Park & KL City Square Centre

Jalan Ampang

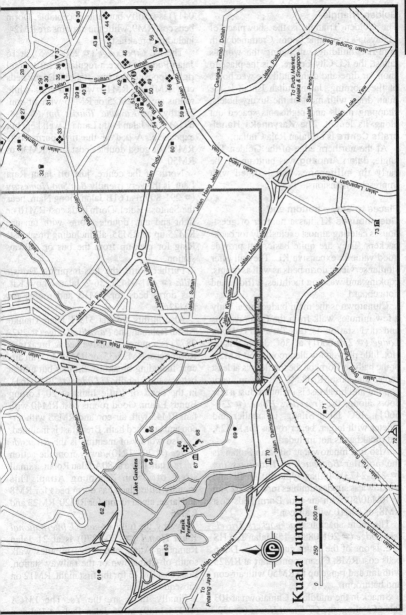

Kuala Lumpur

Golden Triangle

The Golden Triangle is the showpiece of Malaysia's economic boom. Crammed with high-rise buildings, including the world's tallest, the KL City Centre, it is the place to shop, or dine and drink until the wee hours of the morning. Jalan Sultan Ismail is the main drag, with most of the luxury hotels, shopping malls and nightspots spaced out along its length. The **Karyaneka Handicrafts Centre** is on Jalan Raja Chulan.

At the northern edge of the Golden Triangle, **Jalan Ampang** was built up by the early tin millionaires and is lined with impressive mansions.

Places to Stay – bottom end

Guesthouses KL has a number of guesthouses catering almost exclusively for backpackers. They are quite basic, but provide good value in expensive KL. They all offer similar services: dorm beds as well as rooms, cooking and washing facilities, a fridge and noticeboard.

Chinatown is the main budget area. Only a few minutes walk from the Puduraya bus and taxi station is the *Travellers' Moon Lodge* (☎ 230-6601) at 36C Jalan Silang. Hot, little plywood-walled rooms cost RM20, or the hallway dorm on the top floor is at least cooler and costs RM8.50. It's cheap, very popular and breakfast is included. Just a few doors along, the *Travellers Home* (☎ 230-6601), 46C Jalan Silang, is smaller and quieter with larger, better rooms for RM23, but breakfast is not included.

Also in Chinatown, at 60 Jalan Sultan, is the popular *Backpackers Travellers Inn* (☎ 238-2473). It has typically small and windowless singles/doubles for RM22/25 up to RM40/50 with air-con. Dorm beds cost RM8, or RM10 with air-con.

The more spacious *Backpackers Travellers Lodge* (☎ 201-0889), 158 Jalan Tun HS Lee, is one of the better guesthouses. Dorm beds cost RM8. Clean rooms start at RM25 with fan and range up to RM50 with air-con and bathroom.

Smack in the middle of Chinatown at 103 Jalan Petaling, the *CT Guest House* (☎ 232-0417) is scruffy but quite acceptable. Dorm beds cost RM9, while most rooms are RM24, including breakfast.

The *KL City Lodge* (☎ 230-5275), at 16 Jalan Pudu, is more a regular, scruffy hotel right opposite the bus station. Dorm beds cost RM8 or RM10 with air-con, while rooms are RM20/25 or RM35 with air-con. Nearby, the *Kawana Tourist Inn* (☎ 238-6714) at 68 Jalan Pudu Lama is well kept but expensive. A bed in the tiny dorm costs RM12, or good doubles cost from RM30 to RM50.

North of the centre, just off Jalan Raja Laut, is the very friendly *Ben Soo Homestay* (☎ 291-8096) at 61B Jalan Tiong Nam, near the Sentosa Hotel. Dorm beds cost RM10 or light and airy double rooms with fan are RM25 up to RM35, all including breakfast. Ring for pick-up from the bus or railway station.

Further north, the less-inspiring *Transit Villa* (☎ 441-0443), 36-2 Jalan Chow Kit, has dorm beds for RM12 and rooms for RM22/29.

Also in this area, at 319-1 Jalan Tuanku Abdul Rahman, the *Paradise Lodge* (☎ 292-2872) is a more expensive bed & breakfast. Rooms cost RM25/35, or RM35/45 with air-con, including breakfast. Similar but a little better is the friendly *TI Lodge* (☎ 293-0261), in the heart of Little India at 20 Lorong Bunus Enam. Good rooms cost RM40 with fan, RM45 with air-con and RM55 with air-con and attached bath. Breakfast is included.

Also worthy of mention is the *Riverside Lodge* (☎ 201-1210), away from the action but in a quiet area at 80A Jalan Rotan, a small street off Jalan Kampung Attap. This friendly little place has dorm beds for RM8 and large, clean rooms for RM20, RM23 and RM25.

Nearby, the fully air-con *KL International Youth Hostel* (☎ 230-6870) is at 21 Jalan Kampung Attap, about five minutes walk south of Chinatown or the railway station. Beds cost RM15 for the first night, RM12 on subsequent nights.

Finally, there are the Ys. The *YMCA* (☎ 274-1439) at 95 Jalan Padang Belia, a long way south of the centre off Jalan Tun Sambanthan, has good if slightly expensive rooms for RM38/50, up to RM75 for four-bed rooms. Take minibus No 12; ask for the Lido Cinema.

The *YWCA* (☎ 283-225) is much more central at 12 Jalan Hang Jebat. It has plain but acceptable rooms for women at RM30/50, and some for couples from RM50.

Hotels In Chinatown, cheapest of the Chinese cheapies is the well-camouflaged *Wan Kow Hotel* at 16 Jalan Sultan. Very basic rooms with fan and common bath cost RM25. Also very cheap is the *Colonial Hotel* (☎ 238-0336) at 39 Jalan Sultan, where rooms go for RM24/30, or RM34 with air-con. This hotel is more geared towards travellers, but the noisy, wire-topped rooms are very run-down. Check for peepholes.

North of the city on Jalan TAR, the *Coliseum Hotel* (☎ 292-6270) at No 100 is famous for its old planters' restaurant and bar downstairs. The rooms are a little run-down but large, quiet and good value at RM22 with fan, RM30 with air-con. Consequently it is often full. Jalan TAR also has a couple of other basic, cheap hotels. At No 136 the *Tivoli Hotel* (☎ 292-4108) is a reasonable Chinese cheapie which charges RM25 for rooms with fan and common bath. The *Rex Hotel* nearby at No 132 is similar.

Places to Stay – middle
Chinatown has plenty of mid-range hotels. On Jalan Sultan near Jalan Tun HS Lee, the quiet *Hotel City Inn* (☎ 238-9190) has comfortable but small rooms for RM69/80. Just a few doors along, the *Hotel Lok Ann* (☎ 238-9544) at 113A Jalan Petaling has reasonable rooms for RM60/74.

More luxurious options in Chinatown include the *Hotel Malaya* (☎ 232-7722) on Jalan Hang Lekir and the *Hotel Furama* (☎ 230-1777) on Jalan Sultan. Both have rooms from around RM120. The *Swiss Inn* (☎ 232-3333), 62 Jalan Sultan, is a very popular, new hotel. Spotless rooms cost RM136 to RM159 and the hotel has a good

coffee shop popular for its cheap buffet breakfasts.

The *Hotel Pudaraya* (☎ 232-1000), on top of the Pudaraya bus and taxi station, is convenient if overnighting for connections. This large high-rise is a little faded but has very well-appointed rooms for RM104/115.

On Jalan TAR, the *Kowloon Hotel* (☎ 293-4246) at No 142 is another of the older breed of modern hotels. Rooms from RM85/103 are large and well appointed.

Lively Jalan Bukit Bintang, east of the centre at the edge of the Golden Triangle, has a good selection of mid-range hotels. The new *Bintang Warisan* (☎ 248-8111) at No 68 is a larger hotel and a definite grade above the others. Rooms start at RM120/140, plus 15%.

Places to Eat
Hawker Food KL is well endowed with hawker venues, dotted all around the city. In Chinatown, street food can be found everywhere, but Jalan Petaling and Jalan Hang Lekir are good places to start looking. The Central Market also has hawkers' food upstairs.

The Saturday night market on Jalan Tuanku Abdul Rahman has a large collection of food vendors and a great atmosphere, though it's mostly takeaway. The Chow Kit Market, just off Jalan Tuanku Abdul Rahman close to the Asia Hotel, is great for Malay food.

Jalan Alor, one street west of Jalan Bukit Bintang in the Golden Triangle, has open-air tables in the evening serving some of the best Chinese hawkers' fare in KL. Most shopping malls have more expensive, air-con food courts – one of the best is in The Mall shopping centre on Jalan Putra.

Indian Food Little India is a good hunting ground for Indian food. Indian coffee shops and food stalls abound in the Jalan Masjid India/Jalan Tuanku Abdul Rahman area. Upstairs at 60A Jalan TAR, *Bangles* is an Indian restaurant with a good reputation. Further along, the *Shiraz*, on the corner of Jalan TAR and Jalan Medan Tuanku, is a

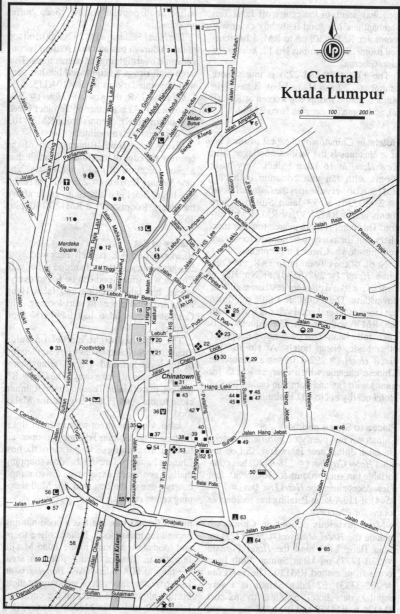

Central
Kuala Lumpur

0   100   200 m

good Pakistani restaurant. Some prefer the similar *Omar Khayyam* next door.

In Chinatown's Central Market, *Hameed's* is a thriving, cafeteria-style restaurant with Indian noodles and curries. Facing the market, *Restoran Yusoof* is popular for roti, biryani etc.

Chinese Food Chinese restaurants can be found everywhere, but particularly around Chinatown and along Jalan Bukit Bintang.

In the Sungei Wang Plaza on Jalan Sultan Ismail near Jalan Bukit Bintang is the *Esquire Kitchen Restoran*, which is very popular for lunch, particularly the RM5 set meals. At the entrance to this plaza is the *Super Noodle House*, which is cheap and popular. The superior *Mayblossom* at No 1/F inside the plaza has more expensive set meals.

Malay Food There are Malay *warungs* (small eating stalls) and *kedai kopis* (coffee shops) throughout KL, but especially along and just off Jalan Tuanku Abdul Rahman. Several of those in the vicinity of the Coliseum Hotel are excellent and cheap; look for the nasi lemak in the early mornings. The *Restoran Imaf*, near the Minerva Bookshop, is a good bet.

The stylish *Kapitan's Club*, 35 Jalan Ampang, has a mixed menu that includes Peranakan food along with Chinese and western dishes. Curry Kapitan is a speciality, as are the savoury Peranakan pastries. Expect to pay RM20 or less per person.

Other KL has a surprising variety of western restaurants, and fast-food chains are found everywhere. Not to be missed is the restaurant in the *Coliseum Hotel* on Jalan TAR, which serves excellent steaks at around RM20. The place is quite a colonial experience and has hardly changed over the years.

Le Coq d'Or is another colonial experience in a fine turn-of-the-century mansion at 121 Jalan Ampang. It's not quite as expensive as the elegant surroundings might indicate.

The set lunch is excellent value for RM9 plus 15%.

KL also has some good, mid-range Thai restaurants. The *Thai Kitchen* in the Central Market on Jalan Hang Kasturi, and the classier *Tamnak Thai*, 74 Jalan Bukit Bintang, are both recommended and moderately priced.

Entertainment

Bars, Discos & Live Music KL's burgeoning nightlife is mostly found in the Golden Triangle on Jalan Sultan Ismail. The *Hard Rock Cafe* in the Concorde Hotel is still the hottest spot in town, with the usual food-and-rock memorabilia blend. A short stroll behind the Hard Rock Cafe, *Brannigans* and the better *Modesto's* are next to each other on Lorong Perak.

The *Shark Club* on Jalan Sultan Ismail near the Istana Hotel is open 24 hours and packs in the crowds. Bands play on weekends.

Popular discos in the Golden Triangle include *Betelnut* on Jalan Penang and *The Jump* in the Wisma Inai on Jalan Tun Razak. At 370B Jalan Tun Razak, *Barn Thai* is a Thai restaurant and long-running jazz/rock joint with a good atmosphere.

The Central Market is popular with travellers – it is quieter but cheaper. Facing the river on the western side of the market, the *Riverbank* has the occasional jazz band or guitar strummer. A few doors away, the *Bull's Head* is an English-style pub with Eagles on the jukebox and Anchor on tap. Or step back in time to the bar at the *Coliseum Hotel* on Jalan Tuanku Abdul Rahman, where you can sip a beer in the planters' chairs or chat to the regulars at the bar.

Cultural Shows The *Malaysian Tourist Information Centre* (☎ 264-3929) on Jalan Ampang has traditional dance performances (RM2) at 3.30 pm on Tuesday, Thursday, Saturday and Sunday. The *Central Market* (☎ 274-6542) has a regular programme of free cultural performances at 7.45 pm on Friday, Saturday and Sunday.

Things to Buy

For handicrafts, check out the Central Market complex in Chinatown. Jalan Petaling in the heart of Chinatown is a colourful shopping street and has some craftwork, cheap clothes and copy watches. Bargain hard. Karyaneka Handicraft Centre, out past the Hilton on Jalan Raja Chulan, displays local craftwork. Jalan Tuanku Abdul Rahman is also worth a browse, especially around the Chow Kit Market.

KL's biggest and most popular shopping malls are in the Golden Triangle on Jalan Sultan Ismail and Jalan Bukit Bintang.

Getting There & Away

Air KL is well served by many international airlines and there are flights to and from Australia, Europe and all regional capitals.

On the domestic network, KL is the hub of MAS services and there are flights to most major towns and cities on the peninsula and in East Malaysia. MAS (☎ 261-0555, 746-3000 for 24-hour reservations) is in the MAS building, Jalan Sultan Ismail.

Bus Most buses operate from the hot and clamorous Puduraya bus and taxi station on Jalan Pudu, just east of Chinatown. There are departures to most places throughout the day, and at night to main towns. Check at the tourist police office or the information counter at the main entrance before you do the rounds of the ticket offices inside. Typical fares from KL are RM18 to Singapore, RM16.50 to Johor Bahru, RM6.50 to Melaka, RM15 to Lumut, RM10 to the Cameron Highlands, RM19 to Penang and RM12.50 to Kuantan. The bus station has a left-luggage office.

Buses to Kelang and Port Kelang (No 793) and Shah Alam (Nos 337 and 338) leave from the Kelang bus station at the end of Jalan Hang Kasturi in Chinatown.

Buses for Jerantut (for Taman Negara) and Kuala Lipis operate from the Pekeliling bus station in the north of the city, just off Jalan Tun Razak. To Jerantut (RM9, 3½ hours) there are four daily and to Kuala Lipis there are at least four departures daily (RM8, four hours).

Though Puduraya has buses to the east coast, Putra bus station (☎ 442-9530), opposite the World Trade Centre, handles more express coach services to Kuantan, Kuala Terengganu and Kota Bharu.

Train KL is also the hub of the railway system. There are daily departures (express trains are marked *) for Butterworth (*7.30 am and *2.15, 10 and 11.30 pm) and Singapore (*7.25 am and *2.30, 9 and 10.25 pm). For the east-coast line to Jerantut (for Taman Negara) and Kota Bharu, you first have to take a southbound train to Gemas and then get another connection – forget it and take a bus.

Taxi Taxis depart from upstairs in the Puduraya bus and taxi station. Per person fares for non-air-con taxis include: Melaka (RM13), Johor Bahru (RM31), Singapore (RM36), Ipoh (RM22), Lumut (RM32), Cameron Highlands (RM32), Penang (RM50), Genting Highlands (RM10), Fraser's Hill (RM18), Jerantut (RM17), Kuala Lipis (RM15), Kuantan (RM25), Kuala Terengganu (RM35) and Kota Bharu (RM35).

Getting Around
The Airport Taxis from the KL international airport, 20 km west of the city, operate on a coupon system (RM22 to Chinatown) from the booth outside the terminal. Avoid non-registered drivers who ask exorbitant rates.

Intrakota air-con buses (RM1.90) and Sri Jaya No 47 (RM1.60) go to the airport every 20 minutes from the Jalan Sultan Mohammed bus stand, opposite the Kelang bus station, from 6.30 am to 10.30 pm. The trip takes 45 minutes, longer if traffic is bad.

Bus KL's bus system is chaotic. City bus companies include Sri Jaya, Len Seng, Len, Foh Hup, Toong Foong and Intrakota (air-con). Air-con services are 50 sen for the first two km and then five sen per km. Pink

minibuses operate on a fixed fare of 60 sen anywhere along their route. Try to have correct change ready when boarding the buses, particularly during rush hours.

Train From the KL railway station, a KTM Komuter service runs along the existing long-distance railway lines, stopping at city stations. It does not connect central KL with any of the city's attractions, but is useful for getting to Port Kelang (via Shah Alam and Kelang) or Seremban, 66 km south of KL.

Light Rail KL's new Light Rail Transit (LRT) system is the city's main answer to alleviate KL's traffic snarls. The only line yet in operation runs from Ampang to Pudu station next to the Puduraya bus station, then through the city centre to Jalan Sultan Ismail. Fares range from 75 sen to RM2.90.

Taxi KL has plenty of taxis and metered fares are RM1.50 for the first two km, then 10 sen for each additional 200 metres. Because of traffic snarls, drivers may be unwilling to use meters and you'll have to bargain. Count on RM3 for a short ride – RM6 should get you halfway across town. At the railway station, buy a taxi coupon from outside platform 4 (the river side of the station).

Car All the major car-rental companies have offices at the airport and in the city. These companies are Avis (☎ 241-7144), Budget (☎ 262-4119), Hertz (☎ 242-1014) and National (☎ 248-0522).

AROUND KUALA LUMPUR
The huge **Batu Caves** are the best known attraction in the vicinity of KL. Just 13 km north of the capital, a short distance off the Ipoh road, the caves are in a towering limestone formation and were little known until about 100 years ago. Later, a small Hindu shrine was built in the major cave and it became a pilgrimage centre during the Thaipusam Festival. Each year in February, thousands of pilgrims flock to the caves to

engage in or watch the spectacularly masochistic feats of Thaipusam devotees.

The major cave, a vast open space known as the Temple Cave, is reached by a straight flight of 272 steps. Beyond the stairs is the main temple. There are a number of other caves in the same formation, including a small museum cave, with figures of the various Hindu gods.

To reach the caves take minibus No 11 from the Central Market or Len bus No 70 from outside the Bangkok Bank bus stand on Jalan Tun HS Lee in Chinatown. During the Thaipusam Festival, special trains run to the caves from KL station.

East of KL, on the road to Ulu Kelang and about 13 km out, is the 62 hectare site of the **National Zoo & Aquarium**. The zoo is laid out around a central lake and the zoo collection emphasises Malaysian wildlife. It is open daily from 9 am to 5 pm and admission is RM5. Take a Len Seng bus No 170 or 177 or minibus No 17 from Lebuh Ampang.

The **Forestry Research Institute of Malaysia (FRIM)** has a jungle park at Sungei Buloh, 15 km north-west of the city centre, with a museum and arboretums explaining the rainforest habitat and flora. A popular picnic spot, it also has jungle trails, from short strolls to a more strenuous walk up to the waterfall. The park is open from 8 am to 6 pm. Take minibus No 31 from the corner of Jalan Ampang and Jalan Gereja.

About 19 km from KL, on the Genting Highlands road, the **Orang Asli Museum** is very informative and gives some good insights into the life and culture of Peninsular Malaysia's 70,000 indigenous inhabitants. It's well worth a look.

Beside the Ipoh road, 22 km north of KL, **Templer Park** was established during the colonial period by the British High Commissioner Sir Gerald Templer. The 1200 hectare park is intended to be a tract of jungle, preserved within easy reach of the city. There are a number of marked jungle paths, swimming lagoons and several waterfalls within the park boundaries. To get there, take bus No 66 from the Puduraya bus and taxi station.

JOHOR BAHRU

The state of Johor comprises the entire southern tip of the peninsula. Its capital is Johor Bahru (known simply as JB), the southern gateway to Peninsular Malaysia as it is connected to Singapore by the 1038-metre-long Causeway.

Johor's history goes back to the mid-19th century when Melaka fell to the Portuguese and the sultans fled and then re-established their capital in this area.

Few people stop for long in JB as both Singapore and Melaka offer better prospects. However, it's worth exploring the **Istana Besar**, the former palace of the Johor royal family and now an impressive museum.

Johor Bahru's area code is 07.

Places to Stay

The best place to stay is the friendly *Footloose Homestay* (☎ 224-2881) at 4H Jalan Ismail, about 20 minutes walk from the Causeway, just off Jalan Gertak Merah. There's one double room for RM24, or just six dorm beds for RM12 per person, all including breakfast.

Of JB's motley collection of Chinese hotels in the centre of town, the cheapest is the basic *Hotel New Chuan Seng*, 35 Jalan Meldrum. Rooms cost RM25 and RM30, the beds at least are clean and it's good value for expensive JB.

For something better, the *Hotel JB* (☎ 223-4788), 80A Jalan Wong Ah Fook, has basic rooms for RM40 with fan, RM49 with fan and bath, and from RM59 with air-con. Jalan Meldrum has plenty of other mid-range hotels, including the quite luxurious *City View Hotel* (☎ 224-9291), where rooms cost RM66, RM82 and RM100.

Places to Eat

The night market, outside the Hindu temple on Jalan Wong Ah Fook, has a great selection of Chinese, Malay and Indian dishes. The *Restoran Medina*, on the corner of Jalan Meldrum and Jalan Siew Niam, serves excellent murtabak, biryani and curries.

Getting There & Away

Air Johor Bahru is well served by MAS (☎ 334-1001) and, as an incentive to fly from JB rather than Singapore, fares to other places in Malaysia are much cheaper than from Singapore. Pelangi Air (☎ 332-4366) also has direct flights to Padang (RM260) and Palembang (RM280) in Sumatra. MAS has a coach service (RM4) from the Puteri Pan Pacific Hotel for the 32 km trip to the airport.

Bus & Taxi JB has more connections to other towns in Peninsular Malaysia than Singapore. JB's new Larkin bus station is five km north of town. The bus from Singapore runs there; taxis want an inflated RM6.

Regular buses go from JB to Melaka (RM10), KL (RM16.50), Butterworth (RM35), Mersing (RM8) and Kuantan (RM16). Melaka buses come through from Singapore, so it pays to book. Long-distance taxis leave from the Larkin bus station, and also from taxi stations on Jalan Wong Ah Fook in central JB. A whole taxi to Singapore costs RM25, about RM10 extra with private taxis that will drop at hotels.

To Singapore, air-con buses operate roughly every 15 minutes until midnight and cost RM1.80. The regular SBS bus No 170 costs RM1. Catch them at the bus station or the Causeway.

Train Daily trains from JB go to KL and Butterworth for west-coast destinations and there is a 9.55 pm direct east-coast train for Taman Negara and Kota Bharu. Through trains also go to Singapore, although a bus or taxi is easier.

Boat Daily ferries operate from Pasir Gudang, about 30 km from Johor Bahru, direct to Batam and Bintan islands in Indonesia's Riau Archipelago. A fortnightly ship goes to Surabaya in Java. Ring SS Holidays (☎ 251-1577) in Pasir Gudang for details. In future, these services may depart from JB's new ferry terminal at Bebas Cukai, two km east of the Causeway, which will also handle ferries to Singapore.

MELAKA

Melaka (Malacca), Malaysia's most historically interesting city, has been the site of some dramatic events over the years. The complete series of European incursions into Malaysia – Portuguese, Dutch and English – occurred here. Yet this was an important trading port long before the first Portuguese adventurers set foot in the city.

In 1405 Admiral Cheng Ho, the 'three-jewelled eunuch prince', arrived in Melaka bearing gifts from the Ming emperor, the promise of protection from arch enemies (the Siamese) and, surprisingly, the Muslim religion. Despite internal squabbles and intrigues, Melaka grew to be a powerful trading state and successfully repulsed Siamese attacks.

In 1511 Alfonso d'Albuquerque took the city for the Portuguese and the fortress of A'Famosa was constructed. In 1641 the city passed into Dutch hands after a siege lasting eight months.

In 1795 the French occupied Holland so the British, allies of the Dutch, temporarily took over administration of the Dutch colonies. In 1824 Melaka was ceded to the British in exchange for the Sumatran port of Bencoolen (Bengkulu today).

Melaka became a sleepy backwater, but it is now stirring from its slumber and new waterfront developments on reclaimed land have seen the historic areas retreat inland. Despite modernisation, it's still a place of intriguing Chinese streets, antique shops, old Chinese temples and cemeteries, and reminders of former European colonial powers.

Information

The helpful tourist office (☎ 283-6538), right in the heart of the city opposite the Christ Church, is open every day from 8.45 am to 5 pm, closed Friday from 12.15 to 2.45 pm. The main post office is three km north of the town centre – take bus No 19 from the bus station.

Melaka's area code is 06.

Town Square & St Paul's Hill

The main area of interest in Melaka is the old

city centred on Town Square, also known as Dutch Square. Behind is St Paul's Hill (Bukit St Paul), site of the original Portuguese fort.

The most imposing relic of the Dutch period in Melaka is the massive red town hall, the **Stadthuys**, built between 1641 and 1660. Believed to be the oldest Dutch building in the east, its typical Dutch architecture features substantial, solid doors and louvred windows. It now houses the excellent **Historical, Ethnographic & Literature Museums**, with detailed explanations of Melaka's history, local culture and traditions. The Stadthuys and its museums are

open daily from 9 am to 6 pm (closed Friday from 12.15 to 2.45 pm).

Facing the square is the bright red **Christ Church**. The pink bricks were brought out from Zeeland in Holland and faced with local red laterite when the church was constructed in 1753.

From the Stadthuys, steps lead up to St Paul's Hill, topped by the ruins of **St Paul's Church**. Originally built by the Portuguese in 1571, it was regularly visited by Francis Xavier. Following his death in China, the saint's body was brought here and buried for nine months before being transferred to Goa

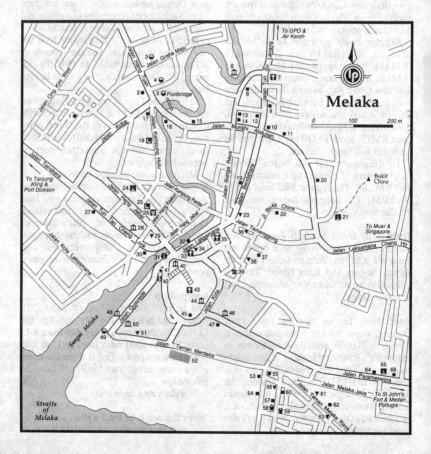

in India where it is to this day. The church has been in ruins for over 150 years, but the setting is beautiful, the walls imposing and fine old Dutch tombstones stand around the interior.

From St Paul's Church, steps lead down to the **Porta de Santiago**. This is the sole surviving relic of the old fort that was originally constructed by Alfonso d'Albuquerque. The Dutch included this gateway in their reconstructed fort of 1670, and it bears the Dutch East India Company's coat of arms.

Nearby, the popular **sound & light show** re-creates Melaka's history each evening at 9.30 pm and costs RM5.

Just along from the Porta de Santiago is a wooden replica of a Melaka sultan's palace which contains the **Muzium Budaya** (Cultural Museum); entry is RM1.50. The small **Proclamation of Independence Hall** has historical displays on the events leading up to independence in 1957.

Back around next to the river, the **Maritime Museum** is housed in a huge re-creation

of a Portuguese ship. Entry (RM2) includes the **Royal Malaysian Navy Museum** across the street.

Chinatown

A walk through Melaka's old Chinatown, just west of the river, is fascinating. Although Melaka has long lost its importance as a port, ancient-looking schooners still sail up the river and moor at the banks. Riverboat trips, leaving from behind the tourist office, operate several times daily, take 45 minutes and cost RM6.

You may still find some of the treasures of the east in the antique shops scattered along Jalan Hang Jebat, formerly known as Jonkers St (Junk St). At 48-50 Jalan Tun Tan Cheng Lock is a traditional Peranakan (Straits-born Chinese) townhouse which has been made into the small **Baba-Nonya Heritage Museum. The Sri Pogyatha Vinoyagar Moorthi Temple**, dating from 1781, and the Sumatran-style **Kampung Kling Mosque** are both in this area. The fascinating **Cheng Hoon Teng**

PLACES TO STAY		66	My Place Guest House	25	Kampung Kling Mosque
1	Malacca Town Holiday Lodge 2			26	Sri Pogyatha Vinoyagar Moorthi Temple
8	Majestic Hotel		**PLACES TO EAT**		
9	City Bayview Hotel	23	Sri Lakshmi Vilas	28	Baba-Nonya Heritage Museum
10	Hotel Accordian	29	Jonkers Melaka Restoran		
11	Emperor Hotel			31	Tourist Office
12	Ramada Renaissance Hotel	34	Restaurant Kim Swee Huat	32	Karyaneka Handicrafts Emporium
13	Hong Kong Hotel	36	Restoran Veni	33	Christ Church
14	Ng Fook Hotel	38	UE Tea House	35	Church of St Francis
15	May Chiang Hotel	51	Glutton's Corner	39	Telekom
16	Plaza Inn	56	New Golden Dragon	40	Stadthuys
17	Visma Hotel	61	Nyonya Makka	41	Tourist Police
19	Central Hotel	63	Ole Sayang	42	Hongkong Bank
20	Palace Hotel			43	St Paul's Church
22	Eastern Heritage Guest House		**OTHER**	44	Cultural Museum
27	The Baba House	2	Immigration	45	Porta de Santiago
30	Heerin House	3	Local Bus Station	46	Proclamation of Independence Hall
37	Apple Guest House	4	Taxi Station		
53	Robin's Nest	5	Express Bus Terminal	47	Sound & Light Show
54	Travellers' Lodge	6	Church of St Peter	48	Maritime Museum
55	Amy Home Stay	7	Church of St Peter	49	Ferries to Dumai (Sumatra)
57	SD Rest House	18	Kampung Hulu Mosque		
58	Melaka Youth Hostel	21	Sam Po Kong Temple & Hang Li Poh Well	50	Royal Malaysian Navy Museum
60	Sunny's Inn			52	Mahkota Parade
62	Malacca Town Holiday Lodge	24	Cheng Hoon Teng Temple	59	Orchid Pub
64	Kancil Guest House			65	Buddhist Temple

Temple on Jalan Tokong Emas is the oldest Chinese temple in Malaysia and has an inscription commemorating Cheng Ho's epochal visit to Melaka.

Other Attractions

In the mid-1400s when the Ming emperor's daughter arrived to wed the sultan of Melaka and seal diplomatic relations, she settled with her entourage at **Bukit China** (China Hill). It has been a Chinese area ever since and is now a Chinese graveyard with views across Melaka. At the base of the hill is the **Sam Po Kong Temple** and the **Hang Li Poh Well**, once an important water supply for Melaka, which was poisoned by various invaders.

The **Villa Sentosa**, near the Majestic Hotel in Kampung Morten, is a Malay house that functions as a museum of sorts. Family members will show you around.

The small Dutch **St John's Fort**, on a hilltop to the east of town, has fine views but only a few walls and cannon emplacements remain.

Air Keroh, 15 km north of Melaka, is home to a number of manufactured tourist attractions, including a small zoo, butterfly park, and **Taman Mini Malaysia/Mini ASEAN**, a theme park with examples of traditional houses from Malaysia and other ASEAN countries.

Melaka's beaches at **Tanjung Kling** and **Pantai Kundor**, to the north-west of town, have plenty of expensive accommodation but the Straits of Melaka have become increasingly polluted over the years. The small island of **Pulau Besar**, reached by boat from Umbai, 10 km south-east of Melaka, has better beaches.

Places to Stay

Guesthouses Melaka has some excellent, well-priced guesthouses. Breakfast is often included in the price. Most are in the new area of Taman Melaka Raya.

In the street directly south of the roundabout, *Robin's Nest* (☎ 282-9142) at No 205B is very clean and well run with a good atmosphere. Rooms range from RM15 to RM25 and dorm beds are RM6. Further down is the similarly priced *Travellers' Lodge* at 214B. This popular place has a large and welcoming common room and a rooftop garden.

One street east, the YHA *Melaka Youth Hostel* (Asrama Belia) (☎ 282-7915) is spotless, well run and has spacious dorms for RM10, then RM7 for each additional night, or RM14 with air-con plus RM10 for each extra night.

At 270A-B, *Sunny's Inn* (☎ 283-7990) is a family-run place with dorm beds for RM7. A tiny single costs RM12, but most rooms are RM15 up to RM30 with air-con.

On Jalan Taman Merdeka, *Amy Home Stay* at 156B is another popular place with dorms for RM7, and rooms from RM15.

Also on Jalan Taman Merdeka, the *Malacca Town Holiday Lodge* (☎ 284-8830) at 148B is well kept and has singles/doubles from RM12/15 (no dorms).

The popular *Eastern Heritage Guest House* (☎ 283-3026), 8 Jalan Bukit China, is housed in a superb old Melaka building near the centre of town. It has typical guesthouse rooms from RM12/15 to RM30 or the dorm costs RM6.

Nearby, the *Apple Guest House* (☎ (010) 667-8744) at 24-1 Lorong Banda Kaba is in a much newer house and costs RM15/18, or RM6 for dorm beds.

Two more guesthouse are on Jalan Parameswara. The *Kancil Guest House* at No 177 is clean, quiet and secure but strictly run. Most rooms cost RM25. At No 205, *My Place Guest House* is run by friendly Indian hosts and is very popular. Slightly cramped rooms start at RM12/15 and the dorm costs RM6.

North of the river, the *Malacca Town Holiday Lodge 2* (☎ 284-6905) at 52 Kampung Empat is further out but has good rooms (no dorms) from RM15 a double, RM25 to RM35 with bath, or RM36 to RM45 with air-con.

Hotels Melaka is also well endowed with hotels in all price ranges.

The very basic *Central Hotel* (☎ 282-2984) is in a very good location at 31 Jalan

Bendahara. Singles/doubles with fan cost RM14/18; doubles with bath are RM25. Though shabby, at these prices it's hard to beat.

The rambling old *Majestic Hotel* (☎ 282-2455) at 188 Jalan Bunga Raya is a classic old hotel with high ceilings, swishing fans and a bar. It could do with a good scrub, but is reasonable value at RM15 for small fan rooms up to RM42 for large air-con rooms.

Other cheap hotels near the bus station include the *Ng Fook*, 154 Jalan Bunga Raya, the nearby *Hong Kong Hotel* and the *New Cathay Hotel*, 100 Jalan Munshi Abdullah. All have rooms for around RM25.

Mid-range options include the *May Chiang Hotel* (☎ 283-9535), 52 Jalan Munshi Abdullah. Immaculately clean air-con rooms cost RM40 with bath. The more modern *Visma Hotel* (☎ 283-8799), 111 Jalan Kampung Hulu, is very good value. Air-con, carpeted rooms cost RM38 and RM45.

Places to Eat

Melaka's food reflects its history, with Nonya cuisine and Portuguese Eurasian food featured among the usual favourites.

Along Jalan Taman Merdeka, on what used to be the waterfront, is a collection of food stalls known as *Glutton's Corner*. The *Bunga Raya* at No 40 has steamed crabs.

On Jalan Laksamana, right in the centre of town, the *Restaurant Kim Swee Huat* at No 38 is a cheap restaurant good for Chinese food and western breakfasts.

Good, if slightly expensive, daytime cafes for Nonya dishes in Chinatown are in the *Heerin House* guesthouse, and the *Jonkers Melaka Restoran*, 17 Jalan Hang Jebat, a craft shop with a few tables.

In the city centre, the *Sri Lakshmi Vilas* and the *Sri Krishna Bavan* next door are good South Indian restaurants. Around the corner at 34 Jalan Temenggong, the *Restoran Veni* is a good Indian place for a roti chanai breakfast.

The Taman Melaka Raya area has a good range of eateries. A hawkers' centre is on Jalan Parameswara opposite the entrance to the sound & light show. The *New Golden Dragon* is a good coffee shop with Chinese hawkers' fare and tables on the pavement. Jalan Taman Merdeka has plenty of other coffee shops and restaurants.

At Medan Portugis (Portuguese Square), you can sample Malay-Portuguese cuisine at tables facing the sea. Excellent seafood is served – a meal will cost around RM30 per person. Pop bands play during the week, and Portuguese/Malay cultural dances are held on Saturdays.

Getting There & Away

Air Pelangi Air (☎ 385-1175) has flights to Singapore, Ipoh and Medan and Pekanbaru in Sumatra.

Bus Most bus companies have their offices near the express bus stand. There are frequent buses to KL (RM6.50, 3½ hours) from 7 am to 7 pm. To Singapore (RM11.50, five hours), buses leave hourly from 8 am to 6 pm; book in advance. Buses to Johor Bahru (RM10, 3½ hours) leave roughly every half hour. To the east coast, two buses per day go to Kuantan (RM14) at 2 pm, and evening buses go to Kuala Terengganu (RM22) and Kota Bharu (RM24).

Taxi Taxis leave from the taxi station just opposite the local bus station. Sample fares are: Port Dickson (RM10), Johor Bahru (RM23), KL (RM13) and Mersing (RM12).

Boat Daily high-speed ferries operate between Melaka and Dumai (RM80, 2½ hours) in Sumatra. Two leave at 10 am and one at 2 pm from the river wharf just past the Maritime Museum. Buy your ticket the day before departure. Dumai is a visa-free entry port into Indonesia for most nationalities.

Getting Around

Melaka is easily explored on foot, but one useful town bus service is No 17 from the local bus station to Taman Melaka Raya and on to Medan Portugis.

A bicycle rickshaw is the ideal way of getting around compact and slow-moving

Melaka. Any one-way trip within the town will cost around RM5. Unmetered taxis cost the same. Many hostels rent bicycles.

PORT DICKSON

Port Dickson is just a port town, but its popular beach resort starts around the Km 8 peg and stretches south of the town to the lighthouse at **Cape Rachado**, 16 km from Port Dickson. Malaysians flock to this mostly upmarket resort on weekends, but it's hard to understand why. The beaches are ordinary, and occasional oil spills from the Straits of Melaka don't help.

Cheap accommodation can be found at the *Port Dickson Youth Hostel* (☎ 647-2188), 6.5 km out of Port Dickson. At Km 13, the Chinese *Kong Ming Hotel* (☎ 662-5683) is right by the beach and has doubles for RM25.

Getting There & Away

By bus, Port Dickson is RM3.80 from Melaka and RM5 from KL. From Port Dickson town, there are buses which will drop you off anywhere along the beach.

SEREMBAN

Seremban, the capital of Negeri Sembilan, is the centre of the Malaysian Minangkabau area, closely related to the Minangkabau area of Sumatra. Seremban is famed for its attractive **Lake Gardens**, and the **State Museum**, three km west of town, has good examples of the Minangkabau style of architecture. Seremban is linked by bus to all major cities in the peninsula, and is on the main train line. Cheap, central hotels include the scruffy *Hotel Nam Yong*, the slightly better but expensive *Oriental Hotel* and the *Happy Hotel*.

From Seremban, a side trip can be made to **Hutan Lipur Ulu Bendol**, a forest park 20 km to the east. The primary dipterocarp rainforest has some excellent short walks. Further east, **Sri Menanti**, just off the Seremban to Kuala Pilah road, is the quiet royal capital first settled over 400 years ago by the Minangkabau from Sumatra.

GENTING HIGHLANDS

The Genting Highlands is a thoroughly modern hill station – casinos are the attraction here rather than the jungle walks. Accommodation is relatively expensive.

It's about 50 km north of KL and buses and taxis go there from the Puduraya bus station.

FRASER'S HILL

Fraser's Hill, set at a cool altitude of 1524 metres, is a quiet and relatively undeveloped hill station. Very few tourists stay here and it's mostly a middle-class Malaysian resort. It retains more colonial charm than the Cameron Highlands and has some delightful, old-fashioned bungalows run by the Fraser's Hill Development Corporation (☎ (09) 362-2201). Bungalow rooms cost RM89.10 (RM99 on weekends), or the FHDC *Puncak Inn* has less inspiring, mid-range rooms from RM58.50 (RM65 on weekends). The *Corona Nursery Youth Hostel* (☎ (09) 362-2225) has very basic rooms for RM10 and is a 40 minute walk from where the bus stops.

Getting There & Away

Fraser's Hill is 103 km north of KL and 240 km from Kuantan on the east coast. The twice-daily bus service from Kuala Kubu Bahru costs RM3.80 and departs at 8 am and 12.30 pm, or a charter taxi is RM45. From KL, take a Tanjung Malim bus to Kuala Kubu Bahru from platform 18 at the Puduraya bus station.

CAMERON HIGHLANDS

Situated about 60 km north from Tapah, off the KL-Ipoh road, this is the best known and most extensive hill station. At an average altitude of 1500 metres, the weather is pleasantly cool, not cold. Jungle walks are the thing to do here and the tourist office and shops in Tanah Rata have somewhat inaccurate maps of the main walks. Most consist of a stroll of an hour or two but some take quite a bit longer and can be tough going.

The only wildlife you are likely to see is the fantastic variety of butterflies. It was here

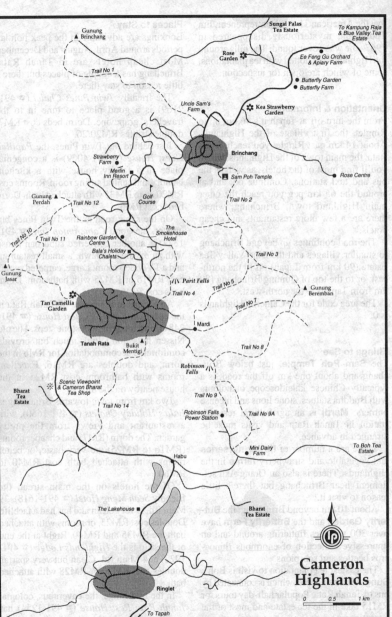

Gunung
Brinchang

To Kampung Raja
& Blue Valley Tea
Estate

Sungai Palas
Tea Estate

Trail No 1

Rose
Garden

Ee Feng Gu Orchard
& Apiary Farm

Butterfly Garden
Butterfly Farm

Uncle Sam's
Farm

Kea Strawberry
Garden

Strawberry
Farm

Brinchang

Merlin
Inn Resort

Sam Poh Temple

Rose Centre

Golf
Course

Gunung
Perdah

Trail No 12

Trail No 2

Gunung
Jasar

Trail No 10

Trail No 11

Rainbow Garden
Centre

The
Smokehouse
Hotel

Trail No 3

Bala's Holiday
Chalets

Parit Falls

Trail No 5

Trail No 4

Gunung
Bereman

Tan Camellia
Garden

Mardi

Trail No 7

Tanah Rata

Bukit
Mentigi

Trail No 8

Scenic Viewpoint
& Cameron Bharat
Tea Shop

Robinson
Falls

Bharat
Tea
Estate

Trail No 14

Robinson Falls
Power Station

Trail No 9

Trail No 9A

To Boh Tea
Estate

Mini Dairy
Farm

Habu

The Lakehouse

Bharat
Tea
Estate

Ringlet

To Tapah

**Cameron
Highlands**

0   0.5   1 km

that the American Thai silk entrepreneur, Jim Thompson, mysteriously disappeared in 1967 – he was never found. The hills around the Highlands are dotted with tea plantations, some of which are open for inspection.

Orientation & Information

From the turn-off at Tapah it's 46 km up to Ringlet, the first village of the Highlands. About 14 km past Ringlet you reach Tanah Rata, the main town of the Highlands, where you'll find most of the hotels, as well as the bus and taxi stations. Continue on, and at around the 65 km peg you reach the other main Highland town, Brinchang, where there are a few more restaurants and cheap hotels.

The road continues up beyond Brinchang to smaller villages and the Blue Valley Tea Estate (90 km from Tapah) off to the north-east, or to the top of Gunung Brinchang (80 km from Tapah) to the north-west.

The area code for the Cameron Highlands is 05.

Things to See

The **Sam Poh Temple**, just below Brinchang and about one km off the road, is a typically Chinese kaleidoscope of colours with Buddha statues, stone lions and incense burners. **Mardi** is an agricultural research station in Tanah Rata and visits must be arranged in advance.

There are a number of **flower nurseries** and vegetable and strawberry **farms** in the Highlands. There is also an Orang Asli settlement near Brinchang but there's little reason to visit it.

About 10 km beyond Brinchang, the **Butterfly Garden** and the **Butterfly Farm** have over 300 varieties fluttering around and an impressive collection of enormous rhinoceros beetles and scorpions.

The easiest tea plantation to visit is Boh's **Sungai Palas Estate**, which is connected by bus to Tanah Rata. Popular half-day tours for RM15 take in the tea estate and most of the attractions.

Places to Stay

Bookings are advisable in the peak holiday periods around April, August and December. Most cheap hotels are in Tanah Rata. Brinchang has a couple of places but there's little reason to stay there.

The friendly *Twin Pines Chalet* (☎ 491-2169) is a good place to tune in to the travellers' grapevine. Dorm beds cost RM7, doubles/triples RM20/26.

Just behind the Twin Pines, the *Papillon Guest House* (☎ 491-4069) is a congenial place in a family house with a kitchen, laundry and central sitting room. Rooms cost RM20 up to RM35 with attached bath. Dorm beds cost RM6.

On the same road as the Twin Pines but quieter, the good *Cameronian Inn* (☎ 491-1327) is another converted suburban house with an expanse of lawn, a small restaurant and a TV/video room. Large, carpeted rooms cost RM16 or RM25 with bathroom. Dorm beds cost RM6.

Also close to the centre of Tanah Rata is the excellent *Father's Guest House* (☎ 491-2484), up a long flight of stone steps. The old Nissen huts don't look much but provide comfortable accommodation for RM6 in the dorm, and doubles are RM16. Excellent rooms with bathroom cost RM25 in the house nearby on the hill.

Two km from town towards Brinchang is *Bala's Holiday Chalets* (☎ 491-1660), with a restaurant and views from the pretty garden. The dorm (RM7) and cheaper rooms (RM16 to RM25) are very basic, or better rooms with attached bath cost RM40 to RM60.

Of the hotels on the main street, the friendly *Seah Meng Hotel* (☎ 491-1618), 39 Main Rd, is very clean and has had a facelift. Doubles cost RM25, or rooms with attached bath are RM35 and RM40. Right at the end of the strip is the *Highlands Lodge* (☎ 491-1922) at 4 Main Rd. Clean but very spartan doubles cost RM20 or RM28 with attached bath.

In the mid-range, the cavernous, colonial *Tanah Rata Rest House* (☎ 491-1254) has seen better days but has very large rooms for

RM60. The *New Garden Inn* (☎ 491-5170) has reasonable but expensive rooms from RM115, or RM81 in quiet periods. The *Cool Point Hotel* (☎ 491-4914) is a new, better appointed hotel with rooms for RM125 and RM180, dropping to RM90 and RM140 in the off season.

Places to Eat

The cheapest food in Tanah Rata is to be found at the row of Malay food stalls along the main street. Stalls include the *Excellent Food Centre*, which has an extensive menu and steaks on Saturday nights. The adjoining *Fresh Milk Corner* sells fresh milk, yoghurt and lassis.

Opposite is the Tanah Rata's lively restaurant strip with tables on the pavement. The *Restaurant Kumar* and the adjacent *Restoran Thanam* both serve good Malay and Indian food. The *Restoran No 14* next to the Malayan Bank also does good Indian food, including the popular masala dosa.

Steamboat, a sort of Oriental variation of a Swiss fondue, is the Highlands' real taste treat. You can try it at the *Orient Restaurant* in the main street.

Further along Main Rd is the Chinese *Jasmine Restaurant*, which has good set meals. The *Roselane Coffee House* serves good breakfasts and set meals for RM7.50.

Getting There & Away

Access to the Highlands is via Tapah, from where buses to Tanah Rata (RM3.50, two hours) run roughly every hour from 8.15 am to 6.15 pm and continue on to Brinchang.

Most long-distance buses leave from Tapah, and these services can be booked at any of the backpacker places, or at CS Travel & Tours (☎ 491-1200), 47 Main Rd. Tanah Rata also has direct services to KL (RM10, five hours) at 8.30 am and 1.30 pm, and to Penang (RM14, six hours) at 9.30 am and 2.30 pm. Book at the bus station. Ekspres Nasional has a bus to KL at 2.30 pm – book at the Downtown Hotel.

From Tanah Rata shared-taxi fares are RM6 to Tapah, RM20 to Ipoh and RM30 to KL, but you may have to charter.

IPOH

The 'city of millionaires', 219 km north of Kuala Lumpur and 173 km south of Butterworth, made its fortune from tin mining. It is a thriving Chinese town with some of the best Chinese food in Malaysia and plenty of colonial architecture dating from its heyday. Interesting cave-temples on the outskirts of the town are the **Perak Tong Temple**, the most important temple, about six km north of town, and the **Sam Poh Temple**, a few km south of town. Both are right on the main road and easy to get to.

Ipoh is also the best take-off point for Lumut and the island of Pangkor.

Ipoh's area code is 05.

Places to Stay

Bottom of the barrel is the *Cathay Hotel* (☎ 241-3322), 88 Jalan CM Yussuf, but what it lacks in ambience is more than made up for by the price and the friendly manager. Large, scruffy rooms cost RM19, RM21 with bathroom or RM32 with air-con.

Of a slightly better standard is the *Embassy Hotel* (☎ 254-9496) at 35 Jalan CM Yussuf, where rooms with fan and bath cost RM28, or RM35 for an air-con double with attached bath.

The *New Hollywood Hotel* (☎ 241-5322) at No 72 Jalan CM Yussuf has rooms with air-con and bath for RM33/40. It's very clean but not such a great deal, though it does have a good restaurant, the Pinang, on the ground floor.

The *Wanwah (Winner) Hotel* (☎ 241-5177), 32 Jalan Ali Pitchay, is a large, spotless hotel – all tiles and polish. The fan rooms with attached bath for RM30 are very good value, and rooms with air-con, TV and hot water cost RM49.

Places to Eat

Ipoh has plenty of restaurants, and the rice noodle dish known as kway teow is reputed to be better in Ipoh than anywhere else in Malaysia. The city's best known place for kway teow is *Kedai Kopi Kong Heng*, on Jalan Bandar Timah between Jalan Pasar and

Jalan Dato Maharajah Lela, a bustling restaurant serving a bit of everything.

Ipoh has plenty of food-stall centres. On Jalan Raja Musa Aziz, the large *Medan Selera Dato Tawhil Azar*, better known as the Children's Playground, has stalls arranged around a small square. It's a very popular place for Malay food in the evening and is open late.

At night, many of the restaurants in the old town are closed, so a good place to head for is Jalan Yau Tet Shin in the new town. On opposite corners, the *Restoran Wong* and *Restoran Onn Kee* specialise in tauge ayam (chicken and bean sprouts) and kway teow.

For Indian food, the *Rahman Restaurant* on Jalan CM Yussuf is very clean and has a wide range of dishes.

Getting There & Away
Air Pelangi Air (☎ 312-4770) flies to KL (RM66), Melaka (RM120), Langkawi (RM107) and to Medan (RM198). MAS also has flights to KL.

Bus The long-distance bus station is in the south-east corner of the city centre, a taxi ride from the main hotel area. Many of the air-con departures to places outside the immediate Ipoh area leave at night. Destinations and fares include Kuala Kangsar (RM3), Butterworth (RM8), Tapah (RM4.50), KL (RM9.50), Lumut (RM3.50), Kuantan (RM23) and Hat Yai (RM28) in Thailand. Tickets should be booked in advance if possible.

Buses to Lumut leave from Syarikat Perak Roadway across Jalan Tun Abdul Rasak from the bus station.

Taxi Long-distance taxis leave from beside the bus station, and there is also another rank directly across the road.

Train All trains between Singapore and Butterworth stop at Ipoh. The 10.40 am and 5.36 pm express trains north stop at Kuala Kangsar (50 minutes) and Taiping (1½ hours) before continuing on to Butterworth (3½ hours).

LUMUT
The Malaysian navy has its principal base in this small river port, but Lumut is little more than a departure point for nearby Pangkor Island or Medan in Indonesia. If you get marooned in Lumut there is a reasonable choice of Chinese hotels.

Getting There & Away
Bus & Taxi Lumut is 101 km from Ipoh, the usual place for Lumut bus connections. Buses to other destinations include Butterworth (RM8.50), KL (RM13) and Tapah (RM8.50) for the Cameron Highlands. Long-distance taxis are RM27.50 to Butterworth, RM10 to Ipoh, RM30 to KL.

Boat Kuala Perlis Langkawi Ferry Service (☎ 683-4258) at the ferry jetty has a high-speed service to Belawan in Sumatra on Thursday at 10 am. It leaves Belawan for Lumut on Wednesday at 11 am. The trip takes 3½ hours and costs RM110/90 one way in 1st class/economy. The price includes the bus ride between Belawan and Medan.

For ferries to Pangkor see the following Pulau Pangkor section.

PULAU PANGKOR
The island of Pangkor is close to the coast, off Lumut, and easily accessible via Ipoh. It's a popular resort island known for its fine beaches, many of which can be reached by an interesting round-island loop on bicycle or motorbike. A visit to the island is principally a 'laze on the beach' operation.

Ferries from Lumut stop on the eastern side of the island at Sungai Pinang Kecil and then Pangkor town, where there are banks, restaurants and shops. The main beaches are on the western side of the island. **Pasir Bogak** is the most developed beach, and the next bay to the north, **Teluk Nipah**, is the main budget accommodation beach. Golden Sands Beach (Teluk Belanga) at the northern end of the island is the preserve of the Pan-Pacific Pangkor Resort. Between these beaches are a number of virtually deserted beaches, the best being **Coral Bay**.

Emerald Bay on nearby Pulau Pangkor Laut is a beautiful little horseshoe-shaped bay but the entire island has been taken over by a luxury hotel conglomerate.

Pangkor's one bit of history, a **Dutch fort** dating from 1670, is three km south of Pangkor village at Teluk Gedong.

Pulau Pangkor's area code is 05.

Places to Stay & Eat
Teluk Nipah Teluk Nipah has the best beach, and though mid-range hotels are popping up everywhere, it still has a few moderately priced options on expensive Pangkor.

The most popular travellers-only place is *Joe Fisherman Village* (☎ 685-2389). Very basic A-frame huts cost RM20 for two, or slightly more substantial cottages cost RM30.

Right next door is *Nazri Nipah Camp* (☎ 685-2014), a friendly place with A-frames for RM20, rooms with bathroom for RM40 and larger chalets for RM50.

The *Coral Beach Camp* (☎ 685-2711) has A-frame huts for RM25, or double rooms for RM50. It lacks atmosphere but the owners arrange reasonably priced boat trips.

Most places to stay have their own restaurants, or the *Bayview Cafe* is a good spot for a meal overlooking the beach. The pleasant *Restoran Takana Juo*, tucked away back from the beach, is a cheap Malay restaurant.

Pasir Bogak Accommodation at Pasir Bogak is mainly aimed at the upper end of the market, and budget options are limited and characterless.

The cheapest option is the *Pangkor Anchor* (☎ 685-1363). Small, ageing A-frame huts in a shady grove with mattresses on the floor cost RM8.50 per person. *Pangkor Village Beach Resort* (☎ 685-2227) has mainly tented accommodation costing RM14 per person, and expensive chalets.

Khoo's Holiday Resort (☎ 685-1164) is a rather ugly concrete conglomeration, but the wooden chalets on the hill behind for RM54.60 and RM78.75 (20% less during the week) are a good mid-range option.

Pasir Bogak has some good seafood restaurants, such as the cheap *Pangkor Restaurant*. More upmarket is the excellent *Restoran Number One*, where a good meal of prawns, fish or crab will cost around RM20 per person.

Getting There & Away
Air Pelangi Air flies to/from KL (RM120), and Singapore's Seletar airport (RM204, S$190 from Singapore).

Boat Pan Silver Ferry has departures from Lumut to Pangkor town every 20 minutes from 6.45 am to 8 pm then at 9 pm, and from Pangkor between 6.30 am and 8 pm. The fare is RM2 each way. Ferries also service the luxury Pan-Pacific Pangkor Resort and the Pangkor Laut Resort on Pulau Pangkor Laut.

Getting Around
Buses run every hour or so from Pangkor village across the island to the far end of the beach at Pasir Bogak and back again. Pangkor also has plenty of minibus taxis costing RM4 from Pangkor to Pasir Bogak, and RM10 to Teluk Nipah.

Motorcycles can be rented for RM30 per day and bicycles for RM10 per day.

KUALA KANGSAR
The royal town of Perak state has the fine **Ubadiah Mosque**, with its onion dome and the minarets squeezed up against it as if seen in a distorting mirror. Other grand buildings of the sultanate in the eastern part of town include the **Istana Kenangan**, now a museum. Kuala Kangsar is where rubber trees were first grown in Malaysia.

The *Double Lion Hotel*, close to the bus station in the centre of town, has good rooms for RM18.

TAIPING
The 'town of everlasting peace' was once a raucous tin-mining town. Its attractive colonial district is centred on the **Lake Gardens**, which has a **zoo**. The oldest **museum** in the country is nearby. Above the town is **Maxwell Hill**, Malaysia's smallest and oldest

hill station. To get there, take a government Land Rover from the station (☎ (05) 807-7243) at the foot of the hill for RM2. You can also walk down in about three hours.

Places to Stay & Eat
The *Hong Kong Hotel* (☎ 807-3824) at 79 Jalan Barrack (the entrance is on Jalan Lim Tee Hooi) is a bargain at RM16/22 for a large room with air-con and bathroom. Nearby, the historic *Town Rest House* (☎ 808-8482), 101 Jalan Stesyen, was once the governor's residence and has a good little cafe. Spartan doubles cost RM20, or large rooms with bathroom cost RM35.

Better still is the *New Rest House (Rumah Rehat Baru)* (☎ 807-2044), overlooking the beautiful Lake Gardens, about a km from the town centre. It's clean, secure and very good value at RM31.50 for large doubles or RM35 with air-con.

Taiping's large night market has many open-air eating stalls and satay is one of the city's specialities.

Getting There & Away
The express bus station is at Kamunting near the north-south highway, seven km from town. Take a bus (60 sen) or taxi (RM3.50) to the centre. Frequent buses go to Butterworth (RM3.80), Ipoh (RM3.80) and KL (RM13.20). The local bus station in the centre of town has non-air-con buses to Kuala Kangsar and Ipoh.

The taxi station near the central market has taxis to Butterworth (RM8.50), Ipoh (RM8) and Kuala Kangsar (RM4).

PENANG
The oldest British settlement in Malaysia, predating both Singapore and Melaka, is also one of Malaysia's major tourist attractions. This is hardly surprising as the 285 sq km island of Penang has popular beach resorts and an intriguing and historically interesting town, Georgetown, which is also noted for its superb food.

Captain Francis Light sailed up and took over the virtually uninhabited island in 1786. Encouraged by free-trade policies, George-

town became a prosperous centre as well as a local mecca for dreamers, dissidents, intellectuals and artists.

Sun Yatsen planned the 1911 Canton uprising in Georgetown, probably in one of the local Hainanese coffee shops. Unmistakably Chinese, it's one of the most likeable cities in South-East Asia. With easy-going *kampungs* (villages), sandy beaches, warm water, good food and plenty of things to see, who wouldn't like Penang?

Orientation
Penang's major town, Georgetown, is often referred to as Penang, although correctly that is the name of the island (the actual Malay spelling is Pinang and it means 'betel nut'). Georgetown is in the north-east of the island, where the straits between the island and the mainland are at their narrowest.

A vehicle and passenger ferry service operates 24 hours a day across the three-km-wide channel between Georgetown and Butterworth on the mainland. South of the ferry crossing is the Penang Bridge – the longest in South-East Asia – which links the island with Malaysia's north-south highway.

Georgetown is a compact city and most places can easily be reached on foot or by bicycle rickshaw. Two important streets to remember are Lebuh Chulia and Lebuh Campbell. You'll find most of Georgetown's popular cheap hotels along Lebuh Chulia or close to it, while Lebuh Campbell is one of the town's main shopping streets. Jalan Penang is another popular shopping street and in this area you'll find a number of the more expensive hotels, including, at the waterfront end of Jalan Penang, the venerable Eastern & Oriental Hotel.

If you follow Jalan Penang south, you'll pass the modern, multistorey blot on the skyline known as the Kompleks Tun Abdul Razak (Komtar).

Information
Tourist Offices The Penang Tourist Association (☎ 281-6665) is on Jalan Tun Syed Sheh Barakbah, close to Fort Cornwallis.

The office is open normal business hours. Tourism Malaysia (☎ 262-0066) has an office a few doors along in the same building.

The best of the tourist offices is the Penang Tourist Guides Association (☎ 261-4461) on the 3rd floor of the Komtar building on Jalan Penang. It is open Monday to Saturday from 10 am to 6 pm and Sunday from 11 am to 7 pm.

Foreign Consulates Visas are not required for most nationalities for entry to Indonesia for up to 60 days, or for a visit to Thailand for a stay of up to four weeks. If you fall outside these requirements, Penang has Indonesian and Thai consulates. The Thai consulate (☎ 282-8029), open weekdays from 9 am to noon and 2 to 4 pm, issues two-month tourist visas for RM33; lots of places up and down Lebuh Chulia will obtain the visa for you for an additional RM10.

Post & Communications The poste restante facility at the GPO is efficient and popular. The Telekom office next door is open 24 hours.

Penang's area code is 04.

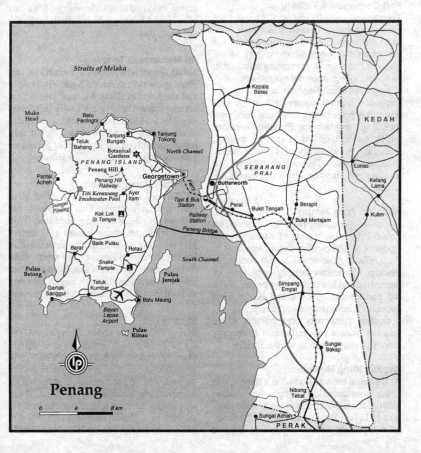

Penang

0   4   8 km

Travel Agencies Silver-Econ Travel (☎ 262-9882) at 436 Lebuh Chulia, MSL (☎ 261-6154) in the Ming Court Hotel on Jalan Macalister near Jalan Rangoon and Happy Holidays (☎ 262-9222) at 442 Lebuh Chulia are all reliable operators.

Warning! Some trishaw riders offer a variety of drugs, but really only sell heroin, a major problem in Georgetown. Malaysia's penalties for drug use are very severe indeed (death for possession of more than 15g of any contraband).

Fort Cornwallis & Padang
The time-worn walls of Fort Cornwallis are one of Penang's oldest sites. Between 1808 and 1810, convict labour was used to replace the original wooden structure with stone. The fort has a small, interesting museum in one of the old gunpowder magazines.

Fort Cornwallis lies next to the Padang – the green, central square laid in colonial times. It is ringed by fine colonial buildings, including the interesting **Penang Museum**, which has exhibits on Penang's history, including gory details of Chinese secret society squabbles. The museum is closed due to structural damage, but may eventually reopen.

Kuan Yin Teng Temple
Just round the corner from the museum, on Lebuh Pitt, is the temple of Kuan Yin, the Goddess of Mercy. The temple was built in the 1800s by the first Chinese settlers in Penang. It's neither terribly impressive or interesting but it's right in the centre of the old part of Georgetown and is the most popular Chinese temple in the city.

Outside stand two large burners where you can burn a few million in Monopoly money to ensure wealth for the afterlife.

Kapitan Kling Mosque
At the same time as Kuan Yin's temple was being constructed, Penang's first Indian Muslim settlers built this mosque at the junction of Lebuh Pitt and Lebuh Buckingham. In a typically Indian-influenced Islamic style, the yellow mosque has a single minaret. Close by on Lebuh Acheh, the **Malay Mosque** has an unusual Egyptian-style minaret.

Khoo Kongsi
The Dragon Mountain Hall is in Cannon Square close to the end of Lebuh Pitt. A *kongsi* is a clan house, a building which is part temple and part meeting hall for Chinese of the same clan or surname.

The present kongsi, dating from 1906 and extensively renovated in the 1950s, is a rainbow of dragons, statues, paintings, lamps, coloured tiles and carvings. It's a part of colourful Penang which definitely should not be missed.

Sri Mariamman Temple
Lebuh Queen runs parallel to Lebuh Pitt, and about midway between the Kuan Yin Temple and the Kapitan Kling Mosque you'll find another example of Penang's religious diversity. The Sri Mariamman Temple is a typical South Indian temple with its elaborately sculptured and painted *gopuram*, or pyramidal gateway tower, soaring over the entrance.

Wat Chayamangkalaram
At Burma Lane, just off the road to Batu Ferringhi, is a major Thai temple – the Temple of the Reclining Buddha. This brightly painted temple houses a 32-metre-long reclining Buddha, loudly proclaimed in Penang as the third longest in the world. Take that claim with a pinch of salt; there's at least one other in Malaysia that's larger, plus one in Thailand (at least) and two in Myanmar.

Penang Hill
Rising 830 metres above Georgetown, the top of Penang Hill provides a cool retreat from the sticky heat below as it's generally about 5°C cooler than at sea level. From the summit, you've got a spectacular view over the island and across to the mainland. There are pleasant gardens, a small cafe and a hotel as well as a Hindu temple and a Muslim mosque on the top. Penang Hill is particularly

pleasant at dusk as Georgetown, far below, starts to light up.

Getting There & Away Take Juara bus No 1, Lim Seng bus No 91 or minibus No 21 from Pengkalan Weld or Lebuh Chulia to Ayer Itam (every five minutes), then MPPP bus No 8 to the funicular station. The ascent of the hill costs RM3/4 one-way/round-trip. There are departures every 15 to 30 minutes from 6.30 am to 9.15 pm from the bottom, until 11.45 pm on weekends. The queues here are often horrendous – waits of half an hour or more are not uncommon on weekends.

The energetic can get to the top by an interesting six km hike starting from the Moon Gate at the Botanical Gardens. The hike takes nearly three hours, so be sure to bring along a water bottle. The easier jeep trail to the top starts beyond the Moon Gate and is closed to private vehicles. Both routes meet near a small tea kiosk.

Kek Lok Si Temple

On a hilltop at Ayer Itam, close to the funicular station for Penang Hill, stands the largest Buddhist temple in Malaysia. The construction commenced in 1890 and took more than 20 years to complete.

The entrance is reached through arcades of souvenir stalls. Go past a tightly packed turtle pond and murky fish ponds until you reach the Ban Po Thar (Ten Thousand Buddhas Pagoda).

A 'voluntary' contribution is the price to climb to the top of the seven tier, 30-metre-high tower, which is said to be Burmese at the top, Chinese at the bottom and Thai in-between.

Beaches

Penang's beaches are not as spectacular as the tourist brochures would have you believe (there are better beaches elsewhere in Malaysia), but they make a pleasant enough day trip from Georgetown and have accommodation for longer stays. They are mainly along the north coast. **Tanjung Bungah** is the first real beach, but it's not attractive for

swimming. **Batu Ferringhi** (Foreigner's Rock) is the resort strip with a string of resort hotels. It has the best beach and the best facilities. **Teluk Bahang** is a less-developed, overgrown fishing village with a dirty beach.

Places to Stay

Hostels Penang has plenty of cheap travellers' hostels which, though spartan, are relatively new, clean and offer good travel information.

The *Plaza Hostel* (☎ 263-0560), 32 Lebuh Ah Quee, is very popular and has an air-con lounge. Beds in the large dorm cost RM7, or small rooms start at RM14/18 and range up to RM35 with air-con, all with common bath.

Another favourite is *D'Budget Hostel* (☎ 263-4794), 9 Lebuh Gereja, close to the ferry terminal and buses. Dorms costs RM7 and RM8. Rooms start at RM15/20. This hostel is big on security and the 5th floor rooftop sitting area is a winner.

The *Paradise Bed & Breakfast* (☎ 2628439) at 99 Chulia St has singles/doubles for RM15/18 or larger rooms for RM29/35, all including breakfast. Rooms are clean and tidy but vary from small windowless boxes to lighter, better rooms.

The *Broadway Hostel* (☎ 262-8550), 35F Jalan Masjid Kapitan Keling, is less popular but has good rooms, many with windows, from RM15/25 to RM40 with air-con. Dorms cost RM7.

GT Guest House (☎ 262-5833), 14 Lebuh China, has large dorms for RM8 and small partitioned rooms for RM15/18.

The *YMCA* (☎ 228-2211) at 211 Jalan Macalister is at the top of this range. Simple but very comfortable singles/doubles with shower cost RM33/35 or RM43/45 with air-con. Rooms with hot water and TV cost RM60 to RM80. To get there, take a No 7 bus.

Hotels Georgetown has a great number of cheap hotels with lots of character but some are long overdue for an overhaul. Stroll down Lebuh Chulia, Lebuh Leith or Love Lane and you'll come across them.

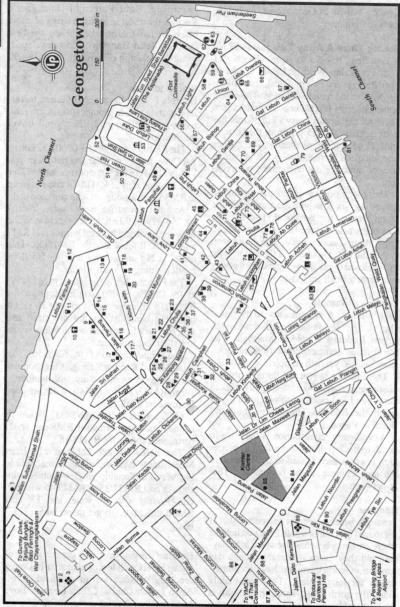

Two very popular places are the *Swiss Hotel* (☎ 262-0133) at 431F Lebuh Chulia and the *Eng Aun* (☎ 261-2333) directly across the road at No 380. They have cafes and are back from the street so are insulated from street noise. The well-run, if sometimes overrun, Swiss Hotel has tidy singles/doubles with fan and common bath at RM17.60/21. The Eng Aun has a variety of decrepit rooms starting at RM14.70 for a single with common facilities, or large doubles with attached showers (toilets shared) from RM19 to RM24.

At 282 Lebuh Chulia, the *Tye Ann Hotel* (☎ 261-4875) is also popular, particularly for its breakfasts downstairs in the restaurant. Run-down rooms are small but private and cost RM16 and there are also RM6 dorm beds.

At 511 Lebuh Chulia is the *Hang Chow Hotel* (☎ 261-0810), a rickety old wooden hotel typical of many with rooms for RM18, but it's well run and has an excellent coffee shop downstairs.

In the streets just off Lebuh Chulia there are a number of other popular places. At 35 Love Lane, the *Wan Hai Hotel* (☎ 261-6853) has dorm beds for RM6 and rooms for RM16 with common bath. It's a friendly, well-run place in a classic Chinese hotel. Rooms are basic and a little noisy but have some style.

The *Tiong Wah Hotel* (☎ 262-2057), close by at 23 Love Lane, is a typical older-style Chinese place in a very quiet area. Rooms with common bath are available for RM18/22.

Also on Love Lane, at No 82 and very close to Lebuh Chulia, is the friendly *Pin*

PLACES TO STAY

2	Sheraton Inn
6	White House Hotel
7	Towne House Hotel
8	Peking Hotel
12	Eastern & Oriental (E&O) Hotel
13	Hotel City Bayview
14	Hotel Continental
15	Malaysia Hotel
16	Merchant Hotel
17	Oriental Hotel
19	Waldorf Hotel
20	Cathay Hotel
21	Lum Thean Hotel
23	Eng Aun Hotel
25	Hang Chow Hotel
36	Swiss Hotel
40	Pin Seng Hotel
41	Wan Hai Hotel
42	Tye Ann Hotel
43	Hon Pin Hotel
44	Hotel Noble
46	Tiong Wah Hotel
56	New Pathe Hotel
57	Hotel Rio
68	D'Budget Hotel
69	GT Guest House
71	Broadway Hostel
77	Paradise Bed & Breakfast
78	Plaza Hostel
84	Shangri-La
87	Sunway Hotel
90	Hotel Grand Continental

PLACES TO EAT

5	Tandoori House
9	Polar Cafe
22	Sin Hin Cafe
24	Yasmee Restaurant
26	Tai Wah Coffee Shop & Bar
28	Taj Restaurant
29	Hameediyah Restaurant
31	Diner's Bakery
33	Green Planet
34	Hong Kong Restaurant
35	Sin Kuan Hwa Cafe
37	Eng Thai Cafe
50	Geethanjali
52	Esplanade Food Centre
55	Dragon King
70	Kaliaman Restaurant
73	Dawood
86	Oriental Restaurant

OTHER

1	Singapore Airlines
3	Penang Plaza
4	Telekom
10	St Georges Church & Cemetery
11	Hippodrome Disco
18	20 Lebuh Leith
27	Reggae Club
30	Chowrasta Bazaar
32	Rock Garden Disco
38	Hong Kong Bar
39	Hot Life Cafe
45	Kuan Yin Teng Temple
47	Penang Museum
48	St George's Church
49	Supreme Court
51	British Council
53	Penang Library & Art Gallery
54	City Hall
58	State Assembly Building
59	Immigration
60	Standard Chartered Bank
61	Victoria Memorial Clocktower
62	Penang Tourist Association & Tourism Malaysia
63	Medan Ferry Offices
64	MS Alley
65	Hongkong Bank
66	GPO
67	Sol Fun Disco
72	Sri Mariamman Temple
74	Kapitan Kling Mosque
75	Post Office
76	Market
79	City Bus Terminal
80	Round Island Buses
81	Railway Booking Office
82	Khoo Kongsi
83	Aacheen St Mosque
85	MAS
88	Thai International
89	Gama Department Store

Seng Hotel (☎ 261-9004), tucked down a little alley. Rooms start at RM17.70 and vary from the crumbling to the presentable, so it pays to check out a few.

The *White House Hotel* (☎ 263-2385) at 72 Jalan Penang is a definite notch up in quality with spotless, large rooms for RM27.50, or RM38.50 with air-con. Those which overlook Jalan Penang are noisy – try to get one at the rear.

For a mid-range hotel, the wonderful-looking *Cathay Hotel* (☎ 262-6271) at 22 Lebuh Leith is a well-maintained, grand colonial hotel. The cavernous lobby nearly equals the exterior. Prices for the huge spotless rooms are RM46 with fan and bath, RM58 with air-con and attached bath.

During peak travel times it can be difficult to find a room, but there are many more cheap Chinese hotels on Lebuh Chulia, Lebuh Campbell and the small connecting streets – a quick wander around will turn up any number of them.

Beach Accommodation Few travellers seem to stay out at the Penang beaches these days though there are some budget places at Tanjung Bungah, Batu Ferringhi and Teluk Bahang.

The only budget offering at Tanjung Bungah is the *Lost Paradise* (☎ 890-7641), at the western end of town. Bungalows for RM20/30 are somewhat run-down but have character. The good restaurant in a garden setting overlooks the beach and Georgetown.

Batu Ferringhi has plenty of big hotels and some budget guesthouses clustered together opposite the beach. The *Baba Guest House* (☎ 881-1686) is a very tidy family home with rooms for RM25, or the RM50 air-con rooms with bath are quite luxurious. Next door *Shalini's Guest House* (☎ 881-1859) is an old, two storey wooden house with a pleasant balcony. Rooms are spartan but cheap for Batu Ferringhi at RM20, more with air-con and bath. Next along is *Ali's Guest House* (☎ 881-1316) with a shady jungle of a garden. The rooms at the back for RM25 are dank, or the better front rooms with bath

cost RM45. The *Ah Beng* (☎ 881-1036) is similar to Shalini's but better maintained. It's an almost identical two storey house with an upstairs balcony and similar prices.

At Teluk Bahang, *Rama's* (☎ 881-1179) has dorm beds for RM6, or double rooms for RM12. It's a very friendly, well kept place run by a Hindu family. *Miss Loh's* is a comfortable, suburban guesthouse off the main road towards the butterfly farm. Dorm beds are RM7, doubles RM15 to RM30. *Fisherman Village Guest House* (☎ 885-2936) is in the Malay fishing kampung and offers simple, tidy rooms for RM18.

Places to Eat
Penang is another of the region's delightful food venues with many local specialities to tempt you. Penang has two types of laksa. Laksa assam is a sour fish soup with tamarind or assam paste, served with white noodles. Originally a Thai dish, laksa lemak has been adopted by Penang and has coconut milk substituted for the tamarind.

Seafood, of course, is very popular in Penang and there are many restaurants that specialise in fresh fish, crabs and prawns – particularly along the northern beach fringe.

Despite its Chinese character, Penang also has a strong Indian presence and there are some popular specialities to savour. Curry kapitan is a Penang chicken curry which supposedly takes its name from a Dutch sea captain asking his Indonesian mess boy what was on that night. The answer was 'curry kapitan' and it's been on the menu ever since.

Murtabak, a thin roti chanai pastry stuffed with egg, vegetables and meat, while not actually a Penang speciality, is done with particular flair on the island.

Hawker Food Georgetown has a big selection of street stalls, with nightly gatherings at places like the seafront Esplanade Food Centre behind the Penang Library. This is one of the best hawkers' centres, as much for the delightful sea breezes as the food.

Gurney Drive, three km further along the coast on the way to Tanjung Bunga is another popular seafront hawker venue.

Lorong Baru, just off Jalan Macalister, is a lively location where food stalls set up in the evenings. Another market good for Malay food springs up every night along Lebuh Kimberley on the corner of Lebuh Cintra, not far from the Komtar centre.

Lebuh Chulia is a great place for noodles after 9 pm. Most stalls are found along the street around the Hon Pin Hotel at No 273.

Indian Food Penang's Little India is along Lebuh Pasar between Lebuh Penang and Lebuh Pitt and along the side streets between. Several small restaurants and stalls in this area offer cheap north (Muslim) and south (vegetarian) Indian food.

Among the more popular Indian restaurants is *Dawood* at 63 Lebuh Queen, opposite the Sri Mariamman Temple. Curry kapitan is just one of the many curry dishes at this reasonably priced restaurant. Beer is not available (since it's run by Indian Muslims), but the lime juice is excellent and so is the ice cream.

Between Lebuh Queen and Lebuh King on Lebuh Pasar is the easy-to-miss *Krishna Vilas*, good for South Indian breakfasts – idli (steamed rice flour cakes) and dosai – and very cheap.

In Chinatown on Lebuh Campbell, the *Taj Restaurant* at 166 and the *Hameediyah Restaurant* at 164A are two Indian Muslim coffee shops with prewar decor, and good curries and murtabak at very cheap prices.

The *Kaliaman Restaurant* on Lebuh Penang is an air-con, South Indian restaurant with banana-leaf meals at lunch time and excellent north Indian food in the evenings.

Chinese Food There are so many Chinese restaurants in Penang that making any specific recommendations is really rather redundant.

At 29 Lebuh Cintra, the *Hong Kong Restaurant* is good, cheap and varied and has a menu in English. One of Georgetown's 'excellent Hainanese chicken-rice' purveyors is the *Sin Kuan Hwa Cafe*, on the corner of Lebuh Chulia and Lebuh Cintra.

One of the most popular outdoor Chinese places is *Hsiang Yang Cafe*, across the street from the Tye Ann Hotel on Lebuh Chulia. It's really a hawkers' centre, with a cheap and good Chinese buffet, plus noodles, satay and popiah vendors.

Breakfast & Western Food Lebuh Chulia has some delightfully old-fashioned coffee shops for a leisurely, cheap breakfast at marble-topped tables while you browse the *New Straits Times*. As well as the coffee, tea and toast served at coffee shops everywhere, those on Lebuh Chulia have much more extensive western breakfast menus, which include muesli, porridge, toast and marmalade and other favourites. Popular hang-outs include the quirky little cafe at the *Tye Ann Hotel* and the tiny *Eng Thai Cafe* at 417B Lebuh Chulia, not far from the Eng Aun and Swiss hotels. Other small Chinese cafes with western breakfast menus include the excellent coffee shop at the *Hang Chow Hotel* at No 511, and the popular little *Sin Hin Cafe* at No 402. At 487 Lebuh Chulia, the very popular *Tai Wah Coffee Shop & Bar* buzzes with activity all day long until late at night. Western breakfasts are also available at the *Eng Aun*, *Swiss* and *Cathay* hotels.

The *Green Planet* at 63 Lebuh Cintra is a popular travellers' restaurant where you can read (and add to) the travel-tips notebooks. It has very stylish decor and good food, but is not the cheapest place in town.

The Komtar complex has western fast food, a good hawkers' centre on the 5th floor and a supermarket.

Getting There & Away
Air The MAS office (☎ 262-0011) in the Komtar building is open from 8.30 am to 6 pm Monday to Saturday, and until 1 pm on Sunday.

See the Getting There & Away section at the start of this chapter for details of flights to other countries in the region.

Bus The main bus terminal is in Butterworth beside the ferry terminal, but some convenient services leave from Georgetown, mostly from the basement of the Komtar centre. Buy tickets at the Komtar ticket offices or from hotels and travel agents on Lebuh Chulia.

Buses go to Kota Bharu (RM20) from the Komtar centre at 9 am and 9 pm – book well in advance. Other east coast buses leave from Butterworth. Only two buses per day go to the Cameron Highlands (RM14) from Georgetown; if full, first take a bus to Tapah (RM10). Other services from either Georgetown or Butterworth are: Alor Setar (RM5), Kuala Perlis (RM7), Taiping (RM4), Lumut (RM9), KL (RM19), Melaka (RM24) and Singapore (RM30 to RM40).

Hotels or travel agents also sell bus and minibus tickets to Hat Yai (RM20), Phuket (RM40), Surat Thani (RM40) and Bangkok (RM65).

Train The railway station is, like the bus and taxi stations, right by the ferry terminal at Butterworth. Trains to KL depart at 7.30 am and 2.35, 10 and 11.55 pm. The 7.30 am train continues on to Singapore; it arrives at 10.35 pm and costs RM60/34 in 2nd/3rd class.

The *International Express* to Hat Yai and Bangkok in Thailand departs at 1.40 pm, arriving in Hat Yai at 4.40 pm and Bangkok the next morning at 8.35 am.

You can make reservations at the Georgetown station (☎ 334-7962) or at the railway booking office (☎ 261-0290) at the ferry terminal, Pengkalan Weld, Georgetown.

Taxi The long-distance taxis also operate from a depot beside the Butterworth ferry terminal. Typical fares for non-air-con taxis include: Alor Setar (RM9), Ipoh (RM15), KL (RM35/41), Kuala Perlis (RM14), Kota Bharu (RM40), Lumut (RM16) and Taiping (RM9).

Boat Kuala Perlis Langkawi Ferry Service (☎ 262-5630) and Ekspres Bahagia (☎ 263-1943), both near the tourist office on Lebuh Light, have ferries to Medan in Sumatra. The journey takes 4½ hours and costs RM110/90 in 1st/2nd class. The boats actually land in Belawan in Sumatra, and the journey to Medan is completed by bus (45 minutes,

included in the price). Both these companies have changing schedules, but between them they will have a departure most days of the week throughout the year.

Getting Around

The Airport Penang's Bayan Lepas airport is 18 km south of Georgetown. A coupon system operates for taxis from the airport. The fare to Georgetown is RM19.

Yellow bus No 83 goes to the airport from Pengkalan Weld or Lebuh China from 6 am to 9 pm. Taxis take about 45 minutes from the centre of town, the bus at least an hour.

Bus There are three main bus departure points in Georgetown, and five bus companies. The city buses (Juara Buses) all depart from the terminal at Lebuh Victoria, which is directly in front of the ferry terminal. Most of these buses also go along Lebuh Chulia, so you can pick them up at the stops along that street.

The other main stand is at Pengkalan Weld, next to the ferry terminal, where the other bus companies operate from – Yellow Bus, Hin Bus, Sri Negara Transport and Lim Seng Bus Co. The new Orient Minibus service has good buses and fares cost a fixed 70 sen anywhere around town. For the beaches take Hin Bus No 93 from Lebuh Chulia.

For around RM5 you can make the circuit of the island by public transport. Start with a Yellow Bus No 66 and hop off at the snake temple, though this run-down temple is easily missed. This Yellow Bus No 66 will take you all the way to Balik Pulau from where you have to change to another Yellow Bus, a No 76 for Teluk Bahang. There are only a few per day, roughly every 2¼ hours from 7.30 am to 7.15 pm, so it's wise to leave Georgetown early and check the departure times when you reach Balik Pulau. At Teluk Bahang you're on the northern beach strip and you simply take a blue Hin Bus No 93 to Georgetown.

Taxi Penang's taxis are all metered, but getting the drivers to use the meters is virtually impossible, so it's a matter of negotiating the fare before you set off. Some sample fares from Georgetown are: Batu Ferringhi, RM14; Botanical Gardens, RM8 to RM10; Penang Hill/Kek Lok Si, RM8; Snake Temple, RM15; and the airport, RM15.

Motorcycle & Bicycle Most of the hotels catering to travellers have bicycles for hire for RM8, as do the shops along Lebuh Chulia. Motorbikes cost from RM20 to RM25.

Trishaw Bicycle rickshaws are ideal on Georgetown's relatively uncrowded streets and cost around RM1 per km, but as with the taxis, agree on the fare before departure. If you come across from Butterworth on the ferry, grab a trishaw to the Lebuh Chulia cheap hotels area for RM3, although you can walk there in five or 10 minutes. For touring, the rate is around RM10 an hour.

Boat There's a 24 hour ferry service between Georgetown and Butterworth on the mainland. Ferries take passengers and cars every eight minutes from 6.30 am to 9.30 pm, then roughly every 15 minutes to an hour. Fares are only charged from Butterworth to Penang; the other direction is free. The adult fare is 40 sen; cars cost around RM7 depending on the size.

ALOR SETAR

The capital of Kedah state is on the mainland north of Penang on the main road to the Thai border, and it's also the turn-off point for Kuala Perlis, from where ferries run to Langkawi Island. People seldom stay very long in Alor Setar but it does have a few places of interest.

The large open town square has a number of interesting buildings around its perimeter. The **Balai Besar** (Big Hall), was built in 1898 and is still used by the sultan of Kedah for ceremonial functions. Next door, the **Muzium Di Raja** is a former royal palace with royal family memorabilia. **Zahir Mosque**, the state mosque completed in 1912, is one the largest and grandest mosques in Malaysia. The **Balai Nobat**, an

octagonal building topped by an onion-shaped dome, houses the *nobat* (royal orchestra).

Places to Stay

There are a number of cheap hotels around the bus and taxi stations in the centre of town. The *Station Hotel* (☎ (04) 733-3786) above the bus station at 74 Jalan Langgar is one of the cheapest in town with rooms from RM17. The *Hotel Mahawangsa* (☎ (04) 733-1433), 449 Jalan Raja, opposite the GPO, is a step up the scale and has air-con rooms at RM49.

Getting There & Away

The central bus station on Jalan Langgar has buses to Butterworth (RM4.25, 1½ hours) and Kuala Kedah (80 sen, half an hour). The small station north of the centre on Jalan Sultan Badlishah has buses to Bukit Kayu Hitam on the Thai border, and Ekspres Tanjung (☎ (04) 731-3329) has two buses daily to Hat Yai for RM10. The main express bus station is two km to the north-east of the centre and has long-distance buses to KL, Melaka, Johor Bahru and Singapore.

The railway station is close to the centre of town. The *International Express* to Hat Yai and Bangkok comes through at 3.30 pm but you'll need to book well in advance. Alternatively, take the 6 am train to Hat Yai (RM8, three hours), a scenic alternative to the buses.

KUALA PERLIS

This small port town in the extreme north-west of the peninsula is visited mainly as the departure point for Langkawi. If you get stuck, the *Asia Hotel*, 1.5 km from the ferry on the road out of town, has basic rooms for RM22. The *Pens Hotel* (☎ (04) 985-4122) is a good mid-range hotel on the main street in the centre of town.

Getting There & Away

Buses and taxis go from the ferry terminal. Most services go to Kangar, but there are also direct buses to Butterworth, Alor Setar, KL and Padang Besar (for Thailand). The short taxi ride into Kangar costs RM1.50, or RM5 to Padang Besar.

The new ferry terminal has a number of companies operating ferries to Langkawi and touts selling accommodation on the island. Ferries leave at least every hour from 8 am to 6 pm and cost RM10.

LANGKAWI

The 104 islands of the Langkawi group are 30 km off the coast from Kuala Perlis, at the northern end of Peninsular Malaysia. They are accessible by boat from Kuala Perlis, Kuala Kedah and Penang and by air from Penang and KL.

Langkawi is pleasant enough and has some good beaches, but the mostly upmarket resorts don't have the atmosphere of the islands on the east coast, though they do have beer, and cheap beer at that, thanks to the island's duty-free status. Langkawi has seen a lot of government-promoted tourist development and luxury hotels are popping up everywhere, but it is not yet totally spoiled.

During school holidays, and at the peak time from November to February, Langkawi gets very crowded, but at other times of the year supply far exceeds demand and the prices come down considerably.

By motorbike you can make a tour of the island taking in **waterfalls** (Telaga Tujuh), a rather pathetic **hot spring**, a legendary **tomb** and other points of interest. The best known beaches are the west coast beaches of **Pantai Cenang** and **Pantai Kok**, on the opposite side of the island from the main town, Kuah.

Langkawi's area code is 04.

Places to Stay & Eat

Kuah Kuah has seen the greatest tourist development in recent years, which is hard to understand given its lack of beaches. If you get stuck, the *Hotel Langkawi* (☎ 966-6248), about a km from the ferry pier, has small windowless boxes for RM20, and better air-con rooms for RM40. Nearby the *Asia Hotel* (☎ 966-6216) has air-con rooms with bathroom for RM50, or RM60 with hot showers.

Pantai Cenang Pantai Cenang is the liveliest beach strip, with a wide range of accommodation, but the budget places are expensive by Malaysian standards.

2020 Chalets (☎ 955-2806) is a reasonable budget place with chalets for RM30 and larger chalets for RM70 with air-con. Further north again are *Suria* (☎ 955-1776) and *Samila* (☎ 955-1964), with cramped and unattractive chalets from RM35 with bath.

The *AB Motel* (☎ 955-1300) is one of the older places on Pantai Cenang, and though dowdy, the big chalets around a lawn are reasonable value at RM30, or RM50 with air-con. Next door, the *Sandy Beach Motel* (☎ 955-1308) is popular but can be very crowded. A-frame chalets cost RM35 for a double with fan and bath, and air-con rooms cost RM80.

Across the road is the *Beach View Motel* (☎ 955-1186), which has a view of nothing at all. Small chalets with fan and attached bath go for RM35.

For mid-range places, two good options are the *Semarak Beach Resort* (☎ 955-1377) and the very pleasant *Beach Garden & Bistro* (☎ 955-1363), both with rooms for around RM100.

Pantai Cenang has some good restaurants. The *Hot Wok Cafe*, opposite the Semarak Resort, has very good Chinese and western food, and seafood is featured.

Pantai Kok Pantai Kok is quieter, slightly cheaper and has a better beach than Cenang, but it is under threat from redevelopment. The best place is *The Last Resort* (☎ 955-1046). There's a choice of rooms with bathroom in a 'longhouse' for RM35, or chalets with air-con go for RM50. It has a good, if slightly expensive, restaurant.

Next door, *Coral Beach Resort* (☎ 955-1000) has better than average little chalets for RM35 with fan and bathroom or RM60 with air-con. Better value is the adjacent *Kok Bay Motel* (☎ 955-1407), where chalets almost identical to the Coral's cost only RM30.

Across the road away from the beach are the *Tropica* (☎ 955-2312) and *Memories* (☎ 955-1118) motels. Tropica has uninspiring chalets with bathroom for RM25. Memories has a shanty at the back with rooms for RM15, but mostly chalets for RM35.

A notch up is the *Idaman Bay Resort* (☎ 955-1212), well back from the beach down a dirt road, but with attractive chalets for RM55 built on stilts around a pond. Best of all is its excellent Thai restaurant.

Getting There & Away

Air MAS (☎ 966-6622) has direct daily flights between Langkawi and KL (RM135), Penang (RM51) and Singapore (RM200).

Boat Ferries between Kuala Perlis and Langkawi (RM10, one hour) leave hourly in either direction between 8 am and 6 pm. Fares can vary depending on the tourist season. Regular ferries also run between Langkawi and the small port town of Kuala Kedah, not far from Alor Setar. Ferries go every 1½ hours from 8 am to 6.30 pm and cost RM13.

Small ferries operate to Satun on the Thai coast from the Kuah jetty daily at 8.45 am and 12.30 and 3.30 pm (RM15). From Satun, buses and taxis go to Hat Yai. During the main tourist season from mid-November until the end of March private yachts also operate between Langkawi and Phuket and offer package trips.

Getting Around

Bus The bus station is opposite the hospital, in the centre of Kuah. The problem with the buses is that services are not that frequent and are limited in scope. Buses run from Kuah to Pantai Cenang (RM1.30), Pantai Kok (RM1.70) and Teluk Ewa.

Taxi Taxis are the main way of getting around the island, and the only way to get to the airport. Fares are fixed and high. From the Kuah jetty fares are: Kuah town (RM4), airport (RM12), Pantai Cenang/Pantai Tengah (RM12) and Pantai Kok (RM16).

Motorcycle & Bicycle The easiest way to get around is to hire a motorbike (usually a Honda 70 step-thru) for RM25 per day or a mountain bike for RM12.

Peninsular Malaysia – East Coast

JOHOR BAHRU TO MERSING

Most travellers head direct to Mersing from Johor Bahru. There are a couple of en-route stops, but they are mainly weekend retreats for Singaporeans.

Around 15 km north-west of **Kota Tinggi**, which is 42 km from JB, are the waterfalls at **Lumbong**. Accommodation at the falls has become expensive, but there are cheaper options in Kota Tinggi.

Johor Lama was the seat of the sultanate following Melaka's fall to the Portuguese. Today the old fort of Kota Batu, overlooking the river, has been restored. It's not easy to get to. You will need to organise a boat in Kota Tinggi for the 30 km trip down the Johor River.

Beach resorts are mainly the preserve of Singaporeans in this part of the world. A turn-off 13 km north of Kota Tinggi leads down 24 km of rather rough road to the sheltered waters of **Jason's Bay**. There are more developed resorts at **Desaru**, 88 km east of JB and also reached via Kota Tinggi. If you're really keen, try the *Desaru Garden Beach Resort* (☎ (07) 822-1101), which has a camping ground at RM5 per head, and dorm beds at RM12 per head. Buses (RM3.50) and taxis run from Kota Tinggi to Desaru.

MERSING

Mersing is a small fishing village on the east coast of Peninsular Malaysia. It's the main departure point for boats to Tioman Island and other islands lying just off the coast in the South China Sea.

The area code for Mersing is 07.

Places to Stay

Sheikh Tourist Agency (☎ 799-3767), 1B Jalan Abu Bakar, is the travellers' place with dorm beds for RM5; the travel agency downstairs provides good information. It's opposite the post office, a few hundred metres before the boat dock. Right next door is *Omar's Backpackers Hostel*, which is less popular but offers near identical accommodation at RM6, or RM14 for a double room.

The *Farm Guest House* (☎ 799-3767) is a rustic retreat a few km from town, where dorm accommodation costs RM15 with all meals. Phone to be picked up from Mersing. *Kali's Guest House* (☎ 799-3613) is another popular place with similar rates (without the meals). The attached pizzeria serves up some very good fare.

There are a couple of Chinese cheapies on Jalan Abu Bakar. The *East Coast Hotel* (☎ 799-1337), at 43A Jalan Abu Bakar, has clean, large rooms from RM14. Next door at 44A is the *Syuan Koong Hotel* (☎ 791-498) with rooms from RM15 to RM28.

Places to Eat

For a roti telur and coffee breakfast, try the *Restoran Keluarga* on Jalan Ismail, or the *E&W Cafe* just around the corner from the Hotel Embassy. For a good selection of fresh cakes and bread, try the *Sri Mersing Cafe* on Jalan Sulaiman.

For cheap Chinese food, there are lots of cafes on Jalan Sulaiman or Jalan Abu Bakar. For cheap, tasty Indian food, try the *Restoran Zam Zam*, next door to Sheikh Tourist agency, and the *Sri Laxmi Restoran* at 30 Jalan Dato Mohammed Ali. For Padang food, there's the restaurant next to the moneychanger on Jalan Abu Bakar.

Getting There & Away

Mersing is 133 km north of JB and 189 km south of Kuantan. The local bus and taxi station is opposite the Country Hotel on Jalan Sulaiman near the river. Long-distance buses for Singapore (RM11), JB (RM7.60), KL (RM16.50), Penang (RM26.50), Ipoh (RM36.50) and Melaka (RM11.20) start and terminate at the R&R Plaza opposite the jetty. The ticket booths are at the back of the plaza.

The taxi station is right next to the bus station. Destinations include: JB (RM12), Kota Tinggi (RM8), Melaka (RM25), Kuantan (RM15) and Pekan (RM12).

TIOMAN ISLAND

Tioman Island is the largest and most spectacular of the east coast islands. It may not be the isolated paradise it once was, but its sheer size (39 km long and 12 km wide) packs in the multiple attractions of laze-away-the-day beaches, crystal clear water thick with coral and fish, as well as jungle-clad mountains complete with waterfalls and fast-flowing streams.

The popular beaches for foreign backpackers are Air Batang, Salang, Juara and Tekek. The southern beaches of Genting and Paya – and Tekek – are popular with Malaysians and Singaporeans during holiday periods. Tioman can get overcrowded at times, but it's certainly one of the prime attractions on the east coast and worth at least a few days.

Places to Stay & Eat

Most foreign travellers gravitate to one of three beaches: Air Batang, Salang or Juara. Salang is the more crowded of the three, but it is the place to be if you want a variety of restaurants and some drinks in the evening. Air Batang is less cluttered and more relaxing, while Juara is the place to get away from it all. Tekek is a bit of a circus these days.

The cheap A-frame accommodation is gradually disappearing and being replaced with chalets. Prices range from RM10 to RM50, though finding something basic from RM10 to RM20 is usually not a problem.

Resort The *Berjaya Tioman Beach Resort* (☎ (09) 414-5445), a massive sprawling place, is the only international-class hotel on the island. Costs are from RM260.

Kampung Tekek Tekek is the largest village on the island and is the administrative centre. The beach here is patchy.

The best places to be based are in the southern part of the beach, though don't expect any bargains. *Sri Tioman* is around 10 minutes walk down the airport road from the jetty. Small huts with mattresses on the floor and mosquito nets cost RM20; chalets cost RM30.

Towards the end of the beach are *Babura* and *Swiss Cottages*. Babura is the better of the two; it has a longhouse setup with rooms with baths, mosquito nets and fans for RM30, and a cluster of beachside chalets for RM35, RM90 with air-con. Its restaurant is one of the more popular on this end of the beach and there's a small bar serving cold beer. *Swiss Cottages* has basic chalets from RM30 and air-con chalets from RM90 – it's not a bargain and the restaurant here is apathetically run.

Accommodation north of the jetty is generally fairly grim, often located away from the beach and with little to recommend it. If you are looking for budget accommodation, you are probably better off heading for Air Batang or Juara. *Ramli's*, a few minutes walk along from the '7 till 7' corner store, is one of the better options, with chalets from RM15. The most popular place is *Mango Grove*, which is a further 10 minutes walk, next door to the new Marine Centre. Chalets here cost from RM20; the restaurant is not bad and it often stays open late. The only drawback of the Mango is that it is sited on a rocky outcrop and you have to walk a fair way to the beach.

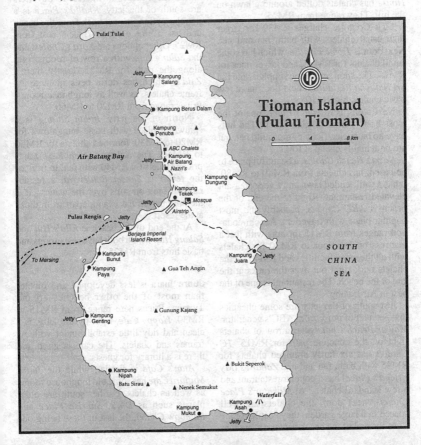

Tioman Island
(Pulau Tioman)

0   4   8 km

Pulai Tulai

Jetty • Kampung Salang

• Kampung Berus Dalam

Kampung Penuba

ABC Chalets
Kampung Air Batang
Nazri's

Air Batang Bay

Jetty

Kampung Dungung

Kampung Tekek
Mosque

Airstrip

Pulau Rengis   Jetty

Berjaya Imperial Island Resort

To Mersing

Kampung Bunut
Kampung Paya

▲ Gua Teh Angin

Kampung Juara   Jetty

SOUTH CHINA SEA

▲ Gunung Kajang

Jetty   Kampung Genting

Kampung Nipah
Batu Sirau ▲   ▲ Nenek Semukut

▲ Bukit Seperok

Waterfall

Kampung Mukut ●   Kampung Asah

Jetty

Air Batang Usually referred to as ABC, Air Batang is a popular beach just over the headland to the north of Tekek. Along with Salang, it's the main travellers' centre, with a lazy string of chalet operations connected by a concrete path that runs the length of the beach. ABC is a more relaxing place to be than Tekek and there's more greenery.

Just north of the jetty is *Aris Huts*, a grotty little place where chalets cost RM25. Close by, over a creek, is the pleasant *South Pacific Chalets*. There are a few chalets right on the beach for RM15, and others on the other side of the path for RM20 to RM30. *Johan's House* has chalets dotted around a lawn on the hill. They range from RM25.

CT's Cottages charges RM30 for larger than usual chalets with bath, fan and net. Next door is *Tioman House*, which has some small chalets for RM15, and larger ones for RM25. The shop sells basic supplies, and the *Sri Nelayan Restaurant* next door has a few basic chalets for RM10.

Next along is *Kartini's Place*, one of the most basic places on this beach. The huts have no bath, electricity or mosquito net, but are undeniably cheap at RM7.

Nazri's Beach Cabins, a beautiful place to be based, has chalets from RM40 to RM80. It has a well-tended lawn and a very pleasant elevated restaurant. Right at the end of the beach is *ABC Chalets*, probably the most popular place with travellers. Accommodation ranges from RM15 for huts with just a mattress on the floor to RM30 for chalets with all the usual facilities and RM40 for the chalets built right out over the rocks at the end of the beach. The restaurant is one of the best in Air Batang.

Just south of the jetty are some cheapies that get a lot of noise from ABC's generator. *Mawar Beach Chalets* has a row of chalets right on the concrete path for RM15. *TC Chalets* has six fairly cramped chalets for RM25 with bath, fan and net. *Zahara's (My Friend's Place)* has a popular restaurant and a few standard chalets. At *Mokhtar's Place Chalets*, next door, the chalets are well spaced in a large garden; they cost RM25.

At the end of the beach is *Nazri's*, another popular travellers' hang-out. It has some very shabby old chalets and A-frames, which cost RM15, and a variety of newer chalets, which cost up to RM85.

Penuba Bay Over the headland from ABC, the *Penuba Bay Cafe* has a few huts for RM15 and some chalets on the hill.

Salang The small bay at Salang is one of the best on the island, but there is sometimes a squeeze on accommodation.

The main places of interest to travellers are south of the jetty. *Khalid's Place* is a popular option. It's set back from the beach and has a nice garden. Chalets cost from RM25. Other options are *Nora's Chalets* and the *Salang Inn*, with a row of rooms right along the path for RM25. Lastly there's *Zaid's*, which has dorm beds in large A-frame chalets, as well as longhouse rooms. Prices range from RM20 to RM60.

North of the jetty, *Indah Salang* is a sprawling place with basic bungalows for RM20 to RM30, four-bed chalets for RM30 to RM50. The *Salang Beach Resort* has pricey chalets for RM40 with fan. In front of the resort is *Sunset Boulevard*, a restaurant/bar built on stilts over the water – it is the only bar on the island, apart from those at the resort.

At the end of the beach is *Ella's Hut* and *Salang Hut*, which both have restaurants and basic huts from RM25.

Juara Juara is less developed and quieter than most of the other beaches around Tioman. Prices here range from RM15 to RM30. *Happy Cafe*, right by the jetty, is a clean and tidy little establishment with A-frames and chalets. The cafe is good and there is a library for guests.

Atan's Cafe is similar, while the *Juara Mutiara Cafe* has some old longhouse rooms as well as chalets. Further south are older places such as *Din's*, *Sunrise Place* and *Rainbow Chalet*, the last of these being one of the cheaper options.

Paradise Point, just north of the jetty, is another good place. It has a good restaurant, and new chalets.

Nipah Nipah has a superb beach, but is very isolated. Ring ahead to the *Nipah Beach Resort* (☎ (07) 799-1012) if you want to stay. Prices range from around RM30, but you may be able to bargain for something cheaper. Only the boats to and from Mersing stop here, by arrangement, and there are no trails to Nipah.

Getting There & Away
Air Silk Air and Pelangi Air have daily flights to/from Singapore for RM132 (S$99). Pelangi also flies daily to KL (RM125, four daily), and to Kuantan (RM77, daily). Berjaya is another small feeder airline, with daily flights to KL for the same price. The booking office for all air tickets is in the Berjaya Tioman Beach Resort.

Boat There are two east-coast entrances to Tioman. Most travellers get to Tioman from Mersing, but for those travelling south down the coast it is easier to get there from Tanjong Gemok, on the border of Pahang and Johor states, 38 km north of Mersing.

From Tanjong Gemok, boats leave twice daily during peak season at 9 am and 2 pm (RM25, 1½ hours). Boats from Tioman back to Tanjong Gemok leave at 11.30 am and 4.30 pm.

From Mersing there are a variety of services to Tioman, though sailing times vary according to the tide. Most boats nowadays are express services (RM25, 1½ hours). Return tickets provide a RM5 discount.

The daily high-speed catamaran service between Singapore and Tioman (S$79, 4½ hours) departs from Singapore daily at 7.55 am, and from the Berjaya Resort jetty at 1.30 pm. Bookings can be made at the desk in the lobby of the Berjaya Resort.

Getting Around
The Sea Bus service operates regular boats between the resort, Tekek, Air Batang and Salang. There is also a 'round island' service stopping in Juara.

OTHER EAST-COAST ISLANDS
Tioman may be the most famous of the islands off Mersing, but there are many others with fabulous beaches. Accommodation tends to be more mid-range and pricier than at Tioman, however. The islands can all be reached by ferry from Mersing.

Pulau Rawa
This tiny island is 16 km from Mersing. The beach is superb and you can snorkel or dive in the crystal-clear waters, though much of the coral around the island itself is dead. Prices for bungalows start at RM110 at the *Rawa Safaris Island Resort* (☎ (07) 799-1204).

Pulau Sibu
Sibu is one of the largest and most popular islands, with good snorkelling and jungle treks across the island. Budget accommodation is available at *O&H Kampung Huts* (☎ (07) 799-3125), which has chalets for RM20 without bathroom, RM50 with.

Pulau Babi Besar
This island is one of the closest to the peninsula. There are some inexpensive chalet operations on Babi Besar with prices from RM10 to RM20, but it would be a good idea to ask around in Mersing as to whether they are still running before heading over to the island. The *Sun Dancer* (☎ (07) 799-4995) is another option, with chalets starting at RM30 (though the deluxe chalets are RM140).

Pulau Tinggi
Tinggi is probably the most impressive island when seen from a distance, as it's an extinct volcano. Accommodation is in expensive resorts, though some locals reportedly supply budget rooms.

KUANTAN
About midway up the east coast from Singapore to Kota Bharu, Kuantan is the capital of the state of Pahang and the start of the

east-coast beach strip which extends all the way to Kota Bharu.

Kuantan is a pleasant enough place but its importance to travellers is mainly as a stop-over en route to other things.

Information

The tourist office (☎ 513-3026) is by the taxi station, opposite the Kompleks Terantum, Kuantan's biggest shopping complex and 22 storey office block. The post office, Telekom office and most of the banks are on Jalan Mahkota near the huge and soaring Sultan Ahmed I Mosque.

The area code for Kuantan is 09.

Things to See

Kuantan's major attraction is **Teluk Chempedak Beach**, about four km from town. It's a small beach bound by rocky headlands. It is popular with locals as a place to eat out.

Places to Stay

On Jalan Mahkota near the taxi station, the *Min Heng Hotel* (☎ 513-5885) is the cheapest in town at RM12/14 for singles/doubles. It's a classic Chinese cheapie.

The *Tong Nam Ah Hotel* (☎ 513-5204), on Jalan Besar near the taxi station, is a good, cheap hotel with rooms for around RM15. Nearby, the *Hotel Baru Raya* (☎ 513-5334)

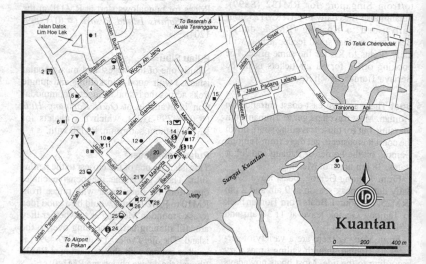

PLACES TO STAY		PLACES TO EAT		10	MAS
5	Hotel Makmur	4	Central Market	12	Immigration
6	Hotel Pacific	7	Restoran Parvathy	13	Post Office
8	New Capitol Hotel	9	Restoran Biryani	14	Maybank
15	Hotel New Meriah	11	Grandy's	18	Standard Chartered
16	Suraya Hotel	19	Tiki's Restoran		Bank
17	Hotel Embassy	21	Food Stalls	20	Mosque Sultan Ahmed I
22	Min Heng Hotel	28	Outdoor Food Stalls	23	Local Bus Station
26	Hotel Baru Raya			24	Tourist Office
27	Tong Nam Ah Hotel	**OTHER**		25	Taxi Station
29	Samudra River View	1	Stadium	30	Kampung Tanjung
	Hotel	2	Hindu Temple		Lumpur
		3	Long-Distance Bus		
			Station		

is better but overpriced at RM29 for a room with fan, or RM39/49 with air-con.

On Jalan Telok Sisek, between Jalan Merdeka and Jalan Bank, there are a number of cheap hotels. The *Hotel Moonlight* (☎ 554-220), 50-52 Jalan Telok Sisek, has good rooms with balcony and attached bath for RM15 and more expensive rooms with bath and air-con for RM30. A few doors along, the *Mei Lai Hotel* is noisy but clean and a good buy at RM12/14 for singles/doubles.

For a room with attached bath, the *New Capitol Hotel* (☎ 513-5222), 55 Jalan Bukit Ubi, is a good choice. It has spotless rooms for RM18, or RM30 with air-con.

The *Hotel New Meriah* (☎ 525-433), at 142 Jalan Telok Sisek, is a good place in this range, with carpeted rooms with attached bath and occasional hot water for RM21/24. Rooms with air-con cost RM28/31 – it's good value.

The only budget accommodation at Teluk Chempedak Beach is the *Sri Pantai Bungalows* (☎ 525-250), which offers good, clean, carpeted rooms with fan for RM25, or with air-con for RM60.

Places to Eat

The small Muslim food stalls dotted along the riverbank, across from the Hotel Baru Raya, are a great place to sit and watch the boats pass by. The seafood is particularly good and the prawns are huge. Another good area for evening food stalls is Jalan Mahkota, not far from the mosque. There are more food stalls set up near the Central Market, with serve-yourself nasi padang places, and good Chinese seafood hot pot.

For breakfast, try *Tiki's Restoran* up the far end of Jalan Mahkota. It's only open during the day, and the two ever-busy brothers who run this place really welcome travellers. There are plenty of good bakeries around, including the one under the Min Heng Hotel, the *Terantum Bakery & Cafe* in the Kompleks Terantum, and several along Jalan Bukit Ubi.

Not far from Tiki's Restoran is the popular *Restoran Cheun Kee*, which serves good Chinese food for around RM3.

At Teluk Chempedak Beach, *Pataya* and *Restoran Massafalah* are pleasant, open-air places specialising in seafood, though the air-con places on the main road are generally better value. There are also a couple of pubs serving Indian food here.

Getting There & Away

Air MAS (☎ 515-7055) has direct flights to Singapore (RM146, four weekly), Kuching (RM233, weekly) and KL (RM74, five daily), and handles Pelangi Air flights to Tioman (RM77, daily).

Bus All the bus companies have their offices on the 2nd floor of the enormous new express bus station on Jalan Stadium. There are buses to KL (RM12.50, five hours), Mersing (RM11, three hours), JB (RM16, five hours) and Singapore (RM16.50, seven hours). For Cherating, take the No 27 Kemaman bus (RM2.50, one hour) from the local bus station.

Taxi Taxis cost RM5 to Pekan, RM15 to Mersing, and RM30 to JB. Heading north it's RM6 to Kemaman or Cherating. To Kuala Terengganu is RM15 and to Kota Bharu, RM25. Across the peninsula a taxi costs RM10 to Temerloh, RM15 to Jerantut, RM18 to Raub and RM20/25 to KL.

AROUND KUANTAN

The coast north of Kuantan is resort territory. The small fishing village of **Beserah**, just 10 km from Kuantan, has some budget accommodation, however. *La Chaumiere* (☎ (09) 544-7662) has French management, is close to the beach and costs RM15 for bed and breakfast. At the other end of the beach is the *Beserah Beach Resthouse* (☎ (09) 544-7492) with similar rates. *Jaafar's Place* is a kampung house about half a km off the road on the inland side. A sign points it out and bus drivers know it. Accommodation costs RM8 a night, or RM15 including all meals.

Buses to Kemaman (No 27), Balok (No 30) and Sungai Karang (No 28) all pass through Beserah. They leave from the main bus station and the fare is 60 sen. Taxis from Kuantan cost RM6.

Gua Charas (Charas Caves) is a limestone outcrop with caves that contain some Thai statuary. Take the Sungai Lembing bus (No 48) from the main bus station in Kuantan and get off at the small village of Panching. From there it's a hot four km walk each way – try hitching.

TASIK CHINI

Tasik Chini is a series of 12 lakes, about 60 km west of Kuantan, and around its shores live the Jakun people, an Orang Asli tribe. It's a beautiful area and you can walk for miles in jungle territory and stay at the nearby Orang Asli village of **Kampung Gumum**.

Places to Stay & Eat

The *Lake Cini Resort* (☎ (09) 456-7897), on the southern shore of the lake, has good cabins with attached bathroom from RM77 for doubles. Some cabins are also set aside for dormitory accommodation – a bed in a 10 bed cabin costs RM18.50, plus a 10% service charge.

A much cheaper option is *Rajan Jones Guest House* in the Orang Asli settlement of Kampung Gumum, a two minute boat ride from the resort or a 30 minute walk. Accommodation is extremely basic – there's no electricity or running water in the village – but it's a rare opportunity to stay near the jungle. The cost is RM15 per person including dinner and breakfast.

Getting There & Away

The tourist information stand in Kuantan can arrange day trips to Tasik Chini for RM50 per person, but the cheapest tours are from Cherating at RM35 per person. Doing it yourself is difficult. From Kuantan catch a bus to Maran and get off at the Tasik Chini turn-off, from where it's 12 km to Kampung Belimbing. You will have to hitch or walk, as bus services to Belimbing no longer operate. Traffic on this road is light. From Belimbing you can hire a boat to Tasik Chini.

The cost is RM40 per boat for the beautiful two hour trip.

The alternative is to take a bus to Felda Chini, south of the lake, from Kuantan or Pekan. Take a Mara No 121 bus marked 'Cini' (RM5.70, two hours) and then hire a motorcycle (RM5) or a taxi to take you the 11 km to the lake.

CHERATING

Cherating is one of the most popular travellers' centres on the east coast. Complete with budget shacks by the sea, a handful of bars, some good restaurants with banana pancake breakfasts, and a reasonable beach with windsurfer breezes, Cherating is as close as the east coast gets to southern Thailand.

Cherating is a good base from which to explore the surrounding area. You can arrange mini-treks and river trips, and most of the places to stay can arrange tours to Tasik Chini (RM35); Gua Charas, Sungai Lembing and Pandan Falls (RM30); and Pulau Ular.

Information

There's no bank in Cherating, but you can change money (at a poor rate) and also make international phone calls at the Checkpoint Cherating shop on the beach road.

Cherating's area code is 09.

Places to Stay

Accommodation ranges from basic A-frame huts for around RM10 to chalets from RM15 to RM50.

On the main road are two of the longest running homestays – *Mak Long Teh's* and *Mak De's*. Mak De's charges RM7, while Mak Teh's charges RM12 per person for accommodation, breakfast and dinner. Both places are less popular than they once were, which is hardly surprising given their proximity to the busy main road.

Matahari Chalets (☎ 581-9126) is on the road to the beachfront and its large rooms with balcony, fridge, and mosquito net are a bargain at RM12/15. You can do batik courses here.

On the beach road there's a group of three places, all with similar facilities and all good. The *Coconut Inn* has a few basic A-frame chalets for RM15 with fan, and RM25/30 with fan and bath. Next door is the attractive *Tanjung Inn* (☎ 581-9081) with chalets for RM40. The *Kampung Inn* (☎ 439-344) is set in a pretty coconut grove and has chalets for RM15 with fan, RM20 with fan and bath, and RM30 for a larger room, also with fan and bath.

Right on the banks of the river, and set in among low trees, is the cosy and rustic *Green Leaves Inn*. The few chalets here are very small and the facilities quite basic, but it's still popular. There's also a small restaurant.

On the same side of the road is the *Payung Cafe*, also on the riverbank. There are a few chalets around a large lawn, and these are quite good at RM15. Next along on the same side of the road is the *Riverside Beach Huts*. It's a friendly place and has chalets with fan at RM20, and with air-con at RM60.

The *Cherating Inn Chalet* (☎ (010) 987-9734) has basic single chalets with fan for RM30 and RM50 with two beds. Across the road is the *Cherating Mini Motel*. It's in a fairly sad state of decay, and not worth the RM35 it charges for the grotty chalets.

On the main access road to Cherating, past the monstrous new *Residence Inn Cherating* is a trail with a sign pointing to *The Moon* (☎ 581-9186). This excellent low-key place has chalets with attached bathroom at RM30/35 and longhouse rooms at RM10/20; weekly and monthly rates are also available. The main attraction is the *Deadly Nightshade Bar & Restaurant*, which usually has a couple of foreigners working in it. It's a unique place.

Places to Eat

Most guesthouses have their own restaurants, but there are also a few restaurants in Cherating, all within easy walking distance of each other. The *Sayang Restaurant* does good Indian food, and *Mimi's*, at the opposite end of the beach, is a popular place. The *Payung Cafe* is a good place for spaghetti and goulash in the evenings.

The *Driftwood Restaurant* on the beachfront near the Kampung Inn is a good place for a beer, and has great food if you feel like splashing out on a lasagne or a pizza.

Getting There & Away

Catch a bus marked 'Kemaman' from the main bus station in Kuantan. Buses leave every hour, the fare is RM2.50 and the journey takes one hour.

RANTAU ABANG

This is the principal turtle beach and the prime area for spotting the great leatherback turtles during the laying season. The long, sandy beach is also good for long, lonely walks. Swimming is possible, but the undertow can be savage.

The **Turtle Information Centre**, close to the main budget accommodation area, has good displays and shows films six times a day. The centre is open every day during the turtle-watching season (May to August) but otherwise closed on Fridays and public holidays. Note that the nearest bank is at Kuala Dungun, 22 km south.

August is the peak egg-laying season, when you have an excellent chance of seeing turtles, but you may also be lucky in June and July. Full moon and high-tide nights are said to be best. The turtles are the east coast's primary tourist attraction. Unfortunately, this has resulted in a decline in turtle numbers. The government is making a concerted effort to protect the turtles and their egg-laying habitat. The beach is now divided into three sections during the season – prohibited, semipublic (where you have to buy tickets) and free access – in an attempt to control the crowds.

Places to Stay & Eat

Right on the beach in front of the Turtle Information Centre are two travellers' places. *Awang's* (☎ (09) 844-3500) is the more popular of the two. Rooms with fan and bath go for RM15/20. The *Ismail Beach Resort* (☎ (09) 844-1054), next door, has similar rooms for RM10 for a double with common bath, RM20 with bath and fan, and RM30 for a large double room with bath and fan.

Dahimah's Guest House (☎ (010) 983-5057) is about one km south towards Kuala Dungun and a popular mid-range option. Rooms with bath and fan are RM30, and RM50 with air-con and bath. It has a good restaurant and arranges trips in the area.

Getting There & Away
Rantau Abang is just over 100 km south of Kuala Terengganu and 138 km north of Kuantan. Dungun-Kuala Terengganu buses run in both directions every hour and there's a bus stop near the Turtle Information Centre. Rantau Abang to Kuala Terengganu costs RM4 and to Dungun costs RM1.50. Heading south you can try to hail down a long-distance bus, or take the bus to Kuala Dungun, from where hourly buses go to Kuantan, as well as to Mersing, Singapore and KL.

MARANG
Marang is a picturesque fishing village on the mouth of the Marang River, though it is being rapidly modernised. The river is dotted with brightly painted boats, the water is crystal clear and thick with fish, and there are good beaches in the south of town, where you will find a couple of budget resort outfits. It is also the departure point for Kapas Island. Marang is a conservative village, however, especially across the river from the main town, and reserve in dress and behaviour is recommended.

Places to Stay & Eat
Most of the guesthouses close to town are on the lagoon, a stone's throw from the beach. *Kamal's Guest House* (☎ (09) 618-2181) is the longest running and one of the best. It's a friendly place with a pleasant garden setting. Dorm beds are RM5, rooms are RM10 and chalets are RM12. The *Island View Resort* (☎ (09) 618-2006) is also good, has free bicycles for guests and charges RM18 for rooms with fan and bathroom. On

the hill behind Kamal's is the *Marang Guesthouse*. It's a notch up from the other guesthouses and has its own restaurant. A dorm bed is RM6, while rooms with fan are RM18. Air-con rooms are available from RM45.

The best of the resort outfits south of the river is the *Bell Kiss Swiss Resort* (☎ (09) 618-1579), formerly known as the Mare Nostrum. It has friendly Swiss management, the restaurant is good, stays open late and serves beer (something of a rarity in this neck of the woods). Simple A-frame chalets are RM20 with common bath, and more luxurious chalets with bath are RM50.

Getting There & Away
Marang is 45 minutes south of Kuala Terengganu, and regular buses run between there (RM1) and Kuala Dungun.

PULAU KAPAS
Six km offshore from Marang is the beautiful little island of Kapas. There are walks and snorkelling, but the island is best avoided during holidays and long weekends, when it is overrun with day-trippers.

Places to Stay & Eat
The *Kapas Garden Resort* (☎ (011) 987-1305) has rooms for RM45 with bath, or RM55 with bath and fan. The *Mak Cik Gemuk Beach Resort* (☎ (09) 618-1221) is similarly priced though not as nice. The *Zaki Beach Chalet* (☎ (09) 612-0258) is the cheapest place, with longhouse rooms for RM15, RM20 with bath, or RM30 for chalets with bath, fan and mosquito nets.

Getting There & Away
Boats shuttle backwards and forwards between Marang and Kapas throughout the day and cost RM7.50 one way.

KUALA TERENGGANU
Standing on a promontory formed by the South China Sea on one side and the wide Terengganu River on the other, Kuala Terengganu is the capital of Terengganu state, and the seat of the sultan. Oil revenue has

transformed Kuala Terengganu from a sprawling oversized fishing village of stilt houses into a medium-sized modern city. There is little to see or do around town and nothing to do by night. Most travellers use it as a staging post to visit nearby attractions such as Lake Kenyir or Marang.

Kuala Terengganu's area code is 09.

Things to See

Kuala Terengganu's compact Chinatown can be found on **Jalan Bandar**. It comprises the usual array of hole-in-the-wall Chinese shops, hairdressing saloons and restaurants, as well as a sleepy Chinese temple and some narrow alleys leading to jetties on the waterfront.

The central **market** is a lively, colourful spot and the floor above the fish section has a good collection of batik and songket. Across the road from the market is a flight of stairs leading up to **Bukit Puteri**, a 200 metre hill with the remains of a fort and good views of the city.

The **Istana Maziah**, the sultan's palace, and the nearby **Zainal Abidin Mosque** make for good photographs. The jetty behind the taxi station is the place for a 40-sen ferry ride

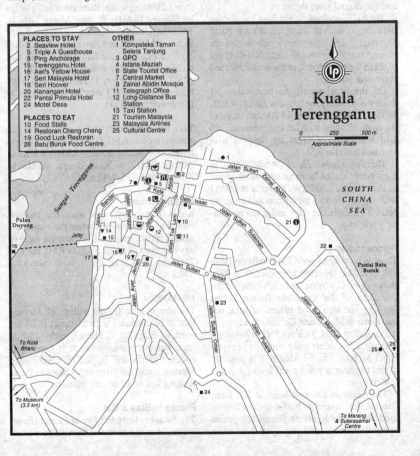

PLACES TO STAY
2 Seaview Hotel
5 Triple A Guesthouse
9 Ping Anchorage
15 Terengganu Hotel
16 Awi's Yellow House
17 Seri Malaysia Hotel
18 Seri Hoover
20 Kenangan Hotel
22 Pantai Primula Hotel
24 Motel Desa

PLACES TO EAT
10 Food Stalls
14 Restoran Cheng Cheng
19 Good Luck Restoran
26 Batu Buruk Food Centre

OTHER
1 Kompeleks Taman Selera Tanjung
3 GPO
4 Istana Maziah
6 State Tourist Office
7 Central Market
8 Zainal Abidin Mosque
11 Telegraph Office
12 Long-Distance Bus Station
13 Taxi Station
21 Tourism Malaysia
23 Malaysia Airlines
25 Cultural Centre

Kuala Terengganu

0   250   500 m
Approximate Scale

SOUTH CHINA SEA

Sungai Terengganu

Pulau Duyung

Jetty

Pantai Batu Buruk

To Kota Bharu

To Museum (3.5 km)

To Marang & Suterasemai Centre

Jalan Sultan Zainal Abidin
Jl Kota
Jalan Bandar
Jalan Banggol
Jl Dato Isaac
Jalan Masjid
Jalan Tok Lam
Jalan Kampong Tok Lam
Jalan Sultan Sulaiman
Jalan Air Jernih
Jalan Sultan Ismail
Jalan Sultan Omar
Jalan Sultan Mahmud
Jalan Sultan Puteri

to **Pulau Duyung**, the largest island in the estuary.

Places to Stay

Ping Anchorage (☎ 622-0851), upstairs at 77A Jalan Dato Isaac, is the No 1 travellers' place. Dorm beds are RM5, rooms are RM12 to RM15, RM20 with attached bath. The rooms are good, but most have wire-topped walls and can be noisy.

The *Triple A Guesthouse* (☎ 622-7372) has dorm beds from RM5 to RM8, while singles/doubles are RM12/15. It's conveniently located close to the state tourist office and the central market.

Awi's Yellow House is a unique guesthouse built on stilts over the river. It's on Pulau Duyung, a 15 minute ferry ride across the river. A bed with mosquito net costs RM5 per night in the open dorm, or the small thatched rooms are RM16.

On the hotel front, the best value for money is probably the *Seaview Hotel* (☎ 622-1911) at 18A Jalan Masjid Abidin, close to the istana. Rooms with fan and common bath cost RM18/28, or there are doubles with attached bath for RM32.

The *Terengganu Hotel* (☎ 622-2900), at the western end of Jalan Sultan Ismail, is one of the cheaper hotels, with rooms at RM33 with fan or RM55 with air-con and attached bath. It's seen better days and is not particularly friendly.

Places to Eat

There is a string of good food stalls on Jalan Tok Lam near the telegraph office. The *Batu Buruk Food Centre* on the beachfront and the 2nd floor of the *Kompleks Taman Selera Tanjung* are also good places to seek out inexpensive Malay and Chinese food.

For Indian food, look out for the *Restoran Thaofiq*, a few doors away from the Seaview Hotel on Jalan Masjid Abidin. It is possible to put together a good meal here for just a few ringgits.

The *Restoran Cheng Cheng*, at 224 Jalan Bandar, has average buffet-style Chinese food at affordable prices. Meals are priced using a colour-coded peg system – when

you've finished eating, take the plate with peg to the counter and pay. It's cheap, and they've got a Lonely Planet recommendation on the wall to prove it.

Getting There & Away

Air MAS (☎ 622-1415), 13 Jalan Sultan Omar, services Kuala Terengganu. There are direct flights to/from KL (RM104, twice daily). A taxi to the airport costs RM15.

Bus Kuala Terengganu has a new bus station on Jalan Masjid Abidin which serves as a terminus for both long-distance and local buses. Heading south, there are regular buses to Marang (RM1), Rantau Abang (RM3), Kuantan (RM9), Mersing (RM18), Johor Bahru (RM22.10) and Singapore (RM23.10). To Kuala Lumpur the fare is RM21.70, and to Melaka RM24. Buses to Kota Bharu (RM7.50) leave every 1½ to two hours from 8.30 am to 7 pm. There are also buses to Butterworth (RM24).

Taxi The main taxi stand is next to the bus station. It costs RM2.50 to Marang, RM8 to Jerteh (for Kuala Besut), RM6 to Rantau Abang, RM12 to Kota Bharu, RM15 to Kuantan and RM35/45 to KL.

Getting Around

Kuala Terengganu was once the trishaw capital of Malaysia, and while their numbers have dropped, they are still the main form of city transport and cost roughly RM1 per km. Taxis are also available – most rides cost RM5.

MERANG

The sleepy little fishing village of Merang (not to be confused with Marang) is 14 km north of Batu Rakit. There's nothing to do here, but the beautiful beach is lined with coconut palms and lapped by clear water. Merang is also the place to get boats to Pulau Redang and other nearby islands.

Places to Stay & Eat

The *Naughty Dragon's Green Planet Home-stay* right in the centre of the village was set to change hands in late 1996, and its fate was uncertain. Check to see if it is still running. It used to be a great place to stay, with doubles at RM15 and dorm beds at RM7. *Razak's Kampung House*, also in the centre of the village, is another option. The cost is RM15 per person.

Getting There & Away
From Kuala Terengganu take one of the three daily Penarek buses (noon, and 4 and 5 pm, RM2.20) or one of the more frequent minibus vans (RM3) from in front of the bookstore on Jalan Masjid.

KUALA BESUT
Kuala Besut, on the coast south of Kota Bharu, has a reasonably pleasant beach but is basically just a staging post for the Perhentian Islands. If you get stranded here, the *Coco Hut Chalet* (☎ (09) 687-2085) has very basic rooms for RM10 and RM15.

Getting There & Away
From the south, take a bus to Jerteh on the main highway, from where buses go every 40 minutes to Kuala Besut. From Kota Bharu it's easier to get off at Pasir Puteh, and take a bus from there. A share taxi from Jerteh or Pasir Puteh to Kuala Besut costs RM1.50. Taxis from Kuala Terengganu cost RM10; from Kota Bharu RM5.

PERHENTIAN ISLANDS
The islands of Perhentian Besar and Perhentian Kecil lie just 21 km off the coast. They are arguably the most beautiful islands in Malaysia. The islands are great for snorkelling and diving, and there is none of the partying that goes on over the border in Thailand – the Perhentian Islands are virtually alcohol-free.

Places to Stay & Eat
Pulau Perhentian Besar Apart from the resort, accommodation is mostly in basic beach huts with rates from around RM20 to RM40. At the northern end of the beach is *Coral View*, with a number of closely bunched chalets, each with attached bath.

Close by is *Mama's Place*, a more basic operation with cheaper prices. Next along is *Cozy*, one of the cheaper setups around.

Coco Hut and *Samudin*, the next two, are unremarkable, while next south is *ABC Chalets*, which is well set up with cheap basic huts right on the beach under the trees. *IBI Huts* and *Abdul's Chalets* are both very popular and have good restaurants.

Over the headland is an easily missed track which leads to Flora Bay. The *Flora Bay Chalets* and (inevitably) *Fauna Bay Chalets* have budget options as well as some very classy chalets up to RM70.

Pulau Perhentian Kecil Accommodation over on Kecil is more basic and prices are generally lower – most places hover at around RM20, though cheaper rates are available (prices vary seasonally), for a chalet with two beds, mosquito net, and washing from a well.

Long Beach is the most popular place to be based. *Chempaka Chalets* has well-spaced chalets and facilities to do your own cooking. *Cottage Huts* has a restaurant right on the beach, but the chalets are cramped together. *Matahari Chalets* is one of the most popular places. Right at the northern end of the beach is the *Moonlight Chalets*, with just a few chalets tucked into the corner of the bay. It's well set up and a good place to stay.

There are a number of small bays around the island, each with just one set of chalets, and often the only access is by boat. *D Lagoon Chalets* is on Teluk Kerma, a small bay on the western side of the island. Also on the western side of the island *Coral Bay Chalets* has been joined by a couple of other chalet operations: *Rajawali* and *Aur Bay*. It's worth taking a look at all three – Rajawali is more upmarket, with prices from RM35. The bay is quiet, gets good sunsets, and the feeding of the huge monitor lizards late every afternoon shouldn't be missed. Further south on the west coast is the *Mira Chalets*. This is another beautiful little beach and there are only a few chalets.

On the south coast at Pasir Petani is *Pleasure Chalets*. Next door is the more upmarket

Pasir Petani Village, which has pleasant chalets, each with attached bath and fan, for RM45.

Getting There & Away

The one-way trip from Kuala Besut to Perhentian costs RM15 and takes 1½ hours. Most boats leave Perhentian early in the morning and return late morning and throughout the afternoon. The boats will drop you off at any of the beaches. When you want to leave it's a good idea to let the owner of your chalets know the day before. Small boats ply between the two islands for RM3 per person.

KOTA BHARU

In the north-east corner of the peninsula, Kota Bharu is the termination of the east-coast road, and a gateway to Thailand. It is the capital of the state of Kelantan, an Islamic stronghold and a centre for Malay culture. It is undoubtedly the most interesting city on the east coast, and many travellers end up staying longer than they planned.

Orientation & Information

The Kota Bharu tourist information centre (☎ 748-5534) is on Jalan Sultan Ibrahim, just south of the clock tower. Like state offices and banks in Kelantan, it is closed Thursday afternoon and Friday, but open on Saturday and Sunday.

The Thai consulate (☎ 744-0867) is on Jalan Pengkalan Chepa and is open from 9 am to 4 pm from Sunday to Thursday, but is usually closed for lunch between 12.30 and 2.30 pm.

Kota Bharu's area code is 09.

Things to See

Padang Merdeka (Independence Square) is a strip of grass that has only some historical associations to claim your attention. The real attraction is the cluster of museums close by. They are all open from 10 am to 6 pm, closed Friday, and charge RM2 or RM3 entry.

The **WWII Memorial Museum** (Bank Kerapu) is dominated by photographic memorabilia. The **Islamic Museum** (Muzium

PLACES TO STAY	
6	Safar Inn
10	City Guest House
12	Ideal Travellers' Guest House
13	Juita Inn
14	Hostel Pantai
15	Star Hostel
16	KB Garden Hostel
17	Johnty's Guest House
19	Mummy's Hitec Hostel
21	Rainbow Inn Guest House
22	Zeck Traveller's Inn
23	Friendly Guest House
24	Kencana Inn
28	Temenggong Hotel
30	Hotel Indah
32	Hotel North Malaysia
34	Thye Ann Hotel
36	Yee Guest House
40	Hitech Hostel/Taxis
42	Kencana Inn City Centre
43	Hotel Murni
44	Hotel Ansar
50	Menora Guest House
52	Rebana House
56	Hotel Perdana

PLACES TO EAT	
1	Food Stalls
11	KFC
25	Night Market Food Stalls
29	McDonald's
32	Restoran Donald Duck
33	Razak Restoran
46	Meena Curry House
55	Food Stalls

OTHER	
2	WWII Memorial Museum
3	Islamic Museum
4	State Mosque
5	Royal Museum
7	Royal Customs Museum
8	Istana Balai Besar
9	Handicraft Village
18	Bird-Singing Place
20	Thai Consulate
26	Central Market
27	Bazaar Buluh Kubu
31	Antique Shop
35	Central Bus & Taxi Station
37	Hongkong Bank
38	Maybank
39	Telekom
41	Old Central Market
45	Clock Tower
47	Malaysia Airlines
48	State Museum
49	Tourist Information Centre
51	Caltex Station
53	Post Office
54	Cultural Centre
57	Silversmith
58	External (Jalan Hamzah) Bus Station
59	Langgar Bus Station

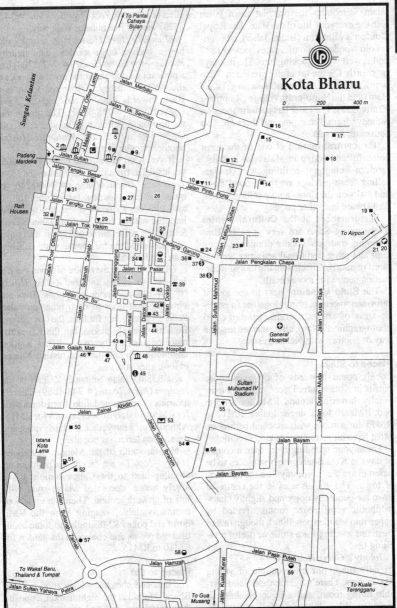

Kota Bharu

0   200   400 m

Islam) celebrates the percolation of Islam into the everyday life of the state. The **Royal Customs Museum** (Istana Jahar), a beautiful old wooden structure, dates back to 1887 and is well worth ducking into. The displays on courtly life are tastefully presented. Also worth a look are the **Royal Museum** (Istana Batu) and the **Handicraft Village** (Kampung Kraftangan). The latter has performances on Sundays from 3 to 6 pm, and there are also souvenirs for sale.

The **central market** is one of the most colourful and active in Malaysia. It is in a modern octagonal building with traders selling fresh produce on the ground floor, and stalls on the floors above selling spices, basketware and other goods.

Performances at the **Cultural Centre** (Gelanggang Seni) are very popular. Top-spinning, traditional dance dramas, *wayang kulit* and other traditional activities are featured regularly. Check with the tourist information centre for more details.

The **State Museum**, next to the tourist information centre, brings together an eclectic array of artefacts, crafts, paintings and photographic displays, all connected in some way or another with Kelantan state.

Places to Stay

Locals count upwards of 60 guesthouse outfits in Kota Bharu. Prices vary only marginally, hovering around RM6 for a dorm bed, RM8/10 for a single/double, RM12 to RM15 for a room with attached bathroom. Most have bicycles and cooking facilities.

For anyone spending more than a couple of days in Kota Bharu, the best places to be based in are the 'homestays' on the outskirts of town. The guesthouses in the centre of town are generally noisy and slightly claustrophobic (coffin-size rooms divided by paper-thin wooden panelling), though few of them are wanting for a smile or useful travelling tips.

Johnty's Guest House (☎ 747-8677) is a friendly place run by a couple of young Malay guys. There's a garden and a comfortable living room, and a basic breakfast is included. When Johnty's is full, many travellers head over to *Zeck Traveller's Inn* (☎ 747-3423), around five minutes walk way.

Mummy's Hitec Hostel is in a funky old house with a large garden. The nearby *Rainbow Inn Guest House* (☎ 747-2708) has a pleasant garden and some great artwork on the walls, courtesy of inspired travellers. Back towards town is the popular *Town Guest House* (☎ 748-5192). The big plus is the rooftop restaurant with good cheap food. Opposite here is the *Windmill Hostel*, another popular place.

If you want to be more centrally located yet insulated from the traffic noise, the *Ideal Travellers' Guest House* (☎ 744-2246) is quiet and has a garden, but is often full. It also runs the *Friendly Guest House*, a few hundred metres away, just off Jalan Kebun Sultan. It's not as attractive, but is also quiet and has good rooms, some with attached bath, for RM15.

Of the places in the centre of town, the *KB Inn* (☎ 744-1786) and *Yee Guest House* (☎ 744-1944) are popular options. They are virtually next door to each other on Jalan Padang Garong, not far from the bus station. Both are friendly places, but the KB is the more popular of the two – it has a good common room and the ever-fussing Nasron to look after you.

At 3338D Jalan Sultanah Zainab is the *Menora Guest House* (☎ 748-1669). There's a variety of accommodation, from dorm beds for RM5 up to large double rooms for RM18. Although on a busy road, it's fairly quiet and the rooftop terrace is popular.

Not far south of the Menora is *Rebana House* – look for the faded sign pointing up an alley next to the Caltex station. It's a lovely house, decorated Malay-style with lots of artwork around. There's a variety of rooms available, ranging from the RM6 dorm and pokey RM8 singles to some beautiful old rooms and chalets in the garden for RM10 to RM15.

Places to Eat

The best and cheapest Malay food in Kota Bharu is found at the night market, opposite the central bus and taxi station. The food stalls are set up in the evenings and there's a wide variety of delicious, cheap Malay food. The whole thing closes down for evening prayers between 7 and 7.45 pm.

There are more good food stalls next to the river opposite the Padang Merdeka, and at the stadium, which has a number of stalls selling ABC (ais batu kacang – the shaved ice dessert). The *Razak Restoran*, on the corner of Jalan Datok Pati and Jalan Padang Garong, is cheap and has excellent Indian Muslim food.

For an excellent lunchtime Malay curry on a banana leaf, try the *Meena Curry House* on Jalan Gajah Mati. For breakfast, the best roti chanai and coffee can be had at the cafe next door to the Hotel Tokyo Baru on Jalan Tok Hakim. Patrons get to sit around a 'bar' and can play with the cigarette lighters dangling from rubber straps.

The *Restoran Vegetarian*, on Jalan Post Office Lama, has good Chinese vegetarian food. The *Restoran Donald Duck* cooks up a very good Cantonese-style duck and rice, and the beer comes in chilled glasses so cold that a block of ice forms in the glass before you can finish the drink.

Getting There & Away
Air The MAS office (☎ 744-7000) is opposite the clock tower on Jalan Gajah Mati. Direct flights go to Penang (RM87), Alor Setar (RM71) and KL (RM104). The airport is eight km from town – take bus No 9 from the old central market. A taxi costs RM11.

Bus The state-run SKMK is the largest bus company, and runs all the city and regional buses, as well as most of the long-distance buses. It operates from the central bus station (city and regional buses) and the Langgar bus station (long-distance buses). All the other long-distance bus companies operate from the Jalan Hamzah external bus station.

SKMK is the easiest to deal with, as it has ticket offices at all the bus stations. Long-distance departures are from the Langgar bus station but, just to make things confusing, a few evening buses also go from the central bus station.

Regular buses go to Kuala Terengganu (RM7.50, three hours) and Kuantan (RM16, six hours). Buses to Johor Bahru (RM29 air-con, 10 hours), Singapore (RM30, 12 hours) and KL (RM25, 10 hours) leave at 8 pm (also 9 pm to KL).

The Thai border is at Rantau Panjang (Sungai Kolok on the Thai side), 1½ hours by bus from Kota Bharu. Bus No 29B departs on the hour from the central bus station and costs RM2.60. From Rantau Panjang walk across the border, and then it's about one km to the station or a trishaw costs RM3. Malaysian currency is accepted in Sungai Kolok.

Train The nearest station to Kota Bharu is at Wakaf Baru, an 80 sen trip on bus No 19 or 27. See the following Kota Bharu to Kuala Lumpur section for more details on this railway.

Taxi The taxi station is on the southern side of the central bus station. Main destinations and costs are: Kuala Terengganu (RM12), Kuantan (RM25), KL (RM35/45), Butterworth (RM38) and Kuala Lipis (RM35).

Getting Around
The airport is eight km from town – take bus No 9 from the old central market. A taxi costs around RM10.

To Pantai Cahaya Bulan (PCB) take bus No 10. It leaves from the Bazaar Buluh Kubu or you can catch it at the bus stand in front of the Kencana Inn.

AROUND KOTA BHARU
Beaches
The beaches around Kota Bharu are nothing special, but are OK for a sunny afternoon. **Pantai Cahaya Bulan** (PCB) used to be known as Pantai Cinta Berahi, the 'Beach of Passionate Love', until local leaders decided it was too raunchy and changed it. Other beaches are **Pantai Irama** (Beach of Melody) at Bachok, and **Pantai Dasar Sabak**, 13 km from Kota Bharu, where the Japanese landed in December 1941, 1½ hours before they bombed Pearl Harbour.

Other Attractions

Also in the Kota Bharu vicinity are **waterfalls** (Pasir Puteh area), a number of Thai temples, including **Wat Phothivihan**, at Kampung Jambu, with its 40 metre reclining Buddha. There are also a number of interesting river trips you can make. At **Kuala Krai**, 65 km south of Kota Bharu, there's a small zoo specialising in local wildlife.

EAST-WEST HIGHWAY

The east-west road starts near Kota Bharu and runs roughly parallel to the Thai border, eventually meeting the little-used road north from Kuala Kangsar to Keroh on the Thai border at Gerik. The highway runs through dense jungle areas and crosses **Pulau Banding**, an island in the middle of Tasik Temengor, a large dam surrounded by jungle and negrito tribes. The *Banding Island Resort* (☎ (05) 791-2076) has mid-range accommodation.

Kota Bharu to Kuala Lumpur

THE JUNGLE RAILWAY

The central railway line goes largely through aboriginal territory. It's an area of dense jungle offering magnificent views.

Commencing near Kota Bharu, the line runs to Kuala Krai, Gua Musang, Kuala Lipis and Jerantut (access point for the Taman Negara National Park) and eventually meets the Singapore-KL railway line at Gemas. Unless you have managed to book a sleeping berth right through, you'll probably find yourself sharing a seat with vast quantities of agricultural produce, babies and people moving their entire homes. Allow for at least a couple of hours delay, even on the expresses.

The line's days are probably numbered, as roads are rapidly being pushed through. The road now goes all the way from Singapore, through Kuala Lipis to Kota Bharu. The train is a lot slower but definitely more interesting.

KUALA LIPIS

The road from Fraser's Hill through Raub meets the railway line at this town. Kuala Lipis is a well-maintained pretty town with fine rows of shops down the main street, and some impressive colonial architecture dating from the time when Kuala Lipis was the state capital.

There's not much to do in Kuala Lipis, but you can arrange good four-day/three-night jungle treks to nearby **Kenong Rimba Park** for RM35 per day, all inclusive. All visitors to the park must be accompanied by a guide.

Places to Stay

The two most popular travellers' hotels, which both organise treks to Kenong Rimba, are on the main street, only 100 metres from the bus station and 200 metres from the train station.

Behind the Sports Toto lottery counter, the *Gin Loke Hotel* (☎ (09) 312-1388) at 64 Jalan Besar has cheap plywood-partitioned rooms for RM12 and is run by a friendly Chinese family. Next door at No 63 is the ever-popular *Appu's Guest House* (☎ (09) 312-3142), which has similar rooms and lots of travel information. Rooms cost RM12 and RM15, or RM30 and RM35 with air-con.

The *Rest House (Rumah Persinggahan Bukit Residensi)* (☎ (09) 312-2599) is a fair hike from the centre on a hill overlooking the town but it has loads of colonial style and a good restaurant. Large rooms (some with balcony) with air-con and attached bath cost RM40 and RM50, or small, uninspiring rooms in the back section cost RM35.

Getting There & Away

There is an express train to Singapore (eight hours) via Jerantut at midnight on Wednesday, Friday and Sunday, or the daily 8 pm train to Gemas also connects to Singapore. Express trains to Wakaf Bharu (for Kota Bharu) leave at 5.10 or 6.50 am. Slow but interesting jungle trains (11 hours) depart at 2.10 and 6.15 pm.

Five buses per day run between Kuala Lipis and KL's Pekeliling bus station from 8 am to 6 pm. Buses and taxis also go to Kuantan, Gua Musang and Kota Bharu.

JERANTUT

Jerantut is the gateway to Taman Negara National Park. Most visitors to the park spend at least one night here, but the town itself has no real attractions.

Places to Stay & Eat

The small, friendly *Green Park Guest House* (☎ (09) 266-3884) on Jalan Besar has four-bed dorms for RM8 and singles/doubles/triples for RM12/20/27. It is an excellent source of information and arranges transport to the Taman Negara. The less-inspiring *Friendly Hostel* (☎ (010) 987-9086) opposite the railway station has large dorms for RM8.

The cheapest hotels can be found on the main road south of the railway station. The best of a bad bunch is the *Hotel Jerantut* (☎ (09) 266-5568), 36 Jalan Besar, with rooms for RM13. Opposite the bus station, the *Hotel Chett Fatt* (☎ (09) 266-5805) is a reasonable place if you can't be bothered walking further. It costs RM15 for a fan room, RM20 to RM28 with air-con.

The *Jerantut Resthouse* (☎ (09) 266-4488), across the railway line on the way to Kuala Lipis, is deservedly the most popular place in town. Pleasant doubles/triples cost RM20/25 with fan and bath or air-con doubles cost RM44 to RM60. Dorm beds cost RM7. The restaurant here is excellent, transport and tours to Taman Negara are offered and every evening an informative briefing is given on the park.

Getting There & Away

Bus Four buses a day go to KL's Pekeliling bus station (RM9, 3½ hours) via Temerloh. Otherwise buses go every half hour to Temerloh (RM2.40, one hour), from where more numerous connections go to KL and other destinations. Buses to Kuantan (RM8.40, three hours) depart up until 3 pm.

Buses to Kuala Tembeling (RM1.20, 45 minutes), for Taman Negara, leave at 8.15 and 11 am, and 1.30 and 5.15 pm, but schedules are unreliable and they don't connect

with the Taman Negara boats. The best bet is to take a chartered taxi to Kuala Tembeling for RM15.

The Jerantut Rest House and the Green Park Guest House also arrange minibuses to Kuala Tembeling for RM4 per person. They can also arrange transport by road all the way to Kuala Tahan.

Train The express train to Singapore (seven hours) leaves at 1 am on Wednesday, Friday and Sunday or the daily 9.20 pm to Gemas connects with another train to Singapore. To Wakaf Bahru (for Kota Bharu) express trains (six hours) leave at 4 or 5.40 am, otherwise the stopping-all-stations 'jungle train' leaves at 12.30 pm and takes 12 hours. All north-bound trains go via Kuala Lipis, and a Kuala Lipis-only train also leaves at 4.40 pm.

TAMAN NEGARA

Peninsular Malaysia's great national park covers 4343 sq km and sprawls across the states of Pahang, Kelantan and Terengganu. The part of the park most visited, however, is all in Pahang. Taman Negara is billed, perhaps wrongly, as a wildlife park. Certainly this vast wilderness area is home to endangered species such as elephants, tigers, panthers and rhinos, but numbers are low and sightings are rare, especially around the heavily trafficked park headquarters. The chances of seeing game are greatest if you do an extended trek away from the more frequented parts of the park, but the main reason to visit is to experience the pristine primary rainforest.

The best time to visit the park is in the dry season between February and September, but it doesn't always rain in the rainy season, when the number of visitors drops dramatically.

Orientation & Information

The park headquarters is at the Taman Negara Resort at Kuala Tahan. There's a Wildlife Department office, restaurant, cafeteria, hostel, some chalets and a shop selling provisions at inflated prices. You can rent camping, hiking and fishing gear. Every night at 8.45 pm there is a free slide show on Taman Negara and its trails. Arrange a guide for trekking or a stay in a hide at the Wildlife Department office. At the resort you can also change money (lousy rate) and make phone calls (expensive). Across the river from the park is the village of Kuala Tahan, which has budget accommodation and restaurants.

Although everyday clothes are quite suitable around Kuala Tahan, you need to be well equipped if heading further afield. River travel in the early morning hours can be surprisingly cold. If overnighting in a hide, you'll need a powerful torch (flashlight).

Mosquitoes can be annoying but you can buy repellent at the park shop. Leeches are generally not a major problem, although they can be a real nuisance after heavy rain.

The kampung of Kuala Tahan, right across the Tembeling River from the park headquarters, also has a couple of basic shops, cafes and two small lodges.

Entrance to the park costs RM1 and a camera permit is RM5. You get these at the office at the Kuala Tembeling jetty.

Hides & Salt Licks

There are several accessible hides and salt licks in the park. A number of them are close to Kuala Tahan and Kuala Trenggan, but your chances of seeing wildlife will increase if you head for the hides furthest from park headquarters. All hides are built overlooking salt licks and grassy clearings.

For overnight stays, take food and your own sleeping bag or sheets from Kuala Tahan (lent free of charge) – you won't need blankets. Each hide costs RM5 per person per night. Even if you're not lucky enough to see any wildlife, the fantastic sounds of the jungle are well worth the time and effort taken to reach the hides. The 'symphony' is at its best at dusk and dawn.

Bumbun Tahan is an artificial salt lick less than five minutes walk from the reception building – no chance of seeing any animals here! Better hides within one to 1½ hours walk from the park HQ are **Bumbun Blau** (you can visit Gua Telinga along the way), **Bumbun Tabing** and **Bumbun**

Cegar Anjing. **Bumbun Yong**, on the Yong River, is about 1½ hours past Blau. **Bumbun Kumbang** is about seven hours from Kuala Tahan, or take the riverboat service up the Tembeling River to Kuala Trenggan and then walk. All these hides have sleeping facilities for six to eight people and nearby fresh water.

Mountains & Walks

Trails around the park headquarters are well marked and heavily trafficked. However, relatively few of the 40,000 visitors the park receives each year venture far beyond the headquarters, and the longer walks are far less trammelled.

Short walks around park headquarters include those to the **Canopy Walkway**, and on to **Bukit Teresik**. You can continue on to **Bukit Indah** or do a loop back via **Lubok Simpon**, a swimming area on the Tahan River.

There's a well-marked, five hour trail along the bank of the Tembeling River for nine km to **Kuala Trenggan**. You can continue on to **Kuala Keniam** for a two day trek.

Gua Telinga is a cave south-west of the park HQ, and it takes about 1½ hours to walk there, after first crossing the Tahan River. It's a strenuous half-hour walk – and crawl – through the cave. Once back at the main path, it's a further 15 minutes walk to the Bumbun Blau hide, where you can spend the night or walk directly back to Kuala Tahan.

The trek for the really adventurous is the ascent of **Gunung Tahan** (at 2187 metres, the highest mountain in Peninsular Malaysia), which is 55 km from the park HQ. It takes nine days, but can be done in seven with a faster descent. A guide is compulsory and costs RM638 for eight people.

A shorter three day walk is **Rentis Tenor** (Tenor Trail). It's quite popular but the trail is not always clear and a guide is recommended.

Places to Stay & Eat

Kuala Tahan All accommodation at park HQ is operated by the privately run *Taman Negara Resort* (☎ (09) 266-3500). Bookings can also be made through its Kuala Lumpur sales office (☎ (03) 245-5585) on the 2nd floor on the Hotel Istana, 73 Jalan Raja Chulan. A 15% tax and service charge is added to all the rates quoted here.

Camping at the park HQ with your own tent costs RM2 per person per night, or you can hire tents. Other camp sites with minimal facilities are scattered throughout Taman Negara. The hostel part of the resort has nine rooms, each clean and comfortable with four bunk beds, overhead fans and personal lockers. The hostel costs RM18 per person.

The resort has luxurious chalets from RM170/200 or RM260/290 with air-con and other mod cons. The resort has one expensive restaurant, and a much cheaper self-service cafeteria. The floating *KT Restoran* is moored on the riverbank.

The village of Kuala Tahan directly across the river from the HQ is slightly less convenient but cheaper for accommodation and food. Crossing the river is easy – simply go down to the park HQ jetty, wave to the restaurants moored on the other bank and a motorised sampan will come and pick you up. Sampans are free if you eat at the restaurants or stay in the village.

In the village, *Liang Hostel* has basic plywood-walled rooms, each with four beds costing RM10 per person. Nearby, the thatch-roofed *Tembeling Hostel* is even more basic, but it has a pleasant lawn area and provides good information on the park. Each room has two single beds with mosquito nets for RM10 per person. Further in the village, *Pakwarin Chalets* has more comfortable accommodation in simple A-frames for RM30. *Teresek View Village* (☎ (09) 266-3065) has large dorms for RM10, small A-frame huts for RM30 and new, mid-range chalets with bath for RM50 and RM60. The small *floating barge restaurants* on the sandbar (more a rockbar) opposite the park HQ are cheap and only a couple of minutes walk away.

Nusa Camp *Nusa Camp*, 15 minutes up the Tembeling River from Kuala Tahan, is much more of a 'jungle camp' than anything at park HQ. Dorm beds cost RM9, A-frames are

RM45 a double, cottages with attached bath are RM60 to RM80 and there is a restaurant. Bookings can be made in KL at the Nusa Camp desk at the tourist centre on Jalan Ampang (☎ (03) 242-3929, ext 112), or at the camp's Jerantut office (☎ (09) 266-2369) at the bus station. It runs its own boat from Kuala Tembeling and the useful riverbus service between Nusa Camp, Kuala Tahan and other places of interest in the park.

Kuala Trenggan & Kuala Keniam About 35 minutes upstream from Kuala Tahan at Kuala Trenggan is the quite luxurious *Trenggan Lodge*. Further upriver is the *Keniam Lodge*. Both are run by the resort and cost RM110 and RM120 respectively.

Getting There & Away

The main entry point into the park is by riverboat from Kuala Tembeling, 18 km from Jerantut. Boats go at 9 am and 2 pm (2.30 pm on Friday). Boats are operated by the resort and Nusa Camp, whose boats also stop at the park HQ before continuing to Nusa Camp. It's a 2½ to three hour boat trip from Tembeling to the park HQ at Kuala Tahan. The trip costs RM18 one way. Leaving the park, boats also depart at 9 am and 2 pm.

Kuala Tembeling is most easily reached by bus or taxi from Jerantut. Kuala Tembeling can also be reached by local train, but it involves arranging in advance for the train to stop at Tembeling Halt, a 2½ km walk from the jetty. Tembeling Halt is just a trackside stop between Jerantut and Kuala Lipis and trains do not normally pick up from there. The nearest station is at Mela, 20 minutes by infrequent bus from the jetty.

From the resort's office at the Hotel Istana in Kuala Lumpur, Reliance Travel has a daily shuttle bus all the way to Kuala Tembeling, leaving at 8 am and costing RM25. Most of the guesthouses in KL can arrange pick-up and drop-off at Kuala Tembeling for the same price.

A rough road now goes all the way to Kuala Tahan village and places to stay in Jerantut can arrange tours via this route.

Getting Around

Nusa Camp has a riverboat service from Kuala Tahan to Nusa Camp (RM5, RM2 for Nusa Camp guests) at 10 am and 12.30 and 6 pm, with more frequent departures in the reverse direction. Other connections are to Kuala Trenggan (RM10), Bumbun Blau and Bumbun Yong. In the wet season services are less frequent or stop altogether.

For charter boats, the Wildlife Department office is helpful in trying to arrange groups for those that want to share costs.

Sarawak

Approximately the same size as Peninsular Malaysia, Sarawak is probably the least visited of all Malaysia's states. This is a shame. Sarawak has some excellent national parks, Kuching is one of the most pleasant cities in all of Asia, and upriver is a fascinating diversity of Dayak tribes and (if one travels far enough) untouched jungle. The politics of logging have injured the state's international reputation to be sure, but there remains much that is worthwhile.

The modern history of Sarawak whiffs of Victorian melodrama. In 1838 James Brooke, a British adventurer with an inheritance and an armed sloop arrived to find the Brunei sultanate fending off rebellion from warlike inland tribes. Brooke put down the rebellion and in reward was granted power over part of Sarawak.

Appointing himself Raja Brooke, he pacified the 'natives', suppressed head-hunting, eliminated the much feared Borneo pirates and founded a dynasty that lasted until after WWII. The Brooke family of 'white rajas' continued to bring ever-growing tracts of Borneo into their control throughout their rule.

Today, Sarawak is an economically important part of Malaysia, accounting for major oil and timber exports. It is also an important producer of pepper, rubber and palm oil. Although the state was hit harder than Peninsular Malaysia by the Communist insurgency, things are peaceful today.

Visas & Permits

See Visas & Documents in the Facts for the Visitor section at the start of this chapter for more information on visa requirements for entering this region.

If you plan to visit any of the longhouses above Kapit on the Rejang or Balleh rivers you will need a permit, which can be obtained in Kapit without fuss or fee. It can be trickier getting a permit for travel in the interior of the north-east. This is the scene of most logging, and where the Dayaks are most active against the government. Permits are required from the District Office in Miri or Marudi for travel to Gunung Mulu, Bario and the upper reaches of the Baram River. It is a time-consuming process, and you will be interviewed to determine your real reason for travelling to the interior, but most travellers don't have any problems, as long as they have absolutely nothing to do with journalism. Tell them you are a carpenter if you think your profession may be a problem.

National park permits are also required but these are largely a formality. They are generally issued as a matter of course when you check in at the park HQ, so there's little point in trying to get one in advance. Bear in mind that the penalty for visiting national parks without a permit is a fine of RM1000 *and* six months in prison (at least it's not death), so always check in at the park HQ before going any further. Permits are required for the Semenggok Wildlife Rehabilitation Centre, but these are issued instantly (along with permits for Bako National Park) at the Tourist Information Centre in Kuching.

Getting There & Away

Air MAS has flights to Sabah and Peninsular Malaysia. The cheapest way to reach Sarawak is to take a flight from Johor Bahru – see the Getting Around section at the beginning of this chapter for details. You can fly to Brunei from Sarawak or skip Brunei by flying from Miri to Kota Kinabalu in Sabah for RM104.

See the following Kuching Getting There & Away section for information on flights to Indonesia.

East Malaysia

LP

0   100   200 km

SULU SEA

CELEBES SEA

SOUTH CHINA SEA

*KALIMANTAN
(INDONESIA)*

Pulau
Balambangan

Pulau
Banggi

Pulau
Malawali

Pulau
Jambongan

Sandakan

Gomantong
Caves

Kunak

Sempoma

Pulau
Sipadan

Lahad Datu

Madai
Caves

Tawau

Tarakan

Tanjung
Selor

Tanjung
Redeb

Sikuati

Kudat

Kota Belud

Mt Kinabalu
(4101 m)

Ranau

Batu 32

Telupid

River

Kinabatangan

SABAH

Tuaran

Tambunan

Keningau

Kota Kinabalu

Beaufort

Tenom

Sipitang

Lawas

Ba Kelalan

Bario

Lio Matoh

Pulau Labuan

Limbang

**BANDAR SERI
BEGAWAN**

Gunung Mulu
National Park

B R U N E I

Sungai
Liang

Baram

Kuala Baram

Miri

Marudi

Lambir Hills
National Park

Niah Caves &
National Park

River

Tubau

Belaga River

Belaga

Badui

River

Baleh

River

Long
Apari

Simanjau
National Park

Bintulu

SARAWAK

Kapit

Putussibau

Rejang River

Sibu

Sarikei

Lubuk Antu

Sri Aman

Simunjan

Bako
National Park

Sematan

Bau

Kuching

MALAYSIA

Land There is no highway linking Sarawak to Sabah. The only land link is between Sabah and Lawas, but there are no road connections between Lawas and the rest of Sarawak. The usual route is to take a bus from Miri to Brunei. From Brunei there are ferry connections with Sabah.

Sea the only regular boat connections from Sarawak are the ferries between Brunei and the isolated outposts of Lawas and Limbang in north-eastern Sarawak.

KUCHING
Kuching is without a doubt the most pleasant and interesting city in Borneo. It's hilly, leafy, has a very pleasant riverside area, and it's very easy to spend a few days exploring the place.

The city contains many beautifully landscaped parks and gardens, historic buildings, an interesting waterfront, colourful markets, one of Asia's best museums, and a collection of Chinese temples, Christian churches and the striking state mosque.

Information
Tourist Offices The Sarawak Tourist Association (STA) office (☎ 240620) is on Main Bazaar, in a new octagonal building on the waterfront. It is a helpful office, and is the place to go with specific queries. Look out for the *Official Kuching Guide*, an excellent freebie.

Foreign Consulates The Indonesian consulate (☎ 241734) is at 5A Jalan Pisang – take a CLL bus No 6 from near the state mosque.

Money The best place to change money is the Hongkong Bank on Jalan Tun Haji Openg. The Standard & Chartered Bank and the Bank of Commerce can also change cash and travellers' cheques.

PLACES TO STAY		
13	Arif Hotel	
31	Anglican Diocesan Resthouse	
33	Kuching Hotel	
34	Metropole Inn	
37	Orchid Inn	
38	Mandarin Lodging House	
39	Goodwood Inn	
40	Hilton Hotel	
44	Riverside Majestic	
49	Holiday Inn	
58	Longhouse Hotel	
59	Kapit Hotel	
60	Ching Hin Hotel	
63	Ban Hua Hin	
67	Borneo Hotel & B & B Inn	
68	Fata Hotel	
70	Telang Usan Hotel	
71	Liwah Hotel	

PLACES TO EAT		
7	Open Air Market (Food Centre)	
9	Jubilee Restaurant	
12	Saujana Food Centre	
26	Green Vegetarian Restaurant	
35	Green Hill Corner	
36	Tiger Garden	
41	Koreana	
43	Stamang BBQ	
48	McDonald's	
52	Suan Chicken Rice	
53	Pizza Hut	
55	Kuching Food Centre	
56	KTS Seafood Canteen	
64	Top Spot Food Court	
66	See Good Seafood Restaurant	
69	San Francisco Grill & Mariner's Pub	

OTHER		
1	Istana	
2	Fort Margherita	
3	STC Bus Station	
4	Taxi Station	
5	Masjid Negeri (State Mosque)	
6	Petra Jaya Bus Station	
8	Electra House	
10	Chin Lian Long Bus Station	
11	Central Police Station	
14	Sikh Temple	
15	Sarawak Tourist Information Centre	
16	Sarawak Museum (New Building)	
17	Muzium Islam Sarawak	
18	Sarawak Museum (Old Building)	
19	Kuching Plaza	
20	Anglican Cathedral	
21	GPO	
22	Court House	
23	Square Tower	
24	Sarawak Tourist Association	
25	Hongkong Bank	
27	Star Bookshop	
28	Borneo Adventure	
29	Chinese History Museum	
30	Hong San Temple	
32	Bishop's House	
34	Concorde Marine Office	
42	De Tavern	
45	Singapore Airlines	
46	Dragonair	
47	Borneo Excursion Travel	
50	Sarawak Plaza	
51	Eeze Trading	
54	Cat City	
57	British Council	
61	Tan Brothers	
62	Ekspres Bahagia	
65	MAS	
72	Hindu Temple	

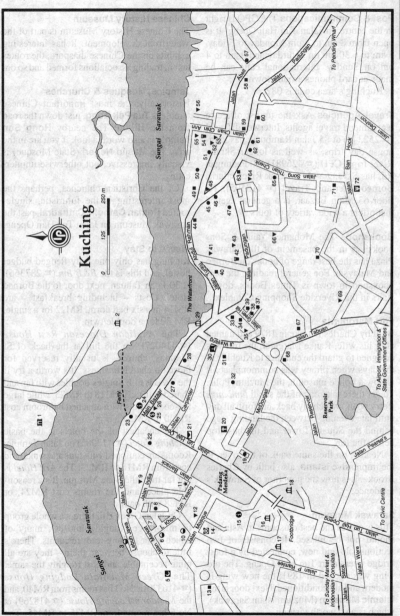

Kuching

0   125   250 m

Sungai Sarawak

Sarawak

The Waterfront

Ferry

Jalan Gambier

Lebuh Jawa

Jalan Bishopgate

Main Bazaar

Jalan Carpenter

Lebuh China

Jalan Mosque

Hlm Yeang

Jalan India

Padang Merdeka

Jalan Tun Haji Openg

Jalan Barrack

Jalan McDougall

Jalan Reservoir

Reservoir Park

Jalan Tabuan

Jl Wayang

Jalan Tabuan

Jalan Padungan

Jalan Song Thian Cheok

Jalan Ban Hock

Chan Chin Ann

Jalan Chin Ann

Jalan Abell

Jalan Padungan

Jalan Deshon

To Pending Wharf

Jalan Abdul Rahman

Jalan P Ramlee

Jalan Satok

Jalan Were

Jalan Tun Hj Openg

To Sunday Market &
Indonesian Consulate

To Airport, Immigration &
State Government Offices

To Civic Centre

Footbridge

To Sunday Market &
Indonesian Consulate

Post & Communications The GPO is right in the centre on Jalan Tun Haji Openg. It is open from 8 am to 4 pm Monday to Friday, 8 am to 6.30 pm on Saturday and 9 am to 4 pm on Sunday. International calls can be made at card phones around town.

Kuching's area code is 082.

Travel Agencies Ask the tourist office to recommend travel agents. Interworld Travel (☎ 252344) at 85 Jalan Rambutan has longhouse day trips, as well as longer Skrang River trips. CPH (☎ 426981), 70 Padungan Rd, has Skrang and Lemanak River safaris. Borneo Interland Travel (☎ 413595), 1st floor 63 Main Bazaar, is a general agency that offers a wide variety of tours.

Bookshops The Mohamed Yahia & Sons bookshop in the basement of the Sarawak Plaza has the best range of books on Borneo and Malaysia. For general reading, the best bookshop in town is Times Books, downstairs in the Riverside Shopping Complex.

Fort Margherita
Built by Charles Brooke in 1879 and named after his wife, Ranee Margaret, the fort was designed to guard the entrance to Kuching in the days when piracy was commonplace. It is now a police museum, the Muzium Polis. To get there take one of the small *tambangs* (ferry boats) which ply back and forth all day until late evening between the landing stage behind the Square Tower and the bus stop below the fort.

Nearby, on the same bank of the river, is the impressive **Istana**, also built by Charles Brooke. It is now the governor of Sarawak's residence.

Sarawak Museum
This is one of the best museums in Asia and should not be missed. It consists of two sections, old and new, connected by a footbridge over Jalan Tun Haji Openg. The old wing was opened in 1891; the new wing is modern and air-conditioned. Next door is the **Islamic Museum** (Muzium Islam Sarawak), which is also worth visiting.

Chinese History Museum
The Chinese History Museum is part of the Waterfront development. It has interesting exhibits on the Chinese diaspora, the routes taken, trading associations formed and so on.

Temples, Mosques & Churches
Historically, the most important Chinese temple is **Tua Pek Kong**, just down the road from the Hilton. The nearby **Hong San Temple** is also worth a look if you are in the area. The **Masjid Negeri** (State Mosque) is visually impressive, but otherwise uninteresting.

Of the Christian churches, perhaps the most interesting is the futuristic, singleroofed **Roman Catholic Cathedral**, past the Sarawak Museum on Jalan Tun Haji Openg.

Places to Stay
Kuching has only one fully fledged budget hostel, and this is the *B&B Inn* (☎ 237366), at 30 Jalan Tabuan, next door to the Borneo Hotel. Costs – including breakfast – are RM14 in a six bed dorm, RM22 for a single, RM 30 for a double/twin.

The *Anglican Diocesan Rest House* (☎ 414027), on the hill at the back of St Thomas' church, is usually reserved for those on church business. It's worth a try if the B&B is full. Singles/doubles with fan and shared bath cost RM18 to RM25, while large fan-cooled flats with attached bathroom cost RM30 to RM35.

The cheapest of the hotels is the basic *Kuching Hotel* (☎ 413985) on Jalan Temple. Rooms are equipped with fans and sinks, and cost from RM18 to RM23. The *Arif Hotel* is not far from the State Mosque. It's a reasonable place, and fan rooms cost RM24, or RM28 with bath.

On Jalan Green Hill there's a whole group of mid-range 'lodging houses', many of which cater to long-term residents. There's little to choose between them – they are all quite acceptable and cost roughly the same. The *Green Mountain Lodging House* (☎ 416320) at No 1 has rooms from RM40, and the *Mandarin Lodging House* (☎ 418269) at No 6 has rooms from RM35 to RM45. The

Orchid Inn (☎ 411417) at No 2, and the *Goodwood Inn* (☎ 244862) at No 16, both have rooms between RM35 and RM45.

Places to Eat

Kuching has the best food in Sarawak, arguably in all of Borneo. The so-called *Open Air Market* (it's covered) on Jalan Market next to the taxi stand is one of the largest and most popular food centres. One section serves mostly Muslim food and the other has mostly Chinese food. The *Top Spot Food Court*, off Jalan Padungan behind the MAS building, is another popular food-stall centre, once again on top of a car park.

The *Green Hill Corner* has a good selection of Malaysian Chinese standards. The *Tiger Garden* has outdoor seating and is a good place to knock back a couple of beers and enjoy a leisurely meal. They're both in the Jalan Green Hill area.

The *Singapore Fried Rice* chain has a few branches around town, including one on Jalan Green Hill, next door to the Hotel Metropole. The advantage of these places is that vegetable dishes are also available along with standards like steamed chicken and rice.

For fast food, check out the area around the Holiday Inn, particularly Sarawak Plaza, where there are branches of *KFC*, *McDonald's*, *Pizza Hut* and local permutations like *Sugar Bun* and *Hertz Chicken*.

Finally, Jalan India has three long-running Indian restaurants: the *Jubilee, Madinah* and *Malaya*. They're all very close to each other on the same side of the street and serve inexpensive Malay curries of the kind widely available in Peninsular Malaysia.

Entertainment

Sarawak has a big drinking culture. Pubs are the best places to meet locals and find out more about Sarawak. Opposite the Hilton car park, look out for *De Tavern*. This extremely friendly place is Kayan-run and frequented by an interesting mix of Malays, Chinese, Indians, Ibans, Kayans and western expats – a couple of nights in here and you'll be on a first-name basis with half of Kuching.

Getting There & Away

Air The MAS office (☎ 244144) is on Jalan Song Thian Cheok and has flights to KL (RM262), Johor Bahru (RM169), Sibu (RM72), Bintulu (RM117), Miri (RM164) and Kota Kinabalu (RM228). MAS also operates two flights per week to Pontianak (RM177) in Indonesia.

Bus The main long-distance Sarawak Transport Company (STC) (☎ 242967) has green-and-yellow buses that depart from the terminus on Lebuh Jawa, which is a continuation of Jalan Gambier. They service the towns of south-west Sarawak around Kuching.

The Petra Jaya buses (☎ 429418) (yellow with red and black stripes) leave from Lebuh Khoo Hun Yeang near Electra House, and these are the buses for Bako National Park and Damai/Santubong.

The blue-and-white Chin Lian Long Company buses leave from Lebuh Gartak near the mosque and have city buses for the airport and wharf. Other long-distance buses for Sarikei, Bintulu and Miri leave from the regional express bus terminal on Jalan Penrissen, five km from town. Tickets can be bought at the Biaramas Express booking office (☎ 429418) on Jalan Khoo Hun Yeang, near Electra House.

Biaramas Express (☎ 452139), Batu 3½, Penrissen Rd, has a bus to Pontianak in Indonesia leaving at 7.30 am; it takes approximately 10 hours. The cost is RM34.50. An Indonesian visa is required for the land border crossing at Tebedu-Entikong.

Boat There are three express boats between Kuching and Sibu, from where you can continue to Niah National Park or head up the Rejang River. They all take around four hours. *Ekspres Pertama* and *Concorde Marine* charge RM29 (RM35 1st class), while *Ekspres Bahagia* charges RM33 (RM38 1st class). Concorde is perhaps the best of the three, as you can sit outside on the ocean leg of the trip. All boats should be booked at least a day in advance to be on the safe side.

The addresses of boat operators and the departure times from Kuching are as follows:

Concorde Marine, Metropole Inn Hotel, Jalan Green Hill (☎ 412551); 8.30 am
Ekspres Bahagia, 50 Padungan Rd (☎ 421948); 1 pm
Ekspres Pertama, 196 Padungan Rd (☎ 414735); 8.30 am

Getting Around

The Airport A taxi between Kuching airport and the city centre costs RM13 (50% more after midnight). STC bus No 12A (green and yellow) costs 90 sen, and operates every 50 minutes from 6.30 am to 6 pm.

Bus City routes are mostly covered by the blue-and-white Chin Lian Long buses, which leave from Lebuh Gartak, near the state mosque, and can be caught at other bus stops around town. The two main services are bus No 6 to the Indonesian consulate, and bus No 17 or 19 to the Pending Wharf.

Taxi There is usually no problem flagging down a taxi on the street, and charges start at RM5, though the taxis are unmetered.

AROUND KUCHING
Semenggok Wildlife Rehabilitation Centre

The Semenggok (also spelt Semenggoh, Semengok and Semengoh!) sanctuary, 32 km south of Kuching, is a rehabilitation centre for orang-utans, monkeys, honey bears and hornbills which have been either orphaned or kept illegally by locals. It's an interesting place, but the Sepilok sanctuary in Sabah is better.

The centre is reached from the Forest Department Nursery along a very pleasant boardwalk through the forest. A permit is required to visit the sanctuary and can be arranged, free of charge, at the Sarawak Tourist Information Centre in Kuching.

To get to the sanctuary, take an STC Penrissen bus No 6 from Kuching (RM1.50, 40 minutes).

Bako National Park

This park is at the mouth of the Bako River,

north of Kuching, and contains some 27 sq km of unspoilt tropical rainforest, beaches, rocky headlands and mangrove swamps. It's a very beautiful area and is well worth a visit. A permit is needed to visit the park, and this, along with accommodation bookings, can be obtained in advance at the Sarawak Tourist Information Centre (☎ (082) 248088) in Kuching.

There are resthouses, hostels and a camping site at the park. Resthouses include fridges, gas burners, all utensils and bed linen. It costs RM80 per resthouse, or RM40 per double room. Hostel cabins sleep four to a room and beds cost RM10 per person. Linen, cooking utensils and a few cups and plates are provided.

The park is 37 km from Kuching and can be reached by Petra Jaya bus No 6 (RM2.10, 45 minutes) and a 30 minute boat ride from Kampung Bako (RM25 for up to 10 people, or RM3 per person if there are more than 10).

Santubong

North of Kuching on the coast, the small fishing village of Santubong has the nearest beach to Kuching. It's average. The main attraction is the **Sarawak Cultural Village** (☎ (082) 422411), a traditionally styled theme park with examples of various types of longhouses, as built by the different peoples of the interior. The result is very touristy, as you would expect, and expensive too (RM45), but well done.

Petra Jaya bus No 2A goes to Santubong.

Kabuh National Park

Just 20 km north-west of Kuching, and opened in 1995, Kabuh National park is an easy day trip from Kuching. Park facilities are still being developed. As yet there is nowhere to stay and there are just three jungle trails. You have less chance of encountering wildlife here than at Bako, but the **Matang Wildlife Centre** should open here sometime over the next couple of years.

Take a Matang No 18 bus (RM3, 50 minutes) from outside the Saujana car park in Kuching.

Gunung Gading National Park

Gunung Gading National Park was opened to the public in mid-1994. The chief attraction is the rafflesia, the world's largest flowering plant. Boardwalks have been laid down, providing access to the areas in which the rafflesia is most likely to be found. The flower has no specific flowering season, so ring the park HQ (☎ (082) 735714) or the national parks booking office (☎ (082) 248088) in Kuching before heading out.

Hostel accommodation is also available at RM10.50 per person, and there are also a couple of hotels in nearby Lundu.

STC bus No 6 runs to Lundu, from where it is only around five minutes drive to Gunung Gading. Take a Pandan bus (ask to be dropped off at the park) or hitch.

UP THE REJANG RIVER

The mighty Rejang River is the main 'highway' of central and southern Sarawak, and most of the trade with the interior is carried out along it. It is also the main trading conduit for logs from the forests in the upper reaches of the river (and its tributaries the Balleh, Belaga and Balui rivers). The number of log-laden barges on the river is astounding and also depressing.

The best time for a trip up the Rejang is in late May and early June, as this is the time of Gawai, the Dayak harvest festival, when there is plenty of movement on the rivers and the longhouses welcome visitors. There are also plenty of celebrations, which usually involve the consumption of copious quantities of arak and *tuak* (rice wine).

On the river there is hotel accommodation only in Song, Kanowit, Kapit and Belaga.

Visiting a Longhouse

The main reason to travel upriver is to visit a longhouse. There is no guarantee, however, that you will succeed. The Orang Uru are generally hospitable, but without an introduction they are not going to invite you into their homes – turning up unannounced is not just bad manners, it can in certain circumstances be a minor catastrophe, particularly if there has been a recent death or certain rituals are under way.

To arrange a visit, the most important commodity you need is time. Most travellers head for Kapit, a small administrative town upriver. Make yourself known around the town – sit in the cafes and get talking to people. If you are not the sociable type, it's unlikely that anyone is going to invite to you their home – unless you bring a couple of bottles of Henessy XO.

If you are invited to a longhouse, don't forget to stock up on gifts to pay for your visit. Alcohol, cigarettes and sweets are most appreciated.

Permits

Before heading upriver from Kapit, you need to get a permit from the state office. This only takes a few minutes, but permits are not available on Saturday afternoon or Sunday. The permit is merely a formality, and chances are you'll never be asked for it. On the top floor of the same building is the Lands & Surveys Department office. It has excellent maps of Sarawak, and for a small charge will photocopy sections of the most detailed ones. These give good detail of the Rejang and Balleh rivers, including many longhouse names.

What to Take

Apart from gifts, other indispensable items include a torch, mosquito repellent, a medical kit with plenty of aspirin and Panadol, and some Lomotil, Imodium or other anti-diarrhoeal.

SIBU

Sibu is the main port city on the Rejang River and will probably be your first stop. There's not a great deal to do in Sibu so most travellers only stay overnight in Sibu and head off up the Rejang the next day. It's worth climbing the tower of the **Chinese temple**, as there are great views of the river from the top of the tower.

Sibu's area code is 084.

Places to Stay

If you can find the caretaker and it's not full, the best place to stay is the Methodist guesthouse, *Hoover House* (☎ 332973), next to the church on Jalan Pulau. It's excellent value at RM10 per person for clean, well-kept rooms.

The bus station area has budget accommodation, but a lot of these places are very seedy. The *Mehung Hotel* (☎ 324852), 17 Maju Rd, has small rooms from RM15, and decent rooms with fan and tiny bathroom from RM20. On the street behind Maju Rd are a couple of grotty hostels with rooms from RM12. The *New Park Hostel* and the *Holiday Hotel* are two of them – not recommended, but OK to crash in for a night.

The town centre has better hotels, though naturally prices are higher. The *Sibu Hotel* (☎ 330784), on Jalan Marshidi Sidek is good for the price and recommended. The rooms cost RM16 with fan, RM20 with fan and bath or RM28 with air-con, bath and TV. The *To-Day Hotel* (☎ 336499), at 40 Jalan Kampung Nyabor, is a well-run place and also home to 'Yeo's Tattoo Artist'. Clean air-con rooms with bath and TV cost RM25/30.

Going up in price and comfort, the *Sarawak Hotel* (☎ 333455), 34 Jalan Cross, has newly renovated singles/doubles from RM30/36. Opposite is the *New World Hotel* (☎ 310311), 1 Jalan Wong Nai Siong, which has rooms from RM30/36, but the Sarawak is slightly better value. *Hotel Capitol 88* (☎ 336444), 19 Jalan Wong Nai Siong, has good rooms for RM30/48.

Places to Eat

There's a small two storey food centre at the end of Market Rd, at the rear of the Palace Cinema, which has stalls selling Malay curries, roti and laksa as well as Chinese food and ais kacang. There are also food stalls on the 2nd floor of the market.

Rex Food Court is a small air-con food centre with a selection of Chinese and western food, including the *Good Morning Sibu* breakfast stall, which does a reasonable western breakfast.

For western fast food, *Sugar Bun* and *McDonald's* are on Jalan Kampung Nyab, and there's a *KFC* outlet on Jalan Wong Nai Siong.

Getting There & Away

Air There are flights to Kapit (RM48), Belaga (RM76), Marudi (RM100), Bintulu (RM64), Miri (RM112), Kuching (RM72) and Kota Kinabalu (RM180).

Bus Syarikat Bus Express has air-con buses to Bintulu for RM18. The Lanang Bus Company has five buses a day to Bintulu between 6 am and 2 pm. The fare is RM16.50 and the trip takes around four hours.

Boat All express boats to Sarikei and Kuching (change at Sarikei) leave from the Sarikei Wharf in front of the Chinese temple. There are three boats operating to Kuching; the trip takes around four hours and costs RM29 to RM33 depending on the company.

Getting to Kapit is the first leg of the journey up the Rejang River. The *ekspres* (RM15) launches which do this trip cover the 130 km or so from Sibu to Kapit in a shade over two hours!

KAPIT

This small town on the eastern bank of the Rejang River dates from the days of the white rajas and still sports an old wooden **fort** built by Charles Brooke.

Information

For travel permits beyond Kapit go to the Pejabat Am office on the 1st floor of the state government complex. It takes around 15 minutes, but bear in mind that the office is only open business hours.

Places to Stay & Eat

The place to head for is the *Rejang Hotel* (☎ (084) 796709), which has good, cheap singles/doubles with fan on the top floor for RM16/20, or with air-con for RM22/26.

If you have no option, the *Kapit Longhouse Hotel* (☎ (084) 796415) and the *Hiap*

Chiong Hotel are two seedy and unwelcoming alternatives.

Food stalls set up in the evening at the night market. The *River View (Ming Hock) Restaurant* on the top floor of the market building is good.

Kapit has a number of good Chinese coffee shops serving the usual Chinese dishes. The *Hua Sin Cafe* serves reasonably priced food, as well as more expensive seafood. The popular *Kah Ping Cafe* on the main square has good pork dishes.

Getting There & Away

Air MAS flies Sibu-Kapit-Belaga and back on Thursday and Sunday. From Kapit, the fare is RM47 to Belaga and RM48 to Sibu.

Boat Ekspres launch departures to Sibu (RM15, 2½ hours) are from 8 am until around 3 pm. During the wet season, ekspres launches leave for Belaga (RM20, six hours) daily from the main jetty. During the dry season, when the river is low, the ekspres boats can't get through the Pelagus Rapids about an hour upstream of Kapit. Small cargo boats (RM50, eight hours) still do the run, however.

There are also boats heading up the Balleh River on a daily basis as far as Interwau – ask at the fuel barges in Kapit.

BELAGA

Belaga is just a small village and government administration centre on the upper reaches of the Rejang, where the river divides into the Belaga and Balui rivers. There are many Kayan and Kenyah longhouses upriver.

Permits

Permits are required for travel beyond Belaga, though it may be restricted to travel as far as the Bakun Rapids, one hour upstream from Belaga. Permits are not required to use the logging road to Tubau and Bintulu.

Places to Stay

The *Belaga Hotel* (☎ (084) 461244) is the most popular with doubles at RM15 with fan

or RM25 to RM40 with air-con. Next door, the *Bee Lian Hotel* (☎ (084) 461416) costs RM25. There's also the *Huan Kilah Lodging House* (☎ (084) 461259), a basic hotel with cheap fan rooms for RM15.

Getting There & Away

From Belaga, ekspres boats go upriver as far as Long Pangai.

In the dry season it's possible to travel overland between Belaga and Bintulu. The journey is not easy; nor is it cheap, unless you get the right connections at the right time. It is possible to do the journey in one day, but allow two in case you get stuck along the way. First take a boat up the Belaga River to the logging camp, just past Long Mitik. It is possible to get an ekspres boat from Belaga for RM5, when there is enough demand; otherwise, hire a longboat for RM90. From the camp, a regular Land Cruiser does the run to Tubau for RM150 per vehicle (RM25 if there are six people). It takes about three hours to Tubau. From Tubau there are ekspres boats to Bintulu (the last leaves at noon) which cost RM14 and take about 3½ hours. If you are stuck in Tubau, there is accommodation for RM10.

BINTULU

Bintulu is a modern, air-conditioned boom town which is best passed through as quickly as possible; there's nothing of interest for the traveller.

Places to Stay

Bintulu is swarming with hotels, but most of them are air-con mid-range places. The *Capital Hotel* (☎ (086) 334667) on Jalan Keppel has a few scruffy rooms with fan for RM15, and a variety of air-con rooms with bath for RM20 to RM45. The *Duong Hing* (☎ (086) 336698), 20 New Commercial Centre, is a small, friendly place, with rooms for RM10/20; air-con singles/doubles cost RM25/28. The *Dragon Inn* (☎ (086) 334223) mostly has air-con rooms with bath and TV for RM30, but also has a couple of cheaper fan rooms with bath for RM20.

MALAYSIA

Places to Eat

The top floor of the new market is the place to go for hawker food. It has dozens of food stalls, and you can sit and look across the river. The night market at the bus station is good for takeaway snacks such as satay, grilled chicken and fish. By the waterfront, the *Seaview Restoran* has standard Chinese food, and does good toasted sandwiches and coffee at breakfast.

Getting There & Away

Air MAS has seven flights daily to Sibu (RM64), six daily to Kuching (RM117), five daily to Miri (RM69) and one daily to Kota Kinabalu (RM127). The airport is smack in the middle of town.

Bus There are frequent buses to Batu Niah (RM10, two hours) and Miri (RM18, four hours). Buses to Sibu (RM18) leave four times daily.

Boat If you're trying to get to Belaga there are ekspres launches that go up the Kemena River as far as Tubau. The journey takes about 3½ hours and costs RM14. Boats leave from the jetty, just a few minutes walk from the bus station, generally between 9 am and noon.

NIAH NATIONAL PARK & NIAH CAVES

A visit to the Niah Caves is one of the most memorable experiences in East Malaysia. The **Great Cave**, one of the largest in the world, is in the centre of the Niah National Park, which is dominated by the 394-metre-high limestone massif of **Gunung Subis**. Archaeologists have found evidence that humans have been living in and around the caves here for 40,000 years.

The swiftlets construct their nests in crevices in the roof of the Great Cave, and it's these nests which are used in the preparation of that famous Chinese dish, bird's-nest soup. Scattered throughout the Great Cave

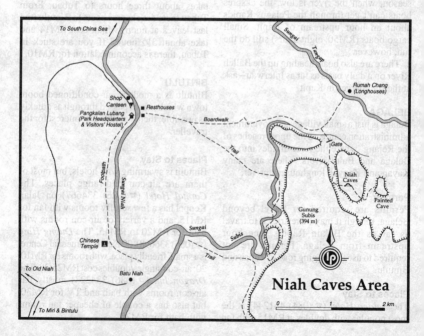

Niah Caves Area

are many flimsy poles, up which the collectors have to scramble to get to the nests.

Another activity which has been going on since 1928 is the collection of guano – bird and bat excrement, which is used as a fertiliser. The millions of winged inhabitants of the caves provide an unforgettable spectacle as evening comes along. Swiftlets are day fliers and bats are nocturnal animals, so if you arrange to be at the mouth of the cave around 6 pm you can watch the shift change as the swiftlets return home and the bats go out for the night.

The park HQ is four km from the village of Batu Niah and the caves themselves are a further three km along a boardwalk – an interesting one hour walk. The boardwalk continues inside the caves, so it's impossible to get lost, though a torch is essential.

Places to Stay
Pangkalan Lubang The *Visitors' Hostel* at the park HQ is a great place to stay. Comfortable four-bed dorms cost RM10 per bed. Also available are four-bed rooms in chalets for RM60.

There are four hotels in Batu Niah. The most popular is the *Niah Caves Hotel* (☎ (085) 737726), which is clean and costs RM22/26 for a single/double.

Getting There & Away
Whether you come from Bintulu or Miri you will end up at Batu Niah, the nearest town to the park. Transport to the park HQ is by taxi or by boat. Boats cost RM2 per person if there are five or more of you, or RM10 per boat. Taxis also cost RM10.

From Batu Niah to Bintulu, buses leave at 6, 7 and 10 am, noon, 1.30 and 3 pm (check with locals to be sure the times haven't changed). The two hour trip to Miri costs RM9 and buses depart six times daily.

LAMBIR HILLS NATIONAL PARK
Lambir Hills is a chain of sandstone hills which reaches a peak of 465 metres at Bukit Lambir. The national park encompassing the hills covers an area of 6952 hectares and, at its closest, is only 20 km from Miri. While it doesn't have the spectacular scenery of Niah and Mulu, or the diversity of Bako, Lambir Hills is an excellent park for short jungle walks, and a good day trip from Miri.

The park HQ is 32 km from Miri. Here you'll find the park office (☎ (085) 36637) and information centre, a canteen and chalets.

Places to Stay & Eat
The new accommodation facilities are very comfortable. Bookings can be made at the national parks office in Miri, or at the office at Niah National Park.

The hostel costs RM10 per person in a four bed room. Standard resthouses cost RM40 per room, while deluxe two bedroom chalets cost RM60 per room or RM120 per chalet. Camping facilities are also available for RM4 per person. The park has a canteen serving fried rice or variations thereof, and the hostel and resthouses have their own cooking facilities. The canteen sells basic provisions, but it is best to bring some fresh food if you will be cooking.

Getting There & Away
From Miri, take the Batu Niah bus for RM2.40, or any nonexpress bus going to Bintulu. From Niah National Park, the buses from Batu Niah to Miri pass Lambir Hills and cost RM6.

MIRI
Miri is another oil boomtown and an R&R retreat for oil workers. It is by no means an unpleasant place but there is little to hold the average traveller. If you've been slogging through the rainforest and are yearning for the bright lights, Miri has plenty of good restaurants and probably the most lively nightlife in all of Borneo.

Information
The post office is about 15 minutes walk from the town centre along Jalan Sylvia, which continues on from Jalan Brooke. The national parks office (☎ (085) 436637) is in the government office complex on Jalan Raja. See the later Gunung Mulu National

Park section for details on obtaining a permit for the area.

Places to Stay

Miri has little in the way of budget accommodation. The cheaper hotels are in the bus station/market area and tend to be noisy and seedy. The *Tai Tong Lodging House* (☎ (085) 411072), at 26 Jalan China, has dorm beds in the lobby for RM8, although the noise and cigarette smoke can make for a restless stay. Other basic but clean rooms in this Chinese cheapie go for RM27/35 with fan and common bath, or RM42 for a double with bath and air-con. The dorm is very insecure – safekeeping of bags costs RM5 per bag.

The *South East Asia Lodging House* (☎ (085) 415488), on the taxi stand square behind the Cathay Cinema, has rooms for RM28 with fan, and RM38 with air-con (all with common bath). The nearby *Fairland Inn* (☎ (085) 4138981) is much better. This friendly hotel has small, clean rooms with windows, air-con, attached bath, and TV for RM30/35.

The *Mulu Inn* has air-con rooms with attached bathroom for RM25/35. It is right by the bus station, and if you are only overnighting for bus connections it is convenient.

Places to Eat

For hawker food there's a small food centre near the Chinese temple where you can choose between Malay food and the usual Chinese dishes. On Jalan Brooke, the *Taman Seroja* is a very pleasant open-air food-stall centre where you can get good satay, more expensive seafood and other dishes. In the Oil Town shopping centre, *The Food Stall* is a small air-con food centre.

For good curries and excellent rotis, *Bilal Restaurant* is one of the better Indian restaurants you'll find in Sarawak. It is on Jalan Persiaran Kabor, a pedestrian mall, and in the evenings the restaurant sets up tables on the pavement.

Entertainment

Miri has a very lively nightlife scene. The only problem is that things really don't get going until around 11 pm. There are no cover charges, but like elsewhere in Sabah and Sarawak beers usually cost around RM9. If you want to sample the action, a good place to start is *The Pub*, which is basically just a friendly watering hole until 11.30 pm, when the deejay turns up. *The Ranch* is just down the road and has live music from around 10.30 pm. It gets packed by around 1 am.

Getting There & Away

Air MAS has Twin Otter services to Marudi (RM29, twice daily), Bario (RM70, daily), Long Lellang (RM66, twice weekly), Long Seridan (RM57, weekly) Limbang (RM45, seven daily), Lawas (RM59, four daily), Labuan (RM57, twice daily) and Mulu (RM69, three daily). There are also flights to Bintulu (RM69, four daily), Kota Kinabalu (RM95, six daily), Kuching (RM164, 15 daily) and Sibu (RM112, eight daily).

Bus There are frequent buses to Bintulu (RM18, 4½ hours). Buses to Batu Niah (RM9, two hours) depart approximately hourly. These buses all pass Lambir Hills (RM2.40) on the highway. Buses to Sibu (RM35, eight hours) leave at 6.45 and 9.30 am.

Getting Around

Bus No 7 runs between Miri and the airport from 6.15 am to 8 pm. It costs RM1. Taxis to and from the airport cost RM12.

Miri itself is easy to get around. It is a small place and everything around town can be reached on foot. For Taman Selera, take bus No 1, 5 or 11; the cost is 40 sen.

MARUDI

Marudi is devoid of attractions, but you will probably find yourself coming through here on your way to or from the interior. Unless you fly from Miri to Bario, you need to get a permit from the District Office here to head further upstream or to Mulu.

Places to Stay

The popular *Grand Hotel* (☎ (085) 755711), Marudi Bazaar, is a good place four or five blocks from where the ekspres launches dock. The cheapest single room is RM16 with fan, but most rooms are air-con and cost RM34 to RM55. The *Alisan* (☎ (085) 755911) also has a few cheap fan rooms for RM17/35. The *Hotel Zola* (☎ (085) 755311) is a notch better and has air-con rooms from RM36 to RM58.

Getting There & Away
Air MAS operates daily Twin Otter flights to Miri (RM29), Bario (RM55), Sibu (RM100), Long Lellang (RM46), Long Seridan (RM42) and Mulu (RM40).

Boat The ekspres boats from Kuala Baram to Marudi operate every hour or so and cost RM15. Upriver, there are ekspres boats to Kuala Apoh or Long Terawan (depending on the water level). They leave when they have enough passengers for RM20 (3½ hours).

GUNUNG MULU NATIONAL PARK
Gunung Mulu National Park is one of the most popular travel destinations in Sarawak. Unfortunately it's also one of the most expensive places to visit, and recent moves to discourage individual travellers means that it is largely the preserve of tour groups. Reports from travellers vary; some feel the expense is worthwhile, others don't.

Gunung Mulu is Sarawak's largest national park, covering 529 sq km of peat-swamp, sandstone, limestone and montane forests. The two major mountains are **Gunung Mulu**, a four day trek, and **Gunung Api**, with its spectacular limestone **Pinnacles**, a three day trek.

The park is noted for its many underground caves. Cave explorers recently discovered the largest cave chamber in the world, the **Sarawak Chamber**, and the 51-km-long **Clearwater Cave**, one of the longest in the world. The **Deer Cave** and the adjoining **Lang Cave** are an easy three km walk from the park HQ along a boardwalk. The more spectacular Clearwater and **Wind** caves can only be reached by boat.

Information
Permits for Gunung Mulu must be obtained from the national parks office (☎ (085) 436637) in Miri, where you will be asked to fill in a form and granted a permit. This permit should then be photocopied along with the information page of your passport and taken to the Resident's office (☎ (085) 433202) on Jalan Raja. Fill another form and hand over the photocopies. Now it is time to obtain police clearance at the police HQ (☎ (085) 432533) on Jalan Pujut. Clearance granted? You can now book accommodation at the national park office.

It's time-consuming but not as bad as it sounds. And bear in mind, if you foolishly forget to organise your permit in Miri, the parks office in Mulu can issue one on the spot when you arrive. You do, however, run the risk of finding all the accommodation booked out if you do it this way.

You cannot go anywhere in the park without a guide. Unless you go with a group, or form a group once you are at the park, costs are prohibitive. For Clearwater and Wind caves, guides cost RM40 per group; for Deer and Lang's caves, guides cost RM20 per group. A guide for trekking costs around RM35 per day. Boat hire costs from RM85 for a visit to Clearwater Cave to RM350 for the Pinnacles trek.

Places to Stay
There is a 15 bed dorm at the hostel, and a bed in one of these costs RM10 per person. A room in the chalets costs RM60, or it costs RM120 for the whole chalet. There's also a VIP resthouse with a six bed room for RM150. The annex has eight five-bed rooms with attached bathroom and fans for RM15 per bed.

Meals at the canteen are slightly expensive. You can cook your own food, as there are gas stoves and you can use the cutlery, crockery, pots and pans. There is a small store at the park HQ selling basic tinned foods, bread, milk, eggs and margarine.

There is private accommodation outside the park at the *Melinau Canteen* (☎ (011) 291641 or (085) 657884 in Miri). It is just a few hundred metres downriver from the jetty at the park HQ, around the bend on the other side of the river. This Berawan-owned place costs RM10 per person in bunk rooms.

Further downriver at Long Pala are more guesthouses owned by the tour companies, such as *Tropical Adventure*, *Seridan Mulu* and *Alo Doda*. It is possible to stay here for around RM15 upwards per night if they are not full, though they are a long way from the park HQ.

Getting There & Away
Air It may well be cheaper to fly from Miri (RM69) than to go by boat. There are also flights from Marudi (RM40) and Limbang (RM40). The airstrip is a few minutes upstream from the park HQ – RM5 by boat.

Bus & Boat With the introduction of regular flights between Miri and Gunung Muru, the overland bus-boat combination has become very hit and miss. From Miri take a bus to Kuala Baram for RM2.20. If you want to try and get to the national park in one day, take the 6 am bus. From Kuala Baram there are express boats to Marudi (RM15, three hours); the first departure is at 7.40 am and they leave at least hourly until 3 pm.

From Marudi, the next stage is Long Terawan (RM20). Travel onwards to the national park from Long Terawan is via charter boat. The official rate is RM150 or RM35 per person if there are more than five of you. In practice, however, few local boat owners are willing to do the trip for RM150 and you may end up paying more or waiting until more people turn up. The journey takes around two hours.

KELABIT HIGHLANDS
If you are planning a long trek into the interior to places such as Bario, Lio Matoh and Long Lellang, the first step is to get a permit from the Resident in Miri. You can also get these permits from the District Officer in Marudi. Bario is the place to arrange treks, and if you do a long trek to Ba Kelalan or Long Semado, you can then fly out to Lawas. Long Lellang is connected by flights to Miri.

Bario
Bario sits on a beautiful high valley floor in the Kelabit Highlands, close to the Indonesian border and makes an ideal base for treks in the highlands. Bario has shops where you can stock up on supplies and gifts to take to the longhouses, as does Ba Kelalan.

There are treks around Bario to places such as Pa Lungan, Ba Kelalan, Long Semado and Lio Matoh. You need to be well prepared and hire local guides.

Places to Stay *Tarawe's* is the place to head for. It's run by a local and his English wife. The cost is RM25 per person, they welcome travellers and provide good trekking information.

Getting There & Away MAS flies Twin Otters from Bario to Miri daily (RM70), usually via Marudi (RM55). The flights are very much dependent on the weather and it's not uncommon for flights to be cancelled, so make sure your schedule is not too tight. These flights are also fully booked well in advance during school holidays.

LIMBANG
This town is the divisional HQ of the Limbang District, sandwiched between Brunei and Sabah. There is nothing of interest in the town itself, but you may well find yourself coming through on the way to or from Brunei or Gunung Mulu.

The *Muhibbah Hotel* (☎ (085) 212153) is one of the cheapest places around, with some older rooms for RM36/42.

Getting There & Away
MAS has flights to Miri (RM45), Gunung Mulu (RM40), Lawas (RM25) and Kota Kinabalu (RM60). The airport is four km from the town centre, and a taxi costs RM4 per person.

An express boat goes to Lawas every morning at 8 am for RM15. There are also frequent boats to Bandar Seri Begawan, the capital of Brunei (RM10, 30 minutes).

LAWAS
Like Limbang, Lawas is essentially a transit town and you may find yourself here while

en route to or from Brunei, on your way up to Bario in the Kelabit Highlands and Ba Kelalan, or in order to take the short flight to Miri skipping clean over Brunei.

The friendly *Hup Guan Lodging House* (☎ (085) 85362) costs RM15/20 for singles/doubles, or the one air-con room costs RM28. All other hotels are air-con and expensive.

Getting There & Away
There are flights to Kota Kinabalu (RM47), Miri (RM59), Limbang (RM25), Ba Kelalan (RM46), Long Semado (RM40) and Labuan (RM31).

The bus to Kota Kinabalu, via Sipitang and Beaufort, leaves at 7.30 am and costs RM20. Otherwise catch a bus to Merapok (RM5), on the Sarawak/Sabah border, and from there you can catch a bus to Sipitang. At the border you have to go through immigration formalities for both states.

For Brunei, the only boat goes at 7.30 am and costs RM20. One boat a day goes to Labuan at 7.30 am for RM20 – book at the Bee Hiong Restaurant (☎ (085) 85137) underneath the Hotel Million. The boat to Limbang goes at 9 am and costs RM15.

Sabah

The chief attractions of Sabah are Mt Kinabalu, the Turtle Islands and the opportunity to see wildlife in the national and state parks. Budget travellers will generally find Sabah more expensive than Peninsular Malaysia, but it is still possible to keep costs to a minimum if you stick to the beaten trail – most of the major attractions have inexpensive accommodation and cheap eats.

Prior to independence Sabah was known as North Borneo and controlled by the British North Borneo Company. Before that, it was part of the Brunei Empire and renowned for its pirates. Kota Kinabalu was at one time known as Api Api (Fire Fire) due to the pirates' tiresome habit of repeatedly putting it to the torch.

Today, Sabah is an integral part of Malaysia. Its economy is based chiefly on oil, timber and agriculture. The road network is generally good, apart from a few horror stretches, and the delightful little railway that meanders from Beaufort to Tenom in the south-west of the state is an interesting jungle trip.

Visas & Permits
For details of the visa requirements of this region, see the Facts for the Visitor section at the start of this chapter.

Getting There & Away
Air MAS has direct flights from Kota Kinabalu to KL and Johor Bahru – see the Getting Around section at the start of this chapter for details. MAS also flies direct to Miri (RM104), Bintulu (RM127) and Kuching (RM228) in Sarawak, and to Labuan (RM52).

Land The only way to leave Sabah by land is via the crossing to Lawas in Sarawak. Unfortunately there are no road connections from Lawas to the rest of Sarawak.

Sea From Lawas, one ferry a day goes to Labuan, but few travellers use this route.

KOTA KINABALU
Known as Jesselton until 1963, Kota Kinabalu was razed during WWII to prevent the Japanese using it as a base. Today it's a modern city of wide avenues and tall buildings, with little in the way of historical charm. All the same, KK, as everyone calls it, is not an unpleasant city; there's just not much to do. It is necessary to stop in KK to book accommodation for the trip to Mt Kinabalu, Sabah's number one attraction.

Orientation
Although the city sprawls for many km along the coast from the international airport at Tanjung Aru to Likas, the centre itself is quite small and most places are within easy walking distance of each other.

Information

Tourist Offices Kota Kinabalu has two excellent tourist offices. Tourism Malaysia (☎ 211732) is on the ground floor of the Wing Onn Life building on Jalan Segunting at the northern end of the city centre. The Sabah Tourism Promotion Corporation (☎ 218620), 51 Jalan Gaya, is housed in a historic building.

Consulates & Immigration The Indonesian consulate (☎ 219110) is on Jalan Karamunsing, south of the city centre.

The immigration office (☎ 216711) is on the 4th floor of the tall government building, near Jalan Tunku Abdul Rahman and around the corner from the Diamond Inn.

Money There are plenty of banks that can change cash and travellers' cheques in the city centre. You'll find moneychangers on the ground floor of Centre Point and Wisma Merdeka.

Post & Communications The post office is right in the centre of town and has an efficient poste restante counter. International calls can be made from card phones around town.

Kota Kinabalu's area code is 088.

National Parks Office The Sabah Parks office (☎ 211585) is very conveniently situated in Block K of the Sinsuran Kompleks on Jalan Tun Fuad Stephens. It handles accommodation bookings for Kinabalu National Park, Tunku Abdul Rahman National Park, Poring Hot Springs, Pulau Tiga, Turtle Islands National Park and Tawau Hills Park.

Things to See

As an example of contemporary Islamic architecture at its best, the **State Mosque** is well worth a visit. It's on the outskirts of town and you'll see it when you're on your way to or from the airport.

The **Sabah Museum** is on the outskirts of town, next to the State Legislative Assembly Hall on Jalan Tunku Abdul Rahman. For a view of the city, head up **Signal Hill** at the eastern edge of the city centre above the former GPO.

The **market** is in two sections – the waterfront area for fish and an area in front of the harbour for fruit and vegetables. Next to the main central market on the waterfront is a market known locally as the **Filipino Market** – the stalls are owned by Filipinos, who sell a wide variety of handicrafts.

Places to Stay

There are three popular travellers' hang-outs in the centre of town and a couple more on the outskirts of town. The *Traveller's Rest Hostel* (☎ 224264) is the most popular travellers' place and is centrally located on the 3rd floor, Block L of the Sinsuran Kompleks. It has dorm beds at RM13. Next door is the *Borneo Wildlife Youth Hostel* (☎ 213668). It's a basic setup with clean dorm rooms for RM12 per bed.

The *Na Balu Lodge* (☎ 262281) is above YBJ Antiques, a block south-west of the Jesselton Hotel. Dorm beds with mosquito nets and fans cost RM20 with breakfast. There's a dining room and kitchen, and a travel service with a wide range of tours.

Jack's Bed & Breakfast (☎ 232367), 17 Block B, 1st floor, Jalan Karamunsing, is a little further out, but is spotlessly clean and well run. It costs RM18 for a dorm bed and breakfast. It's out towards the state mosque, about one km past the cinema complexes on Jalan Tunku Abdul Rahman.

Farida's Bed & Breakfast (☎ 235733), 413 Jalan Saga in Likas, is six km north of the centre of town. Set in a large, quiet, suburban house, it costs RM18 per person for a double room including a great breakfast, or RM12 per person for a bed only.

The *Seaside Travellers Inn* (☎ 750313), H 30 Gaya Park, Jalan Penampang, is 20 km from town past the airport towards Papar. It is not the place to stay if you want to explore KK, but may be ideal if you want a day or two on the beach and you are leaving from the airport. Accommodation ranges from a dorm bed for RM20, single/double rooms for RM40/50, all with a continental breakfast.

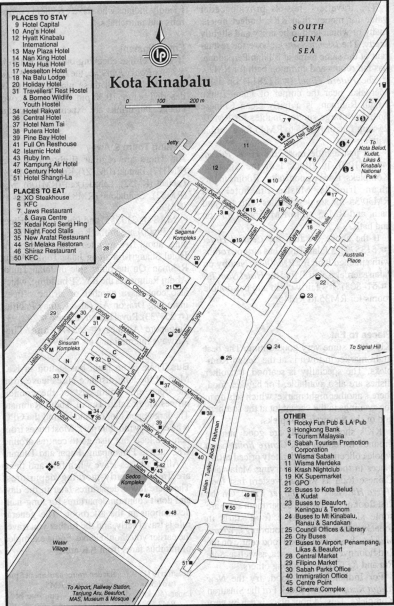

Kota Kinabalu

0   100   200 m

PLACES TO STAY
9 Hotel Capital
10 Ang's Hotel
12 Hyatt Kinabalu
     International
13 May Plaza Hotel
14 Nan Xing Hotel
15 May Hua Hotel
17 Jesselton Hotel
18 Na Balu Lodge
20 Holiday Hotel
31 Travellers' Rest Hostel
     & Borneo Wildlife
     Youth Hostel
34 Hotel Rakyat
36 Central Hotel
37 Hotel Nam Tai
38 Putera Hotel
39 Pine Bay Hotel
40 Full On Resthouse
42 Islamic Hotel
44 Ruby Inn
47 Kampung Air Hotel
49 Century Hotel
51 Hotel Shangri-La

PLACES TO EAT
2 XO Steakhouse
6 KFC
7 Jaws Restaurant
     & Gaya Centre
32 Kedai Kopi Seng Hing
33 Night Food Stalls
35 New Arafat Restaurant
44 Sri Melaka Restoran
46 Shiraz Restaurant
50 KFC

OTHER
1 Rocky Fun Pub & LA Pub
3 Hongkong Bank
4 Tourism Malaysia
5 Sabah Tourism Promotion
     Corporation
8 Wisma Sabah
11 Wisma Merdeka
16 Krash Nightclub
19 KK Supermarket
21 GPO
22 Buses to Kota Belud
     & Kudat
23 Buses to Beaufort,
     Keningau & Tenom
24 Buses to Mt Kinabalu,
     Ranau & Sandakan
26 Council Offices & Library
27 Buses to Airport, Penampang,
     Likas & Beaufort
28 Central Market
29 Filipino Market
30 Sabah Parks Office
45 Immigration Office
45 Centre Point
48 Cinema Complex

SOUTH
CHINA
SEA

To
Kota Belud,
Kudat,
Likas &
Kinabalu
National
Park

Australia
Place

To Signal Hill

Jetty

Segama
Kompleks

Sinsuran
Kompleks

Sedco
Kompleks

Water
Village

To Airport, Railway Station,
Tanjung Aru, Beaufort,
MAS, Museum & Mosque

Jalan Haji Saman
Jalan Datuk Salleh Sulong
Jalan Dr Chong Tain Vun
Jalan Tun Fuad Stevens
Jalan Dua Puluh
Jalan Tun Razak
Jalan Pantai
Jalan Gaya
Jalan Balai Polis
Jalan Bakau
Jalan Tugu
Jalan Merdeka
Jalan Perpaduan
Jalan Laiman Diki
Jalan Tunku Abdul Rahman
Lorong
Jesselton

The travellers' hostels provide better value for money than KK's budget hotels, many of which tend to be noisy and slightly seedy. The *Islamic Hotel*, above the restaurant of the same name at 8 Jalan Perpaduan, has fan rooms and common bath for RM27.

The *Putera Hotel* (☎ 512814) on Jalan Merdeka, near the corner of Jalan Tunku Abdul Rahman, is a fairly clean Chinese hotel with large singles/doubles for RM20/25 with fan, or RM35 to RM45 for a double with air-con.

For just a little more, the *Hotel Rakyat* (☎ 211100), in Block I of the Sinsuran Kompleks, is very good value. Rooms in this clean, friendly, Muslim-run hotel cost RM30/35 for singles/doubles with fan and bath, and RM35 up to RM55 with air-con and bath.

If the above are full, the *Central Hotel* (☎ 513522), 5 Jalan Tugu, has air-con rooms with attached bath for RM40/48. Nearby on Jalan Merdeka, you'll find the *Hotel Nam Tai* (☎ 514803). It's fairly clean and has double rooms for RM35 to RM45.

Places to Eat

KK offers some very good dining. The best night market in town is at the Sedco Kompleks. The speciality is seafood, but other dishes are also available. For hawker food, there's another night market which sets up in the evenings in the vacant lot at the southern end of the Sinsuran Kompleks.

KK's shopping malls are good hunting grounds for cheap fare. *Centre Point* has a whole collection of moderately priced eating places in the basement, serving Malay and Chinese food as well as western fast food (*Pizza Hut*, *KFC* and *Burger King*). On the 2nd floor of the Yaohan department store are some slightly expensive food stalls in squeaky-clean air-con surroundings. *Wisma Merdeka* has a small, good food centre on the 2nd floor overlooking the sea, as well as *Sate Ria* and *KFC* outlets, among others.

For Indian Muslim food, try the *New Arafat Restaurant* in Block I of the Sinsuran Kompleks. This 24 hour place is run by very friendly Indians who serve excellent curries, rotis and murtabaks.

Entertainment

If you feel like checking out what is hip in KK, try *Rocky Fun Pub*, the *LA Pub* or *Krash* (best deejays). All these places tend to be deserted before 10.30 pm. There's no cover charge, but drinks are expensive at around RM9.

Getting There & Away

Air There are regular flights to Brunei (RM117), Bintulu (RM127), Kuching (RM228), Labuan (RM52), Lahad Datu (RM106), Miri (RM82), Sandakan (RM83) and Tawau (RM96).

MAS (☎ 213555) and Philippine Airlines (☎ 239600) are in the Kompleks Karamunsing, about five minutes walk south of the Hotel Shangri-La along Jalan Tunku Abdul Rahman. On the other side of Jalan Tunku Abdul Rahman is the KWSP building, which also contains a number of airline offices, including Dragon Air (also Cathay Pacific) (☎ 254733), Royal Brunei Airlines (☎ 242193), Singapore Airlines (☎ 255444) and Thai Airways International (☎ 232896).

Bus There is no main bus station in KK. Most of the long-distance buses leave from the open area south-east of the council offices along Jalan Tunku Abdul Rahman. The large open plot of land behind the GPO is a very busy minibus park. Most buses from here are local but also go to centres around KK, such as Penampang, Papar and Tuaran.

All minibuses leave when full, and there are frequent early-morning departures. There are fewer departures later in the day, and don't count on departures for long-haul destinations in the afternoon. The general rule is travel early, and the further you travel the earlier you should leave. Some examples of minibus fares from KK are:

Beaufort (97 km), regular departures until about 5 pm, two hours on a very good road, RM5
Papar (50 km), departures until 4 pm, one hour, RM2.50

Lawas (195 km), buses depart at 7.30 am and 1.30 pm, five hours on a paved road except for the 47 km stretch between Beaufort and Sipitang, RM25 to RM30

Tuaran (35 km), departures throughout the day, 45 minutes, RM2

Kota Belud (77 km), departures until 5 pm, two hours, RM10

Kudat (190 km), departures until about 5 pm, three hours, RM12

Ranau (156 km), early morning departures, the last bus leaves at 6 pm and takes about two hours (all buses pass Kinabalu National Park), RM10

Sandakan (386 km), minibus departures early morning only, about six hours, RM35. The big air-con buses, operated by Mizume Enterprise, Lim Sim Siau and Tong Ma, depart at 7 am and are the most comfortable way to do this trip. Fares hover between RM20 and RM25, and it's advisable to book ahead. The road is sealed all the way, except where the new road is already starting to deteriorate.

Keningau (128 km), regular departures to about 1 pm, about 2½ hours on a road which is surfaced all the way, RM10

Tenom, regular departures on a good sealed road, RM25 by taxi, RM20 by minibus

For Kinabalu National Park (RM10, 1½ hours), take the minibuses for Ranau or Sandakan and get off at the park HQ, which is right by the side of the road.

Train The railway station is five km south of the city centre at Tanjung Aru, close to the airport. There are daily trains to Beaufort and Tenom at 8 and 11 am. The train takes four hours to Tenom and seven hours to Beaufort. Minibuses are quicker.

Taxi Besides the minibuses, there are share taxis to most places. They also go when full and their fares are at least 25% higher than the minibuses. Their big advantage is that they are much quicker and more comfortable.

Boat There are three daily boats to Labuan from the jetty behind the Hyatt Hotel. The *Rezeki Murni* and the *Labuan Express* leave at 8 and 10 am and 1.30 and 3 pm. The fare is RM28 in economy class and RM33 in 1st class. There's usually no need to book in advance. The *Kinabalu Express* (☎ 219810)

leaves at 8 and 10 am and 1.30 pm. Economy seats are RM28, 1st class RM32.

Getting Around
The Airport Take a 15 minute taxi ride for RM11, or a red Putatan bus for 65 sen from Jalan Tunku Abdul Rahman, and ask to be dropped at the airport.

Taxi Local taxis are plentiful in the extreme. They are not metered, so it's a matter of negotiating the fare before you set off.

AROUND KOTA KINABALU
Tunku Abdul Rahman National Park
The park has a total area of nearly 4929 hectares and is made up of the offshore islands of Gaya, Mamutik, Manukan, Sapi and Sulug. Only a short boat ride from the centre of the city, they offer some of the best beaches in Borneo, crystal-clear waters and a wealth of tropical corals and marine life.

Places to Stay & Eat Accommodation on the islands is booked through the Sabah Parks office in KK. There are expensive chalets (from RM140) at Manukan and Mamutik, but it is also possible to camp at Gaya, Sulug, Mamutik and Sapi for RM5 per person, if you bring your own tent and you apply for permission in writing from the Sabah Parks office – officially you must do this 'well in advance'.

Getting There & Away Coral Island Tours (☎ (088) 223490) have boats from behind the Hyatt Hotel to the islands at 10 am and 12.30 pm, returning at 1.30 and 3.30 pm, daily. The cost is RM16 return to any of the islands for a minimum of four people.

Sea Quest (☎ (088) 230943), B207 Wisma Merdeka, is another operator that has ferry services to Manukan, Sapi, Mamutik and Gaya for RM15, or to Police Bay for RM20.

RAFFLESIA FOREST RESERVE
The highway from Kota Kinabalu to Tambunan and the central valley region crosses the forested Crocker Range. Near the top of the range on the highway is the

Rafflesia Forest Reserve, devoted to the world's largest flower. The rafflesia is a parasitic plant that is hidden within its host, the stems of jungle vines, until it bursts into bloom and grows up to one metre in diameter.

The Rafflesia Information Centre (☎ (087) 774691), on the highway 59 km from Kota Kinabalu, has interesting displays and information devoted to the rafflesia. From the centre, trails lead into the forest where the rafflesias can be found (if any are flowering – it's a non-seasonal bloom).

Places to Stay

There is no accommodation at the reserve, but *Gunung Emas Highlands Resort* (☎ (011) 811562), Km 52 on the KK-Tambunan road, is perched on the side of the mountain only seven km from the information centre. The views are superb and the climate refreshingly mild, if not downright cold. Simple but comfortable rooms in the main building annex are RM42 per double, or there are four-bed bunk rooms at RM21 per person. On the other side of the highway and a steep climb up the mountain are the hilltop cabins built around tree trunks for RM63. The restaurant is overrun with day-trippers on weekends.

Getting There & Away

From KK take a Tambunan or Keningau minibus to the reserve or the resort for RM8. From Tambunan the cost is RM3.

TAMBUNAN

Across the Crocker Range from Penampang, Tambunan is a small agricultural service town about 81 km from KK. Tambunan can be used as a base to climb Mt Trus Madi, Sabah's second highest peak – it's a much more demanding climb than Mt Kinabalu.

Places to Stay

The *Tambunan Village Resort Centre* (☎ (087) 774076) is a mid-range resort with some basic rooms in three-bedroom chalets for RM30. A camping ground is also available for those with their own equipment – a camp site costs RM3.50. The *Government Rest House* (☎ (087) 774339) costs RM40 per person.

Getting There & Away

There are regular minibuses plying between Tambunan and KK, Ranau, Keningau and Tenom.

BEAUFORT

Beaufort is a quiet provincial town on the Padas River. Its two-storey wooden shophouses have a certain dilapidated charm, and the people go out of their way to make you feel welcome, but the only reason to come here is to catch the train to Tenom or to pass through on the way to eastern Sarawak, Brunei or Labuan.

From Beaufort you can continue on to Menumbok, where frequent ferries go to Labuan. Heading south to Lawas in Sarawak, you pass through Sipitang, which has cheap accommodation and early morning boats to Labuan and Merapok on the Sabah-Sarawak border.

Places to Stay

The three hotels in town are of the same standard and have air-con rooms with TV and attached bathrooms. They all charge RM30/36 for singles/doubles. The *Hotel Beaufort* (☎ (087) 211911) and the *Beaufort Inn* (☎ (087) 211232), 100 metres east, are near each other in town, while the *Mandarin Inn* (☎ (087) 212800) is over the bridge across the river.

Getting There & Away

Bus There are frequent minibus departures for KK (RM5, two hours), and less frequent departures for Sipitang (RM5, 1½ hours). To Menumbok (for Labuan) there are plenty of minibuses until early afternoon for RM9 (one hour).

Train It's a spectacular trip between Beaufort and Tenom, where the train follows the Padas River through steamy jungle. At times the dense jungle forms a bridge over the narrow track. The railcar is quicker and more comfortable and costs RM8.35, while the diesel train costs RM2.75. Book as soon as you arrive in Beaufort or at the Tanjong Aru

Train Departure Times

Beaufort-Tenom

Mon-Sat	8.25 am (R),	10.50 am (D),	noon (G),	1.55 pm (D),	3.50 pm (R)
Sun	6.45 am (D),	10.50 am (D),	2.30 pm (D),	4.05 pm (R)	

Tenom-Beaufort

Mon-Sat	6.40 am (R),	7.30 am (D),	8.00 am (G),	1.40 pm (D),	4.00 pm (R)
Sun	7.20 am (R),	7.55 am (D),	12.10 pm (D),	3.05 pm (D)	

R = Railcar, D = Diesel, G = Goods Train

station in KK (☎ (088) 254611). Departures are listed in the table above.

PULAU LABUAN

Off the coast from Menumbok, Labuan is the jumping-off point for Brunei. The island is a federal territory, governed directly from KL, and its main claim to fame these days is as a duty-free centre. There's very little of interest here for the traveller, and it is best avoided.

Places to Stay

Budget accommodation in Bandar Labuan is very limited. The *Pantai View Hotel* (☎ (087) 411339) on Jalan Bunga Tanjong has large RM25 fan rooms on the top floor if you can get one. Around the corner on Jalan OKK Awang Besar, *Hotel Sri Villa* (☎ (087) 416369) has large fan rooms for RM38, or you might be able to get a smaller room for RM33. The nearby *Melati Inn* (☎ (087) 416307) has small air-con rooms with common bathroom for RM35, but most rooms have attached bathroom and cost from RM45 to RM50.

Getting There & Away

Air There are flights to Kota Kinabalu (RM52), KL (RM372), Kuching (RM199) and Miri (RM66). A taxi to the airport should not cost more than RM5 from Bandar Labuan.

Boat The cheapest option is the slow car ferry to Menumbok which leaves at 8 am and 1 pm, costs RM5 for passengers and takes around 1½ hours. Three launches connect

Labuan and Kota Kinabalu. Tickets can be bought just before departure, or you can book in advance. The *Duta Muhibbah Dua* (RM28, RM33 1st class) leaves Labuan at 8.30 am, and the *Labuan Express Dua* (RM28) departs at 1 pm. These boats can be booked through Sinmatu (☎ (087) 412261) on Jalan Merdeka. *Express Kinabalu* leaves Labuan at 3 pm and can be booked at the Duta Muhibbah Agency. The fare is RM28.

TENOM

Tenom is the home of the friendly Murut people, most of whom are farmers. It's a very pleasant rural town and is also the end of the railway line from Tanjung Aru (KK).

Despite the peaceful setting, there's absolutely nothing to do in the town itself. Just outside of town, however, the **Tenom Agricultural Research Station** makes an interesting diversion, and the train trip to Beaufort is highly recommended.

Places to Stay & Eat

The *Hotel Syn Nam Tai*, on the main street, is the cheapest around with fan rooms for RM17/22. The Indian-run *Sabah Hotel* (☎ (087) 735534) is a definite step up from the Syn Nam Tai. Good, clean fan rooms cost RM22, or air-con rooms are RM37. The *Hotel Kim San* (☎ (087) 735485), set back from the main road, has run-down air-con rooms for RM28 a double.

As usual there are plenty of Chinese kedai kopis all over town selling basic Chinese food. For good Indian food, rotis and murtabak, try the *Bismillah Restaurant* in the

Sabah Hotel, or the *Restoran Istimewa*, which sets up tables outside in the evenings.

Getting There & Away

Most minibuses go to Keningau (RM5), but some also go to KK (RM25). You may as well take the train to Beaufort if you're here.

KOTA BELUD

Kota Belud is the venue of Sabah's largest and most colourful market; it takes place every Sunday – get there as early as possible. It's an easy day trip from KK.

Minibuses go to KK (RM5, two hours) and Kudat (RM5, two hours).

KUDAT

Kudat is right at the far north-eastern tip of Sabah and gets very few foreign visitors. It has a noticeable Filipino influence. The area around Kudat has fine beaches and Rungus longhouses, though it is difficult to get around without your own transport.

Places to Stay

The best buy is the *Restoran dan Hotel Islamik*. Large, clean rooms with fan cost RM15/20 for singles/doubles. All the other hotels are mid-range air-con places. The *Hotel Sunrise* (☎ (088) 613517) is of a good standard and has a few rooms for RM30 without bath, but most have bath and TV and cost from RM40 upwards.

Getting There & Away

There are twice-weekly flights to KK (RM54). Several minibuses a day make the three to four hour trip from Kota Kinabalu for RM10.

MT KINABALU

Sabah's number-one attraction is the highest mountain in South-East Asia. Mt Kinabalu towers 4101 metres above the lush tropical jungles of North Borneo, and is the centre-piece of the vast 750 sq km Kinabalu National Park. Despite its height, it is one of the easiest mountains in the world to climb, and thousands of people of all age groups and fitness levels climb the mountain every

year. All you need is a little stamina, and gear to protect you from the elements – it can get very cold and wet up there.

The climb to the top requires an overnight stop on the way, so bring plenty of warm clothes – you can hire sleeping bags. A RM10 climbing permit is required (RM2 for students). There is also an insurance fee of RM3.50. Hiring a guide is compulsory, and the guide's fee is RM25 per day for one to three people, RM28 for four to six people and RM30 for seven to eight (the maximum). Attach yourself to a group to cut down on costs.

On the first day, you get to within around 700 metres of the summit – there are numerous huts. Set off before dawn to be on the summit before mid-morning, when the clouds roll in. The trip back down to park HQ takes the rest of the day.

It's worth spending a day or so exploring the well-marked trails around the park HQ. At 11.15 am each day there is a guided walk which starts at the administration building and lasts for one to two hours – it's well worth taking.

A slide and video show is presented at the administration building from Friday to Monday at 7.30 pm. It provides an excellent introduction to the mountain.

Places to Stay & Eat

Park Headquarters Advance bookings at the Sabah Parks office in KK are essential. The cheapest places to stay are the 46 bed *Old Fellowship Hostel* and the 52 bed *New Fellowship Hostel*, which cost RM10 per person, or RM5 for anyone under 18 years of age. Both hostels are clean and comfortable, have cooking facilities and a dining area with an open fireplace. The Old Hostel tends to be less cramped.

The rest of the accommodation at park HQ is very good but expensive. The twin-bed cabins are RM50 and annexes for up to four people are RM100. On weekends and during school holidays these rates jump to RM80 and RM160 respectively. There are two-bedroom chalets which can sleep up to six people and they cost RM150 per night (RM200 at weekends/holidays).

The cheaper and more popular of the two restaurants is *Kinabalu Dalsam*, down below reception; it offers Malay, Chinese and western food at reasonable prices. There's also a small shop which sells a limited range of tinned foods, chocolate, beer, spirits, cigarettes, T-shirts, bread, eggs and margarine.

The other restaurant is in the main administration building, just past the hostels. It's more expensive than the Dalsam, but the food is very good. Both restaurants are open from 7 am to 9 pm.

On the Mountain On your way up to the summit you will have to stay overnight at one of the mountain huts at 3300 metres or the 54 bed *Laban Rata Rest House*, which costs RM25 per person in four-bed rooms. It has heating, hot water and a restaurant.

There are three huts at 3300 metres: the 12 bed *Waras* and *Panar Laban* huts, and the 44 bed *Guntin Lagadan Hut*. These cost RM10 per person, or RM5 for those under 18. They are more spartan and unheated, but a sleeping bag is provided and the huts are within walking distance of the restaurant, which is not only open for regular meals but also opens from 2 to 3 am so you can grab some breakfast before attempting the summit. The huts have cooking facilities which you can use if you bring your own food.

As far as sleep is concerned, it doesn't make much difference where you stay; you may sleep quite fitfully – the air is quite thin up there. It's *very* cold in the early mornings (around 0°C!), so take warm clothing with you.

Getting There & Away

There are several minibuses daily from KK to Ranau which depart up to about 1 pm. The 85 km trip as far as the park HQ takes about 1½ to two hours and the fare is around RM10. If you're heading back towards KK, minibuses pass the park HQ until the afternoon, but the best time to catch one is between 8 am and noon. There is a large bus to Sandakan which passes park HQ around

9 am, and there are other minibuses which pass Kinabalu National Park on their way to Ranau, but the last one goes by before 2 pm.

RANAU

Ranau is just a small provincial town halfway between Kota Kinabalu and Sandakan. Few travellers stay overnight since the big attraction is Poring Hot Springs, about 19 km north of the town.

Hotel Ranau (☎ (088) 875351) is the first place you see when entering the town opposite the petrol stations. Singles/doubles with fan cost RM30/45 and range up to RM60 with air-con, TV and bath.

Getting There & Away

Minibuses and taxis depart daily for KK up to about 4 pm, sometimes later, and cost RM10 and take about three hours. It is best to catch them in the morning, as the afternoon services are less reliable. There are large air-con buses to Sandakan (RM25, 3½ hours) from around 7.30 am until noon and they cost RM25. Minibuses go throughout the day but can take a while to fill up, especially in the afternoon.

PORING HOT SPRINGS

The Poring Hot Springs are also part of the Kinabalu National Park but are 43 km away from the park HQ and 19 km north of Ranau.

There are tubs for soaking in, walking trails for some exercise and excellent jungle canopy for a monkey's-eye view of the forest.

Places to Stay & Eat

It is essential to make advance bookings at the Sabah Parks office in KK.

The *Poring Hostel* has two units – one with 24 beds and one with 40 beds. Costs are RM10 per person (RM5 if you are under 18 years of age), and blankets and pillows are provided free of charge. There is a clean, spacious kitchen with gas cookers. A camping ground is also available for RM5 per tent, though you will have to bring your own. Pillows and blankets can be hired for

50 sen each. There are also more expensive cabins from RM60.

There are cooking facilities at Poring (bring your own supplies from Renau), or alternatively there are three inexpensive eating places right opposite the park gate.

Getting There & Away

From Renau, share taxis to Poring cost RM3 on weekends. On weekdays you may need to hitch or charter a taxi (RM15).

SANDAKAN

The former capital city of Sabah, Sandakan is today a major commercial centre where the products of the interior – rattan, timber, rubber, copra, palm oil and even birds' nests – are brought to be loaded onto boats for export.

Sandakan itself is a bit of a dump, and the real attractions lie outside the city. At **Sepilok** is one of the world's four orang-utan sanctuaries. (The others are in Sumatra, west of Medan; Semenggok, Sarawak; and Tanjung Puting National Park in Kalimantan). **Gomantong Caves**, on the other side of the bay, is another worthwhile attraction; it's here that birds' nests are collected. Offshore is one of the world's few **turtle sanctuaries**, where giant turtles come to lay their eggs.

Information

The Sabah Parks office (☎ (089) 273453) is on the 9th floor of Wisma Khoo Siak Chiew at the end of Jalan Tiga. This is where you need to come to make a reservation to visit the Turtle Islands National Park (Taman Pulau Penya).

Sandakan's area code is 089.

Places to Stay

Most travellers head straight for *Uncle Tan's* (☎ 531917), Batu 17½, Labuk Rd, 29 km from town on the main highway. All the bus drivers know this place, so ask to be dropped off there on the way into Sandakan. Coming from town, take a Labuk Rd bus going to Batu 19 or beyond for RM1.70. Tan charges RM20 for a dorm bed, which includes a huge

breakfast, and free tea and coffee throughout the day. Mountain bikes are available for RM2 per day – a good way to visit Sepilok. Uncle Tan also runs very low key and exceedingly cheap tours to both the Turtle Islands and to a jungle camp he has on the lower Kinabatangan River. He also has tours to Tanjung Aru, where you can stay in the stilt village.

The other popular travellers' haunt is the *Travellers' Rest Hostel* (☎ 216454), 2nd floor, Block E, Bandar Ramai-Ramai, over in the west of town. It's a friendly place with dorm beds at RM13 and a couple of simple doubles for RM25. Like Uncle Tan's, the Rest Hostel runs tours to the Turtle Islands and other attractions.

Borneo Bed & Breakfast (☎ 216381), 2nd floor, Lot 12, Block E, Bandar Kim Fung, Batu 4, Jalan Labuk, is around seven km from town, two blocks behind the big Capital supermarket on the main road into Sandakan. There are only three spotlessly clean, spacious rooms with fans – two with twin beds and one with a double bed – and there is a good communal area. It is good value at RM15 per person (RM20 with breakfast), or a double for a couple is RM25 (RM35 with breakfast).

All the other so-called cheap accommodation is in the centre of town and is no great bargain. The *Hotel Hung Wing* (☎ 218895) on Jalan Tiga is a mid-range hotel with a few spacious rooms with attached bathroom and fan for RM25/30. Other air-con rooms range from RM44 to RM65. Also on Jalan Tiga is the *Hotel Paris* (☎ 218488), which has clean rooms from RM25/30 with fan and bath, or RM38/48 with air-con and bath. The *Mayfair Hotel* (☎ 219855) at 24 Jalan Pryer is the best bet for an air-con room with attached bath, costing RM32/40.

Places to Eat

For good Malay food try the *Habeeb Restoran* on Jalan Pryer. It does excellent murtabak, and also has an air-con room upstairs. There are a couple of similar places close by, including the *Cita Rasa* and *Restoran Gane*.

For a western breakfast or a snack, try *Fat Cat* on Jalan Tiga. Nearby, the *Superman Ice Cream Parlour* on Jalan Tiga serves very good ice creams and juices. There is a *KFC* on the opposite corner. Another possibility is the *Apple Fast Food* restaurant on the ground floor of the Hotel Nak on Jalan Edinburgh.

Getting There & Away
Air There are flights to KK (RM83), Kudat (RM54), Lahad Datu (RM48), Semporna (RM50) and Tawau (RM83).

Bus The long-distance bus station is opposite the community centre, out towards the post office. Buses to KK cost RM35, though price wars have seen tickets drop to as low as RM20. Most buses leave at 6.30 and 7 am and take around six hours. The last buses to KK usually leave around 10 or 11 am. There are also buses to Kinabalu National Park HQ for RM25. Minibuses to Ranau cost RM20 and the journey takes about four hours.

There are many minibuses which depart throughout the morning for Lahad Datu, some going on to Tawau. The trip to Lahad Datu takes about three hours and costs RM15. Occasional minibuses also go all the way to Keningau for RM35.

Getting Around
If you're arriving or leaving by air, the airport is about 11 km from the city. A taxi costs RM15. The Batu 7 airport bus runs by the airport, stopping on the main road about 500 metres from the terminal. The fare to/from the city centre is 70 sen.

SEPILOK ORANG-UTAN REHABILITATION CENTRE
Sepilok is one of only four orang-utan sanctuaries in the world, and is one of Sabah's major tourist attractions. The apes are brought here to be rehabilitated to forest life. About 20 still return regularly to be fed. It's unlikely you'll see anywhere near this number at feeding time – three or four is a more likely number.

The apes are fed from two platforms, one in the middle of the forest about 30 minutes

walk from the centre (platform B), and the other close to the HQ (platform A). The latter platform is for the juvenile orang-utans, which are fed daily, usually at 10 am and 2 pm. At platform B the adolescent apes which have been returned to the forest are fed daily at 11 am. For this feeding the rangers leave from outside the Nature Education Centre at 10.30 am daily.

In addition to the orang-utans, there are a couple of Sumatran rhinos and other animals at the centre, as well as some fine walks through the forest. Visiting hours at the centre are Saturday to Thursday from 9 am to noon and 2 to 4 pm; and Friday from 9 to 11.30 am and 2 to 4 pm. To see all the programme, you should arrive at 9 am or 2 pm. Admission is RM10 (RM1 for Malaysians).

Getting There & Away Sepilok is 25 km from central Sandakan. Take the blue Labuk bus marked 'Sepilok Batu 14' from the local bus stand next to the central market on the waterfront (RM1.50, 45 minutes).

TURTLE ISLANDS NATIONAL PARK
The Pulau Penyu National Park comprises three small islands which lie 40 km north of Sandakan. Pulau Selingan, Pulau Bakungan Kecil and Pulau Gulisan are visited by marine turtles which come ashore to lay their eggs, mainly between the months of August and October.

Places to Stay
It's not possible to visit the Turtle Islands on a day trip, so any excursion involves staying overnight. The only accommodation is at the *Sabah Parks Chalet* on Pulau Selingan, which costs RM30 per person per night or RM150 for a two person chalet. Bookings must be made in advance at the Sabah Parks office (☎ (089) 273453) in Sandakan as facilities are limited and tour companies often take bulk bookings. Uncle Tan provides all-inclusive tours to the Turtle Islands for RM180. (See the Sandakan section above for more information.) Accommodation is provided at nearby Pulau Libaran.

Getting There & Away

The Sabah Parks office can arrange transport to the islands and will try to put individuals in with a group. The cost is around RM85 per person. If you have to charter a boat, expect to pay RM350 or more for the return journey. Uncle Tan in Sandakan organises trips out to the islands, and his trips are about as cheap as they come.

KINABATANGAN RIVER

The Kinabatangan River is the largest river in Sabah and flows east from the ranges on the western side of the state and then northeast to enter the sea east of Sandakan. Although logging is widespread along the upper reaches of the river, downriver from the Sandakan-Lahad Datu road some primary forest remains and the forest is home to high concentrations of wildlife. It is an ideal place to observe the wildlife of Borneo, and sightings of the native proboscis monkeys are common along the banks in the morning and evening. Orang-utans and gibbons are also seen from time to time.

This area is virtually inaccessible, but Uncle Tan (see the Sandakan section) has a jungle camp about an hour downstream from the Sandakan-Lahad Datu road, and while it is extremely basic, it does give travellers an opportunity to get out of the towns and stay in the jungle. Tan charges RM15 per person per day for accommodation and meals. Transport there is by bus to where the highway crosses the river, and then by boat to the camp. The charge is RM130 for transport, so obviously it's better if you stay a few days. It's a very popular trip.

LAHAD DATU

Lahad Datu is a plantation and timber service town of 20,000 people. It was once a staging post for the Danum Valley, but now that an expensive resort is the only accommodation in the valley very few individual travellers pass this way. There are frequent minibus departures from Sandakan to Lahad Datu (RM15, 3½ hours).

DANUM VALLEY CONSERVATION AREA

Located on the Segama River 85 km west of Lahad Datu, the Danum Valley Conservation Area was established by the Sabah Foundation and a number of private companies to allow research, education and recreation in untouched rainforest. Unfortunately for budget travellers, accommodation at Danum Valley is only provided by the *Borneo Rainforest Lodge*, where rates start at RM350 for one night. With over 50 km of walking trails in the conservation area, day trips are not really worth the effort.

SEMPORNA

Semporna, between Lahad Datu and Tawau, has a large **stilt village** and a **cultured pearl farm** off the coast. It is rarely visited by individual travellers, however. Most foreigners who pass through Semporna are en route to or from **Sipadan Island**, renowned for its superb diving. Accommodation on the island is provided by expensive resorts.

Places to Stay & Eat

The main hotel in Semporna is the *Dragon Inn Hotel* (☎ (089) 781088), built in traditional floating-village style over the water. The bamboo and thatch rooms cost from RM68/78 for a room with bath, air-con and TV. In town, the *Hotel Semporna* (☎ (089) 781378) is cheaper but poor value. Air-con rooms cost RM45 with shared bathroom, or RM55 with attached bathroom.

Getting There & Away

There are plenty of minibuses between Semporna and Lahad Datu (RM8, 2½ hours, 160 km) and Tawau (RM4, 1½ hours, 110 km). There are also taxis to Tawau for RM10.

TAWAU

A mini-boomtown on the very south-east corner of Sabah close to the Indonesian border, Tawau is a provincial capital and a centre for export of the products of the interior – timber, rubber, manila hemp, cocoa, copra and tobacco. There is virtually nothing of interest in town, and it is generally only visited by travellers en route to or from Tarakan in Kalimantan.

Information

The MAS office (☎ 765533) is in the Wisma SASCO, close to the centre of town. Bouraq, the Indonesian feeder airline, uses Merdeka Travel (☎ 771927) at 41 Jalan Dunlop as its agent. The Indonesian consulate (☎ 772052) is on Jalan Apas, some distance from the centre on the main road coming into town.

Tawau's area code is 089.

Places to Stay

For rock-bottom accommodation, Tawau has a couple of very basic lodging houses, but they are not recommended for women travellers. The cheapest is the *Penginapan Kinabalu Lodging House*, with basic rooms for RM15/20 with a bit of bargaining. The *Hotel Malaysia* is similar and bare, but clean rooms with fan cost RM20 and air-con rooms cost RM30.

Much better is the very clean, well-run *Hotel Soon Yee* (☎ 772447). A fan room costs RM20, and air-con rooms with bath start at RM30. The *Loong Hotel* (☎ 765308), 3868 Jalan Wing Lok, is the best bet for good mid-range facilities. Spotlessly clean air-con singles/doubles with attached bathroom and TV are RM35/45.

The *Hotel Tawau* (☎ 771100) at 73 Jalan Chester has basic fan rooms for RM27 or air-con rooms with attached bath for RM38.50/47.50, but the Loong is better. The *Oriental Hotel* (☎ 761601) has large but scruffy rooms for RM37/45.

Places to Eat

For good Malay food try the *Restoran Sinar Murni* – the chicken curry here is good. For hawker food, there are stalls in the market. Next to the Mosque on Jalan Clinic is a lively area of hawker stalls with inexpensive Indonesian and Malay favourites. For Indian food, the *Restoran Yasin* does good murtabak and curries. *Buddy's Family Restaurant* is the place for western fast food. There are also a couple of branches of *Sugar Bun* and a branch of *KFC* around town.

Getting There & Away

Air MAS has flights between Tawau and Kota Kinabalu (RM96), Sandakan (RM83), Lahad Datu (RM40) and Semporna (RM40).

See the Getting There & Away section at the beginning of this chapter for details of flights to Indonesia.

Bus There are frequent minibuses to Semporna (RM4, 1½ hours). Land Cruisers leave through the morning for Sandakan and cost RM25.

Boat See the Getting There & Away section at the beginning of this chapter for details of boats to Indonesia.

Myanmar

Myanmar, formerly Burma, is one of the world's least western-influenced countries. For the visitor, Myanmar is an enthralling glimpse of a culturally unique country which exists in a social, political and economic time warp. Virtually sealed off from the outside world since 1962, when a dictatorial military regime took control of the government and economy, the country has recently come under increasing international scrutiny following an incremental opening to tourism in the early 90s.

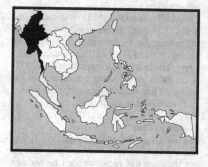

Should You Visit Myanmar?

SLORC (State Law & Order Restoration Council), the latest name for the military junta that has run Myanmar since 1962, is abominable. As a ruling group, it is continuing a tradition that has existed in Myanmar for centuries. Most Burmese monarchs, up to and including the last, King Thibaw, came to power by killing off all persons with claims to the throne. In many regards, Myanmar is still a hundred years behind the rest of South-East Asia. Corvée – involuntary civilian service to the state – was practised in Thailand, Laos, Vietnam and Cambodia until early this century. It is still practised in Myanmar.

Some groups urge non-Burmese not to visit Myanmar, believing that tourism contributes to government repression in Myanmar. Others believe that international visitation helps educate the world as to what's really going on in the country, filling in the gaps left by narrowly focused refugee and activist reports. Almost no one in the international community – certainly not in the international media – seemed to care about what had been going on in Myanmar for the last 35 years until the country began opening up to investment and tourism in 1989.

The National Coalition Government of the Union of Burma, formed by refugee MPs who were elected in 1990 but who weren't permitted to take office, has advised: 'Tourists should not engage in activities that will only benefit SLORC's coffers and not the people of Burma. However, responsible individuals and organisations who wish to verify the facts and to publicise the plight of the Burmese people are encouraged to utilise SLORC's more relaxed tourist policies.' National League for Democracy (NLD) spokesperson Aung San Suu Kyi urged outsiders to boycott Myanmar during Visit Myanmar Year 1996, but stopped short of saying they should never visit as long as the military is still in control.

Anyone contemplating a visit to Myanmar should bear in mind that any contribution they make to the nation's economy may allow Myanmar's repressive government to stay in power that little bit longer. On the other hand, many good-hearted Burmese citizens eke out a living from tourism, however small-scale, and a reduction in tourism automatically means a reduction in local opportunities to earn hard currency. Since the package-tour requirement has been waived, many Burmese citizens believe the potential for ordinary people to benefit from tourist visitation has only increased. Many also believe that keeping the Burmese isolated from international witnesses to the internal oppression may also help cement SLORC's fear-driven control over the people and seal

Myanmar off from the outside world. This is why the government restricts tourism in the first place. Our editorial bias is that if people decide to visit Myanmar to see for themselves, and to support non-government-sponsored tourism, that they'll go with as much advance information as possible. It's your choice!

Facts about Myanmar

HISTORY

The Mon were the first people known to have lived in the area and their influence extended into what is now Thailand. The Mon were pushed back when the Burmans, who now comprise two-thirds of the total population, began arriving from the Tibetan Plateau to the north around the 9th century.

King Anawrahta took the throne of Bagan in 1044 and, with his conquest of the kingdom of Thaton in 1057, inaugurated what many consider to be the golden age of Myanmar's history. The spoils he brought back took Bagan to fabled heights; he also made Theravada Buddhism the state religion and sponsored the establishment of the Burmese alphabet. Today, Myanmar is 90% Buddhist, although belief in *nats*, or animal spirits, still persists.

Despite Anawrahta's efforts, Myanmar entered a period of decline in the 13th century, helped on its way by the vast amounts of money and effort squandered on making Bagan an incredible monument to human vanity. Kublai Khan hastened the decline by ransacking Bagan in 1287, at that time said to contain 13,000 pagodas. In the following centuries, the pattern of Burmese history was basically one of conflict with kingdoms in neighbouring Siam and a series of petty tribal wars.

The coming of Europeans to the east had little influence on the Burmese, who were too busy fighting to be interested in trade. Unfortunately for the Burmese, their squabbles eventually encroached on the Raj in neighbouring Bengal and the British moved in to keep their borders quiet. In three moves (1824, 1852 and 1883) the British took over all of Myanmar. They built railroads, made Myanmar the world's greatest rice exporter and developed large teak markets. Less commendably, they brought in large numbers of Chinese and Indians who exploited the less commercially minded Burmese.

As in other South-East Asian countries, WWII was at first seen as a chance of liberation, an idea which the Japanese, as in Indonesia, soon dispelled. The wartime group of Thirty Comrades was able to form a government after the war, with Aung San as their leader. In 1947 he was assassinated with most of his cabinet. Independence came in 1948 but the uniting of Myanmar proved difficult and ongoing confrontation with breakaway tribes and Communist rebels takes place to this day.

U Nu led the country during the early years of independence, attempting to establish a Buddhist socialism whose objective was 'Social Nibbana'. In 1962 General Ne Win led a left-wing army takeover. After throwing out U Nu's government and imprisoning U Nu for four years, Ne Win set the country on the 'Burmese Way to Socialism'. The path was all downhill. He nationalised everything in sight, including retail shops, and quickly crippled the country economically. The Burmese saw their naturally well-endowed economy stumble as exports of everything plummeted.

Myanmar's crumbling economy reached a virtual standstill when, in 1987 and 1988, after a long period of suffering, the Burmese people had had enough of their incompetent, arrogant government. They packed the streets in huge demonstrations, insisting that Ne Win had to go. He finally did go in July 1988 but in the following month massive confrontations between pro-democracy demonstrators and the military contributed to an estimated 3000 deaths over a six week period.

Ne Win's National Unity Party (formerly the Burmese Socialist Programme Party) was far from ready to give up control and the public protests continued as two wholly

MYANMAR

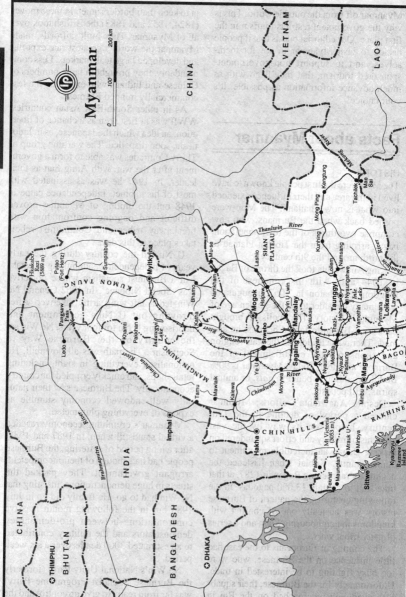

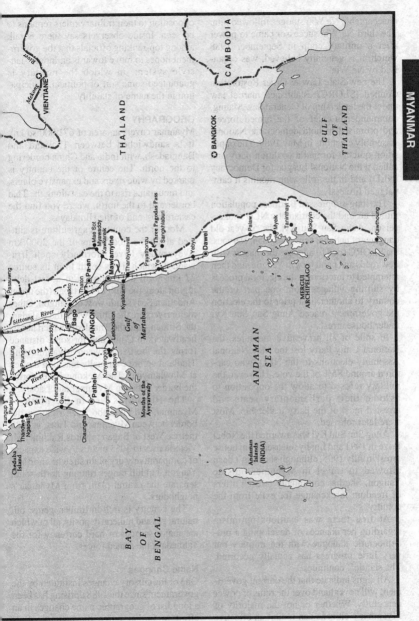

unacceptable Ne Win stooges followed him. The third Ne Win successor came to power after a military coup in September 1988 which, it is generally believed, was organised by Ne Win.

The new State Law & Order Restoration Council (SLORC) established martial law under the leadership of General Saw Maung, commander-in-chief of the armed forces, and promised to hold democratic National Assembly elections in May 1989. The opposition quickly formed a coalition party and called it the National League for Democracy (NLD) and in the following months it campaigned tirelessly.

The long-suppressed Burmese population rallied around the charismatic NLD spokesperson, Aung San Suu Kyi, the 51-year-old daughter of national hero Aung San. Nervous, the SLORC tried to appease the masses with new roads and paint jobs in Yangon, and then attempted to interfere in the electoral process by shifting villages from one part of the country to another. Just prior to the election the government placed Aung San Suu Kyi under house arrest.

In spite of all preventive measures, the National Unity Party lost the May National Assembly elections to the NLD, who captured around 85% of the vote. However, the military refused to allow the opposition to assume their parliamentary seats and arrested most of the party leadership. Most were later released.

Aung San Suu Kyi was awarded the Nobel Prize in 1991 and finally released from house arrest in July 1995, although she hasn't been allowed to travel in Myanmar outside Yangon. She has continually refused offers of freedom in exchange for exile from the country.

At first there was cautious optimism regarding her chances of developing a pro-democratic dialogue with the military but very little progress has actually occurred. The standoff continues.

All signs indicate that the current government will never hand over the reins of power peacefully. Whether or not the majority of Myanmar's citizens can mount an effective opposition to their military rulers remains to be seen. Inside observers say there is talk among top-ranking officials that the government hopes to move towards an Indonesian-style system, in which the military is guaranteed some sort of political participation in the name of stability.

GEOGRAPHY

Myanmar covers an area of 671,000 sq km. It is sandwiched between Thailand and Bangladesh, with India and China bordering to the north. The centre of the country is marked by wide rivers and expansive plains, and mountains rise to the east along the Thai border and to the north, where you find the easternmost end of the Himalayas.

Most of the country's agriculture is situated along the floodplains of the 2000 km Ayeyarwady River (formerly spelt Irrawaddy), which flows south from its source 27 km north of Myitkyina to a vast delta region along the Gulf of Martaban (the upper Andaman Sea) south-west of Yangon. Other major rivers are the Chindwinn, the Kaladan, the Sittoung and the Thanlwin, which has its headwaters in China and for some distance forms the border between Myanmar and Thailand before eventually reaching the sea at Mawlamyine. The Mekong River forms the border between Myanmar and Laos.

The Himalayas rise in the north of Myanmar, and Hkakabo Razi, right on the border between Myanmar and Tibet, is 5889 metres. West of Bagan towards Rakhine, Mt Victoria rises to 3053 metres. A wide expanse of comparatively dry plain stretches north of Yangon, but hill ranges running north-south separate the central plain from Myanmar's neighbours.

The country is rich in timber, gems, oil, natural gas and mineral deposits, all of which are major sources of hard currency for the Tatmadaw, the armed forces.

Name Changes

One of the cursory changes instituted by the government since the 1988 uprising has been a long list of geographic name changes in an effort to further purge the country of its colonial past. The official name of the country has been changed from the Socialist Republic of the Union of Burma to the Union of Myanmar.

According to the government, 'Myanmar' avoids national identification with the Burman ethnic group; 'Burma' is an English corruption of 'Bamar', the Burmese term for that ethnic group. 'Myanmar' has in fact been the official Burmese name for the country since at least the time of Marco Polo's 13th century writings.

In most of the name changes, the new Romanised versions bring the names phonetically closer to the everyday Burmese pronunciation. The 'r' at the end of 'Myanmar' is merely a British English device used to lengthen the preceding 'a' vowel; it is not pronounced. State enterprises that use 'Myanmar' in their titles typically spell the word without an 'r', eg Myanma Airways, Myanma Five Star Line, Myanma Timber Enterprise and so on.

Old Name	New Name
Burma	Myanmar
Rangoon	Yangon
Akyab	Sittwe
Amherst	Kyaikkami
Arakan	Rakhine
Bassein	Pathein
Kengtung	Kyaingtong
Magway	Magwe
Mandalay	no change
Maymyo	Pyin U Lwin
Mergui	Myeik or Beik
Moulmein	Mawlamyine
Myohaung	Mrauk U
Pagan	Bagan
Pegu	Bago
Prome	Pyi, *or more commonly* Pyay
Syriam	Thanlyin
Taunggyi	no change
Tavoy	Dawei
Yaunghwe	Nyaungshwe
Irrawaddy River	Ayeyarwady River
Chindwin River	Chindwinn River
Salween River	Thanlwin River
Sittang River	Sittoung River

CLIMATE

The rainy season lasts from mid-May until mid-October. For the next few months, the weather is quite reasonable. In fact, it is actually cool in Mandalay at night and near freezing in Kalaw. From mid-February, it gets increasingly hot until the rains arrive once more. The Burmese New Year in April, at the peak of the hot season, means much fun and throwing water at all concerned. November to February are the best months to visit.

See the Yangon climate chart in the Appendix.

ECOLOGY & ENVIRONMENT

From the snowcapped Himalayas in the north to the coral-fringed Mergui Archipelago in the south, Myanmar's 2000 km length crosses three distinct ecological regions: the Indian subregion along the Bangladesh and India borders; the Indochinese subregion in the north bordering Laos and China; and the Sundaic subregion bordering peninsular Thailand. Together these regions produce what is quite likely the richest biodiversity in South-East Asia.

Very little natural history research has been carried out in Myanmar due to the country's self-imposed isolation from the academic world since independence. Myanmar claims to have three national parks and 17 wildlife sanctuaries (including two marine and three wetland environments) which together protect about 1% of the nation's total land surface. Compared with international averages, this is a very low coverage (Thailand, by comparison, has 12% coverage); the government reports plans to raise protection to 5% by the end of the century.

At the moment, deforestation by the timber industry poses the greatest threat to wildlife habitats. The state-owned Myanma Timber Enterprise accounts for most of the logging undertaken throughout the country. The latest government plan calls for the complete elimination of all log exports, figuring that the greatest potential revenue comes from processed wood products rather than raw timber. If this plan is carried out, cutting should slow even further. Unfortunately illegal logging in areas of the country controlled by insurgent armies – particularly in the Shan and Kayin states – is not controlled.

These areas – rather than the MTE – are the greatest source of timber smuggled to neighbouring countries.

Wildlife laws are seldom enforced due to corruption and a general lack of manpower. While many animals are hunted for food, tigers and rhinos are killed for the lucrative overseas Chinese pharmaceutical market. Among the Chinese, the ingestion of tiger penis and bone are thought to have curative effects. Taipei, where at least two-thirds of the pharmacies deal in tiger parts (in spite of the fact that such trade is contrary to Taiwanese law) is the world centre for Burmese tiger consumption.

Marine resources are threatened by a lack of long-range conservation goals. For the moment, Myanmar's lack of industrialisation means the release of pollutants into the seas is relatively low. But overfishing, especially in the delta regions, is a growing problem.

FLORA & FAUNA

As in the rest of tropical Asia, most indigenous vegetation in Myanmar is associated with two basic types of tropical forest: monsoon forest (with a distinctive dry season of three months or more) and rainforest (where rain falls more than nine months per year). There is much overlap of the two – some forest zones support a mix of monsoon forest and rainforest vegetation.

In the mountainous Himalayan region above the Tropic of Cancer, Myanmar's flora is characterised by subtropical broadleaf evergreen forest up to 2000 metres; temperate semi-deciduous broadleaf rainforest from 2000 to 3000 metres; and evergreen coniferous and subalpine snow forest passing into alpine scrub above 3000 metres.

The country's most famous flora includes an incredible array of fruit trees, over 25,000 flowering species, a variety of tropical hardwoods and bamboo. Myanmar may possibly contain more species of bamboo than any country outside China. Cane and rattan are also plentiful.

According to the UN's World Development Report, Myanmar currently boasts natural forest cover of 43%, and is ranked 33 among the top 100 countries. It also holds 75% of the world's teak reserves; teak is one of Myanmar's most important exports, for which the biggest consumers are (in descending order) Hong Kong, Singapore, Thailand and India.

When Marco Polo visited Myanmar in the 13th century, he described 'vast jungles teeming with elephants, unicorns and other wild beasts'. Though Myanmar's natural biodiversity has no doubt altered considerably since that time, it's difficult to say just how much because of the lack of scientific data available. Myanmar is rich in bird life, with an estimated 1000 resident and migrating species. Coastal and inland waterways of the delta and the southern peninsula are especially important habitats for South-East Asian waterfowl.

Distinctive mammals of renown – found in dwindling numbers within the more heavily forested areas of Myanmar – include the leopard, jungle cat, fishing cat, civet, Indian mongoose, crab-eating mongoose, Himalayan bear, Asiatic black bear, Malayan sun bear, gaur (Indian bison), banteng, serow (an Asiatic mountain goat), wild boar, sambar deer, barking deer, mouse deer, tapir, pangolin, gibbon, macaque, dolphin and dugong (sea cow). An estimated 2000 tigers are thought to inhabit the primary forests, about four times as many as in neighbouring Thailand. Around 10,000 Asiatic elephants are widely distributed in Myanmar.

Both the lesser one-horned ('Javan') rhinoceros and the Asiatic two-horned ('Sumatran') rhinoceros are believed to survive in very small numbers near the Thai border in the Kayin State. The rare red panda (or cat bear) was last sighted in northern Myanmar in the early 1960s but is still thought to live in the Kachin State forests above 2000 metres.

GOVERNMENT & POLITICS

The Tatmadaw and their political junta, the SLORC, currently rule Myanmar with an iron fist. The only political party with any actual power is Ne Win's National Unity Party.

Burmese citizens have relative economic freedom in all but state-owned trade spheres (naturally these are the big ones, like timber and oil), but their political freedom is strictly curtailed by continued martial law.

Peaceful political assembly is banned and citizens are forbidden to discuss politics with foreigners – though many relish doing so as long as they know potential informers aren't listening. All government workers in Myanmar, regardless of level and status of their occupation, must sign a pledge not to discuss the government among themselves or they risk losing their jobs.

The opposition movement that began in 1988 appears to be quelled now, with the SLORC firmly in control. Amnesty International and UN human rights reports state that the junta has effectively silenced the democracy movement through the systematic use of terror and torture.

The streets in Yangon are festooned with huge red banners bearing slogans: 'Crush All Destructive Elements', 'The Strength of the Nation Lies Only Within', 'Only When There Is Discipline Will There Be Progress' and 'Down With Minions of Colonialism'.

Weekly gatherings at Aung San Suu Kyi's Yangon home, where she speaks to the crowd on the importance of persevering towards democracy, are still well attended, but who knows when there will be another government crackdown.

ECONOMY

In the 1980s, Myanmar was one of the 10 poorest countries in the world. Beginning with the left-wing military takeover in 1962, consumer goods just fell apart, went out of stock or simply became unusable. The official economy went nowhere – though a secondary, black-market economy flourished – until the state finally relinquished control of all industry in 1989. Now everything is available – at a price.

The new open-door economic policy, launched in 1989 to attract foreign investment, has had some success, despite the fact that few investors have been willing to risk their cash while the political situation remains so volatile. Much of the profit the nation takes in is absorbed by the Tatmadaw, which directs all foreign trade in timber, gems, fisheries and oil (the main money-makers), though there is a small but growing middle class in urban areas. Tourism is the only potentially large-scale industry to which ordinary Burmese have access, and the only locally based economic activity besides smuggling that offers them an opportunity to earn hard currency. This is cruelly ironic considering the calls for travel boycotts, which will impact the generals least and the common people the most. Meanwhile Tatmadaw officers live in colonial-style villas in Yangon's best suburbs and are chauffeured about in the latest model Japanese cars. Most conduct multiple business affairs that will ensure their comfortable retirement.

As of 1996 the economy was growing at a rate of 6.5% per year, the highest since before Ne Win took power in the early 1960s. Myanmar now ranks sixth in world rice exports. According to UN statistics, processing and manufacturing have tripled over the last eight years and provide more of the country's GDP than agriculture. Nominal per capita income is US$890, but when adjusted for purchasing power parity amounts to US$676, still the lowest in Asia. Inflation runs at an estimated 30% per annum when adjusted for dollar usage and purchasing power parity (more like 50% if judged by a kyat index alone). For the majority of Myanmar's citizens who don't have access to hard currency, life is still very tough.

Tourism

Tourism, an obvious source of hard currency, was brought to a halt following the 1988 uprising but it is steadily building up again with the new visa regulations and expanding tourist infrastructure. In 1994-95 – the last interval for which statistics were available – around 60,000 foreign visitors came to Myanmar. Yearly receipts earned via tourism so far amount to less than US$1 million, most of which is thought to be spent by business travellers.

During 'Visit Myanmar Year 1996' – which officially runs from October 1996 to October 1997 – the national tourist industry hopes to see a half million visitors. This figure is absurdly unrealistic given the deficiency of the accommodation and transport infrastructure, Myanmar's lack of promotion outside the country and the country's poor human rights image. Observers estimate arrivals won't exceed 160,000 to 200,000 per annum by the end of 1997.

POPULATION & PEOPLE

No reasonably accurate census has been taken since the colonial era but the generally recognised population estimate as of 1996 is 46 million, with an annual growth rate of 2.1%. The population is made up of several racial groupings indigenous to Myanmar, including the Bamar (Burman, around 65%), Shan (10%), Kayin (Karen, 7%), Mon (less than 3%), Kachin (less than 3%), Chin (less than 3%), Kayah (less than 2%) and Rakhine (Arakanese, less than 2%). There are still quite a few Indians and Chinese in Myanmar, but not many other foreigners or immigrants.

The largest cities, in declining order, are Yangon, Mandalay, Pathein, Mawlamyine, Taunggyi and Sittwe.

ARTS

Burmese fine art, at the court level, has not had an easy time since the collapse of the last kingdom – architecture and art were both royal activities which, without royal support, have floundered and faded. On the other hand, at the street level, Burmese culture is vibrant and thriving.

Pwe

Popular drama, one of the keys to understanding modern Burmese culture, is accessible and enjoyable for visitors. The *pwe* (show) is the everyday Burmese theatre; a religious festival, wedding, funeral, celebration, fair, sporting event – almost anything can be a good reason for a pwe. Once under way, a pwe traditionally goes on all night, which is no strain – if the audience gets bored at some point during the performance, they

simply fall asleep and wake up when something more to their taste is on.

Myanmar's truly indigenous dance forms are those that pay homage to the *nats* or members of the spirit world. In special *nat pwes*, one or more nat is invited to possess the body and mind of a medium; sometimes members of the audience are possessed instead, an event greatly feared by most Burmese. Nat dancing styles are very fluid and adaptable, and are handed down from older pwe dancers to their offspring or apprentices.

Marionette Theatre

Yok-thei pwe, or Burmese marionette theatre, presents colourful puppets up to a metre high in a spectacle that many aesthetes consider the most expressive of all the Burmese arts. Developed during the reign of King Bagyidaw in the Konbaung period, it was so influential that it became the forerunner to classical dance as later performed by actors rather than marionettes. The genre's 'golden age' began with the Mandalay kingdoms of the late 18th century and ran through the advent of cinema in the 1930s. Marionette theatre declined following WWII and is now mostly confined to tourist venues in Mandalay and Bagan. Rather less frequently it appears at pwes sponsored by wealthy patrons.

Burmese Music

Traditional Burmese music is primarily two-dimensional in the sense that rhythm and melody provide much of the musical structure, while repetition is a key element in developing this structure. There is also a significant amount of improvisation in live performance, an element traditional Burmese music shares with jazz.

The original inspiration for much of Myanmar's current musical tradition came from Siam after the second conquest of Siam in 1767 when Siamese court musicians, dancers and entertainers from Ayuthaya were brought to Myanmar by the hundreds in order to effect 'cultural augmentation'.

The *saing waing* ensemble accompanies classical dance-dramas which enact scenes from the jatakas or from the Indian epic *Ramayana*. Musical instruments are predominantly percussive, but even the circle of tuned drums, or *pat waing*, may carry the melody. In addition to the pat waing, the traditional Burmese ensemble of seven to 10 musicians will usually play: the *kyaynaung*, a circle of tuned brass gongs; the *saung kauk*, a boat-shaped harp with 13 strings; the *pattala*, a sort of xylophone; the *hne*, an oboe-type instrument related to the Indian shanai; the *palwe*, a bamboo flute; the *michaung*, or crocodile lute; the *patma*, a bass drum; and the *yagwin* (small cymbals) and *wa-let-khoke* (bamboo clappers), which are purely rhythmic in nature and are often played by Burmese vocalists. It is also not uncommon to see a violin or two in a saing, and even the dobro (an American acoustic slide guitar played on the lap) is occasionally used.

Older still is an enchanting vocal folk music tradition still heard in rural areas where the Burmese may sing without instrumental accompaniment while working.

Via radio and cassette tapes, Myanmar's urban ears are fed by a huge pop music industry based in Yangon. Younger Burmese listen to heavily western-influenced sounds – the pervasive power of rock music has even penetrated the SLORC prohibition on western music (except for lyrics, which must always be sung in Burmese). Burmese heavy metal groups with names like Iron Cross, Wild Ones and Emperor have become very successful in recent years.

Art & Architecture

Early Burmese art was always a part of religious architecture – paintings were something you did on the walls of temples, sculpture something to be placed inside them. Since the decline of temple-building, the old painting skills have considerably deteriorated. Modern Burmese paintings in western style reflect only a pale shadow of the former skill and the one painter of any renown, U Ba Kyi, paints murals and canvases commissioned for hotels and government offices.

Burmese woodcarving was mainly reserved for royal palaces, which were always made of timber and were showpieces for the skilful woodcarver. When royal palaces ceased to be built, the woodcarving skills rapidly declined although the new construction boom has brought about a small but growing woodcarving renaissance – again mostly seen in hotels.

Remarkably little research has been carried out on the topic of Burmese religious sculpture other than that from the Bagan and Mandalay eras. A rich Buddhist sculptural tradition in wood, bronze, stone and marble existed among the Shan, Mon and Rakhine peoples, but these have received short shrift from both Burman and foreign scholars. Even Burman sculpture is hard to come by in the country.

It is in architecture that one sees the strongest evidence of Burmese artistic skill and accomplishment. Myanmar is a country of stupas, or Buddhist reliquaries, often called 'pagodas' in English. The Burmese seem unable to see a hilltop without wanting to put a religious monument on top of it. Wherever you are – boating down the river, driving through the hills, even flying above the plains – there always seems to be a stupa in view. It is in Bagan that you see the most dramatic results of this national enthusiasm for religious monuments; for over two centuries a massive construction programme here resulted in thousands of shrines, stupas, monasteries and other sacred buildings.

Paya *Paya* (pa-YAH), the most common Burmese equivalent to the often misleading English term 'pagoda', literally means 'holy one' and can refer to people, deities and places associated with religion. For the most part it's a generic term for what students of Hindu-Buddhist architecture call a 'stupa'. There are basically two kinds of payas: the solid, bell-shaped *zedi* and the hollow square or rectangular *pahto*. A zedi, or stupa, is usually thought to contain 'relics' – either objects taken from the Buddha himself (especially pieces of bone, teeth or hair) or certain holy materials such as Buddha images and other religious objects blessed by a famous *sayadaw* (Burmese Buddhist master). The relics are usually placed inside a *tabena*, or relic chamber, embedded deep in the centre of the zedi. Both zedis and pahtos are often associated with Buddhist monasteries, or *kyaung*.

Payas function basically as a focus for meditation or contemplation. In the case of solid payas (zedis), if there is a need for some sheltered gathering place or a place to house images or other paraphernalia, then this will usually be an ancillary to the paya. There may be small shrines, pavilions, covered walkways or other such places all around a major paya. These are often more heavily ornamented than the zedis themselves.

SOCIETY & CONDUCT

The social ideal for most Burmese citizens – no matter what their ethnic background may be – is a standard of behaviour commonly termed *bamahsan chin*, or 'Burmese-ness'. The hallmarks of bamahsan chin include showing respect for elders; acquaintance with Buddhist scriptures (and the ability to recite at least a few classic verses); the ability to speak idiomatic Burmese; showing discretion in behaviour towards the opposite sex; dressing modestly; and most importantly exhibiting modes of expression and comportment that value the quiet, subtle and indirect rather than the loud, obvious and direct.

Dos & Don'ts

Myanmar is a land of temples, and your visit can begin to feel like a procession from one of them to another. One should dress neatly (no shorts or sleeveless shirts) when visiting religious sites. The Burmese are insistent that you barefoot it in the temple precincts, and that includes the steps from the very bottom of Mandalay Hill, the shop-lined arcades to the Shwedagon Paya and even the ruins of Bagan. Carry your shoes and socks with you.

As elsewhere in Asia it is unseemly to show too much emotion – losing your temper

over problems and delays gets you nowhere, it just amazes people. Stay calm and collected at all times. The Burmese frown on such displays of anger just as much as they frown on too open a display of affection.

As in other Buddhist countries the head is the highest part of the body – spiritually as well as literally. You should never deliberately touch somebody else on the head or pat a child on the head. Equally, the feet are the lowest part of the body – don't point your feet at anyone.

Buddha images are sacred objects, so don't pose in front of them for pictures and definitely do not climb onto them.

Monks are not supposed to touch or be touched by women. If a woman wants to hand something to a monk, the object should be placed within reach of the monk, not handed directly to him.

RELIGION

Around 87% of Myanmar's citizens are Theravada Buddhists, but there is also a strong belief in nats, the animist spirits of the land, and many of the hill tribes are Christian.

Buddhism

For the average Burmese Buddhist everything revolves around the 'merit' (*kutho*, from the Pali *kusala*, or 'wholesome') one is able to accumulate through rituals and good deeds. One of the more typical rituals performed by individuals visiting a stupa is to pour water over the Buddha image at their astrological post (determined by the day of the week they were born) – one glassful for every year of their current age plus one extra to ensure a long life. Asked what they want in their next life, most Burmese will put forth such seemingly mundane and materialistic values as beauty and wealth – or rebirth somewhere beyond the reach of SLORC.

Socially, every Burmese male is expected to take up temporary monastic residence twice in his life: once as a *samanera*, or novice monk, between the ages of five and 15 and again as a fully ordained monk, or *pongyi*, sometime after age 20. Almost all men or boys under 20 years of age participate in the *shinpyu*, or novitiation ceremony – quite a common event since a family earns great merit when one of its sons takes robe and bowl.

Though there is little social expectation to do so, a number of women live monastic lives as *dasasila*, or 'Ten-Precept' nuns. Burmese nuns shave their heads, wear pink robes and take vows in an ordination procedure similar to that undergone by monks.

Nat Worship

The widespread adoption of Buddhism in Myanmar has suppressed but never replaced the pre-Buddhist practice of nat worship. Originally animistic – associated with hills, trees, lakes and other natural features – the Burmese nat has evolved into a spirit that may hold dominion over a place (natural or artificial), person or field of experience.

In spite of King Anawrahta's 12th century attempt to ban it, the nat cult remains strong. The Burmese merely divide their devotions and offerings according to the sphere of influence: Buddha for future lives, and the nats – both Hindu and Burman – for problems in this life. A misdeed, for example, might be redressed by offerings made to the nat Thagyamin (related to the Hindu deity Indra), who once a year records the names of those who perform good deeds in a book made of gold leaves, those who do evil in a book made of dog skin.

A village may well have a nat shrine off in a wooded corner somewhere for the propitiation of the village guardian spirit. Such tree and village shrines are simple dollhouse-like structures of wood or bamboo; their proper placement is divined by a local *saya*, a 'teacher' or shaman trained in spirit lore.

Knowledge of the complex nat world is fading fast among the younger Burmese generation, many of whom pay respect only to the coconut-head house guardian. Red and white are widely known to be nat colours; drivers young and old tie red and white strips of cloth onto the side-view mirrors and hood ornaments of their vehicles for protection from the nats.

Meditation Study

In Yangon there are several centres for the study and practice of *satipatthana vipassana,* or insight-awareness meditation, based on instructions in the Maha Satipatthana Sutta (Sutra) of the Theravada Buddhist canon. The most famous centre in Yangon is the Mahasi Meditation Centre (Mahasi Thathana Yeiktha in Burmese), founded in 1947 by the late Mahasi Sayadaw, perhaps Myanmar's greatest meditation teacher. The Mahasi Sayadaw technique strives for intensive, moment-to-moment awareness of every physical movement, every mental and physical sensation, and ultimately, every thought.

To obtain the necessary 'special-entry visa' for a long-term stay, applicants must receive a letter of invitation from the centre where they would like to study, which may in turn require a letter of introduction from an affiliated meditation centre abroad. This invitation is then presented to a Burmese consulate or embassy, which will issue a visa for an initial stay of six to 12 weeks, as recommended by the centre. This may be extended in Yangon at the discretion of the centre and Burmese immigration.

The special-entry visa takes eight to 10 weeks to be issued and cannot be applied for while a person is in Myanmar on a tourist visa. Food and lodging are provided at no charge at the centres but meditators must follow eight precepts, which include abstaining from food after noon and foregoing music, dancing, jewellery, perfume and high or luxurious beds. Daily schedules are rigorous and may involve nearly continuous practice from 3 am till 11 pm. Westerners who have undergone the training say it is not recommended for people with no previous meditation experience.

For further information, write to:

Chanmyay Yeiktha Meditation Centre
  655-A Kaba Aye Pagoda Rd, Yangon
  (☎ 61479)
International Meditation Centre
  31-A Inya Myaing Rd, Yangon (☎ 31549)
Mahasi Meditation Centre
  16 Thathana Yeiktha Rd, Yangon

Panditarama
  80/A Shwetaunggyaw Rd, Yangon (☎ 31448)

For further information on the teachings of Mahasi Sayadaw, U Ba Khin and Mogok Sayadaw, read *Living Buddhist Masters* by Jack Kornfield.

LANGUAGE

There is a wide variety of languages spoken in Myanmar – fortunately, English is one of them. The Burmese alphabet is most unusual and looks like a collection of interlocked circles. If you would like to tackle Burmese (the main language), look for Lonely Planet's handy *Burmese phrasebook*.

Following are some useful Burmese words and phrases:

Basics

Excuse me.	*kwin pyu baa*
Good morning/ afternoon/evening.	*min ga la baa*
Goodbye. (I'm going)	*pyan dor mai*
Please.	*chay zoo tin baa day*
Thank you.	*chay zoo tin baa dai*
No.	*ma hoke boo*
Yes.	*hoke ket*
How are you?	*mah yeh laa?*
I'm well.	*maa bah day*
Do you understand?	*kin byar har lai tha laa?*
I do not understand.	*chun note nar ma lai boo*
How much?	*bah lout lai?*
Too much.	*myar dai*

Getting Around

Where is the ...?	*... beh mah lai?*
railway station	*boo dah youn*
bus station	*bak skah gait*

Is it far?	*waid thlah?*
left	*bay bet*
right	*nya bet*
straight (ahead)	*tay day*

When will the bus/train leave?
  bak skah/miy tah bai kain?

Accommodation

hotel	*hotay*
guesthouse	*tayko gan*

Can foreigners stay here?
  nain ngan gya thah di mah taylo ya thlah?
How much is the room for one night?
  kahn teh yetko bai lauk lai?

Health & Emergencies

doctor	*syah-woon*
hospital	*sayoun*
Help!	*kaybah!*
Stop!	*yat!*
I am lost.	*lahn pyout thwah bee*

Numbers

1	*tit*
2	*nit*
3	*thone*
4	*lay*
5	*ngar*
6	*howk*
7	*kun nit*
8	*sit*
9	*co*
10	*ta sei*
11	*sair tit*
12	*sair nit*
20	*na sei*
30	*thone sei*
100	*ta yar*
500	*gar yar*

Facts for the Visitor

PLANNING

Maps

Good, up-to-date maps of Myanmar are virtually nonexistent. For a country map, Nelles' *Myanmar* is sufficient for most purposes.

Myanmar Travels & Tours (MTT) publishes very useful and fairly detailed city maps of Yangon, Mandalay and Bagan. All are available from the main MTT office in

Yangon on Sule Pagoda Rd, or from individual MTT offices in the respective cities.

HIGHLIGHTS

Now that visitors may stay nearly a full month (up to two months with extensions), and new areas have been opened up, Myanmar's plentiful attractions are even more accessible.

Historic Temple Architecture
    Bagan, Bago, Salay, Mrauk U, Amarapura, Thayekhittaya
Handicrafts
    Mandalay (kalagas, antiques), Inle Lake (shoulder bags, Shan textiles), Bagan (lacquerware)
Hiking
    Kalaw, Pindaya, Inle Lake, Kyaingtong
Beaches
    Thandwe, Chaungtha, Letkhokkon, Myeik
Traditional Culture
    Yangon, Mandalay, Kyaiktiyo, Mawlamyine

TOURIST OFFICES

Myanmar Travels & Tours, once known as Tourist Burma, is part of the Ministry of Hotels & Tourism, the official government tourism organ in Myanmar. Its main office (☎ 78376, 75328; fax 89588) is at 77/91 Sule Pagoda Rd in Yangon, beside the Sule Paya. MTT has little in the way of brochures or leaflets. The information it has to hand out is sparse and uninteresting, and the officials aren't terribly friendly and helpful, although timetables and costs for places where they do business will usually be right on hand. There are MTT offices in Mandalay, Bagan, Nyaungshwe (Inle Lake) and Taunggyi, but they sometimes give the impression that their purpose is to hinder rather than to be useful.

With the privatisation of the tourist industry, it's no longer difficult to avoid MTT while travelling round Myanmar. Two of their remaining monopolies are express train tickets between Yangon and Mandalay and express boat tickets from Mandalay and Bagan, neither of which can be purchased by a foreigner except through MTT (or its representatives at the station/pier). But in both cases there are alternatives to using MTT transport, so even here you can bypass the bureaucrats.

VISAS & DOCUMENTS
Tourist Visas

The tourist visa situation in Myanmar has been in a state of flux since the upheavals in mid-1988, when the country was briefly closed to all visitors, then reopened under more strict regulations, then opened up wider than it had been at any time since 1962. By early 1994, 28-day tourist visas were being issued with regularity at Burmese embassies abroad; it is no longer necessary to book a package tour in advance.

Once in Yangon, you're free to plan your own itinerary and go almost wherever you like (see Travel Permits later in this section).

The cost of the visa itself is only around US$10 – at least during Visit Myanmar Year 1996 (which lasts through to the end of 1997). After that it may revert to the previous US$16 norm. Tourist visas are readily available through most Myanmar embassies or consulates abroad. At the embassy in Bangkok you can usually receive a visa the same day you apply for it.

Visa Extensions

Although some Myanmar embassies abroad will say tourist visa extensions aren't permitted, once in Myanmar you can usually extend your visa up to 30 days (two week extensions are the norm) beyond the original 28 day validity – at the discretion of the Department of Immigration & Manpower. The usual procedure requires five photos plus payment of a US$36 fee, but this can vary from office to office. If you're refused at one office, try again at another location – in low-tech Myanmar there are no computer checks or other easily communicated records of visa extension applications. Some offices are slower than others; allow two or three days for the extension to go through. The type of permit issued for such extensions is called a 'Stay Permit'.

Travel Permits

The xenophobic government does try to keep tabs on you while you are in Myanmar, though less so than before 1994. In general they don't want you wandering off into 'touchy' regions and that's part of the reason for the 28 day visa. Also, with the emphasis on earning hard currency through the FEC-for-dollars system (see the Money section below), the government obviously wants to keep you within reach of the government banking and tourism system. The further off the beaten track you get, the less likely you'll have to pay for anything in dollars or FECs, which is the only way the government wants your money.

Travel anywhere in the standard tourist quadrangle – Yangon, Mandalay, Bagan, Inle Lake and Taunggyi and to any points between or near these destinations – is freely allowed for anyone holding a valid passport and tourist visa. This includes places a little off the main linking routes such as Bago, Pyay, Shwebo, Magwe, Monywa, Taungoo and Pyinmana – basically anyplace in central Myanmar between the Shan Yoma to the east and the Ayeyarwady River to the west – plus most places in the Ayeyarwady Delta region (Pathein, Twante, Thanlyin, Letkhokkon).

Even for these places, your passport is likely to be checked from time to time. In fact every airport arrival, anywhere in Myanmar, requires a passport and visa check and the filling in of some papers with your name and passport number. Hotel staff also check passports and visas.

Travel to just about anyplace else in Myanmar requires a permit – actually a typed letter stamped with various government seals – issued by the Ministry of Hotels & Tourism (MHT) and approved by the Ministry of Defence. Such permits are available directly from MTT in Yangon or through many private travel agencies. Travel agencies usually require that you contract the services of a guide or driver before they'll arrange for a permit.

The government doesn't publish a list of places that officially require permits or a list of those which don't. So it really becomes sort of a guessing game as to which places you're allowed to visit and which you aren't. Many travellers go to Kyaiktiyo and Lashio

without a permit even though permits are officially required.

Insurgent-controlled territory – eg between Taunggyi and Kengtung in the Shan State or just about anywhere in the Kayin or Tanintharyi states – is absolutely not permitted. Military checkpoints placed at close intervals along every government-controlled road leading into these areas net anyone who tries to enter from Myanmar proper (these areas are in fact more accessible from Thailand – albeit very illegally).

Even *with* a permit, there's no guarantee the local authorities won't give you the boot – as happened to several visitors to Myitkyina in 1995 and 1996. For other places – like Mawlamyine – permits may be easy to get one week and impossible the next, depending on the level of rebel activity in the area.

At some point in your Myanmar travels, you come to realise that the country is still run like a loose-knit collection of warlord states. Even when you're just moving from one Burman-majority division to another, your papers are checked. On top of this, every time you enter a small town or village by car, someone appears to exact tribute from the driver in the form of a 'road tax' (the same thing happens to Burmese road travellers).

All of this could change overnight, especially as Myanmar's frontier areas become more 'secure' following ceasefire agreements with insurgent groups, or military victories over those groups which won't negotiate. By the time you read this, travel restrictions may have loosened considerably – or things could have gone the other way. Most likely the constant passport-checking will persist as long as the ruling junta maintains its warlord mentality – a centuries-old legacy in Myanmar.

Because what is 'officially' open seems to change from week to week, sometimes it's better just to set off for your intended destination rather than ask MTT or wait around for permits. Your fellow travellers on their way out of the country will be the most up-to-date source of info on what's possible and what's not.

EMBASSIES
Myanmar Embassies
Myanmar embassies abroad include:

Australia
22 Arkana St, Yarralumla, ACT 2600
(☎ (06) 273-3811)
Bangladesh
89B Rd No 4, Banani, Dhaka (☎ (2) 60 19 15)
Canada
85 Range Rd, Apt 902-903, The Sandringham, Ottawa, Ont K1N 8J6 (☎ (613) 232-6434/46)
China
6 Dong Zhi Men Wai St, Chaoyang District, Beijing (☎ (010) 532-1584/1425)
UK
19A Charles St, London W1X 8ER (☎ (0171) 629-6966, 499-8841)
USA
2300 'S' St NW, Washington, DC 20008 (☎ (202) 332-9044/5/6)

See the other chapters in this book for Myanmar embassies in those countries.

Foreign Embassies in Myanmar
Myanmar is usually a good place to get visas for other countries. You can often pay for them with free-market kyat (see the Money section below), so they can be very cheap and, as relatively few tourists come to Myanmar, embassy officials can usually issue them quickly. Countries with diplomatic representation in Yangon include:

Australia
88 Strand Rd (☎ 80711)
Bangladesh
56 Kaba Aye Pagoda Rd (☎ 51174)
Canada
See UK Embassy
China
1 Pyidaungsu Yeiktha Rd (☎ 21280)
Indonesia
100 Pyidaungsu Yeiktha Rd (☎ 82550)
Laos
A-1 Diplomatic Quarters, Taw Win Rd (☎ 22482)
Malaysia
82 Pyidaungsu Yeiktha Rd (☎ 20248)
Singapore
287 Pyay Rd (☎ 20854)
Thailand
45 Pyay Rd (☎ 21567)

UK
80 Strand Rd (☎ 81700)
Vietnam
40 Komin Kochin (Thanlwin) Rd (☎ 50361)

Other foreign embassies in Yangon include Egypt, France, India, Japan, Nepal, Pakistan and Sri Lanka.

CUSTOMS
The following items cannot legally be taken out of the country: prehistoric implements and artefacts; fossils; old coins; bronze or brass weights (including opium weights); bronze or clay pipes; kammawas or parabaiks (palm-leaf manuscripts); inscribed stones; inscribed gold or silver; historical documents; religious images; sculptures or carvings in bronze, stone, stucco or wood; frescoes or fragments thereof; pottery; national regalia and paraphernalia.

MONEY
Costs
Travel in Myanmar today is cheaper than it has been at anytime since before the 1988-89 disturbances. Costs depend largely on where you decide to go and which hotels you choose to stay in. Generally speaking the further off the beaten track you go, the cheaper travel becomes.

Goods and services may be priced either in kyat or in US dollars/FECs. Hotel rooms, some train tickets, air tickets, car rental and guide services are generally priced in dollars/FECs – for some of these services dollars/FECs may be the only currencies accepted. Food, taxis, buses and just about everything else in Myanmar are priced in kyat. In keeping with this two-currency system, prices in this chapter are quoted in either US dollars or kyat; anytime dollars are quoted, FECs are equally acceptable.

Daily Expenses Now that the hotel industry has privatised, it's possible to get rooms in well-touristed areas of Myanmar for as low as US$5 per person per night. For shoestring travellers this is high compared with Thailand and Indonesia, but about the same as in

MYANMAR

Laos and Vietnam. In very out-of-the-way places where you can pay entirely in kyat, room rates drop as low as K75 to K200 per person.

Except for those transport services monopolised by MTT (notably tickets for the Yangon-Mandalay express train and Mandalay-Bagan express boat), public ground transport is inexpensive and so slow that you're unlikely to be able to spend more than US$5 a day maximum on long-distance movement.

Although it's difficult to pin down a one-figure travel budget due to all the variables in the equation – particularly whether or not your desired itinerary requires travel permits – you can expect to spend a rock-bottom minimum of about US$10 a day. This assumes always taking the cheapest room available, using public ground transport (avoiding the Yangon-Mandalay express train and Mandalay-Bagan express boat) and eating in local restaurants and teashops rather than hotel restaurants or places geared to foreign tourists.

Inflation It's important to remember that Myanmar has an annual inflation rate of 25 to 30%, so any prices quoted in this book will probably need to be adjusted accordingly. One of the easiest and most accurate ways to calculate overall price increases is to check the price of a cup of tea in a typical Burmese teashop – such prices are more or less standard throughout urban Myanmar. In 1994, for example, you could sip a cup of tea for K6; a year later a sip at the same teashop cost K8. If this formula holds, a cup in mid-1997 would cost about K11. A trishaw ride cited in this guidebook as costing K200 would have increased to around K260 – and so on.

Currency

The kyat (pronounced 'chat') is divided into 100 pyas with a collection of confusing coins which are now rarely seen since the tremendous decrease in the value of the kyat over the last few years. Generally, it's easier to change money at MTT offices, which have longer opening hours than the banks.

The government has a nasty habit of demonetising large denomination notes from time to time. The theory is that anybody who has some large denomination notes sitting around must have obtained them by less than legal means. So the government simply declares that (say) all even-numbered denominations are no longer legal tender.

At present the following kyat banknotes are in use: K1, K5, K10, K15, K20, K45, K50, K90, K100, K200 and K500. Make sure that any K50 or K100 bills you're offered are labelled 'Central Bank of Myanmar' rather than 'Union of Burma Bank'. To discourage the black market, K50 and K100 notes were demonetised in the 1960s, and K25, K35 and K75 notes underwent a similar fate in 1987; unscrupulous money dealers occasionally try to foist these older bills on unsuspecting visitors. Just remember, any note reading 'Myanmar' rather than 'Burma' should be OK.

Foreign Exchange Certificates (FECs) As soon as you exit the immigration check at Yangon international airport you're supposed to stop at a counter and exchange US$300 for 300 FECs – Myanmar's second legal currency. Printed in China, these Monopoly-like notes issued by the Central Bank of Myanmar 'for the convenience of tourists visiting Myanmar' come in denominations equivalent to US$1, US$5, US$10 and US$20.

Payment for FECs is accepted *only* in US dollars or British pound sterling, in the form of cash, travellers' cheques or credit card (at the time of writing, credit cards could not be used at the airport). One US dollar always equals one FEC; the pound equivalent fluctuates according to pound-dollar variance. Reconversion of kyat to dollars or pound sterling is possible only for conversions in excess of US$300 and only when accompanied by the FEC voucher.

FECs can be spent anywhere in Myanmar. No special licence or permit is necessary for a citizen of Myanmar to accept FECs; this is not the case for dollars. Officially approved hotel rooms, airlines, Myanma Railways (some stations) and larger souvenir shops require payment either in dollars or FECs. So the required US$300 purchase of FECs is not something necessarily to avoid since they can be used to pay your hotel costs.

FECs can also be legally exchanged for kyat – at the free-market rate – at shops or from moneychangers that accept FEC. On the other hand, FECs aren't absolutely necessary for Myanmar travel, and if you can get away without having to purchase them you might as well. The staff at the FEC exchange booth at Yangon airport doesn't seem to be too concerned about dragging each and every newly arrived visitor over to the booth and many travellers are able to simply walk past without buying FEC. Upon request, couples are usually permitted to exchange US$300 for both persons rather than US$300 each.

This entire complicated system revolves around the desire of virtually every Burmese – and of course the government – to get their hands on hard currency, commonly referred to as 'FE' (foreign exchange, pronounced like one word, 'effee').

Dollars The 'effee' most desired is the US dollar, Myanmar's third currency – and the most basic to the country's overall economy. Cash dollars can legally be used only at establishments possessing a licence to accept dollars. In reality all merchants are happy to take them. They can also be exchanged for kyat on the black market.

Currency Exchange
With the FEC system in place, it's quite rare – and plain stupid – for any foreign visitor to exchange money at the ridiculously low official exchange rate. Since it's legal for Burmese to possess FECs without any special permit, the visitor no longer needs to consider the official exchange rate and can instead concentrate on getting the best free or 'black' market rate.

This means the old whisky-and-cigarette scheme – buying a bottle of Johnny Walker scotch and a carton of 555s at Bangkok airport's duty-free shop to sell for free-market kyat – is no longer necessary. In fact you'll lose money if you do it! These items

are usually less expensive in Yangon than in Bangkok.

The following table shows official exchange rates:

Australia	A$1	=	K4.67
Canada	C$1	=	K4.32
France	FF10	=	K11.48
Germany	DM1	=	K3.88
Japan	¥100	=	K5.35
New Zealand	NZ$1	=	K4.14
Singapore	S$1	=	K4.19
Thailand	100B	=	K23.00
UK	UK£1	=	K9.21
USA	US$1	=	K5.52

Again, the above rates are basically meaningless since no visitor with any sense changes foreign currency for 'official' kyat. As we went to press the free market rate was running around 140 to 145 kyat per US dollar.

Tipping & Bribes
Minor bribes – called 'presents' in Burmese English (as in 'Do you have a present for me?') – are part of everyday life in Myanmar. Much as tips are expected for a taxi ride or a restaurant meal in the west, extra compensation is expected for the efficient completion of many standard bureaucratic services. A visa extension or customs inspection will move a little more quickly if a 'present' – a little cash, a package of cigarettes, a tube of lipstick, a ballpoint pen – is proffered along with whatever the regular fee is. T-shirts and up-to-date western calendars – basically anything that can be sold for cash – will work minor miracles.

No matter how this system might bruise your sensibilities, you probably won't get through a Myanmar trip without paying at least a couple of minor bribes – even if you're not aware you've paid.

POST & COMMUNICATIONS
Consider yourself incommunicado while in Myanmar, as incoming post and telephone services are notoriously unreliable.

International postage rates are a bargain K5 per letter to the USA and Europe, K4 to

Asia. For registered mail anywhere in the world add K14. Parcels – forget it, unless you have a friend at your embassy or foreign office in Yangon.

Telephone

Domestic Calling other places in Myanmar is relatively simple and very inexpensive from the Central Telephone & Telegraph (CTT) office at the corner of Pansodan and Mahabandoola Sts in Yangon. Only larger cities with area codes can be dialled direct. Smaller towns still use manual switchboards, so you must ask the national operator to connect you to a specific town operator, then request the local number.

International The only public place in the country where international telephone calls can be conveniently arranged is at the CTT office. International calls are charged by three-minute blocks; if you stay on the line for less than three minutes you still pay the full three minute charge. If you want to talk longer than three minutes, you must start all over again for each additional three minute block.

You may have to wait for up to half an hour for a line. The phone office is open Monday to Friday 8 am to 4 pm, weekends and holidays 9 am to 2 pm.

To make international calls from Myanmar, the international access code is 00.

To call Myanmar from outside the country, the country code is 95.

BOOKS

For more information about travelling in Myanmar look for Lonely Planet's *Myanmar – travel survival kit*. The most comprehensive sociopolitical account of pre-1988 Myanmar is *Burma: A Socialist Nation of Southeast Asia* by David Steinberg. *Burma – Insurgency & the Politics of Ethnicity* by Martin Smith contains a well-researched history and analysis of insurgent politics in Myanmar from the 1940s through to 1988.

George Orwell's *Burmese Days* is the book to read in order to get a feel for the country under the British Raj. *Golden Earth*

by Norman Lewis is a reprint of a classic account of a visit to Burma soon after WWII.

Several books offer histories and descriptions of the temple architecture at Bagan. The older *Pictorial Guide to Pagan* contains illustrated descriptions of many of the important Bagan buildings plus a map inside the back cover. It's a useful book that you'll find fairly easily in Myanmar. *Payas of Pagan* is also fairly readily available, but not so detailed or interesting. Top of the line is *Pagan: Art and Architecture of Old Burma* by Paul Strachan. One of the few books available with any information at all about archaeological sites other than Bagan or Mandalay is *A Guide to Mrauk U* by Tun Shwe Khine.

Anyone interested in quickly obtaining a broad understanding of Burmese customs and etiquette should pick up a copy of *Culture Shock! Burma* by Saw Myat Yin. This book simply and accurately explains male and female roles, business protocol, common Burmese ceremonies and festivals, the naming system, how to extend and accept invitations, and even how Burmese perceive westerners.

Outrage: Burma's Struggle for Democracy by journalist Bertil Lintner chronicles the violent suppression of Myanmar's pro-democracy movement from 1987 to 1990, with particular focus on the events of 1988. It is a somewhat polemic look at the student uprisings, but basically it's very informative. *Freedom from Fear & Other Writings* by Aung San Suu Kyi is a collection of essays by and about the Nobel Peace Prize winner.

Yangon has quite a few bookshops, most along Bogyoke Aung San St opposite the Bogyoke Market, where you can find some really interesting books. Also check the Pagan Bookshop at 100, 37th St, quite close to The Strand Hotel. You never know what will turn up in this little shop that specialises in English-language material – much of it is vintage stuff.

NEWSPAPERS & MAGAZINES

The only English-language newspaper readily available in Myanmar is the *New*

Light of Myanmar, a thin, state-owned daily that's chock-full of Orwellian propaganda of the 'War Is Peace' or 'Freedom Is Slavery' nature, mixed in with a fair amount of non-controversial wire news. Recent issues of international magazines like *Time*, *Newsweek* or the *Economist* are quite often available at The Strand Hotel in Yangon. Whenever a feature about Myanmar appears in one of these magazines, however, that issue mysteriously fails to appear. Older issues are sold on the street by sidewalk vendors.

A relatively new tourist-oriented publication called *Today*, available at the MTT office and at many hotels, contains short, noncontroversial articles on Myanmar's culture and the tourism industry, along with useful lists of embassies, current festivals, airlines and long-distance express bus services.

RADIO & TV

All legal radio and television broadcasts are state-controlled. Radio Myanmar broadcasts news in Burmese, English and eight other national languages three times a day. Only music with Burmese-language lyrics goes out on the airwaves.

TV Myanmar operates nightly from 6 to 10 pm via the NTSC system. Regular features include military songs and marching performances, locally produced news and weather reports and a sports presentation.

Educated Burmese generally listen to shortwave BBC and VOA broadcasts for news from the world outside. Every Friday at 12.20 and 4.30 pm, the American Center at 14 Tawwin St, behind the Ministry of Foreign Affairs in Yangon, packs them in for the satellite broadcast of the ABC World News Weekly Highlights. CBS News and the MacNeil/Lehrer Newshour are shown Monday through Friday at 10.30 and 11 am respectively.

PHOTOGRAPHY & VIDEO

Myanmar is a very photogenic place so bring lots of film with you. Colour print film – mostly Kodak, Fuji and Konica brands – is readily and inexpensively available in shops in Yangon and Mandalay. Slide film is harder to find but some shops stock it.

Outside Yangon and Mandalay, film is scarce. Most film you might see on sale in the hinterlands will have come from visitors who sold it while in the country – with no guarantee on age or quality. Photographic processing services are available but quality is erratic. You'll do best to wait until you've returned home – or have your film processed in Bangkok, where decent colour labs are plentiful.

A benefit of Myanmar's low tourist flow is that the Burmese are not overexposed to camera-clicking visitors and are not at all unhappy about being photographed. Even monks like to be photographed although, of course, it's rude to ask them to pose for you and it's always polite to ask anybody's permission before taking photographs.

It is forbidden by law to photograph any military facility or any structure considered strategic – this includes bridges and railway stations – and any uniformed person.

WEIGHTS & MEASURES
Weight

The most common units of weight used in Myanmar are viss *(peiktha)*, pounds *(paun)* and ticals *(kyat tha)*. One viss equals 3.6 pounds (1.6 kg) or 100 ticals. One tical equals 16g.

Volume

At the retail level, rice and small fruits or nuts are sold in units of volume rather than weight; the most common measure is the standard condensed milk can, or *bu*. Eight *bu* equals one small rice basket, or *pyi*, and 16 pyi make a jute sack, or *tin*.

Petrol and most other liquids are sold by the imperial gallon (4.55 litres). One exception is milk, which is sold by the viss.

Length & Distance

Cloth and other items of moderate length are measured by the yard (91.5 cm), called *gaik* in Burmese. A half yard is a *taung* (45.7 cm), which is divided into two *htwa* (22.8 cm).

Half a htwa is a *mait* (11.4 cm), roughly equivalent to an Anglo-American foot.

Road distances are measured in miles (one mile equals 1.61 km). Shorter distances in town or in the countryside may be quoted in furlongs. There are eight furlongs in one mile; thus one furlong equals about two-tenths of a km.

LAUNDRY

Inexpensive laundry services are available through virtually all hotels and guesthouses. In Yangon and Mandalay you'll also find independent laundry shops in the town centres – generally even less expensive than at your lodgings. Techniques employed favour the 'rub and scrub' method, so wash anything delicate yourself.

HEALTH

Myanmar doesn't have the highest of sanitation standards, but then you can't expect very much from one of the world's 10 poorest countries. Frankly, it pays to be very careful with food and drink throughout this country. Only eat food that is cooked, and peel raw fruits or vegetables yourself. All water should be boiled or otherwise treated before consumption, and safe bottled water is available at most tourist destinations.

Dysentery of various types is quite common and you should stock up on appropriate medicines for the prevention and treatment of both the bacillic and amoebic forms (consult a doctor in advance). A supply of diarrhoeal suppressants like Lomotil or Imodium is a must unless you're unusually stoic. If you eat only in the hotels, you'll probably be OK but you'll have to put up with bland, uninspired cooking (The Strand Hotel in Yangon is one exception).

Malaria is not a problem in the areas most frequented by foreign travellers.

See the Health section in the Appendix for more information.

TOILETS & SHOWERS

As in many other Asian countries, the 'squat toilet' is the norm except in hotels and guesthouses geared towards tourists and international business travellers. More rustic toilets in rural areas may simply consist of a few planks over a hole in the ground.

Even in places where sit-down toilets are installed, the plumbing may not be designed to take toilet paper. In such cases the usual washing bucket will be standing nearby or there will be a waste basket where you're supposed to place used toilet paper.

Public toilets aren't very common except in railway stations, larger hotel lobbies and airports. While on the road between towns and villages it is perfectly acceptable to go behind a tree or bush or even to use the roadside when nature calls.

Bathing

Some hotels and most guesthouses in the country do not have hot water, though places in the larger cities will usually offer small electric shower heaters in their more expensive rooms. Very few boiler-style water heaters are available outside larger international-style hotels.

Most rural Burmese bathe at rivers, streams or wells. Those living in towns or cities may have washrooms where a large jar or cement trough is filled with water for bathing purposes. A plastic or metal bowl is used to sluice water from the jar or trough over the body. Even in homes where showers are installed, heated water is uncommon.

If ever you find yourself having to bathe in a public place you should wear a *longyi* (cotton wraparounds for men and women); nude bathing is not the norm.

DANGERS & ANNOYANCES

Theft from tourists seems quite rare in Myanmar, but don't tempt fate by leaving valuables lying around.

PUBLIC HOLIDAYS & SPECIAL EVENTS

Traditionally Myanmar follows a 12 month lunar calendar, so the old holidays and festivals will vary in date, by the Gregorian calendar, from year to year. Myanmar also has a number of more recently originated holidays whose dates are fixed by the Gregorian calendar. Festivals are drawn-out, enjoyable affairs in Myanmar. They generally take place or culminate on full-moon days, but the build-up can continue for days.

Independence Day
4 January – A major public holiday marked by a seven-day fair at Kandawgyi Lake in Yangon. There are fairs all over the country at this time.

Union Day
12 February – Celebrates Bogyoke Aung San's short-lived achievement of unifying Myanmar's disparate racial groups. For two weeks preceding Union Day, the national flag is paraded from town to town, and wherever the flag rests there must be a festival.

Shwedagon Festival
February/March – The largest pagoda festival in Myanmar.

Peasants' Day
2 March

Armed Forces Day
27 March – Celebrated with parades and fireworks. Since 1989 the Tatmadaw has made it a tradition to pardon a number of prisoners on Armed Forces Day.

Buddha's Birthday
April/May – Also celebrates the day of the Buddha's enlightenment and the day he entered nirvana. Thus it is known as the 'thrice blessed day'. One of the best places to observe this ceremony is at Yangon's Shwedagon Paya, where a procession of girls carry earthen jars to water the three banyan trees on the western side of the compound.

Workers' Day
1 May – Although the government renounced socialism in 1989, the country still celebrates May Day.

Buddhist 'Lent'
June/July – Laypeople present monasteries with stacks of new robes for resident monks, since during the three-month Lent period monks are restricted to their monasteries. Ordinary people are also expected to be rather more religious during this time – marriages do not take place and it is inauspicious to move house.

Martyr's Day
19 July – Commemorates the assassination of Bogyoke Aung San and his comrades on that day in 1947. Wreaths are laid at his mausoleum north of the Shwedagon Paya in Yangon.

Festival
July/August – Lots are drawn to see who will have to provide monks with their alms. If you're in Mandalay, try to get to Taungbyone, about 30 km north, where there is a noisy, seven-day festival to keep the nats happy.

Boat Races
September/October – This is the height of the wet season, so boat races are held in rivers, lakes and even ponds all over Myanmar. The best place to be is Inle Lake, where the Buddha images at the Phaung Daw U Kyaung are ceremonially toured around the lake in the huge royal barge, the Karaweik.

Festival of Lights
September/October – Celebrates Buddha's return from a period of preaching. For the three days of the festival all Myanmar is lit by oil lamps, fire balloons, candles and even mundane electric lamps. Every house has a paper lantern hanging outside and it's a happy, joyful time all over Myanmar.

Tazaungdaing
October/November – Another 'festival of lights'. It's particularly celebrated in the Shan State. In Taunggyi there are fire balloon competitions. In some areas there are also speed-weaving competitions during the night – young Burmese women show their prowess at weaving by attempting to produce robes for Buddha images between dusk and dawn. The results, finished or not, are donated to the monks. The biggest weaving competitions occur at Shwedagon Paya in Yangon.

Kathein
October/November – A one-month period at the end of Buddhist Lent during which new monastic robes and requisites are offered to the monastic community. Many people simply donate cash; kyat notes are folded and stapled into floral patterns on wooden 'trees' called *padetha* and offered to the monasteries.

National Day
Late November/early December

Spirit Festivals
November/December

Christmas
25 December – Despite Myanmar's predominantly Buddhist background, Christmas Day is a public holiday in deference to the many Christian Karen.

Karen New Year
December/January – Considered a national holiday. Karen communities throughout Myanmar celebrate by wearing their traditional dress of woven tunics over red *longyis* (the sarong-style cloth covering the lower body) and by hosting folk dancing and singing performances. The largest celebrations are held in the Karen suburb of Insein, just north of Yangon, and in Pa-an, the capital of the Kayin State.

Ananda Festival
December/January – Held at the Ananda Pahto in Bagan.

ACCOMMODATION

Myanmar has been the hottest hotel market in the world for the last two years as dozens of large and small developers have tried to meet the pent-up demand created by years of mismanagement by the Ministry of Hotels & Tourism. MHT is unloading its own properties as fast as it can sell them so by 1996 there were very few government-owned places left in the country.

Technically, any hotel or guesthouse that accepts foreign guests must have a special lodging licence – this is usually displayed somewhere on the wall behind the reception desk. The newer private hotels tend to represent better value than government-owned hotels or hotels that were previously government-owned. Many of the latter are now owned or managed by former MHT hotel managers who have long been accustomed to charging high rates for indifferent service and mediocre room quality. Of the countless new places to stay, among the best are the small, family-run places with fewer than 10 rooms. The situation has actually improved a great deal over previous years when your only choice was low-standard, high-priced MHT-owned hotels – of which there were relatively few.

Rates and overall variety have improved tremendously over the last three or four years, though many of Myanmar's hotels are still a bit overpriced by most South-East Asian standards. Almost all hotels follow a two-tiered pricing system – charging one rate for locals in kyat and another for foreigners in US dollars/FECs. A typical middle-of-the-road, Burmese-owned hotel might charge K900 for Burmese and US$40 for foreigners – over four times the local price figured at the real exchange rate. A dingy guesthouse in the hinterlands might take K75 from locals and US$10 from foreigners – more than a tenfold increase!

Fortunately for travellers on a tight budget there are now a smattering of places in the US$5 to US$10 per person range. Typically this gets a bare cubicle with two beds and a cold-water bathroom down the hall. Rooms with a private cold-water bath cost a few dollars more. A toast-and-egg breakfast is usually included.

You can usually find a few kyat-priced hotels to stay at in out-of-the-way areas, and even in fairly accessible but relatively untouristed Shwebo, Magwe, Myingyan and Pakkoku. We found other towns where guesthouses cost no more than K200 a night, sometimes as low as K50. The rooms in such places are very basic – perhaps two hard beds in a room surrounded by wood partitions that stop 30 cm short of the ceiling. Once the local government begins enforcing the foreign guest licence law this kind of place will become more difficult to find.

FOOD

Despite an international reputation to the contrary, you can eat very well and very inexpensively in Myanmar. Until recently it could often be difficult to find Burmese food in local restaurants, but the economic development in urban areas has brought substantial improvements in the availability and quality of Burmese cuisine. Chinese and Indian food are also quite popular in the larger towns and cities. Street and market stalls tend to provide the regional dishes, but with these you must be a little wary of cleanliness.

Mainstream Burmese cuisine represents an intriguing blend of Burman, Mon, Indian and Chinese influences. Rice *(htamin)* is the core of any Burmese meal, to be eaten with a choice of curry dishes *(hin)*, most commonly fish, chicken, prawns or mutton. Very little beef or pork is eaten by the Burmese – beef because it's considered offensive to most Hindus and Buddhists, pork because the nats disapprove.

Burmese curries are the mildest in Asia in terms of chilli power – in fact most cooks don't use chillies at all in their recipes, just a simple *masala* of turmeric, ginger, garlic, salt and onions, plus plenty of peanut oil and shrimp paste. Heat can be added in the form of *balachaung*, a table condiment made from chillies, tamarind and dried shrimp pounded together, or from the very pungent, very hot *ngapi kyaw* – shrimp paste fried in peanut oil with chilli, garlic and onions. Curries are generally cooked until the oil separates from all other ingredients and floats on top. Some restaurants will add oil to maintain the correct top layer, as the oil preserves the underlying food from contamination by insects and airborne bacteria while the curries sit in open, unheated pots for hours at a time. When you're served a bowl of *hin*, you're not expected to consume all the oil; just spoon the ingredients from underneath.

Almost everything is flavoured with *ngapi*, which is a salty paste concocted from dried and fermented shrimp or fish, and can be very much an acquired taste. A thin sauce of pressed fish or shrimp called *nganpya-yay* may also be used to salt Burmese dishes.

Noodle dishes are most often eaten for breakfast or as light meals between the main meals of the day. By far the most popular is mohinga (pronounced 'moun-hinga'), rice noodles served with a thick, yellow fish soup. Another popular noodle dish, especially at festivals, is *oh-no khauk-swe*, rice noodles with pieces of chicken in a spicy sauce made with coconut milk.

Shan khauk-swe, or Shan-style noodle soup – thin wheat noodles in a light broth with chunks of chilli-marinated chicken – is a favourite all over Myanmar but is most common in Mandalay and the Shan State. A variation popular in Mandalay is made with rice noodles and called *myi shay*. Another Shan dish worth seeking out is *htamin chin*, literally 'sour rice', a turmeric-coloured rice salad.

Some useful words relating to food include:

bread	*pow mohn*
butter	*taw but*
chicken	*kyet (chet) tar*
coffee	*kaw pee*
drinking water	*tao ye*
egg (boiled)	*chet u byok*
egg (fried)	*chet u chor*
fish	*ngar*
hot	*ah poo*
mutton	*seik tar*
noodles	*kaw swe*

restaurant	*sar tao syne*
rice (cooked)	*ta min*
soup	*hin jo*
sugar	*ta jar*
tea	*la bet ye*
teashop	*la bet yea syne*
toast	*pow moh gin*

DRINKS

Nonalcoholic Drinks

Only drink water when you know it has been purified – which in most restaurants it should be. One should be suspicious of ice although we've had lots of ice drinks in Myanmar without suffering any ill effects. Myanma Mineral Water is sold in bottles and is quite safe.

Burmese tea, brewed in the Indian style with lots of milk and sugar, is cheap. Many restaurants, the Chinese ones in particular, will provide as much weak Chinese tea as you can handle – for free. It's a good, safe thirst quencher and some people prefer it to regular Burmese tea. You can always buy some little snack if you'd like a drink but not a meal. Teashops are a good place to drink safely boiled tea and munch on inexpensive snacks like *nam-bya, palata* or Chinese pastries.

Soft drinks are more costly but reasonable by Asian standards. Made-in-Myanmar soft drinks are mostly terrible, but a few come in pleasant flavours – particularly if they're well diluted with ice. One of the better ones is Sparkling Lemon (called 'Lemon Sparkling' by most Burmese). Half-and-half soft drink and soda water is another recommendation. Pepsi and other international brands are becoming increasingly common.

Sugar-cane juice is a very popular streetside drink – cheap, thirst quenching and relatively healthy.

Alcoholic Drinks

Beer Since foreign trade was freed up in the early 1990s, the beer brands most commonly seen in Myanmar are international: Tiger, Bintang, ABC Stout, Singha, San Miguel, Beck, Heineken and other beers brewed in Thailand, Singapore and Indonesia. At one time these brands were available only on the black market; they are now sold freely in shops and restaurants throughout the country and typically cost K65 to K90 per can or bottle.

Myanmar has its own brand, Mandalay beer, which is very similar to Indian or Sri Lankan beer – rather watery but not bad on those hot and dusty occasions when only a beer will do. Unfortunately, considering its low quality, Mandalay beer also happens to be the most expensive beer in Myanmar at K80 to K125 per bottle. Hence few Burmese or foreigners drink the national brew.

Toddy Throughout central Myanmar and the delta, *hta yei*, or 'toddy juice', is the farmer's choice of alcoholic beverage. Hta yei is tapped from the top of a toddy palm, the same tree – and the same sap – that produces jaggery or palm sugar. The juice is sweet and nonalcoholic in the morning, but by mid-afternoon naturally ferments to a weak beer-like strength. By the next day it will have turned. The milky, viscous liquid has a nutty aroma and a slightly sour flavour that fades quickly.

The toddy is sold in the same roughly engraved terracotta pots the juice is collected in for about K60 per pot (or K10 in a bottle to go), and drunk from coconut half-shells set on small bamboo pedestals. Favourite toddy accompaniments include prawn crackers and fried peas. Some toddy bars also sell *hta ayet*, or 'toddy liquor' (also called 'jaggery liquor'), a much stronger, distilled form of toddy sap, for around K22 per bottle.

THINGS TO BUY

Now that free-market kyat may be used openly for purchases, shopping in Myanmar is easier than ever before. Bartering is also quite acceptable and many merchants would love to trade their wares for designer watches, pocket calculators, jeans, T-shirts with English writing on them, and so on.

There is nice lacquerware available, particularly at Bagan. The black and gold items probably aren't as good quality as in Chiang Mai in Thailand, but coloured items are much more vibrant. Look for flexibility in bowls or dishes and clarity of design. Opium weights are cheaper than in Thailand. Beautiful shoulder bags are made by the Shan tribes. *Kalagas*, tapestries embroidered with silver thread, sequins and colourful glass beads, are a good buy.

Be very careful if you decide to buy gems. Many foolish travellers buy fake gemstones. It's another of those fields to dabble in only if you really know what is and what isn't. Precious stones are supposed to be a government monopoly and they are very unhappy about visitors buying stones anywhere except at licensed retail shops. If *any* stones are found when your baggage is checked on departure, they may be confiscated unless you can present a receipt showing they were purchased from a government-licensed dealer. See also the earlier Customs section for information on items which cannot be taken out of the country.

Getting There & Away

Apart from day trips to Three Payas Pass from Thailand, five-day trips from Thailand's Mae Sai to the Burmese town of Kengtung and group travel from China, people who arrive by land or sea are few and far between. That only leaves arriving by air, and even there the choice is fairly restricted since few airlines fly into Yangon.

AIR

There are several major air route options. First, and most commonly, is to travel out and back from Bangkok in Thailand. The second possibility is to slot Myanmar in between Thailand and Bangladesh, India or Nepal – many people travelling from South-East Asia to the subcontinent manage a few weeks in Myanmar in between. The third alternative is to travel out and back from Calcutta. Kuala Lumpur, Singapore and Kunming round out the possibilities.

Bangkok is a good place to look for tickets to Myanmar. Typical costs for Bangkok-Yangon-Bangkok tickets are around US$230 on Thai Airways International, US$220 on Myanma Airways International (MAI), and as low as US$144 on Biman Bangladesh. MAI flies Bangkok-Yangon-Calcutta for a similar figure and Bangkok-Yangon-Kathmandu for around US$200. Round-trip flights to/from Kuala Lumpur, Singapore or Kunming cost around US$250.

Bangkok Airways flew regularly scheduled flights between Chiang Mai and Mandalay for a short time in the early 1990s but is now only doing charters. Air Mandalay, Myanmar's new, privately owned domestic carrier, has its eye set on Chiang Mai and Chiang Rai flights for sometime in the future. For the moment Air Mandalay only runs charter flights to and from these destinations in Thailand.

Thailand

Thai Airways International currently flies Bangkok-Yangon-Bangkok daily. Although slightly more expensive than the equivalent MAI flight, Thai's departure times are much more sane and the service more reliable.

MAI flies from Bangkok to Yangon and vice versa daily, to Hong Kong thrice weekly, Singapore four times weekly, Kuala Lumpur twice weekly and Dhaka once a week.

Bangladesh

Biman Bangladesh flies Bangkok-Yangon-Dhaka (via Chittagong) once a week. It is usually the cheapest operator although not always that reliable. If you plan on overnighting in Dhaka, be sure to get a hotel voucher from Biman before leaving Yangon; in fact it might be best to get it in Bangkok (or wherever you buy the ticket) first, just to be safe.

China

Air China flies 737s between Kunming (Yunnan) and Yangon once a week. If you are travelling around China and then continuing to South-East Asia this can be an economical choice, since from western China

you would not have to backtrack all the way east to Hong Kong, then fly all the way west to Bangkok.

Singapore

Silk Air, a subsidiary of Singapore Airlines, flies to Yangon four times weekly from Singapore.

Reconfirmation

If you are counting on flying out of Yangon on your scheduled date of departure, then you must reconfirm your outbound flight either at the appropriate airport ticket counter or at the relevant airline office in town. This applies regardless of whether your flight is officially confirmed ('OK' status) on the ticket or not. You may notice a sign in the airport waiting lounge which reminds you of this requirement. If you do not reconfirm, the airlines (this goes for any of the airlines flying in and out of Yangon) cannot guarantee your outbound seat. Especially during the height of the tourist season (November-February), most flights out of Yangon seem to be intentionally overbooked.

Departure Tax

A US$6 departure tax, payable in dollars or FECs, is collected at the airport from all ticket-holders before flight check-in.

Getting Around

Travel in Myanmar is not that easy – it's uncertain and often uncomfortable by whatever means of travel you choose.

AIR

Myanmar has 66 airstrips around the country, 23 of which are served by regularly scheduled domestic flights. Most are short, one-strip fields that can land only one plane at a time. None have instrument landing capability, a situation which can be especially tricky during the May to November monsoon season even though all 23 are considered 'all-weather aerodromes'.

A new international airport is under construction outside Yangon near Bago, on a site used by B-29 bombers during WWII. Airports at Mandalay and Heho are soon to add sorely needed runways and expanded passenger facilities.

The Airport

Since 1994 Burmese citizens without special permission or guide licences have been barred from the airport, hence nowadays you usually aren't approached by taxi drivers until you leave the airport. Hotel desks just outside the arrival area can arrange buses into Yangon for US$3 per person, or taxis for US$5 per cab (up to four passengers); most buses and taxis booked this way drop you off at a station on Bogyoke Aung San St. Some hotels will provide free transport if you book a room at their airport hotel desk. You can also book your own taxi from the motley collection of old, battered vehicles parked outside the airport for around US$4 to the destination of your choice.

Coming to the airport from Yangon you can pay in free-market kyat, though the fare works out to be about the same.

Departing from Myanmar is much simpler than arriving, unless you have an early-morning MAI flight out and have to crawl out of bed. MAI make it less pleasant by sending round their bus to collect you at an unnecessarily early hour. The bus starts from The Strand Hotel and crisscrosses all over town on its way to Yangon's international airport in Mingaladon.

For MAI departures, taking a taxi gives you an extra hour (almost) in bed. From downtown Yangon to the airport the going rate for a tiny Mazda is K250 (about US$2.50 at free-market exchange rates) while the more comfortable 'saloon' sedans cost K300 to K350.

If you happen to be flying out of Yangon on Union Day, 12 February, you need to get out to the airport before noon because the road to the airport is closed to non-parade traffic after that time.

Myanma Airways

Myanma Airways' small fleet consists of two Fokker F-28 jets and four F-27 turboprops. Legroom and carry-on luggage space are minimal. All craft are in a decidedly tatty condition and the whole operation seems to be a little on the haphazard side, which does not do wonders for one's nerves when flying with MA.

Schedules for MA don't mean all that much – if the passengers turn up early the flight may go early. If insufficient passengers show up the flight may not go at all. If too many passengers want to fly, another flight may be slotted in. It's wisest in Myanmar to travel as lightly as possible and carry your own baggage out to the aircraft rather than trust that it will find its own way there.

Fares Foreigners must purchase all tickets using Foreign Exchange Certificates (FECs) or US dollars cash. Burmese citizens pay much lower fares in kyat.

Another wrinkle in booking procedures is that you can't take an MA flight that involves an intermediate connection straight through the connecting stop. For example, on Wednesdays MA flight UB 788 goes from Mandalay to Bhamo at 8.30 am and 20 minutes after arrival in Bhamo, the same plane continues northward to Myitkyina. But you can't book this flight straight through from Mandalay to Myitkyina; this is because the MA office in Mandalay apparently can't figure out how many people hold reservations on the Bhamo-Myitkyina leg. So you must stop in Bhamo, and make a new reservation for a seat to Myitkyina. The same goes for flights to Mawlamyine via Dawei, flights from Kengtung to Yangon via Heho, and other such routings.

Air Mandalay

Flying with Air Mandalay (AM) saves visitors a whole list of headaches. In the first place they fly to places for which permits aren't necessary, so that's one layer of bureaucracy eliminated in their ticket lines. Secondly, AM is usually punctual in arrivals and departures and for the most part schedules are

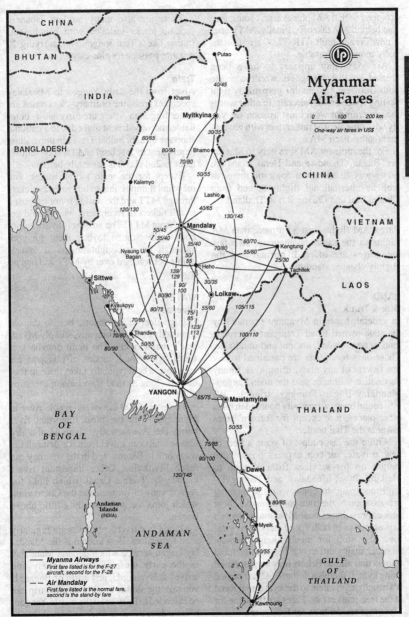

Myanmar Air Fares

One-way air fares in US$

0   100   200 km

CHINA

BHUTAN

INDIA

BANGLADESH

Putao

40/45

Khamti

Myitkyina

60/65

30/35

80/90

Bhamo

Kalemyo

70/80

CHINA

50/55

Lashio

120/130

40/65

130/145

Mandalay

VIETNAM

50/45
35/40

60/70

Kengtung

Nyaung U/
Bagan

65/70

50/55

70/80

55/60

25/30

Tachilek

139/
129

Heho

30/35

Sittwe

90/
100

Loikaw

LAOS

Kyaukpyu

80/90

55/60

105/115

70/80

80/75

75/
85

Thandwe

70/80

50/55

123/
113

100/110

80/90

80/75

YANGON

65/75

Mawlamyine

BAY
OF
BENGAL

THAILAND

50/55

75/85

90/100

Dawei

130/145

35/40

Andaman
Islands
(INDIA)

80/85

ANDAMAN
SEA

Myeik

50/55

GULF
OF
THAILAND

—— *Myanma Airways*
First fare listed is for the F-27
aircraft, second for the F-28

– – – *Air Mandalay*
First fare listed is the normal fare,
second is the stand-by fare

Kawthoung

MYANMAR

arranged so that AM planes aren't waiting on line behind MA takeoffs. Finally, AM planes – new French-built ATR-72s – are substantially more comfortable.

Air Mandalay appears to have been created so that foreigners won't compete with Burmese citizens for perpetually tight seating space on MA aircraft. In other words the government would just as soon see you fly with upscale AM rather than with government-subsidised MA.

For the moment AM flies only to Mandalay, Bagan, Thandwe and Heho. Plans are under way to add more domestic routes as well as international flights to and from Chiang Mai and Chiang Rai in Thailand.

Fares AM flights cost a bit more than MA flights to the same destinations. Two fare categories are offered: normal and the slightly cheaper stand-by.

LAND
Bus & Truck

In general, buses in Myanmar operated by the state-owned Road Transport Enterprise tend to be crowded, ancient and unreliable. These days foreigners are permitted to buy bus tickets of any class, using kyat, to any destination within or near the main Yangon-Mandalay-Bagan-Taunggyi triangle. We also found buses were easily boarded in most other places, too, except for 'brown' areas towards the Thai border.

Within the last couple of years a fleet of new private, air-con express buses have caught on for services from Yangon to Meiktila, Pyay, Mandalay, and Taunggyi – with more sure to come with the ongoing privatisation of the transport industry. These new express buses beat Myanma Railway's express trains in both speed and ticket price; they also stop for meals along the way. Another major difference between bus and train is that all bus tickets may be purchased using kyat; if there's a dollar/FEC fare posted it's usually equivalent to the kyat fare figured at the free-market rate. Fares are the same for Myanmar residents as for foreigners.

There are also many modern Japanese pick-up trucks installed with bench seats (rather like a Thai *songthaew)*, carrying 20 or more passengers plus cargo.

Train

Apart from the daily Yangon to Mandalay special express, the ordinary-class trains are better forgotten – they are dirty, slow, unreliable and very dark at night due to a national shortage of light bulbs! Travel in upper class (equivalent to 1st class) and 1st class (equivalent to 2nd class) is generally better.

Except for the main tourist routes, you may find it impossible to buy railway tickets through MTT and the station is not supposed to sell tickets to foreigners, who should get them from MTT! The answer is to ask somebody at the station to buy them for you, although we've bought tickets at several points not watched over by MTT and had no trouble.

WATER
Riverboat

A huge fleet of riverboats, heir to the old Irrawaddy Flotilla Company, still ply Myanmar's major rivers. The main drawback is speed; where both modes of transport are available, a boat typically takes three to four times as long as road travel along the same route.

There are 8000 km of navigable river in Myanmar, with the most important river being the Ayeyarwady. Even in the dry season boats can travel from the delta all the way north to Bhamo, and in the wet they can reach Myitkyina. Other important rivers include the Twante Canal, which links the Ayeyarwady to Yangon, and the Chindwinn, which joins the Ayeyarwady a little above Bagan.

Only a few riverboat routes are regularly used by visitors. Best known is the Mandalay-Bagan service which departs Mandalay in the early morning twice weekly and arrives at Nyaung U, just north of Bagan. If you take the slower local boats, this trip can be extended to Pyay or all the way to Yangon; it's two days travel downriver from Bagan to

Pyay, where you change boats and have another couple of days travel before reaching Yangon.

Ship

Although the obstacles standing in your way are daunting, it's possible to travel along Myanmar's coastline via Myanma Five Star Line (MFSL), the country's state-owned ocean transport enterprise. MFSL maintains just 21 craft, which sail north and south from Yangon about twice a month. Only eight vessels offer passenger service. Shipping dates vary from month to month and are announced via a public chalkboard at the main MFSL office in Yangon.

Southbound ships sail regularly to Kawthoung, a two night voyage from Yangon, with occasional scheduled calls at Dawei and Myeik. Northbound ships call at Thandwe (a full day from Yangon) and Kyaukpyu (one night) before docking in Sittwe (five more hours) for cargo from India and Bangladesh.

Since to book passage on any MFSL ship you must show an MHT travel permit that specifies travel by ship, and since you must wait around for up to two weeks for a ship going your way, this is by far the most difficult public transport to arrange.

LOCAL TRANSPORT

Larger towns in Myanmar offer a variety of city buses *(kaa)*, bicycle rickshaws or trishaws *(sai-kaa)*, horsecarts *(myint hlei)*, vintage taxis *(taxi)*, more modern little three-wheelers somewhat akin to auto-rickshaws *(thoun bein,* or 'three wheels'), tiny four-wheeled Mazdas *(lei bein,* or 'four wheels') and modern Japanese pick-up trucks (also *kaa)* used like Indonesian bemos or Thai songthaews.

Small towns rely heavily on horsecarts and trishaws as the main mode of local transport. In the five largest cities (Yangon, Mandalay, Pathein, Mawlamyine and Taunggyi), public buses ply regular routes along the main avenues for a fixed per-person rate, usually no more than K2. Standard rates for taxis, trishaws and horsecarts are sometimes

'boosted' for foreigners. A little bargaining may be in order; ask around locally to find out what the going fares are. The supply of drivers and vehicles usually exceeds the demand, so it's usually not hard to move the fare down towards normal levels.

You can rent bicycles in Mandalay, Bagan, Pyin U Lwin and Nyaungshwe.

Yangon (Rangoon)

The capital of Myanmar for less than 100 years, Yangon (formerly called Rangoon) is 30 km upriver from the sea and has an air of seedy decay along with a great pagoda that is one of the real wonders of South-East Asia. A city of wide streets and spacious architecture, it looks run-down, worn-out and thoroughly neglected, although with the roadwork and new coats of paint ordered by the SLORC, your initial impression will probably be favourable. The streets are lively at night with hordes of stalls selling delicious-looking food, piles of huge cigars and those western cigarettes you've just unloaded.

History

As Myanmar's capital city, Yangon is comparatively young – it only became capital in 1885 when the British completed the conquest of Upper Myanmar and Mandalay's brief period as the centre of the last Burmese kingdom ended. Previous to the British conquest, Yangon was very much a small town in comparison with places like Bago, Pyay or Thaton. In 1755 King Alaungpaya conquered Lower Myanmar and built a new city on the site of Yangon, which at that time was known as 'Dagon'. Yangon means 'end of strife': the king rather vainly hoped that with the conquest of Lower Myanmar his struggles would be over. When the British arrived, they rebuilt the capital to its present plan and corrupted the city's name to 'Rangoon'.

Orientation

The city is bounded to the south and west by the Yangon River (also known as the Hlaing

River) and to the east by Pazundaung Canal, which flows into the Yangon River. The whole city is divided into townships, and street addresses are often suffixed with these (eg 126 52nd St, Botataung Township). Addresses in this northern area often quote the number of miles from Sule Paya – the landmark paya (pagoda) in the city's centre. For example, 'Pyay Rd, Mile 8' means the place is eight miles north of Sule Paya on Pyay Rd.

Downtown Yangon's grid-style layout is relatively simple to find your way around and pleasant enough to explore on foot.

Many of the major roadways were renamed after independence, but some of the old names persist and this can be confusing. Mahabandoola Garden St, for example, is still often called Barr St and has both new and old street signs.

Maps The *Yangon Tourist Map,* put out by MTT, is cheap and useful enough for most people. If you anticipate spending a lot of time in the capital, it's worth seeking out the more detailed and more up-to-date *Yangon Guide Map* (Ministry of Forestry, Survey Department).

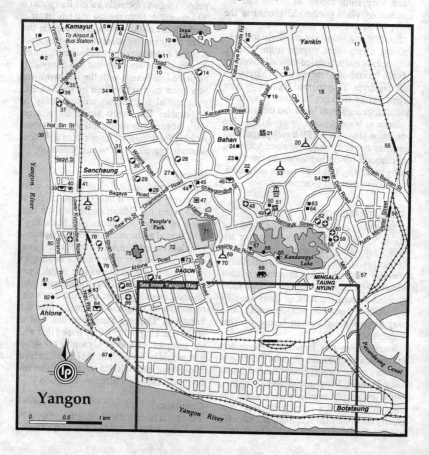

Yangon

Information

Tourist Office The MTT office is right by the Sule Paya at the junction of Sule Pagoda Rd and Mahabandoola St.

Money With the new Foreign Exchange Certificate system in place, no one bothers to change money at the official rate any more. If you're foolish enough to want to, the MTT cashier will gladly take foreign currency. Yangon is the best place in the country for changing money at the free-market rate. Ask around first to establish what the current rate is. If you've bought FECs at the airport, the best place to change them is at a hotel or shop licensed to accept FECs.

Post The GPO is a short stroll east of The Strand Hotel on Strand Rd. It's open Monday to Friday from 9.30 am to 4.30 pm.

Telephone The Central Telephone & Telegraph (CTT) office on the corner of Pansodan and Mahabandoola Sts is the only public place in the country where international telephone calls can be conveniently arranged.

PLACES TO STAY
- 5 Novel Garden Hotel
- 12 State Guest House
- 15 Mya Yeik Nyo Deluxe Hotel
- 24 Mya Yeik Nyo Supreme Hotel
- 25 Mya Yeik Nyo Royal Hotel
- 27 Comfort Inn
- 31 Liberty Hotel
- 34 Aurora Hotel
- 45 Royal Hotel
- 50 Beauty Land Hotel
- 63 Bagan Inn
- 64 Fame Hotel
- 65 Baiyoke Kandawgyi Hotel
- 73 Summit Parkview Hotel

PLACES TO EAT
- 8 Daw Sawyi Restaurant
- 19 Sala Thai Restaurant
- 44 Aung Thuka Restaurant
- 67 Dolphin Restaurant
- 70 Golden View Restaurant

OTHER
- 1 Institute of Marine Technology
- 2 Myanma Dockyards Enterprise
- 3 Hledan Railway Station
- 4 Hledan Zei (Market)
- 6 Judson Baptist Church
- 7 University of Yangon (Main Campus)
- 9 Post Office
- 10 Institute of Foreign Language
- 11 UNICEF
- 13 Tatmadaw Boat Club
- 14 South Korean Embassy
- 16 Sanpya Market
- 17 Bauktaw Railway Station
- 18 Kyaikkasan Grounds (Sports Field)
- 20 Chaukhtatgyi Paya
- 21 Mahasi Meditation Centre
- 22 Air Mandalay
- 23 Home for the Aged Poor
- 26 Vietnamese Embassy
- 28 Yuzana Supermarket
- 29 Singaporean Embassy
- 30 Czech & Slovak Embassy
- 32 Myanma TV & Radio Department
- 33 Institute of Medicine 1
- 35 Police Station
- 36 Hsimmalaik Bus Centre (for Bago, Pathein & Kyaikto)
- 37 Orthopaedic Hospital
- 38 San Pya Fish Market
- 39 Post Office
- 40 Police Station
- 41 Kyemyindaing Railway Station
- 42 Kohtatgyi Paya
- 43 Malaysian Embassy
- 46 Post Office
- 47 Martyrs' Mausoleum
- 48 Jivitdana Hospital
- 49 Japanese Embassy
- 51 Mogok Meditation Centre
- 52 Bogyoke Aung San Museum
- 53 Ngahtatgyi Paya
- 54 Post Office
- 55 Tamwe Railway Station
- 56 Manlwagon Railway Station
- 57 Mingala Zei (Market)
- 58 UNDP & FAO
- 59 Worker's Hospital
- 60 Kandawgyi Clinic
- 61 Eye, Ear, Nose & Throat Hospital
- 62 Nepalese Embassy
- 66 National Aquarium
- 68 Yangon Zoological Gardens
- 69 Maha Wizaya Paya
- 71 Shwedagon Paya
- 72 People's Square
- 74 Thai Embassy
- 75 Pyithu Hluttaw (National Assembly)
- 76 Ahlone Road Railway Station
- 77 Pakistani Embassy
- 78 Panhlaing Railway Station
- 79 People's Hospital
- 80 Thirimingala Zei (Market)
- 81 Myanma Fisheries Enterprise
- 82 Myanma Timber Enterprise
- 83 Police Station
- 84 Post Office
- 85 Chinese Embassy
- 86 Children's Hospital
- 87 Myanma Electric Power Enterprise

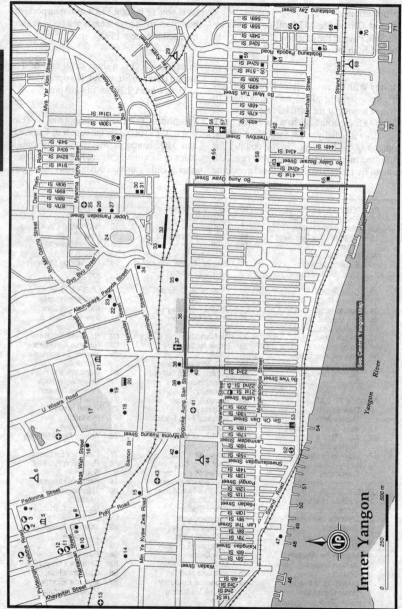

Inner Yangon

Yangon River

See Central Yangon Map

0   250   500 m

The office is open Monday to Friday from 8 am to 4 pm, weekends and holidays from 9 am to 2 pm.

The area code for Yangon is 01.

Shwedagon Paya

Dominating the entire city from its hilltop site, this is the most sacred Buddhist temple in Myanmar. Nearly 100 metres high, it is clearly visible from the air as you fly in or out of Yangon. You may see it as a tiny golden dot while flying over Myanmar to Kathmandu – magic! Visit it in the early morning or evening when the gold spire gleams in the sun and the temperature is cooler. Or see its shimmering reflection from across the Kandawgyi Lake at night. In 1587 a European visitor wrote of its 'wonderful bignesse' and that it was 'all gilded from foote to the toppe'. The Shwedagon has an

equally impressive appearance at night when it glows gold against a velvet backdrop.

A few facts and figures: the current stupa dates from the 18th century, though the site is undoubtedly much older; there are over 8000 gold plates covering the monument; the top of the spire is encrusted with more than 5000 diamonds and 2000 other precious or semiprecious stones; and the compound around the pagoda has 82 other buildings – it is this sheer mass of buildings that gives the place its awesome appeal.

In the compound's north-western corner is a huge bell which the butter-fingered British managed to drop into the Yangon River while carrying it off. Unable to recover it, they gave the bell back to the Burmese, who refloated it by tying a vast number of bamboo lengths to it.

The official admission fee for Shwedagon

	PLACES TO STAY				
30	Sunflower Inn	13	Central Women's Hospital	43	New General Hospital
31	Mann Shwe Gon Guest House	14	Deaf & Dumb School	44	Thayettaw Kyaung
33	Sakhantha Hotel	15	Than Zei (Market)	45	Pickjups to Bago
34	Thamada Hotel	16	School	46	Wadan St Jetty
59	Cozy Guest House	17	Myoma Ground	47	Inland Water Transport Ticket Offices
60	Three Seasons Hotel	18	National Theatre		
62	YMCA	19	Tatmadaw Hall		
63	YWCA (Under Renovation)	20	National Swimming Pool	48	Kaingdan St Jetty
				49	Lan Thit St Jetty
65	Grand Hotel	21	War Museum (Under Construction)	50	Hledan St Jetty
68	Euro Asia Hotel			51	Pongyi St Jetty
		22	Yuzana Pickle Tea	52	Myanma Agricultural Bank
	PLACES TO EAT	23	School		
8	Sei Taing Kya Teashop	24	Aung San Stadium	53	Kheng Hock Keong (Chinese Temple)
		25	Infectious Diseases Hospital		
61	Home Sweet Home			54	Sin Oh Dan St Jetty (Vehicle Ferry to Dalah)
		26	School		
	OTHER	27	School		
1	Egyptian Embassy	28	Theinbyu Zei (Market)	55	School
2	Indonesian Embassy	29	Shwe Pon Pwint Paya	56	Sikh Temple
3	French Embassy	32	Yangon Railway Station	57	Salvation Army Church
4	National Archives				
5	National Museum (Under Construction)	35	Myanma Railways Office	58	Ministers' Offices
				64	Myanma Five Star Lin Office
		36	Bogyoke Aung San Market		
6	Ein Daw Yar Paya	37	St Mary's Cathedral	66	General Hospital
7	No 2 Military Hospital	38	School	67	University of Yangon (Botataung Campus)
9	Ministry of Foreign Affairs	39	School		
		40	Institute of Dental Medicine	69	Botataung Paya
10	American Center & USIS			70	Sawmill
		41	Yangon General Hospital	71	Botataung Jetty
11	Sri Lankan Embassy			72	Myanma Five Star Line Cargo Jetty
12	Lao Embassy	42	Institute of Medicine		

is US$5, which includes an elevator ride to the raised platform of the stupa. There are separate elevators for Burmese and foreigners. If you come before 7 am, you may be able to get in for free.

Sule Paya

Also over 2000 years old and right in the centre of town, 46 metre Sule Paya makes a fine spectacle at night and the inside of the complex is lit up by pulsating neon.

National Museum

The museum, which is on Pansodan (Phayre)

St (around the corner from The Strand Hotel), houses nothing spectacular, but if you have time to kill in Yangon you could do worse.

There are three floors – the stairs to the upper floors are a bit difficult to find. The bottom floor contains jewellery and royal relics and the upper floors feature art and archaeology. Admission is US$5 and it's open from 10 am to 3 pm from Monday to Friday. If you plan to use a camera you must pay an additional K5 for a photography permit.

The government is building a new national museum on Pyay Rd, just around the corner

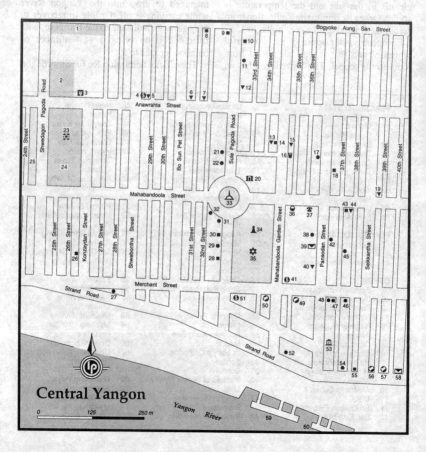

Central Yangon

0   125   250 m

Yangon River

from the Ministry of Foreign Affairs near the Indonesian and French embassies. No word yet as to when it will open but when it does the Pansodan St location will close and all exhibits will be moved to the new site.

Other

There's a mirror maze in the stupa of **Botataung Paya**. Yangon has a fine **open-air market** and the extensive **Bogyoke Aung San Market** is always worth a wander. It's a very pleasant stroll around **Kandawgyi Lake**, where you can visit the huge Karaweik non-floating restaurant. The Karaweik, a local attraction in its own right, is a reinforced concrete reproduction of a royal barge. Yangon has a British-built **zoo** with a collection of Burmese animals, and on Sunday there is a snake charmer and an elephant performance.

Maha Wizaya (Vijaya) Paya, almost opposite the southern gate to Shwedagon Paya, features a well-proportioned zedi built in 1980 to commemorate the unification of Theravada Buddhism in Myanmar. The king of Nepal contributed sacred relics for the zedi's relic chamber and Burmese strongman Ne Win had it topped with an 11-level *hti* (the umbrella or decorated top of a pagoda) – two more levels than the hti at Shwedagon.

The **Kaba Aye Paya** (World Peace Pagoda) is about 11 km north of the city, and was built in the mid-1950s for the 2500th anniversary of Buddhism. The huge reclining Buddha at **Chaukhtatgyi Paya** is also close by.

An interesting excursion from Yangon is a bus trip to **Kyauktan** with its small island pagoda. Another is to take a longer river/canal trip to the famed pottery village of **Twante**, two or three hours away.

Places to Stay

Since the privatisation of the hotel industry in 1993, there has been an explosion of hotel and guesthouse development in Yangon. There now seems to be a general surplus of rooms, so some places may be lowering their rates over the next couple of years. Price

PLACES TO STAY		
8	Central Hotel (Under Construction)	
9	Traders Hotel (Under Construction)	
10	Dagon Hotel	
14	Pyin U Lwin Guest House	
18	Best Inn	
26	White House Hotel	
28	Sofitel (Under Construction)	
30	Garden Hotel	
43	Myanmar Holiday Inn	
47	Zar Chi Win Guest House	
55	The Strand	

PLACES TO EAT	
5	New Delhi Restaurant
6	Simla Restaurant
7	Nila Briyane Shop
12	Golden Chetty Restaurant
13	999 Khauk Swai
15	Theingi Shwe Yee Tea House
19	Bharat Restaurant
40	Nan Yu Restaurant

44	Nilar Win's Cold Drink Shop

OTHER	
1	New Bogyoke Market
2	Open-Air Market
3	Sri Kali Temple
4	Myanma Oriental Bank
11	Inwa Book Store
16	Mr Guitar Cafe
17	Ava Tailoring
20	City Hall
21	Yangon Duty Free Store
22	Myanma Airways International
23	Moseah Yeshua Synagogue
24	Theingyi Zei (Market)
25	Theingyizei Plaza
27	Ministry of Trade
29	Air France
31	Myanma Travel & Tour (MTT)
32	Thai Airways International
33	Sule Paya
34	Independence Monument

35	Mahabandoola Garden
36	Pick-ups to Thanlyin
37	Central Telephone & Telegraph Office
38	Supreme Court
39	Post Office
41	Myanma Foreign Trade Bank
42	Biman Bangladesh
45	Pagan Bookshop
46	Sarpay Beikman Book Centre
48	Silk Air
49	Indian Embassy
50	US Embassy
51	Central Bank of Myanmar
52	Customs
53	National Museum
54	Myanma Airways
56	Australian Embassy
57	UK Embassy
58	GPO
59	Myanma Five Star Line Passenger Jetty
60	Pansodan St Jetty (Passenger Ferry to Dalah)

quotes at the following places almost always include tax and service as well as a rudimentary eggs-and-toast breakfast. Payment is accepted in US dollars cash or FECs only.

The cheapest place to stay in Yangon so far is *Win Guest House* (no phone) at 10 Zay St in Kamayut township. Plain rooms with two beds and little else cost US$7 a single, US$12 a double, with toilet and shower down the hall.

Back in central Yangon, the friendly and popular *White House Hotel* (☎ 71522) at 69/71 Konzaydan St, west of Sule Paya between Merchant and Mahabandoola Sts, offers similar room arrangements for US$10 per person.

The more conveniently located *Zar Chi Win Guest House* (☎ 75407) sits on the western side of 37th St, just south of Merchant St and near the book vendors and Pagan Bookshop. The usual cubicles cost US$15 a single, US$30 a double with shared bath and toilet or US$40 with private bath. Rates include breakfast and a left-luggage service is available. Some travellers have been able to bargain down to US$6 or US$8 per person without breakfast.

Right around the corner on busy Mahabandoola St, between 37th and 38th Sts, the friendly *Myanmar Holiday Inn* (☎ 70016) charges US$12/22 a single/ double without breakfast or US$15/25 with breakfast.

Another downtown place, the *Grand Hotel* (☎ 97493; fax 83360) at 108 Bo Aung Gyaw St, near Merchant St, has a grand facade but little else that deserves the name. A tilting wooden stairway leads to narrow, cluttered rows of not-so-clean cubicles that cost US$10/20 a single/double with shared bath.

Near the railway station at the corner of U Pho Kya Rd and Bo Min Yaung (U Ohn Khine) Rd is one of the best of the budget places. From the street outside it doesn't look like much, but upstairs the *Sunflower Inn* (☎ 76503, 75628) offers very clean if small rooms with communal bath for US$15/20 a single/double including breakfast. Or for US$25/30 you can have a room with private hot-water bath, fridge and TV; there are only a couple of these rooms available and they're often booked.

Places to Eat

There are numerous Indian restaurants around, particularly along Anawrahta St going west from Sule Pagoda Rd. The *New Delhi Restaurant* between 29th St and Shwebontha St serves a wide selection of north and south Indian dishes and is quite good. Some of the smaller Indian places specialise in biryani (which is spiced rice with chicken). Try the *Nila Briyane Shop* between 31st and 32nd Sts. It's crowded but the service is snappy. On Mahabandoola St, at the corner of Seikkhantha (Lewis) St, is the dependable and cheap *Bharat*, which is similar to the New Delhi.

You can get yoghurt or lassi (a delicious yoghurt drink) at *Nilar Win's Cold Drink Shop* at 377 Mahabandoola St, about midway between the YMCA and the Sule Paya. Before 1988, it was quite a travellers' meeting spot and the proprietors have been keeping the premises well scrubbed in preparation for their return.

Try the genuine Burmese food in the *Hla Myanma Rice House* at 27, 5th St, behind the Shwedagon Paya. It's popularly called the Shwe Ba because the famous Burmese actor of the same name had his house nearby. It's a plain and straightforward restaurant, but the food is very good and it also has Chinese and Indian dishes. Figure on spending no more than K250 per person for a full spread, not including beverages.

Back downtown, inexpensive traditional Burmese cuisine can be found at *Danubyu Daw Sawyi* at 194, 29th St, five blocks west of Sule Paya, or at *Khin Than Daw* at No 238 and *Nut Thoke Dar* at No 174 on the same street.

You can sample the whole range of Chinese cuisine in Yangon – from the familiar Cantonese through to the less well-known Shanghai, Sichuan, Beijing or Hokkien dishes. One of the more popular downtown spots these days is the recently remodelled *Nyein Chan Restaurant* at 234 Sule Pagoda Rd near the Dagon Hotel. It's packed nightly with Burmese and Chinese residents enjoying inexpensive but very acceptable southern Chinese food (duck dishes are especially good) and inexpensive, cold beer.

Modest western-style fast-food restaurants with sandwiches, burgers, pizza, spaghetti and the like are multiplying quickly in the city. Typical of the genre are *Home Sweet Home* (☎ 93001), on the corner of Mahabandoola and 52nd Sts, and *Excellent Burgers & Snacks*, on the northern side of Anawrahta St at 33rd St.

Entertainment
Yangon entertainment, never the highlight of any foreigner's Myanmar visit, was dealt a near death-blow by the 11 pm curfew imposed from 1988 to late 1992. The main form of local recreation is hanging out in the teashops or 'cold drink' shops.

Cinema A half dozen or so cinemas along Bogyoke Aung San St, east of Sule Paya, show films for K10 or less per seat. The normal fare is pretty awful; a succession of syrupy Burmese dramas, kungfu smash-ups and European or American action thrillers.

The American Center, behind the Ministry of Foreign Affairs at 14 Taw Win St, shows free American movies every Monday at noon.

Bars & Cafes *The Strand Bar*, far more sophisticated than its funky predecessor, is open from 11 am to 11 pm. Any foreign liquors you may be craving are bound to be among the huge selection of bottles behind the polished wooden bar. Modern watercolours of Burmese scenes decorate the walls and occasionally there's someone around to play the baby grand.

Founded by famous Burmese vocalist Nay Myo Say, *Mr Guitar Cafe* (☎ 85462) at 158-168 Mahabandoola Garden St is a small, two storey cafe-bar decorated with old guitars. Live folk music is featured nightly from 7 to 10 pm. Mr Guitar has a second branch at the back of Bogyoke Aung San Market.

The Nawarat Hotel's popular *Zawgyi Lounge* is a small but pleasant bar decorated with a series of original paintings by well-known Yangon muralist U Ba Kyi. The series depict various episodes in the life of a typical *zawgyi*, or accomplished Burmese alchemist. A Filipino pop band performs Monday through Saturday nights, and on Sunday evening a local jazz band plays. There is no cover charge.

Things to Buy
The sprawling, 70 year old Bogyoke Aung San Market (sometimes called by its British name, Scott Market), appropriately located on Bogyoke Aung San St, has the largest selection of Burmese handicrafts you'll find under one roof (actually several roofs).

Another major market, especially for locals who find Bogyoke Aung San Market a little too pricey, is Theingyi Zei, the biggest market in Yangon. This rambling affair extends four blocks east to west from Konzaydan St to 24th St, and north to south from Anawrahta St to Mahabandoola St. Most of the merchandise for sale represents ordinary housewares and textiles, but the market is renowned for its large section purveying traditional Burmese herbs and medicines.

Yangon isn't a place you would usually think of for tailor-made clothes, but prices for tailoring are among the lowest in South-East Asia. The selection of fabrics at tailor shops, however, is mostly restricted to synthetics. Cotton lengths in prints, plaids, solids and batiks can easily be found in the larger markets, so you may do better to buy cloth at a market and bring it to a tailor shop for cutting and sewing. Try Ava Tailoring (☎ 72973) on Pansodan St near the railway station at the Anawrahta St intersection. If you're measured the day you arrive, they can have clothes ready by the time you return from upcountry. Lain Lain Tailor at 142-143 Bo Galay Bazaar St and Globe Tailoring at 367 Bogyoke Aung San St are also well regarded.

Getting There & Away
Bus Most public and private buses to destinations north of Yangon leave from the Highway Bus Centre at the intersection of

MYANMAR

Pyay and Station Rds, just south-west of Yangon's airport in Mingaladon. Each bus line has its own little office at the station; for the most part these offices are lined up according to general route, eg one section for Nyaung U/Bagan, another for the Mandalay area, another for Taunggyi/Inle Lake and one for Mawlamyine/Dawei. To buy a ticket to any destination which requires a travel permit, you may be asked to show your papers. There are a number of snack shops with rice and noodle plates in case you get hungry while waiting for a departure.

Ordinary government buses are the cheapest and slowest: so slow that the Road Transport Enterprise won't even give arrival times. Private buses generally run better vehicles on tighter schedules for up to twice the government fare. Fares and departure times change with regularity to account for passenger demand; the best way to get a ticket is to show up around 5 am and start asking around (or visit the station the afternoon of the day before you want to go).

Most impressive of all are the new air-con express buses which run to Pyay, Meiktila, Mandalay and Taunggyi. These typically feature large Japanese, Chinese or Korean air-con buses with around 45 reclining seats, and even on-board video. Typical fares are K1300 (or US$10/FEC) for Mandalay, Meiktila or Taunggyi, K450 (or US$4/FEC) to Pyay. These lines also may stop in Bago and Taungoo, where small offices are maintained at roadside restaurants.

The major players on the popular Yangon to Mandalay route are Rainbow Express, Trade Express, Skyline Express and Myanmar Arrow Express, all of whom maintain offices at the Highway Bus Centre as well as in downtown Yangon. Meals are usually provided. Inquire at the offices about hotel pickup; some companies transfer passengers from their hotel to the bus terminal in vans or pick-ups.

Express bus offices downtown include:

Myanmar Arrow Express
    19/25 Aung San Stadium, Southern Wing
    (☎ 74294, 41276)

Rainbow Express
    96/98 Pansodan St (☎ 72250, 83621)
Skyline Express
    284/286 Seikkantha St (☎ 71711)
Trade Express
    9 Yawmingyi St, Dagon (☎ 89291)

Train The 716 km trip from Yangon to Mandalay is the only train trip most visitors consider – there are daily and nightly reserved cars on express trains on this route, where you can be sure of getting a seat. The express trains are far superior to the general run of Burmese trains. First class has reclining seats and is quite comfortable. Sleepers are available but hard to reserve.

In addition to the many trains operated by state-owned Myanma Railways, one private company runs out of Yangon railway station along the Yangon-Mandalay line. Dagon Mann (☎ 71310) reserves just four berths and six upper-class seats for foreigners on its private express train (No 17 Up on the public schedule), which departs Yangon at 3.15 pm on Wednesday, Friday and Sunday, arriving in Mandalay at 5.40 am the next morning. Obviously this is no quicker than the Myanma Railways trains, simply because they use the same engines and tracks. In fact the train really caters to Burmese residents, who pay a good deal less – K200 – for a wooden seat in 64 seat ordinary class. The same seat costs foreigners US$18; in exchange for paying nine times the usual fare, the foreigner is rewarded with a meal choice of hamburger, fried noodles or fried rice, plus one soft drink or beer. More expensive seats and sleepers are available.

Boat Along the Yangon River waterfront, which wraps around southern Yangon, are a number of jetties with boats offering long-distance ferry services. Four main passenger jetties service long-distance ferries headed up the delta towards Pathein or north along the Ayeyarwady to Pyay, Bagan and Mandalay: Pongyi, Lan Thit, Kaingdan and Hledan. Named for the respective streets that extend north from each jetty, all four are clustered in an area just south of Lanmadaw township and south-west of Chinatown. When you purchase a ticket for a particular ferry from the Inland Water Transport Company (IWT) office at the back of Lan Thit St jetty, be sure to ask which jetty your boat will be leaving from.

Myanma Five Star Line ships leave from the MFSL jetty – also known as Chanmayeiseikan jetty – next to Pansodan St jetty.

Getting Around

Bus Over 40 numbered city bus routes connect the townships of Yangon. Many buses date back to the 1940s and carry heavy teak carriages. Often they're impossibly crowded; a Burmese bus is not full until every available handhold for those hanging off the sides and back has been taken. Other routes use newer Japanese and Korean buses that aren't too bad; some routes also use pick-up trucks with benches in the back. If you can find a space you can get anywhere in downtown Yangon for K2 or less. Longer routes cost up to K5.

Train An interesting way of seeing the city, suburbs and surrounding countryside is to take the 'circle line' train from Yangon station. It's crowded with commuters on weekdays but on Saturday morning you can make a 2½ hour loop, allowing you to see the outskirts of the city and surrounding villages.

Taxi Licensed taxis carry red licence plates, though there is often little else to distinguish a taxi from any other vehicle in Yangon. The most expensive are the car-taxis – usually older, mid-sized Japanese cars. Fares are highly negotiable -- most trips around the downtown area shouldn't cost more than K180 one way. You can hire a non-registered cab for the whole day for no more than K2500 or US$25.

Cheaper are the tiny three-wheeled and four-wheeled Mazda taxis, close relatives of the Indian *bajaj* or Thai *tuk-tuks*. A short trip of six to eight blocks or so should cost no more than K50, longer distances downtown K80 to K100 one way.

Trishaw The Burmese-style pedicab or sai-kaa costs roughly K15 per person every km or so. Nowadays trishaws are not permitted on the main streets between midnight and 10 am. They're most useful for side streets and areas of town where traffic is light. As more cars and trucks deluge the roadways, it probably won't be too long before they're banned from the city centre altogether.

Around Yangon

THANLYIN (SYRIAM) & KYAUKTAN

If you've got a morning or afternoon to spare in Yangon, you can make an excursion across the river to Thanlyin and on to the paya (pagoda) at Kyauktan. Thanlyin was the base during the late 1500s and early 1600s for the notorious Portuguese adventurer Philip De Brito.

If you continue 12 km further until the road terminates at a wide river, you can visit the **Yele Paya**, or 'Mid-River Pagoda', at Kyauktan. It's appropriately named since the complex is perched on a tiny island in the middle of the river.

Getting There & Away

With the opening of a Chinese-built bridge over the Bago River a few years ago, the journey from Yangon to Thanlyin no longer involves a ferry trip. Large pick-ups to Thanlyin leave frequently throughout the day from a spot on Sule Pagoda Rd opposite city hall, a little east of Sule Paya. The fare costs K5 per person.

TWANTE

It's an interesting day trip from Yangon to Twante, a small town noted for its pottery and cotton-weaving, and for an old Mon paya complex. One can travel there by public jeep from Dalah (on the opposite bank of the Yangon River) or by ferry along the Yangon River and Twante Canal. The latter mode of transport is slower but provides a glimpse of life on and along the famous canal, which was dug during the colonial era as a short cut across the Ayeyarwady Delta.

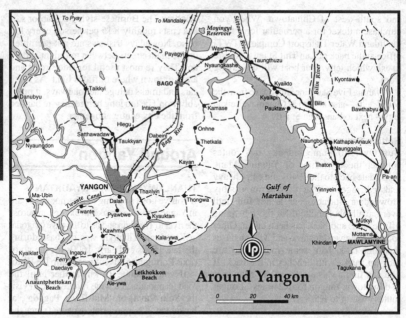

Around Yangon

0   20   40 km

BAGO

Bago is 80 km north-east from Yangon on the Mandalay railway line. Founded by the Mon, the city was a major seaport until the river changed course. This event, coupled with Bago's destruction by a rival Burmese king in 1757, was the city's downfall.

Shwemawdaw Paya

The Great Golden God Pagoda was rebuilt after an earthquake in 1930 and is 14 metres higher than the Shwedagon Paya in Yangon. Murals tell the sad story of the quake. Note the large chunk of the hti (the umbrella or decorated top of a pagoda), which was toppled by a quake in 1917, embedded in the north-eastern corner of the pagoda. Admission to the paya, for foreigners, costs US$3.

Shwethalyaung

This huge reclining Buddha image is nine metres longer than the one in Bangkok and claimed to be extremely life-like. A terrific

signboard gives the dimensions of the figure's big toe and other vital statistics. Foreigner admission is US$3 and worth it.

Other

Bago has other attractions. Beyond the Shwemawdaw is the **Hintha Gon Paya**, a hilltop shrine guarded by mythical swans. On the Yangon side of town, the **Kyaik Pun Paya** has four back-to-back sitting Buddhas. Just before the Shwethalyaung is the **Maha Kalyani Sima** (Hall of Ordination), and a curious quartet of standing Buddha figures.

Carry on beyond the Shwethalyaung and you soon come to the **Mahazedi Paya**, where you can climb to the top for a fine view of the surrounding country. The **Shwegugale Paya**, with 64 seated Buddha images, is a little beyond the Mahazedi.

Places to Stay & Eat

The six storey, modern-looking *Emperor Hotel* (☎ (052) 21349) on the main avenue through town between the railway and the river has a friendly, English-speaking manager. Small but clean rooms cost US$10 a single with fan and attached Asian-style toilet and bath, US$15 with air-con and hot water. The nearby *Htun Hotel* (☎ (052) 21973) at 233, 30th St costs US$10 for a single with shared bath, US$13 with air-con. Only doubles come with attached hot-water bath – a double with fan/air-con costs US$20/25.

Further south-west near the railway crossing, the *San Francisco Guest House* has rooms with shared toilet and bath for US$6 per person, or US$12/15 a single/double with attached bath. It's not particularly clean.

In the centre of town near the market are a number of food stalls, including some good Indian biryani stalls. Indian breakfasts are good at a small, friendly place on a side street south of the main avenue. The *Hadaya Cafe*, opposite the Emperor, is a teashop with a nice selection of pastries, ice cream and good-quality tea.

Getting There & Away

The buses from Yangon operate approximately hourly from 5 or 6 am and depart

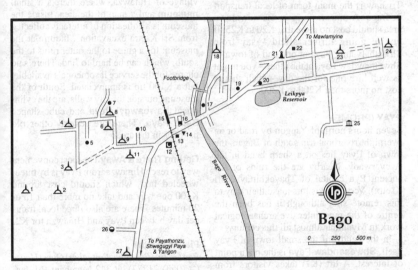

PLACES TO STAY
13 San Francisco Guest House
16 Emperor Motel
22 Shwewatun Hotel

PLACES TO EAT
14 Hadaya Cafe

OTHER
1 Mahagi Paya
2 Gothaingotan Paya
3 Shwegugale Paya
4 Mahazedi Paya
5 Woodcarving Workshop
6 Shwethalyaung
7 Mon Weavers
8 Kyinigan Kyaung
9 Four Figures Paya
10 Three Lions Cheroot Factory
11 Maha Kalyani Sima
12 Mosque
15 Railway Station
17 Market
18 Kha Khat Wain Kyaung
19 Trade Express Office & Liquor Shop
20 Clock Tower
21 Bogyoke Aung San Equestrian Statue
23 Shwemawdaw Paya
24 Hintha Gon Paya
25 Kanbawzathadi Palace Excavation & Museum
26 Bus Terminal
27 Kyaik Pun Paya

from Latha St. The fare is K30 and this can be a manageable bus trip. Avoid Sundays, however, when Bago is a very popular excursion from Yangon and the buses get very crowded. It can also be difficult to get back to Yangon because the buses will be booked out until late in the evening.

If you can't get the bus back to Yangon, try catching the train coming from Mawlamyine back to Yangon, which is supposed to arrive in Bago at 7.30 pm but is often one or two hours late. The fare is K11.

Getting Around

Trishaw is the main form of local transport in Bago. A one-way trip in the downtown area should cost no more than K20 to K25. If you're going further afield – say from Shwethalyaung Paya at one end of town to Shwemawdaw Paya at the other – you might as well hire one for the day, which should cost no more than K200 to K300.

PYAY (PROME)

Seven hours north of Yangon by road or an overnight riverboat trip south of Bagan, the town of Pyay lies on a sharp bend in the Ayeyarwady. Nearby are the ruins of the ancient Pyu capital of Thayekhittaya (Sri Ksetra). Very few visitors make their way to this remote site, although it has been the centre of the most intensive archaeological work in Myanmar almost all this century.

In the centre of the small town of Pyay itself, **Shwesandaw Paya** is the main point of interest. A lift (K1) takes visitors from street level to the elevated main stupa platform which, like the Shwedagon in Yangon, is perched on top of a hill. All in all, it's also one of the country's more impressive zedis, especially on its hillside setting.

Thayekhittaya & Hmawza

The ancient site of Thayekhittaya – known to Pali-Sanskrit scholars as Sri Ksetra – lies eight km north-east of Pyay along a good road that leads to Paukkaung. Taking this road, you'll first come to the towering **Payagyi** (Big Paya), an early, almost cylin-

drical stupa, by the roadside about two km from the edge of the city.

A few km further brings you to the junction where you turn off the Bagan road towards Paukkaung. The road runs alongside the extensive city walls of Sri Ksetra, and ahead on the left you can see the decaying **Payama**, similar in form to the Payagyi, to the north of the road. Surrounded by rice fields, Payama is at its most picturesque in the rainy season. You must walk a half km or so from the highway along a trail which winds through these fields to reach it.

A nearby turn-off south leads into the village of Hmawza, where there's a small **museum** and a map of the area. Inside the museum is a collection of artefacts collected from Sri Ksetra excavations. Inquire at the museum for a guide to the outer ruins to the south, which can be hard to find. There's no charge for the service if someone's available, but a K100 tip is appreciated. South of the museum, outside the city walls, are the cylindrical **Bawbawgyi Paya** and cube-shaped **Bebe Paya**. There are several other old pagodas in the area.

Getting There & Away The most convenient way to reach Hmawza from Pyay is by three-wheeled taxi, which should cost around K100 one way and take no more than 15 or 20 minutes. There are also three local trains per day between Pyay and Hmawza for K2.

Places to Stay

Pan Ga Ba (Pangaba, Pangabar) Guest House (☎ (053) 21277), at 342 Merchant Rd, features basic rooms, with two beds and a mosquito net, in a big house-like building for just K300 per person.

Near the Bogyoke Aung San statue in the middle of town, not far from the railway station, is *Aungapa (Aung Gabar) Guest House* (☎ (053) 21332) at 1463 Bogyoke St. Although the rooms here are a bit small and dark, they're clean and the management is helpful. Bath and toilet are down the hall. Rates run from US$5 per person. Up the road north a bit is the nicer *Shwemyodaw (Golden City) Guest House* (☎ (053) 21990) at 353

High St. Rooms with fan/air-con cost US$15/20, while four-bed air-con rooms are US$25.

Places to Eat

The clean, friendly and inexpensive *Meiywetwar Restaurant* (no English sign), opposite the post office near the Pyay Hotel, serves excellent traditional Burmese food.

The Indian teashop (no name) just south of the Chittee Inn offers decent potato curry and stuffed palatas for breakfast. There are also several Burmese teashops along Bogyoke St, east of the Bogyoke Aung San statue.

Getting There & Away

Bus In Yangon a transport company at the corner of Shwebontha St and Bogyoke Aung San St operates one ordinary bus per day to Pyay that costs just K80 per person; it leaves at 9.30 am and arrives at 4.30 pm. There are more choices from the Highway Bus Centre at the northern end of Yangon, such as Rainbow Express's air-con, 45 seat bus with door-to-door delivery for US$4 or the kyat equivalent.

Boat By riverboat from Bagan it's a two day trip to Pyay with an overnight stop at Magwe. The boat leaves Nyaung U jetty (six km north-east of Old Bagan) every day, except Thursday and Sunday, around 5 am and arrives two evenings later in Pyay around 8 pm. Deck class costs K55, cabins K110. Bring your own food and water, as the food served at the deck canteen is of questionable quality and no bottled water is available.

LETKHOKKON BEACH

Letkhokkon, about three hours by road from Dalah, is the closest beach to the capital. Located in Kunyangon township near the mouth of the Bago River, it's a delta beach facing the Gulf of Martaban with fine powder-beige sand and a very wide tidal bore that tends towards mud flats at its lowest ebb. Copious coconut palms along the beach help make up for the less than crystalline waters.

Getting There & Away

Vehicle ferries cross the Yangon River to Dalah from Sin Oh Dan St jetty between 18th and 19th Sts in Yangon. The road between Dalah and Letkhokkon is in very poor condition in spots. Count on around three hours to complete the journey without stops, more by public conveyance. Near the row of restaurants and teashops on the Dalah side you'll see a cluster of pick-up trucks and jeeps; ask around to see if anyone's going to Letkhokkon. Late morning is probably the best time to bargain – after the drivers have carried all their morning passengers to and fro and before the late afternoon driving circuit begins.

PATHEIN

Situated on the eastern bank of the Pathein River (also known as the Ngawan River) in the Ayeyarwady Delta about 190 km west of Yangon, Pathein is the most important delta port outside the capital despite its distance from the sea.

The scenic waterfront area, markets, umbrella workshops and colourful payas make the city worth a stay of at least a night or two. It also serves as a jumping-off point for excursions to the small beach resort of Chaungtha and further north to Thandwe in the Rakhine State.

Shwemokhtaw Paya, in the centre of downtown Pathein near the riverfront, is a huge golden, bell-shaped stupa. The hti consists of a top tier made from 6.3 kg of solid gold, a middle tier of pure silver and a bottom tier of bronze; all three tiers are gilded and reportedly embedded with a total of 829 diamond fragments, 843 rubies and 1588 semiprecious stones.

Settayaw Paya is perhaps the most charming of the several lesser known payas in Pathein. It is dedicated to a mythical Buddha footprint left by the Enlightened One during his legendary perambulations through mainland South-East Asia. The paya compound wraps over a couple of green hillocks dotted with well-constructed *tazaungs* (shrine buildings).

MYANMAR

Around 25 **parasol workshops** are scattered throughout the northern part of the city, off Mahabandoola Rd. The parasols come in a variety of colours; some are brightly painted with flowers, birds and other nature motifs. One type which can be used in the rain is the saffron-coloured monks' umbrella, which is waterproofed by applying various coats of tree resin over a two day period.

Places to Stay & Eat

Delta Guest House (☎ (042) 22131), at 44 Mingyi Rd, is a good downtown choice.

Small and simple though well-kept rooms cost US$5 per person with common bath downstairs, US$15 for special singles/doubles upstairs with air-con and attached bath.

A little west towards the river, at the corner of Merchant and Myenu Sts, *Koumudra Guest House* offers similar facilities and will probably charge similar prices after it becomes 'licensed lodging' for foreigners.

Among the more well-known and longest-running Chinese places is the *Zee Bae Inn* on Merchant St. The *Morning Star Restaurant* on Mingyi Rd also has decent Chinese food.

PLACES TO STAY	
20	Delta Guest House
21	Koumudra Guest House
28	Erawan Guest House

PLACES TO EAT	
18	Shwezinyaw Restaurant
22	Zee Bae Inn

OTHER	
1	Settayaw Paya
2	Pwo Karen Church
3	Shwezigon Paya
4	School
5	Myanmar Baptist Church
6	Division Office
7	Parasol Workshop
8	Twenty-Eight Paya
9	School
10	Sports Field
11	School
12	Sports Field
13	Clock Tower
14	Post Office
15	Customs House
16	City Hall
17	Shwemoktaw Paya
19	Myanmar Commercial Bank
23	Monastery
24	Mosque
25	Monastery
26	Bandoola Parasol Shop
27	St Peter's Cathedral
29	Hindu Temple

To Pathein Hotel

Bandoola Street

Pathein River

Strand Road

Mahabandoola Road

Merchant Street

Mingyi Road

Hospital

Canal

Shwezedi Street

Central Market

Zegyaung Road

Myenu Road

Victoria Street

Kaladan Street

Station Road

Railway Station

Pathein

0   300   600 m

Shwezinyaw Restaurant, at 24/25 Shwezedi St near Merchant St, is a Burmese/Indian Muslim hybrid with good curries and biryani. It's open from 8 am to 9 pm daily. The biryani at nearby *Mopale* is even better, though the place closes down around 6 or 7 pm.

Getting There & Away
Bus An ordinary bus to Pathein from Yangon's Highway Bus Centre costs just K60 but is crowded and slow – count on around eight hours to cover the distance. Better, if not faster, buses are available from Yangon's Hsimmalaik Bus Centre for K80; there are two departures daily, both at 5 am.

Boat Double-decker 'express' boats leave Yangon's Lan Thit St jetty around 3 and 5 pm daily and arrive at Pathein 16 to 18 hours later. In the reverse direction these boats leave Pathein at 4 and 5 pm daily. Passage costs K54 for upstairs-deck class (with assigned spaces), K48 downstairs and K161 per person for a comfortable two bed cabin. The latter can be difficult to book since there are only eight cabins – you should reserve three days in advance. Along with the two beds, each cabin comes with a washbasin and mirror; a common toilet and shower are shared by all cabin passengers.

There is also one 'ordinary' boat that leaves Yangon at 6 pm, arriving in Pathein 20 hours later. This one costs K44 deck class, K88 per person in the 'saloon' – a single cabin in the upper bow which has four beds. For either type of boat, foreigners must buy tickets from the deputy division manager's office next to Building 63 at Lan Thit St jetty.

CHAUNGTHA BEACH
West of Pathein on the Bay of Bengal coast, Chaungtha Beach has recently opened to foreign tourists. As western coast beaches go, this one fits somewhere between Letkhokkon further south and Ngapali to the north in terms of quality.

Places to Stay & Eat
All accommodation traditionally closes down from 15 May to 15 September. At the overpriced *Chaungtha Beach Hotel* (☎ (042) 22587; 87589 in Yangon) – also known as *New Paradise Hotel* – a bed in a rustic four bed dorm with attached cold-water shower costs US$24 per person. To add insult to high prices, these rooms stand next to an odiferous canal. The main section of the wooden hotel offers 'superior' rooms from US$54 to US$108.

A group of wooden *bungalows* next door go for US$10 per person in four-bed rooms with mosquito nets, high ceilings and attached shower and toilet.

The main street into the village from the beach is lined with rustic seafood restaurants. The better ones include *Pearl, Golden Sea* and *May Khalar*, all of which serve fresh lobster, clams, scallops and fish.

Getting There & Away
The rough 36 km road to Chaungtha from Pathein can be traversed by public bus (actually a large pick-up) in three to four hours. Two passenger trucks leave the Pathein bus terminal daily at 7 and 11 am for Chaungtha for K45 per person. From Pathein you first cross the Pathein River by ferry; the ferry runs roughly every hour from 6 am to 6 pm daily.

Mandalay Region

MANDALAY
Mandalay was the last capital of Myanmar to fall before the British took over, and for this reason it still has great importance as a cultural centre. It is Myanmar's second largest city with a population of around 500,000 and was founded, comparatively recently, in 1857. Dry and dusty in the hot season, Mandalay is a sprawling town of dirt streets, trishaws and horsecarts.

Although Mandalay itself is of some interest, the 'deserted cities' around it are probably even more worthwhile.

The area code for Mandalay is 02.

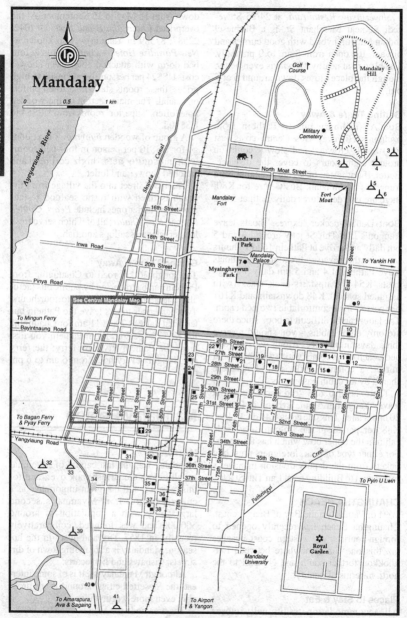

Mandalay

MYANMAR

0   0.5   1 km

Ayeyarwaddy River

Shweta Canal

Golf Course

Mandalay Hill

Military Cemetery

Mandalay Fort

North Moat Street

Fort Moat

Nandawun Park

Mandalay Palace

Myainghaywun Park

To Yankin Hill

East Moat Street

16th Street

18th Street

Inwa Road

20th Street

Pinya Road

See Central Mandalay Map

To Mingun Ferry

Bayintnaung Road

To Bagan Ferry & Pyay Ferry

86th Street
84th Street
83rd Street
82nd Street
81st Street
80th Street

Yangyiaung Road

26th Street
27th Street
28th Street
29th Street
30th Street
31st Street

32nd Street
33rd Street

34th Street
36th Street
37th Street

35th Street

77th Street
76th Street
75th Street
74th Street
73rd Street
71st Street
68th Street
66th Street
62nd Street

78th Street

To Pyin U Lwin

Paleingyi Creek

Royal Garden

Mandalay University

To Amarapura, Ava & Sagaing

To Airport & Yangon

Central Mandalay Map

1
2
3
4
5
6
7
8
9
10
11
12
13
14
15
16
17
18
19
20
21
22
23
24
25
26
27
28
29
30
31
32
33
34
35
36
37
38
39
40
41

Information

Tourist Offices The MTT office (☎ 22540) is in the Mandalay Swan Hotel. It's open from 7 am to 7 pm daily. MTT also has a desk at the airport to meet flights, and at the railway station to meet tourist trains – in order to steer you towards its approved hotels.

MTT's *Mandalay Tourist Map* is useful for getting to the main tourist sites, though it only details four hotels.

Admission Fees The MTT office also collects fees for the various tourist attractions around the city – US$5 per person for Mandalay Palace, US$4 each for Mahamuni Paya and Mandalay Hill; US$3 for Kuthodaw Paya; and US$2 each for Sandamani Paya, Kyauktawgyi Paya and Sagaing Hill. If you visit all these sights, the fees will add up to a steep US$22. Admission fees can also be paid at each site; some people manage to avoid paying by visiting before 7 am or after 5 pm, or by claiming to be on Buddhist pilgrimage.

The Ministry of Hotels & Tourism (MHT) receives a steady trickle of complaints about these relatively high entrance fees and there is talk the fees may be reduced or abandoned in the future.

Mandalay Fort

King Mindon Min ordered the construction of his imposing walled palace compound in 1857. A channel from the Mandalay irrigation canal fills the moat. On 20 March 1945, in fierce fighting between advancing British and Indian troops and the Japanese forces which had held Mandalay since 1942, the royal palace within the fort caught fire and was completely burnt out.

A major reconstruction project begun several years ago is finally finished and the results – mostly concrete construction topped by aluminium roofs – are not that impressive. Because the renovations were notorious for their use of draft labour – most often convict labour, but some local civilian labour as well – many locals as well as visitors refuse to enter the new 'palace'.

Mandalay Hill

An easy half-hour barefoot climb up the sheltered steps brings you to a wide view over the palace, Mandalay and the pagoda-studded countryside.

Kuthodaw Paya

This pagoda's 729 small temples each shelter a marble slab inscribed with Buddhist scriptures. The central pagoda makes it 730.

PLACES TO STAY
10 Inwa Inn
11 Mandalay View Inn
14 Mandalay Swan Hotel
16 Mya Mandalar Hotel
23 Popa II Hotel
24 Popa I Hotel
25 Pacific Hotel
26 Boss Hotel
27 Silver Cloud Hotel
30 Sea Hotel
31 Shanghai Hotel
35 Tiger Hotel
36 Great Guest House
38 Power Hotel

PLACES TO EAT
13 Pyigyimon Restaurant
17 Honey Garden Restaurant
18 Sakantha Restaurant
20 Marie-Min Vegetarian Restaurant
21 Too Too Restaurant
22 BBB Restaurant

OTHER
1 Yadanapon Zoo
2 Kyauktawgyi Paya
3 Kuthodaw Paya
4 Sandamuni Paya
5 Shwenandaw Kyaung
6 Atumashi Kyaung
7 Palace Watchtower
8 Independence Monument
9 School of Fine Arts, Music & Drama
12 Mandalay Marionettes
14 Myanmar Travels & Tours (MTT)
15 Police Academy
19 Mann Swe Gon Handicrafts
28 Gold-Leaf Workshop
29 Judson Baptist Church
32 Shwe In Bin Kyaung
33 Thakawun Kyaung
34 Jade Market
37 Moustache Brothers Pwe Troupe
39 Kin Wun Kyaung
40 Buddha Image Makers
41 Mahamuni Paya

Built by King Mindon around 1860, it is the world's biggest book. Don't confuse it with the **Sandamuni Paya**, which is right in front of it and which also has a large collection of inscribed slabs. The ruins of the **Atumashi Kyaung** (Incomparable Monastery) are also close to the foot of Mandalay Hill.

Shwenandaw Kyaung

Once a part of King Mindon's palace, this wooden building was moved to its present site and converted into a monastery after his death. This is the finest remaining example of traditional wooden Burmese architecture

in Mandalay since all the other palace buildings were destroyed during WWII.

Kyauktawgyi Paya

This pagoda at the base of Mandalay Hill was another King Mindon construction. The marble Buddha is said to have taken 10,000 men 13 days to install in the temple.

Mahamuni Paya

The Mahamuni Paya, or Arakan Pagoda, stands to the south of town. It's noted for its huge, highly venerated, Rakhine-style Buddha image, which is thickly covered in gold leaf.

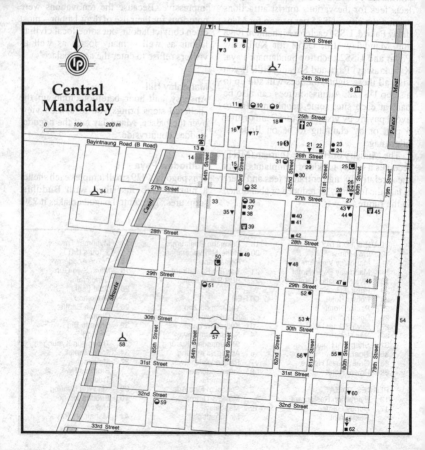

Central Mandalay

Around the main pagoda are rooms containing a huge five tonne gong and Khmer-style bronze figures. Outside the pagoda are streets full of Buddha image makers.

Other

The **Zegyo Market** in the centre of town comes alive at night. The 19th century **Eindawya Paya** and the 12th century **Shwekyimyint Paya** are also close to the centre. The latter is older than Mandalay itself. Several of the town's pagodas have amusing clockwork coin-in-the-slot displays. Mandalay's **museum** is tatty and entry costs US$4.

Places to Stay

Room rates at the bottom end now average US$5 to US$8 per person – high by Burmese standards but the lowest they've been in years. As more hotels and guesthouses obtain licences to accept foreigners, rates may drop even further.

The tidy *Sabai Phyu (Byu) Guest House* (☎ 25377), a multistorey, modern building at 58, 81st St (near Zegyo Market), offers

economy fan rooms with common bath for US$6 to US$10 a single, US$10 to US$15 a double. Another popular place in the same general vicinity is the three storey, 32 room *Royal Guest House* (☎ 22905) at 41, 25th St. Clean, if small, rooms here cost US$6/12 for singles/doubles with common toilet and shower facilities, or US$10/15 with attached toilet and cold-water shower.

Over at 81st and 26th Sts, the 136 room *Taung Za Lat Hotel* (☎ 23210) offers singles/doubles with common bath and toilet for US$6/10, with attached shower and common toilet for US$8/12, or with attached shower and toilet for US$10/15.

The *Garden Hotel* (☎ 25184) at 174, 83rd St is a typical Burmese-style hotel with decent economy rooms for US$6 to US$10 a single, US$15 to US$18 a double and nicer standard rooms for US$10 to US$35. All rooms come with air-con, TV, fridge and breakfast; all except the more expensive standard rooms feature shared toilet and hot-water shower facilities.

The *Coral Rest House* (☎ 24407), on the eastern side of 80th St between 27th and 28th

PLACES TO STAY			
5	Classic Hotel	16	Nylon Ice Cream Bar
6	Thailand Hotel	17	Mann Restaurant
11	Garden Hotel	21	Shells Cafe
18	Royal Guest House	27	Punjab Food House
22	Taung Za Lat Hotel	35	Shwe Let Yar
24	Sabai Phyu Guest		Myanmar Fast
	House		Food
28	Central Hotel &	43	Everest Restaurant
	Dream Hotel	48	Chin Shin Restaurant
29	Ayeyarwady Hotel	56	Htaw Yin Restaurant
37	Moder Hotel	60	Texas Cold Snack Bar
38	Universe Hotel	61	Shwe Wah Restaurant
40	New York Hotel		
41	New Star Hotel	**OTHER**	
42	Bonanza Hotel	2	Mosque
47	Man Ayeyarwady	7	Shwekyimyint Paya
	Hotel	8	Mandalay Museum
49	Hotel Sapphire	9	Buses to Taunggyi
55	Kaung Myint Hotel	10	HMV Pyin U Lwin
62	Palace Hotel		Jeeps
		12	Central Telephone
PLACES TO EAT			Office
1	Rainbow Restaurant	13	Clock Tower
3	Thai Yai Restaurant	14	Zegyo Market
4	Lashio Lay Restaurant	19	Bank
15	Min Min Restaurant	20	Sacred Heart
			Cathedral

23	Myanma Airways
	Office
25	Central Mosque
26	Sikh Temple
30	Air Mandalay Office
31	Main Bus Centre
32	Pick-ups to Monywa
33	Night Market
34	Eindawya Paya
36	Pick-ups to Pyin U
	Lwin
39	Hindu Temple
44	Bamboo Fan
	Factory
45	Hindu Temple
46	Night Market
50	Mosque
51	Pick-ups to
	Amarapura, Ava &
	Sagaing
52	Fire Lookout Tower
53	Police
54	Railway Station
57	Small Pagoda
58	Setkyathiha Paya
59	MMTA Pick-ups to
	Pyin U Lwin

Sts, offers basic rooms with shared facilities for US$5 per person. It's a very local scene and not much English is spoken.

The *Great Guest House* on the northern side of 39th St, between 80th St and the railway, is better; again, it sees few foreigners. This location is convenient to where the Moustache Brothers and other pwe troupes stage their performances.

The cheapest place to stay in Mandalay is also the quietest since it's quite removed from the central downtown area. *Si Thu Tourist Hotel* (☎ 26201), at 29, 65th St, between 30th and 31st Sts, offers the usual cubicles-along-a-corridor setup with shared bath and toilet facilities for US$4 per person; it's not clear whether this is a licensed place or not.

Places to Eat
The long-running *Too Too*, on the southern side of 27th St between 74th and 75th Sts, serves traditional Burmese food from pots lined up on a table, in typical Burmese fashion. The best Shan restaurants are found in the vicinity of 23rd St west of the moat. The popular *Lashio Lay Restaurant*, next to the Classic Hotel on 23rd St, offers a large array of spicy Shan dishes which changes on a daily basis and usually includes four or five vegetarian dishes. There are at least four other Shan places in the area.

There's a selection of Chinese eating places on 83rd St, between 26th and 25th Sts, not far from Zegyo Market. Here you'll find the popular *Mann Restaurant* – one of the city's better Chinese eateries. The nearby *Min Min*, on 83rd St between 26th and 27th Sts, has Chinese Muslim food – it's reasonably cheap, and the food is quite OK.

The strictly vegetarian *Marie-Min Vegetarian Restaurant*, on 27th St between 74th and 75th Sts, serves delicious chapatis, pappadums, curries, pumpkin soup and eggplant dip, plus such non-Indian delights as strawberry lassis (yoghurt shakes), muesli, guacamole, hash-brown potatoes, pancakes and various western-style breakfasts (served all day). The menu, written in eight languages, is priced quite reasonably.

Punjab Food House on 80th St near 27th is a friendly, Sikh-run curry shop with chapatis, rice and vegetarian curries. Across the street from Punjab House, next to the Nepalese temple, is the slightly larger *Everest Restaurant*, with a tasty 'morning nasta' of chapati with vegetables, dosai and aloo puri on occasion.

Shells Cafe, on the northern side of 26th St between 81st and 82nd Sts, serves the best selection of European, Chinese and Burmese pastries in town along with tea, coffee and soft drinks. It's open from 6 am to 6 pm daily.

Entertainment
Mandalay Marionettes (☎ 24581), on 66th St between 26th and 27th Sts, is a small theatre where marionette shows, music and dancing are performed nightly at 8.30 pm. The show lasts around an hour and features selections from the *zat pwe* and *yama pwe* traditions. The admission fee seems to fluctuate between K200 and K400 per person depending on the number of tourists in town.

Things to Buy
Markets Zegyo Market – a redundant term since 'Zegyo' *(zei gyo)* means 'Central Market' – encompasses two large buildings on 84th St; one between 26th and 27th Sts, the other between 27th and 28th Sts. You can find just about anything made in Myanmar here, from everyday consumer goods to jewellery and fine fabrics.

Mandalay is a major crafts centre and you can get some really good bargains if you know what you're looking for. There are many little shops in the eastern part of the city near the Mya Mandalar and Mandalay Swan hotels selling a mixture of gems, carvings, silk, kalaga tapestries and other crafts. If you enter without a tout (most of the younger trishaw or horsecart drivers are into this), you'll get better deals than with a tout, as they are usually paid high commissions.

You can visit a bamboo paper factory on 80th St between 36th and 37th Sts. Here the artisans make fans of paper and bamboo for weddings and banquets.

Getting There & Away

Air Both Myanma Airways and Air Mandalay fly daily to Mandalay from Yangon.

Bus Private buses from Yangon's Highway Bus Centre range in price from K500 to K1200 for a one-way fare, or up to US$10 on the private air-con express buses. For most other destinations outside Mandalay, the usual mode of transport is Japanese pick-up truck. Several companies run pick-ups to Bagan, including Bagan Express at the corner of 82nd and 32nd Sts.

Private pick-ups offering reserved seats to Nyaungshwe (Yaunghwe) are available for US$10 from 23rd St near the Classic Hotel. If you feel like roughing it, you can catch a government bus to Taunggyi for K100 (a large bus) or K300 (an ordinary pick-up) from the bus centre. The trip takes at least seven hours.

From the main bus centre, buses to Lashio cost K100 for the full-day trip. For K400 you can get a nicer pick-up from 23rd St, just north of Rainbow Restaurant. This is also the place to find transport to Mu-se on the Chinese border, although for the latter you'll probably need to show a permit.

Other departures from the main bus centre at the corner of 26th and 82nd Sts include Meiktila (K75, 4½ hours, three times daily), Monywa (K45, 3½ hours, three times daily), Kyauk Padaung (K150, five hours, twice daily), Shwebo (K45 to K60, three hours, three times daily) Pyinmana (K165, seven hours, once daily), Taungoo (K200, 11½ hours, once daily), Bago (K275, 14 to 15 hours, once daily).

Train Although there are a number of trains each day between Yangon and Mandalay, you should only consider the day or night expresses since the other trains represent everything that can be wrong with Burmese rail travel – slow, crowded, uncomfortable and so on. Additionally, it's possible to reserve a seat on the express services, and on these special 'impress the tourists services' you really do get a seat – not a half or a third of a seat. First class even has reclining seats

and is quite comfortable. Sleepers are available but hard to reserve.

Myanma Railways operates daily trains from Mandalay to Myitkyina, Monywa (Ye U) and Lashio.

Boat The Inland Water Transport office (☎ 21144, 21467) is at the Gawwein jetty, at the western end of 35th St (Yangyiaung Rd). For information on ferries to Bagan or Pyay, see the appropriate Getting There & Away sections in the Bagan and Pyay sections.

Getting Around

Bus Mandalay's city buses are virtually always crowded, particularly during the 7 to 9 am and 4 to 5 pm 'rush hours'.

Taxi Around Zegyo Market you'll find hordes of three and four-wheelers. They operate within the city for around K50 to K75 per trip. It's possible to hire cars, jeeps or pick-ups by the day for tours around Mandalay. Count on around K1500 to K2000 for a trip to Amarapura and Sagaing that includes an English-speaking guide; the trucks will take up to eight people so it needn't be expensive.

Trishaw & Horsecart The familiar back-to-back trishaws are the usual round-the-town transport. Count on K25 for a short ride in a trishaw, K40 for a longer one – say, from the Mya Mandalar Hotel to Zegyo Market. Figure on K300 a day per trishaw for all-day sightseeing in the central part of the city, K500 if you include both Mahamuni Paya and Mandalay Hill towards the northern and southern ends of the city. You must bargain for your fare, whether by the trip, by the hour or by the day.

Bicycle There are several places downtown where you can rent bicycles, including a couple of places near the Royal Guest House on 25th St and another place opposite the Mann Restaurant on 83rd St. The average cost is K25 to K35 per hour or K100 to K150 per day, depending on the bike's condition.

AROUND MANDALAY

Close to Mandalay are four 'deserted cities', which make interesting day trips by taxi or bicycle. You can also visit Pyin U Lwin, further to the north-east, which probably requires an overnight stop.

Amarapura

Situated 11 km south of Mandalay, the 'City of Immortality' was the capital of Upper Burma for a brief period of time before the establishment of Mandalay. Among the most interesting sights is the rickety 1.2-km-long **U Bein's Bridge** leading to the **Kyauk-tawgyi Paya**. Just out of town on the road to Sagaing, **Bagaya Kyaung** is one of Myanmar's largest and most active wooden monasteries, dating from the mid-19th century.

Sagaing

If you continue a little further beyond Amarapura, you'll reach the Ava Bridge, the only bridge across the Ayeyarwady River. Built by the British, it was put out of action during WWII and not repaired until 1954. Crossing the bridge will bring you to Sagaing with its temple-studded hill. Sagaing's best known pagoda is not on Sagaing Hill – you have to continue 10 km beyond the town to reach the **Kaungh-mudaw Paya**, which is said to have been modelled on a well-endowed queen's perfect breast.

Ava

The ancient city of Ava, for a long time a capital of Upper Burma after the fall of Bagan, is on the Mandalay side of the Ayeyarwady River close to the Ava Bridge. To get to it, take bus No 8, which runs right down to the Myitnge River, which you must cross by a ferry or canoe; or get off the Sagaing minibus at the Ava Bridge and stroll across the fields to the Myitnge River. There is very little left of Ava today apart from the **Maha Aungmye Bonzan** monastery and a crumbling 27-metre-high watchtower.

Around Mandalay

0   25   50 km

To Mogok & Bhamo

Kyaukmyaung Singu

Shwebo

Hanlin

Wetlet

31

Mayabin

Sedaw

Pai River

Madaya

Sadaung

To Lashio

Ayeyarwady River

To Monywa

Ondaw Mingun

Mandalay

Pyin U Lwin

Ayeyarwady River

Ngazun

Sagaing

Ava

Amarapura

Lema

Myotha

Yeywa

To Myingyan

18

Kyaukse

Ywamonggyi

Zawgyi River

Kanna

Myitta

Natogyi

2

To Thazi & Yangon

Mingun

The fourth of the old cities is Mingun, on the opposite bank from Mandalay, a pleasant 11 km trip upriver. Get a riverboat from the bottom of 26th St (B Rd). The cost is around K10 and the trip takes anything from 45 minutes to two hours. The trip to Mingun is very pleasant and makes a very good introduction to Burmese river travel, particularly if you do not take the boat to Bagan.

Principal sights at Mingun are the huge ruined base of the **Mingun Paya** and the equally grandiose **Mingun Bell**. The pagoda would have been the largest in the world if it had been completed. The bell is said to be the largest uncracked bell in the world – there is a bigger one in Russia but it is badly cracked.

Monywa

The **Thanboddhay Paya** here is one of the largest in Myanmar and is said to contain 582,357 Buddha images. The town of Monywa, a trade centre for the Chindwinn Valley, is 135 km north-west of Mandalay. Buses leave for Monywa regularly from the corner of 83rd St and 27th Rd in Mandalay, cost around K45 and take about three hours. You can also take a Ye U train from Mandalay for only K15, but this trip takes five or six hours.

On the north-eastern side of the main road into town, the *Great Hotel* (☎ (071) 21930) has rooms with good mattresses and attached shower and toilet for US$10 per person.

Pyin U Lwin (Maymyo)

This old British hill station, formerly called Maymyo after the British Colonel May, lies just 60 km north-east of Mandalay and about 800 metres higher.

The chief pleasure of Pyin U Lwin is wandering among the many old Tudor-style mansions and paying a visit to the British bachelor's quarters of Candacraig. You can read a delightful description of Candacraig in Paul Theroux's *Great Railway Bazaar*. There is also a large **botanical gardens**, designed by the British colonialists and built with Turkish POW labour (even the British used draft labour to build tourist attractions!).

Places to Stay & Eat *Golden Dream Hotel*, close to the tower and the HMV pick-up stop, is a rambling place where rooms with shower and toilet down the hall cost US$5 per person. On a side street near a canal, east of Purcell Tower and north of the Mandalay-Lashio road, *Ruby Guest House* charges US$5 for small singles or US$8/15 for larger singles/doubles with shared shower and toilet, US$10/20 for better rooms with private shower and toilet. The *Grace Hotel* at 114A Nann Myaing Rd is a one storey inn,

with rooms costing from US$5 to US$8 per person.

The ex-colonial, teakwood *Candacraig* – now officially known as the *Thiri Myaing Hotel* – has small singles with common bath for US$12, plus larger rooms with attached bathroom for US$24/30 a single/double. Rates include breakfast.

Apart from Candacraig there are a number of assorted eating places in the town centre near the market and clock tower, including several inexpensive Chinese and Indian places.

Getting There & Away From Mandalay, you can take a pick-up truck to Pyin U Lwin for K340 per person. These depart from several places around the centre of Mandalay (there are frequent departures from some markets – see the map) from 5 am until about 3 pm and the trip takes about two to 3½ hours up, two to 2½ down. There is also a daily train but it's more for railway enthusiasts, as it takes four to five hours to negotiate the many switchbacks.

Getting Around Most of the town's famous horsecoaches are stationed near the mosque on the main street downtown. Fares are steep by Myanmar standards: figure on K50 to K60 to travel from the mosque to the Shan market, K150 for the round trip to Candacraig or the Botanical Garden, K500 for all-day sightseeing. You can hire bicycles to explore the town at the Grace Hotel or at either of the two crafts shops on the Mandalay-Lashio road. The going rate is K10 per hour or K70 per day.

Mogok

Famed for the surrounding natural beauty and for the brilliant rubies and sapphires pulled from its red earth, the township of Mogok was until recently completely off limits to foreigners. One is supposed to obtain a travel permit endorsed for Mogok before being permitted to stay overnight. It's roughly 200 km north of Mandalay and there are pick-ups daily between the two towns.

Bagan Region

BAGAN (PAGAN)

One of the true wonders of Asia, Bagan (formerly spelt Pagan) is a bewildering, deserted city of fabulous pagodas and temples on the banks of the Ayeyarwady, to the south-west of Mandalay. Bagan's period of grandeur started in 1057 when King Anawrahta conquered Thaton and brought back artists, artisans, monks and 30 elephant-loads of Buddhist scriptures.

Over the next two centuries, an enormous number of magnificent buildings were erected, but after Kublai Khan sacked the city in 1287 it was never rebuilt. A major earthquake in 1975 caused enormous damage but everything of importance has now been restored or reconstructed. Unhappily, the plunderers who visit places like Bagan to scavenge for western art collectors have also done damage, but it is definitely the place in Myanmar not to be missed.

Orientation

Bagan Archaeological Zone, sometimes known as Old Bang, contains just four hotels, the offices of Myanma Airways and Air Mandalay as well as MTT. The latter is open from 8 am to 8 pm daily; its main function is to administer the admission fee system for the Bagan Archaeological Zone.

Nyaung U is the area's largest settlement, from where most public transport departs, including buses and the Mandalay ferry. Bagan airport is also near Nyaung U.

Information

The entry fee into the Archaeological Zone is US$10 per day for the first two days, US$2 per day thereafter. The fee is collected at the airport from those arriving by air or by the local hotels and guesthouses for everyone else.

Maps You can purchase two useful maps at the MTT office in the Bagan Archaeological Zone, MTT's own *Bagan Tourist Map* and

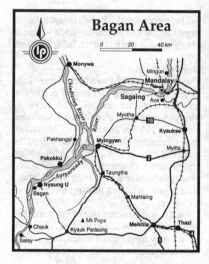

the independently produced *Tourguide Map of Bagan Nyaung U.*

Things to See

Tharaba (Sarabha) Gateway The ruins of the main gate on the eastern wall are all that remain of the old 9th century city wall. Traces of old stucco can still be seen on the gateway. The gate is guarded by highly revered brother and sister nats, the male (Lord Handsome) on the right, the female (Lady Golden Face) on the left.

Ananda Pahto One of the finest, largest, best preserved and most revered of the Bagan temples was built in 1091 and houses four standing Buddhas and two sacred Buddha footprints. Facing outward from the centre of the cube, four 9.5 metre standing Buddhas represent the four Buddhas who have attained nirvana. On the full moon of Pyatho (mid-December to mid-January), a huge pagoda festival attracts thousands to Ananda.

Thatbyinnyu Pahto The highest temple in Bagan, this huge structure consists of two cubes; the lower one merges into the upper

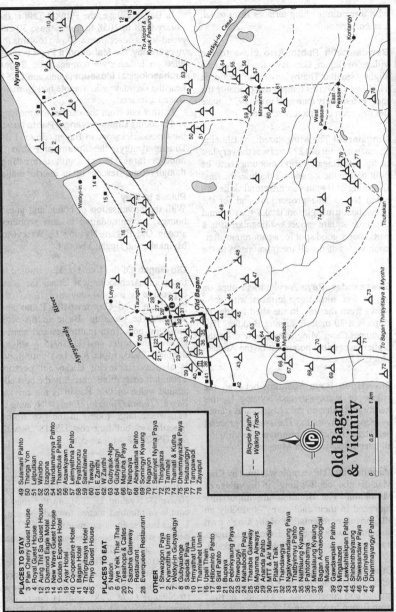

MYANMAR

Old Bagan & Vicinity

PLACES TO STAY
3 Pan Cherry Guest House
4 Royal Guest House
12 Aung Thu Sa Guest House
13 Diamond Eagle Motel
14 New Wave Guest House
15 Golden Express Hotel
19 Ayar Hotel
40 Co-operative Hotel
41 Bagan Hotel
42 Thiripyitsaya Hotel
65 Phyo Guest House

PLACES TO EAT
6 Ayeyeik Thar Thar
20 Teashops & Cafes
27 Saraba Gateway
Restaurant
28 Everqueen Restaurant

OTHER
1 Shwezigon Paya
2 Kyanzittha Umin
7 Wetkyi-in Gubyaukgyi
8 Gubyauknge
9 Sapda Paya
10 Hmyathat Umin
11 Thamiwhet Umin
16 Upali Thein
17 Htilominlo Pahto
18 Sint Pahto
21 Bupaya
22 Pebinkyaung Paya
23 Shwegugyi
24 Mahabodhi Paya
25 Tharaba Gateway
26 Myanma Airways
29 Ananda Pahto
30 MTT & Air Mandalay
31 Pitakat Taik
32 Thandawgya
33 Ngakywenadaung Paya
34 Thatbyinnyu Pahto
35 Nathlaung Kyaung
36 Manuha Kyaung
37 Nanpaya
38 Bagan Archaeological
Museum
39 Gawdawpalin Pahto
43 Mingalazedi
44 Lawkahteikpan Pahto
45 Shinbinthalyaung
46 Shwesandaw Paya
47 Guninyiahma
48 Dhammayangyi Pahto
49 Sulamani Pahto
50 Thinga Yon
51 Lemyethna
53 Winido
53 Izagona
54 Nandamannya Pahto
55 Thambula Pahto
56 Asawkyawn
57 Leimyethna Pahto
58 Payathonzu
59 Sawhlawine
60 Tawagu
61 Wi Zanthi
62 Wi Zanthi
63 Gubyauk-Nge
64 Gubyaukgyi
66 Manuha Paya
67 Nanpaya
68 Abeyadana Pahto
69 Somingyi Kyaung
70 Nagayon
71 Seinnyet Nyima Paya
72 Thingaraza
73 Tarmani
74 Dhammyazika Paya
75 Dhammayazika Paya
76 Hsutaunggyi
77 Tampawadi
78 Zayaput

Bicycle Path/
Walking Track

0   0.5   1 km

To Airport &
Kyauk Padaung

To Bagan Thiripyitsaya & Myothit

To Bagan Thiripyitsaya & Myothit

with three diminishing terraces from which a *sikhara* rises.

Gawdawpalin Pahto Also close to the village of Bagan, Gawdawpalin looks like a slightly smaller Thatbyinnyu. Built between 1174 and 1211, this temple was probably the most extensively damaged in the 1975 quake but has been completely restored.

Mingalazedi The Mingalazedi, or Blessing Stupa, was built in 1277 and was the very last of the late Bagan period monuments to be built before the kingdom's decline, the final flowering of Bagan's architectural skills. It's noted for its fine proportions and for the many beautiful, glazed jataka tiles around the three square terraces. Mingalazedi is a particularly good spot for a panoramic after-noon views of the all the monuments to the east.

Shwesandaw Paya A cylindrical stupa on top of five ultra-steep terraces with good views from the top. In the shed beside the stupa is a 20 metre reclining Buddha. This monument and Mingalazedi now offer the highest accessible points within the Archae-ological Zone.

Shwezigon Paya Standing between the village of Wetkyi-in and Nyaung U, this traditionally shaped gold pagoda was started by King Anawrahta. The stupa's graceful bell shape became a prototype for virtually all later stupas all over Myanmar.

Manuha Paya This temple was built by King Manuha, the 'captive king', in the village of Myinkaba. The Buddhas are impossibly squeezed in their enclosures – possibly an allegorical representation of the king's own discomfort with captivity. Excellent lacquer-ware workshops can be visited in Myinkaba.

Other Sights The **Htilominlo Pahto** was built in 1211 and has fine Buddhas on the ground and upper levels. It's beside the road from Bagan to Nyaung U.

In Bagan village, the **Pitakat Taik** is the library built in 1058 to house those 30 ele-phant-loads of scriptures. Down towards the Ayeyarwady, the **Mahabodhi Paya** is mod-elled on Indian-style temples. The **Bagan Archaeological Museum** (admission US$4) near the Gawdawpalin Temple houses many Bagan artefacts.

Further out from the centre, the massive and brooding **Dhammayangyi Pahto** boasts the finest brickwork in Bagan. Beyond the Dhammayangyi, the **Sulamani Pahto** is another larger temple with interesting, though recent, frescoes on its interior walls.

Places to Stay

With the privatisation of hotels and guest-houses, accommodation is now scattered among Old Bagan, Nyaung U, Wetkyi-in, Myinkaba and Bagan Myothit.

Old Bagan Of the four hotels permitted in the main Archaeological Zone, the least expensive is the *Co-operative Hotel* (no phone) next to Gawdawpalin Pahto and opposite the museum. Basic rooms with mosquito nets, firm mattresses and shared shower and toilet cost US$8/15 a single/double, US$20 a triple. A six bed 'dormitory' is also available for US$6 per person. Though it costs more, currently the best all-around value in Old Bagan is the private *Bagan (Thante/Thande) Hotel* (☎ Nyaung U 12), where large rooms in the two storey 'guesthouse' building cost US$18/26 with fan, US$20/28 with air-con.

Wetkyi-in & Nyaung U This end of the Bagan area is becoming a modest accommo-dation centre. In Wetkyi-in, the *Royal Guest House* (☎ Nyaung U 285), up the road a couple of hundred metres towards Nyaung U, has smaller economy rooms for US$7 per person with shared toilet and cold-water shower, and equally small standard rooms with attached facilities for US$10 per person. Across the road towards Shwezigon is the comfortable *Pan Cherry Guest House* (☎ Nyaung U 74, 228), with 11 fan-cooled singles/doubles with shared bath for US$8/12, three rooms with air-con and attached cold-water shower for US$12/20.

In Nyaung U the *Lucky Seven Guest House* (☎ Nyaung U 77) has rooms with ceiling fans for US$7 a single, US$13 a double. Rates include a substantial breakfast; toilet and cold-water shower facilities are shared. The local-style *Shwe Li Guest House* (☎ Nyaung U 291), on the south side of the road a little west of the traffic circle and central market, features small rooms along a corridor for the same rates. There are several other guesthouses in this area with similar conditions and rates.

Myinkaba Next to Gubyaukgyi at the northern end of the village is the quiet and well-managed *Phyo Guest House*. Eight rooms along an air-con corridor share three bathrooms; the rates are US$8/15 a single/double including breakfast.

Bagan Myothit (New Bagan) This village currently offers more accommodation than any other town or village in the entire Bagan area. The *Queen Hotel* is a somewhat musty local-style place where 10 large rooms with ceiling fans and attached bathrooms (hot water on request) cost US$15/24 a single/double for foreigners. *Bagan Beauty Hotel*, a well-constructed, thick-walled two storey house, has three single rooms and nine double rooms for US$6 per person. On the opposite side of the street, the single-storey *Mya Thida Hotel* has just six rooms with attached hot-water shower and toilet, plus air-con in the corridor, for US$8 per person. This rate can sometimes be negotiated to as low as US$6/8 a single/double if you forego breakfast.

Paradise Guest House offers rooms with ceiling fans and hard beds for US$8/15/21 a single/double/triple with breakfast. The Indian owners of Mandalay's popular Marie Min Restaurant plan to build their own guesthouse on a piece of land opposite the Paradise Hotel.

Places to Eat
Try the *Thiripyitsaya* for a good cold beer as

you watch the sun set over the river from the veranda.

Just outside Tharaba Gateway, the friendly *Sarabha Gateway Restaurant* serves well-seasoned and reasonably priced Burmese, Chinese and Thai food in a simple, quiet, indoor-outdoor setting. Three popular places outside the Archaeological Zone towards Wetkyi-in and Nyaung U are the *Nation* (opposite Shwezigon Paya), *Aye Yeik Thar Yar* (also near Shwezigon) and *Myahadanar* (on the road between Bagan and Nyaung U). The menus at all three are similar, mostly Chinese with some Burmese. There is also a cluster of cheap cafes and teashops next to the boat landing below the Ayar Hotel.

There are a couple of teashops in Myinkaba but nothing else so far. Near Bagan Myothit the *River View* stands above the river off the western side of the road. The menu features both Burmese and Chinese dishes, most of them well prepared. Prices are moderate to high. The nearby *Royal* and *Yar Zar* restaurants aren't quite as upscale but offer similar menus.

Getting There & Away
Air Both Myanma Airways and Air Mandalay fly to Nyaung U-Bagan airport from Yangon, Mandalay and Heho.

Bus, Van & Share Taxi Pick-ups operate daily from Mandalay's main bus centre on 26th St and cost K250 per person. It's a rugged eight hour trip. Share taxis – Toyota hatchbacks – are available to Bagan Myothit for K800 per person.

When spare seats are available, Tiger Head Express will drop passengers off in Meiktila or Thazi on the way to Taunggyi for K250. If there's competition for the seats, Tiger Head sometimes charges the full Taunggyi fare, K500. You could also bus to Meiktila and catch one of several Yangon-bound air-con express buses coming from Mandalay.

Boat A passenger ferry departs Mandalay at 5.30 am every Thursday and Sunday on its down-river cruise to Bagan. The official foreigner fare is US$10 in upper-deck class, US$30 for a cabin. You can get on board the boat the night before departure and grab a piece of deck space, thus saving the cost of a night's accommodation.

A slower, much cheaper ferry does the same route every day except Thursday and Sunday, taking roughly 26 to 29 hours and costing just K40. The slower boat stops one night at Pakkoku, where there are several places to stay including the Myayatanar Inn at 2288 Main Rd.

Getting Around
The Nyaung U-Bagan airstrip is about five km south-east of Nyaung U, which is five km north-east of Old Bagan. Car taxis are available for K200 to K600, depending on the destination.

There is a bus service (pick-up trucks once again) between Nyaung U and Bagan for K3.

You can hire horsecarts from place to place or by the hour; count on an hourly rate of around K50 to K60, K250 for the whole day, or K300 with two passengers.

Bicycles – available for hire at most hotels and guesthouses – are a great way to get around. The usual cost is K80 per day or K50 for half a day.

AROUND BAGAN
Mt Popa
Near Kyauk Padaung, the monastery-topped hill of 1520 metre Mt Popa can be visited as a day trip from Bagan. If you get a group together to charter a taxi-truck to Thazi or Inle Lake, a detour can be made to visit it. It takes 20 minutes or so to make the stiff climb to the top of the hill. This is a centre for worship of the nats.

Salay
During the late 12th and 13th centuries, Salay developed as the expanding spiral of Bagan's influence moved southward along the Ayeyarwady River. Today's Salay is much more of a religious centre than Bagan, with many more working monasteries than found in Bagan today. A trip to Salay is warranted for anyone who develops a passion for Bagan-style architecture.

Among the named sites worth a look is **Payathonzu**, an interconnected complex of three brick shrines with corncob sikharas. In the same area, near the functioning monastery of Thadanayaunggyi Kyaung and the meditation centre of Mogok Vipassana Yeiktha, a 19th century shrine shelters a large lacquer Buddha known as **Nan Paya**. This image, said to date from the 13th century, may be the largest lacquer image in Myanmar; the fingertips alone measure about two metres high.

On the other side of the main road from Kyauk Padaung is **Yoe Soe (Youpson) Kyaung**, the oldest surviving wooden monastery hall in the Bagan area south of Pakkoku.

Getting There & Away By public transport you can catch an early morning pick-up from Nyaung U to Kyauk Padaung (K25, 48 km) and change to a Salay-bound pick-up (K30, 58 km). Salay can easily be visited as a day trip from Bagan if you hire your own vehicle and driver. You could also take a Pyay-bound ferry from Nyaung U, getting off in Salay around midday. The ferry leaves at 5 am every day except Thursday and Sunday and arrives in Salay in the late afternoon; the deck-class fare is around K20.

MEIKTILA
Only a short distance west of Thazi, Meiktila is the town where the Bagan-Taunggyi and Yangon-Mandalay roads intersect. The town sits on the banks of huge Lake Meiktila, bridged by the road from Nyaung U. From one end of this bridge, a wooden pier extends out over the lake to small **Antaka Yele Paya**, a cool spot to rest on warm evenings.

Places to Stay & Eat
Honey Hotel, a converted mansion on Pan Chan St next to the lake, offers large rooms with high ceilings, air-con, private hot showers and good mattresses for US$20/33, or similar rooms with shared bath and air-con for US$10/17. Breakfast is available for US$1.

The *Nawarat Guest House* (no English sign), a two storey green house next to a shop called Mother's House on the main street, rents simple but clean cubicles with shared facilities for K60 per day. Near the market in the centre of town, the *Precious Inn* at 131 Butar Houng (Air Force) St offers unimpressive rooms with shared facilities for US$8/14 a single/double. A busy cafe downstairs serves Chinese and Burmese food.

Most famous of the local restaurants is *Shwe Ohn Pin* on the main street; a couple of the major express buses between Mandalay and Yangon stop here. One of the house specialities is a delicious 'curd curry', big hunks of Indian-style cheese (hlan no kei) mixed with cauliflower and okra in a thick and spicy sauce.

THAZI

Thazi is really nothing more than a place people find themselves in when travelling to or from Bagan or Inle Lake.

In Thazi you're officially allowed to stay at the spartan *Moon-Light Rest House*, upstairs from the Red Star Restaurant, for US$5 per person.

Getting There & Away

Bus The Thazi bus stop is a couple of hundred metres from the railway station. Pick-ups to Kalaw cost K200 for a seat in the back, K300 up the front; there's usually only one departure a day at around 7 am.

If you want to travel between Mandalay and Thazi by bus, you must change buses in Meiktila; this will no longer be the case after the new highway between Mandalay and Thazi is finished. A passenger pick-up between Meiktila and Thazi costs K10 to K15.

Shan State

Nearly a quarter of Myanmar's geographic area is occupied by the Shan State. Before 1989 the area was broken into several administrative divisions collectively known as the 'Shan States'. It's the most mountainous state in the country, divided down the middle by the huge north-south Thanlwin River. About half the people living in the Shan State are ethnic Shan; the state's major ethnic groups include the Palaung, Kachin, Kaw (Akha), Lahu (Musoe), Kokang, Wa, Padaung and Taungthu.

KALAW & PINDAYA

There are several excursions you can make en route to Inle Lake, the main destination of most visitors to the Shan State. The Thazi to Taunggyi road passes through Kalaw, once a popular British hill station.

At Aungban, you can turn off the main road and travel north to Pindaya, where the **Pindaya Caves** are packed with countless Buddha images, gathered there over the centuries.

From either Kalaw or Pindaya, it's possible to make day treks to nearby tribal villages; inquire at guesthouses or hotels for guides, who charge around US$2 a day.

Places to Stay & Eat

In Kalaw the *Pineland Inn*, right on the highway through town, has basic but clean two bed rooms with shared cold-water shower and toilet for US$5 per person.

In Pindaya the only licensed lodging at the time of writing was the *Pindaya Hotel*, a clean and comfortable two storey place about halfway between the town and the caves. Standard singles/doubles with fan and attached shower and toilet cost US$24/30.

Shan-owned *May Pa Laung Restaurant*, three blocks west of the market, offers a good menu of Chinese, Burmese and Shan dishes. For a splurge the famous *Kalaw Hotel* dining room is highly recommended for well-prepared Burmese or European set meals.

Getting There & Away

From Kalaw it costs K25 to Pindaya by public transport.

INLE LAKE

The 22-km-long lake itself is extraordinarily beautiful and famous for its Intha leg rowers, who propel their boats by standing at the

Inle Lake

0   2   4 km

To Shwenyaung

Nyaungshwe
Nanthe
Sizon
In U
Hot Springs
Kaungdine
MTT
Mang Thawk
Kanywa   Lingin
VIP Rest House
Pwezagon
Kyizagon   Pebin Inywa
Shanywa   Inle   Thitseinbin
Lake
Thale U
Nga Phe Kyaung
Kela
Inting
Ywama   Nyaung Win
(Floating Market)   Zayatkyi   Ingyingon
Phaung Daw
U Kyaung
Indein   Yetha   Nampan   Market
Kyibawkon
Inbawkon
Naung Daw
Helon   Maingpyo
Seson
Magyizeik
Inbya
Ban Kan

stern on one leg and wrapping the other leg around the oar. This strange technique has arisen because of all the floating vegetation – it's necessary to stand up to plot a path around all the obstacles.

Half-day boat tours include visits to the floating village of **Ywama**, **Phaung Daw U Kyaung** and a floating market (best on Ywama market days, otherwise it's just souvenir oriented).

One of the best times of the year to be here is during September and October. The ceremonial Phaung Daw U Festival, which lasts for almost three weeks, is closely followed by the Thadingyut Festival, when the Inthas and Shan dress in new clothes and celebrate with fervour the end of Waso, or Buddhist Lent.

You are not allowed to take ordinary water taxis around the lake like the Burmese do. The government, however, tolerates a few entrepreneurs who arrange canoe rides along the canals that run off the lake to villages near Nyaungshwe – check around. In Nyaungshwe, the **Yadana Man Aung Kyaung** and **Shwe Yaunghwe Kyaung** are a couple of temples worth a quick visit.

Orientation

There are four place names to remember in the lake area. First, there's Heho, where the airport is located. Continue east from there and you reach Shwenyaung, where the railway terminates and where you turn south off the road to get to the lake. Continue further east and you reach Taunggyi, the main town in the area. At the northern end of the lake is Nyaungshwe.

Information

To enter the Inle Lake zone, tourists are required to pay a US$3 entry fee at the MTT office near the lake entrance. You're free to canoe to nearby villages without paying the fee, however.

Places to Stay

Nyaungshwe A number of new places have opened in Nyaungshwe since the privatisation of the hotel industry. The friendly *Shwe Hintha Guest House* offers economy rooms with common toilet and hot-water shower for US$5/10 a single/double, while standard rooms with attached cold-water shower and toilet are US$12. All rates include breakfast.

The *Joy Hotel* has 12 basic but clean rooms in a two storey house for US$7/12 with shared toilet and hot-water shower, or US$13/16 with hot-water shower and toilet attached. Breakfast comes with the rooms.

East of Mingala Market on a stream that runs through town is the long, two storey *Evergreen Hotel*. Basic economy rooms here with common toilet and hot-water shower cost US$5 per person. Slightly larger standard rooms with softer mattresses and attached toilet and hot-water shower cost US$12/20 a single/double.

The well-run and quiet *Inle Inn* is one of the oldest privately owned inns in the country. In the back of the main building a thatched wing signed 'Inle Bamboo Lodge' has simple economy rooms with shared toilet and cold-water shower for US$5/8 a single/

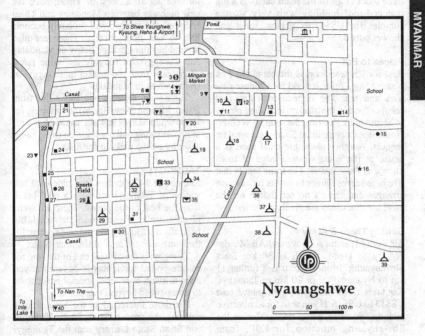

Nyaungshwe

0   50   100 m

PLACES TO STAY		
6	Hu Pin Hotel	
13	Evergreen Hotel	
14	Inle Inn	
21	Joy Hotel	
24	Shwe Hintha Guest House	
30	Pyi Guest House	
31	Golden Express Hotel	

PLACES TO EAT		
2	Hu Pin Restaurant	
4	Shwe Inlay Bakery	
5	Kong Kong Restaurant	
7	Love Village Cafe & Sunflower Restaurant	
8	Golden Crown Restaurant	

9	Teashop	
11	Teashop	
20	Thuka Cafe	
23	Big Drum Restaurant	
40	Four Sisters	

OTHER		
1	Shan Palace Museum	
3	Bank	
10	Stupa	
12	Sri Jagdish Hindu Temple	
15	Township Office	
16	Police	
17	Hlain Kyu Kyaung	
18	Yangon Kyaung	
19	Monastery	
22	Boat Landing	

25	Boat Landing	
26	Moe Ma Kha Boat Hire	
27	Myanmar Travels & Tours (MTT)	
28	Independence Monument	
29	Shwe Zali Paya	
32	Stupas	
33	Yadana Man Aung Kyaung	
34	Stupas	
35	Post & Telegraph Office	
36	Shwe Gu Kyaung	
37	Kan Gyi Kyaung	
38	Monastery	
39	Nigyon Taungyon Kyaung	

double. Better rooms in the main building and in a new wing off to the side come with attached toilet and hot-water shower for US$15/22/33 a single/double/triple. *Pyi Guest House*, in the southern part of town, three blocks east of the main canal, is a big thatched-roof building with very spartan cubicles for US$5 per person, toilet and shower outside.

Places to Eat
Best for Chinese food is the clean *Hu Pin*. Nearby *Shwe Inlay* is good for Chinese pastries and tea. The impecunious can find cheaper food in the market, including plenty of Shan khauk swe (noodle soup). *Pyi Guest House* does a communal Shan-style meal on request. Another place for local food is a house at the south-western edge of town known as *Four Sisters*. The Intha family that live here serves dinner to guests by advance arrangement; there's no set charge for the meal but donations are gladly collected.

Getting There & Away
Air Both Myanma Airways and Air Mandalay fly to Heho, which is 30 km from Shwenyaung, from where it is a further 11 km to Nyaungshwe or 20 km to Taunggyi. Car taxis from Heho to Nyaungshwe cost US$13 to US$15. If you wait for a collective pick-up, you can get a ride as far as the Shwenyaung junction for K30; from Shwenyaung another pick-up goes to Nyaungshwe for K20. If you're continuing on to Taunggyi it's K40 straight through.

Bus & Pick-Up The fare for the better Thazi-Taunggyi trucks varies from K80 to K250 depending on the type of vehicle and number of passengers. If you're heading for Inle Lake, get off at the Shwenyaung junction and catch one of the frequent pick-ups (6 am to 6 pm only) to Nyaungshwe, 11 km south, for K20. There are also a couple of trucks a day between Shwenyaung and Meiktila for K90.

The staging area for most public transport in and out of Nyaungshwe is the street that runs south of the Hu Pin Hotel, one block west of Mingala Market.

Pick-ups and regular buses between Mandalay and the lake area cost K250 to K400 per person depending on the company; all leave between 4 and 6 am and take 10 to 12 hours. At the moment all road transport goes through Meiktila, west of Thazi; once the new highway between Mandalay and Thazi is completed, the trip will probably become half to one hour shorter. There are also several bus lines that go between Mandalay and Taunggyi for roughly the same fares. They leave from the market in Taunggyi or from 25th St in Mandalay.

Tiger Head Express operates a bus from Bagan Myothit (New Bagan) to Taunggyi for K500 which leaves at 4 am; as usual, get off at Shwenyaung and continue on to Nyaungshwe by public pick-up for K20.

TAUNGGYI
Situated at 1430 metres, the pine-clad hill station of Taunggyi provides a cool break from the heat of the plains. There are some pleasant walks if you are in the mood, but basically it's a just a growing trade centre for the south-western area of the Shan State.

Taunggyi is the official end of the line for eastern-bound foreigners in Myanmar; you need difficult-to-receive special permission to go eastward beyond this point.

For those interested in the Shan State's cultures, the modest **Shan State Museum** and **Shan State Library** near the Taunggyi Hotel are worth a visit.

Places to Stay
An old stand-by in Taunggyi, the *May Khu Guest House*, is a rambling wooden structure with foreigner rates of US$10 per person in simple two-bed rooms with common bath. The newer *Khemarat Guest House* at 4B Bogyoke Aung San Rd has economy rooms with shared bath for US$9/12 a single/double plus rooms with attached bath for US$15/18.

The privatised and relatively efficient *Taunggyi Hotel* (☎ (081) 21127, 21302) sprawls over landscaped grounds near the southern end of town. Spacious rooms with attached hot-water bath cost from US$30 to

US$54. The old MHT-style bar and restaurant attract a mix of well-heeled businesspeople and military types.

Places to Eat

A row of small food stalls in the market serve decent Chinese and Shan dishes. On the main street near the Khemarat Guest House, the *Coca Cola Restaurant* has an all-Chinese menu; it's nothing great, but it's popular. The *Lyan You Hotel* – actually only a restaurant – prepares good noodle dishes

Getting There & Away

Trucks to Taunggyi from Inle Lake charge K30 and leave frequently from the Nyaung-shwe market area between 7 am and 5 pm for the 45 minute trip; in the downhill direction the fare is only K15. A taxi along the same route costs US$15 or K2000. There's one pick-up per day from Taunggyi to Pindaya at 2 pm, which arrives at 5.30 pm and costs K40.

From Bagan Myothit and Mandalay, pick-ups cost K250 to K300 per person and take seven or eight hours.

KYAINGTONG (KENGTUNG)

Tucked away in a far eastern corner of the Shan State and surrounded by Wa, Shan, Akha and Lahu villages, Kyaingtong is the sleepy but historic centre for the state's Khün culture. Built around a small lake, and dotted with ageing Buddhist temples and crumbling British colonial architecture, Kyaingtong is possibly the most scenic town in the Shan State.

The rub is that it's only accessible from Thailand. As of 1996 foreigners were again permitted to cross the bridge over the Sai River and proceed north to Kyaingtong via Tachilek. Three-night, four-day excursions may be arranged through any Mae Sai guesthouse or travel agency or you can do it on your own by paying US$18 for a four-day, three-night permit at the border, plus a mandatory exchange of US$100 for Myanmar's Foreign Exchange Certificates. These FECs can be spent on hotel rooms or exchanged on the black market for kyat. The permit can be extended for up to three months at a cost of US$36 at the immigration office in Kengtung.

The road trip allows glimpses of Shan, Akha, Wa and Lahu villages along the way. If current economic and political conditions in Myanmar prevail, the road between Kyaingtong and Taunggyi should soon open to foreign travel. At the moment only Myanmar citizens are permitted to use this road. Fighting between Myanmar's Yangon government and the Shan State's splintered Mong Tai Army makes the Kengtung-Taunggyi journey potentially hazardous.

The drive from Taunggyi takes two long days (sometimes four or five days in wet weather) over a narrow and winding road. The main overnight stops are **Loilem**, **Kunhing** and **Mong Ping**, each of which has rustic guesthouses and rudimentary cafes.

Places to Stay

The *Noi Yee Hotel* in Kengtung costs US$10 per person per night in dorm rooms. MTT tries to steer tourists towards the more expensive, government-run *Kyainge Tong Hotel*, where rooms range from US$30 to US$42.

Harry's Guest House & Trekking at 132 Mai Yang Rd, Kanaburoy Village (☎ (101) 21418), is operated by an English-speaking Kengtung native who spent many years as a trekking guide in Chiang Mai. His simple rooms go for US$5 per person, payable in US, Thai or Burmese currency.

Getting There & Away

The cheapest form of transport to Kyaingtong is the 45B songthaew that leaves each morning from Tachilek. Count on at least six to 10 gruelling hours to cover the 163 km stretch between the border and Kengtung.

The road is currently being improved and will eventually be paved all the way to the Chinese border, 100 km beyond Kengtung.

LASHIO

This township of 103,000 mostly Shan-Chinese and Chinese inhabitants is located at the southern end of the infamous 'Burma

Road'. Until recently Lashio was off limits to foreigners because of its proximity to China – and the hated Chinese Communists – and to ethnic insurgent territory. Shan insurgents are still around, and you're not likely to be allowed beyond the military checkpoints at the north-eastern edge of town without special permission from the regional army command.

Orientation

Lashio is divided into two main districts, Lashio Lay (Little Lashio) and Lashio Gyi (Big Lashio), connected by Theinni Rd. Lashio Lay is the newer and bigger of the two districts.

Things to See

Mansu Paya stands between Lashio Lay and Lashio Gyi on a hill to the western side of Theinni Rd, and is said to be over 250 years old. More impressive is the **Sasana 2500-Year (Pyi Lon Chantha) Paya**, reportedly built by the last Shan *sawbwa* (chieftain) in the area, Sao Hon Phan. More interesting than any of the Buddhist shrines in town is the large and busy **Quan Yin San Temple** in Lashio Lay.

Places to Stay & Eat

Just about any hotel or guesthouse in Lashio seems prepared to accept foreign guests. Rates quoted bounce back and forth between kyat and dollars, or are sometimes quoted in both. *Nadi Ayeyar Guest House* (☎ (082) 21725), on Theinni Rd in Lashio Gyi, one km from the town centre, has clean but small rooms with carpet and good mattresses for US$6/10 a single/double. *Mo Shwe Li Guest House*, near the bus terminal and Mansu Market, charges K200 for a simple single with shared facilities, K300 to K400 for a double, or K700 with attached hot-water shower.

The three storey *Lashio Motel* (☎ (081) 21702, 21738), at the intersection of the Mandalay-Lashio road and Station Rd, charges a hybrid rate of US$9 plus K540 for good rooms with air-con, TV, fridge, toilet

and hot-water shower. The price includes breakfast.

The famous *Lashio Restaurant*, on Theinni Rd just east of the New Asia Hotel, is one of the most reliable for both Chinese and Shan cuisine. Another good restaurant serving both Chinese and Shan meals is *Lite Lite Restaurant*, near the New Asia Hotel on Chinese Temple St. For Yunnanese cuisine, the *Winlight Chinese Muslim Restaurant*, downtown near the Aung Dagon Hotel, is inexpensive and good.

Getting There & Away

Air There are three Myanma Airways flights weekly from Yangon. The airport is north of Lashio Gyi.

Bus, Van & Pick-Up From Mandalay there's a ramshackle RTE bus once daily for K200. Better buses are available from several private companies, some of which operate from the main bus centre in Mandalay, others from the Shan neighbourhood around 23rd St. In either direction the 220 km ride takes a slow nine to 11 hours on a rough, dusty road. To break the trip up, it's a good idea to schedule at least a day's stopover in Pyin U Lwin along the way.

Train Although it's expensive and sometimes takes longer, travel to Lashio by train is definitely more comfortable than by pick-up. The No 131 Up leaves Mandalay at 4.35 am and arrives in Lashio around 6 pm – when it's not delayed by track conditions (9 pm arrivals aren't unusual). Along the way you'll cross the famous Gokteik Bridge and wind around four monumental switchbacks. The Mandalay to Lashio fare costs US$13 in the only upper-class coach on the train. In this car only five seats are under Myanma Railways control; the remainder are controlled by the military. Tickets for this route can be bought 11 days ahead of time, and they sell out fast. From Pyin U Lwin the fare drops to US$11. Apparently, ordinary class isn't available to foreigners, but it might be worth asking.

Kachin State

Myanmar's northernmost state borders India and China to the north and east, the Sagaing Division to the west and the Shan State to the south. The Jingpaw, who are known to the Burmese as 'Kachin', are the majority.

Until the early 1990s the Kachin Independence Organisation (KIO) and its tactical arm, the Kachin Independence Army (KIA), operated with near impunity throughout the state. Following the 1993 signing of a truce with the Yangon government, the KIA have ceased active insurgency. The Burmese government, however, still considers the state a 'sensitive' area and the movements of both foreigners and Burmese are strictly curtailed. The jade trade may also have something to do with travel restrictions in the state.

BHAMO

Bhamo's **daily market** draws Lisu, Kachin and Shan participants from the surrounding countryside. The overgrown city walls of **Sampanago**, an old Shan kingdom, can be seen around five km east of town. **Theindawdye Paya** downtown features an older stupa.

Places to Stay

The *Golden Dragon Hotel* has been known to accept foreigners for K100 a head. The hotel – really more of a guesthouse – can provide a guide to nearby Kachin villages such as Aungtha.

Getting There & Away

Air Myanma Airways flies to Bhamo from Mandalay once a week.

Boat A double-decker ferry plies the Ayeyarwady River between Mandalay and Bhamo twice weekly. Lower-deck class costs K45, upper-deck class K96 and cabins K290. Some foreigners have reported having to pay in dollars to board this boat in Mandalay; you might have better luck paying in kyat from Kyauk Myaung, which is a short road hop

east of Shwebo. The scenery along the upper reaches of the Ayeyarwady is very fine.

MYITKYINA

The waiting time for a Myitkyina permit can extend up to two weeks since authorities in Yangon must check with the regional military command to ensure all is still calm in the state. Set in a flat valley that becomes extremely hot in the hot season and very rainy during the monsoon, the town itself is not that interesting. If permitted to stay in Myitkyina you'll be restricted to a 25 km radius around the city, in basically a flat river valley surrounded by hills. Rice produced in this valley, known as *khat cho*, is considered the best in Myanmar. Highly valued for its delicate texture and fine fragrance, khat cho is scarce and expensive outside the Kachin State.

There are plenty of Kachin villages in the area, and with a guide you may visit those that lie within the 25 km limit. **Myit-son**, the confluence of the Mekha and Malika rivers, 45 km north of town, forms the beginning of the great Ayeyarwady River.

Places to Stay & Eat

The friendly *YMCA* has rooms with common bath for US$15/20 a single/double. It's nothing special but is the best value if you're avoiding government hotels. The *Popa Hotel* at the railway station charges US$20 to US$30 for simple rooms with fan and common bath.

Most of the restaurants in town serve Chinese food. One of the better ones is *Shwe Ainsi (Ein Zay)*, which doesn't look like much but serves quite reasonable food.

Getting There & Away

Air Myanma Airways flies to Myitkyina from Mandalay on Sunday, Monday and Friday; the flight takes 50 minutes and costs US$70 by F-27, US$80 by F-28. MA has one 25 minute flight on Wednesday to/from Bhamo for US$30/35. On Friday there is also a flight between Myitkyina and Putao that lasts 35 minutes and costs US$40/45.

Train Anyone who can afford to fly from Mandalay rather than take the train usually does – the fare difference is not that great considering the time factor. The No 55 Up train from Mandalay leaves daily at 3 pm and is supposed to take 22 hours to reach Myitkyina. In everyday practice it often takes longer – up to 40 hours due to the poor condition of the track. In early 1995 a derailment at the railway bridge near Mohnyin killed more than 100 passengers.

Two private companies run better trains to Myitkyina from the railway station certain days of the week for around US$15 per seat for foreigners, or US$20 for a sleeper.

Road There are no regular public transport services along the road between Mogok and Myitkyina as road conditions are quite bad between Mogok and Bhamo.

PUTAO

The highlands north of Putao are considered among the most pristine Himalayan environments in Asia and could become a major ecotourism destination if made accessible to foreigners. Plans are afoot to bring tourism here; the runway at Putao is being extended so that large jets can land safely. During the late British colonial era, a military post called Fort Hertz was based in Putao. Most of the population of around 10,000 are Kachin and Lisu, followed by Burman, Shan and various other smaller tribal groups.

There is really no reason to go to Putao since you won't be allowed any further north where the real mountains begin. If you go, it's possible to stay at the *Government Guest House* for US$25 per night or at the *Tokyo Guest House* for K75 per person.

Getting There & Away

Foreigners are not allowed to travel to Putao by road. Even with permission the narrow, unsurfaced 356 km road is passable only in dry weather. See the previous Myitkyina section for information on MA flights.

South-Eastern Myanmar

KYAIKTIYO

One of the most interesting formerly 'off-limits' trips is to the incredible balancing boulder stupa at Kyaiktiyo. The small stupa, just 7.3 metres high, sits atop the Gold Rock, a massive, gold-leafed boulder delicately balanced on the very edge of a cliff at the top of Mt Kyaikto. Like Shwedagon Paya in Yangon or Mahamuni Paya in Mandalay, Kyaiktiyo is one of the most sacred Buddhist sites in Myanmar. The permit policy for Kyaiktiyo is vague, though it's clear you're supposed to have a permit to make the trip.

For individual travellers, Bago makes a better starting point for road trips to Kyaiktiyo than Yangon since the hotel staff there are adept at arranging inexpensive alternatives. Also there are no checkpoints along the rail route, so many foreigners travel to Kyaikto by rail without permits.

Once you've reached Kinpun at the base of the mountain, you're supposed to show your permit at a checkpoint placed near the trailhead. In everyday practice the police usually accept a US$10 entry fee if you don't possess a permit, US$4 if you do.

Places to Stay

Although Kyaiktiyo can be visited as a day trip from Bago, the advantage of staying at the top is that you can catch sunset and sunrise – the most magical times for viewing the boulder shrine.

Along the ridge at the top of Mt Kyaikto, the well-situated *Kyaikto Hotel* features a couple of long wooden buildings overlooking the valley below. 'Economy' rooms with two beds and two buckets of water cost US$24/36 a single/double, while simple bamboo huts with mattresses on the floor cost US$10/15. For the latter you bathe outside with bucket and bowl. All rates include the standard toast-and-egg breakfast. When Kyaikto Hotel is full, people have been permitted to sleep on the reception floor for US$5 a head.

In the town of Kyaikto at the foot of the mountain is another *Kyaikto Hotel*. Noisy and not very clean, it charges US$12 per room.

Getting There & Away

Bus Buses straight from Yangon to Kyaikto cost K150 from the Highway Bus Centre; it's much wiser to start from Bago. Buses from Bago to Kyaikto cost K60 and take around five hours.

Train A direct train from Bago to Kyaikto leaves daily at 4.30 am, arriving two and a half to three hours later, substantially quicker than the equivalent bus trip. The foreigner fare is US$3 per seat.

MAWLAMYINE (MOULMEIN)

The atmosphere of post-colonial decay is more palpable here than in fast-developing Yangon or Mandalay; it's also an attractive, leafy, tropical town with a ridge of stupa-capped hills on one side and the sea on the other.

The **Mon Cultural Museum** is dedicated to the Mon history of the region. In the city's east, a hilly north-south ridge is topped with five separate monasteries and shrines. At the northern end is **Mahamuni Paya**, the largest temple complex in Mawlamyine. It's built in the typical Mon style with covered brick walkways linking various square shrine buildings. Further south along the ridge stands **Kyaikthanlan Paya**, the city's tallest and most visible stupa. It was probably here that Rudyard Kipling's poetic 'Burma girl' was 'a-setting' in the opening lines of *Mandalay:* 'By the old Moulmein Pagoda, lookin' lazy at the sea'.

Below Kyaikthanlan is the 100 year old **Seindon Mibaya Kyaung**, a monastery where King Mindon Min's queen, Seindon, sought refuge after Myanmar's last monarch, King Thibaw Min, took power. On the next rise south stands the isolated silver and gold-plated **Aung Theikdi Zedi**. A viewpoint on the western side of the ridge a bit further south looks out over the city and is a favoured

spot for catching sunsets and evening sea breezes.

Mawlamyine's central market, **Zeigyi**, is a rambling area on the western side of Lower Main Rd just north of the main pedestrian jetty for Mottama.

Gaungse Kyun, commonly known in English as 'Shampoo Island', is a picturesque little isle off Mawlamyine's north-western end. You can hire a boat out to the island for K150.

Places to Stay

In the north-western corner of the city, not far from the Mottama vehicle ferry landing, the recently privatised *Mawlamyine Hotel* (☎ (032) 22560) offers well-spaced bunga-lows for a steep (considering the value) US$48/60 a single/double including break-fast, service and tax; Burmese citizens pay one-sixth these rates. The *Thanlwin Hotel* (☎ (032) 21518), on Lower Main Rd, is cur-rently under renovation and will probably run in the US$15 to US$25 range when it reopens – if the requested licence is granted.

At the time of writing, the funky but quite adequate *Breeze Rest House* at 6 Strand Rd was on the verge of receiving its foreigner licence and has rooms with two beds, fan and shared facilities for K120. The English-speaking owner claims he will be adding air-con to at least some of the rooms, for which the rate will be approximately US$10.

Getting There & Away

Air Myanma Airways flies direct from Yangon to Mawlamyine on Wednesday, and via Dawei on Saturday. From Yangon to Mawlamyine the fare for the 35 minute flight is US$65 by F-27, US$75 by F-28. From Dawei, an hour away by plane, the fare is US$50/55.

There are also flights to Mawlamyine from Mandalay on MA for US$75/85.

Bus Mawlamyine's main terminal for south-bound buses or pick-ups is near the southern end of town off the road to Ye. Here you can board public vehicles to Thanbyuzayat (K50, six times daily), Kyaikkami (previously Amherst; K50, six times daily), Dawei (K324, once daily) or Payathonzu on the Thai border (K1500, once daily). Two small indoor restaurants at the terminal serve decent Burmese and Chinese fare.

Train Two express trains run from Yangon to Mottama daily. When the trains are running on time the trip takes seven and a half hours – beating even the fastest bus lines by several hours. The local price for an upper-class seat is K200, while the foreigner price is US$8. Ordinary-class seats cost K75, although they aren't officially available to foreigners. You can then get the ferry across the river to Mawlamyine.

Boat Double-decker passenger ferries depart for Mawlamyine from the Mottama landing on the Thanlwin River every half hour; the fare is K1 and the trip takes 20 to 30 minutes depending on tides. If you don't feel like waiting for a ferry, you can charter a passenger boat across the river for around K300.

Getting Around
Motorised thoun bein (three-wheelers) are the main form of public transport. The going rate is K20 for a short hop within the centre of town, and as much as K50 or K60 for a ride up the ridge to Kyaikthanlan.

AROUND MAWLAMYINE
South of Mudon begins a 'brown area', and most locals will warn against travelling along the roads here after 3 pm due to the possibility of insurgent and/or bandit activity. The authorities frown upon foreigners travelling even as far south as **Kyaikkami** and **Setse**, but the tidal-flat beaches at these towns aren't worth even a moderate risk.

Mottama (Martaban)
The narrow, patched and potholed road from Bago terminates at Mottama, where the wide Thanlwin River empties into the Gulf of Martaban. The railway from Yangon also terminates here, although an extension picks up on the other side in Mawlamyine and continues 145 km to Ye, where a new line leads further south to Dawei. If you're continuing on to Mawlamyine on the other side of the river you must present a travel permit valid for Mawlamyine to immigration authorities at the ferry station.

Getting There & Away See the Mawlamyine Getting There & Away section above for details on transport to Mottama.

Kyaikmaraw
This small but charming town 24 km southeast of Mawlamyine is accessible via a good sealed road. Mon-style **Kyaikmaraw Paya** is well worth a visit.

PA-AN
A new road from Mawlamyine to the Kayin State capital of Pa-an will span the Gyaing River north-east of the city, thus linking Mawlamyine with a Thanlwin River crossing east of Thaton. Tourism authorities in Yangon say Pa-an will soon be added to the list of places foreigners may visit with a permit.

Double-decker ferries from the Pa-an jetty in Mawlamyine leave daily at 6 am and noon for the four hour trip up the Thanlwin River to Pa-an on the river's eastern bank. The fare is K10 and every conceivable inch of deck space is used for cargo and passengers.

DAWEI (TAVOY)
Dawei is a sleepy, tropical seaside town only recently connected to the rest of Myanmar by road and rail. Among local religious monuments, **Shinmokhti Paya** is the most sacred. Reportedly constructed in 1438, this is one of the four shrines in the country that house a Sinhalese Buddha image supposedly made with a composite of cement and pieces of the original bodhi tree.

Beaches & Islands
Few foreigners have been permitted to visit coastal areas around Dawei so details are still sketchy. The best local beach area reportedly lies on the coast around 18 km west of Dawei in Maungmakan township. Here a sand beach stretches eight km, and has some government bungalows usually reserved for VIPs.

Opposite Maungmakan is a collection of three pretty island groups which were named the Middle Moscos Islands by the British – they are now known as Maungmakan, Henze and Launglon (or collectively as the Maungmakan Islands).

Places to Stay & Eat
Sibin Guest House lodges government officials in six-bed rooms with shared facilities for just K15 per person.

Getting There & Away
Air Myanma Airways fields daily flights from Yangon to Dawei and twice weekly flights from Mawlamyine and Kawthoung.

Bus Buses from Mawlamyine may require an overnight at Ye since drivers are loathe to drive in late afternoons or evenings. Even during supposed 'safe hours', dacoits and insurgents sometimes collect a 'road tax' from the drivers along the way.

MYEIK (MERGUI)
The Taninthayi coast, in the extreme south of Myanmar where Myanmar and Thailand share the narrow peninsula, is bounded by the beautiful islands of the Mergui Archipelago. Myeik – known to the colonials as Mergui and locally as Beik or Myeit – sits on a peninsula that juts out into the Andaman Sea.

The city's most venerated Buddhist temple, **Theindawgyi Paya**, contains a European-pose Buddha and a reclining Buddha.

Boats to nearby islands can be chartered for US$60 per day from Myeik's harbour.

Places to Stay
Those with permits may be allowed to stay either at the *Eindaw Pyu Guest House* (K100 per person in tiny bare rooms with shared facilities) at 57 Main Rd or at the government-owned *Annawa* (K500).

Getting There & Away
Air Travel permits valid for Myeik usually stipulate that the bearer arrive by air. Myanma Airways drops in daily from Yangon for

US$90 aboard F-27s, US$100 on F-28s. There are also flights from Mawlamyine, Dawei and Kawthoung.

Bus There are daily buses and pick-ups from Dawei, 249 km north, but it's highly unlikely any foreigner will be permitted to travel by bus to Myeik.

KAWTHOUNG
This small port at the southernmost tip of Taninthayi Division – and the southernmost point of mainland Myanmar – is only separated from Thailand by a broad estuary in the Pakchan River. To the British it was known as Victoria Point and to the Thais it's known as Ko Sawng, which means 'Second Island' in Thai. The main business here is trade with Thailand, followed by fishing. Among the Burmese, Kawthoung is perhaps best known for producing some of the country's best kickboxers!

At the moment Kawthoung is only accessible to foreigners by boat from Ranong, Thailand. It's probably not worth making a special trip to Ranong just to visit Kawthoung, but if you're in the area and decide to cross over, you'll find it's similar to the rest of Myanmar except there are many more motorcycles!

The Mergui Archipelago continues south to Kawthoung and many islands lie tantalisingly offshore in this area. Unfortunately, there is no regular transport to any of these islands and boat charters are expensive.

Visiting Kawthoung
Boats to Kawthoung leave the pier in Ranong regularly for 30B per person. Immediately as you exit the Kawthoung jetty there's a small immigration office on the right, where you must pay US$5 for a day permit. For the same rate you can stay up to three nights but then you're required to buy US$50 worth of Foreign Exchange Certificates. If you want to stay longer, you can extend your permit up to 28 days upon payment of US$36 and the exchange of US$200 into FECs. Whether this will allow you to travel further north is another matter – road travel is impossible

MYANMAR

and boat travel beyond the immediate Kawthoung area is forbidden.

Places to Stay

There's only one place approved for foreigners, the simple *Kawthoung Motel* not far from the waterfront. For simple double rooms with private cold-water bath, Thais pay 350B, foreigners US$25.

Getting There & Away

Air Myanma Airways flies to Kawthoung from Yangon, Myeik and Dawei.

Boat Myanma Five Star Line occasionally sails between Yangon, Dawei, Myeik and Kawthoung but travel is very slow and permits endorsed for ship travel are difficult to obtain, even in Yangon.

See Visiting Kawthoung above for details on boats from Ranong.

Western Myanmar

The Rakhine Yoma (Arakan Range) separates the Rakhine and Chin states from the central Ayeyarwady River plains. Isolated from the Burman heartland, in many ways the inhabitants of both states have more in common with the peoples of eastern India and Bangladesh.

The Rakhine

Rakhine ethnicity is a controversial topic – are the Rakhine actually Burmans with Indian blood, Indians with Burman characteristics or a separate race (as is claimed by the Rohingya insurgents)? Although the first inhabitants of the region were a dark-skinned Negrito tribe known as the Bilu, later migrants from the eastern Indian subcontinent developed the first Hindu-Buddhist kingdoms in Myanmar before the first Christian millennium. These kingdoms flourished before the invasion of the Tibeto-Burmans from the north and east in the 9th and 18th centuries. The current inhabitants of the state

may thus be mixed descendants of all three groups, Bilu, Bengali and Burman.

The earliest Rakhine kingdom, Dhanyawady, arose around the first century AD, possibly even earlier. Dhanyawady was followed by a kingdom known as Wethali ('Vesali' in Pali, 'Waithali' in the Rakhine dialect) in the third century AD. Wethali suffered from invasions by the Mongols in 957 AD, and by Bagan Burmans in the late 11th century. The Burman dominance remained strong until the 15th century when Rakhine came under the influence of the Bengali Islamic kingdom of Gaur. Although the Islamic faith didn't take hold in the area, Islamic ideas regarding maths and science were incorporated into the *Zeitgeist* of the increasingly powerful Mrauk U Dynasty.

In the 16th and 17th centuries, ports along the coast began receiving Arab, Central Asian, Danish, Dutch and Portuguese traders. Growing international trade enabled Mrauk U (Myohaung) to break free of Burman suzerainty once again and the Mrauk U Dynasty came to rule the entire coastline from Chittagong to Yangon, and as far north as Bago.

Rakhine was retaken by the Burmans in 1784 under King Bodawpaya, who sent the crown prince and a force of 30,000 to conquer the region and capture the talismanic Mahamuni image. The British annexed the Rakhine region in 1824 after Rakhine refugees in adjacent Raj territories were attacked by the Burman military.

The Burmese government denies the existence of a Rohingya minority, a group of around three million people who distinguish themselves from the Rakhine majority by their Islamic faith. Many Rakhine Muslims – or Rohingyas as they prefer to be called – have fled to neighbouring Bangladesh and India to escape Burman persecution.

The Chin

The Chin State, to the immediate north, is hilly and sparsely populated. The people and culture exhibit an admixture of native, Bengali and Indian influences similar to that found among the Rakhine, with a much lower Burman presence. As in the Rakhine

State, there have been clear governmental efforts in recent years to promote Burmese culture at the expense of Chin culture, and many Chin have fled west to Bangladesh and India.

Of Tibeto-Burman ancestry, the Chin call themselves Zo-mi or Lai-mi (both terms mean 'mountain people') and share a culture, food and language with the Zo of the adjacent state of Mizoram in India. Outsiders name the different subgroups around the state according to the district in which they live: Tidam Chins, Falam Chins, Hakha Chins etc.

SITTWE

Known to the Bengalis as 'Akyab' and to the Rakhine as 'Saitway', this port city of the Rakhine State sits at the mouth of the Kaladan River, where it empties into the Bay of Bengal. Offshore delta islands form a wide protected channel that has served as an important harbour for many centuries. Sittwe has at least a 2000 year history of habitation, though in its modern form the city started as a trading port around 200 years ago and further developed after the British occupation of 1826.

Highly revered **Payagyi** sits in the centre

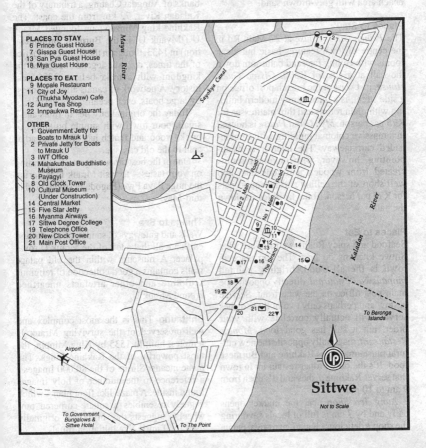

PLACES TO STAY
6 Prince Guest House
7 Gisspa Guest House
13 San Pya Guest House
18 Mya Guest House

PLACES TO EAT
9 Mopale Restaurant
11 City of Joy
   (Thukha Myodaw) Cafe
12 Aung Tea Shop
22 Innpaukwa Restaurant

OTHER
1 Government Jetty for
   Boats to Mrauk U
2 Private Jetty for Boats
   to Mrauk U
3 IWT Office
4 Mahakuthala Buddhistic
   Museum
5 Payagyi
8 Old Clock Tower
10 Cultural Museum
   (Under Construction)
14 Central Market
15 Five Star Jetty
16 Myanma Airways
17 Sittwe Degree College
19 Telephone Office
20 New Clock Tower
21 Main Post Office

Sittwe

Not to Scale

To Baronga Islands

To Government Bungalows & Sittwe Hotel

To The Point

Airport

of town and features a large plain shed supported by pillars decorated with glass mosaic. A large sitting image beneath the shelter was cast in 1900 in the Rakhine style. The **Buddhistic Museum**, on the grounds of Mahakuthala Kyaungtawgyi, is the best place in Myanmar to view Rakhine-style Buddha images.

The **Point** is a land projection at the confluence of the Kaladan River and Bay of Bengal. A large terrace constructed over the flat, shale-and-sandstone point is a good spot to catch the breeze and to cool off on hot afternoons. South-west of The Point is a beach area with grey-brown sand.

Places to Stay

The *Prince Guest House* at 27 Main Rd in the centre of town features basic but clean rooms with ceiling fans and bathroom down the hall at a cost of K500. *Gisspa Guest House*, just west of the branch post office on a side street, is a three storey modern building with plain rooms and thin mattresses for K75 per person. *Mya Guest House* is housed in a massive colonial building with a colonnaded carriageway. The interior is disappointing, however, with unkempt rooms created from wooden partitions that stop well short of the ceiling and mosquito nets for K75 per person. Toilet facilities are down the hall.

Places to Eat

Seafood and spicy Rakhine curries are what Sittwe kitchens do best. The top place in town is the all-wood, brightly painted *Innpaukwa Restaurant*, directly opposite the main post office on the waterfront. Service is slow and perhaps only two of three dishes served will actually correlate with your order, but it still has good food. *Mopale Restaurant*, diagonally opposite the new cultural museum, serves Rakhine and Burmese food. It's the only proper restaurant in town that serves Rakhine dishes and it's open from 9 am to 10 pm.

Aung Tea Shop near the market opens early and by 7 am is full of locals savouring the shop's delicious chapati, nam-bya, palata and potato curry. *Two Stars Tea Garden*, opposite Sittwe Degree College, is popular with students.

Getting There & Away

Air Myanma Airways fields direct flights from Yangon daily except Tuesday, when flights go via Thandwe. The fare is US$80 on F-27s, US$90 on F-28s. Sittwe's tiny airport is only 10 minutes from town.

MRAUK U

Once a centre for one of Myanmar's most powerful kingdoms, Mrauk U straddles the banks of Aungdat Chaung, a tributary of the Kaladan River, 72 km from the coast. The Rakhine king Minzawmun founded Mrauk U ('Myauk U' in the Burmese pronunciation) in 1433, though in the common practice of the times, dynastic legends endowed the kingdom with a make-believe 3000 year history. A network of canals allowed access by large boats, even ocean-going vessels.

Today the original city lies in ruins and a small, poor town with simple buildings of brick, wood and thatch has grown up adjacent to the old city site.

One of the best times – or worst depending on your tastes – to visit Mrauk U is during the huge Paya Pwe (Pagoda Festival) held in mid-May.

Things to See

Walls and gateways of sandstone blocks and earth are all that's left of the Mrauk U royal palace. A museum within the old palace walls contains a good collection of religious sculpture and other artefacts unearthed around Mrauk U.

Shittaung This is the most complex and well-preserved of the surviving Mrauk U temples, built in 1535 by King Minbin, the most powerful of the Rakhine kings. The name means 'Shrine of the 80,000 Images', a reference to the number of holy images found inside. A maze-like floor plan – which vaguely resembles a square-cornered pinwheel – suggests the shrine was originally used for Tantric-like initiation rituals.

Dukkanthein Standing on a bluff 100 metres opposite and to the west of Shittaung, Dukkanthein looks like a huge bunker from the outside. Simple dome-shaped stupas similar to those at Shittaung stand atop receding terraces over a large, slope-sided sanctuary.

Andaw Paya This smaller, eight sided monument features 16 zedis aligned in a square-cornered U-shape around the south, north and west platforms.

Yadanapon (Ratanabon) Paya The largest stupa in the area stands just north of Andaw Paya. Damaged by WWII bombing, only the bottom 'bell' portion and base remain standing. Even minus the original sikhara – now a pile of brick rubble lying to the sides – the brick structure reaches 60 metres in height.

Places to Stay & Eat

The very basic *Myanantheingi Guest House* costs K50 for locals, K200 for foreigners. There are a couple of other places closed to foreigners that cost around K50 per person – the *Dhanyawady* and the *Co-operative* – but the quality is far below that of the Myanantheingi. The *Mrauk U Hotel*, a joint government and private venture, will supposedly be built near the ruins area.

An unnamed restaurant opposite Khite San Tailor on the main street serves fried rice, noodles, fried vegetables and noodle soup. The *Dhanyawady Tea & Cold Drink Shop* (no English sign) opposite the market isn't bad.

Getting There & Away

Both government and private ferries make the river trip between Sittwe and Mrauk U. On the government boat foreigners are supposed to pay US$4 to Inland Water Transport for a round-trip ticket in 'sling-chair class' but if you manage to get the local price you'll pay K11 for the basic passage plus K15 for a sling chair.

The ferries leave from the Mrauk U jetty on Sayokya Chaung at the northern end of Sittwe five days a week. Private ferries sail to Mrauk U on the off days and cost K50 per person.

NGAPALI BEACH

Backed by swaying palms and casuarinas, the Ngapali area is a good place to relax and take a break from the rigours of Myanmar road travel. The very broad, pristine stretch of sand known as Ngapali Beach reaches over three km, and is separated from several more beaches by small, easily negotiated rocky headlands.

If you manage to rent a bicycle (at the Ngapali Beach Hotel, or at one of the restaurants near the hotel or in Thandwe), you can tour several of the villages. Just north of Ngapali Beach are the small villages of **Ngapali** and **Lintha**, both supported by the area's bounteous harvest of fish, coconuts and rice. **Kyiktaw** to the immediate south of Ngapali Beach is similar, followed by **Myabyin**, a larger and more interesting village with a market, a couple of teashops, monasteries and a government rice-storage facility.

Further south still is the village of **Lontha** and an inlet of the same name backed by a sweeping curve of mangrove and sand.

Places to Stay

The mainstay is the *Ngapali Beach Hotel* (☎ Thandwe 28), positioned right on the beach, where two-room wooden bungalows with louvred walls and shaded verandas cost US$25/30 for a 'standard' single/double, US$40/45 for 'superior'.

North of the Ngapali Beach Hotel stands the *Shwer War Kyaing Hotel*, a two storey wooden affair with several large, decaying buildings. It was closed and locked when we visited, even though it was Ngapali's high season; rumours say it's up for sale.

Places to Eat

The Ngapali Beach Hotel has an open-air beachside restaurant with decent and reasonably priced food (kyat acceptable). Almost opposite the New Ngapali Beach Hotel section is *Kyi Nue Yake (Reik) Restaurant*, a small, friendly family-run place with fresh seafood plus Burmese and Chinese dishes – and an English menu. *Zaw Restaurant*, opposite the hotel, is very similar. Prices at both are low to moderate.

Getting There & Away

See the Thandwe section below for details on air and road travel to Thandwe, the transport hub for the region.

Getting Around

A jeep taxi from Thandwe or Thandwe airport to the Ngapali Beach Hotel costs K800. Thandwe, Kyiktaw, Myabyin, Lintha and Lontha are all linked by narrow sealed roads and can be visited by bicycle. Though there are no regular bike rental places, you should be able to make arrangements through the staff at the hotel or through one of the restaurants across the road.

THANDWE (SANDOWAY)

Thandwe (also spelt Thantwe), around 9.5 km north-east of Ngapali Beach, is the seat of a township by the same name. The town boasts a network of sealed and unsealed streets lined with two-storey buildings around 50 to 100 years old, constructed of masonry on the ground floors and wood on the upper floors. A former British jail in the centre of town is now used as a market where vendors sell medicinal herbs, clothes, textiles, hardware and free-market consumer goods. Among the many small shops surrounding the market are a number of gold shops, which suggests that the area is marked by some wealth.

Three stupas perched on hillsides at the edge of town are of mild interest.

Places to Stay & Eat

The *San Yeik Nyein Guest House*, a set of bare but adequate wooden rooms with shared facilities set over a video house a block south of the market, charges K60 per person. This guesthouse was not accepting foreigners when we came along but it may be worth a try.

Next to the market, almost opposite a large mosque, is a very good teashop called *Point*, which offers whitewashed chairs instead of the usual tiny stools. Sticky rice and palatas are usually available here. There are several other tea and cold drink shops in this area, and in the market itself there are a few questionable-looking noodle vendors.

Getting There & Away

Air Air Mandalay flies from Yangon to Thandwe and back thrice a week. The flight takes 50 minutes and costs US$80 confirmed, US$75 stand-by. MA also flies to Thandwe from Yangon on three different days. The fare from Yangon is US$55 by F-28, US$50 by F-27. There are also infrequent flights from Sittwe.

Bus & Taxi A government bus between Thandwe and Yangon costs only K400, with an overnight in Pyay when heading north or Sinde (opposite Pyay) when heading south, but anyone who would endure this 24 hour trip without planning a more appealing stopover must be either crazy or in a very big hurry.

If you decide to break the trip up into sections, there are two different routes to choose from. The longer and more trying, but more scenic, route from the south starts in Pathein, the northern route from Hinthada on the Ayeyarwady River – or better yet use the shorter route from Pyay. Direct buses from Pyay to Thandwe cost K200 – there are only one or two per day, starting early in the morning. It takes around five hours from Pyay to Taungup on the coast, then another three hours from Taungup to Thandwe.

SOUTHERN CHIN STATE

Although it's possible to visit the northern part of the Chin State by road from Kalewa in the Sagaing Division, the true heart of traditional Chin culture is found in the south. **Paletwa**, just over the state line from the Rakhine State, can be reached via boat along the Kaladan River from Sittwe or Kyauktaw. A new road under construction between Mahamuni and Paletwa will also allow vehicle travel direct from Mrauk U when completed.

In the Chin Hills some women still tattoo their faces, though it's a custom that's fading fast. At higher elevations they wear thick, striped cotton blankets draped over the body and ornaments of copper and bronze. Among the Khamui, a sub-tribe that inhabits the lower elevations of southern Chin State, unmarried women wear short skirts and little else. Chin men tend to wear simple western-style dress such as shirts and trousers.

The Philippines

The Philippines are the forgotten islands of this book. Because they're off the regular overland route they've never attracted travellers in great numbers. But if you make the effort to get there you're in for a pleasant surprise: the food's good, accommodation is easy to find and, if island-hopping attracts you, there are over 7000 remarkably diverse islands to choose from. Flights are cheap and boats go everywhere – they are very frequent, remarkably cheap and reasonably comfortable, although not always entirely safe.

Add ease of travel to islands with very friendly people, many of whom speak English, incredibly varied countryside and countless colourful festivals that guests are always welcome to join in, and it's hard not to have a good time. In fact, many travellers reckon the Philippines is their favourite country in the whole region.

Facts about the Philippines

HISTORY

The Philippines is unique among the countries of South-East Asia, both for the variety of its colonisers and for its energetic attempts to cast off the colonial yoke. The Filipinos are a Malay people, closely related to the people of Indonesia and Malaysia. Little is known about their precolonial society, as the Spaniards – who ruled the country for over 300 years – tried to eradicate every trace of what they felt was 'pagan' in the culture.

Ferdinand Magellan, a Portuguese who had switched sides to arch-rival Spain, set off from Europe in 1519 with instructions to sail round the world, claim anything worth claiming for Spain and bring back some spices (a very valuable commodity in Europe). Finding a way round the southern

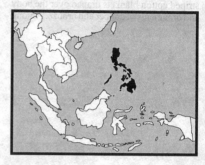

tip of South America took nearly a year but, finally, the small fleet (two of the original four ships) reached the Philippines in 1521.

At the island of Cebu, Magellan claimed the lot for Spain and managed to make a few Christian conversions to boot. Unfortunately, he then decided to display Spanish military might to his newly converted flock by dealing with an unruly tribe on the nearby island of Mactan. Chief Lapu-Lapu managed to kill Magellan. The Cebuanos decided their visitors were not so special after all and the surviving invaders scuttled back to Spain, after collecting a cargo of spices on the way. They arrived in the sole remaining ship in 1522.

The Philippines, named after King Philip II of Spain, was more or less left alone from then until 1565, when Miguel de Legaspi stormed the no-longer-friendly island of Cebu and made the first permanent Spanish settlement. In 1571 Spanish HQ was moved to Manila and from here Spain gradually took control of the entire region – or more correctly converted the region, since Spanish colonial rule was very much tied up with taking the cross to the heathen.

The Spanish were not alone in the area: other European powers and the Japanese and Chinese also made forays into the Philippines and, throughout the Spanish period, the strongly Muslim regions of Mindanao and

Philippines

0   100   200 km

Batanes
Islands

Babuyan
Islands

LUZON

Laoag

Vigan   Tuguegarao

Bontoc   Ilagan
Banaue

San Fernando

Hundred
Islands   Baguio

Dagupan   Baler

Angeles

Olongapo   **MANILA**   Polillo
Islands

*SOUTH
CHINA
SEA*   Lubang
Island   Lucena   **CATANDUANES**

Calapan   **MARINDUQUE**   Naga   Virac
Legaspi   *PHILIPPINE
SEA*

MINDORO   Burias
Island

Roxas   **ROMBLON**

Tablas   Masbate
Island   Sibuyan
Island   Calbayog
**CALAMIAN
GROUP**   **MASBATE**

Boracay   **SAMAR**
Island

Cuyo   **PANAY**   Tacloban
Island   Iloilo
City   Bacolod   **LEYTE**   Dinagat
Cebu   Island

PALAWAN   Puerto Princesa   **CEBU**   Maasin   Siargao
Island
NEGROS   **BOHOL**   Surigao
Tagbilaran

Dumaguete   Camiguin
Siquijor   Island   Butuan
Island

Dipolog   Cagayan
de Oro

Balabac
Island   *SULU SEA*   **MINDANAO**

Davao

Turtle   Zamboanga
Islands
Basilan   General
Sandakan   Island   Santos

**SABAH
(MALAYSIA)**   Jolo
Island

CELEBES SEA

SULU ARCHIPELAGO

the Sulu Archipelago were neither converted nor conquered.

After the defeat of the Spanish Armada by the English in 1588, Spain entered a long period of decline and its control of the region was never fully exploited. The Philippines was generally treated as a subsidiary of Spain's colony in New Spain – Mexico. The colony was a continual drain on the Spanish treasury until the introduction of tobacco in 1782 started to make it profitable.

From 1762, as a result of the Seven Years' War in Europe, the British took control of Manila for over a year, but never extended their rule far into the countryside. Internal events were more threatening to Spanish rule and it is estimated that over 100 revolts against Spanish power were organised. Finally the Spanish sealed their fate by executing Jose Rizal in 1896, after a mockery of a trial. A brilliant scholar, doctor and writer, Rizal had preferred to work for independence by peaceful means, but his execution sparked off the worst revolt to that time.

Nevertheless, it was the USA who finally pushed the Spanish out. The Spanish-American War of 1898 soon spread from Cuba to the Philippines and Spanish power was no match for the USA.

One colonial power, however, was exchanged for another and once the inevitable Filipino revolt had been stamped out, the USA set out to convert the country to the American way of life.

The American colonial period, or 'tutelage' as they preferred to call it, was abruptly ended by WWII, when the Japanese military occupied the islands until General Douglas MacArthur 'returned' in 1944. At the close of the war, independence was granted – it had been promised in 1935 for 10 years later. The American colonial period was considerably more enlightened than that of the Spanish, but it left equally deep impressions, particularly on the economy, since American companies had become firmly entrenched.

In addition, Filipino democracy was modelled on the American pattern and events were to prove that a system wide open to vote-buying in its home environment could

spawn spectacular abuses in Asia. So in the 1950s and 1960s the Philippines bounced from one party to another (usually similar) party until Ferdinand Marcos was elected in 1965.

Marcos was re-elected in 1969 (a feat never previously managed) and declared martial law in 1972, ostensibly to reduce the anarchy which would have inevitably worsened as the 1974 election approached. Also, no doubt, he liked being in control and under the constitution could not run for a third term. Martial law soon became total control and although the previously widespread violence was curtailed, the Philippines suffered from stifling corruption and the economy became one of the weakest in an otherwise booming region.

The assassination of Marcos' opponent Benigno Aquino, in 1983, pushed opposition to Marcos to new heights and further shook the already tottering economy. Marcos called elections for early 1986 and for once the opposition united to support Aquino's widow, Corazon 'Cory' Aquino. With the world's media watching closely, Marcos and Aquino both claimed to have won the election. But 'people power' rallied behind Cory Aquino, and within days Ferdinand and Imelda had slunk off to Hawaii, where the former dictator later died.

Aquino's job on taking power was not easy. The coalition supporting her was an uneasy one and she failed to win the backing of the army and other former pro-Marcos elements. She also failed to come to grips with the NPA (New People's Army), who were pushing for a Communist revolution, and the MNLF (Moro National Liberation Front), fighting for independence in the south. This, coupled with her inability to solve the corruption endemic in the country, eventually led to her own downfall in 1992. She was succeeded by Fidel Ramos, the man whose support had maintained her in power and helped her survive seven attempted coups.

The Protestant Fidel Ramos won the election in 1992 without the support of the Catholic Church and immediately appointed a government clearly intending to fight corruption, revitalise the economy, create jobs and reduce the enormous foreign debt. Equipped with sweeping new powers, he soon moved to secure the ailing energy sector, encourage foreign investment and, in a surprise move, even lifted the ban on the Communist Party in an attempt to end the guerrilla war draining the resources of the country. This policy was vindicated in 1996 when a peace agreement was signed with the MNLF, after much tough negotiating. Ramos has announced his intention to carry out even more political reforms before the end of his period of office in 1998, including the reform of tax laws and the break-up of banking, telecommunications, transport and other cartels. However, many people doubt whether he still has enough time to carry out this ambitious programme, and he can expect opposition from an entrenched oligarchy.

GEOGRAPHY

The official statistics state that the Philippines comprises over 7000 islands – but what is an island and what is a rock that occasionally appears above water level? Together, they make up a land area of about 299,000 sq km, 94% of which is on the 11 largest islands.

The Philippines can be conveniently divided into four areas:

- Luzon, the largest island (site of the capital, Manila), and the nearby islands of Mindoro, Batanes, Catanduanes, Marinduque, Masbate and Mindoro.
- The Visayas – the scattered group of islands south of Luzon.
- Mindanao, the Muslim trouble-centre in the south and the second-largest island in the country, along with the string of islands in the Sulu Archipelago, like stepping stones to Borneo.
- Palawan Island – nearly 400 km long but averaging a width of only 40 km.

CLIMATE

The Philippines is typically tropical – hot and humid year round. The climate can be roughly divided into a January-June dry period and a July-December wet periods. January, February and March are probably the best months for a visit, as it starts to get hotter after March, peaking in May. In some places it seems to rain year round and, in others, it rarely rains at all. From May to November there may be typhoons.

See the Manila climate chart in the Appendix.

ECOLOGY & ENVIRONMENT

A catastrophe on the island of Leyte in November 1991 shook Filipinos out of their complacency over the environment. In the aftermath of a destructive typhoon, masses of water thundered down to the plains from the mountains and caused havoc in the town of Ormoc – killing 5000 and leaving 50,000 homeless. Years of illegal tree felling in the hills above the town had left the slopes bare and incapable of supporting vegetation. There was nothing left to prevent the topsoil from being swept away by floods, a disaster waiting to happen in a country where massive amounts of rain can fall in short periods.

Although there is a long way to go, government agencies like the Department of Environment and Natural Resources (DENR) are trying to reverse the trend of putting the economy before the environment – a problem even developed countries are only now coming to terms with. They have, for example, introduced schemes to re-employ people who lost their jobs after the wood-cutting companies had moved on. The companies may have left behind them a forest denuded of its vegetation, but fertile minds are helping to reshape this landscape in an environmentally conscious way, rehabilitating not only the devastated land but the people who made it that way.

Another serious problem, again made worse because large amounts of money are involved, are fishing methods using cyanide and dynamite. In the former, cyanide is used to stun fish living among coral reefs so they can be collected and shipped off – mostly to Japan. Apart from killing about half of the fish which had been living in the reef, the poison also has a deadly effect on the coral itself. It gradually turns white as it dies and finally becomes an algae-covered corpse. Dynamite has the same effect, but is apparently more destructive because the damage is immediately obvious to the observer. Both destroy coral and the irreplaceable reef habitat of countless other species. On Palawan an attempt has been made to enforce the laws against this wanton destruction, partly as a result of continual warnings from the 'green' newspaper *Bandillo ng Palawan*. However, vested interests, ranging from corrupt government officials, military brass and policemen to the fishermen themselves, are not going to give up such a source of wealth without a fight.

But awareness of the environment is becoming apparent in other parts of the country too. In Manila, no less a figure than First Lady Amelita Ramos kicked off a campaign to save the Pasig River, called 'Piso Para sa Pasig'. Large drums have been placed in department stores where people can throw in money which will be used to clean up the filthy river. The newspaper *Today*, together with other sponsors, has published full-page ads with photos of dead fish, appealing to people to stop polluting 'before toxic wastes lead our rivers and lakes to extinction'. The Department of Interior and Local Government, with the full support of President Ramos, publishes a yearly list of the 'cleanest and greenest towns, cities and provinces'. And it is beginning to matter to people whether their town, city or province comes near the top of the list as clean and green, or at the bottom among the 'dirty dozen'. Palawan, again at the top with its capital Puerto Princesa, is showing it can be done.

As the affluent countries have shown, no country can afford to be complacent about the environment. The Philippines, with their seemingly intractable problems of poverty and unemployment, can only be commended and encouraged by visitors in their attempt to turn things round.

FLORA & FAUNA
Flora
The flora includes well over 10,000 species of trees, bushes and ferns, most of which are endemic to the Philippines. In spite of uncontrolled tree felling in the 80s, the islands of the Philippines are still covered with around 10% tropical rainforest. As well as stands of magnificent giants of the forest and rare tree ferns, over 900 species of orchid make up the astounding variety of jungle flora.

Economically important cash crops include coconut palm, rice and sugar cane, as well as many different kinds of tropical fruits. The narra is the national tree of the Philippines, the sampaguita the national flower. The mango was chosen to be the queen of fruits.

Fauna
Countless species of animal are at home in the Philippines, many of them endemic. A number of smaller mammals, like the rare mouse deer and the fist-sized tarsier, are endangered, as are the tamaraw (a species of dwarf buffalo), the Palawan bearcat and the flying lemur. The best known representative of the bird family is the giant Philippine eagle, of which only 100 are left in the wild. It is the country's national bird. There is a wide range of reptiles, from the little gecko, which is very popular as a house pet, up to the majestic Philippine crocodile, which is also on the list of endangered species. As in all tropical biotopes, the Philippines has a wide variety of snakes, including pythons and poisonous sea snakes. There is an unbelievable array of species of fish, seashells and corals. Dugongs, whale sharks, dolphins and whales are among the largest sea animals in Philippine waters.

Cruelty to Animals
Most Filipinos don't have a close relationship with animals: they don't usually have enough spare money for such luxury. Those they do look after voluntarily are usually only ones that are useful to them, such as pigs, chickens, fish and, in some regions, dogs, which all end up in the pot. Only the lumbering water buffalo, which is set to work, is actually treated in a friendly fashion.

Endangered Species
Apart from those already mentioned under
Fauna, the following animals are on the
endangered list: the scaly anteater, Palawan
Peacock-Pheasant, Luzon Bleeding-heart
Pigeon, flying fox, hawksbill and green sea
turtles, and estuarine crocodile.

National Parks
A visit to one or more of the national parks
is a must for any traveller, especially anyone
who is interested in plants, animals, scenery
or adventure. Nature is still intact, to a large
extent, in Mt Apo National Park on Mindanao and St Paul National Park on Palawan.
On the other hand, illegal wood cutters in
Bicol National Park have left behind a totally
denuded environment.

GOVERNMENT & POLITICS
The Philippines has a constitutional form of
government. The legislative power is vested
in Congress, which is composed of a Senate
(Upper House; 24 Senators) and a House of
Representatives (Lower House; 250 Members
of Congress). The president is elected
directly by the voters for a six-year term.

The Republic of the Philippines is divided
into 12 administrative regions (plus Metro
Manila as the National Capital Region) consisting of 76 provinces. Every province comprises a provincial capital and several
municipalities, which in turn consist of
village communities, or *barangays*.

President Fidel Ramos often has to share
the limelight with his erstwhile opponent
(and would-be president), Miriam Santiago,
who is known for her occasional bluntness
('line them up and shoot them'). The former
actor and present vice-president, Joseph
Estrada ('the poor man's Clint Eastwood'),
is also skilled at getting good media coverage of his activities.

ECONOMY
The economy is principally agrarian. Like
several other countries in the region, the
Philippines is potentially self-sufficient in
rice and other important foods but, because
of poor yields and the evils of absentee land-

lords in a peasant society, it generally ends
up having to import rice, fish and meat. All
of these could conceivably be produced
locally. Slow progress towards much-needed
land reform has been a problem in the Philippines ever since Independence.

Copra, sugar and abaca (a fibre from a
relative of the banana plant), tobacco,
bananas and pineapples are the principal
agricultural exports. Gold and silver mining
are other important economic activities.
There is some industry and it has been
growing in recent years. Widespread corruption and inefficiency have meant that the
boom conditions of other South-East Asian
nations have been slow to rub off on the
Philippines, although this has greatly improved in recent years.

POPULATION & PEOPLE
The population of the Philippines is estimated to be about 67 million and still
growing too fast for comfort. The people are
mainly of the Malay race although there is
the usual Chinese minority and a fair number
of *mestizos* – Filipino-Spanish or Filipino-
American. There are still some remote
pockets of pre-Malay people living in the
hills.

EDUCATION
The Philippine education system is largely
based on the American model: primary education (elementary schools), secondary education (high schools) and higher education
(colleges, universities). Attendance is compulsory for the first four of the six year
elementary school. With an illiteracy rate of
only 12% of the population over fifteen, the
standard of education is high compared with
other developing countries, even if there is a
noticeable drop in standard in non-urban
areas.

ARTS
Dance
Filipinos are talented dancers. They just
can't suppress their enthusiasm for music
and vibrant dancing, whether it be disco
dancing or cha-cha-cha at a fiesta, colourful

folk dancing or modern and classical ballet. Philippine dances are mainly derived from Malay, Spanish and Moslem origins. Among the most beautiful Malay dances are *tinikling* (bamboo or heron dance) and *pandanggo sa ilaw* (dance of lights); the best known Filipino-Muslim dance is *singkil* (court dance). You will also often see performances of the Philippine variations of the Spanish dances *habanera, jota* and *paypay* (the fan dance).

Music

Until recently, traditional Philippine music was considered to be almost exclusively restricted to ethnic minorities; 'civilised' Filipinos had fallen for American and British style pop music and imitated it perfectly. But now more and more musicians are rediscovering their cultural heritage and are bringing old melodies back to life, using traditional instruments like bamboo flutes, gongs and wooden drums, and are singing in Tagalog. The most popular social critic in the Philippines is without a doubt Freddie Aguilar, whose song *Bayan Ko* ('My Country') became the anthem of the Marcos opponents during the uprising of 1986.

Painting

The best known of the Philippine painters of the 19th century are Felix Hidalgo and Juan Luna. Both were honoured with awards on many occasions. The famous painting *Spolarium* by Juan Luna was even awarded a gold medal at the 1884 Madrid Exposition. In the mid-20th century Fernando Amorsolo, Vicente Dizon and Vicente Manansala were all internationally renowned. All three were graduates of the University of the Philippines School of Fine Arts.

SOCIETY & CONDUCT
Traditional Culture

The Philippines has developed a unique mixed culture from the historical blending of foreign influences with indigenous elements. Today, the Muslims and some of the isolated tribes are the only people whose culture remains unadulterated by Spanish and American influences.

The results of this foreign influence can be seen every day in the Philippines. For example, every afternoon even the smallest village square is converted into a basketball court. Ever since American colonial times the entire country has been crazy about this sport of giants – even though the Filipinos themselves tend to be shorter. They also love to gamble, and cockfighting gives them a great chance to indulge in this. It's also not unusual for sums of pesos to change hands after a game of jai alai – the fast ball game from the Basque country, which is also popular here. The average Filipinos are not great savers anyway; they live more to enjoy today and survive it if they can. Tomorrow will take care of itself.

The ability of the Filipinos to improvise and copy from their previous colonial masters is nowhere more apparent than in the jeepney. The army jeeps left behind by the Americans after WWII were converted into colourful, shining-chrome taxis through painstaking detailed work. Nowadays, these vehicles are produced locally by the Filipinos.

The ideas of the New Society, propagated by Marcos, caught the Filipino national consciousness in the 1970s, just as People Power did in the 1980s. Perhaps as a reaction to the residual influence of occupying foreign powers, people began to rediscover their own cultural heritage and began to care about their traditional arts and crafts. As a direct result, the national language began to find more and more favour and is strongly used today in theatre and literature, while *kundimans* – romantic and sentimental love songs – are also popular again.

Dos & Don'ts

In the Philippines, as elsewhere, there are lots of toes you can accidentally tread on unless you're careful. Here are a few tips to help you avoid potentially embarrassing situations while you're travelling:

- If people stare at you, do not get annoyed; they find you interesting – even exotic – and they want to get a good look at you.

- As is usual in more traditional countries, old people are treated with particular respect. Always greet the elderly if there are any present.
- Again, as in other Asian countries, always allow Filipinos a way of extracting themselves from an awkward situation. Above all, they do not want to 'lose face'.
- Whatever is considered polite at home, do not be punctual if you are invited to a social occasion! Turn up at least 30 minutes after the arranged time if you want to be a really polite guest.
- It is normal to remove your shoes before entering someone's home.
- If you are served food, always take at least a taste of it, even if you really can't face it. If you do like it, remember to leave some food on the plate to show you've had plenty.
- If you are in company, silence is taken as a sign you are unhappy with the situation, or don't like somebody present. If you really need peace and quiet, go somewhere you can be alone.

RELIGION

The Philippines is unique for being the only Christian country in Asia – over 90% of the population claims to be Christian and over 80% are Roman Catholic. The Spanish did a thorough job! Largest of the minority religions are the Muslims, who live chiefly on Mindanao and in the Sulu Archipelago.

When the Spanish arrived toting the cross, Islam was just establishing a toehold in the region. It was easily displaced from the northern islands, but in the south the people had been firmly converted and Christianity was never able to make strong inroads.

LANGUAGE

As in Indonesia there is one nominally national language and a large number of local languages and dialects. It takes 10 languages to cover 90% of the population! English and Spanish are still official languages, although the use of Spanish is now quite rare. English is also not as widespread as in the American days, although the English-speaking visitor will not have any trouble communicating – it remains the language of secondary school education and to say someone 'doesn't even speak English' means they've not gone beyond primary school.

Tagalog, or Pilipino, the local language of Manila and parts of Luzon, is now being pushed as the national language. It sounds remarkably like Indonesian – listen to them roll their rrrrs. Lonely Planet's *Pilipino phrasebook* has the full story. The following words are in Pilipino:

Basics

Good morning.	*Magandáng umága.*
Goodbye.	*Paálam.*
Good evening.	*Magandáng gabí.*
Hello.	*Haló.*
Welcome/Farewell.	*Mabúhay.*
How many?	*Ilán?*
How much?	*Magkáno?*
That one.	*Iyón.*
too expensive	*mahál*
Yes.	*Oó.*
No.	*Hindí.*
good	*mabúti*
bad	*masamá*

Getting Around

Where is the ...?	*Násaan ang ...?*
bus station	*terminal ng bus*
train station	*terminal ng tren*
road to Bontoc	*daan papuntang Bontoc*
straight ahead	*dirétso lámang*
to the right	*papakánan*
to the left	*papakaliwá*

Is it far from/near here?
  Maláyó (malápit) ba díto?
What time does the bus leave/arrive?
  Anong óras áalis/dárating ang bus?

Accommodation

camping ground	*kampingan*
guesthouse	*báhay pára sa nga turist*
cheap hotel	*múrang hotél*
price	*halagá*

Do you have any rooms available?
  May bakánte hó ba kayo?
How much for one night?
  Magkáno hó ba ang báyad pára sa isang gabi?

PHILIPPINES

Food & Drinks

beer	*serbésa*
coffee	*kapé*
food	*pagkaín*
milk	*gátas*
restaurant	*restorán*
sugar	*asúkal*
salt	*ásin*
water	*túbig*

Time & Dates

What time is it?	*Anong óras na?*
today	*ngayon*
tomorrow	*búkas*
yesterday	*kahápon*

Health & Emergencies

I'm sick.	*May sakit ako.*
Help!	*Saklólo!*
I'm lost.	*Nawáwalá ako.*
doctor	*doktor*
hospital	*ospital*
chemist	*botíkà*

Numbers

1	*isá*
2	*dalawá*
3	*tatló*
4	*apát*
5	*limá*
6	*ánim*
7	*pitó*
8	*waló*
9	*siyám*
10	*sampú*

Facts for the Visitor

PLANNING
When to Go

Generally, the best time to travel is from the middle of December to the middle of May – that's off season for typhoons. However, you would be well advised not to travel during the Christmas and Easter holiday periods: find yourself a pleasant base to stay at, because the entire country is on the move at these times and you will hardly find a seat on any form of transport.

January and May are the months with the most colourful festivals. In the provinces along the Pacific coast, where vast amounts of rain can fall between November and January, the dry season usually begins in the second half of February at the latest. The rice terraces in North Luzon show themselves at their best in March and April. Those are the pleasant, warm summer months, when island-hopping is the most fun. It really heats up in May, when you'll be glad of the slightest breeze.

Maps

The Nelles Verlag *Philippines* map is an excellent map of the islands at a scale of 1:1,500,000.

What to Bring

The 3rd class on the interisland boats is equipped with bunks or camp beds. A big cloth towel or a thin sleeping bag can really help you feel more comfortable on the rubber sheets covering the bunks.

Trips on outrigger boats can turn out to be quite splashy. A big plastic rubbish bag will protect your bags from the wet.

Especially in country areas electricity cannot be taken for granted, so don't forget to take along a torch (flashlight).

It's almost impossible to buy tampons outside Manila and Cebu City. If you manage to find any, the price might be outrageous. So women travellers should stock up before they go.

HIGHLIGHTS
The Best (and Worst)

Some of the most magnificent scenery in the Philippines is the Central Cordillera in the north of the country. The journey through the mountains from Baguio via Sagada and Bontoc to Banaue, although not the easiest, is unforgettable. And then you have the absolute highlight: the incredible rice terraces of Banaue.

The impressive countryside around Mt Pinatubo was created by the forces of nature. Guided tours operate mostly from Angeles.

The active, cone-shaped Mayon volcano at Legaspi, in South Luzon, is considered to be one of the most beautiful volcanoes in the world.

Despite signs it is moving in the direction of upmarket tourism, the little island of Boracay still has that 'certain something'; in another few years it'll just be one among many.

Lake Sebu in the southern Tiruray Highlands, where the T'boli live, must be the most beautiful inland lake in the Philippines. Unfortunately, this – and other parts of Mindanao – can be an area of conflict and not always safe.

On Palawan, St Paul Subterranean National Park and Underground River as well as El Nido and Bacuit Archipelago are two attractive places worth visiting.

The Philippines without fiestas? Unimaginable. The colourful Ati-Atihan Festival in Kalibo, on the island of Panay, is the most spectacular in the country. But quieter, less 'wild' local town fiestas have an attraction of their own.

Now for the bad news: most Philippine towns don't have much in the way of flair or charm, but of all the tourist attractions in the country, Pagsanjan, south-east of Manila, gets the worst marks. This is not because of the waterfall and the raft ride up to it, but because of the high tips the boat operators demand on top of the fare. They can get quite aggressive and people understandably don't like that.

SUGGESTED ITINERARIES

Anyone who wants to travel intensively around the Philippines needs plenty of time. Days and weeks pass very quickly, particularly if you want to go island-hopping. You should plan a two or three week stay fairly well if you want to experience some of the country's more unusual aspects. If you only have a little time, say a week, and don't particularly want to get to know Philippine airport architecture intimately, you would do

well to restrict yourself to a round trip of North Luzon (eg Manila-Banaue-Sagada-Baguio-Bauang-Manila).

The following is a list of a few of the possibilities, but there are endless opportunities to discover the island world for yourself:

- From Manila to Mindoro via Batangas City (Puerto Galera-Calapan-Roxas), on to Tablas/Romblon, then to Panay via Boracay. From Kalibo back to Manila or from Iloilo City to Manila. You should allow about two weeks for this trip.
- From Panay to Cebu via Negros going south with a detour to Bohol, then back to Manila direct from Cebu City.
- From Panay (Iloilo City) or Cebu (Cebu City) to Palawan (Puerto Princesa), then travel to northern Palawan, returning to Manila from El Nido or from Busuanga.
- From Cebu directly or via Bohol to Leyte and Samar, then through South Luzon to Manila.
- From Cebu to Mindanao (Zamboanga, Davao), then from northern Mindanao (Surigao) on to Leyte and Samar, returning to Manila via South Luzon.

Island-Hopping in the Visayas

With so many islands in the Visayas, such relatively short distances between them and so many ferries and boats, the possibilities for island-hopping are immense.

All things considered, the following route makes an interesting and adventurous loop that takes in most of the Visayan islands with minimal backtracking. Starting from Manila, you could travel south to the Bicol region, and from Matnog at the southern tip of Luzon there are ferries every day to Allen at the northern end of Samar.

The new road down the west coast of Samar means it is now a quick and relatively easy trip through Calbayog and Catbalogan, then across the bridge to Tacloban on the island of Leyte. From Tacloban or Ormoc, or from Bato and Maasin, there are regular ships to Cebu City.

Cebu was where Magellan arrived in the Philippines and there are a number of reminders of the Spanish period. From Cebu there are daily ferries to the neighbouring island of Bohol, famed for its Chocolate Hills. Ferries also cross daily between Cebu and Negros, either in the south of the island to Dumaguete or, closer to Cebu City, from Toledo to San Carlos. You can then continue by bus to Bacolod, from where ferries cross to Iloilo City on Panay.

From Iloilo City, in the south of Panay, you can travel to Caticlan at the north-west tip and make the short crossing by outrigger to the beautiful, relaxing island of Boracay. After a spell of lazing on the beach you can find another outrigger to cross to Tablas Island in the Romblon group, usually to Looc in the south. Take a jeepney to San Agustin and a boat from there to Romblon on Romblon Island. Finally, there are boats twice weekly to Manila.

TOURIST OFFICES
The vast Department of Tourism (DOT) office in Manila could be more aptly called the Temple of Tourism. Computer printouts with completely up to date information on various places are handed out. The regional DOT offices are smaller operations – but the staff are often very knowledgeable and have all the facts at their fingertips and information sheets on their localities.

Local Tourist Offices
Bacolod
City Plaza (☎ (034) 29021)
Baguio
DOT Complex, Governor Pack Rd (☎ (074) 442 7014, 442 6708)
Cagayan de Oro
Pelaez Sports Complex, Velez St (☎ (08822) 723696)
Cebu City
GMC Plaza Building, Plaza Independencia (☎ (032) 91503, 96518)
Cotabato
Elizabeth Tan Building (☎ (064) 211110, 217868)
Davao
Magsaysay Park Complex (☎ (082) 221 6798, 221 6955)
Iloilo City
Bonifacio Drive (☎ (033) 270245)
Legaspi
Peñaranda Park, Albay District (☎ (05221) 44492, 44026)
Manila
T M Kalaw St, Ermita (☎ (02) 523 8411)

San Fernando (La Union)
Matanag Justice Hall, General Luna St, Town Plaza (☎ (072) 412098, 412411)
San Fernando (Pampanga)
Paskuhan Village (☎ (045) 961 2665, 961 2612)
Tacloban
Children's Park, Senator Enage St (☎ (053) 321 2048, 321 4333)
Tuguegarao
2F Tuguegarao Supermarket (☎ (078) 844 1621)
Zamboanga
Lantaka Hotel, Valderroza St (☎ (062) 991 0218)

Tourist Offices Abroad
Overseas offices of the Philippines Department of Tourism include:

Australia
Highmount House, Level 6, 122 Castlereagh St, Sydney, NSW 2000 (☎ (02) 9267-2695/2756)
France
c/o Philippine Embassy, 3 Faubourg Saint Honoré, Paris 75009 (☎ 01 42 65 02 34/02 35)
Germany
Kaiserstrasse 15, 60311 Frankfurt-am-Main (☎ (069) 20893/20894)
Hong Kong
c/o Philippine Consulate, 6F United Centre, 95 Queensway, Central (☎ 2866-6471/7859)
Japan
c/o Philippine Embassy, 11-24 Nampeidai Machi, Shibuya-ku, Tokyo (☎ (03) 3464-3630/3635)
Philippine Tourism Center, 2F Dainan Building, 2-19-23 Shinmachi, Nishi-ku, Osaka 550 (☎ (06) 535-5071/5072)
Korea
1107 Renaissance Building, 1598-3 Socho-dong, Socho-ku, Seoul (☎ (02) 525-1707)
Singapore
c/o Philippine Embassy, 20 Nassim Rd, Singapore (☎ (02) 235 2184/2548)
UK
c/o Philippine Embassy, 17 Albemarle St, London WIX 7HA (☎ (0171) 499-5443/5652)
USA
3660 Wilshire Blvd, Suite 285, Los Angeles, CA 90010 (☎ (213) 487-4527)
447 Sutter St, Suite 507, San Francisco, CA 94108 (☎ (415) 956-4050)
Philippine Center, 556 Fifth Ave, New York, NY 10036 (☎ (212) 575-7915)

VISAS & DOCUMENTS
Visas
Visa regulations vary with your intended length of stay. The easiest procedure is to

simply arrive without a visa, in which case you will be permitted to stay for up to 21 days. However, your passport has to be valid at least six months beyond the 21 day period you intend to stay. If you obtain a visa overseas it will usually allow a 59 day stay. This will normally be granted for about US$35. If you already have a visa on arrival make sure the immigration officers know this or your passport will still be stamped for just 21 days.

Visa Extensions To extend the 21 day stay period to 59 days apply with your passport and the relevant documents to the immigration office in Manila, Cebu City or Angeles. The Manila office is at the Department of Immigration & Deportation, Magallanes Drive, Intramuros, Manila. The extension costs P500 for the Visa Waiver plus P10 for a Legal Research Fee. If you want the four-hour Express Service it costs an additional P250. You must be neatly dressed if you apply in person at the office – rubber thongs/flip-flops will ensure an instant refusal. A number of travel agencies will handle the extension application for a P100 to P200 fee.

After 59 days it gets really complicated, although it's possible to keep on extending for about a year. Further extensions cost P200 per month for the Extension Fee, but you have to add in Alien Head Tax (P200), Alien Certificate of Registration (P400), Emigration Clearance Certificate (P500), plus a whole series of Legal Research fees.

Staying beyond six months also involves a Certificate of Temporary Residence (P700) and after one year there's a Travel Tax (P1620).

Other Documents

Apart from Philippine Airlines (PAL), some other bus and shipping companies offer student discounts. So a student ID card could come in handy.

EMBASSIES
Philippine Embassies

Philippine embassies abroad include:

Australia
    1 Moonah Place, Yarralumla ACT 2600
    (☎ (06) 273 2535)
Canada
    130 Albert St, Ottawa (☎ (613) 233-1121)
France
    3 Faubourg Saint Honoré, Paris 75009
    (☎ 01 42 65 02 34/02 35)
Japan
    11-24 Nampeidai Machi, Shibuya-ku, Tokyo
    (☎ (03) 3496-6555)
New Zealand
    50 Hobson St, Thorndon, Wellington
    (☎ (04) 472-9921)
South Africa
    Southern Life Plaza Building, Schoeman St, Pretoria (☎ (012) 342-6920)
UK
    17 Albemarle St, London WIX 7HA
    (☎ (0171) 499-5443/5652)
USA
    1600 Massachusetts Ave NW, Washington, DC 20036 (☎ (202) 467-9300)

See the other chapters in this book for Philippine embassies in those countries.

Foreign Embassies in the Philippines

Countries with diplomatic representation in the Manila include:

Australia
    Doña Salustiana Ty Tower, 104 Paseo de Roxas, Makati (☎ 817 7911)
Brunei
    Bank of Philippine Islands Building, Ayala Ave, Paseo de Roxas, Makati (☎ 816 2836)
Canada
    Allied Bank Building, 6754 Ayala Ave, Makati (☎ 810 8861)
France
    Pacific Star Building, Gil Puyat Ave, Makati (☎ 810 1981)
Indonesia
    185 Salcedo St, Makati (☎ 892 5961)
Japan
    375 Gil Puyat Ave, Makati (☎ 895 9050)
Malaysia
    107 Tordesillas St, Makati (☎ 817 4581)
New Zealand
    Gammon Center Building, Alfaro St, Makati (☎ 818 0916)
Singapore
    ODC International Building, 219 Salcedo St, Makati (☎ 816 1767)

Thailand
Marie Cristine Building, 107 Rada St, Makati
(☎ 815 4219)
UK
V Locsin Building, 6752 Ayala Ave, Makati
(☎ 816 7116)
USA
1201 Roxas Blvd, Ermita (☎ 521 7116)
Vietnam
554 Vito Cruz, Malate (☎ 500364)

CUSTOMS

Personal effects, a reasonable amount of clothing, toiletries, jewellery for normal use and a small quantity of perfume are allowed in duty-free. Visitors may also bring in 200 cigarettes or two tins of tobacco and two litres of alcohol free of duty.

It is strictly prohibited to bring illegal drugs, firearms and obscene and pornographic media into the country.

Visitors carrying more than US$3000 are requested to declare the amount at the Central Bank counter at the customs area. Foreign currency taken out upon departure must not exceed the amount brought in. Departing passengers may not take out more than P1000 in local currency.

It is strictly forbidden to export drugs. In addition, coral, certain types of orchid, mussels and parts of animals, such as turtle shells and python skins, may not be exported.

MONEY
Costs

'Philippines 2000', the Ramos government's economic and political development programme, was designed to help the country catch up with the rest of Asia's 'tigers' and their growth rates. However, so far it has only brought steep price increases for most of the population. For travellers, eating out and accommodation have become more expensive (about 30% dearer than in Thailand). You will get the best value for your money in the mountains of North Luzon (Banaue, Batad, Sagada), while in the more popular tourist areas, such as the islands of Boracay and Cebu, you will have to dig deeper into your pocket. Some things seem

amazingly cheap – local transport and beer are two good examples. Air fares within the Philippines are also good value, but not as cheap as in past years.

Currency

The unit of currency is the peso (P, also spelt piso), divided into 100 centavos (c). Throughout this section 'c' means centavos, not cents of another currency.

Currency Exchange

The following table shows exchange rates:

Australia	A$1	=	P20.79
Canada	C$1	=	P19.26
France	FF10	=	P50.95
Germany	DM1	=	P17.06
Hong Kong	HK$10	=	P33.94
Japan	¥100	=	P23.69
Malaysia	M$1	=	P10.46
New Zealand	NZ$1	=	P18.36
Thailand	100B	=	P103.29
UK	UK£1	=	P41.02
USA	US$1	=	P26.18

Changing Money

The only foreign currency to have in the Philippines is US dollars – it's no longer true to say that nothing else is considered to exist, only that the US dollar exists more than most.

Furthermore, American Express travellers' cheques are more easily exchanged than other varieties. There are no particular hassles with the peso, although you'll need an exchange receipt if you want to convert any back on departure.

The main problem is that changing travellers' cheques can be slow, particularly away from Manila. Of the banks, the Philippines Commercial International Bank (PCI Bank) is said to offer the best rates for travellers' cheques but American Express is faster. Around Ermita, along Mabini St in particular, there are a great number of moneychangers who are much faster than the banks and give a better rate for cash. The rate varies with the size of the bill – US$100 and US$50 bills are best, US$1 bills are hardly wanted at all.

Rates tend to vary from one changer to another, so shop around. Some of the money-changers will change travellers' cheques as well, but at a worse rate. Even at banks cash tends to get a better rate than cheques, unlike in many other countries.

Well-known international cards, such as American Express, Diner's Club, Master-Card and Visa, are accepted by many hotels, restaurants and businesses in the Philippines. With your Visa and MasterCard you can withdraw cash in pesos at any branch of the Equitable Bank (almost every big city has a branch).

ATM withdrawals are possible on savings account cards, but you must open an account with a Philippine bank first. With your Visa card you can withdraw as much as P20,000 (debited from your account back home) per day from any PCI Bank ATM. Several branch offices have been equipped with ATMs throughout the country.

Black Market

There is said to be a small black market but the rate is only minimally better and it's not worth the risk. The risk is real – there are a lot of money rip-off scams in Manila and any offer of a spectacular exchange rate is bound to be a set-up. There is a wide and interesting variety of tricks involving sleight of hand and other subterfuges.

Tipping & Bargaining

Restaurant staff generally expect a tip (it is part of their wage), even if the menu states that a service charge is included. The money then goes into a kitty and is shared later with the cook and the cashier. If the service was particularly good, a tip of around 5% of the bill will show your appreciation.

Taxi drivers will often try to wangle a tip by claiming not to be able to give change. If the charge on the meter appears to be accurate, the passenger should voluntarily round up the amount: for example, if the fare is P44, then P50 would be appropriate.

When shopping in public markets or even shops, Filipinos try to get a 10% discount.

They almost always succeed. Foreign customers will automatically be quoted a price that is around 20% more than normal or, in places which deal mainly with tourists, up to 50% more.

POST & COMMUNICATIONS
Postal Rates

Air mail letters (per 20g) within the Philippines cost P4 (ordinary/three weeks).

Air mail letters (per 10g) cost P6 to South-East Asia, P7 to Australia and the Middle East, P8 to Europe and North America and P9 to Africa and South America.

Aerograms and postcards cost P5, regardless of their destination.

Sending Mail

So far, all our letters have arrived home safely. If you are sending important items (such as film) by mail, it is best to send it by registered post. Registered express letters will be delivered – all going well – within five days.

Depending on the destination, only parcels weighing less than 10 or 20 kg will be dispatched by the Philippine postal service. They must also be wrapped in plain brown paper and fastened with string. Parcels sent to Europe by surface (sea) mail take from two to four months to reach their destination.

Opening hours in Philippine post offices are not the same everywhere. Many close at noon, others shut on Saturday as well. The following hours can usually be relied upon: Monday to Friday from 8 am to noon, and from 1 to 5 pm.

Receiving Mail

The Philippine postal system is generally quite efficient. Poste restante is available at the GPO in all major towns. Depending on the distance from Manila, it can take up to three weeks to be delivered.

Telephone

You do not find telephones everywhere in the Philippines; in an emergency try the nearest police station, which in many areas will have the only telephone. Telephone numbers are always changing, so obtain a local directory before calling.

In contrast to overseas calls, local calls in the Philippines are full of problems. It can take a ridiculously long time to be connected and the lines over long distances are bad. International calls are simple in comparison.

International telephone calls can be made from many hotels (operator or direct dialling; it depends on their equipment) or from any PLDT (Philippine Long Distance Telephone Company) office.

The access code for making international calls from the Philippines is 00.

To call the Philippines from outside the country, the country code is 63.

Fax, Telegraph & Email

Sending a fax overseas from a hotel can be quite expensive (for example, P350 for one page to Europe). On the other hand, telecommunications companies such as Eastern Telecom and PLDT charge about P95 for the first minute (one page) and P85 for the following minutes.

The international telegram service is reasonably prompt and reliable, but internal telegrams are likely to be delayed. There are two major domestic telegram companies: Radio Communications of the Philippines (RCPI) and Philippine Telegraph & Telephone Corporation (PT&T). To Europe, 12-hour telegrams cost about P14 a word and to Australia they cost P15. Within the Philippines, a telegram to Cebu from Manila, for example, costs about P1.50 a word and takes five hours. To compare, a telex to Europe costs P85 per minute (four lines) through Eastern Telecom.

If you are dying to send some e-mail, so-called cyber-cafes are opening up in many of the larger cities. Manila, Baguio, Cebu City and Davao all have one or more compucafes, with or without drinks, and you can be sure more are on the way. Costs vary, but for about the same money as a short call home you can log onto the Internet and surf the Web, or chat via the keyboard for an hour.

BOOKS

Lonely Planet

For in-depth coverage of travel in the Philippines, look for Lonely Planet's *Philippines – travel survival kit*. The Lonely Planet *Pilipino phrasebook* will come in useful for travel through the islands.

General

Manila has a good selection of bookshops. Unfortunately, most Philippine publications quickly sell out and only rarely is a 2nd edition printed. Notable titles in the last few years have included *A Journey Through the Enchanted Isles* by Amadis Ma Guerrero; *Who's Who in Philippine History* by Carlos Quirino; *In Our Image – America's Empire in the Philippines* by Stanley Karnow; and the excellently researched *Power from the Forest – The Politics of Logging* by Marites Dañguilan Vitug.

NEWSPAPERS & MAGAZINES

After 20 years of press censorship under Marcos, the change of government brought a flood of new national and local newspapers and magazines indulging in a marvellous journalistic free-for-all; many are in English.

There are now about 20 English-language publications, including the *Manila Bulletin*, the *Inquirer*, *Malaya*, *The Manila Chronicle*, the *Manila Standard*, *Newsday*, *Today*, *Daily Globe*, *The Philippine Star*, *The Journal* and the *Evening Star*. If you want to know more you can get *Newsweek, Time, Asiaweek, Far Eastern Economic Review* and the *International Herald Tribune*.

RADIO & TV

Radio and TV operate on a commercial basis, and there are 22 TV channels. Seven of these broadcast from Manila, sometimes in English and sometimes in Tagalog.

Many hotels now offer cable TV with international channels as part of their service.

PHOTOGRAPHY & VIDEO

Take sufficient slide film with you as there is not a lot of choice in the Philippines. This is especially true of the provinces, where the use-by date has often expired. Kodak Ektachrome 100 costs about P170, a 200 costs P215 and a 400 costs P250.

There's no problem with normal colour film, which is often preferred by Filipinos. Development is fast and good value. High gloss prints (nine cm by 13 cm) can be processed in an hour at a cost of P2.50 per print; cheaper processing takes longer.

The usual rules for tropical photography apply in the Philippines. Remember to allow for the intensity of the tropical light, keep your film as cool and dry as possible and have it developed as soon as possible after exposure.

Remember that cameras can be one of the most intrusive and unpleasant reminders of the impact of tourism – it's polite to ask people before you photograph them. A smile always helps.

ELECTRICITY

The electric current is generally 220V, 60 Hz, although the actual voltage is often less. In some areas the standard current is the USA-style 110V.

Blackouts are common even in the tourist centres. A pocket torch (flashlight) is very useful for such occasions.

An adaptor may be needed for Philippine plugs, which are usually like the US flat two-pin type.

LAUNDRY

Only a few of the laundries open to the public in the Philippines are equipped with modern machinery. Self-service laundrettes with coin-operated machines are completely unknown.

If you don't want to wash your clothes yourself, hand them to your hotel or guest-house and you'll get them back within two to three days. They will not always be ironed though. It costs about P15 to have a shirt or blouse washed and ironed.

WEIGHTS & MEASURES

In general, the metric system is in use, although both metric and imperial are normal. Measurements of length are more often given in feet and yards than in centi-metres and metres, while weight is normally expressed in grams and kilograms and tem-perature in Celsius.

If you need to convert from one system to the other, you can use the conversion chart on the inside back cover of this book.

HEALTH

State-owned hospitals and provincial private practices are often badly equipped. In case of an emergency, you should try to reach the nearest town and check into a private hospi-tal. Dental treatment is adequate, at least in the towns and cities. In country areas, on the other hand, dental problems are often simply solved by pulling the tooth.

TOILETS

Toilets are referred to as 'comfort room', or 'CR' for short. In Tagalog, gentlemen are *lalake* and ladies are *babae*. Toilet seats in restaurants and bars are often filthy, and toilet paper is rare. There are no public toilets; it's not unusual to see men relieving themselves in the street.

WOMEN TRAVELLERS

Many Filipinos like to think of themselves as being irresistible macho types, but can also turn out to be surprisingly considerate gentlemen. They are especially keen to show their best side to foreign women. They will address you respectfully as 'Ma'am', shower you with friendly compliments and engage you in polite conversation.

But Filipinas too (for instance if travelling next to a foreign women on a bus) will not miss the chance to ask a few questions out of curiosity: for example, about your home country, reason for and goal of your journey, and of course about your husband, how many children you have etc.

So it would be a good idea to be prepared and have a few polite answers ready. After a few days on the road you'll be grateful for them.

On the other hand, it is best simply to ignore drunken Filipinos if they pester you. Simulated friendliness could easily be mis-understood as an invitation to get to know each other better. If a group of Filipinos is having a drinking session in a restaurant, it is not recommended practice to sit down at a table next to them. You may want to try a different restaurant.

GAY & LESBIAN TRAVELLERS

Homosexuality is viewed tolerantly in the Philippines. Even if jokes are told about them (never meant in an insulting or prejudiced way), gay men (*bakla*) and lesbians (*tomboy*) are almost universally accepted as part of everyday Philippine society. An exception is made in the armed forces: gays and lesbians are banned from military service.

DISABLED TRAVELLERS

Judging by facilities in buildings, the Philippines is really not suited for disabled people. Only a few hotels and guesthouses are equipped with a suitable ramp for wheelchairs, and only rarely has an architect thought of providing roomy toilets with big doors. On the other hand, these deficits are largely made up for by the sheer humanity of the people. When they see a disabled person, Filipinos are not stunned into inaction because they're so concerned, nor do they turn away helplessly. They behave perfectly naturally, without ingratiating themselves in an embarrassing way. And if needed, there's always someone there with a helping hand.

SENIOR TRAVELLERS

The older generation is treated with respect and deference in the Philippines and this applies equally to visitors. On the practical side, if you are over 60 years of age, PAL will give you a 20% rebate on all inland flights. You won't have to pay anything for the boat trip to the Underground River in St Paul National Park.

TRAVEL WITH CHILDREN

A Philippine child is never alone, so a foreign child will definitely never spend a moment without someone to play with. Filipinos are simply crazy about children. If you travel with a child, people will often strike up a conversation with you and you'll have to talk a lot.

DANGERS & ANNOYANCES

The Philippines has rip-offs like anywhere else, but in recent years it has had more. New tricks pop up every year so it's always wise to be on your toes.

Beware of people who claim to have met you before. 'I was the immigration officer at the airport when you came through' is one often-used line. Manila has lots of fake immigration officers ready to dupe the unwary. There are also fake police officers and a favourite scam is to ask to check your money for counterfeit notes. When they return it the money may well be fake, or some of it may be missing.

Don't accept invitations to parties or meals from people who accost you in the street. Drugged coffee is a favourite with these folk and when you wake up your valuables will be long gone. Baguio is a popular place for unexpected invitations.

Beware of pickpockets in crowded areas of Manila or on tightly-packed jeepneys or buses. Favourite places are around Ermita. Sleight-of-hand scams by street moneychangers are another speciality. Invitations to card games are another good way to lose money.

LEGAL MATTERS

If you are arrested, contact your nearest embassy or consulate immediately. However, they may not be able to do much more than provide you with a list of local lawyers and keep an eye on how you are being treated. Remember you are subject to Philippine law when in the Philippines.

Since the early 1980s the laws governing drug abuse have grown increasingly severe in the Philippines. Unauthorised people are absolutely forbidden to handle, own or traffic in drugs. Transgressions are punished very severely and penalties range from six years' imprisonment to death.

BUSINESS HOURS

Businesses first open their doors between 8 and 10 am. Offices, banks and public authorities work a five day week. Some offices are also open on Saturday morning. Banks open at 9 am and close at 3 pm or 3.30 pm. Embassies and consulates are open to the public mainly from 9 am to 1 pm.

Offices and public authorities close at 5 pm. Large businesses like department stores and supermarkets continue until 7 pm, and smaller shops often open until 10 pm.

PUBLIC HOLIDAYS & SPECIAL EVENTS

Offices and banks are closed on public holidays, although shops and department stores stay open. Good Friday is the only time in the year when the entire country closes down. Even public transport stops running, and PAL remains grounded on that day. The public holidays are:

New Year's Day
  1 January
Maundy Thursday, Good Friday and Easter Sunday
  March/April
Bataan Day
  9 April
Labour Day
  1 May
Independence Day
  12 June
All Saints' Day
  1 November
Bonifacio Day
  30 November
Christmas Day
  25 December
Rizal Day
  30 December

ACTIVITIES

A growing number of visitors to the Philippines want to do more than just travel around. The most popular activities are diving and windsurfing, but mountain biking and surfing are also growing in popularity.

Diving

Mindoro (Puerto Galera), Palawan (Puerto Princesa), Bohol (Alona Beach) and Cebu (Moalboal) are the points of departure for the most popular diving places in the archipelago. Boracay is ideal for beginners (there are lots of diving schools), and for wreck divers Subic Bay (Luzon) and Busuanga Island (in the Calamian group) are the places to go.

Windsurfing

The island of Boracay is the Philippine mecca for windsurfers. The best conditions for both beginner and advanced levels can be found on the east coast.

Mountain Biking

The island of Guimaras, between Negros and Panay, looks as if it was made for mountain biking: sparsely populated, with a lack of traffic and other hindrances, its rolling hills and fields are crisscrossed with trails and streams. Enterprising people at Moalboal, on Cebu, are attracting more and more bikers by organising exciting tours.

Surfing

In the early days, practically the only place for surfers to go was the island of Catanduanes. Nowadays, the number one place on their list is Siargao Island, north-east of Mindanao. There is also the so-called Surf Beach at San Juan on the north-west coast of Luzon, which is a bit more accessible.

WORK

Non-resident aliens may not be employed at all, nor theoretically even look for work, without a valid work permit, while foreign residents need the necessary work registration; both can be obtained from the Department of Labor and Employment.

ACCOMMODATION

If your budget for a night's accommodation only stretches up to P100, then there are only a few hotels available. Prices for quite inexpensive accommodation start at around P200.

The cheapest are the guesthouses in the mountains of North Luzon, although some will be pretty basic – with no electricity for example. The best selection of well-equipped, medium-priced hotels can be found in Angeles, near Mt Pinatubo. On the popular little island of Boracay during the on season from December until May, only a handful of resorts offer cottages for less than P500; however, during the off season all sorts of attractive discounts are available.

Reasonably priced accommodation from P150 up to P500 can be found on Palawan, the 'last frontier' of the Philippines.

Maintenance in many hotels is a little lackadaisical so it's worth checking if the electricity and water are working before you sign in. Beware of fires in cheap hotels – Filipino hotels don't close down, they burn down. Check fire escapes and make sure windows will open. Finally, it's often worth asking for a discount or bargaining a little on prices, as they'll often come down.

FOOD
The Filipinos have taken to US fast foods wholeheartedly, so there are plenty of hamburgers and hot dogs. Chinese food is also widely available and menus in many Chinese restaurants are in a mixture of Spanish and English – one of the few reminders of Spain. Filipino food, usually called 'native' food, is a bit like Indonesian *nasi padang* in that it's all laid out on view – and to western palates it would often taste a lot better if it were hot. It's worth a splurge to try good, authentic Filipino food as it can be really delicious. Some popular dishes include:

Adobo – a national standard dish: stewed chicken, pork or squid pieces.
Arroz caldo – boiled rice with chicken, garlic, ginger and onions.
Balut – a popular street-side snack, boiled duck egg containing a partially formed duck embryo – yuck!
Bangus – milkfish, lightly grilled, stuffed and baked.
Crispy pata – crispy fried pig skin, another delicacy or feast dish.
Gulay – vegetable dish, sometimes simmered in coconut milk, particularly gabi leaves.
Inihaw – grilled fish or meat.
Lechon – a feast dish, roast baby pig with liver sauce.
Lumpia – spring rolls filled with meat or vegetables. Lumpia Shanghai are small fried spring rolls filled with meat.
Mami – noodle soup, like mee soup in Malaysia or Indonesia.
Menudo – stew with vegetables and small liver pieces or chopped pork.
Mungos – chick peas, similar to Lebanese humus.
Pancit – noodle dish, either Pancit Canton (thick noodles) or Pancit Guisado (thin noodles).
Pinangat – Bicol vegetable dish laced with very hot peppers – 'the Bicol express'.

DRINKS
There are also a number of Filipino drinks worth sampling (apart from Coke, which they must consume faster than any country apart from the USA):

Halo-Halo – a crushed ice, flavouring and fruit dessert. It means 'all mixed together' and is similar to an *es kacang* in Malaysia.
Iced buko – buko is young coconut.
Kalamansi – the tiny lemons known as kalamansi are served as lemon juice or with black tea. They are thought to have amazing curative effects.
San Mig – San Miguel beer must be one of the cheapest beers in the world and it's also very good.
Tuba – coconut wine; can be very strong.

ENTERTAINMENT
The Filipinos are very keen on their nightlife. There are bars and clubs in every city, as well as cinemas, movies being a popular and inexpensive pleasure. Also popular are karaoke bars, where Filipinos can sing their hearts out and prove how good their voices are.

But there's no doubt that cockfights are what the Filipinos get most excited about. All over the country, every Sunday and public holiday, irritable and expensive fighting birds are let loose on one another. The cockpits are full to bursting point, the audience is high with excitement and a lot of money depends on the outcome of every fight.

SPECTATOR SPORTS
Jai alai and basketball really draw the crowds. Games in the professional league of the Philippine Basketball Association (PBA) take place three times a week. On the other hand, players of jai alai, the fast ball game of Basque origin, have to take an involuntary break now and then because of game-rigging and betting irregularities.

THINGS TO BUY
There are a wide variety of handicrafts available in the Philippines and you will find examples of most crafts on sale in Manila. Clothing, cane and basket work, woodcarving and all manner of regional specialities

can be found. See the various Manila, Luzon and islands sections for more details.

Getting There & Away

AIR

The best way to get to the Philippines is to fly. Although Cebu City, Davao and Laoag now have international airports, Manila is virtually the only international gateway and, for probably 99% of visitors, the first experience of the country.

Hong Kong

Hong Kong is the regional gateway to the Philippines. Fares from Hong Kong to Manila with Air France or Emirates cost around US$130 one way and US$225 return.

Thailand

You can also look for cheap fares from Bangkok. From Bangkok to Manila can cost you around US$225 to US$280 return.

Singapore

Singapore to Manila with Singapore Airlines costs US$270 one way and US$410 return.

Malaysia

From Sabah you can fly from Kota Kinabalu to Manila. On Malaysia Airlines it costs US$180 one way and US$355 return. You can also fly to Manila from Kuala Lumpur for US$260 one way or US$470 return.

Indonesia

There are regular flights now twice a week with Bouraq Airlines between Davao, in the south of Mindanao, and Manado in the north of Sulawesi. The fare is US$150 one way and US$262 return.

Departure Tax

Airport departure tax is P500 in Manila, in Cebu City it's P400 and in Davao P200.

SEA
Malaysia

The Aleson Shipping Lines' MV *Lady Mary Joy* serves the cities of Zamboanga, Mindanao (Philippines) and Sadakan, Sabah (East Malaysia) once a week (US$34; 17 hours).

Getting Around

AIR
Domestic Air Services

Philippine Airlines (PAL) runs a frequent and often economical service to most parts of the country. The only thing that can really be said against it is that there are often flights from Manila to town A, B or C, but rarely flights between towns A, B and C. PAL is pretty security conscious, so expect to be thoroughly frisked.

Student card holders under 26 years of age are eligible for a 20% discount on round-trip domestic flights. PAL also offers a Golden Age Discount of 15% for passengers over 60 years.

PAL flights are often heavily booked and crowded so, unless you can book ahead, you may find it necessary to join the wait-list; fortunately, it is quite efficient in Manila. The wait-list is started each day at the stroke of midnight and as soon as you put your name on the list, you're given a wait-list number.

When a flight is called, they announce down to the number on the list which can be carried. You're wait-listed for a destination, not a flight, so if there are several flights during the day your chances improve with each flight. At midnight the day's wait-list is scrubbed and a new list starts for the next day. The period from 15 December to 4 January is practically hopeless for flights anywhere in the Philippines.

To make reservations, ring PAL at the following number in Manila: ☎ 816 6691.

PAL no longer monopolises all domestic services. There are now a number of smaller operators, such as Air Ads, Air Philippines, Asian Spirit, Cebu Pacific, Grand Air, Pacific

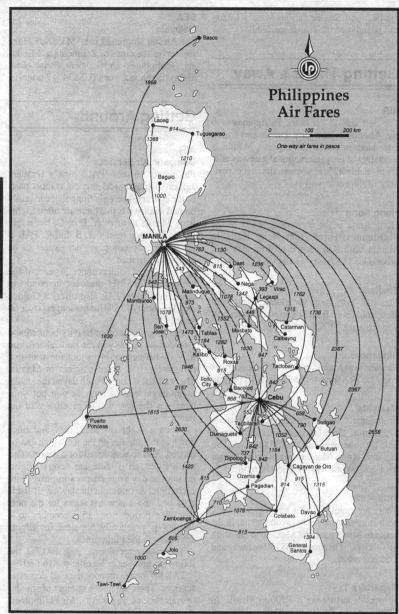

**Philippines
Air Fares**

0   100   200 km

One-way air fares in pesos

Basco

1869

Laoag
814   Tuguegarao
1368

1210

Baguio

1000

MANILA

763 *1130*

815   Daet *1236*

543   Naga *393* Virac
543   Marinduque *1342* *1078* Legaspi *1762*
Mamburao *973*   *448* *1315* *1736*
1078   Masbate   Catarman
San   *1473* Tablas   *1630* Calbayog
Jose *1184* *1262*   *947*   *2367*
1630 Kalibo   Roxas
1948   *815*   Tacloban
2157   Iloilo   *842*   *2367*
City   Bacolod
868 *783* Cebu
552 *395* *658*
Puerto *1815*   Tagbilaran *790* Surigao
Princesa *2630* Dumaguete *1052* *2656*
2551   *842* *1184* Butuan
Dipolog *737* *842*
1420   Cagayan de Oro
815   Ozamis   *814*
Pagadian *915* *1315*
710   Davao
Zamboanga *1078* Cotabato
815   *1394*
605   General
1000 Jolo   Santos

Tawi-Tawi

Airways and Soriano Aviation, and they've become popular since the spate of late-1980s shipping disasters.

Air Passes

PAL passengers can buy an inexpensive Air Pass ('Visit the Philippines Fare') for four, six or eight different Philippine destinations when buying an international ticket (long distance and round trip only). An Air Pass is valid for the same duration as the international ticket. Four coupons cost US$155, six coupons US$182, eight coupons US$198.

BUS

There are an enormous number of bus services running all over the Philippines and they are generally very economical. As a rule of thumb, on a regular bus you cover about 2.5 km per peso and average about 50 km an hour. Thus a 100 km journey will cost about P40 and take about two hours. Air-con buses are more expensive and trips on gravel roads are more expensive than on sealed roads.

Departures are very frequent although buses sometimes leave early if they're full – take care if there's only one bus a day! People like to travel early, when it's cool, so there will probably be more buses going early in the day. Note that on Luzon all roads lead to Manila and so do all bus routes. If you're heading from South Luzon to North Luzon you'll have to take one bus into Manila and another out. The main companies include BLTB, Dangwa Tranco, Victory Liner and Philippine Rabbit.

As well as the regular buses there are more expensive air-con buses (and even more expensive tour buses) operated by companies like Gold Line Tours. Typical fares from Manila for ordinary buses include: Alaminos (237 km, P105), Baguio (250 km, P115), Batangas (110 km, P50), Olongapo (126 km, P60) and Legaspi (544 km, P240).

TRAIN

There were once three passenger rail services in the Philippines, but only one remains and it looks unlikely to last long. The only route left is south from Manila to the Bicol region

of South Luzon. The service is so slow and unreliable that everyone recommends the bus.

CAR & MOTORCYCLE
Road Rules

Cars are driven on the right in the Philippines. Traffic rules are rarely respected, so you should drive defensively at all times. Whatever happens, avoid the temptation to copy the crazy overtaking style of the local drivers.

Rental

Apart from international companies like Avis and Hertz, various local companies can also be found. An important clause in the small print says that rental cars can only be driven on surfaced roads: this really cramps your style in this part of the world. Rentals are made daily or weekly. A Toyota Corolla XL will cost around US$65 per day, or US$390 per week. The driver-renter should be not less than 21 and not more than 65 years of age.

It's only possible to rent a motorcycle in a few tourist places and the prices are relatively high. A 125cc Honda will cost you P350 to P650 per day. Helmets should be worn.

BICYCLE

Touring the Philippines by bike is still a bit unusual. A German couple who rode from Davao in the south of Mindanao via the islands to Manila in four weeks caused quite a stir.

HITCHING

As transport costs are so low, it's hardly worth anyone's while to hitchhike. No Filipino would ever dream of sticking his thumb out for a lift, even if he didn't have the money for a ticket. In any case, drivers usually expect a few pesos if they give lifts 'because of the high price of petrol'.

WALKING

Definitely a good way to meet people and discover the joys of nature. There's always a

PHILIPPINES

way to finish the rest of your journey, as the entire archipelago is crisscrossed with paths and trails. With the right planning, a hiker can avoid practically all contact with cobbles, asphalt and exhaust gases.

BOAT

Getting around by boat is much easier than in Indonesia – it's not so much 'will there be a boat this week?' as 'will there be a boat today?' – and the answer is often 'yes: this morning'. The boats are cheap, usually comfortable and pretty fast, and the Philippine islands are tightly packed together.

The real hub of the shipping services is Cebu – everything seems to run through here, and there are many shipping companies. Apart from the major interisland ships, there are many ferries shuttling back and forth between nearby islands.

Fares differ markedly from company to company. Inquire about student discounts: some shipping lines give 20% or 30%.

Ship travel has its disadvantages. For example, standards vary and some boats are dirty, badly kept and overcrowded. A rough voyage with seasick fellow passengers can be a trial.

The table below shows sample boat fares from Manila to popular destinations in the Philippines:

Destination	Fare (deck class)
Bacolod	P480
Cagayan de Oro	P700
Cebu City	P520
Coron	P300
Davao	P990
Dumaguete	P545
Iloilo City	P510
Kalibo	P400
Puerto Princesa	P455
Roxas	P400
Surigao	P635
Tacloban	P470
Zamboanga	P645

But the most serious problem is safety. The small local boats are often the worst as they may be grossly overloaded and safety equipment is simply nonexistent. Even the very short trips can be risky – there have been some unhappy incidents at Boracay (no deaths, but people have lost all their gear), and the Roxas (Mindoro) to Tablas (Romblon) boats are particularly bad.

Drinks are usually available on board, but on longer trips it's not a bad idea to bring some food supplies. Be prepared for long unscheduled stops at ports along the way. It's important to allow for a flexible schedule if travelling by ship.

At the beginning of 1996 the three biggest Philippine shipping companies, William Lines, Gothong Lines and Aboitiz Lines amalgamated and now trade under the name of WG&A. The most important of their interisland ships were refitted and renamed *Superferry 1*, *Superferry 2* etc. WG&A now have by far the best equipped fleet in the Philippines; their service is well above average, the quality of the food on board has markedly improved and, to top it all off, the ships are relatively punctual.

LOCAL TRANSPORT
Jeepney

The true Filipino local transport is the jeepney. The recipe for a jeepney is: take one ex-US Army jeep, put two benches in the back with enough space for about 12 people, paint it every colour of the rainbow, add tassels, badges, horns, lights, aerials, about a dozen rear view mirrors, a tape deck with a selection of Filipino rock music, a chrome horse (or better a whole herd of them) and anything else you can think of. Then stuff 20 passengers on those benches for 12, add four more in front and drive like a maniac. But they're cheap and you'll find them in cities and doing shorter runs between centres.

At one time it was thought the jeepney was a threatened species and would be replaced by new utility vehicles manufactured in South-East Asia. But now it seems that the Filipinos are simply making brand-new ex-US Army-style jeeps. They're stretched so you can fit more passengers in, but otherwise they're just like jeepneys have always been.

The usual jeepney fare is P1.50 for up to

the first four km and then 50c (sometimes only 25c) a km. You pay as you get out, or anywhere along the way if you prefer and know what it's going to be. To stop a jeepney (when you want to get off) you can rap on the roof, hiss or use the correct term which is *'pára'*, Tagalog for 'stop', or *'báyad'*, meaning 'payment'.

For longer journeys in the country, it's wise to find out what the fare should be before you set off. Beware of 'Special Rides', where you charter the whole vehicle. Try not to be the first person to get into an empty jeepney, because if the driver suddenly takes off you may find you've chartered it. Take care also if several men suddenly get into a jeepney and all try to sit near you. Chances are you're being set up to be pickpocketed – get off and find another vehicle.

Taxi

Taxis are all metered in Manila and they are almost the cheapest in the world. Insist that the meter is used and make sure you have plenty of small change – the driver certainly won't if it's to his advantage. In smaller towns, taxis may not be metered and you will have to negotiate your fare beforehand – tricycles are cheaper. PU-Cabs, found in some larger towns (but not in Manila), are unmetered taxis.

Tricycle

The other local transport, mainly found in smaller towns, is the tricycle: a small Japanese motorcycle with a crudely made sidecar. The normal passenger load should be two or three, but six and seven are not unknown! Fares generally start at P2 per person – longer distances are by negotiation. You will also see some bicycle trishaws.

Calesa

Calesas are two-wheeled horse carriages found in Manila's Chinatown, in Vigan (in North Luzon) and in Cebu City, where they are known as *tartanillas*.

Manila

The capital of the Philippines and by far the largest city, Metro Manila has a population of over 10 million. Manila is not a city of great interest in itself; it's really just an arrival and departure point for the rest of the Philippines. Once you've seen the Spanish ruins in Intramuros you've pretty much seen all Manila has to offer in an historical sense, but a trip around the harbour at sunset will provide an impressive view of the city's modern skyline.

The other attraction is entertainment – there are countless reasonably priced restaurants, pubs, folk music clubs and anything else you could care to ask for.

Orientation

Although it sprawls a great distance along Manila Bay, the main places of interest and/or importance to the visitor are fairly central and concentrated just south of the Pasig River. Immediately south of the river is Intramuros, the old Spanish town, where many of Manila's historic buildings are situated. South of that is the long rectangle of Rizal Park (the Luneta), the lungs of the central area.

Further south again, the districts of Ermita and Malate provide the so-called tourist belt with numerous hotels, restaurants and travel agencies. Here you'll find not only the big international hotels but many of the medium and low-priced places. This is the visitor's downtown Manila; the businessperson's downtown is Makati – several km away.

Maps The Nelles Verlag *Manila* map is an accurate map of the Philippines capital, with a scale of 1:17,500.

Information

Tourist Offices The Department of Tourism's (DOT) grand office (☎ 523 8411) is in Ermita at the Taft Ave end of Rizal Park. The entrance to the Tourist Information Centre is next to the Agrifina Skating Rink in Rizal

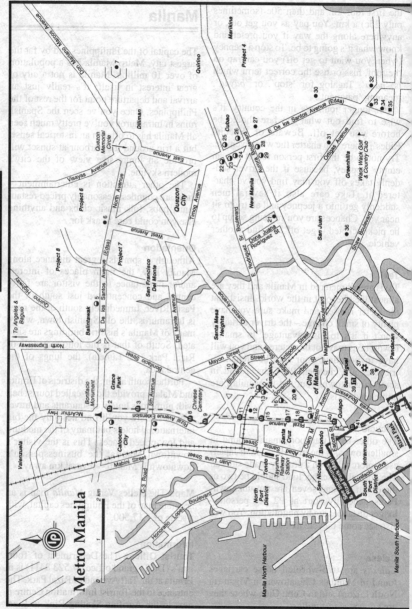
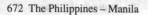

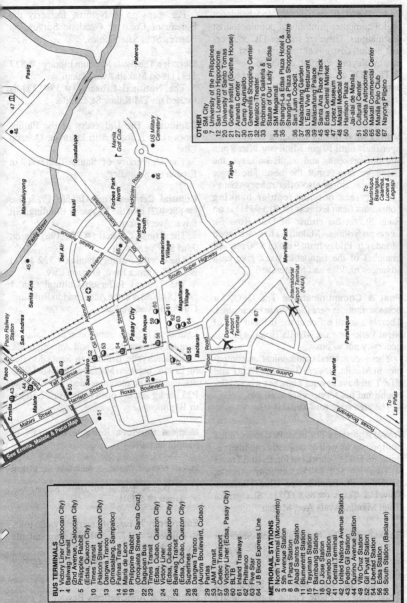

Park. The staff are friendly and hand out useful computer printouts of popular tourist destinations. There are smaller TIC counters just behind customs at the airport and at the nearby Nayong Pilipino complex.

The DOT also maintains a 24 hour tourist assistance hotline (☎ 501660, 501728) for 'travel information, emergency assistance, lost & found and language problems'.

Money Most money-changing facilities are open daily until 10 pm. Mind you, after 9 pm, and on weekends and public holidays, the exchange rate is not the best. The larger department stores also offer money-changing services outside regular banking hours. American Express (☎ 815 9311) is on Rada St, on the corner of Dela Rosa St, Legaspi Village, Makati. They are open Monday to Friday from 9 am to 5.30 pm. All branches of the Equitable Bank give cash advances on Visa and MasterCard.

Post & Communications The GPO, for poste restante, is near the river in Intramuros. There's a small office at the harbour end of Rizal Park, near the Manila Hotel, which is generally not so busy.

There are several communication companies in Manila. Eastern Telecom, PLDT and PT&T all have several branches where telephone and fax services are available.

The area code for Manila is 02.

Travel Agencies For organised tours in the Philippines, as well as domestic and international air tickets, check out Interisland Travel & Tours (☎ 522 1405), Midtown Arcade, Adriatico St, Ermita, and Blue Horizons Travel & Tours (☎ 893 6071), Shangri-La Hotel Manila, Ayala Ave, Makati.

Bookshops The National Book Store, at 701 Rizal Ave in Santa Cruz, is the largest bookstore in the Philippines and has a number of other branches in Metro Manila, eg at the Harrison Plaza. The Solidaridad Book Shop on Padre Faura is particularly good for political books.

For maps go to Namria, formerly the Bureau of Coast & Geodetic Survey, on Barraca St in San Nicolas.

Libraries The Ayala Museum Library (☎ 817 1191) is on Makati Ave, Makati.

The National Library (☎ 599177) is located on TM Kalaw St, Ermita.

Campuses The University of the Philippines (UP) is located in Diliman, Quezon City.

The University of Santo Tomas is in España St, Sampaloc.

Cultural Centres The Alliance Française (☎ 880402) is at the Keystone Building, Gil Puyat Ave, Makati.

The British Council (☎ 721 1981) is on 73rd St, Quezon City.

The Goethe Institut Manila (☎ 722 4671) is at 687 Aurora Blvd, Quezon City.

The Thomas Jefferson Cultural Center (☎ 818 4908) is in the Accelerando Building, Gil Puyat Ave, Makati.

Laundry There's a laundromat in R Salas St, Ermita, between Mabini and Adriatico Sts. The Laundryette Britania in Santa Monica St, Ermita, between Mabini and MH del Pilar Sts, can also be recommended. They charge P25 per kg and are open daily from 7.30 am to 10 pm.

Medical Services Reliable hospitals in Manila include:

Makati Medical Center, 2 Amorsolo St, Makati (☎ 815 9911)
Manila Doctors Hospital, 667 United Nations Ave, Ermita (☎ 503011)

Emergency In case of emergency, the tourist police (☎ 501728, 501660) are available around the clock.

Other useful phone numbers: Emergency police 166, Information 114.

Dangers & Annoyances Beware of overfriendly Filipinos in Manila. Unwary tourists are often picked up around Luneta or simply pickpocketed while wandering the park. Beware of the Manila slum areas too. It is here that 'a mad scramble to pick your pockets ensues', as one visitor commented!

Intramuros

The bitter fighting at the end of WWII did a pretty thorough job of flattening Manila, but there are still some places of interest in Intramuros, the oldest part of the city.

The first Chinese settlement at the site of Manila was destroyed, almost as soon as it sprung up, by Limahong, a Chinese pirate who dropped by in 1574. The Spanish rebuilt this centre as a wooden fort; in 1590 wood was replaced by stone and the fort was gradually extended until it became a walled city called Intramuros. The walls were three km long, 13 metres thick and six metres high. There were seven main gates to the city, in which there were 15 churches, six monasteries and lots of Spanish – who kept the Filipinos at arm's length.

The walls are just about all that was left after WWII finished off what MacArthur had started. During the 1930s he had his HQ there and 'modernised' the place by knocking down lots of old buildings and widening those nasty narrow streets. A few years ago they finally started to renovate the remaining buildings. Worth seeing are the beautifully restored **Casa Manila** in the San Luis complex and **El Amanecer**; both are in General Luna St.

The church and monastery of **San Agustin** is one of the few buildings left from the earliest construction. It was here in 1898 that the last Spanish governor of Manila surrendered to the Filipinos. There is a museum inside which is open daily from 8 am to noon and 1 to 5 pm. Admission is P20.

The **Manila Cathedral** is also in Intramuros and has a history that reads like that of many other Spanish-built churches in the Philippines: built 1581, damaged (typhoon) 1582, destroyed (fire) 1583, rebuilt 1592, partially destroyed (earthquake) 1600, rebuilt 1614, destroyed (earthquake) 1645, rebuilt 1654-71, destroyed (earthquake) 1863, rebuilt 1870-79, destroyed (WWII) 1945, rebuilt 1954-58; on that average an earthquake should knock it down again in 2006. Every Sunday morning, this powerful cathedral provides a glittering background to traditionally-minded couples as they solemnly exchange their vows.

The ruins of the old **Fort Santiago** stand just north of the cathedral. They are now used as a pleasant park – you can climb up top for the view over the Pasig River. The most interesting part of the fort is the **Rizal Shrine Museum**, which contains many items used or made by the Filipino martyr. The room in which he was imprisoned before his execution can be seen. The shrine is open daily, except Mondays and public holidays, from 9 am to noon and 1 to 5 pm.

Fort Santiago's darkest days took place during WWII, when it was used as a prison by the Japanese. During the closing days of the war they went on an orgy of killing, and in one small cell the bodies of 600 Filipinos and Americans were discovered.

Fort Santiago is open daily from 8 am to 10 pm; admission is P15 and includes the museum.

Rizal Park – the Luneta

Intramuros is separated from Ermita, the tourist centre, by Rizal Park, better known as the Luneta. It's a meeting and entertainment place for all of Manila – particularly on Sunday when all kinds of activities are conducted and it's packed with people, ice cream and balloon sellers.

At the bay end of the park is the **Rizal Memorial**. Close by is **Rizal's execution site**, where a firing squad pointing their weapons at Rizal forms the dramatic theme of a group of statues. The site is the centrepiece of a light show based on the execution, which can be seen every evening – at 6.30 pm in Tagalog and 7.30 pm in English – except on rainy days and during power outages. Admission is P30.

The **planetarium** is flanked by a **Japanese** and a **Chinese garden** – favourite meeting spots for young couples, although

PHILIPPINES

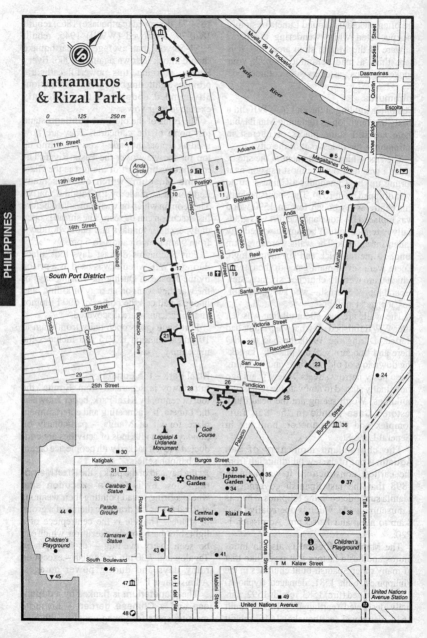

Intramuros
& Rizal Park

0   125   250 m

11th Street

13th Street

Anda
Circle

16th Street

Railroad

Altura

South Port District

20th Street

Boston

Chicago

25th Street

Bonifacio Drive

29

Muelle de la Industria

Pasig   River

Paredes Street

Quintin

Dasmariñas

Escolta

Jones Bridge

Aduana

Magallanes Drive

5

7

6

Postigo

9   8

Archbishop

10

Beaterio

11

12   13

General Luna Street

Cabildo

Real   Street

Magallanes

Solana

Anda

Legaspi

15   14

Muralla

16

17

18   19

Santa Potenciana

Santa Lucia

Basco

20

21

Victoria Street

22

Recoletos

San Jose

23

24

28   26   Fundicion

27   25

Burgos Street

36

Golf
Course

Legaspi &
Urdaneta
Monument

Palacio

30

Katigbak

Burgos Street

31

32   Chinese
Garden

33

Japanese
Garden   35

34

37

Roxas Boulevard

Carabao
Statue

Parade
Ground

42   Central
Lagoon   Rizal Park

39

38

44

Manila Ocosa Street

Tamaraw
Statue

Children's
Playground

43

41

Taft Avenue

Children's
Playground

40

South Boulevard

46

T M Kalaw Street

45

47

M H del Pilar

Mabini Street

48

49

United Nations Avenue

United Nations
Avenue Station

it's a little difficult to hide behind a bonsai tree for a passionate clinch. There's a small admission fee to each of these parks. Further up there are **fountains**, a **roller-skating circuit** and the tourist office.

At the Taft Ave end there's a gigantic pond with a three-dimensional **map of the Philippines**. Once you know a little about the geography of the country it's fascinating to wander around it and contemplate just how many islands there are. There's a three-metre-high viewing platform beside it. Also at this end of the park is a popular **children's amusement park**, with some impressive and fierce-looking dinosaur and monster figures.

Museums

Manila has lots of museums, including the **National Museum** in Burgos St, adjacent to Rizal Park. Admission is free and it's open from Tuesday to Saturday, 9 am to noon and 1 to 5 pm. The **Ayala Museum** on Makati Ave, Makati, is open Tuesday to Sunday from 9 am to 5.30 pm and entry is P30. It has a series of dioramas illustrating events in the Philippines' history. Behind the museum is an aviary and tropical garden.

In Intramuros, there is the **San Agustin Museum** in the Augustine monastery at the San Agustin Church. The **Casa Manila** is a fine old restored colonial-era home right across the road. In the basement there's a partially completed model of Intramuros. The museum is open Tuesday to Sunday from 9 am to noon and 1 to 6 pm, and entry costs P30.

Puerta Isabel II, also in Intramuros, has many liturgical objects, processional carriages and old bells. The Rizal Shrine Museum at Fort Santiago is covered in the Intramuros section above.

The **Cultural Center Museum** is in the bayside Cultural Center in Malate, which is open Tuesday to Sunday from 9 am to 6 pm. Also at the Cultural Center complex there's the **Coconut Palace**, a guesthouse erected for a visit by the pope in 1981. It is open daily except Monday from 9 am to 4 pm and admission costs P100, including a guided tour which takes just under an hour. The **Metropolitan Museum of Manila** in the Central Bank Compound on Roxas Blvd, Malate, has various changing displays. It is open Tuesday to Sunday from 9 am to 6 pm. Admission is free.

PLACES TO STAY		
30 Manila Hotel	13 Bastion de San Gabriel	32 Rizal's Execution Spot
49 Holiday Inn Manila Pavilion	14 Revellin del Parian	33 Planetarium
	15 Puerta del Parian	34 Concerts in the Park & Open-Air Stage
PLACES TO EAT	16 Bastion de Santa Lucia	35 Artificial Waterfall
45 Harbor View Restaurant	17 Puerta de Santa Lucia	36 National Museum
	18 San Agustin Church	37 Department of Finance
OTHER	19 Casa Manila Museum & San Luis Complex	38 Philippines Model
1 Rizal Shrine	20 Bastion de Dilao	39 Agrifina Circle & Skating Rink
2 Fort Santiago	21 Fortin San Pedro	40 Department of Tourism (DOT), Tourist Office & Tourist Police
3 Revellin de San Francisco	22 El Amanecer Building &Tradewinds Bookshop	
4 Seamen's Club	23 Revellin de Recoletos	41 National Library
5 Immigration Office	24 Manila City Hall	42 Rizal Memorial
6 General Post Office	25 Bastion de San Andres	43 Rizal's Fountain
7 Puerta Isabel II	26 Puerta Real	44 Quirino Grandstand
8 Plaza Roma	27 Aquarium	45 Harbour Trips
9 Palacio del Gobernador	28 Bastion de San Diego	46 Army & Navy Club
10 Puerta del Postigo	29 Bureau of Quarantine	47 Museo Pambata
11 Manila Cathedral	31 Rizal Park Post Office	48 US Embassy
12 Letran College		

Ermita, Malate & Paco

0   100   200 m

Other museums include the **Museum of Arts & Sciences** at the University of Santo Tomas in Sampaloc, and the **Philippine Museum of Ethnology** – which has displays depicting Filipino minority groups – at the Nayong Pilipino Complex in Pasay City.

The **Museo ng Malacañang** is in Jose P Laurel St. When you visit the Malacañang Palace in San Miguel, across the Pasig River from central Manila, it seems as if the family of former president Marcos has just left. This impressive place was built by a Spanish aristocrat and was used as a presidential home until Cory Aquino opened the main building as a museum.

It is open for guided groups on Monday and Tuesday from 9 am to noon and from 1 to 3 pm, and Thursday and Friday from 9 am to noon; admission is P200. There is public viewing on Wednesday from 9 am to noon and from 1 pm to 3 pm, and on Thursday and Friday from 1 to 3 pm, at a cost of P20. Sometimes the palace is closed for official functions so call (☎ 521 2307) to check before you go. Jeepneys run from Quiapo Market at Quezon Bridge to the palace.

PHILIPPINES

PLACES TO STAY		
4	Mabini Mansion	
5	San Carlos Mansion	
8	Holiday Inn Manila Pavilion	
17	Hotel Soriente	
18	Birdwatcher's Inn	
19	City Garden Hotel	
20	Richmond Pension	
21	Tadel Apartelle & Yasmin Apartelle	
22	Hotel La Corona	
26	PM Apartelle	
27	Swagman Hotel	
29	Bayview Park Hotel	
32	Aurelio Hotel	
34	Sandico Apartel	
35	Iseya Hotel	
36	Royal Palm Hotel	
37	Pension Filipina & Ralph Anthony Suites	
38	Midtown Inn	
39	The Garden Plaza Hotel & Park Hotel	
41	Robinson's Apartelle	
42	Cherry Lodge Apartelle	
43	Midland Plaza	
45	Casa Blanca I & Si-Kat Inn	
46	Centrepoint Hotel	
47	Hotel Roma	
48	Manila Tourist Inn	
49	Mabini Pension	
52	Boulevard Mansion	
55	Ermita Tourist Inn	
56	Santos Pension House	
57	Manila Midtown Hotel	
58	Tropicana Apartment Hotel	
59	Palm Plaza Hotel	
60	Rothman Inn Hotel	
61	Las Palmas Hotel & Sensation Apartelle	
62	Manila Diamond Hotel	
63	Pension Natividad	
64	Dakota Mansion	
65	Pearl Garden Apartel	
68	APP Mayfair Hotel	
69	Malate Pensionne, Shoshana Tourist Inn & Juen's Place	
70	Victoria Mansion	
72	New Solanie Hotel	
75	Winner Lodge	
77	Hotel Sofitel Grand Boulevard Manila	
78	Euro-Nippon Mansion	
79	Marabella Apartments	
80	Admiral Hotel	
81	Aloha Hotel	
82	Ambassador Hotel	
84	Hotel Royal Co-Co	
85	Victoria Court Motel	
86	True Home	

PLACES TO EAT		
2	Hong Kong Tea House	
3	Maxim's Tea House	
6	McDonald's	
7	KFC	
14	Max's	
16	Barrio Fiesta	
18	Birdwatcher's Bar	
24	Myrna's	
25	Hang's 'N'	
28	Yakiniku Sakura Restaurant	
30	Emerald Garden Restaurant	
33	The Pool	
35	Iseya Restaurant & Rooftop Restaurant	
39	Old Swiss Inn Restaurant	
40	Geosphere Café	
50	Juri's Grand Café & Guernica's	
51	Lili Marleen	
66	Shakey's Malate	
67	Chin Yuen Seafood Palace	
71	Sala Thai	
76	Aristocrat	
83	My Father's Moustache	

OTHER		
1	Museo Pambata	
8	Avis	
9	Manila Doctors Hospital	
10	Tourist Office	
11	Tabacalera	
12	Manila Medical Center	
13	Western Police Station	
14	Hertz	
15	Equitable Bank	
17	International Supermarket	
23	Ermita Church	
31	US Embassy	
37	Sabena Airlines	
39	Mr. Ticket	
44	Robinson's	
53	Philippine Airlines	
54	Gold Line Tours	
55	Scenic View Travel	
73	Malate Church	
74	WG & A	
87	Manila Zoo	
88	Jai-alai de Manila	

Chinatown & Chinese Cemetery

North of the river, Chinatown is interesting to wander through. The luxurious Chinese Cemetery, about two km north of Chinatown near the Abad Santos Metrorail Station, is a bizarre attraction. It's in the north of Santa Cruz, just where Rizal Ave becomes Rizal Ave Extension. A tricycle from the station to the South Gate will be about P5.

Quiapo Church

Quiapo, an older and more traditional part of Manila, has the Quiapo Church by Quezon Bridge. The wooden statue of Christ known as the **Black Nazarene** can be seen here.

Nayong Pilipino

The Nayong Pilipino is the Filipino version of 'the whole country in miniature'. It's out by the international airport, and there are lots of handicraft shops and a good little folk museum with some incredible photographs of various tribes. Entry is P20, and it's open 9 am to 6 pm weekdays and to 7 pm on Saturday and Sunday.

The Extremes – Forbes Park & Tondo

To appreciate the depths of the nation's problems, it's worth visiting Forbes Park and Tondo to see the opposite ends of the Philippines spectrum, from 'haves' to 'have nots'. Forbes Park is a cluster of opulent mansions in the southern part of Makati. Take a taxi from the Makati Commercial Center as you're unlikely to get by the guards on foot.

The slum quarter of Tondo, in North Harbour, is the other side of the equation: about 180,000 Filipinos live here in 17,000 huts in an area of just 1.5 sq km.

Places to Stay

There is a wide variety of accommodation in Manila, and much is close to the central Ermita and Malate areas. Cheapest are the hostels, guesthouses and pension houses, but there are also many cheap hotels.

At times a lot of the cheaper places are full. If you've just arrived in Manila, it might be a good idea to check the DOT information desk at the airport, where there's an exhaustive list of just about everything available in the city. Many of the guesthouses can also be booked through this desk – a few phone calls could save you a lot of walking.

Hostels About three km north of the airport in the direction of Malate and Ermita, you'll find the *Manila International Youth Hostel* (☎ 832 0680) at 4227 Tomas Claudio St, Parañaque, with dorm beds for P100 (YHA members P75). A fridge and cooking facilities are available. The staff have been described as 'somewhat distant'. As it is next to the Excelsior building on the corner of Roxas Blvd, asking for the Excelsior will make taxi trips easier. The hostel is also the office for YSTAPHIL, the Youth & Student Travel Association of the Philippines.

Guesthouses A few of the cheaper guesthouses and pension houses offer dormitory accommodation. There are numerous small places around Ermita and Malate, ranging from rock bottom upwards in standards and price.

The *Town House* (☎ 833 1939) at the Villa Carolina Townhouse, 201 Roxas Blvd, Unit 31, Parañaque, has dorm beds with fan for P80, singles/doubles with fan for P200 and P250, with fan and bath for P300 and P350 and with air-con and bath for P500 and P550. Weekly rates can be arranged. It is pleasant, with a friendly atmosphere created by Bill and Laura, who like travelling themselves. Situated in a small side street called Sunset Drive, it's only about five minutes by taxi from the domestic and international airports. The Town House is a good place to meet people and get information. They also offer currency exchange for guests and the rates are pretty good. There is an airport service for P50 (one or two persons).

There are several inexpensive places to stay in the Remedios Circle area of Adriatico St in Malate. Probably the most popular travellers' centre in Manila is the very good *Malate Pensionne* (☎ 523 8304) at 1771 Adriatico St, Malate. This friendly and remarkably clean place is just off the main road, which means it is quiet; many travellers have praised it for providing excellent accommodation with helpful staff, super service, and pleasant rooms. A dorm bed costs P95 with fan and P110 with air-con. Rooms cost P295 and P360 with fan, P400 with fan and bath, P500 and P600 with air-con and bath and, lastly, P750 with air-con, TV, kitchen and bath. Lockers can be rented and luggage left without charge for up to one week – thereafter it costs P5 per day per piece.

Only a few metres further down the alley, at No 1767 there is the *Shoshana Tourist Inn* (☎ 524 6512), which has cramped, not too inviting rooms with fan for P200 and P250; they also have a cell-like dorm with four beds going for P100 per person.

Right round the corner in the next alleyway leading back to Adriatico St, the unassuming little *Juan's Place* turns out to be an extremely friendly, family-run guesthouse, where you literally live with the family; the atmosphere is decidedly warm-hearted, and they provide cooking facilities. Double rooms go for P110 for one person, or P180 for two – easily the cheapest in Manila.

Joward's Pension House (☎ 521 4845) at 1726 Adriatico St, Malate, also has relatively inexpensive rooms, which, although basic and a bit bare, are OK for the money. Singles with fan cost P280 and with air-con P350. The entrance is directly next to Joward's Hot Pot Restaurant.

The *Pension Natividad* (☎ 521 0524) at 1690 MH del Pilar St, Malate, has provided a constant high standard for years and is a sort of oasis in this sometimes hectic city. You can enjoy a relaxing escape from the chaos all around; also, unlike in most of the other pension houses, you can sit outside. It has dorm beds with fan for P120, doubles with fan and bath for P500 and with air-con and bath for P700. There's a pleasant atmosphere in this well-run place. They have a coffee shop and will look after left luggage.

In central Ermita area the long-established *Mabini Pension* (☎ 524 5404) at 1337 Mabini St, has singles/doubles with fan and bath for P380/450 or with air-con and bath for P650. The rooms are not all necessarily attractive, but the people there are friendly

and helpful. They will take care of visa extensions and look after left luggage. For some reason, Swiss travellers seem to prefer staying here.

There are two self-styled apartelles, or, more appropriately, little pension houses, in Arquiza St between Mabini St and MH del Pilar St in Ermita. The more pleasant of the two is the *Yasmine Apartelle* (☎ 595848), which is quiet with a little courtyard and friendly rooms with air-con for P500, and with air-con and bath for P600. You'll pay just as much for the rooms in the *Tadel Apartelle* (☎ 521 9766) next door, but they also offer little rooms with fan and bath for P350.

Hotels Manila has a number of mid-range hotels; some are only slightly more expensive than the pension houses and guesthouses, but most cost at least twice as much.

The *Sandico Apartel* (☎ 592036) in MH del Pilar St, Ermita, has passable, though ageing, rooms with air-con, bath and TV; a single costs P495 and a double P528.

At 1549 Mabini St, the friendly *Ermita Tourist Inn* (☎ 521 8770) is pleasant and fairly clean; air-con rooms with bath from P530 to P600 are well worth the money.

Directly above the International Supermarket, the *Hotel Soriente* (☎ 599133) is at 595 A Flores St, on the corner of JC Bocobo St, Ermita, and has well-kept air-con rooms with bath for P730.

The *Iseya Hotel* (☎ 592016) at 1241 MH del Pilar St, on the corner of Padre Faura, Ermita, has a roof-top restaurant and quite comfortable singles/doubles with TV, fridge, air-con and bath for P750. Be careful though, the rooms facing MH del Pilar St are quite noisy.

One block further, at 1227 Mabini St, on the corner of Padre Faura, the clean, friendly and accommodating *Royal Palm Hotel* (☎ 522 1515) has recently been renovated. Well maintained, comfortable rooms complete with air-con, bath, fridge and TV start at P1100.

Also in Mabini St, Ermita, the *City Garden Hotel* (☎ 536 1451) is owned by the same company as the Royal Palm. It has immaculate rooms and offers everything as described above for the Royal Palm from P1300, plus a complimentary breakfast. It is often fully booked.

Other places in the middle bracket include the central and convenient *Centrepoint Hotel* (☎ 521 2751) at 1430 Mabini St, Ermita. It has an attractive lobby and is a departure point for tour buses to various locations around Manila, including Puerto Galera. Air-con rooms with fridge and TV are P1640 and P2000.

The *Swagman Hotel* (☎ 599881) at 411 A Flores St, Ermita, is a clean and well-kept place whose rooms have TV, fridge, air-con and bath at P1300. Their own bus leaves three times daily for Angeles. This hotel is a favourite of the Aussies.

Places to Eat

Manila is full of places to eat – with all types of food and all types of prices. Apart from Filipino food and a variety of other Asian cuisines, there are also western fast-food operators and a choice of fixed-price buffets at the best hotels.

The recommendations that follow are essentially in Ermita and Malate because most visitors will be staying there. There are plenty of other restaurants in Makati, Binondo, Santa Cruz and other parts of Manila.

Filipino In Ermita, a good hunting ground for tasty and cheap Filipino food is provided by several *Food Stalls* on JC Bocobo St, between Padre Faura and Robinson's. The average cost of a meal for one, with rice and one vegetable or meat serving, is around P50. On MH del Pilar St, Ermita, *Myrna's* is a popular and often crowded little place appealing essentially to local people rather than the tourist crowds. The speciality here is grilled chicken and milkfish. A meal typically costs about P80; it's closed on Sunday.

Definitely more expensive – but probably worth it – is the *Kamayan* on Padre Faura St in Ermita, near the corner of Mabini St. The name means 'bare hands' because that's what

you eat with – knives and forks aren't used. The food is authentic, delicious and well prepared. Across the back of the restaurant is a line of tapped water jars for you to wash your hands before and after eating. A meal costs about P250.

Despite its name, the *Aristocrat*, on the corner of Roxas Blvd and San Andres St, Malate, is good value. This big Filipino restaurant is the most popular of the six Aristo-crats in Manila and is open 24 hours. Try lapu-lapu fish (expensive) or the fish soup here – a meal costs about P150.

Further down Roxas Blvd, in Pasay City, *Josephine* has superb seafood and live music in the evenings, with folk dances from 8 until 9 pm. A meal in this well-known restaurant costs about P150.

The *Sea Food Market* at JC Bocobo St, Ermita, positively bounces. You select your fish or other seafood from a display area on one side and it's cooked up by a squad of short-order cooks lined up along an open window on the street side. They're all fran-tically stirring woks, scooping pots and jug-gling frying pans while flames leap high. An even larger squad of waiters and waitresses jostle near the counter on the other side. It's wonderful entertainment for passers-by. But beware: fish, shrimps, crabs etc. are sold by weight. The prices given are per 100g! The following cautionary note from a customer may serve as a warning: 'You can spend a lot of money in that place if you are not very careful, as it's by the weight and you may not realise. You are also given wet towels, that seem to be complimentary (you are not told otherwise) and that are later on the bill'.

You can round off a meal here with coffee and cakes in the *Café Alps* next door.

Chinese Manila has a great number of Chinese restaurants. For simple and econom-ical Chinese food try *Mrs Wong Tea House* next to the food stalls near Robinson's, Ermita. A meal will cost from P75 to P100.

Other good, inexpensive Chinese restau-rants include the *Hong Kong Tea House* and *Maxim's Tea House*, both on MH del Pilar St, Ermita. There are even more Chinese restaurants across the river in Chinatown and Binondo.

Japanese For Japanese food, the Y*amato* on Adriatico St in Ermita is good value, especially for sushi and tempura; a regular meal should cost around P175.

Indian Next to the Kamayan Restaurant on Padre Faura there's good north Indian food at *Kashmir* – about P200 for a meal.

Thai In addition to several Thai restaurants in Makati, there is also one in Malate – the *Sala Thai* in JM Napkil St. This popular and relatively inexpensive restaurant has a good selection of Thai curries.

Western There are plenty of western restaurants. For example, the very pleasant *Café Adriatico,* at 1790 Adriatico St, Malate, is a good place for a drink or a meal: there are tables outside and others, upstairs, overlook the Remedios Circle street scene. The food ranges from burgers to pasta. It's not cheap, but it's a very relaxed, stylish place to dine.

Popular German and Swiss restaurants include the *München Grill Pub* on Mabini St, Ermita, where Bavarian dishes and meals of the day with several courses cost about P150, and the much more expensive *Old Swiss Inn Restaurant* in the Garden Plaza Hotel on Belen St, Paco – the place to go for Swiss specialities.

Australian-style food and beer is served at the *Rooftop Restaurant,* on top of the Iseya Hotel at the corner of Padre Faura and MH del Pilar Sts, Ermita. There's a good view over the bay and an Aussie barbecue for P160 on Sundays. Mexican food can be found at *Tia Maria's* in Remedios St, on the corner of Madre Ignacia St, Malate. *Max's* on Maria Orosa St, Ermita, is one of 10 branches around the city and offers a variety of chicken dishes for about P150.

If you prefer organic food on your plate, then the pleasant and inviting *Geosphere Café* is the place for you. In a relaxed atmosphere created by the Filipino owner and his Swiss wife, you'll be served meals prepared with ingredients from their own gardens, eg pasta, sandwiches and cake. (For the uninitiated, organic foods are grown without synthetic fertilisers, pesticides or herbicides.) A meal costs about P100. Occasionally they hold concerts with groups of musicians playing on traditional instruments. The cafe is open from 10 am to 10 pm or later, depending on the atmosphere and the customers.

Vegetarian Vegetarian restaurants are pretty thin on the ground in Manila. The *Kim Wan Garden* on General Malvar St, Malate, serves Chinese and vegetarian food with separate menus for both. The *Bhodi*, inside the Tutuban Mall in Tondo, is a dedicated vegetarian restaurant which serves a wide selection of dishes, including tokwa (tofu), and textured vegetable protein flavoured – and looking like – beef, chicken and pork. The average meal in both places comes to around P80.

Buffets All-you-can-eat breakfast buffets typically cost P200 to P250 at the big hotels in Manila. The *Centrepoint Hotel* on Mabini St, Ermita, offers one at P195.

At the big tourist hotels, lunch buffets typically cost P250 to P350, plus 25% government tax and service. Dinner at one of these places would be P300 to P400.

Fast Food & Cheap Eats Manila has lots of fast-food places, including a selection of *McDonald's, Wendy's, KFCs, Pizza Huts* and *Shakey's Pizzas*. Shakey's is a Philippine institution and they do pretty good pizza; you'll find a branch at the corner of Mabini and Arquiza Sts and another on Remedios St near Roxas Blvd. The Harrison Plaza shopping centre, beside the Century Park Sheraton Hotel, has a *Pizza Hut, McDonald's* and *KFC* all together. *Jollibee* is a local burger chain with numerous branches: there's one on Padre Faura, Ermita.

Entertainment
There is plenty to do after hours in Manila. Mayor Lim's campaign to clean up Ermita has meant most of the lights going out there,

but the entertainment business is flourishing in the parts of Metro Manila where other mayors have their say.

Cinemas Movies are advertised in the daily press. The best cinemas can be found in the modern shopping centres. Admission from P15.

Discos Manila is very much disco-land. Popular places include *Equinox*, on Pasay Rd, Makati, where entry is P100 or P150 (depending on the night).

At the moment the hottest address in Manila is *Zu* in the Shangri-La Hotel Manila on Ayala Ave, at the corner of Makati Ave, Makati. Their idea of combining extravagant fittings with nonstop action seems to be what people are looking for – the guests are certainly enthusiastic about it.

Other popular places include: the *Lost Horizon* in the Philippine Plaza Hotel, Cultural Center complex, Malate; and *Euphoria* in the Hotel Inter-Continental, Ayala Ave, Makati – a modern disco that's very popular with Filipino trendies.

Folk Music Amazing mimics of Bob Dylan, Simon & Garfunkel, James Taylor and other western pop stars often play in the folk clubs. Try the popular *Hobbit House* at 1801 Mabini St, Malate, where the waiters are indeed hobbit-sized – it's entirely staffed by dwarfs. Admission is P50; Mexican dishes are a speciality and after 8.30 pm there's a P60 minimum charge. Further along from Ermita, in Malate, *My Father's Moustache*, at 2144 MH del Pilar St, also has good folk music.

Jazz Jazz can be heard in several of the international hotels. Every Sunday, from 10 am to 1 pm, well-known musicians play at the Jazz Brunch in *The Lobby* in the Manila Peninsula Hotel, Ayala Ave (on the corner of Makati Ave), Makati.

Country & Western Also in Makati, you can hear what must be the best country and western music in Manila at *The Galleon*, in Kalayaan St.

Bars There are plenty of pubs and nightclubs in Makati and Pasay City. Among the best known bars in Makati are *Friday's, Café Mogambo* and *Jool's*, all in Burgos St.

Bistros & Music Lounges Places for a drink and a snack have become very popular. The *Café Adriatico* at 1790 Adriatico St, Malate (on the Remedios Circle), started the craze and is still a favourite. Next door, *Ten Years After* has an aeroplane crashing into the roof and shows rock music videos.

Also on the Remedios Circle is *Moviola*, with a piano bar and restaurant, while nearby on Remedios St is the lively *Penguin Café Gallery*. The popular *Bistro RJ*, in the Olympia building, Makati Ave, features live 50s and 60s music; admission costs vary from P75 to P100 (depending on the night).

Cockfights Cockfights are a popular local activity and there are cockpits at various places which operate on Sunday.

Folk Dances The *Zamboanga Restaurant* on Adriatico St, Malate, has nightly Filipino and Polynesian dancing.

Concerts In idyllic Paco Park, San Marcelino St, *Paco Park Presents* puts on free chamber music at 6 pm on Friday. The free *Concert at the Park* takes place every Sunday at 5 pm in Rizal Park.

Spectator Sports
If not interrupted because of game-rigging and betting irregularities, then *jai alai* games take place seven days a week from 5 pm to 1 am at the *Jai-alai de Manila* stadium on Adriatico St, Malate. The entrance fee is P10. Games of the Philippine Basketball Association (PBA) are played at the *Cuneta Astrodome* on Roxas Blvd, Pasay City, on Tuesday, Friday and Sunday at 5 and 7.30 pm. Admission costs from P15 to P150.

Things to Buy

The Philippines is a great handicraft centre and there are many handicraft shops and centres around Manila – check out the Ilalim ng Tulay Market, next to the Quinta Market, on Carlo Palanca St, Quiapo, and the variety of handicraft places at the Nayong Pilipino. Good buys include cane work, carvings, clothes and hanging-lamps made of shell.

The SM department store, at the Makati Commercial Center, and the Landmark, on Makati Ave, are good for souvenirs if you can't get around the country. Prices are fixed and competitive. Other shopping centres include Harrison Plaza in Malate, Makati Commercial Center, Araneta Center in Cubao, SM City in Quezon City and Greenhills Shopping Center in San Juan.

In Intramuros, there is the El Amanecer building, at 744 General Luna St, which has Silahis for art and crafts, Chang Rong for antiques and Galeria de las Islas for paintings and sculptures. Further up General Luna, opposite San Agustin, is the beautiful Casa Manila complex.

Bargaining is not done as much in the Philippines as in other South-East Asian countries, but you should still haggle a little.

Getting There & Away

Manila is virtually the only entry point to the Philippines. See the Getting There & Away section above for details on flying to the Philippines. Manila is the centre for bus travel to the north and south and for ships from Luzon to the other islands. What little remains of Luzon's railway system also runs from Manila.

Air See the Philippines Getting Around section for details of PAL operations.

Bus The Philippines has a great number of bus companies and they operate from many bus stations in Manila. To further complicate matters, some companies have more than one terminal. There is no single central long-distance bus station in Manila. Several terminals, including those on E de los Santos

Ave (Edsa) in south Manila, can be reached by Metrorail.

Coming into Manila from other centres, buses will generally be signed for their terminal rather than for Manila. The sign may simply announce that the bus is heading for 'Avenida', 'Cubao' or 'Pasay' and it's assumed you know that these are destinations within Manila.

Baliwag Transit (☎ 912 3343) at 33 Edsa, Cubao, Quezon City, has buses going north to Aparri, Bulacan Province, Baliwag, San Jose and Tuguegarao.

BLTB (Batangas-Laguna-Tayabas Bus Company) (☎ 833 5501) is at Edsa, Pasay City (near Victory and Philtranco lines). Buses operate to Nasugbu, Calamba, Batangas, Santa Cruz (for Pagsanjan), Lucena, Naga and Legaspi.

Dagupan Bus (☎ 928 1694) is at New York St, Cubao, Quezon City. Buses operate to Baguio, Dagupan and Lingayen.

Five Star (☎ 833 8339) is at Aurora Blvd (Tramo), Pasay City. Buses go to Alaminos and Dagupan.

Partas (☎ 709820) at Aurora Blvd, Quezon City, has buses going north to Laoag, San Fernando (La Union) and Vigan.

Philippine Rabbit (☎ 711 5819) is at 819 Oroquieta, Santa Cruz (entrance in Rizal Ave). Get a jeepney towards Monumento from Mabini St or Metrorail to D Jose station. This terminal is known as 'Avenida', and if you're coming from the north take a Philippine Rabbit bus marked 'Avenida via Dau'. It takes the Dau Expressway from Angeles and is much faster. Avoid 'Avenida via Caloocan' buses. Buses operate to various destinations in north-west and central Luzon, including Angeles, Baguio, Balanga, Laoag, Mariveles, San Fernando (Pampanga & La Union), Tarlac and Vigan.

Philtranco (☎ 833 5061) is at Edsa, Pasay City. Get a jeepney towards Baclaran from Taft Ave or MH del Pilar St or Metrorail to Edsa station. Buses from here run to Daet, Naga, Tabaco, Legaspi, Sorsogon, Samar, Leyte and Mindanao.

Victory Liner (☎ 361 1514) is at 713 Rizal Avenue Extension, Caloocan City. Jeepneys towards Monumento from Mabini St or Metrorail go to the North terminal. Buses go to Alaminos, Dagupan, Iba, Olongapo and Mariveles from the North terminal.

Train The Philippines' rail operation has contracted to just one route south from Manila to the Bicol region (Ragay). It is

PHILIPPINES

much slower and less reliable than the bus services and its use is not recommended.

Boat The shipping companies generally advertise departures in the Manila English-language dailies. There are plenty of departures from Manila. Although William Lines, Gothong Lines and Aboitiz Lines have formed the new company WG & A, their ships still leave from their respective piers. Scenic View Travel (☎ 522 3495), beside the Ermita Tourist Inn on the corner of Mabini and Soldado Sts, Ermita, sells WG & A tickets, thus saving you a trip to the wharves.

Nearly all interisland departures are made from North Harbour in Manila. If you have trouble finding it, ask a coast guard opposite Pier 8. A taxi from Ermita to North Harbour should cost about P40. Travelling in the other direction – to Ermita – from the harbour after a ship has arrived is likely to be more expensive: nobody's meter seems to work properly and the fare is likely to be between P70 and P100. The jeepney route between the harbour and Ermita is circuitous and slow.

Shipping company offices in Manila are:

Asuncion Shipping Lines
    Pier 2, North Harbour, Tondo (☎ 204024)
    Destinations: Lubang/Mindoro, North Palawan
Negros Navigation Lines
    Pier 2, North Harbour, Tondo (☎ 212691)
    Destinations: Negros, Panay, Romblon
Sulpicio Lines
    Pier 12, North Harbour, Tondo (☎ 201771)
    Destinations: Cebu, Leyte, Masbate, Mindanao, Negros, Palawan, Panay, Samar
WG & A
    Destinations: Bohol, Cebu, Leyte, Masbate, Mindanao, Negros, Palawan, Panay
    Aboitiz Lines, Pier 4, North Harbour, Tondo (☎ 216951)
    Gothong Lines, Pier 10, North Harbour, Tondo (☎ 214121)
    William Lines, Pier 14, North Harbour, Tondo (☎ 219821)

Getting Around

The Airport Manila International Airport (MIA) has officially been renamed Ninoy Aquino International Airport (NAIA). If Manila is your first stop on a first visit to Asia then hold your breath, because it's pure chaos out there. For some reason the Filipinos are unable to make the airport work – in contrast to the efficient, smooth operations at Hong Kong, Bangkok or Singapore.

Domestic and international flights go from the same airport but the terminals are some distance apart. PAL has a shuttle bus to the domestic terminal, but it is free only for its own passengers; passengers on other airlines pay US$10.

At present, only air-con taxis with set fares are allowed to service the airport (eg P220 to Pasay, P350 to Ermita, P350 to Makati and P380 to Quezon City). If you want to get into town for around half the price of the set fare, then you can take the stairs up to the departure level, where you can wait for a taxi that has just dropped off passengers and would otherwise have to head back to town empty. Mind you, lots of sneaky taxi drivers have hit on this trick and now wait for victims at the departure level with bargain 'deals'.

It's only seven km to the Ermita area and since fares are very low it should be pretty cheap to take a taxi there. On the meter the fare between the airport and Ermita should be about P80, but drivers will try for at least P150 – or much more if they can get it.

When going to the airport you can take any taxi. You will probably have better luck at getting a properly working meter.

An economic alternative is to take a taxi to the Metrorail South Terminal in Baclaran for about P30 (providing, that is, one will take you this short distance). From there you can ride the train to Pedro Gil or United Nations Ave station for P6. The Baclaran Terminus is only two km from the airport.

Bus There's a comprehensive bus system around Manila, but it's a little difficult to find your way around until you've got some idea of the city's geography and can recognise the destination names. There are many different bus companies.

Buses, like jeepneys, generally display their destinations on a board in front. This might be a large complex like NAIA, a street name like Ayala (Ayala Ave, Makati) or a whole suburb like Quiapo. Fares are from P1.50 on regular buses.

Metrorail The quick and convenient Metrorail trains run on an elevated line which runs right along Taft Ave beside Ermita. It extends as far as the Bonifacio Monument (Monumento) at Caloocan City in the north and south to Baclaran (Pasay City), quite close to Manila airport.

It's very convenient for getting to the Philtranco/Victory Liner (Edsa) terminals in the south and the Philippine Rabbit and Victory Liner bus terminals in the north. It is also an alternative way of getting to the airport. When traffic is really clogged up you'd probably get to the airport faster (and cheaper) by taking the Metrorail to the South terminal and then taking a taxi from there. However, there is a chance that passengers whose luggage is too large might be turned away. The fare is a flat P6.

Jeepney Jeepneys are very reasonably priced, with fares from P1.50. As with the buses, it can be a little difficult to find your way around, but they're so cheap it's no great loss to get on the wrong one. Most jeepneys pass by the city hall, north of Rizal Park. Heading north, they usually split there and either head north-west to Tondo, straight north to Monumento and Caloocan or north-east to Quezon City, Cubao or various other destinations in that direction.

Heading south, the routes from north of the river converge at City Hall, then split to either go down Taft Ave or MH del Pilar St.

Taxi There are countless metered taxis (make sure the meter is on) and it's generally held that the white Toyota taxis are much better than the more prolific yellow ones. Meters in these cabs are said to 'work better' and the drivers are less inclined to argue about the fares. Always ensure you have plenty of spare change before starting out. Ordinary taxis (those not equipped with air-conditioning) have a flag-down charge of P10, which includes the first 500 metres; thereafter they charge P1 for every 250 metres. However, almost all of the meters still show the old flag-down charge of P2.50, so there will be a surcharge of P7.50. Air-con taxis begin with P16 (the old flag-down charge of P3.50 plus P12.50 surcharge). Nearly all taxis in Manila nowadays are equipped with air-conditioning.

Around Manila

Luzon is the largest island in the Philippines and has a lot to offer apart from Manila. The places in this section can all be visited as day trips from the capital, although a number are worth overnight stops, or can be combined with visits to places further afield. To the north and west of Manila respectively, the attractions are Mt Pinatubo and the WWII battle site of Corregidor at the entrance to Manila Bay. South of Manila there are beach resorts, the Pagsanjan rapids and the Taal Lake volcano. These can be visited en route to South Luzon or to the island of Mindoro.

OLONGAPO & SUBIC
North-west of Manila, on the Bataan Peninsula, Olongapo is where the US Navy used to be stationed. In 1991 the Philippine Senate decided not to extend the Military Bases Agreement (MBA), which had regulated the lease of the bases since the end of WWII.

So, in 1992 the Subic Naval Base was handed back to the Philippine government, who declared the conversion of the base into the Subic Bay Freeport a top national priority. A large area of the former base is covered with virgin rainforest, which was used by the Americans for survival training. After all military restrictions were lifted, the bay itself has been turned into a top-class diving area for wreck divers. There are 20 wrecks on the sea floor, among them the battle cruiser USS *New York*, which was sunk in 1941 and now lies at a depth of 27 metres.

Olongapo is a good starting point for trips to the Mt Pinatubo area or along the Zambales coastline. There are some so-so beaches around Subic, but San Miguel,

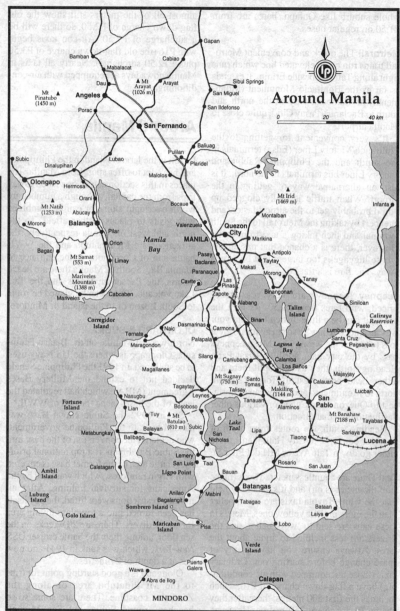

Around Manila

0   20   40 km

slightly north of Subic Bay, is better than any of the beaches between Olongapo and Subic.

The area code for Olongapo is 047.

Places to Stay
There are several hotels of different price ranges in Barrio Barretto, about five km north-west of Olongapo, halfway to Subic. The *Pynes Inn* (☎ 222 5755) is directly on Baloy Beach and has well appointed rooms (good for two) with fan and bath for P250. They also have pleasant balconies overlooking the ocean.

On the National Highway, the *By the Sea Inn* (☎ 222 4560) offers a whole selection of comfortable rooms from P400 to P1200, all with air-con, bath, TV and fridge.

Getting There & Away
Bus It's a two to three-hour bus ride from the Victory Liner station in Manila (P60). From Baguio buses depart hourly (P110; six hours).

Jeepney It's only 12 km from Olongapo to Subic, but watch out for pickpockets on the blue jeepneys.

ANGELES
Angeles has noticeably recovered from the closing of Clark Air Base and the eruption of Mt Pinatubo: the hotels are busier than ever before; restaurants, bars and nightclubs are experiencing an unprecedented boom; and the demand for tours of Pinatubo is still rising. The first signs of economic recovery are definitely there, especially in the Clark Special Economic Zone. The former air base is also due to be reopened soon as Clark International Airport.

Information
The Philippine National Bank (PNB) in Dau changes travellers' cheques. Moneychangers at the checkpoint will change cash.

Britania Launderette and Sunshine Laundry, both at Perimeter Rd, offer a two-hour service. They charge P24 per kg.

The area code for Angeles is 0455.

Places to Stay
Thanks to the former American base, Angeles has a large selection of comfortable hotels with restaurants and swimming pools. The accommodation around here is by far the best value for money in the entire country. All rooms are good for two; there just don't seem to be any single rooms in the whole city. Probably the cheapest place in town is *Some Place Else*, next to the little church in Raymond St, Balibago, where you can get decent rooms with fan for only P120 (there's no swimming pool).

The *New Liberty Inn* (☎ 4588) on MacArthur Highway, Balibago, is set in extensive grounds with a stand of big, old trees. Rooms with fan and bath go for P200 and with air-con and bath from P300. One of the most popular hotels in town is the friendly *Sunset Garden Inn* (cellular ☎ 097-378 1109) in Malabañas Rd, Clarkview. It has tip-top clean rooms with TV, fan and bath for P365 and with air-con for P450. If they are full, there are five more hotels in this price range within walking distance.

Places to Eat
There is an enormous range of international restaurants in Angeles. *Margaritaville* on Fields Ave probably has the widest choice on its menu. In addition to American and Filipino food, they offer excellent Thai dishes from P50.

Getting There & Away
There are several Philippine Rabbit buses daily from Manila (P50; two hours), but make sure the bus is marked 'Expressway/Dau'. Alternatively, there are many bus services operating to North Luzon via Dau, from where you can catch a jeepney (P2) or tricycle (P30) the short distance back to Angeles.

In addition, for P200 there are several daily air-con buses from Manila. Departures from the Swagman Hotel on A Flores St, Ermita, are at 11.30 am, 3.30 pm and 8 pm and from the Centrepoint Hotel, Mabini St, Ermita, at 10.30 am and 5.30 pm (except Monday and Sunday, when it's 7.30 pm).

There are hourly Victory Liner services from Olongapo which take two hours. Victory Liner also have hourly buses from Baguio. They're marked 'Olongapo' and take four hours. Many of the services between Manila and North Luzon go via Dau, a short tricycle ride from Angeles.

AROUND ANGELES
Mt Pinatubo
The unprecedentedly violent eruption of Mt Pinatubo on 15 June 1991 was like a bad dream for many. Clouds of steam and ejecta shot up to 40 km into the stratosphere, darkening the sky, and incredible amounts of ash and sand settled in a wide area around the volcano. West of Angeles, the grey mass of coagulated material reached heights of up to 20 metres and today this impressive terrain is crisscrossed with bizarre ravines, which you can wander through for hours. Other areas are better explored with a vehicle.

Several hotels offer tours to Pinatubo and can arrange guides, eg Sunset Garden Inn, Malabanas Rd; Trend Transport, Field Ave; and R & J at the Wanderer's Inn, Perimeter Rd. Four to five-hour hikes with guide cost about P500 per person.

For flights in ultra-lights contact the Angeles City Flying Club, c/o Woodland Park Resort, Lazares St, Dau, or the Lite-Flite Flying Club, c/o Omni Aviation, Clarkfield. The charter price is P600 for 30 minutes with one passenger. For safety reasons, car tours and hikes should only be attempted in the dry season, the best months being February, March and April.

San Fernando
Not to be confused with San Fernando (La Union), north-west of Baguio, this town is famous for its Easter celebrations, during which about a dozen religious fanatics have themselves nailed to crosses.

CORREGIDOR
This small island, at the mouth of Manila Bay, was the site of the US-Filipino last stand against the invading Japanese. It certainly wasn't impregnable, as planned, but it held

out for a long time. Now it's a national shrine and you can have a look around the underground bunkers and inspect the rusty relics of the fortress armaments.

Today it is run by the Philippine army and there may be someone who will show you some of the less accessible places. There's lots of WWII junk lying around, plus the shattered remains of General MacArthur's pre-war HQ and a museum of the war with a good three-dimensional map. There are stunning views and sunsets from the summit of the highest hill, and a soft drink stand which sells Coke and San Miguel beer.

Getting There & Away
Under the aegis of the Corregidor Foundation (☎ 596487), Sun Cruises (☎ 831 8140) runs daily Corregidor tours. The MV *Island Cruiser* leaves Manila from the PTA Bay Cruise Terminal, next to the Cultural Center, Monday to Friday at 8 am (return trip at 2.30 pm). There are two boats on weekends and holidays, departing Manila at 8 am and 10 am (return trip 2.30 pm and 4.30 pm). Cost is P810 and includes a guided tour. You can pay another P125 for a sound and light show in the shaft of the Malinta Tunnel, and P160 for lunch in the restaurant of the Corregidor Inn.

LAS PIÑAS
On the way to Lake Taal many people stop at Las Piñas to see the Sarao Jeepney Factory and a small church, famous for its pipe organ. The organ, which has over 800 bamboo pipes, was built between 1816 and 1824 and, after restoration in Germany in the early 70s, it still sounds good. On normal weekdays it can only be seen from 2 to 4 pm.

Getting There & Away
Zapote or Cavite buses from Taft Ave in Manila will get you to Las Piñas in half an hour. You can continue to Tagaytay on a Nasugbu bus coming through from Manila.

TAGAYTAY (TAAL VOLCANO)
The volcanic lake of Taal makes a pleasant excursion from Manila. There's a lake in the

cone of the Taal volcano from which emerges a smaller volcano, inside of which is another lake. The view from Tagaytay Ridge is incredible.

You can climb the volcano and there are plenty of boats to the island which can be chartered from **Talisay** for P500 per round trip with guide, or P400 without. As protection against sharp, high grass and pointed lava stones you should wear long trousers and suitable shoes. You can organise boats at Rosalina's Place.

Talisay is easily reached from Batangas or Pagsanjan. It's also possible, but less convenient, to take a jeepney from Tagaytay to the lake and a boat across from there.

Buco, about five km west of Talisay, has an old seismological station, now operated as a Science House, where you can find out about vulcanology and the geological history of the lake.

The area code for Tagaytay is 096.

Places to Stay
Villa Adelaida (☎ 267) at Foggy Heights has rooms for P1000 (up to 20% more on weekends) and a swimming pool and restaurant. When coming from Manila, instead of turning right to Tagaytay, you must turn left. It's near the road going down to the lake towards Talisay.

In Talisay, *Rosalina's Place* at Banga has singles/doubles with fan and bath for P200/250, which is a little overpriced considering the condition of the rooms. It's located just outside town, across from the International Resort and is well placed for a trip to Taal Volcano. A little more expensive, but a recommended alternative, is *Milo's Paradise* (☎ 720318) in Balas, near the turn-off for Tagaytay. This is a relatively new resort with swimming pool; the cottages are roomy (good for four) and quiet, for P600.

Getting There & Away
Take a BLTB bus from Manila heading for Nasugbu – the trip takes one to 1½ hours. It's about 17 km down from Tagaytay to Talisay at the lake side and several jeepneys a day make the dusty journey (P12). Manila to Talisay direct takes about two hours. First, take a BLTB bus marked 'Lemery' or 'Batangas' as far as Tanauan, then a jeepney from the public market to Talisay.

NASUGBU & MATABUNGKAY
Matabungkay is the most popular beach near Manila and gets busy on weekends. Nasugbu has better beaches, including **White Sands**, three or four km north of the town. You can get there by tricycle or outrigger.

Places to Stay & Eat
The *Swiss House Hotel* in Matabungkay has pleasantly furnished double rooms with fan and bath for P650, or there's the *Coral Beach Club* (☎ 318 4868) at P1600 for attractive rooms with air-con and bath. Nasugbu is more expensive.

Getting There & Away
BLTB buses for Nasugbu take about two hours from Manila and leave almost hourly. For Matabungkay get off the bus at Lian and travel the last few km by jeepney.

BATANGAS
Batangas can make a good base for visiting Lake Taal, the nearby old town of Taal and sites along the coast, but the main reason for coming here is to take the ferry across to Mindoro. If you don't leave Manila early enough you won't arrive in Batangas in time to get a boat to Mindoro the same day.

The area code for Batangas is 043.

Places to Stay & Eat
Located on the outskirts of town, the *Alpa Hotel* (☎ 2213) has gone upmarket and rooms with air-con and bath now cost from P850 to P2000. Oh well, at least they have a swimming pool. Most of the inexpensive hotels in town are in poor condition. The relatively centrally located *Avenue Pension House I* (☎ 725 3720) at 30 JP Rizal Ave is acceptable: decent doubles with fan and bath cost P300, with air-con and bath P350. If you stay for 12 hours or less there is a reduction of one third in the bill.

Getting There & Away

Always ask for Batangas City to avoid confusion with Batangas Province, and try to get a Batangas Pier bus if you are heading for Mindoro, otherwise you'll have to take a jeepney for the final stretch. Several buses leave the BLTB terminal in Manila daily for Batangas (P50; 2½ hours). BLTB air-con buses are only a few pesos more expensive, but not all of them go to the pier.

Try to get to Batangas reasonably early if you want to catch one of the boats to Puerto Galera, most of which leave between 12.30 and 1.30 pm. If you don't make it in time, there is another departure at 5 pm. Beware of pickpockets on these buses; they often operate in groups of three.

The Si-Kat Ferry has a daily air-con bus and ship service which departs Manila from the Centrepoint Hotel in Mabini St, Ermita, at 9 am.

LOS BAÑOS & CALAMBA

The **Los Baños Botanic Gardens** has a big swimming pool and the town is noted for its **hot springs** (most resorts are outside of town, along the highway as far as Calamba). Los Baños is also the location of the **International Rice Research Institute**, where the rice varieties that prompted the Asian 'green revolution' were developed.

Just before Los Baños is Calamba, where national hero Jose Rizal was born. **Rizal House** is now a memorial and museum.

Getting There & Away

Buses from Manila for Los Baños or Santa Cruz will get you to both towns. Calamba is the junction town if you're travelling to Batangas, Talisay or Lake Taal.

SAN PABLO & ALAMINOS

San Pablo is a good area for hiking. There's an easy hour's stroll around **Sampaloc Lake**, which is in an extinct volcanic cone. Alternatively, make the longer half-day trip to the twin lakes of **Pandin** and **Yambo**, north-east of San Pablo.

Near here, at Alaminos, **Hidden Valley** is a private park with lush vegetation, natural

springs, a swimming pool and a hefty admission charge of about P1200, which includes a drink on arrival, a buffet lunch and use of facilities such as the pool.

Mt Makiling (1144 metres) is best reached from Alaminos or Los Baños, while from San Pablo you can climb 2188-metre-high **Mt Banahaw**.

The area code for San Pablo is 093.

Places to Stay

There is a beautiful view of Sampaloc Lake from the friendly *Sampaloc Lake Youth Hostel* (☎ 4448) at Efarca Village, on the outskirts of town. It has dorm beds for P120 and doubles with fan and bath for P150. A tricycle from the church or plaza in San Pablo will cost only a few pesos.

Getting There & Away

Bus Buses going from Manila to Lucena, Daet, Naga and Legaspi in South Luzon, or San Pablo direct buses, all run via Alaminos en route to San Pablo (about two hours).

Jeepney From Pagsanjan take a jeepney to Santa Cruz and another from there to San Pablo.

Tricycle It's about five km from Alaminos to Hidden Springs and drivers will firmly demand P100 for this short trip.

PAGSANJAN

Situated 70 km south-east of Manila in the Laguna Province, this is where you can shoot the rapids by canoe. The standard charge for a canoe is P500 for one or two people, including the entry fee. You are paddled upriver to the falls (a good place for a swim) by two *banqueros*, and then go rushing down the rapids – getting kind of wet on the way. At the last major waterfall you can ride on a bamboo raft for an extra P20.

You'll probably get hassled for extra money since plenty of rich tourists come here and throw pesos around. It's reported that if you're unwilling to give in to demands for increased payment, you will not enjoy the rest of the trip. Some boatman aggressively demand P500 or even P1000 as a tip. You have been warned! Banqueros organised by the Youth Hostel, Pagsanjan Falls Lodge or the Willy Flores Guesthouse are reported to be more reasonable, but you're expected at least to tip the boatmen.

The final scenes of *Apocalypse Now* were shot along the river but, despite all the tourist hype, this is no nail-biting white-water maelstrom – more a gentle downriver cruise most of the time. The water level is highest, and the rapids are at their best, in August and September. The best time to go is early in the morning before the tourist hordes arrive, so spend the night in Pagsanjan. The various hotels will all arrange boats for you. On weekends it's terribly crowded.

Places to Stay

Avoid the accommodation 'guides' at Pagsanjan as their commission will cost you extra. There is plenty of accommodation, particularly along Garcia St, which runs along the river and doubles back from beside the post office.

The *Willy Flores Guesthouse* at 821 Garcia St has pleasant rooms for P150/250 and with fan and bath for P250/350. It's a simple, clean place with a homely atmosphere and they'll help you organise boat trips. Miss Estela y Umale's *Riverside Bungalow* (☎ 645 2465) is nearby, at 792 Garcia St. There are two bungalows at P400 with fan and P1200 with air-con. Miss Estela is a good cook.

Places to Eat

There are plenty of good eating places in Pagsanjan, such as the *Me-Lin Restaurant* in Mabini St near the plaza. You'll find good food, nice staff and genuine home-made pizza for P50.

Getting There & Away

Several BLTB buses leave Manila daily for Santa Cruz (P50; two hours), from where jeepneys run the last few km to Pagsanjan.

LUCENA

The capital of Quezon Province, Lucena is a departure point for boats to Marinduque and Romblon. They leave either from Dalahican or from the river harbour of Cotta Port, just outside the town. The **Quezon National Park**, between Lucena and Atimonan, is one of the largest wildlife reserves in Luzon; take along water and food if you intend to go hiking there.

The area code for Lucena is 042.

Places to Stay

The *Lucena Fresh Air Hotel & Resort* (☎ 712424) is in the Isabang district, at the edge of town as you enter from Manila. They have pretty good rooms set in generous grounds: singles/doubles with fan cost P135/155, with fan and bath P220 to P265 and with air-con and bath P385/440. There's also a nice swimming pool, and a restaurant with good meals for about P60.

Places to Eat

The *Casa Arias Garden Restaurant*, in the centre near the BLTB bus station, offers a good choice of meals at reasonable prices.

Getting There & Away

Philtranco, Inland Trailways, Superlines and BLTB buses operate to Lucena from Manila, taking about 2½ hours.

North Luzon

After a spell on the beaches at Hundred Islands, most travellers continue north to the famed rice terraces in the Mountain Province. The Ifugao villages around Banaue and their superb rice terraces have been dubbed the 'eighth wonder of the world'. North Luzon also has the popular summer capital of Baguio and the interesting old town of Vigan, with its many reminders of the Spanish period.

ZAMBALES COAST

The Zambales coast stretches north from Olongapo to Hundred Islands, but, although there are some good stretches of beach, few travellers come this way. **San Antonio**, about an hour north of Olongapo, is a pleasant little town with a market. From nearby Pundaquit, you can arrange trips out to **Camera** and **Capones** islands. **Iba** is the capital of the province and has several beach resorts, most of them rather run-down. Buses run up the Zambales coast from Manila via Olongapo.

HUNDRED ISLANDS, LUCAP & ALAMINOS

The most popular of the west coast resort areas are Hundred Islands, and the nearby towns of Lucap and Alaminos. Actually there are more than 100 islands and if swimming or just lazing around and sunbathing are your thing, then this is a good place.

Unfortunately, the snorkelling and diving aren't as good as they were once because of the long-term use of dynamite for fishing. Lucap, just three km from Alaminos, is the main accommodation centre for the islands and from here you can hire boats to reach them. There are no beaches on the coast and only a few on the islands. However, there are lots of hidden coves, caves and coral reefs. **Quezon**, the largest island, is being developed as a tourist resort. Other popular islands for snorkelling include **Cathedral**, **Parde** and **Panaca**.

There is a tourist office on the Lucap Pier which has a map of the islands and arranges boats.

Places to Stay

Prices vary considerably with the season, jumping up at Easter week and April and May weekends. Most of the accommodation is in Lucap.

While not in the best condition, *Gloria's Cottages* is still acceptable for the money: singles/doubles with fan and bath cost P150/250, or P200/300 with air-con and bath. Right opposite, the *Ocean View Lodge* is clean and has a good restaurant. Rooms start from P200/225 with fan – 250/300 with fan and bath – and a four-bed room with air-con and bath costs P700.

Maxine by the Sea has a beautiful terrace and neat, down-to-earth rooms for P250 with fan and bath or P550 with air-con and bath.

If you want to camp out on the islands, there's a P10 fee on Quezon, Governor's and Children's Islands. Quezon has a *pavilion* for P600; a *cottage* with rooms for six costs P1000 on Governor's; and on Children's there are *huts* for two for P350 and P900. Bring your own food.

Places to Eat

The wharfside canteens are a good place for cheap eats. The *Ocean View Restaurant* is a lodge restaurant with good, inexpensive food. The *Last Resort Restaurant* doesn't close down early in the evening as most of the other places do: Lucap is a quiet place at night. If you're looking for some entertainment, catch a tricycle to nearby Alaminos, where the *Plaza Restaurant* usually has a folk singer.

Getting There & Away

Dagupan Bus, Five Star and Philippine Rabbit buses run hourly from Manila to Alaminos (P105; six hours). You can also catch these buses at Dau, near Angeles (P80; 3½ hours). Victory Liner has several buses daily for the six-hour trip from Olongapo to Alaminos. A few Dagupan and Byron buses operate to Alaminos from Baguio (four hours).

Getting Around

Tricycle From Alaminos, it's just a short tricycle ride to Lucap at P20 to P25 for up to four passengers.

Boat An outrigger from Lucap to the Hundred Islands costs P275 for up to six people, plus a P5 entry fee per person. For about P100 extra you can be dropped off and picked up later. Four or five hours is enough for most people, especially where there is no shade. Quezon is the most popular island and you can get drinks at the kiosk there.

LINGAYEN, DAGUPAN & SAN FABIAN

Located at the southern end of Lingayen Gulf, Dagupan is mainly a transport hub. There are also some beaches in the vicinity, none of them particularly memorable. Between Lingayen and Dagupan you could try **Lingayen Beach** (15 km from Dagupan) and **Blue Beach** (three km away at Bonuan), while **White Beach** is 15 km north-east at San Fabian. White Beach is really brownish-grey.

AGOO & ARINGAY

Between San Fabian and Bauang is Agoo, where a **basilica**, rebuilt after an 1892 earthquake, is worth going to see. It is probably the most beautiful church in La Union Province. In Aringay you can visit the small **Don Lorenzo Museum**, opposite the old church.

BAUANG

Further north on the coast, Bauang has a long stretch of beach with many resort hotels. There are better beaches in the Philippines, but Bauang is only an hour or two's travel from Baguio in the hills and this probably accounts for its popularity. San Fernando (La Union) is just six km north of Bauang and the beach area is between the two – about two km north of Bauang and four km south of San Fernando. Lots of jeepneys shuttle back and forth.

The area code for Bauang is 072.

Places to Stay

Bauang's hotels are mainly along the grey-sand beach between Baccuit and Paringao. Prices at most of these places are quite high, but often negotiable.

The *Jac Corpuz Cottages*, next to the Leo Mar resort at Baccuit, have rooms with bath from P250. This place is nothing special, but it's relatively inexpensive for Bauang. At the *Leo Mar Beach Resort* simple but well-kept rooms with fan and bath cost from P400. Also at the southern end of the beach, the *Hide Away Beach Resort* is a large house where spacious rooms with fan cost from P300, or from P400 with air-con. Unlike some other accommodation in Bauang, the price is appropriate for what you get.

Situated next to each other at the north end of the beach are several attractive resorts with swimming pools and comfortable, pleasantly furnished, air-conditioned rooms and cottages for around P850. Among them are: *China Sea Beach Resort* (☎ 414821); *Coconut Grove Resort* (☎ 414276); *Cabaña Beach Resort* (☎ 412824); *Bali Hai Beach Resort* (☎ 412504); and *Southern Palms Beach Resort* (☎ 415384).

Places to Eat

Food in the resort hotels tends to be expensive. The *Villa Estrella, Fisherman's Wharf* and *Bali Hai* are all pretty good. On the National Highway, a few metres back from the beach opposite the Long Beach Hotel, the *Jasmin Restaurant* offers inexpensive Filipino dishes for about P75.

Getting There & Away

Bus The many buses from Manila to Bauang take over six hours and some continue north to Vigan and Laoag. It takes over an hour from Baguio on Philippine Rabbit or Eso-Nice Transport and slightly less by jeepney (P25). It's a nice trip down the winding road to the coast, but try to sit on the left side for the best views.

Jeepney Jeepneys take about 30 minutes to get from Bauang to San Fernando.

SAN FERNANDO (LA UNION)

The 'city of the seven hills' is the capital of La Union Province, and the **Museo de La Union** next to the Provincial Capitol building gives a cultural overview of the region. The Chinese **Ma-Cho Temple** on the northern edge of town is also well worth a visit.

Information

The tourist office (☎ 412098, 412411) is in the Matanag Justice Hall, General Luna St, Town Plaza.

The area code for San Fernando (La Union) is 072.

Places to Stay

The centrally located *Plaza Hotel* (☎ 412996) on Quezon Ave (which becomes the main highway) has a wide variety of passable, clean rooms – something for everybody, so to speak. Doubles with fan and bath cost P280 and with air-con and bath P500. Somewhat better (and newer) is the *Hotel Mikka* (☎ 415737) on Quezon Ave, across and down from the Ma-Cho Temple. Immaculate, pleasant rooms with air-con, bath and TV cost P400 (single) and P500 (double).

Three km north of San Fernando, *Shalom Beach Cottages* on Santo Niño Road, in Lingsat, has spacious rooms with veranda, fan and bath for P350. There is a nice garden and they offer weekly and monthly rates.

Places to Eat

The *Mandarin Restaurant* has reasonably priced food and there are lots of cheap snack places around, a number of which offer complete fixed-price meals for about P60. Places to try include the *New Society Restaurant*, opposite the market in Burgos St, the *Crown Restaurant* and the *Garden Food Center*.

Getting There & Away

There are numerous daily buses from Manila (P120; seven hours). See the Bauang section above for other transport information.

SAN JUAN

About 10 km north of San Fernando, the small town of San Juan is situated on an elongated bay. The beach here is wider and cleaner than the one in Bauang and it has become known as a surfing beach; from November until February you may come across some surfers, but otherwise there's not much going on.

About two km north of San Juan there are a few potteries. The decorative earthenware they make is on sale at the side of the road.

Places to Stay

About one km south of San Juan, in Urbiztondo, the *Surf Camp* offers good accommodation at reasonable rates. Dorm bunks are P100, cottages with fan, fridge and

cooking facilities can be had for P500. They have favourable weekly and monthly rates. Not far from there, the *Monaliza Resort* has small rooms with fan from P250 to P500, the more expensive ones with fridge and cooking facilities. The place has a pleasant, big veranda overlooking the ocean. Just as at the Surf Camp they have surf boards to rent (at P100 for two hours).

About 500 metres north of San Juan, in Montemar Village, the *Sunset German Beach Resort* (☎ 414719) has rugged little stone cottages. Friendly rooms with fan and bath cost P400. This is a small, well-tended place with lots of plants.

Getting There & Away

Jeepneys from San Fernando to San Juan leave from Burgos St at the corner of Quezon Ave. The fare to Urbiztondo is P3, to Montemar Village P5 (get off at the turn-off in Ili Norte – it's about 200 metres from there to the beach).

BAGUIO

Situated at an altitude of about 1500 metres, Baguio is much cooler than Manila and for this reason once served as a summer capital. Still popular as an escape from the lowland heat, this laid-back town has plenty of parks and an interesting market. It's also good for buying handicrafts (although you have to bargain aggressively to get a good price).

Baguio is also famed for its faith healers, to whom many people flock each year. To most travellers, however, the town serves mainly as a gateway to the mountain provinces of the Central Cordillera and the amazing rice terraces.

Information

The tourist office (☎ 442 7014) is at the DOT complex on Governor Pack Rd.

The area code for Baguio is 074.

Things to See

The **City Market** has local produce and crafts, including basketwork, textiles, wood carvings and jewellery. There's a small **Mountain Provinces Museum** in Club (formerly Camp) John Hay, a well-kept recreation area in the south-eastern suburbs of town. When you're there don't miss the **Cemetery of Negativism**, with its amusing gravestones; it's right next to **Liberty Park**. **Burnham Park** is in the town and the **Baguio Botanic Gardens** are a km out. There are scenic views of the surrounding countryside from **Mines View Park** at the east end of town (P2 by jeepney).

In **La Trinidad**, the provincial capital just to the north of the city, visit the governor's offices and see the **Kabayan mummies**. These remarkably well-preserved mummified bodies were brought from burial caves in the north.

Places to Stay

The simple but well-kept *Baguio Goodwill Lodge* (☎ 442 6634) at 58 Session Rd, right in the centre of town, has decent singles/doubles for P200/280, or P350/420 with bath. The *Benguet Pine Tourist Inn* (☎ 442 7325), at 82 Chanum St on the corner of Otek St, is a clean and quiet place and has dorm beds for P150 and singles/doubles for P250/P350, P500 with bath. This is a very popular place to stay.

For P160 you can get a bed in the clean dorm at the *Baden Powell Inn* (☎ 442 5836) at 26 Governor Pack Rd. Singles/doubles with bath go for P800. The rooms are clean and look downhill at the back, away from the noise of the street. This place is conveniently located for some of the bus terminals.

About one km east of the town centre, the *Mountain Lodge* (☎ 442 4544) at 27 Leonard Wood Rd has singles/doubles with bath for P600. This pleasant, friendly hotel is cosy, comfortable and good value.

The *Swagman Attic Inn* (☎ 442 5139) at 90 Abanao St has nicely furnished rooms with TV and bath for P765 and P1055. This pleasant accommodation near the town hall is managed by Australians.

Places to Eat

The *Dangwa Tranco Bus Terminal* has a good, cheap restaurant (P50). The so-called *Slaughterhouse Restaurants* on Balajadia St are also simply furnished, but offer excellent meat dishes at good prices (P60). At both the *New Ganza* and the *Solibao* in Burnham Park you can eat outside.

There are various other restaurants along Session Rd, Baguio's main street, like the *Sizzling Plate*, a good place for a proper breakfast, and the *Kowloon House*, where you can get dim sum 24 hours a day. If you'd like to try out traditional Cordillera cooking and drinks, then the *Café by the Ruins* opposite the town hall is the place to go (P150).

Entertainment

There are a number of good music places in town. Jazz freaks meet at the *Songs Music Gallery* in Session Rd. The *Café Legarda* in the Mount Crest Hotel, in Legarda Rd at the corner of Urbano St, is a chic and trendy bar always filled with students; solo singers and bands take turns every night. The *Music Box Pizza House* on Zandueta St has a very 'different' atmosphere, if you're not turned off by plastic chairs and large jugs of beer; the music is more raw and passionate here. By far the most popular disco is called *Spirits* and is in a magnificent building in Otek St.

Things to Buy

In Baguio look for Ifugao wood carvings and for interesting hand-woven fabrics. The cottons are produced in such limited quantities that they rarely even reach Manila. They're much cheaper in Bontoc or Banaue than in Baguio. The baskets and wooden salad bowls are remarkably cheap, but a little bulky to carry home.

Getting There & Away

Air PAL has 50-minute flights from Manila to Baguio five times a week. Jeepneys to the airport leave from Mabini Rd, between Session and Harrison Rds.

Bus Philippine Rabbit, Victory Liner, Dangwa Tranco and Dagupan Bus all operate daily from Manila to Baguio (P115; six hours); Victory Liner has the most extensive schedule and comfortable buses. You can also catch these buses from Dau, near Angeles.

PHILIPPINES

PHILIPPINES

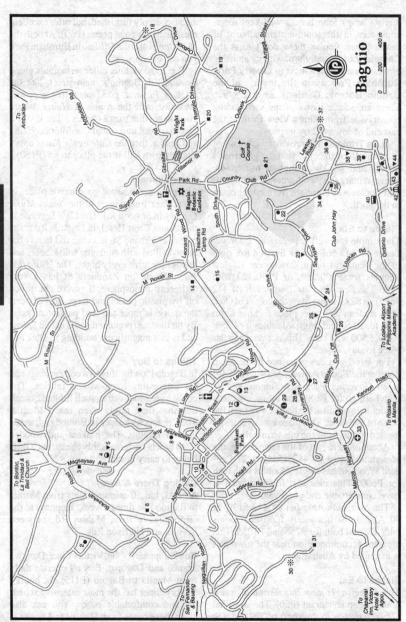

Baguio

0   200   400 m

There are hourly Victory Liner buses from Olongapo to Baguio (six hours), a few Dagupan Bus and Byron buses from Dagupan (two hours) and several Philippine Rabbit and Eso-Nice Transport buses from San Fernando (P25; two hours).

Dangwa Tranco has two daily bus services to Banaue (nine hours) which depart early in the morning. Departures to Bontoc are also in the morning (eight hours). Dangwa Tranco is also the operator to Sagada, with a daily early morning bus (P115; seven hours).

CENTRAL CORDILLERA

The main provinces of the Cordillera mountain ranges, Mountain Province and Ifugao, start 100 km north-east of Baguio and are famed for interesting tribes and spectacular rice terraces. If you've spent much time in South-East Asia, going to a place just to see more rice terraces may seem a little weird, but these are definitely special.

Some 2000 to 3000 years ago the Ifugao people carved terraces out of the mountainsides around Banaue, which are as perfect today as they were then. They run like stepping stones to the sky – up to 1500 metres high – and if stretched end to end would extend over 20,000 km. In more remote areas, the Ifugao still practice traditional ways – this no longer includes head-hunting.

Getting There & Away

You can approach the Central Cordillera from two directions. The more spectacular route, the Halsema Rd, climbs up from Baguio to Bontoc, the capital of Mountain Province. Halsema Rd reaches a height of 2255 metres and is the highest road in the Philippines. Try to get a seat on the right-hand side to get the best views. Expect rough, winding mountain roads in buses which are robust but lack the most comfortable suspension. The trip takes about seven hours and from Bontoc you can make side trips to places like Sagada, or continue to Banaue, the main town for rice terraces and another three or four hour trip.

The faster alternative route is direct from Manila via Nueva Viscaya Province – on occasionally good roads the bus trip takes 10 hours. The Baguio-Bontoc-Banaue road is often cut off during the wet season, but it's far more interesting so you should try to

PLACES TO STAY		OTHER		27	Convention
1	Hotel Supreme	2	Easter School of		Center
3	Baguio Village Inn		Weaving	28	University of the
6	Skyview Lodge	4	Times Transit Bus		Philippines (UP)
14	Mountain Lodge		Terminal	29	Tourist Office
16	Vacation Hotel Baguio	7	St Louis University	30	Lourdes Grotto
19	Villa La Maya Inn	8	City Market	31	Dominican Hill
20	Mansion House	9	City Hall	32	Baguio Medical
26	Woods Place Inn	10	Eso-Nice Transport		Center
31	Diplomat Hotel		Bus Terminal	33	Baguio General
35	Igorot Lodge	11	Cathedral		Hospital
		12	Dagupan Bus	34	Snider Hall
PLACES TO EAT			Terminal &	36	Tennis Courts
5	Slaughterhouse		Philippine Rabbit	37	MacArthur Park
	Restaurants		Bus Terminal		View Point
23	Halfway House	13	Victory Liner Bus	39	Main Club
25	Uncle's Music		Terminal	40	Swimming Pool
	Lounge &	15	Teacher's Camp		& Tennis Courts
	Restaurant,	17	St Joseph Church	41	Cemetery of
	Session Bistro	18	Mines View Park		Negativism &
	Music Lounge &	21	Baguio Country Club		Liberty Park
	Restaurant	22	Mile-Hi	42	Mountain
38	19th Tee Patio		Recreational		Provinces
44	Lone Star Steak		Center		Museum
	House & Mexican	24	Club John Hay	43	Tennis Courts
	Restaurant		Main Gate		

make the trip in at least one direction by this route. July to September is the wettest period.

BONTOC

Bontoc is the first major town you come to from Baguio and the main town of the area. It's possible to walk from here to the villages of the Igorot people – they build their rice terraces with stone dikes, unlike the earth terraces of Banaue. Take food and water for yourself and dried fish or other gifts for the villagers.

The village of **Malegcong** is a two or three hour walk into the mountains. You have to follow a narrow creek for about 200 metres before you reach the footpath leading to the village. Always ask permission before taking photographs of the people here. There is a chance that one or two jeepneys a day will make the trip between Bontoc and the rice terraces. Because of the high fare (P40) most locals decide to walk instead.

After a long hike through the mountains, there's nothing better than a good massage. Blind masseurs in the Bontoc massage centre will give you a 1st class treatment lasting over an hour for P150.

The excellent **Bontoc Museum** is run by the local Catholic mission and includes head-hunting relics, Chinese vases and photos of the mountain tribes; admission is P20.

Places to Stay

Let's put it this way: accommodation in Bontoc was obviously at its best a long time ago. The *Pines Kitchenette & Inn* is the only reasonably acceptable place; doubles cost P140, or P300 with bath. It's about five minutes walk from the bus stop.

Places to Eat

Food is pretty good in Bontoc – try the great cinnamon rolls in the local bakery. The *Pines Kitchenette* is a good, roomy restaurant where, among other things, you can get a decent breakfast.

Things to Buy

Bontoc is a good place to buy locally woven materials, woodcarvings and other handicrafts of Mountain Province.

Getting There & Away

There are five Dangwa Tranco buses daily between Baguio and Bontoc, generally departing in the early morning.

The 150 km trip takes about eight hours (P130). On from Bontoc to Banaue there is usually a daily jeepney at 6.30 to 7.30 am and a daily (except Sunday) bus at 7.30 to 8 am. As elsewhere in the Central Cordillera, transport is somewhat unreliable. If you can't find regular transport you can charter a jeepney.

SAGADA

Only 18 km from Bontoc, the tranquil little village of Sagada is famed for its **burial caves** and **hanging coffins**. The people are friendly and it's a good place to buy local weaving. You'll probably need a local guide and some sort of light to explore the more extensive caves, like the **Sumaging Cave** (Big Cave) south of Sagada. Guides can be arranged through the Sagada Environmental Guides Association (SEGA) in the tourist information center.

About 500 metres from the town centre, heading towards Bontoc, the **Eduardo Masferré Studio** has photographs of life in Mountain Province from the 30s to the 50s.

Places to Stay

All the places to stay in this popular little town seem to have a policy of charging around P75 per person. In most you must order a bucket of hot water for P10 the evening before if you don't want a cold shower in the morning – and when they say cold water in Sagada they really mean cold!

Masferrés Inn is very popular – 'quaint, charming, cosy and rustic' was how one traveller described it. Other places include the *St Joseph Resthouse*, across from the hospital where the bus stops. It's also friendly and well kept and the food is superb value. The *Mapiyaaw Pensione* is idyllically located in a natural rock garden 600 metres from the town centre heading towards Bontoc. It's a three storey building, but it manages to be cosy with a fireplace and big balcony on each floor. Or there's the *Rocky Valley Inn*, which once again is a pleasant place and does good meals.

Places to Eat

Both *Café Bilig* and the *Village Bistro* are good and inexpensive restaurants (P50); in the latter you can sit outside comfortably. The *Shamrock Café* and the small, pleasantly fitted out *Log Cabin* will also feed you well. The food at the Log Cabin is excellent, although it is advisable to reserve a table. Banana cake is a Sagada speciality and is served in all these places.

Getting There & Away

Bus There are about five Dangwa Tranco and Lizardo Trans buses daily from Baguio in the early morning (P135; seven hours).

Jeepney A jeepney from Bontoc to Sagada only takes an hour (P20); there are only three or four a day, usually leaving early in the morning or in the afternoon.

BANAUE

From Bontoc the road turns south and runs through incredibly spectacular countryside to Banaue, the heart of the terrace scenery. It's a narrow, rough road and travel is slow – but what a view. Take the right side of the bus to appreciate it best.

There are many hiking trails in the vicinity of Banaue.

Information

Tourist Office The tourist information office has a good map of Banaue's surroundings for P6.

Money There is no bank in Banaue but, if you're really stuck, you can probably change money at the Banaue Hotel (at a bad rate) or in the RSR Store across from the Sanafe Lodge.

Telephone The area code for Banaue is 073.

Places to Stay

There are plenty of small places to stay here, the cheapest from around P50 to P75 per person. The *Jericho Guest House* is basic, but has clean rooms for P60/100. The popular *Wonder Lodge* (☎ 386 4017) is a cosy place and has singles/doubles for P75/150, as does the *Half Way Lodge*. Another good place to stay is the pleasant *Stairway Lodge* (☎ 386 4030). Singles/doubles are P75/150 and doubles with bath are P250.

The *People's Lodge* (☎ 386 4014) is a wonderful place with a bakery and restaurant. There is a lovely balcony with a great view. Rooms are friendly and cost P75/100, and with bath P350. At the *Green View Lodge* (☎ 386 4021) the rooms are very clean, tastefully decorated and have a beautiful view over the terraces. They cost P100/200 for singles/doubles and P350/400 with bath. You will also find good accommodation at the *Sanafe Lodge* (☎ 386 4085), which has dorm beds for P120 (students P60) or quite comfortable rooms with bath for P450/650.

Finally, the expensive Banaue Hotel administers the *Banaue Youth Hostel*, where dorm beds are P150 (students P125). You can use the hotel swimming pool.

Places to Eat

Most hotels have small restaurants or offer meals – the *Stairway, Half Way, Cool Winds* and *Las Vegas* restaurants are all good and cheap (P75), although most close around 9 pm.

The restaurant at the *Banaue Hotel* is excellent and, if there are enough guests, Ifugao dances are held at night. Entry is P20.

Getting There & Away

You can reach Banaue from either direction but, while the Bayombong route is faster, the Bontoc route is much more interesting.

From Baguio, there are two daily Dangwa Tranco buses via Bayombong (P135; nine hours). They leave early in the morning, but at busy times they will leave when they're full.

From Baguio, via Bontoc, you must overnight in Bontoc en route; from there it takes about three hours on the bus, which departs daily (except Sunday) early in the morning. Arrive very early for a good seat. There's also a daily jeepney (P60; 2½ hours).

From Manila, the daily Dangwa Tranco bus leaves at 7 am (P160; 10 hours). If you miss this direct bus, take a Baliwag Transit bus to Solano, just before the Banaue turn-off. From there, jeepneys run to Lagawe and then to Banaue, and take another two or three hours.

BATAD

The wonderful village of Batad is surrounded by breathtakingly beautiful rice terraces – for which it is one of the best viewpoints. It's a two hour, sometimes steep, walk to Batad after a 12 km jeepney ride from Banaue. There are a number of small, inexpensive places to stay in Batad and near the village there's a delightful waterfall with good swimming.

Places to Stay

Accommodation in Batad is spartan, but the atmosphere is friendly and it's worth staying here, rather than just day-tripping from Banaue. The *Hillside Inn, Rita's Mount View Inn, Batad Pension, Cristina's Guest House, Foreigner's Inn, Shirley's Inn* or *Simon's Inn* all cost around P30 per person.

Getting There & Away

You can get transport 12 km of the way to Batad from Banaue (P25), but you must walk the rest of the way. Buses which ply the route between Banaue and Mayoyao pass the turn-off for Batad. It takes about two hours along the signposted path from between Dalican and Bangaan. Beware of self-appointed, but expensive, 'guides'.

VIGAN

About 130 km north of San Fernando (La Union), this interesting old town was second only to Manila during the Spanish era and today is the best-preserved Spanish town in the country. If you're interested in old Spanish architecture and ancient-looking

churches, this region of Ilocos is a prime hunting ground.

It's fascinating just wandering around the town very early in the morning, taking in the narrow streets around Mena Crisologo St, listening to the clip-clop of horse-drawn calesas.

The area code for Vigan is 077.

Things to See

The house where Jose Burgos was born now houses the **Ayala Museum**. He was executed by the Spanish in 1872. The museum is behind the Capitol building, has lots of antiques, old paintings and photographs and the curator is delighted to tell tourists the history of the area. The **Cathedral of St Paul** dates from 1641 and is one of the oldest and largest churches in the country.

Places to Stay

At 1 Bonifacio St, *Grandpa's Inn* might be the cheapest place in town, but it's not too inviting. Rather run-down rooms with fan are P130, with fan and bath P200 or with air-con and bath P350. You'd be better off at the *Vigan Hotel* (☎ 722 3001), on Burgos St, with its old-style rooms with fan for P275/375 and with air-con and bath for P495/675.

If you're interested in catching a bit of historical atmosphere – and there's nowhere in the Philippines better for this than Vigan – then checking in at one of the restored colonial-style hotels is the way to go. The *RF Aniceto Mansion* (☎ 722 2382) in Mena Crisologo St has the most inexpensive rooms in this category. Singles/doubles with fan and bath are P250/350 and with air-con and bath P550/650. However, the most attractive of them all is the *Villa Angela* (☎ 722 2914) diagonally across from the El-Juliana Hotel, between Quirino Blvd and Ventura de Los Reyes St. This is a beautiful old villa with a well preserved interior, furniture from colonial times and a magnificent garden. Singles/doubles with fan and bath go for P250/500 and doubles with air-con and bath for P800.

Places to Eat

The *Victory Restaurant* on Quezon Ave offers different menus each day. The *Cool Spot Restaurant* is a lovely half-open-air place at the Vigan Hotel and is known for its good Ilocano cooking. But if you want really outstanding food and big portions the place to go is the *888 Restaurant* in Del Pilar St, which is open until after midnight. They also offer cheap pool at P2 per game.

While you're in Vigan you should try *empanadas* at least once; these are tasty vegetable-filled pasties of Spanish origin. You can get them from around 4 pm until quite late at night at the Plaza Burgos for P3 each.

Getting There & Away

From Manila, the trip takes about eight hours (P180) with Partas Lines, Philippine Rabbit, Times Transit, Farinas Trans or Maria de Leon. Some buses continuing north to Laoag bypass the town, in which case you will have to take a tricycle from the highway for P5. Buses also connect from San Fernando, Aparri and Laoag. You can reach Vigan from Baguio via San Fernando, or by the coast from Hundred Islands and Dagupan, again via San Fernando.

It's about two hours beyond Vigan to Laoag and you can continue right around the north of Luzon to Claveria, Aparri, Tuguegarao and back down to Manila.

LAOAG

In 1818, when Ilocos Province was divided in two, Laoag, on the Laoag River, became the capital of Ilocos Norte, one of Luzon's most beautiful provinces.

The area code for Laoag is 077.

Things to See

There are many old Spanish churches in the Ilocos Norte Province and Laoag has **St William's Cathedral**, built between 1650 and 1700. Near Laoag, in **Bacarra**, the town's church has a massive, earthquake-damaged bell tower.

South-east of the town is **Sarrat**, birthplace of the former president, Ferdinand

Marcos. In the centre of town is the restored **Sarrat Church & Convent**, built in 1779 by Augustinian monks. Marcos memorabilia, including the refrigerated remains of the former president, can be found at the **Marcos Mansion** in Batac, south of Laoag. A few km south-west of Batac is the fortress-like **Paoay Church** in a style referred to as 'earthquake baroque'. The coastline between Laoag and Paoay, with its extensive sand dunes, is most impressive.

Places to Stay

The *Texicano Hotel* (☎ 722 0606) on Rizal St has singles/doubles with fan in the old building for P110/132, with fan and bath for P143/165 and with air-con and bath for P462/495. In the new building air-con rooms with TV are P680/765. The rooms are acceptable and this is the best of the less expensive hotels; the staff are friendly. The *Casa Llanes Pension* (☎ 722 1125) on Primo Lazaro Ave is also OK for the money. It has spacious rooms with fan and bath for P165 and with air-con and bath for P270. They give a 20% discount if you stay for twelve hours or less.

Places to Eat

The *City Lunch & Snack Bar*, on the corner of General Antonio Luna and Nolasco Sts, has good cheap Chinese and Filipino dishes and reasonably priced breakfasts. The *Peppermint Brickside Café* on Don Severo Hernando Ave is good, although meals are more expensive; they have live music in the evenings. The *Colonial Fast Food* on FR Castro Ave is an air-con restaurant which serves tasty Filipino food. The *Town Bakery* on Jose Rizal St between Balintawak St and Bagumbayan St has lots of good biscuits and pastries – as well as donuts for one peso!

Getting There & Away

Air PAL has three weekly flights between Manila and Laoag.

Bus Buses from Manila take 10 hours and from Vigan two hours. Less frequent buses travel around the north coast to Claveria (three hours), Aparri (five hours) and Tuguegarao (seven hours).

TUGUEGARAO
In an area known for its many caves, the **Callao Cave** can be found 15 km north-east of Tuguegarao, about nine km north of Peñablanca. There are some good walks in the **Sierra Madre**.

The area code for Tuguegarao is 078.

Places to Stay
The *Pensione Abraham* (☎ 844 1793) on Bonifacio St has acceptable rooms at a reasonable price: singles/doubles with fan cost P80/110, with fan and bath P150/280 and with air-con and bath P250/350.

The best accommodation in town is the pleasant *Pensione Roma* (☎ 844 1057) on the corner of Luna and Bonifacio Sts. Friendly rooms with fan and bath are P300 and with air-con and bath P600/650.

At Peñablanca you can stay in the *Callao Cave Resort*, where rooms cost P200 to P400, or there are cottages for P500 to P700.

Places to Eat
Opposite Pensione Abraham, the *Pampanguena Restaurant* changes its menu daily and has a large choice of cakes.

Getting There & Away
PAL flies between Manila and Tuguegarao three times a week.

Baliwag Transit buses from Manila take 11 hours and depart hourly (P170).

BALER & EAST LUZON
Much of *Apocalypse Now* was shot near Baler on the wild east coast of North Luzon. The town itself is not very interesting, but you can visit the surrounding country and the coast. In December, the strong surf should attract surfers.

Places to Stay
The *Amihan Hotel*, on Bitong St, has rooms with fan for P90/180 and with fan and bath for P200. There are various places along the beach in Sabang.

Getting There & Away
It takes 2½ hours to get from Manila to Cabanatuan and then another four hours from there to Baler. If coming south from Tuguegarao, you also change buses at Cabanatuan.

South Luzon

With its impressive contours and countless bays and inlets, the south of Luzon meanders its way from Manila in the direction of Samar, the most easterly island of the Visayas. The major attraction of Bicol, as South Luzon is also called, is the majestic Mayon volcano at Legaspi, claimed to be the most perfectly symmetrical volcano cone in the world. Between Sorsogon and Matnog lies the so-called 'Switzerland of the Orient': beautiful Mt Bulusan with its extensive foothills.

SAN MIGUEL BAY
San Miguel Bay, with its beaches and islands, is an interesting detour on the route south. **Daet** is a good overnight stop en route to the bay. **Mercedes**, a small coastal village about 10 km north-east of Daet, has a lively fish market from 6 to 8 am, and from here you can reach **Apuao Grande Island**, with its white sand beach, in San Miguel Bay.

Places to Stay
In Daet the centrally located *Karilagan Hotel* (☎ 721 2314) has quite good rooms with fan and bath for P150/200 and with air-con and bath for P400/550.

On the white sand beach on Apuao Grande Island, the *TS Resort* has dorm accommodation for P100 and a good number of attractive cottages with fan and bath from P350 to P700. They also offer facilities like a swimming pool, golf course and tennis courts.

Places to Eat
Near the Karigalan Hotel, a pleasant place with good food is the *Sandok at Palayok*. It's on the second floor, so you have to manage

a few stairs. A few streets away, the *Golden House Restaurant* is recommended for its Chinese dishes.

Getting There & Away

Air PAL has flights to Daet from Manila twice a week.

Bus Buses from Manila take about seven hours to Daet and some continue to centres further south. It's three to four hours further south to Legaspi via Naga.

Jeepney Jeepneys go to Mercedes, the jumping-off point for the San Miguel Bay islands.

NAGA

In late September this friendly and noticeably clean town holds the **Peñafrancia Festival**, which includes a huge and colourful procession. Hotel prices at this time can be twice or three times as much as normal.

The area code for Naga is 054.

Places to Stay

The friendly and fairly good *Sampaguita Tourist Inn* (☎ 214810) on Panganiban Drive has singles with fan and bath for P145 (good value), singles with air-con and bath for P235 and doubles with air-con and bath for P325 and P450.

A little bit more expensive, but noticeably better, the *Moraville Hotel* (☎ 811 1807) is on Dinaga St. It has singles/doubles with fan and bath for P175/275 and with air-con, bath and TV for P400/500. The rooms are quiet and comfortably furnished.

Places to Eat

The *Ming Chun Foodhouse* on Peñafrancia Ave serves good Filipino and Chinese dishes. The *New China Restaurant* on General Luna St offers daily specials for about P60, and *Carl's Diner* at Plaza Rizal is a clean, inexpensive and popular 50s-style fast food restaurant.

Things to Buy

Pili nuts are a popular favourite in the Bicol region. There is a shop in the market at Naga which sells all varieties of pili nuts.

Getting There & Away

PAL has a daily flight from Manila which takes one hour. Buses take 8½ hours from Manila and there are also buses from Daet (1½ hours) and Legaspi (two hours).

LEGASPI

The main city of the Bicol region hugs the waterfront in the shadow of the Mayon volcano.

Orientation & Information

Legaspi is actually divided into two parts. Inland from the port area is the Albay district of the town. The two areas are linked by Rizal St.

The tourist office (☎ 44492, 44026) is in the Albay district beside Peñaranda Park, near the cathedral. It has been announced that the tourist office will move sometime in 1997 to Rizal St near the Victoria Hotel.

The area code for Legaspi is 05221.

Things to See

Kapuntukan Hill, south-east of the city, provides a fascinating panoramic view of Legaspi harbour with the impressive Mayon in the background. In the **St Rafael Church**, on Aguinaldo St across from the Rex Hotel, the altar is a 10 tonne volcanic rock from Mayon.

The '**headless monument**' (in front of the post office) to those who died at the hands of the Japanese in WWII is sadly neglected.

Places to Stay

There are plenty of cheap hotels around Legaspi, but none will win any prizes for high standards.

There is quite a choice along Peñaranda St, parallel to the waterfront. *Catalina's Lodging House* is a friendly place with basic rooms with fan for P80/120, with fan and bath for P140 and with air-con and bath for P300/400. On the same street, the *Hotel*

Xandra (☎ 22688) has reasonable, clean rooms with fan for P120/150, with fan and bath for P180/200, or with air-con and bath for P220/300.

More expensive places include the *Legaspi Plaza Hotel* (☎ 23344), on Lapu-Lapu St, which has slightly shabby rooms with fan and bath for P355/340 and better ones with air-con and bath for P500/600. The *Hotel Casablanca* (☎ 23130) on Peñaranda St has pretty good air-con rooms with bath for P700, some with a big balcony. They provide a free shuttle service to and from the airport.

Places to Eat

Legaspi offers a wide choice of places to eat – like the *New Legaspi Restaurant* on Lapu-Lapu St, where the special meal for about P60 can be recommended. The food is basically Chinese with some Filipino dishes. Try the New Legaspi's pineapple pie for a treat.

The *Mamalola Bakery & Snack House* on Peñaranda St will surprise you not only with its plucky karaoke singers but also with its excellent cooking. The *Legaspi Ice Cream House* in Magellanes St makes wonderful ice cream.

Things to Buy

In South Luzon, *abaca* products are the main craft. Abaca is a fibre produced from a relative of the banana tree. It's best known end-product was the rope known as Manila hemp (as opposed to Indian hemp, produced from the fibre of the marijuana plant), but today it's made into all manner of woven products, including bags and place mats.

Getting There & Away

Air PAL has daily fights from Manila which take 50 minutes.

Bus Buses from Manila to Legaspi all pass through Naga. BLTB, Inland Trailways and Philtranco buses depart from their terminals on Edsa in Pasay City and the trip takes 11 to 12 hours. The fare to Legaspi is about P240, depending on the bus.

Buses to Tabaco take about 45 minutes.

Direct buses to Matnog generally come through from Manila and may well be full. It's probably easier to take local services to Sorsogon or Irosin and change there.

AROUND LEGASPI
Santo Domingo

This long black-sand beach is 15 km northeast of Legaspi and sometimes has quite high surf. Jeepneys run from Legaspi to Santo Domingo and tricycles run from there to the resorts along the beach.

Daraga & Cagsawa

The eruption of Mayon in 1814 totally destroyed the villages of Camalig, Cagsawa and Budiao on its southern side. The **Cagsawa Church** was rebuilt in a baroque style at nearby Daraga. It's just a 15 minute jeepney ride from Legaspi. The **Cagsawa ruins** are a short distance west of Daraga. There are also some ruins at **Budiao**, about two km from Cagsawa, but they are not so interesting.

Camalig

The interesting **Hoyop-Hoyopan Caves** are about 10 km from Camalig – hire a tricycle there and back or take a jeepney. The church in Camalig has artefacts that were excavated from the caves in 1972. Camalig is about 14 km from Legaspi and is reached by jeepneys and buses.

MAYON

Derived from the word 'beautiful' in the local dialect, Mayon is claimed to be the world's most perfect volcano cone. You can best appreciate it from the ruins of Cagsawa church. In 1814 Mayon erupted violently and killed 1200 people, including those who took shelter in the church. To get to Cagsawa, take a jeepney bound for Camalig and alight at the Cagsawa sign, from where it's a few minutes walk.

Mayon is said to erupt every 10 years and recently it's been doing even better than that. A spectacular eruption in 1968 was followed by another in 1978 and then another in late 1984. The last serious eruption was in February 1993. Seventy people died and a further 50,000 were evacuated.

If you want to appreciate Mayon from closer up, you can climb it in a couple of days – the tourist office in Legaspi will fix you up. The usual cost for two people is US$60, including a guide, a porter and a tent. Take warm clothing and a sleeping bag; provisions are extra – take enough for two days. Count on P300 per person for food and for a second porter if you don't want to carry your own food and gear.

You take a jeepney to Buyuhan (extra cost) and then climb 2½ hours to Camp 1 (Camp Amporo), at about 800 metres. If you start late you spend the night in the simple hut there. Another four hours takes you to Camp 2 (Camp Pepito), at about 1800 metres. Here you have to use a tent as there is no hut. The night can be fairly cold and from here it's a four hour climb to the summit.

The last 250 metres is a scramble over loose stones and steep rocks; it's advisable to be roped. Going down takes three hours from the crater to Camp 2, two hours to Camp 1 and two hours to the road.

You can try hiring a guide and porter in Buyuhan for about P500 a day. To try the ascent without a guide is reckless and irresponsible because many of the harmless-looking canyons turn out to be dead ends with sheer drops.

The Mayon Vista Lodge (which is no longer open) provides a good viewpoint 800 metres up the 2450-metre-high volcano. To get there, take a Ligao-bound jeepney from Tabaco to the turn-off, from where it's an eight km walk (or hitch) to the lodge. Alternatively, hire a jeepney from Tabaco or, more economically, persuade the regular Ligao jeepney, for a consideration, to make the detour to the lodge. The tourist office advises people not to climb the north slope of the volcano as it is considered too dangerous.

TABACO

Tabaco is just a departure point for the Catanduanes ferry.

Getting There & Away

Buses go direct to Tabaco from Manila or it's just 45 minutes from Legaspi and another half-hour on to Tiwi.

SORSOGON, GUBAT & BULAN

Sorsogon, the capital of the southernmost province of Luzon, is really just a transit region to the Visayas. The long and wide **Rizal Beach** at nearby Gubat is OK but nothing to get excited about. Ferries cross to Masbate from Bulan.

Places to Stay

The *Dalisay Hotel* at 182 VL Peralta St, Sorsogon, is simple and fairly clean; rooms are P75/130 with fan and P100/150 with fan and bath.

The *Rizal Beach Resort* at Gubat, although beginning to show its age, has passable singles/doubles with fan and bath for P450/550. Their restaurant is open until 10 pm.

Mari-El's Lodging House, by the pier in Bulan, is a straightforward place with rooms with fan for P60/120.

Getting There & Away

Buses to Sorsogon, from Legaspi, leave every half hour and take 1½ hours. It's 3½ hours from Legaspi to Bulan.

BULUSAN & IROSIN

Mt Bulusan is a 1560-metre-high volcano at the centre of the triangle between Juban, Bulusan and Irosin. It is a fascinating area: hundreds of different kinds of trees, giant ferns, rare orchids and other flora cover its slopes and there's a small crater lake of the same name a pleasant six km walk from Bulusan. Apart from Bulusan, there is another good base for a stay in the so-called 'Switzerland of the Orient': the Mateo Hot & Cold Springs Resort. This pleasant establishment is in a forest about four km northeast of Irosin (three km in the direction of Sorsogon and then one km north-east). There is a signpost at the point where the path leaves the road. The resort has two pools (one lukewarm and one hot).

Places to Stay

The family-run *Bartilet's Lodging House* behind the town hall in Bulusan has clean rooms at P100/200 with fan. At the pleasant *Villa Luisa Celeste Resort* in Dancalan, Bulusan, the rooms are clean and spacious, with fan and bath for P250/350 and with air-con and bath for P450. They have a swimming pool. At the peaceful *Mateo Hot & Cold Springs Resort* in Irosin, the rooms are basic but passable, and cost P100/200.

Getting There & Away

Buses from Legaspi go to Irosin or to Bulan via Irosin in about 2½ hours.

MATNOG

Right at the southern tip of Luzon, this is the departure point for boats to Allen, on Samar.

Places to Stay

Mely's Snack House costs P30 per person. It's a basic place and the only one left in Matnog. If they miss the last ferry, most Filipinos prefer to sleep in the big waiting room at the pier.

Getting There & Away

Buses run to Irosin from Legaspi, from where you continue by jeepney. You can do the trip with all connections in 3½ hours. There are also direct Philtranco and BLTB buses, but they come straight through from Manila so it can be difficult to get a seat. Coming from Allen there are usually jeepneys waiting to meet the ferry.

Islands Around Luzon

Although Luzon is the main island of the Philippines and offers a lot of things to see and do, it is only the start – there are still nearly 7000 islands left to explore. Islands around Luzon include the Batanes, which are scattered off the far northern coast; Catanduanes, off the south-eastern coast near Legaspi; the smaller islands of Masbate and Marinduque; and lastly, the large island of Mindoro, which has become a very popular escape because of its beautiful beaches and relaxing accommodation possibilities.

BATANES

The Batanes Islands are surprisingly unspoilt and different; they display a raw beauty, varying greatly with the tides. Many houses here are built of solid rock and have roofs thickly thatched with grass. There is next to no traffic on the roads, which makes the islands ideal for hiking.

Places to Stay

In Basco, *Mama Lily's Inn* offers unpretentious but pleasant and friendly accommodation; clean rooms with fan will cost you P400 per person, including three meals.

Getting There & Away

PAL flies to Basco from Laoag on Monday and from Tuguegarao on Wednesday.

CATANDUANES

There are some excellent beaches and pleasant waterfalls on this island, but few tourists come here. The main town and accommodation centre is **Virac**. About 30 km north-east, **Puraran** has a wonderful long, white beach.

The area code for Virac is 052.

Places to Stay

Sandy's Blossoms Pension House (☎ 811 1762) at Piersite, Virac, has basic rooms with fan for P100/200; they have a little garden restaurant where they serve snacks. The more expensive *Catanduanes Hotel* on San Jose St has rooms with fan and bath for P290/400. It is unpretentious but quite cosy, and has a good restaurant on the roof. Both places are located within walking distance of the pier.

On the beach at Puraran, the *Puting Baybay Resort* charges P350 per person for a simple room, including three meals.

Getting There & Away

PAL flies daily to Virac from Manila and on Monday, Wednesday and Friday from Legaspi.

The ferry to Virac, on Catanduanes, departs Tabaco daily (P50; four hours).

MASBATE

The small island of Masbate is between Luzon and the main Visayan group. It's noted for its large cattle herds, but very few travellers come here.

Getting There & Away

Air PAL has daily flights between Masbate and Manila, and flights four times a week between Masbate and Legaspi.

Boat There are a couple of ships a week from Cebu to Cataingan (11 hours) and a daily boat makes the four hour trip from Bulan in South Luzon. Boats go from Mandaon on Masbate to Sibuyan Island in Romblon Province, and from the town of Masbate to Manila and back.

Masbate Town

Masbate is also the main town on the island. **Bitu-on Beach**, a few km south-east, has some cottages which make a good alternative to staying in town.

The area code for Masbate is 056.

Places to Stay The *St Anthony Hotel* (☎ 180) on Quezon St has simple rooms with fan for P110/150, with fan and bath for P200/250 and with air-con and bath for P300/350. It's the only half-decent hotel in town.

Places to Eat Try the *Peking House* in the port area for good food, or the *Petit Restaurant* opposite the St Anthony Hotel in Quezon St.

MARINDUQUE

The small island of Marinduque is sandwiched between Mindoro and Luzon. It's noted for its Easter Moriones festivals, in particular at Boac. On Good Friday, the *antipos* (flagellants) engage in a little religious masochism as they flog themselves with bamboo sticks.

From Buenavista, on the south coast, you can climb **Mt Malindig**, a 1157-metre-high dormant volcano. The weekend **Buenavista Market** is worth seeing. The **Tres Reyes Islands** are 30 minutes by outrigger from Buenavista – **Gaspar Island** has a small village and a nice coral beach. **White Beach**, near Torrijos, is probably the best beach on Marinduque. The towns of **Gasan** and **Mogpog** are also heavily involved in the Easter passion play.

Getting There & Away

Air PAL has daily flights to Marinduque from Manila.

Boat There are usually one or two boats daily from Lucena in Luzon to Balanacan (P62; three hours). Jeepneys meet the boats and go to Boac. Crossings are also made between Lucena and Buyabod, the harbour for Santa Cruz.

There's a daily service from Gasan, between Boac and Buenavista, to Pinamalayan on Mindoro. The crossing takes three hours.

Boac

One of the most colourful religious ceremonies in the Philippines takes place at Boac from Good Friday until Easter Sunday. Dressed as Roman centurions wearing large carved masks, the participants capture Longinus, the centurion who was converted after he had stabbed Christ in the side with his spear. The festival ends with a *pugutan* (mock beheading) of the hapless Longinus.

The area code for Boac is 042.

Places to Stay On Nepomuceno St, the *Boac Hotel* is probably the best of the handful of places offering basic accommodation in the town. Singles/doubles with fan cost P100/200 and with fan and bath P180/350.

Directly on the sea front at Balaring, five km south of Boac, the *Marinduque Marine* dive resort has immaculate rooms with fan and bath for P400. About one km further south, on the pebbly beach at Caganhao between Boac and Cawit, is the *Cassandra Beach Resort*, where cottages with fan and bath cost P175; use of the kitchen is possible.

MINDORO

The relatively undeveloped island of Mindoro is the nearest 'last frontier' to Manila – the Philippines has quite a few last frontiers. The population is concentrated along the coastal strip and inland is mainly dense jungle and mountains. Because you can get to Mindoro very easily from Manila, many travellers make the trip to try the beautiful beaches of Puerto Galera on the north-east tip of the island. Another, albeit less popular, destination is the small island of North Pandan just off the west coast.

Getting There & Away

Air PAL has flights from Manila to Mamburao and San Jose.

Bus & Boat The usual route to Mindoro is from Batangas, on Luzon, to Calapan or Puerto Galera. Buses run directly to Batangas from the BLTB terminal in Manila (P60, three hours), but beware of pickpockets – they work overtime on this route.

The ferry crossing takes about two hours; there are at least five Batangas to Calapan services daily, and seven Batangas to Puerto Galera services. The services to Puerto Galera are at 8.30 am and 12.30 and 5 pm (Viva ferry to Balatero Pier; P40); at 9.30 am, noon and 1.30 pm (big outrigger to Sabang; P50); and at noon (Si-Kat ferry to Puerto Galera; P150).

From the Centrepoint Hotel on Mabini St, Ermita, a daily Si-Kat Ferry air-con bus departs at 9 am to connect with the company's noon Si-Kat ferry from Batangas to Puerto Galera (P300, bus and ferry).

On Mindoro you can continue from Pinamalayan to Marinduque, and from Roxas on to Boracay (Panay) or Romblon. The Mindoro to Boracay route is becoming quite popular and combines the two beach destinations of Puerto Galera and Boracay. Be careful, as some of the boats on this route are leaky tubs and are often dangerously overloaded.

There's a big outrigger from Roxas to Boracay on Monday and Thursday (P250; six hours). From December to May it can leave as often as every other day.

Puerto Galera

For some time now, the fine beaches and excellent snorkelling around Puerto Galera have been attracting travellers as well as divers (in Sabang and La Laguna there are around 20 dive shops). There are also some pleasant walks and the whole area is starting to become very popular, especially with Germans (at White Beach) and Australians (at Sabang).

There are many places to stay at the various beaches, which include **La Laguna**, **Sabang** and **White Beach** at San Isidro (seven km out of town), **Aninuan Beach**, and **Talipanan Beach**. Sabang offers the biggest choice of accommodation, although the beach there has completely disappeared over the years.

Information The Rural Bank in Puerto Galera changes cash and may also change travellers' cheques.

Places to Stay – In Town Inexpensive rooms in Puerto Galera generally cost from around P100 to P200. The modest *Melxa's Greenhill Nipa Hut* has rooms with fan for P100/150, as does the friendly *Malou's Hilltop Inn*.

Right at the wharf, the *Coco Point* has rooms with fan and bath which are good value for P250.

About 1.5 km out of town, towards Sabang, the idyllically located *Tanawin Lodge*, near Encenada Beach, has beautiful, fully furnished two-storey houses with living rooms and bedrooms from P700 to P1800. There is a swimming pool and the view of Varadero Bay is fantastic.

Places to Stay – At the Beaches Out on the beaches there are lots of cottages with fan and bath from around P250 to as much as

P600 a day. Most of the prices quoted are for double occupancy. The places that follow are just a small selection of the numerous possibilities.

Sabang can get very loud at night around the discos and bars. Cottages at *Seashore Lodge* and at *Al Can's Inn* are P250 to P400; the more expensive ones have cooking facilities. The nicely laid-out *Terraces Garden Resort* has quiet rooms on a slope above the beach at P300.

You can walk around the coast from here to the La Laguna beaches, which are better for sunbathing and snorkelling. At Small La Laguna, *Nick & Sonia's Cottages* and *Full Moon* both have pleasant, quite comfortable cottages from P200. The *El Galleon Beach Resort* has spacious rooms at P500. Up the hill, *Carlo's Inn* has rooms for P650 and apartments for P850; there's a nice view thrown in.

At Big La Laguna there's the *Paradise Lodge*, with rooms for P350 and P550; the *El Oro Resort* has a beautiful garden and cottages cost P400; and at *La Laguna Beach Club*, which has a swimming pool, comfortable, well-furnished rooms cost P650, or P900 with air-con.

Further afield, at White Beach, the *White Beach Nipa Hut* has lots of little cottages with fan and bath for P350. *Summer Connection* is a quiet little place at the western end of White Beach and has cottages for P400. Or try the popular *White Beach Lodge*, where fairly spacious cottages go for P250/350; they have a good restaurant.

At Aninuan Beach, next one along from White Beach, the popular *Tamaraw Beach Resort* has cottages for P350 and P650.

Places to Eat Restaurants around the docks in the town include *Coco Point*, *Harbour Point* and *Typhoon*. The *Pier Pub Pizza* doesn't just make pizza, they also have tasty seafood. Most of the beach cottages have restaurants.

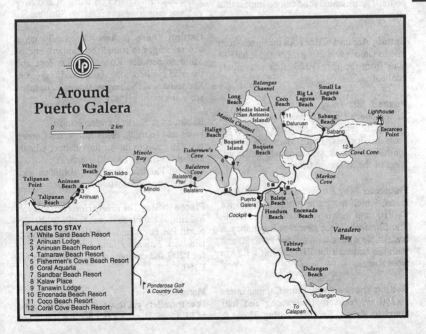

Around Puerto Galera

0   1   2 km

PLACES TO STAY
1 White Sand Beach Resort
2 Aninuan Lodge
3 Aninuan Beach Resort
4 Tamaraw Beach Resort
5 Fishermen's Cove Beach Resort
6 Coral Aquaria
7 Sandbar Beach Resort
8 Kalaw Place
9 Tanawin Lodge
10 Encenada Beach Resort
11 Coco Beach Resort
12 Coral Cove Beach Resort

PHILIPPINES

Getting There & Away – Bus Southward to San Jose from Puerto Galera requires several stages – two hours to Calapan, four hours to Roxas (P100), two hours to Bulalacao (P75) and another four hours on a rough road to San Jose (P80).

Getting There & Away – Jeepney There are several jeepneys daily between Calapan and Puerto Galera (P30; two hours). The road does not continue westward from Puerto Galera to Wawa, the port of Abra de Ilog. (Two or three ferries a day travel between Batangas and Wawa).

Getting Around – Jeepney Several jeepneys run daily between Puerto Galera and White Beach in San Isidro (P10) and some go on to Talipanan Beach for P15. It's a 45 minute walk from White Beach to Talipanan Beach.

A jeepney from Puerto Galera to Sabang costs P10, or you can walk it in about 1½ hours. The unsealed road can be impassable after heavy rains.

Getting Around – Boat An outrigger from Puerto Galera to Sabang takes about half an hour from the pier (P150; four passengers per boat).

Roxas & Mansalay

Roxas doesn't exactly make you feel like staying for long, but from there you can get boats to Boracay. From Mansalay, further south from Roxas, you can walk to the villages of the Mangyan tribes.

Places to Stay Roxas has the *Santo Niño Hotel*, which has basic rooms with fan for P80/160 and with fan and bath for P150/200. The *Catalina Beach Resort* at Bagumbayan has simple rooms with fan for P60/120 and with fan and bath for P100/200; it's 1.5 km from Roxas.

Getting There & Away From Calapan buses take three hours to Bongabong and four hours to Roxas. See the Getting There & Away section of the Mindoro section above for boat information.

San Jose

From the not very inviting town of San Jose, it may be possible to visit the Mangyan tribes or you can rent a boat to **Ambulong** or **Ilin Island** for swimming and snorkelling. **Apo Reef**, a popular diving spot well offshore, can be reached from San Jose or Sablayan.

The area code for San Jose is 046.

Places to Stay The *Sikatuna Town Hotel* (☎ 697) on Sikatuna St is simple but fairly good. Rooms with fan cost P70/100, P145 with fan and bath, or P410 with air-con and bath. You would actually be better off at their *Sikatuna Beach Hotel*, which is a little bit out of town on the way to the airport and charges roughly the same.

Places to Eat San Jose has only a few acceptable places to eat. You could try the *Emmanuel Panciteria* on Rizal St and *Nice & Spice*, which serves pizzas, on Sikatuna St.

Getting There & Away It usually takes several stages to round the southern end of Mindoro between Roxas and San Jose and the road is often none too good. Progress to Mamburao, via Sablayan, is tough and takes six hours by bus (P80).

Sablayan & North Pandan Island

From this friendly, clean little coastal town you can cross to one of the offshore islands in Pandan Bay (P100; 30 minutes).

North Pandan Island is a gorgeous spot and has a beautiful white-sand beach.

Places to Stay The *Emely Hotel* in Sablayan has simple but clean rooms for P60/120. On North Pandan Island, the pleasant and very laid-back *Pandan Island Resort* has rooms for P200 and cottages with fan and bath for P350.

Mamburao

Few travellers get this far up the west coast of Mindoro. But it's a fair bet that it will not be long before the northern stretch of the coastline from Mamburao to Sablayan becomes a centre for tourism.

Places to Stay The *Traveller's Lodge* in Mamburao has basic rooms with fan for P100/160, or with fan and bath for P160/270.

Four km north-west of Mamburao, the sizeable *Tayamaan Palm Beach Club* has stone cottages with fan and bath for P500. They are located in a beautiful bay with a good beach.

Getting There & Away PAL flies between Mamburao and Manila.

Cebu

Between the islands of Luzon in the north and Mindanao in the south lies the largest island group of the Philippines: the Visayas. The Visayan islands include Cebu, Bohol, Leyte, Biliran, Samar, Romblon, Panay, Guimaras, Negros and Siquijor.

The most visited of the Visayan islands, Cebu is the major travel hub of the southern Philippines and flights and shipping services radiate in all directions. This is also where Magellan introduced Christianity to the Philippines with the erection of a cross – and where he was killed in a skirmish on Mactan Island on 27 April 1521.

Getting There & Away
Air PAL flies from Cebu City to Manila and Legaspi on Luzon. There are also flights between Cebu City and Bohol (Tagbilaran), Leyte (Tacloban), Mindanao (almost all big cities), Negros (Bacolod, Dumaguete), Palawan (Puerto Princesa) and Panay (Iloilo City, Kalibo).

Boat Shipping company addresses in Cebu City include:

Bullet Express Corporation
    Pier 1 (☎ 91272)

Cebu Ferries Corporation
    Pier 4, Quezon Blvd (☎ 253 1181, 253 1196)
Cokaliong Shipping Lines
    46 Jakosalem St (☎ 212262)
George & Peter Lines
    Jakosalem St (☎ 75914, 74098)
K&T Shipping Lines
    MacArthur Blvd (☎ 62359, 90633)
Lite Shipping Corporation
    Lavilles St (☎ 253 7776, 253 6857)
Socor Shipping Lines
    MacArthur Blvd (☎ 78225)
Sulpicio Lines
    1st St, Reclamation Area (☎ 73839, 99723)
Trans-Asia Shipping Lines
    MJ Cuenco Ave (☎ 254 6491)

Bohol There are several departures daily between Cebu City and Tagbilaran (P70, four hours/regular boat; P150, 1½ hours/speed boat) and Tubigon (P45, 2½ hours) on Bohol.

Camiguin The usual route is by air or ship from Cebu City to Cagayan de Oro or Butuan, in Mindanao, then a bus to Balingoan. From there ferries run across to Benoni, on Camiguin, three times daily. Or you can take another ship from Cagayan de Oro. Sometimes there's a ship on Sunday directly from Cebu City to Mambajao.

Leyte A variety of ships operate between Cebu City and Baybay, Maasin, Ormoc, Tacloban and other ports on Leyte. The fastest are the connections by speed boat from Cebu City to Maasin (P200; two hours) and Ormoc (P200; two hours).

Luzon Lots of ships operate between Cebu City and Manila (P520; 22 hours).

Mindanao An enormous number of ships operate between Cebu and Mindanao. It takes 10 to 12 hours between Cebu City and Butuan (P154), Cagayan de Oro (P145), Dipolog (P145), Iligan (P145), Ozamis (P145) or Surigao (P125). Zamboanga is about 16 hours away and Davao (P450) about 24 hours.

Negros There are four departures daily between Toledo on Cebu and San Carlos on Negros; the trip takes 30 minutes. There are connecting buses between San Carlos and Bacolod. Other less regular routes between these narrowly separated islands include Bato, in the far south of Cebu, to Tampi; from Tangil to Guihulngan on the west coast; and from Hagnaya in the north to Cadiz, via Bantayan Island. Ships also operate between Dumaguete and Cebu City (P95, five hours/regular boat; P200, two hours/speed boat).

Other Places There are also connections between Cebu and Panay, Samar and Siquijor.

Getting Around

Buses run from Cebu City's Southern bus terminal to Toledo and the other west-coast departure points for nearby Negros.

CEBU CITY

Cebu City is the capital and main town, and Colon St is claimed to be the oldest street in the Philippines. The city is currently undergoing considerable redevelopment and modernisation. It's an easy-going place with plenty of places to stay and eat.

Information

Tourist Office The tourist office (☎ 96518, 82329) is in the GMC building at Plaza Independencia.

Money The Philippine National Bank, near Cebu City Hall, and some department stores (eg Gaisano Metro on Colon St) are good places to change money. American Express (☎ 253 7059) has moved to Metrobank Plaza, 6th floor, Osmeña Blvd. It is open Monday to Friday from 8.30 am to 4 pm. All branches of the Equitable Bank give cash advances on Visa and MasterCard. Citibank, Osmeña Blvd, has an ATM for Visa and MasterCard.

Telephone The area code for Cebu City is 032.

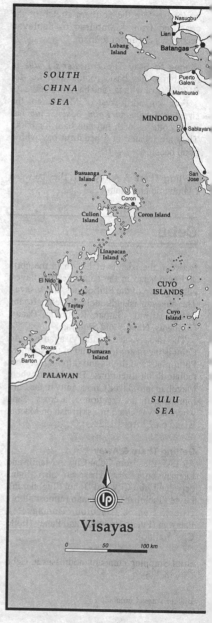

Visayas

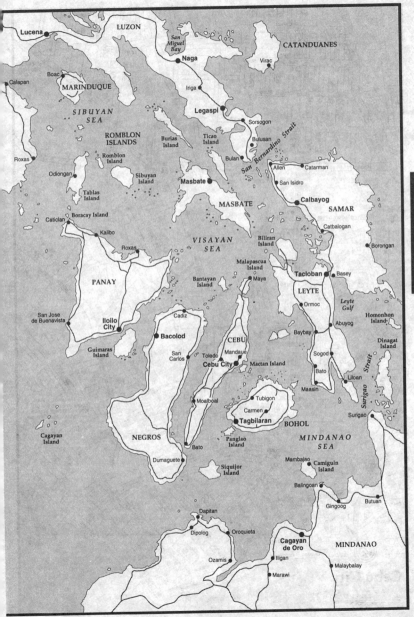

Cebu City

0   250   500 m

PLACES TO STAY

2	Mayflower Pension House
6	Cebu Mintel
7	Cebu Grand Hotel & The Apartelle
9	Kukuk's Nest Pension House & Tonros Apartelle
12	Myrna's Pensionne
15	West Gorordo Hotel
20	St Moritz Hotel
23	Gali Pension House
25	Casa Loreto Pension House
26	Jasmine Pension
27	Verbena Pension House
30	Elegant Circle Inn
31	Park Place Hotel
32	Fuente Pension House
48	Cebu Midtown Hotel
49	Kan-Irag Hotel
51	Emsu Hotel
53	Jasmine Pension
54	Arbel's Pension House
57	Jovel Pension House
59	YMCA
60	Diplomat Hotel
66	Teo-Fel Pension House
67	Cebu Elicon House
72	Golden Valley Inn
74	Hotel de Mercedes & McSherry Pension House
75	Century Hotel
81	Cebu Hallmark Hotel
84	Hotel Victoria de Cebu
85	Ruftan Pensione
86	Centrepoint Hotel
87	Pacific Tourist Inn
90	Patria de Cebu

PLACES TO EAT

3	Food Street
4	Boulevard Restaurant
9	Kukuk's Nest Restaurant
13	Pistahan Seafood Restaurant
14	Coffee House 24 & Maiko Nippon Restaurant
15	Family Choice Restaurant
16	Europa Delicatessen & Butcher Shop
18	Royal Concourse Restaurant
20	L' Oasis Garden Restaurant
22	Govinda's
29	Dunkin Donuts
33	Ginza Restaurant & McDonald's
34	Old Cebu Restaurant
35	Mikado Japanese Restaurant
36	Ding Qua Qua Dimsum House
37	Swiss Restaurant
40	Alavar's Seafoods House
41	Grand Majestic Restaurant
42	Lighthouse Restaurant
44	Shakey's Pizza
45	La Dolce Vita Restaurant & Vienna Kaffee-Haus
46	Mister Donut
47	Ric's Food Express
50	Sammy's Restaurant
51	McDonald's
55	Cosia sa Cebu Restaurant
60	Europa Delicatessen & Butcher Shop
61	Café Adriatico
70	Our Place Restaurant
76	Pete's Kitchen & Mini Food Center
77	Snow Sheen Restaurant
78	Snow Sheen Restaurant
84	Visayan Restaurant
85	Ruftan Café

OTHER

1	Provincial Capitol
5	Cebu Doctors Hospital
7	Bouraq Airlines, Grand Air, KLM & Philippine Airlines
8	Qantas Airways & Singapore Airlines (Silk Air)
9	Duty-Free Shop
10	Frankfurter Hof Folkhouse
11	Cebu Holiday & Fitness Center
16	Q C Pavilion, Continental Airlines, Northwest Airlines, Qantas Airways, Scandinavian Airlines & Thai Airways International
17	PCI Bank & US Consulate
19	Avis
20	St Moritz Disco-Nightclub
21	Ayala Center
24	Rizal Memorial Library & Museum
28	Fruit Stalls
35	Mango Plaza & National Book Store
36	Rustan's Department Store
37	Ball's Disco, Cities Music Lounge & Robinson's Foodorama
38	Iglesia Ni Kristo Church
39	Cathay Pacific Airways & The Rivergate Mall
43	Steve's Music Bar
44	Puerto Rico Bar
48	Robinson's Department Store, American Express & Metrobank Plaza
49	Bachelor's Too, Love City Disco & Thunderdome
50	Silver Dollar Bar
52	Anzar Coliseum
56	Sacred Heart Hospital
58	Bookmark
62	ABC-Liner Bus Terminal
63	Caretta Cemetery
64	Old Northern Bus Terminal
65	Chinese Cemetery
68	Southern Bus Terminal
69	Central Bank
71	San Carlos University
73	Casa Gorordo Museum
79	Minibuses to Argao
80	Gaisano Metro Department Store
82	Gaw Department Store
83	Gaisano Main Department Store
88	Carbon Market
89	Cebu Cathedral
91	Basilica Minore del Santo Niño
92	Magellan's Cross
93	City Hall & Philippine National Bank (PNB)
94	Plaza Independencia
95	Tourist Office
96	Fort San Pedro
97	Immigration Office
98	General Post Office

PHILIPPINES

Emergency In case of emergency, the tourist police (☎ 221136) are available around the clock.

Fort San Pedro

This is the oldest Spanish fort in the country. It was built in 1565, by Legaspi, to keep out marauding pirates. It is currently being restored and the main entrance is very impressive. Entry is P10.

Magellan's Cross

A small circular building, opposite the town hall, houses a hollow cross which is said to contain fragments of the cross brought here by Magellan and used in the first conversions to Christianity.

Basilica Minore del Santo Niño

Not far from the Magellan shrine, the Santo Niño statuette is the main attraction in this basilica, built in 1740. This image of Jesus as a child was said to have been given to Queen Juana of Cebu by Magellan on the queen's baptism in 1521. It's the oldest religious relic in the country.

Taoist Temple

Overlooking the town, in the ritzy Beverly Hills residential area, is a magnificent Taoist temple. To get to the temple take a Lahug jeepney and ask to stop at Beverly Hills – you've then got a 1.5 km walk uphill. Alternatively, take a taxi for about P40.

Casa Gorordo Museum

In the downtown Parian district, the impressive Casa Gorordo Museum is a beautifully restored and period-furnished home dating from the turn of the century. Admission costs P15; it is closed on Sunday.

Places to Stay

The amiable *Ruftan Pensione* (☎ 79138), on Legaspi St, is close to the centre. It's a nice place and has unassuming but clean rooms with fan from P135 to P440. A good bet is the *Cebu Elicon House* (☎ 253 0367), on the corner of P del Rosario and General Junquera Sts: a dorm bed costs P95 with air-con, and rooms cost P130/200 with fan and P360/430 with air-con and bath.

Also in the acceptable price range, the *McSherry Pension House* (☎ 254 4792) has rooms with fan and bath for P250/300 and with air-con and bath for P350/450. It's a pleasant central place in a quiet lane off Pelaez St, next to the Hotel de Mercedes.

The peaceful *Mayflower Pension House* (☎ 253 7233) on Villalon Drive, East Capitol Site, has rooms with fan for P180/230 or with air-con and bath for P350/410.

If you're looking for a pleasant, old-style place to stay, check out the *Kukuk's Nest Pension House* (☎ 231 5180) at 157 Gorordo Ave. Its cosily furnished rooms with fan cost P224/392 and P616 with air-con and bath. There's a nice garden restaurant, too. Finally, the *Verbena Pension House* (☎ 253 4440) at 584A Don Gil Garcia St has clean, really nice rooms of various sizes, all with air-con and bath for P370/430.

If you're looking for cheaper accommodation, it's worth asking if they've got rooms without air-con at the better quality places in Cebu City. They'll always try to steer you towards air-con first.

Places to Eat

There are lots of places to eat at in Cebu City, many of them along Colon St – you can, of course, eat much more cheaply off this beaten track. Notable for its excellent, inexpensive food, the *Visayan Restaurant* in V Gullas St has big portions and friendly service. The *Snow Sheen Restaurant*, near the corner of Osmeña Blvd and Colon St, has very good, low-priced Chinese and Filipino food for about P80. *Pete's Kitchen*, on Pelaez St, also has reasonably priced Chinese and Filipino food. Nearby is *Pete's Mini Food Center*, a big, partly open-air restaurant.

The *Food Center* on the top floor of the Gaisano Metro department store gives you the opportunity to wander around and try something unusual.

For a good breakfast try the *Ruftan Café* on Legaspi St, and for affordable western food (P80) and cold beer *Our Place* in Pelaez St is the place to go.

Maxilom Ave (it used to be called Mango Ave) has lots of places to eat, including a *Shakey's Pizza*, the *Lighthouse* for Filipino food (P150) and the *Swiss Restaurant* with excellent, although not exactly cheap, European food. About five minutes walk from Maxilom Ave, on Don Ramon Aboitiz St near the corner of Juana Osmeña St, *Govinda's* serves well cooked, tasty vegetarian dishes at reasonable prices (student meal P30).

The *Royal Concourse* on Gorordo Ave is a big, very clean, self-service restaurant with inexpensive Filipino, Chinese and Japanese dishes. For fresh seafood, try the *Pistahan Seafood Restaurant* on the same street.

Things to Buy
In Cebu you'll find lots of shell jewellery and guitars. The interesting Carbon Market, south of Magellanes St, sells produce and handicrafts. Making guitars is a big business on Mactan Island near Cebu City; they vary widely in price and quality.

Getting There & Away
There are several buses daily from the Southern bus terminal on Bacalso Ave for the 1½ hour trip from Cebu City to Toledo on the other coast. You also find buses at the Southern bus terminal for Bato (another departure point for Negros) and Moalboal. If you want to travel to northern Cebu (eg Hagnaya for Bantayan Island or Maya for Malapascua Island), Cebu City's new Northern bus terminal on Soriano St is where you will normally get on the bus, although some buses still leave from the old Northern bus terminal on MJ Cuenco Ave.

Getting Around
The Airport There are shuttle buses to the city (P40; one hour). They stop at the Park Place Hotel at Fuente Osmeña. Alternatively, you can take a taxi for P150 or take a tricycle from near the terminal to the Mactan Bridge (P10) and a jeepney into the city (P4.50) from there.

Jeepney Jeepneys around Cebu City cost P1.50.

Taxi There are also lots of taxis, which cost P10 (air-con taxis cost P16) for the first 500 metres and P1 for every additional 200 metres.

AROUND CEBU
Mactan Island
The island where Magellan met Lapu-Lapu (and lost) is now the site of Cebu's airport and is joined to Cebu by a bridge. Guitars, one of the big industries in Cebu, are manufactured here and there are monuments to both Lapu-Lapu and Magellan.

Places to Stay Around the island there are now a number of fine but expensive (US$100) beach resorts.

In Lapu-Lapu, near Mactan Bridge, there are a couple of less expensive hotels. The small *Mactan Bridgeside Hotel* (☎ 340 1703) has rooms with TV, fan and bath for P385, and with air-con and bath for P700. They also have motorcycles for rent.

Getting There & Away Several jeepneys ply between Cebu City and Lapu-Lapu daily (P4.50).

Bantayan Island
Beautiful Bantayan Island, off the northwest coast of Cebu, has some good beaches on its south coast. The island can also be used as a stepping stone to Negros.

Places to Stay The *Santa Fe Beach Club* in Talisay, just north of Santa Fe, has basic, fairly small cottages with fan and bath for P300 and nice rooms with air-con and bath for P900. Just south of Santa Fe, the well-appointed *Kota Beach Resort* has rooms with fan from P480, cottages with fan and bath for P720 and with air-con and bath for P1080. Next to it, right on the beach, you'll find the *Budyong Beach Resort* has slightly cheaper cottages. The *Saint Josef Lodge* and the *Admiral Lodging House* are cheapies (P90 per person) of the basic variety in the town of Bantayan.

Getting There & Away Buses run from Cebu City's Northern bus terminal to San Remedio and Hagnaya (P65; three hours). There are four boats daily from Hagnaya to Santa Fe on Bantayan (P44; one hour). A daily boat connects Bantayan with Cadiz on Negros.

Malapascua Island

Beautiful little Malapascua Island is about eight km north-east of Cebu and 25 km west of Leyte. The blindingly white Bounty Beach on the south coast is a gorgeous bathing beach.

Places to Stay In Logon village, *Bebe's Lodging House* offers basic accommodation for P100/150. The *Cocobana Beach Resort* will set you back a bit more: roomy, generously appointed cottages with bath cost P650, although in the off season, from May to November, they cost P450.

Places to Eat The best places to eat on the island are *La Isla Bonita* and *Ging Ging's Flower Garden*.

Getting There & Away Buses leave from Cebu City's Northern bus terminal for Maya early in the morning (P50; 3½ hours). Outrigger boats leave Maya for Malapascua between 10.30 and 11.30 am (P25; 40 minutes). There is a boat connection between Maya and San Isidro on Leyte.

Moalboal

There's good, reasonably priced scuba diving at **Pescador Island**, near Moalboal, and a number of beach resorts near the town along **Panagsama Beach**. In Moalboal, tours with mountain bikes are getting more and more popular.

Places to Stay There's a fairly wide range of accommodation available, from simple huts right through to comfortable, air-conditioned rooms. At the lower end of the price scale, with rooms from P100/200, try *Pacita's Nipa Hut, Eve's Kiosk, Sunshine Pension House* and *Pacifico's Cottages*. Of a better standard, starting from P300, there are *Kukuk's Nest, Cora's Palm Court* and *Sumisid Lodge*.

Places to Eat There's good Filipino food at *Ising's Place* and *Emma's Store*. Slightly more expensive, but delicious, dishes can be found at *Hannah's Place* and *Visaya Bar*. The *Last Filling Station* can be recommended for a healthy breakfast and proper coffee.

Getting There & Away Numerous buses make the daily 90 km trip from Cebu City (P26; 2½ hours). A friendly bus driver may even take you right down to the beach, so it's worth asking. Otherwise take a tricycle from Moalboal for about P20.

Buses run regularly to Bato, at the southern end of the island, from where ships make the short crossing to Negros.

Bohol

It's a short ferry trip from Cebu City to the island of Bohol. The famous Chocolate Hills here are strangely rounded and look rather like chocolate drops when the vegetation turns brown in the dry season. They are about 60 km north-east of Tagbilaran, the main town. Bohol is an easy-going, quiet sort of place with some fine beaches, relatively untouched forests and interesting old churches.

There's some superb diving around Bohol. **Balicasag Island**, just 10 km south-west of Panglao Island, is surrounded by a coral reef. **Pamilacan** is a beautiful little island, 20 km south-east, that gets very few visitors. **Cabilao Island**, 30 km north-west of Tagbilaran, has excellent diving and snorkelling.

Getting There & Away

Air Most people get to Bohol via Cebu. There are PAL flights daily from Cebu City to Tagbilaran and from Manila to Tagbilaran.

Boat From Cebu City there are four fast, air-conditioned daily ferries to Tagbilaran

(P200; 1½ hours), a number of daily ferries to Tubigon (P45; three hours) and a couple to Talibon (four hours).

There are daily boats from Ubay (in the north-east of Bohol) to Bato and Maasin on Leyte (P50; three hours); a weekly ship to Manila (P550; 26 hours); and a number of services to ports in Mindanao.

TAGBILARAN

There's not much in Tagbilaran, the capital and main port, but you can make worthwhile day trips from the city.

The area code for Tagbilaran is 038.

Places to Stay

On Lesage St, the *Tagbilaran Vista Lodge* (☎ 411 3072) is fairly good, with rooms from P75/95, with fan and bath for P100/120 and with air-con and bath for P250/275. The *Nisa Travelers Inn* (☎ 411 3731) on Carlos P Garcia Ave has slightly better rooms with fan for P120/150, with fan and bath for P160/180 or with air-con and bath for P350.

On the other side of Carlos P Garcia Ave, the *Charisma Lodge* (☎ 411 3094) is your best bet among the cheaper hotels: passable, clean rooms with fan cost P100/150, P175/200 with fan and bath, and P330/350 with air-con and bath – good value.

Just off Carlos P Garcia Ave, on MH del Pilar St, the pleasant and small *Gie Garden Hotel* (☎ 411 3182) has reasonable rooms with air-con and bath for P330/480, although some of them are dark and a bit musty. The *Hotel La Roca* (☎ 411 3179) is on Graham Ave, on the northern edge of town towards the airport, and has comfortable rooms with air-con and bath from P530/660. There is a swimming pool as well.

Places to Eat

The restaurant at the *Gie Garden Hotel* has good, cheap food, as does the highly recommended *BQ Garden Restaurant* at the south end of town on Gallares St. They have a disco after 7 pm. The *Garden Café* is a pleasant place next to the church.

AROUND TAGBILARAN

The old **Punta Cruz pirate watchtower** is 15 km north, near Maribojoc. **Loon**, a few km north-west of Maribojoc, has a beautiful old church dating from 1753. **Antequera**, about 10 km north-east of Maribojoc, has a Sunday market where basketwork is sold.

At **Bool**, three km east of Tagbilaran, there's a monument commemorating the blood compact between Legaspi and Rajah Sikatuna. **Baclayon**, four km east of Bool, is the oldest town in Bohol and has one of the oldest churches in the Philippines, dating from 1595. Boats go from there to nearby Pamilacan Island.

Loay has an old church. Outrigger boats go up the Loboc River. The large **San Pedro Church** in Loboc dates from 1602 and there is a remarkable naive painting on its ceiling.

PANGLAO ISLAND

Two bridges connect Bohol to Panglao Island, where there are now several beach resorts. Located on the south-west coast, **Alona Beach** is the most popular, especially for diving. Unfortunately, bathing is spoilt a bit by the sea urchins that lurk in the sea grass and care is required. **Doljo Beach** is also good, although the water is very shallow. **Hinagdanan Cave** at Bingag in the north-east of the island is worth a look.

Places to Stay

There are about a dozen resorts to choose from at Alona Beach. Best offering for a room with fan, at P150/200, is the *Alonaville*. It has good rooms with fan and bath for P300/400 and with air-con and bath for P400/600. There's a pleasant, family-like atmosphere at *Peter's House*, where they offer spacious rooms for P200/400. A really nice place to spend the night is the *Alona Tropical*, which also has a deservedly popular restaurant. Their cottages with fan and bath cost P350.

If you like to be surrounded by lots of greenery, try the *Alona Kew White Beach*. It has fairly extensive grounds and offers cottages with fan and bath from P650 to P900 (depending on size), and with air-con and bath for P1400. They have a fine, big restaurant and also arrange excursions.

Getting There & Away

Bus JG Express buses go several times a day from Tagbilaran to the island. Those marked 'Panglao' go right across the island to Panglao town, near Doljo Beach. Those marked 'Panglao-Tauala' go along the southern coast and detour to Alona Beach (P10; 45 minutes).

Tricycle From Tagbilaran to Alona Beach by tricycle costs P100 and takes about an hour.

CHOCOLATE HILLS

Legend has it that the Chocolate Hills (there are more than 1000 of them, up to 50 metres high) are either the teardrops of a heartbroken giant or the debris from a battle between two giants. The scientific explanations for these curious, similarly shaped hills are more mundane: some think they are the result of volcanic eruptions when the area was submerged; others believe they were formed by the weathering of marine limestone over impermeable claystone.

Hiking in the area is best in the dry season, from December to May, when the vegetation has turned brown and the hills are at their most 'chocolate'-like.

Places to Stay

The *Hostel Chocolate Hills* is right in among the hills, about 53 km from Tagbilaran. It's a km off the main road at the top of one of the higher hills. Dorm beds are P75 and double rooms with bath and balcony (beautiful view) are P200. The hostel has been neglected and looks a bit run-down at the moment, but there are plans to have it renovated. There's a restaurant and a swimming pool, though the latter is unusable most of the time.

Getting There & Away

Carmen, the town for the Chocolate Hills, is 58 km from Tagbilaran. You must get out four km before Carmen, so don't forget to tell the driver. It is about a one km walk from the main road to the Chocolate Hills

complex. There are several St Jude Bus and Arples Line buses a day from Tagbilaran to Carmen (P20; two hours). It's about two hours by bus between the Chocolate Hills and Tubigon.

TUBIGON, TALIBON & UBAY

Tubigon is a small town from where ships operate to and from Cebu. Talibon also has shipping services to Cebu and is the jumping-off point for nearby Jao Island. From Ubay, on the east coast, boats run to Leyte.

Places to Stay

The *Cosare Lodging House* in Tubigon has simple but clean rooms with fan for P60/120. The friendly people at the *Lapyahan Lodge*, at Pasil Beach in Talibon, have OK rooms with fan for P70/120 and with fan and bath for P100/180. In Ubay, you can stay at the *Royal Orchid Pension House*, where rooms with fan are P100, or at the *Casa Besas Pension House*, where rooms cost P160 with fan and bath, and P300 with air-con and bath.

Getting There & Away

From Tubigon buses to Carmen take two hours, and to Tagbilaran, 1½ hours. Buses from Tagbilaran to Talibon take four hours and go via Carmen and the Chocolate Hills. Tagbilaran to Ubay buses also go via Carmen.

Leyte

Another of the Visayan Islands, Leyte is notable for being the island where MacArthur fulfilled his promise to return to the Philippines: towards the end of WWII Allied forces landed here and started to push out the Japanese. Like the neighbouring island of Samar, few westerners get to Leyte, so you can expect to be stared at a lot. Although there are some outstanding national parks and an impressive mountain region there is little tourist development.

Getting There & Away
Air PAL flies to Tacloban daily from Cebu City and Manila.

Bus The San Juanico Bridge connects Leyte with neighbouring Samar. There are daily buses from Tacloban, via Catbalogan and Calbayog in Samar, right through Luzon to Manila – a 28 hour trip in total.

Boat Ships operate between Cebu City and a variety of ports around Leyte, eg Ormoc (P76, six hours/regular boat; P200, two hours/speed boat), Maasin (P86, six hours/regular boat; P200, two hours/speed boat) or Palompon (P67, five hours). Outriggers operate daily between Carmen on Cebu and Isabel on Leyte (four hours) and between Maya in northern Cebu and San Isidro (two hours).

Daily outriggers connect Ubay on Bohol with Bato and Maasin (P100; four hours). Buses to Mindanao run from Tacloban to Liloan in the south of the island; from there a ferry takes you across to Lipata, 10 km north-west of Surigao, and buses continue to Cagayan de Oro or Davao. The ferry crossing takes three hours. There are also ships from Maasin to Surigao.

Getting Around
Buses go hourly between Tacloban and Ormoc (P40; 2½ hours). Ormoc to Baybay and Tacloban-Baybay-Maasin also have regular bus services.

TACLOBAN
The small port of Tacloban is the main city of Leyte and home town of the great shoe collector, Mrs Marcos. Seven km out of town, **Red Beach** (it isn't red – that was just its WWII code name) is the spot where General Douglas MacArthur fulfilled his famous 'I shall return' pledge in October 1944. There's a memorial showing MacArthur wading ashore. Take a jeepney there, but return by getting another jeepney in the same direction; it loops back via Palo

Information
The tourist office (☎ 321 2048, 321 4333) is in Senator Enage St, at Children's Park.

The area code for Tacloban is 053.

Places to Stay
Tacloban offers a wide variety of places to stay. *Cecilia's Lodge* (☎ 321 2815) at 178 Paterno St is basic but reasonably good value: from around P100 – more expensive with bathroom or air-con. *Manabó Lodge* (☎ 321 3727) on Zamora St has fairly good rooms from P160/250. *Leyte Normal University House* (☎ 321 3175) on Paterno St is pricier, with rooms from around P200 to P350.

More expensive places include the value-for-money *Tacloban Plaza Hotel* (☎ 321 2444) on Justice Romualdez St and the *Manhattan Inn* (☎ 321 4170) on Rizal Ave. Both are good, clean places with comfortable, similarly priced air-con rooms for P350 to P600.

Places to Eat
You can start the day at the *Good Morning Restaurant*, with its adjoining bakery, on Zamora St. Feel like some Italian food for a change? Then check out *Giuseppe's* on Avenida Veteranos. But if it's seafood you're after, the inexpensive but excellent *Angus Restaurant* is a must. You can find it on the southern outskirts of town, about two km from the centre, on San Pedro Bay.

ORMOC
Ormoc is just the jumping-off point for boats to Cebu. The 40 km **Leyte Mountain Trail** starts near Ormoc. It crosses right over the island from Lake Danao, at about 700 metres altitude, to Lake Mahagnao. From there you can go down to Burauen, where there's a bus connection to Tacloban (last bus leaves about 3 pm).

The area code for Ormoc is 05351.

Places to Stay
The *Hotel Don Felipe* (☎ 64661) on Bonifacio St has immaculate rooms with fan and bath for P190/290; the more expensive

rooms with air-con are the best you'll find in Ormoc. On the same street, the *Pongos Hotel* (☎ 2482) has pretty good rooms with fan and bath for P200/310, or with air-con and bath for P385/550.

Places to Eat

The *Bahia Coffee Shop* at the Hotel Don Felipe is a good restaurant, or try the *Magnolia Sizzler* on the corner of Bonifacio and Lopez Jeana Sts.

Biliran

Biliran was a sub-province of Leyte until 1992, when it became an independent province with Naval as the capital. The island is connected by bridge with the main island of Leyte.

The densely vegetated interior is mountainous and full of extinct volcanoes up to 1200 metres high. It's no use looking for dream beaches here, but countless waterfalls offer a refreshing chance to cool down instead.

Places to Stay

Only a handful of places in Naval offer accommodation in the basic category. At the *Bayview Lodge* in Castin St, passable rooms with fan go for P50/110 and with bath for P150. Air-con rooms with bath cost P250/350 and are a bit overpriced. The small veranda is a nice place to relax. Expect real hospitality and a family atmosphere at the *LM Lodge* in Vincentillo St, where they have basic but clean rooms with fan for P70/140, and with fan and bath for P140/200.

The pleasant little *Agta Beach Resort* is located on a pretty bay a few km north of Almeria. Basic rooms with fan and bath cost P75/150 and clean, well-furnished rooms with air-con and bath cost P350. The beach here is not really suitable for swimming, as the water is too shallow, but the beautiful, natural swimming pool in Masagongsong, three km further north, has cool spring water; admission is P2.

Places to Eat

While enjoying the friendly, pleasant surroundings of the *Gemini Coffee Shop* near the jetty in Naval, you can get Filipino food as well as a small selection of cakes. It's open until 8.30 pm.

Getting There & Away

Biliran Island can be reached by taking a bus from Tacloban to Naval (P50; three hours) or from Ormoc to Naval (2½ hours).

Samar

The large Visayan island of Samar acts as a stepping stone from Luzon to Leyte. There is a regular ferry service from Matnog, at the southern end of Luzon, to Allen and San Isidro at the northern end of Samar. From there, the Pan-Philippine Highway runs along the picturesque coast and a bridge connects Samar with Leyte.

This recently constructed road has made transport through Samar much easier. Elsewhere the island is fairly undeveloped so finding transport can be hard going. Samar also experiences guerrilla activity so check the situation before venturing there. The northern part of Samar and the west coast are usually OK. The **Sohoton National Park**, near Basey in southern Samar, is the island's outstanding attraction.

Getting There & Away

Bus Buses between Catbalogan and Tacloban, in Leyte, take two hours.

Boat There are a number of ferries daily between Matnog and Allen, and between Matnog and San Isidro. The crossing takes 1½ to two hours.

CALBAYOG

Calbayog is just another 'through' town, although the road there from Allen runs along the coast almost the entire way. The views are especially fine around **Viriato**, between Allen and Calbayog. The **Blanca**

Aurora Falls are about 50 km south-east of Calbayog. They're reached by riverboat to Buenavista (one hour) from near the village of Gandara.

Places to Stay

At the *San Joaquin Inn*, at the market on the corner of Nijaga and Orquin Sts, basic rooms with fan cost P70/140 and with fan and bath P280/350. Their restaurant serves very good food, despite its appearance; and it's cheap too.

The best hotel in Calbayog is the *Central Inn* on Navarro St, where very clean rooms with air-con and bath cost P500. It also has a rooftop restaurant.

Getting There & Away

There are a couple of daily Philippine Eagle buses and several jeepneys between Catarman and Calbayog, via Allen. Several buses a day go from Catbalogan to Calbayog (two hours). There are some slower jeepneys.

CATBALOGAN

There are beaches around Catbalogan, but it's really just a stepping stone to Tacloban on Leyte. Buses cross to the east coast from here.

Places to Stay

Now that the inaptly named Fortune Hotel has been closed down and Tony's Hotel has burned down, there is no longer a big choice in Catbalogan. If it's still open, *Kikay's Hotel* on Curry Ave will have basic singles/doubles with fan for P100/170 and one double room with air-con and bath for P280.

At the southern end of town right on the seafront, you can find the quite new *Maqueda Bay Hotel*, where you can spend the night in clean, spacious air-con rooms with bath for P500, P600 with TV. There's a gorgeous view of the ocean from the restaurant.

Getting There & Away

At least four buses run daily from Catbalogan, via Borongan (P30; three hours), to Guiuan on the south-east coast of Samar (P60; five hours).

Romblon

This scattering of small islands in the Visayan group is in the middle of the area bordered by South Luzon, Masbate, Panay and Mindoro. It's noted for its marble: quality marble is exported and an extensive range of carved marble souvenirs is produced. There are some good beaches and the tranquil town of Romblon has a notable cathedral. The three main islands of the group are Romblon and the larger islands of Sibuyan and Tablas.

Getting There & Away

Air PAL flies three times a week between Manila and Tugdan on Tablas Island.

Boat Regular boats operate between Lucena on Luzon and Magdiwang on Sibuyan, and between Lucena and Romblon town on Romblon. There are also services twice a week between Manila and Romblon town. Other boats, some of them large outriggers, operate between Romblon ports and Masbate, Mindoro and Panay.

Mindoro to Tablas and Tablas to Boracay travel, used by some intrepid travellers as a route between the two popular beach centres of Puerto Galera and Boracay, can be a bit risky. There have been some unhappy incidents at Boracay (no deaths, but people have lost all their gear), and the Roxas (Mindoro) to Tablas (Romblon) boats are particularly bad.

ROMBLON ISLAND

The small port of **Romblon** on Romblon Island is the capital of the province. **San Andres** and **Santiago Hill forts** were built by the Spanish in 1640, while **San Joseph's Cathedral** dates from 1726 and houses a collection of antiques. There are good views from the **Sabang** and **Apunan lighthouses**. **Lugbung Island** shelters the bay and has a beautiful white beach, as does nearby **Kobrador Island**.

Places to Stay

The *Moreno Seaside Lodge*, by the harbour, has rooms of the most basic variety for P60/120. A much better choice in town is the *Marble Hotel*, where rooms with fan and bath cost P120/150.

You can stay at the *Palm Beach Resort* at Lomas Beach, four km south of Romblon town; it's P150 per person for a cottage with fan and marble bath. *D'Marble Beach Cottages* in San Pedro is a well-looked-after place with neat cottages for P170 and P220.

Places to Eat

The *Kawilihan Food House* is by the harbour, but the *Tica Inn* is probably the best restaurant in town.

Getting There & Away

Boats go about four times weekly between Romblon town and Sibuyan in two hours. Daily outriggers to San Agustin, on Tablas, take 45 minutes.

TABLAS ISLAND

Tablas is the largest island in the Romblon group. The main towns are San Agustin, Odiongan, Looc and Santa Fe.

Places to Stay

The *Kamella Lodge* in San Agustin has rooms with fan for P100/200, with fan and bath for P350 and with air-con and bath for P450/650. In Odiongan, the *Shellborne Hotel* costs P125/250 with fan and bath. In Looc, *Tablas Pension House* across from the market costs P100/200. Tugdan has the *Airport Pension House*, where modest but clean rooms with fan and bath cost P150/300.

Getting There & Away

Air Flights to Tugdan from Manila are almost always heavily booked. Jeepneys meet the plane and go to San Agustin (one hour), Santa Fe (one hour) and Looc (45 minutes).

Boat San Agustin is the port for boats to Romblon town. Odiongan's small harbour is just outside the town and, from here, boats go to Batangas on Luzon and Roxas on Mindoro. Looc is the port for boats to Boracay, and there's a connecting jeepney service from the airport in Tugdan. There's also a daily boat from Santa Fe to Carabao (the island between Tablas and Boracay), Boracay and Caticlan on Panay. The two hour trip to Boracay costs P70.

SIBUYAN ISLAND

Sibuyan is more mountainous and less developed than the other islands. There are several **waterfalls** and the 2050-metre-high **Mt Guiting-Guiting**.

Panay

The large, triangular island of Panay in the Visayan group has a number of decaying forts and watchtowers – relics from the days of the Moro pirates. There are also some interesting Spanish churches, especially on the south coast, which stretches from Iloilo City around the southern promontory at Anini-y to San Jose de Buenavista. The Ati-Atihan Festival in January, in Kalibo, is one of the most popular in the Philippines. Last, but far from least, the delightful little island of Boracay, off the north-western tip of the island, is one of the Philippines' major travellers' centres.

Getting There & Away

Air There is a variety of flight services to Panay from Manila, Cebu City and other major centres. Air Philippines flies from Manila to Iloilo City; PAL flies from Manila to Iloilo City, Kalibo and Roxas, and from Cebu City to Iloilo City and Kalibo; and Air Ads, Asian Spirit and Pacific Airways fly from Manila to Caticlan. Travellers bound for Boracay head for Kalibo or Caticlan, but the Kalibo flights are often heavily booked.

Boat You can reach Panay by boat from Cebu, Leyte, Luzon, Mindanao, Mindoro, Negros, Palawan and Romblon. The shortest crossing is the two hour trip from Bacolod in Negros to Iloilo City. There are several boats daily.

It's possible (with some difficulty) to travel from Mindoro to Boracay, but this can be a dangerous trip as the outrigger boats are often no match for severe conditions in the Tablas Strait.

ILOILO CITY

Iloilo City is the capital of Iloilo Province and the main city on Panay. It is a large town which was very important during the Spanish era. There's the small but interesting **Museo Iloilo** ('window on the past') in the city, plus the coral **Molo Church**. Iloilo City is noted for its *jusi* (raw silk) and *piña* (pine-apple-fibre) weaving. Today, Sinamay Dealer on Osmeña St has the only remaining loom. The very colourful Dinagyang festival is held in January.

Information

The tourist office (☎ 270245) is on Boni-facio Drive.

The area code for Iloilo City is 033.

Places to Stay

The popular *Family Pension House* (☎ 27070), on General Luna St, has clean, acceptable rooms with fan and bath for P175/225, or air-con doubles with bath from P350 to P700.

The *Original River Queen Hotel* (☎ 270176), on Bonifacio Drive, needs some mainte-nance but is still OK for the price: rooms with fan and bath are P220/300 or with air-con and bath P400/500. Other middle-bracket places include *The Castle Hotel* (☎ 81021) on Bonifacio Drive, close to the River Queen Hotel. It's an older, renovated building with an impressive façade. The rooms are small but clean. Singles with fan and bath cost P280, with air-con and bath P450, doubles with air-con and bath are available from P550.

Centrally situated in a lane between JM Basa and Iznart Sts, *Centercon Hotel* (☎ 73431) has rooms with fan for P300 (noisy) and com-fortable air-con rooms with bath for P390/455.

Places to Eat

You can get good Chinese and Filipino meals for about P75 in JM Basa St: upstairs in the *Mansion House Restaurant* and in *The Summer House*, which also serves a proper western breakfast. The airy *Tree House Res-taurant*, belonging to the Family Pension House, has a pleasant atmosphere and is well known for its good steaks.

Batchoy is a speciality of the western Visayas and consists of beef, pork and liver in noodle soup; the *Oak Barrel* on Valeria St is one of the best of the batchoy restaurants. You can eat Filipino food with your fingers at *Nena's Manokan* restaurant in General Luna St. However, the most popular, and probably the best, local restaurant is called *Tatoy's Manokan & Seafood*; it is located at Villa Beach on the western edge of town, about eight km from the city centre.

Things to Buy

Apart from fabrics, such as *barong* shirts made from *piña*, Iloilo City is known for shellcraft and is a good town in which to look for 'santos', antique statues of the saints.

Getting There & Away

Buses from Iloilo City to Kalibo and Caticlan (where boats run to Boracay) leave from the Tanza bus terminal on the corner of Rizal and Ledesma Sts.

Getting Around

The airport is about seven km out and a PU-Cab there costs about P50.

KALIBO

The only real interest here is the annual **Ati-Atihan Festival** in January – the Mardi Gras of the Philippines. Similar festivals are held elsewhere in the country but this one is the most popular.

The area code for Kalibo is 036.

Places to Stay

Gervy's Lodge (☎ 3081) on R Pastrada St has simple, clean rooms for P80/160. In the same street the *RB Lodge* (☎ 2604) has basic and fairly good rooms with fan for P100/200, or doubles with air-con and bath for P350.

There are a couple of passable hotels on S Martelino St. The *Glowmoon Hotel* (☎ 3193) has acceptable rooms with fan for P250/400 and rooms with air-con and bath for P700. Also in this price category, but with better rooms, is the spruce *Garcia Legaspi Mansion* (☎ 662 3251) on the third floor at 159 Roxas Ave. Rooms with fan and bath cost P350/450 and with air-con and bath from P500 to P850.

During the Ati-Atihan Festival, prices in Kalibo may triple and it can be almost impossible to find a hotel room.

Places to Eat

The *Peking House Restaurant* on Martyrs St has outstanding Chinese food; the set menu for P65 can be recommended. The *Glowmoon Hotel* also has a restaurant with excellent, if not so cheap, food.

Getting There & Away

Air PAL flights between Manila and Kalibo are very heavily booked, so make reservations well ahead of time and reconfirm as early as possible. PAL also flies between Cebu City and Kalibo.

Bus Ceres Liner buses operate from Iloilo City to Kalibo daily (P60; five hours). From Kalibo the buses leave from the service station on the southern edge of town.

From Kalibo to Caticlan, where boats cross to Boracay, takes about two hours by jeepney from Roxas Ave (P30). If you arrive by plane from Manila in the early afternoon you might be able to get to Boracay before sunset. After the flight from Manila arrives, comfortable air-con buses leave the airport for Caticlan. The trip takes about 1½ hours (P150, including the boat transfer, which costs P15).

CATICLAN

Outrigger boats cross from Caticlan to Boracay and there's also a small airport for the increasingly popular flights from Manila. Sunday – market day – merits a trip from Boracay.

Getting There & Away

Bus There are direct buses from Iloilo City to Caticlan but it takes seven hours – five to Kalibo and two more to Caticlan.

Jeepney Jeepneys from Kalibo leave several times daily (P30; two hours).

BORACAY

This superb little island, off the north-western tip of Panay, has beautiful clear water and splendid beaches. It is about nine km long, only a km wide in the middle, and you can walk across it in just 15 minutes.

Beach and water activities, general lazing and watching the sunset are daily attractions at this popular spot. Although electricity has arrived on Boracay it's still a good idea to bring along a torch (flashlight).

Information

The DOT runs a small office in Manggayad, at about the middle of White Beach. The Allied Bank along the main road will change travellers' cheques and cash.

Things to See

Besides the snorkelling spots and wonderful sunsets, there are two minor attractions at the northern end of the island: the **Museum of Shells & Native Costumes** at Ilig-Iligan, and a **cave** inhabited by fruit bats between Ilig-Iligan and Yapak.

Places to Stay

There are three little villages connected by walking tracks – Yapak at the north, Balabag in the middle and Manoc-Manoc in the south. Accommodation is in comfortable cottages for two with a veranda and, usually, with a bathroom. Recently the prices have gone up dramatically, and the cheapest accommodation is now P250, although hard to find. But in the off season, from June to October, Boracay seemed a real bargain and some places go down to P100 for a cottage. There are also now a handful of much flashier places, some of them at the more remote beaches.

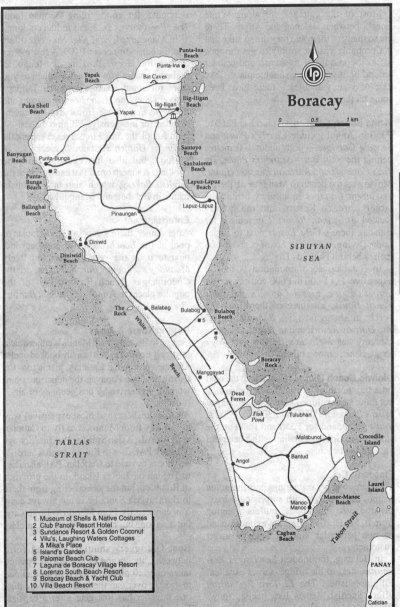

Boracay

1. Museum of Shells & Native Costumes
2. Club Panoly Resort Hotel
3. Sundance Resort & Golden Coconut
4. Vilu's, Laughing Waters Cottages & Mika's Place
5. Island's Garden
6. Palomar Beach Club
7. Laguna de Boracay Village Resort
8. Lorenzo South Beach Resort
9. Boracay Beach & Yacht Club
10. Villa Beach Resort

Most of the cottages are along White Beach, between Balabag and Angol. There are so many of them and they are so alike that it's probably easiest simply to get dropped off in the middle of the beach and wander around until you find a suitable place. Take care of your valuables – there have been some thefts.

White Beach Good cheap places at P250 to P350 in Angol include *Charly's Place* and *Seaside Cottages* – both about 100 metres behind the Sulu Bar – *Moreno's Place*, *Tin Tin's Cottages* and *Austrian Pension House*. Moving up the beach to Manggayad, there's *St Vincent Cottages* in an alley behind the larger Lorenzo Resort, and the quietly located *Ati-Atihan Resort*. Convenient for Balabag there's *GP's Resort* next to Lapu-Lapu Diving, and *Villa Lourdes* about 100 metres behind Nautilus Diving.

In Balabag, accommodation is mostly expensive. For P400 to P600 you can stay at *Serina's Place*, *Fiesta Cottages* and *Bans Beach House*, all three of them near the beach; in Manggayad, it's *Bahay Kaibigan* and *Dalisay Resort*; and in Angol, this price category has *Melinda's Garden* and *Roy's Rendezvous*, among others.

Diniwid Beach Diniwid Beach is in the next little bay north of White Beach; tourism is not quite so developed here. You can stay at *Mika's Place* for P250 and P300, for P300 at *Vilu's Place*, and for P350 and P500 on the slope at the *Golden Coconut* with a beautiful view of the beach.

Places to Eat
There are so many restaurants here that some tempt customers in with surprisingly inexpensive, yet sumptuous, buffets (ranging from P75 to P120). Others have concentrated on one particular kind of food to attract customers.

In Balabag, the modest *Sea Lovers Restaurant*, next to the bridge, serves excellent Filipino dishes. The *El Toro Restaurant* offers Spanish dishes like paella; *Jony's Place* has Mexican; and *Zur Kleinen Kneipe* is popular for good, filling German food. *True Food* serves excellent Indian cooking.

In Manggayad, *Nigi Nigi Nu Noos* offers a four-course dinner for P100. A few metres further, the *Green Yard* has a Mongolian barbecue where you can eat as much as you want for about P130. Along the Talipapa market street, the *Honeybee Restaurant* and the *Nene Bell Foods House* can be recommended for inexpensive Filipino dishes.

In Angol, the *Star Fire* serves cheap meals. *Melindas Garden Restaurant* specialises in seafood, but also has excellent Filipino cooking. A superb breakfast can be had at the *English Bakery*, which also has establishments in Balabag and Manggayad.

Entertainment
After dinner, there's dancing, good music or pool at the *Beachcomber* at Balabag and, next to it, at the very popular and lively *Moondog's Shooter Bar* belonging to the Cocomangas Beach Resort. Two of the popular places in Angol are the *Sulu Bar* and *The Jungle*.

Getting There & Away
Getting to Boracay from Manila is either quick, relatively expensive and heavily booked or else it's time-consuming. Caticlan, just across the narrow strait on Panay, is the departure point whether you arrive by bus, jeepney or air.

Air The quickest (and most expensive) way to Boracay from Manila is to fly to Caticlan with Air Ads, Asian Spirit or Pacific Airways (P1700). PAL flies to Kalibo, from where it's two hours by road to Caticlan. PAL also flies to Tugdan on Tablas Island, in the province of Romblon, but the sea crossing from there to Boracay via Santa Fe is not always easy. You can also fly from Manila to Iloilo City, but it's a long bus ride from there to Caticlan.

Boat Outriggers shuttle back and forth between Caticlan and Boracay. The crossing takes only 20 minutes, but they're inclined to grossly overload the boats and more than one traveller has lost gear after a capsize. From June to November, during the south-western monsoons, the sea on the west side of Boracay can get too rough for outriggers. They then tie up on the east coast, at or near Bulabog.

There's a big outrigger between Boracay and Looc, on Tablas, twice a week, which takes about two hours in good conditions. There's also a daily one to Santa Fe on Tablas (1½ hours). There are jeepneys from Santa Fe and Looc to Tugdan, the airport on Tablas. The boat departs from Tablas when passengers arrive from the airport.

There are also several ports in north Panay, including Dumaguit and New Washington, both near Kalibo.

Guimaras

Guimaras, an island province between Panay and Negros, makes a pleasant day trip from nearby Iloilo City. **Alubihod Beach**, with its white sand, is good for swimming; it's about 45 minutes walk from Nueva Valencia. The walk to **Daliran Cave** from Buenavista is pleasant, although the cave is not that memorable. There's a beautiful view over Iloilo Strait from Bondulan Point, near Jordan, which has a giant cross standing on it.

Places to Stay
The *Colmenaras Hotel & Beach Resort* has rooms with fan and bath for P120 or cottages for P100/200; there's no bathing beach here, although there is a pool.

At Alubihod Beach the native-style cottages of the *Raymen Resort* cost P600.

Getting There & Away
Boat Small ferries cross from Iloilo City to the island almost hourly (P5; 30 minutes).

Negros

Sandwiched between Cebu and Panay, and well connected by ferry services in both directions, is the sugar island of the Philippines. Kanlaon volcano may, it is hoped, become a similar tourist attraction to the famous Mayon volcano in South Luzon. The east and south-east coasts can offer Spanish-style charm – perhaps a reason why foreigners often spend a few days in and around the pleasant little town of Dumaguete.

Getting There & Away
Air PAL flies to Bacolod and Dumaguete from Cebu City and from Manila.

Boat There are four ferry departures daily between Toledo in Cebu and San Carlos in Negros. The crossing takes just 30 minutes. Other regular services across the comparatively narrow waters between the two islands are from Tampi to Bato in the far south; Tangil to Guihulngan in the centre; and Hagnaya via Bantayan Island to Cadiz in the north. Ships also operate between Cebu City and Dumaguete.

The next island north is Panay; the popular route from Negros to Panay is the Bacolod to Iloilo City boat service, but you can also go via Guimaras Island. The Bacolod to Iloilo City ferry operates two or three times daily (P50; two hours). Allow an hour to get by jeepney from Bacolod to the Banago wharf. Other Negros to Panay connections include the daily boats from Victorias to Culasi and Malayu-an, both near Ajuy, on the east coast of Panay.

There are also frequent shipping connections between Negros and other islands, including Siquijor, Luzon (a 20 hour trip) and Mindanao.

Getting Around
Along the north and east coasts it's 313 km between Bacolod and Dumaguete, which are at opposite ends of the island. The trip takes 7½ hours (P150) and it's wise to take an express bus as it avoids the many small village stops. Bacolod to San Carlos takes four hours. The route along the west coast, from Bacolod to Dumaguete and then cutting across the island via Mabinay, is shorter and faster (5½ hours).

BACOLOD

Bacolod is a typical Filipino city of no great interest. You can visit the huge **Victoria's Milling Company**, one of the world's largest sugar refineries, 35 km north of the city. Bacolod is also one of the major ceramics centres of the Philippines.

Information

The tourist office (☎ 29021) in the city plaza has first-hand information for climbing Mt Kanlaon.

The area code for Bacolod is 034.

Places to Stay

The *Pension Bacolod* (☎ 23883) on peaceful 11th St offers good value for money: immaculate singles/doubles with fan cost P95/145, P155/200 with fan and bath, and with air-con and bath P260/335. No wonder it's often fully booked. The small, well-managed *Ester Pension* (☎ 23526) in Araneta St has tiny rooms with fan and bath for P150/200 and with air-con and bath from P300. It's OK for the money.

The centrally located *Bacolod Pension Plaza* (☎ 27076) on Cuadra St has more than 60 friendly, quiet rooms with air-con and bath from P575 to P790. Finally, the *Bascon Hotel* (☎ 23141) on Gonzaga St is neat and clean, and has comfortable air-con rooms at P550/650.

Places to Eat

Reming's & Sons Restaurant in the city plaza serves good Filipino fast food, as does the air-con *Gaisano Food Plaza* on Luzuriaga St. The *Ang Sinugba Restaurant* on San Sebastian St is clean, well kept and does 1st class native food, while *Mira's Café* on Locsin St serves native coffee.

You can get barbecues and beer at the many all-night restaurants at the *Manokan Country*, in the Reclamation Area.

Getting There & Away

Bus There are a number of Ceres Liner buses daily between Bacolod and Dumaguete via San Carlos, and two Royal Express buses via Mabinay.

Jeepney Jeepneys run to Ma-ao, Silay and Victorias.

Getting Around

The Airport A PU-Cab from the airport to the centre shouldn't cost more than P30 or you can stop a passing jeepney, as they all go to the city plaza.

Bus After the arrival of a ferry from Iloilo City, air-con shuttle buses will take you to the city plaza for P20.

Jeepney Banago Wharf is about seven km north, say P7 by jeepney or P40 by PU-Cab. The Northern bus terminal is a P2 trip on a jeepney labelled 'Shopping'.

AROUND BACOLOD
Sugar Plantations

Old steam locomotives, used on the sugar cane fields until recently, can possibly be seen at the **MSC** (Ma-ao Sugar Central) – check at the tourist office in Bacolod. Ma-ao is an hour by jeepney from Bacolod. The **Hawaiian-Philippine Sugar Company** in Silay has a 180 km rail network and some fine steam engines. Silay is only half an hour from Bacolod.

Informative and efficient guided tours of the **Vicmico** (Victorias Milling Company) plant are operated from Tuesday to Friday. Arrangements can be made at their Public Relations building. Again, there are some fine old steam locomotives, but Victorias also has the quirky **St Joseph the Worker Chapel** with its famous mural of the Angry Christ. Victorias is an hour by bus (P13) or jeepney (P8) from Bacolod and it's a further 15 minutes by jeepney (P1.50) to the 'VMC'.

DUMAGUETE

Dumaguete is a very pleasant little town, centred on the large Silliman University campus, where there's a very interesting **anthropological museum** and a cheap cafeteria. South of Dumaguete you come to a few passable beaches. **Silliman Beach**, not far from town, is fine for swimming but nothing special.

The area code for Dumaguete is 035.

Places to Stay

Jo's Lodging on Silliman Ave provides basic accommodation in rooms with a fan for P80/100. The fairly comfortable *Opena's Hotel* (☎ 225 0595) on Katada St has singles with fan at P150 and rooms with bath and TV for P350, or P450 with air-con. The *OK Pensionne House* (☎ 225 4636) on Santa Rosa St is well frequented. It has clean rooms with fan and bath for P275 and a variety of rooms with air-con and bath from P385 to P1320.

The *Insular Flintlock Hotel* (☎ 3495) on Silliman Ave near the university has excellent rooms from around P400 to P600.

Along the coast south of Dumaguete there are a few nice resorts, including the *El Dorado Beach Resort* in Dauin, *Hans & Nenita's Malatapay Cottages* in Maluay, the *Salawaki Beach Resort* in Zamboanguita and the *Kookoo's Nest Beach Resort* on Tambubo Bay.

Places to Eat

There's excellent food at the Chinese *Chin Loong Restaurant* on Rizal Blvd; particularly recommended is the special menu for P60. *N's Pizza Plaza* on Percides St is a student hang-out with fruit juices, cakes and pizzas. The roof-garden restaurant *Aldea*, on the corner of Percides and San Juan Sts, is extremely pleasant and offers good Filipino and Chinese food.

Getting There & Away

The fastest bus connection from Bacolod to Dumaguete is with Royal Express via Mabinay (5½ hours). There are also Ceres Liner buses round the southern end of the island via Hinoba-an (12 hours).

Siquijor

The island of Siquijor lies about 20 km east of southern Negros and is one of the smallest provinces in the Philippines. A surfaced road encircles this hilly island, connecting its tidy villages and small towns. Larena is its main port, Siquijor is the capital. The most popular

beaches are at Sandugan, six km north of Larena, and along the west coast at Paliton, two km north of San Juan.

Among Filipinos, Siquijor is known for its 'witches and magicians and healers with wondrous powers'. Indeed, many strange events take place on this island, especially in the mountain village of San Antonio.

Places to Stay

In Larena, the *Luisa & Son's Lodge* near the noisy wharf has basic rooms with fan for P100/150. The *Larena Pension House*, just a few minutes walk uphill from the wharf, has unpretentious but fairly good rooms with fan for P75/150.

On Sandugan Beach, you can stay for P300/350 in pleasantly decorated cottages with fan and bath at *Casa de la Playa*, *Kiwi Dive Resort* and *Paradise Beach*.

On Paliton Beach, the peaceful *Sunset Beach Cottages* have rooms for P120/150 and cottages with bath for P250.

Getting There & Away

There are two boats daily between Dumaguete on Negros and Larena (three hours), three boats weekly between Cebu City and Larena (seven hours), three boats a week between Plaridel on Mindanao and Larena (five hours) and one boat weekly between Tagbilaran on Bohol and Larena (four hours).

Getting Around

Jeepneys and tricycles are the main means of transport. A tricycle from Siquijor to Larena costs P5 per person.

Mindanao

South of the Visayas is Mindanao, the second largest of the Philippine islands and also the country's biggest trouble spot. The predominantly Muslim population has long chafed at Christian rule: Islam had already gained a toehold by the time the Spanish arrived, and throughout the Spanish era the situation varied from outright rebellion to uneasy truce. More recently, the Mindanaoans have campaigned hard for separation from the rest of the country. Armed at one time by Libya's fervent (and oil-rich) Gaddafi, the Mindanao guerrilla force (the Moro National Liberation Front, or MNLF) staged a long-running battle with government forces. Although the government and the MNLF concluded a peace agreement in 1996, it is by no means certain that peace will follow. Both radical Christian and Moslem splinter groups were against the agreement and promptly announced they would oppose it with violence if necessary. It is wise to inquire carefully and think twice before travelling through troubled areas.

The little volcanic island of Camiguin, a little offshore from Mindanao, features an easy-going, provincial lifestyle.

Getting There & Away
Air You can fly to Mindanao from Cebu City or Manila. There are flights to a number of major cities in Mindanao, including Zamboanga, Davao, Cagayan de Oro and Surigao.

Boat There are several ships weekly from Cebu City to various Mindanaoan ports and also from Leyte, Negros and Panay. From Manila there are a couple of ships each week to Zamboanga (P645; 32 hours).

There are also regular weekly ships to neighbouring Bohol, and Leyte is connected by the Liloan to Lipata (10 km north-west of Surigao) ferry service with through buses to and from Tacloban. Balingoan on Mindanao is the departure point for visits to Camiguin Island.

Getting Around
Bus It is wise to be careful when travelling by bus in Mindanao – guerrilla shoot-ups still may occur and bus travel is none too safe in any case. The tourist office will advise you on which routes are safe and which ones to forget.

From Zamboanga, there are buses to Pagadian and Dipolog. From Pagadian, you can continue to Iligan, from where another bus ride will take you to Cagayan de Oro.

Buses continue from Cagayan de Oro to Surigao, from where you cross to Leyte. Davao can be reached from Cagayan de Oro, Butuan or Surigao.

Boat There are shipping services around the coast.

SURIGAO & SIARGAO ISLAND
There are a number of beautiful small islands east of Surigao, which is located on the north-eastern tip of Mindanao. They can best be reached from General Luna on the island of Siargao, where foreigners usually head for. It's the number one destination for surfers in the Philippines.

The area code for Surigao is 08681.

Places to Stay
The *Garcia Hotel* (☎ 658) on San Nicolas St, is a fairly good place with a variety of rooms from P60/120. On Borromeo St, the *Tavern Hotel* (☎ 293) starts at P60/90 for the simplest, fan-cooled rooms and goes up to around P600 for an air-con double with bath. It's a pleasant place with a seaside restaurant.

There are a number of places to stay on Siargao Island. In General Luna, the *BRC Beach Resort* has wooden cottages, set in grassy grounds, with bath for P50 per head or P250 full board. The *Latitude 9 Beach Resort* is in a beautiful location, in Union on the south coast of Siargao. The owner's wife takes care of the cooking; P50 per meal.

Getting There & Away
Bus Several buses travel daily from Surigao to Butuan (P48; two hours), Cagayan de Oro (P125; six hours) and Davao (P155; eight hours).

From Surigao, you can travel by bus, taking the ferry across to Leyte, and on through Leyte, Samar and right through Luzon to Manila.

Boat A ferry operates daily from Surigao to Siargao Island (P40; 4½ hours).

Getting Around
The Airport A tricycle between the airport and town is about P10.

Tricycle Most boats use the wharf south of town, but the ferries to and from Leyte operate from the Lipata wharf, about 10 km north-west. A regular tricycle trip should be less than P5 per person (P50 for a 'special ride') but there are also buses.

BUTUAN
Butuan is just a junction town two hours south of Surigao by bus. It's thought that this might be the oldest settlement in the Philippines.

The area code for Butuan is 08521.

Places to Stay
The immaculately run *Hensonly Plaza Inn* (☎ 225 1340) on Villanueve St has basic, clean, but windowless, rooms for P85, more expensive rooms with fan and bath for P150/200, or with air-con and bath for P250/350. Just round the corner, on San Francisco St, the *Emerald Villa Hotel* counts as one of the best in town. Excellent rooms with fan, bath and TV cost P300/400 and are worth the money.

Getting There & Away
Butuan is about two hours by bus from Surigao with onward connections to Davao (P107; six hours), Cagayan de Oro (P75; 3½ hours) and Iligan.

BALINGOAN
Situated midway between Butuan and Cagayan de Oro, this is the port for ferries to nearby Camiguin Island.

CAGAYAN DE ORO
On the north coast, Cagayan de Oro is a friendly, clean, prospering university town. It's also the centre of the Philippines' pineapple industry. The **Xavier University Folk Museum** (Museo de Oro) is worth a visit, but otherwise there's not much to see. The giant pineapple fields are located 34 km outside of town, at Camp Phillips.

Information
The tourist office (☎ 723696) can be found just north of the town centre, in the Pelaez Sports Complex on A Velez St.

The area code for Cagayan de Oro is 08822.

Places to Stay
The *Parkview Lodge* (☎ 723223) is on T Neri St in a quiet area next to the Golden Friendship Park. It's newly renovated and the interior is pleasantly light. Rooms cost P210/270 with fan, and P480 with air-con and bath.

The *Nature's Pensionne* (☎ 723718) on T Chavez St is more expensive; clean rooms with air-con and bath cost from P460 to P790.

Places to Eat
You can get big, cheap meals at the *Bagong Lipunan Restaurant* on A Velez St. About 100 metres south of there you will find the *Persimmon Fastfoods & Bakeshoppe*, an inexpensive self-service restaurant with good, standard Filipino dishes.

Getting There & Away
There are buses almost hourly to Balingoan (P35; two hours) and Butuan. Davao is 10 hours away (P185) and Iligan only an hour. Zamboanga is a 16 hour bus trip; buses depart when full.

Getting Around
The Airport The airport is 10 km from town and P75 by taxi.

Jeepney The main bus terminal is on the edge of town beside the Agora Market and jeepneys run between there and the town centre. Look out for a Divisoria jeepney from the station or a Gusa/Cugman jeepney from the town. By taxi it's P30. The wharf is five km out.

DIPOLOG & DAPITAN
Close to the city of Dipolog, Dapitan is where Jose Rizal spent his period of exile from 1892 to 1896. The city waterworks and a grass-covered relief map of Mindanao, in

the town square, were made by Rizal. A few km away from the city is the place he stayed in, which has a dam he built to create a swimming pool. Other attractions include a fruit-bat roost and some good swimming and diving areas.

The area code for Dipolog is 065.

Places to Stay

Ranillo's Pension House (☎ 3030) on Bonifacio St in Dipolog is the best of the cheaper places, and has quite good rooms with fan for P80/100, more with bathroom or air-con. On Magsaysay St, the *Ramos Hotel* (☎ 3299) costs from P120/240 for the simplest rooms with fan.

More expensive places include the good *CL Inn* (☎ 3491) on Rizal Ave, which has comfortable rooms with air-con and bath from P300/450. The *Village Hotel* (☎ 415 2338) is at Sicayab near the beach, about three km outside Dipolog towards Dapitan. It has basic but spotless rooms of various sizes with fan and bath for P300, and with air-con and bath for P400.

Getting There & Away

Air PAL flies between Dipolog and Zamboanga.

Bus Buses from Zamboanga take about 13 hours via Pagadian, where you may have to change buses.

ZAMBOANGA

One of the most visited cities in Mindanao is Zamboanga, which acts as the gateway to the Sulu Archipelago. In early 1996 there was a series of bombings right in town, so if you intend to go there check the latest situation first.

Information

The tourist office (☎ 991 0218) is in the Lantaka Hotel, east of the town centre towards Fort Pilar and Rio Hondo.

The area code for Zamboanga is 062.

Fort Pilar & Rio Hondo

Fort Pilar is an old Spanish fort on the water-front south of the city. Some restoration is going on and there's now a **Marine Life Museum**. From the fort battlements, you get a good view to Rio Hondo, the Muslim village on stilts a little further down the coast.

Markets & Shops

The colourful **fish market** at the docks is busy in the late afternoon. In the alleys of the public markets next door there are lots of little flea-market-style shops.

Parks

The **Pasonanca Park** is a large park in the hills, a little beyond the airport – the main attraction here is a famous tree house. Nearby is **Climaco Freedom Park**, named after a murdered mayor of Zamboanga.

Islands

Ten minutes across the bay by outrigger is the island of **Santa Cruz**, which has good swimming and a beautiful beach. It costs around P200 to rent a boat for the round trip. The island of **Basilan**, about a two hour boat ride away, is the centre for the colourful Yakan tribe.

Places to Stay

Atilano's Pension House (☎ 991 4225), on Mayor Jaldon St, is a comfortable place with big rooms from P140 to P280.

About 200 metres further south and also on Mayor Jaldon St, the *L'Mirage Pension House* (☎ 991 3962) is of a better standard; well-kept rooms with fan cost P175/225, P225/275 with fan and bath, and with air-con and bath, P350/385. This is immaculate accommodation and well worth the money.

The centrally located *Paradise Pension House* (☎ 991 1054) on the corner of Barcelona and Tomas Claudio Sts has reasonable rooms with air-con, bath and TV for P500.

Places to Eat

There are lots of places to eat around the centre of Zamboanga. Right next to the George & Peter Lines office on Valderroza St is the inexpensive *Flavorite Restaurant*. The *Food Paradise* on Tomas Claudio St is

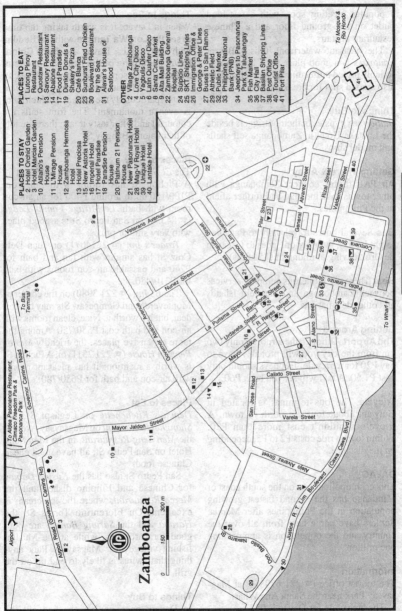

Zamboanga

PLACES TO STAY
2 Hotel Orchid Garden
3 Hotel Marcian Garden
10 Atilano's Pension House
11 L'Mirage Pension House
12 Zamboanga Hermosa Hotel
13 Hotel Preciosa
15 New Astoria Hotel
16 Imperial Hotel
17 Hotel Paradise
18 Paradise Pension House
20 Platinum 21 Pension House
21 New Pasonanca Hotel
28 Mag-V Royal Hotel
39 Unique Hotel
40 Lantaka Hotel

PLACES TO EAT
1 Lutong Pinoy Restaurant
7 Quostaw Restaurant
13 Savoury Restaurant
14 Abalone Restaurant
17 Food Paradise
19 Dunkin Donuts & Shakey's Pizza
20 Café Blanca
23 Sunburst Fried Chicken
30 Boulevard Restaurant by the Sea
31 Alavar's House of Seafood

OTHER
4 Village Zamboanga
5 Lovia City Disco
6 Yagpulis Disco
6 Latin Quarter Disco
8 Santa Cruz Market
9 Alta Mall Building
22 Zamboanga General Hospital
24 Sulpicio Lines
25 SKT Shipping Lines
26 Immigration Office & George & Peter Lines
27 Buses to San Ramon
29 Athletic Field
32 Public Market
33 Philippine National Bank (PNB)
34 Jeepneys to Pasonanca Park & Taluksangay
35 Fish Market
36 City Hall
37 Basilan Shipping Lines
38 Post Office
40 Tourist Office
41 Fort Pilar

PHILIPPINES

a popular meeting spot, with a fast-food outlet on the ground floor and a Chinese restaurant upstairs.

The pleasant waterfront Talisay Bar at *Lantaka's* is a good place for a beer; a reasonably priced buffet dinner is served and it's also a good spot for breakfast.

Things to Buy

Badjao sea gypsies in their outriggers beside the Lantaka Hotel in Zamboanga sell shells and model ships.

Getting There & Away

Air PAL flights connect Zamboanga with other towns in Mindanao and further afield in the Philippines.

Bus Several buses travel daily to Pagadian (eight hours), but only one goes to Cagayan de Oro, leaving at midnight (15 hours).

Boat There are numerous shipping services between Zamboanga and the Sulu Islands and other destinations.

Getting Around

The Airport Although the airport is only two km from the city you will probably have to pay P20 for a tricycle. Jeepneys should only cost P1.50. A taxi will set you back P60.

Tricycle The bus terminal is located in Guiwan, about four km north of town. A tricycle shouldn't cost more than P20. Within town a ride costs P2 to P5, depending on the distance.

DAVAO

This cosmopolitan city on the south coast of Mindanao has the second fastest growing population in the Philippines after Manila. Settlers have come here from all over the country and the population is approaching one million.

Information

The tourist office (☎ 221 6798) is at Magsaysay Park near the Santa Ana Wharf.

The area code for Davao is 082.

Things to See

When in Davao, it is worth taking the time to see the **Lon Wa Temple** with its 'Buddha with 1000 hands'. Davao also has a **Chinatown**, the **Shrine of the Holy Infant Jesus of Prague** and some pleasant parks. The city is renowned for its wide variety of tropical fruits – particularly the durian, to which there is even a monument! The fruit stalls are colourful and offer tasty treats; there are lots of them along Bangoy St.

Places to Stay

The *El Gusto Family Lodge* (☎ 73662) at 51 A Pichon St has rooms with fan from P100/180 up to around P400 for an air-con room with bath. *Le Mirage Family Lodge* (☎ 84334) on San Pedro St is a good place with very similar prices.

Trader's Inn (☎ 2214071) on Juan Dela Cruz St has singles with fan and bath for P240 and passable air-con rooms with bath for P310/420.

The *BS Inn* (☎ 221 3980) on the corner of Monteverde and Gempesaw Sts may be a bit dear, but it's worth it. Nice, clean rooms with air-con and bath cost P550/750. Among the more expensive places, the friendly *Manor Pension House* (☎ 221 2511) on A Pichon St is worth a mention: it has pleasant rooms with air-con and bath for P650/780.

Places to Eat

Dencia's Kitchenette on Legaspi St, the *Shanghai Restaurant* on Magsaysay Ave and the *Men Seng Restaurant*, in the Men Seng Hotel on San Pedro St, all have good cheap Chinese food.

San Pedro St also has the *Kusina Dabaw* for Chinese and Filipino dishes and the *Merco Restaurant*, where the ice cream is excellent. On Florentino Torres St, the *Harana* and the *Sarung Banggi* are both good for barbecues, while at the Muslim fishing village near Magsaysay Park anything that swims is likely to end up on the grill.

Things to Buy

In Davao, once you've checked out the

brassware, jewellery and handicrafts, devote your time to sampling the amazing variety of fruits – durians are the Davao speciality.

Getting There & Away
Air PAL flies from Cagayan de Oro, Zamboanga and further afield.

Bus Buses take about six hours from Butuan, 10 from Cagayan de Oro, four from General Santos (P67) and more than eight from Surigao.

Boat There's one weekly ship between General Santos (P90; 9 hours) and Davao, and between Surigao and Davao (P160; 17 hours).

Getting Around
The airport is 12 km north-east of the centre – say P50 by taxi or P2 by a tricycle to the main road, from where you can get a jeepney for P3.50. To town, take the jeepney 'San Pedro'; from town to the airport junction, take the 'Sasa' jeepney.

AROUND DAVAO
Beaches
There are a variety of black beaches around the city, like **Talomo** (eight km south), but probably the best beach is the white **Paradise Island Beach** on Samal Island. **Samal Island** is only a short banca ride away (outriggers leave near Sasa Bridge – shortly before Lanang towards the airport).

Mt Apo
At 2954 metres, Mt Apo is the highest mountain in the Philippines. It overlooks Davao and can be climbed in four to five days. On your way to the top you'll pass waterfalls, hot springs and pools of boiling mud and you might even spot the rare Philippine eagle. No special equipment is needed for the climb. March to May are the driest (hence best) climbing months and the tourist office can offer advice and arrange guides.

GENERAL SANTOS (DADIANGAS)
There's not a great deal of interest in this city in the south-west of Mindanao. It's in a major fruit-producing area (bananas and pineapple). About 50 km west of General Santos as the crow flies beautiful Lake Sebu nestles in the Tiruray Highlands. The T'boli, a cultural minority group who maintain their traditions, live on its shores. The weekly market on Saturdays is worth visiting.

The area code for General Santos is 083.

Places to Stay
The unpretentious *Concrete Lodge* (☎ 552 4876) on Pioneer Ave has rooms with fan and bath for P130/160. The *South Sea Lodge I* (☎ 552 5146) on Pioneer Ave is very similarly priced. Close by, also on Pioneer Ave, the clean *Hotel Sansu* (☎ 552 2422) has good air-con rooms with bath for P460/580.

On Lake Sebu there are a few basic places which offer accommodation for about P75 per person, eg the *Ba-ay Village Inn* and the *Hillside View Park Lodge*.

Getting There & Away
Bus Buses take four hours to Davao or an hour to Koronadel (Marbel). From Koronadel to Lake Sebu via Surallah it's another 1½ hours (bus and jeepney).

Boat There are two ships weekly from General Santos to Zamboanga (P290; 12 hours) and one weekly ship to Iloilo City (P600; 22 hours).

Camiguin

Located off the many bays on the north coast of Mindanao, Camiguin is an idyllic, small, get-away-from-it-all sort of place. The tiny island actually has seven volcanoes; Hibok-Hibok, the best known, last erupted in 1951. The beaches are nothing special but the people are great.

Getting There & Away
There may be occasional ships from other islands, but the usual route is from Balingoan

in Mindanao to Benoni on Camiguin. A ferry crosses seven times daily (P15; 1½ hours).

If you leave Cebu City in the evening you can reach Cagayan de Oro on Mindanao in about 10 hours, make the 1½ hour bus trip to Balingoan and then ferry across to Camiguin, arriving by the early forenoon.

A boat leaves from Cagayan de Oro on Tuesday, Thursday and Saturday at 8 am for Guinsiliban on the southern tip of Camiguin (P50; three hours).

Getting Around

The 65 km circuit of the island takes about three hours actual travelling time. While it is possible to travel around the island on jeepneys and tricycles, there are not many vehicles between Yumbing and Catarman. You are more independent of public transport with a hired motorcycle. Many resorts rent out mountain bikes for P150 and motorcycles for P350 a day.

MAMBAJAO

Mambajao is the capital and main town of Camiguin.

Information

You'll find the Camiguin tourist office in the Provincial Capitol building. The Philippine National Bank will change your travellers' cheques.

The area code for Mambajao is 088.

Places to Stay

Tia's Pension House (☎ 871045), near the town hall, has rooms with fan for P75/150. There is also *Tia's Beach Cottages*, just a few minutes from the centre, where cottages with bath cost P300; and straight across from there is the beautiful *Shore Line Cottages*, with rooms for P85 per person.

Between Kuguita and Bug-ong there are several beach bungalows.

AROUND THE ISLAND

Starting from Mambajao, and travelling anticlockwise, at **Kuguita** there's a beach and some coral where you can snorkel. The *Turtles Nest Beach Cottages* cost P350 with

bath. They have trim grounds with a garden. Another four km takes you to **Agoho**, where the *Caves Resort* (☎ 879040) is a beautiful dive resort near the beach with rooms from P150 to P500. The food here is also good value. Some other possibilities are the *Camiguin Seaside Lodge* and the *Morning Glory Cottages*, both with dorm beds, rooms and cottages. In Bug-ong, the pleasant *Jasmine by the Sea* (☎ 879015) has cottages with bath for P300 and P400.

Continuing beyond Yumbing, **Bonbon** has some interesting church ruins and a huge cross in the sea marking a sunken cemetery. Near Catarman, a track leads to the **Tuwasan Falls**. Down at the southern end of the island, there's a 300-year-old **Moro watchtower** at Guinsiliban.

Benoni is near the artificial Tanguine Lagoon, where the peaceful *JA's Fishpen Lodge* has basic but attractive cottages, with big verandas, standing on piles in the water. With fan and bath they cost P200. The rather run-down *Mychellin Beach Resort* is opposite Mantigue (Magsaysay) Island in Mahinog and has rooms for P150.

Hibok-Hibok Volcano

The 1320-metre-high Hibok-Hibok volcano can be climbed in the dry season; from Ardent Hot Spring it takes at least four hours. A guide (P350) is useful as the weather on the mountain is changeable and you can easily get lost. The volcano erupted disastrously in 1951 and it's now monitored from the Comvol station.

Katibawasan Waterfall

The waterfall, with good swimming, is three km from Pandan, which in turn is only two km from Mambajao. Near here the Ardent Hot Spring, a favourite for weekend outings, has a beautifully designed swimming pool.

White Island

Three km off Agoho, this small island is just a sand bar. There is no shade but there is good swimming and snorkelling. Count on P200 to rent a boat for the round trip, but arrange a definite time to be picked up.

Sulu Islands

The countless little islands that dribble from Zamboanga, in Mindanao, to Sabah in north Borneo are home to some of the most fervently Muslim people in the country. The Spanish and Americans never dominated them and even now things aren't under total control. Things happen on these islands – they are definitely not free of conflict, but are incredibly exciting to visit.

The main towns are **Jolo**, on the island of the same name; **Bongao**, capital of the province of Tawi-Tawi; and, in the deep south, **Sitangkai**, also called the 'Venice of the east'. The people of the archipelago are great seafarers – many, particularly the Badjao, or 'sea gypsies', live on houseboats or in houses built on stilts over the water. Smuggling and piracy occur in the area and some of the practitioners are reputed to be very well equipped and armed.

Getting There & Away
Air PAL flies daily from Zamboanga to Jolo and Tawi-Tawi.

Boat Ships sail six times a week from Zamboanga to Sitangkai (45 hours) and back, via Jolo (10 hours), Siasi (22 hours) or Bongao (36 hours).

Palawan

Off to the west of the Visayas, Palawan is the long thin island stretching down to the Malaysian state of Sabah. Things to do and see here are mainly connected with nature: islands, scuba diving and caves with underground rivers and wildlife. On no other island in the Philippines are people as attuned to nature and aware of the environment as on Palawan. The protection of wildlife and commitment to the environment is a serious way of life for many Palaweños.

Getting There & Away
Air There are daily PAL flights between Manila and Puerto Princesa, and twice weekly between Cebu City and Puerto Princesa (via Iloilo City). Air Ads and Pacific Airways fly from Manila to Busuanga, and Soriano Aviation flies from Manila to El Nido.

Boat Ships sail to Puerto Princesa (P455; 23 hours) twice a week, and three times a week to Coron (P300; 22 hours). Ships sail twice weekly (P300; 18 hours) from Batangas to Coron. Finally, ships sail six times a month from Iloilo City via Cuyo to Puerto Princesa (P360; 38 hours).

Getting Around
Puerto Princesa, the capital, is roughly halfway down the island. Buses and jeepneys run up and down: south, as far as Brooke's Point (P90; four hours), or north to Roxas (P55; four hours), Port Barton (P80; six hours), Taytay (P95; nine hours) and El Nido (P180; 12 to 15 hours).

PUERTO PRINCESA
The remarkably clean capital of Palawan has a population of about 120,000 and is a good base for excursions to elsewhere on the island.

Information
There's a City Tourist Office (☎ 433 2983) at the airport, and a Provincial Tourist Office in the Provincial Capitol building on Rizal Ave, at the corner of Fernandez St.

The area code for Puerto Princesa is 048.

Places to Stay
The pleasant *Duchess Pension House* (☎ 433 2873) on Valencia St is a popular place and has attracted a steady stream of travellers for years. It has clean, fan-cooled rooms for P100/150 and more expensive doubles with bathrooms.

Abelardo's Pension (☎ 433 2049), 63 Manga St, has reasonably good rooms with fan for P150/250, with fan and bath for P300, or with air-con and bath for P450. This place is a good source of tips about Palawan. The tastefully designed, family-run *Puerto Pension* on 35 Malvar St is a good alternative. Rooms are decorated native-style using lots of bamboo. Those with fan and shared bath cost P175/225, with fan and bath P275, and with air-con and bath P490. There is a nice garden and a roof deck drinking lounge with a view of Puerto Bay.

The *Trattoria Terrace Pensionhouse* (☎ 433 2719) on 353 Rizal Ave has good rooms with fan from P190/290 and with air-con and bath for P550/650. The owner is very helpful and the staff are friendly. More expensive places include the charming *Casa Linda* (☎ 433 2006) on Trinidad Rd about 80 metres off Rizal Ave. This is a pleasant place with a garden tended by someone who cares. It has native-style rooms with fan and bath for P375/455 and with air-con and bath for P525/595. The nearby *Badjao Inn* (☎ 433 2761) on 350 Rizal Ave is a clean, well-kept place (even if it doesn't look like it from the street) with comfortable rooms from P260 to P600. There is a tidy garden.

Places to Eat
There's a cosmopolitan selection of restaurants along Rizal Ave. Try the attractive *Café Puerto* for French food or the *Roadside Pizza Inn* for Italian. The *Pink Lace* prepares everything from Filipino, Chinese, Indian and Mexican to Vietnamese! At the *Kamayan Folkhouse & Restaurant*, you can try Filipino dishes and have a choice of sitting on the terrace or in a tree house.

The pleasant and busy *Swiss Bistro Valencia* at the back of the Trattoria Terrace Pensionhouse has excellent steaks and European dishes, together with what must be the best music in town. Head to the charmingly rustic *Ka Lui Restaurant* for fresh seafood. At the entrance to the Vietnamese refugee camp, two km out of town behind the airport, the *Pho Vietnamese Restaurant* has well cooked – if a bit pricey – Vietnamese food and freshly baked, French-style bread.

The self-serve *NCCC Fast Food Restaurant*, on the ground floor in the shopping mall of the same name in A Lacson St, offers a wide choice of inexpensive Filipino dishes.

Getting Around
There are plenty of tricycles for getting around town for P2, and they will take you out to the airport for P15 to P20.

AROUND PUERTO PRINCESA
There are various places within day-trip distance of Puerto Princesa. For example, **Irawan** has the Irawan Crocodile Farming Institute and **Iwahig** has Iwahig Prison and Penal Farm.

The diving is good at **Honda Bay**, off Tagburos (Santa Lourdes Pier), only 10 km from Puerto Princesa. There are many small islands in the bay. White **Nagtabon Beach** lies on a beautiful, calm bay on the west coast and is another good swimming spot.

Sabang is famed for the long **Underground River** in St Paul Subterranean National Park – a highlight of Palawan. From the beach in Sabang you can either take a boat for P200 or walk over the monkey trail through the beautiful jungle of the national park to the mouth of the river – it takes about two hours.

Places to Stay
Even if the trip from Puerto Princesa to the Underground River can be done in a day, the long journey there and back, plus the incredible countryside, mean you should plan on staying at least one or two nights in Sabang.

The cheapest accommodation is available at the *Ranger Station* in the national park, where a bed can be had for P75; for P50 you can sleep in a tent. There are four other places offering accommodation on the beach at Sabang; among them *Robert's Beach Cottages* has basic cottages for P175 and better ones with bath for P200 and P250. A bit to one side, situated on a little bay at the east end of the beach, you'll find *Mary's Beach Resort* – definitely the best place to go. Cottages without bath are P150 and with bath P250.

Places to Eat

You can get excellent Filipino food, various salads and a good breakfast at good prices in the pleasant *Gonzalez Restaurant* near the Sabang pier.

SOUTH PALAWAN

Unlike the north of Palawan, the south of the island doesn't have too much to offer the traveller.

Quezon, halfway from Puerto Princesa to the southern end of the island, is the jumping-off point for the **Tabon Caves**. There's a small **National Museum** in Quezon and the caves have yielded some interesting stone-age finds. It takes half an hour by boat to the caves.

Places to Stay

In Quezon you can stay in basic little rooms for P70 per person at the *New Bayside Lodging House*. The nicely laid out *Tabon Village Resort* at Tabon Beach, about four km north-east of Quezon, has rooms at P100/120 and cottages with bath for P250/350.

Getting There & Away

More than a dozen buses travel between Puerto Princesa and Quezon (P55; three hours) daily.

NORTH PALAWAN

On the west coast, **Port Barton** on Pagdanan Bay is something of a travellers' hang-out. There are a number of fine islands in the bay, some beautiful beaches and good snorkelling.

After a half-day journey north-east of Port Barton you come to **Taytay**, the former capital of Palawan. Here you can visit the ruins of a fort built in 1667 by the Spaniards.

Right up in the north-west of Palawan, there's beautiful **El Nido**. This picturesque little village is surrounded by rugged, steep limestone cliffs; It's not easy to get to, but it's well worth the effort. A boat trip to the offshore islands of the **Bacuit Archipelago** is fascinating.

The northernmost part of Palawan consists of the **Calamian Group**, whose main islands are Busuanga, Culion and Coron. Wreck diving is a big attraction in this beautiful island world and improvements to the travel links with other islands and towns, together with the expansion in overnight accommodation, have caused a modest upsurge in tourism. There are some dive shops in **Coron**, the main town in Busuanga.

Places to Stay

Port Barton At the beach in Port Barton you can stay at *Summer Homes* in rooms for P100 per person or cottages with bath for P150 (good for two). It's a small place with a family atmosphere. The cottages are right on the beach and the rooms are in the garden behind. The little cottages at *Elsa's Place* are pleasant; with a bath they cost P250. Right next door, the *Swissippini Lodge & Resort* is the biggest place on the beach and has attractive cottages of various sizes and fittings, all with bath from P350 to P600.

Taytay In Taytay, you can stay cheaply at *Publico's International Guest House*, where basic rooms surround the plants of the inner courtyard and cost P60/120. The price is just right for what you get. *Pem's Pension House* on the bay at the fort is a little more expensive. There the basic rooms cost P75/150 and cottages with fan and bath P250 to P500.

El Nido There is a wide choice of accommodation in El Nido. You can get rooms for around P100 per person at *Austria's Guesthouse* and *Bayview Lodging House*, and at *Lualhati Cottage*, which is right at the entrance to the community and is a particularly good deal. Many places also offer a variety of different cottages with fan and bath for between P300 and P500, eg *Marina Garden Beach Cottages*, *Gloria's Beach Cottages*, *Dara Fernandez Cottages*, *Tandikan Cottages* and *Lally & Abet Beach Cottages*.

Coron There are several guesthouses in Coron town on Busuanga, some of them built on stilts over the water. In the *Sea Breeze Lodging House* the cheapest, and admittedly spartan, rooms cost P60 per person; better doubles with fan, bath and their own veranda cost P300. Next to the market, the attractively designed *L&M Pe Lodge* has small rooms for P100/200, or with fan and bath for P250. About 15 minutes on foot from Coron you'll come to the peaceful *Kokosnuss Resort* with its big garden. Com-

fortable cottages with or without bath cost P240 to P480.

Getting There & Away.
The only reliable connection between mainland Palawan and the Calamian Group is from Taytay to Coron. A big outrigger makes the trip every Wednesday and Saturday (P350; 8 hours); the return journey is on a Monday or a Friday.

Singapore

Singapore is a small island at the tip of the Malay Peninsula. It thrives on trade and, through a combination of hard work and efficient, if at times repressive, government, has become one of the most affluent countries in Asia. It's a crossroads for travellers but also offers a wide variety of places to visit, things to buy and some of the best food in Asia.

Singapore, with its preoccupation with cleanliness and orderliness, can be a pleasant break from the more hectic travelling you find elsewhere in the region. But it's also less traditional and more antiseptic.

Facts about Singapore

HISTORY

Singapore's improbable name, which means Lion City, came from a Sumatran prince who thought he saw a lion when he landed on the island – it was much more likely a tiger. Singapore would have drifted on as a quiet fishing village if Sir Stamford Raffles had not decided, in 1819, that it was just the port he needed. Under the British it became a great trading city and a military and naval base, but that didn't save it from the Japanese in 1942.

In 1959 Singapore became internally self-governing, in 1963 it joined Malaysia and, in 1965, this federation was in tatters and Singapore became independent. The reason behind this was a basic conflict of interest between 'Malaysia for the Malays' and Singapore's predominantly Chinese population. Under Prime Minister Lee Kuan Yew, Singapore made the best of its independence. Trade, tourism and industrialisation soon made up for the loss of British military bases.

Mr Lee's somewhat iron-fisted government also turned Singapore into a green, tidy garden city where no one dares to litter the streets, or even carelessly drop cigarette ash.

The economy is dynamic, the water from the taps is drinkable, smoking in public places is forbidden, cars are heavily taxed and all drivers are discouraged from venturing into the city centre during rush hour.

Singapore's progressive attitudes have another side: criticism of the government is not a recommended activity, the press is tightly controlled and the minuscule elected opposition has always had a hard time. It has even been loudly mooted as to whether the country actually needs any opposition to the People's Action Party (PAP). Lee Kuan Yew finally stepped down from the leadership in 1990 and handed over the reigns to Goh Chok Tong, though Lee is still Special Minister and exerts a major influence.

Goh Chok Tong instituted a series of liberalising reforms. Goh's social reforms saw a relaxation of censorship laws, a flourishing in the arts and a greater awareness of the quality-of-life issues that concern most modern, industrialised nations. However, few real steps have been made towards democratisation, despite growing calls for increased freedom.

GEOGRAPHY

The population squeezes itself into a low-lying 646 sq km island at the tip of the Malay peninsula, not much more than 100 km north of the equator. A km-long Causeway connects

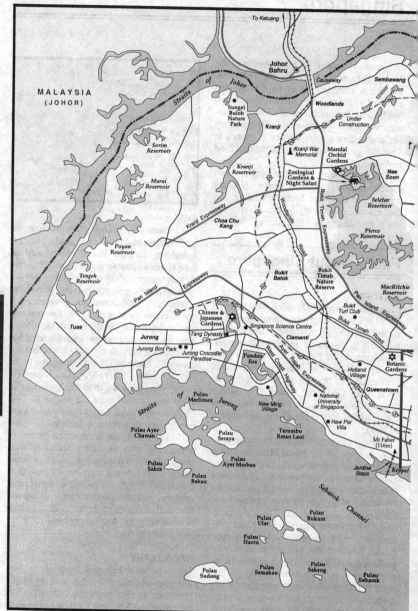

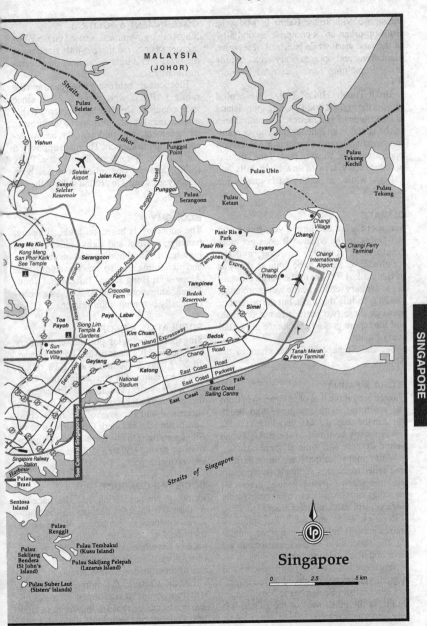

MALAYSIA
(JOHOR)

Straits

of

Johor

Pulau
Seletar

Punggol
Point

Pulau Tekong
Kechil

Pulau
Tekong

Yishun

Seletar
Airport

Jalan Kayu

Punggol

Road

Punggol

Pulau
Serangoon

Pulau
Ketam

Pulau Ubin

Sungei
Seletar
Reservoir

Changi
Village

Changi

Changi Ferry
Terminal

Ang Mo Kio

Kong Meng
San Phor Kark
See Temple

Serangoon

Serangoon Road

Pasir Ris
Park

Pasir Ris

Loyang

Changi
International
Airport

Central

Upper

Expressway

Tampines

Expressway

Changi
Prison

Crocodile
Farm

Tampines

Bedok
Reservoir

Simei

Toa
Payoh

Siong Lim
Temple &
Gardens

Paya Labar

Kim Chuan

Pan Island Expressway

Bedok

Tanah Merah
Ferry Terminal

Sun
Yatsen
Villa

Serangoon Road

Geylang

Changi

Road

Katong

East Coast

Road

Parkway

National
Stadium

East Coast

Park

East Coast

East Coast
Sailing Centre

See Central Singapore Map

Straits of Singapore

Singapore Railway
Station

Harbour

Pulau
Brani

Sentosa
Island

Pulau
Renggit

Pulau Tembakul
(Kusu Island)

Pulau
Sakijang
Bendera
(St John's
Island)

Pulau Sakijang Pelepah
(Lazarus Island)

Pulau Suber Laut
(Sisters' Islands)

Singapore

0   2.5   5 km

SINGAPORE

Singapore with Johor Bahru in Malaysia. Built-up urban areas comprise around 50% of the land area, while parkland, reservoirs, plantations and open military areas occupy 40%. Remaining forest accounts for only 4%.

Bukit Timah (Hill of Tin), in the central hills, is the highest point on Singapore Island at an altitude of 162 metres. The central area of the island is an igneous outcrop, containing most of Singapore's remaining forest and open areas. The western part of the island is a sedimentary area of low-lying hills and valleys, while the south-east is mostly flat and sandy.

CLIMATE

Singapore is hot and humid year-round as it is so close to the equator. It does get more comfortable at night, however, and the weather never seems to be quite as sticky as in Bangkok, 1500 km to the north. November to January tend to be the wettest months, and May to July the driest, but the difference between these two periods is not dramatic and Singapore gets an abundance of rainfall every month.

See the Singapore climate chart in the Appendix.

FLORA & FAUNA

Though Singapore was once covered in tropical rainforest, with mangrove and beach forest in the coastal areas, very little remains and is mostly confined to the Bukit Timah Nature Reserve and some offshore islands.

While many animals are now extinct, long-tailed macaques, squirrels, flying squirrels, tree shrews, flying lemurs, civet cats (musang) and the distinctive pangolin (scaly anteater) still exist in forest areas.

Reptiles, frogs and toads are common. Snakes are still found in urban areas, including the reticulated python, poisonous pit viper and black spitting cobra.

Singapore has over 300 bird species and migrant species are observed in the migratory season from September to May. Sungei Buloh, in the north-west of the island, is a new bird sanctuary.

GOVERNMENT & POLITICS

Singapore's government is based on the Westminster system, but there is little freedom of the press and a tight lid is held on government criticism.

Elections are held every five years, and the ruling PAP has won every election since independence. The PAP has delivered stable government and impressive economic advancement, and undoubtedly has widespread popular support. The main opposition party is the Singapore Democratic Party (SDP), and the opposition vote has been steadily growing – to around 40% in the last election.

ECONOMY

The economy is based on trade, shipping, banking, tourism and light industry (often high-tech). Shipbuilding and maintenance and oil refining are also important industries. Along with Hong Kong, Taiwan and South Korea, Singapore is one of East Asia's economically booming 'mini-dragons'.

POPULATION & PEOPLE

Singapore's polyglot population numbers 2.95 million. It's made up of 77.5% Chinese, 14.2% Malay, 7.1% Indian and 1.2% of any and every nationality you can imagine. Curiously, after years of promoting birth control, the government has decided it's been too successful and the joys of the three child family are now extolled. Of course, it has a Singapore twist to it – there are extra incentives to having children if the parents have university degrees.

SOCIETY & CONDUCT

Growing westernisation and the pace of modern life has seen changes in the traditional customs in Singapore. While some traditional customs are given less importance or have been streamlined, the strength of traditional religious values and the practice of time-honoured ways remain.

For the Chinese, the moment of birth is strictly recorded; it is essential for astrological consultations that are important in later life. Funerals are traditional, colourful and expensive affairs. Paper houses, cars, TV sets and even paper servants are offered and burnt so that the deceased can enjoy all these material benefits in the next life. The importance of the grave and its upkeep remains, and most Chinese will pay their respects to the elders on All Souls Day. The major Chinese celebration is Chinese New Year.

Islam provides the focus for Malays, but *adat* (customary law) guides the important ceremonies and events in life, such as birth, circumcision and marriage. Many aspects of adat exhibit Hindu and even pre-Hindu influences. The most important festival for Malays is Hari Raya Puasa, the end of the fasting month.

Most Singaporean Indians come from southern India, so the customs and festivals that are more important in the south, especially Madras, are the most popular in Singapore. Deepavali, the Festival of Lights, is the major Indian festival in Singapore and homes are decorated with oil lamps to signify the victory of light over darkness. The spectacular Thaipusam is the most exciting festival.

RELIGION

The variety of religions found in Singapore is a direct reflection of the diversity of races living there. The Chinese are predominantly followers of Buddhism and Shenism (deity worship), though a significant number are Christian. Malays are overwhelmingly Muslim, and most Indians are Hindus from southern India, though a significant number are Muslim.

LANGUAGE

English is widely spoken, as is Malay, Tamil and a number of Chinese dialects. After a spell in Singapore, you may come to the conclusion that Chinese is not a language to be whispered or even spoken. It is a language to be howled, yowled, shrieked and screamed. In any Chinese restaurant, you will witness just how. The 'official' Chinese dialect is Mandarin – you may see public signs urging Chinese citizens to 'Speak Mandarin, Not Dialect!'.

Facts for the Visitor

PLANNING
When to Go

Anytime. Climate is not a major consideration, as Singapore gets a fairly steady annual rainfall. Your visit may coincide with various festivals – Singapore has something happening every month. Thaipusam is one of the most spectacular festivals, or if shopping and eating are your major concerns, July is a good month as the Singapore Food Festival and Great Singapore Sale are held.

Maps

Various good giveaway maps are available at tourist offices, the airport on arrival, some hotels and shopping centres. Nelles and Periplus are the best of the commercial maps. The best reference of all is the *Singapore Street Directory*, a bargain at S$9 plus GST. It's available at most bookshops.

HIGHLIGHTS

The best way to get a feel for Singapore is to wander around its inner city. Though the ethnic areas are quickly becoming dining and drinking venues rather than repositories of traditional culture, **Chinatown, Little India** and **Arab St** are still fascinating areas to explore.

The historic **Singapore River** is a lively stretch of restoration and redevelopment, especially in the evening when the restaurants and bars of Boat Quay and Clarke Quay are packed.

The **Singapore Zoo** is one of Singapore's most popular attractions, and nothing like the animal jails you normally find in South-East Asia. Highly recommended is the **Night Safari** next to the zoo, which allows you to view animals along jungle paths at night. The **Jurong Bird Park** has a huge variety of birdlife and similarly well-tended enclosures.

Green and clean Singapore also has plenty of gardens, the pick of which is the **Botanic Gardens**. For a walk in the jungle, **Bukit**

SINGAPORE

Timah Nature Reserve is about as far away from the city as you can get.

The theme park island of **Sentosa** is Singapore's answer to Disneyland, though the comparison is a loose one. The fun park activities are mostly for families, but it has enough to keep adults amused.

Last but not least, every visitor ends up at **Orchard Rd**, a dazzling strip of modern delights. Singapore has plenty of other attractions to keep you amused from a day in transit to a week's exploration.

TOURIST OFFICES

The Singapore Tourist Promotion Board (STPB) has a Tourist Information Centre at its head office at 1 Orchard Spring Rd (☎ 1800-738 3778), off Cuscaden Rd in the Orchard Rd area. Another is conveniently located at 02-34 Raffles Hotel Arcade (☎ 1800-334 1335) on North Bridge Rd in the colonial district. Both can answer most queries and have a good selection of handouts. Pick up a copy of the excellent *Singapore Official Guide*, which is updated monthly.

VISAS & DOCUMENTS

Most western nationalities do not require visas. You are granted an initial two weeks on entry and a one month stay permit is usually not a problem if you ask for it. You can easily extend a 14 day stay permit for another two weeks, but extensions beyond a month become increasingly hard. The government obviously feels that a month is long enough for anybody to do their shopping. Inquire at the Immigration Department (☎ 532 2877), Pidemco Centre, 95 South Bridge Rd (see the Central Singapore map).

An international student card is not of much use as student discounts are almost invariably for Singaporeans only, and Singapore has no YHA hostels to use a Hostelling International card.

EMBASSIES

Singapore is generally a good place to get visas. Regional foreign embassies in Singapore include:

Australia
    25 Napier Rd (☎ 737 9311)
Brunei
    325 Tanglin Rd (☎ 733 9055)
India
    31 Grange Rd (☎ 737 6777)
Indonesia
    7 Chatsworth Rd (☎ 737 7422)
Malaysia
    301 Jervois Rd (☎ 235 0111)
Myanmar (Burma)
    05-04 BN building, 133 Middle Rd (☎ 338 1073)
Philippines
    20 Nassim Rd (☎ 737 3977)
Thailand
    370 Orchard Rd (☎ 235 4175)

CUSTOMS

Visitors to Singapore are allowed to bring in one litre of wine, beer or spirits duty-free, and most other goods are already duty-free. Singapore does not allow duty-free concessions for cigarettes and tobacco. The importation of chewing gum was banned after anti-social elements started gumming up the doors of the Mass Railway Transit (MRT) subway system. Duty-free concessions are not available if you come from Malaysia or if you leave Singapore for less than 48 hours.

The importation or exportation of illegal drugs carries the death penalty for more than 15g of heroin, 30g of morphine, 500g of cannabis or 200g of cannabis resin, or 1.2 kg of opium. Trafficking in lesser amounts ranges from a minimum of two years jail and two strokes of the rotan to 30 years and 15 stokes of the rotan.

MONEY
Costs

Singapore is much more expensive than other South-East Asian countries. The only cheap accommodation is in guesthouse dormitories, which will cost around US$4, or a double room in a cheap hotel or guesthouse costs from US$15 to US$35. Singapore has plenty of cheap dining possibilities, public transport is cheap and many attractions are free. It is possible to stay in Singapore for as little as US$15 per day, but be prepared to spend a lot more if you want to indulge in some of the luxuries you may have craved in less developed countries.

Currency & Changing Money

Singapore uses 1c, 5c, 10c, 20c, 50c and S$1 coins, while notes are in denominations of S$2, S$5, S$10, S$50, S$100, S$500 and S$1000; Singapore also has a S$10,000 note – not that you'll see too many.

There are no pitfalls in changing money in Singapore but if you're watching every cent it is worth shopping around the banks – exchange rates tend to vary and many banks also make a small service charge on a per-cheque or per-transaction basis.

Singapore is one of the major banking centres of Asia so it is a good place to transfer money. Moneychangers can supply currency from almost anywhere, and they delightfully calculate complicated double exchanges – the conversion of Thai bahts into Indonesian rupiah, for example. They are found everywhere – almost every shopping centre has one – and generally, they're better than banks for changing cash.

All major credit cards are accepted and cash advances on Visa and MasterCard can be readily obtained over the counter at banks, or through the many ATMs that display credit symbols. Some banks are connected to international networks that allow you to withdraw funds from overseas savings accounts if you have a card with a PIN number (check with your home bank).

Currency Exchange

The following table shows the exchange rates:

Australia	A$1	=	S$1.11
Canada	C$1	=	S$1.03
France	FF10	=	S$2.73
Germany	DM1	=	S$0.92
Indonesia	Rp1000	=	S$0.61
Japan	¥100	=	S$1.27
New Zealand	NZ$1	=	S$0.98
Thailand	100B	=	S$5.54
UK	UK£1	=	S$2.20
USA	US$1	=	S$1.41

Tipping & Bargaining

Tipping is not usual in Singapore. Most expensive hotels and restaurants have a 10% service charge, in which case tipping is discouraged.

Many shops are fixed price and it is unnecessary to bargain for everyday goods or transport, as in many Asian countries. A fair number of small shops in the tourist areas, especially electronic shops, don't display prices. In this case bargaining is almost always required. For handicrafts and other tourist-oriented items, a price tag doesn't mean you can't bargain, and you often should.

Taxes & Refunds

Singapore's has a 3% GST applied to all goods and services. Visitors purchasing goods worth S$500 or more through a shop participating in the GST Tourist Refund Scheme can apply for a refund of GST, but it's a hassle.

In addition to the 3% GST, a 10% service charge and 1% 'cess' (government entertainment tax) is added to the more expensive hotel and restaurant bills, as well as at most nightspots and bars. Most of the cheaper establishments don't add taxes but absorb them into the quoted price.

POST & COMMUNICATIONS

The GPO on Fullerton Rd, close to the Singapore River, is open 24 hours for basic postal services, including fax service. The efficient poste restante service is only open during normal business hours. The Comcentre, 31 Exeter Rd, very near the Somerset MRT station on Orchard Rd, is also open 24 hours. Singapore is an efficient place from which to send parcels, and rates are good compared with many other South-East Asian countries.

There are several Telecom centres, such as the one in the GPO, where it is easy to make international calls. The phone centres also have Direct Home phone (press a country button for direct connection with your home country operator and then reverse the charges) and credit-card phones. International calls can also be dialled from public payphones with a stored-value phone card. They cost from S$2 to S$50 and are available at Telecom centres and retail outlets.

To make international calls from Singapore, the international access code is 001.

To call Singapore from outside the country, the country code is 65.

For directory information call ☎ 03; the police emergency number is ☎ 999.

BOOKS

The Lonely Planet *Singapore city guide* is a detailed and compact guidebook to the city-state and includes detailed, colour maps.

Singapore has experienced something of a literary boom, especially after Goh Chok Tong's relaxation of censorship laws, and bookshops are packed with Singaporean titles. *A History of Singapore* by CM Turnball is the best choice for a detailed overview of Singapore's history. Books on politics range from the pro-government *Governing Singapore* by Raj Vasil to *Dare to Change: an Alternative Vision for Singapore* by Chee Soon Juan, the leader of the opposition Singapore Democratic Party.

Singapore probably has the best bookshops in South-East Asia. The main MPH shop on Stamford Rd, in the colonial district, is excellent, but there are numerous other good bookshops around the city, including other MPH branches, Times and Kinokuniya bookshops. Centrepoint shopping complex on Orchard Rd has branches of Times and MPH.

NEWSPAPERS & MAGAZINES

Singapore has three Chinese daily newspapers with a combined daily circulation of over 450,000 and three English newspapers with a slightly higher circulation. There is also a Malay daily and an Tamil daily. The English daily newspapers are the establishment *Straits Times*, the *Business Times* and the tabloid *New Paper*. *Time*, *Newsweek* and many other foreign magazines are readily available.

HEALTH

Health worries are not so much of a problem in Singapore, though heat exhaustion and dehydration apply as in any tropical country. Singapore possesses the best medical facilities in the region and many people come here from neighbouring countries if they need medical attention.

DANGERS & ANNOYANCES

Singapore is a very safe country with low crime rates. The usual precautions apply and pickpockets are not unknown, but in general crime is not a problem.

The importation of drugs carries the death penalty and, quite simply, drugs in Singapore should be avoided at all costs, not that you are likely to come across them.

BUSINESS HOURS

In Singapore, government offices are usually open from Monday to Friday and Saturday mornings. Hours vary, starting around 7.30 to 9.30 am and closing between 4 and 6 pm. On Saturday, closing time is between 11.30 am and 1 pm. Banks are open from 9.30 am to 3 pm weekdays and until 11.30 am on Saturday.

Shop hours are variable. Small shops are generally open Monday to Saturday from 10 am to 6 pm, while department stores and large shopping centres are open from 10 am to 9 or 9.30 pm, seven days a week. Most small shops in Chinatown and Arab St close on Sunday, though Sunday is the big day in Little India.

PUBLIC HOLIDAYS & SPECIAL EVENTS

The following days are public holidays. For those not based on the western calendar, the months they are likely to fall in are given:

New Year's Day
    1 January
Chinese New Year
    January or February
Hari Raya Puasa
    January
Good Friday
    April

Hari Raya Haji
 April
Vesak Day
 April or May
Labour Day
 1 May
National Day
 9 August
Deepavali
 November
Christmas Day
 25 December

Singapore's polyglot population celebrates an amazing number of festivals and events. Chinese New Year is the major festival, and even Chinese who profess no religion will clear out the old and bring in the new. The house is given a spring clean and all business affairs and debts brought up to date before the new year. It falls in late January or early February and goes on for a week. It's more a stay-at-home holiday than one offering lots of attractions, and hotels will be packed out, taxis scarce, restaurants often closed and prices temporarily higher.

Other Singapore-only special events include the biennial Singapore Festival of Arts, held around May. It alternates with Festival of Asian Performing Arts held every odd year. Around July, the month-long Singapore Food Festival celebrates the national passion with special offerings at everything from hawker centres to gourmet restaurants. During the Great Singapore Sale, also held around July, merchants are encouraged by the government to drop prices in an effort to boost Singapore's image as a shopping destination.

ACCOMMODATION

Singapore's hotels run the full range from dormitories in travellers' guesthouses to five star high-rises and old world luxury at the Raffles. See Places to Stay later in this chapter for a rundown on budget and mid-range accommodation, but if you want to splash out and stay in luxury, Singapore has scores of international standard hotels, and Orchard Rd has the biggest concentration. When competition hots up, the big hotels

offer large discounts – if you arrive by air check out the latest rates at the airport.

FOOD

Singapore is far and away the food capital of Asia. When it comes to superb Chinese food, Hong Kong may actually be a step ahead but it's Singapore's sheer variety and low prices which make it so good. Equally important, Singapore's food is so accessible – you don't have to search out obscure places, you don't face communication problems and you don't need a lot of money. Cheap, hygienic hawker centres are everywhere or, if you have the cash, Singapore has a mind-boggling array of restaurants serving cuisine from all over the world.

Singapore has all the favourites found in Malaysia (see the Food section in that chapter for details), such as roti chanai (Indian) and satay (Malay), though the availability and variety of Chinese food is greater. If Singapore has a national dish, then it is Hokkien fried mee, otherwise known as Singapore noodles. Thick, yellow egg noodles are fried with prawns, pork, bean sprouts and vegetables in a rich stock and served with chilli and lime.

Getting There & Away

AIR

Singapore is a major travel hub and flights operate in and out of Changi airport at all hours. There are direct flights to all the capital cities in South-East Asia and to regional centres, such as Phuket and Hat Yai in Thailand, Cebu in the Philippines and many destinations in Malaysia and Indonesia.

Travel Agents

Singapore is a very good place to look for cheap airline tickets. Some typical rock-bottom discount fares being quoted in Singapore include South-East Asian destinations like Bangkok from S$200 one way, Denpasar from S$220 and Jakarta S$120. To the subcontinent, you can fly to Delhi or

Kathmandu for S$450 one way, Madras for S$400.

Fares to Australia include Sydney or Melbourne for S$500 one way or S$600 excursion return, Perth from $400 one way or S$500 return. London, or other European destinations, costs from S$550 one way with the Eastern European airlines and from S$620 one way with the better airlines. One-way fares to the US west coast are around S$650 direct or with a stop in Manila.

For good travel agents, STA Travel (☎ 734 5681) is in the Orchard Parade Hotel, 1 Tanglin Rd, and a branch office is at 127 Bencoolen St, under the Why Not Homestay. Also on Bencoolen St is Harharah Travel (☎ 337 2633) at 171-C in the same building as Hawaii Hostel. Airpower Travel (☎ 337 1392), B1-07 Selegie Centre, 189 Selegie Rd, and 26 Sultan Gate (☎ 294 5664) near Arab St, is recommended by many travellers

Malaysia

Singapore International Airlines (SIA) has flights to the main cities, though Malaysian Airlines (MAS) is the main carrier. Flights from Singapore include: Kota Kinabalu (S$391, RM418), Kuala Lumpur (S$147, RM159), Kuantan (S$136, RM146), Kuching (S$193, RM205), Langkawi (S$204, RM218) and Penang (S$170, RM182). Pelangi Air and Silk Air have flights to other destinations, including Tioman Island (S$99, RM132), Melaka and Ipoh. Almost all flights go from Changi airport, but a few regional flights, such as those to Tioman, leave from Seletar airport.

There is no discounting on flights between Malaysia and Singapore, but note that it's much cheaper to fly from Malaysia to Singapore than Singapore to Malaysia – the Malaysian ringgit is worth around 50% less than the mighty Singapore dollar.

It's much cheaper to fly to Malaysian destinations from Johor Bahru, just across the Causeway from Singapore, than directly from Singapore. MAS operates a connecting bus service for S$10 from the Novotel Orchid, 214 Dunearn Rd (see the Central Singapore map), to the Johor Bahru airport.

In Singapore, tickets for internal flights originating in Malaysia are only sold by MAS (☎ 336 6777), 02-09 Singapore Shopping Centre, 190 Clemenceau Ave (see the Orchard Road Area map).

Indonesia

The most popular flight is from Singapore to Jakarta. Many airlines do this route for around S$120 one way, S$200 return. There are also direct flights between Singapore and Medan, Padang, Palembang, Pekanbaru, Pontianak, Surabaya and Ujung Pandang. Garuda is the main carrier.

Departure Tax

The airport departure tax (Passenger Service Charge; PSC) from Changi airport is S$15, payable at check-in or you can purchase PSC coupons in advance at airline offices, travel agencies and major hotels.

LAND
Malaysia

Bus For Johor Bahru, buses leave from the terminal on the corner of Queen and Arab Sts; the Bugis MRT station is within walking distance. Air-con express buses (S$1.80) depart every 15 minutes between 6.30 am and midnight, or take public SBS bus No 170 (90c). Buses stop at the Singapore checkpoint, but don't worry if yours leaves while you clear immigration – keep your ticket and just hop on the next one that comes along. Three buses per day also go to Kuala Lumpur (KL) from this terminal.

Long-distance buses to Melaka, KL and the east coast of Malaysia leave from the bus terminal on the corner of Lavender St and Kallang Bahru, near the top end of Jalan Besar (the continuation of Bencoolen St). Pan Malaysia Express (☎ 294 7034) has buses to KL (S$17.80), Kuantan (S$16.50), Kota Bharu (S$30.10) and Mersing (S$13.10). Hasry (☎ 294 9306) has buses to KL (S$17) and Melaka. Melacca-Singapore Express (☎ 293 5915) has eight buses daily to Melaka (S$11; 4½ hours). It is preferable to buy your tickets the day before departure. Many travel agents also sell bus tickets.

To Thailand and northern Malaysian destinations on the way, such as Ipoh, Butterworth, Penang and Alor Setar, most buses leave from the Golden Mile Complex, 5001 Beach Rd, at the north-east end near Arab St. The Lavender MRT station is 0.5 km away. Buses to Penang cost around S$35 and most leave in the afternoon and evening. Bus agents line the outside of the building, or Morning Star Travel (☎ 292 9009) is another agent at the Lavender MRT station.

Train Singapore is the southern termination point for the Malaysian railway system. The Singapore railway station (☎ 222 5165 for fare and schedule information) is on Keppel Rd, south-west of Chinatown.

Four trains go every day to KL. Fares range from S$19 in 3rd class to S$68 in 1st class on the express trains, and from S$14.80 to S$60 on the ordinary trains. Express trains leave at 7.30 am (arriving 1.50 pm) and 2.25 pm (arriving 8.55 pm) and limited express trains leave at 8 pm (arriving 5.10 am) and 10.30 pm (arriving 6.05 am). The 7.30 am *Ekspres Rakyat* continues on to Butterworth, arriving at 10.35 pm. There is also an express train to Tumpat (in the very north-east of Malaysia) at 11.30 pm, which reaches Jerantut at 4 am for Taman Negara National Park.

Taxi For Johor Bahru, long-distance taxis leave from the terminal on the corner of Queen and Arab Sts. They cost S$6 per person, but as foreigners take longer to clear the border you will most likely have to charter a whole taxi for S$24. The bus is quicker if there are delays at the Causeway.

SEA
Malaysia
The overwhelming majority of travellers coming to or from Malaysia will either be coming through Changi airport or crossing the Causeway by road or rail, but a few ferry services exist.

Take bus No 2 from central Singapore out to Changi Village, near Changi airport, and take a bumboat ferry across to Pengerang in Malaysia for S$5.

A car and passenger ferry operates from north Changi (take a taxi from Changi Village) to Tanjung Belungkor, east of Johor Bahru. The 11 km journey takes 45 minutes, and costs S$15/24 (RM15/27) one way/return. From the Tanjung Belungkor jetty, two bus services operate to Desaru, and a Kota Tinggi service is planned.

To Tioman Island, Kalpin Tours (☎ 271 4866), 02-40 World Trade Centre (WTC), is the agent for the high-speed catamaran that does the trip in 4½ hours. Departures are at 7.55 am from the WTC, and the fare is S$79/140 one way/return. Sailings usually don't run in the monsoon season from November to March. Kalpin Tours also has ferries from the WTC to the fishing village of Kukup in Johor on weekends.

Indonesia
Curiously, there are no direct shipping services between any of the major towns of Indonesia and its near neighbour, Singapore. You can, however, travel by sea between the two countries via the Riau Archipelago, the Indonesian islands to the south of Singapore, and then on to Sumatra or Java.

Numerous high-speed ferry services go from the WTC, opposite Sentosa Island, to Batam and Bintan, the two major islands closest to Singapore. Ferries go every day to Sekupang (S$16; half an hour) on Batam, at least every half hour from 7.35 am to 9.15 pm. From Sekupang, high-speed ferries go to Pekanbaru and other destinations in Sumatra. This is a popular route to Sumatra.

For Bintan, ferries go to Tanjung Pinang (S$51; 1½ hours) from the WTC at 9, 9.50 and 10.10 am, 1.30, 3 and 5.10 pm. From Bintan, Pelni boats and the MV *Samudera Jaya* go to Jakarta. Ferries also go to Bintan from the Tanah Merah Ferry Terminal on Tanah Merah Ferry Rd, near Changi airport, but only to the big Bintan Resort on the north-west of the island. Ships go from Bintan to Jakarta.

You don't require a visa to enter Indonesia via Batam or Bintan. For full details of onward travel from Batam and Bintan, see under Sumatra in the Indonesia chapter.

Getting Around

THE AIRPORT

Singapore's ultramodern Changi airport, 20 km east of the city, is one of those efficient miracles that Singapore specialises in. It has banking, money changing, post and telephone facilities, hotel reservation counters, left-luggage facilities, nearly 100 shops, hotel rooms, a fitness centre and a business centre. There are free films, audiovisual shows, bars with entertainment, hairdressers, medical facilities and a mini Science Discovery Museum, and if you're in transit for a long time you can even take a free two hour tour of the city.

Changi is divided into Terminal 1 and Terminal 2 – each in themselves international airports to match the world's best, connected in less than two minutes by the Changi Skytrain.

If you are one of the many air travellers fed up with overpriced and terrible food at airports, then Changi airport has a myriad of excellent restaurants serving food at normal prices. Even better, Changi has hawker centres in the basement of Terminal 1 and just outside Terminal 2.

Leaving the airport, catch public buses from the basement bus stop. Public buses No 16 and 16 E (express) stop on Stamford Rd for the Bencoolen St-Beach Rd cheap accommodation enclave and continue on to Orchard Rd. The fare is a flat S$1.30 and you have to tender correct money, so get some coins when you change money on arrival. Going to the airport, catch these buses on Orchard or Bras Basah Rds. The buses operate every eight to 12 minutes from 6 am to midnight, and take about half an hour.

Alternatively, the convenient Airbus service runs roughly every 20 minutes from 6 am to midnight. Three routes service all the big hotels in the colonial district (it also drops off on Bencoolen St) and Orchard Rd. The cost is S$5.

Taxis from (but not to) the airport are subject to a S$3 supplementary charge on top of the metered fare, which is around S$12 to S$15 to most places.

Singapore has another 'international' airport – forgotten Seletar, which handles a few services for the smaller regional airlines, such as Pelangi flights to Tioman in Malaysia. It is in the north of the island, and the easiest way to get there is to take a taxi; the nearest MRT station is Yio Chu Kang.

BUS

Singapore has a comprehensive bus network with frequent buses. You rarely have to wait more than a few minutes for a bus and they go almost everywhere. If you intend to do a lot of travelling by public transport in Singapore, a copy of the *Transitlink Guide*, S$1.20 from bookshops, listing all bus and MRT services, is a good investment.

Bus fares start from 50c (60c for air-con buses) for the first 3.2 km and go up in 10c increments for every 2.4 km to a maximum of S$1 (S$1.30 air-con). Drop the exact fare into the change box when boarding – change is not given.

Singapore Explorer bus passes cost S$5 for one day or S$12 for three days of unlimited travel, but you have to do a lot of bus travelling to get your money's worth.

MASS RAPID TRANSIT (MRT)

Singapore's ultramodern MRT system is the easiest, fastest and most comfortable way of getting around the city. The Somerset, Orchard and Newton MRT stations are all close to Orchard Rd. The Dhoby Ghaut station is closest to Bencoolen St. The Bugis and City Hall stations straddle Beach Rd.

Tickets vary from 60c to S$1.50, and are bought at ticket vending machines at MRT stations. You can also buy Transitlink stored-value tickets for S$10 (plus S$2 deposit); the exit machine electronically deducts fares from the encoded card and returns the card to you until its full value has been utilised. The cards can also be used in some buses that have validator machines.

Trains run from around 6 am to midnight and operate every three to eight minutes.

TAXI

Singapore has plenty of taxis, all air-con, metered, neat and clean, with drivers who know their way around and have been taught to be polite, believe it or not!

Taxis cost S$2.40 for the first one km then 10c for each additional 240 metres. From midnight to 6 am, there is a 50% surcharge over the metered fare. NTUC (☎ 452 5555) is one of the biggest companies.

Cars entering Singapore's Central Business District (CBD) between 7.30 am and 6.30 pm Monday to Friday, and 10.15 am and 2 pm on Saturday, have to purchase a special CBD licence, so you will have to pay the S$3 fee for a taxi if a passenger hasn't already done so. A S$1 surcharge also applies for trips from the CBD in afternoon peak times.

OTHER TRANSPORT

You still see a few bicycle rickshaws in Chinatown and on Orchard Rd. Always agree on the fare beforehand.

You can easily rent cars in Singapore, although it is rather pointless when you consider the excellent public transport available. Expensive surcharges apply if you take a rental car into Malaysia, where rental rates are cheaper anyway.

Check the following Things to See section for details on the ferries out to various islands.

Cycling in Singapore may not have too much appeal but if you want a bicycle to ride further afield, Singapore could be a good place to buy it. Check the yellow pages of the phone directory. Bicycles can be hired at a number of places on the East Coast Parkway, but they are intended mostly for weekend jaunts along the foreshore.

ORGANISED TOURS

A wide variety of tours are available in Singapore. Operators are listed in the tourist office's *Singapore Official Guide*. Most half-day tours cost between S$20 and S$40, while full-day tours can range up to S$70. Some of the most popular tours are river boat and harbour tours (see Things to See).

Things to See & Do

THINGS TO SEE

Singapore offers an accessible selection of varied Asian flavours in a small package. There's a modern CBD, the nearby but fast-disappearing old Chinatown and relics of a British colonial past, as well as colourful Little India and Arab St.

River & Central Business District

The Singapore River is no longer the city-state's commercial artery but it's still in the heart of Singapore, flanked by the business district, Chinatown and the colonial district.

Start at Raffles Place, the trading centre of a city that thrives on trade. The banks, offices and shipping companies are clustered around here. At the southern end of the business district, **Lau Pa Sat** (see the Central Singapore map) is a 'festival market', with souvenir shops and a host of food stalls housed in the restored Telok Ayer Centre, a fine old cast-iron Victorian marketplace. From **Clifford Pier**, you can get a good view over the teeming harbour or take a harbour boat tour. From there, walk along to **Merlion Park**, where Singapore's Merlion symbol spouts water over the Singapore River (see the Colonial District map).

The Singapore River has been comprehensively cleaned up and is now a recreational stretch of colonial restoration and photo opportunities. The old **Empress Place** building is now a museum. Nearby is **Raffles' Statue**. On the south bank, **Boat Quay** is a picturesque area of restored old shops housing restaurants and bars. It's the liveliest nightspot in the city. North Boat Quay leads upriver to **Clarke Quay**, where the restored old *godowns* (warehouses) and shopfronts house a variety of shops and restaurants. One of the best ways to see the river is to take a river boat tour (S$7) from Clarke Quay.

Colonial District

The centre of colonial Singapore is north of the river. Near Empress Place is the **Victoria**

SINGAPORE

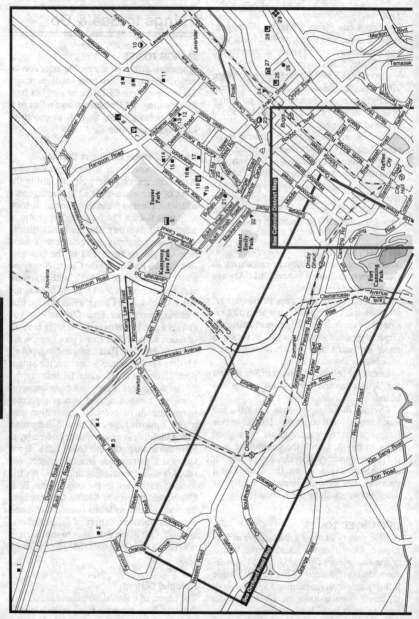

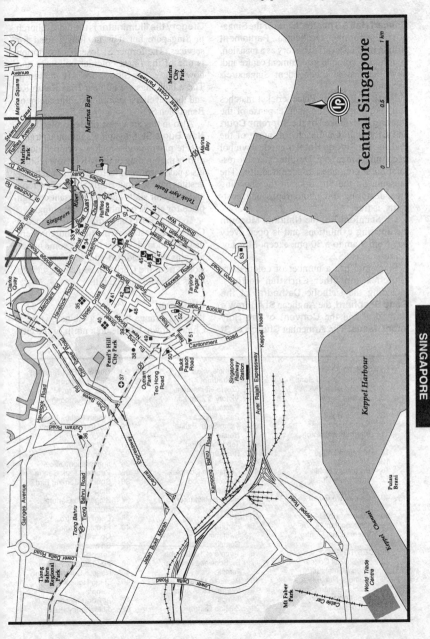

Central Singapore

Concert Hall & Theatre, home of the Singapore Symphony Orchestra. **Parliament House** has had a varied history as a mansion, courthouse, colonial government centre and, now, the seat of independent Singapore's parliament.

North of Empress Place, cricket matches still take place on the open expanse of the **Padang**, overlooked by the **Supreme Court** and **City Hall**. On Beach Rd, north of the Padang, the **Raffles Hotel** is another symbol of colonial Singapore. Despite extensive restoration, it continues to ooze tradition. The museum on the 3rd floor in the shopping area, featuring old photographs and postcards, is free.

On Stamford Rd, the **National Museum** has rotating exhibitions and is open every day from 9 am to 5.30 pm, except Monday. Admission is S$2.

Singapore has a number of colonial-era churches and other Christian edifices, including the Catholic **Cathedral of the Good Shepherd**, the Anglican **St Andrew's Cathedral** and the **Convent of the Holy Infant Jesus**. The Armenian **Church of St Gregory the Illuminator** is the oldest church in Singapore but it is no longer used for services. The former St Joseph's Institution is one of the finest colonial buildings and now houses the **Singapore Art Museum**. These buildings are all near Bras Basah Rd and the travellers' accommodation centre of Bencoolen St.

Also in this area, east of Bencoolen St, is **New Bugis St**, Singapore's infamous transvestite playground which was ripped down during the building of the MRT. Now rebuilt, it's a pale shadow of its former self and transvestites have left, but Bugis St has a few food and souvenir stalls and is a pleasant enough place for alfresco dining in the evening.

To reach **Fort Canning Hill**, continue up Coleman St past the Armenian Church where there's a good view over the city, some minor remains of the old fort and poignant gravestones from the Christian cemetery, set into walls at the foot of the hill.

Chinatown

It seems strange to have a Chinatown in a Chinese town, but the area north of the city

PLACES TO STAY		20	Komala Vilas	23	Ban San Bus Terminal
1	Novotel Orchid Hotel		Restaurant	25	Sultan Mosque
2	Metropolitan YMCA	22	Selera Restaurant	26	Airpower Travel
3	Garden Hotel	24	Victory & Zam Zam	27	Istana Kampong
4	Hotel VIP		Restaurants		Glam
8	Palace Hotel	33	Pasta Fresca	28	Hajjah Fatima Mosque
9	Kam Leng Hotel	39	Tiong Shan Eating	29	Golden Mile Complex
11	International Hotel		House	30	GPO
13	Tai Hoe Hotel	41	Teo Hiang Hing	31	Clifford Pier
14	Marajam Lodge		Restaurant	32	Harry's
15	Ali's Nest	44	Lau Pa Sat	34	Immigration Office
16	Broadway Hotel	48	Chinatown Complex	35	People's Park Centre
17	Little India Guest		Market & Food	36	Sunday Morning Bird
	House		Centre		Singing
49	Chinatown Guest	51	Hillman Restaurant	37	Singapore General
	House				Hospital
50	Majestic Hotel	**OTHER**		38	Pearl's Centre
53	Metropolitan YMCA	5	Farrer Park	40	People's Park
	International Centre		Swimming		Complex
			Complex	42	Sri Mariamman
PLACES TO EAT		6	Temple of 1000 Lights		Temple
12	Fut Sai Kai Coffee	7	Sri Srinivasa Perumal	43	Fuk Tak Ch'i Temple
	Shop & Restaurant		Temple	45	Nagore Durgha Shrine
19	Muthu's, Nur Jehan,	10	Buses to Malaysia	46	Thian Hock Keng
	Delhi & Banana	18	Veerama Kali Amman		Temple
	Leaf Apolo		Temple	47	Al-Abrar Mosque
	Restaurants	21	Zhujiao Centre	52	JJ Mahoney Pub

SINGAPORE

centre as far as New Bridge Rd (which runs south-west from the Singapore River) is just that. Much of this area, one of the most picturesque in Singapore, was ploughed over for development but more recently many of the old shophouses have been restored. In the process, a number of traditional businesses have been replaced by fashionable restaurants, bars and expensive shops. Despite the gentrification, this traditional heart of Singapore still holds plenty of interest.

There's a whole dictionary of religions in Singapore, so you'll find a lot of temples. A walk around Chinatown will take you to the **Wak Hai Cheng Bio** Chinese temple, the **Nagore Durgha Shrine**, the **Thian Hock Keng Temple**, dating from 1840 and one of the most colourful in Singapore, and the **Al-Abrar Mosque**. Also in this intriguing area is the **Sri Mariamman Temple** on South Bridge Rd, a technicolour Hindu shrine with brilliant statuary on the tower over the entrance. It was originally built in 1827 and its present form dates from 1862. Several times a year there are fire-walking ceremonies inside – the firewalkers start at a slow ceremonial pace but soon break into a sprint.

There's always something interesting to see as you wander the convoluted 'five foot ways' of Chinatown. A five foot way, which takes its name from the fact that it is roughly five feet wide, is a walkway at the front of the traditional Chinese shophouses which is enclosed, veranda-like, at the front of the building. The difficulty with them is that every shop's walkway is individual – one may well be higher or lower, or closer to or further from the street, than the next.

The **Tanjong Pagar** conservation area, the first major restoration project in Chinatown (wedged between Neil and Tanjong Pagar Rds) is the showpiece of restored Chinatown.

Little India

Although Singapore is predominantly Chinese, there's a colourful Indian district around Serangoon Rd, just north of the colonial district. The smell of spices and curries wafting through the area is as much a part of the district's flavour as the colours and noises.

Attractions in Little India include the **Zhujiao Centre** market, the restored **Little India Arcade** and the backstreets off Serangoon Rd, with their exotic little shops and temples, including the **Veerama Kali Amman** and **Sri Srinivasa Perumal** temples. The **Temple of 1000 Lights** on Race Course Rd at the northern edge of Little India has a fine 15-metre-high seated Buddha, illuminated, for a small fee, by the promised 1000 lights. There is also a mother-of-pearl replica of the Buddha's footprint.

The seedy alleyways behind Desker Rd house Singapore's most infamous brothels and the coffee shops with outdoor tables do a roaring trade. It is the successor to old Bugis St, without the tourists and carnival atmosphere, and later in the evenings the transvestites strut their stuff.

Arab St

South-east of Little India is Arab St, the Muslim centre, especially along North Bridge Rd. Here you'll find old shops with Malaysian and Indonesian goods, and the **Sultan Mosque** on North Bridge Rd, the biggest mosque in Singapore. It was originally built in 1825 but was totally replaced a century later. The **Istana Kampong Glam** was the centre for Malay royalty, resident here before the arrival of Stamford Raffles.

It's always interesting to wander around the picturesque streets, with evocative names like Baghdad St, Kandahar St and Haji Lane. Bussorah St is newly renovated and it comes to life during Ramadan, when food stalls set up after dark for the faithful who fast during the day.

Orchard Rd Area

This area is a corridor of big hotels and busy shopping centres. Beyond Orchard Rd are the fine old colonial homes where the wealthy elite of Singapore still live. Holland Village is an expat enclave out on the western continuation of Orchard Rd.

Peranakan Place, at Orchard and Emerald Hill Rds, is one old-fashioned exception to

SINGAPORE

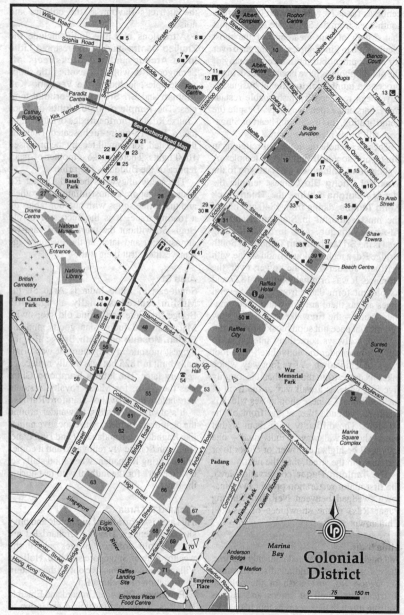

SINGAPORE

Wilkie Road
Sophia Road
Prinsep Street
Albert Street
Albert Complex
Rochor Centre

Selegie Road
Middle Road
Waterloo Street
Albert Centre
New Bugis St
Cheng Yan Place
Manila St.
Johore Road
Blanco Court
Bugis
Fraser Street

Paradiz Centre
Kirk Terrace
See Orchard Road Map
Fortune Centre
Bugis Junction
Tan Quee Lan Street
Farquhar Street

Cathay Building
Hardy Road
Orchard Road

Bras Basah Park
Bencoolen Street
Bras Basah Road
Queen Street
Bain Street
Rochor Road
Liang Seah Street
To Arab Street

Drama Centre
National Museum
Fort Entrance
National Library

Victoria Street
Middle Road
Cashin St.
Purvis Street
North Bridge Road
Seah Street
Shaw Towers

British Cemetery
Fort Canning Park
Cox Terrace
Canning Rise

Armenian Street
Stamford Road
Raffles Hotel
Beach Road
Beach Centre

Nicoll Highway

Raffles City
Suntec City
War Memorial Park

City Hall
Coleman Street
Raffles Boulevard

Hill Street
North Bridge Road
Colombo Court
St Andrew's Road
Padang
Raffles Avenue
Marina Square Complex

Singapore
High Street
Elgin Bridge
River
Hallpike Street
Parliament Lane

Carpenter Street
South Bridge Road
Hong Kong Street

Raffles Landing Site
Empress Place Food Centre
Empress Place

Connaught Drive
Esplanade Park
Queen Elizabeth Walk

Anderson Bridge
Fullerton Road
Merlion

Marina Bay

Colonial District

0   75   150 m

the glass and chrome gloss of Orchard Rd. In recent times, there has been a resurgence of interest in Peranakan culture in Singapore. Peranakan is the term for Straits-born Chinese, also called *nonyas* (women) and *babas* (men). Traditionally, the Straits-born Chinese have spoken their own patois and practiced their own customs, a hybrid of Chinese and Malay. This is probably the nearest Singapore comes to having a cultural identity. Peranakan Place is a lane of restored shophouses, one of which is a small, interesting museum (entry S$4).

The **Istana** (President's Palace) is open to the public on selected public holidays, such as New Year's Day. The recently rebuilt **Chettiar Hindu Temple** is on Tank Rd near the intersection of Clemenceau Ave and River Valley Rd. It's a short walk from Orchard Rd and most active during the spectacular Thaipusam festival.

Jurong

Jurong town, west of the city centre, is a huge industrial complex but it also has a few tourist attractions.

On the way out to Jurong is **Haw Par Villa** (formerly the Tiger Balm Gardens), originally built with the fortune amassed from the Haw Par brothers' miracle medicament. Fun park additions have changed much of the gory and crazy charm of the old gardens, though some of the grotesque statuary telling tales from Chinese mythology survives. Entry is an overpriced S$16.50.

Out at Jurong, there are the adjoining **Chinese Gardens** and **Japanese Gardens**, right by the Chinese Garden MRT station.

The **Jurong Bird Park** is interesting, even if you're not a feathered-friend freak. The impressive enclosures and beautifully landscaped gardens house over 8000 birds. The bird park is open Monday to Friday from 9

SINGAPORE

PLACES TO STAY		
5	Sun Sun Hotel	
6	Why Not Homestay	
8	Goh's Homestay & Hawaii Hostel	
11	South-East Asia Hotel	
14	New 7th Storey Hotel	
15	New Backpackers Lodge	
16	Backpackers' Cozy Corner	
17	Ah Chew Hotel	
18	Waffles Home Stay	
19	Hotel Inter-Continental	
20	Hotel Bencoolen	
21	Lee Boarding House, Peony Mansions & Latin House	
22	Bencoolen House	
23	San Wah Hotel	
24	Strand Hotel	
25	Bayview Inn	
27	YMCA International House	
30	Allson Hotel	
34	Lido Hotel	
35	Das Travellers' Inn	
36	Lee Travellers' Club & Willy's Guest House	
37	Shang Onn Hotel	
40	Metropole Hotel	
41	Carlton Hotel	
47	Mayfair City Hotel	

50	Westin Plaza Hotel	
51	Westin Stamford Hotel	
52	Marina Mandarin Hotel	
60	Excelsior Hotel	
61	Peninsula Hotel	

PLACES TO EAT		
7	Sahib Restaurant	
9	Fatty's Wing Seong Restaurant	
26	Regency Palace	
29	Koh Fong Restaurant	
31	Xiang Man Lou Food Court	
33	Swee Kee Restaurant	
38	Yet Con Restaurant	
39	Tropical Makan Palace Food Stalls	
59	Hill Street Food Centre	

OTHER		
1	Selegie Complex	
2	Peace Mission	
3	Peace Centre	
4	Parklane Shopping Mall	
10	Fu Lou Shou Complex	
12	Kuan Yin Temple	
13	Mosque	
28	Singapore Art Museum	
32	Bras Basah Complex	

42	Cathedral of the Good Shepherd	
43	National Museum Shop	
44	Substation	
45	Asian Civilisations Museum	
46	MPH Bookshop	
48	Stamford House	
49	Singapore Tourist Promotion Board Office	
53	St Andrew's Cathedral	
54	Telecom	
55	Peninsula Plaza	
56	US Embassy	
57	Church of St Gregory the Illuminator	
58	Singapore Philatelic Museum	
62	Funan Centre	
63	High Street Centre	
64	Riverwalk Galleria	
65	City Hall	
66	Supreme Court	
67	Singapore Cricket Club	
68	Parliament House	
69	Victoria Concert Hall & Theatre	
70	Raffles' Statue	
71	Empress Place Building	

am to 6 pm and on weekends from 8 am to 6 pm. Admission is S$9.27. Get there on bus No 194 or 251 from the Boon Lay MRT station. Right opposite the bird park is **Jurong Crocodile Paradise**, open from 9 am to 6 pm daily and costing S$6.

The **Singapore Science Centre**, on Science Centre Rd, has handles to crank, buttons to push and levers to pull – all in the interest of making science come alive. It is open Tuesday to Sunday from 10 am to 6 pm, and admission is S$3. Take the MRT to the Jurong East station and then walk 0.5 km west or take bus No 66 or 335 from the station.

Tang Dynasty City, about two km south of the Chinese and Japanese gardens, is a

huge theme park re-creation of old Chang'an, China's Tang Dynasty capital from the 6th to 8th centuries AD. It is open every day from 9.30 am to 6.30 pm. Admission is S$15.45.

East Coast & Changi

The East Coast district, out towards the airport, has a popular beach with recreational and dining facilities along the foreshore. **East Coast Park** has swimming, windsurfing and bicycle rentals.

If you want to find the Malay influence within Singapore, head inland from East Coast Park to the **Katong** district. Along East Coast Rd you'll find old terraces, excellent Nonya restaurants and antique shops.

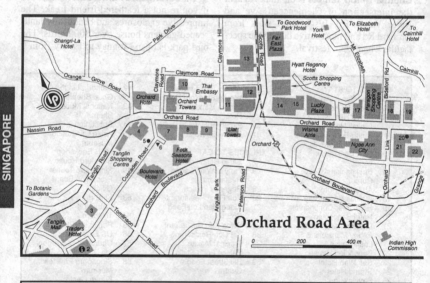

Orchard Road Area

PLACES TO STAY
1 Omni Marco Polo Hotel
3 Regen Hotel
4 Orchard Parade Hotel
8 Hilton International Hotel
10 Hotel Negara
13 Royal Holiday Inn Crowne Plaza
15 Marriott Hotel
18 Crown Prince Hotel
21 Mandarin Hotel
34 Holiday Inn Park View
40 Hotel Grand Central
41 Supreme Hotel
44 Imperial Hotel

PLACES TO EAT
6 Hard Rock Cafe
27 Azizas Restaurant
31 Saxophone Bar & Grill
32 Cuppage Thai Food Restaurant
38 Snackworld & Selera Cuppage Food Centre
39 Istanbul Corner

OTHER
2 Singapore Tourist Promotions Board Office
5 Ming Arcade
7 Forum Shopping Centre

Nearby **Geylang Serai**, a Malay residential area, is easily accessed by the Paya Lebar MRT station. On Geylang Rd is the **Malay Cultural Centre**, a Malay theme park with a museum and entertainment for kids, or you can wander around the shops for free. Next door is the interesting, old-fashioned Geylang Serai market.

At the far eastern end of the island is **Changi**, the village from which the airport takes its name. There's a half-decent beach and Changi Prison has a fascinating little museum about the prisoner-of-war camp operated by the Japanese during WWII. The museum is open Monday to Saturday from 9.30 am to 4.30 pm. Bus No 2 runs to Changi from the Bencoolen St and Raffles city area.

Islands, Beaches & Watersports

Singapore's sprinkling of islands to the south have undergone a lot of development over the past few years. **Sentosa** has been the most developed – it's rather plastic, although very popular as a local weekend escape. Entry to the island is S$5 and the ferry trip from the WTC costs 80c or there are buses. Alternatively, you can take the cable car to the island from Mt Faber or the WTC for S$5.50. The cable-car ride, with its spectacular views, is one of the best parts of a visit to Sentosa.

Most attractions on the island cost extra but monorail and bus transport on the island is included in the entry cost. Attractions here

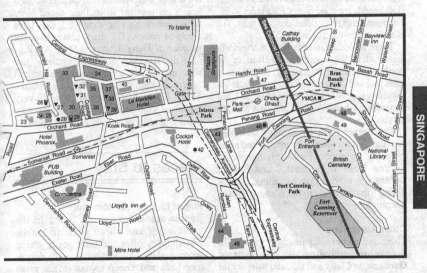

9	Far East Shopping Centre	23	Faber House	37	Orchard Plaza
11	International Building	24	Midpoint Orchard	42	House of Tan Yeok Nee
12	Shaw Centre	25	Orchard Emerald	43	Singapore Shopping
14	Tang's	26	No 5, Que Pasa		Centre
16	Tang Building		& The Den	45	Chettiar Hindu
17	Promenade Shopping	28	Peranakan Place		Temple
	Centre	29	Papa Joe's	46	Supreme House
19	Yen San Building	30	Centrepoint	47	MacDonald House
20	Singapore Airlines	33	Cuppage Centre	48	National Museum
22	Orchard Theatre	35	Cuppage Plaza	49	Drama Centre
		36	Orchard Point		

include the informative Pioneers of Singapore, Surrender Chamber and Festivals of Singapore museum, with waxworks figures showing Singapore's history and festivals. Underwater World is a spectacular aquarium where the marine life swims around and over you while you move along an acrylic tunnel. Entry is S$12. Fort Siloso with its WWII displays is worth a visit, or there are plenty of fun rides and other theme park attractions. Sentosa also has sports facilities and Singapore's best beaches.

Other islands are not as developed as Sentosa. There are ferry trips several times a day (much more frequently on weekends) to **St John's Island** and **Kusu Island**. Tiny Kusu has a Chinese temple and a Malay shrine. Both islands are good places for a quiet swim. The round-trip ferry ticket costs S$6.20. The islands are crowded on weekends.

There are other islands both to the north and south of Singapore. **Pulau Ubin**, to the north, is the most interesting. It still has a rural feel and can be explored by bicycle – a good day trip. Bumboat ferries to Pulau Ubin leave from Changi Village and cost S$2 per person.

The **Farrer Park Swimming Complex** (see the Central Singapore map) is the nearest public swimming pool to the Bencoolen St area. Head to the **East Coast Sailing Centre** for windsurfing or sailing. Scuba-diving trips are made to the islands south of Singapore.

Other Attractions

There are numerous parks and gardens in Singapore, including the fine **Botanic Gardens** on Cluny and Holland Rds, not far from Tanglin Rd (west of the city centre – see the Singapore Island map). Or you can climb **Mt Faber** (116 metres; west of the city centre) or **Bukit Timah** (north-west of the Botanic Gardens), about as high as you can get in Singapore. The nature reserve at Bukit Timah has the only large area of primary rainforest left in Singapore and some good walking trails traverse the jungle. **Sungei Buloh Nature Park**, in the north-west of the island, is a wetland nature reserve for bird-spotting.

The world-class **Zoological Gardens**, on Mandai Lake Rd in the north of the island, is one of Singapore's most popular attractions. The orang-utan colony and the Komodo dragons are major attractions. The zoo is open daily from 8.30 am to 6 pm. Admission is S$9.27. Take the MRT to the Ang Mo Kio MRT station, and then bus No 138. Next to the zoo is the **Night Safari**, open from 7.30 pm to midnight nightly. Walking trails through the park allow a unique opportunity to view nocturnal animals under special lighting. This excellent attraction costs S$15.45. The **Mandai Orchard Gardens** are beside the zoo.

Sunday morning **bird-singing** sessions are one of Singapore's real pleasures. Bird lovers get together to let their caged birds have a communal sing-song while they have a cup of coffee. The main centre is at the junction of Tiong Bahru and Seng Poh Rds, near the Havelock Rd hotel enclave (just west of the city centre – see the Central Singapore map). It's a half-km walk from the Tiong Bahru MRT station. It's all very organised – tall pointy birds go in tall pointy cages and little fat ones in little fat cages.

Places to Stay

Places to Stay – bottom end

Budget accommodation is found in the guesthouses and cheap Chinese hotels. Guesthouses offer the only really cheap accommodation in Singapore, with dormitory beds and cheap rooms (often small spartan boxes with a fan). Free tea and coffee are standard offerings, and a basic breakfast is usually thrown in. They are the best places to meet other travellers.

Most of the cheap hotels have seen better days, but they do have more character than the guesthouses. Rooms range from around S$25 to S$60. This will get you a fairly spartan room with a bare floor, a few pieces of furniture, a sink and a fan. Couples should always ask for a single room – a single usually means just one double bed, whereas a double has two.

The main area for budget accommodation is in the colonial district. Bencoolen St and Beach Rd have the most options. Other cheap possibilities are found further north in Little India and nearby Jalan Besar, and in Chinatown (south of the river).

Bencoolen St Area Singapore's original and biggest backpackers' centre is at 46-52 Bencoolen St. There's no sign at all; go around the back and take the lift.

At the top, at least in elevation, *Lee Boarding House* (☎ 338 3149) has its reception at room No 52 on the 7th floor. It's a large place with dorms for S$8 or less crowded air-con dorms for S$9. Singles/doubles cost S$19/29 with fan, S$29/35 with air-con, or good hotel-style rooms with air-con and bathroom cost S$45 to S$70. *Peony Mansions* (☎ 338 5638), one of the original guesthouses, is on the 4th floor. Dormitory beds cost S$8, singles cost S$20 and doubles are S$30 to S$45. The dorms aren't great but many of the rooms are quite good.

On the other side of Bencoolen St, between the Strand and Bencoolen hotels, is *Bencoolen House* (☎ 338 1206) at No 27. The reception area is on the 7th floor. Dorm beds cost S$7, a few singles cost S$20 but most rooms cost from S$25 to S$45 with air-con. It's a bit run-down but OK.

In the thick of things, the *Why Not Homestay* (☎ 338 8838), 127 Bencoolen St, is a popular place with an excellent 24 hour Indian coffee shop downstairs. It has a variety of reasonable rooms from S$25 to S$50 with air-con and shower. *Green Curtains* (☎ 334 8597) next door at No 131A is an offshoot of Peony Mansions with well-maintained rooms. The S$20 fan rooms are small and dark but better rooms range up to S$45.

Another centre for guesthouses is at 171 Bencoolen St. *Goh's Homestay* (☎ 339 6561), up a long flight of stairs to the 3rd floor at 171A, has a pleasant eating/meeting area. The rooms are clean but small, without windows and expensive at S$34/44 or S$12 in the dorm. *Hawaii Hostel* (☎ 338 4187) on

the 2nd floor at 171B is an impersonal place, with eight bed dorms for S$10, pokey singles for S$25 and better air-con doubles for S$35.

Redevelopment in the area has seen the demise of most of the old hotels. The *San Wah* (☎ 336 2428) at 36 Bencoolen St is a little better than the cheapest Chinese hotels. Singles/doubles cost S$45/50, S$5 more with air-con. At 260-262 Middle Rd, the good, spotlessly clean *Sun Sun Hotel* (☎ 338 4911) has rooms for S$40/48, or air-con doubles cost S$54.

Beach Rd Area *Lee Traveller's Club* (☎ 339 5490), on the 6th floor of the Fu Yeun building at 75 Beach Rd, is a large, popular place but not as cramped as some others. The air-con dorm costs S$8, singles start at S$15 and air-con doubles cost S$30 and S$35. *Willy's* (☎ 337 0916), in the same building on the 3rd floor, is reasonable but packed with rooms. Small dorms cost S$7, tiny windowless singles are S$20 or better air-con doubles cost S$28 and S$30.

Waffles Home Stay (☎ 334 1608), on the 3rd floor of 490 North Bridge Rd, is a friendly place with dorms for S$8 and S$10, and a few basic double rooms for S$26.

Liang Siah St, which runs onto Beach Rd, has a couple of good guesthouses. The popular *New Backpackers Lodge* (☎ 334 8042) at No 18A has dorm beds for S$8 and most rooms go for S$25. *Backpackers' Cozy Corner* (☎ 296 8005) at No 2A tries harder and offers a slightly better standard of rooms. Dorms cost S$7 and rooms range from S$15 to S$28 with fan, S$32 to S$40 with air-con and bathroom.

The traditional Chinese hotels are run-down but good for the price. The *Shang Onn* (☎ 338 4153), 37 Beach Rd, is a little more expensive at S$30/34/45 for single double/ triple rooms. The rooms are very clean and have character but not much else. The *Lido* (☎ 337 1872) at 54 Middle Rd is a rickety, old wooden hotel but immaculately kept. Large rooms for S$24/28 are good value, but the management is less than welcoming. At the corner of Liang Seah St and North Bridge Rd, the *Ah Chew Hotel* (☎ 336 3563) is very basic but friendly. The S$30 rooms are

SINGAPORE

decrepit, but at least the eyeball-sized holes have been taped over.

Little India & Jalan Besar A couple of good guesthouses have sprung up in Little India, both on Roberts Lane. The most popular is the friendly *Ali's Nest* (☎ 291 2938) at No 23. Dorms cost S$7, a few small singles go for S$15 or better doubles cost S$25. *Marajam Lodge* (☎ 293 5251) at No 30 is a bigger place with a variety of rooms scattered around for S$15 to S$25, S$30 with air-con. The hallway dorm costs S$7, or a two bed shared room costs S$11 per person.

The *Little India Guest House* (☎ 294 2866), 3 Veerasamy Rd, is more a small hotel than a guesthouse. Small, well-appointed rooms with shared bathrooms cost S$38/50.

Jalan Besar has a few cheap hotels, convenient for the Malaysia bus station but not much else. The pick of the bunch is the spotlessly clean *Palace Hotel* (☎ 298 3108) at 407A-B Jalan Besar. Large, balconied double rooms for S$25 are good value. This is a hotel with history – Tony Wheeler wrote the 1st edition of this book in a back room. Further south down Jalan Besar at No 383, the *Kam Leng* (☎ 298 2289) is a run-down old hotel with rooms for S$28, S$35 with air-con. At No 290A, the architecturally interesting *International Hotel* (☎ 293 9238) has large doubles for $40, or S$48 with bath.

Chinatown The friendly *Chinatown Guest House* (☎ 220 0671), 5th floor, 325D New Bridge Rd, has dorm beds for S$10 and reasonable rooms for S$30 up to S$45 with air-con. It's about the cheapest option in Chinatown and handy to the Outram Park MRT station.

One of the better cheap hotels in Singapore is the *Majestic Hotel* (☎ 222 3377), 31 Bukit Pasoh Rd, but this popular hotel is often full. Air-con singles/doubles are S$47/55 or S$59/69 with bath. The rooms without bath are the most pleasant.

Other Areas The *Mayfair City Hotel* (☎ 337 4542) is at 40-44 Armenian St near Orchard Rd, behind the National Museum in the colo-

nial district. Good rooms with air-con, shower and TV cost S$60/70 for singles/doubles.

Mitre Hotel (☎ 737 3811) at 145 Killiney Rd is the cheapest hotel anywhere near Orchard Rd (half a km to the north). It would have to be the most dilapidated flea pit in Singapore, but it does have a good deal of character. It is in an old villa set back off the street in large grounds and has a dingy bar popular with oil-rig workers. Rough singles cost S$24 or passable doubles with air-con and attached bath cost S$36.

The Ys Singapore has three YMCAs, which take men, women and couples, and provide mostly mid-range accommodation. Though expensive, they are still very popular, so advance bookings in writing with one night deposit are usually essential. Non-YMCA members pay a small charge for temporary membership.

The *YMCA International House* (☎ 336 6000), 1 Orchard Rd, is in a handy position with good facilities, including a fitness centre, swimming pool, restaurant and a McDonald's. Average mid-range singles/doubles with air-con, TV and bathroom cost S$80/90, plus 13% tax and service charge. A bed in a four bed dorm costs S$25.

The *Metropolitan YMCA* (☎ 737 7755), 60 Stevens Rd, also has well-appointed rooms, a pool and a cafe. It is a good 15 minute walk north of Orchard and Tanglin Rds. Singles/doubles/triples with bathroom, TV and air-con range from S$78/87/100 to S$91/100/118.

The well-equipped *Metropolitan YMCA International Centre* (☎ 222 4666), 70 Palmer Rd, is a little far out, but close to Chinatown, the railway station and the Tanjong Pagar MRT station. Singles with common shower are S$34, but these are for men only. Doubles/triples with attached bathrooms are S$71/80.

Places to Stay – Middle
While Singapore has dozens of high-rise, luxury hotels with all mod-cons, mid-range hotels are in short supply. Most rooms in

these hotels will have air-con, TV, telephone and bathroom attached. In the major hotels, a 14% government tax and service charge is added to your bill, but many mid-range hotels, like those in the bottom end, include this in the price.

The *New 7th Storey Hotel* (☎ 337 0251) at 229 Rochor Rd, at the northern end of the colonial district, is an upmarket cheapie with rooms for S$59, or S$75 with attached bathroom. The *South-East Asia Hotel* (☎ 338 2394) at 190 Waterloo St is quiet and good for the money. Doubles cost S$63, or S$79 with two double beds.

Smaller modern hotels include the *Hotel Bencoolen* (☎ 336 0822), 47 Bencoolen St. The rooms are cheaply put together and cost S$88 and S$93. Much better is the *Strand Hotel* (☎ 338 1866), 25 Bencoolen St, with rooms for S$95.

The new *Beach Hotel* (☎ 336 7712), 95 Beach Rd, has a better class of rooms for $95 to S$120.

The *Broadway Hotel* (☎ 292 4661), 195 Serangoon Rd, in Little India, is an older hotel with singles/doubles for S$80/90 and S$90/100, plus 4% tax. The new *Tai Hoe Hotel* (☎ 293 9122), 163 Kitchener Rd, is the pick of the new hotels that have sprung up in Little India. Excellent rooms cost a reasonable S$74/88.

You can find a few reasonably priced hotels around Orchard Rd. On Kramat Rd, one block north of Orchard Rd, the *Supreme Hotel* (☎ 737 8333) is central and a good deal for the position. Doubles cost S$85. *Lloyd's Inn* (☎ 737 7309), 2 Lloyd Rd, is a small, attractive hotel less than a 10 minute walk from Orchard Rd in a quiet street among the old villas of Singapore. Lee Kuan Yew is a neighbour. Well-appointed doubles cost S$85 a double or S$95 with fridge.

In the quiet residential area to the north of Orchard and Tanglin Rds, the *Hotel VIP* (☎ 235 4277), 5 Balmoral Crescent, has a swimming pool and rooms for S$99. The *RELC International House* (☎ 737 9044), 30 Orange Grove Rd, is a quality hotel edging into the top-end category. Large doubles with balcony and fridge are S$110.

Places to Eat

Hawker Food

Traditionally, hawkers had mobile food stalls (pushcarts), set up their tables and stools around them and sold their food right on the streets. Real, mobile, on-the-street hawkers have now been replaced by hawker centres, where a large number of stationary hawkers can be found under the one roof. These centres are the baseline for Singapore food, where the prices are lowest and the eating is possibly the most interesting.

Scattered among the hawkers are tables and stools, and you can sit and eat in any area you choose – none of them belong to a specific stall. A group of you can sit at one table and all eat and purchase drinks from a variety of different stalls.

One of the wonders of food-centre eating is how the various operators keep track of their plates and utensils – and how they manage to chase you up with the bill. The real joy of these food centres is the sheer variety; while you're having Chinese food, your companion can be eating a biryani and across the table somebody else can be trying the satay. As a rough guide, most single dish meals cost from S$2 to S$3; the price is higher for more elaborate dishes.

City Centre In the business centre, *Empress Place*, beside the Singapore River, is a busy lunchtime centre and a pleasant place to have a meal.

Near the waterfront is the trendy *Lau Pa Sat*, on Raffles Quay near the Raffles Place MRT station. Hawkers inside serve Nonya, Korean and western food, as well as more usual fare. Quasi-mobile hawkers set up in the evenings on Boon Tat St, and a more traditional hawkers' centre is just on the other side of Raffles Quay

Orchard Rd Area Hawker food is mostly found in slightly more expensive air-conditioned food courts in the shopping centres.

The *Scotts Picnic Food Court* in the Scotts

Shopping Centre on Scotts Rd, just off Orchard Rd by the Hyatt Hotel, is glossier and more restaurant-like than the general run of food centres, and the stalls around the dining area are international. Similar food centres are the *Orchard Emerald Food Court*, in the basement of the Orchard Emerald shopping centre, and the *Food Life Food Court*, on the 4th floor of the Wisma Atria. The busy hawker centre on the 6th floor of *Lucky Plaza* (near the Orchard MRT station) has a good range of cheap hawkers' favourites.

Colonial District The *Albert Centre*, on Albert Rd between Waterloo and Queen Sts, is an extremely good, busy and very popular centre which has all types of food at low prices. On the corner of Bencoolen and Albert Sts, in the basement of the Sim Lim Square complex, is the *Tenco Food Centre*, a very clean establishment.

Victoria St Food Court, next to the Victoria Hotel, has an air-con section at the back and a bar with draught beer. The *Tropical Makan Palace* in the basement of the Beach Centre, 15 Beach Rd, is close to the Raffles Hotel. It has food stalls in the air-con section or you can eat outside.

The famous *Satay Club* has finally fallen to redevelopment, but many of the hawkers have moved from the waterfront to Clarke Quay by the river where the satay is still superb. Specify how many sticks (35c each) you want or they'll assume your appetite is much larger than it is.

Chinatown The Chinatown area has a number of excellent food centres. The *People's Park Complex* has a good, large food centre, and the *Maxwell Food Centre* is an old-fashioned centre on the corner of South Bridge and Maxwell Rds (near the Tanjong Pagar MRT station – see the Central Singapore map).

Some of the best Chinese food stalls in town are on the 2nd floor at the *Chinatown Complex*, on the corner of Sago and Trengganu Sts, where there is also a market. Try the *Fu Ji Crayfish*, stall No 02-221,

where a superb crayfish or prawn claypot with vegetables and rice costs around S$5.

The *Fountain Food Court* at 51 Craig Rd is more upmarket, with nouveau decor and air-con comfort. It has satay and other Malay food, popiah and kueh, and good congee.

Chinese

Singapore has plenty of restaurants serving everything from a south Indian rice plate to an all-American hamburger, but naturally it's Chinese restaurants that predominate.

Colonial District The famous *Fatty's Wing Seong Restaurant* at 01-33 Albert Complex on Albert St, near the corner of Bencoolen St, has an extensive menu and consistently good food. Most dishes cost around S$5 to S$8, and go up to S$20 or more for crab.

The *Esquire Kitchen* (☎ 336 1802), 02-01 Bras Basah Complex, is another moderately priced place with air-con, Chinese decor and good food. Good value set lunches and dinners cost S$18 for two people.

Chicken-rice is a common and popular dish all over town. Originally from Hainan in China, chicken-rice is a dish of elegant simplicity, and in Singapore they do it better than anywhere. *Swee Kee*, 51 Middle Rd, close to the Raffles Hotel, is a long-running specialist with a very high reputation. Chicken and rice served with chilli, ginger and thick soya sauce is S$3.50. It also serves steamboats. A stone's throw from Swee Kee you'll find *Yet Con*, 25 Purvis St, which some claim is the best of all Singapore's chicken-rice places.

On Bencoolen St, the Fortune Centre (a few blocks north-west of the Raffles Hotel) is a good place for cheap vegetarian food. On the ground floor you'll find the *ABC Eating House* and *Yi Song* food stalls, which have cheap vegetarian food in air-con surroundings. Upstairs on the 4th floor is the *Eastern Vegetarian Food* coffee shop.

Chinatown The *Hillman*, 159 Cantonment Rd, near the Outram Park MRT station at the edge of Chinatown, is a straightforward Cantonese restaurant where you can have a good meal for under S$15 per person.

For dim sum a good bet is the *Tiong Shan Eating House*, an old-fashioned coffee shop on the corner of New Bridge and Keong Saik Rds. A plate of dim sum is around S$1.50, and as good as you'll find anywhere.

Teochew food is a widely available cuisine, and the coffee shops on Chinatown's Mosque St are good places to try it. Menus are hard to come by but a request for suggestions and prices will be readily answered, and the prices are low. *Teo Hiang Hing* at 47 Mosque St is good Teochew eatery.

Chinatown has some moderately priced vegetarian restaurants, including the *Happy Realm* on the 3rd floor of Pearl's Centre on Eu Tong St (see the Central Singapore map), one of the best around. Mains cost around S$5 to S$6, and it serves good claypot dishes.

Coast Singapore has another local variation on Chinese food. Seafood in Singapore is simply superb, whether it's prawns or abalone, fish-head curry or chilli crabs. Seafood isn't cheap, and a whole fish, crab or prawns start at just under S$20 per dish. Many of the seafood places don't have set prices but base dishes on 'market price' and the size of the fish. Make sure you check the price first.

The *UDMC Seafood Centre*, at the beach on East Coast Parkway (several km east of the city centre), has a number of seafood restaurants and is very popular in the evenings. The food and the setting are good, but some places tend to hustle a bit, so definitely check the prices first.

Indian

To sample eat-with-your-fingers south Indian vegetarian food, the place to go is the Little India district off Serangoon Rd (just north of the colonial district – see the Central Singapore map). The famous and very popular *Komala Vilas*, 76 Serangoon Rd, has an open downstairs area where you can have masala dosa (S$1.50) and other snacks. The upstairs section is air-conditioned and you can have

its all-you-can-eat rice meal for S$4.50. Remember that it is customary to wash your hands before you start and use your right hand to eat with – ask for eating utensils only if you really have to!

Another main contender in the local competition for the best southern Indian food is the *Madras New Woodlands Cafe* at 14 Upper Dickson Rd off Serangoon Rd, around the corner from Komala Vilas. A branch of the well-known Woodlands chain in India, prices are about the same as at Komala Vilas.

Race Course Rd, a block north-west from Serangoon Rd, is the best area in Singapore for nonvegetarian curry. Try the *Banana Leaf Apolo* at 56 Race Course Rd for superb nonvegetarian Indian food, including Singapore's classic fish-head curry, or the very popular *Muthu's Curry Restaurant* at No 78. *Delhi Restaurant* (☎ 296 4585) at No 60 is an excellent north Indian restaurant, with tandoori food and curries from S$7 to S$10. Expect to pay around S$20 per person with bread and side dishes. Similar places on Race Course Rd are *Nur Jehan* at No 66 and *Maharajahs's Tandoor* at No 70.

For Indian Muslim food (chicken biryani for S$3.50, as well as murtabak and fish-head curry), there are fine establishments on North Bridge Rd, near the corner of Arab St, opposite the Sultan Mosque. The *Victory* and *Zam Zam* are two of the most well known.

Sahib Restaurant at 129 Bencoolen St, near Middle Rd (see the Colonial District map), is a small, basic Indian restaurant with very good food, including fish-head curry. Meals are around S$4 and it is open 24 hours. At the other end of the scale, *Maharani* (☎ 235 8840) is on the 5th floor of the Far East Plaza, 14 Scotts Rd (near the Hyatt Hotel – see the Orchard Rd map). The northern Indian food and the service are good in this casual restaurant. You can eat well for S$20 per person.

Malay, Indonesian & Nonya

The Orchard Rd area has a number of good restaurants. *Bintang Timur* (☎ 235 4539), 02-13 Far East Plaza, 14 Scotts Rd, has excellent Malay food and you can try a good range of dishes and eat your fill for under S$20. *Tambuah Mas* (☎ 733 3333), 04-10/13 Tanglin Shopping Centre, 19 Tanglin Rd, is a moderately priced Indonesian restaurant with a good selection of seafood dishes and Indonesian favourites, such as rendang, gado gado and cendol. If you like the fiery food of northern Sumatra, a good nasi padang specialist is the cheap *Rumah Makan Minang* on the corner of Muscat and Kandahar Sts, behind the Sultan Mosque on Arab St (see the Central Singapore map), in a renovated shophouse.

Nonya & Baba Restaurant (☎ 734 1382) is one of the best restaurants to try Nonya food at reasonable prices. Most mains cost around S$6 for small claypots and up to S$15 for large serves. A variety of snacks and sweets are also available. It is at 262-64 River Valley Rd, near the corner of Tank Rd and directly behind the Imperial Hotel (see the Orchard Rd map).

East Coast Rd in Katong is also a great place to try Nonya food. The *Peranakan Inn & Lounge*, 210 East Coast Rd, is one of the cheapest places in Singapore to eat Nonya food in an air-con setting. Most dishes cost S$4 to S$6, or more expensive seafood dishes cost S$12 to S$20. During the day, try the Nonya kueh (cakes) and curry puffs at the wonderfully old-fashioned *Katong Bakery & Confectionary*, 75 East Coast Rd. The best bus for East Coast Rd is No 14, which goes along Orchard and Bras Basah Rds in the colonial district.

Other Asian Cuisine

The Golden Mile Complex at 5001 Beach Rd (see the Central Singapore map) is a modern shopping centre catering to Singapore's Thai community where you'll find a number of small coffee shops serving Thai food and Singha beer. A good meal will cost S$4 to S$5. On Orchard Rd, *Parkway Thai* (☎ 737 8080) in Centrepoint, 176 Orchard Rd, has an extensive menu – small mains range from S$8 up to S$15 for seafood.

Singapore has experienced a Japanese restaurant boom, but you don't have to spend a small fortune at a Japanese restaurant. A few food courts also have Teppanyaki grills with a dining bar. At the Bugis Junction shopping centre on North Bridge Rd in the colonial district, grills cost around S$6 to S$10, or set meals are S$15. *Teppanyaki Place* in the Tanglin Mall Food Court on Tanglin Rd (see the Central Singapore map) is similar.

Western

Yes, you can get western food in Singapore too. *McDonald's*, *KFC*, *Burger King*, *Pizza Hut* etc are in profusion.

The *Hard Rock Cafe*, 50 Cuscaden Rd, near the corner of Orchard and Tanglin Rds, is popular for American-style steaks, BBQ grills and ribs. Main meals cost around S$20.

On Bencoolen St, the *Golden Dragon Inn* is a Chinese coffee shop on the 2nd floor of the Fortune Centre that does a reasonable job of western grills. Steak or prawns with chips and eggs served on a sizzler cost only S$6, or cholesterol breakfasts cost S$3.

Singapore has plenty of Italian restaurants. Boat Quay has a good selection. *Pasta Fresca* at 30 Boat Quay is one of the better value places, with a huge range of authentic pastas from S$10 and small pizzas from S$12 to S$15.

Breakfast, Snacks & Delis

The big international hotels have their large international breakfast buffets (around S$18 to S$20), of course, but there are still a few old coffee shops which do cheap Chinese and Indian breakfasts – take your pick of dosa and curry or yu-tiao and hot soy milk.

Many places do a fixed-price breakfast – Continental or American. Try the *Silver Spoon Coffee House* at B1-05 Park Mall on Penang Rd near Orchard Rd. One of the nicest breakfasts is undoubtedly *Breakfast with the Birds* (☎ 265 0022) at Jurong Bird Park west of the city centre (see the Singapore Island map). The buffet breakfast costs S$12.36 (admission is extra), the waffles are great and the birds will tell your fortune for free.

Old Chang Kee is a chain with outlets all over town that specialises in that old favourite – curry puffs. The *Selera Restaurant*, 15 McKenzie Rd, near Selegie Rd in the colonial district, is a great place for curry puffs. Try its range, washed down with coffee in an old-style kopi tiam (coffee shop).

Singapore has plenty of delis that cater for lunching office workers and snacking shoppers in the CBD and Orchard Rd. In the Orchard Rd area, *Aroma's Deli*, 01-05 Tanglin Shopping Centre on Tanglin Rd, has good coffee and a changing deli menu.

Entertainment

At night, eating out is one of the favourite Singaporean occupations and it takes place at the hundreds of restaurants and countless hawker-centre stalls. Chinese street-operas still take place around the city, especially around September during the Festival of Hungry Ghosts, with fantastic costumes and (to western ears) a horrible noise. Lion dance troupes are increasingly popular and perform at special events, but otherwise traditional entertainment is hard to see. The *Straits Times* lists cultural performances, and Singapore has a growing local theatre scene and plenty of cinema complexes showing the latest offerings from overseas.

Singapore's nightlife is burgeoning. It's not of the Bangkok sex and sin variety, nor does a wild club scene exist, but the huge number of bars and discos are becoming increasingly sophisticated. *Eight Days*, the weekly TV and entertainment magazine, has the best listings.

Cover charges at discos and clubs are typically S$15 to S$25, but usually include the first drink. A glass of beer will cost around S$8, less during happy hours from around 5 to 8 pm. Many of the bars have bands and no cover charge.

The Orchard Rd area is still the main centre for live music. *Sparks*, level 7, Ngee Ann City on Orchard Rd, is a huge disco with the biggest music system in town, a dazzling laser show and other bars that get some interesting bands. The *Hard Rock Cafe*, 50 Cuscaden Rd, has the usual rock memorabilia and some good bands.

Some good places don't usually have a cover charge. *Anywhere* in the Tanglin Shopping Centre, 19 Tanglin Rd (near the Orchard Parade Hotel), is a long-running rock'n'roll place with a casual atmosphere. The *Saxophone Bar & Grill*, 3 Cuppage Terrace near the corner of Orchard Rd, is a small place with blues and jazz music. Emerald Hill Rd row has a collection of bars in the renovated terraces just up from Orchard Rd. *No 5* at 5 Emerald Hill Rd is very popular with a largely tourist clientele. Next door at No 7, *Que Pasa* is a popular tapas bar with a Spanish theme.

The renovated banks of the Singapore River in the centre of town are the happening place in Singapore, especially the incredibly popular Boat Quay. Upmarket *Harry's* at No 28 Boat Quay is popular with corporate highfliers and has jazz bands. Around the corner, *Molly Malone's*, 42 Circular Rd, is an Irish pub with Guinness on tap and traditional Irish bands. Back on Boat Quay, *Culture Club* at No 38 sometimes has decent bands, as does the faster paced *Zappa Rock Bar* at No 45. Right at the end of Boat Quay near the bridge, *cafe@boatquay* at No 82 is a cyber cafe with banks of terminals for surfing the net. Further up river, Clarke Quay is less frenetic but also has its fair share of popular bars. The most happening bar is the *Crazy Elephant*.

The Tanjong Pagar area in Chinatown has plenty of quieter bars in the restored terraces. The pick of the bars here is the *JJ Mahoney Pub* at 58 Duxton Rd. It has a large range of beers, bands, a games-room bar and a karaoke bar. The liveliest night spot in Tanjong Pagar is *Moon*, 62 Tanjong Pagar Rd, a small but happening place with a lively dance floor and a club atmosphere. A cover charge of S$23 (including two drinks) applies on weekends.

Of course you can have a drink at the Raffles, at the *Long Bar* or the *Bar & Billiard Room*. A Singapore Sling, invented at the Raffles, will set you back S$16. A less pretentious and much cheaper place to drink is

SINGAPORE

at *New Bugis St*. You can have a beer at the food stalls under the stars, and a couple of places have karaoke and bad Filipino bands. The *Boom Boom Room*, 3 New Bugis St, has Singapore's only regular stand-up comic.

If you're wondering what happened to the transvestites, *Desker Rd*, just off Serangoon Rd in Little India, is the successor to Bugis St. The back alleys are a highly active red-light district, and the coffee shops nearby do a roaring trade in noodles and beer. It doesn't have the atmosphere of old Bugis St, but it is lively and the transvestites come out later in the evening.

Things to Buy

Shopping is a big attraction in Singapore, though with free-market policies applying in many countries around the world it is not the bargain centre it used to be. Duty-free prices for most goods still make shopping in Singapore attractive, but it pays to know prices at home before you seize on anything as a great bargain.

For electronics, Hong Kong may have a slight edge on prices, but Singapore is still the cheapest in South-East Asia and the range is fabulous. Singapore also has a great range for clothes, shoes, sporting goods etc, but prices may be higher than at home (depending on where 'home' is). Crafts from all over South-East Asia can be found but they are all imported and prices are high.

In Singapore, fixed-price shops are increasingly becoming the norm but bargaining is still often required, especially in the tourist areas. Many of the small shops, particularly electronic and souvenir shops, don't display prices and you should bargain at these outlets. Even when prices are displayed it doesn't always mean that prices are fixed, especially for souvenirs. Fixed-price department stores will give you a rough idea of true prices, but with so many fixed-price discount shops around it hardly seems worth the hassle of bargaining.

Make sure that guarantees are international. It's no good having to bring something back to Singapore for repair. Check that electronic goods are compatible with your home country – voltages vary, and TVs and VCRs made for Japan and the USA operate on a different system to most other countries.

As for where to shop, the answer is almost anywhere. Orchard Rd and its periphery has the biggest proliferation of ultramodern shopping centres. The People's Park Complex and the People's Park Centre, huge shopping centres in Chinatown, sell almost everything but beware of tourist prices. For modern consumer goods, the fixed-price shops at Changi airport offer surprisingly competitive prices.

For oddities and handicrafts, try Arab St, the Singapore Handicraft Centre in Chinatown Point, Chinatown, or Serangoon Rd in Little India. The Serangoon Plaza department stores on Serangoon Rd and the large Mustafa Centre around the corner have electrical and everyday goods as cheap as you'll find anywhere. For luxury goods, it's Orchard Rd again. The Funan Centre on North Bridge Rd and Sim Lim Square on Bencoolen St (see the Colonial District map) have inexpensive computer peripherals and software. Film and developing are cheap, as is camera gear, and shops are found everywhere.

Thailand

Thailand has much to interest the traveller: historic culture, lively arts, exotic islands, nightlife, a tradition of friendliness and hospitality to strangers and one of the world's most exciting (and hottest!) cuisines. And if you've got the slightest interest in monastic ruins, restored temples and Buddhism, Thailand is the place to go.

Thailand's economic boom of the last few years has been accompanied by an equally spectacular tourist boom, but this ease of travel, excellent and economic accommodation and some of the finest beach centres in Asia still make Thailand a very good country to visit.

Facts about Thailand

HISTORY

Thailand's history often seems very complex – so many different peoples, kings, kingdoms and cultures have had a hand in it. The earliest civilisation in Thailand was probably that of the Mon, who brought a Buddhist culture from the Indian subcontinent. The rise of the Davaravati kingdoms in central Thailand was ended by the westward movement of the energetic Khmers, whose influence can be seen in Thailand at Phimai and Lopburi. At the same time, the Sumatran-based Sriwijaya Empire extended up through Malaya and into southern Thailand.

Kublai Khan's expansion in China speeded up a southern migration of the Thai people and, in 1220 Thai princes took over Sukhothai, their first Siamese capital. Other Thai peoples migrated to Laos and the Shan states of Burma. Another Thai kingdom, called Lanna Thai (Million Thai Rice-Fields), formed under King Mengrai in Chiang Rai in the north and later moved to Chiang Mai. In 1350 the Prince of U Thong founded yet another Thai capital – at Ayuthaya – which eventually overshadowed Sukhothai. Ayuthaya was unsurpassed for two centuries: the Khmers were pushed right out of Siam and the Khmer capital of Angkor was abandoned to the jungles, which hid it almost to this century.

In the 16th century the Burmese – archrivals of the Thais – who had become disunited after Kublai Khan's sacking of Bagan, regrouped and wrought havoc in Thailand. Chiang Mai, which Ayuthaya had never absorbed, was captured by the Burmese in 1556, and in 1569 Ayuthaya also fell. However, their success was short lived and the Thais recaptured Chiang Mai in 1595. European influences first appeared in Thailand during the next century, but the execution of Constantine Phaulkon, Greek emissary of the French, ended that little episode.

In the 18th century the Burmese attacked again and in 1767, after a prolonged siege, took and utterly destroyed Ayuthaya. The Siamese soon regrouped and expelled the Burmese, but Ayuthaya was never reconstructed. In 1782 the new capital at Thonburi was moved across the river to its present site at Bangkok, and the still-ruling Chakri Dynasty was founded under King Rama I. In the 19th century, while all the rest of South-East Asia was being colonised by the French, Dutch and British, Siam managed to remain independent. By deftly playing off one European power against another, King Mongkut

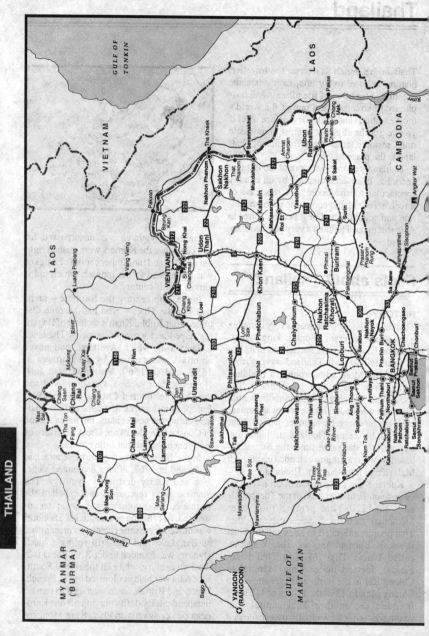

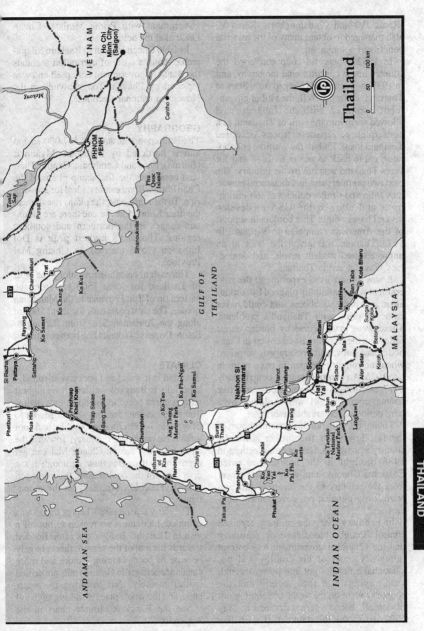

(Rama IV) and Chulalongkorn (Rama V) also managed to obtain many of the material benefits of colonialism.

In 1932 a peaceful coup converted the country into a constitutional monarchy, and in 1939 the name was changed from Siam to Thailand. During WWII, the Phibul government complied with the Japanese and allowed them into the Gulf of Thailand; as a consequence, Japanese troops occupied Thailand itself. Phibul, the wartime collaborator, came back to power in 1948 and for years Thailand was run by the military. The next two premiers also had dictatorial power; they followed similar policies of self-enrichment and allowed the USA to develop several bases within Thai borders in support of the American campaign in Vietnam. In 1973 Thanom was given the boot in an unprecedented student revolt, and democracy was restored in Thailand.

It was a short-lived experiment: the government was continually plagued by factionalism and party squabbles, and could never come to grips with Thailand's problems. These were made worse by border unrest following the Communist takeovers in Cambodia and Laos, and nobody was surprised when the military stepped in once more in late 1976. An abortive counter-coup in early 1977, elections in 1979 and another abortive counter-coup in 1981 were followed by a long period of remarkable stability.

Thailand's remarkable economic boom of the last few years has further aided the country's prospects. Democratic elections in 1988 brought in the business-oriented Chatichai Choonvahan, who shifted power from the military to the business elite and relentlessly pursued pro-development policies.

In February 1991 the military regained control through a bloodless coup, reasoning that the Chatichai government was corrupt (allegedly most of his cronies – if not Chatichai himself – got into power through vote-buying) and that society and the economy were on the verge of spinning out of control. Bloody demonstrations in May 1992 led to the reinstalment of a civilian government with Prime Minister Chuan Leekpai at the helm.

In 1996 Chuan lost out to Banharn Silapa-archa. Amid a spate of corruption scandals the Banharn government collapsed and was replaced by Chavalit Yongchaiyudh in the November national elections.

GEOGRAPHY

Thailand covers an area of 517,000 sq km and is bordered by Malaysia, Myanmar (Burma), Laos and Cambodia. Central Thailand comprises the flat, damp plains of the Chao Phraya River estuary, ideal for growing rice. To the north-east, the plains rise to meet the drier Khorat Plateau and there are mountain ranges in the northern and southern regions. Thailand's highest peak is Doi Inthanon (2596 metres), in Chiang Mai Province.

The eastern coastline runs along the Gulf of Thailand for some 1500 km from the eastern tip of Trat Province to the Malaysian border. The west coast runs for about 560 km along the Andaman Sea, from Ranong to Satun. Dozens of islands hug both coastlines.

CLIMATE

Thailand is tropical and sticky year-round – especially in Bangkok – although the highest temperatures occur in the north-east plains. The three seasons are: hot – from March to May; rainy – from June to October; and cool – from November to February. Towards the end of the hot season Chiang Mai can get even hotter than Bangkok, although it's a drier heat. In the cool season, the north can almost get 'cold', especially in the mountains.

The rainy season rarely brings things to a complete halt and is no reason to put off a visit to Thailand. Bangkok is often flooded towards the end of the season; this is largely because of poor planning – more and more canals are being filled in and wells are drilled indiscriminately, thus lowering the water table, and the whole place is sinking anyway!

See the Bangkok climate chart in the Appendix.

ECOLOGY & ENVIRONMENT

Unique in South-East Asia because its north-south axis extends some 1800 km from mainland to peninsular South-East Asia, Thailand provides habitats for an astounding variety of flora and fauna.

Like all countries with a high population density, there is enormous pressure on Thailand's ecosystems: 50 years ago about 70% of the countryside was forest; by 1995 an estimated 25% of the natural forest cover remained. Logging and agriculture are mainly to blame for this decline, and the loss of forest cover has been accompanied by dwindling wildlife. Notable species extinct in Thailand include the kouprey (a type of wild cattle), Schomburgk's deer and the Javan rhino, but innumerable smaller species have also fallen by the wayside.

In response to environmental degradation, the Thai government has created a large number of protected areas since the 1970s. Legislation has been enacted to protect specific plants and animals – Thailand has also become a signatory to the UN Convention on International Trade in Endangered Species (CITES) – and the government hopes to raise total forest cover to 40% by the middle of the next century.

It is now illegal to sell timber felled in Thailand, and all imported timber is theoretically accounted for before going on the market. The illegal timber trade has further diminished with Cambodia's recent ban on all timber exports and the termination of all Thai contracts by the Burmese. Laos is now the number one source for timber imported into Thailand – both legal and illegal.

Corruption impedes government attempts to shelter species coveted by the illicit global wildlife trade and to preserve Thailand's sensitive coastal areas. The Forestry Department is currently under pressure to take immediate action in those areas where preservation laws have gone unenforced, including coastal zones where illegal tourist accommodation has flourished. There has also been a crackdown on restaurants serving 'jungle food' (aahãan pàa), which consists of often endangered wildlife, such as barking deer, bear, pangolin, civet and gaur.

As elsewhere in the region, the tiger is one of the most endangered of large mammals. Tiger hunting or trapping is illegal, but poachers continue to kill the cats for the lucrative overseas Chinese pharmaceutical market. Around 200 to 300 wild tigers are thought to be hanging on in the national parks of Khao Yai, Kaeng Krachan, Thap Lan, Mae Wong and Khao Sok.

Air and water pollution are problems in urban areas. The passing of the 1992 Environmental Act was an encouraging move by the government; it provides environmental quality standards and establishes national authority to designate conservation and pollution control areas. Pattaya and Phuket became the first locales to be decreed pollution control areas, thus making them eligible for government clean-up funds. With such assistance, officials in Pattaya now claim they'll be able to restore Pattaya Bay – exposed to improper waste disposal for at least the last 20 years – to its original purity by the end of this decade.

FLORA & FAUNA

Flora

Monsoon forests account for about a quarter of all remaining natural forest cover; they feature a variety of deciduous trees which shed their leaves during the dry season to conserve water. About half of all forest cover consists of rainforests, which are typically evergreen. Although central, north, eastern and north-eastern Thailand mainly contain monsoon forests and the south is predominantly rainforest, there is much overlap – some zones support a mixture of both monsoon forest and rainforest.

The remaining quarter of the country's forest cover consists of freshwater swamp forests in the delta regions, forested crags amid the karst topography of both north and south, and pine forests at higher altitudes in the north. Thailand's most famous flora includes an incredible array of fruit trees, bamboo (more species than any country outside China and possibly Myanmar), tropical hardwoods and over 27,000 flowering species, including many examples of the national floral symbol – the orchid.

Fauna

The indigenous fauna of Thailand's northern half is mostly of Indochinese origin while that of the south is generally Sundaic (ie typical of Malaysia, Sumatra, Borneo and Java). There is a large overlap of habitat for plants and animals from both zones, extending from around Prachuap Khiri Khan on the southern peninsula to Uthai Thani in the lower north.

Thailand is particularly rich in bird life: over 1000 resident and migrating species have been recorded – approximately 10% of all world bird species. Indigenous mammals – mostly found in dwindling numbers in national parks and wildlife sanctuaries – include the tiger, leopard, elephant, Asiatic black bear, Malayan sun bear, gaur (Indian bison), banteng (wild cattle), serow (an Asiatic goat-antelope), sambar deer, barking deer, mouse deer, tapir, pangolin, gibbon, macaque, dolphin and dugong (sea cows). Forty of Thailand's 300 mammal species, including the clouded leopard, Malayan tapir, tiger, Irrawaddy dolphin, jungle cat, dusky langur and pileated gibbon, are on the International Union for Conservation of Nature (IUCN) list of endangered species.

National Parks

Despite Thailand's rich diversity of flora and fauna, it has only been in recent years that most of the 79 national parks (only 50 of which receive an annual budget), 89 'non-hunting areas' and wildlife sanctuaries and 35 forest reserves have been established. Eighteen of the national parks are marine parks that protect coastal, insular and open-sea areas. Together these cover 13% of the country's land and sea area, one of the highest ratios of protected to unprotected areas of any nation in the world (compare this figure with India's 4.2%, Japan's 6.5%, France's 8.8% and the USA's 10.5%).

GOVERNMENT & POLITICS

Since 1932 the government of the Kingdom of Thailand has nominally been a constitutional monarchy, inspired by the bicameral British model but with myriad subtle differences; frequent military coups d'etât and occasional vote-buying sprees stretch the definition considerably.

The Thai monarchy, though constitutionally only a figurehead institution, in reality wields considerable decision-making power during times of crisis. Born in 1927, His Majesty Bhumibol Adulyadej (pronounced 'Phumíphon Adunyádèt') is the ninth king of the Chakri Dynasty. Since 1988 Bhumibol has been the longest-reigning king in Thai history; he also claims the longest current reign of any monarch worldwide.

For administrative purposes, Thailand is divided into 76 *jangwàat*, or provinces. Each province is subdivided into *amphoe*, or districts, which are further subdivided into *king-amphoe* (subdistricts), *tambon* (communes or village groups), *mùu-bâan* (villages), *sukhãaphibaan* (sanitation districts) and *thêtsàbaan* (municipalities). Urban areas with more than 50,000 inhabitants and a population density of over 3000 per sq km are designated *nákhon*; those with populations of 10,000 to 50,000, and not less than 3000 per sq km, are *muang* (or *meuang*). The term is also used loosely to mean metropolitan area (as opposed to an area within strict municipal limits).

A provincial capital is an *amphoe muang*. An amphoe muang takes the same name as the province of which it is capital, eg amphoe muang Chiang Mai (often abbreviated as 'muang Chiang Mai') means the city of Chiang Mai, capital of Chiang Mai Province.

ECONOMY

Agriculture remains the mainstay of the Thai export economy. Thailand is the world's number-one rice exporter and the first in rubber production. Other major export products are tapioca, coconut, maize, sugar, tin, cement, pineapple, tuna, sugar, soybean, jute, processed food products, textiles and electronics. Since 1987 tourism has become a leading earner of foreign exchange, occasionally surpassing even Thailand's largest single export, textiles

Many economists are painting a bright economic future for Thailand, saying that it will join the ranks of the NICs (Newly Industrialised Countries) like Korea and Taiwan within five to 10 years. Others say that the infrastructure hasn't yet caught up with the current rate of growth (about 8% per annum) and change. Average annual per capita income is about US$2680, but there is a wide gap between affluent Bangkok and the much less affluent countryside.

POPULATION & PEOPLE

Thailand's population is about 54 million. Although basically homogeneous, there are many hill tribes in the northern area and some Malays in the south, as well as numbers of Lao, Mon, Khmer, Phuan and other common South-East Asian ethnic groups. About 10% of the population is Chinese, but they're so well assimilated that almost no one bothers to note the difference.

EDUCATION

The literacy rate in Thailand runs at 93.8%, one of the highest in mainland South-East Asia. In 1993 the government raised compulsory schooling from six to nine years. Although a high social value is placed on education as a way to achieve material success, at most levels the system itself favours rote learning over independent thinking.

Thailand's public school system is organised around six years at the pràthōm (primary) level beginning at age six, followed by three years of mátháyom (middle) and three years of udom (high) school. In reality less than nine years of formal education is the national norm. These statistics don't take into account the monastic schooling at Buddhist wats (Thai Buddhist temple-monasteries), which may provide the only formal education available in remote rural areas.

ARTS

Traditional Sculpture & Architecture

A visit to the Bangkok National Museum is a good way to acquaint yourself with Thailand's canonical art periods: works from each of the periods are on display. Then, as you travel upcountry and view old monuments and sculpture, you'll know what you're seeing, as well as what to look for.

Since 1981 the Thai government has made the restoration of nine key archaeological sites part of its national economic development plan. As a result, the Fine Arts Department, under the Ministry of Education, has developed nine historical parks: Sukhothai and Si Satchanalai Historical Parks in Sukhothai Province; Phra Nakhon Si Ayuthaya HP in Ayuthaya Province; Phanom Rung HP in Buriram Province; Si Thep HP in Phetchabun Province; Phra Nakhon Khiri HP in Phetburi Province; Phimai HP in Nakhon Ratchasima Province; Muang Singh HP in Kanchanaburi Province; and Kamphaeng Phet HP in Kamphaeng Phet Province.

Painting

Apart from prehistoric and historic cave or rock-wall murals found throughout the country, not much formal painting predating the 18th century exists in Thailand. Presumably a great number of temple murals in Ayuthaya were destroyed by the Burmese invasion in 1767. The earliest surviving temple examples are found at Ayuthaya's Wat Ratburana (1424), Wat Chong Nonsii in Bangkok (1657-1707) and Phetburi's Wat Yai Suwannaram (late 17th century).

Nineteenth-century religious painting has fared better; Ratanakosin-style temple art is in fact more highly esteemed for painting than for sculpture or architecture. Typical temple murals feature rich colours and lively detail. Some of the finest are found in Wat Phra Kaew's Wihan Phutthaisawan (Buddhaisawan Chapel) in Bangkok, and at Wat Suwannaram in Thonburi.

Music

Traditional Music From a western perspective, traditional Thai music is some of the most bizarre on the planet. However, acquiring a taste for it is well worth the effort: classical, central Thai music is spicy, like Thai food, and features an incredible array of textures and subtleties, hair-raising tempos and pastoral melodies.

THAILAND

The classical orchestra is called the *pìi-phâat* and can include as few as five players or more than 20. Among the more common instruments is the *pìi*, a woodwind instrument with a reed mouthpiece; it is heard prominently at Thai boxing matches. The pii is a relative of a similar Indian instrument, while the *phin*, a banjo-like stringed instrument whose name comes from the Indian *vina*, is considered native to Thailand. A bowed instrument, similar to examples played in China and Japan, is aptly called the *saw*. The *ranâat èk* is a bamboo-keyed percussion instrument resembling the western xylophone, while the *khlui* is a wooden flute.

The pii-phaat ensemble was originally developed to accompany classical dance-drama and shadow theatre, but these days can be heard in straightforward performance in temple fairs and concerts.

In the north and north-east there are several popular reed instruments with multiple bamboo pipes, which function basically like a mouth-organ. Chief among these is the *khaen*, which originated in Laos; when played by an adept musician it sounds like a rhythmic, churning calliope. The funky *lûuk thûng*, or 'country' (literally 'children of the fields') style, which originated in the north-east, has become a favourite throughout Thailand.

Modern Music Popular Thai music has borrowed much from the west, particularly its instruments, but retains a distinct flavour. The best example of this is the famous rock group Carabao. Recording and performing for nearly 20 years now, Carabao is by far the most popular musical group Thailand has ever seen and has even scored hits in Malaysia, Singapore, Indonesia and the Philippines. This band and others have crafted an exciting fusion of Thai classical and luuk thung forms with heavy metal.

Another major influence on Thai pop was a 1970s group called Caravan. They created a modern Thai folk style known as *phleng phêua chii-wít*, or 'songs for life', which feature political and environmental topics rather than the usual moonstruck love themes. During the dictatorships of the 1970s many of Caravan's songs were officially banned by the government.

Yet another inspiring movement in modern Thai music is the fusion of international jazz with Thai classical and folk motifs.

Theatre & Dance

Traditional Thai theatre consists of six dramatic forms: *khŏn*, formal masked dance-drama depicting scenes from the *Ramakian* (the Thai version of India's *Ramayana)* and originally performed only for the royal court; *lákhon*, a general term covering several types of dance-dramas (usually for non-royal occasions) as well as western theatre; *lí-khe* (likay), a partly improvised, often bawdy folk play featuring dancing, comedy, melodrama and music; *mánohra*, the southern Thai equivalent of li-khe, but based on a 2000-year-old Indian story; *năng*, or shadow plays, limited to southern Thailand; and *hùn lŭang* or *lákhon lék*, puppet theatre.

SOCIETY & CONDUCT

Thai culture' is rooted in the history of Thai migration throughout South-East Asia, and shares features with the Lao of neighbouring Laos, the Shan of north-eastern Myanmar and the numerous tribal Thais found in isolated pockets from Dien Bien Phu, Vietnam, all the way to Assam, India.

Although Thailand is the most 'modernised' of the existing Thai (more precisely, Austro-Thai) societies, the cultural underpinnings are evident in virtually every facet of everyday life. Those aspects that might be deemed 'westernisation' – eg the wearing of trousers instead of *phâkhamāa*, the presence of automobiles, cinema and 7-elevens – show how Thailand has adopted and adapted tools invented elsewhere.

Dominant hallmarks of Thai culture include the three concepts of *sanuk* (fun), *naa* (face) and *phuu yai – phuu nawy* (big person – little person). In Thailand anything worth doing – even work – should have an element of sanuk, otherwise it automatically becomes drudgery. Thais believe strongly in the concept of 'saving face' – that is, avoiding confrontation and endeavouring not to embarrass themselves or other people (except when it's sanuk to do so!). Finally, all relationships in traditional Thai society – and virtually all relationships in the modern Thai milieu as well – are governed by connections between phuu yai and phuu nawy. Phuu nawy are supposed to defer to phuu yai following simple lines of social rank defined by age, wealth, status and personal and political power.

Conduct

Monarchy and religion are the two sacred cows in Thailand. Thais are tolerant of most kinds of behaviour as long as it doesn't insult one of these.

Monarchy The monarchy is held in considerable respect and visitors should be respectful too – avoid disparaging remarks about the king, queen or anyone in the royal family. One of Thailand's leading intellectuals, Sulak Sivarak, was arrested in the early 80s for describing the king as 'the skipper' – a passing reference to his fondness for sailing.

While it's OK to criticise the Thai government and even Thai culture openly, it's considered a grave insult to Thai nationhood – as well as to the monarchy – not to stand when you hear the royal anthem (composed by the king, incidentally).

Religion Correct behaviour in temples entails several guidelines, the most important of which is to dress neatly (no shorts or tank tops) and to take your shoes off when you enter any building that contains an image of the Buddha. Buddha images are sacred objects, so don't pose in front of them for pictures and definitely do not clamber upon them.

Monks are not supposed to touch or be touched by women. If a woman wants to hand something to a monk, the object should be placed within reach of the monk and not handed directly to him.

When sitting in a religious edifice, keep your feet pointed away from any Buddha images. The usual way to do this is to sit in the 'mermaid' pose: fold your legs to the side with the feet pointing backwards.

Social Gestures

Traditionally, Thais greet each other not with a handshake but with a prayer-like palms-together gesture, known as a *wai*. If someone wais you, you should wai back (unless wai-ed by a child).

The feet are the lowest part of the body (spiritually as well as physically), so don't point your feet at people or point at things with your feet. In the same context, the head is regarded as the highest part of the body, so don't touch a Thai on the head.

Thais are often addressed by their first name with the honorific *Khun* or a title preceding it. Friends often use nicknames or kinship terms like *phii* (elder sibling) or *nong* (younger sibling).

Dress & Attitude

Beach attire is not considered appropriate for trips into town and is especially counter-productive if worn to government offices (eg when applying for a visa extension). As in most parts of Asia, anger and emotions are rarely displayed and generally get you nowhere. Remember the paramount rule in any argument or dispute is to keep your cool.

RELIGION

Buddhism is the dominant religion, and practised by about 95% of the population. Orange-robed monks, and sitting, standing or reclining Buddhas made of gold, marble and stone are common sights. The prevalent form of Buddhism practised is the Theravada (Council of the Elders) school. Also known as Hinayana, it is the same as that found in Sri Lanka, Myanmar, Laos and Cambodia. Theravada Buddhism emphasises the potential of the individual to attain Nibbana (Nirvana) without the aid of saints or gurus.

Every Thai male is expected to become a monk for a short period in his life, optimally

THAILAND

between the time he finishes school and the time he starts a career or marries. Men or boys under 20 years of age may enter the Sangha (Buddhist brotherhood) as novices, and it is not unusual, since a family earns great merit when a son takes robe and bowl. Traditionally, the length of time spent in a wat is three months, during the Buddhist lent (*phansāa*), which begins in July and coincides with the rainy season. However, nowadays men may spend as little as a week or 15 days to accrue merit as monks. There are about 32,000 monasteries – and 200,000 monks – in Thailand.

In Thailand's four southernmost provinces – Yala, Narathiwat, Pattani and Satun – there's a large Muslim minority.

LANGUAGE

Although Thai is a rather complicated language with a unique alphabet, it's fun to try at least a few words. The *Thai phrasebook* by Lonely Planet gives a handy basic introduction to the language and contains many helpful words and phrases.

The main complication with Thai is that it is tonal; the same word could be pronounced with a rising, falling, high, low or level tone and could theoretically have five meanings!

Several different words can be used to mean 'I' but the safest are *phóm* for men and *dîichán* for women. You can also omit the pronoun altogether and say, for example, *mâi khâo jai* (do not understand).

Mâi pen rai is a very useful phrase, although it actually has far more meanings than simply 'it doesn't matter': it can also mean 'don't bother', 'forget it', 'leave it alone', 'take no notice', or even 'that's enough'.

The 'ph' in a Thai word is always pronounced like an English 'p', not as an 'f'.

Basics
Hello.	*sawàt dii*
How are you?	*pen yangai?*
I'm fine.	*sabàay dii*
Excuse me.	*khăw thôht*
Please.	*kaa-ru-naa/pròht*

Thank you.	*khàwp khun*
foreigner of European descent	*farang*
Yes. (female)	*khâ*
Yes. (male)	*khráp*
No.	*mâi*
How much?	*thâo rai?*
toilet	*hâwng sûam*

Getting Around
I want to go to ...	*yàak pai ...*
Where is the ...?	*... yûu thîi nǎi?*
bus	*rót meh*
train	*rót fai*
hotel	*rohng raem*
post office	*praisanii*
station	*sathaanii*
beach	*ao*
island	*ko*
house/village	*ban*

How far?	*klai thâo rai?*
here/there	*thîi-nîi/thîi-nûun*
near/far	*klâi/klai*
left/right	*sái/khwaa*
straight ahead	*trong pai*

Accommodation
guesthouse	*bâan phák*
hotel	*rohng raem*

Do you have a room?	*mii hâwng mǎi?*
How much per night?	*kheun-lá thâo rai?*

Time & Dates
When?	*mêu-arai?*
What time?	*kìi mohng?*
today	*wan níi*
tomorrow	*phrûng níi*
yesterday	*mêua waan*

Health & Emergencies
doctor	*măw*
chemist/pharmacy	*ráan khǎai yaa*
Help!	*chûay dûay!*
Go away.	*pai láew*
police	*tam-ruat*

Numbers

1	*nèung*
2	*sǎwng*
3	*sǎam*
4	*sìi*
5	*hâa*
6	*hòk*
7	*jèt*
8	*pàet*
9	*kâo*
10	*sìp*
11	*sìp èt*
20	*yîi sìp*
21	*yîi sìp èt*
30	*sǎam sìp*
100	*nèung roi*
200	*sǎwng roi*
1000	*nèung phan*

Facts for the Visitor

PLANNING
Maps

Lonely Planet publishes the 1:1,150,000 scale *Thailand travel atlas*, a 44-page country map booklet designed to combine maximum accuracy with maximum portability. The atlas includes place names in both Thai and roman script, travel information in five languages (English, French, German, Spanish and Japanese), topographic shading and a complete geographic index. It has been spot-checked on the ground for accuracy and currency by this author. The atlas is readily available for around US$9 at many Bangkok bookshops.

Nelles and Bartholomew each publish decent 1:500,000 scale maps of Thailand with general topographic shading. The Bartholomew map is more up-to-date and accurate than the Nelles, though both maps could use updating and corrections.

The large-format Roads Association of Thailand publishes a 48-page, bilingual road atlas called *Thailand Highway Map*. The atlas includes 1:1,000,000 Highway Department maps reduced to a manageable size and includes dozens of city maps, driving dis-

tances and lots of travel and sightseeing information. It costs 100 to 120B depending on the vendor, but beware of inferior knock-offs.

TOURIST OFFICES

The Tourist Authority of Thailand (TAT) has an office at the airport in Bangkok, another in central Bangkok and quite a few in regional centres around the country. They have a lot of useful brochures, booklets and maps and will probably have an information sheet on almost any Thai subject that interests you. The TAT is probably the best tourist office in South-East Asia for the production of useful information sheets rather than (often useless) pretty colour brochures.

Each regional office also puts out accommodation guides that include cheap places to stay. In Bangkok, they sell the invaluable bus map which lists all the Bangkok bus routes. The flip side of the bus map has a pretty good map of Thailand with Thai script as well. Make sure any map you get has names on it in Thai as well as English.

Local Tourist Offices

Locations of TAT offices in Thailand include:

Ayuthaya
    Si Sanphet Rd (temporary office), Ayuthaya 13000 (☎ (36) 422768; fax 422769)
Bangkok
    372 Bamrung Meuang Rd, Bangkok 10100 (☎ (2) 226-0060/72; fax 224-6221)
Cha-am
    500/51 Phetkasem Highway, Amphoe Cha-am, Phetburi 76 (☎ (32) 471005; fax 471502)
Chiang Mai
    105/1 Chiang Mai-Lamphun Rd, Chiang Mai 50000 (☎ (53) 248604/7; fax 248605)
Chiang Rai
    Singhakai Rd, Chiang Rai 57000 (☎ (53) 717433; fax 717434)
Hat Yai
    1/1 Soi 2, Niphat Uthit 3 Rd, Hat Yai, Songkhla 90110 (☎ (74) 243747; fax 245986)
Kanchanaburi
    Saengchuto Rd, Kanchanaburi 71000 (☎ /fax (34) 511200)
Khon Kaen
    15/5 Prachasamoson Rd, Khon Kaen 40000 (☎ (43) 244498; fax 244497)

Lopburi
HM the Queen's Celebration Building (temporary office), Provincial Hall, Narai Maharat Rd, Lopburi 15000 (☎ (36) 422768; fax 422769)

Nakhon Phanom
184/1 Sonthonvichit Rd, Nakhon Phanom 48000 (☎ (42) 513490, 513491; fax 513492)

Nakhon Ratchasima (Khorat)
2102-2104 Mittaphap Rd, Nakhon Ratchasima 30000 (☎ (44) 213666; fax 213667)

Nakhon Si Thammarat
Sanam Na Meuang, Ratchadamnoen Klang Rd, Nakhon Si Thammarat 80000 (☎ (75) 346515; fax 346517)

Narathiwat (Sungai Kolok)
Asia Highway 18 (temporary office), Sungai Kolok, Narathiwat 96120 (☎ (73) 612126; fax 615230)

Pattaya
382/1 Chai Hat Rd, Pattaya Beach, South Pattaya 21000 (☎ (38) 427667; fax 429113)

Phitsanulok
209/7-8 Surasi Trade Centre, Boromtrailokanat Rd, Phitsanulok 85000 (☎ (55) 252743; fax 252742)

Phuket
73-75 Phuket Rd, Phuket 83000 (☎ (76) 212213, 211036; fax 213582)

Rayong
153/4 Sukhumvit Rd, Rayong 21000 (☎ /fax (38) 655420; fax 655422

Surat Thani
5 Talaat Mai Rd, Ban Don, Surat Thani 84000 (☎ /fax (77) 282828)

Trat (Laem Ngop)
100 Muu 1, Trat-Laem Ngop Rd, Laem Ngop, Trat 23120 (☎ /fax (38) 597255)

Ubon Ratchathani
264/1 Kheuan Thani Rd, Ubon Ratchathani 34000 (☎ (45) 243770; fax 243771)

Udon Thani
Provincial Education Office (temporary office), Phosi Rd, Udon Thani 41000 (☎ /fax (42) 241968)

Tourist Offices Abroad

TAT offices can be found in the following countries:

Australia
7th floor, Royal Exchange Building, 56 Pitt St, Sydney NSW 2000 (☎ (02) 9247-7549; fax 251-2465)

Malaysia
c/o Royal Thai Embassy, 206 Jalan Ampang, 50450 Kuala Lumpur (☎ (03) 248-0958; fax 241-3002)

Singapore
c/o Royal Thai Embassy, 370 Orchard Rd, Singapore 0923 (☎ (02) 235-7694; fax 733-5653)

UK
49 Albemarle St, London W1X 3FE (☎ (0171) 499-7679; fax 629-5519)

USA
5 World Trade Center, Suite 3443, New York, NY 10048 (☎ (212) 432-0433; fax 912-0920)
3440 Wilshire Blvd, Suite 1100, Los Angeles, CA 90010 (☎ (213) 382-2353; fax 389-7544)
303 East Wacker Drive, Suite 400, Chicago, IL 60601 (☎ (312) 819-3990; fax 565-0359)

VISAS & DOCUMENTS

You've got a variety of choices in the visa game for Thailand. First of all, citizens of 56 different countries can enter Thailand without any visa and be granted a 30 day stay. (Those from Sweden, Denmark, New Zealand and South Korea take note: you can travel in Thailand for up to 90 days without a visa.) Officially, you must have an outward ticket but in practice this does not always seem to be rigidly enforced.

The one month visa is free. Next in length of validity is the tourist visa, which is good for 60 days and costs US$15. Three passport photos must accompany all applications.

Visa Extensions

Sixty-day tourist visas may be extended up to 30 days at the discretion of Thai immigration authorities. The Bangkok office (☎ 287-3101) is on Soi Suan Phlu, Sathon Tai Rd, but you can apply at any immigration office in the country – every province that borders a neighbouring country has at least one. The usual fee for extension of a tourist visa (up to one month) is 500B. Bring along one photo and one copy each of the photo and visa pages of your passport. Normally only one 30-day extension is granted.

The 30 day visa can be extended for 7 to 10 days (depending on the immigration office) for 500B. You can also leave the country and return immediately to obtain another 30-day stay. There is no limit on the number of times you can do this, nor is there a minimum interval you must spend outside the country.

EMBASSIES
Thai Embassies
Embassies include:

Australia
   Royal Thai Embassy, 111 Empire Circuit, Yarralumla, Canberra, ACT 2600 (☎ (06) 273-1149, 273-2937)
Canada
   Royal Thai Embassy, 180 Island Park Dr, Ottawa, Ontario K1Y 0A2 (☎ (613) 722-4444)
France
   Royal Thai Embassy, 8 Rue Greuze, 75116 Paris (☎ 01 47 27 80 79)
Germany
   Royal Thai Embassy, Ubierstrasse 65, 53173 Bonn (☎ (228) 355065)
Nepal
   Royal Thai Embassy, Jyoti Kendra Building, Thapathali, Kathmandu (☎ (01) 213910)
New Zealand
   Royal Thai Embassy, 2 Cook St, Karori, Wellington 5 (☎ (04) 476-8618)
UK
   Royal Thai Embassy, 29-30 Queen's Gate, London SW7 5JB (☎ (0171) 589-0173/2944/2857)
USA
   Royal Thai Embassy, 1024 Wisconsin Ave NW, Washington, DC 20007 (☎ (202) 944-3600)
   Royal Thai Consulate, 801 N La Brea Ave, Los Angeles, CA 90038 (☎ (213) 937-1894)

See the other chapters in this book for Thai embassies in those countries.

Foreign Embassies in Thailand
Countries with diplomatic representation in Bangkok include:

Australia
   37 Sathon Tai Rd (☎ 287-2680)
Canada
   Boonmitr Building, 138 Silom Rd (☎ 234-1561/8, 237-4126)
China
   57 Ratchadaphisek Rd (☎ 245-7032/49)
India
   46 Soi Prasanmit (Soi 23), Sukhumvit Rd (☎ 258-0300/6)
Indonesia
   600-602 Phetburi Rd (☎ 252-3135/40)
Laos
   193 Sathon Tai Rd (☎ 254-6963, 213-2573)
Malaysia
   35 Sathon Tai Rd (☎ 286-1390/2)

Myanmar (Burma)
   132 Sathon Neua Rd (☎ 233-2237, 234-4698)
Nepal
   189 Soi Phuengsuk (Soi 71), Sukhumvit Rd (☎ 391-7240)
New Zealand
   93 Withayu Rd (☎ 251-8165)
Singapore
   129 Sathon Tai Rd (☎ 286-2111, 286-1434)
Vietnam
   83/1 Withayu Rd (☎ 251-7201/3, 251-5835/8)

CUSTOMS
Like most countries, Thailand prohibits the import of illegal drugs, firearms and ammunition (unless registered in advance with the Police Department) and pornographic media. Visitors are permitted to bring the following into the country without paying duty: a reasonable amount of clothing and toiletries for personal use; professional instruments; one movie/video camera with three rolls of film/videotape or one still camera with five rolls of film; up to 200 cigarettes, or up to 250g of other smoking materials; and one litre of wine or spirits.

Electronic goods like personal stereos, calculators and computers can be a problem if customs officials have reason to believe you're bringing them in for resale. As long as you don't carry more than one of each, you should be OK. Occasionally, customs will require you to leave a hefty deposit for big-ticket items (eg a lap-top computer or midi-component stereo), which is refunded when you leave the country with the item in question. If you make the mistake of saying you're just passing through and don't plan to use the item while in Thailand, they may ask you to leave it with the Customs Department until you leave the country.

MONEY
Costs
Thailand is an economical country to visit: transport is reasonably priced, comfortable and reliable; finding a place to stay is rarely difficult, although the tourist boom has created some problems in the 'on' seasons (December-January and July-August); costs are low and you get good value for your

THAILAND

money; and as long as you can stand a little spice, the food is also very good and cheap.

Bangkok is more expensive than elsewhere in the country, partly because lots of luxuries are available there which you simply won't be tempted with upcountry. However, so many cheap guesthouses have sprung up in the Banglamphu area of the city that accommodation needn't necessarily be more expensive than elsewhere. Of course, the Bangkok hassles – noise and pollution being the main ones – may drive you to look for extra comfort, and air-conditioning can be very nice.

One good way to save money is to travel in the off season, which in Thailand means from April to June or from September to October. During these periods, tourist destinations are less crowded and prices for accommodation are generally lower. In the remainder of the year, hotels and guesthouses often raise their prices to whatever the traffic will bear.

Budget-squeezers should be able to get by on 200B per day outside Bangkok if they really watch their expenses. This estimate includes basic guesthouse accommodation, food, nonalcoholic beverages and local transport, but not film, souvenirs, tours, long-distance transport or vehicle hire. Add another 50 to 75B per day for every large beer (25 to 35B for small bottles) you drink.

Currency

The baht (B) is divided into 100 satang, although 25 and 50 satang are the smallest coins you'll see. Coins come in 1B (three sizes), 5B (two sizes) and 10B denominations. Notes are in 10B (brown – but gradually being phased out of circulation), 20B (green), 50B (blue), 100B (red) and 500B (purple) and 1000B (beige) denominations of varying shades and sizes. A 10,000B bill is on the way. Changing a note larger than 100B can be difficult in small towns and villages.

In upcountry markets, you may hear prices referred to in saleng – a saleng is equal to 25 satang.

Currency Exchange

The following table shows the exchange rates:

Australia	A$1	=	20.12B
Canada	C$1	=	18.62B
France	FF10	=	49.33B
Germany	DM1	=	16.67B
Japan	¥100	=	22.93B
New Zealand	NZ$1	=	17.77B
Singapore	S$1	=	18.05B
UK	UK£1	=	39.71B
US	US$1	=	25.28B

The baht is aligned with the US dollar, and the US$-baht rate fluctuates only slightly from day to day. Baht rates against other currencies will, of course, fluctuate relative to the US dollar.

Banks give the best exchange rates and are generally open from 8.30 am to 3.30 pm Monday to Friday (except in Bangkok, where they're open 10 am to 4 pm). Avoid hotels, which give the worst rates. In the larger towns and tourist destinations, there are also foreign exchange kiosks that are open longer hours, usually from around 8 am to 8 pm. All banks deduct a 7 to 10B service charge per cheque – thus you can save money by using larger denomination travellers' cheques (eg cashing a US$100 cheque will cost you 7 to 10B while cashing five US$20 cheques will cost 35 to 50B).

There is no black market for US dollars, but Bangkok is a good centre for buying Asian currencies, particularly those of neighbouring countries where black market money changing flourishes (eg Laos and Myanmar) – try the moneychangers on New (Charoen Krung) Rd for these.

Credit cards are becoming widely accepted at hotels, restaurants and other business establishments. Visa and MasterCard are the most commonly accepted, followed by American Express and Diners Club. Cash advances are available on Visa and MasterCard at many banks and exchange booths.

All major Thai banks offer ATM (automatic teller machine) services; many of the machines will accept foreign ATM cards and/or debit cards.

Tipping

Tipping is not customary except in the big tourist hotels of Bangkok, Pattaya, Phuket and Chiang Mai. Even here, if a service charge is added to the bill, tipping isn't necessary.

Bargaining

Bargaining is mandatory in almost all situations. Arab and Indian traders brought bargaining to Thailand early in the millennium and the Thais have developed it into an art. Nowhere in South-East Asia is it more necessary not to accept the first price, whether dealing with Bangkok non-metered taxi drivers or village weavers. While bargaining, it helps to stay relaxed and friendly – gritting your teeth and raising your voice is almost always counter-productive.

POST & COMMUNICATIONS

The Thai postal system is relatively efficient and few travellers complain about undelivered mail or lost parcels. Poste restante can be received at any town in the country that has a post office, and most hotels and guesthouses will gladly hold mail for guests as long as the envelopes are so marked.

Telephone

The telephone system is also fairly modern and efficient – larger amphoe muang (provincial capitals) are connected with the IDD system. The central post office in any amphoe muang will usually house, or be located next to, the international telephone office. There is generally someone at this office who speaks English. In any case, the forms are always bilingual.

The access code for making international calls from Thailand is 001.

To call Thailand from outside the country, the country code is 66.

BOOKS

Bangkok has some of the best bookshops in South-East Asia. See under Bookshops in the Bangkok section later in this chapter for details.

Lonely Planet

Lonely Planet's *Thailand – travel survival kit* provides much more detail on the country than can be squeezed into this chapter. Lonely Planet also publishes a *Bangkok city guide*, a *Thailand travel atlas* and a *Thai phrasebook* and *Thai Hill Tribes phrasebook*.

Guidebooks

Discovering Thailand (Oxford University Press) by Clarac & Smithies is good for architectural and archaeological points of interest, although it's a bit dated.

Arts

Several books on Thai arts have appeared over the years. Perhaps the easiest to find (if not necessarily the most accurate) is *Arts of Thailand* (hardback) by Bangkok's dynamic duo, writer Steve Van Beek and photographer Luca Invernizzi Tettoni. William Warren and Tettoni have authored a worthy book on Thai design called *Thai Style* (hardback).

Culture

Denis Segaller's *Thai Ways* and *More Thai Ways* (both paperbacks) are readable collections of cultural vignettes relating to Thai culture and folklore. *Mai Pen Rai* by Carol Hollinger (paperback) is often suggested as an introduction to Thai culture but is more a cultural snapshot of Thailand in the 1960s. More useful as a cultural primer is Robert & Nanthapa Cooper's *Culture Shock! Thailand*, part of a series that attempts to educate tourists and business travellers in local customs.

Hill Tribes

The Hill Tribes of Northern Thailand by Gordon Young (Monograph No 1, The Siam Society, paperback) covers 16 tribes, including descriptions, photographs, tables and maps. Young was born of third-generation Christian missionaries among Lahu tribespeople, speaks several tribal dialects and is an honorary Lahu chieftain. *From the Hands of the Hills* by Margaret Campbell (hardback) has beautiful pictures of hill tribe handicrafts. The photo-oriented *Peoples of the Golden Triangle* by Elaine & Paul Lewis (hardback) is also good – but expensive.

History & Politics

The Indianized States of South-East Asia (paperback) by George Coedes, *The Thai Peoples* by Erik Seidenfaden (hardback, out of print), *Siam in Crisis* (paperback) by Sulak Sivarak and *Political Conflict in Thailand: Reform, Reaction, Revolution* (hardback) by David Morrell & Chai-anan Samudavanija are all worth reading. Two of the best modern histories are David Wyatt's *Thailand: A Short History* (paperback) and *The Balancing Act: A History of Modern Thailand* (paperback) by Joseph Wright Jr.

Thailand's role in the international narcotics trade is covered thoroughly in Alfred McCoy's *The Politics of Heroin in Southeast Asia* and Francis Belanger's *Drugs, the US, and Khun Sa*.

The fictional *Red Bamboo*, by ex-prime minister Kukrit Pramoj, vividly portrays and predicts the conflict between the Thai Communist movement and the establishment during the 60s and 70s. His book *Si Phaendin: Four Reigns* (1981), the most widely read novel ever published in Thailand, covers the Ayuthaya era. Both novels are available in English.

FILMS

Probably the most famous movie associated with Thailand is *The Bridge on the River Kwai*, a 1957 Academy Award-winning production based on Pierre Boulle's book of the same name and starring Alec Guinness. Although based on events in Thailand during WWII, much of the film was shot on location in Sri Lanka (then Ceylon). Another early film of some notoriety was 1962's *The Ugly American*, a vehicle for Marlon Brando based on the novel by William J Lederer. In this muddled picture Thailand stands in for the fictionalised South-East Asian nation of Sarkan. Part-time Thai politician and academic Kukrit Pramoj enjoyed a substantial role as the fictitious nation's prime minister. Kukrit went on to become Thailand's prime minister in 1974.

The Man with the Golden Gun, a pedestrian 1974 James Bond film starring Roger Moore and Christopher Lee, brought the karst islands of Ao Phang-Nga to international attention for the first time. A year later the French soft-porn movie *Emmanuelle* ('Much hazy, soft-focus coupling in downtown Bangkok', wrote *the Illustrated London News*) added to the myth of Thailand as sexual idyll and set an all-time box office record in France. A half dozen or so Emmanuelle sequels, at least two of which returned to Thailand for script settings, were produced over the next decade.

Virtually every film set during the Vietnam War has been shot either in the Philippines or in Thailand. Relative logistical ease means Thailand tends to be the location of choice. The first such movie shot in Thailand was *The Deer Hunter*, which starred Robert DeNiro and relative newcomer Meryl Streep; it won the 1978 Academy Award for best picture. Oliver Stone's *Heaven and Earth* (1993) is one of the more recent pictures to paint Vietnam on a Thai canvas.

There is now a substantial Thai contingent of trained production assistants and casting advisers who work on location with foreign companies – mainly from Japan, Hong Kong and Singapore.

NEWSPAPERS & MAGAZINES

Two English-language newspapers – the *Bangkok Post* (morning) and *The Nation* (afternoon) – are published daily in Thailand and distributed in most provincial capitals. *The Post* is the better of the two for international news and, in fact, is regarded by many journalists as the best English daily in South-East Asia. *The Nation* has better local and regional news coverage.

A third English-language daily, the less widely available *Thailand Times*, is owned by an investment company with an obvious bias towards growth and development.

Though mostly devoted to domestic and regional business, the English-language *Manager* occasionally prints very astute, up-to-date cultural pieces. *Bangkok Metro*, a slick lifestyle magazine started in 1995, brings a new sophistication to Bangkok publications dealing with art, culture and music.

Many popular magazines from the UK, USA, Australia and Europe – particularly those about computer technology, autos, fashion, music and business – are available in bookstores which specialise in English-language publications.

RADIO & TV

Thailand has more than 400 radio stations, including 41 FM and 35 AM stations in Bangkok alone. Radio Thailand broadcasts English-language programmes at 97 FM from 6 am to 11 pm. Most of the programmes comprise local, national and international news, sports, business and special news-related features. Another public radio station, 107 FM, is affiliated with Radio Thailand and Channel 9 on Thai public television. It broadcasts Radio Thailand news bulletins at the same hours as Radio Thailand (7 am, 12.30 pm and 7 pm).

Between 6 and 8 pm several FM stations provide soundtracks in English for local and world satellite news on TV Channel 3 (105.5 FM), Channel 7 (103.5 FM), Channel 9 (107 FM) and Channel 11 (8 pm, 88 FM).

Thailand's five public and private TV networks are all based in Bangkok, and satellite and cable services are swiftly multiplying. Of the many regional satellite operations aimed at Thailand, the most successful so far are Satellite Television Asian Region (STAR), Channel V (a Hong Kong-based music video telecast), Zee TV (Hindi programming) and Thailand's own IBC.

Turner Broadcasting (CNN International), ESPN, HBO and various telecasts from Indonesia, Malaysia, the Philippines, Brunei and Australia are available via Indonesia's Palapa C1 satellite. Other satellites tracked by dishes include China's Apstar 1 and soon-to-be-launched Apstar 2.

Tourist-class hotels in Thailand often have one or more satellite TV channels (plus in-house video), including a STAR 'sampler' channel that switches from one STAR offering to another.

PHOTOGRAPHY

Print film is inexpensive and widely available throughout Thailand. Slide film is also inexpensive but it can be hard to find outside Bangkok and Chiang Mai – be sure to stock up before heading upcountry. Film processing is generally quite good in the larger cities and also quite inexpensive. Kodachrome must be sent out of the country for processing, which can take up to two weeks.

Hill tribespeople in some frequently visited areas expect money if you photograph them, while certain Karen and Akha flee a pointed camera. Use discretion when photographing villagers anywhere in Thailand because a camera can be a very intimidating instrument. You may feel better leaving it behind when visiting certain areas.

CALENDAR

The official year in Thailand is reckoned from 543 BC, the beginning of the Buddhist Era, so that 1997 AD is 2540 BE.

ELECTRICITY

Electric current is 220V, 50 Hz. Electrical wall outlets are usually of the round, two-pole type; some outlets also accept flat, two-bladed terminals, and some will take either flat or round terminals. Any electrical supply shop will carry adaptors for any international plug shape and voltage converters.

WEIGHTS & MEASURES

Dimensions and weight are usually expressed in the metric system in Thailand. The exception is land measure, which is often quoted using the traditional Thai system of *waa*, *ngaan* and *râi*. Old-timers in the provinces will occasionally use traditional weights and measures in speech, as will boat builders, carpenters and other craftspeople when talking about their work.

THAILAND

Here are some conversions to use for such occasions:

1 sq *waa*	=	4 sq metres
1 *ngaan* (100 sq waa)	=	400 sq metres
1 *râi* (4 ngaan)	=	1600 sq metres
1 *bàht*	=	15g
1 *taleung* or *tamleung* (4 baht)	=	60g
1 *châng* (20 taleung)	=	1.2 kg
1 *hàap* (50 chang)	=	60 kg
1 *níu*	=	about 2 cm (or 1 inch)
1 *khêup* (12 niu)	=	25 cm
1 *sàwk* (2 kheup)	=	50 cm
1 *waa* (4 sawk)	=	2 metres
1 *sén* (20 waa)	=	40 metres
1 *yôht* (400 sen)	=	16 km

LAUNDRY

Virtually every hotel and guesthouse in Thailand offers a laundry service. Rates are generally geared to room rates; the cheaper the accommodation, the cheaper the washing and ironing. Cheapest of all are public laundries, where you pay by the kg.

Many Thai hotels and guesthouses also have laundry areas where you can wash your clothes at no charge; sometimes there's even a hanging area for drying. At accommodation where a laundry area isn't available, do-it-yourself-ers can wash their clothes in the sink and hang clothes out to dry in their rooms. Laundry detergent is readily available in supermarkets and shops selling general merchandise.

HEALTH

In Thailand, malaria is mostly restricted to a few rural areas – notably the islands of the eastern seaboard (Rayong to Trat) and the provinces (but not the capitals) of Kanchanaburi, Chaiyaphum, Phetchabun, Mae Hong Son and Tak. Virtually all strains of malaria in Thailand are resistant to chloroquine and mefloquine, so it's advisable to take an alternative.

There are small epidemics of Japanese encephalitis in northern Thailand each rainy season. Mosquitoes carry the disease and the risk is said to be greatest in rural zones.

People who may be at risk of contracting Japanese encephalitis are those who will be spending long periods of time in rural areas during the rainy season (June to October).

As of January 1996 the World Health Organisation (WHO) estimated there were approximately 600,000 HIV-positive cases in Thailand, a number also supported by research by the Thai Ministry of Health. An estimated 6% of these are thought to be full-blown AIDS cases, but the number will undoubtedly have increased by the time you read this. In spite of rumours to the contrary, the Thai government keeps all AIDS-related records open to public scrutiny and is trying to educate the general public about AIDS prevention. In Thailand, the disease is most commonly associated with intravenous heroin use, but is also known to be transmitted through sexual contact, both heterosexual and homosexual. If you're going to have sex in Thailand, use condoms.

Opisthorchiasis Opisthorchiasis is caused by 'liver flukes', tiny worms that are occasionally present in freshwater fish. The main risk comes from eating raw or undercooked fish. Travellers should in particular avoid eating *plaa ráa* (sometimes called *paa daek* in north-east Thailand), an unpasteurised fermented fish used as an accompaniment for rice in the north-east. Plaa ráa is not commonly served in restaurants but is common in rural areas of the north-east, where it's considered a great delicacy. The Thai government is currently trying to discourage north-easterners from eating plaa ráa or other uncooked fish products. A common roadside billboard in the region these days reads *isāan mâi kin plaa dìp*, or 'north-eastern Thailand doesn't eat raw fish'.

Liver flukes *(wiwâat bai tàp* in Thai) are endemic to villages around Sakon Nakhon Province's Nong Han, the largest natural lake in Thailand. Don't swim in this lake! (As with blood flukes, liver flukes can bore into the skin.) A much less common way to contract liver flukes is through swimming in rivers. The only other known area where the flukes might be contracted by swimming in contaminated waters is in the southern reaches of the Mekong River.

See the Health section in the Appendix for more information.

TOILETS & SHOWERS

As in many other Asian countries, the 'squat toilet' is the norm in Thailand – except in hotels and guesthouses geared towards tourists and international business travellers. Next to a typical squat toilet there's a bucket or cement reservoir filled with water; a plastic bowl usually floats on the surface or sits nearby. This water supply has a two-fold function: the toilet-goer scoops water from the reservoir with the plastic bowl and uses it to clean their nether regions while still squatting over the toilet. Since there is usually no mechanical flushing device attached to a squat toilet, a few extra scoops must be poured into the toilet bowl to flush waste into the septic system. In larger towns, mechanical flushing systems are becoming increasingly common, even with squat toilets. More rustic toilets in rural areas may simply consist of a few planks over a hole in the ground.

Even in places where sit-down toilets are installed, the plumbing may not be designed to take toilet paper. In such cases the usual washing bucket will be standing nearby or there will be a waste basket where you're supposed to place used toilet paper.

Public toilets are common in cinema houses, department stores, bus and railway stations, larger hotel lobbies and airports. While on the road between towns and villages it is perfectly acceptable to go behind a tree or bush, or even to use the roadside when nature calls.

Some hotels and most guesthouses in the country do not have hot water, though places in the larger cities will usually offer small electric shower heaters in their more expensive rooms. Very few boiler-style water heaters are available outside larger international-style hotels.

Guesthouses may have wash rooms where a large jar or cement trough is filled with water for bathing; a plastic or metal bowl is used to sluice water from the jar or trough over the body. Even in homes where showers are installed, heated water is uncommon. Most Thais bathe at least twice a day.

WOMEN TRAVELLERS

Foreign women have been attacked while travelling alone in remote parts of Thailand. Everyday incidents of sexual harassment are much less common than in India, Indonesia or Malaysia, and this may lull women who have recently travelled in these countries into thinking that travel in Thailand is safer than it is. If you're a woman travelling alone, try to pair up with other travellers when travelling at night or in remote areas. Urban areas seem relatively safe; the exception is Chiang Mai, where there have been several reports of harassment. Make sure hotel and guesthouse rooms are secure at night – if they're not, demand another room or go somewhere else.

GAY & LESBIAN TRAVELLERS

Thai culture is very tolerant of homosexuality, both male and female. The nation has no laws that discriminate against homosexuals and there is a fairly prominent gay/lesbian scene around the country. There is no 'gay movement' in Thailand, since there's no anti-gay establishment to move against. Whether speaking of dress or mannerism, 'butch' women and 'feminine' men are generally accepted without comment.

Public displays of affection – whether heterosexual or homosexual – are frowned upon.

DISABLED TRAVELLERS

Thailand presents one large, ongoing obstacle course for the mobility-impaired. With its high kerbs, uneven sidewalks and nonstop traffic, Bangkok can be particularly difficult – many streets must be crossed via pedestrian bridges flanked by steep stairways, while buses and boats don't stop long enough for even the mildly handicapped. Rarely are there any ramps or other access points for wheelchairs.

Only Hyatt International, Novotel, Sheraton, Holiday Inn and Westin hotels – none of them in the shoestring budget range – offer

THAILAND

some measure of access for the mobility-impaired.

Travel in the streets is still possible, and enjoyable, providing you have a strong, ambulatory companion. Some obstacles may require two carriers; Thais are by nature helpful and could generally be counted on for assistance.

For wheelchair travellers, any trip to Thailand will require a good deal of advance planning; fortunately a growing network of information sources can put you in touch with those who have wheeled through Thailand before. There is no better source of information than someone who's done it.

In Thailand you can contact:

Assn of the Physically Handicapped of Thailand
    73/7-8 Soi Thepprasan (Soi 8), Tivanon Rd,
    Talaat Kawan, Nonthaburi 11000
    (☎ (2) 951-0569; fax 580-1098 ext 7)
Disabled Peoples International – Thailand
    78/2 Tivanon Rd, Pak Kret, Nonthaburi 11120
    (☎ (2) 583-3021; fax 583-6518)
Handicapped International
    87/2 Soi 15, Sukhumvit Rd, Bangkok 10110.
Thai Disability Organisations
    David Lambertson, Ambassador
    (☎ /fax (2) 254-2990)

SENIOR TRAVELLERS

Senior discounts aren't generally available in Thailand, but the Thais more than make up for this in the respect they typically show for the elderly. In traditional Thai culture status comes with age; there isn't as heavy an emphasis on youth as there is in the west. Thais will go out of their way to help older people in and out of taxis or with luggage, and – usually but not always – in waiting on them first in shops and post offices.

DANGERS & ANNOYANCES

There's always a lot of talk about safety in Thailand – guerrilla forces along two out of four international borders, muggings, robberies and who-knows-what get wide publicity. Communist insurgency in the north and north-east was wiped out in the early 1980s, and in the south it came to an official end in 1989. The remaining danger areas are along the Burmese (drug-smuggling and ethnic insurgents) and Cambodian (Khmer Rouge) border areas. Take extra care when travelling in these areas and avoid travelling at night.

Robberies and hold-ups, despite their publicity, are relatively infrequent. If there is a rule of thumb, however, it's that the hold-up gangs seem to concentrate more on tour buses than on the ordinary buses or the trains, probably assuming that the pickings will be richer.

Precautions

Theft in Thailand is still usually a matter of stealth rather than strength – you're more likely to be pickpocketed than mugged. Take care of your valuables, don't carry too much cash around with you and watch out for razor artists (they slit bags open in crowded quarters) and the snatch-and-run experts in Bangkok. Don't trust hotel rooms, particularly in the beach-hut places like Ko Samui and Ko Pha-Ngan. Try not to place your bag on the roof of buses or in under-floor luggage compartments.

Also, take care when leaving valuables in hotel safes. Many travellers have reported unpleasant experiences after leaving valuables in Chiang Mai guesthouses: on their return home, they received huge credit card bills for purchases (usually jewellery) charged to their cards in Bangkok. The cards had, supposedly, been secure in the hotel or guesthouse safe while the guests were out trekking!

Women in particular, but men also, should ensure their rooms are securely locked and bolted at night. Inspect cheap rooms with thin walls for strategic peepholes.

Thais are a friendly lot and their friendliness is usually genuine. Nevertheless, on trains and buses, particularly in the south, beware of strangers offering cigarettes, drinks or chocolates. Several travellers have reported waking up with a headache sometime later to find their valuables have disappeared. Travellers have also encountered drugged food or drink from friendly strangers in bars, and from prostitutes in their own hotel rooms.

Keep zippered luggage secured with small locks, especially while travelling on buses and trains. This will not only keep out most sneak thieves, but prevent con artists posing as police from planting contraband drugs in your luggage. That may sound paranoid, but it happens.

Armed robbery appears to be on the increase in remote areas of Thailand, but the risk should still be considered fairly low. Avoid going out alone at night in remote areas and, if trekking in north Thailand, always walk in groups.

Scams

Over the years, LP has received dozens of letters from victims who've been cheated of large sums of money by con men posing as 'friendly Thais'. All of the reports have come from Bangkok and Chiang Mai, and they always describe invitations to buy gems at a special price or participate in a card game. The con artist usually strikes up a friendship on the street (often near Wat Pho, Wat Phra Kaew or Jim Thompson's House), then invites the foreigner to observe a gem purchase or card game in which the friendly stranger will participate. After explaining how easy it is to make heaps of money in the gem or card scheme, the foreigner is invited to invest. It may be hard to believe, but lots of visitor fall for it and always end up losing a lot of money.

If you become involved in one of these scams, the police (including the tourist police) are usually of little help: it's not illegal to sell gems at outrageously high prices and everyone's usually gone from the card game by the time you come back with the police.

Remember: gems and card games are this year's scam so, no doubt, some totally new and highly original scheme will pop up next year. The contact men are usually young, friendly, personable, smooth-talking 'students'. They prey on younger travellers – if you're in your 20s you're a prime target. We've even heard of combining the old drugging games with the new selling ones – 'I never thought of buying gems until I drank that soft drink they gave me'.

If you avoid gem shops, you'll avoid much potential trouble. Yes, there are some honest ones, but if you avoid them all you'll stay closer to your shoestring budget anyway.

Tuk-Tuks

Any *tuk-tuk* (three-wheeled motorcycle taxi) driver in Bangkok that offers you a ride for only 10 or 20B is a tout who will undoubtedly drag you to one or more 'factory' showrooms selling gems, clothes or handicrafts – no matter that you've already agreed on another destination in advance! To avoid this extremely frustrating situation, avoid tuk-tuks in Bangkok and use metered taxis instead – they're just as cheap.

Drugs

Penalties for drug offences are stiff: if you're caught using marijuana, you face a fine and/or up to one year in prison; for heroin use, the penalty can be anywhere from six months' to 10 years' imprisonment, or worse. Remember that it is illegal to buy, sell or possess opium, heroin or marijuana in any quantity (although the possession of opium is legal for consumption, but not for sale, among hill tribes).

BUSINESS HOURS

Most businesses are open from Monday to Friday. Many retailers and travel agencies are also open on Saturday. Government offices are open from 8.30 am to 4.30 pm and some close for lunch from noon to 1 pm.

PUBLIC HOLIDAYS & SPECIAL EVENTS

There's always a festival happening somewhere in Thailand. Many are keyed to Buddhist or Brahmanic rituals and follow a lunar calendar. Thus they fall on different dates (by the western solar calendar) each year, depending on the phases of the moon.

Such festivals are usually centred on the wats and include: Makkha Bucha (full moon in February – commemorating the gathering, without prior summons, of 500 monks to hear the Buddha speak); Wisakha Bucha (full moon in May – commemorating the birth, enlightenment and death of the Buddha); Asanha Bucha (full moon in July – commemorating the Buddha's first public discourse); and Khao Phansaa (full moon in July – celebrating the beginning of the Buddhist Rains Retreat). For other holidays, the Thai government has assigned official dates that don't vary from year to year, as follows:

New Year's Day
    1 January
Chakri Memorial Day
    6 April
Songkran Festival (Thai New Year)
    12-14 April
National Labour Day
    1 May
Coronation Day
    5 May
Queen's Birthday
    12 August
Chulalongkorn Day
    23 October
King's Birthday
    5 December
Constitution Day
    10 December
New Year's Eve
    31 December

Government offices and banks close on the above dates; some businesses will also choose to close. As in any other country, the days before and after a national holiday are marked by heavy air and road traffic, and full hotels.

Regional Holidays

Many provinces hold annual festivals or fairs to promote their specialities, eg Chiang Mai's Flower Festival, Kamphaeng Phet's Banana Festival, Yala's Barred Ground-Dove Festival and so on. A complete, up-to-date schedule of events around the country is available from TAT offices in each region or from the central Bangkok TAT office.

ACTIVITIES

Thailand isn't all temples and museums. Those interested in outdoor activities can take up diving, snorkelling, windsurfing, canoeing, kayaking, trekking and cycling –

either independently or in the company of guides and groups.

Diving & Snorkelling

Thailand's two coastlines and countless islands are popular among divers for their mild waters and colourful marine life. The biggest diving centre – in numbers of participants, not dive operations – is still Pattaya, simply because it's less than two hours drive from Bangkok. There are several islands with reefs a short boat ride from Pattaya and this little town is packed with dive shops.

Phuket is the second biggest jumping-off point – the largest if you count dive operations – and offers the largest choice of places, including small offshore islands less than an hour away; Ao Phang-Nga (a one to two hour boat ride), with its unusual rock formations and clear green waters; and the world-famous Similan and Surin islands in the Andaman Sea (about four hours away by fast boat). Reef dives in the Andaman are particularly rewarding – some 210 hard corals and 108 reef fish have so far been catalogued in this understudied marine zone, where probably thousands more species of reef organisms live. In recent years dive operations have multiplied rapidly on the palmy islands of Ko Samui, Ko Pha-Ngan and Ko Tao off Surat Thani, in the Gulf of Thailand. Chumphon Province, another up-and-coming area just north of Surat Thani, has a dozen or so islands with undisturbed reefs. Newer frontiers include the so-called Burma Banks (north-west of Mu Ko Surin), Khao Lak and islands off the coast of Krabi and Trang provinces. All of these places, with the possible exception of the Burma Banks, are suitable for snorkelling and scuba diving, since many reefs are no deeper than two metres.

Masks, fins and snorkels are readily available for rent at dive centres and through guesthouses in beach areas. However, if you're particular about the quality and condition of the equipment you use, you might be better off bringing your own mask and snorkel: some of the stuff for rent is second-rate and people with large heads may have difficulty finding masks that fit, since most are made or imported for Thai heads.

Windsurfing

The best combinations of rental facilities and wind conditions are found on Pattaya and Jomtien beaches in Chonburi Province, on Ko Samet, on the west coast of Phuket and on Chaweng Beach on Ko Samui. Some rental equipment is also available on Hat Khao Lak (north of Phuket), Ko Pha-Ngan, Ko Tao and Ko Chang. In general, the windier months on the Gulf of Thailand are mid-February to April. On the Andaman Sea side of the Thai-Malay peninsula winds are strongest from September to December.

Windsurfing gear for rent at Thai resorts is generally not the most complete or up-to-date. Original parts may be missing, or may have been replaced by improvised, Thai-made parts. For the novice windsurfer this probably won't matter, but hot-doggers may be disappointed in the selection. Bring your own if you have it.

Sea Canoeing/Kayaking

Touring the islands and coastal limestone formations around Phuket and Ao Phang-Nga by inflatable canoe or kayak has become an increasingly popular activity over the last five years. A typical sea canoe tour seeks out half-submerged caves called 'hongs' (*hâwng*, Thai for 'room'), and is timed so you can paddle into the caverns at low tide. Several outfits and guesthouses in Phuket and Krabi offer equipment and guides.

Trekking

Wilderness walking or trekking is one of northern Thailand's biggest draws. Typical treks run for three or four days (though it is possible to arrange everything from one to 10-day treks) and feature daily walks through forested mountains and overnight stays in hill tribe villages to satisfy both ethno and eco-touristic urges.

Other trekking opportunities are available in Thailand's larger national parks, where rangers may be hired as guides and cooks for a few days at a time at reasonable rates.

Cycling

Details on pedalling your way around Thailand can be found in the Getting Around chapter.

COURSES
Thai Language Study

Several language schools in Bangkok, Chiang Mai and other places where foreigners congregate offer courses in Thai language. Tuition fees average around 250B per hour. Some places will let you trade English lessons for Thai lessons; if not, you can usually teach English on the side to offset tuition costs.

If you have an opportunity to 'shop around' it's best to enrol in programmes that offer lots of linguistic interaction, rather than rote learning or the 'natural method', which has been almost universally discredited for the over-attention paid to teacher input.

The *AUA Language Centre* (☎ 252-8170) at 179 Rajadamri (Ratchadamri) Rd, Bangkok, is one of the most popular places to study Thai; in fact it's the largest private language school in the world! AUA also has branches in Chiang Mai, Lampang, Phitsanulok, Khon Kaen, Udon, Mahasarakham, Ubon, Songkhla and Phuket. Most of these are housed on Thai college or university campuses. Not all AUAs schedule regular Thai classes, but study can usually be arranged on an ad hoc basis. Teaching methodologies in upcountry AUAs tends to be more flexible than at the Bangkok unit.

The YWCA's *Siri Pattana Thai Language School* (☎ 286-1936), 13 Sathon Tai Rd, Bangkok, gives Thai language lessons and preparation for the Baw Hok exam necessary for public school teaching certification in Thailand. Siri Pattana has a second branch at 806 Soi 38, Sukhumvit Rd, Bangkok.

Meditation Study

Thailand has long been a popular place for western students of Buddhism, particularly those interested in a system of meditation known as *vipassana* (Thai: *wí-pàt-sa-nãa*), a Pali word which roughly translated means

THAILAND

'insight'. Foreigners who come to Thailand to study vipassana can choose among dozens of temples and meditation centres (*sǎmnák wípàtsanǎa*) which specialise in these teachings. Teaching methods vary from place to place, but generally emphasise learning to observe mind-body processes from moment to moment. Thai language is usually the medium of instruction but several places also provide instruction in English. Details on some of the more popular meditation-oriented temples and centres are given in the relevant sections. Instruction and accommodation are free of charge at temples, though donations are expected.

Short-term students will find that two-month tourist visas are ample for most courses of study. Long-term students may want to consider getting a three or six-month Non-Immigrant Visa. A few westerners become ordained as monks or nuns to take full advantage of the monastic environment; they are generally (but not always) allowed to stay in Thailand as long as they remain in robes.

Some places require lay persons staying overnight to wear white clothes. For even a brief visit, wear clean, polite clothing, ie long trousers or skirt, and sleeves which cover the shoulder.

For a detailed look at vipassana study in Thailand, including visa and ordination procedures, read *The Meditation Temples of Thailand: A Guide* (Spirit Rock Center, PO Box 909, Woodacre, CA 94973, USA, or Silkworm Publications, Chiang Mai) or *A Guide to Buddhist Monasteries & Meditation Centres in Thailand* (available from the World Federation of Buddhists in Bangkok).

Useful pre-meditation course reading includes Jack Kornfield's *Living Buddhist Masters*: it contains short biographies and descriptions of the teaching methods of 12 well-known Theravada teachers, including six Thais (Ajaans Buddhadasa, Jamnien, Thammatharo, Naep, Chaa and Maha Bua). Half these teachers have died since the book's publication, but their methods have been preserved and propagated by younger teachers around the country.

Thai Boxing Training

Many westerners have trained in Thailand (especially since the release of Jean-Claude Van Damme's martial arts flick *The Kickboxer*, which was filmed on location in Thailand), but few last more than a week or two in a Thai camp – and fewer still have gone on to compete on Thailand's pro circuit.

An Australian, Patrick Cusick, occasionally directs muay thai seminars for farangs in Thailand. Contact him at Thai Championship Boxing (☎ 234-5360; fax 237-6303), Box 1996, Bangkok. The Pramote Gym (☎ 215-8848) at 210-212 Phetburi Rd, Ratthewi, offers training in Thai boxing as well as other martial arts (judo, karate, tae kwon do, krabi-krabong) to foreigners and locals.

Those interested in training at a traditional muay thai camp might try the Sityodthong-Payakarun Boxing Camp in Naklua (north of Pattaya) or Fairtex Boxing Camp outside Bangkok (c/o Bunjong Busarakamwongs, Fairtex Garments Factory, 734-742 Trok Kai, Anuwong Rd, Bangkok). The newer Lanna Boxing Camp in Chiang Mai (64/1 Soi Chang Kian (Soi 1), Huay Kaew Rd, Chiang Mai 50300, ☎ /fax (53) 273133) and Patong Boxing Club in Phuket (59/4 Muu 4, Na Nai Rd, Patong Beach, ☎ (01) 978-9352; fax (76) 292189) specialise in training for foreigners.

Be forewarned, though, that muay thai training is gruelling and features full-contact sparring, unlike tae kwon do, kenpo, kungfu and other East Asian martial arts. For more information about Thai boxing, see the Spectator Sports section later in this chapter.

Thai Massage

Thailand offers ample opportunities to study its unique tradition of massage therapy. Wat Pho in Bangkok is considered the master source for all Thai massage pedagogy, although northern Thailand boasts its own, 'softer' version. Chiang Mai has become a major centre for Thai massage instruction; practically every guesthouse in town offers or can arrange for lessons.

Thai Cooking Schools

More and more travellers are coming to Thailand just to learn how to cook. Recommended schools include:

Oriental Hotel Cooking School – features five-day courses under the direction of well-known chef Chali (Charlie) Amatyakul; Soi Oriental, Charoen Krung Rd (☎ 236-0400/39)

Chiang Mai Cookery School – three-day courses include market and herb garden visits; 1-3 Moon Meuang Rd (☎ 206388, 490456)

WORK

Thailand's steady economic growth has provided a variety of work opportunities for foreigners, although in general it's not as easy to find a job as it is in more developed countries. The one exception is English teaching: as in the rest of East and South-East Asia, there is a high demand for English speakers to provide instruction to Thai citizens. This is not because of a shortage of qualified Thai teachers with a good grasp of English grammar; rather, it represents the desire to have native speaking models in the classroom.

Voluntary and paying positions with organisations that provide charitable services in education, development or public health are available for those with the right educational and/or experiential backgrounds.

ACCOMMODATION

For consistently good value, the cheap Thai hotels are among the best in the region. Almost anywhere in Thailand, even Bangkok, you can get a double for 150B or less. In fact, Bangkok has had such a proliferation of small guesthouses that it's become easier to find rooms in the rock-bottom price category.

There can be an amazing variation in prices at the same hotel. You'll find fancy air-con rooms at over 400B and straightforward fan-cooled rooms at a third of that price. There will be a choice of hotels in even the smallest towns, although 'hotel' will often be the only word written on them in English. Finding a specific place in some smaller towns can be a problem if you don't speak Thai.

A typical 150B Thai hotel room is plain and spartan, but will include a toilet, a shower and a ceiling fan. Rooms with a common toilet can cost from 70 to 140B. Guesthouses vary from 50 to 100B for a single, 100 to 120B a double, and are likely to be a little more basic and not have bathrooms. At the less touristic beach centres in southern Thailand, you'll find pleasant individual beach cottages for less than 200B.

As in Malaysia, many of the hotels are Chinese-run and couples can often save money by asking for a single – a single means one double bed, a double means two.

FOOD

Thai food is like Chinese with a sting – it can be fiery. Eating Thai style involves knowing what to get, how to get it and how to get it for a reasonable price. Outside of tourist areas, few places have a menu in English, and as for having prices on a menu... To make matters worse, your mangled attempts at asking for something in Thai are unlikely to be understood. Make the effort, for there are some delicious foods to be tried. Lonely Planet's *Thai phrasebook* contains and extensive food section with English descriptions, roman transliteration and Thai script.

Khâo phàt (fried rice) is a common dish – a close cousin to Chinese fried rice or Indonesian nasi goreng. It usually comes with sliced cucumber, a fried egg on top if you ask for *phii-sèht* (special) and some super hot peppers to catch the unwary. When you don't know what else to order, this will almost always be available. *Kài phàt bai ka-phrao*, a fiery stir-fry of chopped chicken, chillies, garlic and fresh basil, is another Thai favourite. *Phàt thai* is fried noodles, bean sprouts, peanuts, eggs, chillies and often prawns – good value at any street stall.

Many Thai restaurants are actually Chinese – serving a few of the main Thai dishes among the Chinese, or some Thai-influenced Chinese ones. In the south, look for delicious seafood and thick, coconut-laced curries, while in the north and north-east there are various local specialities centred on 'sticky rice' *(khâo niaw)*.

Other examples of Thai food include:

fried rice	*khâo phàt*
with chicken	*khâo phàt kài*
with pork	*khâo phàt mũu*
with prawns	*khâo phàt kûng*
spicy lemon soup	*tôm yam*
Indian-style curry	*kaeng kari*
Thai curry	*kaeng phèt*
curried chicken	*kaeng kài*
stir-fried vegetables	*phàt phàk ruam mít*
fried prawns	*kûng thâwt*
grilled fish	*plaa phão*
fine-noodle salad	*yam wún sên*
fried eggs	*khài dao*
scrambled eggs	*khài kuan*
omelette	*khài jii oh*

For vegetarians:
I eat only vegetarian food.
   Phõm/dii-chãn kin jeh.
I can't eat pork.
   Phõm/dii-chãn kin mũu mâi dâi.
I can't eat beef.
   Phõm/dii-chãn kin néua mâi dâi.

cabbage	*phàk kà-làm*
cauliflower	*dàwk kà-làm*
corn	*khâo phôht*
cucumber	*taeng kwaa*
eggplant	*mákhẽua mûang*
garlic	*kràtiam*
lettuce	*phàk kàat*
long bean	*thùa fák yao*
okra (ladyfingers)	*krà-jíap*
onion (bulb)	*hũa hãwm*
onion (green)	*tôn hãwm*
peanuts (ground nuts)	*tùa lísõng*
potato	*man faràng*
pumpkin	*fák thawng*
taro	*pheùak*
tofu	*tâo-hûu*
tomato	*mákhẽua thêt*

DRINKS

Soft drinks are cheaper than almost anywhere in South-East Asia. Tea and coffee are prepared strong, milky and sweet. Thais prefer to drink most fruit juices with a little salt mixed in. Unless a vendor is used to serving farangs, your fruit juice or shake will come slightly salted. If you prefer unsalted fruit juices, specify *mâi sài kleua* (without salt). Sugar cane juice *(náam âwy)* is a Thai favourite and a very refreshing accompaniment to curry-and-rice plates. Many small restaurants or food stalls that don't offer any other juices will have a supply of freshly squeezed náam âwy on hand.

More dairy products are available in Thailand than anywhere else in South-East Asia – including very good yoghurt.

Water

Water purified for drinking purposes is simply called *náam dèum* (drinking water), whether boiled or filtered. *All* water offered to customers in restaurants or to guests in an office or home will be purified, so you needn't fret about the safety of taking a sip. In restaurants you can ask for *náam plào* (plain water), which is always either boiled or taken from a purified source; it's served by the glass at no charge or you can order by the bottle. A bottle of carbonated water (soda) costs about the same as a bottle of plain purified water but the bottles are smaller.

hot water	*náam ráwn*
boiled water	*áam tôm*
cold water	*áam yen*
ice	*náam khãen*
Chinese tea	*chaa jiin*
weak Chinese tea	*náam chaa*
iced Thai tea with milk & sugar	*chaa yen*
iced Thai tea with sugar only	*chaa dam yen*
no sugar (command)	*mâi sài náam-taan*
hot Thai tea with sugar	*chaa dam ráwn*
hot Thai tea with milk & sugar	*chaa ráwn*
hot coffee with milk & sugar	*kafae ráwn*
iced coffee with sugar, no milk	*oh-liang*

orange soda	*náam sôm*
plain milk	*nom jèut*
iced lime juice with sugar (usually with salt too)	*náam mana*
no salt (command)	*mâi sài kleua*
soda water	*náam sõh-daa*
bottled drinking water	*náam dèum khùat*
bottle	*khùat*
glass	*kâew*

ENTERTAINMENT
Cinemas

Movie theatres are found in towns and cities throughout the country. Typical programmes include US and European shoot-em-ups mixed with Thai comedies and romances. Violent action pictures are always a big draw; as a rule of thumb, the smaller the town, the more violent the film offerings. English-language films are shown with their original soundtracks only in a few theatres in Bangkok, Chiang Mai and Hat Yai; elsewhere all foreign films are dubbed in Thai. Ticket prices range from 10 to 70B. Every film in Thailand begins with a playback of the royal anthem, accompanied by projected pictures of the royal family. Viewers are expected to stand during the anthem.

Bars & Nightclubs

Urban Thais are night people and every town of any size has a selection of nightspots. For the most part they are male-dominated, though the situation is changing rapidly in the larger cities, where young couples are increasingly seen in bars. Of the many types of bars, probably the most popular continues to be the 'old west' style, patterned after Thai fantasies of the 19th century American west – lots of wood and cowboy paraphernalia.

The 'go-go' bars seen in lurid photos published by the western media are limited to a few areas in Bangkok, Chiang Mai, Pattaya and Phuket's Patong Beach. These are bars in which girls typically wear swimsuits or other scant apparel. In some bars they dance to recorded music on a narrow raised stage.

To some visitors it's pathetic, to others paradise. Under a new law passed in 1995, all bars and clubs which don't feature live music or dancing are required to close by 1 am. Many get around the law by bribing local police.

Coffee Houses

Apart from the western-style cafe, which is becoming increasingly popular in Bangkok, there are two other kinds of cafes or coffee shops in Thailand. One is the traditional Hokkien-style coffee shop (*ráan kaa-fae*), where thick, black, filtered coffee is served in simple, casual surroundings. These coffee shops are common in the Chinese quarters of southern provincial capitals, though less common elsewhere. Frequented mostly by older Thai and Chinese men, they provide a place to read the newspaper, sip coffee and gossip about neighbours and politics. The other type, called *kaa-feh* (cafe) or 'coffee house', is more akin to a nightclub, where Thai men consort with a variety of Thai female hostesses. This is the Thai counterpart to farang go-go bars, except girls wear dresses instead of swimsuits. A variation on this theme is the 'sing-song' cafe, in which a succession of female singers take turns fronting a live band. Cafes which feature live music are permitted to stay open till 2 am.

Discos

Discotheques are popular in larger cities; outside Bangkok they're mostly attached to tourist or luxury hotels. The main disco clientele is Thai, though foreigners are welcome. Some provincial discos retain female staff as professional dance partners for male entertainment, but for the most part discos are considered fairly respectable nightspots for couples. Thai law permits discotheques to stay open till 2 am.

SPECTATOR SPORTS
Thai Boxing (Muay Thai)

Almost anything goes in this martial sport, both in the ring and in the stands. If you don't mind the violence in the ring, a Thai boxing match is worth attending purely for the spectacle – the wild musical accompaniment, the ceremonial beginning of each match and the frenzied betting around the stadium.

Bouts are limited to five three-minute rounds separated with two-minute breaks. Contestants had to wear international-style gloves and trunks (always either in red or blue) and their feet are taped. As in international-style boxing, matches take place on a 7.3 sq metre canvas-covered floor with rope retainers supported by four padded posts, rather than the traditional dirt circle. All surfaces of the body are still considered fair targets and any part of the body except the head may be used to strike an opponent. Common blows include high kicks to the neck, elbow thrusts to the face and head, knee hooks to the ribs and low crescent kicks to the calf. A contestant may even grasp an opponent's head between his hands and pull it down to meet an upward knee thrust. Punching is considered the weakest of all blows and kicking merely a way to 'soften up' one's opponent; knee and elbow strikes are decisive in most matches. Matches are held every day of the year at the major stadiums in Bangkok and the provinces (there are about 60,000 full-time boxers in Thailand), and they are easily found.

Takraw

Tàkrâw, sometimes called Siamese football in old English texts, refers to games in which a woven rattan ball about 12 cm in diameter is kicked around. The rattan (or sometimes plastic) ball itself is called a lûuk tàkrâw. The traditional way to play takraw in Thailand is for players to stand in a circle (the size of the circle depends on the number of players) and simply try to keep the ball airborne by kicking it. Points are scored for style, difficulty and variety of kicking manoeuvres. A popular variation on takraw – and the one used in intramural or international competitions – is played with a volleyball net, using all the same rules as in volleyball except that only the feet and head are permitted to touch the ball. It's amazing to watch the players perform aerial pirouettes, spiking the ball over the net with their feet. Another variation

has players kicking the ball into a hoop 4.5 metres above the ground – basketball with feet, but without a backboard!

THINGS TO BUY

Many bargains await you in Thailand if you have the space to carry them back. Always haggle to get the best price, except in department stores. And don't go shopping in the company of touts, tour guides or friendly strangers as they will inevitably – no matter what they say – take a commission on anything you buy, thus driving prices up.

Textiles are possibly the best all-round buy in Thailand. Thai silk is considered the best in the world and is very inexpensive. Cottons are also a good deal – common items like the phâakhamǎa (reputed to have over a hundred uses in Thailand) and the phâasîn (the slightly larger female equivalent) make great tablecloths and curtains. The north-east is famous for mát-mìi cloth – thick cotton or silk fabric woven from tie-dyed threads, similar to Indonesia's ikat fabrics. Tailor-made and ready-made clothes are relatively inexpensive.

Thai shoulder bags (yâam) are generally quite well made. They come in many varieties, some woven by hill tribes, others by northern Thai cottage industry.

Real antiques cannot be taken out of Thailand without a permit from the Department of Fine Arts. No Buddha image, new or old, may be exported without permission – again, refer to the Fine Arts Department, or, in some cases, the Department of Religious Affairs, under the Ministry of Education. Too many private collectors smuggling and hoarding Siamese art (Buddhas in particular) around the world have led to strict controls. Some antiques (and many fakes) are sold at the Weekend Market in Chatuchak Park. Objects for sale in the tourist antique shops are fantastically overpriced, as can be expected. In recent years northern Thailand has become a good source of Thai antiques – prices are about half what you'd typically pay in Bangkok.

Thailand is one of the world's largest exporters of gems and ornaments, rivalled only by India and Sri Lanka. Although rough stone sources in Thailand itself have decreased dramatically, stones are now imported from Australia, Sri Lanka and other countries to be cut, polished and traded here. Gold ornaments are sold at a good rate because labour costs are low. The best bargains in gems are jade, rubies and sapphires.

Warning For gems, shop around and *don't be hasty*. Remember: There's no such thing as a 'government sale' or a 'factory price' at a gem or jewellery shop; the Thai government does not own or manage any gem or jewellery shops. Buy from reputable dealers only, unless you're a gemologist. Never make purchases in the company of a newly found Thai 'friend'. The Asian Institute of Gemological Sciences (☎ 513-2112; fax 236-7803), 484 Ratchadaphisek Rd (off Lat Phrao Rd in the Huay Khwang District, north-east Bangkok), offers short-term courses in gemology as well as tours of gem mines for those interested. See the Dangers & Annoyances section earlier in this chapter for detailed warnings on gem fraud.

In Chiang Mai there are shops selling handicrafts. It's worth shopping around for the best prices and bargaining. The all-round best buys of northern hill tribe crafts are at the Chiang Mai Night Bazaar – if you know how to bargain. Thailand produces some good lacquerware, much of it made in Myanmar and sold along the northern Burmese border; try Mae Sot, Mae Sariang and Mae Sai for the best buys.

In Bangkok, Chiang Mai and all the tourist centres, there is a flourishing black market street trade in fake designer goods; particularly Benneton pants and sweaters, Lacoste (crocodile) and Ralph Lauren polo shirts, Levi's jeans, and Rolex, Dunhill and Cartier watches. Tin-Tin T-shirts are also big. No-one pretends they're the real thing, at least not the vendors themselves. The European and American manufacturers are applying heavy pressure on the Asian governments involved to get this stuff off the street, so it may not be around for much longer.

Getting There & Away

AIR

You can fly to Bangkok from various other Asian cities, such as Hong Kong, Manila, Singapore, Kuala Lumpur, Penang, Colombo, Yangon, Dhaka, Calcutta and Kathmandu. Bangkok is a major access point for Myanmar, Nepal, Vietnam, Laos and Cambodia. Although Bangkok is the main entry point for Thailand, you can also fly into Chiang Mai from Hong Kong, Mandalay (Myanmar) and Kunming (China), and to Hat Yai from Penang (Malaysia).

Bangkok is a popular place for buying airline tickets, although it's no longer the number-one bargain centre of the region. Some typical discounted one-way fares available from Bangkok include: Kuala Lumpur, US$110; Hong Kong, US$126; Manila, US$230; Penang, US$100 to US$132; Phnom Penh, US$100 to US$130; Singapore, US$74 to US$120; Taipei, US$220 to US$373; Yangon, US$100 to US$126; and Vientiane, US$80 to US$100.

Over the years, we have had a lot of letters complaining about various travel agencies in Bangkok – and a few saying what a good deal they got. Remember nothing is free, so if you get quoted a price way below other agencies, be suspicious. In smaller agencies, insist on getting the ticket before handing over your cash. And don't sign anything.

A favourite game of some agents has been getting clients to sign a disclaimer saying that they will not request a refund under any circumstances. Then, when the client picks their ticket up, they find it is only valid for one week or something similar – not very good when you're not planning to leave for a month or two. Alternatively, the ticket may only be valid within certain dates, or other limitations may be placed upon it.

Another catch is you may be told that the ticket is confirmed (OK) only to find on closer inspection that it is only on request (RQ) or merely open. Or even worse, the ticket actually has OK on it when in fact no

THAILAND

reservation has been made at all. So read everything carefully and remember – *caveat emptor*, buyer beware.

Reconfirmation

Flights in and out of Thailand are often overbooked these days so it's imperative that you reconfirm any return or ongoing flights you have as soon as you arrive there. If you don't, there's a very good chance you'll be bumped from your flight at the airport. It never hurts to reconfirm more than once.

Departure Tax

The departure tax on international flights is 250B. You're exempted from paying it if you're only in transit and have not left the transit area. Domestic departure tax is 30B.

LAND
Malaysia

West Coast The basic land route between Penang and Hat Yai is by taxi. It is fast, convenient and, for around RM30 or 300B, not expensive. The taxis that operate this route are generally big old Chevrolets or Mercedes, all Thai-registered. From Penang, you'll find them at the various travellers' hotels around Georgetown. In Hat Yai, they'll be at the railway station or along Niphat Uthit 2. Magic Tour, downstairs from the Cathay Guest House in Hat Yai, has buses for only 200B which leave twice daily and take five hours. This is the fastest way to cross the border by land and involves a minimum of fuss.

You can also easily walk or take a taxi across the border at Sadao (Bukit Kayu Hitam on the Malaysian side) or Padang Besar. At both places, buses run from either side; from Padang Besar there's also a train from Butterworth to the border.

The *International Express* train will take you from Padang Besar to Hat Yai and Bangkok without a change of trains. There are also connecting services to or from Singapore and Kuala Lumpur. The train operates every day and, it appears, without the border delays which used to be a problem.

The *International Express* departs Bangkok at 3.15 pm daily, arrives in Hat Yai at 7.04 the next morning and in Padang Besar at 8 am the same day. Everyone disembarks at Padang Besar, proceeds through immigration, then boards 2nd class KTM train No 99 to arrive in Butterworth at 12.40 pm Malaysian time (one hour ahead of Thai time). From Malaysia, the train leaves Padang Besar at 5 pm, arrives in Hat Yai at 6.10 pm and in Bangkok at 9.50 am the next day. Fares from Padang Besar to Hat Yai are 13B for 2nd class and 30B for 1st. From Padang Besar to Bangkok is 326B and 694B respectively.

There is an additional express surcharge on the *International Express* of 100B. For berth charges see the Getting Around section below. Altogether these charges, plus the basic fares, really add up; if you're looking for the cheapest way across the border, take the bus.

East Coast From Kota Bharu (Malaysia), you can take a share taxi to Rantau Panjang – 45 km for about RM6. It's then just a half km (maybe nearer one km) stroll across the border to the town of Sungai Kolok. From here, trains run to Hat Yai and Bangkok. The border is only open from 6 am to 6 pm.

Laos

Official Thai-Lao border crossings that are open to foreigners include Chong Mek (near Pakse), Mukdahan (opposite Savannakhet), Nakhon Phanom (opposite Tha Khaek), Nong Khai (near Vientiane) and Chiang Khong (opposite Huay Xai). Exits from Laos into Thailand at any of these crossings can be arranged in Vientiane, but only the Nong Khai-Vientiane crossing is regularly used to enter Laos from Thailand.

Cambodia

At the moment, no land or sea crossings between Cambodia and Thailand are officially allowed. Sometimes special permission to enter Cambodia from Aranyaprathet, Thailand (opposite Poipet, Cambodia), is granted by Thailand's Interior Ministry.

Eventually – if and when Cambodia stabilises – this may become a common way to reach Phnom Penh from Thailand. A railway links Poipet with the Cambodian capital.

Myanmar

Day trips into Myanmar are allowed from Three Pagodas Pass (for Payathonzu), Mae Sot (for Myawaddy) and Mae Sai (for Thachilek and Chiangtung/Kyaingtong). At present overland travel to Yangon from Thailand is not permitted.

SEA

Malaysia

There are also some unusual routes between Malaysia and Thailand. For example, go to Kuala Perlis (the jumping-off point for Langkawi Island) and take a long-tail boat for about RM4 to Satun (or Satul), just across the border in Thailand. These are legal entry and exit points, with immigration and customs posts. On arrival in Satun, it costs about 10B for the three km ride from the docks to immigration. You can then bus into Hat Yai. Again, make sure you get your passport properly stamped.

You may also be able to get a boat to Satun via Langkawi, a large Malaysian island on the Thai-Malaysian marine border. When they're running, boats to Langkawi leave Satun about every one or 1½ hours and cost from RM10 to 15. Though it's cheaper to go straight to Satun from Kuala Perlis, Langkawi is worth a stop if you have the time.

Another possibility is to take a yacht between Penang and Phuket; at times they run back and forth regularly.

Getting Around

AIR

Thai Airways International (THAI) operates both international and domestic routes. They have a useful flight network around Thailand. It's not much used by budget travellers because ground-level transport is generally

so good. THAI's domestic flights use Boeing 737 and Airbus 300 aircraft.

The internal fares are generally fixed, but you might be able to find cheaper tickets for international sectors, such as Bangkok to Penang. Both propjet and jets operate on some sectors; in these cases, fares will be lower on the prop aircraft. The fares shown on the air fares chart are all for jet travel.

Bangkok Airways has five main routes: Bangkok-Sukhothai-Chiang Mai; Bangkok-Samui-Phuket; Bangkok-Ranong-Phuket; Bangkok-Hua Hin-Samui; and U Taphao (Pattaya)-Samui. The mainstay of the Bangkok Airways fleet is the Franco-Italian ATR-72.

Orient Express Air, formerly a carrier in Cambodia known as SK Air, is a relative newcomer that uses B727-200s for all flights. It operates charter and tour package flights between Chiang Mai and Phuket, and 20 scheduled domestic routes link the north with the south and north-east without Bangkok stopovers.

Air Passes

THAI offers special four-coupon passes – available only outside Thailand for purchases in foreign currency – in which you can book any four domestic flights for one fare of US$259 as long as you don't repeat the same leg. Unless you plan carefully this isn't much of a savings, since it's hard to avoid repeating the same leg in and out of Bangkok.

If you were to buy separate tickets from Bangkok to Hat Yai, then Hat Yai to Phuket, Phuket to Bangkok and finally Bangkok to Chiang Mai, you'd spend 6625B (US$265), a savings of only US$6. However, if you were to fly from Bangkok to Phuket, Phuket to Bangkok, Bangkok to Chiang Mai – then continue overland to Sakon Nakhon and fly back to Bangkok from there, you'd save approximately US$60 over the total of the individual fares.

For information on the four-coupon deal, known as the 'Discover Thailand fare', inquire at any THAI office outside Thailand.

THAILAND

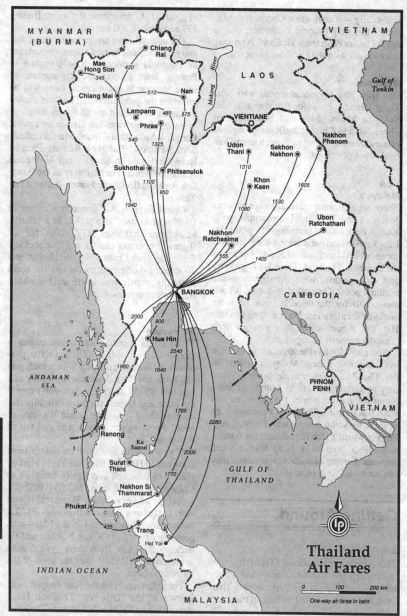

MYANMAR
(BURMA)

VIETNAM

Chiang
Rai

Mae
Hong Son
345

420

LAOS

Gulf of
Tonkin

Mekong River

Chiang Mai

510

Nan

575

Lampang

485

Phrae

1325

VIENTIANE

540

Udon
Thani

1310

Sakhon
Nakhon

Nakhon
Phanom

Sukhothai

1100

Phitsanulok

950

Khon
Kaen

1605

1940

1080

1530

Ubon
Ratchathani

Nakhon
Ratchasima

555

1405

BANGKOK

CAMBODIA

2000

900

Hua Hin

2540

1980

1640

PHNOM
PENH

ANDAMAN
SEA

1785

2280

VIETNAM

Ranong

Ko
Samui

2005

GULF OF
THAILAND

Surat
Thani

1770

Nakhon Si
Thammarat

Phuket

690

435

Trang

Hat Yai

INDIAN OCEAN

MALAYSIA

**Thailand
Air Fares**

0   100   200 km

One-way air fares in baht

THAILAND

BUS

The Thai bus service is widespread and phenomenally fast – terrifyingly so, much of the time. There are usually air-con buses as well as 'normal' ones, and on major routes there are also private, air-con tour buses. The air-con buses are so cold that blankets are handed out as a matter of routine and the service is so good it's embarrassing. You often get free drinks, pillows, free meals and even 'in-flight movies' on some routes! There are often a number of bus stations in a town – usually public and private stations.

Warning

Beware the low-priced 'VIP' buses and minivans that leave from the Khao San Rd area. Rarely do these bus lines provide the services promised in advance; Khao San Rd buses have even left passengers stranded alongside the highway halfway between Bangkok and the supposed destination. The government buses from the official bus terminals are generally safer and more reliable.

TRAIN

The government-operated trains in Thailand are comfortable, frequent, punctual and moderately priced – but rather slow. On comparable routes, the buses can often be twice as fast, but the relatively low speed of the train means you can often leave at a convenient hour in the evening and arrive at your destination at a pleasant hour in the morning.

Train fares plus sleeping-berth charges make train travel appear a bit more expensive than bus travel. However, with a sleeping berth you may save over the cost of the bus fare plus one night's hotel costs. The trains have a further advantage over the buses in that they're far safer and there's more room to move around. All in all, Thailand's railways are a fine way to travel. One caveat: food served on trains is rather expensive by Thai standards; you'll save considerable baht by bringing your own food on board.

There are four main railway lines plus a few minor side routes. The main ones are: the northern line to Chiang Mai; the southern line to Hat Yai (where the line splits to enter Malaysia on the west coast via Padang Besar and to terminate near the east coast at Sungai Kolok); the eastern line to Ubon Ratchathani; and the north-eastern line to Nong Khai.

Very useful condensed railway timetables are available in English at the Hualamphong railway station in Bangkok. These contain schedules and fares for all rapid and express trains, as well as a few ordinary trains.

Bookings

Unfortunately, the trains are often heavily booked, so it's wise to book ahead. At the Hualamphong station in Bangkok, you can book trains on any route in Thailand. The advance booking office is open from 8.30 am to 4 pm Monday to Friday, and from 8.30 am to noon on Saturday, Sunday and holidays. Seats, berths or cabins may be booked up to 90 days in advance.

Charges

There is a 50B surcharge for express trains and a 30B surcharge for rapid trains – the greater speed is gained mainly through fewer stops. Some 2nd and 3rd class services are air-con, in which case there is a 70B surcharge (note that there are no 3rd class cars on either rapid or express trains).

Sleeping berths also cost extra. In 2nd class, upper berths are 100B, lower berths are 150B. For 2nd class sleepers with air-con add 250/320B per upper/lower ticket. No sleepers are available in 3rd class. The lower berths are cooler since they have a window, which upper do not. In 1st class, the berths cost 520B per person in two-berth or single-berth cabins. Sleepers are only available in 1st and 2nd class, but apart from that, 3rd class is not too bad.

Fares are roughly double for 2nd class over 3rd and double again for 1st class over 2nd. Count on around 180B for a 500 km trip in 2nd class. You can break a trip for two days for each 200 km travelled, but the ticket must be endorsed by the station master, which costs 1B.

CAR & MOTORCYCLE

Cars, jeeps or vans can be rented in Bangkok and large provincial capitals. The best deals are usually on 4WD Suzuki Caribians, which can be rented for as low as 700 to 800B per day for long-term rentals or during low seasons. Check with travel agencies or large hotels for rental locations. Always verify that a vehicle is insured for liability before signing a rental contract and ask to see the dated insurance documents. If you have an accident while driving an uninsured vehicle you're in for some major hassles.

Motorcycles can be rented in major towns and in many smaller tourist centres, including Krabi, Ko Samui, Ko Pha-Ngan, Mae Sai, Chiang Saen and Nong Khai. Since there is a surplus of motorcycles for rent in Chiang Mai and Phuket these days, they can be rented in these towns for as little as 100B per day. A substantial deposit is usually required to rent a car; motorcycle rental usually requires that you leave your passport.

Permits

Foreigners who wish to drive a motor vehicle (including motorcycles) in Thailand need a valid international driver's licence. If you don't have one, you can apply for a Thai driver's licence at the Police Registration Division (PRD) (☎ 513-0051/5) on Phahonyothin Rd in Bangkok. Provincial capitals also have PRDs. If you present a valid foreign driver's licence at the PRD you'll probably only have to take a written test; other requirements include a medical certificate and three passport-sized colour photos. The forms are in Thai only, so you'll also need an interpreter.

Motorcycle Touring

Motorcycle travel is a popular way to get around Thailand, especially in the north. Dozens of places along the guesthouse circuit, including many guesthouses themselves, have set up shop with no more than a couple of motorbikes for rent. It is also possible to buy a new or used motorbike and sell it before you leave the country – a good used 125cc bike costs around 20,000B. Daily rentals range from 100 to 120B a day for a 100cc step-through (eg Honda Dream, Suzuki Crystal) to 500B a day for a good 250cc dirt bike.

The legal maximum size for motorcycles manufactured in Thailand is 150cc, though in reality few on the road exceed 125cc. Anything over 150cc must be imported, which means an addition of up to 600% in import duties. The odd rental shop specialises in bigger motorbikes (average 200 to 500cc), which were either imported by foreign residents and sold on the local market, or came into the country as 'parts' then discreetly assembled, and licensed under the table.

While motorcycle touring is one of the best ways to see Thailand, it is undoubtedly one of the easiest ways to cut your travels short – permanently. You could also run up very large repair and/or hospital bills in the blink of an eye. But with proper safety precautions and driving conduct adapted to local standards, you can see parts of Thailand inaccessible by other modes of transport and still make it home in one piece. Some guidelines to keep in mind:

- If you've never driven a motorcycle before, stick to the smaller 80 to 100cc step-through bikes with automatic clutches. If you're an experienced rider but have never done off-the-road driving, take it slow the first few days.
- Always check a machine over thoroughly before you take it out. Look at the tyres to see if they still have tread, look for oil leaks, test the brakes. You may be held liable for any problems that weren't duly noted before your departure. Newer bikes cost more than clunkers, but are generally safer and more reliable. Street bikes are more comfortable and ride more smoothly on paved roads than dirt bikes; it's silly to rent an expensive dirt bike if most of your riding is going to be along decent roads. A two-stroke bike suitable for off-roading generally uses twice the fuel of a four-stroke bike with the same engine size, thus lowering your cruising range in areas where roadside pumps are scarce (eg the 125cc Honda Wing gives you about 300 km per tank while a 125cc Honda MTX gets about half that).
- Wear protective clothing and a helmet (most rental places will provide a helmet with the bike if asked). Without a helmet, a minor slide on gravel can leave you with concussion, cuts or bruises. Long pants,

long-sleeved shirts and shoes are highly recommended as protection against sunburn and as a second skin if you fall. If your helmet doesn't have a visor, then wear goggles, glasses or sunglasses to keep bugs, dust and other debris out of your eyes. It is practically suicidal to ride on Thailand's highways without taking these minimum precautions for protecting your body. Gloves are also a good idea – to prevent blisters from holding on to the twist-grips for long periods of time.

- For distances of over 100 km or so, take along an extra supply of motor oil and, if riding a two-stroke machine, carry two-stroke engine oil. On long trips, oil burns fast.
- You should never ride alone in remote areas, especially at night. There have been incidents where farang bikers have been shot or harassed while riding alone, mostly in remote rural areas. When riding in pairs or groups, stay spread out so you'll have room to manoeuvre or brake suddenly if necessary.
- In Thailand the de facto right of way is determined by the size of the vehicle, which puts the motorcycle pretty low in the pecking order. Don't fight it and keep clear of trucks and buses.
- Distribute whatever weight you're carrying on the bike as evenly as possible across the frame. Too much weight at the back of the bike makes the front end less easy to control and prone to rising up suddenly on bumps and inclines.
- Get insurance with the motorcycle if at all possible. The more reputable motorcycle rental places insure all their bikes; some will do it for an extra charge. Without insurance you're responsible for anything that happens to the bike. If an accident results in a total loss, or if the bike is somehow lost or stolen, you can be out 25,000B plus. To be absolutely clear about your liability, ask for a written estimate of the replacement cost for a similar bike – take photos as a guarantee. Some agencies will only accept the replacement cost of a new bike.

Health insurance is also a good idea – get it before you leave home and check the conditions that apply to motorcycle riding.

BICYCLE

Bicycles can also be hired in many locations; guesthouses often have a few for rent at only 20 to 30B per day. Just about anywhere outside Bangkok, bikes are the ideal form of local transport because they're cheap and non-polluting and keep you moving slowly enough to see everything. Carefully note the condition of the bike before hiring; if it

breaks down you are responsible and parts can be very expensive.

Many visitors are bringing their own touring bikes to Thailand these days. Gradients in most of the country are moderate; exceptions include the far north, especially Mae Hong Son and Nan provinces, where you'll need iron thighs. There is plenty of opportunity for dirt-road and off-road pedalling, especially in the north, so a sturdy mountain bike would make a good alternative to a touring rig. Favoured touring routes include the two-lane roads along the Mekong River in the north and the north-east – the terrain is mostly flat and the river scenery is inspiring.

No special permits are needed to bring a bicycle into the country, although bikes may be registered by customs – which means if you don't leave the country with your bike you'll have to pay a huge customs duty. Most larger cities have bike shops – there are several in Bangkok and Chiang Mai – but they usually stock only a few Japanese or locally made parts. All the usual bike trip precautions apply – bring a small repair kit with plenty of spare parts, a helmet, reflective clothing and plenty of insurance.

HITCHING

Although hitching is not the relatively easy proposition it is in Malaysia, it is possible to hitch through Thailand. In places, traffic will be relatively light and the wait for a ride can be quite long, but it is certainly done (see the section on hitching in the introductory Getting Around chapter).

BOAT

There are lots of opportunities to travel by river or sea. You can take boats to offshore islands and many riverboats operate on Thailand's numerous waterways. The traditional Thai runabout for river trips is the long-tail boat, so called because the engine operates the propeller via a long, open tail shaft. The engines are often car engines mounted on gimbals – the engine is swivelled to steer the boat.

THAILAND

LOCAL TRANSPORT

A wide variety of local transport is available in Thailand. In the big cities you'll find taxis, although they only have meters in Bangkok. Always negotiate your fare before departure. Then there are *samlors*, Thai for 'three wheels'. There are regular bicycle samlors (cycle rickshaws) and motorised samlors, which are usually known as tuk-tuks because of the nasty noise their woefully silenced two-stroke engines make. You'll find bicycle samlors in all the smaller towns throughout Thailand; tuk-tuks can be found in all the larger towns, as well as in Bangkok. In Bangkok they are notoriously unreliable – either the drivers can't find the destination you want or make time-consuming detours to shops, where they are hoping for commissions. You must bargain and agree on a fare before taking samlors and tuk-tuks, but in many towns there is a more-or-less fixed fare anywhere in town.

Songthaew literally means 'two-rows' and these small pick-ups with a row of seats down each side serve a similar purpose to tuk-tuks or minibuses. In some cities, certain regular routes are run by songthaews or minibuses.

Finally, there are regular bus services in certain big cities. In Thailand fares are usually fixed for any route up to a certain length – in Bangkok up to 10 km.

Of course, there are all sorts of unusual means of getting around – horse-drawn carriages in some small towns, and ferries and riverboats in many places.

Bangkok

Thailand's coronary-inducing capital has a surprising number of quiet escapes if you make your way out of the busy streets. But before you leave, you will have to put up with noise, pollution and some of the worst traffic jams in Asia. Add annual floods and sticky weather and it's hardly surprising that many people develop an instant dislike for the place.

However, beneath the surface Bangkok has plenty to offer, including cheap accommodation, excellent food and great nightlife. There are lots of sights – step out of the street noise and into the calm of a wat, for example. The Chao Phraya River is refreshing compared with the anarchy of the streets, and a canal cruise through Thonburi will show you how delightful the *khlongs* (canals) were and, occasionally, still are.

Bangkok, or Krung Thep as it is known to Thais, became the capital of Thailand after the Burmese sacked Ayuthaya in 1767. At first, the Siamese capital was shifted to Thonburi, across the river from Bangkok, but in 1782 it was moved to its present site.

Orientation

The Chao Phraya River divides Bangkok from Thonburi. Almost the only reason to cross to Thonburi (apart from the Southern bus terminals or the Bangkok Noi railway station) is to see Wat Aran (Temple of the Dawn).

The main Bangkok railway line virtually encloses a loop of the river; within that loop is the older part of the city, including most of the interesting temples and the Chinatown area, and the popular travellers' centre of Banglamphu.

East of the railway line is the new area of the city, where most of the modern hotels are located. Rama IV Rd is one of the most important roads: it runs right in front of the Hualamphong railway station and eventually gets you to the Malaysia Hotel area. A little to the north, and approximately parallel to Rama IV, is Rama I Rd; it passes Siam Square and eventually becomes Sukhumvit Rd, where many popular hotels, restaurants and entertainment spots are located.

Small streets or lanes are called *sois*.

Maps One thing to buy as quickly as possible is a Bangkok bus map. *Bangkok Thailand Tour'n Guide Map* has the most up-to-date bus map of Bangkok on one side and a fair map of Thailand on the other. The bus map is necessary if you plan to use Bangkok's very economical bus system. It usually costs around 40B and is available at most bookstores in Bangkok which carry English-language materials. *Nancy Chandler's Map of Bangkok* is a colourful map of the unusual attractions. It has all the *Chao Phraya River Express* stops in Thai script and costs 70B.

Information

Tourist Offices There are tourist offices at the airport and in Bangkok – the Thai tourist office is very good for detailed leaflets and information sheets. You'll find the city office of the Tourist Authority of Thailand (TAT) (☎ 226-0060) at 327 Bamrung Muang Rd. It's open from 8.30 am to 4.30 pm every day. Smaller TAT offices, with fewer materials, can be found at Chatuchak Market (Weekend Market) and opposite Wat Phra Kaew on Na Phra Lan Rd; these two are open daily 8.30 am to 7.30 pm.

Money Thai banks have currency exchange kiosks in many parts of Bangkok, though they are particularly concentrated in the Sukhumvit Rd, Khao San Rd, Siam Square and Silom Rd areas. Hours vary from location to location, but most are open from 8 am to 8 pm daily. Regular bank hours in Bangkok are now 10 am to 4 pm – a schedule instituted in 1995 in an effort to relieve traffic congestion.

A number of moneychangers along Charoen Krung (New) Rd, close to the GPO, are good if you want to buy another Asian currency, such as Burmese kyats.

Post & Communications The GPO is on Charoen Krung (New) Rd and has a very efficient poste restante service, open from 8 am to 8 pm on weekdays and from 8 am to 1 pm on weekends and holidays. Every single letter is recorded in a large book and you're charged 1B for each one. They also have a packing service here if you want to send parcels home.

When the GPO is shut you can send letters from the adjacent central telegraph office, which is open 24 hours. You can also make international telephone calls here at any time of day or night. Hotels and guesthouses usually make service charges on every call, whether they are collect or not.

Branch post offices throughout the city also offer poste restante and parcel services. In Banglamphu, the post office at the east end of Trok Mayom, near Sweety Guest House, is very conveniently located; packaging services are available here as well.

At the airport, and in some post offices and shopping centres, special telephones with Home Direct service are available. On these you can simply push a button for a direct connection with long-distance operators in 20 countries, including Australia, Canada, Denmark, Germany, Hong Kong, Italy, Japan, New Zealand, the UK and the USA.

The area code for Bangkok is 2.

Travel Agencies Bangkok is packed with travel agents of every manner and description, but if you're looking for cheap airline tickets it's wise to be cautious. Ask other travellers for advice about agents. The really bad ones change their names frequently, so saying J Travel, for example, is not to be recommended is useless when it's called something else next week. Wherever possible, try to see the tickets before you hand over the money.

STA Travel has Bangkok branches at Wall Street Tower (☎ 233-2582), 33 Surawong Rd, Room 1405, and in the Thai Hotel (☎ 281- 5314), 78 Prachatipatai Rd, Banglamphu. They sell discount air tickets and seem reliable – we have yet to receive a negative report about them.

Three agents that are permitted to do Thai railway bookings at regular State Railway of Thailand (SRT) fares are Airland (☎ 252-5432), 866 Ploenchit Rd; Songserm Travel Centre (☎ 255-8790), 121/7 Soi Chalermnit, Phayathai Rd, and 172 Khao San Rd (☎ 282-8080; and Thai Overland Travel & Tour (☎ 635-0500), 407 Sukhumvit Rd, between Sois 21 and 23. Other agencies can arrange rail bookings but will slap on a surcharge of 50 to 100B per ticket. The TAT head office has the addresses of all the different sales agencies.

THAILAND

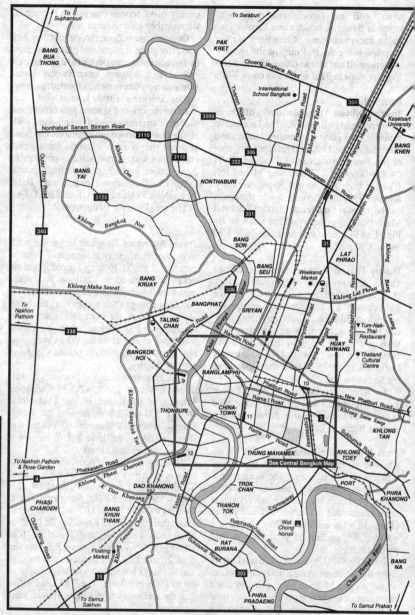

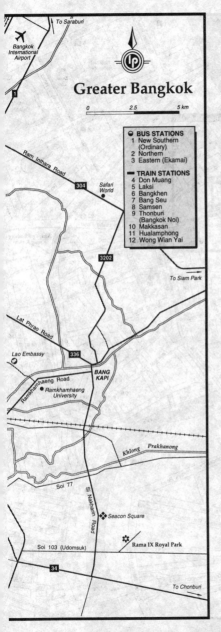

Greater Bangkok

0   2.5   5 km

BUS STATIONS
1 New Southern
   (Ordinary)
2 Northern
3 Eastern (Ekamai)

TRAIN STATIONS
4 Don Muang
5 Laksi
6 Bangkhen
7 Bang Seu
8 Samsen
9 Thonburi
   (Bangkok Noi)
10 Makkasan
11 Hualamphong
12 Wong Wian Yai

Bookshops Bangkok has some of the best bookshops in South-East Asia. Asia Books at Soi 15-17, Sukhumvit Rd, has an excellent selection of English-language books. There are also branches in the Landmark Hotel on Sukhumvit Rd, opposite Soi 5; on the 3rd floor of the World Trade Centre, Ploenchit Rd; on the 3rd floor of Thaniya Plaza, Silom Rd; and in the Peninsula Plaza on Ratchadamri Rd. Duang Kamol (DK) Books, with branches in Siam Square, the Mahboonkrong Centre, Patpong Rd and Soi 8, Sukhumvit Rd, also has a wide selection.

On Patpong Rd, The Bookseller is another good place for browsing. You can also find decent book departments in various branches of the Central department store (306 Silom Rd, Ploenchit Rd and Wang Burapha) and in many of the better hotels.

On Khao San Rd in Banglamphu, at least three streetside vendors specialise in used paperback novels and guidebooks, including many Lonely Planet titles. Shaman Books (☎ 629-0418) at 71 Khao San Rd carries a good selection of guidebooks, maps and books on spirituality in several languages.

Medical Services There are several good hospitals in Bangkok:

Bangkok Adventist (Mission) Hospital
    430 Phitsanulok Rd (☎ 281-1422, 282-1100)
Bangkok Christian Hospital
    124 Silom Rd (☎ 233-6981/9, 235-1000)
Bangkok General Hospital
    Soi 47, New Phetburi Rd (☎ 318-0066)
Bumrumgrad Hospital
    33 Soi 3, Sukhumvit Rd (☎ 253-0250)
Chao Phraya Hospital
    113/44 Pinklao Nakhon-Chaisi Rd, Bangkok Noi
    (☎ 434-6900)
Phayathai Hospital
    364/1 Si Ayuthaya Rd (☎ 245-2620)
    or 943 Phahonyothin Rd (☎ 270-0780)
Samitivej Hospital
    133 Soi 49, Sukhumvit Rd (☎ 392-0010/9)
Samrong General Hospital
    Soi 78, Sukhumvit Rd (☎ 393-2131/5)
St Louis Hospital
    215 Sathon Tai Rd (☎ 212-0033/48)

Emergency All of the hospitals listed above offer 24 hour service. Bangkok does not have

THAILAND

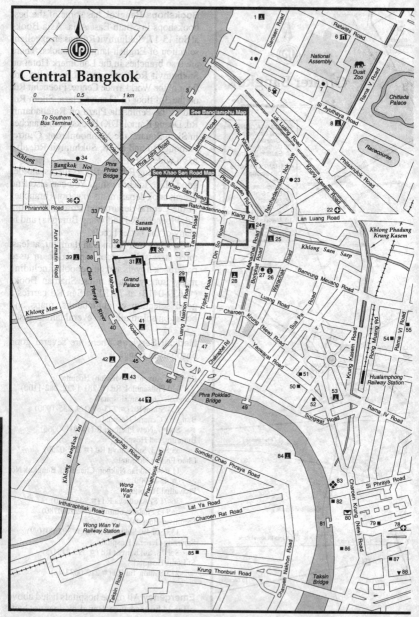

Central Bangkok

0   0.5   1 km

To Southern
Bus Terminal

See Banglamphu Map

See Khao San Road Map

Khao San Road

Ratchadamnoen

Grand
Palace

Sanam
Luang

Chao Phraya River

National
Assembly

Dusit
Zoo

Chitlada
Palace

Racecourse

Hualamphong
Railway Station

Phra Pokklao
Bridge

Wong
Wian Yai

Wong Wian Yai
Railway Station

Taksin
Bridge

an emergency phone system staffed by English-speaking operators. Between 8 am and midnight your best bet for English-speaking assistance is the Tourist Assistance Centre (☎ 281-5051, 282-8129). After midnight you'll have to rely on your own resources or on English-speaking hotel staff.

Temples

Bangkok has about 400 wats and those described in this section are just some of the most interesting. Remember to take your shoes off before entering the *bot* (the central sanctuary or chapel in a Thai temple). Dress and behave soberly in the wats, because Thais take Buddhism seriously.

Wat Phra Kaew & the Grand Palace Consecrated in 1782, the so-called Temple of the Emerald Buddha is the royal temple within the palace complex. It has a variety of buildings and frescoes of the *Ramakian* (the Thai *Ramayana)* around the outer walls. The Emerald Buddha (made of jasper) stands in the main chapel. The image was discovered at Chiang Rai inside a stucco Buddha. It was later moved to Lampang then Chiang Mai, before being carried off to Luang Prabang and Vientiane by the Lao, from where it was later recaptured by the Thais.

The admission fee of 125B includes entry to the Royal Thai Decorations and Coin Pavilion (on the same grounds), and to

THAILAND

Vimanmek, 'the world's largest golden teak mansion', near the Dusit Zoo (next to the National Assembly). Wat Phra Kaew's opening hours are from 8.30 to 11.30 am and from 1 to 3.30 pm; a strict dress code requires long pants or skirts, covered shoulders and shoes with enclosed heels.

Wat Pho The Temple of the Reclining Buddha (the name actually means Temple of the Bodhi Tree) has an extensive collection of panels, bas reliefs, *chedis* (stupas) and statuary to view, as well as the celebrated 46 metre reclining Buddha, which looks like a beached whale with mother-of-pearl feet. This is the oldest and largest wat in Bangkok, and it's from here that all those Thai temple rubbings come. Admission is 10B and the reclining Buddha can be seen from 8 am to 5 pm daily.

Wat Traimit A large stucco Buddha that had been in temporary storage here for 20 years was dropped from a crane while being moved to a permanent site – revealing over five tons of solid-gold Buddha under the stucco. The stucco covering was probably intended to hide it during one of the Burmese invasions. The wat is now known as the Temple of the Golden Buddha. Admission is 10B and the golden image can be seen from 8 am to 5 pm daily. It's a short walk from the Hualamphong railway station.

Wat Arun The Temple of the Dawn stands on the Thonburi side of the Chao Phraya River. It's seen at its best from across the river, especially at night when the 82 metre *prang* (Khmer-style tower), decorated with ceramics and porcelain, is lit by spotlights. You can climb halfway up the tower. This wat is open daily from 8.30 am to 5.30 pm; admission is 10B. To get there, hop on a 1B ferry from the pier at the end of Na Phra Lan Rd (near Wat Phra Kaew) or at Thai Wang Rd (near Wat Pho).

Wat Benchamabophit The Marble Temple is relatively new (built by Rama V in 1899) and has a huge collection of Buddha images

from all periods of Thai Buddhist art. There is a pond full of turtles beside the temple. Admission is 10B.

Wat Saket The Golden Mount is a rather unattractive lump of masonry atop an artificial hill. As Bangkok is pancake flat, it provides a fine view from the top. Admission is free, but it costs 5B to get to the top terrace.

Other Temples Across Mahachai Rd from Wat Saket is **Wat Ratchanatda**, the site of a popular market selling Buddha images, amulets and charms. **Wat Bowonniwet** (Bovornives) on Phra Sumen Rd is the headquarters of the minority Thammayut monastic sect. **Wat Intharawihaan**, just north of Banglamphu on Wisut Kasat Rd (near the junction with Samsen Rd), has an enormous standing Buddha image. The 'giant swing', **Sao Ching Cha**, used to be the centre for a spectacular festival which is no longer held.

A small Hindu Shaiva temple, **Maha Uma Devi Temple**, sits on the corner of Pan and Silom Rds. It contains three main deities: Khanthakumara, Ganesh and Uma Devi (Parvati), although a whole pantheon of Hindu and Buddhist statuary lines one wall.

National Museum

Supposedly the largest museum in South-East Asia, this is a good place for an overview of Thai art and culture before you start exploring the former Thai capitals. All the periods and styles of Thai history and art are shown here. Located on Na Phrathat Rd, the museum is open from 9 am to 4 pm, but is closed on Monday and Tuesday – admission is 20B. There are free tours of the museum, conducted in English, on Wednesday (Buddhism) and Thursday (Thai art, religion, culture) – each begins at 9.30 am from the ticket pavilion.

Jim Thompson's House

Located on Soi Kasem San 2, Rama I Rd, this is the beautiful house of the American Thai silk entrepreneur Jim Thompson, who disappeared without trace back in 1967 in the Cameron Highlands in Malaysia. His house, built from parts of a number of traditional wooden Thai houses and furnished with a superb collection of Thai art and furnishings, is simply delightful. Pleasantly sited on a small khlong, it is open daily from 9 am to 5 pm. Admission is 40B for anyone under 25 and 100B for everyone else.

Floating Markets

The Wat Sai floating market in Thonburi is really a tourist trap – all the boats here are now tourist boats. The trip to the market is picturesque, but with the tourist shops, snake farms and the like it all looks very artificial.

We recommend skipping the Wat Sai market for the less touristic floating market at Khlong Damnoen Saduak, beyond Nakhon Pathom. See under Nakhon Pathom in the Bangkok Region section later in this chapter for details.

Other Attractions

An interesting **river tour** can be made by taking a Chao Phraya River taxi from Wat Ratchasingkhon pier (lots of buses go there) as far north as Nonthaburi. This is a three hour, 15B trip with plenty to see along the way. The Klong Bangkok Noi canal taxi route

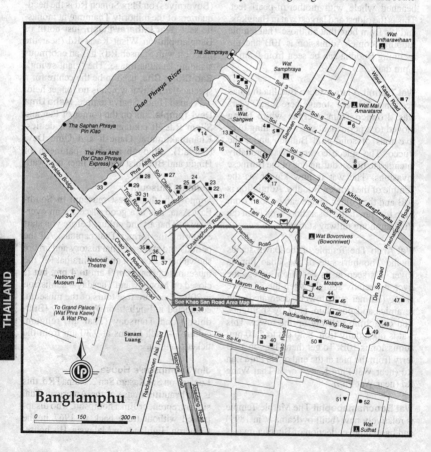

Banglamphu

0   150   300 m

from Tha Phra Chan, next to Thammasat University, only costs 10B and takes you along a colourful 45 minute route, seemingly far from Bangkok.

All sorts of oddities can be found at the enormous **Weekend Market** which takes place opposite the Northern bus terminal. Take an air-con bus No 2, 3, 9, 10 or 13. It's open all day Saturday and Sunday, and you can find almost anything there from opium pipes to unusual posters. It also has lots of other activities to watch. There are a number of other interesting markets around Bangkok.

Bangkok also has a **Chinatown**, with a thieves' market and an Indian district on its periphery. This area is around Chakrawat Rd, midway between the Grand Palace and the Hualamphong train station.

At the **Queen Saovabha Memorial Institute (Snake Farm)** on Rama IV Rd, snakes are milked of their venom every day at 10.30 am and 2 pm (10.30 am only on weekends and holidays) – admission is 70B.

The **Oriental Hotel** is an attraction in its own right. It's the Raffles of Bangkok and is consistently voted the best hotel in Asia. Somerset Maugham and Joseph Conrad are among the Oriental's historic guests (commemorated in the hotel's Authors' Wing). Be sure to dress nicely or you may be barred from entering the lobby.

Lumphini Park, situated at Rama IV and Ratchadamri Rds, offers a shady respite from the city's noise and traffic. Likewise for the **Dusit Zoo** on Rama V Rd, which is open from 9 am to 6 pm daily; admission is 20B for adults, 5B for children, 10B for those over 60.

One of Bangkok's more unusual sights is the **Brahma shrine**, outside the Grand Hyatt Erawan Hotel, where people come to seek help for some wish they want granted – like their girlfriend to marry them. The person promises that if the grant is made they will pay for something to be done – a favourite promise is to pay for 20 minutes dancing by the Thai dancers who are always ready and waiting for such commissions.

Another hotel shrine worth seeing is the **lingam (phallus) shrine**, behind the Hilton International in Nai Loet Park off Withayu (Wireless) Rd. Clusters of carved stone and wooden lingam surround a spirit house and shrine built by a millionaire businessman to honour Jao Mae Thapthim, a female deity thought to reside in the old banyan tree on the site.

PLACES TO STAY		
1	Home & Garden Guesthouse	
2	Clean & Calm Guesthouse	
3	River House	
4	Villa Guesthouse	
5	Truly Yours Guesthouse	
6	AP Guesthouse	
7	Trang Hotel	
8	Vimol Guesthouse	
9	New World House Apartments & Guesthouse	
11	Banglamphu Square Guesthouse	
12	Gipsy Guesthouse	
13	PS Guesthouse	
15	Apple II Guesthouse	
16	KC Guesthouse	
20	Canalside Guesthouse	
21	Sawasdee House/Terrace Guesthouse	
22	Chusri Guesthouse	
23	Super Siam Guesthouse	
24	My House	
25	Merry V Guesthouse	
26	Green Guesthouse	
27	New Siam Guesthouse	
28	New Merry V	
29	Beer & Peachy Guesthouses	
30	Apple Guesthouse	
31	Rose Garden Guesthouse	
32	Mango Guesthouse	
35	Chai's House	
37	Charlie's House	
38	Royal Hotel	
39	P Guesthouse	
40	Palace Hotel	
41	Central Guesthouse	
42	PC Guesthouse	
43	Srinthip Guesthouse	
45	Nat II Guesthouse	
46	Sweety Guesthouse	
47	Prasuri Guesthouse	
50	Hotel 90	
PLACES TO EAT		
14	Roti Mataba	
34	Wang Ngar Restaurant	
48	Vijit Restaurant	
51	Arawy Restaurant	
OTHER		
10	Siam Commercial Bank	
17	New World Shopping Centre	
18	Banglamphu Department Store	
19	Post Office	
33	UNICEF	
36	National Gallery	
44	Post Office	
49	Democracy Monument	
52	City Hall	

THAILAND

Places to Stay

There are all sorts of places to stay in Bangkok, with a wide range of prices, mainly concentrated in distinct areas.

Banglamphu is the number one travellers' centre and has a simply amazing number of budget-priced guesthouses, plus restaurants, snack bars, travel agents and all the other back-up facilities. A big advantage of Banglamphu is that it's central to many of Bangkok's major tourist attractions.

Soi Ngam Duphli is quieter and slightly more expensive; at one time it was the main travellers' centre and it still attracts many visitors. Then there's the Sukhumvit Rd area, which has some travellers' hotels among the more expensive places. Much more central are the noisy Hualamphong station, Chinatown and Siam Square areas.

Competition in the Banglamphu area is so fierce that you can still get a room in Bangkok for scarcely more than it was 10 years ago. The cheapest rooms start at 80B for a single or 120B for a double in the Banglamphu and Hualamphong areas. The air-con places in Soi Ngam Duphli and along Sukhumvit Rd now begin at around 400 to 500B. Some hotels give student discounts if you ask.

If you have to stay near the airport, the least expensive option is *We-Train Guest House* (☎ 566-1774, 566-2288; fax 566-3481) at 501/1 Mu 3, Dechatung Rd, Sikan, Don Muang. Simple but clean fan rooms with private bath cost 450B single/double or 770B with air-con (extra beds cost 150B). You can also get a bed in a fan-cooled dorm for 150B, air-con 200B. Right across the road from the airport terminal (take the Airport Hotel pedestrian bridge), the Don Muang town area has lots of little shops, a market, many small restaurants and food stalls, and even a wat.

There's a hotel booking desk at the airport which can book you into many of the cheaper (but not rock-bottom) hotels.

Banglamphu Also known as the Khao San Rd area, Banglamphu is over towards the river, near the Democracy Monument and on the route to the airport. Banglamphu is central, particularly for the various wats and the National Museum. Most of the guesthouses are basic but they can be excellent value: the standard price is around 70B or 80B for a single, and from 100 to 120B for a double. Some very basic guesthouses are

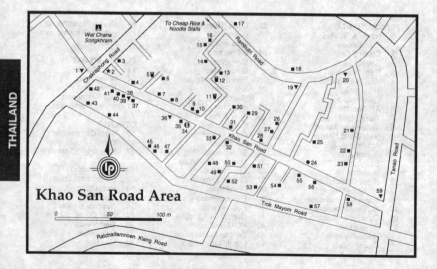

Khao San Road Area

even cheaper in the off season, so it doesn't hurt to try bargaining.

It's quite difficult to recommend any of them since names and management change periodically. Check your room first because, in some cases, a 'room' is just a tiny cubicle, partitioned off with cardboard. Like losmen at Kuta Beach on Bali, there are so many places around Khao San Rd that it's just a case of wandering about until you find one that suits. The map shows many, but not all, of them.

Popular places along Khao San Rd, or on the alleys just off it, include the *Bonny* (☎ 281-9877), *Top* (☎ 281-9954), *Hello* (☎ 281-8579), *Lek* (☎ 281-2775), *VIP* (☎ 282-5090), *Marco Polo (160) Guesthouse, Good Luck, Chada, Nat* and many others, all very similar. A couple of places do not fit the usual guesthouse mould. The *Khaosan Palace Hotel* (☎ 282-0578) at 139 Khao San Rd is Chinese-owned and costs from 250/350B for a room with a fan and bath. Next door is the popular *New Nith Jaroen Hotel* (☎ 281-9872), which has similar rooms and rates but slightly better service.

On the soi parallel and just south of Khao San Rd, which connects with Chakraphong Rd via Trok Mayom, you'll find the *J & Joe, New Joe, Ranee Guest House, 7-Holder* and, by now, probably several other guesthouses.

There's a small soi east off Tanao Rd (at the end of Khao San) that offers several more cheapies, including the plain and basic *Central* (☎ 282-0667), *PC, Sweety* (☎ 281-6756), *CH II* and *Nat II* guesthouses, all at the usual Khao San rates. This network of alleys is fairly quiet since it's off the main road.

Another relatively quiet area is the network of sois and alleys between Chakraphong Rd and Phra Athit Rd, to the west of Khao San Rd, including Soi Rambutri, Soi Chana and Trok Rong Mai. Good choices include the *New Siam* (Soi Chana; ☎ 282-4554), *Merry V* (Soi Rambutri), *Mango* (Soi Rambutri), *Apple* (Soi Rambutri), *Rose Garden* (Trok Rong Mai; ☎ 281-8366) and the *Golf* (Trok Rong Mai). On Phra Athit Rd, near the river, the *Peachy* (☎ 281-6471) and *New Merry V* guesthouses are slightly upmarket for Banglamphu, with rates from 140 to 350B.

The guesthouses along Chakraphong Rd tend to be a bit noisy as it's a fairly large thoroughfare.

PLACES TO STAY		30	Khaosan Palace Hotel	57	7-Holder Guesthouse
3	Siam Guesthouse	31	Grand Guesthouse	58	Chada Guesthouse
4	Sitdhi Guesthouse	32	Dior Guesthouse		
6	Chart Guesthouse	35	PB Guesthouse	**PLACES TO EAT**	
7	Hello Guesthouse	37	Chart Guesthouse	1	Gaylord Indian
8	Mam's Guesthouse	39	Prakorb's House		Restaurant
9	Lek Guesthouse	40	NS Guesthouse	7	Hello Restaurant
10	Buddy Guesthouse	41	Thai Guesthouse	19	Chabad House
13	Doll Guesthouse &	42	Ploy Guesthouse	20	Pizza Hut
	Others	43	J Guesthouse	27	Best Aladdin
14	Suneeporn	44	Joe Guesthouse		Restaurant
	Guesthouse	45	Ranee Guesthouse	36	Royal India Restaurant
15	AT, Leed & Jim's	46	New Joe Guesthouse	38	Hello Restaurant
	Guesthouses	47	Kaosarn Privacy	59	Arawy Det
16	Green House		Guesthouse		
17	Viengtai Hotel	48	Bonny & Top	**OTHER**	
18	Orchid House		Guesthouses	2	Chana Songkhram
21	VS Guesthouse	49	Marco Polo (160		Police Station
22	Nisa Guesthouse		Guesthouse)	5	Paradise, No-Name &
23	Harn Guesthouse	50	Good Luck Guesthouse		Hotel in the Wall
25	New Royal	51	VIP Guesthouse	11	Buddy Beer
	Guesthouse	52	Tong Guesthouse	12	Artsy Fartsy Bar & Art
26	Marco Polo Hostel	53	Neo Guesthouse		Gallery
27	Best Guesthouse	54	Nana Plaza Inn	24	Central Minimart
28	Nat Guesthouse	55	Siri Guesthouse	33	Shops
29	New Nith Jaroen Hotel	56	CH II Guesthouse	34	Krung Thai Bank

THAILAND

Around Banglamphu Guesthouses continue to pop up around the Banglamphu area. Go up Chakraphong Rd and then Samsen Rd (it changes names) north from Banglamphu and after about a km, just before the National Library, Phitsanulok Rd dead-ends on Samsen Rd and Si Ayuthaya Rd crosses it.

On two parallel sois off Si Ayuthaya Rd towards the river (west from Samsen) are five guesthouses run by various members of the same extended family: *Tavee Guest House* (☎ 282-5983), *Sawatdee Guest House* (☎ 282- 5349), *Backpacker's Lodge* (☎ 282-3231), *Shanti Lodge* (☎ 281-2497) and *Original Paradise Guest House* (☎ 282-4094/8673). All are clean, well kept, fairly quiet and cost 50B for a dorm bed, and from 100/150B for singles/doubles. There's a lot of friendly family competition between these places. This area has the distinct advantage of being a short walk from Tha Thewet, a *Chao Phraya River Express* pier; from the pier you walk east along Krung Kasem Rd to Samsen Rd, turn left, cross the canal and then take another left into Si Ayuthaya Rd.

Close by here is the *Bangkok International Youth Hostel* (☎ 282-0950) at 25/2 Phitsanulok Rd. It has a 70B fan dorm, 80B air-con dorm and air-con singles/doubles with toilet and shower at 250/300B if you have a youth hostel card. Non-members can purchase a temporary membership for 50B or a full annual membership for 300B. Several readers have written to say that the hostel staff can be quite rude to guests.

Chinatown-Hualamphong Station This is one of the cheapest areas in Bangkok but also one of the noisiest. The traffic along Rama IV Rd has to be heard to be believed. There are a few hotels alongside the station, but these station-area cheapies are no bargain compared with the even cheaper places over in Banglamphu, and it's nowhere near as pleasant a place to stay.

The *Sri Hualamphong Hotel* (☎ 214-2610) at 445 Rong Muang Rd is one of the better ones, with rooms at 120B with fan. The *Sahakit (Shakij) Hotel* is a few doors down towards Rama IV Rd and has rooms

for 100B up. There are numerous good, cheap eating places around the station, but take care: some of Bangkok's best pickpockets and razor artists work the station area.

Across Rama IV near Wat Traimit, the *New Empire Hotel* (☎ 234-6990) at 572 Yaowarat Rd has air-con doubles from 450B up to 800B. It's a bit noisy, but in a good Chinatown location, near the intersection of Yaowarat and Charoen Krung (New) Rds. There are a number of other Chinatown hotels around, but most don't have signs in English.

The *TT 2 Guest House* (☎ 236-2946) is about a 10 minute walk south from the station, at 516-518 Soi Sawang, Si Phraya Rd near the junction with Mahanakhon Rd. It's a short walk from the GPO and river. From the station, turn left and walk a block along Rama IV Rd, then turn right (south) down Mahanakhon Rd. There will be signs close to Si Phraya Rd. It's worth the effort to find this comparatively large, well-kept and popular place. Single/double rooms cost 180B; there's a strict midnight curfew. To find the more hidden *TT 1 Guest House* (☎ 236-3053; 138 Soi Wat Mahaphuttharam, off Mahanakhon Rd) from the station, cross Rama IV Rd, walk left down Rama IV and then right on Mahanakhon, and follow the signs for TT 1. It's only about a 10 minute walk from the station. Dorm beds are just 40B and singles/doubles go for 150B.

Siam Square On Soi Kasem San 1, off Rama I Rd opposite the National Stadium, there are several places which are good value, though they tend towards mid-range rather than low-budget accommodation. Right on the corner of this soi and Rama I Rd is the *Muangphol Building* (☎ 215-3056/0033), which offers decent air-con singles/doubles for 450/550B and has a restaurant downstairs. The *Pranee Building* next door has 300 to 350B fan rooms, air-con rooms starting at 400B, but no restaurant.

More home-like are the family-run *A-One Inn* (☎ 215-3029) and the *Bed & Breakfast Inn* (☎ 215-3004), both of which are at the end of Soi Kasem San 1 and cost 400 to 500B for air-con rooms; rates may drop 100B in the low season. Both have small dining areas on the ground floor. Rates at the Bed & Breakfast Inn include breakfast but rooms are a bit larger at the A-One. The *Wendy House* and *White Lodge*, opposite the A-One Inn, offer clean, modern rooms in the 400 to 500B range. Avoid the *Reno* and *Star* hotels on this soi; both are overpriced and rather unfriendly.

Soi Ngam Duphli Just off Rama IV Rd, this was for many years the travellers' centre of Bangkok, though overall the places are no longer the best value. To get there take an ordinary bus No 4, 13, 14, 22, 27, 46, 47, 74, 109 or 115 or a No 7 air-con bus, and get off just after the roundabout on Rama IV Rd.

Once, the prime attraction here was the *Malaysia Hotel* (☎ 286-3582) at 54 Soi Ngam Duphli – this was one of the hotels quickly thrown together for the R&R trade back in the Vietnam War. It is multistorey and has air-con, a swimming pool and all that sort of thing. When the war ended they decided to cut prices to the bone and fill it with the travellers who were invading the region. For a while the Malaysia was a sort of working test on how long a building could hang together with much abuse and no care.

Now it has been cleaned up and is just another mid-range hotel. There are 120 rooms with air-con and bathroom, costing 498B for a standard single or double, 586B with a TV and small fridge or 700B with a TV, larger fridge and carpet.

Today there are also many smaller guest-houses around Soi Ngam Duphli – in that respect, it's a quieter version of Khao San Rd. At the unimpressive but OK *Anna Guest House*, 21/30 Soi Ngam Duphli, rooms start at 100B. At the northern end of Soi Ngam Duphli, near Rama IV Rd, the *ETC Guest House* (☎ 286-9424, 287-1478) is an efficiently run, multistorey place with a travel agency downstairs. Rooms are small but clean; rates are 120B with shared bath, 160/200B for singles/doubles with private bath. All rates include a light breakfast.

One of the best deals in this area is *Sala Thai Daily Mansion* (☎ 287-1436), a well-run place with very clean rooms for 150 to 200B; it's on an alley that runs north off Soi Si Bamphen. Also in this alley are the similarly priced *Lee 4 Guest House* and *Madame*. Apart from the hotels and guesthouses there are also lots of travel agencies, restaurants, bars and all manner of other 'services' in the area.

The *YWCA* (☎ 286-1936) is close to the Soi Ngam Duphli area at 13 Sathon Tai (South) Rd. Rooms have air-con and baths, and cost from 567B. This Y takes only women guests and has a restaurant, swimming pool and other facilities. At 27 Sathon Tai Rd is the more expensive *YMCA* (☎ 286-5134), where rooms start at 1377B – both men and women can stay here.

Sukhumvit Rd North of Rama IV Rd and running out from the centre, much like Rama IV Rd, this is a major tourist centre. Take an ordinary bus No 2, 25, 40 or 48, or an air-con bus No 1, 8, 11 or 13. The hotels here are not Bangkok's top-notch places: most are out of the budget traveller's price range, but there are a few worthwhile places scattered about. Staying in this area puts you in the newest part of the city and the furthest from old Bangkok. All the lanes running off Sukhumvit Rd are called Soi, and have a number – the bigger the number, the further up (east) Sukhumvit Rd it is. All even numbers are to the south and odd to the north.

Starting at the Rama I end (Rama I changes into Sukhumvit Rd), you'll find the historic *Atlanta Hotel* (☎ 252-1650) at 78 Soi 2. Owned since its construction in the 1950s by Dr Max Henn, a former secretary to the maharajah of Bikaner and sometime Indochina agent, the Atlanta is a simple but reliable stand-by, with clean, comfortable rooms in several price categories. Simple but well-kept rooms cost from 300/400B with fan and private bath, and up to 450/550/600B with air-con. Facilities include a small coffee shop and a swimming pool. The heavily annotated coffee shop menu offers a crash course in Thai cuisine that could prove very useful upcountry.

THAILAND

Further up, at Soi 13, the *Miami Hotel* (☎ 255140) is one of the cheaper tourist hotels. It's all air-con now and costs 500/550B. After taking a long, slow dive through the 80s, the Miami is looking a bit better – the pool is even clean enough to swim in again! Still, ask to see a room first and get a reduction if it's not up to par.

Guesthouses are also beginning to appear on Sukhumvit Rd, just like everywhere else in Bangkok. Try the *Disra House* (☎ 258-5102) between Soi 33 and Soi 33/1 (off the access street to the Villa cinema). Clean, comfortable rooms range from 80 to 150B. Of similar standard is the *SV Guest House* (☎ 253-0606) at 19/35-36 Sukhumvit Rd, Soi 19.

Thonburi *The Artists Place* (☎ 852-0056; fax 862-0074) at 63 Soi Thiam Bunyang, off Soi Krung Thonburi 1 (near Wong Wian Yai), was recently opened by Thai artist Charlee Sodprasert as a place for visiting artists to congregate and work. Singles and doubles cost 80 to 120B, while more expensive rooms go for 350B. Studio space is available.

Places to Eat
Banglamphu & Around There are lots of cheap eating places around Banglamphu, including several on the ground floors of guesthouses in Khao San Rd. For the most part they serve western food and Thai food prepared for western palates. Popular places include the two *Hello Restaurants, Wally House, Orm* and the *Prakorp's House.*

For more authentic fare, try the many Thai places along Rambutri Rd, just north of Khao San Rd. Of outstanding value and selection is the 8th floor food mall in the *New World Shopping Centre*, three blocks north of Khao San Rd. For an all-vegie menu at low prices, seek out the *Vegetarian Restaurant* at 117/1 Soi Wat Bowon, near Srinthip Guest House.

The *Yok Yor* on Samphraya pier has good seafood, a menu in English and main dishes costing from around 50B. The Yok Yor also operates a dinner cruise that offers the same menu with a reasonable 50B surcharge for

boat service. Nearby is the similar *Chawn Ngoen*; it has no English sign, but there is an English menu.

Phra Athit Rd, over towards the river where you find the Trok Rong Mai guesthouses, has some inexpensive restaurants and food stalls.

Hualamphong Lots of good cheap restaurants, mostly Chinese, can be found along Rong Muang Rd by the station.

Pahurat The *Royal India* at 392/1 Chakraphet Rd is one of the better places in the Pahurat District; it's much better than the one on Khao San Rd. The *ATM Shopping Centre*, on Chakraphet Rd opposite the Royal India, has an Indian food centre on the top floor. The alley alongside the centre features cheap Indian food stalls as well.

Siam Square The Siam Square sois have plenty of good places in varying price ranges. Try the big noodle restaurant *Coca* on Henri Dunant Rd, close to Rama I Rd. At 93/3 Soi Lang Suan, Ploenchit Rd, the *Whole Earth Restaurant* does good, if somewhat expensive, Thai and Indian vegetarian food. The Whole Earth has a second branch on Soi 26, Sukhumvit Rd.

Directly opposite the Siam Centre on Rama I Rd, there's a *KFC*, a *Dunkin' Donuts* and a string of other American-style fast-food eateries. *Uncle Ray's* has some of the best ice cream in Bangkok.

The 7th floor of the *MBK*, or *Mahboonkrong Centre* (on the south-west corner of Rama I and Phayathai Rds), there's a good Singapore-style food centre with everything from steak and salad to Thai vegetarian fare. It's open from 10 am to 9 pm daily. On the 4th floor of the same building are a number of other food vendors, as well as several slightly upmarket restaurants serving western or Japanese food. At street level there's a host of fast food places.

At the intersection of Soi Kasem San I and Rama I Rd there's the excellent, inexpensive *Thai Sa-Nguan* restaurant, where curry and rice is 15 to 20B a plate. Good kuaytiaw (rice noodles) and khao man kai (chicken rice) are also available here.

Silom & Surawong Rds At 30/37 Patpong 2, the *Thai Room* has reasonable Thai-Chinese-Mexican food. Try the *Bobby's Arms* on Patpong Rd for a good Aussie-Brit pub. *Mizu's Kitchen* on Patpong Rd 1 has a loyal Japanese and Thai following for its inexpensive but good Japanese food, including Japanese steak. Silom and Surawong Rds are south-west of Lumphini Park.

Opposite the Silom Rd entrance to Patpong Rd, in the CP Tower building, there's a cluster of air-con American and Japanese-style fast food places: *McDonald's, Pizza Hut, Chester's Grilled Chicken, Suzuki Coffee House* and *Toplight Coffee House*. Several are open late to catch the night-time Patpong traffic.

Halfway down Silom Rd, across from the Narai Hotel, you can get good Indian snacks near the Tamil temple. For south Indian food, try the basic *Madras Cafe* (☎ 235-6761) in the Madras Lodge at 31/10-11 Vaithi Lane (Trok 13), off Silom Rd near the Narai Hotel; it serves idlis, dosas and a few other south Indian snacks and a selection of north Indian dishes. There are several other interesting possibilities along parallel Suriwong Rd; the reliable and moderately priced *Maria Bakery & Restaurant* at No 311/2-4 serves all manner of Thai and Vietnamese dishes, as well as pizza and pastries.

Sukhumvit Rd The *Yong Lee Restaurant* at 211 Sukhumvit Rd, near Soi 15 and Asia Books, does standard Thai and Chinese food.

The ground floor of the *Ambassador Hotel*, between Sois 11 and 13, has a good food centre. It offers several varieties of Thai, Chinese, Vietnamese, Japanese, Muslim and vegetarian food at 20 to 40B per dish using a coupon system.

On Soi 12, *Cabbages & Condoms*, famous for its name alone, is run by Thailand's hyperactive family planning association. The famous *Djit Pochana* (☎ 258-1578) has a branch on Soi 20 and is one of the best-

value restaurants in town for traditional Thai dishes. The all-you-can-eat lunch buffet is 90B. By Soi 17, there's the fancy *Robinson's Department Store* with a branch of *McDonald's* at street level and a basement supermarket and food centre, which features everything from *Dunkin' Donuts* to frozen yoghurt, ice cream, noodles and a variety of Thai food stands.

Entertainment

Thai Classical Dance The *National Theatre* periodically hosts classical Thai dance performances – call ☎ 224-1342 weekdays between 8.30 am and 4.30 pm for the current schedule. Special exhibition performances by the *Chulalongkorn University Dance Club* are offered once a month – ask at TAT for the latest schedule.

To see Thai classical dancing for free, hang out at the *Lak Muang Shrine* near Sanam Luang, or the *Erawan Shrine*. Another good venue is the *Centre for Traditional Performing Arts* on the 4th floor of the Bangkok Bank, just off Ratchadamnoen Rd in Bangkok. Free public performances are given every Friday at 5 pm – arrive at least an hour early for a seat.

Several Bangkok restaurants sponsor dinner performances that feature a mix of dance and martial arts, all very touristy (the food is usually nothing special), for around 250 to 500B.

Live Music Along Soi Lang Suan and Sarasin Rd, between Rama IV and Ploenchit Rds, are several bars that feature live western pop, folk, blues, and jazz played by Thai bands. Among the most popular (and better) music bars are *Blue's Bar* and *Old West*. Opposite the Asia Hotel on Phayathai Rd is the *Rock Pub*, a hang-out for Thai metalheads. Bangkok has its own *Hard Rock Cafe*, with live music nightly, at Siam Square Soi 11. The three storey *Saxophone Pub Restaurant*, south-east of the Victory Monument circle at 3/8 Victory Monument, Phayathai Rd, has become an institution for musicians of several genres. The *Magic Mushroom* at 212/33 Sukhumvit Rd (next to Soi 12) hires

THAILAND

a variety of rock and blues acts nightly, including some of Bangkok's biggest names.

Massage & Go-Go Bars Bangkok is, of course, known as the Oriental sin-city extraordinaire (though Manila and Taipei each have more sex workers per capita) and hordes of (male) package tourists descend simply to sample its free-wheeling delights. Patpong Rd, just off Silom Rd, is the centre for the city's spectator sports, while massage parlours are found at many hotels and in the tourist ghettos like Sukhumvit Rd and, of course, Patpong Rd.

In Thailand, a 'body massage' means the masseuse's, not yours. Avoid Bangkok's large massage parlours along Phetburi Tat Mai Rd, which cost as much as US$40 for a lukewarm bath and massage. Go-go bar ghettos include infamous Patpong Rd I and II (between Silom and Surawong Rds); the Nana Plaza group on Soi 4, Sukhumvit Rd; and the alley known as Soi Cowboy, parallel to Sukhumvit Rd between Sois 21 and 23. Alongside the railway tracks, opposite Soi 1, there's a collection of very rustic open-air bars. Or, there are coffee-bar pick-up joints, like the infamous *Thermae Coffee House* on Ploenchit Rd.

Many visitors find that indulgence in the pleasures of sin-city lead to social diseases or worse. In addition to all the usual STDs, such as gonorrhoea and syphilis, Thailand also has a serious AIDS problem: the use of condoms – or total abstinence – is imperative. Less physical problems also occasionally befall revellers – wallets have disappeared while pants were down, and hookers have been known to spike patrons' drinks with knockout drugs.

Of course, Bangkok also has plenty of 'straight' nightspots. Not every bar is a pick-up joint and even in those that are you can just have a drink if that's all you want.

Other Bars Three locales compete to see who can be the trendiest and pack in the most weekend hipsters. Royal City Avenue (Soi Sunwichai, north off New Phetburi Rd) is chock-a-block with clubs like *Absolute Zero*, *Baby Hand Pub, Bar Code, Chit, Cool Tango, Radio Underground, Relax, Shit Happens* and *Why Art?*, most with recorded music.

A string of small dance clubs on Soi 2 and Soi 4, both parallel to Patpong 1 and 2 off Silom Rd, attract a more mixed crowd, in terms of age, gender, nationality and sexual orientation.

Thai Boxing This sport, where they kick as well as punch, is quite a scene. There are two stadiums: *Lumphini* on Rama IV Rd near Soi Ngam Duphli and *Ratchadamnoen* on Ratchadamnoen Nok Ave. Admission prices start at around 180B and go up to 800B for ringside seats. The out-of-the-ring activity is sometimes even more frenzied and entertaining than that within the ring.

Things to Buy

Anything you can buy out in the country you can also get in Bangkok – sometimes the prices may even be lower. Silom Rd and Charoen Krung (New) Rd are two good shopping areas that cater to tourists.

Better deals are available in Bangkok's large open-air markets at Chatuchak Park (Weekend Market), Yaowarat (Chinatown), Pratunam and Pahurat. Things to look for include:

Cotton & Silk Lengths of cotton and the beautifully coloured and textured Thai silk can be made into clothes or household articles. There are some good shops along Silom Rd but the fabric stalls in the Indian district of Pahurat are cheaper.

Temple Rubbings Charcoal on rice paper or coloured on cotton, these rubbings used to be made from temple bas reliefs. Today they're made from moulds taken from the temple reliefs. Wat Pho is a favourite place with a very wide choice, but check prices at shops in town before buying at Wat Pho because they often ask too much.

Clothes The Thais are very fashion-conscious and you can get stylish clothes ready made or made to measure at attractive prices.

The Mahboonkrong Shopping Centre near Siam Square and New World Centre in Banglamphu are two of the best places to shop for inexpensive clothes – also check the Siam Square alleys and the Weekend Market.

Gems Buyer beware. Unless you know stones, Bangkok is no place to seek out 'the big score'. *Never* accept an invitation from a tout or friendly stranger to visit a gem store, as the visit will soon turn into a confidence game in which you're the pigeon. See Dangers & Annoyances in the Thailand Facts for the Visitor section for more details on gem scams.

If you want to learn about gemstones before having a look around (a very sensible idea), visit the Asian Institute of Gemological Sciences (☎ 513-2112; fax 236-7803) at 484 Rachadaphisek Rd, in the Huay Khwang District north-east of Bangkok. The institute offers reputable, reasonably priced gemology courses of varying lengths. The staff can also assess the authenticity and quality of stones (but not their value) that are brought to them.

Other Silver, bronze and nielloware (silver inlaid with black enamel) items include a variety of jewellery, plates, bowls and ornaments. Antiques are widely available but you'd better know what you're looking for. Temple bells and carved wooden cow bells are nice souvenirs. There is a string of art galleries along Charoen Krung (New) Rd from the GPO where you will find those attractive little leaf paintings – nicely framed and small enough to make handy presents.

The Weekend Market, opposite the Northern bus terminal is, of course, a great place to look for almost any oddity. Behind the Chalerm Thai Theatre at Wat Ratchanatta, there's an amulet market, where you can buy protection against almost anything.

Getting There & Away

Bangkok is the travel focus of Thailand. Unless you cross the border from Malaysia, this is the place where you're most likely to arrive. It's also the centre from where travel routes fan out across the country.

Air Bangkok is a major centre for international ticket discounting. It's also the centre for Thai Airways International's domestic flight schedules.

Some airline offices:

Air France
    Ground floor, Chan Issara Tower, 942/51 Rama IV Rd (☎ 234-1330/9; reservations ☎ 233-9477)
Air India
    16th floor, Amarin Tower, Ploenchit Rd (☎ 256-9620; reservations ☎ 256-9614/8)
Air New Zealand
    1053 Charoen Krung Rd (☎ 233-5900/9, 237-1560/2)
All Nippon Airways (ANA)
    2nd floor, CP Tower, 313 Silom Rd (☎ 238-5121)
American Airlines
    518/5 Ploenchit Rd (☎ 254-1270)
Bangkok Airways
    Queen Sirikit National Convention Centre, New Ratchadaphisek Rd, Khlong Toey (☎ 229-3434, 253-4014)
    1111 Ploenchit Rd (☎ 254-2903)
Bangladesh Biman
    Chongkolnee Building, 56 Surawong Rd (☎ 235-7643/4, 234-0300/9)
British Airways
    Chan Issara Tower, Rama IV Rd (☎ 236-0038)
Canadian Airlines International
    Maneeya Building, 518/5 Ploenchit Rd (251-4521, 254-8376)
Cathay Pacific Airways
    11th floor, Ploenchit Tower, Ploenchit Rd (☎ 263-0606)
Delta Air Lines
    7th floor, Patpong Building, 1 Surawong Rd (☎ 237-6855; reservations ☎ 237-6838)
EVA Airways
    3656/4-5 2nd floor, Green Tower, Rama IV Rd (☎ 367-3388; reservations 240-0890
Garuda Indonesia
    27th floor, Lumphini Tower, 1168 Rama IV Rd (☎ 285-6470/3)
Japan Airlines
    254/1 Ratchadaphisek (☎ 274-1400, 274-1435)
KLM-Royal Dutch Airlines
    Maneeya Building, 518/5 Ploenchit Rd (☎ 254-8834; reservations 254-8325)
Lao Aviation
    Silom Plaza, 491/17 Silom Rd (☎ 236-9821/3)

Malaysia Airlines
    98-102 Surawong Rd
    (☎ 236-5871; reservations ☎ 236-4705/9)
    20th floor, Ploenchit Tower, Ploenchit Rd
    (☎ 263-0565)
Myanmar Airways International
    Charn Issara Tower, Rama IV Rd (☎ 267-5078)
Northwest Airlines
    Peninsula Plaza, 153 Ratchadamri Rd
    (☎ 254-0789)
Philippine Airlines
    Chongkolnee Building, 56 Surawong Rd
    (☎ 234-2483, 233-2350/2)
Qantas Airways
    Chan Issara Tower, 942/51 Rama IV Rd
    (☎ 267-5188, 236-0307)
Royal Air Cambodge
    c/o Malaysia Airlines
Royal Nepal Airlines
    Sivadon Building, 1/4 Convent Rd
    (☎ 233-3921/4)
Scandinavian Airlines (SAS)
    Soi 25, Sukhumvit Rd (☎ 260-0444)
Silk Air
    12th floor, Silom Centre Building, Silom Rd
    (☎ 236-0303; reservations ☎ 236-0440)
Singapore Airlines
    12th floor, Silom Centre Building, 2 Silom Rd
    (☎ 236-0303; reservations ☎ 236-0440)
South African Airways
    Maneeya Building, 518/5 Ploenchit Rd
    (☎ 254-8206)
Swissair
    1 Silom Rd
    (☎ 233-2930/4; reservations ☎ 233-2935/8)
Thai Airways International (THAI)
    89 Vibhavadi Rangsit Rd
    (☎ 513-0121; reservations ☎ 233-3810)
    485 Silom Rd (☎ 234-3100/19)
    6 Lan Luang Rd (☎ 280-0060, 628-2000)
    Asia Hotel, 296 Phayathai Rd (☎ 215-2020/4)
United Airlines
    9th floor, Regent House, 183 Ratchadamri Rd
    (☎ 253-0558)
Vietnam Airlines (Hang Khong Vietnam)
    3rd floor, 572 Ploenchit Rd (☎ 251-4242)

Bus The Bangkok bus terminals are:

North & North-East
    Northern & North-Eastern Bus Terminal, Phahon-
    yothin Rd (☎ 279-4484). On the road to the airport;
    go there for buses to Ayuthaya, Sukhothai, Chiang
    Mai and Chiang Rai, plus the towns in the north-
    east.

East
    Eastern Bus Terminal, Soi 40 (Ekamai),
    Sukhumvit Rd (☎ 391-2504). For Pattaya and all
    points east.
South
    Southern Bus Terminal, Highway 338 and Phra
    Pinklao Rd (☎ 434-5558 ordinary, 391-9829 air-
    con). For buses to Nakhon Pathom, Kanchanaburi,
    Hua Hin, Surat Thani, Phuket, Hat Yai and all
    other points south.

All terminals have good left-luggage facilities.

Train There are two main railway stations.
The big Hualamphong station on Rama IV
Rd handles services to the north, north-east
and most of the services to the south. The
Thonburi, or Bangkok Noi, station handles
some services to the south. If you're heading
south ascertain from which station your train
departs.

Getting Around
The Airport Bangkok airport is 25 km north
of the city centre and there is a variety of
ways of getting back and forth.

Bus Just a few steps outside the airport
there's a highway that leads straight into the
city. Air-con bus No 29 costs 16B and plies
one of the most useful, all-purpose routes
into town because it goes to the Siam Square
and Hualamphong areas. After entering the
city limits via Phahonyothin Rd (which turns
into Phayathai Rd), the bus passes Phetburi
Rd (where you get off to change buses for
Banglamphu), then Rama I Rd at the Siam
Square/Mahboonkrong intersection (for
buses out to Sukhumvit Rd, or to walk to Soi
Kasem San 1 for Muangphol Lodging, Reno
Hotel etc) and finally turns right on Rama IV
Rd to go to the Hualamphong District. You'll
want to go the opposite way on Rama IV for
the Soi Ngam Duphli lodging area. No 29
runs only from 5.45 am to 8 pm, so if you
arrive on a late-night flight you'll miss it.

Air-con bus No 4 (16B, 5.45 am to 8 pm)
begins with a route parallel to that of the No
29 bus – down Mitthaphap Rd to Ratchaprarop
and Ratchadamri Rds (Pratunam District),

crossing Phetburi, Rama I, Ploenchit and Rama IV Rds, then down Silom, left on Charoen Krung, and across the river to Thonburi.

Alternatively, bus No 13 from the airport goes down Phahonyothin Rd, turns left at the Victory Monument to Ratchaprarop Rd, then travels south to Ploenchit Rd and east on Sukhumvit Rd all the way to Bang Na. These air-con buses stop running at 8 pm.

A THAI minibus goes to most major hotels (and some minor ones, if the driver's in the mood) for 100B per person. It seems to depart erratically.

Minibuses depart regularly for the airport from the Khao San Rd accommodation enclave. They charge 50B.

Airport Bus In mid-1996 a new airport express bus service began operating from Bangkok International to three different Bangkok districts for 70B per person. Buses run every 15 minutes from 5 am to 11 pm. Since this service is quite new, the routes, fares and hours could change during the first year or two of operation.

A-1 goes to the Silom Rd business district via Pratunam and Ratchadamri Rd, stopping at big hotels like the Indra, Grand Hyatt Erawan, Regent Bangkok and Dusit Thani.

A-2 goes to Sanam Luang via Phayathai Rd, Lan Luang Rd, Ratchadamnoen Klang Rd and Tanao Rd; this is the one you want if you're going to the Siam Square or Banglamphu areas.

A-3 goes to the Phrakhanong District via Sukhumvit Rd.

Train The railway into Bangkok runs near the airport. You can get a train straight to Hualamphong station for 10B in 3rd class, 50B if you happen onto a rapid or express train. Walk over the enclosed pedestrian bridge from the international terminal to the Amari Airport Hotel. The railway station is right in front of the hotel. The departure times aren't always that convenient, however, and of course you have to lug your bag(s) a long way. It's timed for commuters to or from work, not for passengers to or from the airport.

Taxi Greedy Thai Airways International touts try to steer all arriving passengers towards one of their expensive limousine services, which are just glorified air-con taxi services costing a flat 350B – definitely a rip-off. Just ignore them and head straight for the city taxi counter. Metered taxis from the airport are around 150B, or 250B if you buy a ticket at the city taxi counter tucked away at the far end of the arrival hall. Between three or more people, it's as cheap as the airport bus and rather more convenient.

If it's your first time in Bangkok, try the 250B taxi fare, particularly if there are several of you to split the cost.

Bus The Bangkok bus service is frequent and frantic – a bus map is an absolute necessity. Get one from the tourist office or from bookshops and news stands for 35 to 40B. Buses are all numbered and the map is easy to follow. Don't expect it to be 100% correct though – routes change regularly. Fares for ordinary buses vary according to the type of bus: from 2.50B (green or blue buses) to 3.50B (red buses) for any journey under 10 km; over 10 km it jumps as high as 5B – out to the airport for example. The No 17 bus does a useful circuit of the city attractions and terminates near the National Museum and Emerald Buddha.

There are also a number of public air-con buses with numbers that may cause confusion with the regular buses. They start at 6B but jump to 16B on the long trips. Apart from the cool comfort, the air-con buses are less crowded, especially in comparison with the mayhem on the regular buses. Even less crowded are the red Microbuses, which stop boarding passengers once every seat is filled and collect a 30B flat fare.

Taxi & Tuk-Tuks Bangkok recently instituted a metered taxi service, a welcome change from the days when kerbside haggling added to the stress of moving around crowded streets. Around central Bangkok, metered taxi fares should generally run from 50 to 75B (35B at flagfall, plus 2B for each additional time/distance increment). Although detours may be

THAILAND

necessary to avoid traffic snarls some drivers try to pad fares by driving around in circles, so keep an eye on a map to make sure your driver is proceeding in the right direction.

You must fix fares in advance for other taxis or the tuk-tuks. The latter are really only useful for shorter trips. When the distances get longer they often become more expensive than regular taxis. You often need real endurance to withstand a long tuk-tuk trip – and half the time the drivers don't know their way around Bangkok anyway.

Motorcycle Taxi Motorcycle taxis have moved from the sois to the main avenues. Fares for a motorcycle taxi are about the same as tuk-tuks except during heavy traffic, when they may cost a bit more. Keep your legs tucked in – the drivers are used to carrying passengers with shorter legs than those of the average farang and they pass perilously close to other vehicles while weaving in and out of traffic.

Boat River travel through and around Bangkok is not only much more interesting and peaceful than fighting your way through town in a bus or taxi, it is also much faster. There are a number of regular services along the Chao Phraya River and adjoining khlongs. Boats also buzz back and forth across the river from numerous points.

Easiest to use and understand is the *Chao Phraya River Express* – a big, long boat with a number on the roof – that runs up and down the river, although it only stops at certain landing stages, like the Oriental Hotel. This river-bus service costs 5 to 10B, depending on the distance you travel, and you buy your ticket on the boat.

Bangkok still has quite a few khlongs but it's no longer the 'Venice of the east'. Routes still open include Khlong Saen Saep, the canal between the Democracy Monument area and the Ramkhamhaeng University area, along which long-tailed boats run. The boat from Banglamphu to the University costs 10B and takes only 20 minutes; a bus would take nearly an hour under normal traffic conditions.

Bangkok Region

There are a number of interesting places within day-trip distance of Bangkok – some also make interesting stepping stones on your way north, east or south. You can stop at Ayuthaya on your way north, for example, or Nakhon Pathom on your way south.

The **Ancient City** (Muang Boran) (☎ 226-1936/7, 323-9252) is an 80 hectare complex with scaled-down replicas of Thailand's more famous historic sites. It's 33 km south of Bangkok. Admission is a reasonable 50B and you can get there by taking bus No 25 or air-con bus No 7, 8 or 11 from Sukhumvit Rd to Pak Nam, and then taking a small local bus. It's open daily 8 am to 5 pm.

There is also a **Crocodile Farm** in the same area and the **Rose Garden Country Resort**. About 15 km out of the city, there's an excellent swimming pool complex at **Siam Park**. Bus No 27 gets you there, although not every No 27 goes to Siam Park. Entry is 60B, which ensures it is not very crowded.

AYUTHAYA

This was the Thai capital until its destruction by the Burmese in 1767. It is 86 km north of Bangkok. Built at the junction of three rivers, an artificial channel has converted the town into an island. To find your way around, get a copy of the excellent guidebook and map available from the Chan Kasem Museum here or in Bangkok.

During the 10 days leading to the Songkran Festival in mid-April, there is a sound and light show with fireworks over the ruins. This is a great time to visit Ayuthaya, but you might want to take refuge in a smaller town during the final water-throwing days of Songkran itself – unless you fancy staying wet for the day! Loi Krathong – when tiny votive boats are floated in rivers and ponds as tribute to the River Goddess – is another good time to be in Ayuthaya.

The telephone code for Ayuthaya is 35.

On the Island

Places to see are either 'on the island' or 'off the island'. There's a 10 to 20B admission charge to some of the ruins between 8 am and 4.30 pm. The best way to see the ruins is by bicycle, which can be rented at guesthouses. Tuk-tuk tours cost 200 to 300B for a day's sightseeing.

The **Chao Sam Phraya National Museum** is open daily from 9 am to 4 pm. Admission is 10B. There's a second national museum at the **Chan Kasem Palace**; the opening hours and admission are the same.

The **Wat Phra Si Sanphet** is the old royal temple and has three restored chedis. The adjacent **Wihaan Phra Mongkon Bophit** houses a huge bronze seated Buddha. **Wat Thammikarat** is particularly appealing because of its overgrown, deserted feeling and the stone lions which guard a toppling chedi.

Wat Suwannawat was built towards the close of the Ayuthaya period and has been completely and very colourfully restored. **Wat Ratburana** and **Wat Phra Mahathat** are both extensively ruined but majestic.

Off the Island

The **Wat Phra Chao Phanan Choeng** was a favourite of Chinese traders and has a big seated Buddha. **Wat Chai Wattanaram** used to be one of Ayuthaya's most overgrown, evocative-of-a-lost-city type of ruins, with stately lines of disintegrating Buddhas. Today, some hard restoration work (and the wonders of modern cement) has produced a row of lookalike brand-new Buddhas! It's still a lovely wat with nice gardens.

The **Golden Mount** to the north of the city has a wide view over the flat country. Also to the north is the **elephant kraal** – the last of its kind in Thailand. **Wat Yai Chai Mongkon** to the south-east has a massive ruined chedi, which contrasts with surrounding contemporary Buddha statues.

For a historical overview of the Ayuthaya period, check out the **Ayuthaya Historical Study Centre** near Wat Yai Chai Mongkon. Japanese-funded, this ambitious facility houses hi-tech displays that cover not only

art and archaeology but also the social and political history of the period.

Wat Na Phra Men (Meru), opposite the old royal palace *(wang luang)* grounds via a bridge, is notable because it escaped destruction in 1767. The main *bot* (chapel) was built in 1546 and features fortress-like walls and pillars.

Places to Stay

Guesthouses The *Ayuthaya Guest House* (☎ 251468) is down a soi off Naresuan Rd, near the bus terminal and the Sri Smai Hotel. Rates are 100B single/double. Next door a branch of the same family runs the *Old BJ Guest House* (☎ 251526) at slightly lower rates. Both offer food service and bike rentals.

The *New BJ Guest House* (☎ 244046) at 19/29 Naresuan Rd has clean rooms for 60B dorm, 100B single/double, and a nice eating area in front.

Almost directly across the river from the train station in an old teak house is the *Ayuthaya Hostel* (☎ 241978), also known as Reuan Derm, at 48/2 U Thong Rd. Plain rooms with ceiling fans and shared bath cost 200B for small rooms, 250B for larger ones.

Hotels The *U Thong Hotel* (☎ 251136), on U Thong Rd near the boat landing and the Chan Kasem Palace, is noisy but otherwise tolerable; rooms are 180/250B with fan or 300/400B with air-con. A few shops down, the *Cathay Hotel* (☎ 251562) is a better choice at 150/270B with fan, 300B air-con.

At 13/1 Naresuan Rd, the *Thai Thai Bungalow* (☎ 251505) has basic but OK rooms with bath from 120B up to 300B with air-con.

Sri Smai (Si Samai) Hotel (☎ 252249), 12 Thetsaban Soi 2, just off Naresuan Rd, is a more upmarket place that charges 400B for rooms with fan and bath, 550B with air-con and 600B with air-con and hot water.

Places to Eat

There are lots of places to eat in Ayuthaya, including the *night market* opposite the Chan

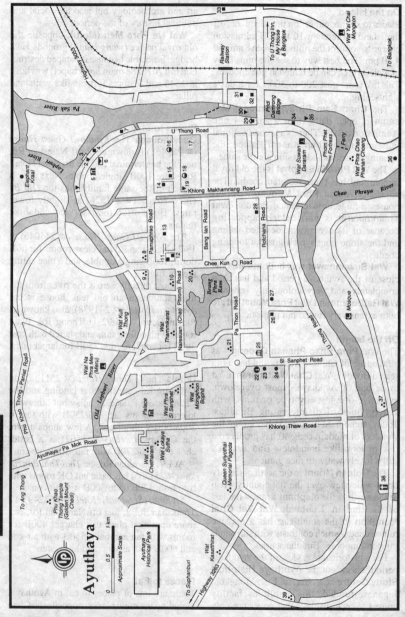

THAILAND

Ayuthaya

0   0.5   1 km
Approximate Scale

Ayuthaya Historical Park

Kasem Palace. The *Chainam*, opposite Chan Kasem Palace next to the Cathay Hotel, has tables on the river, a bilingual menu and friendly service; it's also open for breakfast.

There are a couple of *floating restaurants* on the river near the Pridi Damrong Bridge, worth considering for a splurge. The *Phae Krung Kao* has a good local reputation – it's on the south side of the bridge on the west bank.

PLACES TO STAY
4	U Thong Hotel
7	Cathay Hotel
11	Thongchai Guesthouse
12	New BJ Guesthouse
13	Thai Thai Bungalow
14	Ayuthaya & Old BJ Guesthouses
15	Sri Smai (Samai) Hotel
26	Suan Luang (Royal Garden) Hotel
28	Wieng Fa Hotel
29	Ayuthaya Hostel
31	Tevaraj Tanrin Hotel
32	Krungsri River Hotel
33	Ayuthaya Grand Hotel
34	Pai Thong Guesthouse (Under Reconstruction)

PLACES TO EAT
1	Hua Raw Night Market
2	Night Market
19	Duangporn Restaurant
30	Floating Restaurants
35	Phae Krung Kao

OTHER
3	Pier (Boat Landing)
5	Chan Kasem Palace
6	GPO
8	Chinese Shrine
9	Wat Suwannawat
10	Wat Ratburana
16	Air-Con Minivans to Bangkok
17	Chao Phrom Market
18	Bus Terminal
20	Wat Phra Mahathat
21	Wat Phra Ram
22	Tourist Office
23	Future TAT
24	City Hall
25	Chao Sam Phraya National Museum & TAT Office
27	Ayuthaya Historical Study Centre
36	Ayuthaya Historical Study Centre (Annex)
37	Wat Phutthaisawan
38	St Joseph's Cathedral
39	Wat Chai Wattanaram

Getting There & Away

Bus There are buses to Ayuthaya from the Northern bus terminal in Bangkok every 10 minutes; the 1½ hour trip costs 22B. The first bus is at 5 am and the last at 7 pm.

Train There are frequent trains from the Hualamphong station; the 3rd class fare is 15B and the travelling time is the same as the buses. The Ayuthaya station is some distance from the town centre, but at the Bangkok end, taking the train saves you trekking out to the Northern bus terminal. After getting off at Ayuthaya, the quickest way to reach the old city is to walk straight west to the river, where you can catch a short ferry ride across to the Chao Phrom pier for 1B.

A tuk-tuk from the Ayuthaya railway station into town will cost no more than 20B.

Boat There are no longer any scheduled or chartered boat services between Bangkok and Ayuthaya.

Several companies in Bangkok operate luxury cruises to Bang Pa In with side trips by bus to Ayuthaya for around 1000 to 1200B per person, including a lavish luncheon.

Getting Around

The cheapest way to see the town is by rented bicycle – 40 to 50B per day from the Ayuthaya or New BJ guesthouses. You can also hire a taxi or samlor by the hour (150B) or by the day (400B) to explore the ruins. Or get a group of people together and hire a boat from the Palace pier to do a circular tour of the island and see some of the less accessible ruins. Figure on about 300B for a three hour trip with a maximum of eight passengers. During the Songkran Festival in April, the local government runs daily boat tours from the U Thong pier for a bargain 50B per person.

Songthaews and shared tuk-tuks ply the main routes for 3 to 5B per person.

BANG PA IN

The **Royal Palace** in Bang Pa In has a strange collection of buildings in Chinese, Italian and Gothic style, and a Thai-style pavilion in a small lake. It's not all that interesting, but makes a pleasant riverboat trip from Ayuthaya, which is 20 km to the north. Admission is 50B and the palace is open daily from 8.30 am to 3.30 pm. Across the river from the palace is an unusual church-like wat reached by a trolley-cum-cable-car – the crossing is free.

Getting There & Away
There are minibuses (or large songthaew trucks) between Bang Pa In and Ayuthaya every 15 minutes. The short trip costs 8B.

From Bangkok, there are ordinary buses to Bang Pa In every half hour from 6 am to 6 pm; the fare is 17B.

LOPBURI
Situated 154 km north of Bangkok, this former capital of the Khmer Lavo period (10th century) shows strong Hindu and Khmer influences in its temple and palace ruins.

Orientation & Information
The new town of Lopburi is some distance east of the old fortified town and is centred on two large roundabouts. There is really nothing of interest in the new section, so try to stay at a hotel in the old town if you're interested in the palace and temple ruins.

The area code for Lopburi is 36.

Tourist Office There's a TAT office (☎ 422768) in the Sala Jangwat (Provincial Hall) in new Lopburi. This office may move to a more permanent location in the next couple of years. You can get a good map of Lopburi from the tourist office.

Phra Narai Ratchaniwet
This former palace of King Narai is a good place to begin a tour of Lopburi. Built between 1665 and 1677, it was designed by French and Khmer architects – an unusual blend that works quite well. The main gate is off Sorasak Rd, opposite the Asia Lopburi Hotel. Inside the grounds are the remains of the royal elephant stables, a reservoir, a reception hall, various pavilions and residence halls, and the **Lopburi National Museum**.

The museum is housed in three separate buildings, which contain an excellent collection of Lopburi period sculpture, as well as an assortment of Khmer, Dvaravati, U Thong and Ayuthaya art, traditional farm implements and dioramas of farm life. It's open Wednesday to Sunday from 8.30 am to noon and from 1 to 4 pm. Admission into the palace grounds is free; museum entry is 10B.

Other Ruins
Most important is the **Prang Sam Yot**, or Sacred Three Spires, which was originally built as a Hindu shrine and is reckoned to be the finest Khmer structure in the region. **Prang Khaek** and **Wat Phra Si Ratana Mahathat** are also notable.

Phaulkon's House, the home of the Greek adviser to Ayuthaya during its heyday, is also in Lopburi. Phaulkon was beheaded by the king's ministers when he began courting French influence in the area.

Places to Stay & Eat
You can do a day trip to Lopburi from Ayuthaya. If you want to stay, the hotels on Na Kala Rd, close to the railway station, are about the cheapest. On Na Kala Rd, opposite Wat Nakhon Kosa, the *Indra* costs 120B for clean, spacious rooms with fan and bath or 260B air-con. On the same road, but closer to the railway station, the *Julathip* (which doesn't have a sign in English) has rooms with fan and bath for 100B – but ask to see them first.

Still on Na Kala Rd, the *Suparaphong* is not far from Wat Phra Sri Ratana Mahathat and the railway station. It's similar in price and standard to the Julathip. Overlooking King Narai's palace, the *Asia Lopburi* (☎ 41 1892) is on the corner of Sorasak and Phra Yam Jamkat Rds. It's clean and comfortable and has two Chinese restaurants downstairs. Rooms are 130/180B with fan and bath, and up to 350B with air-con. *Muang Thong* (☎ 411036), across from Prang Sam Yot, has noisy but adequate rooms for 100/120B with fan and bath, plus some cheaper rooms without bath for 80B.

There are several *Chinese restaurants* along Na Kala Rd, parallel to the railway line, but they tend to be a bit pricey. The places on the side streets of Ratchadamnoen and Phra Yam Jamkat Rds are better value.

At 26/47 Soonkangkha Manora, near the Australian Education Placement Centre, there's a *Sala Mangsawirat* (vegetarian pavilion) with inexpensive Thai vegie food; like most Thai vegetarian restaurants, it's only open from around 9 am to 2 pm.

Getting There & Away

Bus Ordinary buses leave about every 10 minutes from Ayuthaya or every 20 minutes from Bangkok – the three hour trip costs 40B; less frequent air-con ones are 72B. From Kanchanaburi, you can get to Lopburi via Suphanburi and Singhburi on a series of public buses or share taxis.

Train You can reach Lopburi from Bangkok by train for 28B in 3rd class, and 57B in 2nd. One way of visiting Lopburi on the way north is to take the train from Ayuthaya (or Bangkok) early in the morning, leave your gear at the station for the day while you look around and then continue north on the night train.

Getting Around

Samlors go anywhere in old Lopburi for 20B. Songthaews run a regular route between the old and new towns for 3B per person.

SARABURI

There's nothing of interest in Saraburi itself, but between here and Lopburi you can turn off to the **Phra Phutthabat**. This small, delicate and beautiful shrine houses a revered Buddha footprint. Like all genuine Buddha footprints, it is massive and identified by its 108 auspicious distinguishing marks. In February and March there are pilgrimage festivals at the shrine.

The area code for Saraburi is 36.

Places to Stay

Try the *Thanin* or *Suk San* at Amphoe Phra Phutthabat – both cost 100 to 160B for fan rooms. In town, the *Kyo-Un (Kiaw An)* (☎ 222022) on Phahonyothin Rd has nicer rooms from 420B. Other hotels include the slightly cheaper *Saraburi* (☎ 211646/ 211500) opposite the bus stand.

SUPHANBURI

This very old Thai city has some noteworthy Ayuthaya-period chedis and one Khmer prang. **Wat Phra Si Ratana Mahathat** (is there a more popular name for a wat in Thailand?) is set back off Malimaen Rd close to the city centre. A staircase inside its Lopburi-style prang leads right to the top.

About seven km west of Suphan town is **Don Chedi**, a pagoda that commemorates the 16th century mounted elephant duel between Thailand's King Naresuan and the Prince of Burma. Naresuan won, thus freeing Ayuthaya from Pegu's rule. During the week of 25 January, there's an annual **Don Chedi Monument Fair** in which the elephant battle is re-enacted in full costume.

The area code for Suphanburi is 35.

Places to Stay

The *King Pho Sai* (☎ 521412) at 678 Nane Kaew Rd has rooms from 140B. The *KAT* (☎ 521619/39) at 433 Phra Phanwasa and the *Suk San* (☎ 511668) at 1145 Nang Pim Rd are similarly priced.

NAKHON PATHOM

At 127 metres, the gigantic orange-tiled **Phra Pathom Chedi** is the tallest Buddhist monument in the world. It was begun in 1853 to cover the original chedi of the same name. Nakhon Pathom is regarded as the oldest city in Thailand – it was conquered by Angkor in the early 11th century and in 1057 was sacked by Anawrahta of Bagan (Burma). There is a museum near the chedi and outside the town is the pleasant park of **Sanam Chan** – the grounds of the palace of Rama VI. In November, there's a **Phra Pathom Chedi Fair** that packs in everyone from fruit vendors to fortune tellers.

From Nakhon Pathom, you can make an excursion to the **floating market** at Klong Damnoen Saduak. This has become a popular, less-touristic alternative to the over-commercialised Bangkok floating market. All you have to do to get there is hop on a bus bound for Samut Songkhram to the south and ask to be let off in Damnoen Saduak or *talaat nam* (floating market). Go early in the morning (around 6 or 7 am is best) to avoid the tourist hordes from Bangkok.

Places to Stay & Eat

On Lungphra Rd, near the railway station, the *Mitsamphan Hotel* (☎ 242422) has rooms for 150B with fan and bath – more with air-con. The *Mitrthaworn (Mittaowan)*, on the right as you walk towards the chedi from the train station, has rooms at 200/220B with fan and bath, 300B for air-con.

The *Mitphaisan* (its English sign says 'Mitr Paisal') is further down the alley to the right from the Mittaowan and has rooms from 250B. All three 'Mit' hotels are owned by the same family. The Mitphaisan seems best this time around.

There's an excellent *fruit market* along the road between the train station and the Phra Pathom Chedi. *Song Saen*, on Ratchadamnoen Rd a few blocks directly west of Phra Pathom Chedi, offers a pleasant Thai sala setting with good, medium-priced Thai food.

Getting There & Away

Nakhon Pathom is 56 km west of Bangkok. Every weekend there's a special rail trip to Nakhon Pathom and on to Kanchanaburi. Otherwise, you can get there by bus from the Southern bus terminal in Bangkok, or by rail. Buses leave every 10 minutes and cost 16B for the one hour trip. The rail fare is 14B in 3rd class.

RATCHABURI

More often abbreviated Rat-buri, this provincial capital is on the way south from Nakhon Pathom, well before you get to the coast and Hua Hin. Ratchaburi is well-known among Thais for its ceramics indus-

try, particularly the large brown-glazed water jars etched with cream-coloured dragon motifs (from which they get their common farang name, 'dragon jars').

The *Kuang Hua Hotel* (☎ (32) 337119) at 202 Amarin Rd has reasonable but basic rooms for 120B with fan and bath, or 100B with shared facilities.

KANCHANABURI

Kanchanaburi (pronounced Kan-cha-NA-buri) is often referred to as Kan. The infamous bridge over the River Kwai (actually Khwae) was built here, 130 km west of Bangkok, during WWII.

The graves of thousands of Allied soldiers can be seen in Kanchanaburi or you can take a train across the bridge and continue further west, where there are caves, waterfalls and a Neolithic burial site. The bridge that stands today is not the one constructed during the war – that was destroyed by Allied air raids – though the curved portions of the structure are original.

The town was founded by Rama I as protection against Burmese invasion over the Three Pagodas Pass, which is still a major smuggling route into Myanmar. Today it's a favourite vacation spot for Thais and foreigners alike.

Information

There's a good TAT office near the bus station.

The area code for Kanchanaburi is 34.

Death Railway Bridge

The bridge made famous by the film *Bridge on the River Kwai* spans the Khwae Yai River, a tributary of the Mae Klong River, a couple of km north of town. The bridge was a small but strategic part of the Death Railway to Burma and was in use for 20 months before the Allies bombed it in 1945.

During the first week of December every year there's a nightly sound and light show at the bridge. It's a pretty impressive scene, with the sounds of bombers and explosions and fantastic bursts of light. The town gets a lot of tourists during this week, so book early if you want to attend.

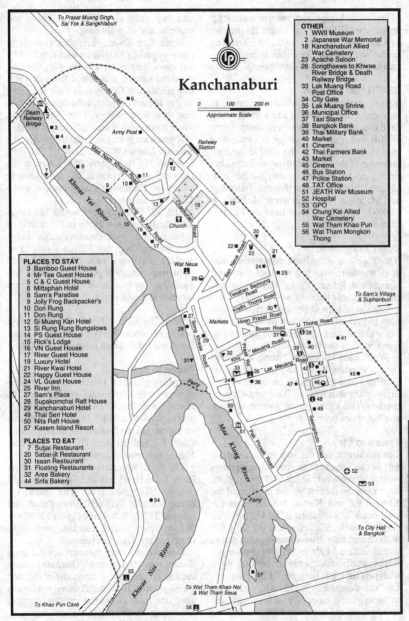

Kanchanaburi

To Prasat Muang Singh, Sai Yok & Sangkhlaburi

Saengchuto Road

Death Railway Bridge

Army Post

Railway Station

Mae Nam Khwae Road

Khwae Yai River

Rong Hip Awy Road

Chaokunen Road

Church

Wat Neua

Ban Neua Road

Tesaban Bamrung Road

Krathi Thong Road

Hiran Prasat Road

Markets

Song Khwae Road

Khu Meuang Road

Bovon Road

U Thong Road

Prasat Road

Lak Meuang Road

Saengchuto Road

Ferry

Mae Klong River

Pak Phraek Road

Ferry

To Sam's Village & Suphanburi

To City Hall & Bangkok

To Wat Tham Khao Noi & Wat Tham Seua

To Khao Pun Cave

0   100   200 m
Approximate Scale

OTHER
1 WWII Museum
2 Japanese War Memorial
18 Kanchanaburi Allied War Cemetery
23 Apache Saloon
26 Songthaews to Khwae River Bridge & Death Railway Bridge
33 Lak Muang Road Post Office
34 City Gate
35 Lak Muang Shrine
36 Municipal Office
37 Taxi Stand
38 Bangkok Bank
39 Thai Military Bank
40 Market
41 Cinema
42 Thai Farmers Bank
43 Market
45 Cinema
46 Bus Station
47 Police Station
48 TAT Office
51 JEATH War Museum
52 Hospital
53 GPO
54 Chung Kai Allied War Cemetery
55 Wat Tham Khao Pun
56 Wat Tham Mongkon Thong

PLACES TO STAY
3 Bamboo Guest House
4 Mr Tee Guest House
5 C & C Guest House
6 Mittaphan Hotel
8 Sam's Paradise
9 Jolly Frog Backpacker's
10 Don Rung
11 Don Rung
12 Si Muang Kan Hotel
13 Si Rung Rung Bungalows
15 PS Guest House
15 Rick's Lodge
16 VN Guest House
17 River Guest House
19 Luxury Hotel
21 River Kwai Hotel
22 Happy Guest House
24 VL Guest House
25 River Inn
27 Sam's Place
28 Supakornchai Raft House
29 Kanchanaburi Hotel
49 Thai Seri Hotel
50 Nita Raft House
57 Kasem Island Resort

PLACES TO EAT
7 Sutjai Restaurant
20 Sabai-jit Restaurant
30 Isaan Restaurant
31 Floating Restaurants
32 Aree Bakery
44 Srifa Bakery

THAILAND

Get to the bridge from town by catching a songthaew (5B) along Pak Phraek Rd (parallel to Saengchuto Rd, close to the river) heading north. You can also take a train from the Kanchanaburi train station to the bridge for 2B.

JEATH War Museum

This interesting little outdoor museum is run by monks. It's set up just like a POW camp on the actual site of a war-time camp. Entry is 20B and it's worth seeing. It's estimated that 16,000 western POWs died in the construction of the Death Railway to Burma but the figures for labourers, many forcibly conscripted from Thailand, Burma, Indonesia and Malaysia, were even worse. As many as 100,000 to 150,000 may have died in this area during WWII.

Other Attractions

There are two Allied **war cemeteries** near Kanchanaburi, one just north of town, off Saengchuto Rd near the railway station, and the other across the river west of town, a few km down the Khwae Noi tributary. The town also has an interesting **Lak Muang**, or city pillar shrine, on Lak Muang Rd, two blocks north-west of the tourist office.

Wat Tham Mongkon Thong is famous for its 'Floating Nun', who meditates while floating in a pool of water, an attraction that draws daily busloads of Thai and Chinese tourists. This cave temple is some distance south-west of town.

Places to Stay

Guesthouses You can stay on the river in a raft house (or over the river in bungalows built on piers) for 30 to 50B per person, depending on the raft. At the junction of the Khwae Yai and Khwae Noi rivers is the well-run *Nita Raft House* (☎ 514521), where singles/doubles with mosquito net are 100B with shared bath. Two other popular places of this sort are the *River* and *VN* guesthouses, where small, basic rooms are 50/70B, more with private bath. Both are on the river, not far from the railway station. One drawback to these places, especially on weekends and holidays, is the presence of floating disco

rafts that cruise up and down blasting pop music nearly all night long.

North of the VN and River guesthouses is the very popular *Jolly Frog Backpacker's* (☎ 514579) – it costs 50/90B for a room with veranda, mosquito screens and shared bath, or 130B with private bath. Other places come and go but they're all pretty similar. In the floating restaurant area there's the well-run *Sam's Place*, where rooms with shared bath start at 100B.

If you want to stay out near the bridge, the *Bamboo House* (☎ 512532) at 3-5 Soi Vietnam, on the river about a km before the Japanese War Memorial, has quiet double rooms for 100B with shared bath, or up to 450B with air-con.

The *VL Guest House*, across the street from the River Kwai Hotel in the middle of town, is good value: clean, spacious rooms with fan and bath are 150B for singles or doubles, and larger rooms holding four to eight people cost 50B per person. The VL has a small dining area downstairs and they rent bicycles and motorbikes.

Hotels The *Luxury Hotel* (☎ 511168) is a couple of blocks north of the River Kwai Hotel and offers clean rooms from 100B.

Places to Eat

There are plenty of places to eat along the northern end of Saengchuto Rd near the River Kwai Hotel. The quality generally relates to the crowds! Good, inexpensive eating can also be found in the *markets* along Prasit Rd and between U Thong and Lak Muang Rds, east of Saengchuto Rd.

The *Sabai-jit* restaurant, just north of the River Kwai Hotel, has an English menu and consistently good food. The *Isaan*, on Saengchuto Rd between Hiran Prasat and Krathai Thong Rds, serves great kài yâang (whole spicy grilled chicken) and other north-eastern Thai specialities.

Down on the river, there are several large *floating restaurants* where it's hard not to enjoy the atmosphere, even if the quality of the food varies. Across from the floating restaurants along the road are several smaller, cheaper *food stalls* which open in the evenings.

The *Aree Bakery* near the Lak Meuang has excellent baked goods, ice cream, coffee, tea and sandwiches. There are tables and chairs for a sit-down.

Getting There & Away

Bus Regular buses leave Bangkok every 20 minutes daily for Kanchanaburi from the Southern bus terminal in Thonburi. The trip takes about three hours and costs 34B. Aircon buses leave every 15 minutes and cost 62B. The last bus back to Bangkok leaves Kan around 10 pm.

Train The regular train costs 25B for 3rd class. There are only two a day and they both leave from the Bangkok Noi station in Thonburi, not from Hualamphong.

Share Taxi & Minivan You can take a share taxi from Saengchuto Rd to Bangkok for 50B per person. Taxis leave throughout the day whenever five passengers accumulate at the taxi stand. These taxis will make drops at Khao San Rd or in the Pahurat District. Guesthouses in Kanchanaburi also arrange daily minivans to Bangkok for 80B per person, with drop-offs at Khao San Rd.

Getting Around

You can hire motorbikes from the Suzuki dealer near the bus station. The cost is 150B per day and they are a good way of getting to the rather scattered attractions around Kanchanaburi.

Samlors within the city are 10 to 15B a trip. Regular songthaews in town are 3B, but be careful you don't accidentally 'charter' one, because it'll be a lot more.

AROUND KANCHANABURI

Numerous interesting excursions can be made from Kanchanaburi.

Waterfalls

The **Erawan Falls** make an interesting bus trip (1½ to two hours) beyond Kanchanaburi. There's a 25B admission charge to a two km footpath which goes along the river and past seven waterfalls. There are plenty of good plunge pools, so take along your swimming gear.

To get to the falls take an early morning bus from the station; it costs 19B to the end of the line, from where you have to walk a couple of km to the start of the waterfall trail. Make an early start since the last bus back is at 4 pm. For the lazy – or those with the money – minibuses cruise by the river guesthouses at around 9 am daily and take passengers right into Erawan Park for 60B per person – they return around 3.30 pm.

Other waterfalls are generally too far from Kanchanaburi for a day trip. For overnighters, the **Huay Khamin** falls are one of the most interesting.

Other Attractions

There are a few places of interest along the road to Sangkhlaburi. From Kanchanaburi, take the Nam Tok Sai Yok road. A few km past the river you can visit the **Phu Phra Cave**. Another pause can be made at the **Prasat Muang Singh Temple**, a western outpost of the Khmer Empire. The **Sai Yok Falls** are 60 km out (overnight raft trips head down the Khwae Noi River from here) and another 44 km takes you past the **Sai Yok Yai National Park**. Around 107 km out, there's the **Hin Dat Hot Springs**, but dress discreetly if you decide to try them out – don't swim in the nude.

SANGKHLABURI & THREE PAGODAS PASS

These days it's relatively easy to travel up to the pass (Chedi Sam Ong in Thai) and have a peek into Myanmar. Getting there requires an overnight pause in Sangkhlaburi, 223 km north from Kan. The village on the Myanmar side of the pass has been the scene of firefights between the Mon and Karen insurgents – both armies want to control the collection of 'taxes' levied on smuggling.

In March 1990, the Burmese government regained control of the area, rebuilt the bamboo village in wood and concrete and renamed it Payathonzu. A row of tourist shops have been built and tourists are allowed over the border for day trips; there is an entrance fee of 130B. There is talk of reopening the road all the way to Mawlamyine. The three pagodas themselves are rather inconspicuous, small and whitewashed monuments.

Places to Stay

At Thong Pha Phum, the last town before Sangkhlaburi, there are several places to stay for around 120 to 150B a night.

In Sangkhlaburi, the *Phornphalin Hotel* is on the first street to the left when you enter town and has rooms from 160B. Two km east of the bus station, near the lake, the *Burmese Inn*, has lakeview rooms for 60B single, 80B double. The similar *P Guest House*, a bit further on, has cheaper rooms for 30 to 50B.

Getting There & Away

Four buses a day go to Sangkhlaburi from Kanchanaburi between 6 am and 1 pm; the ride takes 4½ hours and costs 70B. More expensive, faster air-con minivans are also available. You can also get to Sangkhlaburi by a rented motorbike from Kan. This is not a road for the inexperienced motorcyclist – it has lots of dangerous curves, steep grades and long stretches where there is no assistance. If you go by motorbike, refuel in Thong Pha Phum, 150 km north of Kan – there isn't another fuel stop before Sangkhlaburi, another 70 km away. From Sangkhlaburi, there are hourly songthaews (30B, 40 minutes) to Three Pagodas Pass all day long.

PATTAYA

Thailand's biggest and once most popular beach resort is a long way from being its nicest. Situated 154 km south of Bangkok, a fourth 'S' (for sex) can be added to Sun, Sea & Sand in this gaudy and raucous resort. Pattaya is designed mainly to appeal to European package tourists, and there are plenty of snack bars along the beach strip proclaiming 'bratwurst mit brot' is more readily available than khao phat.

Pattaya consists of a long beach strip of mainly expensive hotels. The beach is drab and dismal and if you venture into the equally uninviting water you run the risk of being mowed down by a lunatic on a ski-boat, an out-of-control jet-ski or simply dropped on from above by a parasailor. Its one real attraction is the rather beautiful offshore islands, where the snorkelling is good.

The area code for Pattaya is 38.

Places to Stay & Eat

Although Pattaya is basically a package-tourist, big-hotel deal, there are a handful of cheaper places squeezed in the small sois, back off the main beach road. Cheap in Pattaya would be expensive just about anywhere else in Thailand. This is true even when compared with Ko Samui or Phuket.

Most of the less expensive places are concentrated along and just off Pattaya 2 Rd, near sois 6, 10, 11 and 12. *Lucky House*, between sois 8 and 10, has simple but clean rooms for 100B – you may have to bargain for this price – with fan and bath. Most other low-end places cost 300 to 400B. The *U-Thumphorn*, opposite Soi 10 on Pattaya 2 Rd, has fan rooms for 150 to 250B. One of the best value-for-money places in Pattaya is the modern *Apex Hotel* (☎ 429233) at No 216/2 near Soi 11; it has older rooms with air-con, TV and fridge for 250 to 300B.

Nearby Jomtien Beach is a bit quieter and nicer than Pattaya Beach; the *RS Guest House* (☎ 231867/8) rents smallish rooms for 250B with fan, or 350B with air-con.

Most food in Pattaya is expensive – cheap eating here means *Pizza Hut* or *Mister Donut*! Shops along the back street on Pattaya 2 Rd have decent Thai food. Look for cheap rooms back here, too.

Getting There & Away

Air Bangkok Airways has a daily flight between nearby U-Taphao and Ko Samui for 1660B each way.

Bus There are departures every half hour from the Eastern bus terminal in Bangkok for the two hour, 37B trip to Pattaya. Air-con buses are 66B. There are also all sorts of air-con tour buses to Pattaya run by a number of tour companies. At 9 am, noon and 7 pm,

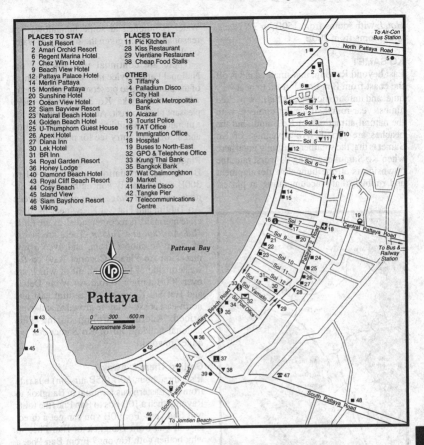

Pattaya

PLACES TO STAY
1 Dusit Resort
2 Amari Orchid Resort
6 Regent Marina Hotel
7 Chez Wim Hotel
9 Beach View Hotel
12 Pattaya Palace Hotel
14 Merlin Pattaya
15 Montien Pattaya
20 Sunshine Hotel
21 Ocean View Hotel
22 Siam Bayview Resort
23 Natural Beach Hotel
24 Golden Beach Hotel
25 U-Thumphorn Guest House
26 Apex Hotel
27 Diana Inn
30 Lek Hotel
31 BR Inn
34 Royal Garden Resort
36 Honey Lodge
40 Diamond Beach Hotel
43 Royal Cliff Beach Resort
44 Cosy Beach
45 Island View
46 Siam Bayshore Resort
48 Viking

PLACES TO EAT
11 Pic Kitchen
28 Kiss Restaurant
29 Vientiane Restaurant
38 Cheap Food Stalls

OTHER
3 Tiffany's
4 Palladium Disco
5 City Hall
8 Bangkok Metropolitan Bank
10 Alcazar
13 Tourist Police
16 TAT Office
17 Immigration Office
18 Hospital
19 Buses to North-East
32 GPO & Telephone Office
33 Krung Thai Bank
35 Bangkok Bank
37 Wat Chaimongkhon
39 Market
41 Marine Disco
42 Tangke Pier
47 Telecommunications Centre

Pattaya Bay

0   300   600 m
Approximate Scale

To Air-Con Bus Station
North Pattaya Road
Central Pattaya Road
To Bus & Railway Station
South Pattaya Road
To Jomtien Beach

there are buses direct from Bangkok airport for 200B one way.

Getting Around
Songthaews cruise Pattaya Beach and Pattaya 2 Rds for 5B per person, or go to Jomtien for 10B. Don't ask the fare first or drivers will think you want a charter.

RAYONG
Most of Thailand's *náam plaa* (fish sauce) comes from Rayong. For most travellers it is just a quick bus change on the way to Ko Samet, but there are a few pleasant beaches

at this 'real' Thai resort beyond Pattaya. Prices aren't much lower than in Pattaya (for beach places), though they are better value.

Places to Stay & Eat
The *Rayong Hotel* at 65/3 Sukhumvit Rd and the *Rayong Otani* at No 169 have rooms from 150B. There are good cheap eats at the *market* near the Thetsabanteung cinemas, and at the string of restaurants and noodle shops on Taksin Maharat Rd, just south of Wat Lum Mahachaichumphon.

If you get stuck in Ban Phe, the port town for Ko Samet, you can stay at the *Queen*

THAILAND

Hotel, with rooms from 150B, or *TN Place*, with rooms from 200B.

KO SAMET

East beyond Rayong, this small island is off the coast from Ban Phe. It used to be a very quiet and untouristic place but is now packed almost year-round. It cannot compete with the natural attractions of Ko Samui, but the beaches are superb. An advantage of Ko Samet is that the weather is usually good here when Ko Samui is getting its worst rain; the downside is all the bungalow development and rubbish that's accumulating in places.

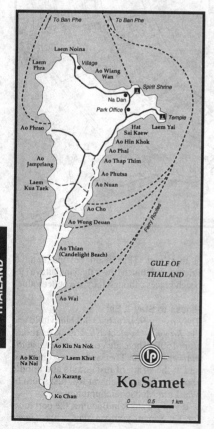

Ko Samet

Water is rationed at some bungalows – a reasonable policy given the scarcity of water on the island.

There are continual rumours that the National Park Service may close down most of the bungalows to preserve the environment, which could make Ko Samet a far more pleasant place to visit. At the moment there is a moratorium on building new accommodation and a 50B park entry fee for non-Thais.

Places to Stay

Beach accommodation costs from 80 to 300B and is mainly concentrated along the north-east coast. *Naga Bungalows*, between Ao Tubtim and Hat Sai Kaew near the concrete mermaid, is recommended, as are *Little Hut, Ao Phai* and *Tubtim*. There are plenty of others to choose from, and even a few places on Ao Phrao (Coconut Bay) on the western side of the island, all of which are over 300B a night. Avoid Ao Wong Deuan and Hat Sai Kaew on the central east and north-east coast – they're crowded and over-priced. Another warning: during Thai national holidays all of Ko Samet can get quite crowded.

Getting There & Away

It's a three hour, 50B (85B air-con) bus ride from the Eastern bus terminal in Bangkok to Rayong, then a 10B bus to Ban Phe (the touts will find you). For 90B you can get a direct air-con bus from Bangkok to Ban Phe, so why bother with Rayong? From Ban Phe, a fishing boat will take you out to Na Dan on the north end of Ko Samet for 30B. Other boats go to Ao Wong Deuan or Ao Thian, on the central east coast, for the same price. A boat to Ao Wai will cost 40B.

Many Khao San Rd agencies in Bangkok organise round-trip transport to Ko Samet for around 150 to 160B one way, including the boat fare. Not only is this more expensive than doing it on your own, you won't have a choice of which boat to take or where it stops.

Getting Around

Taxi trucks on the island cost from 10 to 50B per person, depending on how far you're going. There are trails all the way to the southern tip of the island, and a few cross-island trails as well.

TRAT PROVINCE

Located about 400 km south-east of Bangkok, the province of Trat borders Cambodia. Gem-mining and smuggling are the most important occupations, though tourism is growing at Ko Chang National Marine Park. You'll find gem markets at the Hua Thung and Khlong Yo markets in Bo Rai District, about 40 km north of Trat town. You can make good buys if (and only if) you know what you're buying. The largest gem market is in neighbouring Chanthaburi.

As Highway 318 goes east and then south on the way to Khlong Yai, the province of Trat thins to a sliver between the Gulf of Thailand and Cambodia. Along this sliver are a number of little-known beaches, including **Hat Sai Si Ngoen**, **Hat Sai Kaew**, **Hat Thap Thim** and **Hat Ban Cheun**.

The provincial capital has nothing much to offer – it is a jumping-off point for Ko Chang and other islands. You can get information about Ko Chang National Marine Park in **Laem Ngop**, a small coastal town approximately 20 km south-west of Trat. This is also where you get boats to Ko Chang.

The area code for Trat is 39.

Places to Stay

Trat The friendly *NP Guest House* (☎ 512564) at 1-3 Soi Luang Aet, Lak Meuang Rd (in a lane which is a south-easterly continuation of Tat Mai Rd), offers beds in a clean three bed dorm for 50B, or private rooms for 80/100B single/double with shared bath.

The *Trat Inn* (☎ 511028) at 66-71 Sukhumvit Rd and *Thai Roong Roj (Rung Rot)* (☎ 511141) at 196 Sukhumvit Rd have rooms from around 110 to 200B. Also good is the *Foremost Guest House* (☎ 511923) at 49 Thana Charoen Rd, towards the canal. Rooms here are 60/80/100B for single/double/triple rooms. The same family runs the *Windy Guest House* across the road on the canal.

Laem Ngop There's really no reason to stay here since most boats to Ko Chang leave in the afternoon and it's only 20 km from Trat, but the cosy *Chut Kaew Guest House* has rooms from 60/120B.

Places to Eat

The municipal *market* in the centre of town will satisfy your nutritional needs cheaply, day or night. On the Trat River, north-east of town, is a smaller *night market* which sells seafood. *Max & Tick Breakfast Cafe* (☎ 520-799) at 1-3 Soi Luang Aet, Lak Meuang Rd, near NP Guest House, offers good coffee and western breakfasts from 6.30 to 11 am.

Getting There & Away

Regular buses from Bangkok's Eastern terminal to Trat cost 80B and take seven to eight hours. By air-con bus, it's 140B and takes about five hours. Ordinary buses between Chanthaburi and Trat are 22B and take about 1½ hours.

Share taxis to Laem Ngop leave Trat from a stand along Sukhumvit Rd next to the municipal market; these cost 10B per person shared or 100B to charter. They depart regularly throughout the day, but after dark you will have to charter.

Getting Around

Samlors around town cost 10B per person, while Mazda taxi trucks are 5B and motorbike taxis are 10B. A door-to-door minibus from Trat to Bo Rai is 35B.

HAT LEK TO CAMBODIA

The small Thai border outpost of Hat Lek is the southernmost point on the Trat mainland. Small boats are available from Hat Lek to Pak Khlong on the island of Ko Kong – on the Cambodian side of the border – for 100B per person or 800B charter. If you plan to continue further, you can take a passenger ferry from Pak Khlong to Sao Thong for 10B, then change to a three hour speedboat ride (500B per boat) to Sihanoukville. From Sihanoukville it's a three hour, 40B share taxi ride to Phnom Penh. You may also be able to catch a once-daily bus all the way to Phnom Penh.

A Cambodian visa is necessary and can be obtained in Bangkok, not at the border. As far as the Thai authorities are concerned this is semi-illegal, and while in Cambodia you are technically in Thailand!

KO CHANG NATIONAL MARINE PARK

Ko Chang is the second largest island in Thailand after Phuket; the park actually covers 47 of the islands off Trat's coastline. The main island has a few small villages supported by coconuts, fishing and smuggling, but increasing numbers of tourists are attracted to the small bays and beaches, especially along the island's west coast. In the interior there's a series of scenic waterfalls called **Than Mayom Falls**, or Thara Mayom.

Places to Stay

Ko Chang Starting at the northern end of the island at pretty Hat Sai Khao, there's a string of fairly inexpensive beach bungalows, including *Rock Sand, KC, Yaka, Tantawan Bamboo, Cookie* and *Haad Sai Khao*; all start at 100B for basic huts with shared facilities. There's also a sprinkling of nicer, more expensive huts.

Further south, on Ao Khlong Phrao, you'll

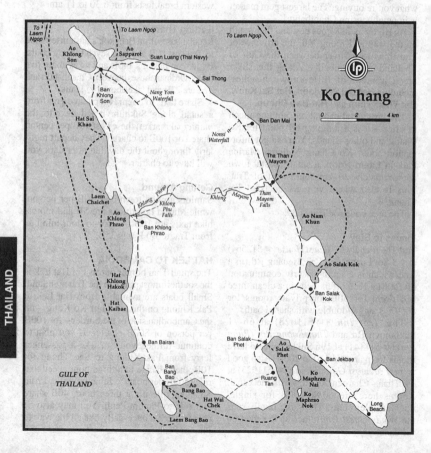

find huts for 80 to 100B at the *Chaichet Bungalows*. Further south yet, at Ao Kaibae, *Erawan, Magic, Good Luck, Chokdee, Coral Resot, Kaibae Hut* and others have cheaper huts at 50 to 150B, plus more expensive ones.

Down along the south coast at Ao Bang Bao are the *Bang Bao Blue Wave* and *Bang Bao Lagoon* for 80 to 300B. You may also be able to rent rooms cheaply in nearby Ban Bang Bao. The next bay along the coast, Ao Salak Phet, features the on-again, off-again *Ban Salakpetch Bungalow* with typical thatched huts for 40 to 60B.

Other Nearby islands with bungalow accommodation include Ko Kut, Ko Kradat, Ko Kham and Ko Mak.

Getting There & Away
Ko Chang Take a songthaew (10B) from Trat south-west to Laem Ngop on the coast, then a ferry to Ko Chang. Ferry fares differ according to the beach destination: 40B to Ao Sapparot (the main year-round pier), 70B to White Sand (Hat Sai Khao) and Ao Khlong Phrao, and so on. Ferries to the beachless east coast are less expensive: Tha Than Mayom 35B, Ao Salak Kok 35B and Ao Salak Phet 50B. Departures for Ao Sapparot are three or four times daily and the 70B fare includes a truck ride to the west coast beach of your choice. Departures for other bays are once daily, usually in the afternoon.

Air-con minibuses leave daily from Khao San Rd in Bangkok and go direct to Laem Ngop for 250B. The fare includes a ferry ride to Ao Khlong Son.

Other Islands Two or three fishing boats a week go to Ko Kut from the Tha Chaloemphon pier, on the Trat River towards the eastern side of Trat town. The fare is 80B per person. Coconut boats go to Ko Kut once or twice a month from a pier on the canal.

During the November to May dry season boats to Ko Mak leave daily from the Laem Ngop pier in the afternoon; the fare is 150B per person. Coconut boats go to Ko Mak from the Canal pier once or twice a month –

the trip takes five hours and costs 100B per person.

Daily boats to Ko Kham and Ko Wai depart around 3 pm for 150B and 70B respectively.

Getting Around
Songthaews meeting the boats at Ao Sapparot charge 30B per person to any beach along the west coast, although if you paid 70B for the boat your songthaew fare is already paid for. Between Ao Salak Kok and Ao Salak Phet, a daily jeep service costs 10B per person.

Northern Thailand

The northern area was where early Thai kingdoms (Lanna Thai, Hariphunchai and Sukhothai) first developed, so it's full of interesting temples and ruins. Most visitors tend to cluster around the northern capital of Chiang Mai, while the more adventurous head for the somewhat remote provinces of Chiang Rai, Mae Hong Son, Nan and Phrae. From here, you can make treks through the area inhabited by Thailand's many hill tribes. This too is the region of the infamous Golden Triangle – where Thailand, Laos and Myanmar meet and from where much of the world's opium originates.

Hill Tribe Treks
One of the most popular activities from Chiang Mai, Chiang Rai or Mae Hong Son is to take a trek through the tribal areas in the hills to the north. The best known tribes in this region are the Hmong (Meo), Karen, Lisu, Lahu (Musoe), Mien (Yao) and Akha, but tribal groups are also found across the border in Myanmar and Laos: lines on the political map have little meaning to them. Although pressure is being applied to turn them to more acceptable types of agriculture, opium is still a favourite crop here.

Unfortunately, these treks have become a bit too popular over the last decade or so and some areas are simply over-trekked. A little care is needed to guarantee a good experience.

THAILAND

Finding a good tour guide is probably the key to a good trek: a guide who cannot speak English, let alone the hill tribe languages, is hardly a ticket to an interesting trip. It's also important to check out your fellow trekkers – try to organise a meeting before departure. The best guides will be conversant with the tribes and their languages and have good contacts and easy relations with them. The best way of finding a good operator is simply to ask other travellers in Chiang Mai. People just back from a trek will be able to give you the low-down on how theirs went.

Treks normally last four days and three nights, although longer treks are also available, and the usual cost is around 1500B. Bring a water bottle and medicines, and money – for lunch on the first and last day and for odd purchases.

For an up-to-date list of trek operators, visit the TAT office. Making a recommendation here would be meaningless because guides often change companies, and operators open and close with alarming frequency. Some useful questions to ask include:

- How many people will there be in the group? Six to 10 is a good maximum range.
- Can the organiser guarantee that no other tourists will visit the same village on the same day, especially overnight?
- Can the guide speak the language of each village to be visited (this is not always necessary, as many villagers can speak Thai nowadays)?
- Exactly when does the tour begin and end? Some three-day treks turn out to be less than 48 hours in length.
- Do they provide transport before and after the trek or is it just by public bus (often with long waits)?

You can also just head off on your own or hire a guide or porter by yourself, but treks aren't that expensive and there are some areas where it is unwise to go.

Most people who go on these treks have a thoroughly good time and reckon they're great value. Comments include 'the best experience of my life...I hope we left the villages as we found them', and 'the area we covered was only recently opened for trekking and the guides were some of the nicest people I have ever met'.

Warning There have been a number of hold-ups and robberies over the years. This area of Thailand is relatively unpoliced, with a 'wild west' feel. Ask around that everything is OK before setting blithely off into the wilds. People who run into trouble often discover afterwards that their guide didn't really know where they were going, or went into areas they should have known were not safe.

Don't bring too much money or other valuables with you. You can leave your gear behind in Chiang Mai with your hotel or the trek operator.

Conduct Once on a trek, there are several other guidelines for minimising the negative impact on the local people:

- Always ask permission before taking photos of tribal people and/or their dwellings. You can ask through your guide or by using sign language. Because of traditional belief systems, many individuals – and even whole tribes – may object strongly to being photographed.
- Show respect for religious symbols and rituals. Don't touch totems at village entrances or any other object of obvious symbolic value without asking permission. Keep your distance from ceremonies being performed unless you're asked to participate.
- Practise restraint in giving things to tribespeople or bartering with them. Food and medicine are not necessarily appropriate gifts if they result in altering traditional dietary and healing practices. The same goes for clothing. Tribespeople will abandon hand-woven tunics for printed T-shirts if they are given a steady supply. If you want to give something to the people you encounter on a trek, the best thing is to make a donation to the village school or other community fund. Your guide can help arrange this.

Some guides strictly forbid the smoking of opium on treks. This seems to be a good idea, since one of the problems trekking companies have is dealing with opium-addicted guides. Volunteers who work in tribal areas also say opium smoking sets a bad example for young people in the villages.

Hill Tribe Directory
The term hill tribe refers to ethnic minorities living in the mountainous regions of north-

ern and western Thailand. The Thais refer to them as *chao khao*, literally meaning mountain people. Each hill tribe has its own language, customs, mode of dress and spiritual beliefs.

Most are of semi-nomadic origin, having migrated to Thailand from Tibet, Burma, China and Laos during the past 200 years or so, although some groups may have been in Thailand much longer.

The Tribal Research Institute in Chiang Mai recognises 10 different hill tribes but there may be up to 20 in Thailand. The institute's 1993 estimate of their total population was 550,000.

The following descriptions cover the largest tribes, which are also the groups most likely to be encountered on treks. Linguistically, they can be divided into three main groups: the Tibeto-Burman (Lisu, Lahu, Akha); the Karenic (Karen, Kayah); and the Austro-Thai (Hmong, Mien). Comments on ethnic dress refer mostly to the female members of each group as hill tribe men tend to dress like rural Thais. Population figures are 1986 estimates.

The Shan *(Thai Yai)* are not included as they are not a hill tribe group per se; they live in permanent locations, practice Theravada Buddhism and speak a language very similar to Thai.

Lonely Planet's *Thai Hill Tribes phrasebook* gives a handy, basic introduction to the culture and languages of a number of tribes.

Akha (Thai: *I-kaw*)
Population: 33,600
Origin: Tibet
Present locations: Thailand, Laos, Myanmar, Yunnan (China)
Economy: rice, corn, opium
Belief system: animism, with an emphasis on ancestor worship
Distinctive characteristics: head dresses of beads, feathers and dangling silver ornaments. Villages are along mountain ridges or on steep slopes 1000 to 1400 metres in altitude. The Akha are among the poorest of Thailand's ethnic minorities and tend to resist assimilation into the Thai mainstream. Like the Lahu, they often cultivate opium for their own consumption.

Hmong (Thai: *Meo* or *Maew*)
Population: 80,000
Origin: southern China
Present locations: southern China, Thailand, Laos, Vietnam
Economy: rice, corn, opium
Belief system: animism
Distinctive characteristics: simple black jackets and indigo trousers with striped borders or indigo skirts, and silver jewellery. Most women wear their hair in a large bun. They usually live on mountain peaks or plateaus. Kinship is patrilineal and polygamy is permitted. They are Thailand's second-largest hill tribe group and are especially numerous in Chiang Mai Province.

Karen (Thai: *Yang* or *Kariang*)
Population: 265,600
Origin: Myanmar
Present locations: Thailand, Myanmar
Economy: rice, vegetables, livestock
Belief system: animism, Buddhism, Christianity – depending on the group
Distinctive characteristics: thickly woven V-neck tunics of various colours (unmarried women wear white). Kinship is matrilineal and marriage is endogamous. They tend to live in lowland valleys and practice crop rotation rather than swidden (slash and burn) agriculture. There are four distinct Karen groups – the White Karen (Skaw Karen), Pwo Karen, Black Karen (Pa-o) and Kayah. These groups combined are the largest hill tribe in Thailand, numbering a quarter of a million people or about half of all hill tribe people. Many Karen continue to migrate into Thailand from Myanmar, fleeing Burmese government persecution.

Lahu (Thai: *Musoe*)
Population: 58,700
Origin: Tibet
Present locations: southern China, Thailand, Myanmar
Economy: rice, corn, opium
Belief system: theistic animism (supreme deity is Geusha); some groups are Christian
Distinctive characteristics: black and red jackets with narrow skirts for women. They live in mountainous areas at about 1000 metres. Their intricately woven shoulder bags *(yaam)* are prized by collectors. There are four main groups – Red Lahu, Black Lahu, Yellow Lahu and Lahu Sheleh.

Lisu (Thai: *Lisaw*)
Population: 24,000
Origin: Tibet
Present locations: Thailand, Yunnan (China)
Economy: rice, opium, corn, livestock
Belief system: animism with ancestor worship and spirit possession

THAILAND

Distinctive characteristics: the women wear long multi-coloured tunics over trousers and sometimes black turbans with tassels. Men wear baggy green or blue pants pegged in at the ankles. They wear lots of bright colours. Premarital sex is said to be common, along with freedom in choosing marital partners. Patrilineal clans have pan-tribal jurisdiction, which makes the Lisu unique among hill tribe groups (most tribes have power centred at the village level with either the shaman or a village headman). Their villages are usually in the mountains at about 1000 metres.

Mien (Thai: *Yao*)
Population: 35,500
Origin: central China
Present locations: Thailand, southern China, Laos, Myanmar, Vietnam
Economy: rice, corn, opium
Belief system: animism with ancestor worship and Taoism
Distinctive characteristics: women wear black jackets and trousers decorated with intricately embroidered patches and red fur-like collars, along with large dark blue or black turbans. They have been heavily influenced by Chinese traditions and use Chinese characters to write the Mien language. They tend to settle near mountain springs at between 1000 and 1200 metres. Kinship is paal and marriage is polygamous.

Getting There & Away
The straightforward way of getting to the north is simply to head directly from Bangkok to Chiang Mai either by bus, train or air. From Bangkok, you can visit the ancient capitals of Ayuthaya, Lopburi and Sukhothai on your way to Chiang Mai. If you visit these ancient cities southbound, rather than northbound, you'll hit them in chronological order. Or, you could take a longer, 'off-the-beaten-track' route by first heading west to Nakhon Pathom and Kanchanaburi, then back-tracking and travelling north-east by bus to Suphanburi and Lopburi.

From Chiang Mai, you can head north to Fang and take the daily riverboat down the Kok River (a tributary of the Mekong) to Chiang Rai. Or do the Mae Song loop through Mae Sariang and Pai. From there, you can head back through Chiang Mai, get off at Lampang, and either catch a bus via Tak to Sukhothai or take the train to Phitsanulok. From Phitsanulok, you can bus it to Lom Sak and then Loei and Udon Thani.

There is also a road between Lom Sak and Khon Kaen. Udon Thani and Khon Kaen are both on the rail and bus routes back to Bangkok, but there are a number of other places worth exploring in the north-east before you head back to the capital.

CHIANG MAI
Thailand's second-largest city is a bit of a tourist trap – full of noisy motorbikes and souvenir shops – but it offers interesting contrasts with the rest of the country and there is plenty to see. It's also a useful base for trips further afield.

Founded in 1296, Chiang Mai was at one time part of the independent Lanna Thai (Million Thai Rice-Fields) kingdom, much given to warring with kingdoms in Burma and Laos, as well as Sukhothai to the south. You can still see the moat that encircled the city at that time, but the remaining fragments of the city wall are mainly reconstructions. Chiang Mai fell to the Burmese in 1556 but was recaptured in 1775.

Orientation
The old city of Chiang Mai is a neat square bounded by moats. Moon Muang Rd, along the east moat, is one of the main centres for cheap accommodation and places to eat. Tha Phae Rd runs east from the middle of this side and crosses the Ping River, where it changes name to Charoen Muang Rd. The railway station and the GPO are both further down Charoen Muang Rd, a fair distance from the centre.

Information
Tourist Office The TAT (☎ 248604/07) is in an office (not shown on some Chiang Mai maps) on Chiang Mai-Lamphun Rd, a couple of hundred metres south of the Nawarat Bridge. They have piles of useful hand-outs on everything from guesthouse accommodation to trekking.

Maps Finding your way around Chiang Mai is fairly simple. A copy of Nancy Chandler's *Map Guide to Chiang Mai* is worth its 70B price. If you're planning to get around by city bus, you ought also to have a copy of P&P's *Tourist Map of Chiang Mai: Rose of the North*, which has a good bus map on one side and a very detailed highway map of northern Thailand on the other.

Foreign Consulates Chiang Mai has several foreign consular posts where you may be able to arrange visas or extend passports. The Indian consulate here is a common stopping-off point for travellers on their way to India; they take about four days to process a visa.

Canada
     51 Chiang Mai-Lamphun Rd (☎ 850147)
China
     111 Chang Law Rd (☎ 276135)
India
     344 Faham (Charoenrat) Rd, Faham
     (☎ 243066, 242491)
UK
     139/2 3rd floor, IBM Building, Huay Kaew Rd
     (☎ 894189, 894140)
USA
     387 Wichayanon Rd (☎ 252629/31)

Money All major Thai banks have several branches throughout Chiang Mai; most are open 8.30 am to 3.30 pm. In the well-touristed areas – Tha Phae Rd, Moon Muang Rd, Chiang Mai Night Bazaar etc – they also operate foreign exchange booths that are open after bank hours as late as 8 pm.

Post & Communications The main post office in Chiang Mai is on Charoen Muang Rd near the railway station. It is open Monday to Friday from 8.30 am to 4.30 pm, Saturday and Sunday from 9 am to 1 pm. Overseas calls, telexes; faxes and telegrams can be arranged here from 7 am to 10 pm.
     The area code for Chiang Mai is 53.

Bookshops & Libraries The best book-shops in Chiang Mai are the DK Book House on Kotchasan Rd and the Suriwong Book Centre on Si Donchai Rd. Check Suriwong's 2nd floor for books on Thailand and South-East Asia, along with various other English-language selections.
     The USIS/AUA library on Ratchadamnoen Rd inside the east gate has a selection of English-language newspapers and maga-zines.

Cultural Centres Several foreign cultural centres in Chiang Mai host film, music, dance, theatre and other socio-cultural events.

Alliance Française
     138 Charoen Prathet Rd (☎ 275277); French films (subtitled in English) every Tuesday at 4.30 pm, Friday at 8 pm; admission is free to members, 10B students, 20B general public.
USIS/AUA
     24 Ratchadamnoen Rd (☎ 278407, 211377); USIS shows US films every second and fourth Saturday at 2 pm and 7 pm; admission is free. AUA also offers English and Thai language courses.
British Council
     198 Bamrungrat Rd (☎ 242103); free British movies every Thursday at 7 pm.

Immigration The immigration office (☎ 277510) is off Route 1141 near the airport (bus No 6 will take you there).

Medical Services The McCormick Hospital (☎ 241107) on Kaew Nawarat Rd is the traveller's best bet. Another good one is the modern Chang Puek Hospital (☎ 220022; fax 218120) at 1/7 Chang Pheuak Rd Soi 2.

Tourist Police The tourist police can be reached in Chiang Mai by dialling ☎ 248974 from 6 am to midnight or ☎ 491420 after hours. Their office is attached to the TAT office on Chiang Mai-Lamphun Rd.

Dangers & Annoyances Beware of drug busts in Chiang Mai. Some guesthouses and samlor drivers have been known to supply you with dope and then turn you in. Also take care with valuables stored at guesthouses while out trekking. A few years ago, Thai-land was swept by a range of credit-card scams: a favourite was to borrow credit cards from trekkers' baggage while they were away. Months later, back in their home country, they would discover enormous bills had been run up.

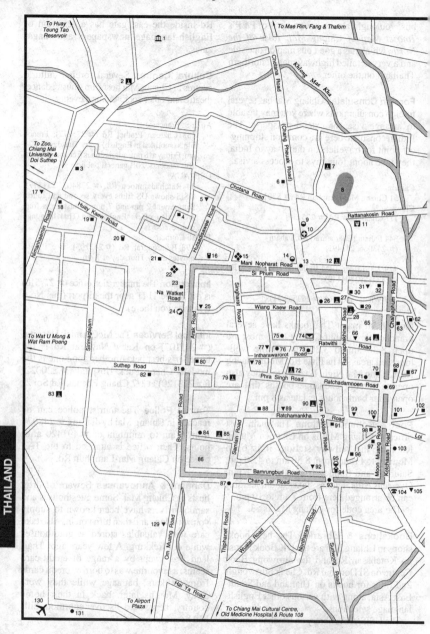

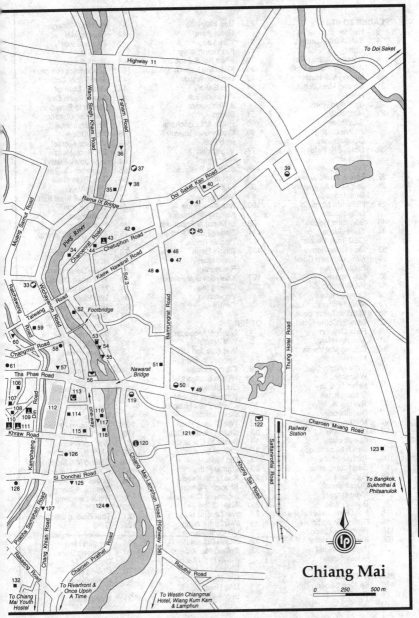

Chiang Mai

0   250   500 m

THAILAND

PLACES TO STAY
3 Holiday Inn
4 YMCA International Hotel
6 Novotel Chiang Mai
18 Amari Rincome Hotel
19 Muang Mai Hotel
21 Chiang Mai Orchid Hotel
23 Sri Tokyo Hotel
29 Northland, Sawatdee & Lam Chang Guesthouses
30 Libra, SK, Peter & Supreme Guesthouses
32 Tanya Guesthouse
34 Je t'Aime & Cowboy Guesthouses
35 Hollanda Montri Guesthouse
40 Sunshine House
44 The rePlace
51 C&C Teak House
52 Mee Guesthouse
59 New Mitrapap Hotel
62 Eagle House
63 Lek House
67 VK Guesthouse
68 Daret's House
70 Montri House
80 Manit's Guesthouse
82 Chiang Come Hotel
88 Felix City Inn
91 Anodard Hotel
94 Chiang Mai Youth Hostel
96 Jame, North Star, Welcome, Kritsada & Toy Guesthouses
97 Top North Guesthouse
98 Muang Thong Hotel
101 Little Home Guesthouse
102 Sarah Guesthouse
106 Taphae Place
107 Baan Jongcome
108 Ratchada Guesthouse
114 Night Bazaar Guesthouse
115 Porn Ping Tower Hotel
116 Galare Guesthouse
118 River View Lodge
123 Poy Luang Hotel
132 Paradise Hotel & Guesthouse

PLACES TO EAT
5 Sa-Nga Choeng Doi
17 The Pub

25 Uan Heh-Haa Restaurant
31 Wira Laap Pet & Kai Yaang Isaan
36 Khao Soi Samoe Jai
38 Khao Soi Lam Duan
49 Lim Han Nguan
54 The Gallery
55 Riverside Bar & Restaurant
57 Bacco
60 Ruam Mit Phochana
66 Crusty Loaf Bakery & Irish Pub
77 Vegetarian Restaurant
78 Si Phen Restaurant
89 Heuan Phen
92 Night Market
99 Mitmai Restaurant
100 Kuaytiaw Reua Koliang Restaurant
105 Si Donchai Phochana
114 Galare Food Centre
117 Piccola Roma
125 Whole Earth Vegetarian Restaurant
127 Khao Soi Suthasinee
129 Chiang Mai Vegetarian Centre

OTHER
1 National Museum
2 Wat Jet Yot
7 Wat Kuu Tao
8 Sports Stadium
9 Chang Pheuak (White Elephant) Bus Station (Provincial Buses)
10 Chang Puek Hospital
11 Devi Mandir
12 Wat Chiang Yuen
13 Chang Pheuak Gate
14 Buses to Doi Suthep
15 Cathay Square
16 Old West
20 Marble Pub
22 Kad Suan Kaew Shopping Centre
24 Japanese Consulate
26 THAI Office
27 Wat Chiang Man
28 Wat Lam Chang
33 US Consulate
37 Indian Consulate
39 Chiang Mai Arcade (New) Bus Station (Buses to Chiang Rai, Mae Sariang, Mae Hong Son & Bangkok)

41 Phayap College
42 Chiang Mai International School
43 Wat Chetuphon
45 McCormick Hospital
46 Thai Tribal Crafts
47 British Council
48 Sara Health Club
50 Buses to Baw Sang & San Kamphaeng
53 The Brasserie
56 Post Office
58 Warorot Market
61 DK Book House
64 Wat Dawk Euang
65 Somphet Market
69 Tha Phae Gate
71 USIS\AUA
72 Wat Chai Phra Kiat
73 Three Kings Monument
74 Post Office
75 Chiang Mai Central Prison
76 District Offices
79 Wat Phra Singh
81 Suan Dawk Gate
83 Wat Suan Dawk
84 Mengrai Kilns
85 Wat Pheuak Hong
86 Buak Hat Park
87 Suan Prung Gate
90 Wat Chedi Luang & Wat Phan Tao
93 Chiang Mai Gate
95 Buses to Hot, Chom Thong, Doi Inthanon & Hang Dong
103 DK Book House
104 International Telephone Offices
109 Wat Chang Khong
110 Wat Phan Thong
111 Wat Loi Khraw
112 Night Bazaar
113 Chiang Mai Mosque (Ban Haw Mosque)
119 Buses to Lamphun, Pasang, Chiang Rai & Lampang
120 TAT Office
121 Thai Boxing Stadium
122 GPO
124 Alliance Française
126 Anusan Market
128 Suriwong Book Centre
130 Chiang Mai International Airport
131 Immigration

THAILAND

Wat Chiang Man

This is the oldest wat within the city walls and was erected by King Mengrai, Chiang Mai's founder, in 1296. Two famous Buddha images – Buddha Sila and the Crystal Buddha – are kept here in the *wihan* (smaller chapel) to the right of the main bot. Like Bangkok's Emerald Buddha, the Crystal Buddha was once shuttled back and forth between Siam and Laos.

Wat Phra Singh

Situated in the centre of town, this well-kept wat was founded in 1345. There are a number of interesting buildings here; the supposedly 1500-year-old Phra Singh Buddha image is a subject of some controversy and its exact history is unknown.

Wat Chedi Luang

Originally constructed in 1411, this wat contains the ruins of a huge chedi which collapsed during an earthquake in 1545. A partial restoration has preserved its 'ruined' look while ensuring it doesn't crumble further.

Other Wats

The **Wat Jet Yot** has seven (*jet*) spires (*yot*) and was damaged by the Burmese in 1566. It's near the National Museum and is modelled (imperfectly) after the Mahabodhi Temple in Bodh Gaya, India, where the Buddha attained enlightenment. **Wat Kuu Tao** has a peculiar chedi that looks like a pile of diminishing spheres.

The **Wat Suan Dawk** was built in 1383. It contains a 500-year-old bronze Buddha image and colourful Jataka murals showing scenes from the Buddha's lives. **Wat U Mong**, a forest temple outside the city to the west, also dates from Mengrai's rule and has a fine image of the fasting Buddha.

National Museum

The National Museum has a good display of Buddha images and northern Thai handicrafts. It is open from 9 am to 4 pm Wednesday to Sunday; admission is 10B.

Other Attractions

The **Tribal Research Centre** at Chiang Mai University has a small but good museum of hill tribe artefacts. Head out west from the city centre – it's two blocks north once you get to the university. **Old Chiang Mai** is a touristy 'instant hill tribes' centre. There are Thai and hill tribe dance performances here every night.

You'll often see local hill tribes people in Chiang Mai – check the **night bazaar** just off Tha Phae Rd. Chiang Mai's **jail**, in the centre of town, has a large, resident population of foreigners – most of whom were incarcerated after drug busts.

Courses

Thai Massage Study Chiang Mai has become a centre for Thai massage studies. The oldest and most popular place to study is the Old Medicine Hospital (☎ 275085) on Soi Siwaka Komarat off Wualai Rd, opposite the Old Chiang Mai Cultural Centre. The 11 day course costs around 2500B, including all teaching materials.

Other places with similar instruction include: Chaiyuth Priyasith's School of Thai Remedial Massage at 52 Soi 3, Tha Phae Rd; International Training Massage (☎ 218632) at 171/7 Morakot Rd in Santitham; and The rePlace (☎ 248838) at 1 Chetuphon Rd (next to Wat Chetuphon).

Muay Thai Lanna Muay Thai (☎ /fax (53) 273133) at 64/1 Soi Chiang Khian, off Huay Kaew Rd, is a boxing camp that offers kickboxing instruction to foreigners as well as Thais. Rates are 100B a day or 2500B a month.

Festivals

The annual dry-season **Songkran** (Water Festival) takes place, with particular fervour, in mid-April in Chiang Mai. The late-December to early-January **Winter Fair** is also a great scene, with all sorts of activities and lots of interesting visitors from the hills. The biggest festival of all is the **Flower Festival**, held during the first week of February. This festival features parades in which the various *amphoes*, or districts, throughout

THAILAND

Chiang Mai Province compete for the best flower-bedecked float and enter their most beautiful young women in the Queen of the Flower Festival contest.

Places to Stay

Guesthouses In Chiang Mai, travellers' accommodation is usually in guesthouses. There are plenty of them, ranging from 40B per person for a dorm bed to 300B for a room with private toilet and shower; most places run at 80 to 150B. Many of the guesthouses are along Moon Muang Rd and on the other side of the east moat. Others can be found along Charoenrat Rd, on the east side of the Ping River, and on Charoen Prathet Rd, on the west side of the river. The latter streets are some distance from the city centre, but convenient for the railway station and Chiang Rai buses.

TAT lists over 100 guesthouses at last count – so if you don't like one, move. During peak periods (from December to March and from July to August), it may be best to go to the TAT office first, pick up a free copy of the guesthouse list and make a few calls to find out where rooms are available. All guesthouses now have phones.

Banana Guest House (☎ 206285) at 4/9 Ratchapakhinai Rd (near Chiang Mai Gate) is a small place with dorm beds for just 40B, plus single rooms with shared facilities for 60B and doubles with private bath for 120B. *Nat Guest House* (☎ 212878) at 7 Soi 6, Phra Pokklao Rd, is a comfortable, long-established place with 24 rooms for 100/150B. *Visaj Guest House* (☎ 214016) is a new place at 104 Ratchadamnoen Rd, near Wat Phra Singh, that shows promise. Rooms with private shower and toilet cost 90B single/double, or 120B including breakfast; there's a good view of Wat Phra Singh from the rooftop.

Changmoi House (☎ 233184) on Chang Moi Kao Rd, a half block north of Tha Phae Rd, offers simple, clean rooms in a narrow shophouse for 50B a dorm bed, 60B a single, 80 to 100B a double, or 120 to 150B a triple, all except the dorm room with fan and hot shower. Also on Chang Moi Rd is the comfortable *Eagle House* (☎ 235387) at 80/

100B. The long-standing *VK Guest House*, down an alley off Chang Moi Rd near Tha Phae Rd, is quiet and friendly – it costs 60/80B for basic but clean rooms; a triple with bath costs 35B per person.

On Chaiyaphum Rd, in the same area, is the popular *Daret's House*. Rooms cost 80/100B and it's almost always full – simply because it's so visible. Further north, inside the moat along Soi 9, are a number of decent places with rooms for 80/100B with shared bath, or 150/180B with private bath: *Libra, SK House, Supreme House, SUP Court* and *Peter*.

The *Chiang Mai Youth Hostel* (☎ 272169) at 63A Bamrungburi Rd, behind Chiang Mai Gate, has single rooms with shared facilities for 80B, doubles with fan and bath for 120B (YHA card required). There is another branch on Changklan Rd with rates of 120/150B with fan and bath or 250/300B with air-con.

On Soi 4, off Tha Phae Rd further east towards the river, there are several newer, two-storey brick guesthouses with downstairs sitting areas: *Midtown House, Tapae, Thana, Sarah, Flamingo* and *Baan Jongcome* (☎ 274823), each with good rooms in the 80 to 200B range.

C&C Teak House (☎ 246966) at 39 Bamrungrat Rd, between the train station and the Ping River, has quiet, comfortable rooms in a 100-year-old teak house for 50B a single, 60/80B a single/double with fan downstairs, or 120B a double with fan upstairs.

Two pleasant places along Charoenrat Rd next to the Ping River are *Mee Guest House* at No 193/1, where doubles with bath cost 60B, and *Pun Pun* (☎ 243362) at No 321, where fan rooms are 130B and upgraded air-con rooms 250B. There are lots of others tucked away throughout Chiang Mai.

Hotels There are plenty of hotels, in all price ranges. In Chiang Mai's small Chinatown, the basic *Sri Ratchawongse* (☎ 235864) at 103 Ratchawong Rd, between the east moat and the Ping River, has singles/doubles with fan and bath for 120/180B. Nearby at 94-98 Ratchawong Rd is the nicer *New Mitrapap*

(☎ 235436), where rooms are 130 to 200B. Both hotels are close to several good, inexpensive Chinese restaurants, as well as the Warorot Market.

The funky *Muang Thong* (☎ 278438) at 5 Ratchamankha Rd costs 100/150B, and the *Nakhorn Ping* (☎ 23 6024), 43 Taiwang Rd between the east moat and the river, costs 120 to 170B.

Moon Muang Golden Court (☎ 212779), off the street at 95/1 Moon Muang, is good value for 150B with fan and hot shower.

The *Roong Ruang Hotel* (☎ 232017/18) at 398 Tha Phae Rd, near the east side of the moat, has a good location and clean, spacious rooms at 270B with fan and private bath.

Places to Eat

Thai South of Tha Phrae Rd, on the moat, the big, open-air *Aroon Rai* specialises in northern Thai food and is a great place to try sticky rice and other northern specialities. Get a group together in order to try the maximum number of dishes – some of them are *very* hot and spicy. Nearby on Chaiyaphum Rd, just up from Tha Phae Gate, the *Thanam Restaurant* is smaller but even better for local food. It's very clean and no alcohol is served.

The highly regarded *Si Phen* (no English sign) at 103 Intharawarorot Rd, near Wat Phra Singh, specialises in both northern and north-eastern style dishes.

The *Riverside Bar & Restaurant* on Charoenrat Rd, on the banks of the Ping River, features home-style Thai cooking and country/folk music. On weekend nights it's quite the scene.

Chiang Mai is famed for its fine noodles. Khâo sòi, a concoction of spicy curried chicken with flat wheat noodles, is the true Chiang Mai speciality. The oldest area for khâo sòi is the Jiin Haw (Yunnanese Muslim) area around the Ban Haw Mosque on Soi 1, Charoen Prathet Rd, not far from the Night Bazaar. Yunnanese-run *Khao Soi Fuang Fah* and *Khao Soi Islam*, both on this soi, serve khâo sòi for 20 to 25B as well as Muslim curries and Thai-style biriyani. Most khâo sòi places are open from around 10 am till 3 or 4 pm, although Khao Soi Islam and Khao Soi Fuang Fah are open 5 am to 5 pm.

Galare Food Centre, opposite the main Night Bazaar building on Chang Khlan Rd, is a large and very good outdoor food centre; free Thai classical dancing is featured on some evenings.

Western Along either side of the east moat near Tha Phae Gate there are a number of places that pack in the travellers attracted to western food and fruit drinks. The long-running *Daret's House* does some great drinks and westernised Thai food, but service can be slow when it's crowded.

The *American Restaurant & Bar* on Tha Phae Rd near the Roong Ruang Hotel specialises in pizza, burgers, deli sandwiches, breakfast and Tex-Mex. *Firenze Pizzeria Steak House* next door does good pizzas, pastas, steak, fruit juices and espresso drinks at moderate prices.

The *JJ Bakery* under the Montri Hotel has a good menu of Thai, Chinese and western food at very reasonable prices and is air-conditioned.

The friendly *Dara Steak Shop*, next to Queen Bee Car Rental, at the corner of Moon Muang and Ratchamankha Rds, has a very good and reasonably priced Thai and western menu.

The slightly more expensive *Crusty Loaf Bakery & Irish Pub* (the main sign merely reads 'Irish Pub') on Ratwithi Rd offers baked goods, good coffee, yoghurt, muesli, sandwiches, pasta, vegetarian dishes, baked potatoes, ice cream, some Thai food, beer on tap, fruit and vegetable juices and a two-for-one paperback swap.

Chinese Chiang Mai has a small Chinatown centred on Ratchawong Rd, north of Chang Moi Kao Rd, where you'll find a whole string of Chinese rice and noodle shops. Most offer variations on Tae Jiu (Chao Zhou) or Yunnanese cooking.

Vegetarian Chiang Mai has several vegetarian places. There's a traveller-oriented vegetarian place on Moon Muang Rd called

AUM Vegetarian Restaurant. Reports are mixed on this one – we liked it but some people think the food's not so great.

The Asoke Foundation-sponsored *Chiang Mai Vegetarian Centre* (☎ 271262) operates a dirt-cheap Thai vegetarian restaurant on Om Muang Rd south of the south-west corner of the city walls; it's open Sunday through Thursday from 6 am to 2 pm only.

Markets The *Somphet Market* on Moon Muang Rd, north of the Ratwithi Rd intersection, sells cheap take-away Thai food. On the opposite side of the moat, along Chaiyaphum Rd north of Lek House, is a small but thriving *night market* where you can get everything from noodles and seafood to Yunnanese specialities. The *Warorot Market*, at the intersection of Chang Moi and Changklan Rds, is open from 6 am to 5 pm daily. Upstairs, inside the market, vendors serve excellent and very cheap Chinese rice and noodle dishes.

Entertainment

Cinema Movies with English soundtracks are frequently shown at the Vista chain of cinemas at the shopping centres of Airport Plaza (Om Muang Rd), Kad Suan Kaew (Huay Kaew Rd) and Vista Chotana Mall (Chang Pheuak Rd).

Live Music At 37 Charoenrat Rd, near the river, *The Brasserie* has become a favourite late nightspot (11.15 pm to 2 am) to listen to a talented Thai guitarist named Took play energetic versions of Pink Floyd, Hendrix, Cream, Dylan, Marley and other 1960s/70s gems.

Gay Venues Chiang Mai has several gay men's bars, including the relaxed *Coffee Boy Bar* in a 70-year-old teak house at 248 Thung Hotel Rd, not far from the Arcade bus terminal; on weekends there's a cabaret show. Other popular gay meeting places include low-key *Danny's Bar* (☎ 225171) at 161 Chang Phukha Rd Soi 4 and *Kra Jiap Bar & Restaurant* at 18/1 Wualai Rd Soi 3.

Things to Buy

There are a lot of things to attract your money in Chiang Mai, but basically it is a very commercial and touristy place. A lot of junk is churned out for the undiscerning – so buy carefully. The Chiang Mai Night Bazaar, on Chang Khlan Rd, is a great place to find almost anything, from handicrafts to cheap jeans, but you'll have to bargain hard.

Warorot Market (also locally called Kaat Luang, or 'Great Market') is the oldest market in Chiang Mai. A former royal cremation grounds, it has been a marketplace site since the reign of Chao Inthawararot (1870-97). Although quite dilapidated, it's an especially good market for Thai fabrics.

For ceramics, Thai Celadon, about six km north of Chiang Mai, turns out ceramics modelled on the Sawankhalok pottery that used to be made at Sukhothai and exported all over the region hundreds of years ago. Other ceramics can be seen close to the Old Chiang Mai Cultural Centre.

Getting There & Away

Air THAI has flights to Chiang Mai several times daily from Bangkok. The flight takes an hour and the normal fare is 1940B – a special night fare is less. There are also flights between Chiang Mai and other towns in the north, including Chiang Rai, Mae Hong Son and Nan, and to Phuket in the south. Bangkok Airways also operates three flights per week to/from Bangkok via Sukhothai for 1640B.

Orient Express Airlines (☎ 818092, 818120) is headquartered at the airport and offers several flights a week to/from Surat Thani, Hat Yai, Khon Kaen, Ubon and Udon.

Bus Regular buses from Bangkok take 10 or 11 hours to reach Chiang Mai and cost from 161 to 164B (depending on the route); aircon buses cost around 300B and take about nine to 10 hours. Lots of buses leave from the Northern bus terminal between 5.30 am and about 10 pm. A variety of more expensive tour buses also make the trip – a 'VIP' bus with 30 reclining seats is 370 to 400B.

Several travel agencies on Bangkok's Khao San Rd offer air-con bus tickets from 200B which include a free night's accommodation in Chiang Mai. Some of these trips work out OK, but others are rip-offs in which the Chiang Mai guesthouse charges bathroom and electricity fees in lieu of a room charge. The only real advantage to these trips is that they depart from Khao San Rd, saving you a trip to the Northern bus terminal. But the entire bus will be loaded with foreigners – not a very cultural experience.

If you intend to hop from town to town on your way north, Chiang Mai buses operate via Phitsanulok, Sukhothai, Uttaradit and Lampang.

Train Trains to Chiang Mai from Bangkok are rather slower than buses, although this is no problem on the overnight service if you have a sleeper. There are four express trains and three rapid trains per day. A 2nd class ticket on the express costs 281B, plus sleeper and express charges. Third class tickets are only available on the rapid trains and cost 151B. Whether travelling by bus or train, you should book in advance if possible.

Getting Around
The Airport A taxi from the airport costs 80B, or 100B for a 'limousine'. The airport is only two or three km south-west of the city centre.

Local Transport City buses operate from 6 am to 6 pm and cost 3B in town. Nos 1, 2 and 3 (yellow) cover the whole city, No 5 (red) does a loop around the moat and No 6 (red) goes around the highway loop. There are plenty of red songthaews around the city with standard fares of 5B, but drivers often try and get you to charter (50B or less).

You can rent bicycles (20 to 30B a day) or motorbikes (from 150 to 250B) to explore Chiang Mai – check with your guesthouse or one of the rental services along Moon Muang Rd near the Tha Phae Gate.

Hordes of songthaew jockeys meet incoming buses and trains at Chiang Mai – they wave signs for the various guesthouses and if the one you want pops up you can have a free ride.

AROUND CHIANG MAI
Doi Suthep
From the hill-top temple of **Wat Phra That Doi Suthep**, 16 km west of Chiang Mai, there are superb views over the city. Choose a clear day to make the hairpin-curved ascent to the temple. A long flight of steps, lined by ceramic-tailed *nagas* (dragons), leads up to the temple from the car park. Or you can take a short, steep tram ride.

The **Phu Ping Palace** is five km beyond the temple – you can wander the gardens on Friday, Saturday and Sunday. Just before the palace car park, a turn to the left will lead you to a **Hmong village**, four km away. It's very touristic since it's so close to Chiang Mai, but the opium 'museum' is worth a visit if you're in the vicinity.

Getting There & Away Minibuses to Doi Suthep leave from the west end of Huay Kaew Rd and cost 30B – downhill it's 20B. For another 5B, you can take a bicycle up with you and zoom back downhill.

Baw Sang & San Kamphaeng
The 'umbrella village' of Baw Sang is nine km east of Chiang Mai. It's a picturesque though touristy spot where the townspeople engage in just about every type of northern Thai handicraft. Beautiful paper umbrellas are hand-painted. A huge garden one is around 500B, but postage and packing can add a fair bit more. Attractive framed leaf paintings are also made here. Four or five km further down Highway 1006 is San Kamphaeng, which specialises in cotton and silk weaving. Pasang, however, is probably better for cotton.

Getting There & Away Buses to Baw Sang (sometimes spelled Bo Sang or Bor Sang) leave from the north side of Charoen Muang Rd in Chiang Mai, between the river and the GPO, every 15 minutes. The fare is 5B to Baw Sang and 6B to San Kamphaeng.

Elephants
A daily 'elephants at work' show takes place near the Km 107 marker on the Fang road

north of Chiang Mai. Arrive around 9 am or earlier to see bath-time in the river. It's really just a tourist trap, but probably worth the admission price. Once the spectators have gone, the logs are all put back in place for tomorrow's show!

It's a good idea to have a picture of an elephant to show the bus conductor, or 'elephant' may be interpreted as 'Fang', the town further north. There's a northern Thailand elephant meeting in November each year – hotel and food prices go up at that time.

Elephants can also be seen at the **Young Elephant Training Centre** at Thung Kwian (Km 37) on the road from Chiang Mai to Lampang. This place is set up for tourists and has seats and even toilets, but nobody seems to know about it. When the trainer feels like it, sometime between 8 am and noon, the show begins and you'll see the elephants put through their paces. The elephants appreciate a few pieces of fruit – 'it feels like feeding a vacuum cleaner with a wet nozzle,' reported one visitor. Any bus on the main road south-east will take you to Lampang.

Doi Inthanon

Thailand's highest peak, Doi Inthanon (2595 metres), can be visited as a day trip from Chiang Mai. There are some impressive waterfalls and pleasant picnic spots here. Between Chiang Mai and Doi Inthanon, the small town of Chom Thong has a fine Burmese-style temple, **Wat Phra That Si Chom Thong**.

Getting There & Away Buses run regularly from Chiang Mai to Chom Thong for 15B. From there, you take a songthaew the few km to Mae Klang for about 15B and another to Doi Inthanon for 35B.

Lamphun

This town, only 26 km south of Chiang Mai, has several interesting wats. **Wat Phra That Haripunchai** has a small museum and a very old chedi, variously dated at 897, 1044 or 1157 AD. There are some other fine buildings in the compound, and the world's largest

bronze gong hangs in a reddish pavilion on the grounds. **Wat Chama Thevi**, popularly known as Wat Kukut, has an unusual chedi with 60 Buddha images set in niches. Another Haripunchai-era wat in the town, **Wat Mahawan**, is a source of highly reputable Buddhist amulets.

Places to Stay *Si Lamphun* (☎ (53) 511-1760) on the town's main street, Inthayongyot Rd, has rather grotty rooms for 80 to 140B. *Tareerat Court* (☎ (53) 560224), on Chama Thewi Rd near Wat Kukut, is a clean apartment-style place with rooms for 130 to 150B.

Getting There & Away Buses depart Chiang Mai regularly from the south side of Nawarat Bridge on Lamphun Rd. The fare is 7B. A bus on to Pasang will cost 5B.

Lampang

South-east of Chiang Mai, this town was another former home for the Emerald Buddha. The old town's fine wats include **Wat Si Rong Meuang, Wat Si Chum** and **Wat Phra Kaew Don Tao** on the bank of the Wang River north of town. In the village of Koh Kha, 20 km to the south-west, **Wat Lampang Luang** was originally constructed in the Haripunchai period and restored in the 16th century. It's an amazing temple with walls like a huge medieval castle. Getting there is a little difficult, so start out early in the day.

Places to Stay & Eat The on-again, off-again *No 4 Guest House*, a large old teak house in the pleasant residential Wang Neua area, north of the river, has basic rooms for 80/100B a single/double. Friendly *Sri Sangar (Si Sa-Nga)* (☎ (54) 217070) at 213-215 Boonyawat Rd has large rooms with fan and bathroom for 100B up. There are a number of other hotels along Boonyawat Rd, most with rooms starting at 140 to 160B.

In the vicinity of the Kim and Asia hotels along Boonyawat Rd there are several good rice and noodle shops. *Mae Hae Restaurant*, on Upparat Rd, is a diminutive, clean place with cheap and good northern Thai food.

Getting There & Away There are regular buses between Lampang and Chiang Mai (29B), Chiang Rai, Phitsanulok or Bangkok. The bus station in Lampang is some way out of town. It's 10B by songthaew, more if you arrive late at night. To book an air-con bus from Lampang to Bangkok or Chiang Mai there is no need to go to the bus station as the tour bus companies have offices in town along Boonyawat Rd near the roundabout.

Pasang
Only a short songthaew ride south of Lamphun, Pasang is a centre for cotton-weaving. The Nantha Khwang shop has fine locally made cotton goods.

PHITSANULOK
This vibrant lower northern city is mainly used as a stepping stone to other places. It's on the rail line between Bangkok and Chiang Mai, and you get off here for Sukhothai. **Wat Phra Si Ratana Mahathat** (known locally as Wat Yai) is an interesting old wat, and contains one of the most revered Buddha images in Thailand, the Phra Jinnarat.

The area code for Phitsanulok is 55.

Places to Stay & Eat
The comfortable *Phitsanulok Youth Hostel* (☎ 242060) at 38 Sanam Bin Rd (take bus No 3 from the railway station) has rooms for 100/140/210B a single/double/triple; dorm beds are 40B. A Hostelling International membership is mandatory (temporary one-night memberships are 50B; annual membership is 300B). The hostel has a modest restaurant and there are several cheap eateries in the vicinity. At 11/12 Ekathotsarot Rd, the *Green House* offers simple comfort and a casual atmosphere for 80B single, or 100 to 120B for a double with shared bath.

If you come straight out of the railway station and turn left by the expensive *Amarin Nakhon Hotel*, on the corner of the first and second right turns you'll find some cheaper hotels. The recently renovated *Unachak* on Phayalithai Rd has decent rooms for 150B. Further towards the river on Phayalithai Rd, the run-down *Chanprasert* has plain fan rooms for 90 to 120B. Better value than either of these are the 150/200B rooms at the clean and friendly *Siam Hotel* (☎ 258844) at 4/8 Athitayawong Rd, a half block from the river and main post office.

At any of the *flying vegetable* restaurants in town, cooks fling fried morning glory vine through the air from the wok to a plate held by a waiter who has climbed onto the shoulders of two colleagues (or onto a truck in the night market)! *Floating restaurants* along the river are also popular.

Getting There & Away
Buses for Sukhothai go from the town centre, but the stations for buses to the east or north are on the other (east) side of the railway tracks, on the outskirts of town. From Chiang Mai or Bangkok, you can reach Phitsanulok by bus or rail. Buses from Bangkok cost 96B, or 163B with air-con. You can also fly here with THAI from Bangkok, Chiang Mai, Lampang, Mae Sot or Nan.

Getting Around
City buses run between the town centre and the airport or bus station for 3B. Samlor rides within the town centre should cost 20 to 30B per person.

SUKHOTHAI
Although Sukhothai was Thailand's first capital it only lasted a little over 100 years from its foundation, in 1257, before being superseded by Ayuthaya, in 1379. But if its period of glory was short, its achievements in art, literature, language and law, apart from the more visible evidence of great buildings, were enormous. In general, the ruins visible today at Sukhothai and other cities of the kingdom, like Kamphaeng Phet and Si Satchanalai, are more appealing than Ayuthaya because they are less urbanised and more off the beaten track.

Orientation & Information
Old Sukhothai, known as Meuang Kao, is spread over quite an area. New Sukhothai is 12 km from the old town and has a good market, but otherwise it's an uninteresting

THAILAND

place. Sukhothai is 55 km east of the Bangkok to Chiang Mai road from Tak. A map, available at the old town entrance, is essential for exploring the scattered ruins. The ruins are divided into five zones and there is a 20B admission fee into each. Bicycles can be hired to get around.

The area code for Sukhothai is 55.

Ramkhamhaeng National Museum
This museum provides an introduction to Sukhothai history and culture, and is a good place to begin your explorations. They also sell guides to the ruins here. It's open daily from 9 am to 4 pm and admission is 10B.

Wat Mahathat
This vast assemblage, the largest in the city, once contained 198 chedis – apart from various chapels and sanctuaries. Some of the original Buddha images remain, including a big one among the broken columns. A large ornamented pond gives fine reflections.

Wat Si Chum
A massive seated Buddha figure is tightly squeezed into this open, walled building. A narrow tunnel inside the wall leads to views over the Buddha's shoulders and on to the top. Candle-clutching kids used to guide you up and point out the 'Buddha foot' on the way, but the tunnel has been closed to visitors in recent years.

Other Attractions
The **Wat Si Sawai** has three prangs and a moat and was originally intended as a Hindu temple. It's just south of Wat Mahathat. **Wat Sa Si** is a classically simple Sukhothai-style wat set on an island. **Wat Trapang Thong**, next to the museum, is reached by the footbridge crossing the large lotus-filled pond which surrounds it. It is still in use. Somewhat isolated to the north of the city, **Wat Phra Pai Luang** is similar in style to Wat Si Sawai. **Wat Chang Lom** is to the east; the chedi is surrounded by 36 elephants. **Wat**

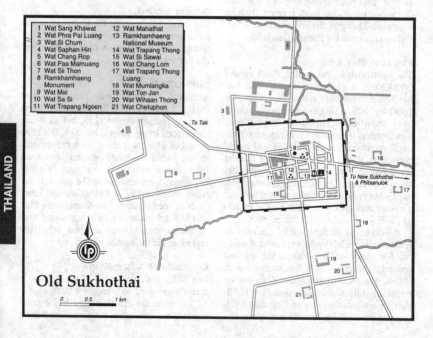

1	Wat Sang Khawat	12	Wat Mahathat
2	Wat Phra Pai Luang	13	Ramkhamhaeng
3	Wat Si Chum		National Museum
4	Wat Saphan Hin	14	Wat Trapang Thong
5	Wat Chang Rop	15	Wat Si Sawai
6	Wat Paa Mamuang	16	Wat Chang Lom
7	Wat Sii Thon	17	Wat Trapang Thong
8	Ramkhamhaeng		Luang
	Monument	18	Wat Mumlangka
9	Wat Mai	19	Wat Ton Jan
10	Wat Sa Si	20	Wat Wihaan Thong
11	Wat Trapang Ngoen	21	Wat Chetuphon

To Tak

To New Sukhothai & Phitsanulok

Old Sukhothai

0   0.5   1 km

Saphan Hin is a couple of km west of the old city walls on a hillside and features a large standing Buddha looking back to Sukhothai.

Places to Stay
New Sukhothai is a dull town, although there are some decent hotels and restaurants.

Guesthouses Guesthouses include the *Anasukho Guest House* (☎ 611315) in a large house at 234/6 Charot Withithong Rd, Soi Panitsan, near the Rajthanee Hotel. Dorm beds are 40B and single/double rooms cost 50/80B.

Yupa House (☎ 612578) is near the west bank of the Yom River at 44/10 Prawet Nakhon Rd, Soi Mekhapatthana. The family that runs Yupa are friendly and often invite guests to share meals. They have 30B dorm beds, plus rooms of various sizes from 60 to 100B. The nearby *Somprasong Guest House* and *Ban Thai* are similarly priced.

Lotus Village (☎ 621484; fax 621463) at 170 Ratchathani Rd, on the east bank of the Yom River, is set in spacious grounds with a garden sitting area, and is suitable for long-term stays. Some rooms are in teak houses on stilts over a lotus pond in back. Rates are 100 to 150B per person, depending on room size.

Hotels Near the town centre, the *Sukhothai Hotel* (☎ 611133) at 5/5 Singhawat Rd has a sign in English, Thai and Chinese. The rooms are in the 150 to 180B range (more expensive with air-con).

Other places include the *Sawaddiphong* (☎ 611567) at 56/2 Singhawat Rd, which has rooms from 180 to 250B and isn't bad. The traveller-oriented *Chinnawat Hotel* at 1-3 Nikhorn Kasem Rd has large single rooms with a double bed, ceiling fan and bathroom for 80 to 150B.

Places to Eat
Both the *night market* and the *municipal market* near the town centre are good and cheap places to eat. The *Chinnawat Hotel* restaurant isn't bad. *Fah Fah (F&F) Fast Food* (no English sign) on Charot Withithong Rd, beyond the Rajthanee Hotel, is a two-storey air-con restaurant attached to a department store; it has an extensive menu of Thai, Chinese and western foods.

Getting There & Away
Air Bangkok Airways recently began operating flights from Bangkok three times a week; the fare is 1100B and the flight takes an hour and 10 minutes.

Bus Air-con buses to Sukhothai from Chiang Mai cost 125B, and from Bangkok are 102B without air-con or 142B with. Most services go via Phitsanulok. From Phitsanulok, buses to Sukhothai depart regularly and cost 16B; the trip takes about an hour. Phitsanulok is also the nearest point on the Bangkok to Chiang Mai railway line. Alternatively, you can approach Sukhothai from Tak – the fare is 23B. Buses to Chiang Rai now go by a more direct route and take about six hours.

Buses to Sawankhalok and Si Satchanalai (20B) leave regularly from the intersection across from the Sukhothai Hotel.

Getting Around
It's 5B for a songthaew or bus between the new town and the ruins. They leave from across the bridge and along a bit on the left-hand side, a fair distance from where other buses depart in the hotel and shopping area.

In old Sukhothai, you can hire bicycles from opposite the museum. They cost 20B a day and tend to be brakeless and shaky but they're OK for the tracks between the ruins. Alternatively, the park operates a tram service through the old city for 20B per person.

AROUND SUKHOTHAI
Si Satchanalai – Chaliang Historical Park
More isolated and less touristic than the Sukhothai ruins, these stand 56 km to the north of new Sukhothai. Climb to the top of the hill supporting **Wat Khao Phanom Phloeng** for a view over the town and river. **Wat Chedi Jet Thaew** has a group of stupas

in classic Sukhothai style. **Wat Chang Lom** has a chedi surrounded by Buddha statues in niches and guarded by the fine remains of elephant buttresses. Walk along the riverside for two km or go back down the main road and cross the river to **Wat Phra Si Ratana Mahathat**, a very impressive temple with a well-preserved prang and a variety of seated and standing Buddhas. There's a separate 10B admission for this wat.

Sawankhalok Pottery Sukhothai was famous for its beautiful pottery, much of which was exported. The Indonesians were once keen collectors and fine specimens can be seen in the National Museum in Jakarta. Much of the pottery was made in Si Satchanalai. Rejects – buried in the fields – are still being found. Several of the old kilns have been carefully excavated and can be viewed along with original pottery samples at the **Si Satch-analai Centre for Study & Preservation of Sangkalok Kilns**.

Places to Stay In Sawankhalok, the *Muang In* (☎ (55) 642622) at 21 Kasemrat Rd has rooms from 160B. The more centrally located *Sangsin Hotel* (☎ (55) 641259) at 2 Thetsaban Damri 3 Rd (the main street through town) has clean, comfortable rooms with fan for 180B. There are some newer, more expensive *bungalows* next to the Si Satch ruins – it's not really worth staying there overnight but it's not a bad place for food and drink.

Getting There & Away Take a bus to Sawan-khalok and then change to a Si Satchanalai bus. The ruins are 11 km before the new town – tell the bus conductor '*muang kao*' (old city) and look for a big corn cob-shaped prang. The river is less than a km off the road and there is now a suspension bridge across it. The last bus back leaves at around 4 pm.

KAMPHAENG PHET

This town is only a couple of km off the road from Bangkok to Chiang Mai. There are a number of temple ruins within the old city

and the very fine remains of the long city wall. Outside the wall is **Wat Phra Si Ariyabot**, which has the shattered remains of standing, sitting, walking and reclining Buddha images. **Wat Chang Rop**, or 'temple surrounded by elephants', is just that – a temple with an elephant-buttressed wall.

Kamphaeng Phet National Museum, across the road from these temples, displays artefacts from the Kamphaeng Phet area, including terracotta ornamentation from ruined temples and Buddha images in the Sukhothai and Ayuthaya styles. The museum is open Wednesday to Sunday from 8.30 am to 4 pm. Admission is 10B.

The area code for Kamphaeng Phet is 55.

Places to Stay & Eat

It can be a little difficult to find places here since few signs are in English. *The Guest House* (☎ 712295) at Soi 2, Thesa Rd opposite the police station, is a new guesthouse run by a Thai-farang couple with dorm beds for 80B and rooms for 120 to 250B; services include a restaurant, bike rental and book swap.

At 114 Ratchadamnoen Rd, the *Ratcha-damnoen Hotel*, in the newer part of the city, has adequate rooms for 120/140B as well as more expensive air-con ones. Better value, if you can afford the extra baht, is the *Gor Choke Chai (Kaw Chokchai) Hotel* (☎ 711247) at 7-31 Ratchadamnoen Rd (Soi 6) – fan-cooled rooms cost 170 to 190B.

A small *night market* sets up every evening in front of the provincial offices, near the old city walls, and there are some cheap restaurants near the roundabout.

Getting There & Away

The bus fare from Bangkok is 87B, or 157B with air-con. Most visitors come here from Sukhothai (25B), Phitsanulok (35B) or Tak (20B).

TAK

This is just a junction town from Sukhothai on the way north to Chiang Mai or west to Mae Sot. It's pronounced 'Tahk' not 'Tack'.

The southern section of the city harbours a few old teak homes.

Information

TAT (☎ 514-4341) has an office in a beautiful new building at 193 Taksin Rd, where you can pick up info hand-outs and hotel brochures.

The area code for Tak is 55.

Places to Stay & Eat

If you have to stay here, then try the *Tak* (☎ 514422) at 18/10 Mahat Thai Bamrung Rd. It's off the road down a long alley; rooms with fan and shower cost 155 to 220B. The *Mae Ping* (☎ 511807) is very similar but a little more worn; large rooms with fan and bath are an economical 70 to 100B, air-con 250B.

MAE SOT

This outpost sits on Thailand's border facing the Burmese town of Myawaddy and is a big centre for smuggling between the two countries. The area used to be a hotbed of Communist guerrilla activity in the 1960s and 70s, but is now merely a relay point for the highly profitable trade in guns, narcotics, teak and gems. The local population is an interesting mixture of Thais, Chinese, Indians, Burmese and Karen tribespeople.

Songthaews can take you right to the Moei River border from Mae Sot for 7B. If the border is open you may be permitted to cross the footbridge to Myawaddy for the day. The Pan-Asian Highway (Asia Route 1) continues from here all the way to Istanbul – if only you were allowed to follow it.

Highway 1085 runs north from Mae Sot to Mae Hong Son, Province and makes an interesting trip.

The area code for Mae Sot is 55.

Places to Stay & Eat

At the east end of town towards the river, the *Mae Sot Guest House* at 736 Intharakhiri Rd has single/double rooms with shared bath for 100B. They also hand out helpful area maps. The *No 4 Guest House*, a large house well off the road at 736 Intharakhiri Rd, charges 30B for a dorm bed, 60B for a room with shared bath.

Close to the main market in the south part of town, the new *West Frontier Guest House* (☎ 532638) at 18/2 Bua Khun Rd, near Pha-Waw Hospital, has six rooms in a two storey brick and wood house for 70 to 100B per person, with a 20B discount when two people share a room. There are also several hotels in town, the cheapest of which is the *Suwannavit Hotel* (☎ 531162) on Soi Wat Luang. OK rooms with bath cost 80B in the old wing and 100B in the new building.

There is a good *food centre* next door to the Siam Hotel. The *market* also has good take away food, and opposite the mosque are several interesting *Burmese food stalls*. There are also several OK *food vendors* at the Mae Moei border market.

Getting There & Away

Air THAI flies to Mae Sot from Bangkok (1865B) four times a week via Phitsanulok (495B) and Chiang Mai (590B).

Bus Air-con minibuses (28B) and share taxis (50B) to Mae Sot leave hourly, 6 am until 6 pm, from the Tak bus station. The trip takes 1½ hours. There is a daily 1st class air-con bus to Mae Sot from Bangkok's Northern bus terminal that leaves at 10.15 pm for 224B; 2nd class air-con buses cost 174B.

MAE HONG SON

North-west of Chiang Mai – 368 km away by road and close to the Burmese border – Mae Hong Son is a crossroads for Burmese visitors, opium traders, local hill tribes and tourists seeking out the 'high north'. There are several Shan-built wats in the area and a fine view from the hill by the town. It's a peaceful little place that's also a travellers' centre. Treks booked out of this town are generally less expensive than out of Chiang Mai or Chiang Rai.

Information

Tourist brochures and maps can be picked up at the tourist police office (☎ 611812) on Singhanat Bamrung Rd. Open 24 hours, this

THAILAND

is also the place to report mishaps such as theft or to lodge complaints.

The area code for Mae Hong Son is 53.

Places to Stay

All the hotels are on the two main streets, Khunlum Praphat and Singhanat Bamrung Rds. *Siam* (☎ 611148) and *Methi (Mae Tee)* (☎ 611121), both on Khunlum Praphat Rd, are rather dismal at 150B for a room with fan and bath, 300 to 350B for air-con.

The plethora of inexpensive guesthouses scattered around town are better value. About a km north-west of town is the new location of the long-running *Mae Hong Son Guest House*, along with *Sang Tong Huts*, *Paradise* and *Khon Thai*. Mae Hong Son Guest House is the best deal, 60 to 100B for a room without bath, 200B for a bungalow with private bath.

In the Jong Kham Lake area there are several very pleasant guesthouses, including *Jong Kham*, *Holiday House* and *Johnnie House*. All are friendly little places with rates starting at 50 to 80B.

Places to Eat

Many guesthouses cook western-style meals and also offer northern Thai food. *Paa Dim* on Khunlum Praphat Rd is a warehouse-like restaurant with dishes from every region in Thailand; it's popular with Thai and farang alike because of its reasonable prices and good-sized portions. *Lucky Bakery Kitchen*, west of Khunlum Praphat Rd on Singhanat Bamrung Rd, does 'cowboy steak' and baked goods.

Getting There & Away

Air There are daily flights between Mae Hong Son and Chiang Mai for 345B.

Bus By bus, it's nine hours from Chiang Mai to Mae Hong Son via Mae Sariang. There are about five departures a day along two different routes: the northern, through Pai (90B ordinary, 175B air-con, 7 to 8 hours), and the southern, through Mae Sariang (115B ordinary, 205B air-con, 8 to 9 hours). The southern route is more comfortable. Although the

Pai route is slow and windy, recent road improvements mean the trip can take as little as seven hours (don't count on it to be on time, however). The scenery is quite spectacular in parts and you can break the trip by staying overnight in Pai.

PAI

This little town between Chiang Mai and Mae Hong Son is a mildly interesting, somewhat remote kind of place. It is a good base for exploring the surrounding country and especially for doing self-guided treks. For a view of the town, climb the hill to nearby **Wat Phra That Mae Yen**.

Places to Stay & Eat

Guesthouses line the two main streets in Pai. Across from the bus terminal is the *Duang Guest House*, where clean rooms with shared hot-water shower cost 40 to 50B a single and 80 to 100B a double.

On the main road through town are *Charlie's House* and *Nunya's*, with rooms from 50B single with shared bath to 200B double in a bungalow with private bath.

Spacious rooms are available at the *Wiang Pai Hotel*, a traditional wooden hotel with rooms from 50 to 100B.

There are several bungalow operations along the Pai River east of town, including the *Riverside*, *Pai River Lodge* and *Pai Guest House*, all with accommodation in the 50 to 80B range.

Peter & Vandee Hut, near the village of Mae Yen, about two km from the bridge over the Pai River (the turn-off is only 1.2 km from the bridge), offers 15 simple thatched huts spread over a slight slope for 30B single, 50B double.

Most of the eating places in Pai line the main north-south and east-west roads. Many serve farang food, like felafel, hummus and tacos. The *Thai Yai* does a good farang breakfast, plus a few Thai and Shan dishes. For authentic local food, try the *Muslim Restaurant* for noodle and rice dishes, or the *Khun Nu*, which has a variety of Thai dishes.

Getting There & Away

The Chiang Mai to Pai road is now completely paved. It takes just four hours to travel between the towns – the bus fare is 50B.

FANG & THA TON

Fang was founded by King Mengrai in 1268 but there is little of interest today apart from the earth ramparts of his old city. Tha Ton is, however, a good base for hill tribe visits or for the downriver ride to Chiang Rai. It's 152 km north of Chiang Mai and there are some points of interest along the way, apart from the elephant camp mentioned in the Around Chiang Mai section. It's probably better not to stay in Fang itself but at Tha Ton, from where the boats run to Chiang Rai.

Places to Stay

Fang If you must stay in Fang, then the *Fang Hotel* has rooms from 90B. Alternatives are the friendly *Wiang Kaew Hotel*, behind the Fang Hotel, and the *Ueng Khum (Euang Kham) Hotel* around the corner on Thaw Phae Rd; both have rooms in the 110 to 180B range.

Tha Ton *Thip's Travellers Guest House* continues to get good reports and costs 50/80B for singles/doubles with shared bath, 80/100B with private shower. Further on the road nearest the pier, the *Chan Kasem Guest House* has rooms from 60B.

Lou-Ta, about 15 km to the north-east, is the nearest Lisu village to Tha Ton. *Asa's Guest Home* offers two basic bamboo-walled rooms for 150B per person per night, including two meals. The friendly family who own the house can arrange one and two-day jungle trips in the area. To get there take a yellow songthaew from Tha Ton for 10B (or motorcycle taxi for 20B) and ask to be let off in Lou-Ta.

Getting There & Away

It takes three hours from Chiang Mai to Fang by bus and the fare is 43B – buses go from the new bus station north of White Elephant (Chang Phuak) Gate. It's 11B, 40 minutes from Fang to Tha Ton.

AROUND FANG & THA TON

Trekking & Rafting

There are pleasant walks along the river near Tha Ton. Treks and raft trips can be arranged through Thip's Travellers Guest House or Mae Kok River Lodge. Thip's arranges economical bamboo house-rafts with pilot and cook for three days for 1200B per person (four person minimum), including all meals, lodging and rafting. The first two days are spent visiting villages and hot springs near the river, and on the third day you dock in Chiang Rai.

You could also pull together a small group of travellers and arrange your own house-raft with a guide and cook for a two or three day journey downriver, stopping off in villages of your own choosing along the way. A house-raft generally costs around 350 to 400B per person per day, including all meals, and takes up to six people – so figure on 1000 to 1200B for a three day trip with stops at Shan, Lisu and Karen villages along the way.

River Trip to Chiang Rai

The downriver trip from Tha Ton to Chiang Rai is a bit of a tourist trap these days – the villages along the way sell Coke and there are lots of TV aerials. But it's still fun. The open, long-tail boat departs Tha Ton at around 12.30 pm. To catch it straight from Chiang Mai, you must leave at 7 or 7.30 am at the latest and make no stops on the way, or take the 6 am bus. The fare on the boat is an expensive 160B and the trip takes about three to five hours. The length of the trip depends on the height of the river.

You get an armed guard on the boat, but he seems to spend most of the time asleep with his machine gun in a plastic sack. The trip finishes just in time to catch a bus back to Chiang Mai, so it can really be a day trip from Chiang Mai. It's better to stay in Tha Ton, however, and then travel on through Chiang Rai or Chiang Saen. You may sometimes have to get off and walk. It's also possible to make the trip (much more slowly) upriver, despite the rapids.

These days, some travellers are getting off the boat in **Mae Salak**, a large Lahu village about a third of the way to Chiang Rai from Tha Ton. From here, it is possible to trek to dozens of tribal villages south in the Wawi area. The fare as far as Mae Salak is 50B.

Other Attractions

The **Chiang Dao Caves**, filled with old Buddha images and bizarre cave formations, are five km off the road and 72 km north of Chiang Mai. The **Mae Sa Cascades** are seven km off the road from Mae Rim, a further 13 km north.

CHIANG RAI

Although this town was once the home of the Emerald Buddha, it's of no intrinsic interest – just a stepping stone for other places like Tha Ton, Chiang Saen and Mae Sai. However, it is an alternative starting point for hill tribe treks. Chiang Rai is 105 km north of Chiang Mai.

The area code for Chiang Rai is 53.

Places to Stay

Chat House (☎ 711481) near the Kok River pier at 1 Trairat Rd has rooms with shared hot-water shower for 50 to 80B, dorm beds for 40B and rooms with private hot-water shower for 100 to 150B.

Also near the Kok River boat pier (for boats from Tha Ton), at 445 Singhakai Rd, is the *Mae Kok Villa*, which has dorm accommodation for 40B and single/double rooms with fan and hot water for 120/150B.

North of here are a couple of places on a large island separated from the city by a Kok River tributary. *Chian House* (☎ 713388) at 172 Si Bunruang Rd has simple but nicely done rooms from 80/100B with hot shower, 100 to 200B for bungalows with hot shower. Also on the island is *Pintamorn Guest House* (☎ 713317, 714161), where comfortable singles/ doubles are 80/120B with hot water. There are also doubles with air-con in a separate house for 150/250B and a few cheaper rooms with shared facilities for 50/80B and 70/100B, plus a dorm that costs just 10B per bed.

The *Boonbundan Guest House* (☎ 712914) is in a walled compound in the southern part

of town at 1005/13 Jetyot Rd. Here there's a choice of accommodation to suit virtually every budget: in small rooms off the garden, in huts or in a new air-con building overlooking the garden. They range from 60B for small cubicles to 350B for large air-con rooms. The *New Boonyoung* at 1054/5 Sanam Bin Rd has a similar arrangement, minus the new building.

Near the clock tower and district government buildings on Suksathit Rd, the *Chiengrai Hotel* has rooms from 140B. Around the corner from the Chiang Rai Hotel, at 424/1 Banphraprakan Rd, the *Suknirand Hotel* costs 300B and up for air-con rooms.

The clean and efficient *Krung Thong Hotel* (☎ 711033; fax 711848) at 412 Sanambin Rd has large one/two-bed rooms with fan and bath for 200/240B; air-con rooms cost 320B.

Places to Eat

Many restaurants are strung out along Banphraprakan and Thanarai Rds. Near the bus station there are the usual *food stalls* offering cheap and tasty food. Near the clock tower on Banphraprakan Rd are the *Phetburi* and *Ratburi* restaurants, with excellent selections of curries and other Thai dishes.

The *Bierstube*, on Phahonyothin Rd south of the Wiang Inn, has been recommended for German food. There are several other western-style pubs along here and on the street in front of the Wiang Come Hotel. *La Cantina* (☎ 716808), operated by an Italian expat and situated on a small soi called Clocktower Plaza (also Sapkaset Plaza), offers an extensive selection of pizza, pasta, Italian regional specialities and wines.

Noi is a small family-run Thai vegetarian place at the corner of Utarakit and Ngam Meuang Rds – an English sign simply reads 'Vegetarian'.

Heuan Kao (Old House), diagonally opposite the Chiengrai Hotel on Suksathit Rd, has live music nightly from 7 pm till midnight. The decor and atmosphere is 'Thai classic' (lots of B&W photos of Rama VI) and there's a reasonable Thai-Chinese menu for munchies, also good ice cream.

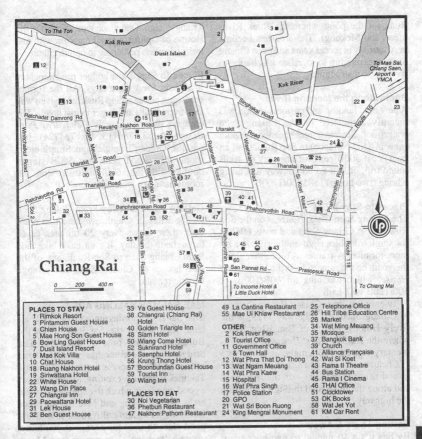

Chiang Rai

0   200   400 m

PLACES TO STAY
1   Rimkok Resort
3   Pintamorn Guest House
4   Chian House
5   Mae Hong Son Guest House
6   Bow Ling Guest House
7   Dusit Island Resort
9   Mae Kok Villa
10 Chat House
19 Ruang Nakhon Hotel
19 Siriwattana Hotel
22 White House
23 Wang Din Place
27 Chiangrai Inn
29 Paowattana Hotel
31 Lek House
32 Ben Guest House

33 Ya Guest House
38 Chiengrai (Chiang Rai) Hotel
40 Golden Triangle Inn
48 Siam Hotel
50 Wiang Come Hotel
52 Suknirand Hotel
54 Saenphu Hotel
56 Krung Thong Hotel
57 Boonbundan Guest House
59 Tourist Inn
60 Wiang Inn

PLACES TO EAT
30 Noi Vegetarian
36 Phetburi Restaurant
47 Nakhon Pathom Restaurant

49 La Cantina Restaurant
55 Mae Ui Khiaw Restaurant

OTHER
2   Kok River Pier
8   Tourist Office
11 Government Office & Town Hall
12 Wat Phra That Doi Thong
13 Wat Ngam Meuang
14 Wat Phra Kaew
15 Hospital
16 Wat Phra Singh
17 Police Station
20 GPO
21 Wat Sri Boon Ruong
24 King Mengrai Monument

25 Telephone Office
26 Wat Ming Meuang
28 Market
34 Wat Ming Meuang
35 Mosque
37 Bangkok Bank
39 Church
41 Alliance Française
42 Wat Si Koet
43 Rama II Theatre
44 Bus Station
45 Rama I Cinema
46 THAI Office
51 Clocktower
53 DK Books
58 Wat Jet Yot
61 KM Car Rent

Getting There & Away

Air The new Chiang Rai international airport, about 10 km north of town, fields daily flights from Bangkok for 1855B, from Chiang Mai for 420B. THAI hopes to establish routes between Chiang Rai and other Asian capitals – possibly Luang Prabang (Laos) and Kunming (China) – over the next few years.

Bus Buses between Chiang Mai and Chiang Rai are 57B (regular), 79B (air-con) or 102B (with air-con and video). Be sure to get the *sãi mài* (new route) buses, which take only

four hours – by the old road (via Lampang) the trip takes seven hours.

CHIANG SAEN

Only 61 km north of Chiang Rai, this interesting little town on the banks of the Mekong River has numerous ruins of temples, chedis, city walls and other remains from the Chiang Saen period. There is also a small national museum.

Laos is across the river from Chiang Saen and the official apex of the Golden Triangle – where the borders of Myanmar, Laos and Thailand all meet – is further north at Sop

Ruak (at the point where the Ruak River meets the Mekong). The area has become very touristy in recent years and even Chiang Saen is beginning to sacrifice its charms to riverside construction.

Boats along the Mekong River

A new boat landing and customs station was recently completed on the Chiang Saen waterfront. Six-passenger speedboats *(reua raew* in Thai parlance) to Sop Ruak (half an hour) cost 300B per boat one way or 400B round trip, or will go all the way to Chiang Khong (two hours) for 1200/1700B.

Places to Stay & Eat

The *Chiang Saen Guest House* is on the Sop Ruak Rd in Chiang Saen and costs 60/70B for singles/doubles right on the river – a bit more for nicer A-frames. A bit further along this road, on the same side, is the *Siam Guest House*, which has huts for 60B/100B, or 100/120B with bath.

Twenty km from Chiang Rai on the way to Chiang Saen, via Highway 1129, is the lively Hmong village of Ban Khiu Khan, where the *Hmong Guest House* offers rudimentary huts for 70B a night.

Cheap noodle and rice dishes are available in and near the *market* – on the river road and along the main road through town from the highway.

Getting There & Away

By bus it's a 40 minute to two hour (very variable!) trip from Chiang Rai to Chiang Saen for 17B. Returning to Chiang Mai from Chiang Saen is faster (4½ hours versus nine) if you don't take the direct Chiang Mai bus. Instead, go back to Chiang Rai first and take a Chiang Mai bus from there. The Chiang Saen to Chiang Mai buses take a roundabout route over poor roads.

AROUND CHIANG SAEN
Sop Ruak

Nowadays Sop Ruak, nine km north of Chiang Saen, is besieged daily by busloads of package tourists who want their pictures taken in front of the 'Welcome to the Golden

Triangle' sign. One place worth a visit is the **House of Opium**, a small museum with historical displays pertaining to opium culture.

Places to Stay Most budget travellers stay in Chiang Saen these days. All the former shoestring places in Sop Ruak have given way to souvenir stalls and larger tourist hotels. The cheapest place to stay is *Debavalya Park Resort* (☎ (53) 784113; fax 784224), just past the 'Golden Triangle' sign. Simple clean rooms with good beds cost 500B single/double with fan, 600B with air-con; all rooms have hot-water showers.

Getting There & Away From Chiang Saen to Sop Ruak, a songthaew/share taxi costs 10B; these leave every 20 minutes or so throughout the day. It's an easy bike ride from Chiang Saen to Sop Ruak; any of the guesthouses in Chiang Saen can arrange bicycle rentals.

MAE SAI-MAE SALONG AREA

Mae Sai is the northernmost point in Thailand, right across the Sai River from the Burmese trading post of Takhilek. The bridge over the river has recently been opened to foreigners for day trips. Although Takhilek is not very exciting, Mae Sai makes a good base from which to explore mountain areas like Doi Tung and Mae Salong, once infamous for opium cultivation. It is also a good place to shop for gems – if you know what you're doing – lacquerware from Myanmar, and other crafts.

Cross-Border Trips to Takhilek & Kyaingtong

Foreigners may cross the Sai River into Takhilek (spelt Tachilek in Myanmar) upon payment of a US$10 fee and the deposit of their passports at the immigration post on the Thai side. Besides shopping for Shan and Burmese handicrafts (which are about the same price as on the Thai side) and eating Shan/Burmese food, there's little to do on the other side.

Three-night/four-day excursions 163 km north to the town of Kyaingtong (usually spelt Chiang Tung by the Thais) may be arranged through any guesthouse or travel agency in Mae Sai. You can do it on your own by paying US$18 for a three night permit at the border, plus a mandatory exchange of US$100 for Myanmar's Foreign Exchange Certificates (FECs). These FECs can be spent on hotel rooms or exchanged on the black market for real kyat (the Burmese currency – see the Myanmar chapter for details on the money system).

Kyaingtong is a sleepy but historic capital of the Shan State's Khün culture – the Khün speak a northern Thai language related to Shan and Thai Lü, and call their town 'Kengtung'. It's a bit more than half-way between the Thai and Chinese borders – eventually the road will be open all the way to China but for now Kyaingtong is the limit. Travel westward to Taunggyi, capital of the Shan State, is also off limits.

There's even less to do in Kyaingtong than in Takhilek, but it's a scenic town dotted with

Buddhist temples around a small lake. You can catch glimpses of small Shan, Akha, Wa and Lahu villages along the way. The *Noi Yee Hotel* costs US$10 per person per night in multi-bed rooms. *Harry's Guest House & Trekking* at 132 Mai Yang Rd, Kanaburoy Village, is operated by an English-speaking Kengtung native who spent many years as a trekking guide in Chiang Mai. His simple rooms go for US$5 per person, payable in US, Thai or Burmese currency.

As with the Takhilek day trips, you must leave your passport at the border. You can rent a jeep on either side: Thai vehicles are charged a flat rate of US$50 for vehicles with a capacity of five or fewer passengers and US$100 for vehicles with a capacity of over five; Burmese vehicle hire is more expensive and requires the use of a driver. The cheapest form of transport to Kyaingtong is on the songthaews (44B) that leave each morning from Takhilek. Whatever the form of transport, count on at least six to ten gruelling

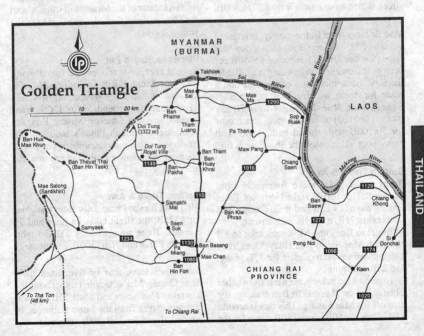

hours (depending on road conditions) to cover the 163 km stretch between Takhilek and Kyaingtong.

Places to Stay & Eat

Mae Sai Near the town entrance is the *Chad Guest House* (☎ (53) 732054), which is run by a friendly Shan family and has rooms for 100 to 150B, plus a bamboo rowhouse for 50B per person. They also have a good kitchen. The *Mae Sai Guest House* is right on the Sai River, a couple of km from the bridge. Bungalows cost from 100/120B a single/double with shared facilities, but recent reports are nearly unanimous in condemning the rude, surly staff. Much better is the nearby *Mae Sai Plaza Guest House*, with a variety of rooms from 60 to 120B. Also on the river are the *Northern Guest House* and *Sai Riverside*, with secure, comfortable rooms for 80 to 200B.

Other budget places include the *Sin Wattana* and *Mae Sai* hotels, along the main street, which have rooms from 180 to 300B.

Mae Salong Area In the mostly Yunnanese village of Mae Salong, the old wooden *Shin Sane (Sin Sae) Hotel* has rooms for 50B per person. Information on trekking is available; there is also a nice little eating area and a place for doing laundry. Next to the Shin Sane, *Akha Mae Salong Guest House* (☎ (53) 765103) offers cramped, bare rooms for 50/100B with shared bath, 150B with bath – poor value unless the Shin Sane is full.

Getting There & Away

Buses to Mae Sai leave frequently from Chiang Rai for 18B and take 1½ hours. From Chiang Saen it's 16B and from Chiang Mai a bus costs 71B, or 121B with air-con.

To get to Doi Tung Mountain, take an 8B bus from Mae Sai to Ban Huay Khrai, then a songthaew up the mountain for 35B going, and 25B returning.

To get to Mae Salong, get a bus from either Chiang Rai or Mae Sai to Ban Basang, the turn-off for Mae Salong. This bus is around 12B. Then it's 50B up and 40B down for the

hour-long songthaew trip to Mae Salong. You can also bus from Tha Ton to Mae Salong for 60B. The modern name for this town is Santikhiri.

PHRAE

Both Phrae and Nan have been neglected by tourists and travellers because of their seeming remoteness from Chiang Mai. But Phrae is easily reached from Den Chai (a town on the Bangkok-to-Chiang Mai rail line) by bus along Highway 101.

Phrae is probably most famous for producing the distinctive, indigo dyed cotton farmer's shirt seen all over Thailand. Temple architecture in Phrae is a bit unusual since you'll find both Burmese and Lao styles – see **Wat Jom Sawan** for Shan-style, and **Wat Phra Non** and **Wat Luang** for Lanna-style.

Phae Muang Phi, or Ghost Land, is a strange geological phenomenon, about 18 km north of Phrae, where erosion has created bizarre pillars of soil and rock. Phrae is also the last habitat of the Mrabri hill tribe, whom the Thais call *phii thong leuang* (spirits of the yellow leaves).

Places to Stay & Eat

Several cheaper hotels can be found along Charoen Muang Rd, including *Ho Fa*, *Siriwattana* and *Thep Wiman*, all of which have rooms for around 80 to 120B. Yantarakitkoson and Charoen Muang Rds, the main streets through Phrae's modern half, are dotted with *small restaurants*. The rustic, open-air *Malakaw* on Ratsadamnoen Rd offers good Thai food.

Getting There & Away

Air THAI flies to Phrae daily from Bangkok for 1325B; the flight takes an hour and 20 minutes. There are also daily THAI flights between Phrae and Nan (300B, 25 minutes).

Bus Buses leave four or five times daily from Chiang Mai's Arcade bus station; the trip takes four hours and costs 55B. An aircon bus leaves from the same station at 10 am and 10 pm for 76B (98B 1st class).

Train Trains to Den Chai from Bangkok are 188B in 2nd class or 90B in 3rd class, plus supplementary charges as they apply. Blue songthaews leave Den Chai frequently for Phrae and cost 20B.

NAN

Nan was a semi-autonomous kingdom until 1931 and it is still one of the least 'developed' and underpopulated provinces in Thailand. **Wat Phumin** and **Wat Phra That Chae Haeng** are two important temples in Nan. In October and November, boat races on the river feature 30-metre wooden boats with crews of up to 50 rowers. The **Nan National Museum** is one of the best curated provincial museums in the country.

It's possible to trek out of Nan to mountainous **Doi Phu Kha National Park** and adjacent Thai Lü, Htin, Khamu and Mien villages. Ask at any of the hotels or guesthouses for information.

The area code for Nan is 54.

Places to Stay

Doi Phukha Guest House (☎ 771422), 94/5 Sumonthewarat Rd (actually on a soi off Sumonthewarat), offers rooms in an old teak house for 70/900B. *Wiangtai House* (☎ 710-247) at 21/1 Soi Wat Hua Wiang Tai (off Sumonthewarat Rd near the Nara department store) has rooms in a large modern house for 120B (one large bed), 150B (two beds) and 180B (three beds).

Nan Guest House (☎ 771849) is in another large house at 57/16 Mahaphrom Rd (actually at the end of a soi off Mahaphrom Rd) near the THAI office. Singles/doubles/triples with shared bath cost 60/80/100B; for rooms with private bath, add 20B per person.

Among Nan's hotels, the least expensive is the *Amorn Si* at 97 Mahayot Rd, where very basic rooms go for 150B. *Sukkasem* at 29/31 Anantaworarittidet Rd has better rooms from 150 to 170B with fan and bath, 300B with air-con.

Places to Eat

One of the most dependable downtown restaurants is the old brick and wood *Siam Phochana* on Sumonthewarat Rd. It's a very popular spot all day long for rice and noodle dishes, open 7 am to 9 pm. *Miw Miw*, opposite the Nan Fah Hotel, is a bit cleaner than Siam Phochana and has good jók, noodles and coffee.

Getting There & Away

Buses run to Nan from Chiang Mai (83B, and 115 to 146B for air-con) and Chiang Rai (74B). The most direct way to Nan is from Den Chai via Phrae. You can also fly there from Bangkok, Chiang Mai, Phrae and Phitsanulok.

North-Eastern Thailand

The north-east is the least visited region of Thailand, although there are a number of places of interest here, and in many ways it is the most 'Thai'. The lack of tourists can be attributed to the region's proximity to Laos and Cambodia, and the history of hold-ups and Communist guerrilla actions in the 1970s and early 1980s. Nowadays it's as safe to travel in as any other part of the country.

Among north-easterners, this region is known as Isaan, from the Sanskrit name for the Mon-Khmer Isana kingdom – a pre-Angkor culture that flourished in what is now north-eastern Thailand and Cambodia. Isaan culture and language is marked by a mixture of Lao and Khmer influences.

Points of major interest in the north-east include the scenic Mekong and the many Khmer temple ruins, especially those from the Angkor period.

Getting There & Away

Railway lines operate from Bangkok to Udon Thani and Nong Khai on the Lao border, in the north-east, and to Ubon Ratchathani, near the Cambodian border, in the east. You can make an interesting loop through the north-east by travelling first to Chiang Mai and other centres in the north and then to Phitsanulok, Khon Kaen, Loei and Udon Thani. Several north-eastern cities are also accessible by air from Bangkok.

THAILAND

NAKHON RATCHASIMA (KHORAT)

Also known as Khorat, Nakhon Ratchasima is mainly thought of as a place from which to visit the Khmer ruins of Phimai and Phanom Rung, although it also has a few attractions in its own right. They include the **Mahawirawong Museum**, in the grounds of Wat Sutchinda, which has a fine collection of Khmer art objects. It's open from 9 am to noon and 1 to 4 pm Wednesday to Sunday. The **Thao Suranari Memorial** is a popular shrine to Khun Ying Mo, a heroine who led the local inhabitants against Lao invaders during the reign of Rama III.

Information

The TAT office in Nakhon Ratchasima can supply you with a map of the city and a list of hotels, restaurants and other useful information. The office is on Mittaphap Rd at the western edge of town, beyond the railway station. A tourist police contingent (☎ 213333) is attached to the TAT office.

The area code for Nakhon Ratchasima is 44.

Places to Stay

The *Doctor's House* (☎ 255846) at 78 Seup Siri Rd Soi 4 is quiet and comfortable and has four large rooms for 80 to 160B. The new

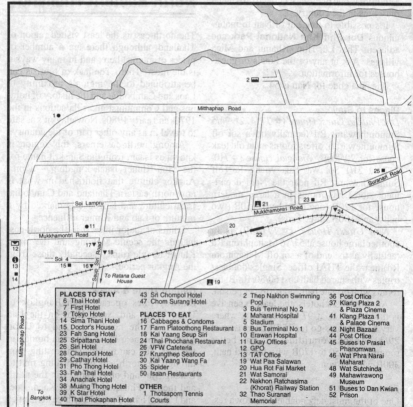

PLACES TO STAY	43 Sri Chompol Hotel	2 Thep Nakhon Swimming	36 Post Office
6 Thai Hotel	47 Chom Surang Hotel	Pool	37 Klang Plaza 2
7 First Hotel		3 Bus Terminal No 2	& Plaza Cinema
9 Tokyo Hotel	PLACES TO EAT	4 Maharat Hospital	41 Klang Plaza 1
14 Sima Thani Hotel	16 Cabbages & Condoms	5 Stadium	& Palace Cinema
15 Doctor's House	17 Farm Platoothong Restaurant	8 Bus Terminal No 1	42 Night Bazaar
23 Fah Sang Hotel	18 Kai Yaang Seup Siri	10 Erawan Hospital	44 Post Office
25 Sripattana Hotel	24 Thai Phochana Restaurant	11 Likay Offices	45 Buses to Prasat
26 Siri Hotel	26 VFW Cafeteria	12 GPO	Phanomwan
28 Chumpol Hotel	27 Krungthep Seafood	13 TAT Office	46 Wat Phra Narai
29 Cathay Hotel	30 Kai Yaang Wang Fa	19 Wat Paa Salawan	Maharat
31 Pho Thong Hotel	35 Spider	20 Hua Rot Fai Market	48 Wat Sutchinda
33 Fah Thai Hotel	50 Isaan Restaurants	21 Wat Samorai	49 Mahawirawong
34 Anachak Hotel		22 Nakhon Ratchasima	Museum
38 Muang Thong Hotel	OTHER	(Khorat) Railway Station	51 Buses to Dan Kwian
39 K Star Hotel	1 Thotsaporn Tennis	32 Thao Suranari	52 Prison
40 Thai Phokaphan Hotel	Courts	Memorial	

THAILAND

Ratana Guest House (☎ (01) 927-0354), a bit further south along Seup Siri Rd on Soi Suksan 39, offers clean rooms in a modern, two storey house for 80 to 150B.

At 68-70 Mukkhamontri Rd, near the railway station, the *Fah Sang* has OK fan rooms for 130 to 230B. The *Siri Hotel* at 167-8 Phoklang Rd is central and friendly; rooms start at 120B. The *Tokyo Hotel* on Suranari Rd has good, big singles with bath for 100B. The cheapest place on Phoklang Rd – *Chumpol Hotel* at No 701-2 – costs just 100B for a basic but clean room in a classic Thai-Chinese hotel.

Places to Eat

There are lots of good places to eat around the western gates to the town centre, near the Thao Suranari Memorial. Several inexpensive *Thai-Chinese restaurants* can also be found along Ratchadamnoen Rd in this vicinity. At night, the *Hua Rot Fai Market* on Mukkhamontri Rd and the Manat Rd *night bazaar* offer a great selection and cheap prices; both are at their best from 6 to 10 pm.

Next to the Siri Hotel, the infamous *VFW Cafeteria*, a hang-out for American ex-GIs who live in the area, has real American breakfasts plus steak, ice cream, pizza and

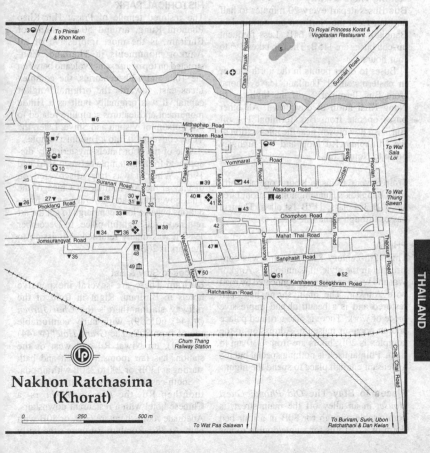

Nakhon Ratchasima (Khorat)

salads. For the best kài yâang and sômtam (Isaan-style grilled chicken and green papaya salad) in town, try *Kai Yaang Seup Siri*, near Doctor's House on Seup Siri Rd.

Things to Buy

Khorat has many shops specialising in Khorat silk. Several are found along Ratchadamnoen Rd near the Thao Suranari Shrine, including Ratri, Thusnee (Thatsani) and Today. Over on Chomphon Rd are a couple of others – Chompol and Jin Chiang.

Getting There & Away

Bus Buses depart every 20 minutes to half an hour from the Northern bus terminal in Bangkok – the fare is 64B. Less frequent air-con buses are 115B. The trip takes 3½ to four hours.

Buses to other points in the north-east or in eastern central Thailand leave Khorat from Bus Terminal 2, off the highway to Nong Khai north of downtown. All other buses operate from Bus Terminal 1 – off Burin Rd downtown, near the intersection of the Mittaphap Rd loop and the highway north to Nong Khai.

Train Several trains to Khorat operate daily from Bangkok's Hualamphong station; fares are 51B 3rd class, 117B 1st class. The trip passes through some fine scenery.

PHIMAI

This 12th century Khmer shrine was constructed in the style of Cambodia's Angkor Wat and was once directly connected by road with Angkor. The main shrine has been restored and is a beautiful and impressive piece of work. There is also a ruined palace and an open-air museum. Admission to the complex is 20B; hours are from 7.30 am to 6 pm. Phimai itself is nothing special but it's a pleasant enough place to spend the night.

Places to Stay The *Old Phimai Guest House*, in an alley off the main street, is comfortable enough for 80B in a four bed dorm or 120/150B for single/double rooms

with shared bath. Opposite is the similar *S&P New Phimai Guest House*.

Around the corner from the bus terminal, the adequate *Phimai Hotel* has rooms ranging from 120B without bath to 400B for an air-con double with bath.

Getting There & Away There are buses every half hour from Nakhon Ratchasima's main bus station, behind the Erawan Hospital on Suranari Rd. The trip takes one to 1½ hours and costs 16B.

PRASAT HIN KHAO PHANOM RUNG HISTORICAL PARK

The restored temple of Prasat Hin Khao Phanom Rung, around 50 km south of Buriram, is the most impressive of all Angkor monuments in Thailand. Constructed on top of an extinct volcano between the 10th and 13th centuries, the complex faces east, towards the original Angkor capital. It was originally built as a Hindu monument and features sculpture related to the worship of Vishnu and Shiva. Later, the Thais converted it into a Buddhist temple.

One of the door lintels mysteriously disappeared from the temple between 1961 and 1965. When it was later discovered on display at the Art Institute of Chicago, the Thai government and several private foundations began a long campaign to get the art returned to its rightful place. In December 1988 it was finally returned. Admission to the park is 20B.

Places to Stay & Eat

Buriram There are several inexpensive hotels in Buriram. Right in front of the railway station there's the *Chai Jaroen* (π (44) 601559), with fairly comfortable rooms from 80B. The *Grand Hotel* (π (44) 611089), up Niwat Rd and west of the station, has fair rooms with fan and bath starting at 130B, or 200 to 250B with air-con.

South-east of the railway station on Sunthonthep Rd, the *Prachasamakhi* is a Chinese hotel with a restaurant downstairs. Adequate rooms here are 60B, or 80B with bath. At 38/1 Romburi Rd there's the fairly nice *Thai Hotel* (☎ (44) 611112), where clean rooms start at 140B with fan and bath and go as high as 550B for a deluxe room.

A small *night market*, with good, inexpensive food, is held in the evenings in front of the railway station. At the intersection of Samattakan and Thani Rds there's a larger *night market*, with mostly Chinese – but also a few Isaan – vendors.

Nang Rong *Honey Inn* (☎ (44) 671131) at 8/1 Soi Ri Kun is run by a local schoolteacher who speaks English. Large, clean rooms cost 100/150B single/double.

Getting There & Away

Prasat Hin Khao Phanom Rung can be approached from Nakhon Ratchasima, Buriram or Surin. From Nakhon Ratchasima, take a Surin-bound bus and get out at Ban Ta-Ko, which is just a few km past Nang Rong. The fare is about 20B. From the Ta-Ko intersection, occasional songthaews go as far as the foot of Khao Phanom Rung (12 km, 15B), or you can catch any one going south to Lahan Sai. Songthaews at the foot of Khao Phanom Rung make the final leg for 5B.

If you take a Lahan Sai truck, get off at the Ban Don Nong Nae intersection (there are signs here pointing to Phanom Rung) – this leg is 3B. From Ban Don Nong Nae, you can get another songthaew to the foot of the hill for 10B, charter a pick-up for 40B one way, or hitch. A motorbike taxi all the way from Ta-Ko to Phanom Rung costs 60 to 70B. You may have to bargain hard to get these rates, as the drivers will ask for as much as 200B.

There are also a couple of morning songthaews from Buriram Market that go directly to Ban Don Nong Nae; these are met by songthaews that go straight to the ruins.

From Surin, you take a Nakhon Ratchasima-bound bus and get off at the same place on Highway 24, Ban Ta-Ko, then follow the directions above.

Buses from Nakhon Ratchasima to Buriram leave every half an hour during the day; they take about 2½ hours and the fare is 35B.

KHON KAEN

The midpoint between Nakhon Ratchasima and Udon Thani, Khon Kaen is also the gateway to the north-east from Phitsanulok. The branch of the **National Museum** here has an excellent Thai sculpture collection. Otherwise it's just one big, busy town.

The area code for Khon Kaen is 43.

Consulates

The Lao People's Democratic Republic recently opened a consulate (☎ 223698, 221961) at 123 Photisan Rd. Foreigners have successfully obtained 15-day tourist visas here in three days time for 750 to 1000B, depending on nationality. Apparently this is an experimental programme, since the Lao embassy in Bangkok does not issue such visas directly.

There is also a Vietnamese consulate (☎ 241586; fax 241154) in Khon Kaen at 65/6 Chatapadung Rd.

Places to Stay & Eat

There are plenty of hotels in Khon Kaen but not all have their names up in English. Among the least expensive places is the *Suksawat* (☎ 239611), off Klang Meuang Rd, where rooms are 70B with shared facilities, 90 to 140B with fan and bath. At the *Si Mongkon Hotel*, No 61-67 Klang Muang Rd, grungy rooms cost 90B with fan, 400B with air-con. The *Saen Samran Hotel* at 55-59 Klang Muang Rd costs 160 to 200B with fan, 250B with air-con

Khon Kaen has a lively *night market*, with plenty of good food stalls, next to the air-con bus terminal. Moderately priced *Khrua Weh* (Tiam An Hue in Vietnamese) is an excellent Vietnamese restaurant in an old house on Klang Meuang Rd, near Prachasamoson Rd. *Ob-Un Vegetarian Restaurant* (a sign in English reads 'Vegetarian Food') off the north side of Si Chan Rd serves Thai vegetarian dishes for 15 to 25B each and is open daily 8 am to 9 pm. The *Vegetarian Restaurant* on Lang Muang Rd is similar.

Getting There & Away

Air THAI flies four times daily between Bangkok and Khon Kaen (55 minutes,

1080B one way). Orient Express Air flies daily from Chiang Mai for 1115B one way, from Udon Thani twice a week for 800B and from Ubon on Saturday for 1100B.

Bus From Nakhon Ratchasima, it's 2½ hours to Khon Kaen by bus and the fare is 48B. Ordinary buses to Khon Kaen from Phitsanulok take about five hours and cost 92B.

Rail Khon Kaen is on the Bangkok-Nakhon Ratchasima-Udon Thani rail line, but buses are much faster along this section.

UDON THANI

This was one of the biggest US Air Force bases in Thailand during the Vietnam era – one of those places from where they flew out to drop thousands of tons of bombs into the jungle in the hope that somebody might be standing under one of the trees. Aside from massage parlours and ice-cream parlours, there are a few shops selling Isaan handicrafts.

Ban Chiang, 50 km east, has some interesting archaeological digs – the excavations at **Wat Pho Si Nai** are open to the public, and there's a recently constructed national museum (admission 10B).

Places to Stay

The *Queen Hotel* at 6-8 Udon-Dutsadi Rd has rooms with fan and bath from 100B. At 123 Prajak Silpakorn Rd, the *Sriswast (Si Sawat)* has rooms in an old building for 100B, in a newer building for 140 to 280B.

The nicer *Tang Porn Dhiraksa Hotel* (☎ (42) 221032) on Mak Khaeng Rd has large, fairly quiet fan rooms for 120B with shared bath, 180B with attached bath.

Places to Eat

Udon Thani has plenty of restaurants – many with western food – but you can also find places that specialise in the Isaan food of the north-east region. *Yawt Kai Yang* at the corner of Pho Si and Mukkhamontri Rds is a good spot to try Isaan-style grilled chicken

(kài yàang) with spicy papaya salad and sticky rice.

Try the *Rung Thong* at the west side of the clock tower for good curries (it closes around 5 pm, though). In the new *Charoensi Complex*, at the south-eastern end of Prajak Silpakorn Rd, there's a good food centre and a couple of modern coffee shops.

Getting There & Away

There are regular flights to Udon Thani from Bangkok, Chiang Mai and Khon Kaen. Buses from Bangkok depart frequently and cost 134B – the trip takes about nine hours. A bus from Nakhon Ratchasima to Udon Thani is 64B and takes four to five hours. There are regular buses between Udon Thani and Ban Chiang throughout the day for 22B.

Trains from Bangkok cost 219B in 2nd class and take 11 hours overnight. Take a sleeper – it's worthwhile on this long trip.

NONG KHAI

Right on the Mekong River, this is the major crossing point to the Lao capital, Vientiane. It's 624 km from Bangkok and only 55 km north of Udon Thani. The city is developing fast as it gears up for trade with Laos – a bridge now joins the two countries.

Visas for Laos are available from travel agencies in Nong Khai.

Information

Bookshop Wasambe Bookshop (☎ /fax (42) 460717), on the soi leading to Mutmee Guest House, sells new and used English-language novels, guidebooks (especially for Thailand and Laos), maps, and books on spirituality, plus a small but growing collection of German, French and Dutch titles. Fax and Email services are also available here.

Places to Stay

Guesthouses Long-established *Mutmee (Mat-mii)*, on the river off Meechai Rd, has rooms with shared facilities from 70 to 120B, with private bath from 200B. They have a pleasant garden restaurant overlooking the river. Also on Meechai Rd, there's the newer *Sawadee*, with small but clean rooms for

THAILAND

80/120B, and the *Mekong*, with rooms overlooking the river for 50 to 130B.

Several blocks further east, off Meechai Rd on the river, is *Tommy's* – dorm beds are 30B and rooms cost from 50 to 70B.

Hotels Two cheapies on Banthoengjit Rd are the *Banthoengjit* and the *Kheng Houng (Huang)*, with somewhat dismal rooms for 100 to 150B. *Pongvichita (Phongwichit)* at 1244/1-2 Banthoengjit Rd is fairly clean and businesslike and costs 200/350B for a one/two-bed room with fan and bath, 450/500B with air-con.

Places to Eat

Overlooking the Laos ferry pier, *Udom Rot* has good food and a pleasant atmosphere. Another riverside choice is the *Rim Nam Khong*, next to the Mekong Guest House. Two doors south of Pongvichita Hotel, the *Thai Thai Phochana* has all the usual Thai and Chinese dishes; it's open all night. The French influence in Laos has crept over the border and into the local *pastry shops.*

Getting There & Away

By bus, it's 146B (263B with air-con) from Bangkok and takes nine or ten hours. Udon is only 1¼ hours away, and the fare is 15B.

Nong Khai is the end of the rail line which runs from Bangkok through Nakhon Ratchasima, Khon Kaen and Udon Thani. The basic fare is 238B in 2nd class, not including supplementary charges.

Laos Shuttle buses ferry passengers back and forth across the bridge from a designated terminal near the Thai-Lao Friendship Bridge for 10B per person; there are departures every 20 minutes from 8 am to 5.30 pm. From the Lao side of the bridge you can get a taxi to Vientiane for 100B.

AROUND NONG KHAI

Twelve km to the south-east of Nong Khai is **Wat Phra That Bang Phuan**. It is one of the most sacred temple sites in the north-east because of a 2000-year-old Indian-style stupa originally found here (it was replaced or built over by a Lao-style chedi in the 16th century). **Wat Hin Maak Peng**, 60 km north-west, is a quiet and peaceful place on the banks of the Mekong.

Sala Kaew Ku, also called **Wat Khaek** (Indian temple) by locals, is a strange Hindu-Buddhist sculpture garden established by a Brahmanic yogi-priest-shaman of Lao birth who merges Hindu and Buddhist philosophy, mythology and iconography into a cryptic whole. It's four or five km south-east of town on the road to Beung Kan.

NONG KHAI TO LOEI

Following the Mekong River from Nong Khai into Loei Province, you'll pass through Si Chiangmai, Sangkhom, Pak Chom and Chiang Khan. Each of these small towns has a couple of guesthouses with accommodation from 60 to 100B. Although there are no major attractions along this route, it's a nice area to take a break from the road. Relaxing walks along the Mekong are just the thing for frazzled nerves.

LOEI

From Loei you can climb the 1500 metres **Phu Kradung** mountain, about 75 km to the south. The mountain is in a national park with trails, and cabins are available if you want to stay. The climb takes about four hours if you're reasonably fit.

Places to Stay

Guesthouses *Muangloei Guest House* is within walking distance of the bus terminal, at 103/72 Soi Aw Daw Ruamjai. Basic singles/doubles cost 60/90B.

For stays of more than one night, a better choice is the *Friendship Guest House* (☎ (42) 832408), south of the post office, or *Cotton Inn* at 257/41 Soi Buncharoen: rooms here in a wooden building by the river cost 80B or, in a modern house, 200B in a large room that will sleep up to five.

Hotels The *Sarai Thong* on Ruamjit Rd has rooms from 90 to 160B, all with fan and bath; it's off the street, quiet and clean. The *Srisawat*, nearby on Ruamjit Rd, is similar

THAILAND

but slightly cheaper. The *Di Phakdi* (☎ (42) 811294) on Ua Ari Rd, around the corner from the more expensive Thai Udom Hotel and opposite the cinema, has minimalist rooms from 120B with fan and bath.

Just off Chumsai Rd, the *PR House* (☎ (42) 811416) offers modest apartments for rent: with fan and solar-heated shower they cost 180 to 240B per night, or 350B with air-con, and less for long-term stays.

Places to Eat
The *market* at the intersection of Ruamjai and Charoen Rat Rds has cheap eats, including some local specialities. Near the Bangkok Bank on Charoen Rat Rd, the *Chuan Lee* and the *Sawita* are two pastry/coffee shops that also sell a range of Thai and western food. There's a good Thai *vegetarian restaurant* near PR House.

Getting There & Away
Buses run directly from Bangkok to Loei, or you can get there from Udon Thani for 38B and from Phitsanulok via Lom Sak for 58B. Buses to Phu Kradung leave the Loei bus station in the morning. Direct ordinary buses to Chiang Mai cost 136B.

LOM SAK
It's an interesting trip from Phitsanulok to this colourful small town on the way to Loei and Udon Thani. It's also a pleasant trip from here to Khon Kaen. Near the bus stop, the noisy *Sawang Hotel* has rooms for 80 to 110B, and a Chinese coffee shop.

BEUNG KAN
This small dusty town on the Mekong River, 185 km east of Nong Khai, has a Vietnamese influence. Nearby is **Wat Phu Thawk**, a remote forest wat built on a sandstone outcrop.

NAKHON PHANOM
There's a great view across the Mekong towards Tha Khaek, in Laos, from this otherwise dull city. **Renu Nakhon**, a village south of Nakhon Phanom on the way to That Phanom, is renowned for its daily handicraft market (biggest on Saturday).

Information
Tourist Office The TAT (☎ (42) 513492) has a new office, in a beautiful colonial-style building, at the corner of Sala Klang and Sunthon Wijit Rds. The staff distribute information on Nakhon Phanom, Mukdahan and Sakon Nakhon provinces.

Places to Stay
The *Charoensuk Hotel* (692/45 Bamrung Muang Rd), *First Hotel* (370 Si Thep Rd) and *Grand Hotel* (corner of Si Thep and Ruamjit Rds) offer similarly simple accommodation, in multistorey buildings downtown, for around 140 to 200B per room with fan and private shower, more for air-con. For 200 to 400B you can get something a bit nicer at either the *Si Thep Hotel* (708/11 Si Thep Rd) or the *Windsor Hotel* (692/19 Bamrung Meuang Rd).

Places to Eat
Most of the town's better *Thai* and *Chinese restaurants* are along the river on Sunthon Wijit Rd. There are several good, *inexpensive shops*, serving dishes like noodles and curry and rice, along Bamrung Meuang Rd, north of the Windsor and Charoensuk hotels.

Getting There & Away
There are regular buses from Nong Khai to Nakhon Phanom, via Sakon Nakhon, for 50B. All the way from Udon Thani it's 64B by ordinary bus, 114B air-con.

THAT PHANOM
This remote north-eastern town, on the banks of the Mekong River, has the famous **Wat Phra That Phanom**, which is similar in style to Pha That Luang in Vientiane, Laos. There's also some interesting French-Chinese architecture around the town, again showing the Lao influence. A Lao market gathers by the river Monday and Thursday from around 8.30 am to noon.

THAILAND

Places to Stay & Eat

The pleasant *Niyana Guest House* is on a soi near the That Phanom pier. Dorm beds are 50B, singles are 70B and a double is 90B. Niyana also does bicycle rentals and short boat trips on the river.

Chai Von (Wan) Hotel, on Phanom Phanarak Rd to the north of the arch (turn left as you pass under the arch), is an old wooden hotel with rooms from 60B with shared bath, 80B with bath. There are a couple of *Thai restaurants* near the Chai Von Hotel.

Getting There & Away

Songthaews from Nakhon Phanom to That Phanom cost 15B and take about 1½ hours. Stay on until you see the chedi on the right. Sakon Nakhon is two to three hours northwest by bus at a cost of 20B. Buses to Ubon Ratchathani cost 54B ordinary, 99B air-con.

YASOTHON

Although it's a bit out of the way if you're doing the Mekong circuit, the two hour bus trip from Ubon Ratchathani is worth making to witness the annual **Rocket Festival** (8-10 May). This popular north-eastern rain-and-fertility festival is celebrated with particular fervour in Yasothon.

Places to Stay

The *Udomphon Hotel* at 169 Uthairamrit Rd and *Surawet Wattana* at 128/1 Changsanit Rd each cost 150 to 200B for rooms with fan and bath. The *Yot Nakhon* (☎ (45) 711122) at 169 Uthairamrit Rd costs from 180B for fan rooms, 300B with air-con.

Getting There & Away

A bus to Yasothon from Ubon Ratchathani costs 27B.

MUKDAHAN

Fifty-five km south of That Phanom, 170 km north of Ubon Ratchathani and directly opposite the city of Savannakhet in Laos, Mukdahan is known for its beautiful Mekong scenery and as a Thai-Lao trade centre. According to agreements between the Thai and Lao governments, a bridge between Mukdahan and Savannakhet will be built within six years.

A road east from Savannakhet ends at Lao Bao on the Vietnamese border, where it's possible to cross into Vietnam if you hold a valid Vietnamese visa.

Places to Stay

The *Hua Nam Hotel* at 20 Samut Sakdarak Rd charges 150B for rooms with fan and shared bath or 300B with air-con and private bath. On the same road is the cheaper *Banthom Kasem Hotel*, but it's a real dive. *Hong Kong Hotel*, over at 161/1-2 Phitak Santirat Rd, is similar in design to the Hua Nam but a bit nicer; rates are 150 to 190B. Better is *Saensuk Bungalow* at 2 Phitak Santirat Rd, which offers clean, quiet rooms for 120 to 200B fan, more for air-con.

Getting There & Away

There are frequent buses from either direction – 29B ordinary (48B air-con) from Nakhon Phanom, half that from That Phanom, or 34B (77B air-con) from Ubon.

Savannakhet Ferries cross the Mekong between Savan and Mukdahan frequently – between 8.30 am and 5 pm weekdays and 8.30 am and 12.30 pm Saturday – for 30B from Thailand, 850 kip from Laos.

UBON (UBOL) RATCHATHANI

This was the site of another major US Air Force base during the Vietnam War. **Wat Paa Nanachat** at nearby Warin Chamrap has a large contingent of foreign monks in residence. **Wat Thung Si Muang** in the centre of town and **Wat Phra That Nong Bua** on the outskirts are also interesting; the latter has a good copy of the Mahabodhi stupa in Bodh Gaya, India.

Information

Tourist Office The TAT (☎ 243770) has a very helpful branch office at 264/1 Kheuan Thani Rd, opposite the Sri Kamol Hotel.

The area code for Ubon Ratchathani is 45.

THAILAND

Places to Stay

Suriyat Hotel at 47/1-4 Suriyat Rd has bare rooms with fan for 130 to 180B, or 300B with air-con. A better choice in this range is the *Si Isaan (Far East)* (☎ 254204) at 220/6 Ratchabut Rd: singles/doubles are 150/180B with fan and private bath, or in a separate building there are air-con rooms for 300B.

The *New Nakornluang Hotel* (☎ 254768) at 84-88 Yutthaphan Rd has decent fan rooms with private bath for 150 to 250B, air-con for 250B.

Places to Eat

Several inexpensive *rice and noodle shops* can be found along Kheuan Thani Rd, including the *Chiokee*, which is very popular among local office workers and offers Thai, Chinese and western-style breakfasts.

The family-run *Piak Laap Pet* on Jaeng Sanit Rd (next to a radio relay station) and *Suan Maphrao*, near Km 288 on the road to Yasothon, have the best Isaan food in Ubon. Try the knockout laap pet (spicy duck salad).

Getting There & Away

Air THAI has two daily flights from Bangkok to Ubon. The fare is 1405B and the flight takes an hour. Orient Express Air (☎ 264832) flies from Chiang Mai to Ubon via Khon Kaen for 1950B, and from Udon for 1180B. In the reverse direction Khon Kaen flights stop over in Udon.

Bus By bus, there are frequent departures daily from the Northern bus terminal in Bangkok; fares are 161B on the regular buses, 290B air-con. Air-con buses from Nakhon Phanom take six to seven hours and cost 98B.

Train An express train and two rapid trains leave daily from Bangkok. Fares are 95B in 3rd class (rapid and ordinary trains only) and 221B in 2nd class (rapid and express), not including rapid or express surcharges.

SURIN

Surin is best known for the elephant roundup held in late November every year. There are elephant races, fights, tug-of-wars and anything else you can think of to do with a couple of hundred elephants. If you've ever had an urge to see a lot of elephants at one time, this is a chance to get it out of your system! Several minor Khmer ruins can also be visited nearby. A lot of day or overnight trips are available from Bangkok during this time.

The area code for Surin is 45.

Places to Stay

Pirom's House (☎ 515140) at 242 Krung Si Nai Rd has dorm beds for 50B per person and singles/doubles for 70/120B. Pirom can suggest day trips around Surin, including excursions to nearby villages and Khmer temple sites. Run by an expat Texan and his wife, *Country Roads Cafe & Guesthouse* (☎/fax 515721) is a bit out of the centre at 165/1 Sirirat Rd, behind the bus terminal; rooms cost 100B.

Hotel prices soar during roundup time, but normally the *Krung Si* (☎ 511037) on Krung Si Rd has rooms from 120 to 200B. *Thanachai Hotel*, just off the roundabout on Thetsaban 1 Rd near the post office, has somewhat dark and dingy rooms for 60/80B.

Getting There & Away

Regular buses from the Northern bus terminal in Bangkok cost 108B. There are many special tour buses at roundup time. You can also get there on the Ubon Ratchathani express and rapid trains for 169B in 2nd class, not including surcharges. Book seats well in advance during November.

Southern Thailand

The south of Thailand offers some of the most spectacular scenery in the country – plus beautiful beaches, good snorkelling, fine seafood and a good selection of things to see. There are roads along the east and west coasts; the east-coast road runs close to the railway line.

Both the geography and the people of the south are very different from the rest of the country. The rice paddies of central Thailand give way to rubber and oil palm plantations, which can be seen right down through Malaysia. Many of the people are related to the Malays in both culture and religion. This 'difference' has long promoted secessionist rumblings and the Thai government still has to grapple with occasional outbreaks of violence in the south.

The two main attractions of the south are the world-famous islands of Phuket and Ko Samui. Both offer a wide range of accommodation (Phuket less so than Ko Samui) and some superb beaches. Other attractions include the awesome limestone outcrops which erupt from the green jungle and the sea between Phang-Nga and Krabi, and the nearly deserted beaches of Trang, Pattani and Narathiwat. Chaiya has some archaeologically interesting remains and, deep in the south, Hat Yai is a rapidly-growing, modern city with a colourful reputation as a weekend getaway from Malaysia.

Getting There & Away
You can travel south from Bangkok by air, bus or rail. The road south runs down the east coast as far as Chumphon, where you have a choice of climbing over the narrow mountain range and going down the west coast (for Ranong, Phuket, Krabi, Trang and Satun) or continuing south on the east coast (for Surat Thani, Ko Samui, Nakhon Si Thammarat, Pattani and Narathiwat).

The railway follows the eastern route and both routes meet again at Hat Yai. From Hat Yai, rail and roads split and you can follow either route to Malaysia: down the west coast to Alor Setar and then Penang, or head to the east and cross the border from Sungai Kolok to Kota Bharu.

PHETBURI (PHETCHABURI)
Phetburi, 160 km south of Bangkok, has a number of interesting old temples. A walking tour can take in six or seven of them in two or three hours, including the old Khmer site of Wat Kamphaeng Laeng and the Ayuthaya-era Wat Yai Suwannaram.

On the outskirts of town, next to the Phetkasem Highway, is **Khao Wang**, a hill topped by a restored King Mongkut palace. You can walk up the hill to the historical park or take a cable car for 10B one way. Entry to the park is 20B.

The **Phra Nakhon Khiri Fair** takes place in early February and lasts about eight days. Centred on Khao Wang and the city's historic temples, the festivities include a sound and light show at the Phra Nakhon Khiri Palace, temples festooned with lights and performances of Thai classical dance-drama.

Places to Stay & Eat
The *Chom Klao* is on the east side of Chomrut Bridge and has rooms for 100 to 130B. The *Nam Chai*, a block further east, is similarly priced but not such good value. The *Phetburi* is on the next street north of Chomrut Bridge and behind the Chom Klao; it has overpriced rooms at 150B with fan and bath. The *Ratanaphakdi Hotel* on Chise-In Rd is better – clean rooms with private bath cost 200B single/double.

There are several good *restaurants* in the vicinity of Khao Wang serving a variety of standard Thai and Chinese dishes. The cheapest food – with plenty of variety – is at the *night market* at the southern end of Surinluechai Rd, under the digital clock tower.

Getting There & Away
Buses leave regularly from the Southern bus terminal in Thonburi, Bangkok, for 36B or 65B with air-con, and take about three hours. Buses to Phetburi from Hua Hin are 20B.

AROUND PHETBURI
The nearby **Kaeng Krachan National Park** is Thailand's largest. There is public transport from Phetburi as far as Kaeng Krachan village for 20B. From there, you must hitch or charter a truck for the four km to the park entrance.

HUA HIN
This town, 230 km south of Bangkok, is the oldest Thai seaside resort. Hua Hin is still a popular weekend getaway for Thais, but has

recently been discovered by a rash of Europeans, who have brought high-rise hotels and western restaurants. Rama VII had a summer residence here and the royal family still uses it.

The **Hotel Sofitel Central Hua Hin** is fronted by trees and shrubs trimmed to resemble roosters, ducks, women opening umbrellas, giraffes and snakes.

Places to Stay

Accommodation in Hua Hin tends to be a bit on the expensive side since it's so close to Bangkok. Rates are usually higher on weekends and holidays, so go during the week for the best deals.

The cheapest places are found along or just off Naretdamri Rd. Rooms at *Khun Daeng House*, on Naretdamri Rd, cost 100 to 150B with private bath. *Maple Leaf Bed & Breakfast* and *Europa* each have rooms in the 150 to 200B range. Further south-east along Naretdamri there's a string of other guesthouses, most costing 200B or more.

On Phetkasem Rd, there's the *Chaat Chai* at No 59/1 with fan rooms from 140 to 220B, or the *Damrong* at No 46, which has slightly lower prices for fan rooms, more for air-con.

If you can afford it, the *Hotel Sofitel Central Hua Hin* (☎ 512021/40) is a fine experience. Formerly the Railway Hotel, this delightfully old-fashioned place was built by German railway engineers and leased by a French conglomerate in 1986. It's just off the beach on Damnoen Kasem Rd. The rooms are big, the ceilings are high and the service is polished. Rooms in the old colonial wing start at 3100B. Movie buffs may recognise the place as the Hotel Le Phnom from the film *The Killing Fields*.

Places to Eat

Hua Hin is noted for its seafood, available near the pier at the end of Chomsin Rd or at the *night market* (always settle the price before ordering). Along Naretdamri Rd there are a number of touristy restaurants with touristy prices, such as the *Beergarden*, *Headrock Cafe* and *La Villa*.

Getting There & Away

Buses run from the Southern bus terminal in Bangkok. There are frequent departures for the four hour trip and the cost is 51B, or 92B with air-con. Buses from Phetburi are 20B.

Trains en route to Hat Yai in the south also stop at Hua Hin. The trip takes around 4½ hours and costs 44B in 3rd class and 92B in 2nd class.

Getting Around

Samlors from the railway station to the beach cost 20B; from the bus terminal to Naretdamri Rd, 20 to 25B; and from Chatchai Market to the fishing pier, 20 to 30B.

PRACHUAP KHIRI KHAN

This provincial capital is sleepy compared with Hua Hin, but some fine seafood can be found here. South of Ao Prachuap, around a small headland, scenic **Manao Bay** is ringed by limestone mountains and islets.

A few km north of town there's another bay, **Ao Noi**, where a small fishing village has a few rooms to let.

Places to Stay & Eat

The centrally located *Yuttichai* at 35 Kong Kiat Rd has fair rooms with fan and bath from 100 to 200B. Around the corner on Phitak Chat Rd, *Inthira Hotel* is similarly priced but noisier; it's currently undergoing renovation so rates – and comfort – may increase. The *King Hotel* (☎ 611170), further south on the same street, has rooms from 200 to 250B.

On Chai Thale Rd, near the top-end Hadthong Hotel, is a small *night market* that's quite good for seafood.

Getting There & Away

From Bangkok, buses are 72B, 130B with air-con. Buses from Hua Hin are 30B and leave the bus station on Sasong Rd frequently between early morning and mid-afternoon.

It's also possible to catch a train from Hua Hin to Prachuap for 19B in 3rd class.

THAILAND

THAP SAKAE & BANG SAPHAN

These two districts are south of Prachuap Khiri Khan, near the border with Chumphon Province. Both have minor beach areas that are fairly undeveloped.

The town of Thap Sakae is set back from the coast and isn't much – north and south of town, however, are the beaches of **Hat Wanakon** and **Hat Laem Kum**. There are a couple of guesthouses here and you can ask permission to camp at Wat Laem Kum, 3½ km from Thap Sakae. You can buy food at the fishing village of Ban Don Sai, nearby and to the north.

Bang Saphan isn't much either, but the long beaches here are beginning to attract some development. You can seek out the **beaches** of Hat Sai Kaew, Hat Ban Krut, Hat Ban Nong Mongkon, Hat (Ao) Baw Thawng Lang, Hat Pha Daeng, Hat Khiriway and Hat Bang Boet.

Getting around can be a problem since there isn't much public transport between the beaches.

Places to Stay & Eat

Thap Sakae Near the sea in a small fishing village about 2½ km east of town, the *Talay Inn* (☎ (32) 671417) is in a cluster of bamboo huts on a lake fed by a waterfall; it costs 100B per person. Also in the vicinity are a few concrete-block places, such as the *Chan Reua*, with rooms for 200 to 400B. The *Chaowarit (Chawalit)*, right off the highway near the south end of town, has simple but clean rooms for 120B with shared bath, 150 to 200B with fan and bath.

Hat Khiriwong *Tawee Beach Resort* has bungalows with private bath for 70 to 120B.

Bang Saphan Along the bay of Ao Bang Saphan, the *Boonsom Guest House* and *Van Veena Bungalows* are tourist bungalows in the 200 to 300B range. *Karol L's*, six km south of Bang Saphan, has bungalows for 80 to 100B.

The new *Suan Luang Resort* (☎ (01) 2125687; fax (32) 691054) at 97 M 1 is 600 metres from the beach, just up from Karol's.

They will pick up customers from the railway station if you give them a call. Their spacious bungalows with mosquito proofing are 200B for wooden ones, 350B for concrete; there are discounts for longer stays.

The *Krua Klang Ao* restaurant is a good place for seafood.

Getting There & Away

Buses from Prachuap to Thap Sakae are 12B, and 8B from Thap Sakae to Bang Saphan. If you're coming from further south, buses from Chumphon to Bang Saphan are 25B.

You can also get 3rd class trains between Prachuap, Thap Sakae and Bang Saphan for a few baht on each leg.

RANONG

Ranong is 600 km south of Bangkok and 300 km north of Phuket. Only the Chan River separates Thailand from Kawthaung (Victoria Point), in Myanmar, at this point. There's a busy trade supplying Burmese needs – the focus of the sea trade is the Saphaan Plaa pier, which is eight km south-west of town (5B on a No 2 songthaew).

Much of the town centre has a Hokkien Chinese flavour. Just outside of town is the 42°C (107°F) **Ranong Mineral Hot Springs** at Wat Tapotaram.

The area code for Ranong is 77.

Places to Stay & Eat

Along Ruangrat Rd in Ranong there are a number of cheap places, including the *Rattanasin* (150B single/double) and the *Suriyanon* (80 to 100B). The *Asia* (☎ 811113) and *Sin Tavee* (☎ 811213) on the same road are in the 200 to 280B range for fan rooms, more with air-con.

The somewhat expensive *Jansom Thara Hotel*, up on the main road, is the place to stay for mineral bathing – all the hotel's water is piped in from the hot springs. Rooms start at 1400B, but sometimes they offer discounted rooms for as low as 771B.

For inexpensive Thai and Burmese breakfasts, try the *morning market* on Ruangrat Rd, along which there are also several traditional Hokkien *coffee shops* with marble-topped tables. A couple of km north of town on the highway, between the Caltex and PT petrol stations, the *Mandalay* specialises in Burmese and Thai seafood.

Getting There & Away
Air Ranong airport, 20 km south of town off Highway 4, opened in November 1995. Bangkok Airways is the main carrier, with daily two-hour flights from Bangkok for 1980B each way.

Bus Buses from Chumphon are 35B or from Surat Thani 60B (80B air-con). Buses from Takua Pa are 45B, or 80B from Phuket. The bus terminal in Ranong is outside town near the Jansom Thara Hotel. To/from Bangkok, ordinary buses cost 140B, air-con 250B.

AROUND RANONG
Along the coast at the southern end of Ranong Province is **Laem Son National Park**, a wildlife and forest reserve consisting of mangrove swamps, sandy beaches and mostly uninhabited islands. On nearby **Ko Chang**, several beach places are open November to April, including *Rasta Baby*, *Ko Chang Contex*, *Sabai Jai* and *Cashew Resort*, all with simple huts for 100 to 200B a night. Boats to Ko Chang leave from Ranong's Saphaan Plaa twice daily; fares are negotiable depending on how many passengers board.

For **Victoria Point**, boats leave the same pier regularly from around 7 am till 3 pm for 30B per person. Immediately as you exit the Victoria Point jetty there's a small immigration office on the right, where you must pay US$5 for a day permit.

CHAIYA
Just north of Surat Thani, Chaiya is one of the oldest cities in Thailand and has intriguing ruins from the Sumatran-based Sriwijaya Empire. Indeed, some scholars believe this was the real centre of the empire, not Palembang. The name is a Thai abbreviation of 'Siwichaiya'. The restored **Boromathat Chaiya** stupa is very similar in design to the *candis* (shrines) of central Java. A national museum next to the stupa contains artefacts from the Sriwijaya era.

Outside of town, **Wat Suanmok** is a complete contrast, a modern forest monastery established by Thailand's most famous Buddhist monk, the late Ajaan Phutthathat (Buddhadasa).

Places to Stay & Eat
There are guest quarters in *Wat Suanmok* for those participating in monthly 10-day meditation retreats, but most visitors make Chaiya a day trip from nearby Surat Thani. Too many travellers treat Suanmok and other forest wats as open zoos – visit it only if you are genuinely interested in Buddhism or meditation. *Udomlap Hotel*, just off the main road and close to the railway station in Chaiya, has rooms with fan for 80 to 100B.

There are several places to eat in the vicinity of the railway station. About 10 minutes from town there's a long pier with two *restaurants*.

Getting There & Away
Chaiya is on the railway line only 20 km north of Surat Thani – you can get there by rail, bus or even taxi. Wat Suanmok is about seven km out of Chaiya. Buses run there directly from Surat Thani bus station so it isn't necessary to go right into Chaiya. Until late afternoon there are songthaews from Chaiya train station to Wat Suanmok for 8B per passenger, or you can get there from the station by motorbike for 20B.

SURAT THANI
This busy port is of interest for most travellers only as a jumping-off point for the island of Ko Samui, 30 km off the coast.

Places to Stay & Eat
Many of Surat Thani's hotels are transient specialists and you're likely to sleep better on the night ferry, without all the disturbances of nocturnal customers coming and going. With the rail, bus and boat combination tickets, there's no reason to stay in Surat Thani at all.

Within walking distance of the Ban Don pier are the *Surat, Thanfa, Ban Don* and *Thai* hotels, each with rooms in the 120 to 300B range.

In nearby Phun Phin, near the railway station, the simple *Tai Fah* and *Sri Thani* hotels have rooms for around 100B.

The *market* near the bus station has good, cheap food or, in Ban Don, try the places on the waterfront.

Getting There & Away
Air THAI flies to Surat Thani from Bangkok (1785B), Chiang Mai (3115B), Nakhon Si Thammarat (340B), Hat Yai (1200B), Phuket (475B) and Ranong (485B).

Bus & Minivan From the Southern bus terminal in Bangkok, the trip to Surat Thani takes 11 hours and costs 158B, or 285B for an air-con bus. From Surat Thani, buses run to Songkhla, Hat Yai, Phuket and other towns around the south. There are also cramped air-con minivans to tourist centres like Krabi and Phuket; these cost about the same as an air-con bus but are usually a lot less comfortable.

Train By train the fare from Bangkok to Surat Thani is 224B in 2nd class, but Surat Thani station is 14 km out of town, at Phun Phin. If you're heading south to Hat Yai you may decide it is easier to take a bus than to risk getting to the station to find there are no seats left.

Getting Around
From the railway station to the pier for Ko Samui ferries, buses leave every five minutes and cost 6B. The buses that meet the night express are free, but if you arrive at a time when the buses aren't running, a taxi to Ban Don costs about 60 to 70B.

KO SAMUI
This beautiful island, off the east coast, is very much on its way to becoming a fully fledged tourist resort. An airport was finally opened here in 1987 and car ferries have been in operation for several years, so it's hardly 'untouched', but at least you can't drive there over a bridge (as you can to Phuket). For now, there's still accommodation at nearly every budget level.

Orientation
Ko Samui is the largest island on the east coast and the third largest in Thailand. It's about 25 km long and 21 km wide and is surrounded by 80 other islands, all except six of which are uninhabited. The main town is Na Thon, and most of the population is concentrated there or at a handful of other towns scattered around the coast. Coconut plantations are still an important source of income, and visitors go relatively unnoticed outside the beach areas, especially outside the high tourist seasons (December to March and July to August).

Information
The best time to visit Ko Samui is from February to late June. July to late October is very wet and from then until January it can be very windy. During the on season, from December to March and from July to August, accommodation can get a little tight.

There are several foreign exchange services in Na Thon, Chaweng and Lamai. Mail can be sent to poste restante at the GPO, Na Thon.

The area code for Ko Samui is 77.

Medical Services A new medical facility, Bandon International Hospital (☎ 425382/3; fax 425342) has recently opened in Bo Phut.

Things to See
The beaches are beautiful and, naturally, the main attraction, but note the water is not as clear on the north or west coasts as along the east and south. Ko Samui also has a number of scenic waterfalls in the centre of the island – particularly **Hin Lat**, three km east of Na Thon, and **Na Muang**, 10 km south-east of Na Thon. Although Hin Lat is closer to Na Thon, Na Muang is the more scenic.

Near the village of Bang Kao, there's an interesting old chedi at **Wat Laem Saw**. The **Wat Phra Yai** (Big Buddha Temple), with its

THAILAND

12-metre-high Buddha image, is at the north-eastern end of the island, on a small rocky islet joined to the main island by a causeway. The monks are pleased to have visitors, but proper attire (no shorts) should be worn on the temple premises.

Environmental Message

Samui's visitors and inhabitants produce over 50 tonnes of garbage a day, much of it plastic. Not all of this is disposed of properly, and much – including quite a few plastic bottles – ends up in the sea, where it wreaks havoc on marine life. Remember to request recyclable glass water bottles instead of plastic, or to try and fill you own water bottle from the large, reusable canisters used in the restaurants of guesthouses and hotels.

Places to Stay & Eat

There are over 200 places to stay at the beaches, most ranging in cost from 100 to 400B a night, plus a smattering of luxury places ranging from 1000 to 3000B and over. Hat Chaweng and Hat Lamai are the two most popular spots, and both have beautiful sands and clear, sparkling water. Lamai has a coral reef; Chaweng has the largest beach,

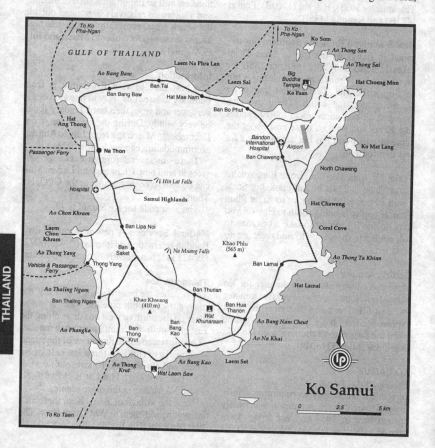

Ko Samui

GULF OF THAILAND

To Ko Pha-Ngan

Ko Som

Ao Thong Son

Ao Thong Sai

Laem Na Phra Lan

Ao Bang Baw

Laem Sai

Big Buddha Temple

Hat Choeng Mon

Ban Tai

Ban Bang Baw

Hat Mae Nam

Ko Faan

Hat Ang Thong

Ban Bo Phut

Bandon International Hospital

Airport

Ko Mat Lang

Passenger Ferry

Na Thon

Ban Chaweng

North Chaweng

Hin Lat Falls

Hospital

Samui Highlands

Hat Chaweng

Ao Chon Khram

Coral Cove

Laem Chon Khram

Ban Lipa Noi

Khao Phlu (565 m)

Ao Thong Yang

Ban Saket

Na Muang Falls

Ao Thong Ta Khian

Vehicle & Passenger Ferry

Thong Yang

Ban Lamai

Ao Thaling Ngam

Ban Thurian

Hat Lamai

Ban Thaling Ngam

Khao Khwang (410 m)

Wat Khunaraam

Ban Hua Thanon

Ao Phangka

Ban Thong Krut

Ban Bang Kao

Ao Bang Nam Cheut

Ao Na Khai

Ao Thong Krut

Ao Bang Kao

Laem Set

Wat Laem Saw

To Ko Taen

0   2.5   5 km

with probably the best water, and a small island opposite. Both are now dotted with discos/beer bars, so are not especially quiet during the high season.

Bo Phut and Big Buddha beaches are on the bay which encloses Ko Faan (the Big Buddha island), and these are rather quieter. Thong Yang is also very quiet, as are the little coves and tidal flats along the south shore. You can get further away from it all on the neighbouring island of Ko Pha-Ngan.

Na Thon If you want to stay in the town, there are a number of hotels to choose from. The *Palace Hotel* on the waterfront has clean, spacious rooms starting at 250 to 280B with fan, or 350 to 400B with air-con. Less expensive is the *Seaview Guest House* on Wattana Rd, which has Khao San-style rooms with fan and bath for 150 to 200B. On the southern edge of town, *Jinta Bungalows* has basic rooms for 150 to 250B.

Several *restaurants* face Na Thon's harbour and offer a combination of western food and Thai seafood; one of the oldest and best is the *Chao Koh*. On the next street back there are two or three *bakeries*, a *pizza joint*, a good *curry shop*, and a Hokkien *coffee shop* that has somehow managed to withstand the tourist onslaught.

Chaweng The island's longest beach offers the largest number and variety of places to stay, though they are constantly upgrading themselves to drive room rates higher. The cheaper ones are all much the same and cost from 80 to 150B a night for a small bungalow – knock it down a bit for a longer stay or during the off season, when some will go as low as 50B. In North Chaweng, you'll find *Matlang Resort, Venus, Blue Lagoon, Marine, Moon, Family* and *K John Resort*.

Towards the centre of the beach, prices rise a bit to the 100 to 350B range, as at *Lucky Mother, Coconut Grove, Charlie's Hut, Viking* and *Joy Resort*. Around the small headland at the south end, the only surviving budget place is *Chaweng Noi*, which costs 100 to 150B for a hut. Everything else on Chaweng is upscale and beyond the shoestring budget.

Lamai Samui's second most popular beach is finally succumbing to bigger tourist developments and is feeling the price squeeze, although overall it's still less expensive than Chaweng. Cheaper huts at the north-east end of the beach are at *New Hut, Thong Gaid Garden, Island Resort, Rose Garden* and *Suksamer*, all in the 150 to 300B range. New Hut also has a few 80B rooms, but the proprietors have been known to eject guests who don't eat in their restaurant.

Lamai's central section begins with a string of 100 to 600B places: *Mui, Utopia, Magic, Coconut Villa* and the *Weekender*. The Weekender has a wide variety of bungalows and activities to choose from, including a bit of nightlife. The *Coconut Beach* is a find at the bay's centre – it still charges only 80 to 200B.

Next comes *Thai House Inn, Marina Villa, Sawatdi, Mira Mare, Sea Breeze* and *Varinda Resort* – 100 to 600B places with elaborate outdoor dining areas. At the southern end of central Lamai Beach is a mixture of 50 to 200B places, including the long-standing *Paradise, Bill's Resort, White Sand, Palm, Nice Resort* and *Sun Rise*.

Beyond a headland, between Hat Lamai and Bang Nam Cheut, are some of Ko Samui's cheapest digs, including *Swiss Chalets, Noi, Chinda House* and *Rocky*, all with huts from 80 to 300B.

Big Buddha *Family Village* gets good reviews and costs from 200 to 700B. *Big Buddha Bungalows*, from 200 to 350B, is still OK. *Sun Set* is about the cheapest place here now, with simple huts at 80 to 300B. *Como's, Champ Resort, Beach House, Kinnaree* and *Number One* are in the 150 to 300B range.

Bo Phut Although there are about 20 places to stay here, this area manages to stay fairly quiet. At the north end, *Bo Phut Guesthouse, Sandy Resort, World Resort, Samui Palm Beach, Calm Beach Resort* and *Peace* have bungalows in the 80 to 300B range.

Towards the village is *Boon Bungalows*, a small operation with 50 to 100B huts. West of Boon is *Ziggy Stardust*, a clean place with huts from 500 to 1500B. Cheaper in this area are *Smile House*, *Miami* and *Oasis*, all with huts in the 50 to 200B range.

The village has a couple of cheap local-style *restaurants* and a couple of farang places.

Hat Mae Nam At this beach 14 km north-east of Na Thon, the *Friendly, New La Paz Villa* and *Silent* are all economical beach places with huts in the 80 to 200B range. Moving towards Bo Phut you'll find *Moon Hut Bungalows*, *Rose Bungalows*, *Laem Sai Bungalows*, *Maenam Villa* and *Rainbow Bungalows*, all with old-style Samui huts for 80 to 150B a night. While the scene at Mae Nam is not quite as picturesque as at Chaweng or Lamai, the swimming and sand are quite OK.

Other Along the southern end of the island you'll find bungalows tucked away into smaller bays and coves. If the development along Chaweng and Lamai is too much for you, this area might be just the ticket – all you need is a motorbike and a Ko Samui map. As at Lamai, the places along the southern end are pretty rocky – which means good snorkelling but not such good swimming.

Try Ao Na Khai and Laem Set, just beyond the village of Hua Thanon, for the best southern beaches. Other possibilities include Ao Thong Krut and Ao Bang Kao. Bungalows here start at 60 to 400B with bath.

At Ao Thong Yang and other seaside areas along Samui's west coast, bungalows are springing up everywhere because the car ferry from Don Sak docks on this side. None of them are anything special, nor are they cheap, and the beaches tend to become mud flats during low tide.

Getting There & Away
You can fly directly to Ko Samui from Bangkok with Bangkok Airways (2540B), or there are three ferry companies running boats from Surat Thani. Altogether, there are four ferry piers on the Surat coast (Ban Don, Tha Thong, Khanom and Don Sak – only three are in use at one time) and two piers on Ko Samui (Na Thon and Thong Yang). This can make things a bit confusing at times, but if you just follow the flow of travellers everything will work out.

The State Railway of Thailand does rail, bus and ferry tickets straight through to Ko Samui from Bangkok or the reverse. You end up paying about 50 to 80B more this way than if you book all the segments yourself.

Be cautious when using local agents to make mainland train and bus bookings – they don't always get made, or are not for the class you paid for. Several travellers have written to complain of rip-offs here.

Express Boats from Tha Thong From November to May, three daily express boats leave for Samui's Na Thon pier from Tha Thong in Surat and take 2 to 2½ hours to reach the island. Departure times are usually 7.30 am, noon and 2.30 pm – these are subject to change according to weather conditions. From June to October, there are only two express boats a day – at 7.30 am and 1.30 pm – because the seas are usually too high in the late afternoon for a third sailing in this direction. Passage is 105B one way and 170B return. This fare see-saws from season to season; if any rivals to Songserm, the main ferry company, appear on the scene (as happened twice before in the last fours years), Songserm drops its fares immediately – to as low as 50B one way – to drive the competition out of business.

From Na Thon back to Surat, there are departures at 7.15 am, noon and 2.45 pm from November to May, or at 7.30 am and 2.45 pm from June to October. The morning boat includes a bus ride to the train station in Phun Phin. The afternoon boats include a bus ride to the train station and to the Talaat Kaset bus station in Ban Don.

Night Ferry There is also a slow boat for Ko Samui that leaves the Ban Don pier each night at 11 pm, reaching Na Thon around 5 am. This one costs 70B for the upper deck (with pillows and mattresses) and 50B down below (straw mats only). The night ferry back to the mainland leaves Na Thon at 9 pm and arrives at 3 am.

Vehicle Ferry From Talaat Mai Rd in Surat Thani, you can get bus and ferry combination tickets straight through to Na Thon. These cost 70B, or 90B for an air-con bus. Pedestrians, cars and motorbikes can also take the ferry directly from Don Sak. It leaves at 6.50 am, 8 am, 10 am, 2 pm and 5 pm, and takes one hour to reach the Thong Yang pier on Ko Samui. Excluding bus fares, the fares are: pedestrians 50B, motorbikes and driver 75B, and a car and driver 190B.

Don Sak, in Surat Thani Province, is about 60 km from Surat Thani. A bus from the Surat bus station is 14B and takes 45 minutes to an hour to arrive at the Don Sak ferry. If you're coming north from Nakhon Si Thammarat, this might be the ferry to take, although from Surat the Tha Thong ferry is definitely more convenient.

Tour buses run directly from Bangkok to Ko Samui, via the Don Sak car ferry, for around 330B. From Ko Samui, air-con buses to Bangkok leave from near the pier in Na Thon twice daily, arriving in Bangkok in the early morning (there's a dinner stop in Surat the evening before). Through buses are also available from Ko Samui to Hat Yai and other points south. Check with the travel agencies in Na Thon for the latest routes.

Getting Around

It's about 19 km from Na Thon to Bo Phut on the north coast, and 23 km to Chaweng in the east. Minibuses and songthaews operate all day. Official fares from Na Thon are 10B to Mae Nam or Bo Phut, 15B to Big Buddha and 20B to Chaweng or Lamai. Farangs are often charged 5B extra because their backpacks take up so much room. From the car-ferry landing in Thong Yang, rates are 20B for Lamai, Mae Nam and Bo Phut/Big Buddha, 25B for Chaweng.

Often you'll be met in Na Thon (even on the ferry at Ban Don) and offered free transport if you stay at the place doing the offering.

You can rent motorbikes on Ko Samui – these are better value at Na Thon than at the beaches. Smaller 100cc bikes cost 150B a day and larger ones are 200B – ask for discounts for multi-day rentals.

KO PHA-NGAN

The island of Ko Pha-Ngan is north of Ko Samui and although nearly as big, it is generally more quiet and tranquil. It also has beautiful beaches, some fine snorkelling and the **Than Sadet Falls**. The lack of an airport and relative lack of paved roads has so far spared it from tourist-hotel and package-tour development.

At **Wat Khao Tham**, on a hilltop on the south-west side of the island, 10-day Buddhist meditation retreats are conducted by an American-Australian couple during the latter half of most months. The cost is 1800B; write in advance to Khao Tham, Ko Pha-Ngan, Surat Thani, for information, or pre-register in person.

Ferries from Surat, Ko Samui and Ko Tao dock at Thong Sala on Pha-Ngan's west coast; there are also smaller boats from Mae Nam and Bo Phut on Ko Samui to Hat Rin on the island's southern end.

Places to Stay

The beaches here are not among the island's best, but since they're close to Thong Sala, people waiting for an early boat back to Surat Thani or on to Ko Tao sometimes stay here. On Ao Bang Charu, the *Petchr Cottage*, *Sundance*, *Pha-Ngan Villa* and *Moonlight* are all in the 60 to 120B range.

Just north of Thong Sala are the *Phangan* (60 to 300B), *Charn* (80 to 120B), *Siripun* (100 to 400B) and *Tranquil Resort* (60 to 200B). Further north, at the southern end of Ao Wok Tum, the basic *Tuk, Kiat, OK* and *Darin* are all from 40 to 80B. A little further down around the cape of Hin are *Porn Sawan*, *Cookies* and *Beach*, with the same rates and facilities.

Places to Eat

Unlike Ko Samui, Ko Pha-Ngan isn't known for fabulous cuisine. Virtually all beach accommodations have their own simple cafes with typical 'farang-ised' versions of Thai food plus the usual muesli-yoghurt, sandwiches and so on. In Thong Sala, several cafes near the pier cater to farang tastes and also sell boat tickets. *Cafe de la Poste*, opposite the post office, offers imported cheeses, coffee, sandwiches, pizza, pasta and vegetarian dishes.

Ban Tai & Ban Khai Between the villages of Ban Tai and Ban Khai there's a series of sandy beaches with well-spaced collections of bungalows, most in the 50 to 100B range. They include *Dewshore, P Park, Liberty Birdville, Jup, Bay Hut, Lee's Garden* and *Golden Beach.*

Laem Hat Rin This long cape has beaches along both its western and eastern sides. They're getting very crowded these days,

especially on the eastward side (which has the best beach) – the all-night 'full moon' parties here are legendary and have recently begun attracting the attention of the local police. Most of the places on the eastward beach start at 150B a night; they include *Paradise, Beach Blue, Haadrin Resort, Tommy* and *Palita Lodge*; a couple of slightly cheaper ones, like *Sunrise* and *Sea Garden Bungalows*; and the upscale *Pha-Ngan Bayshore Resort*. Built into the rocky headland at the north end of Hat Rin, *Mountain Sea Bungalows* and *Serenity* have huts for 80 to 200B.

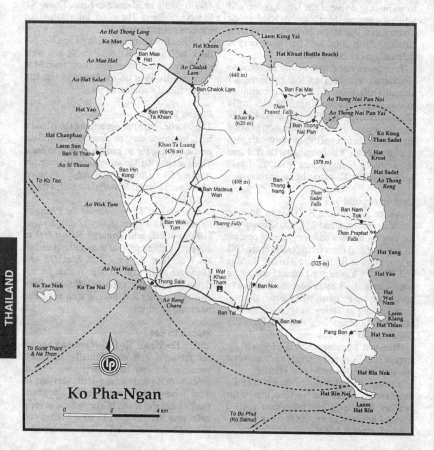

Ko Pha-Ngan

Along the western side are the long-running *Palm Beach* and *Sunset Bay Resort*, both of which cost from 50 to 200B. Other places that offer similarly priced accommodation are *Rainbow, Coral, Bird, Star, Bang Son Villa, Sun Beach, Sea Side, Sooksom, Laidback Shack, Dolphin, Sandy* and, down near the tip of the cape, the *Lighthouse* and *Leela Bungalows*.

Ao Chalok Lam & Hat Khuat These two pretty bays on the northern end of Pha-Ngan are still largely undeveloped. Chalok Lam has *Try Tong Resort* and *Fanta* at 50 to 200B. Huts at Hat Kuat's *Bottle Beach, Bottle Beach II, OD Bungalows* and *Sea Love* cost 60 to 250B. West of Hat Khuat, 2½ km across Laem Kung Yai, is Hat Khom, where the *Coral Bay* charges 40 to 50B.

Ao Mae Hat The beach at Ao Mae Hat isn't fantastic, but there is a bit of coral offshore. *Maehaad Bungalows* has simple huts for 50B plus wood-and-thatch huts with private bath for up to 150B; the *Mae Hat Bay Resort* and *Crystal Island Garden* have small wooden huts in the same price range. Moving southwestward, nicer wooden huts at the *Island View Cabana* cost from 50 to 250B; there's also a good restaurant.

Ao Si Thanu The *Laem Son* starts at 40B while the *Sea Flower, Seetanu* and *Great Bay* all have huts costing from 50 to 180B, depending on facilities. Several other places come and go in this area with the seasons.

East Coast On the beach at Ao Thong Nai Pan Yai, near Ban Thong Nai Pan on the island's north-east coast, are the *White Sand, AD View* and *Nice Beach* for 60 to 300B. Up on Thong Nai Pan Noi are the very nicely situated and well-maintained *Panviman Resort* (300B and up) and *Thong Ta Pan Resort* (80 to 150B).

Getting There & Away
There are regular ferries from Na Thon, on Ko Samui, to Thong Sala for 50B (60B in the opposite direction) and occasional boats

from Bo Phut to Hat Rin for 50 to 60B. The latter trip requires wading in from the boat to the beach in hip-deep water. The crossing takes about 45 minutes.

The night ferry from Ban Don in Surat stops in Thong Sala – the fare is 100B on the upper deck and 60B on the lower deck for the six hour trip.

A new company called Rossarin Tour has 35-passenger speedboats that go between Hat Mae Nam, on Ko Samui, and Thong Sala for 150B; this boat only takes about half an hour to reach Thong Sala. From January to September, there is also a slower boat between Hat Mae Nam and Ao Thong Nai Pan, on Pha-Ngan; the fare is 60B.

Subject to weather conditions, there are daily express boats between Thong Sala and Ko Tao, 47 km north, at 2.30 pm. The trip takes 2½ hours and costs 150B one way.

Rossarin Tour operates speedboats between Thong Sala and Ko Tao a couple of times a day for 350B per person; the crossing only takes about an hour.

KO TAO
Ko Tao, or Turtle Island, is only 21 sq km in area and lies 44 km north of Ko Pha-Ngan. Like Ko Pha-Ngan, the island is mostly mountainous with only a few dirt tracks here and there for roads. It has developed very quickly in the past few years and because of its popularity among divers it is now considerably more touristed – and a bit more expensive – than Ko Pha-Ngan.

Places to Stay
Accommodation on the island fits more or less between Samui and Pha-Ngan in terms of costs and amenities. Most bungalows now cost 80 to 150B a night, though some are 150 to 600B. During the peak season – December to March – it can be difficult to find accommodation anywhere on the island and people sleep on the beach or in restaurants until a hut becomes available.

Ao Mae On Ao Mae beach, north of the main pier, *Dam* has nice thatched huts for 100 to 150B. There's also *Crystal* (150 to 600B),

Queen Resort (100 to 200B) and *Tommy Resort* (80 to 500B). On Hat Sai Ri, the *Haad Sai Ree Resort, Ko Tao Cabana* and *SP Cabana* all cost 200 to 250B. *Sai Ri Cottage, New-Way* and *O-Chai* are all in the 80 to 250B price range.

Ao Laem Thian & Ao Tanot On the cape which juts out over the north end of Ao Tanot, *Laem Thian* has huts built among the rocks from 60B. Ao Tanot, at the southern end of Ko Tao, is one of the best spots for snorkelling and has good bungalow operations. *Tanote Bay Resort* charges 50 to 100B for simple but well-maintained huts, while *Poseidon* has rather shabby huts for 50 to 80B. The friendly *Diamond Beach* offer huts from 50 to 100B. *Bamboo Hut*, a new place, has decked bungalows for 100B.

Ao Chalok Ban Kao & Laem Tato This nicely situated coral beach, about 1.7 km south of Ban Mae Hat by road, has become quite crowded. On the hill overlooking the western part of the bay, you'll find *Laem Khlong* (100 to 500B, no beach) and *Viewpoint*, with lots of bungalows for 80 to 350B and a grumpy staff. Next are *Sunshine* and *Buddha View Dive Resort*, with bungalows in the 140 to 400B range.

Laem Tato can only be reached on foot and at low tide. *Tatoo Lagoon* offers basic huts for 60B, and more elaborate ones for up to 300B. On the hillside are the basic *Banana Rock* and *Aud Bungalow* for 100 to 200B.

Getting There & Away

Every third day, depending on the weather, a boat runs between Surat Thani (Tha Thong) and Ko Tao, a seven to eight hour trip for 220B one way.

Depending on the weather, boats make the three hour trip from Ko Pha-Ngan to Ko Tao daily for 150B. There are also boats daily from Chumphon's Tha Saphan Tha Yang (on the mainland). The trip takes five to seven hours, depending on the boat, and costs 200B. All boats dock at Ban Mae Hat on the island's west side.

A faster speedboat to Ko Tao leaves Chumphon at 8 am, arriving at 10.30 am, for 400B per person.

NAKHON SI THAMMARAT

Nakhon Si Thammarat has the oldest wat in the south, **Wat Phra Mahathat**. Reputed to be over 1000 years old and rebuilt in the mid-13th century, the wat has a 78-metre-high chedi topped by a solid-gold spire. The town also has an interesting **National Museum** with a good 'Art of Southern Thailand' exhibit.

Nakhon Si Thammarat is also noted for its nielloware (a silver and black alloy-enamel jewellery technique) and for the making of leather shadow puppets and dance masks.

Information

A TAT office (☎ 346516) is housed in a 70-year-old building in the north-west corner of the Sanaam Naa Meuang (City Field) off Ratchadamnoen Rd, near the police station.

The area code for Nakhon Si Thammarat is 75.

Places to Stay

Most hotels are near the train and bus stations. The best budget value is the friendly *Thai Lee Hotel* at 1130 Ratchadamnoen Rd, where clean rooms with fan and private shower cost 120 to 200B. On Yommarat Rd, across from the railway station, the *Si Thong* has adequate rooms from 120B with fan and bath. Alternatively, try the similar *Nakhon* at 1477/5 Yommarat Rd.

On Jamroenwithi Rd (walk straight down Neramit Rd opposite the station for two blocks and turn right), the *Siam Hotel* at No 1407/17 is a large hotel with rooms from 130B with fan and bath. Across the street at No 1459/7, the *Muang Thong* has rooms from 100B. Near the Siam Hotel, on the same side of the street, the *Thai Fa* has similar rates and ambience.

Places to Eat

There are lots of funky old *Chinese restaurants* along Yommarat and Jamroenwithi Rds. At night the entire block running south from the Siam Hotel is lined with *cheap food vendors*. Muslim stands opposite the hotel sell delicious roti klûay (banana pancake), khâo mók (chicken biryani) and mátàbà (pancakes stuffed with chicken or vegetables) in the evening, and by day there are plenty of *rice and noodle shops*.

Bovorn Bazaar offers several culinary delights, including *Hao Coffee* and the adjacent *Khrua Nakhon*, a large open-air restaurant serving real Nakhon cuisine.

Getting There & Away
From the Southern bus terminal in Bangkok, it takes 12 hours to Nakhon Si Thammarat; the fare is around 190B, or 342B by air-con bus. Daily buses from Surat Thani cost about 37B (air-con 60B). You can also get buses and share taxis to/from Songkhla, Krabi, Trang, Phuket or Hat Yai; share taxi fares are about twice ordinary bus fares.

PHATTALUNG
The major rice-growing centre of the south, Phattalung is also noted for its shadow puppets. The town has a couple of interesting wats, and **Lam Pang** is a pleasant spot for eating and relaxing beside the 'inland sea' on which Phattalung is situated. **Thale Noi Wildlife Preserve** – primarily a waterbird sanctuary – is 32 km to the north-east, and the **Tham Malai** cave is just outside town.

Places to Stay
The *Phattalung Hotel* at 43 Ramet Rd is the cheapest place in town, at 100B with fan and bath, although the rooms are dark and dirty. The larger and friendlier *Thai Hotel*, on Disara-Nakarin Rd, off Ramet Rd near the Bangkok Bank, has spacious rooms for 150/180B single/double with fan and bath, up to 350B with air-con.

The *Hoa Far (Haw Fa) Hotel*, on the corner of Poh Saat and Khuhasawan Rds, has large, clean rooms with fan and bath for 140 to 170B, air-con for 250B.

Places to Eat
One of the best Thai restaurants in Phattalung is *Khrua Cook* on Pracha Bamrung Rd. Also

on Pracha Bamrung Rd look for *Khrua Muang Lung*, a place with Muslim curries.

Getting There & Away
Buses from Phattalung to Nakhon Si Thammarat or Hat Yai take 2 hours and costs 30B. Air-con buses and minivans to/from Hat Yai are 27B and 30B respectively and take about the same time. There is one mini-van a day to/from Songkhla, for 35B.

There are also 3rd class trains to Phattalung from Surat Thani (42B) and Nakhon Si Thammarat (22B).

SONGKHLA
Not much is known about the pre-8th century history of Songkhla, a name derived from the Yawi 'Singora' – a mutilated Sanskrit reference to a lion-shaped mountain (today called Khao Daeng) opposite the harbour. The settlement originally lay at the foot of Khao Daeng, where two cemeteries and the ruins of a fort are among the oldest structural remains. Today it sits on a peninsula between Thale Sap Songkhla (an 'inland sea') and the Gulf of Thailand.

Things to See
Offshore are two islands known as 'cat' and 'mouse'. Although the beach is not very interesting, Songkhla has an active **waterfront**, with a smattering of historic architecture and brightly painted fishing boats; an interesting **National Museum** (admission 10B); an **old chedi** at the top of Khao Tan Kuan hill; and **Wat Matchimawat**, which has frescoes, an old marble Buddha image and a small museum. The National Museum, open from 9 am to noon and 1 to 4 pm Wednesday to Sunday, has a collection of Burmese Buddhas and various Sriwijaya artefacts. The building is an old Thai-Chinese palace.

Places to Stay
The popular and clean *Amsterdam* at 15/3 Rong Muang Rd has nice rooms with shared bath and toilet for 150 and 180B. It's run by a friendly Dutch woman.

THAILAND

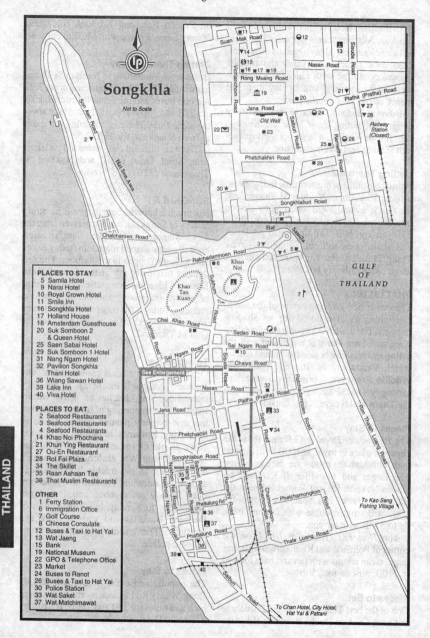

Songkhla

Not to Scale

GULF
OF
THAILAND

PLACES TO STAY
5 Samila Hotel
9 Narai Hotel
10 Royal Crown Hotel
11 Smile Inn
16 Songkhla Hotel
17 Holland House
18 Amsterdam Guesthouse
20 Suk Somboon 2
   & Queen Hotel
25 Saen Sabai Hotel
29 Suk Somboon 1 Hotel
31 Nang Ngam Hotel
32 Pavilion Songkhla
   Thani Hotel
36 Wiang Sawan Hotel
39 Lake Inn
40 Viva Hotel

PLACES TO EAT
2 Seafood Restaurants
3 Seafood Restaurants
4 Seafood Restaurants
14 Khao Noi Phochana
21 Khun Ying Restaurant
27 Ou-En Restaurant
28 Rot Fai Plaza
34 The Skillet
35 Raan Aahaan Tae
38 Thai Muslim Restaurants

OTHER
1 Ferry Station
6 Immigration Office
7 Golf Course
8 Chinese Consulate
12 Buses & Taxi to Hat Yai
13 Wat Jaeng
15 Bank
19 National Museum
22 GPO & Telephone Office
23 Market
24 Buses to Ranot
26 Buses & Taxi to Hat Yai
30 Police Station
33 Wat Saket
37 Wat Matchimawat

See Enlargement

Khao Tan Kuan

Khao Noi

To Kao Seng
Fishing Village

To Chan Hotel, City Hotel,
Hat Yai & Pattani

Railway
Station
(Closed)

Old Wall

THAILAND

The *Songkhla Hotel* is on Vichianchom Rd across from the fishing station; rooms cost 140B or from 180B with bath. At the foot of Khao Tan Kuan (the hill overlooking town), the *Narai Hotel*, 14 Chai Khao Rd, is a long walk from the bus station (take a trishaw), though it's a pleasant and friendly place; rooms start at 110B with shared bath.

Places to Eat

As you might expect, Songkhla has a reputation for seafood and there's a string of beach-front seafood specialists. None of them are particularly cheap and eating here is mainly a lunchtime activity. Try curried crab claws or fried squid.

At night, the food scene shifts to Vichianchom Rd in front of the *market*, where there is a line of food and fruit stalls. *Khao Noi Phochana*, on Vichianchom Rd near the Songkhla Hotel, has a good lunchtime selection of Thai and Chinese rice dishes. Along Nang Ngam Rd in the Chinese section there are several cheap *Chinese noodle and congee shops*.

There are several fast-food spots at the intersection of Sisuda and Platha Rds, including *Jam's Quik* and *Fresh Baker*, both with burgers, ice cream and western breakfasts.

Getting There & Away

Buses from Surat Thani to Songkhla cost 120B. Air-con buses from Bangkok take 19 hours and cost 425B. Regular buses are 224B, but add a few baht to get to Hat Yai. By train, you have to go to Hat Yai first. There are buses and share taxis from Hat Yai to Songkhla – 9B by bus and 15B by minivan or share taxi.

Although the usual route north from Songkhla is to backtrack to Hat Yai and then take the road to Phattalung and Trang, you can also take an interesting backroads route. There's a bus trip to Ranot, 63 km north at the end of the Thale Sap lagoon, and further buses connect to Hua Sai (32 km) and then Nakhon Si Thammarat (56 km).

Getting Around

Motorcycle taxis around Songkhla cost 10B and songthaews are 5B for anywhere on their routes.

AROUND SONGKHLA

On **Ko Yaw**, an island on the inland sea, you can see local cotton weaving and a **Folklore Museum** that emphasises Southern Thai culture. Buses to the island from either Songkhla or Hat Yai cost 8B.

The **Khu Khut Waterbird Sanctuary** is on the eastern shore of Thale Sap Songkhla near Sathing Phra, about 30 km north of Songkhla town. This 520 sq km sanctuary is a habitat for over 200 species of waterbirds.

HAT YAI

This is a busy commercial centre where the east and west coast roads and the railway line all meet. Apart from being the south's business capital, Hat Yai is also a popular 'sin centre' for Malaysians who pop across the border on weekends to partake of Thailand's flesh trade.

Orientation & Information

The three main streets – Niphat Uthit 1, 2 and 3 – all run parallel to the railway line. The TAT office (☎ 243747) is at 1/1 Soi 2, Niphat Uthit 3 Rd.

The immigration office (☎ 243019, 233760) is on Rattakan Rd near the railway bridge, in the same complex as a police station.

The area code for Hat Yai is 74.

Things to See

A few km out of town, towards the airport and just off Phetkasem Rd, **Wat Hat Yai Nai** has a large reclining Buddha image – get a samlor heading in that direction and hop off after the U Thapao Bridge. On the first Saturday of each month, **bullfights** (bull versus bull) are held at Hat Yai. There's always heavy betting among the Thai spectators.

Places to Stay

Hat Yai has dozens of hotels within walking distance of the train station. During Chinese New Year most room rates at the lower end double. Many places cater for the Malaysian dirty-weekend trade – it's not a traveller's dream town.

Still very popular with travellers is the *Cathay Guest House*, on the corner of Niphat

THAILAND

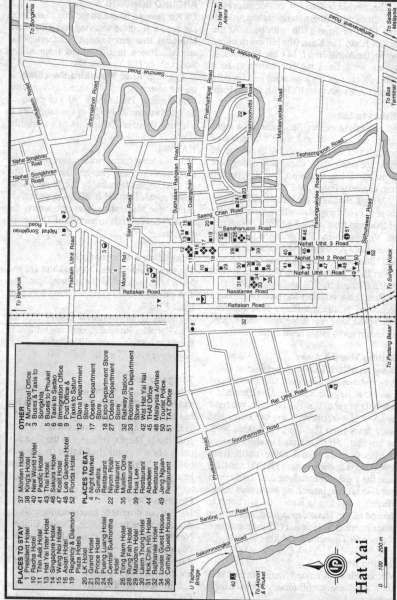

Uthit 2 and Thamnoonvithi Rds. Rooms here start at 120B and there is also a 60B dorm. The management is quite helpful with information on local travel and travel to Malaysia or further north in Thailand, and there is a reliable bus ticket agency downstairs.

The *Tong Nam Hotel* at 118-120 Niphat Uthit 3 Rd is a basic Chinese hotel with good rooms for 150B with fan, up to 300B with air-con and private bath. *Kim Hua*, opposite and further south on the same road, is 200 to 270B for fan and attached bath. The friendly *Thin Aek Hotel* at 16 Duangchan Rd (behind Diana Department Store on Niphat Uthit 3 Rd) is another old Chinese relic; rooms are 80B with shared bath, 100B with shower, 120B with shower and two large beds. The toilet is outside for all rooms.

On Niphat Uthit 1 Rd there's the *Mandarin Hotel*, where standard rooms are 170B for a double with fan and bath, 250B a triple, and 270B with air-con. The *Weng Aun* is an old Chinese Hotel across from King's Hotel on Niphat Uthit 1 Rd, four doors down from the Muslim Ocha restaurant; very basic singles start at 110B. Another good deal is the *Hok Chin Hin Hotel* (☎ 243258) on Niphat Uthit 1 Rd, a couple of blocks from the railway station. Very clean rooms with bath and fan cost 150B single, 240B double; there's a good coffee shop downstairs.

Places to Eat

Hat Yai has plenty of good places to eat, including lots of shops selling cakes, confectionery, fruit and ice cream. Across from the King's Hotel, the popular *Muslim Ocha* is still going strong, with roti and curry dip in the mornings and rice and curries all day. This is one of the few Muslim cafes in town where women – even non-Muslim – seem welcome; discreet dress is recommended for both sexes.

The extensive *night market* along Montri 1 Rd, across from the Songkhla bus station, specialises in fresh seafood. Inexpensive morning dim sum is available at *Shangrila* on Thamnoonvithi Rd near the Cathay Guest House. In the evenings the Chinese-food action moves to *Hua Lee* on the corner of

Niphat Uthit 3 and Thamnoonvithi Rds; it's open till the wee hours.

Getting There & Away

See the Thailand Getting There & Away section earlier in this chapter for details of travel between Hat Yai and Malaysia.

Air There are at least two flights daily from Bangkok, and Hat Yai is also connected by air with Phuket, Penang, Surat Thani, Chiang Mai and Singapore.

Bus There are many agencies for buses to Bangkok and for taxis to Penang: along Niphat Uthit 2 Rd, towards the Thai Airways and Malaysia Airlines offices, and around the railway station. The travel agency below the Cathay Guest House is reliable and also books tour buses.

Buses from Bangkok cost 227B, or 428B with air-con. Buses to Phuket are 122B ordinary, 220B with air-con, 200B by minivan. Ordinary buses to Satun cost 27B. Buses to Krabi (air-con only) are 125B, while ordinary buses to Surat Thani cost 86B (120B air-con).

It's 18B for a bus, 25B for a share taxi, to Padang Besar on the Malaysian border. If you're going to the other side, buses to Sungai Kolok (air-con only) cost 96B.

Train Fares from Bangkok – without rapid or express supplements – are 313B in 2nd class. There is no 3rd class on express trains to/from Bangkok. Third class trains to Hat Yai start only as far north as Chumphon (99B) and Surat Thani (55B).

Getting Around

The Airport The THAI van costs 40B per person for transport to the city; count on about 150B for a private taxi or about 50 or 60B for a songthaew.

Local Transport Songthaews cost 5B anywhere around town.

AROUND HAT YAI

The **Ton Nga Chang Waterfall**, 24 km west of the city, features 1200-metre, seven-tiered cascades in the shape of a pair of elephant tusks. October to December is the best time to visit. To get to the falls take a Rattaphum-bound songthaew (10B) and ask to get off at the *náam tòk* (waterfall).

SATUN

There's little of interest in this province in the south-west corner of Thailand, but from here you can take boats to Kuala Perlis or Langkawi Island in Malaysia, or visit the Tarutao islands offshore.

Places to Stay

In Satun, the *Rian Thong Hotel* ('Rain Tong' on the English sign) at the end of Samanta Prasit Rd has large rooms for 120B. The more modern *Satun Thani* in the town centre is 190B but it's noisy. The *Udomsuk* (☎ (74) 711006), near the municipal offices on Hatthakam Seuksa Rd, is better value at 120 to 130B.

Places to Eat

There are several cheap Muslim *food shops* near the gold-domed Bambang Mosque in the centre of town. For Chinese food, wander about the little Chinese district near the Rian Thong Hotel.

Getting There & Away

Share taxis between Hat Yai and Satun cost 40B; buses cost 27B. Satul Transport Co, a half km north of the Wang Mai Hotel on the same side of the road, sells THAI tickets (for flights out of Trang or Hat Yai), and also operates buses to Trang (37B) and Hat Yai (27B, 30B air-con).

Frequent boats to Kuala Perlis in Malaysia leave from the Tammalang pier south of town between 9 am and 1 pm for 40B (RM4 in the reverse direction). There are also three boats daily to/from Langkawi Island for 150B or RM15 each way.

Getting Around

An orange songthaew to Tammalang pier costs 10B from Satun.

KO TARUTAO NATIONAL MARINE PARK

Pak Bara, 60 km north of Satun, is the usual jumping-off point for the Ko Tarutao archi-pelago, just north of the Malaysian border. A regular boat services only five of the 51 islands (Tarutao, Adang, Lipe, Rawi and Klang), of which only the first three are generally visited by tourists.

Places to Stay

Officially the park is only open from November to May. Visitors who show up on the islands during the monsoon season can stay in *park accommodation*, but they must transport their own food from the mainland unless staying on Ko Lipe, where *private accommodation* and restaurants are available. Even during other times of year it's advisable to bring extra food for Ko Tarutao and Ko Adang, as the park canteens are a little pricey and not that good.

Park accommodation on Ko Tarutao is in several locations and costs 400B for a large 'deluxe' two room *bungalow*, or 600B for one of eight *cottages* that sleep up to eight people. A four bed room in a *longhouse* costs 280B. All rooms and bungalows must be paid for in full, even if only one person rents it. You may pitch your own tent for 10B per person in designated *camping grounds* at Ao San and Ao Jak.

At Laem Son, on Ko Adang, a bed in a privately owned *longhouse* costs 40B per person, while two-person *bungalows* are 200B. On Ko Lipe you can stay at *Pattaya Beach Bungalow* for 100B per room with shared facilities, 200 to 270B with attached toilet. *Shaolea* has a longhouse with rooms for 50/80B single/double, and huts for 150B with shared bath, or 200B with attached bath.

Getting There & Away

From Satun to Pak Bara, you first take a bus (15B) or share taxi (25B) to La-ngu and then a songthaew (8B) to Pak Bara. Boats to Tarutao cost 100B per person each way, or you can charter a boat large enough for 8-10 people for 800B. Boats continue to Lipe and Adang for 180B one way. They run between November and April – the park is closed for the remainder of the year.

PHUKET

Thailand's largest island is barely an island, since it's joined to the mainland by a bridge. Once known as 'Junk Ceylon', Phuket was a major trade entrepôt and tin-mining centre in the 19th century, but these days its well-developed resort role has come to the fore. The town of Phuket is pleasant enough – in the town centre you'll see plenty of Sino-Portuguese architecture – but it's the beautiful beaches and the offshore islands which are the main attraction.

Virtually all transport radiates from Phuket town and popular beaches are scattered all over the island. The island is very hilly, and many of the hills drop right into the sea. Beach accommodation is becoming downright high-class these days, with international-class resorts on nearly every beach.

Information

The TAT office, on Phuket Rd, has a list of standard songthaew charges to the various beaches. The THAI office is on Ranong Rd and the post office is on Montri Rd.

The area code for Phuket is 76.

Phuket Beaches

Patong Ao Patong, 15 km west of Phuket town, is the most developed and most crowded of the many beaches. As a result it has a greater variety of accommodation than most of the others, although food is a little more expensive than at Ao Kata Yai or Ao Karon. There's also more going on at night here, including a thriving hostess bar scene. The beach itself is long, white, clean and lapped by picture-postcard clear waters. Jetskis are a major nuisance, however.

Karon & Kata Ao Karon is only a little south of Ao Patong and 20 km from Phuket town. This is really a triple beach: there's the long golden sweep of Ao Karon, then a small headland separates it from the smaller but equally beautiful Ao Kata Yai. Another small headland divides this from Ao Kata Noi, where you'll find good snorkelling. Offshore, there's the small island of **Ko Pu**. All

have beautiful beaches with that delightful, squeaky-feeling sand.

Most of the development is centred on the two Kata beaches and the southern end of Karon beach. Development is creeping north, but local hoteliers say they're determined it won't become as saturated as Ao Patong. A new beach promenade with street lights adds a touch of class.

Nai Han South again from Ao Kata Noi is Hat Nai Han, a small, pleasant beach which was one of the last hold-outs for cheap bungalows until the Phuket Yacht Club moved in. Although it's now more of a scene it's still pleasant and very sparsely developed, thanks to monastic holdings at the beach's centre.

You can walk along a coastal track from Ao Karon to Hat Nai Han in about two hours. In fact, you could probably walk right around the island on coastal tracks. The roads radiate from Phuket town and you have to backtrack into town and out again to get from one beach to another by road – even though they are just a couple of km apart along the coast. **Ao Saen** is a pleasant little place between Kata Noi and Nai Han.

Rawai If you go round the southern end of the island from Hat Nai Han you'll come to Hat Rawai, another tourist development. Again these are mostly more expensive places and the beach is not so special. At low tide, there's a long expanse of mud exposed before you get to the sea. People staying at Rawai often travel out to other beaches to swim. Rawai is a good place to get boats out to the islands scattered south of Phuket. There is good snorkelling at **Ko Hae**.

Other Beaches Between Rawai and Phuket town, there are more places to stay dotted along the nicely beached south-east stretch of coast. A little north of Ao Patong is **Hat Surin**, a long beach which is less sheltered and where the water is a little rougher than the normal Phuket calm. **Ao Kamala** has a wide calm bay but not such a good beach. It is just a km or so south of Hat Surin. Between the two there's an absurdly beautiful little

THAILAND

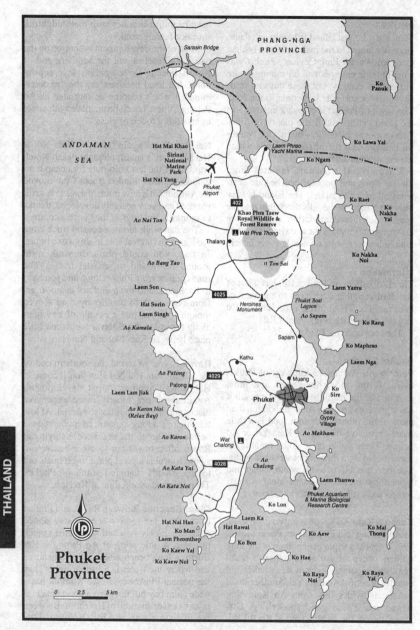

PHANG-NGA
PROVINCE

Sarasin Bridge

Ko
Panuk

ANDAMAN

SEA

Hat Mai Khao
Sirinat
National
Marine
Park
Hat Nai Yang

Laem Phrao
Yacht Marina

Ko Lawa Yai

Ko Ngam

Phuket
Airport

402

Ko Raet

Ko
Nakha
Yai

Ao Nai Ton

Khao Phra Taew
Royal Wildlife &
Forest Reserve
Wat Phra Thong

Thalang

Ko Nakha
Noi

Ao Bang Tao

Ton Sai

Laem Son

4025

Heroines
Monument

Laem Yamu

Hat Surin
Laem Singh

*Phuket Boat
Lagoon*

Ao Kamala

Ao Sapam

Ko Rang

Sapam

Ko Maphrao

Kathu

Laem Nga

Ao Patong

4029

Muang

Laem Lam Jiak

Patong

Phuket

Ko
Sire

*Ao Karon Noi
(Relax Bay)*

Sea
Gypsy
Village

Ao Karon

Wat
Chalong

Ao Makham

4028

Ao Kata Yai

*Ao
Chalong*

Ao Kata Noi

Laem Phanwa

Phuket Aquarium
& Marine Biological
Research Centre

Ko Lon

Hat Nai Han
Ko Man
Laem Phromthep
Ko Kaew Yai
Ko Kaew Noi

Laem Ka

Hat Rawai

Ko Bon

Ko Aew

Ko Mai
Thong

Ko Hae

**Phuket
Province**

0   2.5   5 km

Ko Raya
Noi

Ko Raya
Yai

THAILAND

beach, **Laem Singh** – the very image of a tropical paradise.

At the north-west tip of the island, attractive **Hat Nai Thon** has only one resort, while lengthy **Hat Nai Yang** and **Hat Mai Khao** are protected by Sirinat National Marine Park. Turtles come ashore to lay their eggs from late October to February at Hat Mai Khao.

Other Attractions

If the attraction of beaches starts to pall, Phuket also has a number of waterfalls and other novelties. The **Thai-Danish Marine Biological Research Centre** has an interesting fish collection. It's open from 8 am to noon and 2 to 4 pm – take a songthaew to Ao Makham.

There is good snorkelling at many points around Phuket. **Ko Hae** is said to be particularly good, as are **Ko Raya Yai**, **Ko Raya Noi** and **Ko Yai** – all accessible by boat from various piers at Rawai and Ao Paw (Bang Rong).

Places to Stay & Eat – Phuket Town

Most people head straight out to the beaches, but should you want to stay in town – on arrival or departure night for example – there are some pleasant places. At 19 Phang-Nga Rd, the 1929-vintage *On On* has rooms from 100 to 220B and a lot of character. The *Pengman* nearby at 69 Phang-Nga Rd, above a Chinese restaurant, costs just 100B for basic but clean single/double rooms with fan and bath.

The *Thara* on Thepkasatri Rd has rooms with fan and bath for 120B. About 100 metres south of the Thara, the *Suksabai Hotel* is good value with clean, well-kept rooms for 120B.

The big eating centre in town is the *Mae Porn* restaurant, on the corner of Phang-Nga Rd and Soi Pradit, near the On On Hotel. They have a vast selection of fresh Thai, Chinese and western food at good prices. Even cheaper is the *Raan Jee Nguat*, around the corner on Yaowarat Rd and across from the closed Siam cinema – fine Phuket-style noodles with curry are 10B; it opens early and closes around 2 pm. The *night market* on Phuket Rd is also good.

Places to Stay & Eat – Phuket Beaches

The two main centres for travellers are Ao Patong and Ao Kata/Ao Karon. Ao Patong is more developed and more expensive; Ao Kata/Ao Karon is a bit more laid-back in spite of its Club Med. It's initially a little confusing, since the name Kata seems to encompass places at both the Kata beaches and the south end of Karon. There are numerous other beaches of course, some of them very quiet and peaceful. Nai Han still has the cheapest beach accommodation.

Ao Patong This was the original beach development and is now full of hotels, restaurants, snack bars, motorbike-hire places, dive shops, girlie bars and all manner of things to do. If you want a little more night-time activity, then Ao Patong may appeal to you more than the other, sleepier places. The accent here is on the more expensive places – there are also a number of cheapies, but they cost a bit more than elsewhere.

Bottom end for Patong hotels and guesthouses is now 300 to 500B during the high season. During the low season from May to October, you should request a discount of 30% to 50%. Among the least expensive places to stay are *Asia, Boomerang, Capricorn Villa* and *Club Oasis*.

Ao Kata & Karon Although resort rates of 1000 to 3000B now predominate, there are still a few places in the 150 to 400B range. They're all rather similar – pleasant little wooden or cement bungalows with their own toilet, shower and veranda. Popular places include the *Kata Tropicana* or, right next to it, the *Happy Hut* – which is very similar or even a little nicer – with rooms from 150B; they're both a bit off the beach. The same goes for *Bell Guest House*, which costs 100 to 200B. *Cool Breeze* at Kata Noi has a few bungalows from 150B.

Along Karon, there are a number of places with prices from 300B, including *Karon Seaview Bungalow, My Friend* and *Fantasy Hill*.

The accommodation area is backed up with a whole collection of very similar *beach restaurants*, featuring the usual traveller's

THAILAND

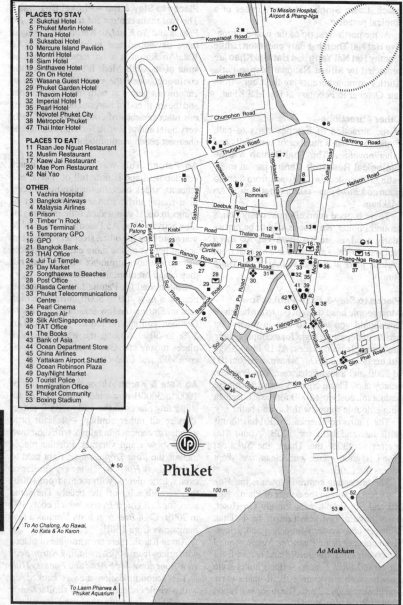

PLACES TO STAY
2 Sukchai Hotel
5 Phuket Merlin Hotel
7 Thara Hotel
8 Suksabai Hotel
10 Mercure Island Pavilion
13 Montri Hotel
18 Siam Hotel
19 Sinthavee Hotel
22 On On Hotel
25 Wasana Guest House
29 Phuket Garden Hotel
31 Thavorn Hotel
32 Imperial Hotel 1
35 Pearl Hotel
37 Novotel Phuket City
38 Metropole Phuket
47 Thai Inter Hotel

PLACES TO EAT
11 Raan Jee Nguat Restaurant
12 Muslim Restaurant
17 Kaew Jai Restaurant
20 Mae Porn Restaurant
42 Nai Yao

OTHER
1 Vachira Hospital
3 Bangkok Airways
4 Malaysia Airlines
6 Prison
9 Timber 'n Rock
14 Bus Terminal
15 Temporary GPO
16 GPO
21 Bangkok Bank
23 THAI Office
24 Jui Tui Temple
26 Day Market
27 Songthaews to Beaches
28 Post Office
30 Rasda Center
33 Phuket Telecommunications
   Centre
34 Pearl Cinema
36 Dragon Air
39 Silk Air/Singaporean Airlines
40 TAT Office
41 The Books
43 Bank of Asia
44 Ocean Department Store
45 China Airlines
48 Yattakan Airport Shuttle
49 Ocean Robinson Plaza
49 Day/Night Market
50 Tourist Police
51 Immigration Office
52 Phuket Community
53 Boxing Stadium

To Mission Hospital,
Airport & Phang-Nga

Komarapat Road

Nakhon Road

Chumphon Road

Damrong Road

Thungkha Road

Thepkasatri Road

Yaowarat Road

Satool Road

Soi Rommani

Deebuk Road

Narison Road

Suthat Road

Phang-Nga Road

To Ao Patong

Krabi   Road

Thalang Road

Fountain
Circle

Ranong Road

Rasada Road

Takua Pa Road

Montri Road

Bangkok Road

Phuntphon Road

Phuket Road

Ong Sim Phai Road

Sol Phuntphon

Sol 9

Sol Talingchan

Kra Road

Phunphon Road

Phuket

0   50   100 m

To Ao Chalong, Ao Rawai,
Ao Kata & Ao Karon

To Laem Phanwa &
Phuket Aquarium

Ao Makham

THAILAND

dishes from porridge or pancakes to fruit drinks and banana fritters. Prices for accommodation and food go hand in hand at Phuket – Kata is cheaper than Patong for both accommodation and food.

Nai Han South of Kata and west of Rawai, this used to be a more remote, get-away-from-it-all beach. Now the Phuket Yacht Club has come to the north end, although the centre has remained undeveloped. If you follow the road through the Yacht Club and beyond to the next cape, you'll come to the simple *Ao Sane Bungalows* (☎ 288306), which cost 100 to 300B, depending on the season and condition of the huts.

Other Beaches Not all the beaches have accommodation, but if you want to get away from it all you can certainly find more remote places. Camping is allowed on both Nai Yang and Mai Khao beaches. The park accommodation on Nai Yang costs 200B in a dorm-like longhouse, 300B in a four bed bungalow, 600B in a 12 bed one. Two-person tents can be rented for 60B a night.

Getting There & Away
Air You can fly to Phuket from Bangkok, Hat Yai, Narathiwat, Nakhon Si Thammarat and Surat Thani. Bangkok Airways also flies between Ko Samui and Phuket daily. THAI flies between Phuket and several international destinations, including Penang, Langkawi, Kuala Lumpur, Singapore, Hong Kong, Taipei and Sydney.

Bus From Hat Yai to Phuket, it's eight hours by bus for 112B (192 to 202B air-con). Buses from the Southern bus terminal in Bangkok take 13 or 14 hours, and cost 210B or 368B with air-con, 570B VIP. Buses from Bangkok usually go overnight, which probably helps reduce the scare quota. Other buses from Phuket include: Phang-Nga in two hours for 26B; Krabi in four hours for 47B (80B air-con); Surat Thani in six to seven hours for 77B; Nakhon Si Thammarat in eight hours for 93B; and Trang in six hours for 78B.

Boat Phuket has become a popular yachting centre. It's sometimes possible to get yacht rides from here to Penang, Sri Lanka or further afield. Try Laem Phrao Yacht Marina (☎ /fax 327109) at Laem Phrao, on the island's north-east tip; Phuket Boat Lagoon (☎ 239055; fax 239056) at Ao Sapam, about 20 km from Phuket town on the east shore; and Ao Chalong, south-west of town on the island's south-eastern edge.

Getting Around
The Airport The airport is 11 km out of town. Yuttakarn Co runs an airport shuttle bus service between the town and airport (29 km) for 70B per person. The drop-off point in town is a bit out of the way, on a soi off Phunphon Rd. There's a similar service to Patong, Kata or Karon beaches for 100B.

Local Transport When you first arrive in Phuket, beware of the local rip-off artists who will be on hand to tell you the tourist office is five km away, that the only way to get to the beaches is to take a taxi, or that a songthaew from the bus station to the town centre will cost you a small fortune.

Actually, songthaews run all over the island from a central area on Ranong Rd, near the market. The tourist office (which is also in the town centre) puts out a list of the standard charges to all the beaches and other popular destinations, plus the recommended charter costs for a vehicle. Around town, the standard fare is 7B. Out of town, the standard fares to all the beaches vary from 10B (Kata, Karon, Patong and Rawai) to 20B (Nai Han) to 30B (Nai Thon, Nai Yang).

You can also hire motorbikes (usually 100cc Japanese bikes) from around 150B a day at various places at the beaches or in Phuket town.

KHAO SOK NATIONAL PARK
Situated about midway between Phuket and Surat Thani, this 646 sq km national park has wonderful jungle, foliated limestone cliffs and some crystal-clear rivers. You can stay at the national park lodge for 350B per room, or rent tents for 50B per person. Private

treehouse bungalows are also available at *Khao Sok River Huts* (200 to 400B), *Bamboo House* (100 to 250B), *Art's Riverview Jungle Lodge* (200 to 600B) and *Our Jungle House* (400B). All places have guides for jungle trips. Meals are available for 40 to 60B.

To get to the park, take a Takua Pa-Surat Thani bus; the park is 1.5 km off Route 401 between Takua Pa and Surat Thani at Km 109.

PHANG-NGA

Situated 94 km from Phuket town on the route to Hat Yai, Phang-Nga makes a good day trip from Phuket by motorbike. On the way to the town, turn off just five km past the small town of Takua Thung and visit **Wat Tham Suwankhuha**, a cave shrine full of Buddha images. Tha Dan (with the Phang-Nga customs pier), between here and Phang-Nga, is where you hire boats to visit **Phang-Nga Bay**, which has Muslim fishing villages on stilts, strangely shaped limestone outcrops soaring out of the sea and water-filled caves. Tours from the pier vary from 150 to 400B; from Phuket they cost at least 300 to 600B per person. The best tours are run by Sayan Tour, which has a small office next to the bus terminal in Phang-Nga.

Places to Stay & Eat

The hotel with the most character and facilities is *Thawisuk*, the place with the blue facade in the middle of Phang-Nga; it has clean rooms for 100B single/double. Along Phetkasem Rd, Phang-Nga's main street, you'll also find the *Rak Phang-Nga* and the *Lak Muang* (☎ (76) 411125/288), two typical places with rooms for 200 to 280B.

You can buy good seafood and khanom jiin at the *stalls* across from the movie theatre in Phang-Nga's main market. South-west of the market, not far from the bus terminal, the new and clean *Nawng James* serves very good and inexpensive khao man kai, won-ton and noodles.

KRABI

This small town offers similar offshore excursions to Phang-Nga, but there are good local **beaches** to check out as well: Noppharat

Thara, Ao Nang, Phra Nang and Raileh are the most popular. The longest beach is along Ao Nang, a lovely spot easily reached from Krabi. Phra Nang Bay is perhaps the most beautiful of all the beaches in this area. World-class rock-climbing has become a major activity along the coast near Tham Phra Nang.

Places to Stay & Eat – Town

Guesthouses New guesthouses are popping up all over town. Most offer little cubicles over shophouses for 80 to 120B. *Riverside Guest House* and *Swallow Guest House* are among the better ones, followed by *K L, S & R* and *Grand Tower*.

Guesthouses just south-west of the town centre are quieter. Out on Jao Fah Rd, the *Chao Fa Valley* costs from 150 to 300B. On the same side of Jao Fah Rd, *KR Mansion & Guest House* offers a dorm with 50B beds; rooms for 120 to 150B with fan and shared bath; and single to quad rooms with fan and private bath for 200 to 400B.

Hotels The *New Hotel* on Phattana Rd has somewhat seedy rooms for 150/250B with fan and bath. The *Thai* on Itsara Rd is overpriced, so give it a miss. The *Riverside Hotel* at 287/11 Utarakit Rd is the best hotel deal in town at 230/350B (fan/air-con) for spacious, clean rooms. The same owners operate the friendly *City Hotel* at 15/2-3 Sukhon Rd, with sparkling rooms for 250/480B fan/air-con.

At night, *food vendors* set up along the waterfront and there is a good *morning market* in the centre of town. *Thammachart*, below the Riverside Guest House, serves good vegetarian food oriented towards farang palates.

Places to Stay – Beaches

Ao Nang This has been a centre for budget accommodation, though rates are gradually increasing with demand. Near the turn-off for the pricey Krabi Resort, but well away from the beach, *Ao Nang Ban Lae* has huts for 150 to 250B. Down on the beach heading south you'll come to *Ao Nang Beach*, *Wanna's Place* and *Sea Breeze*, all 100 to

150B for fairly simple huts, and *Gift's*, a nicer spot where larger huts with bath cost 250 to 350B

Up Route 4203, a hundred or so metres from the beach, the small *BB Bungalow* has relatively modern, if simple, huts for 150 to 350B. *Ya Ya* next door is similar. Further up the road, away from the beach, are the quite decent *Green Park* (80 to 150B) and *Jungle Hut* (70B to 200B with private bath). During the low season you may be able to get the cheaper huts for 50B a night.

Rai Leh Beach (West) This beach is accessible by boat only and is very crowded December to March. *Railay Bay Bungalows* packs in nearly a hundred huts right across the peninsula to East Hat Rai Leh; rates range from 200 to 400B, depending on size. Nicer *Railay Village* and *Sand Sea* fall in the 300 to 500B range.

Tham Phra Nang Beach This beach is also accessible by boat only and is entirely occupied by the very upmarket *Dusit Rayavadee Resort*. The beach is not Dusit's exclusive domain – a wooden walkway has been left around the limestone bluff so that you can walk to Hat Tham Phra Nang from East Rai Leh. From West Rai Leh a footpath leads through the forest around to the beach.

Rai Leh Beach (East) This beach is accessible by boat (or on foot from Tham Phra Nang or West Rai Leh). In addition to Railay Bay Bungalows, this mangrove-lined beach features the treehouse-style *Ya-Ya* for 100 to 200B, *Coco Bungalows* for 100 to 150B and *Diamond Cave Bungalows* for 80B and up. This beach tends towards mud flats at low tide. Tex Rock Climbing offers instruction, equipment and guided climbs.

Places to Eat – Beaches
Aside from the simple cafes attached to beach accommodations, the only place to find food at Krabi's beaches is along the north end of the beach at Ao Nang, past where Highway 4203 turns inland. Here

you'll find a short string of thatched-roof bars and restaurants.

Getting There & Away
Government buses to/from Bangkok cost 193B ordinary, 368 to 377B air-con or 440B VIP. Buses from Phuket to Krabi are 46B and leave hourly from the terminal on Phang-Nga Rd. There are several buses a day from Phang-Nga to Krabi for 25B. From Surat Thani, it's 60B and the trip takes four hours.

Buses to and from Krabi arrive and depart at Taalat Kao, just outside Krabi proper – a songthaew into town is 5B.

Getting Around
Boats to the various beaches at Rai Leh and Phra Nang leave from the Jao Fa pier on the Krabi waterfront and cost 40B per person. Noppharat Thara Beach and Ao Nang can be reached by songthaew for 15B.

AROUND KRABI
The **Than Bokkharani National Park** near Ao Luk, a 10B songthaew ride from town, makes an interesting excursion with its forest and small waterfalls. About five km north and then two km east of Krabi, **Wat Tham Seua** (Tiger Cave Temple) is one of southern Thailand's most famous forest wats.

KO PHI PHI
Ko Phi Phi, four hours south-west of Krabi by boat, has white beaches, good diving and a huge cavern where the nests for bird's-nest soup are collected. There are actually two islands: Phi Phi Don is inhabited and has lots of accommodation. Phi Phi Le is uninhabited and is the site for the licensed collecting of the nests of swiftlets (often erroneously called swallows); one of the nest caverns has some curious paintings.

Unfortunately, and despite the island being part of a designated national marine park, runaway growth has almost completely spoiled the atmosphere on Phi Phi Don. Phi Phi Le remains protected – not because it's part of the park (it isn't) but because the birds' nest collectors make sure no one interferes with the ecology. Because all the

THAILAND

accommodation is on Phi Phi Don, it can only be recommended these days if you're quite keen on snorkelling at nearby reefs. Otherwise, give it a miss.

Places to Stay & Eat

During high season, all accommodation on Phi Phi Don tends to be booked solid. *Chong Khao* is set inland, with a path leading to both Lo Dalam and Ton Sai beaches. Rooms in a rowhouse or bungalow range from 100 to 200B with shared facilities, 250B with attached bath. Off by itself on a little cove at the south-east end of Hat Hin Khao, *Maphrao Resort* offers thatched A-frame huts in a natural setting for 100 to 320B.

On the other side of the peninsula at Hat Yao, *PP Long Beach, Coral Bay Resort* and *Pee Pee Paradise Pearl* offer a wide variety of beach accommodation – from 100B for simple huts to 800B for more elaborate ones.

A little village of sorts has developed in the interior of the island near Ao Ton Sai and Hat Hin Khom. Among the gift shops, scuba shops and cafes there are a several budget-oriented places to stay in the 100 to 400B range, none of them very special. For the most part they just take the overflow when all the beach places are full.

Getting There & Away

Ko Phi Phi is equidistant from Phuket and Krabi, but Krabi is the more economical point of departure. From Krabi's Jao Fah pier, there are usually four boats a day, costing 125B one way for the two hour boat, 150B for the faster, one hour boat. Boats run regularly from November to May, but schedules depend on the weather during the monsoon.

There are also daily boats to Ko Phi Phi from Ao Nang, west of Krabi, from October/ November to April/May for 150B per person.

TRANG

The town of Trang, between Krabi and Hat Yai, has a history that goes back to the 1st century AD, when it was an important centre for seagoing trade. Trang probably reached its peak during the 7th to 12th centuries, at the height of the Sriwijaya Empire. Today it's a bustling little place and known as the cleanest city in Thailand. The Vegetarian Festival is celebrated fervently in September/October.

Places to Stay & Eat

A number of hotels are located along the city's two main thoroughfares, Phra Ram VI Rd and Visetkul (Wisetkun) Rd, which run from the clock tower. The *Wattana Hotel*, Phra Ram VI Rd, offers rooms for 230 to 280B with fan and bath, more for air-con. Over on Ratchadamnoen Rd, the *Phet Hotel* (☎ (75) 218002) has fair rooms with fan and shared bath for 80B, or with attached bath for 100 to 150B. They also have a restaurant downstairs.

On Visetkul Rd, the *Queen Hotel* features large clean rooms with fan for 230B, or 350B with air-con.

Adjacent to the Queen's Hotel, the *Image Restaurant* has a very broad selection of rice and noodle dishes, plus a few vegetarian specials. Two khao tom places on Phra Ram VI Rd, *Khao Tom Phui* and *Khao Tom Jai Awn*, serve all manner of Thai and Chinese standards from the evening until 2 am. The *Muslim Restaurant*, opposite the Thamrin Hotel on Phra Ram VI Rd, serves inexpensive roti kaeng, curries and rice.

Getting There & Away

A bus from Satun or Krabi to Trang is 37B; from Hat Yai it's 40B. A share taxi from the same cities is around 70B. Air-con buses from Krabi cost 70B and take three to four hours. From Phattalung it's 15B by bus, 30B by share taxi.

Air-con buses to/from Bangkok are 375B (203B for an ordinary bus) or 565B for a VIP bus. The air-con buses take about 12 hours.

Getting Around

Samlors around town cost 10B per trip, tuk-tuks 20B. Honda 100cc motorbikes can be rented from a shophouse at 44A Phra Ram VI Rd for 200B per day.

AROUND TRANG

The geography of the surrounding province is similar to that of Krabi and Phang-Nga, but it's much less frequented by tourists. Trang's coastline has several sandy beaches and coves, especially in the Sikao and Kantang districts. From the road between Trang and Kantang there's a turn-off west onto an unpaved road that leads down to the coast. At the coast, a road south leads to Hat Yao, Hat Yong Ling and Hat Jao Mai. The road north leads to Hat Chang Lang and Hat Pak Meng. There are also several small islands just off the coast, including Ko Muk, Ko Kradan, Ko Ngai (Hai) and Ko Sukon.

SUNGAI KOLOK & BAN TABA

Sungai Kolok in the south-east is the departure point for the east coast of Malaysia. Another border crossing at Ban Taba, 32 km east, is a shorter and quicker route to Kota Bharu, Malaysia. Eventually, this crossing is supposed to replace Sungai Kolok, but it looks like Sungai Kolok will remain open for a long time.

Information

There are a couple of banks in the town centre; Malaysian dollars can be changed at the bus station or in shops. It's easier to buy baht from a Malaysian bank or moneychanger before you cross into Thailand, although it's also possible to change money on the Thai side of town. There's a TAT office next to the immigration post on the Thai side. The border is open from 5 am to 5 pm (6 am to 6 pm Malaysian time).

Places to Stay

There are few English signs in Sungai Kolok. There are a number of places to stay in the centre of town, although they are a bit grotty. The town is just a 10B trishaw ride from the border or a five minute walk straight ahead from the railway station.

The most inexpensive places are along Charoenkhet Rd. Cheapies include the *Savoy Hotel* and, next door, the *Thailiang Hotel*, which has rooms from 120 to 150B. Over on the corner of Thetpathom and Waman Amnoey Rds is the pleasant *Valentine* at 180B with fan and 330B with air-con. There's a coffee shop downstairs and free fruit and coffee is provided to guests.

Places to Eat

There's a good Chinese *vegetarian restaurant* between the Asia and Savoy hotels that's open daily 7 am to 6 pm. A cluster of reliable *Malay food vendors* can be found at the market and in front of the railway station.

Getting There & Away

When you cross the border from Malaysia, the railway station is about a km straight ahead on the right-hand side – 10B by motorcycle taxi. The bus station is a further km beyond the railway station, down a turning to the left.

Bus & Share Taxi Air-con buses to Hat Yai cost 98B and leave from the Valentine Hotel four times daily. The trip takes about four hours. Share taxis to Hat Yai cost 120B and leave from next to the Thailiang Hotel.

Train From Hat Yai, the 3rd class rail fare is 31B. From Bangkok, fares are 180B in 3rd class and 378B in 2nd class, before the rapid, express or sleeper supplements.

Ferry A ferry across the river into Malaysia is 5B. The border crossing here is open the same hours as in Sungai Kolok. From the Malaysian side you can get buses direct to Kota Bharu for RM1.50.

THAILAND

Vietnam

After the fall of South Vietnam to Communist forces in 1975, Vietnam was virtually isolated from the world. But in 1989 Vietnam flung open the doors to foreign tourists and investors. This now-popular travel destination offers a rich, unique culture and outstanding scenic beauty.

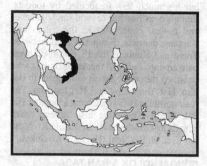

Facts about Vietnam

HISTORY

About 1000 years of Chinese rule over the Red River Delta (all of Vietnam at the time), marked by tenacious Vietnamese resistance and repeated rebellions, ended in 938 AD when Ngo Quyen vanquished the Chinese armies at the Bach Dang River.

During the next few centuries, Vietnam repulsed repeated invasions by China and expanded in a southward direction along the coast at the expense of the kingdom of Champa, which was wiped out in 1471.

The first contact between Vietnam and the west took place in Roman times. Recent European contact with Vietnam began in the 16th century, when European merchants and missionaries arrived. Despite restrictions and periods of persecution, the Catholic Church eventually had a greater impact on Vietnam than on any country in Asia except the Philippines.

In 1858 a joint military force from France and the Spanish colony of the Philippines stormed Danang after the killing of several missionaries. Early the next year, they seized Saigon. A few years later, Vietnam's Emperor Tu Duc signed a treaty that gave the French part of the Mekong Delta region. In 1883 the French imposed a Treaty of Protectorate on Vietnam.

French rule often proved cruel and arbitrary. Ultimately, the most successful resistance came from the Communists. The first Marxist group in Indochina, the Vietnam Revolutionary Youth League, was founded by Ho Chi Minh in 1925.

During WWII, the only group that did anything significant to resist the Japanese occupation was the Communist-dominated Viet Minh. When WWII ended, Ho Chi Minh – whose Viet Minh forces already controlled large parts of the country – declared Vietnàm independent. French efforts to reassert control soon led to violent confrontations and full-scale war. In May 1954 Viet Minh forces overran the French garrison at Dien Bien Phu.

The Geneva Accords of mid-1954 provided for a temporary division of the country into two zones at the Ben Hai River. When the leader of the southern zone, an anti-Communist Catholic named Ngo Dinh Diem, refused to hold elections scheduled for 1956, the Ben Hai line became the de facto border between the Democratic Republic of Vietnam (North Vietnam) and the Republic of Vietnam (South Vietnam).

In about 1960, the Hanoi government changed its policy of opposition to the Diem regime from one of 'political struggle' to one of 'armed struggle'. The National Liberation Front (NLF), a Communist guerrilla group better known as the Viet Cong (VC), was founded to fight against Diem.

Diem was a brutal ruler and was assassinated in 1963 by his own troops. After Hanoi

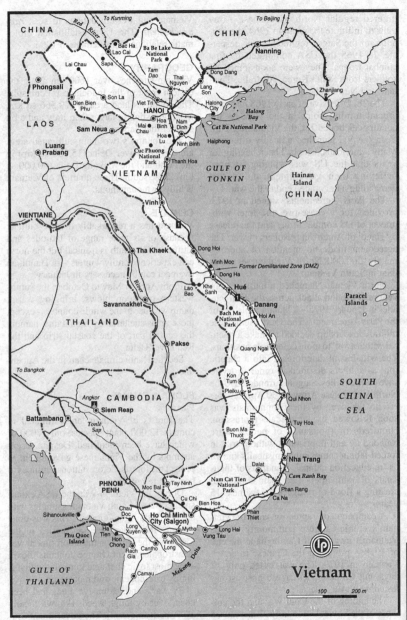

Vietnam

ordered regular North Vietnamese Army units to infiltrate the south in 1964, the situation for the Saigon regime became desperate. In 1965 the USA committed its first combat troops. They were soon joined by soldiers from South Korea, Australia, Thailand and New Zealand.

The Tet Offensive of early 1968 marked a crucial turning point in the war. As the country celebrated Tet, the Vietnamese New Year, the VC launched a deadly offensive. Many Americans, who had been hearing for years that the US was winning, stopped believing their government and started demanding a negotiated end to the war.

The Paris Agreements, signed in 1973, provided for a cease-fire, the total withdrawal of US combat forces and the release by Hanoi of American prisoners of war. The agreement made no mention of approximately 200,000 North Vietnamese troops then in South Vietnam.

North Vietnam launched a massive conventional ground attack across the 17th Parallel in January 1975 – a blatant violation of the Paris Agreements. The South Vietnamese military leadership decided to make a 'tactical withdrawal' to more defensible positions. The withdrawal deteriorated into a chaotic rout as soldiers deserted in order to try to save their families. Saigon surrendered to the North Vietnamese Army on 30 April 1975.

The takeover by the Communists was soon followed by large-scale repression. Hundreds of thousands of people were rounded up and imprisoned without trial in forced-labour camps euphemistically known as 're-education camps'. Hundreds of thousands of southerners fled their homeland, creating a flood of refugees for the next 15 years.

A campaign of repression against Vietnam's ethnic-Chinese community – plus Vietnam's invasion of Cambodia at the end of 1978 – prompted the Chinese to attack Vietnam in 1979. The war lasted only 17 days, but Chinese-Vietnamese mistrust has lasted well over a decade.

The ending of the Cold War and the collapse of the Soviet Union in 1991 has caused Vietnam and western nations to seek *rapprochement*. The USA established diplomatic relations with Vietnam in 1995.

GEOGRAPHY

Vietnam stretches over 1600 km along the eastern coast of the Indochinese Peninsula. The country's land area is 329,566 sq km, making it slightly larger than Italy and a bit smaller than Japan.

The country's two main cultivated areas are the Red River Delta (15,000 sq km) in the north and the Mekong Delta (60,000 sq km) in the south. Three-quarters of Vietnam is hilly or mountainous.

CLIMATE

Vietnam has a remarkably diverse climate because of its wide range of latitudes and altitudes. The south is tropical but the north can experience chilly winters – in Hanoi, an overcoat can be necessary in January.

From April or May to October, the southwestern monsoon blows, bringing warm, damp weather to the whole country – except those areas sheltered by mountains, namely the central part of the coastal strip and the Red River Delta.

See the Hanoi climate chart in the Appendix.

FLORA & FAUNA
Flora

The forests of Vietnam are estimated to contain 12,000 plant species, only 7000 of which have been identified. Despite recent attempts by the Vietnamese government to protect the forests, deforestation continues to be a severe problem.

During the Vietnam War, the USA extensively sprayed South Vietnam's jungles with the herbicide Agent Orange. This was done to deny the Viet Cong sanctuaries in the forest, but the effect on the environment was catastrophic. Agent Orange contains dioxin – the most toxic chemical known – which is highly carcinogenic and mutagenic.

By war's end, extensive areas had been taken over by tough weeds (known locally as 'American grass'). The government estimates that 20,000 sq km of forest and farmland were lost as a direct result of the American war effort. A reafforestation programme has helped, but the forests of Vietnam may never return to their prewar grandeur.

Fauna

Vietnam's wild fauna is enormously diverse. The country is home to 273 species of mammals, 773 species of birds, 180 species of reptiles, 80 species of amphibians, hundreds of species of fish and thousands of kinds of invertebrates. Larger animals of special importance in conservation efforts include the elephant, rhinoceros, tiger, leopard, black bear, honey bear, snub-nosed monkey, douc langur (remarkable for its variegated colours), concolour gibbon, macaque, rhesus monkey, serow (a kind of mountain goat), flying squirrel, kouprey (a blackish-brown forest ox), banteng (a kind of wild ox), deer, peacock, pheasant, crocodile, python, cobra and turtle.

Endangered Species

Tragically, Vietnam's wildlife is in a precipitous decline as forest habitats are destroyed and waterways become polluted. In addition, uncontrolled illegal hunting has exterminated the local populations of various animals, in some cases eliminating entire species. Officially, the government has recognised 54 species of mammals and 60 species of birds as endangered.

In coastal areas, the locals sell colourful live coral dredged up from the sea floor, which of course goes white and dead in a few hours anyway. Thus, tourists buying this stuff are helping to deplete the scarce coral reefs. In the Central Highlands, rare animals are often trapped for sale to restaurants or to make exotic trophies. True, the local people need the money, but there are better ways to pass it over to them. Think about it.

National Parks

At the present time, Vietnam has five national parks: Cuc Phuong, Cat Ba and Ba Be Lake in the north; Bach Ma National Park in the centre; and Nam Cat Tien National Park in the south.

GOVERNMENT & POLITICS

The Socialist Republic of Vietnam (SRV) came into existence in July 1976 as a unitary state comprising the Democratic Republic of Vietnam (North Vietnam) and the territory of the defeated Republic of Vietnam (South Vietnam). Despite the rapid pace of economic reforms in the 1990s, the government shows no sign of moving towards democracy and political control remains firmly in the hands of the Communist Party.

ECONOMY

Vietnam is poor, with an estimated per capita income of US$200 per year. As has long been the case, bureaucracy and corruption remain the most significant impediments to Vietnam's economic development. However, there are signs that things are improving.

The economy was devastated in the 1960s and 1970s by war, but even the government has admitted that the present economic fiasco is mainly the result of the collectivisation policies that followed reunification and bloated military budgets.

Limited private enterprise was reintroduced in 1986. Since 1991 the loss of trade and aid from the former Eastern bloc has caused Vietnam to greatly accelerate the pace of free-market economic reform. The reforms have breathed new life into an economy that was moribund. Ironically, the recent flood of money from foreign investors has propped up the state sector, causing it to expand. The bloated bureaucracy is resisting privatisation, and plans to open a stock market have been postponed until some unspecified time in the future. Still, there are many who believe that Vietnam has all the potential to become one of Asia's economic 'tigers'.

POPULATION & PEOPLE

In 1995 Vietnam's population reached 74.6 million, making it the 12th most populous country in the world. There is virtually no government-orchestrated family planning policies and people may have as many children as they wish. Annual population growth is 2.3%.

The population is 84% ethnic-Vietnamese and 2% ethnic-Chinese; the rest is made up of Khmers, Chams (a remnant of the once-mighty Champa kingdom) and members of some 60 ethno-linguistic groups (also known as Montagnards, which means 'Highlanders' in French).

EDUCATION

Although university education is out of reach for most Vietnamese, the country's literacy rate is estimated at 88.6%. Unlike in many other poor countries, women generally receive the same access to education as men.

ARTS

Sculpture

Vietnamese sculpture has traditionally centred on religious themes and functioned as an adjunct to architecture, especially that of pagodas, temples and tombs.

The Cham civilisation produced spectacular carved sandstone figures for its Hindu and Buddhist sanctuaries. The largest single collection of Cham sculpture in the world is at the Cham Museum in Danang.

Architecture

The Vietnamese have not been great builders like their neighbours the Khmers, who erected the monuments of Angkor in Cambodia. Most of what the Vietnamese have built has been made of wood and other materials that proved highly vulnerable in the tropical climate.

The grand exception is the stunning towers built by Vietnam's ancient Cham culture. These are most numerous in central Vietnam. The Cham towers at My Son are a major tourist drawcard.

Water Puppetry

Water puppetry (*roi nuoc*) is a uniquely Vietnamese art form found mostly in the north, though there are shows put on in Saigon.

SOCIETY & CONDUCT

Traditional Culture

The family is the basic unit of Vietnamese society, and one who is not married is pitied rather than envied. Most foreigners are asked if they are married – if you're single and under age 30, the best response is 'not yet'. If you're over 30, perhaps you simply should say 'yes, and I have one child' even if this is not so. Trying to explain that you are happily single will not go down well with most Vietnamese.

Dos & Don'ts

Shoes are removed inside most Buddhist temples and often in people's homes, but this is not universal so watch what others do. Don't point the bottoms of your feet towards other people or towards Buddhist statues.

In general, shorts are considered inappropriate wear for all but children or men labouring in the sun. However, the recent influx of foreigners has influenced Vietnamese tastes, and women in fashionable Saigon have started wearing shorts. However, such changes have not yet filtered to the hinterlands.

Leaving a pair of chopsticks sticking vertically in a rice bowl looks similar to the incense sticks which are burned for the dead. This powerful death sign is not appreciated anywhere in the Orient.

RELIGION

Four great philosophies and religions have shaped the spiritual life of the Vietnamese people: Confucianism, Taoism, Buddhism and Christianity.

Over the centuries, Confucianism, Taoism and Buddhism have fused with popular Chinese beliefs and ancient Vietnamese animism to form what is known collectively as Tam Giao (Triple Religion), which is sometimes referred to as Vietnamese Buddhism. The religious life of the Vietnamese is also profoundly influenced by ancestor worship, which dates from long before the arrival of Confucianism or Buddhism.

Muslims, mostly ethnic-Khmers and Chams, constitute about 0.5% of the population.

VIETNAM

Vietnam has the highest percentage of Catholics (8% to 10% of the population) in Asia outside of the Philippines.

Caodaism is an indigenous Vietnamese sect that was founded with the intention of creating the ideal religion by fusing the secular and religious philosophies of both east and west. It was established in the early 1920s based on messages revealed in seances to Ngo Minh Chieu, the group's founder. The sect's colourful headquarters is in Tay Ninh, 96 km north-west of Saigon. There are currently about two million followers of Caodaism in Vietnam.

LANGUAGE
Perhaps the trickiest aspect of spoken Vietnamese for westerners is learning to differentiate between the six tones, each of which is represented by a different diacritical mark. Thus, every syllable in Vietnamese can be pronounced six different ways. Depending on the tones, the word *ma* can be read to mean 'phantom', 'mother', 'rice seedling', 'tomb' or 'horse'.

Most of the names of the letters of the Latin-based *quoc ngu* alphabet are the same as the names of the letters in French. Dictionaries are alphabetised as in English except that each vowel/tone combination is treated as a different letter. The consonants of the Vietnamese alphabet are pronounced much as they are in English with a few exceptions.

đ	With a crossbar; like a hard 'd'
d	Without a crossbar; like a 'z' in the north and a 'y' in the south
gi	Like a 'z' in the north and a 'y' in the south
ng	Like the '-ng a-' in 'long ago'
nh	Like the Spanish 'ñ' (as in *mañana*)
ph	Like an 'f'
r	Like 'z' in the north and 'r' in the south
s	Like an 's' in the north and 'sh' in the south
tr	Like 'ch' in the north and 'tr' in the south
th	Like a strongly aspirated 't'
x	Like an 's'
ch	Like a 'k'
ơ	As in 'bird'
ư	Between the 'i' in 'sister' and the 'u' in sugar

Basics
Hello.	Chao.
Good night.	Chuc ngu ngon.
Thank you.	Cam on.
Thank you very much.	Cam on rat nhieu.
Excuse me. (often used before questions)	Xin loi.
Yes.	Vang. (north) Co, phai. (south)
No.	Khong.
I don't understand.	Toi khong hieu.
How much (price)?	Cai nay bao nhieu tien?

Getting Around
I want to go to ...	Toi muon đi ...
Is it far?	Co xa khong?
Where is the ...?	... ơ đau?
bus station	ben xe
railway station	ga xe lua
post office	buu dien
telephone	dien thoai
What time does the ... leave/arrive?	May gio ... khoi hanh/den?
bus	xe buyt
train	xe lua

Accommodation
hotel	khach san
guesthouse	nha khach
cheap hotel	khach san re tien
air-con	quat lanh
toilet	nha ve sinh
bathroom	nha tam

Do you have any rooms available?
  Ong co phong nao trong khong?
How much is it per night/per person?
  Bao nhieu moi dem/moi nguoi?

Time & Dates
What time is it?	May gio roi?
today	hom nay
tomorrow	ngay mai
yesterday	hom qua

Health & Emergencies

I'm sick.	*Toi bi benh.*
Please call a doctor.	*Lam on goi bac si.*
hospital	*benh vien*
chemist/pharmacy	*nha thuoc tay*
dizziness	*chong mat*
headache	*nhuc dau*
vomiting	*oi, mua*
Help!	*Cuu toi voi!*
Thief!	*Cuop/Cap!*
police	*cong an*

Numbers

first	*nhat*
second	*nhi*
1	*mot*
2	*hai*
3	*ba*
4	*bon*
5	*nam*
6	*sau*
7	*bay*
8	*tam*
9	*chin*
10	*muoi, chuc*
11	*muoi mot*
19	*muoi chin*
20	*hai muoi*
21	*hai muoi mot*
30	*ba muoi*
90	*chin muoi*
100	*mot tram*
200	*hai tram*
900	*chin tram*
1000	*mot nghin*
10,000	*muoi nghin*
100,000	*tram nghin*
1 million	*mot trieu*

From three upwards, the cardinal and ordinal numbers are the same.

Facts for the Visitor

PLANNING
Maps

Basic road maps of Vietnam are readily available, though fine details are lacking.

Lonely Planet's *Vietnam travel atlas* gives an in-depth view of towns, highways and topographic features.

It's easy to find good maps of the major cities such as Hanoi, Saigon, Hué, Danang and Nha Trang. However, maps of most small to mid-sized cities are rare indeed.

HIGHLIGHTS

Some places which have proven particularly popular with travellers include Dalat, Nha Trang, Hoi An, Hué, Hoa Lu, Cat Ba Island, Halong Bay and Sapa.

TOURIST OFFICES

Vietnam doesn't have tourist offices as such. Rather, there are state-run travel agencies which masquerade as tourist offices. The names they use, such as Vietnam Tourism and Saigon Tourist, are misleading. They are not in the business of promoting Vietnam as a tourist destination. In fact, they have little information that they're willing to give for free – essentially, they are in business to book pricey tours. Booking tours through private agencies is of course another possibility, and is often cheaper.

Local Tourist Offices

Every province has a regional tourist office cum travel agency. Although selling tours is their primary function, the staff might be willing to part with some useful travel information if you approach them in a friendly manner. See the listing for individual cities for the location of local 'tourist offices'.

Tourist Offices Abroad

Some Vietnamese 'tourist offices' abroad include:

France
> Vietnam Tourism, 4, Rue Cherubini, Paris 75002 (☎ 01 42 86 86 37; fax 01 42 60 43 32)
> Saigon Tourist, 24, Rue des Bernadins, Paris 75005 (☎ 01 40 51 03 02; fax 01 43 25 05 70)

Germany
> Saigon Tourist, 24 Dudenstrasse 78 W, 1000 Berlin 61 (☎ (030) 786-5056; fax 786-5596)

Japan
    Saigon Tourist, IDI 6th floor, Crystal Building, 1-2, Kanda Awaji-cho, Chiyoda-ku, Tokyo 101 (☎ (03) 3258-5931; fax 3253-6819)
Singapore
    Vietnam Tourism, 101 Upper Cross St, No 02-44 People's Park Centre, Singapore 0105 (☎ (02) 532-3130; fax 532-2952; pager 601-3914)
    Saigon Tourist, 131 Tanglin Rd, Tudor Court, Singapore 1024 (☎ (02) 735-1433; fax 735-1508)

VISAS & DOCUMENTS

While Vietnamese bureaucracy is legendary, completing the necessary paperwork to obtain a visa is not all that daunting. Bangkok seems to be the fastest and most popular place to get a Vietnamese visa, though Hong Kong is a viable alternative. Keep plenty of visa photos handy – you need at least two to apply for a visa (sometimes three or four), and occasionally a couple more photos to get through immigration upon arrival in Vietnam.

Tourist Visas

Tourist visas are only valid for a single 30 day stay. To make matters worse, the visa specifies the exact date of arrival and departure. Thus, you must solidify your travel plans well in advance. You cannot arrive even one day earlier than your visa specifies. And if you change your plans and postpone your trip by two weeks, then you'll only have 16 days remaining on your visa instead of 30 days.

Vietnamese visas specify where you are permitted to enter and leave the country – usually Ho Chi Minh City's Tan Son Nhat or Hanoi's Noi Bai airports. Other options worth considering are the Chinese border at Huu Nghi Quan (Friendship Gate) or Lao Cai, or the Cambodian border at Moc Bai and the Laotian border at Lao Bao. Make sure this is made clear on your visa application. If you later decide to exit from a place not listed on your visa, amendments can be made at the Foreign Affairs Ministry in Hanoi or Saigon, or even at the local immigration police (Hué is popular for this).

You usually have the choice of getting your visa issued on a separate piece of paper or else stamped into your passport. Having it stamped into your passport is generally *not* a good idea. The reason is that in most towns, hotels are required to register their guests – foreign and domestic – with the police. To do this, they need your visa and locals' identity papers. If the visa is stamped into your passport, you may need to hand it over, thus exposing yourself to the possibility of it getting lost. When you apply for a visa, it's best to give the travel agency photocopies of your passport rather than the original – this will ensure that the visa comes back on a separate paper.

Prices for single-entry tourist visas are around US$45 to US$60. In Bangkok they can be issued in about four days, in Hong Kong five days, but in other places (Taiwan, for example) as long as 10 working days. An 'express visa' takes half the time and is arranged by fax to Hanoi – the drawback is a greater chance of things going awry (paperwork not done properly on the Vietnamese end and the visa being declared 'invalid' on arrival). Many travel agencies offer package deals with visa and air ticket included. In Bangkok, the place to look for competitive prices is Khao San Rd. Vista Travel at 24/4 Khao San Rd claims a large share of the budget travel market. In Hong Kong, a travel agency specialising in visas and air tickets to Vietnam is Phoenix Services (☎ 2722-7378; fax 2369-8884) in Room B, 6th floor, Milton Mansion, 96 Nathan Rd, Tsimshatsui, Kowloon.

Visas can also be obtained in Australia through STA Travel for around A$90 or from other travel agencies. They take about two weeks to issue.

The Vietnamese embassy in Beijing has had some bad reviews from travellers – sometimes it's cooperative, but usually not.

Business Visas

There are several advantages in having a business visa: such visas are usually valid for three months; they can be issued for multiple-entry journeys; you are permitted to work in Vietnam; and the visas can be extended with relative ease. Business visas

VIETNAM

are arranged at travel agencies, who can also normally arrange the requisite 'sponsor'. Trying to obtain the visa yourself through a Vietnamese embassy is more troublesome.

There is another category of business visa which remains valid for six months. To get these, you must apply in Vietnam. If approved, you must then go abroad (most travellers go to Phnom Penh or Vientiane) to pick up the visa from a Vietnamese embassy.

Warning
You might think that after you've obtained your visa and entered Vietnam, all is well. Unfortunately, Vietnamese immigration authorities may arbitrarily give you a shorter stay than what your visa calls for. Thus, your 30 day tourist visa might only be validated for one week, or your six month business visa may only net you a three month stay. No matter what it says on the front side of your visa, immediately after it's been stamped by the immigration officer, look on the back side and see how many days they've given you. If you've only been given a week, sometimes you can get it changed right at the airport or border checkpoint – otherwise, you might be forced to visit the Foreign Affairs Ministry and apply for an extension.

Visa Extensions
In mid-1995 the Vietnamese authorities suddenly stopped issuing visa extensions to tourists. However, they can issue extensions in 'emergencies', but this is probably more trouble than it's worth. When your 30 days is up, you'd best leave the country.

When visa extensions are granted, they are granted for 15 days at a time and you can get extensions up to a maximum stay of three months. The cost is US$20 or US$30, depending on whether the relevant officials in charge of such matters need a new colour TV or a new refrigerator. Either way, visa extensions are not usually easy to handle yourself. Rather, a Vietnamese travel agent or your hotel can make the arrangements. Many hotels have a sign on the front desk indicating that they have a visa extension

service. The procedure takes one or two days and one photo is needed. You can apply for your extension even several weeks before it's necessary. This process is only readily accomplished in major cities – Hanoi, Saigon, Danang or Hué. At the time of this writing, the Hué office was the most friendly, but that can easily change when officials get reshuffled.

Re-Entry Permits
If you plan a side trip to Cambodia, you can use your original Vietnamese visa (if it hasn't expired) to re-enter Vietnam, but you must first secure a re-entry permit (US$10). Travel agencies in Saigon or Hanoi can usually get these permits much faster than you can yourself, but if you're patient you can try applying directly to the Interior Ministry. If you fly to Phnom Penh, you can get a Cambodian visa on arrival for free if you stay less than 15 days – for overland crossings, you'll need to apply for a Cambodian visa.

Travel Permits
Since 1993 internal travel permits supposedly have been abolished. However, local authorities make up their own rules. Currently, travel permits are required for the following places: Lat Village and Lang Bian Mountain in Dalat; minority villages around Buon Ma Thuot and Pleiku in the Central Highlands; and villages around the Demilitarised Zone (DMZ).

However, policies change frequently. Furthermore, there have been reports of con artists insisting that police permits are required when in fact this is not the case. Many unsuspecting foreigners have paid for bogus 'permits' which were little more than a photocopied piece of paper with someone's signature scribbled on it.

EMBASSIES
Vietnamese Embassies
Vietnamese embassies abroad include:

Australia
    6 Timbarra Crescent, O'Malley, Canberra, ACT 2603 (☎ (06) 286-6059)

China
   32 Guanghua Lu, Jianguomenwai, Beijing
   (☎ (010) 532-1125)
   Guangzhou Consulate
   (☎ (020) 776-9555 ext 101, 604)
France
   62-66 Rue Boileau, Paris 16 (☎ 01 44 14 64 00)
UK
   12-14 Victoria Rd, London W8 5RD
   (☎ (0171) 937-1912)
USA
   Vietnamese Liaison Office, Washington, DC
   (☎ (800) 874-5100). Visa processing is done by
   Travel Documents Inc, 734 15th St NW, Suite
   400, Washington, DC 20005 (☎ (202) 638-3800)

See the other chapters in this book for Vietnamese embassies in those countries.

Foreign Embassies in Vietnam
Useful embassies in Hanoi include:

Australia
   66 Ly Thuong Kiet St (☎ 825-2703)
Cambodia
   71A Tran Hung Dao St (☎ 825-3789)
Canada
   31 Hung Vuong St (☎ 823-5500)
China
   46 Hoang Dieu St (☎ 825-3736)
France
   57 Tran Hung Dao St (☎ 825-2719)
Germany
   29 Tran Phu St (☎ 843-0245)
Laos (Consular Section)
   40 Quang Trung St (☎ 826-8724)
Malaysia
   Building A3, Van Phuc Diplomatic Quarters
   (☎ 825-3371)
Myanmar (Burma)
   Building A3, Van Phuc Diplomatic Quarters
   (☎ 825-3369)
Philippines
   27B Tran Hung Dao St (☎ 825-7873)
Thailand
   63-65 Hoang Dieu St (☎ 823-5092)
UK
   16 Ly Thuong Kiet St (☎ 825-2510)
USA (liaison)
   7 Lang Ha St, but will move in 1997
   (☎ 843-1500)

CUSTOMS
Travellers occasionally report trouble with Vietnamese customs. Some travellers have even had their Lonely Planet books seized! Ditto for video tapes. It's best to keep such dangerous items buried deep down in your luggage or else in your coat pocket.

You are not permitted to take antiques or other 'cultural treasures' out of the country. If you purchase fake antiques, be sure that you have a receipt and a customs clearance form from the seller. Suspected antiques will be seized, or else you'll have to pay a 'fine'.

MONEY
Costs
Vietnam is very cheap compared with any western country, but not so cheap compared with some travel bargains in Asia, such as Indonesia and India. It would be dirt cheap if you could pay the same as the locals, but special 'foreigners only' prices are often charged. In hotels, foreigners are normally charged double the price a Vietnamese would pay for the same room. For airline tickets, foreigners pay triple; for trains, foreigners are charged five times the Vietnamese price!

Nevertheless, since hotels, food and buses are so cheap, ascetics can get by on less than US$10 a day. For US$15 to US$20, a backpacker can live fairly well.

Currency
The dong is the currency of Vietnam. Banknotes in denominations of 200d, 500d, 1000d, 2000d, 5000d, 10,000d, 20,000d and 50,000d are presently in circulation. There are no coins.

The US dollar virtually acts as a second local currency, and hotels, airlines and travel agencies all normally quote their prices in dollars. This is in part because Vietnamese prices are so unwieldy, since US$100 is over one million dong! For this reason, we also quote prices in US dollars. However, realise that you can, and should, pay dong. Indeed, Vietnamese law requires that all transactions be in dong, though in practice many people will accept dollars.

Currency Exchange

The following table shows exchange rates:

Australia	A$1	=	8727d
Canada	C$1	=	8076d
France	FF10	=	2141d
Germany	DM1	=	7239d
Japan	¥100	=	9959d
New Zealand	NZ$1	=	7722d
Thailand	100B	=	43,408d
UK	UK£1	=	17,216d
USA	US$1	=	11,000d

Changing Money

Large-denomination bills (US$100) are preferred when changing into dong, but a small supply (say US$20 worth) of ones and fives will prove useful on arrival to hire a taxi into the city.

Travellers' cheques in US dollars can be exchanged for dong at certain banks – most hotels and airline offices will not accept travellers' cheques. Lost or stolen travellers' cheques cannot be replaced in Vietnam.

Be very careful with your money – travellers' cheques and large-denomination cash belongs in a money belt or pockets sewn inside your trousers.

Visa, MasterCard and JCB credit cards are now acceptable in major cities. Getting a cash advance from a credit card is also possible, but you'll be charged a 4% commission.

Money can be cabled into Vietnam quickly and cheaply and the recipient can be paid in US dollars. However, sending money by wire is fast only if the overseas office is a 'correspondent bank' with Vietcombank. The list of correspondent banks is not extensive, but growing. At the time of writing, only the branches of Vietcombank in Saigon and Hanoi are equipped to handle wire transfers.

Black Market

There is really no black market in Vietnam. However, black market 'moneychangers' may approach you on the street and offer a fantastic exchange rate. You can be sure that such exchanges will wind up with you getting cheated or robbed.

During major public holidays when the banks are closed, the only place you can legally change money is at the airports in Hanoi and Ho Chi Minh City. Otherwise, you'll have to change US dollars cash in a small shop. Jewellery shops are the best places for this, but you will be charged a hefty commission (at least 5%).

Tipping & Bargaining

Tipping is not expected but it's enormously appreciated. For someone making under US$50 per month, 10% of the cost of your meal can equal half a day's wages.

Bargaining is common, even with the police if you are fined! Always be polite and smiling when bargaining – nastiness will cause the other party to lose face, in which case they'll dig in their heels and you'll come out the loser.

POST & COMMUNICATIONS

Postal Rates

International postal service from Vietnam is not unreasonably priced when compared with most other countries. However, international telecommunications charges are among the highest in the world.

Sending Mail

Take your letters to the post office yourself and make sure that the clerk cancels them *while you watch* so that someone for whom the stamps are worth a day's salary does not soak them off and throw your letters away.

Receiving Mail

Poste restante works in the larger cities but don't count on it elsewhere. There is a small surcharge for picking up poste restante letters. All post offices are marked with the words 'Buu Dien'.

Telephone

The cheapest and simplest way by far to make an international direct dial (IDD) call is to buy a telephone card, known in Vietnam as a 'UniphoneKad'. They are on sale at the telephone company. UniphoneKads can only be used in special telephones which are mainly found only in Hanoi and Ho Chi Minh City (and mostly in hotel lobbies). The cards are issued in three denominations; 30,000d, 150,000d and 300,000d. The 30,000d card will only work for domestic calls.

To call international long distance, first dial 00 followed by the country code, area code and phone number. To call domestic long distance, dial 0 plus the area code and phone number.

To call Vietnam from abroad, the country code is 84.

Fax, Telegraph & Email

Most GPOs and many tourist hotels in Vietnam offer domestic and international fax, telegraph and telex services. Hotels are likely to charge more than the post office.

To access Email, you'll have to make an international phone call. Vietnam's packet-switching network, Vietpac, is so expensive and takes so long to set up that it's not a viable option even for foreign residents. Access to the Internet is currently restricted to government agencies, though there is talk of opening service to businesses.

BOOKS

Lonely Planet's *Vietnam – travel survival kit* has the full story on the country. Two classic books from the French colonial period are Graham Greene's novel *The Quiet American* and Norman Lewis' account of travels in the region in the early 1950s, *A Dragon Apparent*. One of the finest books about the war written by a Vietnamese is *The Sorrow of War* by Bao Ninh. *Brother Enemy* by Nayan Chanda is an excellent book about the war's aftermath.

FILMS

There are heaps of videos dealing with America's war experience in Vietnam. Some titles to look for include *Rambo, Apocalypse Now, Full Metal Jacket, Platoon, The Deer Hunter, Good Morning Vietnam, Born on the 4th of July, Air America* and *Heaven & Earth*. Films set during the French colonial period include *The Lover* and *Indochine*. More contemporary films include *Scent of the Green Papaya* and *Cyclo*.

NEWSPAPERS & MAGAZINES

The English-language *Vietnam News* is published daily in Saigon but is little more than a pamphlet – don't bother. Of far more interest is the *Vietnam Investment Review* (published weekly) and the *Vietnam Economic Times* (published monthly). *What's On in Saigon* is a monthly freebie magazine (look for it in pubs) which gives the rundown on Saigon's nightlife.

RADIO & TV

Foreign radio services such as the BBC World Service, Radio Australia and Voice of America can be picked up on short-wave frequencies.

Vietnamese TV broadcasts little of interest to foreigners, but satellite dish antennae are rapidly proliferating and many hotels now offer Hong Kong's Star TV, BBC, CNN and other channels.

PHOTOGRAPHY & VIDEO

New film-safe machines have replaced the ancient dental x-ray machines which were at one time notorious for destroying film upon arrival at the airport.

For videos, on both arrival and departure, you are supposed to get a certificate of clearance from the 'Cultural Department'. Of course, the Cultural Department doesn't have branch offices in the airport or at land border crossings. Some travellers have even been hassled over laser disks and music cassette tapes. Usually, the payment of a small 'fine' causes these problems to evaporate.

ELECTRICITY

About 95% of the electric current in Vietnam is 220V at 50 Hz, but you can still find 110V (also at 50 Hz). Looking at the shape of the outlet on the wall gives no clue as to what voltage is flowing through the wires, so try to find a light bulb to check.

WEIGHTS & MEASURES

Vietnam subscribes to the international metric system.

LAUNDRY

Virtually every hotel offers a cheap laundry service, but they dry clothes in the sun so this may not work well in the rainy season.

HEALTH

Malaria is a serious threat and chloroquine resistance has been widely reported in Vietnam. There have been outbreaks of Japanese encephalitis in the south, so a vaccination is highly recommended.

TOILETS

The toilets in hotels catering to foreigners are of the familiar western 'throne' variety. The toilets in restaurants and other public places are generally the less aesthetic squat variety and toilet paper is seldom provided. Public toilets are scarce anyplace in Vietnam, and in cities you'll often have to visit a restaurant or cafe to take care of business. Out in the hinterlands, just find some bushes.

WOMEN TRAVELLERS

While it always pays to be prudent (avoid dark, lonely alleys at night), western women very rarely have problems in Vietnam. But it can be a different story for an Asian woman.

An Asian woman accompanied by a western male will automatically be labelled a 'Vietnamese whore'. The fact that the couple could be married (or just friends) doesn't seem to occur to anyone, nor does it seem to register that the woman might not be Vietnamese at all. If she's Asian then she's Vietnamese, and if she's with a western male then she must be a prostitute.

Women in this situation can expect considerable verbal abuse, though it will be spoken entirely in Vietnamese, which means she may not realise that insults are being hurled at her if she doesn't speak the language. However, there will be no mistaking the hateful stares and obscene gestures. All this abuse will come from Vietnamese men (including teenagers) rather than Vietnamese women.

For racially mixed couples wanting to visit Vietnam, no easy solution exists. Of course, public intimacy (holding hands etc) is best avoided, but even just walking down the street together invites abuse. Four people travelling together are less likely to encounter trouble than just two. In an actual confrontation, the woman should shout some abuse at the antagonist in any language *other* than Vietnamese – this might make the vigilante realise that he is confronting a foreigner rather than a 'Vietnamese whore'. If this revelation sinks in, he might suddenly apologise!

Hopefully, this dismal situation will improve with time as Vietnamese get more used to the idea of Asian tourists visiting their country.

USEFUL ORGANISATIONS

Hanoi

Chamber of Commerce & Industry
    33 Ba Trieu St (☎ 825-2961)
Culture & Information Ministry
    51 Ngo Quyen St (☎ 825-3231)
Entry-Exit Permit Department
    40A Hang Bai St (☎ 825-5798)
Foreign Affairs Ministry
    1 Ton That Dam St (☎ 825-8201)
Trade & Tourism Ministry
    31 Tran Tien St (☎ 825-4950)

Saigon

Chamber of Commerce & Industry, 171 Vo Thi Sau St, District 3 (☎ 823-0339)
Tax Bureau, 140 Nguyen Thi Minh Khai St, District 3 (☎ 829-2141)

DANGERS & ANNOYANCES

Since 1975 many thousands of Vietnamese have been maimed or killed by rockets, artillery shells, mortars, mines and other ordnance left over from the war. *Never* touch any relics of the war you may come across – such objects can remain lethal for decades. Remember, one bomb can ruin your whole day.

Although the amount pinched by snatch thieves and pickpockets pales in comparison with what is raked in by high-ranking kleptocrats, it's the street crime that most worries travellers. The good news is that violent crime is still relatively rare in Vietnam. The bad news is that just about every other kind of crime is not rare at all. Drive-by bag snatchers are common – thieves on motorbikes have been known to snatch bags through the open windows of cars and buses. Travellers on the trains report that on slow sections, gear can be grabbed straight through the windows. Skilled pickpockets work the crowds.

LEGAL MATTERS

The police in Vietnam are the best that money can buy. Don't expect much help from them unless you pay. Travellers report being charged US$35 to obtain a simple loss report needed to make an insurance claim for stolen property. If you have a traffic accident, your vehicle is likely to be confiscated by the police and you'll have to pay to get it back (regardless of whose fault the accident was). Most Vietnamese never call the police – they settle legal disputes on the spot (either with cash or fists). If you lose something really valuable (like your passport or visa), then you'll need to contact the police. Otherwise, it's better not to bother.

BUSINESS HOURS

Offices, museums etc are usually open from 7 or 8 am to 11 or 11.30 am and from 1 or 2 pm to 4 or 5 pm. Most museums are closed on Monday.

PUBLIC HOLIDAYS & SPECIAL EVENTS

Tet (Tet Nguyen Dan), the Vietnamese lunar New Year, is the most important annual festival. The Tet holiday officially lasts three days, but many Vietnamese take the following week off work and all hotels, trains and buses are chock-a-block. It's a good time to avoid Vietnam. For the rest of this century, Tet falls on the following dates: 7 February 1997, 28 January 1998, 16 February 1999 and 5 February 2000.

The date on which Saigon surrendered to Hanoi-backed forces in 1975, 30 April, is commemorated nationwide as Liberation Day.

ACTIVITIES
Hiking

No doubt the most popular venue for hiking is the north-west region of the country (the Sapa area). Travellers also have good things

to say about hikes in Cuc Phuong National Park near Hanoi. The hiking trails in Bach Ma National Park and Nam Cat Tien National Park are in poor shape so you'll need a guide. The hike up Lang Bian Mountain in Dalat gets good reviews, but the local government requires you to hire a guide and obtain a permit. Fortunately, Vietnamese trekking guides can be hired cheaply.

Watersports

Without a doubt, Nha Trang is the place to head for if you're interested in windsurfing, snorkelling, scuba diving and boating.

COURSES
Language

To qualify for student visa status, you need to study at a bona fide university (as opposed to a private language centre or with a tutor). Universities require that you study 10 hours per week. Lessons usually last for two hours per day, for which you pay tuition of around US$5.

You should establish early on whether you want to study in northern or southern Vietnam, because the regional dialects are very different.

In the south, the vast majority of foreign language students enrol at the General University of Ho Chi Minh City (Truong Dai Hoc Tong Hop) at 12 Binh Hoang, District 5. It's near the south-west corner of Nguyen Van Cu St and Tran Phu St.

Other options in the south include Ho Chi Minh City Polytechnic (☎ 865-4087) and Lotus College (☎ 829-0841) at 53 Nguyen Du St, District 1.

In the north, Hanoi National University (☎ 858-1468) has the largest market share. The Vietnamese Language Centre is actually inside the Polytechnic University, not at the main campus of Hanoi National University at 90 Nguyen Trai St. There is a dormitory at the Polytechnic University for foreign students (Nha A-2 Bach Khoa) and this is a good place to inquire about tuition.

Hanoi's other place to study is the Hanoi Foreign Language College's Vietnamese Language Centre (☎ 826-2468). The main campus is nine km from downtown, but there is a smaller campus closer to the city centre at 1 Pham Ngu Lao St.

WORK

At least 90% of foreign travellers seeking work in Vietnam wind up teaching English, though there is some demand for French teachers too. Pay can be as low as US$2 per hour at a university and up to US$5 per hour at a private academy. Some travellers even manage US$10 per hour for private tutoring. However, there are plenty of hurdles to overcome, starting with the visa (you'd best get a business visa) to finding a place to live (the Vietnamese authorities don't allow foreigners to rent inexpensive rooms with a family). Many people report being short-changed on their pay. Working in Vietnam will also attract the attention of the local tax authorities.

ACCOMMODATION
Hotels

The good news is that the tourism boom has been accompanied by a boom in high-standard hotel construction. The bad news is that prices are rising. Foreigners are usually not permitted to stay in the really grotty dumps, but finding hotels priced at around US$10 is still fairly easy. Many hotels throw in a simple free breakfast of coffee and baguettes.

Guesthouses

Many Vietnamese have opened up guesthouses in their own homes. These places are licensed by the government and are expected to meet certain standards for cleanliness and security. Prices are in the range of US$5 to US$25 depending on facilities. In some places you must share the bath with others, but often your room will have its own bath.

There are a growing number of bottom-end guesthouses providing dormitory beds for foreigners only at about US$3 to US$4 per person. These are not to be confused with the ultra-cheap dormitories for Vietnamese nationals only – staying in these places is considered dangerous and foreigners are prohibited.

FOOD

One of the delights of visiting Vietnam is the amazing cuisine – there are said to be nearly 500 traditional Vietnamese dishes – which is, in general, superbly prepared and very cheap.

Snacks

The Vietnamese bake the best French bread (baguettes) in South-East Asia. A loaf typically costs US$0.10.

Main Dishes

Pho is the Vietnamese name for the noodle soup that is eaten at all hours of the day. *Com* means rice dishes. You'll see signs saying 'Pho' and 'Com' everywhere.

A Vietnamese speciality is spring rolls (*nem* in the north, *cha gio* in the south). These are normally dipped in *nuoc mam* (a foul-smelling fish sauce), though most foreigners prefer soy sauce (*xi dau* in the north, *nuoc tuong* in the south).

Because Buddhist monks of the Mahayana tradition are strict vegetarians, Vietnamese vegetarian cooking (*an chay*) is an integral part of Vietnamese cuisine.

Desserts

Vietnamese sweets tend to be a little too sweet for foreign palates. However, you may want to try *banh it nhan dau*, a gooey pastry made of pulverised sticky rice, beans and sugar. Most foreigners prefer the ice cream (*kem*) or yoghurt (*yaourt*), which are generally good quality.

Fruit

Aside from the usual delights of South-East Asian fruits, Vietnam chips in with its own unique green dragon fruit (*trai thanh long*) grown only in the Nha Trang area.

DRINKS
Nonalcoholic Drinks

Whatever you drink, make sure that it's been boiled or bottled. Ice is generally safe in Saigon and Hanoi, but not guaranteed elsewhere. Vietnamese coffee is fine stuff but the tea is disappointing. Foreign soft drinks like Coca-Cola and Pepsi are widely available.

An excellent local treat is carbonated mineral water with lemon and sugar (soda chanh).

Alcoholic Drinks

Memorise the words bia hoi, which mean 'draught beer'. There are signs advertising it everywhere, and most cafes have it on the menu. Quality varies but is generally OK and very cheap (US$0.32 per litre!). Places that serve bia hoi usually also have good but cheap food.

There are a number of foreign brands which are brewed in Vietnam under licence. This includes BGI, Carlsberg, Heineken and Vinagen.

ENTERTAINMENT

Discos

These are popping up all over the country, though they are especially numerous in Hanoi and Saigon. The most popular places feature a Filipino band and taped music. Interestingly, when the band starts to play, everyone sits down to watch and listen – they get up to dance when the music tapes are played! It's still good fun, and prices are reasonable except at the fancy five star hotels.

Karaoke

That bizarre Japanese phenomena, karaoke, has taken Vietnam by storm. Most westerners find it about as entertaining as watching concrete dry. However, many Asian travellers wax apoplectic as they sing along with a video featuring a bikini-clad model with a faraway gaze. If you sit in a karaoke bar for over an hour, you too will have a faraway gaze, caused no doubt by being blasted with music at 100 decibels.

Classical Music

It's not Vienna, but both Hanoi and Saigon boast a Conservatory of Music (Nhac Vien). Performances are given about twice weekly, but not throughout the year. Make local inquiries.

Rock Music

This is a sore spot with western travellers. The good news is that there are nightly con-

certs in Saigon and (to a lesser extent) Hanoi. The bad news is that the music is almost entirely western bubble-gum pop hits from the 60s and 70s. It's perhaps telling that the most popular band in Vietnam today is Boney M (remember them?).

An essential difference from western-style performances is that each vocalist (accompanied by a house band) gets to perform one or two songs each. The singers seem to have a uniform of sorts – a sequins-and-satin outfit with a perma-press hairdo. The best bands (if there are any) always play at the end of the concerts, forcing you to sit through the rest.

Pubs

Again, Hanoi and Saigon are the only places to have a significant pub scene that can appeal to western tastes. Some of these places feature very elaborate motifs – everything from Bavarian tavern to Aussie pub or American heavy-metal bar with a large-screen TV.

THINGS TO BUY

Handicrafts available for purchase as souvenirs include lacquerware items, mother-of-pearl inlay, ceramics (including enormous elephants), colourful embroidered items (hangings, tablecloths, pillowcases, pyjamas and robes), greeting cards with silk paintings on the front, wood-block prints, oil paintings, watercolours, blinds made of hanging bamboo beads (many travellers like the replica of the Mona Lisa), reed mats (rushes are called coi in the north, lac in the south), Chinese-style carpets, jewellery and leatherwork.

In places frequented by tourists, it's easy to buy what looks like equipment left over from the Vietnam War. However, almost all of these items are reproductions and your chances of finding anything original is slim. The 'Zippo' lighters seem to be the hottest selling item.

The graceful Vietnamese national dress – these days worn almost exclusively by women – is known as the ao dai. It consists of a close-fitting blouse with long panels in the front and back that is worn over loose black or white trousers.

VIETNAM

Getting There & Away

AIR

The best deal is the 'open jaws' ticket, which allows you to fly into Saigon and exit from Hanoi (or vice versa). This saves you the time and expense of backtracking.

Cambodia

Phnom Penh-Saigon one way costs US$60. Phnom Penh-Hanoi one way is US$220. Return fares are exactly double.

Hong Kong

Hong Kong to Saigon costs US$291 one way, US$555 return. There are also Hong Kong-Hanoi flights (US$264 one way; US$500 return). The open jaws ticket costs US$535.

Laos

Vientiane-Hanoi one way costs US$90. Vientiane-Saigon is US$250. Return fares are exactly double.

Malaysia

Kuala Lumpur-Saigon one-way/return is US$150/290.

Philippines

Manila-Saigon one-way/return is priced at US$185/350.

Singapore

Singapore-Saigon one-way/return is priced at US$213/400.

Thailand

Bangkok, only 80 minutes flying time from Saigon, has emerged as the main port of embarkation for air travel to Vietnam. Bangkok-Saigon tickets are US$165 one way; round-trip tickets cost exactly double. There are also direct Bangkok-Hanoi flights (US$176 one way; US$341 return trip).

Departure Tax

The airport departure tax is US$7, which can also be paid in dong.

LAND

To enter or exit Vietnam overland your visa must indicate the correct border crossing. Once you've obtained your visa you can still have it amended at the immigration police or Foreign Affairs Ministry.

The Vietnamese police at the land border crossings are known to be particularly problematic. They may only give you a one week stay rather than the one month indicated on your visa. Most travellers find that it's easier to exit Vietnam overland than to enter the country that way.

China

Vietnam's two land border crossings with China can be reached from either side by train. The busiest border crossing is at Dong Dang (20 km north of Lang Son in north-east Vietnam), and the nearest Chinese town to this border crossing is Pinxiang. Nanning, capital of China's Guangxi Province, is about four hours by bus or train from the border. The crossing point is known in Vietnamese as Huu Nghi Quan (Friendship Gate). There is a twice-weekly direct Beijing-Hanoi train which passes through Friendship Gate.

There is also an 851 km metre-gauge railway, inaugurated in 1910, linking Hanoi with Kunming in China's Yunnan Province. It crosses the border at Lao Cai in north-west Vietnam. The Chinese town opposite Lao Cai is Hekou. Officials have announced that a direct Kunming-Hanoi train will be operating soon.

Cambodia

Buses run daily except Sunday between Phnom Penh and Saigon via the Moc Bai border checkpoint. The air-conditioned bus costs US$12, the bus without air-con is US$5.

Laos

You can travel overland by bus between the southern Lao province of Savannakhet and central Vietnam via the border crossing at Lao Bao, which is on Vietnam's national highway 9, 80 km west of Dong Ha. There is a cross-border bus running between Danang (Vietnam) and Savannakhet. In Vietnam, you can catch this bus in Danang, Dong Ha or Lao Bao. In Laos, the only place you are likely to board is Savannakhet. Dong Ha to Savannakhet on this bus costs US$15 for foreigners. From the Vietnamese side, departure from Danang is at 4 am, from Dong Ha at 10 am, Lao Bao at 2 pm and arrival in Savannakhet is at 7 pm. Border guards (both Lao and Vietnamese) have been known to ask for bribes.

There are also local buses which just go up to the border from the Vietnamese side, and also from the Lao side.

Getting Around

AIR

All air travel within Vietnam is handled by Vietnam Airlines and Pacific Airlines. The booking system is now fully computerised, so you can even reconfirm your international flight from some quiet backwater like Hué.

Soviet-made aircraft are known for vibration, noise and falling out of the sky, but Vietnam Airlines has recently done a good job of overhauling its aging fleet. New western-made engines have been installed into the rust-bucket Soviet planes, which accounts for the remarkably smooth and quiet ride.

BUS

Vietnam's extensive bus network reaches virtually every corner of the country. Almost all Vietnamese buses suffer from frequent breakdowns, tiny seats or benches, almost no legroom and chronic overcrowding. Prices are so cheap that bus travel is almost free, but foreigners are always overcharged – if you pay only double, you've done well. There is no such thing as a reservation until you've bought and paid for a ticket, and once you've paid you can forget about refunds.

The salvation for foreigners are the minibuses. These are pricier, faster and more comfortable – you can even pay for two seats on these if you want more legroom.

We feel compelled to specifically warn travellers about the so-called US$35 'open ticket' sold by Sinh Cafe in Saigon. The bus isn't much better than the Vietnamese public buses, but it's often full (in which case you get left behind or sent on the public bus). And for your trouble, you save a big US$6 compared with making the same journey (Saigon-Hué) on a tourist minibus.

Most intercity buses and minibuses depart very early in the morning.

TRAIN

The 2600 km Vietnamese railway system runs along the coast between Saigon and Hanoi and links the capital with Haiphong and points north. Odd-numbered trains travel southward; even-numbered trains go northward.

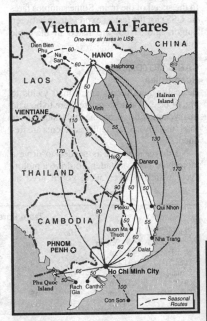

Vietnam Air Fares
One-way air fares in US$

VIETNAM

Even the fastest trains in Vietnam are very slow, averaging 30 km/h and slowing to five or 10 km/h in some sections. The quickest rail journey between Saigon and Hanoi takes 36 hours at an average speed of 48 km/h, but most trains are slower than this.

Children frequently throw rocks at the trains – this can easily cause injury and conductors will insist you keep the metal shields down, which spoils the view.

Classes

There are five classes of train travel in Vietnam: hard seat, soft seat, hard berth, soft berth and super berth. Conditions in hard seat and soft seat can be horrible, often worse than the bus. Hard berth has three tiers of beds (six beds per compartment). Because the Vietnamese don't seem to like climbing up, the upper berth is cheapest.

Costs

Foreigners are charged five times the Vietnamese price, and prices also vary according to the speed of the train. Some samples fares (in US$) for the fastest express train between Saigon and Hanoi are listed in the table below.

CAR & MOTORCYCLE
Road Rules

Basically there aren't any. Small yields to big, or else. Traffic cops are there to be paid off. Vehicles drive on the right side of the road (usually). Spectacular accidents are frequent.

No driver's licence is needed to drive a motorbike 50cc or under. To drive a motorcycle which is over 50cc, you'll need an international driver's licence endorsed for motorcycle operation to be legal. In practice, many people drive motorcycles without a licence.

Rental

Vietnamese labour is so cheap that many foreigners rent the vehicle complete with driver. This can apply to motorcycles as well as cars. Figure on giving the driver at least US$5 per day, plus US$5 to US$10 for the bike depending on engine size. Hiring a car costs about US$0.35 to US$0.70 per km, usually with a driver included. Travel agencies and some cafes handle vehicle rentals.

If you want to rent a motorcycle and drive it yourself, you'll normally be asked to leave your passport as security. You will almost never be given the owner's registration certificate (you'll be given a photocopy instead). This means that if the police pull you over (likely), they will have a ready-made excuse to fine you because your papers won't be in order. There is nothing you can do other than to bargain for a cheaper 'fine'.

Warning Beware of a motorcycle rental scam which some travellers have encountered in Saigon. What happens is that you rent a bike and the owner supplies you with an excellent lock and suggests you use it. What he doesn't tell you is that he has a key too, and somebody follows you and 'steals' the bike at the first opportunity. You then have to pay for a new bike or forfeit your passport, visa, deposit or whatever security you left. And the person who rented the bike to you still has it!

Train Fares (US$)								
Station	Distance from Saigon	Hard Seat	Soft Seat	High Berth	Mid Berth	Low Berth	Soft Berth	Super Berth
Nha Trang	411 km	9	16	22	24	26	28	31
Dieu Tri	631 km	13	24	34	37	40	43	47
Danang	935 km	18	36	50	54	59	64	69
Hué	1038 km	20	39	55	60	65	70	77
Dong Hoi	1204 km	23	45	64	70	76	82	89
Hanoi	1726 km	33	65	91	99	108	117	127

Purchase

Except for bona-fide foreign residents, buying a motorcycle for touring Vietnam is illegal. However, some travellers have reported that so far the authorities have turned a blind eye to the practice. Apparently, you buy a bike but register it in the name of a trusted Vietnamese friend. Some shops which sell motorcycles will let you keep the bike registered in the shop's name. This requires that you trust the shop owners, but in most cases this seems to work out OK. The big issue is what to do with the bike when you are finished with it. If you return to the city where you originally purchased the bike, you can simply sell it back to the shop you bought it from (at a discount, of course). Another possible solution is to sell it to another foreigner travelling in the opposite direction. But, remember, buying a motorcycle is illegal and a crackdown may come at any time.

BICYCLE

Long-distance cycling is becoming a popular way to tour some parts of Vietnam. The main hazard is the traffic. To get around this, it's wise to avoid certain areas (the Mekong Delta and national highway 1). The best cycling seems to be in the Central Highlands, though you'll have to cope with some big hills.

Purchasing a good touring bike in Vietnam is hit or miss. You'd be wise to bring one from abroad.

HITCHING

Westerners have reported great success at hitching. In fact, the whole system of passenger transport in Vietnam is premised on people standing along the highways and flagging down buses or trucks. To get a bus, truck or other vehicle to stop, stretch out your arm and gesture towards the ground with your whole hand. Drivers will expect to be paid for picking you up – negotiate the fare before getting on board.

BOAT

Vietnam's only commercial hydrofoil connects Saigon with Vung Tau.

The extensive network of canals in the Mekong Delta makes getting around by boat feasible in the far south. Day cruises on Halong Bay and nearby Cat Ba Island (near Haiphong in the north) are extremely popular.

LOCAL TRANSPORT

Bus

Inner city bus transport exists in Saigon and Hanoi, and nowhere else. Most foreigners rarely use these local buses.

Taxi

Western-style taxis with meters are readily available in Hanoi, Saigon, Danang and Hué. Elsewhere, ask around travel agencies, cafes and hotels about hiring a car.

Honda Om

The *Honda om* is an ordinary motorbike on which you ride seated behind the driver. There is no set procedure for finding a driver willing to transport you somewhere. You can either try to flag someone down (most drivers can always use a bit of extra cash) or ask around. In places frequented by tourists, the drivers will be looking for you.

Cyclo

Travelling by *cyclo* (pedicab) is the most practical and fun way to get around cities. Always agree on a price before setting off. Bargaining with fingers is not a good idea. Some cyclo drivers have tried to cheat travellers by simply holding up one finger, which travellers interpret as US$1, but upon arrival at your destination the driver interprets as US$10. Since cyclo drivers often don't speak English, have a pen and paper available to write down prices.

ORGANISED TOURS

Cafes catering to foreigners are usually the cheapest places to organise budget tours. You can also ask at travel agencies – some are cheap, but others charge hefty prices. When shopping for tours, be sure that you aren't comparing apples and oranges – a cafe that offers you a dirt cheap tour may also be offering you dirt cheap accommodation in a dormitory. That may or may not be what you want.

Ho Chi Minh City (Saigon)

Vietnam's largest population centre, Ho Chi Minh City covers an area of 2056 sq km, but it's a cartographer's creation – 90% is rural. The 'real city' is downtown (District 1), also known as Saigon, a name still used by most people to refer to the whole city. Cholon (District 5) is the Chinese section.

The huge numbers of people and their obvious industriousness give Saigon, capital of South Vietnam for nearly 20 years from 1956 to 1975, a bustling, dynamic and spirited atmosphere.

Orientation

Ho Chi Minh City is divided into 12 urban districts (*quan*, derived from French *quartier*) and six rural districts (*huyen*).

Maps Maps of the city are on sale everywhere. Be aware that a number of maps sold have pre-1975 Saigon printed on one side and post-1975 Ho Chi Minh City on the other. Don't get confused and use the wrong side or you'll have a hard time matching street signs with the map!

Information

Foreign Consulates The addresses and telephone numbers of some of Ho Chi Minh City's consulates are as follows:

Australia
    Rooms 326-327, New World Hotel, 76 Le Lai St, District 1 (☎ 829-6035; fax 829-6031)
Cambodia
    41 Phung Khac Khoan St, District 1 (☎ 829-2751)
Canada
    203 Dong Khoi St, Room 303 (☎ 824-2000 ext 3320)
China
    39 Nguyen Thi Minh Khai St (☎ 829-2457/63)
France
    27 Xo Viet Nghe Tinh St, District 3 (☎ 829-7231)
Germany
    126 Nguyen Dinh Chieu St, District 3 (☎ 829-1967)

Indonesia
    18 Phung Khac Khoan St, District 1 (☎ 822-3799)
Laos
    181 Hai Ba Trung St, District 3 (☎ 829-7667)
Malaysia
    53 Nguyen Dinh Chieu St, District 3 (☎ 829-9023)
Singapore
    5 Phung Khac Khoan St, District 1 (☎ 822-5173)
Thailand
    77 Tran Quoc Thao St (☎ 822-2637)
UK
    261 Dien Bien Phu St, District 3 (☎ 829-8433)

Money The airport bank gives the legal exchange rate, but beware of short-changing. The bank is sometimes closed when you'd expect it to be open, so you'd be wise to have sufficient US dollar notes in small denominations to get yourself into the city.

Vietcombank (☎ 829-7245) occupies two adjacent buildings at the intersection of Ben Chuong St and Nguyen Thi Minh Khai (Pasteur St). The east building is the one that does foreign exchange.

Sacombank at 211 Nguyen Thai Hoc St (the corner of Pham Ngu Lao St) is right in the heart of budget traveller territory.

Post & Communications Saigon's French-era GPO (Buu Dien Thanh Pho Ho Chi Minh) is at 2 Cong Xa Paris, next to Notre Dame Cathedral. Postal services are available daily from 7.30 am to 7.30 pm.

The area code for Ho Chi Minh City is 8.

Travel Agencies High recommendations go to Ann's Tourist, Kim's Cafe and Linh Cafe.

Ann's Tourist
    58 Ton That Tung St, District 1 (☎ 833-2564, 833-4356)
Ben Thanh Tourist
    121 Nguyen Hue St, District 1 (☎ 829-8597)
Dalat Tourist
    21 Nguyen An Ninh St, District 1 (☎ 823-0227)
Fiditourist
    195 Pham Ngu Lao St, District 1 (☎ 835-3018)
    71-73 Dong Khoi St, District 1 (☎ 829-6264)
Kim's Cafe
    270 De Tham St, District 1 (☎ 839-8177)
Linh Cafe
    235 Pham Ngu Lao St (☎ 836-0643)

VIETNAM

Saigon Tourist
49 Le Thanh Ton St, District 1 (☎ 829-8914)
Vietnam Tourism
234 Nam Ky Khoi Nghia St, District 3
(☎ 829-0776)
Youth Tourist Company
292 Dien Bien Phu St, District 3 (☎ 829-4580)
c/o Kim's Cafe, 270-272 De Tham St, District 1
(☎ 835-9859; fax 829-8540)

Bookshops Hieu Sach Xuan Thu (☎ 822-4670) at 185 Dong Khoi St, District 1, is currently the best in town.

Lao Dong Shop (☎ 825-1951), 104 Nguyen Hue St, District 1, has a good selection of magazines. Ditto for Song Huong (☎ 822-3040), 100A Nguyen Thi Minh Khai St, District 1.

Expats looking to subscribe to foreign magazines should contact Xunhasaba (☎ 825-2860), 25B Nguyen Binh Khiem St, District 1.

Medical Services Travel Medical Consultancy (☎ 835-7644), 10 Nguyen Canh Chan St, District 1, is staffed by foreign doctors and caters to expats and visitors. This clinic is closed at night and on weekends.

The French Consulate operates a clinic (☎ 829-7231/5) at 27 Nguyen Thi Minh Khai St, District 3. You do not need to be a French national, and the doctor speaks English and French. Call for an appointment. This is *not* a 24 hour clinic and is closed on weekends.

Emergency Cho Ray Hospital or Benh Vien Cho Ray (☎ 855-4137/8, 855-8074) has 1000 beds and is one of the best medical facilities in Vietnam. It's at 201B Nguyen Chi Thanh St, District 5 (Cholon). There is a section for foreigners on the 10th floor. About a third of the 200 doctors speak English. There are 24 hour emergency facilities.

The Emergency Centre (☎ 822-5966, 829-1711, 829-2071), 125 Le Loi St, District 1, operates 24 hours. Doctors speak English and French.

Asia Emergency Assistance (☎ 829-8520), Hannam Office building, 65 Nguyen Du St,

District 1, has a medical services programme for resident expats.

Dangers & Annoyances Saigon has the most determined thieves in all of Vietnam. The pickpockets in the Dong Khoi St area are so good that they can snatch your underwear without you even noticing. Beware of the 'under the newspaper trick', practised by cute little children who want to sell you maps, postcards, newspapers and magazines. The kids can relieve you of your wallet while playing with you too. Snatch thieves on motorbikes may steal the sunglasses right off your face. Ben Thanh Market is another favourite venue for pickpockets.

While it's probably safe to take cyclos during the daytime, it may not be at night – in Saigon, cyclo drivers have been known to take their passengers down some dark, deserted alley and mug them.

Things to See & Do

Giac Lam Pagoda This pagoda dates from 1744 and is believed to be the oldest in the city. The architecture and style of ornamentation have not changed since the 19th century. It is open to visitors from 6 am to 9 pm.

Giac Vien Pagoda The pagoda is right next to Dam Sen Lake in District 11 and is in a more rural setting. Giac Vien was founded by Hai Tinh Giac Vien about 200 years ago. The pagoda is open from 7 am to 7 pm.

Emperor of Jade Pagoda This pagoda, known in Vietnamese as Phuoc Hai Tu and Chua Ngoc Hoang, was built in 1909 by the Canton congregation, and is a gem of a Chinese temple. Filled with colourful statues of phantasmal divinities and grotesque heroes, it's one of the most spectacular pagodas in the city.

The statues, which represent characters from both the Buddhist and Taoist traditions, are made of reinforced papier-mâché. It is at 73 Mai Thi Luu St in a part of Saigon known as Da Kao (or Da Cao). To get there, go to 20 Dien Bien Phu St and walk half a block north-westward.

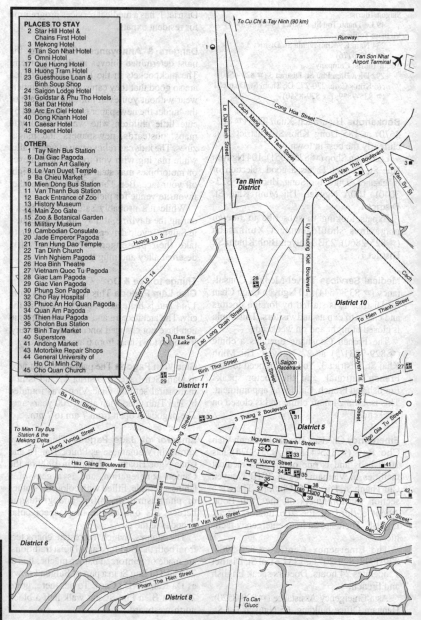

PLACES TO STAY
2 Star Hill Hotel &
   Chains First Hotel
3 Mekong Hotel
4 Tan Son Nhat Hotel
5 Omni Hotel
17 Que Huong Hotel
18 Huong Tram Hotel
23 Guesthouse Loan &
   Binh Soup Shop
24 Saigon Lodge Hotel
31 Goldstar & Phu Tho Hotels
38 Bat Dat Hotel
39 Arc En Ciel Hotel
40 Dong Khanh Hotel
41 Caesar Hotel
42 Regent Hotel

OTHER
1 Tay Ninh Bus Station
6 Dai Giac Pagoda
7 Lamson Art Gallery
8 Le Van Duyet Temple
9 Ba Chieu Market
10 Mien Dong Bus Station
11 Van Thanh Bus Station
12 Back Entrance of Zoo
13 History Museum
14 Main Zoo Gate
15 Zoo & Botanical Garden
16 Military Museum
19 Cambodian Consulate
20 Jade Emperor Pagoda
21 Tran Hung Dao Temple
22 Tan Dinh Church
25 Vinh Nghiem Pagoda
26 Hoa Binh Theatre
27 Vietnam Quoc Tu Pagoda
28 Giac Lam Pagoda
29 Giac Vien Pagoda
30 Phung Son Pagoda
32 Cho Ray Hospital
33 Phuoc An Hoi Quan Pagoda
34 Quan Am Pagoda
35 Thien Hau Pagoda
36 Cholon Bus Station
37 Binh Tay Market
40 Superstore
43 Andong Market
43 Motorbike Repair Shops
44 General University of
   Ho Chi Minh City
45 Cho Quan Church

VIETNAM

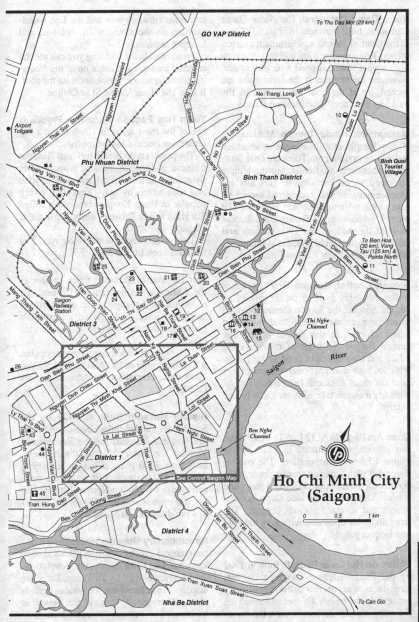

Ho Chi Minh City (Saigon)

See Central Saigon Map

VIETNAM

Notre Dame Cathedral The Notre Dame Cathedral, built between 1877 and 1883, is in the heart of Saigon's government quarter. Its neo-Romanesque form and two 40 metre high square towers, tipped with iron spires, dominate the skyline. If the front gates are locked, try at the door on the side of the building that faces Reunification Palace.

Mariamman Hindu Temple Mariamman Hindu Temple is a little piece of southern India in central Saigon. There are only 50 to 60 Hindus here, all Tamils, but the temple (referred to in Vietnamese as Chua Ba Mariamman), is also considered sacred by many ethnic Vietnamese and Chinese. The temple, which is at 45 Truong Dinh St, was built at the end of the 19th century and dedicated to the Hindu goddess Mariamman. It is open daily from 7 am to 7 pm.

Saigon Central Mosque Built by south Indian Muslims in 1935 on the site of an earlier mosque, the Saigon Central Mosque is an immaculately clean and well-kept island of calm in the middle of bustling central Saigon. In front of the sparkling white and blue structure at 66 Dong Du St, with its four nonfunctional minarets, is a pool for ritual ablutions before prayers. As with any mosque, take off your shoes before entering.

Quan Am Pagoda At 12 Lao Tu St, Cholon, this pagoda was founded in 1816 by the Fujian Chinese congregation. The roof is decorated with fantastic scenes, rendered in ceramic, from traditional Chinese plays and stories. The tableaus include ships, houses, people and several ferocious dragons. The front doors are decorated with very old gold and lacquer panels.

Phuoc An Hoi Quan Pagoda Built in 1902 by the Fujian Chinese congregation, this pagoda is one of the most beautifully ornamented in the city. Of special interest are the many small porcelain figures, the elabo-rate brass ritual objects and the fine wood-carvings on the altars, walls, columns and hanging lanterns.

From outside the building you can see the ceramic scenes, each made up of innumerable small figurines, which decorate the roof. It is at 184 Hung Vuong St in Cholon.

Thien Hau Pagoda Thien Hau Pagoda is one of the most active in Cholon and a big hit with overseas Chinese tourists.

The pagoda is dedicated to Thien Hau, the Chinese goddess of the sea, who protects fisherfolk, sailors, merchants and anyone else who travels by sea. Thien Hau is very popular in Hong Kong (where she's called Tin Hau) and in Taiwan (where her name is Matsu).

Thien Hau Pagoda is at 710 Nguyen Trai St and is open from 6 am to 5.30 pm.

War Remnants Museum Once known as the 'Museum of American War Crimes', the name has been changed so as not to offend the sensibilities of American tourists. It's housed in the former US Information Service building.

This museum is Vietnam's most popular. It's on the corner of Le Qui Don and Vo Van Tan Sts near central Saigon. Admission costs US$0.70.

History Museum Built in 1929 by the Société des Études Indochinoises and once the National Museum of the Republic of Vietnam, the History Museum displays arte-facts from 3300 years of human activity in what is now Vietnam. Just inside the main entrance to the zoo (on Nguyen Binh Khiem St), it is open from 8 to 11.30 am and from 1 to 4 pm daily except Monday.

Revolutionary Museum Housed in a white neoclassical structure built in 1886 and once known as Gia Long Palace, the Revolution-ary Museum is at 27 Ly Tu Trong. There are displays of artefacts from the various periods of the Communist struggle for power in Vietnam. The museum is open from 8 to

11.30 am and from 2 to 4.30 pm, Tuesday to Sunday.

Reunification Palace Built in 1966 to serve as South Vietnam's Presidential Palace, it was towards this building – then known as Independence Hall – that the first Communist tanks in Saigon rushed on the morning of 30 April 1975, the day Saigon surrendered. The building has been left just as it looked on that momentous day.

Reunification Palace is open for visitors from 7.30 to 10 am and 1 to 4 pm daily except when official receptions or meetings are taking place. English and French-speaking guides are on duty during these hours. The visitors' office and entrance is at 106 Nguyen Du St. Admission is a steep US$4.

Zoo & Botanical Garden The zoo and its surrounding gardens, founded by the French in 1864, are a delightful place for a relaxing stroll under giant tropical trees. The History Museum is just inside the main gate, which is at the intersection of Nguyen Binh Khiem and Le Duan Sts.

Cong Vien Van Hoa Park Next to the old Cercle Sportif, an elite sporting club during the French period, the bench-lined walks of Cong Vien Van Hoa Park are shaded with avenues of enormous tropical trees.

This place is still an active sports centre but now you don't have to be French to visit. There are tennis courts, a swimming pool and a clubhouse which have a grand colonial feel about them. It's worth a look for the pool alone. There are Roman-style baths with a coffee shop overlooking the colonnaded pool. There is a dressing room but no lockers.

Cong Vien Van Hoa Park is adjacent to Reunification Palace. There are entrances across from 115 Nguyen Du St and on Nguyen Thi Minh Khai St.

Binh Quoi Tourist Village Built on a small peninsula in the Saigon River, the Binh Quoi Tourist Village (Lang Du Lich Binh Quoi) is a slick tourist trap. The 'village' is essentially a park featuring boat rides, water-puppet shows, a restaurant, a swimming pool, tennis courts, a camping ground, a guesthouse and amusements for the kiddies. The park puts in a plug for Vietnam's ethnic minorities by staging traditional-style minority weddings accompanied by music. From 5 to 10 pm, there is a traditional music performance and boat rides along the river.

Binh Quoi Tourist Village is eight km north of central Saigon in the Binh Thanh District. The official address is 1147 Xo Viet Nghe Tinh St.

Boat Tours To see Saigon from the water, you can easily hire a motorised five metre boat and cruise the Saigon River. Warning – there have been quite a few unpleasant bag snatching and pickpocketing incidents at the docks at the base of Ham Nghi St. It's better to go to the area just south of the Saigon Floating Hotel where you see the ships offering dinner cruises. Around that area, you'll always see someone hanging around looking to charter a boat.

The price should be US$5 per hour for a small boat, or US$10 to US$15 for a larger and faster craft. Two hours is easily enough.

Places to Stay – bottom end

Pham Ngu Lao, De Tham and Bui Vien Sts form half a rectangle which is the heart of the budget traveller haven. These streets and the adjoining alleys are bespeckled with a treasure trove of cheap accommodation and cafes catering to the low-end market. Unfortunately, a major construction project to redevelop the northern side of Pham Ngu Lao St into a luxury tourist area is due to begin soon. Until that happens, popular places in this neighbourhood include:

Guesthouse 70, 70 Bui Vien St (☎ 833-0569), US$8 to US$14, add US$2 for air-con

Hoang Vu Hotel, 265A Pham Ngu Lao St (☎ 839-6522), doubles US$12 to US$35 (161 rooms)

Hoang Yen Mini-Hotel, 83A Bui Thi Xuan St (☎ 839-1348), rooms cost US$16 to US$21

Hotel 211, 211 Pham Ngu Lao St (☎ 835-2353), singles/twins US$8/12 with fan, or US$12/16 with air-con

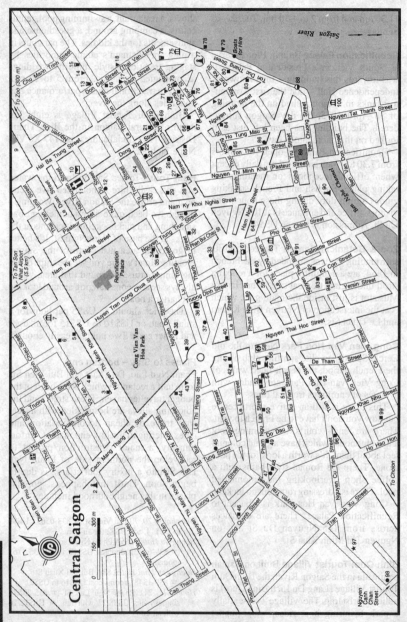

Central Saigon

My Man Mini-Hotel, 373/20 Pham Ngu Lao St (but actually in a side alley) (☎ 839-6544), rooms with fan US$10 to US$14, with air-con US$14 to US$18 (10 rooms)

Prince Hotel, 193 Pham Ngu Lao St (☎ 832-2657), singles/doubles US$6/11 (66 rooms)

Thai Binh Hotel, 325 Pham Ngu Lao St (☎ 839-9544), doubles with fan US$5 to US$7 (28 rooms)

Thanh Thanh 2 Hotel, 205 Pham Ngu Lao St (☎ 832-4027), dorm beds US$3.50, doubles US$8 to US$9

Vien Dong Hotel, 275A Pham Ngu Lao St (☎ 839-3001), singles US$12 with fan, US$32 to US$70 with air-con

An alternative to the Pham Ngu Lao St area is a string of wonderful guesthouses on an alley connecting Co Giang and Co Bac Sts. The first hotel to appear here and probably still the best is *Miss Loi's Guesthouse* (☎ 835-2973), 178/20 Co Giang St. Room

PLACES TO STAY		PLACES TO EAT			
3	Saigon Star Hotel	14	Tex Mex	25	Phnom Penh Bus Garage
4	Bao Yen Hotel	17	Mogambo Bar & Restaurant	30	Revolutionary Museum
5	Sol Chancery Hotel			31	Saigon Intershop & Minimart
6	International Hotel	18	Sapa Bar & Restaurant		
8	Victory Hotel			33	Ben Thanh Market
16	Orchid Hotel	27	Kem Bach Dang (Ice Cream Parlour)	36	Mariamman Hindu Temple
21	Continental Hotel				
26	Rex Hotel	28	Kem Bach Dang (Ice Cream Parlour)	37	Bicycle Shops
29	Norfolk Hotel			38	Bus Stop (to Cambodia)
32	Tan Loc Hotel	43	Annie's Pizza		
34	Embassy Hotel	53	Linh Cafe	45	Ann's Tourist
35	Tao Dan Hotel	54	Lotus Cafe & Saigon Cafe	47	Thai Binh Market
39	Hoang Gia Hotel			58	Sacombank
40	New World Hotel	55	Kim's Cafe & Madras House	61	Ben Thanh Bus Station
41	Palace Saigon Hotel				
42	A Chau Hotel	56	Zen Vegetarian Restaurant	62	Tran Nguyen Hai Statue
44	Rang Dong Hotel				
46	Hoang Yen Mini-Hotel	59	Tin Nghia Vegetarian Restaurant	63	Ar Museum
48	My Man Mini-Hotel			70	Saigon Central Mosque
49	Thai Binh Hotel				
50	Vien Dong Hotel	71	Indian Restaurant	72	Vung Tau Bus Stop
51	Guesthouse 70 & 72	73	Hien & Bob's Place		
52	Hoang Vu Hotel	79	Floating Restaurants	74	Apocalypse Now
57	Prince (Hoang Tu) Hotel	82	Lemon Grass Restaurant	75	Ton Duc Thang Museum
60	Van Canh Hotel				
64	Champagne Hotel	**OTHER**		77	Me Linh Square & Tran Hung Dao Statue
65	Kimdo Hotel	1	Xa Lo Pagoda		
66	Century Saigon Hotel	2	Thich Quang Duc Memorial	85	Huynh Thuc Khang Street Market
67	Palace Hotel				
68	Bong Sen & Mondial Hotels	7	War Crimes Exhibition	86	The Old Market
		9	Former US Embassy (1967-75)	87	Pre-1967 US Embassy
69	Caravelle Hotel				
72	Saigon Hotel	10	GPO	88	Ferries across Saigon River & to Mekong Delta
76	Bach Dang Hotel	11	Notre Dame Cathedral		
78	Saigon Floating Hotel				
80	Riverside Hotel	12	Asia Emergency Assistance	89	Vietcombank
81	Dong Khoi Hotel			90	An Duong Vuong Statue
83	Majestic Hotel	13	Stephanie' Bar		
84	Saigon Prince Hotel	15	Chi Chi's Bar	94	Phung Son Tu Pagoda
91	Rose 2 Hotel	19	Municipal Theatre		
92	Thai Binh Duong Hotel	20	Q Bar	97	Immigration Office
		22	Saigon Tourist	98	Travel Medical Consultancy
93	Phong Phu Hotel	23	Vietnam Airlines		
95	Windsor Hotel	24	Hotel de Ville (People's Committee)	100	Uncle Ho's Museum for Momentos
96	Metropole Hotel				
99	Miss Loi's Guesthouse				

VIETNAM

prices are around US$8 to US$10 for a double. Many of Miss Loi's neighbours are jumping into this business and the area seems destined to develop into another budget travellers' haven.

Other budget hotels spread about town include:

A Chau Hotel, 92B Le Lai St (☎ 833-1814), singles/twins with fan US$7/10, air-con twins US$15

Rang Dong Hotel, 81 Cach Mang Thang Tam St (☎ 839-8264), doubles US$15 to US$45

Tao Dan Hotel, 35A Nguyen Trung Truc St (☎ 823-0299), US$12 to US$16 with fan, air-con US$20 to US$24 (94 rooms)

Van Canh Hotel, 184 Calmette St (☎ 829-4963), singles US$5 to US$13, twins US$7 to US$15 (33 rooms)

Places to Stay – middle

District 1 By far and away, this is the most popular neighbourhood with travellers.

Bong Sen Hotel, 117-119 Dong Khoi St (☎ 829-1516), twins US$27/36 to US$190

Caravelle Hotel, 19-23 Lam Son Square (☎ 829-3704), singles/twins with air-con cost from US$51/63 to US$180

Champagne Hotel, 129-133 Ham Nghi St (☎ 822-4922), also known as *Que Huong Hotel*, singles US$38 to US$48, twins US$35 to US$45

Embassy Hotel, 35 Nguyen Trung Truc St (☎ 829-1430), doubles US$60 to US$100

Hoang Gia Hotel, 12D Cach Mang Thang Tam St (☎ 829-4846), singles/twins go for US$30/35

Huong Sen Hotel, 70 Dong Khoi St (☎ 829-1415), doubles US$35/50 to US$90

Majestic Hotel, 1 Dong Khoi St (☎ 829-5515), singles/twins US$35/47 to US$120/140

Metropole Hotel, 148 Tran Hung Dao St (☎ 832-2021), singles/doubles US$86/95 to US$119/128, suites US$149

Mondial Hotel, 109 Dong Khoi St (☎ 829-6291), singles/twins US$56/86 to US$101/117

Norfolk Hotel, 117 Le Thanh Ton St (☎ 829-5368), singles/twins US$75/90 to US$150/165

Orchid Hotel, 29A Don Dat St (☎ 823-1809), doubles US$40

Palace Hotel, 56-64 Nguyen Hue St (☎ 829-2860), singles/twins US$40/55 to US$120/140

Palace Saigon Hotel, 82 & 108 Le Lai St (☎ 833-1353, 835-9421), doubles US$25 to US$35

Phong Phu Hotel, 105 Ky Con St (☎ 822-2020), doubles US$25 to US$35

Riverside Hotel, 18 Ton Duc Thang St (☎ 822-4038), singles/twins US$45/60 to US$200/230

Rose 2 Hotel, 141 Nguyen Thai Binh St (☎ 823-1573), doubles US$25

Saigon Hotel, 47 Dong Du St (☎ 829-9734), singles/twins from US$36/44 to US$69/79

Tan Loc Hotel, 177 Le Thanh Ton St (☎ 823-0028), singles/twins US$45/58 to US$86/100

Thai Binh Duong Hotel, 92 & 107 Ky Con St (☎ 832-2674), doubles US$20 to US$25

District 3 This area seems to attract many French travellers.

Bao Yen Hotel, 9 Truong Dinh St (☎ 829-9848), doubles US$12 to US$14 (12 rooms)

Guesthouse Loan, 3 Ly Chinh Thang St (☎ 844-5313), doubles US$18 to US$25 (30 rooms)

Huong Tram Hotel, 24/9 Pham Ngoc Thach St (☎ 829-6086), singles US$30, twins US$43 to US$53

Que Huong Hotel, also known as the *Liberty Hotel*, 167 Hai Ba Trung St (☎ 829-4227), singles/twins US$20/30 to US$30/40

Victory Hotel, 14 Vo Van Tan St (☎ 829-4989), doubles US$26 to US$50

Tan Binh & Phu Nhuan Districts This is the area out towards the airport.

Chains First Hotel, 18 Hoang Viet St (☎ 844-1199), singles/twins US$65/75 to US$125

Mekong Hotel, 261 Hoang Van Thu St (☎ 844-1024), singles/twins US$35/40, suites US$45

Tan Son Nhat Hotel, 200 Hoang Van Thu St (☎ 844-1039), doubles US$25 to US$50

District 5 District 5 is Cholon, Ho Chi Minh City's Chinatown. Most of the hotels here pack out with travellers from Hong Kong, Taiwan and Singapore, but it's a good neighbourhood if you want to get off the backpacker circuit.

Arc En Ciel Hotel, also known as the *Rainbow Hotel*, 52-56 Tan Da St (☎ 855-4435), singles/doubles US$44/55 to US$55/66, suites US$88

Bat Dat Hotel, 238-244 Tran Hung Dao B St (☎ 855-5819), doubles US$65 to US$120

Caesar Hotel, 34-36 An Puong Vuong St (right inside Andong Market) (☎ 835-0677), doubles US$80 to US$150

Dong Khanh Hotel, 2 Tran Hung Dao B St (☎ 835-2410), singles/doubles are US$55/69 to US$129/157 (81 rooms)
Regent Hotel, 700 Tran Hung Dao St (☎ 835-3548), doubles US$40 to US$68

Places to Eat

Cafes Pham Ngu Lao St supplies everything you need in life, from steak and salad to banana pancakes and ice-cream sundaes. Oh yes, and there's some Vietnamese food too (be sure to try the spring rolls). And all at bargain basement prices.

Highly recommended places in this league include: *Kim's Cafe*, 270 De Tham St; *Linh Cafe*, 235 Pham Ngu Lao St; *Lotus Cafe* at 197 Pham Ngu Lao St and *Saigon Cafe* at 195 Pham Ngu Lao St.

Vegetarian *Tin Nghia Vegetarian Restaurant* is a small place about 200 metres from Ben Thanh Market at 9 Tran Hung Dao St. Meals cost less than US$1.

On the first and 15th days of the lunar month, food stalls around the city – especially in the markets – serve vegetarian versions of non-vegetarian Vietnamese dishes.

Ice Cream The best ice cream (kem) in Ho Chi Minh City is served at the two shops called *Kem Bach Dang*, which are on Le Loi St on either side of Nguyen Thi Minh Khai (Pasteur St). Kem Bach Dang 2 is at 28 Le Loi St. Both are under the same management and serve ice cream, hot and cold drinks and cakes for very reasonable prices. A US$2 speciality is ice cream served in a baby coconut with candied fruit on top (kem trai dua).

Dozens of little ice cream and yoghurt places line Dien Bien Phu St between Nos 125 and 187.

Entertainment

Downtown Saigon is *the* place to be on Sunday and holiday nights. The streets are jam-packed with young Saigonese, in couples and groups, cruising the town on bicycles and motorbikes, out to see and be seen.

Dinner Cruise Wining and dining while floating around the Saigon River is not the worst way to spend an evening. The floating restaurants dock just opposite the Riverside Hotel. They open at 6 pm, depart the pier at 8 pm and return at 10 pm. Prices vary from US$4 to US$6 for dinner à la carte, though you could spend significantly more if you go heavy on the booze. Tickets for the cruise can be bought at the pier and you can call for information (☎ 822-5401). Most of the boats feature live music and dancing.

Discos There is dancing with a live band at the *Rex Hotel*, 141 Nguyen Hue St, nightly from 7.30 to 11 pm.

Cheers is the disco inside the Vien Dong Hotel at 257 Pham Ngu Lao St. Admission to Cheers costs US$8 and things start to roll from 8 pm onwards.

The *Starlight Nightclub* is on the 11th floor of the Century Saigon Hotel (☎ 231818 ext 46) at 68A Nguyen Hue St, District 1. It's open nightly from 7 pm until 2 am.

The Saigon Floating Hotel is where you'll find the *Down Under Disco*. Men must pay a cover charge of US$20, but women are permitted to enter for free. The excellent band keeps the audience rocking.

The *Palace Hotel* at 56 Nguyen Hue St, District 1, has a nightclub open from 8 to 11 pm. Ditto for the *Caravelle Hotel* at 19 Lam Son Square, District 1.

The *Venus Club* is in the Saigon Star Hotel, 204 Nguyen Thi Minh Khai St, District 3. It's notable for its disco and karaoke rooms. Cover is US$3.

Water Puppets The History Museum (just inside the zoo) is where you'll find occasional water puppet performances for just US$1.

The Binh Quoi Tourist Village has water puppet shows in the evening.

There is a water puppet theatre at 28 Vo Van Tan St, District 3, offering daytime performances only.

Pubs *Apocalypse Now*, 2C Thi Sach, comes alive at 6 pm and keeps rolling until at least 2 am.

Guitar Bar (☎ 822-2166), 62 Hai Ba Trung St, boasts a deejay and music videos. It's open from 5 pm to 1 am.

Ice Blue (☎ 822-2664), 54 Dong Khoi St, is an English-style pub featuring imported beers, popcorn and darts.

The *Saxophone Bar* in the New World Hotel has no cover charge and offers such attractions as live jazz piano.

Things to Buy

In the last few years the free market in tourist junk has been booming – you can pick up a useful item like a lacquered turtle with a clock in its stomach or a ceramic Buddha that whistles the national anthem. But even if you're not the sort of person who buys tourist kitsch, Saigon is a good shopping city and there is sure to be something that catches your eye.

Ben Thanh Market (Cho Ben Thanh) is perhaps the best place to start your search. Part of the market is devoted to normal everyday items like vegetables and laundry detergent, but the locals have not overlooked the lucrative tourist trade either. Some items have price tags and some don't – polite bargaining should help. Warning – there are *plenty* of pickpockets in this market.

Dong Khoi St is the big arts and crafts tourist bazaar, but prices are outrageous. In this neighbourhood you'd better try to get a 50% or more discount, or else don't even bother and go someplace else.

In the Pham Ngu Lao St budget travellers' zone, there are a few small shops plugging T-shirts and other backpacker paraphernalia. Be sure to check out adjacent De Tham and Bui Vien Sts for more small shops.

Getting There & Away

Air Airline offices include:

Air France
    130 Dong Khoi St, District 1 (☎ 829-0981)
Asiana Airlines
    141-143 Ham Nghi St, District 1 (☎ 822-2665)
Cathay Pacific Airways
    58 Dong Khoi St, District 1 (☎ 822-3203)

China Airlines (Taiwan)
    132 Dong Khoi St (Continental Hotel), District 1
    (☎ 825-1387)
China Southern Airlines
    52B Pham Hong Thai St, District 1
    (☎ 829-1172, 829-8417)
EVA Airways
    129 Dong Khoi St, District 1 (☎ 822-4488)
Garuda Indonesia
    106 Nguyen Hue St, District 1 (☎ 829-3644)
Korean Air
    141 Nguyen Hue St, District 1 (☎ 829-6042)
KLM-Royal Dutch Airlines
    244 Pasteur St, District 3 (☎ 823-1990)
Lao Aviation
    39/3 Tran Nhat Duat St (☎ 844-2807)
Lufthansa Airlines
    132 Dong Khoi St (Continental Hotel), District 1
    (☎ 829-8529)
Malaysia Airlines
    116 Nguyen Hue St, District 1 (☎ 823-0695)
Philippine Airlines
    132 Dong Khoi St (Continental Hotel), District 1
    (☎ 823-0502, 823-0544)
Qantas Airways
    311 Dien Bien Phu St, District 3 (☎ 839-6194)
Royal Air Cambodge
    16 Ho Huan Nghiep St, District 1
    (☎ 829-9462, 890-7302)
Singapore Airlines
    6 Le Loi St, District 1 (☎ 823-1583)
Thai Airways International
    65 Nguyen Du St, District 1
    (☎ 822-3365, 829-2810)
Vietnam Airlines
    116 Nguyen Hue St, District 1 (☎ 829-2118)
    15B Dinh Tien Hoang St (☎ 829-2118, 823-0697)

Bus Intercity buses depart from and arrive at a variety of stations around Ho Chi Minh City. *Ben xe* means 'bus station', so if you need to ask for any of these stations just put 'ben xe' first followed by the station name.

Cholon station is the most convenient place to get buses to Mytho and other Mekong Delta towns. The Cholon bus station is at the very western end of Tran Hung Dao B St in District 5, close to the Binh Tay Market.

Less conveniently located than Cholon station, Mien Tay station nevertheless has even more buses to points south of Ho Chi Minh City (basically the Mekong Delta). This enormous station (☎ 825-5955) is about

10 km west of Saigon in An Lac, a part of Binh Chanh District (Huyen Binh Chanh).

Buses to places north of Ho Chi Minh City leave from Mien Dong bus station (☎ 829-4056), which is in Binh Thanh District about five km from downtown Saigon on national highway 13.

Buses to Tay Ninh, Cu Chi and points north-east of Ho Chi Minh City depart from the Tay Ninh bus station, which is in Tan Binh District.

Vehicles departing from Van Thanh bus station serve destinations within a few hours of Ho Chi Minh City. For foreign travellers, the most popular destination is probably Vung Tau.

Just next to the Saigon Hotel and the mosque on Dong Du St is where you catch minibuses (not big buses) to Vung Tau. This is a bus stop, not an official bus station.

Train The Saigon railway station, or Ga Sai Gon (☎ 824-5585), is in District 3 at 1 Nguyen Thong St. The ticket office is open from 7.15 to 11 am and from 1 to 3 pm daily.

Boat Passenger and goods ferries to the Mekong Delta depart from the Nguyen Kiem pier at the river end of Ham Nghi St near the Majestic Hotel. Hydrofoils to Vung Tau depart from the same wharf.

Getting Around
The Airport Tan Son Nhat international airport is seven km from the centre. The taxis for hire outside the customs hall will try to overcharge, so bargain (a fair price into town is about US$7). Cyclos can be hailed outside the gate to the airport, which is a few hundred metres from the terminal building – a ride to central Saigon should cost about US$1 or US$2.

Bus Few foreigners use the skeletal bus system, but the adventurous or truly destitute might want to consider the following:

Saigon – Cholon Buses depart Central Saigon from opposite the Saigon Floating Hotel and continue along Tran Hung Dao St to Binh Tay Market in Cholon, then return along the same route. The fare is US$0.20.

Mien Dong – Mien Tay Buses depart Mien Dong bus station (north-east Ho Chi Minh City), pass through Cholon and terminate at Mien Tay bus station on the western edge of town. The fare is US$0.40.

Van Thanh – Mien Tay Buses depart Van Thanh bus station (eastern Ho Chi Minh City), pass through Cholon and terminate at Mien Tay bus station (western Ho Chi Minh City). The fare is US$0.40.

Taxi Taxis can be occasionally hailed on the street. If you don't find one straight away, ring up and one will be dispatched in less time than it takes to say 'Ho Chi Minh City'. Companies in this business include: Airport Taxi (☎ 844-6666); Cholon Taxi (☎ 822-6666); Davi Taxi (☎ 829-0290); Gia Dinh Taxi (☎ 822-6699); Saigon Taxi (☎ 842-4242); Saigon Tourist Taxi (☎ 822-2206); and Vina Taxi (☎ 842-2888).

Bicycle Rental bicycles are widely available from many budget hotels and cafes, especially in the Pham Ngu Lao St backpacker ghetto.

Cyclo Cyclos are the most interesting way of getting around town, but avoid them at night and always agree on fares beforehand.

Around Saigon

CU CHI TUNNELS
The tunnel network of Cu Chi District, now part of Greater Ho Chi Minh City, became legendary during the 1960s for its role in facilitating Viet Cong control of a large rural area only 30 km from Saigon. At its height, the tunnel system stretched from the South Vietnamese capital to the Cambodian border.

In the district of Cu Chi alone, there were over 200 km of tunnels. After ground operations against the tunnels claimed large numbers of casualties and proved ineffective, the

Americans turned their artillery and bombers on the area – this turned the area into a moonscape.

Parts of this remarkable tunnel network have been reconstructed in the interests of promoting Vietnamese patriotism and mass foreign tourism.

Getting There & Away

Minibuses operated by budget cafes charge around US$5 per person. Tourist hotels and Saigon Tourist run minibus tours to the area at considerably higher prices.

TAY NINH

Tay Ninh town, capital of Tay Ninh Province, serves as the headquarters of one of Vietnam's most interesting indigenous religions, Caodaism. The **Caodai Great Temple** was built between 1933 and 1955.

The Religion of Caodai

Caodaism is the product of an attempt to create the ideal religion through the fusion of secular and religious philosophies from both east and west. The result is a colourful and eclectic potpourri that includes bits and pieces of Buddhism, Confucianism, Taoism, Hinduism, native Vietnamese spiritism, Christianity and Islam. Victor Hugo is among the westerners especially revered by the Caodai; look for his likeness at the Great Temple.

Caodaism was founded in 1926 after messages were communicated to the group's leaders by spirits. By the mid-1950s, one in eight southern Vietnamese was a Caodai. Today, the sect has about two million followers. All Caodai temples observe four daily ceremonies, which are held at 6 am, noon, 6 pm and midnight.

Getting There & Away

Tay Ninh is 96 km north-west of Ho Chi Minh City. The Caodai Holy See complex is four km east of Tay Ninh. Many travellers book a one day minibus tour from the cafes in Saigon, which includes both Tay Ninh and the Cu Chi Tunnels.

VUNG TAU

Vung Tau is a beach resort 128 km south-east of Saigon. Vung Tau's beaches are not Vietnam's best, but are the most accessible from Saigon and therefore the town packs out on weekends. Although Vung Tau is a relaxing place and worth visiting, the beaches are marred by pollution from raw sewage and nearby offshore oil drilling platforms.

The area code for Vung Tau is 64.

Things to See & Do

Beaches The main bathing area on the peninsula is **Back Beach** (Bai Sau, also known as Thuy Van Beach), an eight-km-long stretch of sand. The northern end of this beach is reasonably pretty, but the southern end is a tacky collection of shops, restaurants and hotels. The water here is the cleanest in Vung Tau, which isn't saying much.

Front Beach (Bai Truoc, also called Thuy Duong Beach) is near the centre of town. It's prettier than Back Beach, but the water is really too dirty for swimming.

Bai Dau, a quiet coconut palm-lined beach, is probably the prettiest stretch of shoreline, though there is little sand. The beach, which is about three km north of town, stretches around a small bay.

Bai Dua (Roches Noires Beach) is a small beach about two km south of the town centre.

Walks The six km circuit around Small Mountain (Nui Nho) begins at the southern end of Front Beach and continues on Ha Long St along the rocky coastline. The 10 km circuit around Large Mountain begins at the northern end of Front Beach.

Other Sights The **Hon Ba Temple** is on a tiny island just south of Back Beach. It can be reached on foot at low tide. **Niet Ban Tinh Xa**, one of the largest Buddhist temples in Vietnam, is on the western side of Small Mountain. Built in 1971, it is famous for its five tonne bronze bell, a huge reclining Buddha and intricate mosaic work.

The 30-metre-high figure of **Jesus** (Thanh Gioc) with arms outstretched is reminiscent of Rio de Janeiro and gazes across the South

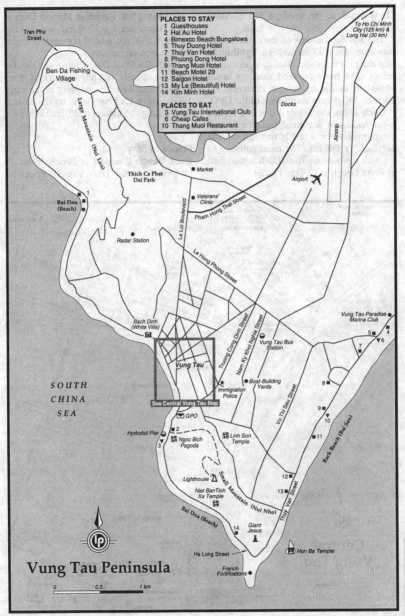

PLACES TO STAY
1 Guesthouses
2 Hai Au Hotel
4 Bimexco Beach Bungalows
5 Thuy Duong Hotel
7 Thuy Van Hotel
8 Phuong Dong Hotel
9 Thang Muoi Hotel
11 Beach Motel 29
12 Saigon Hotel
13 My Le (Beautiful) Hotel
14 Kim Minh Hotel

PLACES TO EAT
3 Vung Tau International Club
6 Cheap Cafes
10 Thang Muoi Restaurant

To Ho Chi Minh
City (125 km) &
Long Hai (30 km)

Tran Phu
Street

Ben Da Fishing
Village

Docks

Large Mountain (Nui Lon)

Thich Ca Phat
Dai Park

Market

Airstrip

Bai Dau
(Beach)

Veterans'
Clinic

Airport

Pham Hong Thai Street

Le Loi Boulevard

Radar Station

Le Hong Phong Street

Vung Tau Paradise
Marina Club

Bach Dinh
(White Villa)

Truong Cong Dinh Street

Nam Ky Khoi Nghia Street

Vung Tau Bus
Station

5
4
7
6

Vung Tau

SOUTH
CHINA
SEA

Boat-Building
Yards

Vo Thi Sau Street

8

Immigration
Police

See Central Vung Tau Map

GPO

9
10

Hydrofoil Pier

2

Linh Son
Temple

11

3
Ngoc Bich
Pagoda

Back Beach (Bai Sau)

Lighthouse

Small Mountain
(Nui Nho)

12

Niet BanTinh
Xa Temple

13

Thuy Van Street

Bai Dua (Beach)

14
Giant
Jesus

Ha Long Street

Hon Ba Temple

Vung Tau Peninsula

French
Fortifications

0   0.5   1 km

China Sea from the southern end of Small Mountain.

The 360 degree view of the entire peninsula from the 197-metre-high **lighthouse** *(hai dang)* is truly spectacular, especially at sunset. The narrow paved road up Small Mountain to the lighthouse intersects Ha Long St 150 metres south-west of the GPO.

Bach Dinh, the White Villa, is a former royal residence set amid frangipanis and bougainvilleas on a lushly forested hillside overlooking the sea. The main entrance to the park surrounding Bach Dinh is just north of Front Beach at 12 Tran Phu St.

The **Vung Tau Paradise Marina Club** at Back Beach has a golf course and driving range. A 1500 room hotel is currently under construction on the site.

Thich Ca Phat Dai, a must-see site for domestic tourists, is a hillside park of monumental Buddhist statuary built in the early 1960s. Thich Ca Phat Dai is on the eastern side of Large Mountain at 25 Tran Phu St.

Places to Stay

Back Beach Cheapest is *Beach Motel 29* (☎ 853481) at 29 Thuy Van St. Prices on

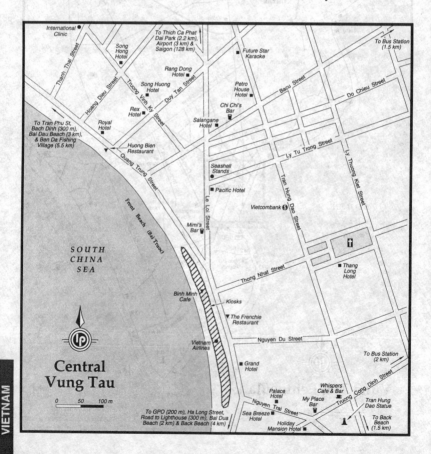

International Clinic

To Thich Ca Phat Dai Park (2.2 km), Airport (3 km) & Saigon (128 km)

To Bus Station (1.5 km)

Thanh Thai Street

Song Hong Hotel

Future Star Karaoke

Hoang Dieu Street

Truong Vinh Ky Street

Rang Dong Hotel

Song Huong Hotel

Duy Tan Street

Petro House Hotel

Bacu Street

Do Chieu Street

Chi Chi's Bar

Rex Hotel

To Tran Phu St, Bach Dinh (300 m), Bai Dau Beach (3 km), & Ben Da Fishing Village (5.5 km)

Royal Hotel

Salangane Hotel

Huong Bien Restaurant

Quang Trung Street

Ly Tu Trong Street

Ly Thuong Kiet Street

Seashell Stands

Le Loi Street

Pacific Hotel

Tran Hung Dao Street

Front Beach (Bai Truoc)

Vietcombank

SOUTH CHINA SEA

Mimi's Bar

Thong Nhat Street

Thang Long Hotel

Binh Minh Cafe

Kiosks

The Frenchie Restaurant

Nguyen Du Street

Vietnam Airlines

To Bus Station (2 km)

Central Vung Tau

0 50 100 m

Grand Hotel

Palace Hotel

Whispers Cafe & Bar

My Place Bar

Cong Dinh Street

Tran Hung Dao Statue

Nguyen Trai Street

Sea Breeze Hotel

Truong

To GPO (200 m), Ha Long Street, Road to Lighthouse (300 m), Bai Dua Beach (2 km) & Back Beach (4 km)

Holiday Mansion Hotel

To Back Beach (1.5 km)

VIETNAM

weekdays are US$3 to US$6, but on weekends rise to US$4 and US$8.

The prettiest budget accommodation is up at the northern end of Back Beach. Here you'll find the *Bimexco Beach Bungalows* (☎ 859916). Bungalows for two persons cost US$10 to US$15, while a four person beach house is US$18 to US$25. Be aware that some of the bungalows in this area belong to the nearby *Thuy Duong Hotel* and cost from US$40 to US$60. Rooms at the Thuy Duong itself cost between US$25 and US$30.

Close to the beach with large spacious grounds is the *Saigon Hotel*. Rooms are also large and, complete with terrace and private bath, cost US$9 with fan only, or US$18 to US$31 with air-con.

Thang Muoi Hotel (☎ 852665), 4-6 Thuy Van St, is one of the older places in Back Beach but also boasts an alluring garden-like environment. Doubles with fan cost US$11 or US$12. With air-con the price is US$25 to US$29.

Everything else in Back Beach is pricey. The selection includes the following:

My Le Hotel, Thuy Van St (☎ 852177), doubles US$35 to US$75

Phuong Dong Hotel, 2 Thuy Van St (☎ 852593), doubles US$30 to US$40

Thuy Van Hotel, Thuy Van St (93 rooms), doubles US$18 to US$35

Front Beach The only cheap place in this neighbourhood is the Thang Long Hotel (☎ 852175) at 45 Thong Nhat St. Doubles with fan are US$10 to US$20. Air-con will set you back US$15 to US$20.

Everything else in Front Beach is relatively pricey. The line-up includes:

Grand Hotel, 26 Quang Trung St (☎ 856164), rooms with fan US$15, with air-con US$20 to US$46

Hai Au Hotel, 100 Ha Long St (☎ 856178), doubles are US$25 to US$45, suites US$60 to US$85

Holiday Mansion Hotel, Truong Cong Dinh St (☎ 856169), US$27 to US$32 (15 rooms)

Pacific Hotel, 4 Le Loi St (☎ 852279), doubles US$27 to US$29 (53 rooms)

Palace Hotel, Nguyen Trai St (☎ 852265), doubles US$40 to US$55, suites US$70 to US$100

Petro House Hotel, 89 Tran Hung Dao St (☎ 852014), standard rooms US$53 to US$60, suites US$85 to US$195

Rang Dong Hotel, 5 Duy Tan St (☎ 852133), currently closed for renovation

Rex Hotel, 1 Duy Tan St (☎ 852135), doubles US$35 to US$100

Royal Hotel, 48 Quang Trung St (☎ 859852), doubles US$46 to US$120

Salangane Hotel, also called *Hai Yen Hotel*, 8 Le Loi St (☎ 852571), doubles US$20 to US$40

Sea Breeze Hotel, 11 Nguyen Trai St (☎ 852392), doubles US$40 to US$60

Song Huong Hotel, 10 Truong Vinh Ky St (☎ 852491), doubles US$30 to US$40

Places to Eat

Kiosks lining the beach do cheap noodle dishes. Opposite the kiosks on Front Beach is *The Frenchie Restaurant*, 26 Quang Trung St, which does fine French food.

Entertainment

Expat bars that get moving in the evening include: *My Place* (☎ 856028), 14 Nguyen Trai St; *Whispers Cafe & Bar* (☎ 856762), 438 Truong Cong Dinh St; *Chi Chi's Bar* (☎ 853948), 236 Bacu St; and *Mimi's Bar*, Le Loi St.

Getting There & Away

Bus Private minibuses to Vung Tau from Saigon leave every 15 to 30 minutes from opposite the mosque on Dong Du St (near the Saigon Hotel) and cost US$4. Large public air-conditioned buses depart from Saigon's Van Thanh bus station.

Boat The best way to reach Vung Tau is by hydrofoil. These depart Saigon from the Nguyen Kiem pier near the Majestic Hotel, cost US$10 and take 75 to 80 minutes to complete the journey. In Vung Tau you board the hydrofoil at Cau Da pier opposite the Hai Au Hotel (Front Beach).

LONG HAI

To avoid the crowds, backpackers are increasingly heading to Long Hai, which is 30 km north-east of Vung Tau.

The area code for Long Hai is 64.

Places to Stay

Places to stay in Long Hai include:

Huong Bien Motel (☎ 868430), beach bungalows (10 rooms), doubles with fan US$15, with air-con US$20

Long Hai Green Hotel (Khach San Xanh Long Hai) (☎ 868337), doubles with fan US$7, doubles with air-con US$11 to US$14

Long Hai Guesthouse (Nha Nghi Long Hai) (☎ 868312), doubles US$20

Long Hai Hotel (Khach San Long Hai) (☎ 868010), doubles US$20 to US$30 (25 rooms)

Military Guesthouse (Nha Nghi Quan Doi) (☎ 868316), beach bungalows, doubles with fan US$7 (28 rooms)

Palace Hotel (☎ 868364), doubles US$26 to US$32

Rang Dong Hotel (☎ 868356), doubles US$20 to US$30

CON SON ISLAND

The Con Dao Archipelago is a group of 14 islands and islets 180 km south of Vung Tau. The largest island in the group, whose total land area is 20 sq km, is partly forested Con Son Island, which is ringed with bays, bathing beaches and coral reefs. This scenic island has peaks reaching up to 600 metres high. The island's population is only 2000 persons plus an undetermined number of chickens, pigs and ducks.

Under the French, Con Son was used as a prison for opponents of French colonialism, earning a fearsome reputation for the routine mistreatment and torture of prisoners. In 1954 the prison was taken over by the South Vietnamese government, which continued the tradition of holding political prisoners in horrifying conditions. The island's **Revolutionary Museum** tells part of the story.

The only place to stay is the *Phi Yen Hotel* (☎ 830168), where doubles are US$20 to US$30. From Saigon, there are flights (US$100 one way) on Vasco Airlines (☎ 844-5999), which has its office in Ton Son Nhat airport.

Mekong Delta

Flat as a billiards table but lusciously green and beautiful, the Mekong Delta is the southernmost region of Vietnam. It's a rich agri-cultural region, the breadbasket (or perhaps 'ricebasket') of the nation. The delta is a thick patchwork of rice paddies, swamps and remnant forest interlaced with canals and rivers – an intriguing place to explore.

MYTHO

Mytho is a quiet city of 100,000 easily reached as a day trip from Saigon, and serves as a good introduction to the delta region.

Things to See & Do

Boat Trips Visiting the islands of the Mekong River is the main attraction. However, the Mytho police do not permit foreigners to rent boats cheaply from the locals. Instead you are forced to rent a boat from the government at around US$25 per hour.

Dong Tam Snake Farm About 10 km from Mytho is this interesting snake farm where you can wrap yourself in a python (if you dare) or watch the Vietnamese snake handlers milk poison from cobras.

Getting There & Away

Bus Mytho is served by regular (non-express) buses which leave Saigon's Mien Tay bus station.

The Mytho bus station (Ben Xe Khach Tien Giang) is several km west of town – take Ap Bac St westward and continue on to national highway 1.

Boat A passenger ferry to Mytho leaves Ho Chi Minh City daily at 11 am from the dock at the end of Ham Nghi St; the trip should take about six hours.

OTHER SIGHTS

Other places to consider visiting include: **Cantho** (the political, economic and cultural centre of the Mekong Delta); **Chau Doc**, which has a well-known mosque across the river in Chau Giang District and a number of pagodas and temples at Sam Mountain; **Rach Gia** on the Gulf of Thailand (where boats depart for Phu Quoc Island); **Phu Quoc Island**, a beautiful island with white-sand beaches; **Ha Tien**, a coastal town almost on the Cambodian border near which there are a number of grottoes and beaches; **Hon Chong** (32 km from Ha Tien), which has the best beach in the otherwise muddy Mekong Delta.

All these places have cheap accommodation and are served by buses and, in some cases, scheduled ferry services. Cantho and Phu Quoc Island have air service from Ho Chi Minh City.

Central Highlands

The Central Highlands covers the southern part of the Truong Son Mountain Range. The most accessible place is Dalat. The region, which is home to many ethno-linguistic minority groups (Montagnards), is renowned for its cool climate, beautiful mountain scenery and innumerable streams, lakes and waterfalls.

DALAT

Dalat (elevation 1475 metres) is in a temperate region dotted with lakes and waterfalls and surrounded by evergreen forests. Dalat is often called the 'City of Eternal Spring' – days are pleasant and nights are cool enough for wearing a light jacket. The economy is based on tourism and some agriculture, and it's Vietnam's most favoured honeymoon spot.

Information

Dalat's travel agency/tourist office is Dalat Tourist (☎ 822520), 4 Tran Quoc Toan St.

The area code for Dalat is 63.

Things to See & Do

Dalat's **Central Market** is in the Mai building – the street level is the place to find dried fruits and upper levels are a great place to buy clothing. Behind the Mai building is a modern **Vegetable Market**, which offers the finest vegetables in Vietnam (as well as cut flowers and the usual merchandise).

Xuan Huong Lake in the centre of Dalat was created in 1919 by a dam. Paddleboats that look like giant swans can be rented. The

Dalat Golf Course occupies 50 hectares on the northern side of the lake near the **Flower Gardens**.

About 500 metres east of Xuan Huong Lake is a railway station, and though you aren't likely to arrive in Dalat by train, the station is worth a visit. The **Crémaillère** (cog railway) linked Dalat and Thap Cham (Phan Rang) from 1928 to 1964 – it was closed in 1964 because of repeated Viet Cong attacks. The line has now been partially repaired and is operated as a tourist attraction. For US$3 you can ride five km down the tracks to the suburbs of Dalat and back again.

The **Flower Gardens** (Vuon Hoa Dalat) were established in 1966 by the South Vietnamese Agriculture Service.

Five km north of Xuan Huong Lake is the **Valley of Love** (Thung Lung Tinh Yeu), so named in 1972 by romantically minded students from Dalat University. This place is heavy on the tourist kitsch – you'll see Vietnamese models dressed up as cowboys for photo opportunities (for a fee). You too can get dressed up as a cowboy and have your picture taken while riding a horse.

Cam Ly Falls is one of those must-see spots for domestic visitors. The grassy areas around the 15-metre-high cascades are decorated with stuffed jungle animals, which Vietnamese tourists love to be photographed with. Plenty of 'cowboys' wander around here too.

The **Lake of Sighs** (Ho Than Tho) is a natural lake enlarged by a French-built dam. Horses can be hired near the restaurants. The lake is six km north-east of the centre of Dalat.

Datanla Falls is south-east of Dalat off Highway 20 about 200 metres past the turnoff to Quang Trung Reservoir. From the road, it's a pleasant walk downhill.

Prenn Falls is one of the largest and most beautiful falls in the Dalat area. The entrance to Prenn Falls is 13 km from Dalat towards Phan Rang; the entrance fee is US$0.50.

The nine hamlets of **Lat Village** are about 12 km north-west of Dalat at the base of Lang Bian Mountain. The inhabitants are ethnic minorities. A police permit is required to visit Lat Village.

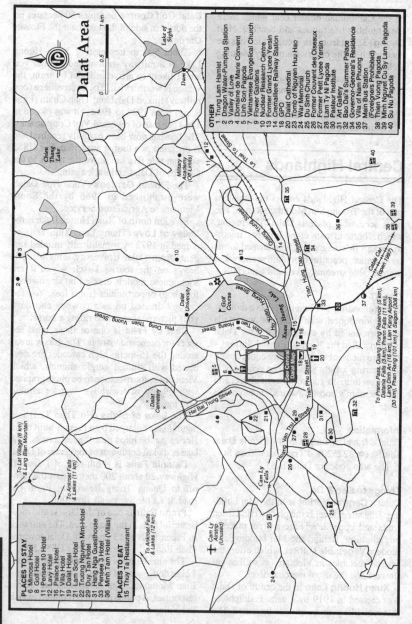

Dalat Area

0 0.5 1 km

PLACES TO STAY
6   Mimosa Hotel
8   Golf Hotel
11   Pensee 10 Hotel
12   Lavy Hotel
16   Palace Hotel
17   Villa Hotel
19   Dalat Hotel
21   Lam Son Hotel
22   Truong Nguyen Mini-Hotel
29   Duy Tan Hotel
31   Hang Nga Guesthouse
33   Pensee 3 Hotel
36   Minh Tam Hotel (Villas)

PLACES TO EAT
15   Thuy Ta Restaurant

OTHER
1   Trung Lam Hamlet
2   Dragon Water-Pumping Station
3   Valley of Love
4   Domaine de Marie Convent
5   Linh Son Pagoda
7   Vietnamese Evangelical Church
9   Flower Gardens
10   Nuclear Research Centre
13   Former Grand Lycee Yersin
14   Cremallère Railway Station
18   GPO
20   Dalat Cathedral
23   Tomb of Nguyen Huu Hao
24   War Memorial
25   Du Sinh Church
26   Former Couvent des Oiseaux
27   Former Petit Lycee Yersin
28   Lam Ty Ni Pagoda
30   Pasteur Institute
31   Art Gallery
32   Bao Dai's Summer Palace
34   Governor-General's Residence
35   Villa Ong Tinh Phuong
37   Main Bus Station
       (Foreigners Prohibited)
38   Thien Vuong Pagoda
39   Minh Nguyet Cu Sy Lam Pagoda
40   Su Nu Pagoda

Hang Nga Guesthouse & Art Gallery, nicknamed the 'Crazy House' by locals, is notable for its Alice-in-Wonderland architecture.

Lang Bian Mountain (also called Lam Vien) has five volcanic peaks ranging in altitude from 2100 to 2400 metres. The scenic hike up to the top of Lang Bian Mountain takes three to four hours from Lat Village. A guide and special permit from the police are required to climb the mountain.

Lang Dinh An (also known as the 'chicken village') is a minority area 18 km from Dalat. The village gets its name from an enormous concrete chicken which towers over the huts and fields.

For information about paragliding, contact the Peace Hotel or the Trade Union (Cong Doan); ☎ 822173) at 1 Yersin St.

Places to Stay

Cheap hotels currently in vogue with budget travellers include the Cam Do, Highland, Mimosa I & II, Peace I & II and the Phu Hoa. The complete list of hotels which can accept foreigners is as follows:

Anh Dao Hotel, 50 Hoa Binh Square (☎ 822384), singles US$29 to US$45, doubles US$35 to US$55

Cam Do Hotel, 81 Phan Dinh Phung St (☎ 822732), dorm beds US$4, doubles US$10 to US$30

Duy Tan Hotel, 82 3 Thang 2 St (☎ 822216), singles US$30 to US$42, doubles US$36 to US$48

Golf Hotel, 11 Dinh Tien Hoang St (☎ 824082), doubles US$35 to US$65

Haison Hotel, 1 Nguyen Thi Minh Khai St (☎ 822622), doubles US$25 to US$40

Hang Nga Guesthouse, 3 Huynh Thuc Khang St (☎ 822070), doubles US$20 to US$60

Highland Hotel, also called the *Cao Nguyen Hotel*, 90 Phan Dinh Phung St (☎ 823738), singles US$4 to US$6, doubles US$7 to US$10

Lam Son Hotel, 5 Hai Thuong St (☎ 822362), singles US$8 to US$10, doubles US$12 to US$14

Lavy Hotel, also called *Lam Vien Hotel*, 20 Hung Vuong St (far from the centre) (☎ 822507), singles US$8 to US$15, doubles US$12 to US$20

Mimosa Hotel, 170 Phan Dinh Phung St (☎ 822656), singles US$5 to US$9, doubles US$8 to US$15

Mimosa II Hotel, also called *Thanh The Hotel*, 118 Phan Dinh Phung St (☎ 822180), singles US$4 to US$9, doubles US$7 to US$15

Minh Tam Hotel, 20A Khe Sanh St (☎ 822447), doubles US$50

Ngoc Lan Hotel, 42 Nguyen Chi Thanh St (☎ 822136), singles US$30 to US$42, doubles US$36 to US$48

Peace Hotel, also called *Hoa Binh Hotel*, 64 Truong Cong Dinh St (☎ 822787), singles US$5 to US$7, doubles US$8 to US$12

Peace II Hotel, also called *Hoa Binh II Hotel*, 67 Truong Cong Dinh St (☎ 822982), doubles US$8

Pensee 2 Hotel, 2 Lu Gia St (far from the centre) (☎ 822933), doubles US$10

Pensee 3 Hotel, 3 Ba Thang Tu St (☎ 822286), doubles US$20

Pensee 10, 10 Phan Chu Trinh St (☎ 822937), singles/twins US$15/20

Phu Hoa Hotel, 16 Tang Bat Ho St (☎ 822194), singles US$7, doubles US$10 to US$12

Thanh Binh Hotel, 40 Nguyen Thi Minh Khai St (☎ 822909), singles US$8 to US$22, doubles US$12 to US$28

Thuy Tien Hotel, Duy Tan and Khoi Nghia Nam Ky Sts (☎ 821731), singles US$25 to US$30, doubles US$30 to US$36

Trixaco Hotel, 7 Nguyen Thai Hoc St (☎ 822789), singles US$8, doubles US$10 to US$30

Truong Nguyen Mini-Hotel, 74 Hai Thuong St (☎ 821772), singles US$10, doubles US$15 to US$25

Villa Hotel, 8A Ho Tung Mau St (☎ 821431), doubles US$25 to US$40

Places to Eat

The Chinese restaurant in the *Mimosa Hotel* is excellent and cheap. Ditto for the *Dong A Restaurant* at 82 Phan Dinh Phung St. Other budget places favoured by travellers include the *Long Hoa Restaurant* on Duy Tan St, *Hoang Lan Restaurant* on Phan Dinh Phung St and the *Shanghai Restaurant* at 8 Khu Hoa Binh Quarter.

European fare can be had at *La Tulipe Rouge Restaurant* at 1 Nguyen Thi Minh Khai St. *Thanh Thanh Restaurant* at 4 Tang Bat Ho St is an upscale eatery with fine French food. Even more upscale is the pricey *Thuy Ta Restaurant*, 2 Yersin St, which is built on pilings in Xuan Huong Lake.

Stop 'n Go Cafe, across from the Rap 3/4 Cinema, is an intriguing place to sip coffee and talk to the chatty owner.

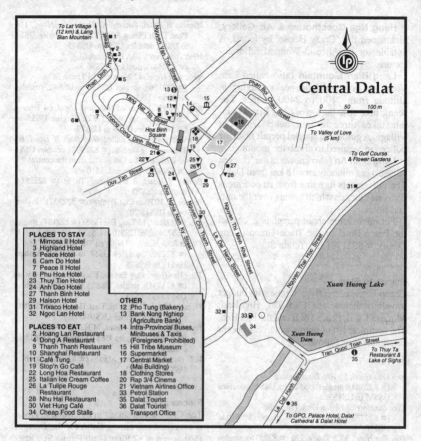

Central Dalat

0   50   100 m

To Lat Village
(12 km) & Lang
Bian Mountain

To Valley of Love
(5 km)

To Golf Course
& Flower Gardens

Hoa Binh
Square

Duy Tan Street

Xuan Huong Lake

Xuan Huong
Dam

Tran Quoc Toan Street

To Thuy Ta
Restaurant &
Lake of Sighs

To GPO, Palace Hotel, Dalat
Cathedral & Dalat Hotel

PLACES TO STAY
1 Mimosa II Hotel
3 Highland Hotel
5 Peace Hotel
6 Cam Do Hotel
7 Peace II Hotel
8 Phu Hoa Hotel
23 Thuy Tien Hotel
24 Anh Dao Hotel
27 Thanh Binh Hotel
29 Haison Hotel
31 Trixaco Hotel
32 Ngoc Lan Hotel

PLACES TO EAT
2 Hoang Lan Restaurant
9 Dong A Restaurant
9 Thanh Thanh Restaurant
10 Shanghai Restaurant
11 Café Tung
15 Stop'n Go Café
22 Long Hoa Restaurant
25 Italian Ice Cream Coffee
26 La Tulipe Rouge
   Restaurant
28 Nhu Hai Restaurant
30 Viet Hung Café
34 Cheap Food Stalls

OTHER
12 Pho Tung (Bakery)
13 Bank Nong Nghiep
   (Agriculture Bank)
14 Intra-Provincial Buses,
   Minibuses & Taxis
   (Foreigners Prohibited)
15 Hill Tribe Museum
16 Supermarket
17 Central Market
   (Mai Building)
18 Clothing Stores
20 Rap 3/4 Cinema
21 Vietnam Airlines Office
33 Petrol Station
35 Dalat Tourist
36 Dalat Tourist
   Transport Office

Getting There & Away

Air There are flights to and from Saigon twice weekly for US$40 one way.

Bus Foreigners are not permitted to take the local Vietnamese buses when arriving in or departing from Dalat.

Tourist minibuses to Dalat can be booked from the cafes on Pham Ngu Lao St in Saigon. In Dalat, hotels and Dalat Tourist sell tickets to Nha Trang (US$8).

Getting Around

For vehicle rentals, visit the Dalat Tourist Transport Office (☎ 822479) at 9 Le Dai Hanh St.

Foreigners are not permitted to rent a private taxi, but travel by motorbike is permitted. Many hotels offer bicycle rentals and there are places in the tourist scenic spots where you can rent a horse.

Tours are offered through Dalat Tourist and the hotels.

BUON MA THUOT, PLEIKU & KON TUM

The big three towns of the Western Highlands are Buon Ma Thuot, Pleiku and Kon Tum. Ethnic Vietnamese make up the major-

VIETNAM

ity in these towns, but the surrounding countryside is dominated by Montagnards. There are many small, fascinating villages to explore here, but watch out for the rapacious police (especially in Buon Ma Thuot) as they like to force foreigners to buy 'travel permits' (a hand-scribbled note from the police chief costing US$50).

Kon Tum seems to be the area of most interest to travellers. Cyclists are also most enthralled with this area as motorised traffic is light, the scenery fine and the climate cool.

South-Central Coast

PHAN THIET

Phan Thiet is best known for its smelly nuoc mam (fish sauce) and fishing industry. The river flowing through the centre of town creates a small **fishing harbour**, which is always chock-a-block with boats and makes for charming photography.

The big attractions are the two nearby beaches. Closest to town is impressive **Phan Thiet Beach**. A project is under way to construct a four star hotel and golf course near the sea. To get to the beach, turn east (right if you're heading north) at Victory Monument, an arrow-shaped, concrete tower with victorious cement people at the base.

Much more impressive is **Mui Ne Beach**, known for its enormous sand dunes. This could easily rate as Vietnam's best beach. It's 22 km east of Phan Thiet proper, near a fishing village at the tip of Mui Ne Peninsula.

The area code for Phan Thiet is 62.

Places to Stay

The most attractive place by far is the *Hai Duong Resort* (☎ 848401) at Mui Ne Beach. It offers villas, windsurfing, sailing, motorbikes and bicycles for rent. There is a bar and restaurant too. This place fills up fast so call for reservations.

The *Vinh Thuy Hotel* (☎ 821294) is right on Phan Thiet Beach at Ton Tuc Thang St. Doubles with air-con cost US$27 to US$34.

Staying in town is much less inspiring. You can try the *Phan Thiet Hotel* (☎ 82573) at 40 Tran Hung Dao St. Doubles are US$15 and US$18.

The *Khach San 19-4* (☎ 82460) is across from the Phan Thiet bus station at 1 Tu Van Tu St. Doubles cost US$12.

CA NA

This small town, 312 km from Saigon, consists of two hotels and a restaurant along a white-sand beach dressed up by attractive giant boulders. It's a wonderful spot to relax. Buses along national highway 1 can drop you off in Ca Na. Double rooms at the hotel start at US$10.

NHA TRANG

Nha Trang has what is probably the nicest municipal beach in all of Vietnam. The turquoise waters around Nha Trang are almost transparent, making for excellent fishing, snorkelling and scuba diving.

The area code for Nha Trang is 58.

Things to See & Do

The **Po Nagar Cham Towers** were built between the 7th and 12th centuries on a site used by Hindus for worship. The towers are two km north of Nha Trang on the left bank of the Cai River.

Hon Chong Promontory is a scenic collection of granite rocks jutting out into the South China Sea. The promontory is 3.5 km north of central Nha Trang.

Long Son Pagoda is about 500 metres west of the railway station. The **Giant Seated Buddha** is on the hill behind the pagoda.

The **Oceanographic Institute** has an aquarium and specimen room. The nearby **Bao Dai's Villas** (Cau Da Villas) is also worth a visit.

A **boat cruise** to the offshore islands is one of the highlights of Nha Trang. Almost every hotel in town can book you onto one of the boat tours run by Mama Linh for US$7. There is a separate boat tour to **Monkey Island**.

The best place for travellers to rent **watersports** equipment (except scuba gear) is the Sailing Club (☎ 826528), 72-74 Tran Phu St. For scuba diving, check out the Blue Diving

Nghe Mountain
(Hon Nghe)

To Qui Nhon (238 km)
& Danang (541 km)

Son Mountain
(Hon Son)

Cai River

2 Thang 4 Street

Nguyen
Dinh
Chieu

Po Nagar
Cham
Towers

Nha Nghi
Hon Chong

Ha Ra
Bridge

Xom Bong
Bridge

Red Island
(Hon Do)

To Phan
Rang (104 km)
& Saigon (448 km)

See Central Nha Trang Map

To Dong
Bo

Nha Trang Beach

Nha Trang

0   400   800 m

Nha
Khach 78

Hai Dang
Mini-Hotel

Police
Station

To
Dong Bo

Hai Au III Hotel
& Mini-Hotel 86

Huong Duong
Centre

Thanh Thanh
Hotel

Ana Mandara
Resort

SOUTH
CHINA
SEA

Oil
Storage
Tanks

Bao Dai's Villas

Oceanographic
Institute

Seashell
Shop

Nha Trang Ship Dock
(Cang Nha Trang)

Chut Mountain
(Nui Chut)

Cau Da
Dock

Cau Be

Outdoor
Aquarium
(Ho Ca Tri
Nguyen)

Bai Mieu
Fishing Village

Mieu Island
(Hon Mieu)

VIETNAM

Club (☎ 825390) at the Coconut Cove Resort, on the beach opposite the Hai Yen Hotel.

Places to Stay – bottom end

Ecpco Hotel, 14 Tran Phu St (☎ 825861), doubles US$18 to US$27

Hai Au I Hotel, 3 Nguyen Chanh St (☎ 822862), doubles US$12 to US$22

Hai Au II Hotel, 4 Nguyen Chanh St (☎ 823644), doubles with fan US$12, with air-con US$22

Hai Au III Hotel, 88 Tran Phu St (☎ 822826), doubles with fan US$15, with air-con US$20 to US$25

Hai Dang Mini-Hotel, 84 Tran Phu St (☎ 825203), doubles US$14 to US$23

Mini-Hotel 86, 86 Tran Phu St (☎ 824074), singles/doubles with fan US$10/12, with air-con US$20/22

Nha Khach 58, also called *Hai Quan Guesthouse*, 58 Tran Phu St (☎ 826304), doubles with fan US$7, with air-con US$13 to US$18

Nha Khach 62, 62 Tran Phu St (☎ 825095), singles with fan US$7, with fan and hot water US$10

Nha Khach 78, 78 Tran Phu St (☎ 826342), doubles with fan US$8 to US$12, with air-con US$14 to US$25

Nha Trang I Hotel, 129 Thong Nhat St (☎ 826645), doubles with fan US$8, with air-con US$12 to US$25

Nha Trang II Hotel, 21 Le Thanh Phuong St (☎ 822956), doubles with fan US$8, with air-con US$12 to US$15

Nha Trang III Hotel, 22 Tran Hung Dao St (☎ 823933), doubles with fan US$10, with air-con US$17 to US$25

Royal Hotel, 40 Thai Nguyen St (☎ 822298), doubles US$6 to US$20

Thong Nhat Hotel, 5 Yersin St (☎ 822966), singles with fan US$9, with air-con US$11 to US$20

Places to Stay – middle

Ana Mandara Resort, beach villas under construction

Bao Dai's Villas, also called *Cau Da Villas*, Tran Phu St (☎ 881049), doubles US$25 to US$70

Duy Tan Hotel, 24 Tran Phu St (☎ 822671), doubles US$23 to US$50

Grand Hotel, also called *Nha Khach 44* (☎ 822445), doubles US$18 to US$63

Hai Yen Hotel, 40 Tran Phu St (☎ 822828), doubles US$20 to US$100

Huu Nghi Hotel, 3 Tran Hung Dao St (☎ 827005), under renovation

Khatoco Hotel, 9 Biet Thu St (☎ 823724), doubles US$30 to US$70

Post Hotel (☎ 821250), doubles US$33 to US$50

Thang Loi Hotel, 4 Pasteur St (☎ 822241), doubles US$20 to US$40

Thanh Thanh Hotel, Tran Phu St, under construction

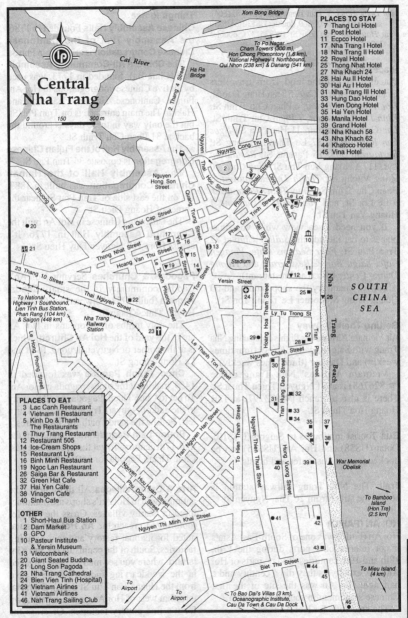

Central Nha Trang

0   150   300 m

Cai River

Xom Bong Bridge

Ha Ra Bridge

To Po Nagar
Cham Towers (300 m),
Hon Chong Promontory (1.6 km),
National Highway 1 Northbound,
Qui Nhon (238 km) & Danang (541 km)

2 Thang 4 Street

Nguyen Cong Tru St

Nguyen Hong Son Street

Thai Hoc Street

Phan Boi Chau Street

Dinh Phung Street

Le Loi Street

Quang Trung Street

Tran Qui Cap Street

Phan Chu Trinh Street

Hai Ba Trung Street

Pasteur Street

Thong Nhat Street

Hoang Van Thu Street

Le Thanh Phuong Street

Yet Kieu Street

Stadium

Yersin Street

23 Thang 10 Street

Thai Nguyen Street

Ly Thanh Ton Street

To National
Highway 1 Southbound,
Lien Tinh Bus Station,
Phan Rang (104 km)
& Saigon (448 km)

Nha Trang Railway Station

Nguyen Trai Street

Le Thanh Ton Street

Ly Tu Trong St

Nguyen Chanh Street

Nha Trang Beach

SOUTH CHINA SEA

Tran Hung Dao Street

Hoang Hoa Tham Street

Tran Phu Street

Le Hong Phong Street

Tran Nguyen Han Street

Phu Dong Street

Nguyen Huu Huan Street

To Hien Thanh Street

Nguyen Thien Thuat Street

Hung Vuong Street

Nguyen Thi Minh Khai Street

War Memorial Obelisk

To Bamboo Island
(Hon Tre)
(2.5 km)

To Airport

To Airport

Biet Thu Street

To Mieu Island
(4 km)

< To Bao Dai's Villas (3 km),
Oceanographic Institute,
Cau Da Town & Cau Da Dock

PLACES TO STAY
7   Thang Loi Hotel
9   Post Hotel
11 Ecpco Hotel
17 Nha Trang I Hotel
18 Nha Trang II Hotel
22 Royal Hotel
25 Thong Nhat Hotel
27 Nha Khach 24
28 Hai Au II Hotel
30 Hai Au I Hotel
31 Nha Trang III Hotel
33 Hung Dao Hotel
34 Vien Dong Hotel
35 Hai Yen Hotel
36 Manila Hotel
39 Grand Hotel
42 Nha Khach 58
43 Nha Khach 62
44 Khatoco Hotel
45 Vina Hotel

PLACES TO EAT
3   Lac Canh Restaurant
4   Vietnam II Restaurant
5   Kinh Do & Thanh
    The Restaurants
6   Thuy Trang Restaurant
12 Restaurant 505
14 Ice-Cream Shops
15 Restaurant Lys
16 Binh Minh Restaurant
19 Ngoc Lan Restaurant
26 Saiga Bar & Restaurant
32 Green Hat Cafe
37 Hai Yen Cafe
38 Vinagen Cafe
40 Sinh Cafe

OTHER
1   Short-Haul Bus Station
2   Dam Market
8   GPO
10 Pasteur Institute
    & Yersin Museum
13 Vietcombank
20 Giant Seated Buddha
21 Long Son Pagoda
23 Nha Trang Cathedral
24 Bien Vien Tinh (Hospital)
29 Vietnam Airlines
41 Vietnam Airlines
46 Nah Trang Sailing Club

VIETNAM

Vien Dong Hotel, 1 Tran Hung Dao St (☎ 821606), singles US$25 to US$60, doubles US$30 to US$70
Vina Hotel, 66 Tran Phu St (☎ 825137), doubles US$22 to US$27

Places to Eat

Places that get the nod from travellers include: *Green Hat Cafe*, 5 Tran Hung Dao St; *Hoan Hai Restaurant*, 6 Phan Chu Trinh St; *Kinh Do Restaurant*, 7 Phan Chu Trinh St; *Lac Canh Restaurant*, 11 Hang Ca St; *Ngoc Lan Restaurant*, 37 Le Thanh Phuong St; *Restaurant 505*, 15 Pasteur St; *Restaurant Lys*, 117A Hoang Van Thu St; *Sinh Cafe*, 10 Hung Vuong St; *Thanh The Restaurant*, 3 Phan Chu Trinh St; *Thuy Trang Restaurant*, 9 Le Loi St; and *Vietnam II Restaurant*, 7 Hoang Van Thu St.

If you need a sea view while you dine, places to eat include the *Sailing Club* at 72 Tran Phu St, *Four Seasons Cafe*, *Vinagen Cafe*, *Saiga Bar & Restaurant* and *Huong Duong Centre* (disco and restaurant).

For ice cream try the shops at 58 and 60 Quang Trung St (corner Le Thanh Ton St).

Getting There & Away

Air Vietnam Airlines has flights connecting Nha Trang with Saigon (daily), Hanoi (four times weekly) and Danang (three times weekly).

Vietnam Airlines' Nha Trang office (☎ 826768) is at 91 Nguyen Thien Thuat St. There is also a branch (☎ 823797) at 12B Hoang Hoa Tham St.

Bus Tourist minibuses to Saigon (US$10), Dalat (US$8) and Hoi An (US$15) can be booked from tourist cafes and hotels.

Train The Nha Trang railway station is across the street from 26 Thai Nguyen St.

HOI AN (FAIFO)

Hoi An (Faifo) was one of South-East Asia's major international ports during the 17th, 18th and 19th centuries. Today, parts of Hoi An look exactly as they did a century and a half ago. Hoi An was the site of the first Chinese settlement in southern Vietnam.

The area code for Hoi An is 51.

Things to See

Chinese Assembly Halls Founded in 1786, the **Assembly Hall of the Cantonese Chinese Congregation** is at 176 Tran Phu St.

The **Chinese All-Community Assembly Hall** (Chua Ba), founded in 1773, was used by all five Chinese congregations in Hoi An: Fujian, Cantonese, Hainan, Chaozhou and Hakka. The main entrance is on Tran Phu St, but the only way in these days is around the back at 31 Phan Chu Trinh St.

The **Assembly Hall of the Fujian Chinese Congregation** is opposite 35 Tran Phu St.

The **Assembly Hall of the Hainan Chinese Congregation** was built in 1883. It's on the east side of Tran Phu St, near the corner of Hoang Dieu St.

The Chaozhou Chinese in Hoi An built the **Chaozhou Assembly Hall** in 1776. It's across from 157 Nguyen Duy Hieu St.

Pagodas & Churches Serving Hoi An's Caodai community is the small **Caodai Pagoda** (built 1952) between Nos 64 and 70 Huynh Thuc Khang St.

The only tombs of Europeans in Hoi An are in the yard of the **Hoi An Church**, which is at the corner of Nguyen Truong To St and Le Hong Phong St.

Chuc Thanh Pagoda was founded in 1454, making it the oldest pagoda in Hoi An. To get to Chuc Thanh Pagoda, go all the way to the end of Nguyen Truong To St and turn left. Follow the sandy path for 500 metres.

Phuoc Lam Pagoda was founded in the mid-17th century. To get there, continue past Chuc Thanh Pagoda for 350 metres.

Arts & Crafts Villages All those neat fake antiques sold in Hoi An's shops are manufactured in nearby villages. Cross the An Hoi footbridge to reach the **An Hoi Peninsula**, noted for its boat factory and mat weaving factories. South of the peninsula is **Cam Kim Island**, where you see many people engaged in the woodcarving industry (take a boat from the Hoang Van Thu St dock). **Cam Ha**, three km west of Hoi An, is a village known for it's fine pottery factories. Or cross the

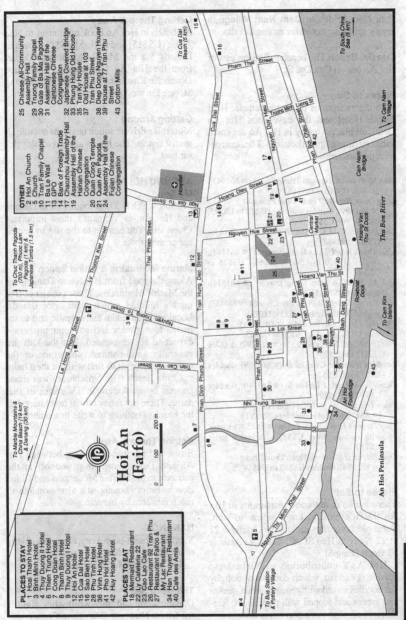

PLACES TO STAY

1 Hoai Thanh Hotel
4 Binh Minh Hotel
6 Thuy Duong II Hotel
7 Thien Trung Hotel
8 Trong Doan Hotel
9 Thanh Binh Hotel
9 Thuy Duong I Hotel
12 Hoi An Hotel
15 Cua Dai Hotel
16 Sao Bien Hotel
28 Phu Tinh Hotel
36 Vinh Hung Hotel
41 Pho Hoi Hotel
42 Huy Hoang Hotel

PLACES TO EAT

18 Mermaid Restaurant
23 Ly Cafeteria 22
23 Cao Lao Cafe
26 Restaurant 92 Tran Phu
27 Restaurant Faifoo &
     My Lac Restaurant
34 Han Thuyen Restaurant
40 Cafe des Amis

OTHER

2 Hoi An Church
5 Church
10 Tran Family Chapel
11 Ba Le Wall
13 GPO
14 Bank of Foreign Trade
17 Chaozhou Assembly Hall
19 Assembly Hall of the
     Hainan Chinese
     Congregation
20 Quan Cong Temple
21 Quan Am Pagoda
24 Assembly Hall of the
     Fujian Chinese
     Congregation
25 Chinese All-Community
     Assembly Hall
29 Truong Family Chapel
30 God of Ba Mu Pagoda
31 Assembly Hall of the
     Cantonese Chinese
     Congregation
32 Japanese Covered Bridge
33 Phung Hung Old House
35 Tan Ky House
37 Old House at 103
     Tran Phu Street
38 Diep Dong Nguyen House
39 House at 77 Tran Phu
     Street
43 Cotton Mills

Hoi An (Faifo)

0   100   200 m

To Marble Mountains &
China Beach (19 km)
& Danang (30 km)

To Chuc Thanh Pagoda
(700 m), Phoc Lam
Pagoda (1 km) &
Japanese Tombs (1.5 km)

Le Hong Phong Street

Nguyen Truong To Street

Ly Thuong Kiet Street

Thai Phien Street

Tran Cao Van Street

Phan Dinh Phung Street

Nhi Trung Street

Le Loi Street

Tran Hung Dao Street

Nguyen Hue Street

Hoang Dieu Street

Ngo Gia Tu Street

Hospital

Cua Dai Street

Pham Thai Street

Truong Minh Luong St

Nguyen Duy Hieu Street

Phan Boi Chau Street

To Cua Dai Beach (5 km)

To South China Sea (5 km)

To Cam Nam Village

Cam Nam Bridge

Thu Bon River

Hoang Van Thu St Dock

Central Market

Rowboat Dock

Nguyen Thai Hoc Street

Bach Dang Street

Tran Phu Street

Thai Hoc Street

Hoang Van Thu St

Phan Chu Trinh Street

An Hoi Footbridge

To Cam Kim Island

An Hoi Peninsula

Nguyen Thi Minh Khai Street

To Bus Station
& Pottery Village

VIETNAM

Cam Nam bridge to **Cam Nam Village**, a lovely spot also noted for arts and crafts.

Cua Dai Beach The beach is five km east of Hoi An out on Cua Dai St.

Places to Stay
With the exceptions of the unaesthetic Hoai Thanh Hotel and the cavernous Hoi An Hotel, all places to stay in Hoi An are small and charming guesthouses. The current selection includes:

Binh Minh Hotel, Nguyen Truong To St (☎ 861943), doubles US$10 to US$16

Cong Doan Hotel, 50 Phan Dinh Phung St (☎ 861899), doubles with fan US$10 to US$15, with air-con US$20

Cua Dai Hotel, 18 Cua Dai St (☎ 861722), doubles US$20 to US$35

Hoai Thanh Hotel, 23 Le Hong Phong St (☎ 861242), singles US$10 to US$15, doubles US$25 to US$40

Hoi An Hotel, 6 Tran Hung Dao St (☎ 861574), doubles US$7 to US$50

Huy Hoang Hotel, 73 Phan Boi Chau St (☎ 861453), singles US$12, doubles US$15 to US$30

Pho Hoi Hotel, 7/2 Tran Phu St (☎ 861633), dorm beds US$4, doubles US$10 to US$25

Phu Tinh Hotel, 144 Tran Phu St (☎ 861297), doubles US$12 to US$25

Sao Bien Hotel, 15 Cua Dai St (☎ 861589), doubles US$18 and US$28

Thanh Binh Hotel, 1 Le Loi St (☎ 861740), doubles US$12 to US$25

Thien Trung Hotel, 63 Phan Dinh Phung St (☎ 861720), singles/doubles US$10/15

Thuy Duong I Hotel, 11 Le Loi St (☎ 861574), rooms with outside toilet US$8, with inside toilet US$10

Thuy Duong II Hotel, 68 Hunh Thuc Khang St (☎ 861394), doubles US$10 to US$14

Places to Eat
There are so many good restaurants in Hoi An that it's hard to know where to start. Some old favourites include *Ly Cafeteria 22* at 22 Nguyen Hue St and *Cafe des Amis* at 52 Bach Dang St.

Hoi An's contribution to Vietnamese cuisine is cao lau, which consists of doughy flat noodles mixed with croutons, bean sprouts and greens and topped with pork slices. Restaurants all over town serve this dish.

Getting There & Away
All hotels in Hoi An book minibuses to Nha Trang (US$15) and to Hué (US$8). Buses to Danang via the Marble Mountains depart from the Hoi An bus station (Ben Quoc Doanh Xe Khach) at 74 Huynh Thuc Khang St, one km west of the town centre.

Getting Around
Motorbike drivers solicit business outside all tourist hotels. The hotels also have bicycles for rent.

AROUND HOI AN
My Son
My Son, which is 60 km south-west of Danang and Hoi An, is Vietnam's most important Cham site. You can get to the site by rented car or motorbike.

Marble Mountains & China Beach
Along the road from Hoi An to Danang are the Marble Mountains. These consist of five marble hillocks which were once islands. Local children make enthusiastic and unsolicited tour guides and souvenir pushers – expect to be surrounded. But the kids are generally good-natured, and some of the caves are difficult to find without their help.

China Beach (Bai Non Nuoc) was made famous by an American TV series of that name. There is a fancy tourist hotel here, but the beach is nothing to write home about.

Getting There & Away
Buses and minibuses running between Hoi An and Danang can drop you off at the entrance to the Marble Mountains and China Beach. From Danang, it's also possible to reach this area by bicycle.

DANANG
Vietnam's fourth-largest city, Danang is chiefly of interest to travellers as a transit stop.

The area code for Danang is 51.

Things to See
Danang's one and only worthwhile sight is the **Cham Museum** (Bao Tang Cham).

Places to Stay – bottom end

Ami Hotel, 7 Quang Trung St (☎ 824494), doubles US$12 to US$26

Dai A Hotel, 27 Yen Bai St (☎ 827532), doubles US$15 to US$65

Danang Hotel, 3 Dong Da St (☎ 821986), doubles US$6 to US$30

Hai Van Hotel, 2 Nguyen Thi Minh Khai St (☎ 821300), doubles US$12 to US$20

Hoai Huong Travel Shop & Guesthouse, 105 Tran Phu St (☎ 824874), doubles US$7

Huu Nghi Hotel, 7 Dong Da St (☎ 821021), cold-water rooms US$5 to US$12, rooms with air-con and hot water are US$8 to US$10

Marble Mountains Hotel, 5 Dong Da St (☎ 823258), doubles US$6 to US$30

Minh Tam II Mini-Hotel, 63 Hoang Dieu St (☎ 826687), doubles US$17 to US$35

Pacific Hotel, also called *Thai Binh Duong Hotel*, 93 Phan Chu Trinh St (☎ 822137), singles US$20 to US$32, doubles US$23 to US$36

Thanh Thanh Hotel, 50 Phan Chu Trinh St (☎ 821230), doubles US$7 to US$12

Thu Do Hotel, 107 Hung Vuong St (☎ 823863), singles US$4, doubles US$6 to US$12

Vinapha Hotel, 80 Tran Phu St (☎ 825072), doubles US$16 to US$18

Places to Stay – middle

Bach Dang Hotel, 50 Bach Dang St (☎ 823649), doubles US$40 to US$70

Binh Duong Mini-Hotel, Tran Phu St (☎ 821930), doubles US$25 to US$35

Hai Au Hotel, 177 Tran Phu St (☎ 822722), doubles US$40 to US$60

Marco Polo Hotel, 11C Quang Trung St (☎ 823295), singles US$50 to US$90, doubles US$60 to US$100

Peace Hotel, 3 Tran Quy Cap St, also called the *Hoa Binh Hotel* (☎ 823984), doubles US$25 to US$50

Phuong Dong Hotel, 93 Phan Chu Trinh St (☎ 821266), singles US$40 to US$46, doubles US$51 to US$57

Song Han Hotel, 36 Bach Dang St (☎ 822540), doubles US$25 to US$40

Thu Bon Hotel, 10 Ly Thuong Kiet St (☎ 821101), singles US$24 to US$27, doubles US$30 to US$32

Places to Eat

Café Lien, directly opposite the Danang Hotel, draws in a lot of the backpacker traffic. The *Tu Do Restaurant* at 172 Tran Phu St does excellent food but is not cheap. The *Hoang Ngoc Restaurant* at 106 Nguyen Chi Thanh St gets good reviews from travellers.

Getting There & Away

Air One of the best reasons to come to Danang is to fly out of it. There are daily flights to Hanoi and Saigon; four times weekly to Pleiku; three times weekly to Haiphong, Nha Trang and Qui Nhon. Vietnam Airlines (☎ 821130) is at 35 Tran Phu St.

Bus The Danang intercity bus station (Ben Xe Khach Da Nang) is about three km from the city centre. The ticket office for express buses is across the street from 200 Dien Bien Phu St.

Train Danang train station (Ga Da Nang) is about 1.5 km from the city centre on Haiphong St.

Pick-up Xe Lams and small passenger trucks to places in the vicinity of Danang leave from the short-haul pick-up truck station opposite 80 Hung Vuong St.

HUÉ

Hué served as Vietnam's political capital from 1802 to 1945 under the 13 emperors of the Nguyen Dynasty. Traditionally, the city has been one of Vietnam's cultural, religious and educational centres. Today, Hué's main attractions are the splendid tombs of the Nguyen emperors, several notable pagodas and the remains of the citadel.

Most of the city's major sights have an admission charge of at least US$5.

The area code for Hué is 54.

Things to See

The Citadel Construction of the moated citadel (Kinh Thanh), whose perimeter is 10 km, was begun in 1804 by Emperor Gia Long. The emperor's official functions were carried out in the **Imperial Enclosure** (Dai Noi, or Hoang Thanh), a 'citadel within the citadel' which has a six-metre-high wall 2.5 km in length.

Within the Imperial Enclosure is the **Forbidden Purple City** (Tu Cam Thanh), which was reserved for the private life of the emperor.

The beautiful hall which houses the **Imperial Museum** was built in 1845 and restored in 1923.

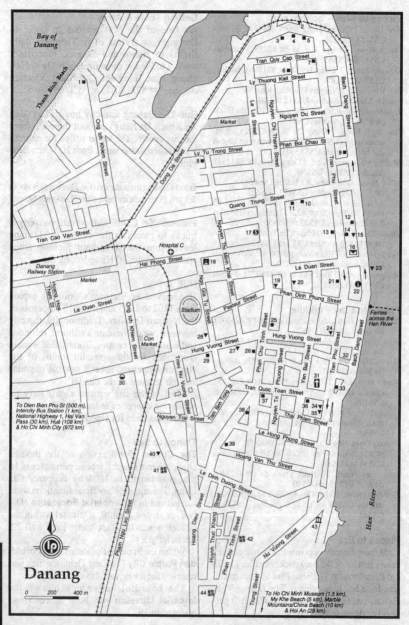

Bay of
Danang

Thanh Binh Beach

Tran Quy Cap Street

Ly Thuong Kiet Street

Bach Dang Street

Dong Da Street

Ong Ich Khiem Street

Market

Le Loi Street

Nguyen Chi Thanh Street

Nguyen Du Street

Phan Boi Chau St

Ly Tu Trong Street

Tran Phu Street

Quang Trung Street

Nguyen Thi Minh Khai Street

Tran Cao Van Street

Hospital C

Hai Phong Street

Danang
Railway Station

Market

Le Duan Street

Ong Ich Khiem Street

Ngo Gia Tu Street

Pasteur Street

Stadium

Con
Market

Le Duan Street

Phan Dinh Phung Street

Phan Chu Trinh Street

Hung Vuong Street

Trisimeu Nu Vuong Street

Hung Vuong Street

Yen Bai Street

Tran Phu Street

Bach Dang Street

Ferries
across the
Han River

To Dien Bien Phu St (500 m),
Intercity Bus Station (1 km),
National Highway 1, Hai Van
Pass (30 km), Hué (108 km)
& Ho Chi Minh City (972 km)

Hoang Hoa Tham St

Nguyen Trai Street

Yen Bai Street

Tran Quoc Toan Street

Phan Chu Trinh Street

Nguyen Tri Phuong Street

Thai Phien Street

Le Hong Phong Street

Hoang Van Thu Street

Le Dinh Duong Street

Hoang Dieu Street

Huynh Thuc Khang Street

Phan Chu Trinh Street

Phan Ngu Lao Street

Han River

Danang

0   200   400 m

To Ho Chi Minh Museum (1.5 km),
My Khe Beach (5 km), Marble
Mountains/China Beach (10 km)
& Hoi An (29 km)

Nu Vuong Street

Trung Street

VIETNAM

Royal Tombs The Tombs of the Nguyen Dynasty (1802-1945) are seven to 16 km south of Hué.

Nam Giao (Temple of Heaven) was once the most important religious site in Vietnam.

Dong Khanh's Mausoleum, the smallest of the Royal Tombs, was built in 1889. Construction of the **Tomb of Thieu Tri**, who ruled from 1841 to 1847, was completed in 1848.

Perhaps the most majestic of the Royal Tombs is the **Tomb of Minh Mang**, who ruled from 1820 to 1840. The tomb is 12 km from Hué on the west bank of the Perfume River (there's a ferry from a point about 1.5 km south-west of Khai Dinh's Tomb).

The gaudy and crumbling **Tomb of Emperor Khai Dinh**, who ruled from 1916 to 1925, was begun in 1920 and completed in 1931.

Pagodas, Temples & Churches The **Thien Mu Pagoda** (also called Linh Mu Pagoda) is one of the most famous structures in all of Vietnam. The pagoda, founded in 1601, is on the banks of the Perfume River, four km south-west of the citadel.

The **Bao Quoc Pagoda** was founded in 1670. **Notre Dame Cathedral** (Dong Chua Cuu The) at 80 Nguyen Hue St is an impressive modern building.

There are quite a few pagodas and Chinese congregational halls in Phu Cat and Phu Hiep subdistricts, which are across the Dong Ba Canal from Dong Ba Market. The entrance to **Dieu De National Pagoda** (Quoc Tu Dieu De), built under Emperor Thieu Tri (ruled 1841-47), is along Dong Ba Canal at 102 Bach Dang St. Hué's Indian Muslim community constructed the **mosque**, at 120 Chi Lang in 1932.

Chieu Ung Pagoda (Chieu Ung Tu) opposite 138 Chi Lang St was founded by the Hainan Chinese congregation in the mid-19th century and was rebuilt in 1908.

The **Cantonese Chinese Congregation Assembly Hall** (Chua Quang Dong) is at 176 Tran Phu St.

Tang Quang Pagoda (Tang Quang Tu), just down the road from 80 Nguyen Chi Thanh St, is the largest of the three Hinayana (Theravada) pagodas in Hué.

Thuan An Beach Thuan An Beach (Bai Tam Thuan An), 13 km north-east of Hué, is on a splendid lagoon near the mouth of the Perfume River.

Boat Cruises All-day boat trips on the Perfume River take in many of the aforementioned sights. Look for boats on the east bank of the river just north of the Trang Tien Bridge.

PLACES TO STAY				
1	Khach San Du Lich Thanh Binh	37	Phuong Dong Hotel	40	Thanh An Vegetarian Restaurant
3	Huu Nghi Hotel	38	Pacific Hotel		
4	Marble Mountains Hotel	39	Minh Tam II Mini-Hotel		
5	Danang Hotel	**PLACES TO EAT**		**OTHER**	
6	Thu Bon Hotel	2	Café Lien	14	Vietnam Airlines
7	Peace Hotel	15	Thanh Lich Restaurant	16	GPO
8	Hai Van Hotel	19	Tuoi Hong Cafe	17	Vietcombank
9	Song Han Hotel	20	Hoang Ngoc Restaurant	18	Caodai Temple
10	Ami Hotel	23	Christie's Restaurant	22	Danang Tourist
11	Marco Polo Hotel	24	Thanh Huong Restaurant	25	Municipal Theatre
12	Bach Dang Hotel	27	Dac San Restaurant	30	Short-Haul Pick-Up Truck Station
13	Binh Duong Mini-Hotel	28	Chin Den Restaurant	31	Danang Cathedral
21	Vinapha Hotel	34	Tiem An Binh Dan Restaurant	32	Cho Han (Market)
26	Thanh Thanh Hotel	35	Tu Do & Kim Do Restaurants	41	Phap Lam Pagoda
29	Thu Do Hotel			42	Tam Bao Pagoda
33	Hai Au Hotel			43	Cham Museum
36	Dai A Hotel			44	Pho Da Pagoda

VIETNAM

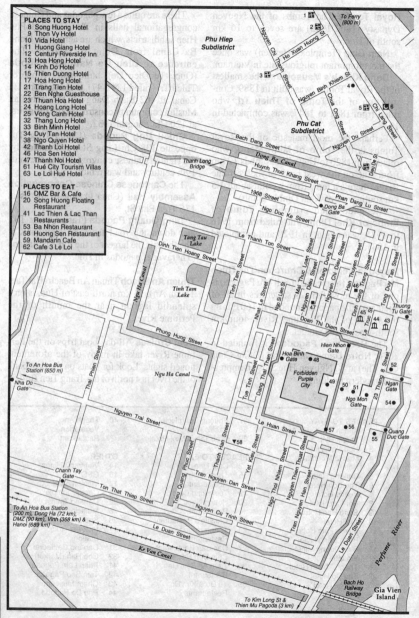

PLACES TO STAY
8 Song Huong Hotel
9 Thon Vy Hotel
10 Vida Hotel
11 Huong Giang Hotel
12 Century Riverside Inn
13 Hoa Hong Hotel
14 Kinh Do Hotel
15 Thien Duong Hotel
17 Hoa Hong Hotel
21 Trang Tien Hotel
22 Ben Nghe Guesthouse
23 Thuan Hoa Hotel
24 Hoang Long Hotel
25 Vong Canh Hotel
32 Thang Long Hotel
33 Binh Minh Hotel
34 Duy Tan Hotel
38 Ngo Quyen Hotel
42 Thanh Loi Hotel
46 Hoa Sen Hotel
47 Thanh Noi Hotel
61 Hué City Tourism Villas
63 Le Loi Hué Hotel

PLACES TO EAT
16 DMZ Bar & Cafe
20 Song Huong Floating Restaurant
41 Lac Thien & Lac Than Restaurants
53 Ba Nhon Restaurant
54 Huong Sen Restaurant
59 Mandarin Cafe
62 Cafe 3 Le Loi

VIETNAM

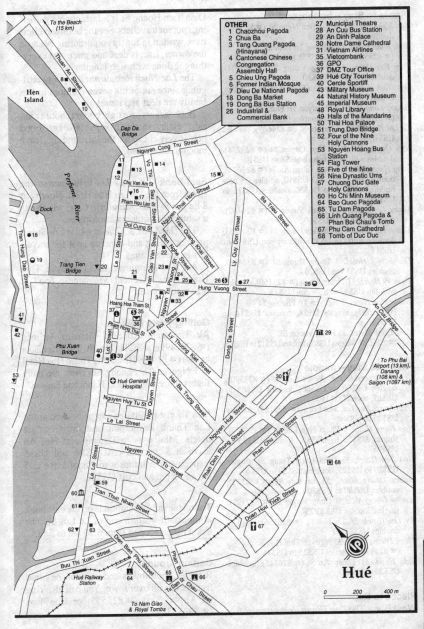

To the Beach
(15 km)

Thuan An Street

Hen Island

Perfume River

Dock

Dap Da Bridge

Nguyen Cong Tru Street

Vo Thi

Chu Van Am St

Pham Ngu Lao Street

Doi Cung St

Le Loi Street

Tran Cao Van Street

Ben Nghe St

Nguyen Thai Hoc Street

Tran Quang Khai Street

Ba Trieu Street

Ly Quy Don Street

Hung Vuong Street

Tran Hung Dao Street

Trang Tien Bridge

Hoang Hoa Tham St

Pham Hong Thai St

Ha Noi St

Nguyen Tri Phuong St

Phu Xuan Bridge

Le Loi Street

Ly Thuong Kiet Street

Dong Da Street

An Cuu Bridge

Hué General Hospital

Nguyen Huy Tu St

Ngo Quyen Street

Le Lai Street

Hai Ba Trung Street

Nguyen Hue Street

To Phu Bai Airport (13 km), Danang (108 km) & Saigon (1097 km)

Nguyen Truong To Street

Phan Dinh Phung Street

Phan Chu Trinh Street

Le Loi Street

Tran Thuc Nhan Street

Dien Bien Phu Street

Buu Thi Xuan Street

Hué Railway Station

Tu Dam Street

Phan Boi Chau Street

Doan Huu Trinh Street

To Nam Giao & Royal Tombs

Hué

0   200   400 m

VIETNAM

OTHER
1 Chaozhou Pagoda
2 Chua Ba
3 Tang Quang Pagoda (Hinayana)
4 Cantonese Chinese Congregation Assembly Hall
5 Chieu Ung Pagoda
6 Former Indian Mosque
7 Dieu De National Pagoda
18 Dong Ba Market
19 Dong Ba Bus Station
26 Industrial & Commercial Bank
27 Municipal Theatre
28 An Cuu Bus Station
29 An Dinh Palace
30 Notre Dame Cathedral
31 Vietnam Airlines
35 Vietcombank
36 GPO
37 DMZ Tour Office
39 Hué City Tourism
40 Cercle Sportiff
43 Military Museum
44 Natural History Museum
45 Imperial Museum
48 Royal Library
49 Halls of the Mandarins
50 Thai Hoa Palace
51 Trung Dao Bridge
52 Four of the Nine Holy Cannons
53 Nguyen Hoang Bus Station
54 Flag Tower
55 Five of the Nine
56 Nine Dynastic Ums
57 Chuong Duc Gate Holy Cannons
60 Ho Chi Minh Museum
64 Bao Quoc Pagoda
65 Tu Dam Pagoda
66 Linh Quang Pagoda & Phan Boi Chau's Tomb
67 Phu Cam Cathedral
68 Tomb of Duc Duc

Places to Stay – bottom end

Ben Nghe Guesthouse, 4 Ben Nghe St (☎ 823687), doubles US$8 to US$15

Binh Minh Hotel, 12 Nguyen Tri Phuong St (☎ 825526), doubles US$8 to US$40

Duy Tan Hotel, 12 Hung Vuong St (☎ 825001), doubles US$10 to US$30

Gia Dinh Hotel, Vo Thi Sau St (☎ 826461), singles/doubles US$6/8

Hoang Long Hotel, 20 Nguyen Tri Phuong St (☎ 828235), singles/doubles US$10/15

Le Loi Hué Hotel, 2 Le Loi St (☎ 824668), doubles US$10 to US$20

Ngo Quyen Hotel, 11 Ngo Quyen St (☎ 823278), doubles with outside bath US$8 to US$10

Song Huong Hotel, 51-66 Thuan An St (☎ 823675), doubles (in old annex) US$10, singles (in new building) US$20 to US$30, doubles US$25 to US$35

Thang Long Hotel, 16 Hung Vuong St (☎ 826462), doubles US$10 to US$40

Thanh Loi Hotel, 7 Dinh Tien Hoang St (☎ 824803), doubles with fan US$5, with air-con US$10 to US$15

Thanh Noi Hotel, 3 Dang Dung St (☎ 822478), doubles US$15 to US$20

Thon Vy Hotel, 37 Thuan An St (☎ 825160), doubles with fan US$8, with air-con US$15

Thuan Hoa Hotel, 7 Nguyen Tri Phuong St (☎ 822553), singles US$8, doubles US$14 to US$75

Vong Canh Hotel, 25 Hung Vuong St (☎ 824130), singles US$8, doubles US$12 to US$15

Places to Stay – middle

Century Riverside Inn, 49 Le Loi St (☎ 823390), singles US$60 to US$80, doubles US$65 to US$85, suites US$150

Guesthouse 5 Le Loi, 5 Le Loi St (☎ 822155), doubles US$25 to US$60

Hoa Hong Hotel, 1 Pham Ngu Lao St (☎ 824377), singles US$30 to US$80, doubles US$35 to US$90

Hoa Sen Hotel, 33 Dinh Cong Trang St, singles US$20 to US$25, doubles US$30 to US$40

Huong Giang Hotel, 51 Le Loi St (☎ 822122), doubles US$50 to US$200

Huong Giang Villa, 3 Hung Vuong St (☎ 822122), singles/doubles US$20/25

Ky Lin Hotel, 58 Le Loi St (☎ 826556), singles/doubles US$25/30

Thien Duong Hotel, 33 Nguyen Thai Hoc St (☎ 825976), doubles US$25 to US$45

Vida Hotel, 31 Thuan An St (☎ 826145), doubles US$20 to US$50

Places to Eat

West Bank The *Lac Thanh Restaurant* at 6A Dien Tien Hoang St is a fashionable gathering spot for travellers. See the book travellers have written in for tips on ordering because the owner, Lac, is deaf and mute and everything is done with sign language.

The *Lac Thien Restaurant* is equally intriguing since six of the seven children in this family are deaf and mute!

Backpackers on a tight budget should consider eating in the *Dongba Market*. Food here is very cheap but the surroundings leave much to be desired.

East Bank *Cafe 3 Le Loi* is just across the street from the Le Loi Hué Hotel. Nearby at 8 Le Loi St is the *Mandarin Cafe*, which has a salubrious outdoors atmosphere.

The *DMZ Bar & Cafe* at 44 Le Loi St is a popular eating and dancing spot for travellers in the evenings.

Am Phu Restaurant at 35 Nguyen Thai Hoc St has excellent Vietnamese food at reasonable prices.

Getting There & Away

Air The main office of Vietnam Airlines (☎ 823249) is at 12 Ha Noi St. There is also a branch (☎ 824709) inside the Thuan Hoa Hotel at 7 Nguyen Tri Phuong St. There are daily flights connecting Hué to Hanoi and Saigon.

Bus Tourist minibuses can be booked at the Lac Thanh Restaurant and most budget hotels. Minibuses to Danang and Hoi An leave at 8 am and cost US$4 and US$5 respectively. Minibuses to Hanoi leave at 5 am and 5 pm and cost US$22.

Train Hué railway station is on the east bank at the south-western end of Le Loi St. The ticket office is open from 6.30 am to 5 pm.

Getting Around

Bicycles, motorbikes and cars can be hired from hotels all over town. You can also ring up Airport Taxi (☎ 825555) or Hué Taxi (☎ 833333).

AROUND HUÉ
DMZ & Vicinity

From 1954 to 1975, the Ben Hai River served as the demarcation line between South Vietnam and North Vietnam. The Demilitarised Zone (DMZ) consisted of an area five km to either side of the demarcation line.

Most of what you can see nowadays in the DMZ are places where historical things happened. To make sense of it all you really need a guide who can explain just what you're looking at. Budget tours (about US$15 per person) can easily be booked in Hué. Most hotels in Hué and some cafes (check the Lac Thanh Restaurant) are good places to look for tours. Foreigners need a travel permit to visit the DMZ, but this should be included in the quoted tour price.

Things to See

The remarkable **Tunnels of Vinh Moc** are similar to the ones at Cu Chi, but these are the real thing, not rebuilt for mass tourism.

Truong Son National Cemetery (Nghia Trang Liet Si Truong Son) is a memorial to the tens of thousands of North Vietnamese soldiers killed along the Ho Chi Minh Trail. Row after row of white tombstones stretch across the hillsides.

The gargantuan 175 mm cannons at **Camp Carroll** were used to shell targets as far away as Khe Sanh, over 30 km away. These days, there is not much to see here except a few overgrown trenches and the remains of their timber roofs.

Set amid beautiful hills, valleys and fields at an elevation of about 600 metres, the town of **Khe Sanh** (Huong Hoa) is a pleasant district capital once known for its French-run coffee plantations. **Khe Sanh Combat Base**, site of the most famous siege of the Vietnam War, sits silently on a barren plateau surrounded by vegetation-covered hills often obscured by mist and fog.

Lao Bao, 18 km from Khe Sanh, is right on the Tchepone River (Song Xe Pon), which marks the Vietnam-Laos border. Towering above Lao Bao on the Lao side of the border is Co Roc Mountain, once a North Vietnamese artillery stronghold. Two km towards Khe Sanh from the border crossing (now open to foreigners) is the lively Lao Bao Market.

Hanoi

Hanoi, capital of the Socialist Republic of Vietnam, is different things to different people. Most foreigners find Hanoi to be slow-paced, pleasant and even charming. It's a city of lakes, shaded boulevards, embassies and holy shrines dedicated to the late, great Ho Chi Minh.

But things are changing fast. New highrises are crowding out the charming French colonial houses, the number of cars and motorbikes increases daily while postcard vendors and cyclo drivers buzz around tourists like flies. On the other hand, the hotels have improved dramatically, once bare shelves in the state stores are now overflowing with goods and even the staid socialist restaurants have improved their menus. What better place than the national capital to witness all the growth, progress, foibles and follies of Vietnam's new economic reforms?

Information

Visas The immigration police office is at 87 Tran Hung Dao St. The Foreign Affairs Ministry is at 1 Ton That Dam St, near Ho Chi Minh's Mausoleum.

Money Vietcombank is at 78 Nguyen Du St. ANZ Bank is at 14 Le Thai To St on the western shore of Hoan Kiem Lake. Credit Lyonnais at 10 Trang Thi St changes money, but imposes a US$5 service charge unless you change over US$200.

Post & Communications The GPO (☎ 825-7036; fax 825-3525) is at 75 Dinh Tien Hoang St.

The area code for Hanoi is 4.

Travel Agencies There are plenty of travel agencies in Hanoi, both government and private, which can provide cars, book air tickets and arrange tours. A partial list follows:

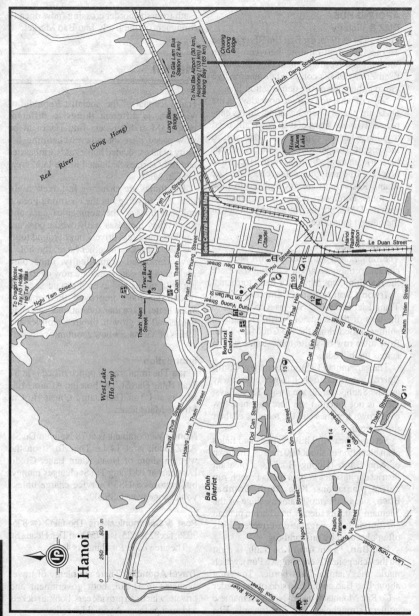

Hanoi

0   250   500 m

Red River (Song Hong)

West Lake (Ho Tay)

Trac Bach Lake

Hoan Kiem Lake

The Citadel

Botanical Gardens

Ba Dinh District

Radio Transmitter

To Gia Lam Bus Station (2 km)

To Noi Bai Airport (30 km), Haiphong (103 km) & Halong Bay (165 km)

Chuong Duong Bridge

Long Bien Bridge

Bach Dang Street

See Central Hanoi Map

Le Duan Street

Hanoi Railway Station

Nghi Tam Street

To Dragon Hotel, Tay Ho Hotel & Ho Tay Villas

Yen Phu Street

Thanh Nien Street

Quan Thanh Street

Phan Dinh Phung Street

Thuy Khue Street

Hoang Hoa Tham Street

Dien Bien Phu Street

Hoang Dieu Street

Hung Vuong Street

Ton That Dam St

Nguyen Thai Hoc Street

Cat Linh Street

Ton Duc Thang Street

Kham Thien Street

Doi Can Street

Kim Ma Street

Ngoc Khanh Street

La Thanh Street

Giang Vo Street

Lang Trung Street

Buoi Street

To Lich River

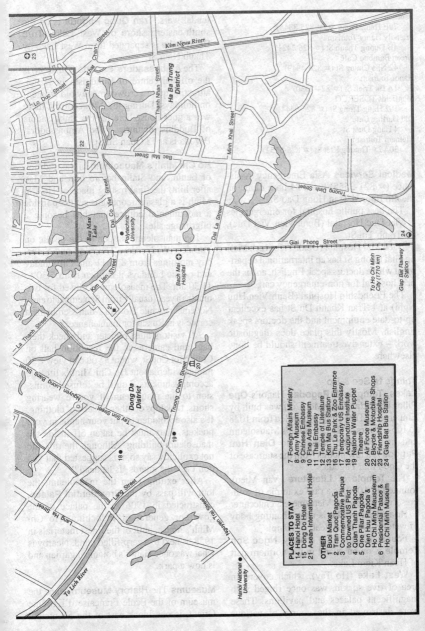

PLACES TO STAY
14 Hanoi Hotel
15 Dong Do Hotel
21 Asean International Hotel

OTHER
1 Buoi Market
2 Tran Quoc Pagoda
3 Commemorative Plaque to Downed US Pilot
4 Quan Thanh Pagoda
5 One Pillar Pagoda,
   Dien Huu Pagoda &
   Ho Chi Minh Mausoleum
6 Presidential Palace &
   Ho Chi Minh Museum
7 Foreign Affairs Ministry
9 Army Museum
10 Fine Arts Museum
11 Thai Embassy
12 Temple of Literature
13 Kim Ma Bus Station
16 Thu Le Park & Zoo Entrance
17 Temporary US Embassy
18 Acupuncture Institute
19 National Water Puppet
   Theatre
20 Air Force Museum
22 Bicycle & Motorbike Shops
23 Friendship Hospital
24 Giap Bat Bus Station

VIETNAM

Especen
79E Hang Trong St (☎ 825-8845)
Friendly Hanoi Tourism
4B Duong Thanh St (☎ 826-7421)
Green Bamboo Café
42 Nha Chung St (☎ 826-4949)
Hanoi Tourism
1A Ba Trieu St (☎ 824-2330)
Manfields TOSERCO
102 Hang Trong St (☎ 826-9444)
Old Darling Cafe
4 Hang Quat St
Vietnam Tourism
30A Ly Thuong Kiet St (☎ 825-5552)

Medical Services Asia Emergency Assistance (☎ 821-3555) has a 24 hour clinic on the 4th floor, 4 Tran Hung Dao St.

The best public hospital for emergencies is Viet Duc Hospital (Benh Vien Viet Duc), 48 Tranh Thi St.

Bach Mai Hospital (Benh Vien Bach Mai) on Giai Phong St has an international department where doctors speak English, and is the best hospital for non-emergency care.

The Friendship Hospital (Benh Vien Huu Nghi) at 1 Tran Khanh Du St has excellent up-to-date equipment and the doctors speak English. Mostly this place does diagnostic work – extensive treatment should be done elsewhere.

Things to See & Do
Lakes, Temples & Pagodas Hanoi's **One Pillar Pagoda** (Chua Mot Cot) was built by Emperor Ly Thai Tong, who ruled from 1028 to 1054. Tours of Ho Chi Minh's Mausoleum end up here. The entrance to **Dien Huu Pagoda** is a few metres from the staircase of the One Pillar Pagoda.

The **Temple of Literature** (Van Mieu), founded in 1070, is a rare example of well-preserved traditional Vietnamese architecture.

Hoan Kiem Lake is an enchanting body of water right in the heart of Hanoi.

Founded in the 18th century, **Ngoc Son Temple** is on an island in the northern part of Hoan Kiem Lake.

West Lake (Ho Tay), which covers an area of five sq km, was once ringed with magnificent palaces and pavilions. These were destroyed in the course of various

feudal wars. **Tran Quoc Pagoda** is on the south-eastern shore of West Lake. **Truc Bach Lake** is separated from West Lake by Thanh Nien St.

The **Ambassadors' Pagoda** (Quan Su) is the official centre of Buddhism in Hanoi, attracting quite a crowd (mostly old women) on holidays. During the 17th century, there was a guesthouse here for the ambassadors of Buddhist countries. The Ambassadors' Pagoda is at 73 Quan Su St.

Ho Chi Minh's Mausoleum In the tradition of Lenin, and Stalin before him and Mao after him, the final resting place of Ho Chi Minh is a glass sarcophagus set deep inside a monumental edifice that has become a pilgrimage site.

The mausoleum is open to the public on Tuesday, Wednesday, Thursday and Saturday mornings from 8 to 11 am. On Sunday and public holidays it is open from 7.30 to 11.30 am. The mausoleum is closed for two months a year (usually from September to early November) while Ho Chi Minh's embalmed corpse is in Russia for maintenance.

All visitors must register and check their bags and cameras at the reception hall on Chua Mot Cot St, where a you can view a 20 minute video about Ho Chi Minh's life and accomplishments. You'll be refused admission to the mausoleum if you're wearing shorts, tank tops or other 'indecent' clothing. It's also forbidden to put your hands in your pockets. Hats must be taken off inside the mausoleum building. Although the rules do not explicitly say so, it is suggested that you don't ask the guards 'Is he dead?'

After exiting from the mausoleum, the tour will pass by the **Presidential Palace**, constructed in 1906 as the palace of the governor general of Indochina. Ho Chi Minh's house, built of the finest materials in 1958, is next to a carp-filled pond. Nearby is what was once Hanoi's botanical garden and is now a park.

Museums The **History Museum**, once the museum of the École Française d'Extrême Orient, is one block east of the Municipal

VIETNAM

Theatre at 1 Pham Ngu Lao St. The **Army Museum** is on Dien Bien Phu St; it is open daily except Monday from 7.30 to 11.30 am only. The displays include scale models of various epic battles from Vietnam's long military history, including Dien Bien Phu and the capture of Saigon.

The **Ho Chi Minh Museum** is divided into two sections, 'Past' and 'Future'. You start in the past and move to the future by walking in a clockwise direction downwards through the museum from the top of the stairs (right-hand side). The displays are very modern and all have a message (eg peace, happiness, freedom etc). Some of the symbolism is hard to figure out (did Ho Chi Minh have a cubist period?). The 1958 Ford Edsel bursting through the wall (an American commercial failure to symbolise America's military failure) is a knockout. Photography is forbidden. Upon entering, all bags and cameras must be left at reception.

Many of the exhibits at the **Air Force Museum** are outdoors. This includes a number of Soviet MiG fighters, reconnaissance planes, helicopters and anti-aircraft equipment. Inside the museum hall are other weapons, including mortars, machine guns and some US-made bombs (hopefully defused). There is a partially truncated MiG with a ladder – you are permitted to climb up into the cockpit and have your photo taken. The museum is on Truong Chinh St.

The works in the **Fine Arts Museum** (Bao Tang My Thuat) are fascinating. The museum is at 66 Nguyen Thai Hoc St and is open from 8 am to noon and 1.30 to 4 pm Tuesday to Sunday.

St Joseph Cathedral Stepping inside St Joseph Cathedral (inaugurated in 1886) is like being instantly transported to medieval Europe. The cathedral is noteworthy for its square towers, elaborate altar and stained-glass windows. The first Catholic mission in Hanoi was founded in 1679.

The main gate to St Joseph Cathedral is open daily from 5 to 7 am and from 5 to 7 pm – the hours when masses are held.

Places to Stay – bottom end

In general, hotels in Hanoi are more expensive than in Saigon. Complicating the issue is the fact that most of the budget guesthouses only have a few rooms each and are scattered throughout the city. There is no travellers' haven equivalent to Saigon's Pham Ngu Lao St. This means that you might have to spend quite a long time traipsing from one place to another if you want something cheap.

Lotus Guesthouse is sort of a backpacker centre because it's the only place to offer dormitories. Other good bets are Especen, the Tong Dan Guesthouse and New Tong Dan Guesthouse. A partial list of bottom-end places to stay follows:

Especen operates nine mini-hotels which you book from its main office at 79E Hang Trong St (☎ 825-8845); doubles cost US$12 to US$50

Green Bamboo Café, 42 Nha Chung St (☎ 826-4949), doubles US$15

Hoa Long Hotel, Hang Trong St (☎ 826-9319), doubles US$15

Khach San 30-4, 115 Tran Hung Dao St (☎ 825-2611), doubles with shared bath US$8, with attached bath US$35

Lotus Guesthouse, 42V Ly Thuong Kiet St (☎ 826-8642), dorm beds US$4, singles US$8

Mai Lien Hotel, 31A Mai Hac De St (☎ 822-8385), doubles US$20 to US$30

Mango Hotel, 118 Le Duan St (☎ 824-3754), doubles US$25 to US$40

Nam Phuong Hotel, 16 Bao Khanh St (☎ 825-8030), doubles US$15 to US$45

New Tong Dan Guesthouse, Tran Quang Khai St (☎ 825-2219), doubles US$9 to US$30

Orient Hotel, 72 Tran Xuan Soan St (☎ 822-6811), singles/doubles US$20/40

Phu Gia Hotel, 136 Hang Trong St (☎ 825-7512), doubles US$25 to US$48

Phung Hung Hotel, 2 Duong Thanh St (☎ 826-5555), doubles US$25

Queen Cafe, 65 Hang Bac St (☎ 826-0860), singles/doubles US$5/7

Sophia Hotel, 6 Hang Bai St (☎ 826-6848), doubles US$20

Tong Dan Guesthouse, 17 Tong Dan St (☎ 826-5328), doubles US$9 to US$30

Viet My Hotel, 21 Mai Hac De St (☎ 822-6220), doubles US$25 to US$55

Vinh Quang Hotel, 24 Hang Quat St (☎ 824-3423), doubles US$25 to US$40

Win Hotel, 27 Tong Duy Tan St (☎ 823-3275), doubles US$25 to US$70

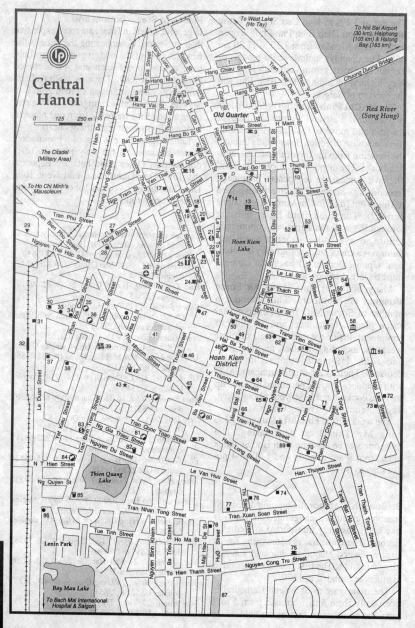

Central Hanoi

0   125   250 m

Places to Stay – middle

Binh Minh Hotel, 27 Ly Thai To St (☎ 826-6441), doubles US$30 to US$50

Dien Luc Hotel, also called the *Energy Hotel*, 30 Ly Thai To St (☎ 825-0457), top-floor rooms cost US$25, other rooms are US$40 to US$60

Dong Loi Hotel, 94 Ly Thuong Kiet St (☎ 825-5721), doubles US$45 to US$68

Freedom Hotel, 57 Hang Trong St (☎ 826-7119), doubles US$35 to US$69

Hoan Kiem Hotel, 25 Tran Hung Dao St (☎ 826-4204), doubles US$40 to US$74

Hong Ngoc Hotel, 34 Hang Manh St (☎ 828-5053), doubles US$35 to US$45

Las Vegas Hotel, 7 Le Van Huu St (☎ 824-8958), doubles US$40 to US$120

Rose Hotel, also called *Khach San Hoa Hong*, 20 Phan Boi Chau St (☎ 825-4438), doubles US$48 to US$72

Spring Song Hotel, 27 Mai Hac De St (☎ 822-9169), doubles US$50 and US$70

Trang Tien Hotel, 35 Trang Tien St (☎ 825-6341), doubles US$35 to US$60

Places to Eat

After the delectable cuisine of Saigon, Hanoi is disappointing. Restaurants in the capital tend to be more expensive than elsewhere, the food lousier and the service lethargic. But things have been gradually improving.

Restaurants Old favourites for backpackers are the 'two darlings' – the *Old Darling Café* at 4 Hang Quat St and the *Real Darling Café* on the same street at No 33. Both do reasonable Vietnamese dishes and light western food like pancakes and fruit shakes.

The *Queen Cafe* at 65 Hang Bac St does light food (plenty of baguettes, fried eggs

VIETNAM

and coffee). The situation is very similar at the *Tourist Meeting Cafe*, 59 Ba Trieu St.

The *Green Bamboo Café* at 42 Nha Chung St is moving into the mid-price range, but you can still eat very well for under US$5. This place has become a sort of unofficial travel centre – this is where you can book trips to Halong Bay, Sapa etc, and the travel noticeboard here is also the best in Hanoi. The cafe operates a book exchange.

Café de Paris (☎ 821-2701) at 16A Nguyen Cong Tru St is an outstanding cafe proud of its Parisian atmosphere (including an accordion player on Saturday night). Homesick French travellers come here in droves.

The Little Italian (☎ 825-8167) at 81 Tho Nhuom St does superb pizza, pasta and cocktails. It's expensive (US$8 for a pizza), but you can get it delivered to your hotel.

Le Bistrot (☎ 826-6136), 34 Tran Hung Dao St, is notable for fine French food.

Club Opera (☎ 826-8802) at 59 Ly Thai To St is not a concert hall but rather an excellent western-food restaurant.

Hué-style cooking is the speciality at the *Hué Restaurant*. The restaurant's slogan is that their food is 'more Hué than Hué'. This place is at the eastern end of Ly Thuong Kiet St.

The large Chinese restaurant on the ground floor of the *Hoa Long Hotel* (☎ 826-9319) on Hang Trong St near the western shore of Hoan Kiem Lake is well worth checking out.

Dog meat, a Hanoi delicacy, is available from kerbside vendors a few hundred metres north of the History Museum on Le Phung Hieu St near Tran Quang Kha St.

A few other restaurants serving a mostly foreign clientele include: *Cha Ca Restaurant*, 14 Cha Ca St; *Phuc Fish & Chips*, 3 Le Thai To St; *Piano Restaurant*, 50 Hang Vai St; and *Restaurant Bistrot*, 34 Tran Hung Dao St.

Ice Cream The best ice-cream bar is inside the *Trang Tien Hotel* at 35 Trang Tien St, but it's down in the basement and is not immediately obvious.

The *Thuy Ta Restaurant* has so-so food, but the ice cream is superb. The restaurant is at 1 Le Thai To St.

The best ice-cream sundaes can be found at *Kem Tra My*, which is on Nguyen Thai Hoc St near Ho Chi Minh's Mausoleum.

For some of the best French pastries and coffee in Vietnam, visit the *Pastry & Yogurt Shop* (☎ 825-0216) at 252 Hang Bong St.

Entertainment

Cinema Fanslands Cinema (☎ 825-7484), 84 Ly Thuong Kiet St, offers the best movies in town. French speakers will also be pleased with what's on offer at Alliance Française (☎ 826-6970), 42 Yet Kieu St. Another possibility is the New Age Cinema at 52 Hang Bai St.

Disco The *VIP Club* (☎ 825-2690), in the Boss Hotel at 60-62 Nguyen Du St, Hai Ba Trung District, is a thoroughly modern disco with thumping music, strobe lights and large-screen video. The VIP Club also has slot machines and karaoke cubicles. There is no cover charge but beer costs US$3 a glass while gin & tonic goes for US$6!

Water Puppets This fantastic art form is unique to Vietnam, and Hanoi is one of the best places to see it. Just on the shore of Hoan Kiem Lake is the Municipal Water Puppet Theatre (Roi Nuoc Thang Long). Performances are given from 8 to 9 pm every night except Monday. Admission is US$2.

Even better is the National Water Puppet Theatre (Nha Hat Mua Roi Trung Uong), eight km south of the centre at 32 Truong Chinh St. Admission costs US$2. There are four performances weekly on Tuesday, Thursday, Saturday and Sunday at 7.45 pm. Some of the cafes catering to foreigners book a low-cost bus to the theatre which departs central Hanoi at 6.50 pm and also brings you back.

Pubs *Apocalypse Now* at 46 Hang Vai St calls itself a 'restaurant and dive bar'. It's about as good a dive as you'll find in Hanoi. It opens at 5 pm and closes whenever.

Tintin Pub at 14 Hang Non St serves only drinks (no food), though the management has plans to introduce snacks. It's open from 8 pm until 2 am.

There is a cosy pub in the upstairs portion of the Green Bamboo Café at 42 Nha Chung St.

Hanoi's expat community often gets together at the *Lan Anh Bar* (☎ 826-7552), 9A Da Tuong St.

Sunset Pub, 10 Giang Vo St, atop the Dong Do Hotel, has a live jazz band Thursday and Saturday nights from 7 to 10.30 pm.

Things to Buy

Lots of western customers seem to like the Ho Chi Minh T-shirts. However, it might be worth keeping in mind that neither Ho Chi Minh T-shirts nor VC headgear are popular apparel with Vietnamese refugees and certain war veterans living in the west. Wearing such souvenirs while walking down a street in Los Angeles or Melbourne might offend someone, possibly endangering your relationship with the Overseas Vietnamese community, as well as your dental work.

Hang Gai St and its continuation, Hang Bong St, are a good place to look for embroidered tablecloths and hangings. Hanoi is a good place to have informal clothes customtailored. There are also a number of antique shops in the vicinity.

A good shop for silk clothing is Khai Silk (☎ 825-4237), 96 Hang Gai St. You can also try nearby Duc Loi Silk at 76 Hang Gai St.

Greeting cards with traditional Vietnamese designs hand-painted on silk covers are available around town for US$0.10 or so.

There is an outstanding shoe market along Hang Dau St at the north-eastern corner of Hoan Kiem Lake.

Souvenir water puppets, costumery and paraphernalia can be purchased from the theatres which do these performances.

For philatelic items, try the philatelic counter at the GPO (in the main postal services hall).

Watercolour paints and brushes are available at a store at 216 Hang Bong St (corner Phung Hung St). Musical instruments can be purchased from shops at 24 and 36 Hang Gai, and 76 and 85 Hang Bong.

Getting There & Away

Air Vietnam Airlines has nonstop international flights between Hanoi and Bangkok, Dubai, Guangzhou (China), Hong Kong, Seoul, Singapore, Taipei and Vientiane. There are other international flights via Saigon. China Southern Airlines flies Hanoi-Beijing via Nanning.

Domestic and international airline offices found in Hanoi are as follows:

Air France
    1 Ba Trieu St (☎ 825-3484)
Cathay Pacific
    27 Ly Thuong Kiet St (☎ 826-7298)
China Southern Airlines
    Binh Minh Hotel, 27 Ly Thai To St (☎ 826-9233)
Malaysia Airlines
    15 Ngo Quyen St (☎ 826-8820)
Pacific Airlines
    100 Le Duan St (☎ 851-5356)
Singapore Airlines
    17 Ngo Quyen St (☎ 826-8888)
Thai Airways International
    25 Ly Thuong Kiet St (☎ 826-6893)
Vietnam Airlines
    1 Quang Trung St (☎ 825-0888)

Pacific Airlines is the only company besides Vietnam Airlines to offer domestic flights.

Bus Hanoi has several main bus terminals. There are frequent minibuses throughout the day to Haiphong from Hang Thung St near Tran Quang Kha St. Service begins at around 5 am and the last one leaves Hanoi about 6 pm. These minibuses depart when full (and they really mean 'full'). The cost will typically be around US$2 to US$3 per person. In Haiphong, you catch the minibuses at the government-owned bus station on Nguyen Duc Canh St.

It's a rather different story on governmentowned buses. You should purchase your tickets the day before departure. The so-called 'express buses' leave daily at 5 or 5.30 am. Most nonexpress (regular) buses depart between 4.30 and 5.30 am, though some, especially on shorter routes, leave later in the day.

Gia Lam bus station (Ben Xe Gia Lam) is where you catch buses to points north-east of Hanoi. This includes Halong Bay and the China border near Lang Son. The bus station is two km north-east of the centre – you have to cross the Red River to get there. Cyclos won't cross the bridge so you need to get there by motorbike or taxi.

Giap Bat bus station (Ben Xe Giap Bat) serves points south of Hanoi, including Saigon. The station is seven km south of the Hanoi railway station.

Kim Ma bus station (Ben Xe Kim Ma) is opposite 166 Nguyen Thai Hoc St (corner Giang Vo St). This is where you get buses to the north-west part of Vietnam, including Lao Cai and Dien Bien Phu.

Train The Hanoi railway station, or Ga Ha Noi (☎ 852628), is opposite 115 Le Duan (at the western end of Tran Hung Dao St). The ticket office is open from 7.30 to 11.30 am and from 1.30 to 3.30 pm only.

Getting Around

The Airport Hanoi's Noi Bai airport is about 35 km north of the city, which means you aren't going to get there by cyclo.

Minibuses from Hanoi to Noi Bai airport depart from the Vietnam Airlines booking office on Quang Trung St. The schedule depends on the departure and arrival times of domestic and international flights, but in any case the buses are scheduled to meet arriving and departing flights. You should make your booking the day before departure. The trip to Noi Bai typically takes 50 minutes.

At Noi Bai airport, arriving passengers will be asked by a woman in a booth near the exit to purchase minibus tickets.

Taxi drivers congregate at the Vietnam Airlines booking office in Hanoi. Needless to say, they are numerous at the airport itself. Drivers will start their opening bid at around US$25, but this can easily be bargained to US$15.

Bus Better tourist maps of Hanoi include bus lines marked in red. Service on most of the bus routes is infrequent.

Motorcycle & Cyclo You'll find cyclos parked every five to 10 metres in central Hanoi, and each driver will enthusiastically try to arm wrestle you into his vehicle. The quoted price is usually three times the real price.

The situation is much the same with motorbikes. You can rent a bike with driver for about US$10 per day.

Bicycle Most budget hotels have bicycles for rent at about US$1 to US$2 per day.

AROUND HANOI
Perfume Pagoda
The Perfume Pagoda (Chua Huong) is a complex of pagodas and Buddhist shrines built into the limestone cliffs of Huong Tich Mountain.

Pilgrims and other visitors spend their time here boating, hiking and exploring the caves.

The Perfume Pagoda is about 60 km south-west of Hanoi in Hoa Binh Province, accessible first by road and then by river. There is an obligatory US$7 admission fee which includes a 1½ hour river trip. Some of the cafes in Hanoi book day trips to the Perfume Pagoda for US$15 (which does not include the admission fee).

Thay Pagoda
Thay Pagoda (Master's Pagoda) is dedicated to Thich Ca Buddha (Sakyamuni, the historical Buddha). Visitors enjoy watching water-puppet shows, hiking and exploring caves in the area.

Thay Pagoda is about 40 km south-west of Hanoi in Ha Tay Province. Some of Hanoi's cafes catering to budget travellers offer combined day tours of the Thay and Tay Phuong pagodas.

Tay Phuong Pagoda
Tay Phuong Pagoda (Pagoda of the West) consists of three parallel single-level structures built on a hillock said to resemble a buffalo. The 76 figures carved from jackfruit wood, many from the 18th century, are the pagoda's most celebrated feature.

Tay Phuong Pagoda is approximately 40 km south-west of Hanoi in Tay Phuong hamlet, Ha Tay Province. A visit here can easily be combined with a stop at Thay Pagoda.

The North

Stretching from the Hoang Lien Mountains (Tonkinese Alps) eastward across the Red River Delta to the islands of Halong Bay, the northern part of Vietnam (Bac Bo), known to the French as Tonkin, includes some of the country's most spectacular scenery. The mountainous areas are home to many distinct hill-tribe groups.

HOA LU

Known to travellers as Vietnam's 'Halong Bay without the water' (see the Halong Bay section), Hoa Lu boasts breathtaking scenery. While Halong Bay has huge rock formations jutting out of the sea, Hoa Lu has them jutting out of the rice paddies.

Hoa Lu was the capital of Vietnam under the Dinh Dynasty (ruled 968-980) and the Early Le Dynasty (ruled 980-1009). The ancient citadel of Hoa Lu, most of which has been destroyed, covered an area of about three sq km.

Today there are two sanctuaries at Hoa Lu. **Dinh Tien Hoang**, restored in the 17th century, is dedicated to the Dinh Dynasty. The second temple, **Dai Hanh**, or Dung Van Nga, commemorates the rulers of the Early Le Dynasty.

Bic Dong Grotto is in the village of Van Lam, a short boat trip away. Other popular sights include the Tam Coc Caves and Xuyen Thuy Grotto.

The area code for Hoa Lu is 30.

Places to Stay

There are currently no places to stay in Hoa Lu itself, but nearby (12 km) Ninh Binh serves as the local bedroom community for travellers. Places to stay include:

Bien Bach Hotel, 195 Le Dai Hanh St (☎ 871449), doubles US$15 to US$25
Hoa Lu Hotel, Tran Hung Dao St (☎ 871217), singles US$15 to US$30, doubles US$20 to US$35
Ninh Binh Hotel, 2 Tran Hung Dao St (☎ 871337), doubles US$20 to US$25
Queen Mini-Hotel, 30 metres from Ninh Binh railway station (☎ 871874), doubles US$10 to US$15

Song Van Hotel II, 86 Van Giang St (☎ 871860), doubles US$10 to US$25
Song Van Hotel, Le Hong Phong St (☎ 871974), doubles US$21
Thuy Anh Mini-Hotel, Van Giang St (☎ 871602), doubles US$8 to US$20

Getting There & Away

Hoa Lu is 120 km due south of Hanoi and the journey takes about two hours by car. No train stops in Hoa Lu, but the *Reunification Express* stops in nearby Ninh Binh. From there you can rent a car, motorbike or bicycle to complete the 12 km journey to Hoa Lu.

CUC PHUONG NATIONAL PARK

Cuc Phuong National Park is one of Vietnam's most important nature preserves. Ho Chi Minh personally took time off from the war in 1963 to dedicate this national park, Vietnam's first.

The elevation of the highest peak in the park is 648 metres, and the hills are laced with many grottoes. At the park's lower elevations, the climate is subtropical. During the rainy season (summer), leeches are everywhere, making trekking impossible.

A guide is not mandatory for short walks, but it would be foolish and risky to attempt a long trek alone through the dense jungle. There are three-day treks to Hmong villages.

Admission to the national park costs US$5.

Places to Stay

There are two guesthouses, one by the park entrance gate and another 20 km away in the park's centre. The guesthouse by the gate costs US$30 to US$40, and has the great advantage of being located near a few restaurants. By contrast, the guesthouse in the park's centre has no food unless ordered a day or two in advance.

Getting There & Away

Cuc Phuong National Park is 140 km from Hanoi (via Ninh Binh); sections of the road are in poor condition. There is no public transport, but with a car or motorbike it is possible to visit the forest as a day trip from Hanoi.

VIETNAM

HAIPHONG

Haiphong, Vietnam's third most populous city, is the north's main industrial centre and one of the country's most important seaports. There is precious little to see here, but some travellers use it as a staging post for visiting Halong Bay and Cat Ba Island.

Potentially prosperous, Haiphong remains a backwater, though foreign investors are now showing much interest.

The area code for Haiphong is 31.

Places to Stay

Budget travellers tend to head for the Thanh Lich Hotel. The full accommodation menu follows:

Bach Dang Hotel, 42 Dien Bien Phu St (☎ 842444), doubles US$17 to US$45

Cat Bi Hotel, 30 Tran Phu St (☎ 846306), doubles US$15 and US$30

Cau Rao Hotel, 460 Lach Tray St (far from the centre) (☎ 847021), doubles US$10 to US$40

Dien Bien Hotel, 67 Dien Bien Phu St (☎ 842264), doubles US$25 to US$40

Duyen Hai Hotel, 5 Nguyen Tri Phuong St (☎ 842157), doubles US$30 to US$35

Hoa Binh Hotel, 104 Luong Khanh Thien St (☎ 846907), doubles US$25

Hong Bang Hotel, 64 Dien Bien Phu St (☎ 842229), doubles US$39 to US$65

Hotel du Commerce, 62 Dien Bien Phu St (☎ 842706), doubles US$25 to US$40

Nha Khach Thanh Pho, opposite the main ferry pier on the Cam River (☎ 842524), doubles US$25

Thang Nam Hotel, 55 Dien Bien Phu St (☎ 842818), doubles US$10 to US$20

Thanh Lich Hotel, 47 Lach Tray St in a park-like compound one km from the centre (☎ 847361), doubles with shared bath US$8, with attached bath US$12

Getting There & Away

Air Both Pacific Airlines and Vietnam Airlines fly Haiphong-Saigon. Vietnam Airlines also offers three flights weekly on the Haiphong-Danang route.

Bus & Train Haiphong is 103 km from Hanoi and the journey by road takes about three hours. The two cities are also linked by rail.

AROUND HAIPHONG
Do Son Beach

Palm-shaded Do Son Beach, 21 km southeast of Haiphong, is the most popular seaside resort in the north and a favourite of Hanoi's expat community. This is also the site of Do Son Casino, the first casino to open in Vietnam since the Communists 'liberated' the south in 1975.

HALONG BAY

Magnificent Halong Bay, with its 3000 islands rising from the clear, emerald waters of the Gulf of Tonkin, is one of the natural marvels of Vietnam. The vegetation-covered islands are dotted with innumerable beaches and grottoes created by the wind and the waves.

To see the islands and grottoes, a boat trip is mandatory.

Orientation & Information

Food, accommodation and all other life-support systems are to be found in the town of Halong City. The town is bisected by a bay – the west side was formerly called Bai Chay but is now officially Halong City West. A short ferry ride takes you to Halong City East, formerly known as Hon Gai. Accommodation can be found on both sides of the bay, but Halong City West is more scenic and more well endowed with hotels and restaurants.

The area code for Halong City is 33.

Places to Stay

Vuon Dao St in the centre of Halong City West has a solid row of mini-hotels with little to choose between them. Most budget travellers head for this area. From west to east, the hotel line-up is as follows:

Thanh Nien Hotel, US$12

Postal Hotel, also called *Khach San Buu Dien* (☎ 846205), doubles US$30 to US$35

Ngoc Mai Mini-Hotel (☎ 846123), US$14 to US$11

Thu Thuy Mini-Hotel (☎ 846295), US$6 to US$9

Phuong Vi Mini-Hotel, doubles US$7 to US$9

Sun Flowers Mini-Hotel, also called *Khach San Hoa Huong Duong*, 14 Vuon Dao St (☎ 846153), US$8 to US$10

Van Nam Mini-Hotel (☎ 846593), US$8 to US$10

VIETNAM

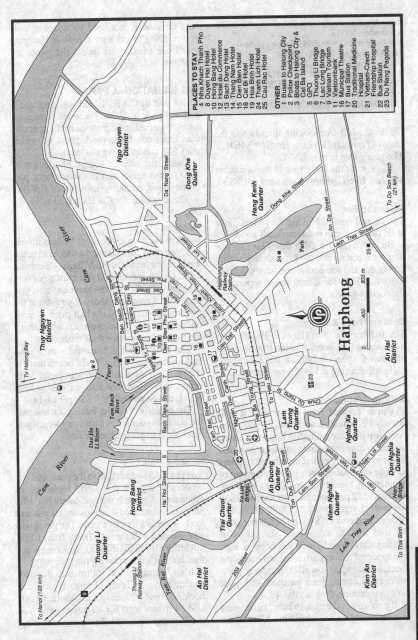

PLACES TO STAY
4 Nha Khach Thanh Pho
8 Duyen Hai Hotel
10 Hong Bang Hotel
12 Hotel du Commerce
13 Bach Dang Hotel
14 Thang Nam Hotel
15 Dien Bien Hotel
18 Cat Bi Hotel
19 Hoa Binh Hotel
24 Thanh Lich Hotel
25 Cau Rao Hotel

OTHER
1 Buses to Halong City
2 Police Checkpoint
3 Boats to Halong City & Cat Ba Island
5 GPO
6 Thuong Li Bridge
7 Lac Long Bridge
9 Vietnam Tourism
11 Vietcombank
16 Municipal Theatre
17 Bus Station
20 Traditional Medicine Hospital
21 Vietnam-Czech Friendship Hospital
22 Bus Station
23 Du Nang Pagoda

Haiphong

Ngo Quyen District

Dong Khe Quarter

Hang Kenh Quarter

Da Nang Street

Dong Khe Street

To Do Son Beach (21 km)

Lach Tray Street

Park

Cam River

Thuy Nguyen District

To Halong Bay

Le Loi Street

Haiphong Railway Station

An Da Street

Cau Dat Street

Tam Bach River

Ferry

Dao Ha Li River

Bach Dang Street

Cam River

Hong Bang District

Ha Noi Street

To Hanoi (103 km)

Thuong Li Quarter

Thuong Li Railway Station

Tam Bac River

Trai Chuoi Quarter

203 Street

An Hai District

Kien An District

Xa Lua Bridge

Nguyen Duc Canh Street

Tran Nguyen Han Street

Ton Duc Thang Street

Lam Son Street

An Duong Quarter

Niem Nghia Quarter

Don Nghia Quarter

Niem Bridge

Lach Tray River

To Thai Binh

Lam Tuong Quarter

Nghia Xa Quarter

An Hai District

Chua Du Hang Street

Hai Ba Trung Street

Tran Phu Street

Dien Bien Phu Street

Hoang Dieu St

Dao Street

Phu Street

Tran Quang Khai St

Minh Khai Street

Ben Binh Dang Street

Nguyen Tri Phuong St

800 m

400

0

VIETNAM

Peace Hotel, also called *Hoa Binh Hotel* (☎ 846009), doubles US$12
Hai Trang Hotel (☎ 846094), doubles US$10
Thanh Lien Hotel, US$8 to US$10
Vina Lyn Hotel, US$10
Rose Hotel, doubles US$10 to US$12
Cuu Long Hotel doubles US$8 to US$12
Viet Nhat Hotel, doubles US$10
Dung Tien Hotel, doubles US$8 to US$9

Up on the hill overlooking the town is the large (47 rooms) *Tien Long Hotel* (☎ 846042). The going rate here is US$22.

Right near the ferry pier is the upmarket *Van Hai Hotel*, where rooms start at US$30.

Places to Eat
The central area of Halong City West has a solid line of cheap restaurants, all good.

Be aware that the *Dien Bun Thit Cho* is a dog-meat restaurant. No English sign warns you of this and some travellers have unknowingly had Fido for dinner (most report that the food is good).

Getting There & Away
The 165 km trip from Hanoi to Halong Bay takes about five hours by bus. Budget cafes and travel agencies book a three-day/two-night trip starting at US$25 per person.

Getting Around
If you're booked into a tour a boat will already be provided no doubt. If you're on your own it's easy enough to hire a motorised launch to tour the islands and their grottoes. You can probably round up other foreigners to share the boat or even go with a group of Vietnamese tourists. A mid-sized boat can hold six to 12 persons and costs around US$6 per hour. Larger boats can hold 50 to 100 persons and cost US$10 to US$20 per hour. To find a boat, ask around the quays of Halong City West. There has been at least one reported robbery from a small boat – the foreign passengers lost all their money, passports etc. Leaving your passport with your hotel's reception desk is advised.

If you've got the cash to burn, helicopters can be chartered for whirlwind tours of the bay. Of course, it's hard to imagine how you're going to get a good look at the grottoes from a helicopter unless the pilots are *really* skilled.

CAT BA NATIONAL PARK
About half of Cat Ba Island was declared a national park in 1986. There are numerous lakes, waterfalls and grottoes in the spectacular limestone hills, the highest of which rises 331 metres above sea level.

Today, the island's human population of 12,000 is concentrated in the southern part of the island, including the town of Cat Ba.

The area code for Cat Ba Island is 31.

Beaches
Much to the consternation of budget travellers, you must pass through a tunnel to reach the beaches from Cat Ba Village – there is a US$1 charge for this and you must pay *every* time you pass through the tunnel, even if you do it several times in one day. If you stay at the government-run hotel it's half price, – most unfair to the private hotel owners who cannot get this concession for their customers.

The beach itself is beautiful – nice sand and crystal-clear water. At the beach there is simple food available (French bread with drinks etc). There are also six cabins here which can be rented for US$8 per night.

The beach is in a cove. Facing out towards the water, to your left is a pathway which you can follow to yet another beach.

National Park
You pay US$1 admission to the park, and the services of a guide cost US$3 regardless of group size. A guide is not mandatory but definitely recommended – otherwise, all you are likely to see is a bunch of trees. The guide will take you on a walk through Trung Trang Cave, but bring a torch (flashlight). Trekking is not feasible if it's raining (too slippery).

It's 17 km from Cat Ba town to the park headquarters at Trung Trang. Hotels can book you onto a 12 seat minibus which costs US$30 (round trip) for 12 passengers. You must arrange the time with the driver to come and pick you up at the end of the day. Motorbike drivers want about US$5. There have been cases of drivers demanding more than the agreed amount or else they refuse to bring you back to town.

Places to Stay

All the hotels are fairly noisy due to adjacent karaokes and the drone of generators, which operate from around 5 pm until 10 pm. Rumour has it that next year the electricity will be on for 24 hours – hopefully, this does not mean that those infernal generators will run all night! The four hotels currently on offer are:

Chua Dong Hotel (☎ 888243), huge state-owned place, doubles US$6 to US$20
Hoang Huong Hotel (☎ 888274), privately owned, doubles US$12 to US$15
Lan Ha Hotel (☎ 888299), newly opened private hotel, doubles US$15 to US$20
Quang Duc Hotel (☎ 888231), private but not too good, doubles US$8 to US$10

Getting There & Away

Cat Ba National Park is 133 km from Hanoi and 30 km east of Haiphong. A boat to Cat Ba departs from Haiphong every day at 11 am and returns the next day at 6 am; the trip takes about 3½ hours and costs US$3.

An alternative (though not recommended) way to reach Cat Ba is via the island of Cat Hai, which is closer to Haiphong. A boat departs Haiphong for Cat Hai, makes a brief stop and continues on to the port of Fulong on Cat Ba Island. A bus connects Fulong to Cat Ba Village, a distance of 30 km.

Chartered private boats run trips between Cat Ba and Halong Bay. Make inquiries at the pier at either end.

Getting Around

Motorbikes are available for rent in the town for US$1.50 per hour or US$5 per day. Hotels and restaurants book boat tours around the island.

BA BE LAKE NATIONAL PARK

This incredibly beautiful area boasts waterfalls, rivers, deep valleys, lakes and caves set amid towering peaks. The area is inhabited by members of the Dai minority who live in homes built on stilts.

There are actually several lakes here, the largest of which is called Ba Be and is about 145 metres above sea level and surrounded by steep mountains up to 1754 metres high.

Ba Be (Three Bays) is the name of the southern part of a narrow body of water seven km long; the northern section of the lake, separated from Ba Be by a 100-metre-wide strip of water sandwiched between high walls of chalk rock, is called **Be Kam**. The Nam Nang River is navigable for 23 km between a point four km above Cho Ra and the **Dau Dang Waterfall**, which consists of a series of spectacular cascades between sheer walls of rock.

An interesting place is **Puong Cave**. The cave is 300 metres long and passes completely through a mountain. A navigable river flows through the cave, making for an interesting boat trip. You can also organise boat trips to some nearby tribal villages.

Foreigners are charged a US$6 entry fee to the park.

Places to Stay

The town of Cho Ra boasts the *Ba Be Hotel* (☎ (26) 876115), where rooms cost US$15.

Getting There & Away

Ba Be Lake is 240 km (eight hours) from Hanoi, 61 km from Bach Thong (Bac Can) and 18 km from Cho Ra. Most visitors to the national park go from Hanoi by chartered vehicle. Some of the cafes in Hanoi have started organising bus trips.

Reaching this national park by public transport is possible but not easy. The way to do it is to take a bus from Hanoi to Bach Thong (Bac Can), and from there another bus to Cho Ra.

In Cho Ra you can take a wonderful boat ride to the park for US$16 per person (the boat holds 15 to 20 persons).

HOA BINH

The city of Hoa Binh (Peace) is 74 km southwest of Hanoi. This area is home to many Montagnard people.

VIETNAM

Unfortunately, Hoa Binh is the minority village for packaged tours. Hill-tribe clothing is on sale in the market, but in large sizes specially made for tourists. Some of the other genuine Montagnard souvenirs look as if they should have a 'Made in Taiwan' sticker on the bottom. Maybe they do. Give them another year and the Montagnards will be selling banana-muesli pancakes.

All this having been said, there's no reason why you shouldn't stop in and have a look. However, to get a look at the traditional Montagnard lifestyle, this begins about 50 km to the west and continues right up to the border with Laos and beyond.

The area code for Hoa Binh is 18.

Places to Stay
Although the outside is ugly, the *Thai Binh Hotel* (☎ 852001) has good rooms for US$28. Your other option is the *Hoa Binh I Hotel* (☎ 852051), where doubles cost US$35.

MAI CHAU
One of the closest places to Hanoi where you can see a real hill-tribe village is Mai Chau. It's a beautiful place, very rural with little in the way of a downtown – rather, it's a collection of farms and huts spread out over a large area. The people here are ethnic Tai (Thai), though only distantly related to tribes in Thailand.

Foreigners must pay an admission fee of US$0.50 to enter Mai Chau.

The area code for Mai Chau is 18.

Places to Stay
The only hotel in town is the *Mai Chau Guesthouse* (☎ 867262), where rooms are US$9 to US$15. However, most travellers prefer to stay in a real minority house (US$5 per person) at Lac Village (Ban Lac).

Getting There & Away
Mai Chau is a little to the south of national highway 6, which is the direct Hanoi-Dien Bien Phu route. So getting there requires a slight detour.

You'll be hard-pressed to find any direct public transport to Mai Chau from Hanoi. If you're not on a tour or don't have your own chartered vehicle, your best hope would be to take a public bus from Hanoi to Hoa Binh, followed by a motorcycle taxi to Mai Chau.

Some cafes in Hanoi run trips to Mai Chau. All transport, food and accommodation is provided for as low as US$28 per person.

LAO CAI
Lao Cai is the major town at the end of the railway line and right on the Chinese border. The border crossing slammed shut during the 1979 war between China and Vietnam and remained closed until 1993. Its reopening has changed Lao Cai into a major destination for travellers journeying between Hanoi and Kunming, the latter being the capital of China's scenic Yunnan Province.

The border town on the Chinese side is called Hekou, separated from Vietnam by a river and a bridge. The bridge and border crossing is open daily from 8 am until 5 pm and you must pay a small toll to cross.

The area code for Lao Cai is 20.

Orientation
The border is three km from Lao Cai railway station. Making this journey is best accomplished on a motorbike, which costs around US$0.50.

Places to Stay
In Hekou, on the Chinese side, budget accommodation is available at the old *Hekou Hotel* or the new, relatively upmarket *Dongfeng Hotel*. In Lao Cai, the situation is as follows:

Post Office Guesthouse, also called *Nha Khach Buu Dien* (☎ 830033), doubles US$10 to US$13
Red River Guest House, also called *Nha Khach Song Hong*, doubles US$8 to US$12
Red River Hotel, also called *Khach San Hong Ha* (☎ 830007), doubles US$6 to US$8

Getting There & Away
There are two trains daily in each direction on the Lao Cai-Hanoi run. One train runs at night and one during the day. The morning

train departs Hanoi at 8.20 am and the evening one at 8.20 pm, and travelling time is 10 to 12 hours. Tickets for foreigners cost US$10 but are usually only sold on the day of departure. There is no soft sleeper, just hard seat, soft seat and (on night trains) hard sleeper. The toilets are pretty bad, so dehydrate before boarding. Once the train is under way, go to the attendant at the end of your car for a pillow and blanket – if you don't need the blanket for warmth, you can still use it as extra padding beneath your bottom.

International trains which actually cross the border are planned, and might be running by the time you read this.

SAPA

Sapa is an old hill station in a beautiful valley at 1600 metres elevation. Don't forget your winter woollies – Sapa is known for its cold, foggy winters (down to 0°C). Thanks to the chilly climate, the area boasts temperate-zone fruit trees (peaches, plums etc) and gardens for raising medicinal herbs. The dry season for Sapa is approximately January through June – afternoon rain showers in the mountains are frequent.

Surrounding Sapa are the Hoang Lien Mountains. These mountains include **Fansipan**, which at 3143 metres is Vietnam's highest. The trek from Sapa to the summit and back can take four days.

The market on Saturday is a major attraction. Check out some of the hats on sale.

Some of the more well known sights around Sapa include Thac Bac (Silver Falls) and Cau May (Cloud Bridge), which spans the Muong Hoa River.

The area code for Sapa is 20.

Places to Stay

Auberge Hotel, doubles US$12, good restaurant
Bank Guest House, inside the bank, doubles US$5 to US$7
Forestry Hotel, generally overpriced, doubles US$10 to US$25
Green Bamboo Hotel, has a bar in the evenings, dorm beds US$4, doubles US$15 to US$25
Trade Services Guest House, also called *Nha Khach Thuong Nghiep*, doubles US$5 to US$8

Trade Union Guest House, beautiful building but cold water only, doubles US$5

Getting There & Away

The gateway to Sapa is Lao Cai, 30 km from Sapa. Trains arriving from Hanoi at Lao Cai railway station are met by buses which can take passengers directly to Sapa for US$2.

Locals are also very willing to drive you up the mountain by motorbike for US$5, but travellers have reported problems with drivers taking them halfway and then asking for more money to complete the journey. If you don't cough up the cash, they threaten to leave you stranded.

Driving a motorbike from Hanoi to Sapa takes two days over roads which are often muddy or flooded. The total distance between Hanoi and Sapa is 370 km.

Some of the cafes in Hanoi now offer four-day bus trips to Sapa for US$50. This is probably the most hassle-free way to do the journey.

BAC HA

The highlands around Bac Ha are about 900 metres above sea level, making the area somewhat warmer than Sapa. Ten minority groups live around Bac Ha: Dzao, Giay, Han, Hmong, Lachi, Nung, Phula, Tay, Thulao and Kinh (Viet).

One of Bac Ha's main industries is the manufacture of alcoholic brews (rice wine, manioc wine and corn liquor). Some of this stuff is so potent that it can ignite (literally). Harvesting opium also used to be a major source of revenue, but the Communists put a stop to that several years ago.

There are many plum trees around Bac Ha, and during the springtime the countryside is white with **plum blossoms**. The season for eating plums is June and July.

There are three big markets in the area, all within 20 km of each other. The **Can Cau Market** is the best market, but it's only open on Saturday. You'll see plenty of 'flower Hmong' here, so called because the women embroider flowers on their skirts. Items on sale include water buffalos, pigs, horses, chickens etc. The market is 16 km north of

Bac Ha town and eight km south of the Chinese border.

Bac Ha Market is in Bac Ha Town itself and gets very crowded, but it's lively and interesting. The market only operates on Sunday.

About 10 km from Bac Ha Town on the way to Can Cau Market, **Lungphin Market** is the least beautiful of the three markets, but it runs on both Saturday and Sunday.

Getting There & Away

A bus departs Lao Cai for Bac Ha (63 km) daily at 1 pm. Bac Ha is 230 km (10 hours) from Hanoi. Some cafes in Hanoi offer four-day bus trips to Bac Ha for around US$60.

DIEN BIEN PHU

History is the main attraction here. Dien Bien Phu seems to hold the same fascination for the French as the DMZ does for North Americans.

Dien Bien Phu was the site of that rarest of military events, a battle that can be called truly decisive. On 6 May 1954, Viet Minh forces overran the beleaguered French garrison at Dien Bien Phu after a 57 day siege, shattering French morale and forcing the French government to abandon its attempts to re-establish colonial control of Indochina.

The **Military Museum** (open daily) tells the story. Admission is US$2.

The area code for Dien Bien Phu is 23.

Places to Stay & Eat

The *Dien Bien Phu Mini-Hotel* (☎ 824319) offers rooms with attached bath for US$12 to US$18.

About three km from the centre in the direction of Hanoi is the *Trade Union Guesthouse* (☎ 824841), also known as *Nga Nghi Cong Doan*. Doubles cost US$6 to US$20.

The best food in town is at the *Lien Tuoi Restaurant* near the Military Museum.

Getting There & Away

During the tourist season (roughly April through September) Vietnam Airlines operates flights between Dien Bien Phu and Hanoi three times a week.

Some travellers rent motorbikes in Hanoi and do a loop trip – Hanoi to Dien Bien Phu, onwards to Sapa, Lao Cai and then back to Hanoi. This takes about 10 days and the roads are sometimes rough or flooded, but it is possible to put the motorcycle on the train from Lao Cai to Hanoi. The route passes through a number of towns where the majority are hill tribes (notably the Black Tai and Hmong) who still live as they have for generations.

Religions of South-East Asia

Buddhism

Buddhism was founded by Siddhartha Gautama, an Indian prince, in the 6th century BC. After years of ascetic wanderings and contemplation he became the 'enlightened' or 'awakened one', the Buddha. His message is that the cause of life's suffering is the illusory nature of desire, and that by overcoming desire we can free ourselves from suffering. Desire can be conquered by following the Eightfold Path, consisting of right understanding, thought, speech, conduct, livelihood, effort, attentiveness and concentration. The ultimate goal is *nirvana*, the escape from the endless round of births and rebirths and their lives of suffering.

Buddhism is essentially a Hindu reform movement, and its philosophy owes much to the Hindu notions of *maya* (the illusory nature of existence) and *moksha* (enlightenment). The big difference is that Buddhism shunned the Hindu pantheon of gods and the caste system. It was initially not a religion but a practical, moral philosophy free from the priestly Brahman hierarchy.

Buddhism gained wide adherence in India with its adoption by Emperor Ashoka in the 3rd century BC, but later split into two sects: Mahayana (greater path) and Hinayana (lesser path), also known as Theravada (teaching of the elders). Mahayana Buddhism showed greater mysticism and the *bodhisattva*, or saint who attains nirvana, reintroduced the idea of divinity to Buddhism. It spread north to Tibet, China and Japan, and then down to Vietnam. The more scholarly, philosophical Theravada sect found less favour in the royal courts, but continued to thrive in Sri Lanka and lower Burma even after a resurgent Hinduism virtually eliminated Buddhism in India by the end of the first millennium AD.

In South-East Asia, Buddhism, along with Hinduism, was adopted by kingdoms in Indochina, Sumatra and Java in the first millennium. The major change came in the 11th century when the Burmese adopted Theravada Buddhism, and this later spread to Thailand, Laos and Cambodia. Theravada Buddhism remains the dominant faith in these countries today while Vietnam, with its strongly Chinese influence, follows a form of Mahayana Buddhism.

Hinduism

Today, the tiny island of Bali is the only place in the region where Hinduism dominates, but Hinduism has strongly influenced the other cultures of South-East Asia.

Hinduism is a complex religion, but at its core is the mystical principle that the physical world is an illusion *(maya)* and until this is realised through enlightenment *(moksha)* the individual is condemned to a cycle of rebirths and reincarnations. Brahma is the ultimate god and universal spirit, but Hinduism has a vast pantheon of gods that are worshipped on a day-to-day level.

The two main gods are Shiva, the Destroyer, and Vishnu, the Preserver. Shivaism represents a more esoteric and ascetic path, and with Shiva's *shakti*, or female energy (represented by his wives Kali and Parvati), destruction and fertility are intertwined. Shivaism found greater acceptance in South-East Asia, perhaps because it was closer to existing fertility worship and the appeasement of malevolent spirits. Vishnuism places greater emphasis on devotion and duty, and Vishnu's incarnations, Krishna and Rama, feature heavily in South-East Asian art and culture through the stories of the *Ramayana* epic.

Hinduism and Buddhism were often intertwined in South-East Asia and many empires accepted the principles and iconography of both religions. Hinduism's rigid caste system had much less relevance in South-East Asia, but the notions of the god-king and the elitist nature of Hindu society were readily accepted by South-East Asian rulers.

Islam
In the early 7th century in Mecca, Mohammed received the word of Allah (God) and called on the people to submit to the one true God. His teachings appealed to the poorer levels of society and angered the merchant class. In 622 Mohammed and his followers were forced to flee Medina, and this migration – the *hijrah* – marks the beginning of the Islamic calendar, year 1 AH, or 622 AD. By 630 Mohammed returned to take Mecca.

Islam is the Arabic word for 'submission', and the duty of every Muslim is to submit to Allah. This profession of faith is the first of the Five Pillars of Islam, the five tenets in the Koran which guide Muslims in their daily lives. The other four are to pray five times a day, give alms to the poor, fast during Ramadan and make the pilgrimage to Mecca.

In its early days Islam suffered a major schism into two streams – the Sunnis and the Shi'ites. The Sunnis comprise the majority of Muslims today, including most Muslims in South-East Asia.

Islam came to South-East Asia with Indian traders and was not of the more orthodox Islamic tradition of Arabia. Islam was adopted peacefully by the coastal trading ports of South-East Asia, and was established in northern Sumatra by the end of the 13th century. The third ruler of Melaka adopted Islam in the mid-14th century, and Melaka's political dominance in the region saw the religion spread throughout Malaysia and Indonesia to Mindanao in the southern Philippines. By the time the Portuguese arrived in the 16th century, Islam was firmly established and conversion to Christianity was difficult. Pre-Islamic traditions exist side by side with Islam in South-East Asia, but with the rise of Islamic fundamentalism, the cries to introduce Islamic law and purify the practices of Islam have increased, especially in Malaysia.

Christianity
Christianity first came with the Portuguese in the 15th century. The Portuguese spread Christianity in a few pockets of Indonesia, notably Flores and Timor, but it was the Spanish that were the most successful missionary force. Their former colony, the Philippines, is still the stronghold of Catholicism in Asia today.

The English and the Dutch were mostly pragmatic traders, not proselytisers, and, apart from an obsession with converting headhunters, generally had little desire to spread Christianity. Missionaries were active in Borneo, Irian Jaya and the Batak lands in north Sumatra, and these are the strongholds of Christianity, mixed with animism, in Indonesia and Malaysia. Vietnam has long had contacts with Christianity, first through the Portuguese and Spanish, and then under French patronage when the Catholic church flourished.

Other
Animism is in some ways the most pervasive of all religions. The rituals of indigenous religions can still be seen in many levels of belief throughout South-East Asia and pockets of animist worship can be found everywhere. The outer areas of Indonesia, such as Kalimantan, Irian Jaya, Sulawesi and Sumba, and the northern hill tribe areas are the strongholds of nature and spirit worship.

South-East Asia has other religions and different shades of established ones. Of note is the , which is the major form of non-Buddhist worship in Laos.

Climate

Bandar Seri Begawan

mm	Rainfall	in	°C	Temperature	°F
600		24	40		104
500		20	30		86
400		16			
300		12	20		68
200		8	10		50
100		4			
0	J F M A M J J A S O N D	0	0	J F M A M J J A S O N D	32

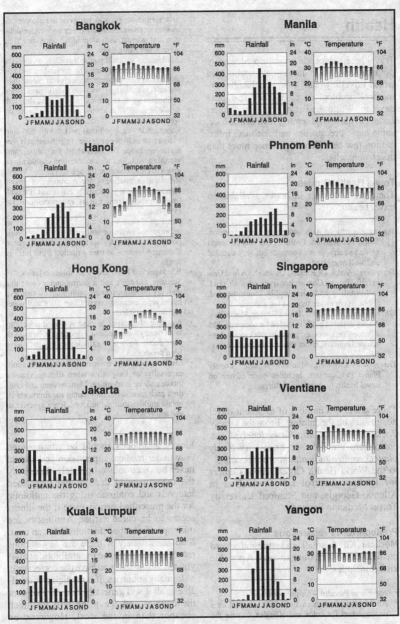

Health

Travel health depends on your predeparture preparations, your day-to-day health care while travelling and how you handle any medical problem or emergency that does develop. While the list of potential dangers can seem quite frightening, with a little luck, some basic precautions and adequate information few travellers experience more than upset stomachs.

Travel Health Guides

There are a number of books available on travel health:

Staying Healthy in Asia, Africa & Latin America, Moon Publications. Probably the best all-round guide to carry, as it's compact but very detailed and well organised.

Travellers' Health, Dr Richard Dawood, Oxford University Press. Comprehensive, easy to read, authoritative and also highly recommended, although it's rather large to lug around.

Where There Is No Doctor, David Werner, Macmillan. A very detailed guide intended for someone, like a Peace Corps worker, going to work in an undeveloped country, rather than for the average traveller.

Travel with Children, Maureen Wheeler, Lonely Planet Publications. Includes basic advice on travel health for younger children.

There are also a number of excellent travel health sites on the Internet. From the Lonely Planet home page *http://www.lonelyplanet. com*, there are links, at *http://www.lonely planet.com/health/health.htm/h-links.htm*, to the World Health Organisation, Centers for Disease Control and Prevention in Atlanta, Georgia, and Stanford University Travel Medicine Service.

Predeparture Preparations

Medical Kit A small and straightforward medical kit is a wise thing to carry. A possible kit list includes:

- Aspirin or Panadol – for pain or fever.
- Antihistamine (such as Benadryl) – useful as a decongestant for colds and allergies, to ease the itch from insect bites or stings or to help prevent motion sickness. Antihistamines may cause sedation and interact with alcohol, so care should be taken when using them.
- Antibiotics – useful if you're travelling well off the beaten track, but they must be prescribed and you should carry the prescription with you. Some individuals are allergic to commonly prescribed antibiotics such as penicillin or sulpha drugs. It would be sensible to always carry this information when travelling.
- Loperamide (eg Imodium) or Lomotil for diarrhoea; prochlorperazine (eg Stemetil) or metaclopramide (eg Maxalon) for nausea and vomiting. Antidiarrhoea medication should not be given to children under the age of 12.
- Rehydration mixture – for treatment of severe diarrhoea. This is particularly important if travelling with children, but is recommended for everyone.
- Antiseptic such as Betadine, which comes as impregnated swabs or ointment, and an antibiotic powder or similar 'dry' spray – for cuts and grazes.
- Calamine lotion – to ease irritation from bites or stings.
- Bandages and Band-aids – for minor injuries.
- Scissors, tweezers and a thermometer (note that mercury thermometers are prohibited by airlines).
- Insect repellent, sunscreen, Chap Stick and water purification tablets.
- A couple of syringes, in case you need injections in a country with medical hygiene problems. Ask your doctor for a note explaining why they have been prescribed.
- Multivitamins are a worthwhile consideration, especially for long trips when dietary vitamin intake may be inadequate. Men, women and children each have different vitamin requirements so obtain multivitamin tablets which are specific to age and gender.

Ideally antibiotics should be administered only under medical supervision and should never be taken indiscriminately. Take only the recommended dose at the prescribed intervals and continue using the antibiotic for the prescribed period, even if the illness seems to be cured earlier. Antibiotics are quite specific to the infections they can treat. Stop immediately if there are any serious reactions and don't use the antibiotic at all if you are unsure that you have the correct one.

In many countries, if a medicine is available at all it will generally be available over the counter and the price will be much cheaper than in the west. However, be careful when buying drugs in developing countries, particularly where the expiry date may have passed or correct storage conditions may not have been followed. Bogus drugs are common and it's possible that drugs which are no longer recommended, or have even been banned, in the west are still being dispensed in many Third World countries.

In many countries it may be a good idea to leave unused medicines, syringes etc with a local clinic, rather than carrying them home.

Health Preparations Make sure that you're healthy before you start travelling. If you are embarking on a long trip, make sure your teeth are OK; there are lots of places where a visit to the dentist would be the last thing you'd want.

If you wear glasses, take a spare pair and your prescription. Losing your glasses can be a real problem, although in many parts of Asia you can get new spectacles made up quickly, cheaply and competently.

If you require a particular medication, take an adequate supply, as it may not be available locally. Take the prescription or, better still, part of the packaging showing the generic rather than the brand name (which may not be locally available), as it will make getting replacements easier. It's a wise idea to have a legible prescription with you to show you legally use the medication – it's surprising how often over-the-counter drugs from one place are illegal without a prescription or even banned in another.

Immunisations Vaccinations provide protection against diseases you might meet along the way. For some countries no immunisations are necessary, but the further off the beaten track you go the more necessary it is to take precautions. Smallpox has now been wiped out worldwide, so immunisation is no longer necessary.

Currently yellow fever is the only vaccine required by international health regulations to enter a country, and only then when coming from an infected area. Occasionally travellers face bureaucratic problems regarding cholera vaccine even though all countries have dropped it as a health requirement for travel. Other vaccinations are not required by law, but many are highly recommended for your own personal protection.

All vaccinations should be recorded on an International Health Certificate, which is available from your physician or government health department, for your own records as much as for any legal requirements.

Plan ahead for getting your vaccinations: some of them require an initial shot followed by a booster, while some vaccinations should not be given together. It is recommended you seek medical advice at least six weeks prior to travel.

Most travellers from western countries will have been immunised against various diseases during childhood, but your doctor may still recommend booster shots against measles or polio, diseases still prevalent in many developing countries. The period of protection offered by vaccinations differs widely and some are contraindicated if you are pregnant.

In some countries immunisations are available from airport or government health centres. Travel agents or airline offices will tell you where. The vaccinations you should consider for a trip to South-East Asia are:

- *Polio* A booster of either the oral or injected vaccine is required every 10 years to maintain your immunity from childhood vaccination. Polio is a very serious, easily transmitted disease. Polio cases continue to be reported from Cambodia, Indonesia, Laos, Myanmar and Vietnam. The incidence of polio is low in Malaysia, the Philippines and Thailand.
- *Tetanus & Diphtheria* Boosters are necessary every 10 years and protection is highly recommended.
- *Typhoid* Available either as an injection or oral capsules. Protection lasts from one to five years depending on the vaccine and is useful if you are travelling for long in rural, tropical areas. You may get some side effects such as pain at the injection site, fever, headache and a general unwell feeling. A new single-dose injectable vaccine, Typhim Vi, which appears to have few side effects, is now available but is more expensive. Side effects are unusual with the oral form but occasionally an individual will have stomach cramps.

• *Hepatitis A* The most common travel-acquired illness which can be prevented by vaccination. Protection can be provided in two ways – either with the antibody gamma globulin or with the vaccine Havrix 1440. Havrix 1440 provides long-term immunity (possibly more than 10 years) after an initial injection and a booster at six to 12 months. It may be more expensive than gamma globulin but certainly has many advantages, including length of protection and ease of administration. It is important to know that being a vaccine it will take about three weeks to provide satisfactory protection – hence the need for careful planning prior to travel.

Gamma globulin is not a vaccination but a ready-made antibody which has proven very successful in reducing the chances of hepatitis infection. Because it may interfere with the development of immunity, it should not be given until at least 10 days after administration of the last vaccine needed; it should also be given as close as possible to departure because it is at its most effective in the first few weeks after administration and the effectiveness tapers off gradually between three and six months.

• *Hepatitis B* Travellers at risk of contact (see Infectious Diseases section) are strongly advised to be vaccinated, especially if they are children or will have close contact with children. The vaccination course comprises three injections given over a six month period, then boosters every three to five years. The initial course of injections can be given over as short a period as 28 days, then boosted after 12 months if more rapid protection is required.

• *Rabies* Pretravel rabies vaccination involves having three injections over 21 to 28 days and should be considered by those who will spend a month or longer in a country where rabies is common, especially if they are cycling, handling animals, caving or travelling to remote areas. Also consider vaccinating children (who may not report a bite). If someone who has been vaccinated is bitten or scratched by an animal, they will require two booster injections of vaccine.

• *Tuberculosis* TB risk should be considered for people travelling more than three months. As most healthy adults do not develop symptoms, a skin test before and after travel to determine whether exposure has occurred is usually all that is required. Vaccination for children who will be travelling for more than three months is recommended

• *Japanese B Encephalitis* Vaccination is usually considered for those spending a month or longer in a risk area, those making repeated trips to a risk area or those visiting during an epidemic. The vaccination course consists of three injections given over 30 days. The vaccine has been associated with serious allergic reactions, so the decision to have it should be balanced against the risk of contracting the illness.

• *Meningococcal Meningitis* Vaccination should be considered by travellers to Vietnam. A single injection will give good protection against the A, C, W and Y groups of the bacteria for at least a year. The vaccine is not, however, recommended for children under 2 years because they do not develop satisfactory immunity from it.

Basic Rules

Care in what you eat and drink is the most important health rule; stomach upsets are the most likely travel health problem (between 30% and 50% of travellers in a two week stay experience this) but the majority of these upsets will be relatively minor. Don't become paranoid; trying the local food is definitely part of the experience of travel, after all.

Water The number one rule is *don't drink the water unless you are certain it is safe*, and that includes ice. In some places, such as Singapore, tap water is safe but if you don't know for certain that the water is safe always assume the worst. Reputable brands of bottled water or soft drinks are generally fine, although in some places bottles refilled with tap water are not unknown. Only use water from containers with a serrated seal – not tops or corks. Take care with fruit juice, particularly if water may have been added. Milk should be treated with suspicion, as it is often unpasteurised. Boiled milk is fine if it is kept hygienically and yoghurt is always good. Tea or coffee should also be OK to drink, since the water should have been boiled.

Water Purification The simplest way of purifying water is to boil it thoroughly. Vigorous boiling for five minutes should be satisfactory even at high altitude. Remember that at high altitude water boils at a lower temperature, so germs are less likely to be killed.

Simple filtering will not remove all dangerous organisms, so if you cannot boil water it should be treated chemically. Chlorine tablets (Puritabs, Steritabs or other brand names) will kill many but not all pathogens. They will not kill giardia and amoebic cysts. Iodine is very effective in purifying water and is available in tablet form (such as Potable Aqua), but follow the directions carefully and remember that too much iodine can be harmful.

If you can't find tablets, tincture of iodine (2%) can be used. Four drops of tincture of iodine per litre or quart of clear water is the recommended dosage; the treated water should be left to stand for 20 to 30 minutes before drinking. Iodine loses its effectiveness if exposed to air or damp, so keep it in a tightly sealed container. Flavoured powder will disguise the taste of treated water and is a good idea if you are travelling with children.

Food There is an old colonial adage which says: 'If you can cook it, boil it or peel it you can eat it...otherwise forget it'. Salads and fruit should be washed with purified water or peeled where possible. Ice cream is usually OK if it is a reputable brand name, but beware of Third World street vendors and of ice cream that has melted and been refrozen. Thoroughly cooked food is safest but not if it has been left to cool or if it has been reheated. Shellfish such as mussels, oysters and clams should be avoided as well as undercooked meat, particularly in the form of mince. Steaming does not make shellfish safe for eating.

If a place looks clean and well run and if the vendor also looks clean and healthy, then the food is probably safe. In general, places that are packed with travellers or locals will be fine, while empty restaurants are questionable. Busy restaurants mean the food is being cooked and eaten quite quickly with little standing around and is probably not being reheated.

Nutrition If your food is poor or limited in availability, if you're travelling hard and fast and therefore missing meals, or if you simply lose your appetite, you can soon start to lose weight and place your health at risk.

Make sure that your diet is well balanced. Eggs, tofu, beans, lentils and nuts are all safe ways to get protein. Fruit you can peel (bananas, oranges or mandarins for example)

is usually safe and a good source of vitamins. Try to eat plenty of grains (rice) and bread. Remember that although food is generally safer if it is cooked well, overcooked food loses much of its nutritional value. If your diet isn't well balanced or if your food intake is insufficient, it's a good idea to take vitamin and iron pills.

In hot climates make sure you drink enough – don't rely on feeling thirsty to indicate when you should drink. Not needing to urinate or very dark yellow urine is a danger sign. Always carry a water bottle with you on long trips. Excessive sweating can lead to loss of salt and therefore muscle cramping. Salt tablets are not a good idea as a preventative, but in places where salt is not used much adding salt to food can help.

Everyday Health A normal body temperature is 37°C (98.6°F); more than 2°C (4°F) higher is a 'high' fever. A normal adult pulse rate is 60 to 100 per minute (children 80 to 100, babies 100 to 140). You should know how to take a temperature and a pulse rate. As a general rule the pulse increases about 20 beats per minute for each 1°C (2°F) rise in fever.

Respiration (breathing) rate is also an indicator of illness. Count the number of breaths per minute: between 12 and 20 is normal for adults and older children (up to 30 for younger children, 40 for babies). People with a high fever or serious respiratory illness (like pneumonia) breathe more quickly than normal. More than 40 shallow breaths a minute usually means pneumonia.

In western countries with safe water and excellent human waste disposal systems we often take good health for granted. In years gone by, when public health facilities were not as good as they are today, certain rules attached to eating and drinking were observed, like washing your hands before a meal. It is important for people travelling in areas of poor sanitation to be aware of this and adjust their own personal hygiene habits.

Clean your teeth with purified water rather than straight from the tap. Avoid climatic extremes: keep out of the sun when it's hot, dress warmly when it's cold. Avoid potential diseases by dressing sensibly. You can get worm infections through walking barefoot or dangerous coral cuts by walking over coral without shoes. You can avoid insect bites by covering bare skin when insects are around, by screening windows or beds or by using insect repellents. Seek local advice: if you're told the water is unsafe due to jellyfish, crocodiles or bilharzia, don't go in. In situations where there is no information, discretion is the better part of valour.

Medical Problems & Treatment

Self-diagnosis and treatment can be risky, so wherever possible seek qualified help. Although we do give treatment dosages in this section, they are for emergency use only. Medical advice should be sought where possible before administering any drugs.

An embassy or consulate can usually recommend a good place to go for such advice. So can five-star hotels, although they often recommend doctors with five-star prices. (This is when that medical insurance really comes in useful!) The ill-equipped village hospital may be cheap, but it is often better to pay for the best. In some places standards of medical attention are so low that for some ailments the best advice is to get on a plane and go somewhere else. You can usually find good medical facilities in Asia, especially in the major cities.

Climatic & Geographical Considerations

Sunburn In the tropics and at high altitude you can get sunburnt surprisingly quickly, even through cloud. Use a sunscreen and take extra care to cover areas which don't normally see sun – eg, your feet. A hat provides added protection, and you should also use zinc cream or some other barrier cream for your nose and lips. Calamine lotion is good for mild sunburn.

Remember that too much sunlight, whether it's direct or reflected (glare), can damage your eyes. If your plans include being near water, sand or snow, then good sunglasses are doubly important. Good quality sunglasses are treated to filter out ultraviolet

radiation, but poor quality sunglasses provide limited filtering, allowing more ultraviolet light to be adsorbed than if no sunglasses were worn at all. Excessive ultraviolet light will damage the surface structures and lens of the eye.

Prickly Heat Prickly heat is an itchy rash caused by excessive perspiration trapped under the skin. It usually strikes people who have just arrived in a hot climate and whose pores have not yet opened sufficiently to cope with greater sweating. Keeping cool but bathing often, using a mild talcum powder or even resorting to air-conditioning may help until you acclimatise.

Heat Exhaustion Dehydration or salt deficiency can cause heat exhaustion. Take time to acclimatise to high temperatures and make sure you drink sufficient liquid. Salt deficiency is characterised by fatigue, lethargy, headaches, giddiness and muscle cramps and in this case salt tablets may help. Vomiting or diarrhoea can deplete your liquid and salt levels. Anhydrotic heat exhaustion, caused by an inability to sweat, is quite rare. Unlike the other forms of heat exhaustion it is likely to strike people who have been in a hot climate for some time, rather than newcomers.

Heat Stroke This serious, sometimes fatal, condition can occur if the body's heat-regulating mechanism breaks down and the body temperature rises to dangerous levels. Long, continuous periods of exposure to high temperatures can leave you vulnerable to heat stroke. You should avoid excessive alcohol or strenuous activity when you first arrive in a hot climate.

The symptoms are feeling unwell, not sweating very much or at all and a high body temperature (39°C to 41°C, or 102°F to 106°F). Where sweating has ceased the skin becomes flushed and red. Severe, throbbing headaches and lack of coordination will also occur, and the sufferer may be confused or aggressive. Eventually the victim will become delirious or convulse. Hospitalisation is essential, but meanwhile get victims out of the sun, remove their clothing, cover them with a wet sheet or towel and then fan continuously.

Fungal Infections Hot weather fungal infections are most likely to occur on the scalp, between the toes or fingers (athlete's foot), in the groin (jock itch or crotch rot) and on the body (ringworm). You get ringworm (which is a fungal infection, not a worm) from infected animals or by walking on damp areas, like shower floors.

To prevent fungal infections wear loose, comfortable clothes, avoid artificial fibres, wash frequently and dry carefully. If you do get an infection, wash the infected area daily with a disinfectant or medicated soap and water, and rinse and dry well. Apply an antifungal powder like the widely available Tinaderm. Try to expose the infected area to air or sunlight as much as possible and wash all towels and underwear in hot water as well as changing them often.

Cold Too much cold is just as dangerous as too much heat, particularly if it leads to hypothermia. Sub-zero temperatures are rare in Asia, but if you are trekking at high altitudes be prepared. Expect it to get below 0°C on top of Mt Kinabalu, but it can be uncomfortably cold on lower peaks. In the north of the region – in the mountain areas of Vietnam and Laos, for example – temperatures do get down to freezing.

Hypothermia occurs when the body loses heat faster than it can produce it and the core temperature of the body falls. It is surprisingly easy to progress from very cold to dangerously cold due to a combination of wind, wet clothing, fatigue and hunger, even if the air temperature is above freezing. It is best to dress in layers; silk, wool and some of the new artificial fibres are all good insulating materials. A hat is important, as a lot of heat is lost through the head. A strong, waterproof outer layer is essential, as keeping dry is vital. Carry basic supplies, including food containing simple sugars to generate heat quickly and lots of fluid to

drink. A space blanket is something all travellers in cold environments should carry.

Symptoms of hypothermia are exhaustion, numb skin (particularly toes and fingers), shivering, slurred speech, irrational or violent behaviour, lethargy, stumbling, dizzy spells, muscle cramps and violent bursts of energy. Irrationality may take the form of sufferers claiming they are warm and trying to take off their clothes.

To treat mild hypothermia, first get the person out of the wind and/or rain, remove their clothing if it's wet and replace it with dry, warm clothing. Give them hot liquids – not alcohol – and some high-kilojoule, easily digestible food. Do not rub victims, instead allow them to slowly warm themselves. This should be enough to treat the early stages of hypothermia. The early recognition and treatment of mild hypothermia is the only way to prevent severe hypothermia, which is a critical condition.

Altitude Sickness Acute Mountain Sickness, or AMS, occurs at high altitude and can be fatal. The lack of oxygen at high altitude (over 2500 metres) affects most people to some extent.

It is very rare to contract AMS in South-East Asia, but you should be careful at Mt Kinabalu in Sabah and the peaks of Irian Jaya in Indonesia, such as Puncak Jaya. There is no hard and fast rule as to how high is too high: AMS has been fatal at altitudes of 3000 metres, although 3500 to 4500 metres is the usual range. It is always wise to sleep at a lower altitude than the greatest height reached during the day, and generally acclimatise as much as you can.

It may be mild (benign AMS) or severe (malignant AMS) and occurs because less oxygen reaches the muscles and the brain at high altitude, requiring the heart and lungs to compensate by working harder. Symptoms usually develop during the first 24 hours at altitude but may be delayed up to three weeks. Symptoms of benign AMS include headache, lethargy, dizziness, difficulty sleeping and loss of appetite. Malignant AMS may develop from benign AMS or without warning and can be fatal. These symptoms include breathlessness, a dry, irritative cough (which may progress to the production pink, frothy sputum), severe headache, lack of coordination and balance, confusion, irrational behaviour, vomiting, drowsiness and unconsciousness.

In benign AMS the treatment is to remain resting at the same altitude until recovery, usually a day or two. Paracetamol or aspirin can be taken for headaches. If symptoms persist or become worse, however, descent is necessary; even 500 metres can help. The treatment of malignant AMS is immediate descent to a lower altitude. There are various drug treatments available but they should never be used to avoid descent or enable further ascent by a person with AMS.

To prevent acute mountain sickness, you should ascend slowly, have frequent rest days and drink extra fluids. Eat light, high-carbohydrate meals for more energy, and avoid alcohol and sedatives.

Motion Sickness Eating lightly before and during a trip will reduce the chances of motion sickness. If you are prone to motion sickness try to find a place that minimises disturbance – near the wing on aircraft, close to midships on boats, near the centre on buses. Fresh air usually helps, reading or cigarette smoke doesn't. Commercial anti-motion-sickness preparations, which can cause drowsiness, have to be taken before the trip commences; when you're feeling sick it's too late. Ginger is a natural preventative and is available in capsule form.

Infectious Diseases

Diarrhoea A change of water, food or climate can all cause the runs; diarrhoea caused by contaminated food or water is more serious. Despite all your precautions you may still have a bout of mild travellers' diarrhoea but a few rushed toilet trips with no other symptoms is not indicative of a serious problem. Moderate diarrhoea, involving half-a-dozen loose movements in a day, is more of a nuisance. Dehydration is the main danger with any diarrhoea, particularly for children, where dehydration can occur quite quickly. Fluid replacement remains the mainstay of management. Weak black tea with a little sugar, soda water, or soft drinks allowed to go flat and diluted 50% with water are all good. With severe diarrhoea a rehydrating solution is necessary to replace minerals and salts. Commercially available ORS (oral rehydration salts) is very useful; add the contents of one sachet to a litre of boiled or bottled water. In an emergency you can make up a solution of eight teaspoons of sugar to a litre of boiled water and provide salted cracker biscuits at the same time. You should stick to a bland diet as you recover.

Lomotil or Imodium can be used to bring relief from the symptoms, although they do not actually cure the problem. Only use these drugs if absolutely necessary – eg if you *must* travel. For children under 12 years, Lomotil and Imodium are not recommended. Under all circumstances fluid replacement is the main message. Do not use these drugs if the person has a high fever or is severely dehydrated.

In certain situations, a need for antibiotics may be indicated:

- Diarrhoea with blood and mucous. (Gut-paralysing drugs like Imodium or Lomotil should be avoided in this situation.)
- Watery diarrhoea with fever and lethargy.
- Persistent diarrhoea for more than five days.
- Severe diarrhoea (Use antibiotics if it is logistically difficult to stay in one place.)

The recommended drugs (adults only) would be either norfloxacin (400 mg twice daily for three days) or ciprofloxacin (500 mg twice daily for three days).

The drug bismuth subsalicylate has also been used successfully. It is not available in some countries, including Australia. The dosage for adults is two tablets or 30 ml and for children it is one tablet or 10 ml. This dose can be repeated every 30 minutes to one hour, with no more than eight doses in a 24 hour period.

The drug of choice in children would be co-trimoxazole (Bactrim, Septrin, Resprim) with dosage dependent on weight. A five day course is given.

Giardiasis The parasite causing this intestinal disorder is present in contaminated water. The symptoms are stomach cramps, nausea, a bloated stomach, watery, foul-smelling diarrhoea and frequent gas. Giardiasis can appear several weeks after you have been exposed to the parasite. The symptoms may disappear for a few days and then return; this can go on for several weeks. Tinidazole, known as Fasigyn, or metronidazole (Flagyl) are the recommended drugs for treatment. Either can be used in a single treatment dose. Antibiotics are of no use.

Dysentery This serious illness is caused by contaminated food or water and is characterised by severe diarrhoea, often with blood or mucous in the stool. There are two kinds of dysentery. Bacillary dysentery is characterised by a high fever and rapid onset; headache, vomiting and stomach pains are also symptoms. It generally does not last longer than a week, but it is highly contagious.

Amoebic dysentery is often more gradual in the onset of symptoms, with cramping abdominal pain and vomiting less likely; fever may not be present. It is not a self-limiting disease: it will persist until treated and can recur and cause long-term health problems.

A stool test is necessary to diagnose which kind of dysentery you have, so you should seek medical help urgently. In case of an emergency the drugs norfloxacin or ciprofloxacin can be used as presumptive treatment for bacillary dysentery, and metronidazole (Flagyl) for amoebic dysentery.

For bacillary dysentery, 400 mg of norfloxacin twice daily for seven days or 500 mg of ciprofloxacin twice daily for seven days are the recommended dosages.

If you're unable to find either of these drugs then a useful alternative is co-trimoxazole 160/800 mg (Bactrim, Septrin, Resprim) twice daily for seven days. This is a sulpha drug and must not be used in people with a known sulpha allergy.

In the case of children the drug co-trimoxazole is a reasonable first-line treatment.

For amoebic dysentery, the recommended adult dosage of metronidazole (Flagyl) is one 750 mg to 800 mg capsule three times daily for five days. Children aged between eight and 12 years should have half the adult dose; the dosage for younger children is one-third the adult dose.

An alternative to Flagyl is Fasigyn, taken as a 2g daily dose for three days. Alcohol must be avoided during treatment and for 48 hours afterwards.

Cholera Cholera vaccination is not very effective. The bacteria responsible for this disease are waterborne, so that attention to the rules of eating and drinking should protect the traveller.

Outbreaks of cholera are generally widely reported, so you can avoid such problem areas. The disease is characterised by a sudden onset of acute diarrhoea with 'rice water' stools, vomiting, muscular cramps and extreme weakness. You need medical help – treat for dehydration, which can be extreme, and if there is an appreciable delay in getting to hospital it will be necessary to begin taking tetracycline. The adult dose is 250 mg four times daily. It is not recommended in children aged eight years or under nor in pregnant women. An alternative drug would be Ampicillin. People allergic to penicillin should not take Ampicillin. Remember that while antibiotics might kill the bacteria, it is a toxin produced by the bacteria which causes the massive fluid loss. Fluid replacement is by far the most important aspect of treatment.

Typhoid Typhoid fever is another gut infection that travels the faecal-oral route – ie contaminated water and food are responsible. Vaccination against typhoid is not totally effective and typhoid is one of the most dangerous infections, so medical help must be sought.

In its early stages typhoid resembles many other illnesses: sufferers may feel like they have a bad cold or flu on the way, as early symptoms are a headache, a sore throat and a fever which rises a little each day until it is around 40°C (104°F) or more. The victim's pulse is often slow relative to the degree of fever present and gets slower as the fever rises – unlike a normal fever where the pulse increases. There may also be vomiting, diarrhoea or constipation.

In the second week the high fever and slow pulse continue and a few pink spots may appear on the body; trembling, delirium, weakness, weight loss and dehydration are other symptoms. If there are no further complications, the fever and other symptoms will slowly go during the third week. However, you must get medical help before this because pneumonia (acute infection of the lungs) or peritonitis (perforated bowel) are common complications, and because typhoid is very infectious.

The fever should be treated by keeping the victim cool and dehydration should also be watched for.

The drug of choice is ciprofloxacin at a dose of 1g daily for 14 days. It is quite expensive and may not be available. The alternative, chloramphenicol, has been the mainstay of treatment for many years; the adult dosage is two 250 mg capsules four times a day. Children aged between eight and 12 years should have half the adult dose; younger children should have one-third the adult dose.

Viral Gastroenteritis This is caused not by bacteria but, as the name suggests, by a virus. It is characterised by stomach cramps and diarrhoea, and sometimes by vomiting and/or a slight fever. All you can do is rest and drink lots of fluids.

Hepatitis Hepatitis A is a very common problem among travellers to areas with poor sanitation. The disease is spread by contaminated food or water. The symptoms are fever, chills, headache, fatigue, feelings of weakness and aches and pains, followed by loss of appetite, nausea, vomiting, abdominal pain, dark urine, light-coloured faeces and jaundiced skin; the whites of the eyes may also turn yellow. You should seek medical advice, but in general there is not much you can do apart from rest, drink lots of fluids, eat lightly and avoid fatty foods. People who have had hepatitis must forego alcohol for six months after the illness, as hepatitis attacks the liver and it needs that amount of time to recover.

Hepatitis B, which used to be called serum hepatitis, is spread through contact with infected blood, blood products or bodily fluids (for example, through sexual contact, unsterilised needles and blood transfusions, or via small breaks in the skin). Other risk situations include having a shave or tattoo in a local shop, or having your body pierced. The symptoms of type B are much the same as type A except that they are more severe and may lead to irreparable liver damage or even liver cancer.

Persons who should receive a hepatitis B vaccination include anyone who anticipates contact with blood or other bodily secretions, either as a health care worker or through sexual contact with the local population, particularly those who intend to stay in the country for a long period of time.

Hepatitis Non-A Non-B is a blanket term formerly used for several different strains of hepatitis, which have now been separately identified. Hepatitis C is similar to B but is less common. Hepatitis D (the 'delta particle') is also similar to B; its occurrence is currently limited to IV drug users. Hepatitis E, however, is similar to A and is spread in the same manner, by water or food contamination.

Tests are available for these strands, but are very expensive. Travellers shouldn't be too paranoid about this apparent proliferation of hepatitis strains; they are fairly rare (so far) and following the same precautions as for A and B should be all that's necessary to avoid them.

Opisthorchiasis Travellers in Laos, Cambodia and Thailand should be on guard against liver flukes (opisthorchiasis). These are tiny worms that are occasionally present in freshwater fish. The main risk comes from eating raw or undercooked fish – in particular, avoid eating *pa dek*, which is fermented fish used as an accompaniment to rice. A much less common way to contract liver flukes is by swimming in lakes and rivers.

Symptoms depend very much on how many of the flukes get into your body. They can range from no symptoms at all to fatigue, a low-grade fever and a swollen or tender liver (or general abdominal pains), along with worms or worm eggs in the faeces.

People suspected of having liver flukes should have a stool sample analysed by a competent doctor or clinic in Vientiane, Bangkok or Phnom Penh. The usual medication is 25 mg per kg of body weight of praziquantel (often sold as Biltricide) taken three times daily after meals for two days.

Worms These parasites are most common in rural, tropical areas and a stool test when you return home is not a bad idea. They can be present on unwashed vegetables or in undercooked meat and you can pick them up through your skin by walking in bare feet. Infestations may not show up for some time, and although they are generally not serious, if left untreated they can cause severe health problems. A stool test is necessary to pinpoint the problem and medication is often available over the counter.

Tetanus This potentially fatal disease is found in undeveloped tropical areas. It is difficult to treat but is preventable with immunisation. Tetanus occurs when a wound becomes infected by a germ which lives in the soil and in the faeces of horses and other animals, so clean all cuts, punctures or animal bites. Tetanus is also known as lockjaw, and the first symptom may be discomfort in swallowing, or stiffening of the jaw and neck; this is followed by painful convulsions of the jaw and whole body.

Rabies Rabies is a fatal viral infection found in many countries and is caused by a bite or scratch by an infected animal. Dogs are noted carriers, as are monkeys and cats. Any bite, scratch or even lick from a warm-blooded, furry animal should be cleaned immediately and thoroughly. Scrub with soap and running water, and then clean with an alcohol solution. If there is any possibility that the animal is infected, medical help should be sought immediately. Even if the animal is not rabid, all bites should be treated seriously as they can become infected or can result in tetanus. A rabies vaccination is now available and should be considered if you are in a high-risk category – eg, if you intend to explore caves (bat bites could be dangerous) or work with animals.

Meningococcal Meningitis This very serious disease attacks the brain and can be fatal – recurring epidemics have occurred in Vietnam. A scattered, blotchy rash, fever, severe headache, sensitivity to light and neck stiffness which prevents forward bending of the head are the first symptoms. Death can occur within a few hours, so immediate treatment is important.

Treatment is large doses of penicillin given intravenously, or, if that is not possible, intramuscularly (ie in the buttocks). Vaccination offers good protection for over a year, but you should also check for reports of current epidemics.

Tuberculosis There is a world-wide resurgence of TB. It is a bacterial infection which is usually transmitted from person to person by coughing but may be transmitted through consumption of unpasteurised milk. Milk that has been boiled is safe to drink, and the souring of milk to make yoghurt or cheese also kills the bacilli. Typically many months of contact with the infected person are required before the disease is passed on. The usual site of the disease is the lungs, although other organs may be involved. Most infected people never develop symptoms. In those who do, especially infants, symptoms may arise within weeks of the infection occurring and may be severe. In most, however, the disease lies dormant for many years until, for some reason, the infected person becomes physically run-down. Symptoms include fever, weight loss, night sweats and coughing.

Schistosomiasis Known as bilharziasis, or more commonly bilharzia, this disease is carried in water by minute worms. The larvae infect certain varieties of freshwater snails found in rivers, streams, lakes and particularly behind dams. The worms multiply and are eventually discharged into the water surrounding the snails.

They attach themselves to your intestines or bladder, where they produce large numbers of eggs. The worm enters through the skin, and the first symptom may be a tingling and sometimes a light rash around the area where it entered. Weeks later, when the worm is busy producing eggs, a high fever may develop. A general feeling of being unwell may be the first symptom; once the disease is established abdominal pain and blood in the urine are other signs. The infection often causes no symptoms until the disease is well established (several months to years after exposure) and damage to internal organs irreversible.

The disease is endemic in the southern Philippines, central Sulawesi and parts of Vietnam.

Avoiding swimming or bathing in fresh water where bilharzia is present is the main method of preventing the disease. Even deep water can be infected. If you do get wet, dry off quickly and dry your clothes as well. Seek medical attention if you have been exposed to the disease, even if you don't have any symptoms, and tell the doctor your suspicions, as bilharzia in the early stages can be confused with malaria or typhoid. If you cannot get medical help immediately, praziquantel (Biltricide) is the recommended treatment. The recommended dosage is 40 mg/kg in divided doses over one day. Niridazole is an alternative drug.

Diptheria Diphtheria can be a skin infection or a more dangerous throat infection. It is spread by contaminated dust contacting the skin or by the inhalation of infected cough or sneeze droplets. Frequent washing and keeping the skin dry will help prevent skin infection. A vaccination is available to prevent the throat infection.

Sexually Transmitted Diseases Sexual contact with an infected sexual partner spreads these diseases. While abstinence is the only 100% preventative, using condoms is also effective. Gonorrhoea, herpes and syphilis are the most common of these diseases; sores, blisters or rashes around the genitals and discharges or pain when urinating are common symptoms. In some STDs, such as wart virus and chlamydia, symptoms may be less marked or not observed at all in women. Syphilis symptoms eventually disappear completely but the disease continues and can cause severe problems in later years. The treatment of gonorrhoea and syphilis is by antibiotics.

There are numerous other sexually transmitted diseases, for most of which effective treatment is available. However, there is no cure for herpes.

HIV/AIDS HIV, the Human Immunodeficiency Virus, may develop into AIDS, Acquired Immune Deficiency Syndrome. HIV is a problem in countries such as Thailand and the Philippines, and head-in-the-sand attitudes from some South-East Asian countries help make it a growing problem throughout the region. In these countries transmission is predominantly through heterosexual sexual activity, primarily in the sex industry. The second highest risk group is IV drug users. Any exposure to blood, blood products or bodily fluids may put the individual at risk. Apart from abstinence, the most effective preventative is always to practice safe sex using condoms. It is impossible to detect the HIV-positive status of an otherwise healthy-looking person without a blood test.

HIV/AIDS can also be spread through infected blood transfusions and dirty needles – they are as dangerous as intravenous drug use if the equipment is not clean. If you do need an injection, it may be a good idea to buy a new syringe from a pharmacy and ask the doctor to use it. You may also want to take a couple of syringes with you, in case of emergency.

Do not let the fear of contracting HIV/AIDS through blood transfusions or inappropriate medical practices stop you from seeking medical advice. The risk is very small, and many good facilities are found throughout the region. Some countries, such as Thailand, have extensive blood-screening programs.

Insect-Borne Diseases

Malaria This serious disease is spread by mosquito bites. Malaria is endemic throughout South-East Asia and it is extremely important to take malarial prophylactics. Parts of the region are low risk – malaria is virtually unheard of in Singapore, Hong Kong, Brunei, Peninsular Malaysia and many of the major cities – but there are malarial areas throughout South-East Asia, including the remote parts of East Malaysia, Thailand, the Philippines, and much of Indochina and Indonesia. In South-East Asia, Irian Jaya is the most dangerous area. Anyone contemplating an extensive trip in South-East Asia should seek medical advice on the appropriate antimalarials to take. Antimalarial drugs do not prevent you from being infected but kill the parasites during a stage in their development.

Symptoms include headache, fever, chills and sweating, which may subside and recur. In its initial stages malaria can resemble flu symptoms of chills and shakes, high fever and possibly vomiting and delirium. Without treatment malaria can develop more serious, potentially fatal effects. If you think you have malaria, seek treatment immediately. Major hospitals in Asia can provide good quality care and have expertise in dealing with malaria. Almost all deaths from malaria are a result of delay in diagnosis.

There are a number of different types of malaria. The one of most concern is falciparum malaria. This is responsible for the very serious cerebral malaria. Falciparum is the predominant form in many malaria-prone areas of the world, including parts of South-East Asia. Contrary to popular belief cerebral malaria is not a new strain.

The problem in recent years has been the emergence of increasing resistance to commonly used antimalarials like chloroquine,

maloprim and proguanil. Newer drugs such as mefloquine (Lariam) and doxycycline (Vibramycin, Doryx) are now recommended for chloroquine and multidrug-resistant areas. Expert advice should be sought on antimalarials. Try to consult a doctor with expertise in tropical diseases – they should be able to inform you about high risk and resistant areas, and appropriate antimalarials for these areas and for the individual (eg, some antimalarials have been known to produce side effects, and some are inappropriate for pregnant women or for long-term use).

The main messages are:

- Primary prevention must always be in the form of mosquito-avoidance measures. The mosquitoes that transmit malaria bite from dusk to dawn and during this period travellers are advised to:
  1. wear light-coloured clothing
  2. wear long pants and long-sleeved shirts
  3. use mosquito repellents containing the compound DEET on exposed areas
  4. avoid highly scented perfumes or aftershave
  5. use a mosquito net – it may be worth taking your own.
- While no antimalarial is 100% effective, taking the most appropriate drug significantly reduces the risk of contracting the disease.
- No one should ever die from malaria. It can be diagnosed by a simple blood test, so a traveller with a fever or flu-like illness should seek examination as soon as possible.

Contrary to popular belief, once a traveller contracts malaria he/she does not have it for life. Two species of the parasite may lie dormant in the liver but this can also be eradicated using a specific medication. Malaria is therefore curable, as long as the traveller seeks medical help when symptoms occur, either at home or overseas.

Dengue Fever There is no prophylactic available for this mosquito-spread disease; the main preventative measure is to avoid mosquito bites. A sudden onset of fever, headaches and severe joint and muscle pains are the first signs before a rash starts on the trunk of the body and spreads to the limbs and face. After a further few days, the fever will subside and recovery will begin. Serious complications are not common.

Japanese B Encephalitis This viral infection of the brain is transmitted by mosquitoes. It is usually a severe illness with a high mortality rate. Most cases occur in rural areas because part of the life cycle of the virus takes place in pigs or wading birds. Symptoms include fever, headache, vomiting, neck stiffness, pain in the eyes when looking at light, alteration in consciousness, seizures or paralysis or muscle weakness. Correct diagnosis and treatment require hospitalisation. Vaccination is recommended for those intending to spend more than a month in a rural risk area during the rainy season, for those making repeated trips into a risk area or who are planning to stay for a year or more in a risk area, and for those visiting an area where there is an epidemic. The disease is not common in travellers.

Filariasis This is a mosquito-transmitted parasitic infection which is found in many parts of Asia. There is a range of possible manifestations of the infection, depending on which filarial parasite species has caused the infection. These include fever, pain and swelling of the lymph glands; inflammation of lymph drainage areas; swelling of a limb or the scrotum; skin rashes; and blindness. Treatment is available to eliminate the parasites from the body, but some of the damage they cause may not be reversible. Medical advice should be obtained promptly if the infection is suspected.

Typhus Typhus is spread by ticks, mites or lice. It begins with fever, chills, headache and muscle pain, followed a few days later by a body rash. There is often a large painful sore at the site of the bite and nearby lymph nodes are swollen and painful.

Tick typhus is spread by ticks. Scrub typhus is spread by mites that feed on infected rodents and exists mainly in Asia and the Pacific Islands. You should take precautions if walking in rural areas in South-East Asia. Seek local advice on areas where ticks pose a danger and always check your skin carefully for ticks after walking in a danger area, such as a tropical forest. A strong insect repellent can help, and serious walkers in tick areas should consider having their boots and trousers impregnated with benzyl benzoate and dibutylphthalate.

Cuts, Bites & Stings

Cuts & Scratches Skin punctures can easily become infected in hot climates and may be difficult to heal. Treat any cut with an antiseptic such as povidone-iodine (Betadine). Where possible avoid bandages and Band-aids, which can keep wounds wet. Coral cuts are notoriously slow to heal, as the coral injects a weak venom into the wound. Avoid coral cuts by wearing shoes when walking on reefs, and clean any cut thoroughly with hydrogen peroxide if available.

Bites & Stings Bee and wasp stings are usually painful rather than dangerous. Calamine lotion or Stingose will give relief, or ice packs will reduce the pain and swelling. There are some spiders with dangerous bites but antivenins are usually available. There are various fish and other sea creatures which can sting or bite dangerously or which are dangerous to eat. Again, local advice is the best suggestion.

Snakes To minimise your chances of being bitten always wear boots, socks and long trousers when walking through undergrowth where snakes may be present. Don't put your hands into holes and crevices, and be careful when collecting firewood.

Snake bites do not cause instantaneous death and antivenins are usually available. Keep the victim calm and still, wrap the bitten limb tightly, as you would for a sprained ankle, and then attach a splint to immobilise it. Then seek medical help, if possible with the dead snake for identification. Don't attempt to catch the snake if there is even a remote possibility of being bitten again. Tourniquets and sucking out the poison are now comprehensively discredited.

Jellyfish Local advice is the best way of avoiding contact with these sea creatures with their stinging tentacles. The box jellyfish is found mostly in inshore waters around Australia, but is occasionally found in Borneo. It is potentially fatal, but stings from most jellyfish are simply rather painful. Dousing in vinegar will deactivate any stingers which have not 'fired'. Calamine lotion, antihistamines and analgesics may reduce the reaction and relieve the pain.

Bedbugs & Lice Bedbugs live in various places, but particularly in dirty mattresses and bedding. Spots of blood on bedclothes or on the wall around the bed can be read as a suggestion to find another hotel. Bedbugs leave itchy bites in neat rows. Calamine lotion may help.

All lice cause itching and discomfort. They make themselves at home in your hair (head lice), your clothing (body lice) or in your pubic hair (crabs). You catch lice through direct contact with infected people or by sharing combs, clothing and the like. Powder or shampoo treatment will kill the lice and infected clothing should then be washed in very hot water.

Leeches & Ticks Leeches may be present in damp rainforest conditions; they attach themselves to your skin to suck your blood. Trekkers often get them on their legs or in their boots. Salt or a lighted cigarette end will make them fall off. Do not pull them off, as the bite is then more likely to become infected. Leech socks are a worthwhile investment for those contemplating a lot of jungle trekking. An insect repellent may keep them away.

You should always check your body if you have been walking through a tick-infested area, as they can spread typhus.

Women's Health
Gynaecological Problems Poor diet, lowered resistance due to the use of antibiotics and even contraceptive pills can lead to vaginal infections when travelling in hot climates. Maintaining good personal hygiene and wearing skirts or loose-fitting trousers and cotton underwear will help to prevent infections.

Yeast infections, characterised by a rash, itch and discharge, can be treated with a vinegar or even lemon-juice douche or with yoghurt. Nystatin, miconazole or clotrimazole suppositories are the usual medical prescription. Trichomonas and gardnerella are more serious infections; symptoms are a smelly discharge and sometimes a burning sensation when urinating. Male sexual partners must also be treated, and if a vinegar-water douche is not effective medical attention should be sought. Metronidazole (Flagyl) is the prescribed drug.

Pregnancy Most miscarriages occur during the first three months of pregnancy, so this is the most risky time to travel as far as your own health is concerned. Miscarriage is not uncommon, and can occasionally lead to severe bleeding. The last three months should also be spent within reasonable distance of good medical care. A baby born as early as 24 weeks stands a chance of survival, but only in a good modern hospital. Pregnant women should avoid all unnecessary medication, but vaccinations and malarial prophylactics should still be taken where possible. Additional care should be taken to prevent illness and particular attention should be paid to diet and nutrition. Alcohol and nicotine, for example, should be avoided.

Women travellers often find that their periods become irregular or even cease while they're on the road. Remember that a missed period in these circumstances doesn't necessarily indicate pregnancy. There are health posts or family planning clinics in many small and large urban centres in developing countries, where you can seek advice and have a urine test to determine whether you are pregnant or not.

History Chart

	Indonesia	Malaysia & Singapore	Thailand	Myanmar (Burma)	Vietnam	Cambodia & Laos	Philippines
BC	Java Man 500,000 BC	Proto Malay migration from China 2500 BC		Mon arrive 2000 BC Asoka's Buddhist missionaries arrive 3rd C BC	Rise of Dong Son culture 300 BC Chinese rule 111 BC - 938 AD		
AD 0				Burmans arrive from Tibet 3rd C	Hindu Champa kingdom 2nd C Mahayana Buddhism	Hindu Funan kingdom 1st - 6th C	
500	Hindu-Buddhist Sriwijaya Empire in Sumatra 7th C Buddhist Sailendras in Java 8th C – Borobudur built 782-824 Hindu Mataram kingdom Java 9th C	Malay peninsula under loose control of Sriwijaya		Bagan founded 849	Chinese overthrown – 1st Viet dynasty 938	Chenla kingdom 6th C Sailendras invade Chenla Angkor founded 889 – Hindu rule	
1000	Sriwijaya defeats Mataram 1006 Cholas attack Sriwijaya 1025 Decline of Sriwijaya 13th C Majapahit Empire founded in Java 1292 – Gajah Mada prime minister 1331-64 Rise of Islam and decline of Majapahits 15th C	Islam comes to Sumatran and Malay peninsular ports Melaka founded 1402 Melaka sultanate converts to Islam	Sukhothai kingdom 1238-1376 – Theravada Buddhism and Thai script adopted Ayuthaya founded 1350 Thais attack Khmers and control Malay states 15th C	Bagan dynasty 1044-1287 – Theravada Buddhism adopted Mongols sack Bagan 1287	Ly dynasty 1010-1225 – Theravada Buddhism promoted Tran dynasty 1225-1400 – Mongol invasion repelled	Angkor Wat built 1112-52 Theravada Buddhism replaces Hinduism 14th C Angkor occupied by Thais 1431, Phnom Penh becomes capital	Islam introduced to Mindanao 15th C

History Chart

	Indonesia	Malaysia & Singapore	Thailand	Myanmar (Burma)	Vietnam	Cambodia & Laos	Philippines
1500	Fall of Majapahits 1520 Portuguese in Ternate 1511 Javanese Muslim Mataram kingdom founded 1582	Portuguese conquer Melaka 1511	Burmese invasions				Magellan arrives 1521 Spanish settle Cebu 1565 Legaspi conquers Manila 1571
1600	Dutch VOC founded 1602 – Macassar, Moluccas, Java conquered	Dutch conquer Melaka 1641			French missionaries arrive		
1700	Dutch divide Mataram into Solo and Yogyakarta 1755	Francis Light arrives in Penang 1786	Burmese sack Ayuthaya 1767		Tay Son rebellion 1771-1802		British occupy Manila 1762-63
1800	British occupy Java 1811-16 Diponegoro's Java War 1825-30 Ethical Policy 1870-1900	Raffles founds Singapore 1819 British intervention in sultanates Malay Federation 1895	Mongkut (1851-68) and Chulalongkorn (1868-1910) reforms and modernisation	British wars of 1824, 1852 and 1883 sees Britain annex Burma	French seize Saigon (1859), occupy Cochinchina (1862), then Annam and Tonkin (1885)	Cambodia becomes French protectorate 1863	Rizal executed 1896 Independence from Spain, then US annexation 1898
1900	Nationalist movements of Sarekat Islam (1912), PKI (1920) and PNI (1927)	Rubber introduced	Coup sees end of absolute monarchy 1932		Nationalism suppressed	French gain Lao and Mekong territories from Thais 1904	Internal self-government 1935
World War II and Japanese interregnum 1939-45	Republic of Indonesia proclaimed 1945 War against Dutch 1946-49 Untung coup and massacre 1965 Soeharto president 1965-	Federation of Malaya 1948 Communist Emergency 1948-1960 Independence 1957 Singapore goes it alone 1965	Elections restored 1946 but civilian government interrupted by military coups Student riots 1973 Democracy comes to Thailand 1992	Independence 1948, accompanied by Communist and Karen rebellions Ne Win seizes power in left-wing army coup 1962 Democracy movement crushed 1988	Ho Chi Minh declares north independent 1945 Franco-Viet Minh War 1946-54 Vietnam divided 1955 US bombing of north 1965 Saigon falls 1975	Khmer Rouge 'killing fields' 1975-78 Vietnam invades Cambodia 1978 UN-sponsored elections 1993	Independence 1946 Marcos president 1965-86 Marcos ousted, Aquino becomes president 1986

Glossary

BRUNEI

adat – customary law

khalwat – 'close proximity', or exhibition of public affection between the sexes

CAMBODIA

apsaras – shapely dancing women, found on Khmer sculpture

asuras – devils

devaraja – god-king

devas – gods

hols – variegated silk shirts

kramas – checked scarves

moto – motorcycle taxi

prasat – tower

remorque-moto – transport; a trailer pulled by a motorbike

vihara – sanctuary

HONG KONG

dim sum – series of Cantonese dishes, served only for breakfast or lunch

kaido – small to medium-sized ferry

KCR – Kowloon-Canton Railway

MTR – Mass Transit Railway

sampan – small motorised launch

walla walla – water taxi; bigger than a sampan but smaller than a kaido

INDONESIA

air panas – hot springs

alun alun – main public square of a town

andong – four-wheeled horse-drawn cart

bajaj – motorised three-wheeled taxi found in Jakarta

balolang – large outrigger with sails

batik – coloured cloth made by waxing and dyeing process

becak – bicycle rickshaw

bemo – pick-up truck or minibus, often with two rows of seats down the side; also known as an *angkot*

bendi – two-person horse-drawn cart

bis air – river ferry in Kalimantan

bisnis – 'business' class on trains

candi – Javanese shrine

dokar – two-wheeled horse-drawn cart

ekonomi – 'economy' class on trains

eksekutif – 'executive' (ie 1st) class on trains

gamelan – traditional Javanese and Balinese orchestra with large xylophones and gongs

gang – alley, lane

ikat – cloth in which pattern is produced by dyeing individual threads before weaving

kantor pos – post office

klotok – motorised canoe

kraton – palace

kretek – clove-flavoured cigarette

lepa-lepa – small outrigger canoes

losmen – basic accommodation

mandi – Indonesian bathing facility

opelet – small minibus; also called a *mikrolet* or a *colt*

pasar – market

Pelni – national shipping line

pencak silat – martial art popular throughout Indonesia

penginapan – simple lodging house

perahu – outrigger

rumah makan – restaurant or food stall (lit. 'eating house')

warung – food stall, cheap restaurant

wartel – telephone office

wayang kulit – shadow-puppet play

wayang orang – masked dance drama playing scenes from the *Ramayana*

wisma – guesthouse or lodge

LAOS

héua phai – rowboat

héua hãng nyáo – long-tail boat

héua wái – speedboat

jumbo – large, motorised three-wheeled taxi

khwaeng – province

muang – district

paa – fish

phíi – spirits; phíi worship is the main non-Buddhist religion of Laos

sim – main sanctuary in a Lao Buddhist monastery where monks undergo ordination

talàat – market

thàek-sii – 'taxi', passenger trucks with two

benches in the back; also known as *sāawng-thâew*
thâat – Buddhist stupa or reliquary
thanõn – street

MACAU

lorcha – type of sailing cargo-vessel
pastelaria – small cake shop
vila – cheap hotel; often called *hospedaria* or *pensão*

MALAYSIA

air – water
alor – groove, furrow, main channel of river
batu – stone, rock, milepost
gunung – mountain
istana – palace
jalan – road
kampung – village
kongsi – clan house
kota – fort or city
kuala – river mouth, or place where a tributary joins a larger river
padang – open grassy area (usually the city square)
pulau – island
tuak – rice wine

MYANMAR

hti – pronounced 'tee', the umbrella or decorated top of a pagoda
longyi – Burmese sarong
nats – guardian spirit beings
pwe – festival
stupa – pagoda containing relics of Buddha
tonga – two-wheeled horse-drawn cart

PHILIPPINES

abaca – a local plant; its leafstalks are the source of Manila hemp
banqueros – boatmen
calesas – two-wheeled horse-drawn carriages; known as *tartanillas* in Cebu City
mestizos – Filipino-Spanish or Filipino-American people

MNLF – Moro National Liberation Front; Muslim guerilla army in Mindanao
NPA – New Peoples Army; communist guerrilla movement

SINGAPORE

godown – warehouse
MRT – Mass Rapid Transit metro system
Peranakan – Straits-born Chinese

THAILAND

ao – bay or gulf
bot – central sanctuary or chapel in a Thai temple
chedi – stupa; monument erected to house a Buddha relic
farang – foreigner of European descent
hat – beach
khlong – canal
ko – island
muang – city
prang – Khmer-style tower on temples
samlor – three-wheeled pedicab
soi – lane or small street
songthaew – small pick-up truck with two benches in the back, used as buses/taxis
talaat nam – floating market
tuk-tuk – motorised samlor
wang – palace
wat – Buddhist temple-monastery

VIETNAM

ao dai – Vietnamese national dress
buu dien – post office
Caodaism – Vietnamese religious sect
cyclo – pedicab
Honda om – motorbike taxi
kem – ice cream
khach san – hotel
nha khach – guesthouse
nuoc mam – fish sauce
pho – noodle soup
Tet – lunar New Year
xe lam – three-wheeled motorised vehicle

Index

TEXT

LONELY PLANET JOURNEYS

JOURNEYS is a unique collection of travel writing – published by the company that understands travel better than anyone else. It is a series for anyone who has ever experienced – or dreamed of – the magical moment when they encountered a strange culture or saw a place for the first time. They are tales to read while you're planning a trip, while you're on the road or while you're in an armchair, in front of a fire.

JOURNEYS books catch the spirit of a place, illuminate a culture, recount a crazy adventure, or introduce a fascinating way of life. They always entertain, and always enrich the experience of travel.

ISLANDS IN THE CLOUDS
Travels in the Highlands of New Guinea
Isabella Tree

Isabella Tree's remarkable journey takes us to the heart of the remote and beautiful Highlands of Papua New Guinea and Irian Jaya – one of the most extraordinary and dangerous regions on earth. Funny and tragic by turns, *Islands in the Clouds* is her moving story of the Highland people and the changes transforming their world.

Isabella Tree, who lives in England, has worked as a freelance journalist on a variety of newspapers and magazines, including a stint as senior travel correspondent for the *Evening Standard*. A fellow of the Royal Geographical Society, she has also written a biography of the Victorian ornithologist John Gould.

'One of the most accomplished travel writers to appear on the horizon for many years . . . the dialogue is brilliant' – Eric Newby

---

SEAN & DAVID'S LONG DRIVE
Sean Condon

Sean Condon is young, urban and a connoisseur of hair wax. He can't drive, and he doesn't really travel well. So when Sean and his friend David set out to explore Australia in a 1966 Ford Falcon, the result is a decidedly offbeat look at life on the road. Over 14,000 death-defying kilometres, our heroes check out the re-runs on tv, get fabulously drunk, listen to Neil Young cassettes and wonder why they ever left home.

Sean Condon lives in Melbourne. He played drums in several mediocre bands until he found his way into advertising and an above-average band called Boilersuit. *Sean & David's Long Drive* is his first book.

'Funny, pithy, kitsch and surreal . . . This book will do for Australia what Chernobyl did for Kiev, but hey you'll laugh as the stereotypes go boom'
– Time Out

LONELY PLANET PHRASEBOOKS

Building bridges,
Breaking barriers,
Beyond babble-on

Listen for the gems

Speak your own words

Ask your own
questions

Master of
your
own
image

- handy pocket-sized books
- easy to understand Pronunciation chapter
- clear and comprehensive Grammar chapter
- romanisation alongside script to allow ease of pronunciation
- script throughout so users can point to phrases
- extensive vocabulary sections, words and phrases for every situations
- full of cultural information and tips for the traveller

'...vital for a real DIY spirit and attitude in language learning' – Backpacker

'the phrasebooks have good cultural backgrounders and offer solid advice for challenging situations in remote locations' – San Francisco Examiner

'...they are unbeatable for their coverage of the world's more obscure languages' – The Geographical Magazine

---

Arabic (Egyptian)
Arabic (Moroccan)
Australia
  *Australian English, Aboriginal and
  Torres Strait languages*
Baltic States
  Estonian, Latvian, Lithuanian
Bengali
Burmese
Brazilian
Cantonese
Central Europe
  *Czech, French, German, Hungarian,
  Italian and Slovak*
Eastern Europe
  *Bulgarian, Czech, Hungarian, Polish,
  Romanian and Slovak*
Egyptian Arabic
Ethiopian (Amharic)
Fijian
Greek
Hindi/Urdu

Indonesian
Japanese
Korean
Lao
Latin American Spanish
Malay
Mandarin
Mediterranean Europe
  *Albanian, Croatian, Greek, Italian,
  Macedonian, Maltese, Serbian,
  Slovene*
Mongolian
Moroccan Arabic
Nepali
Papua New Guinea
Pilipino (Tagalog)
Quechua
Russian
Scandinavian Europe
  *Danish, Finnish, Icelandic, Norwegian
  and Swedish*

South-East Asia
  *Burmese, Indonersian, Khmer, Lao,
  Malay, Tagalog (Pilipino), Thai and
  Vietnamese*
Sri Lanka
Swahili
Thai
Thai Hill Tribes
Tibetan
Turkish
Ukrainian
USA
  *US English, Vernacular Talk,
  Native American languages and
  Hawaiian*
Vietnamese
Western Europe
  *Basque, Catalan, Dutch, French,
  German, Irish, Italian, Portuguese,
  Scottish Gaelic, Spanish (Castilian)
  and Welsh*

LONELY PLANET TRAVEL ATLASES

Lonely Planet has long been famous for the number and quality of its guidebook maps. Now we've gone one step further and in conjunction with Steinhart Katzir Publishers produced a handy companion series: Lonely Planet travel atlases – maps of a country produced in book form.

Unlike other maps, which look good but lead travellers astray, our travel atlases have been researched on the road by Lonely Planet's experienced team of writers. All details are carefully checked to ensure the atlas corresponds with the equivalent Lonely Planet guidebook.

The handy atlas format means no holes, wrinkles, torn sections or constant folding and unfolding. These atlases can survive long periods on the road, unlike cumbersome fold-out maps. The comprehensive index ensures easy reference.

- full-colour throughout
- maps researched and checked by Lonely Planet authors
- place names correspond with Lonely Planet guidebooks
  – no confusing spelling differences
- legend and travelling information in English, French, German, Japanese and Spanish
- size: 230 x 160 mm

Available now:
Chile & Easter Island • Egypt • India & Bangladesh • Israel & the Palestinian Territories • Jordan, Syria & Lebanon • Laos • Thailand • Vietnam • Zimbabwe, Botswana & Namibia

---

LONELY PLANET TV SERIES & VIDEOS

Lonely Planet travel guides have been brought to life on television screens around the world. Like our guides, the programmes are based on the joy of independent travel, and look honestly at some of the most exciting, picturesque and frustrating places in the world. Each show is presented by one of three travellers from Australia, England or the USA and combines an innovative mixture of video, Super-8 film, atmospheric soundscapes and original music.

Videos of each episode – containing additional footage not shown on television – are available from good book and video shops, but the availability of individual videos varies with regional screening schedules.

Video destinations include: Alaska • American Rockies • Australia – The South-East • Baja California & the Copper Canyon • Brazil • Central Asia • Chile & Easter Island • Corsica, Sicily & Sardinia – The Mediterranean Islands • East Africa (Tanzania & Zanzibar) • Ecuador & the Galapagos Islands • Greenland & Iceland • Indonesia • Israel & the Sinai Desert • Jamaica • Japan • La Ruta Maya • Morocco • New York • North India • Pacific Islands (Fiji, Solomon Islands & Vanuatu) • South India • South West China • Turkey • Vietnam • West Africa • Zimbabwe, Botswana & Namibia

The Lonely Planet TV series is produced by:
Pilot Productions
Duke of Sussex Studios
44 Uxbridge St
London W8 7TG UK

Lonely Planet videos are distributed by:
IVN Communications Inc
2246 Camino Ramon
California 94583, USA

107 Power Road, Chiswick
London W4 5PL UK

Music from the TV series is available on CD & cassette.
For video availability and ordering information contact your nearest Lonely Planet office.

PLANET TALK

Lonely Planet's FREE quarterly newsletter

We love hearing from you and think you'd like to hear from us.

*When...*is the right time to see reindeer in Finland?
*Where...*can you hear the best palm-wine music in Ghana?
*How...*do you get from Asunción to Areguá by steam train?
*What...*is the best way to see India?

For the answer to these and many other questions read PLANET TALK.

Every issue is packed with up-to-date travel news and advice including:

* a letter from Lonely Planet co-founders Tony and Maureen Wheeler
* go behind the scenes on the road with a Lonely Planet author
* feature article on an important and topical travel issue
* a selection of recent letters from travellers
* details on forthcoming Lonely Planet promotions
* complete list of Lonely Planet products

To join our mailing list contact any Lonely Planet office.

Also available: Lonely Planet T-shirts. 100% heavyweight cotton.

LONELY PLANET ONLINE

Get the latest travel information before you leave or while you're on the road

Whether you've just begun planning your next trip, or you're chasing down specific info on currency regulations or visa requirements, check out the Lonely Planet World Wide Web site for up-to-the-minute travel information.

As well as travel profiles of your favourite destinations (including interactive maps and full-colour photos), you'll find current reports from our army of researchers and other travellers, updates on health and visas, travel advisories, and the ecological and political issues you need to be aware of as you travel.

There's an online travellers' forum (the Thorn Tree) where you can share your experiences of life on the road, meet travel companions and ask other travellers for their recommendations and advice. We also have plenty of links to other Web sites useful to independent travellers.

With tens of thousands of visitors a month, the Lonely Planet Web site is one of the most popular on the Internet and has won a number of awards including GNN's Best of the Net travel award.

http://www.lonelyplanet.com

LONELY PLANET PRODUCTS

Lonely Planet is known worldwide for publishing practical, reliable and no-nonsense travel information in our guides and on our web site. The Lonely Planet list covers just about every accessible part of the world. Currently there are eight series: *travel guides, shoestring guides, walking guides, city guides, phrasebooks, audio packs, travel atlases* and *Journeys* – a unique collection of travel writing.

EUROPE

Austria • Baltic States & Kaliningrad • Baltic States phrasebook • Britain • Central Europe on a shoestring • Central Europe phrasebook • Czech & Slovak Republics • Denmark • Dublin city guide • Eastern Europe on a shoestring • Eastern Europe phrasebook • Finland • France • Greece • Greek phrasebook • Hungary • Iceland, Greenland & the Faroe Islands • Ireland • Italy • Mediterranean Europe on a shoestring • Mediterranean Europe phrasebook • Paris city guide • Poland • Prague city guide • Russia, Ukraine & Belarus • Russian phrasebook • Scandinavian & Baltic Europe on a shoestring • Scandinavian Europe phrasebook • Slovenia • St Petersburg city guide • Switzerland • Trekking in Greece • Trekking in Spain • Ukrainian phrasebook • Vienna city guide • Walking in Switzerland • Western Europe on a shoestring • Western Europe phrasebook

NORTH AMERICA

Alaska • Backpacking in Alaska • Baja California• California & Nevada • Canada • Florida • Hawaii • Honolulu city guide • Los Angeles city guide • Mexico • Miami city guide • New England • New Orleans city guide • Pacific Northwest USA • Rocky Mountain States • San Francisco city guide • Southwest USA • USA phrasebook

CENTRAL AMERICA & THE CARIBBEAN

Bermuda • Central America on a shoestring • Costa Rica • Cuba • Eastern Caribbean • Guatemala, Belize & Yucatán: La Ruta Maya • Jamaica

SOUTH AMERICA

Argentina, Uruguay & Paraguay • Bolivia • Brazil • Brazilian phrasebook • Buenos Aires city guide • Chile & Easter Island • Chile & Easter Island travel atlas • Colombia • Ecuador & the Galápagos Islands • Latin American Spanish phrasebook • Peru • Quechua phrasebook • Rio de Janeiro city guide • South America on a shoestring • Trekking in the Patagonian Andes • Venezuela

Travel Literature: Full Circle: A South American Journey

ANTARCTICA

Antarctica

ISLANDS OF THE INDIAN OCEAN

Madagascar & Comoros • Maldives & Islands of the East Indian Ocean • Mauritius, Réunion & Seychelles

AFRICA

Arabic (Moroccan) phrasebook • Africa on a shoestring • Cape Town city guide • Central Africa • East Africa • Egypt • Egypt travel atlas• Ethiopian (Amharic) phrasebook • Kenya • Morocco • North Africa • South Africa, Lesotho & Swaziland • Swahili phrasebook • Trekking in East Africa • West Africa • Zimbabwe, Botswana & Namibia • Zimbabwe, Botswana & Namibia travel atlas

Travel Literature: The Rainbird: A Central African Journey • Songs to an African Sunset: A Zimbabwean Story

MAIL ORDER

Lonely Planet products are distributed worldwide. They are also available by mail order from Lonely Planet, so if you have difficulty finding a title please write to us. North American and South American residents should write to Embarcadero West, 155 Filbert St, Suite 251, Oakland CA 94607, USA; European and African residents should write to 10 Barley Mow Passage, Chiswick, London W4 4PH; and residents of other countries to PO Box 617, Hawthorn, Victoria 3122, Australia.

NORTH-EAST ASIA

Beijing city guide • Cantonese phrasebook • China • Hong Kong, Macau & Guangzhou• Hong Kong city guide • Japan • Japanese phrasebook • Japanese audio pack • Korea • Korean phrasebook • Mandarin phrasebook • Mongolia • Mongolian phrasebook • North-East Asia on a shoestring • Seoul city guide • Taiwan • Tibet • Tibet phrasebook • Tokyo city guide

Travel Literature: Lost Japan

MIDDLE EAST & CENTRAL ASIA

Arab Gulf States • Arabic (Egyptian) phrasebook • Central Asia • Iran • Israel & the Palestinian Territories • Israel & the Palestinian Territories travel atlas • Istanbul city guide • Jerusalem city guide • Jordan & Syria • Jordan, Syria & Lebanon travel atlas • Middle East • Turkey • Turkish phrasebook • Yemen

Travel Literature: The Gates of Damascus • Kingdom of the Film Stars: Journey into Jordan

ALSO AVAILABLE:

Travel with Children • Traveller's Tales

INDIAN SUBCONTINENT

Bangladesh • Bengali phrasebook • Delhi city guide • Hindi/Urdu phrasebook • India • India & Bangladesh travel atlas • Indian Himalaya • Karakoram Highway • Nepal • Nepali phrasebook • Pakistan • Rajasthan • Sri Lanka • Sri Lanka phrasebook • Trekking in the Indian Himalaya • Trekking in the Karakoram & Hindukush • Trekking in the Nepal Himalaya

Travel Literature: In Rajasthan • Shopping for Buddhas

SOUTH-EAST ASIA

Bali & Lombok • Bangkok city guide • Burmese phrasebook • Cambodia • Ho Chi Minh city guide • Indonesia • Indonesian phrasebook • Indonesian audio pack • Jakarta city guide • Java • Laos • Lao phrasebook • Laos travel atlas • Malay phrasebook • Malaysia, Singapore & Brunei • Myanmar (Burma) • Philippines • Pilipino phrasebook • Singapore city guide • South-East Asia on a shoestring •South-East Asia phrasebook • Thailand • Thailand travel atlas • Thai phrasebook • Thai audio pack • Thai Hill Tribes phrasebook • Vietnam • Vietnamese phrasebook • Vietnam travel atlas

AUSTRALIA & THE PACIFIC

Australia • Australian phrasebook • Bushwalking in Australia • Bushwalking in Papua New Guinea • Fiji • Fijian phrasebook • Islands of Australia's Great Barrier Reef • Melbourne city guide • Micronesia • New Caledonia • New South Wales & the ACT • New Zealand • Northern Territory • Outback Australia • Papua New Guinea • Papua New Guinea phrasebook • Queensland • Rarotonga & the Cook Islands • Samoa • Solomon Islands • South Australia • Sydney city guide • Tahiti & French Polynesia • Tasmania • Tonga • Tramping in New Zealand • Vanuatu • Victoria • Western Australia

Travel Literature: Islands in the Clouds • Sean & David's Long Drive

THE LONELY PLANET STORY

Lonely Planet published its first book in 1973 in response to the numerous 'How did you do it?' questions Maureen and Tony Wheeler were asked after driving, bussing, hitching, sailing and railing their way from England to Australia.

Written at a kitchen table and hand collated, trimmed and stapled, *Across Asia on the Cheap* became an instant local bestseller, inspiring thoughts of another book.

Eighteen months in South-East Asia resulted in their second guide, *South-East Asia on a shoestring*, which they put together in a backstreet Chinese hotel in Singapore in 1975. The 'yellow bible', as it quickly became known to backpackers around the world, soon became *the* guide to the region. It has sold well over half a million copies and is now in its 9th edition, still retaining its familiar yellow cover.

Today there are over 180 titles, including travel guides, walking guides, language kits & phrasebooks, travel atlases and travel literature. The company is one of the largest travel publishers in the world. Although Lonely Planet initially specialised in guides to Asia, we now cover most regions of the world, including the Pacific, North America, South America, Africa, the Middle East and Europe.

The emphasis continues to be on travel for independent travellers. Tony and Maureen still travel for several months of each year and play an active part in the writing, updating and quality control of Lonely Planet's guides.

They have been joined by over 70 authors and 170 staff at our offices in Melbourne (Australia), Oakland (USA), London (UK) and Paris (France). Travellers themselves also make a valuable contribution to the guides through the feedback we receive in thousands of letters each year.

The people at Lonely Planet strongly believe that travellers can make a positive contribution to the countries they visit, both through their appreciation of the countries' culture, wildlife and natural features, and through the money they spend. In addition, the company makes a direct contribution to the countries and regions it covers. Since 1986 a percentage of the income from each book has been donated to ventures such as famine relief in Africa; aid projects in India; agricultural projects in Central America; Greenpeace's efforts to halt French nuclear testing in the Pacific; and Amnesty International.

'I hope we send the people out with the right attitude about travel. You realise when you travel that there are so many different perspectives about the world, so we hope these books will make people more interested in what they see. These are guidebooks, but you can't really guide people. All you can do is point them in the right direction.'
 – Tony Wheeler

LONELY PLANET PUBLICATIONS

Australia
PO Box 617, Hawthorn 3122, Victoria
tel: (03) 9819 1877 fax: (03) 9819 6459
e-mail: talk2us@lonelyplanet.com.au

USA
Embarcadero West, 155 Filbert St, Suite 251,
Oakland, CA 94607
tel: (510) 893 8555 TOLL FREE: 800 275-8555
fax: (510) 893 8563
e-mail: info@lonelyplanet.com

UK
10 Barley Mow Passage, Chiswick,
London W4 4PH
tel: (0181) 742 3161 fax: (0181) 742 2772
e-mail: 100413.3551@compuserve.com

France:
71 bis rue du Cardinal Lemoine, 75005 Paris
tel: 1 44 32 06 20 fax: 1 46 34 72 55
e-mail: 100560.415@compuserve.com

World Wide Web: http://www.lonelyplanet.com